51ST EDITION

KOVELS'®
Antiques &
Collectibles
PRICE GUIDE 2019

BLACK DOG
& LEVENTHAL
PUBLISHERS
NEW YORK

Cover design by Carlos Esparza and Frances Soo Ping Chow

Front cover photographs, from left to right:
Furniture, chest, Sheraton, mahogany
Doll, Margot of Italy, felt
Haviland, vase, man reading under tree

Back cover photographs, top to bottom:
Furniture, chair, fireside, Kindt-Larsen
Jewelry, pin, parakeet
Toy, car, taxi, yellow cab
Handel, lamp, domed shade, birds of paradise

Spine:
Silver-English, dish, entree, lid

Authors' photographs © Kim Ponsky (top) and Alex Montes de Oca (bottom)

Black Dog & Leventhal Publishers
Hachette Book Group
1290 Avenue of the Americas
New York, NY 10104

www.hachettebookgroup.com
www.blackdogandleventhal.com

First Edition: September 2018

Black Dog & Leventhal Publishers is an imprint of Running Press, a division of Hachette Book Group.
The Black Dog & Leventhal Publishers name and logo are trademarks of Hachette Book Group, Inc.

The publisher is not responsible for websites (or their content) that are not owned by the publisher.
The Hachette Speakers Bureau provides a wide range of authors for speaking events.
To find out more, go to www.HachetteSpeakersBureau.com or call (866) 376-6591.

Print book interior design by Sheila Hart Design, Inc.

ISBN: 978-0-316-48604-0

Printed in the United States of America

WW
10 9 8 7 6 5 4 3 2 1

BOOKS BY RALPH AND TERRY KOVEL

American Country Furniture, 1780–1875

A Directory of American Silver, Pewter, and Silver Plate

Kovels' Advertising Collectibles Price List

Kovels' American Antiques 1750–1900

Kovels' American Art Pottery

Kovels' American Collectibles 1900–2000

Kovels' American Silver Marks, 1650 to the Present

Kovels' Antiques & Collectibles Fix-It Source Book

Kovels' Antiques & Collectibles Price Guide (1968–2009)

Kovels' Bid, Buy, and Sell Online

Kovels' Book of Antique Labels

Kovels' Bottles Price List (1971–2006)

Kovels' Collector's Guide to American Art Pottery

Kovels' Collector's Guide to Limited Editions

Kovels' Collectors' Source Book

Kovels' Depression Glass & Dinnerware Price List (1980–2004)

Kovels' Dictionary of Marks— Pottery and Porcelain, 1650 to 1850

Kovels' Guide to Selling, Buying, and Fixing Your Antiques and Collectibles

Kovels' Guide to Selling Your Antiques & Collectibles

Kovels' Illustrated Price Guide to Royal Doulton (1980, 1984)

Kovels' Know Your Antiques

Kovels' Know Your Collectibles

Kovels' New Dictionary of Marks— Pottery and Porcelain, 1850 to the Present

Kovels' Organizer for Collectors

Kovels' Price Guide for Collector Plates, Figurines, Paperweights, and Other Limited Edition Items

Kovels' Quick Tips: 799 Helpful Hints on How to Care for Your Collectibles

Kovels' Yellow Pages: A Resource Guide for Collectors

The Label Made Me Buy It: From Aunt Jemima to Zonkers— The Best-Dressed Boxes, Bottles, and Cans from the Past

BOOKS BY TERRY KOVEL AND KIM KOVEL

Kovels' Antiques & Collectibles Price Guide (2010–2019)

INTRODUCTION

Kovels' Antiques & Collectibles Price Guide 2019 has current, reliable price information and makers' marks. The book has 16,000 prices, 2,500 new color photographs, more than 700 categories, black and white pictures, plus a center section on "What's Hot and What's Not in Antiques & Collectibles" that includes record prices for the year. We are frequently asked questions like "How old is my grandmother's dish?" This year, to help with identification, more than 100 categories include three marks and the years they were used. The history, location, and other important information can still be found in the category introduction. (More dated marks are online at Kovels.com and in our book, *Kovels' New Dictionary of Marks—Pottery and Porcelain.*) You will also find more than 200 added facts of interest and tips about care and repair. Each photograph is shown with a caption that includes the description, price, and source. The book has color tabs and color-coded categories that make it easy to find listings, and it uses a modern, readable typestyle. Each of the categories has its own introduction that gives the history and descriptions to help identify an unknown piece. We update these introductory paragraphs every year to indicate new owners, new distributors, or new information about production dates. This year we made updates to 145 paragraphs, many of which tell of the sale or closing of a company. All antiques and collectibles priced here were offered for sale during the past year, most of them in the United States, from June 2017 to June 2018. Other prices came from sales that accepted bids from all over the world. Almost all auction prices given include the buyer's premium since that is part of what the buyer paid. Very few include local sales tax or extra charges such as phone bids, online bids, credit cards, or shipping.

Most items in our original 1968 price book were made before 1860, so they were more than a century old. Today in *Kovels' Antiques & Collectibles Price Guide* we list pieces made as recently as 2010, as there is great interest in furniture, glass, ceramics, and good design made since 1950.

The book is more than 500 pages long and crammed full of prices and photographs. We try to include a balance of prices and do not include too many items that sell for more than $5,000. By listing only a few very expensive pieces, you can realize that a great paperweight may cost $10,000 but an average one is only $25. Nearly all prices are from the American market for the American market. Only a few European sales are reported. We don't include prices we think result from "auction fever" but we do list verified bargains.

There is an index with cross references. Use them often. It includes categories and much more. For example, there is a category for "Celluloid." Most celluloid will be there, but a toy made of celluloid may be listed under "Toy" and also indexed under "Celluloid." There are also cross-references in the listings and in the category introductions. But some searching must be done. For example, Barbie dolls are in the Doll category; there is no Barbie category. And when you look at "Doll, Barbie," you find a note that "Barbie" is under "doll, Mattel, Barbie" because Mattel makes Barbie dolls and most dolls are listed by maker.

All the photographs and the prices are new. Antiques and collectibles pictured are items that were offered for sale or sold for the amount listed, inclusive of the buyer's premium, from

Toy, Henry & Henrietta, celluloid
Bertoia Auctions

June 2017 to June 2018. Wherever we had extra space on a page, we filled it with tips about the care of collections and other useful information. Don't discard this book. Old Kovels' price guides can be used in the coming years as a reference source for price changes and for tax, estate, and appraisal information.

The prices in this book are reports of the general antiques market. As we said, every price in the book is new. We do not estimate or "update" prices. Prices are either realized prices from auctions or completed sales or curated asking prices. We know that a buyer may have negotiated a lower price. We do not pay dealers, collectors, or experts to estimate prices. If a price range is given, at least two identical items were offered for sale at different prices. Price ranges are found only in categories like "Pressed Glass," where identical items can be identified. Some prices in *Kovels' Antiques & Collectibles Price Guide* may seem high and some low because of regional variations, but each price is one you could have paid for the object somewhere in the United States. Internet prices from sellers' ads or listings are avoided. Because so many non-collectors sell online but know little about the objects they are describing, there can be inaccuracies in descriptions. Sales from well-known Internet sites, shops, and sales, carefully edited, are included.

If you are selling your collection, do not expect to get retail value unless you are a dealer. Wholesale prices for antiques are 30 to 40 percent of retail prices. The antiques dealer must make a profit or go out of business. Internet auction prices are less predictable; because of an international audience or "auction fever," prices can be higher or lower than retail.

Time has changed what we collect, the prices we pay, what is "best," and what has dropped in price. There are also laws about endangered species, not a concern when we started, and many changes in tax laws, estate problems, and even more and better reproductions and fakes that make buying more difficult. But there are many more ways to buy and sell. When we started, it was house sales, flea markets, and a few formal antiques auctions. Now, computers and the Internet have made it possible for anyone to buy and sell any day of the week, in every price range. There seem to be more shows closing or joining other shows, auction houses merging, and many more auction bidders. Almost every auction is online as well as available by phone to buyers around the world. And, there are frequently live bidders at the more expensive sales. But many auctions end up with unsold pieces, some offered for sale at a set price after the auction. Even eBay is selling only about one-third of the offered antiques. And there are thousands of places to look for prices!

READ THIS FIRST

This is a book for the buyer and the seller. It is an organized, illustrated list of average pieces, not million-dollar paintings and rare Chinese porcelains. Everything listed in this book was sold within the last

Indian, basket, Paiute, beaded
Allard Auctions

12 months. We check prices, visit shops, shows, and flea markets, read hundreds of publications and catalogs, check Internet sales, auctions, and other online services, and decide which antiques and collectibles are of most interest to most collectors in the United States. We concentrate on average pieces in any category. Prices of some items were very high because a major collection of top-quality pieces owned by a well-known collector or expert was sold. Fame adds to the value. Many catalogs now feature the name and biography of the collector and advertise the auction with the collector's name in all the ads. This year there

were major sales of toys, banks, guns, art pottery, advertising, clock, military collectibles, Joseff costume jewelry and another of Boucher costume jewelry, metal lunch boxes, Nakashima furniture, American Indian items, Hot Wheels, Fiesta dinnerware, John Prip silver, movie posters, irons, corkscrews, cigarette lighters, Blenko glass, sewer tile figures, *Star Wars* memorabilia, and personal collections of famous people. Single collector auctions of dolls, Victorian glass, and Tiffany of all types were well-advertised and prices were high. Some of these prices are reported. The most important bottle auctions are run by major bottle auction companies that feature rare bottles and American flasks. Some of these high prices are also reported, along with less expensive inkwells and bitters bottles.

Most listed pieces are less than $10,000. The lowest price is $3 for a paper milk bottle cap used by the Cedarside Dairy of Waterloo, Iowa. The highest price, $252,000, was for a piece of scrimshaw, a whale's tooth engraved with the ship "Pacific of Nantucket," only 4¾ inches long. The smallest item is a pair of ½-inch goldtone cufflinks with a profile of a Roman man's head in relief, sold for $65. The largest item is a 1970s double cabinet by Paul Evans made of chromed steel, other metals, and rosewood. It is 33 by 180 by 90 inches and cost $12,500.

Many unusual, unique, and even weird things were auctioned this year. We list a nineteenth century taxidermied mermaid, 44 inches long. It is a fish tail topped with the torso and head of a monkey, mounted on a stand. It was made for a sideshow and sold for $6,517. Other oddities: a pair of leather and wood pony lawn shoes, $277; a 1920s prison uniform with a striped shirt, pants, and metal buttons stamped "N.C. Prison," $1,000; and a bronze "Lunar Eclipse" clock made by Wendell Castle with stacked geometric shapes, $4,250.

Clock, Lunar Eclipse by Wendell Castle
Rago Arts and Auction Center

HOW TO USE THIS BOOK

There are a few rules for using this book. Each listing is arranged in the following manner: CATEGORY (such as Silver), OBJECT (such as vase), and DESCRIPTION (as much information as possible about size, age, color, and pattern). Some types of glass, pottery, and silver are exceptions to this rule. These are listed CATEGORY, PATTERN, OBJECT, DESCRIPTION, PRICE. All items are presumed to be in good condition and undamaged, unless otherwise noted. In most sections, if a maker's name is easily recognized, like Gustav Stickley, we include it near the beginning of the entry. If the maker is obscure, the name may be near the end.

- To save space, dollar amounts do not include dollar signs, commas, or cents at the end, so $1,234.00 is written 1234.
- You will find silver flatware in either Silver Flatware Plated or Silver Flatware Sterling. There is also a section for Silver Plate, which includes coffeepots, trays, and other plated hollowware. Most solid or sterling silver is listed by country, so look for Silver-American, Silver-Danish, Silver-English, etc. Silver jewelry is listed under Jewelry. Most pottery and porcelain is listed by factory name, such as Weller or Wedgwood; by item, such as Calendar Plate; in sections like Dinnerware or Kitchen; or in a special section, such as Pottery-Art, Pottery-Contemporary, Pottery-Midcentury, etc.

- Sometimes we make arbitrary decisions. Fishing has its own category, but hunting is part of the larger category called sports. We have omitted guns except for toy guns. These are listed in the toy category. It is not legal to sell weapons without a special license, so guns are not part of the general antiques market. Air guns, BB guns, rocket guns, and others are listed in the Toy section. Everything is listed according to the computer alphabetizing system.

- We made several editorial decisions. A butter dish is a "butter." A salt dish is called a "salt" to differentiate it from a saltshaker. It is always "sugar and creamer," never "creamer and sugar." Where one dimension is given, it is the height; if the object is round, it's the diameter. The height of a picture is listed before width. Glass is clear unless a color is indicated.

- Some antiques terms, such as "Sheffield" or "Pratt," have two meanings. Read the paragraph headings to know the definition being used. All category headings are based on the vocabulary of the average person, and we use terms like "mud figures" even if not technically correct. Some categories are known by several names. Pressed glass is also called pattern glass or EAPG (Early American Pattern Glass). We use the name "pressed glass" because much of the information found in old books and articles use that name.

- This book does not include price listings for fine art paintings, antiquities, stamps, coins, or most types of books. Comic books are listed only in special categories like Superman, but original comic art and cels are listed in their own categories.

- Prices for items pictured can be found in the appropriate categories. Look for the matching entry with the abbreviation "Illus." The color photograph will be nearby.

- Thanks to computers, the book is produced quickly. The last entries are added in June; the book is available in September. But human help finds prices and checks accuracy. We read everything at least five times, sometimes more. We edit more than 35,000 entries down to the 16,000 entries found here. We correct spelling, remove incorrect data, write category paragraphs, and decide on new categories. We proofread copy and prices many times, but there may be some misspelled words and other errors. Information in the paragraphs is updated each year, and this year more than 145 updates and additions were made.

- Prices are reported from all parts of the United States, Canada, Europe, and Asia, and converted to U.S. dollars at the time of the sale. The average rate of exchange on June 1, 2018, was $1 to about $1.30 Canadian, €0.86 (euro), and £0.75 (British pound). Meltdown price for silver was $13.82 per ounce in June 2018. Prices are from auctions, shops, Internet sales, shows, and even some flea markets. Every price is checked for accuracy, but we are not responsible for errors. We cannot answer your letters asking for price information, or where to sell, but please write if you have any requests for categories to be included or any corrections to the paragraphs or prices. You may find the answers to your other questions at Kovels.com or in our newsletter, *Kovels On Antiques & Collectibles*.

- When you see us at shows, auctions, house sales, flea markets, or even the grocery store, please stop and say hello. Don't be surprised if we ask for your suggestions. You can write to us at P.O. Box 22192, Beachwood, OH 44122, or visit us on our website, Kovels.com.

TERRY KOVEL AND KIM KOVEL
July 2018

ACKNOWLEDGMENTS

The world of antiques and collectibles is filled with people who share knowledge and help, tell stories of the record prices, amazing sales and news, and make books like this possible. Dealers, auction galleries, antiques shops, serious collectors, clubs, publications, and even museum experts have given advice and opinions, sent pictures and prices, and made suggestions for changes. Thank you to all of them! Each picture is labeled with the name of the source. We list a phone number, postal address, and Web address at the end of the book, so you can learn more about any pictured piece. And we also include the names of many of the people or places that reported some prices.

And, we want to give special thanks to the staff at Kovels' and at Hachette, our publisher. They deserve the most credit. They helped gather the 16,000 prices, 2,500 pictures, marks, tips on care of collections, and hotlines (bits of information too important to ignore) put it all together, and made it work.

Our thanks to the Hachette staff:

- J. P. Leventhal, who was with us from the start at Crown Publishing (our first publisher) through today as part of the Hachette Book Group.
- Lisa Tenaglia, who is editing her eighth edition of Kovels', knows all the changes and improvements, and encouraged new ideas.
- Lillian Sun in production and Mike Olivo, managing editor, and Kara Thornton, publicity, and the others at Hachette who did all the things we never see and never have to worry about that add to the quality of the book.
- Mary Flower, Robin Perlow, and Cynthia Schuster Eakin are the proofreaders who find all sorts of errors we missed. They seem to know how to spell every foreign name and the dates of every battle or World's Fair or change in a country's name. They even knew some pictures were given the wrong captions. If the copy is perfect or nearly perfect, it is because they are so talented.
- And Sheila Hart, who has done the layout and design for many editions and kept up with our changes that often made her job even harder. She has to get all the prices and all the pictures into position in alphabetical order near the captions, so readers can see both. She creates a great design out of the required order. Her assistant, Malcolm Bellew, helped with the unusual requirements.

And to those on the Kovels' staff:

- Janet Dodrill, art director, who makes improvements to the look and quality of the pictures. She outlines every picture, checks the color, and does all sorts of magic things to make the pictures and marks look perfect.
- Our in-house price staff of Mozella Colon, Beverly Malone, Renee McRitchie, Dorothy Conrad, and Sarah Marino who use secret ways to get ranges of prices from all parts of the country and translate them into our listings. And to Tina McBean, assistant, and Lauren Rafferty, who worked on parts of the project for part of the year.
- Cherrie Smrekar, who is able, cheerful, and willing to do extra work on any part of the project in addition to her other writing jobs.
- Liz Lillis, our proofreader, writer, and researcher who tells us all where the commas and periods go—before or after a final parenthesis mark—and other grammar problems. She also seems to know every date and the spelling of every name and how to write a homepage.

- And last, but definitely not least, Gay Hunter, who watches every entry and picture. She records the price, where a picture is found, who did the work, then records all the many documents and pictures, keeps count, runs spellchecks, and understands our complicated identification codes. But most of all, she keeps us to our deadlines.

CONTRIBUTORS

The world of antiques and collectibles is filled with people who have answered our every request for help. Dealers, auction houses, and shops have given advice and opinions, supplied photographs and prices, and made suggestions for changes. Many thanks to all of them:

Photographs and information were furnished by: Ahlers & Ogletree Auction Gallery, Alex Cooper Auctioneers, Allard Auctions, AntiqueAdvertising.com, Antiques & Art International, Bertoia Auctions, Blackwell Auctions, Brunk Auctions, Bunch Auctions, Bunte Auction Services, Burchard Galleries, Clars Auction Gallery, Copake Auction, Cordier Auctions, Cottone Auctions, Cowan's Auctions, Crescent City Auction Gallery, DuMouchelles, Early American History Auctions, eBay, Eldred's Auctioneers and Appraisers, Etsy, Fisher-Price, Fontaine's Auction Gallery, Forsythe's Auctions, Fox Auctions, Freedom Auction Company, Freeman's Auctioneers & Appraisers, Garth's Auctioneers & Appraisers, Glass Works Auctions, Hake's Americana & Collectibles, Heritage Auctions, Hess Auction Group, Humler & Nolan, I.M. Chait, James D. Julia Auctioneers, Jeffrey S. Evans & Associates, Julien's Auctions, Kaminski Auctions, Keystone Auctions, Leland Little Auctions, Leslie Hindman Auctioneers, Los Angeles Modern Auctions, Martin Auction Co., Michann's Auctions, Mike Clum Auctions, Milestone Auctions, Morning Glory Jewelry, Morphy Auctions, Morton Subastas, Myers Auction Gallery, Naudeau's Auction Gallery, Neal Auctions, New Orleans Auction Galleries, Palm Beach Modern Auctions, Pook & Pook, Potter & Potter Auctions, Rachel Davis Fine Arts, Rafael Osona Auctions, Rago Arts and Auction Center, Replacements Ltd., Rich Penn Auctions, Richard D. Hatch & Associates, RSL Auction, Ruby Lane, SCP Auctions, Selkirk Auctioneers & Appraisers, Skinner, Inc., Soulis Auctions, Specialists of the South, Stony Ridge Auction, Strawser Auction Group, Susanin's Auctioneers & Appraisers, The Stein Auction Company, Theriault's, Thomaston Place Auction Galleries, Inc., Treadway, Uniques & Antiques, Weiss Auctions, Willis Henry Auctions, Wm Morford Auctions, Woody Auction, and Wright. The contact information for these people is at the back of the book starting on page 502.

Record price pictures courtesy of Christie's, Copley Fine Art Auctions, Crocker Farm, Henry Aldridge & Son, John McInnis Auctioneers, Phillips, and WestLicht Photographica Auction.

To the others who knowingly or unknowingly contributed to this book, we say thank you: Anderson Americana, Aspire Auctions, Auction Gallery of the Palm Beaches, Auction Team Breker, Berner's Auction Gallery, Bonhams, Bremo Auctions, Burchard Galleries, Charleston Estate Auctions, Christie's, Concept Art Gallery, Crocker Farm, Dallas Auction Gallery, Danica's Antiques, Don's Antiques, Doyle New York, Garden Party Collection Vintage Jewelry, Great Vintage Jewelry, Hill Auction Gallery, Hill House Wares, Horst Auction Center, iCollect, Jackson's, Jasper52, John Moran Auctioneers, Kennedy's Auction Service, Leland Little Auctions, Leonard Auction, Lewis & Maese, M. Schon Art & Design, Malleries Luxuries, Michelle's Vintage Jewelry, Mroczek Brothers Seattle Auction House, Norman C. Heckler, Open-Wire Insulator Services, Quinn's Auction Galleries, Rich Penn, Richard Opfer, Ripley Auctions, Rush Antiques, Showtime Auction Services, Sotheby's, The Internet Antique Shop, Touch of Glass, Trocadero, Ultimate Adornment, Vintage Treasures, Weschler & Son, and Westport Auction.

A. WALTER made pate-de-verre glass under contract at the Daum glassworks from 1908 to 1914. He decorated pottery during his early years in his studio in Sevres, where he also developed his formula for pale, translucent pate-de-verre. He started his own firm in Nancy, France, in 1919. Pieces made before 1914 are signed *Daum, Nancy* with a cross. After 1919 the signature is *A. Walter Nancy.*

Bowl, Crab, Mottled Brown, Yellow, Signed, 9 In. .... *illus*	3509
Night-Light, Cone Shape, Shade, Yellow Ground, Red & Pink Flowers, 8½ In.	2722
Paperweight, Green Crayfish, Light Green Base, Signed, 4¼ In.	3025
Vase, Green To Blue, Leaves, Berry, Bees, 5¾ In.	3125

ABC plates, or children's alphabet plates, were most popular from 1780 to 1860 but are still being made. The letters on the plate were meant as teaching aids for children learning to read. The plates were made of pottery, porcelain, metal, or glass. Mugs and other items were also made with alphabet decorations. Many companies made ABC plates. Shown here are marks used by three English makers.

Charles Allerton & Sons
c.1890–1912

Enoch Wood & Sons
1818–1846

William E. Oulsnam & Sons
c.1880–1892

Mug, Alphabet, Rafts, Houseboats, Brownhills Pottery, c.1880, 2¾ x 2¾ In.	125
Mug, Little Bo Peep, Sheep, Silver, Loop Handle, William Kerr & Thiery, c.1880, 2¾ In.............	720
Mug, Nursery Characters, Birds, Animals, Silver Plate, Homan Silver Co., c.1920, 2½ In.	113
Plate, Alphabet, Brown Transferware, 2 Girls, Tea Party In Garden, c.1890, 6⅝ In. .... *illus*	149
Plate, Bulldog, Glass, 8-Sided, Central Well & Footring, Raised Letters, Martinsville, c.1910, 6 In. .	98
Plate, Civil War Soldiers, Staffordshire, 1870s, 7½ In.	210
Plate, Crusoe Finding The Foot Prints, Brownhills Pottery, c.1890, 7 In.	96
Plate, Girl's Portrait, Glass, Aqua, 6⅜ In.	40
Plate, Horse Scenes, Red Transferware, Raised Letters, Staffordshire, 1800s, 6¾ In.	125
Plate, Nickel, Alphabet Border, Embossed, c.1870, 6¼ In.	65
Plate, Polar Bear, Cubs, Brownhills Pottery, c.1880, 7¼ In.	248
Plate, Riding Hood Meets Wolf, Brownhills Pottery, c.1880, 7¼ In.	315
Plate, Who Killed Cock Robin?, Poem, Tin, c.1900, 7⅞ In..	65

ABINGDON POTTERY was established in 1908 by Raymond E. Bidwell as the Abingdon Sanitary Manufacturing Company. The company started making art pottery in 1934. The factory ceased production of art pottery in 1950.

Vase, Delta, Yellow Satin Glaze, 2 Handles, c.1938, 10 In. .... *illus*	85
Vase, Pink, Shaped Mouth, Fluted, Round Domed Base, 10¾ In.	30
Vase, Trojan Warrior Head, Art Deco, Gray, 7¼ x 2 In.	62

ADAMS china was made by William Adams and Sons of Staffordshire, England. The firm was founded in 1769 and became part of the Wedgwood Group in 1966. The name *Adams* appeared on various items through 1998. All types of tablewares and useful wares were made. Other pieces of Adams may be found listed under Flow Blue and Tea Leaf Ironstone.

William Adams & Co.
1905–1917

William Adams & Sons
1917–1965

Adams under Wedgwood
1966–1975

Bowl, Vegetable, Adams' Rose, Pearlware Beaded Rim, Oval, 1825, 1⅝ x 8¾ x 11 In.	130

A. Walter, Bowl, Crab, Mottled Brown, Yellow, Signed, 9 In.
$3,509

James D. Julia Auctioneers

ABC, Plate, Alphabet, Brown Transferware, 2 Girls, Tea Party In Garden, c.1890, 6⅝ In.
$149

Ruby Lane

TIP
Carry your keys and use the flashlight on your phone when walking at night.

Abingdon, Vase, Delta, Yellow Satin Glaze, 2 Handles, c.1938, 10 In.
$85

Ruby Lane

Adams, Plate, Adams' Rose, Spatter, Ironstone, 8¾ In.
$83

Hess Auction Group

Adams, Soup, Dish, Head Waters Of The Juniata, Red Transfer, 10½ In.
$35

Hess Auction Group

Advertising, Banner, Ringling Bros. Barnum & Bailey, Elephant Walk, Canvas, 2-Sided, 56 x 52 In.
$780

Freedom Auction Company

They Might Have Been Clara Rolls

Tootsie Roll candy was first made in 1896 in New York City by Leo Hirshfield. He named the candy for his daughter Clara, whose nickname was Tootsie.

Creamer, Adams' Rose, Spatter, Helmet Shape, 4 In.	189
Gravy Boat, Chusan, Oriental Flare, Celadon, 1970-79	75
Jug, Silver Rim, Brown Neck, Handle Above, Rabbit Hunt, Stoneware, 1798, 8¼ In.	400
Jug, Silver Rim, White Relief, Classical Figures, Arched Panels, Blue Jasper, 1700s, 7 In.	431
Plate, Adams' Rose, Spatter, Ironstone, 8¾ In. .... *illus*	83
Plate, Salad, Singapore, Pale Green, Blue & Yellow Bird, 8 In.	15
Plate, Soup, Adams' Rose, Spatter, 9 In.	236
Salt, Boat Shape, Turtle Base, Green, c.1874, 2 x 3 In.	70
Soup, Dish, Head Waters Of The Juniata, Red Transfer, 10½ In. ..... *illus*	35
Tureen, Tray, Lid, Flow Blue, Staffordshire, House, River, 7½ In.	192

ADVERTISING containers and products sold in the old country store are now all collectibles. These stores, with crackers in a barrel and a potbellied stove, are a symbol of an earlier, less hectic time. Listed here are many advertising items. Other similar pieces may be found under the product name, such as Planters Peanuts. We have tried to list items in logical places, so enameled tin dishes will be found under Graniteware, auto-related items in the Auto category, paper items in the Paper category, etc. Store fixtures, cases, signs, and other items that have no advertising as part of the decoration are listed in the Store category. The early Dr Pepper logo included a period after "Dr," but it was dropped in 1950. We list all Dr Pepper items without a period so they alphabetize together. For more prices, go to kovels.com.

Ashtray, Matchbox Holder, Howard Johnson's, Porcelain, W.H. Coon Co., Scranton, c.1935, 4 x 5 In.	45
Ashtray, Pennsylvania Rubber Co., Balloon Tire, Blue, Glass, Match Holder, 1920s, 4½ x 4 In.	95
Banner, Ringling Bros. Barnum & Bailey, Elephant Walk, Canvas, 2-Sided, 56 x 52 In. ..... *illus*	780
Bank, Vending, Reading Biscuits, Tin Lithograph, Huntley & Palmer, 9 In.	660
Beer Tap Knob, Golden Age Beer, Brass, Fernwood Brewing Co., Fernwood, Pa., 2 In.	120
Bench, Red Goose Shoes, Wood, Painted, Zeppelin, Shaped Edges, 3 Dividers, 33 x 72 In.	840
Billhook, Hunt's Perfect Baking Powder, Woman, Apron, Cardboard Lithograph, 7 x 3 In.	106
Bin, Havenner's Takoma Bread, Pine, Green, Yellow, Hasp, Lock, Chain, c.1900, 28 x 27 In.	438
Books may be included in the Paper category.	
Bottles are listed in the Bottle category.	
Bottle Openers are listed in the Bottle Opener category.	
Bottle Topper, Orange Crush, Girl, Seated, Drinking, Oranges, 9 x 7 In.	377
Bowl, Hershey's, Red & White Stripes, 1900s	25
Box, see also Box category.	
Box, Candy, Hildreth's Velvet Molasses, Monkeys, Sleeping Child, Velvet, Cardboard, 1940, 4 x 10 In.	25
Box, Cereal, Nabisco Shredded Wheat, Stainless Steel Kitchenware Offer On Front, 6 x 7 x 4 In.	55
Box, Cereal, Portage Rolled Oats, Cardboard, Cylindrical, Figures Carrying Canoe, 3 Lb.	265
Box, Crate, Milk Bottle, St. Louis Business, Wood, 1900s	25
Box, D.M. Ferry Seeds, Man Holding Tomato, Metal Clasp, Wood, 4½ x 13 x 6½ In.	184
Box, Display, Canadian Baking Powder, Indian Label, Wood, Pearce, Duff & Co., 7 x 10 In.	315
Box, Display, Canadian Baking Powder, Indians & Teepees, Hinged Lid, 7¾ x 11 x 2¾ In.	316
Box, Display, Monkey Links, 22 Boxes Of Tire Chain Links, 8⅞ x 13 x 7¼ In.	374
Box, Display, Tryalax, Chocolate Laxative, 3 Faces, Countertop, c.1925, 3 x 5 In.	125
Box, Display, Winchester Gun Oil, Cardboard, 6 Cans Of Oil, 11 x 7 x 2½ In.	891
Box, J.H. Mohlman, Ground Spices, Lid, Wood, 16 x 8½ x 4½ In.	242
Box, Log Cabin Smoking Tobacco, Black Man Sitting By Cabin, Wood, c.1875, 8 x 14 x 9 In.	776
Box, Mamma's Choice Rolled Oats, Girl, Bow In Hair, Cardboard, 3 Lb. 7 Oz., 9 x 5 In.	345
Box, Massasoit Collars, Round, Green, Indian Brave, 1870-80s, 2 x 3 In.	547
Box, Putnam Dyes, Wood, Embossed Paper Labels, Hinge, Varnish, 21 In.	120
Box, Rice's Flower Seeds, Children Playing, Outdoor Scene, Wood, 3⅞ x 11 x 6⅝ In.	246
Box, Seal Of North Carolina Plug Cut, Tobacco, Wood, Marburg Co., 1880s, 7 x 5 x 4 In.	130
Box, Yankee Oats, Uncle Sam Image, Quaker Oats Co., Cardboard, 9 x 3 In. .... *illus*	224
Broadside, Broadway Trunk Store, John Monson, c.1910, 15 x 23 In.	960
Cabinet, Diamond Dyes, Baby, Feathers, Tulips, Doors Slide, 20 In.	420
Cabinet, Diamond Dyes, Evolution Of Woman, Tin Litho Panel, Oak Case, 30 x 23 In. ..... *illus*	472
Cabinet, Diamond Dyes, Redheaded Fairy With Wand, Tin Lithograph, 30 In.	420
Cabinet, Dr. Lesure, Veterinary, Horse Head Through Opening In Wall, 6⅞ x 21 x 6¾ In.	6440

Advertising, Box, Yankee Oats, Uncle Sam Image, Quaker Oats Co., Cardboard, 9 x 3 In.
$224

AntiqueAdvertising.com

Advertising, Cabinet, Diamond Dyes, Evolution Of Woman, Tin Litho Panel, Oak Case, 30 x 23 In.
$472

Hess Auction Group

Advertising, Cabinet, Needle, Walnut, Drawers, Best Quality Of Sewing Machine Needles, 24 In.
$560

Hess Auction Group

Advertising, Dispenser, Drink Dr. Swett's Root Beer, Original Pump, 13 ½ In.
$5,228

Morphy Auctions

> **TIP**
> *Display groups of at least three of your collectibles to get decorating impact.*

Advertising, Dispenser, Drink Hires Rootbeer, Hires Boy, Original Spigot, 18 In.
$18,450

Morphy Auctions

Advertising, Dispenser, Jim Dandy Root Beer, Old Ball Pump, 2-Sided Decoration, 15 In.
$11,430

Morphy Auctions

Advertising, Dispenser, Ward's Lemon Crush, 13 x 11 In.
$1,600

Woody Auction

Advertising, Dispenser, Ward's Orange Crush, 14 In.
$1,700

Woody Auction

ADVERTISING

Advertising, Display, Box, Frank Siddalls Soap, Wood, Flip-Up Lid, 16 x 10½ x 6 In.
$59

AntiqueAdvertising.com

Advertising, Display, Sun-Ray Cigar, Pleasing To All, Plate Glass, 4¼ x 17 In.
$800

Woody Auction

Advertising, Egg Crate, Wood, Black Stencil, John E. Gonce, Elkton, MD, 11 x 13 x 12 In.
$236

Hess Auction Group

Advertising, Figure, General Electric, Bandleader, Wood, Composition, Jointed, Parrish, 19 In.
$649

Wm Morford Auctions

4

Cabinet, Humphrey's Remedies, Gold Lettering, Product Listing, 22 x 28 In.	175
Cabinet, Needle, Walnut, Drawers, Best Quality Of Sewing Machine Needles, 24 In. *illus*	560
Cabinet, Wear Airmaid Hosiery, In Flying Colors, Wing-Walking Girl, 19 x 19½ x 9 In.	490
Calendars are listed in the Calendar category.	
Can, Sears Oil Cream, Separator Machine, 11 x 6 x 3¾ In.	316
Can, Whiz Metal Polish, Packard Limo, Hand Soldered, 7½ x 3½ In.	488
Canisters, see introductory paragraph to Tins in this category.	
Cards are listed in the Card category.	
Case, Bunte Cough Drops, 40 Full Boxes, 1912.	350
Case, Display, Mrs. Robbinson's Pies, Table Talk Pies, Racks, 1930s, 23 x 15 In.	710
Change Receiver, see also Tip Tray in this category.	
Charger, Jim Bean, Workers Making Whiskey, Tin Lithograph, Frame, c.1905, 31 x 32 In.	1200
Chest, Pine, Lift Top, Painted, Cowdray Polo Tournament, Handles, 1935, 21 x 20 In.	580
Cigar Cutter, Habana Flor Fina, Metal, Mechanical, Cigar Box Shape, 1¾ x 1¾ In.	71
Clocks are listed in the Clock category.	
Cooler, Royal Crown Cola, Embossed, Stainless Steel Lids, Ideal Co., 1940s, 42 x 36 x 22 In.	660
Creamer, Borden's, Elsie The Cow, Head, Pink Necklace, Blue Bell, Japan, 1940s, 3¾ In.	20
Dispenser, Drink Dr. Swett's Root Beer, Original Pump, 13½ In. *illus*	5228
Dispenser, Drink Hires Rootbeer, Hires Boy, Original Spigot, 18 In. *illus*	18450
Dispenser, H.J. Peck Select Spices, Tin, Hinged Lids, 8 Bins, Women On Front, 32 x 21 In.	925
Dispenser, Jim Dandy Root Beer, Old Ball Pump, 2-Sided Decoration, 15 In. *illus*	11430
Dispenser, Mission Orange Juice, Patterned Glass, Art Deco, Black, Red, Orange, 16¼ In.	129
Dispenser, Ward's Lemon Crush, 13 x 11 In. *illus*	1600
Dispenser, Ward's Lemon Crush, Lemon Form, Pump Nozzle, 15 In.	480
Dispenser, Ward's Orange Crush, 14 In. *illus*	1700
Display, Beech-Nut Chewing Gum, Peppermint, 5 Cents, Wire Stand, Tin Lithograph, 8 x 6 In.	210
Display, Bottle, Ironbrew Syrup, Arm Holding Hammer, Metal Cap, 10 x 3½ In.	1121
Display, Box, Frank Siddalls Soap, Wood, Flip-Up Lid, 16 x 10½ x 6 In. *illus*	59
Display, Corona Wool Fat For Horses & Cows, Glass Door, Gold Lettering, 23½ In.	270
Display, Dr. West's Miracle-Tuft, Toothbrush, Red Bakelite, Bristles, 1950s, 18 In.	245
Display, Gurn-Z-Gold Milk, Milk Carton, Paper, Wax Inside & Out, Barnum, Minn., c.1960, 10 In.	5
Display, Indian Head Radiator Cement, Cardboard, Countertop, 11 x 11 x 1¼ In.	546
Display, Levi's, Figural Cowboy, Hat, Standing, Saddle Over Shoulder, Composition, 29 In.	975
Display, Luden's Menthol Cough Drops, Slant Glass, Image Of Boxes, 9 x 5 x 5 In.	805
Display, Philip Morris, Johnny, Bellhop, No Cigarette Hangover, Cardboard, 44 x 15 In.	265
Display, Stroh's Beer, Truck, Red, Black, Yellow, Metal Piece, Steps Included, 1900s, 14 x 9 In.	30
Display, Sun-Ray Cigar, Pleasing To All, Plate Glass, 4¼ x 17 In. *illus*	800
Display, Window, California Syrup Of Figs, Children's Laxative, Cardboard, 31 x 43 In.	547
Dolls are listed in the Doll category.	
Door Push, Buy Dr. Daniels' Medicines, Please Close The Door, Tin, Embossed, 9 x 3 In.	1380
Door Push, Hercules Overalls, Blue, White Letters, Porcelain, 6 x 4 In.	1150
Door Push, Holsum Bread, Tin Lithograph, Adjustable Bracket, 3 x 31 x 1⅜ In.	460
Door Push, Millbrook Bread, Loaf, Adjustable Mounting Bracket, 8½ x 27 In.	518
Door Push, Pull, Majors Cement, Mends Everything, Navy, White, 6½ x 3⅞ In.	413
Door Push, Sunbeam Batter Whipped, Girl, Loaf Shape, Tin Lithograph, c.1950, 8½ x 27 In.	310
Door Push, Sweet Heart Products, Flour, Heart Shape, Porcelain, 1900s, 5¼ x 5 In.	325
Egg Carton, Bloomer Bros., Chickens, Inner Dividers, Cardboard, 1930s, 6 x 7 In.	25
Egg Crate, Wood, Black Stencil, John E. Gonce, Elkton, MD, 11 x 13 x 12 In. *illus*	236
Fans are listed in the Fan category.	
Figure, General Electric, Bandleader, Wood, Composition, Jointed, Parrish, 19 In. *illus*	649
Figure, Mellin's Baby Food, Girl, Seated, Pink Cheeks, White Dress, Bisque, 6 x 3 In.	47
Figure, Pig, Rice's Country Sausage, Incised, Chalkware, 5 x 9 In.	241
Jar, Acme Quality Paints Inc., Glass, Copper Top, Patented, USA, 1965, 8¾ In.	35
Jar, Borden's, Metal Lid, Opaque Glass Label, Countertop, 9 In.	540
Lamps are listed in the Lamp category.	
Lunch Boxes are also listed in the Lunch Box category.	
Lunch Box, Red Indian Cut Plug Tobacco, Tobacco Pack Images, Train, 5 x 7¾ In.	632
Matchbox Cover, Chippewa Shoes, Indian Head, 1 x ½ x 2 In.	122
Menu Holder, Soda Fountain, Piper Ice Cream, Celluloid, 4-Page Menu Inside, 7¼ x 5 In.	415

Advertising mirrors of all sizes are listed here. Pocket mirrors range in size from 1 ½ to 5 inches in diameter. Most of these mirrors were given away as advertising promotions and include the name of the company in the design.

Mirror, Airline Bee Products, Pure Honey, Bees, 2⅛ In.	236
Mirror, Arndt Co. Good For Trade, Woman, Auburn Hair, Celluloid, 2 In.	389
Mirror, Carson City, Nevada, Celluloid, Showgirl Image, 2¼ In. ..... *illus*	1770
Mirror, Churchill Drug Co., Wholesale Druggists, Buildings, Blue, 4 In.	200
Mirror, Cincinnati & Suburban Bell Telephone Co., Celluloid, 2¾ In. ..... *illus*	3304
Mirror, Dayton Overalls, Celluloid, Woman Dressing, 2⅛ In. ..... *illus*	2478
Mirror, Finck's Detroit-Special Overalls, Celluloid, 1909-60, 3 In. ..... *illus*	300
Mirror, He-No Tea, Woman, Hat, Flowers, Holding Packer Of Tea, Celluloid, 2¾ x 1¾ In.	4025
Mirror, Juliette Shoes, Celluloid, Woman Holding Shoe, 2¾ In. ..... *illus*	1092
Mirror, Keystone Overalls, The Masquerader, Cleveland & Whitehill Co., 2¾ x 1¾ In.	401
Mirror, Ludlow Ambulance Service, Holmes Auto Co., Tinted Photo, Celluloid, Holmes, c.1920, 3½ In. .	250
Mirror, Patterson Mfg. Co., Woman On Couch, Celluloid, c.1900, 2¾ In. ..... *illus*	679
Mirror, Turkey Gin, Straus, Gunst & Co., Richmond, Celluloid, c.1910, 2¾ In. ..... *illus*	738
Mirror, United States Music Company, Building, Red, 3½ In.	283
Mirror, Vander Espt's Medicinal Cure, Nude Woman, 4-Day Cure, Celluloid, 1¾ In. ..... *illus*	531
Mirror, West End Brewing, Celluloid, 2¼ In.	236
Mug, Glass, A & W, Decal, Clear, Handle, c.1973, 6 In.	9
Ornaments, Kellogg's, Snap, Crackle, Pop, Pewter, c.1990, 2 In., 3 Piece	18
Pails are also listed in the Lunch Box category.	
Pail, Coffee, Jersey Farm, Milk Pail, Red Cow, Black, Tin Lithograph, 9⅞ x 5½ In.	3220
Pail, Jumbo Peanut Butter, Elephant, 3⅜ x 3⅞ In.	165
Pail, Rio Chewing Tobacco, Lid, Plantation Workers, Paper On Wood, 10 Lb., 11 x 13 In.	242
Pail, Sunny Boy Peanut Butter, Handle, Brundage Bros., Toledo, Ohio, Tin, c.1925, Lb.	175
Pail, Tobacco, Spaulding & Merrick Co., Scenery, 5¼ x 5½ In.	4600
Pail, Uncle Daniel Tobacco, Smoking Man, Lake, 6½ x 7⅜ In.	165
Pail, Velvet Tobacco, Girl, Old-Fashioned Dress, Lorillard & Co., 10 Lb., 1888, 11 x 11 In.	196
Pail, Virgin Smoking Tobacco, Paper Wraparound Label, Marburg Bros., 3⅞ x 4¼ In.	431
Paperweight, Shackamaxon Worsted Co., Clothing & Tailoring, Hand Blown, 2 x 3⅜ In.	59
Pin, Apple Valley Pow-Wow, Indian Chief, Pinback, 1955, 1¾ In. Diam.	10
Rack, Gulf Batteries, Service Station Stand, Metal, Painted In Orange, Gulf Batteries, 38 x 22 x 17 In.	240
Rack, Tom's Peanuts, Metal, 2 Shelves, Red & Silver, 1950s, 14 x 9 In.	165
Sack, American Lady Self-Rising Flour, Amelia Earhart, c.1935, 24 x 17 In.	165
Salt & Pepper Shakers are listed in the Salt & Pepper category.	
Scales are listed in the Scale category.	
Shadowbox, Display, Bug-A-Boo, Super Insect Spray, Light-Up, 8 x 16 x 4 In.	2875
Sign, Abbott's Ice Cream, Woman, Bonnet & Dress, Metal, 2-Sided, Hanging, 32 x 36 In.	530
Sign, Acme, Beer, Howdy Stranger, Pinup Girl, Cowboy Outfit, 11 x 17 In.	690
Sign, Aetna, Coast-To-Coast, Yellow, Red, Blue Ground, Square, c.1920, 20 x 15 In.	263
Sign, American Wringer Co.'s, Tin Lithograph, Embossed, Self-Framed, 9¾ x 13 In. ..... *illus*	1711
Sign, Archie Allen, Camp YWCA, Sheet Metal, 24 x 27 In.	316
Sign, Arco Gas Station, Daily Pricing, Pole Mounted, Blue, 1960, 50 x 38 x 2 In.	650
Sign, Arm & Hammer Soda, Arm Holding Hammer, Yellow, White, Black, Tin, 13 x 6⅝ In.	776
Sign, Beech-Nut Mints, They Melt On Your Tongue, Flavors, Boy, 26 x 17 In.	247
Sign, Beech-Nut, Amelia Earhart, Plane, Photo, Black, White, Cardboard, 22 x 28 In.	604
Sign, Buckingham Cigarettes, Porcelain Over Steel, 1970, 94 x 58 x 1 In.	4800
Sign, Bull Durham Smoking Tobacco, Cardboard Litho, Uncut, Trademark Bull, 35 x 30¾ In.	1215
Sign, Bull Durham Smoking Tobacco, Statue Of Woman, Bull, 24 In.	2128
Sign, C. Terrot Dijon Bicycles, Man, Bike, Horses, Paper Lithograph, Cardboard Mount, 13 x 16 In.	241
Sign, Call For Philip Morris, Woman, Phone, Cigarette, Yellow, Red, 8 x 27½ In.	247
Sign, Calumet Insurance, Chicago, Indian Smoking Long Pipe, Tin, Embossed, 20 x 14 In.	1898
Sign, Campy's, Camp, Sheet Metal, Wood, 22 x 10 x 8 In.	128
Sign, Carlton Cafe Confectionery, Reverse Painted, Glass, 9 x 23 In.	176
Sign, Champion Cigars, Havana, Cheroots, Girl, Goat, Lithographed Cloth, Matted, 22 x 15 In.	460
Sign, Champlain Gas Station, 2-Sided, Quebec, 1960, 54 x 76 x 1¼ In.	3400
Sign, Chancellor Cigar, Reverse Painted Glass, Gilt Frame, 32 x 43 In.	2204
Sign, Clapp & Jones Steam Fire Engines, Figural, Top Hat, Painted Wood, 24 x 25 In.	2420
Sign, Clown Rowing Boat, Large Glass Of Beer In Boat, Linen Backed, Germany, 1970, 26 x 34 In. .	490

Advertising, Mirror, Carson City, Nevada, Celluloid, Showgirl Image, 2¼ In.
$1,770

Advertising, Mirror, Cincinnati & Suburban Bell Telephone Co., Celluloid, 2¾ In.
$3,304

Advertising, Mirror, Dayton Overalls, Celluloid, Woman Dressing, 2⅛ In.
$2,478

TIP
Keep basement windows locked at all times.

A

Advertising, Mirror, Finck's Detroit-Special Overalls, Celluloid, 1909-60, 3 In.
$300

Wm Morford Auctions

Advertising, Mirror, Juliette Shoes, Celluloid, Woman Holding Shoe, 2¾ In.
$1,092

Wm Morford Auctions

Advertising, Mirror, Patterson Mfg. Co., Woman On Couch, Celluloid, c.1900, 2¾ In.
$679

Wm Morford Auctions

Sign, Columbia Records, Enameled Metal, 2-Sided, Round, 28 In. *illus*	1500
Sign, Columbia Records, On Sale Here, Thermometer, Enameled Metal, Wood, 61 x 18 In.	1000
Sign, Congress Tires, Die Cut Tire Graphic, Tin Flange, 24 x 16 In.	3600
Sign, Construction Warning, Industrial Theme, Orange, 1970, 33 x 80 In.	850
Sign, Cork Distilleries Co., Bottle Of Old Irish Whisky, Tin Lithograph, 12 x 16 In. *illus*	165
Sign, Delco Batteries, Battery Graphic, Tin, 20 x 14 In.	762
Sign, Devlish Good Cigars, 5 Cents, Box Of Cigars, Tin Lithograph, 9⅞ x 13 In.	207
Sign, Dr. Daniels Dog Condition Tablets, Yellow, 6 x 9 In.	106
Sign, Dr Pepper, Good For Life, Red, White, Porcelain, 10 x 24 In.	776
Sign, Dr. Tutt's Liver Pills, Doctor, Mother, Children, Cardboard, 11½ x 7 In.	345
Sign, Drink Kemp's Fine Old Fashioned Root Beer, Yellow, Green, Brown, 13⅞ x 19¾ In.	401
Sign, Drink Smile, Smiling Orange, 2-Sided, Bottom Flange, Mount, 12 x 10 In.	845
Sign, Drink Trefz, Taste Tells, Bottled At The Brewery, Cardboard Lithograph, 10 x 13 In.	177
Sign, Duke's Mixture, Tobacco Pack, Raised Convex, Porcelain, 12 x 8⅞ In.	1121
Sign, Dutch Masters Paints, Dutch Man, Red, White, Black, Porcelain, 26 In.	374
Sign, El Producto Cigars, Scranton Tobacco Co., Yellow, Red, Black, Porcelain, 20 x 24 In.	604
Sign, Excelsior Fireworks, Fireworks Display, Crowd, Red, White, Blue, Paper, 31 x 21 In.	2185
Sign, Fire Escape, Hand Pointing, Porcelain, Raised Volcano Grommet Holes, 4 x 20 In.	661
Sign, Firth & Hall Pianoforte & Music Co., Painted Wood, c.1910, 22 x 97 In. *illus*	840
Sign, Flan Lyonnais, Kitchen Piece, Pastry Chef, Dessert, Linen Back, 1930, 15 x 22 In.	350
Sign, Gibson Christmas Cards, Santa Claus, Die Cut, Paper Lithograph, 22 x 13 In. *illus*	413
Sign, Giusti's Master Loaf, The Guardian Of Health, Navy, Yellow, Red, 9 x 20 In.	719
Sign, Good-Grape Soda, Banner, Red, Yellow, Embossed, 5⅜ x 19⅝ In.	247
Sign, Goodyear Tires, Globe Graphic, Porcelain Flange, 30 x 26 In.	3000
Sign, Grand Republic, Flour, Woman Kneading Dough, Man At Door, 22 x 16 In.	719
Sign, Grape Smash, Carbonated, 5 Cents, Bunch Of Grapes, Tin Litho, 1926, 9⅜ x 13⅜ In.	489
Sign, Grape-Nuts, To School Well Fed, Girl & Dog, Tin, Self-Framed, 30½ x 20 In. *illus*	6608
Sign, Greensmith's Derby Dog Biscuits, 18¾ x 23¾ In.	613
Sign, Greyhound Lines, Bus Depot, Enameled Porcelain, 20 x 30 In.	805
Sign, Grimston, Tumble Down Dick, Steward & Patteson, Painted, 2-Sided, Iron, Trade, 9½ x 33 In.	708
Sign, Harley-Davidson, Orange, Black, Gold, Tin Lithograph, c.1940, 18 x 24 In.	2714
Sign, Heinz Mince Meat, Can, Jar, Cardboard, c.1925, 11 x 21 In.	134
Sign, Hi-Country Beef Jerky, Montana, Wood, Metal Frame, 5 x 8½ In.	65
Sign, Hires Root Beer, R-J, For Real-Juices, Green, Black, Red Circle, 2-Sided, Metal, 16 In.	300
Sign, Hires Root Beer, With Lunch, Bottle & Glass Of Hires, Lithograph, 11 x 10 In.	150
Sign, Hires, Visit Our Fountain, Enjoy A Delicious Hires Float, Soda Jerk, Frame, 4 x 17 In.	60
Sign, Honey Moon, Tobacco, Can, Couple Holding Hands, Moon & Stars, Tin, 9 x 6 In.	460
Sign, Hood Tires, Flagman Graphics, Tin, 24 x 12 In.	2400
Sign, Hoosier Seed Drills, Farm Scene, Horses, Celluloid, Cardboard, Frame, 20 x 24 In. *illus*	1770
Sign, Howard, Dustless Dusters, Woman Holding Up Dusting Cloth, Paper, Frame, 29 x 20 In.	1323
Sign, Iron Fireman, Automatic Coal Burner, Roboman Logo, Porcelain, 6 In.	834
Sign, Kayo, K-O Your Thirst, Boxer, Hat, Bottle, Red, White Text, 9¾ x 27¾ In.	401
Sign, Lemp Brewing, Woman, Holding Glass Of Beer, Tin Lithograph, 16 In.	74
Sign, Little Savage, Domestic Sewing Machines, Island Girl, Paper, Roll-Down, 27 x 12 In.	317
Sign, Mack Trucks, Bulldog, Enameled, Porcelain, 28 x 36 In.	5865
Sign, Maestro Cigars, Man In Tuxedo, Cardboard, Frame, 32 x 48 In.	122
Sign, Mail Pouch Tobacco, Stagecoach, Lithograph, c.1915, 92 x 78 In.	29000
Sign, Mastiff, Tobacco, When Golfing Smoke Mastiff, Golfer, Cardboard, 13 x 7 In.	374
Sign, Miles, Texas Steer Shoes For Men, Steer Head, Tin, Embossed, 19 x 13 In.	1208
Sign, Milk, Food For The Nerves, Tin, Embossed, Black, Red, 19½ x 13 In.	456
Sign, Nesbitt's Soda, Bottle, Black Circle, Yellow Ground, Stout Sign Co., 23½ In.	198
Sign, Novelty Woven Corsets, Mother & Daughter, Lithograph, c.1875, 13 x 16 In.	300
Sign, O Boy Gum, Goudey Gum Company Tin, Stains, 1930, 16 x 7¼ In.	420
Sign, Okito Cigar, Cardboard Lithograph, Red & Black, Woman, 18 x 10 In.	679
Sign, Old Gold Cigarettes, Boating, 1930, 16 x 27 In.	374
Sign, Old North State Tobacco That Is Tobacco, Cloth, Navy, 20 x 28 In.	401
Sign, Old Quaker Rye Whiskey, Men, After Dinner Drinks, Paper, Frame, 1900, 21 x 28 In.	495
Sign, Old Town Canoe, Canoe & Crossed Paddles Shape, Wood, 16 x 14⅛ In.	4025
Sign, Old Virginia Cheroots, A Great Smoke, Red, Yellow, Blue, Tin Lithograph, 16 x 10 In.	283
Sign, OshKosh B'Gosh, Uncle Sam, Die Cut, Cardboard, c.1935, 27 x 45 In. *illus*	420

Advertising, Mirror, Turkey Gin, Straus, Gunst & Co., Richmond, Celluloid, c.1910, 2¾ In.
$738

Wm Morford Auctions

Advertising, Mirror, Vander Espt's Medicinal Cure, Nude Woman, 4-Day Cure, Celluloid, 1¾ In.
$531

AntiqueAdvertising.com

Advertising, Sign, American Wringer Co.'s, Tin Lithograph, Embossed, Self-Framed, 9¾ x 13 In.
$1,711

Wm Morford Auctions

Advertising, Sign, Columbia Records, Enameled Metal, Double Sided, Round, 28 In.
$1,500

Rago Arts and Auction Center

Advertising, Sign, Cork Distilleries Co., Bottle Of Old Irish Whisky, Tin Lithograph, 12 x 16 In.
$165

Hess Auction Group

Advertising, Sign, Firth & Hall Pianoforte & Music Co., Painted Wood, c.1910, 22 x 97 In.
$840

Garth's Auctioneers & Appraisers

Advertising, Sign, Gibson Christmas Cards, Santa Claus, Die Cut, Paper Lithograph, 22 x 13 In.
$413

AntiqueAdvertising.com

Snapp!
In 1932, Snapp!, a small gnome wearing a baker's cap and carrying a spoon, was the first gnome to be featured on Kellogg's Rice Krispies.

Advertising, Sign, Grape-Nuts, To School Well Fed, Girl & Dog, Tin, Self-Framed, 30½ x 20 In.
$6,608

Wm Morford Auctions

Advertising, Sign, Hoosier Seed Drills, Farm Scene, Horses, Celluloid, Cardboard, Frame, 20 x 24 In.
$1,770

Wm Morford Auctions

Advertising, Sign, OshKosh B'Gosh, Uncle Sam, Die Cut, Cardboard, c.1935, 27 x 45 In.
$420

Cowan's Auctions

Advertising, Sign, Sweet, Orr & Co., Pants, Shirts & Overalls, Tin Lithograph, c.1890, 20 x 28 In.
$6,150

Cowan's Auctions

Advertising, Sign, Three Feathers Whiskey, Ask The Bartender, Sheet Metal, Die Cut, 10 x 7 In.
$142

Hess Auction Group

Tinware

After 1850 canisters and spice boxes, cans that held tea, coffee, and spices, were japanned and stenciled with the name of the product. By 1880 names and designs were printed directly on metal cans and boxes.

Advertising, Sign, Uncle Sam's Boys Eat Wheatlet, Cardboard, Franklin Mills, 15 x 22 In.
$802

AntiqueAdvertising.com

Sign, Painted, Gold Lettering, 2 Crossed Rifles, Black Ground, Alfred Gun Club, 13 x 46 In.	1750
Sign, Peco Hen Feed, Pheasant, Pittsburg Elev. Co., Painted, Wood, 1930-40, 34 x 20 In.	1265
Sign, Philip Morris, No Cigarette Hangover, Johnny, Cardboard, Easel Back, 44 x 15 In.	263
Sign, PNP Peinture National Paint, Shield, 2-Sided, Porcelain, Canada, 1950s, 24 x 20 In.	275
Sign, Poll-Parrot, Figural, Parrot, Colors, Porcelain, Hanging, 36 x 13 x 3 In.	3565
Sign, Quality Candies, Pinup Girl, Boxing Ring, Blue, Yellow, 9 x 16 ¼ In.	247
Sign, R. & H. Bottle Beer, Seminude Woman Next To Water, Cardboard Litho, 16 x 8 In.	4140
Sign, Rex Flour, Red, White Letters, Porcelain, 4 x 20 In.	518
Sign, Ringling Bros., Barnum & Bailey, Leopard, Cardboard, Wood Frame, 47 x 35 In.	240
Sign, Ringling Bros., Barnum & Bailey, Hanging Rope, Cardboard, 48 x 38 In.	300
Sign, Round Oak, Stoves, Ranges & Furnaces, Easel Back, Die Cut, Doe-Wah-Jack, 7 x 7 In.	306
Sign, Royal Crown Cola, Tin, Die Cut, Nehi Corporation, 1936, 58 x 15 In.	400
Sign, Sealshipt Oyster System, Cobalt Blue On White, Porcelain Flange, 2-Sided, c.1915, 15 x 13 In.	875
Sign, Sherwin-Williams, Paint, 3-Dimesional, French Lettering, 1950s, 30 x 60 x 3 In.	2950
Sign, Silsby Manufacturing Co., Badge Shape, Wood, Gold Lettering, 48 x 23 ½ In.	3025
Sign, Socony Aircraft Motor Oil, Airplane Graphics, 30 x 20 In.	4200
Sign, Socony Aircraft Oil No. 1, White, Blue, Red, Porcelain, 10 ½ x 7 ⅝ In.	920
Sign, Speedway Coils, Race Car, Tin, Embossed, 13 x 9 In.	1440
Sign, Sunbeam, Energy Packed Bread, Girl Eating Bread, Red, 54 ½ x 19 In.	375
Sign, Sunkist Oranges-Lemons, Blue, Red, 10 x 18 In.	743
Sign, Sweet, Orr & Co., Pants, Shirts & Overalls, Tin Lithograph, c.1890, 20 x 28 In. ...... *illus*	6150
Sign, Three Feathers Whiskey, Ask The Bartender, Sheet Metal, Die Cut, 10 x 7 In. ...... *illus*	142
Sign, Turkey, Spanish Onion Crate, Linen Backed, Lithograph Label, 9 x 7 In.	80
Sign, Uncle Sam's Boys Eat Wheatlet, Cardboard, Franklin Mills, 15 x 22 In. ...... *illus*	802
Sign, Watertite Paints & Enamels, Buoy, Red, Green, White, Embossed Tin, 1950s, 12 x 24 In.	295
Sign, We Use Sherwin-Williams Automotive Enamels, 22 ½ x 30 ¼ In.	519
Sign, West Berkley Express & Draying Company, Porcelain, Enameled, 15 x 20 In.	604
Sign, Weyman's Smoking Tobacco, For Sale, Scale, Paper Litho, c.1880-90, 9 x 24 In.	184
Sign, Whistle In Bottles, Bottle, Embossed, Nail Holes, 4 ½ x 19 In.	210
Sign, World Wide Secret Service, Nick Zella Detective Agency, Sheet, Tin, 14 x 20 In.	99
Sign, Yankee Screwdriver, Spiral Ratchet, Screwdriver, Tin Lithograph, 4 ⅜ x 9 ⅞ In.	863
Syphon, Chromed, Enamel Metal, Rechargeable, Soda King, Box, c.1938, 10 x 4 In. ...... *illus*	1125
Tap Knob, Aimes Beer, Mt. Carmel Brewery, 3 In.	210
Tap Knob, Blackhawk Beer, Blackhawk Brewing Co., 2 ¼ In.	523
Tap Knob, Coors Beer, Celluloid, 2 ½ In.	523
Tap Knob, Fell Brewery Beer, Carbondale, Brass, 2 ¼ In.	150 to 210
Tap Knob, Fort Mason Beer, Celluloid, 2 ⅜ In.	461
Tap Knob, Goenner & Co., New Life Beer, 2 ¾ In.	185
Tap Knob, Golden Age Beer Tap, Brass Face, 2 ¼ In.	120
Tap Knob, Indiana Beer, Polished Metal, 2 ¼ In.	2091
Tap Knob, Kuebler Ale Beer, Easton, 2 In.	660
Tap Knob, Lackawanna Beer & Ale, Scranton, 2 ½ In.	450
Tap Knob, Moersch-Bacher, Old German Beer, Brass, 2 ¼ In.	660
Tap Knob, Old Dobbin Beer, Erie Brewing Co., 2 ½ In.	510
Tap Knob, Old German Beer, Ashland Brewing Co., 2 In.	240
Tap Knob, Pixie Ale, Dubois Brewing Co., 2 ½ In.	660
Tap Knob, Rooney's Beer, Celluloid, 2 ¼ In.	210
Tap Knob, Schmidt's Beer, Celluloid, 2 ½ In.	120
Tap Knob, Silver Dime, Special Beer, 2 ¼ In.	270
Tap Knob, Wiedemanns Royal Amber Beer, Celluloid, 2 ¼ In.	185
Textile, Shakespeare Rye, Cards, Book, What Bard Knew About Poker, Frame, 24 In.	216
Thermometers are listed in the Thermometer category.	
Tile, Hamm's Beer, Tavern Wall, Lakeside Plastics, Oshkosh, 1970s, 8 x 4 In., 11 Piece	275

Advertising tin cans or canisters were first used commercially in the United States in 1819 and were called tins. Today the word *tin* is used by most collectors to describe many types of containers, including food tins, biscuit boxes, roly poly tobacco containers, gunpowder cans, talcum powder sprinkle-top cans, cigarette flat-fifty tins, and more. Beer Cans are listed in their own category. Things made of undecorated tin are listed under Tinware.

Tin, 1860, Old Virginia Smoke Tobacco, 2 Men, 1 Holding Hat & Banjo, 4 x 3 x 4 In.	604

Tin, Bambino Smoking Tobacco, Babe Ruth, Batting, Pocket, 4 x 3 x ⅞ In.	1840
Tin, Bell Co. Spice, Poultry Seasoning, Turkey, Red, Blue, 2¾ x 2⅜ In.	271
Tin, Big Chief, Cigar, Indians, On Horseback, Paper Label, 5⅜ x 4¾ In.	604
Tin, Birchwood Coffee, Brave, Canoe, Copps Co., 5¼ x 4¼ In.	212
Tin, Biscuit, Barnum & Bailey, Portraits, Circus Acts, 5½ x 8¾ x 6½ In.	317
Tin, Biscuit, Fry Chocolate, Bus, 8 In.	840
Tin, Biscuit, Royal Telephone Booth, Crumpsall & Cardiff, 7 In.	270
Tin, Biscuit, Wild West, Buffalo Bill, Cowboys & Indians, Lithographed, 3 x 8 x 2 In.	345
Tin, Bulldog Smoking De Luxe, Tobacco, Bulldog, Pipe, 2¾ x 2⅜ In.	354
Tin, Buster Brown Cigar, Outcault's Cartoon Characters, 5 x 5 In.	4025
Tin, Cadette Talc, Soldier Shape, Blue-Gray Uniform, Tin Litho, 7 x 2¼ In. *illus*	200
Tin, Cafe Savoy Coffee, Blue, White, 1¼ x 2 In.	59
Tin, Campfire Marshmallows, Boy Scout Camping, 2⅛ x 8 In.	106
Tin, Challenge Mills Brand Canela, Ostrich, Egg, Trees, 3⅜ x 2¼ In.	177
Tin, Cigar, Apache Trail, Indian On Horseback, Multicolor, 5¾ x 6 x 4 In.	2645
Tin, Continental Cubes Tobacco, Washington, Looking At Map, Pocket, 3⅞ x 3¼ x 1 In.	184
Tin, Convention Hall Coffee, Building, Lb., 6¼ x 4⅜ In.	460
Tin, Drum Major Marshmallows, Willard Chocolates, Toronto, 5⅛ x 11 In.	242
Tin, Educator Crackers, Ark, Animal Images, White, Red Roof, Johnson's, 4½ x 11 x 3 In.	604
Tin, Farmer's Pride Coffee, Steel Cut, Man & Child, Paper Lithograph, 6⅛ x 4¼ In.	306
Tin, Gubec Square, Tobacco, Cairo, Egypt Scenes, Multicolor, 4⅞ x 3⅜ x 2¼ In.	776
Tin, Hannover Coffee, Brave, Headdress, Green, 5½ x 4⅜ In.	247
Tin, Hazard Co., Spice, Stunning, Detailed, 3¾ x 2¼ x 1¾ In.	253
Tin, Hoadley's Chewing Gum, Factory Building Shape, 4 x 6 In., 2 Piece	3660
Tin, Irvins Animal Crackers, Drum Shape, Circus Parade, Tin Litho, Lid, 3¾ x 7¼ In.	184
Tin, Island Hash Mixture Tobacco, Daniel Scotten & Co., Lithographed, 4¾ x 3⅝ x 2 In.	776
Tin, Ivins Big Show, Cookies, Crackers, Drum Shape, Strap, Lid, 1930s, 4 x 7 In.	185
Tin, Jule Cars Cut Plug, Tobacco, Blackwell Durham, Lithographed, 3 x 4½ x 1½ In.	489
Tin, Kamargo Coffee, Indian Chief Head, Teepees, Trees, Lithographed, 6 x 4 In.	1955
Tin, King Of All Coffee, Hinged Lid, Ginna & Co. Lithograph, Red Orange, 4½ x 3⅛ In.	106
Tin, Liberty Mills Coffee, Miss Liberty, American Flag, 2 Lb., 7⅛ x 5½ In.	403
Tin, Long's Covered Wagon Syrup, Absolutely Pure, 4 x 4 In.	7980
Tin, Loyl Coffee, Teal, Red Text, 3⅜ x 4⅛ In.	118
Tin, Lucky Spots, Cigar, Cards, 4 Aces, 50 Ct., 5¼ x 5½ In.	165
Tin, Lucky Strike, Roll Cut Tobacco, White, 4⅜ x 3 In.	377
Tin, Mastiff Cut Plug Tobacco, 2 Mastiff Dogs, Yellow, Red Letters, Lb., 6 x 4 x 5¼ In.	2760
Tin, Missouri, Ensign Perfection Cut Tobacco, Pennant, Pocket, 4½ x 3 x ⅞ In.	1265
Tin, Mother Goose Talc, Baby Powder, Light Blue, 6¼ x 2½ In.	295
Tin, Mother's Brand Salted Peanuts, Pry Lid, Cream, Red, 8 x 6½ In.	3220
Tin, Nickleplate Spices, Mace, Man Riding Horse, 2¼ x 1⅞ In.	129
Tin, Old Judge Coffee, 3 Lb., 10 x 5¼ In.	210
Tin, Pocono Brand Coffee, Woman, Headdress, 6¼ x 4⅝ In.	200
Tin, Poppy Cigar, Woman, Yellow Flowers, Tin Lithograph, 5¾ x 5⅛ In.	1150
Tin, Pride Of Arabia Coffee, Beige, Horse, Rider, Tin Lithograph, 2⅞ x 4¼ In.	70
Tin, Pure Honey, Hualclo Apiary, Paint Can, Roses & Honeybees, Gilt, 1920s, Gal.	95
Tin, Red Wing Cigar, Indian Maiden, Lid, 5⅜ x 6⅛ x 3⅞ In.	546
Tin, Richmond Mixture, Carl Braff, Brave, Headdress, Red, Tin Lithograph, 3 x 4¼ In.	118
Tin, Rose-O-Cuba Cigars, Woman, Lacy Headdress, Flowers, Tin Lithograph, 5 x 5 In.	138
Tin, Scissors Cut Plug Tobacco, Pictures Scissors, Oval, Pocket, 4⅝ x 3 x 1⅜ In.	6555
Tin, Seminole Coffee, Red, Paper Lithograph, 5½ x 4¼ In.	129
Tin, Smoke Mastiff Plug Cut, Tin Litho, Lid, 2 Dogs, Tobacco Pack, J.B. Pace Co., 6 x 4 x 5 In.	2760
Tin, Spice, Dining Car Mustard, Waiter, Railroad Dining Car, Tin Litho, 3½ x 2¼ In. *illus*	472
Tin, Spice, Fairway Mustard, 2 Children, Grass, 1½ Oz., 3 x 2⅜ In.	161
Tin, Spice, Fiesta Brand Mustard, Spice Of Life, Dancer, Tambourine, Litho, c.1910, 2 Oz.	80
Tin, Spice, Honest Brand, Cinnamon, Gilles Coffee Co., 7¼ x 3¼ In.	35
Tin, Spice, Red Turkey, Red Pepper, Tin Lithograph, 3¾ x 2¼ In. *illus*	307
Tin, Spice, Red Turkey Pure Spices, Cloves, Lithograph, Maltby Co., 3¾ x 2¼ In.	271
Tin, Strawberry Oberon Marshmallows, Red, Gold, Loose Wiles Co., 1930s, 4 In.	90
Tin, Strong-Heart Brand Coffee, Indian, Yellow Ground, 5¾ In.	915
Tin, Sweet Violet Cube Cut, Will Not Bite The Tongue, 4½ x 3 In.	483

Advertising, Syphon, Chromed, Enamel Metal, Rechargeable, Soda King, Box, c.1938, 10 x 4 In.
$1,125

Rago Arts and Auction Center

Advertising, Tin, Cadette Talc, Soldier Shape, Blue-Gray Uniform, Tin Litho, 7 x 2¼ In.
$200

AntiqueAdvertising.com

Advertising, Tin, Spice, Dining Car Mustard, Waiter, Railroad Dining Car, Tin Litho, 3½ x 2¼ In.
$472

Advertising, Tin, Spice, Red Turkey, Red Pepper, Tin Lithograph, 3¾ x 2¼ In.
$307

Advertising, Tin, Tiger Mills Special Pepper, Tin, Paper Lithograph, Wood, Canister, c.1890, 15 x 12 In.
$472

Tin, Tiger Mills Special Pepper, Tin, Paper Lithograph, Wood, Canister, c.1890, 15 x 12 In. *illus*	472
Tin, Vanko Tobacco, Horse, Green, Gold, 5½ x 6¼ In.	120
Tin, W.G. Bell & Co., Spiced Seasoning, Boston, Lithograph, Hinged Lid, 2½ x 1½ In.	130
Tin, Warrior Coffee, Indian Head, Pry-Lid Top, Lb., 5¾ x 4⅜ In.	460
Tin, White Lilac Coffee, Blue, Orange, White, Lilacs, 6 x 4¼ In.	188
Tin, Wilbur's Breakfast Cocoa, Cherub Stirs In Cup, 6⅞ x 3¾ In.	47
Tin, Winner Cut Plug Tobacco, Car Race, Top Handle, Rectangular, 8 In.	1245

Advertising tip trays are decorated metal trays less than 5 inches in diameter. They were placed on the table or counter to hold either the bill or the coins that were left as a tip. Change receivers could be made of glass, plastic, or metal. They were kept on the counter near the cash register and held the money passed back and forth by the cashier. Related items may be listed in the Advertising category under Change Receiver.

Tip Tray, Cottolene, Black Woman & Child, 4¼ In.	240
Tip Tray, Grapico Soda, Distinctively Individual, Red, 4¼ In.	354
Tip Tray, Lehnert Beer, Dog, Glasses, Smoking Cigar, Tin Litho, American Art Work, Round, 1910, 4 In.	270
Tip Tray, Leinbach Box Co., Woman, Gold Headband, Gold Dress, 4¼ In.	165
Tip Tray, Oak Stoves & Ranges, Copper, Embossed, c.1900, 3⅛ x 4¾ In.	142
Tobacco Cutter, Mule, Iron, Cast, R.J.R. Tobacco Co., 7 x 9 In.	165
Toy, Clown Juggler, Black Baby, Bucahn Soaps, Wood, Mechanical, 9¾ x 9¼ In.	150
Tray, Baker's Breakfast Cocoa, Woman, House, 6 In.	236
Tray, Bevo, All Year-Round Soft Drink, Team Of Horses, Delivery Wagon, Tin, 1920, 6½ In.	150
Tray, Clysmic Mineral Waters, Buck, Topless Girl, Holding Large Bottle, 16 x 13 In.	834
Tray, Crystal Spring Brewing Co., Blue, Round, 15 In.	5980
Tray, Crystal Spring Brewing Co., Girls At Spring, Porcelain, Brass Rim, Round, 15 In.	5980
Tray, East Buffalo Beer, White, Blue Text, Buffalo, On Range, 11⅛ x 13¾ In.	2415
Tray, Fred Miller Brewing Co., Eagle, Blue, 12 In.	1475
Tray, Galliker's Ice Cream, Boy & Girl, Under Umbrella, Beach, Tin, Round, 13 In.	265
Tray, Gunther's Beer, Couple, Waiter, Small Dog, Eleanor Lee Templeman, 1934, 14 In.	75
Tray, Tip, see Tip Trays in this category.	

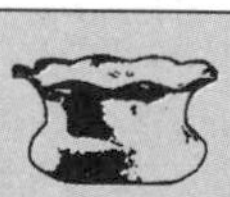

AGATA glass was made by Joseph Locke of the New England Glass Company of Cambridge, Massachusetts, after 1885. A metallic stain was applied to New England Peachblow, which the company called Wild Rose, and the mottled design characteristic of agata appeared. There are a few known items made of opaque green with the mottled finish.

Bowl, Peachblow, Metallic Mottling, Ruffled Rim, Ground & Polished Pontil, 1800s, 2½ In.	120
Finger Bowl, Peachblow, Ruffled Rim, New England Glass Co., Late 1800s, 2½ In. *illus*	120
Spooner, Cylindrical, Squared Mouth, Purple Stain, Crimped Rim, 6 In.	987
Tumbler, Peachblow, Rose To White, Glossy, 1875-99, 3¾ In. *illus*	234
Vase, Lily, Amber Satin, Glass, Purple, Trifold Rim, Trumpet, New England, 8½ In.	334

AKRO AGATE glass was founded in Akron, Ohio, in 1911 and moved to Clarksburg, West Virginia, in 1914. The company made marbles and toys. In the 1930s it began making other products, including vases, lamps, flowerpots, candlesticks, and children's dishes. Most of the glass is marked with a crow flying through the letter *A*. The company was sold to Clarksburg Glass Co. in 1951. Akro Agate marbles are listed in this book in the Marble category.

Bowl, Large Heart, Carved, Natural Mineral, 5 x 11 x 9 In.	100
Dish, Fish Shape, Jade Green, 5 x 3½ In.	28
Flowerpot, Blue, Marbleized, Ribbed Collar, 2½ x 2 In.	25
Planter, Blue, Marbleized, Jonquil, Marked, 5 x 3 x 2 In.	17
Smoking Set, Ashtray, Cigarette Holder, Box, Green, Marbleized, Box, 5 Piece	295
Sugar & Creamer, Yellow, Octagonal, Child's	35

ALABASTER is a very soft form of gypsum, a stone that resembles marble. It was often carved into vases or statues in Victorian times. There are alabaster carvings being made even today.

Bust, Apollo Belvedere, Marble Plinth & Socle, Signed, O. Scheggi, 18 In. *illus*	2196

Bust, Cupid, Bow In Right Hand, Quiver Of Arrows, C. Lapini, 20 x 10 x 14 In.	4235
Bust, Jeanne D'Arc, Marble, Shift, Head Scarf, 9½ x 10 In.	295
Bust, Joan Of Arc, Head Covering, Rectangular Base, 1900s, 15 In.	308
Bust, Woman, Downcast Eyes, Hair Pinned By Ears, 14 x 13 In.	354
Bust, Woman, Scarf Around Head & Neck, Downcast Eyes, Enrico Castellucci, 11 x 10 In.	153
Bust, Young Girl, Scarf, Lace Edge, 17½ In.	192
Chandelier, Carved, Lobed Sides, Carved Rosettes Border, Bronze Chain, Italy, c.1900, 41 In.	1750
Ewer, Dragon, Rose, Leaves, Stepped Base, 22½ x 5 In.	165
Figure, Buddha, Gilt, Standing On Lotus Base, Holding Pearl, 1900s, 41 In.	240
Lamp, Electric, Art Deco, Woman, Roman Costume, Rock, Nautilus Shell, Waves, 25 In.	1003
Lamp, Electric, Girl Seated, With Cat, Under Umbrella, Emilio Fiaschi Style, 30 In.	390
Lamp, Electric, Lion, Lying Down, On Edge Of Mountain, Roaring, 12½ x 16 In.	1134
Lamp, Electric, Tiger, Crouching, Under Palm Tree, Emilio Fiaschi Style, 26 In.	375
Lamp, Electric, Woman, Nude, Hand Stretched Out, Roses, Robe, Globe Shade, 42 x 17 In.	5670
Lamp, Figure, Engraved Garments, Globe Top, Single Socket, 29 x 9 x 9½ In.	545
Lamp, Nude Figure, Female Fairy, Butterfly Wings, Lily Flower Shape Fountain, 16 x 12 x 8½ In.	787
Lamp, Nude Woman, Inverted Bell, Gadrooned Edges, Giovanni Brogi, 36 x 12 In.	3025
Lamp, Polar Bears, Red Highlighted Eyes, Igloo Globe, Single Socket, 7 x 8½ x 10 In.	726
Pedestal, Carved Spiral, Squat Lotus Leaf Knop, Faceted Base, Italy, c.1900, 37 x 9 In.	458
Sculpture, 2 Children, Walking On Log, Girl's Chin On Boy's Shoulder, c.1900, 17 In. ... illus	236
Sculpture, Lovers, Seminude, Standing, Kissing, A. Cipriani, 27 x 14½ In.	2750
Sculpture, Man, In Armor, Astolfo Vagioli, Signed Verso Truncation, 1800s-1900s, 21 In.	1920
Sculpture, Pope Pius X, Affixed Marble Base, 13 In.	177
Sculpture, Winged Cupid, Amour De La Terre, Signed, C. Lapini, 25 x 15 x 17 In.	4840
Urn, Grapes & Vine Carved Handle, Wavy Grooved Body, Square Base, 17½ x 6 In.	119
Vase, Star Crimped Top, Strong Color, 2¾ In.	330

ALUMINUM was more expensive than gold or silver until the 1850s. Chemists learned how to refine bauxite to get aluminum. Jewelry and other small objects were made of the valuable metal until 1914, when an inexpensive smelting process was invented. The aluminum collected today dates from the 1930s through the 1950s. Hand-hammered pieces are the most popular.

Bread Tray, Rabbits, Arthur Court, 1966, 14 In.	35
Briefcase, Green, Lines, Handle, Rivets, 1920s ... illus	141
Egg, Chromed, Red, Transparent Coat, Jeff Koons, 2008, 4¾ x 3 x 3 In.	562
Sculpture, Abstract Applied Shape On Rectangular Plaque, D. Wagner, 1973, 36 x 28½ In.	1062
Sculpture, Flying Ribbon, Gold Colored, Clear Acrylic Base, Dan Murphy, 1978, 21 x 20 In.	542
Sculpture, Sun Scoop, Powder Coated, Enamel, Yellow, Poles, Tubes, 73 x 67 In.	1875

AMBER, see Jewelry category.

AMBER GLASS is the name of any glassware with the proper yellow-brown shading. It was a popular color just after the Civil War and many pressed glass pieces were made of amber glass. Depression glass of the 1930s–1950s was also made in shades of amber glass. Other pieces may be found in the Depression Glass, Pressed Glass, and other glass categories. All types are being reproduced.

Bottle, Tapered Neck, Applied, Crimped Collar, Below Plain Rim, Free-Blown, 8⅞ x 3¼ In.	900
Bowl, Peacocks, Palms, 6 x 11½ In.	211
Pitcher, Brown, Swirls, 7⅜ In.	25
Pitcher, Coin Spot, Applied Rope Twist Clear Handle, 8 x 6¼ In.	33
Vase, Fish & Seaweed, Enamel, Pinched Sides, Footed, 7½ In. ... illus	71
Vase, Ruffled Flared Mouth, Painted Flower, Leaves, Butterfly, Handles, 9 In., Pair	38

AMBERINA, a two-toned glassware, was originally made from 1883 to about 1900. It was patented by Joseph Locke of the New England Glass Company but was also made by other companies and is still being made. The glass shades from red to amber. Similar pieces of glass may be found in the Baccarat, Libbey, Plated Amberina, and other categories. Glass shaded from blue to amber is called *Blue Amberina* or *Bluerina*.

Agata, Finger Bowl, Peachblow, Ruffled Rim, New England Glass Co., Late 1800s, 2½ In.
$120

Garth's Auctioneers & Appraisers

Agata, Tumbler, Peachblow, Rose To White, Glossy, 1875-99, 3¾ In.
$234

Jeffrey S. Evans

Alabaster, Bust, Apollo Belvedere, Marble Plinth & Socle, Signed, O. Scheggi, 18 In.
$2,196

I.M. Chait

This is an edited listing of current prices. Visit Kovels.com to check thousands of prices from previous years and sign up for free information on trends, tips, reproductions, marks, and more.

Alabaster, Sculpture, 2 Children, Walking On Log, Girl's Chin On Boy's Shoulder, c.1900, 17 In. $236

Cottone Auctions

Aluminum, Briefcase, Green, Lines, Handle, Rivets, 1920s $141

RSL Auction Co.

Amber Glass, Vase, Fish & Seaweed, Enamel, Pinched Sides, Footed, 7 ½ In. $71

Hess Auction Group

Censer, Carved, Animal Finial Lid, Double Handle, Tripod, Chinese, 4 ½ x 4 ½ In.	225
Pitcher, Diamond Optic, Square Neck & Mouth, Reeded Handle, 6 ¾ In.	59
Pitcher, Faceted, Rope Twist Handle, 6 ½ In.	25
Pitcher, Fuchsia At Top, Amber At Bottom, Ribbing, Amber Glass Handle, 7 In.	7260
Syrup, Fuchsia At Top, Amber At Bottom, Ribbing, Silver Collar & Handle, 5 ½ In.	6655
Tankard, Art Glass, Thumbprint Design, Enamel Flowers, 10 In.	30
Tumbler, Plated, Fuchsia Color At Top, Color Gradation, Ribbing, 4 In.	726
Vase, Applied Pulled Twist, Ruby Flowers, 12 In. .... illus	70
Vase, Diamond-Quilted, 3 Ribbed Amber Glass Applied Feet, 6 In.	180
Vase, Satin Glass, Purple, Red, Yellow, White, 10 ½ x 4 ½ In.	48

AMERICAN DINNERWARE, *see Dinnerware.*

AMERICAN ENCAUSTIC TILING COMPANY was founded in Zanesville, Ohio, in 1875. The company planned to make a variety of tiles to compete with the English tiles that were selling in the United States for use in fireplaces and other architectural designs. The first glazed tiles were made in 1880, embossed tiles in 1881, faience tiles in the 1920s. The firm closed in 1935 and reopened in 1937 as the Shawnee Pottery.

Paperweight, Pencil Holder, Ram, Crystalline Glaze, Impressed, 3 ½ In. .... illus	200
Tile, Cavalier, Frame, Brown Glaze, 18 x 6 In.	125
Tile, Medieval Priest, Squeezebag Decoration, Terra-Cotta, Multicolor, 14 ¼ x 9 In. .... illus	600
Tile, Persian Prince, Kneeling, Blue, Green, Brown, c.1882, 14 x 10 In.	500

AMETHYST GLASS is any of the many glasswares made in the dark purple color of the gemstone amethyst. Included in this category are many pieces made in the nineteenth and twentieth centuries. Very dark pieces are called *black amethyst.*

Bowl, Globe Form, Circle Decoration, Diamond Pattern, 1900s, 6 In.	24
Decanter, White Dot Flowers, Green Leaves, Stopper, 13 ¾ x 4 ¾ In.	22
Marmalade, Ruffled Rim, 7 x 6 ½ In.	133
Rose Bowl, Pedestal, Clear Foot, Gold Trim, Applied Colored Jewel Highlights, 8 x 6 In.	84
Vase, Cut To Clear, Petal Shape Fluting, 10 x 9 ¾ In., Pair	238
Amethyst Glass, Vase, Gilt, Courting Couple, Treen, Acanthus Scroll, 7 ¼ x 4 In., Pair.... illus	695
Vase, Trumpet, Scalloped Rim, 6-Sided Base, Bull's-Eye, Oval, Sandwich, 1800s, 8 In.	431

AMPHORA *pieces are listed in the Teplitz category.*

ANDIRONS *and related fireplace items are included in the Fireplace category.*

ANIMAL TROPHIES, such as stuffed animals (taxidermy), rugs made of animal skins, and other similar collectibles made from animal, fish, or bird parts, are listed in this category. Collectors should be aware of the endangered species laws that make it illegal to buy and sell some of these items. Any eagle feathers, many types of pelts or rugs (such as leopard), ivory, rhinoceros horn, and many forms of tortoiseshell can be confiscated by the government. Related trophies may be found in the Fishing category. Ivory items may be found in the Scrimshaw or Ivory categories.

Atlantic Sailfish, Caught Off Miami, Mounted On Wave Base, 1990s, 96 In.	840
Bear, Cinnamon Black, Full Wall Mount, 60 In.	531
Bear, Rug, Brown, Claws, Black Felt Border, c.1960, 66 x 56 In.	390
Black Bear, Head, Shoulders, Front Legs, Wall Mount With Branch, c.1935, 33 In.	625
Blue Wildebeest, Botswana, Shoulder Mount, 1990s, 29 x 26 In.	240
Brook Trout, Head Left Mount, Walnut Plaque, 12 x 27 In.	726
Brook Trout, Head Right Mount, Oval Plaque, David Footer, 11 x 24 In.	847
Brook Trout, Real Skin, Mounted, Mahogany Back, Nash Of Maine, 1903, 26 In.	360
Cape Boar, Head, Shoulder Wall Mount, 20 In.	94
Cape Buffalo, Head, Shoulder Wall Mount, Horn Spread, 6 x 35 In.	165
Elk Hooves, Pair, Mounted Wood Display, 23 x 8 In.	24
Elk, Shoulder Mount, 6-Point Antlers, c.1950, 58 x 56 In.	484
Salmon, Carved, Painted, On Plaque, Signed, Lawrence C. Irvine, 15 x 34 In. .... illus	1150

Salmon, Carved, Painted, White Birch Bark Backboard, Lawrence C. Irvine, 15 ½ In.	*illus*	1452
Trout, Glass Eyes, Pine Backboard, Marked Mike Borrett, 24 In.		780
Turkey, Full Wall Mount, Wide Fan, 10 x 25 In.		71
Walleye, Lake Erie, 14 Lb., 1990s, Wall Mount, 31 In.		48
Wild Boar, Shoulder Mount, 20 x 14 In.	*illus*	127

ANIMATION ART collectibles include cels that are painted drawings on celluloid needed to make animated cartoons shown in movie theaters or on TV. Hundreds of cels were made, then photographed in sequence to make a cartoon showing moving figures. Early examples made by the Walt Disney Studios are popular with collectors today. Original sketches used by the artists are also listed here. Modern animated cartoons are made using computer-generated pictures. Some of these are being produced as cels to be sold to collectors. Other cartoon art is listed in Comic Art and Disneyana.

Cel, Charlie Brown Christmas, Peanuts, Charles Schulz, Promotional Production, 10 x 7¾ In.	311
Cel, Charlie Brown, Red Background, Peanuts, Charles Schulz, 4¼ x 3½ In.	147
Cel, Disney, Demonstration, 5-Step Process, Pencil Drawing To Painting, 1993, 7½ x 11 In.	102
Cel, Disney, Scrooge McDuck, Ratty, Moley, Mickey's Christmas Scene, 1983, 10 x 13 In.	226
Cel, Donald Duck, Chips Ahoy, Clarence Nash Autograph, 8¼ x 11 In.	90
Cel, Hand Drawn, Jose Carioca, Donald Duck, 10 x 13 In.	170
Cel, Owl & Piglet, Piglet Whispering To Owl, Hand Painted, Disney, 1977	280
Drawing, Br'er Rabbit, Song Of The South, Graphite On Paper, Disney, 6 x 6½ In.	124
Illustration, Mr. Toad, Adventures, Gouache, Disney, Signed, Don Williams, 1986, 7 x 18 In.	254
Illustration, Uncle Scrooge, 7 Panels, Original Art Page, Signed, Carl Barks, 14 x 9¾ In.	396
Serigraph, Jetsons Original, Inscribed & Signed, Bill Hanna & Joe Barbera, 10 x 13 In.	124

ANNA POTTERY was started in Anna, Illinois, in 1859 by Cornwall and Wallace Kirkpatrick. They made many types of utilitarian wares, bricks, drain tiles, and giftware. The most collectible pieces made by the pottery are the pig-shaped bottles and jugs with special inscriptions, applied animals, and figures. The pottery closed in 1894.

Anna Pottery

Flask, Pig, Reclining, Incised Poem, Shortest, Quickest, Cheapest, 1880, 6¼ In.	5227
Pitcher, Frog, Tree Stump, Oak Branches, Acorns, Monkey Handle, 1885, 13⅝ In.	2091

APPLE PEELERS *are listed in the Kitchen category under Peeler, Apple.*

ARABIA began producing ceramics in 1874. The pottery was established in Helsinki, Finland, by Rörstrand, a Swedish pottery that wanted to export porcelain, earthenware, and other pottery from Finland to Russia. Most of the early workers at Arabia were Swedish. Arabia started producing its own models of tiled stoves, vases, and tableware about 1900. Rörstrand sold its interest in Arabia in 1916. By the late 1930s, Arabia was the largest producer of porcelain in Europe. Most of its products were exported. A line of stoneware was introduced in the 1960s. Arabia worked in cooperation with Rörstrand from 1975 to 1977. Arabia was bought by Hackman Group in 1990 and Hackman was bought by Iittala Group in 2004. Fiskars Corporation bought Iittala in 2007 and Arabia is now a brand owned by Fiskars.

ARABIA FINLAND

Cup & Saucer, Demitasse, Blue Finn Flower Pattern	20
Figurine, Giraffe, Cream, Brown Spots, Marked, 10 In.	170
Pitcher, Brown Cow, Kkaj Franck, Finland, 4 In.	58
Plaque, Bird, Barbed Wire Fence, Iridescent Glaze, Marked, 8 x 6 In.	75
Teapot, Infuser, Brown Matte Glaze, Mottled, Squat, 5 Cup	45
Vase, Ball Shape, Raised Rings, Blue Bands, Gilt, 6½ In.	77
Vase, Black, Gray, Peach Marbleized, Luster, c.1930, 6 x 5 In. ..... *illus*	60

ARCHITECTURAL antiques include a variety of collectibles, usually very large, that have been removed from buildings. Hardware, backbars, doors, paneling, and even old bathtubs are now wanted by collectors. Pieces of the Victorian, Art Nouveau, and Art Deco styles are in greatest demand.

Arch, Terra-Cotta, Relief, Figural Putti, Heavy Filigree, 2 Sections, 45 x 52 x 9 In.	605

Amberina, Vase, Applied Pulled Twist, Ruby Flowers, 12 In.
$70

Woody Auction

American Encaustic, Paperweight, Pencil Holder, Ram, Crystalline Glaze, Impressed, 3½ In.
$200

Humler & Nolan

American Encaustic, Tile, Medieval Priest, Squeezebag Decoration, Terra-Cotta, Multicolor, 14¼ x 9 In.
$600

Thomaston Place Auction Galleries

Amethyst Glass, Vase, Gilt, Courting Couple, Treen, Acanthus Scroll, 7¼ x 4 In., Pair
$695

Ruby Lane

Animal Trophy, Salmon, Carved, Painted, On Plaque, Signed, Lawrence C. Irvine, 15 x 34 In.
$1,150

James D. Julia Auctioneers

Animal Trophy, Salmon, Carved, Painted, White Birch Bark Backboard, Lawrence C. Irvine, 15½ In.
$1,452

James D. Julia Auctioneers

Animal Trophy, Wild Boar, Shoulder Mount, 20 x 14 In.
$127

DuMouchelles

Bathtub, Bronzed, Iron, Pottery Tile, Mahogany Rim, Legs, c.1900, 28 x 68 In.	4250
Corbel, Wood, Seahorse, Stylized, White, 28 In., Pair	409
Door Handle, Bronze, Mask, Mythical Beasts, Double Scroll Handle, 13¼ In.	406
Door Handle, Steel, Lunar Surface, Polished, Blacked, James Bearden, 19½ x 3 In., Pair	1000
Door, Farmhouse, Pine, Iron Grate Panel, Blue Paint, France, c.1800, 71 x 19 In., Pair ... *illus*	726
Door, Walnut, Entryway, Carved, Iron, Giltwood Frame, Phil Powell, 86½ In. *illus*	33750
Door, Wood, 2 Panels, 4 Bars, Side Clasping Lock, Green, France, c.1775, 69 x 20 In., Pair	1920
Door, Wood, Amusement Ride Pan, Pinstripe, Rose Bouquet, Metal Fittings, France, 1900s, 26 x 48 In.	113
Door, Wood, Arched, Rococo Style, Painted, Gilt, Scrollwork, Pair, 1800s, 91 x 57 In.	3500
Door, Wood, Cabinet, Gilt, Carved, Religious Portraits, Italy, Pair, c.1925, 67 In.	4000
Door, Wood, Carved, 8 Panels, Animals, Nailheads, Ring Pulls, 85½ x 24 In., Pair *illus*	1098
Door, Wood, Carved, Geometric, Lizard, Dogon People, Mali, 22 x 16 In.	125
Doorknocker, Metal, Half Circle, Radiating Rivets, Ring, 17 x 9 In., Pair	175
Doorknocker, Metal, Mask, Grotesque, Horned Head, Knocker Ring In Mouth, 14 x 8¼ In.	188
Doorway, Wood, Fretwork, Stick & Ball Border, Chain-Link Panels, Fan, 24 x 81 In. *illus*	938
Element, Giltwood, Leaves, Flowers Flanked By Scrolls, France, c.1850, 10 x 57 In.	2375
Elevator Grate, Cast Iron, Grid, Scrolls, Flaherty Iron Works, 80 x 12 In., Pair	153
Fireboard, Wood, Farm Scene, American Flag, Applied Trim, Arched Top, 1900s, 26 x 32 In.	330
Fireplace Surround, Carved Marble, Floral & Scroll Design, Louis XV Style, 48 x 68 In.	1188
Fireplace Surround, Marble, Carved, Shell, Leaves, Louis XV Style, c.1900, 46 x 58 In.	8125
Fireplace Surround, Marble, Molded Edge, Serpentine Frieze, Louis XVI, c.1900, 46 x 58 In.	5000
Fireplace Surround, Wood, George III, Carved, Stained, 54½ x 68¼ In.	406
Gate, Iron, Arched, Fleur-De-Lis, Scrolls, White Paint, 1900, 68 x 33 In., Pair	1750
Gate, Iron, Post, Ball Finial, 44 In.	532
Gate, Lock, Iron, Violin Shape, Continental, c.1900, 14½ In.	469
Gate, Neoclassical, Gilt Bronze, Peryton Center, Leaves, Scrolls, 1800s, 31 x 29 In., Pair .. *illus*	3965
Gate, Wood, Automatic, Weight Counter-Balance, Patent, Harry Stauffer, 1923, 37 x 21 x 10 In.	100
Gate, Wrought Iron, Spear Finials, 5½ In.	60
Grate, Iron, Demilune, Circles, Leaves, 21 x 41½ In.	30
Lamp Post, Maidens Holding Shade, Electrified, M. Vance & Co., c.1875, 60 x 13 In., Pair	4250
Mailbox, Front Door, Latch, Slant Roof, Newspaper Loops, Iron Griswold, c.1895, 13 x 6 In.	350
Mantel, Fireplace, Herter Brothers, Bird's-Eye Maple, Inlay, Columns, c.1880, 46 x 84 In. *illus*	4800
Mantel, Hood, Renaissance Revival, Walnut, c.1880, 124 x 73 In. *illus*	2500
Mantel, Marble, Rococo, Serpentine, Scrolled Flower Corners, c.1850, 49 x 75 In.	5795
Mantel, Walnut, Serpentine Shelf, Raised Panel, Flowers, c.1775, 44¾ x 81¾ In.	1920
Model, Staircase, Metal, Patinated, Wrought Railing, Wood Base, c.1890, 18 x 20½ In.	500
Molding, Wood, Angel, Wings, Face, Shelf, Ebonized, 1800s, 11 x 30 In.	96
Molding, Wood, Carved, Gesso, Accent, 1700s, 7 x 9 x 1¼ In.	30
Ornament, Cast Iron, Star, Round, Red, 1800s, 8 In.	95
Ornament, Copper, Gilt, Full Bodied American Eagle, Massachusetts, 1880, 31 x 32 In.	1750
Ornament, Sailor, Figural, Acanthus Instead Of Legs, 55 x 21 In., Pair	9375
Overmantel Mirror, Giltwood, Leaves & Acorns, 3 Sections, 1800s, 25 x 66 In. *illus*	300
Padlock, Figural, Hunchback, Open Mouth, Key	2052
Panel, Iron, Alternating Squares & Crosses, Openwork, J. Royere, 98 x 68 In., Pair	8750
Railing, Wrought Iron, Geometric Design, 117 x 54 In.	3545
Roof Tile, Lion, Miry, Buddhist, C.K. Chan, Chinese, 1900s	444
Screens are listed in the Fireplace and Furniture categories.	
Shield, Iron, Rosette, Sun Form, Dug, Continental, 1200s, 5¾ In.	60
Wall Bracket, Wood, Stylized Ferns, Conical, Continental, 15 x 13½ In.	32
Wall Bracket, Wood, Wood Knots, Arched, Circle Cutouts, Arts & Crafts, 42 x 16 In., Pair	64

AREQUIPA POTTERY was produced from 1911 to 1918 by the patients of the Arequipa Sanatorium in Marin County, north of San Francisco. The patients were trained by Frederick Hurten Rhead, who had worked at Roseville Pottery.

Vase, Cherry Blossoms, Microcrystalline Glaze, Globular, c.1910, 4 x 6 In.	875
Vase, Incised Stylized Flowers, Brown, Green, F. Rhead, c.1911-13, 5¼ x 3¾ In. *illus*	1342
Vase, Squeezebag Decoration, Heart Shape Leaves, Brown, Cream, F. Rhead, 3½ x 3 In.	5625

Arabia, Vase, Black, Gray, Peach Marbleized, Luster, c.1930, 6 x 5 In.
$60

Ruby Lane

Architectural, Door, Farmhouse, Pine, Iron Grate Panel, Blue Paint, France, c.1800, 71 x 19 In., Pair
$726

James D. Julia Auctioneers

Architectural, Door, Walnut, Entryway, Carved, Iron, Giltwood Frame, Phil Powell, 86 ½ In.
$33,750

Rago Arts and Auction Center

Architectural, Door, Wood, Carved, 8 Panels, Animals, Nailheads, Ring Pulls, 85 ½ x 24 In., Pair
$1,098

Neal Auction Co.

Architectural, Doorway, Wood, Fretwork, Stick & Ball Border, Chain-Link Panels, Fan, 24 x 81 In.
$938

Garth's Auctioneers & Appraisers

Architectural, Gate, Neoclassical, Gilt Bronze, Peryton Center, Leaves, Scrolls, 1800s, 31 x 29 In., Pair
$3,965

Neal Auction Co.

Architectural, Mantel, Fireplace, Herter Brothers, Bird's-Eye Maple, Inlay, Columns, c.1880, 46 x 84 In.
$4,800

Naudeau's Auction Gallery

Architectural, Mantel, Hood, Renaissance Revival, Walnut, c.1880, 124 x 73 In.
$2,500

Heritage Auctions

Architectural, Overmantel Mirror, Giltwood, Leaves & Acorns, 3 Sections, 1800s, 25 x 66 In.
$300

Brunk Auctions

A

Arequipa, Vase, Incised Stylized Flowers, Brown, Green, F. Rhead, c.1911-13, 5 ¼ x 3 ¾ In.
$1,342

Rago Arts and Auction Center

Auto, Hood Ornament, Boyce Moto-Meter, Chromed Winged Base, Mercury, Metal, 6 x 6 x 10 In.
$531

AntiqueAdvertising.com

Auto, Hood Ornament, Indian Chief Head, Pontiac, Metal, 1920s, 2 ⅜ x 5 x 4 In.
$838

AntiqueAdvertising.com

ARGY-ROUSSEAU, *see G. Argy-Rousseau category.*

 ARITA is a port in Japan. Porcelain was made there from about 1616. Many types of decorations were used, including the popular Imari designs, which are listed under Imari in this book.

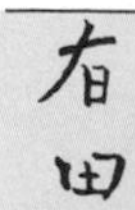

Charger, Blue, White, Flower Garden, 16 In.	480
Jar, Lid, Scholars, Immortals, Landscape, Reclining Figure Finial, White, Blue, Japan, 8 ½ In.	375
Jar, Temple, Blue, White, Embossed, Coastal Villages, Mountains, 20 In.	219
Vase, Bushes, Trees, Flowers, Rocks, Blue, White, 1700s, 9 ½ In.	125

 ART DECO, or Art Moderne, a style started at the Paris Exposition of 1925, is characterized by linear, geometric designs. All types of furniture and decorative arts, jewelry, book bindings, and even games were designed in this style. Additional items may be found in the Furniture category or in various glass and pottery categories, etc.

Ashtray, Woman, Nude, Backward Bending, Holding Tambourine, Amber Glass Insert, 36 In.	224
Bowl, Glass, Mottled Pink, Yellow & Amber, Impressed Art Verrier St, 1920s, 3 x 11 In.	1200
Bowl, Opalescent, 2 Handles, Footed Base, Embossed Signature, Pierre D'Avesn, 10 x 7 In.	158
Case, Cigarette, Yellow Gold, Monogram Opening, 1900s	36
Cigar Box, Rectangular Silver Plate, Female, Arms Outstretched, Radiant Sky, 2 x 7 x 5 In.	215
Figurine, Antelope, Green Patinated Cast Metal, Marble & Slate Base, 13 x 22 x 4 ¾ In.	354
Figurine, Dancing Girls, White Glaze, Porcelain, Signed On Base, Karl Menser, 12 x 7 ¼ x 6 ¾ In.	136
Figurine, Pear, Painted, Polished Gourd, Helen Harrison, 16 In.	59
Figurine, Woman Holding Flowers, Signed, Ernest Gazan, 1930, 9 ¾ x 6 x 4 ½ In.	124
Vase, Black, White Body, Pale Orange, Classical Figures, Man, Phrygian Cap, 1800s, 10 In.	1046
Vase, Bulbous, Bulls & Leaves, Incised Base, Primavera, France, 18 x 13 In.	649
Vase, Large Orange Flowers, Black Accents, Signed, 1900s, 5 ¼ x 5 In.	113
Vase, Translucent Blue, Geometric Decoration, Etched Signature, 6 x 9 ½ In.	565

ART GLASS, *see Glass-Art category.*

 ART NOUVEAU is a style of design that was at its most popular from 1895 to 1905. Famous designers, including Rene Lalique and Emile Galle, produced furniture, glass, silver, metalwork, and buildings in the new style. Ladies with long flowing hair and elongated bodies were among the more easily recognized design elements. Copies of this style are being made today. Many modern pieces of jewelry can be found. Additional Art Nouveau pieces may be found in Furniture or in various glass and porcelain categories.

Bowl, Iridescent Amethyst, Loetz Style, Bronze Fitted Pedestal & Handles, 5 ½ x 11 In.	240
Ewer, Patinated Metal, Figural Handle, Female Nudes, Ch. Perron, c.1900, 8 In.	192
Letter Opener, Woman's Head, Flowing Hair Handle, Wording Embossed, 8 ¾ In.	82
Perfume Bottle, Emerald Green Glass, Silver Overlay, Globular, Flared Rim, 1900, 3 x 3 x 3 In.	94
Perfume Vial, Sterling Silver, Crystal, Silver Lid, Pendant, 1900s, 3 In.	60
Vase, Metal, Hydrangea, Stems, Relief, Yellow, Green Tint, Marked H. Sibeud, 12 In.	295
Vase, Ruby, 2 Handles, Gilt Metal Holder, Marked, Orivit, 9 In.	212

ART POTTERY, *see Pottery-Art category.*

 ARTS & CRAFTS was a design style popular in American decorative arts from 1894 to 1923. In the 1970s collectors began to rediscover Mission furniture, art pottery, metalwork, linens, and light fixtures from this period. The interest has continued. Today everything from this era is collectible, including jewelry, graphics, and silverware. Additional items may be found in the Furniture category and other categories.

Box, Lid, Lotus Blossom, Copper, Blue & Green Enamel, Frank J. Marshall, 2 ¾ x 1 In.	1500
Frame, Louis XIV Style, Carved & Gilded, 25 x 31 In.	176
Garden Bowl, Pottery, Florals, Dark Blue, Matte Glaze, Leaves, Pinholes, 1920, 8 ½ x 3 ¼ In.	24

AURENE PIECES *are listed in the Steuben category.*

AUSTRIA *is a collecting term that covers pieces made by a wide variety of factories. They are listed in this book in categories such as Royal Dux or Porcelain.*

AUTO parts and accessories are collectors' items today. Gas pump globes and license plates are part of this specialty. Prices are determined by age, rarity, and condition. Collectors say "porcelain sign" for enameled iron or steel signs. Packaging related to automobiles may also be found in the Advertising category. Lalique hood ornaments may be listed in the Lalique category.

Button, Member Liberty Motor League, ⅞ In.	9
Can, Bomber Motor Oil, Airplane, Confederate Flag, Rebel Oil Co. Flag, Qt., 5½ x 4 In.	1896
Can, Golden Lion Motor Oil, Tin Lithograph, Lion Image On Both Sides, Full, Qt.	910
Can, Monogram Motor Oil, Stands Up, Red, Row Of Soldiers, Qt.	165
Can, Motor Manor Motor Oil, Knight In Armor, Red, Black, 5⅝ x 4 In.	424
Can, Motor Seal, Highly Refined Motor Oil, Cream, Green, Qt.	129
Can, Sears & Roebuck, Lube Oil, Graphic Image Of Machine, Early, 11 x 6 In.	325
Can, Skunk Oil Motor Oil, Qt.	1427
Can, Whiz, Clutch & Belt Compound, Car, Blue, Yellow, 12 Oz.	153
Clip, Braender Tires, Bulldog, Tied To Tire, Red, 2⅞ x 2⅝ In.	177
Display, Driving Gloves, Aris, Automotive Graphics, Black, Metal Hands, 13 x 10 x 6 In.	38
Display, Hoffman Valves, Man In Front Of Large Radiator, Valves, 16 x 10 x 3⅝ In.	403
Display, Lightbulb, Goodrich Tires, Red, Blue Letters, White, Solar Electric Co., 4 x 3 In.	1208
Engine Compression Chamber, Salesman's Sample, Willys-Knight Automotive Co., 4 x 3 In.	680
Gas Pump, Black Gold Alabama, Red, Metal Frame, Miniature, 33 x 7 x 7 In.	126
Gas Pump, Phillips 66, Ethyl, Lighted Globe, Decal, Black & White Accents, 57 x 23 x 21 In.	1071
Gas Pump, Sinclair, Metal Tag, White, Green, 2-Sided, Tokheim, 1947, 59 x 39 x 16 In.	4800
Gas Pump, Texaco Gilbarco, Firetruck Colors, Stainless Steel Rim, Restored, 1953, 60 x 28 x 16 In.	3000
Hood Ornament, Boyce Moto-Meter, Chromed Winged Base, Mercury, Metal, 6 x 6 x 10 In.. *illus*	531
Hood Ornament, Centaur, Art Deco, 5¾ x 8 In.	306
Hood Ornament, Falcon, Chromed Metal, 3 x 6½ In.	259
Hood Ornament, Ford, Flying Quail, 3¼ x 4¾ In.	236
Hood Ornament, Indian Chief Head, Pontiac, Metal, 1920s, 2⅜ x 5 x 4 In. *illus*	838
Hood Ornament, Mack Trucks, Dog, Light-Up Eyes, Chromed Metal, 4 x 4¾ In.	59
Hood Ornament, Policeman, Rotating Arms, Swivel Base, Cast Aluminum, 8 In. *illus*	270
License Plate Attachment, I Fly At Beckerman Field, Airplane, 1950s, 5⅝ x 9⅞ In.	236
License Plate Attachment, Pilots Association, Wings, Embossed, Chrome Finish, 3 x 8 In.	318
License Plate, National Recovery Act, Eagle Design, Trucking Industry, 1934	72
License Plate, Tennessee, Dealer, 2D-3647, 1949	55
License Plate, Tennessee, Orange, 44-64, White Letters, 1951	55
Light, Taxicab, White Cylinder, Amber Lights On Ends, 3 x 12 In. *illus*	720
Parking Meter, Coin-Operated, Dual Mode Features, Carl C. Magee, 1935, 51 x 16 In.	246
Ring, Packard, Gold, Executive Presentation, Bloodstone, 1⅛ x ¾ In.	6900
Service Station Globe, Air, Tire Pump, White, Red Letters, Lenses Both Side, 11 x 5 x 10 In.	1064
Shift Knob, Ford, Plastic, Embossed Brass Logo, San Diego Ford Building, 1935, 1½ x 1⅝ In.	165
Sign, AC, Service, Auto Products, 1940, 21 x 10 In.	3220
Sign, Auto-Lite, Authorized Electric Service, Porcelain, Flange, 2-Sided, 12 x 15 In.	1610
Sign, BMW, Logo, Round, Blue, Black, White, Metal, 12 In.	62
Sign, Esso, 2-Sided, Oval Frame, Complete Support, 1950, 66 x 90 x 2 In.	3800
Sign, Exide, Car, Batteries, Pictures Battery, Flange, Tin Lithograph, 14 x 14 In.	1265
Sign, Firestone Tire, Tire Graphic, Porcelain Strip, 48 x 20 In.	2040
Sign, Francisco Auto Heater, Tin Lithograph, Self-Framed, 18 x 40 In. *illus*	3658
Sign, Gillette Tires, Batteries, Bear, Tire, Metal, Embossed, Self-Framed, c.1952, 19 x 73 In.	265
Sign, Kendall Motor Oils, Red, White, Round, 24 In.	684
Sign, Majestic Garage, Racing, Car, 12 x 22 In.	489
Sign, Marathon Tires, Touring Car, Tin Lithograph, Clear Coated, 1915, 23 x 17 In.	9225
Sign, Maserati, Logo, Blue, Red, Round, 12 In.	187
Sign, Mobil Gas, Logo, Red, Blue, 12 x 12¼ In.	389
Sign, Mobil Oil, Ask For Gargoyle, White, Red Gargoyle, Black Letters, Porcelain, 24 x 19 In.	1323
Sign, Mobil Pegasus, In Shape Of Flying Horse, Red, Porcelain, 40 x 56 In.	4370
Sign, No Parking Here, Silver, Cast Metal, Oval, 40½ In.	204

Auto, Hood Ornament, Policeman, Rotating Arms, Swivel Base, Cast Aluminum, 8 In.
$270

Rich Penn Auctions

Auto, Light, Taxicab, White Cylinder, Amber Lights On Ends, 3 x 12 In.
$720

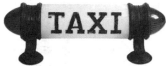

Rich Penn Auctions

Auto, Sign, Francisco Auto Heater, Tin Lithograph, Self-Framed, 18 x 40 In.
$3,658

Wm Morford Auctions

Auto, Sign, Tire Tag, Bicycle, Yellow Kid, Puncturoid, 2-Sided, Cardboard, 3 x 1⅝ In.
$425

AntiqueAdvertising.com

Autumn Leaf, Cookie Jar, Lid, Finial, Handles, 9¼ In.
$30

Specialists of the South

Autumn Leaf, Teapot, Aladdin, 10¼ In.
$60

Ruby Lane

Autumn Leaf, Vase, Wall Pocket, Thailand, 8½ In.
$47

Replacements, Ltd.

Sign, Odell Tires, Tin Lithograph, Flange, 13 x 17 In.	1064
Sign, Pennfield Motor Oils, Finest From Pennsylvania Fields, 13¾ x 19¾ In.	672
Sign, Phillips 66, Red, White, Black, 2-Sided, 70 x 70 In.	357
Sign, Pump, Texaco, Green T In Red Star, Porcelain Base, 2-Sided, 17 x 15 In.	3105
Sign, Richlube Motor Oil, Shield & Car, Porcelain, 24 In.	4800
Sign, Seaside Gasoline, Sea Gull, Die Cut, Porcelain, 44 x 44 In.	4500
Sign, Security Oils & Greases, Anchor Graphics, Porcelain, 22 x 18 In.	2700
Sign, Signal Gasoline Stoplight, Globe Lenses, 15 In.	7380
Sign, Sinclair HC Gasoline, Green, Red, White, Porcelain, 14 x 14 In.	1955
Sign, Texgas, Pump Plate, White, Red & Blue Letters, Enameled Porcelain, 7 x 14 In.	316
Sign, Tire Tag, Bicycle, Yellow Kid, Puncturoid, 2-Sided, Cardboard, 3 x 1⅝ In. _illus_	425
Sign, Veedol, Motor Oil, Can Is King, Pictures King On Top Of Can, 60 x 28 In.	1436
Tire Gauge, Buick Logo, Navy, White, US Gauge Co., 3¼ x 2 In.	153
Traffic Light, Green, One-Way, Iron, Aluminum, Lacquer, Brick-Like Pattern, 90 x 16 x 18 In.	510
Watch, Packard Motor Car Co., Executive Presentation, c.1940, 2 x 1¾ In.	603
Weather Vane, Pontiac, Dealership, Indian Head Silhouette, Iron, 32 x 28 In.	1380

AUTUMN LEAF pattern china was made for the Jewel Tea Company beginning in 1933. Hall China Company of East Liverpool, Ohio, Crooksville China Company of Crooksville, Ohio, Harker Potteries of Chester, West Virginia, and Paden City Pottery, Paden City, West Virginia, made dishes with this design. Autumn Leaf has remained popular and was made by Hall China Company until 1978. Some other pieces in the Autumn Leaf pattern are still being made. For more prices, go to kovels.com.

Bowl, Salad, 9 In.	14
Bowl, Vegetable, Oval, 10⅜ In.	22
Cake Plate, 9½ In.	28
Coffeepot, 9½ x 6 x 8½ In.	50
Coffeepot, Hall's Superior, Gold Trim, 9½ x 6 x 8½ In.	50
Cookie Jar, Lid, Finial, Handles, 9¼ In. _illus_	30
Cup & Saucer	9
Jug, Ball, 80 Oz.	37
Jug, Utility, 40 Oz.	21
Pitcher, Ball Jug, Marked	87
Platter, 11¼ In.	35
Platter, 13 In.	27
Teapot, Aladdin, 10¼ In. _illus_	60
Tray, Stenciled, Tole, 9 x 11 In.	59
Vase, Wall Pocket, Thailand, 8½ In. _illus_	47

AVON _bottles are listed in the Bottle category under Avon._

AZALEA dinnerware was made for Larkin Company customers from about 1915 to 1941. Larkin, the soap company, was in Buffalo, New York. The dishes were made by Noritake China Company of Japan. Each piece of the white china was decorated with pink azaleas.

Cachepot, Green, 5½ x 6¼ In.	20
Dinner Plate, 10½ In.	29
Milk Jug, Pink & Turquoise, 5¾ x 18 In.	122
Platter, Ironstone, 14½ x 18 In.	45
Platter, Noritake, 8¾ x 11¾ In.	55

BACCARAT glass was made in France by La Compagnie des Cristalleries de Baccarat, located 150 miles from Paris. The factory was started in 1765. The firm went bankrupt and began operating again about 1822. Cane and millefiori paperweights were made during the 1845 to 1880 period. The firm is still working near Paris making paperweights and glasswares.

Candelabrum, 4-Light, 3 Arms, Swirled Stem, Vase Base, Prisms, 19 x 12 In., Pair	1500

Caviar Set, Bowl & Ice Basin, 1900s, 4 x 7 In.	300
Decanter, Whiskey, Crystal, Harmonie, Stoppers, Signed, Box, Pair, 1900s, 10 x 3½ In.	750
Dresser Box, Lid, Cranberry, Apple Green, Acid Cut Flowers & Lattice, Round, 3½ x 6 In.	270
Figurine, Madonna, Robed, Cross For Face, Marked, 1900s, 7 In. .... *illus*	365
Figurine, Panther, Seated, 6 x 3 In.	94
Figurine, Sphinx, 3¾ x 4¾ In.	187
Lamp, Opaline Glass, Painted Japonisme Birds, Moon, Rosewood Base, 1880, 18 x 18 x 13 In.	336
Lamp, Photophore, Rope Twist Stem, Spread Foot, Leafy Shade, 1800s, 14 x 5 In., Pair	366
Paperweight, Blue Dahlia, 29 Petals, 5 Green Leaves, 1972, 2¼ In.	225
Paperweight, Concentric, Millefiori, 1971, 3½ In.	700
Paperweight, Zodiac, Gemini, Blue, Faced, 2¾ In.	54
Vase, Flared Rim, Tapered Fluted Body, Brass Bottom Collar, Cut Glass Foot, 12 x 8½ In.	148
Vase, Round, Amber, 5½ In.	125

BADGES have been used since before the Civil War. Collectors search for examples of all types, including law enforcement and company identification badges. Well-known prison or law enforcement badges are most desirable. Most are made of nickel or brass. Many recent reproductions have been made.

Deputy Sheriff, Washington State, Shield, Eagle, George F. Cake Co., c.1935, 3 x 3 In.	705
Detective, Inspector Post's, J.D.C., General Foods Premium, 1932, 1⅝ In.	20
Employee, Gillette Tire Co., Logo, Cloisonne, Enamel Number 1399, 1⅝ x 1⅜ In.	153
Labor Day-Hawthorne Park, Bronze, Bullion Border, Pacific Regalia Mfg., c.1920s	110
Police, Apache Indian Nation, 6-Point Star, 3½ In.	80
U.S. Marshal, Brass, 3¼ In.	45
Visitor, Harley-Davidson Factory, 1950s Bike, Red, Chromed, 1¼ x 1⅜ In.	165
Visitor, Harley-Davidson Factory, c.1949 Pan Head Bike, Blue, 1⅜ In.	118

BANKS of metal have been made since 1868. There are still banks, mechanical banks, and registering banks (those that show the total money deposited on the face of the bank). Many old iron or tin banks have been reproduced since the 1950s in iron or plastic. Some old reproductions marked *Book of Knowledge, John Wright,* or *Capron* may be listed. Pottery, glass, and plastic banks are also listed here. Mickey Mouse and other Disneyana banks are listed in Disneyana. We have added the M numbers based on *The Penny Bank Book: Collecting Still Banks* by Andy and Susan Moore and the R numbers based on *Coin Banks by Banthrico* by James L. Redwine.

Alphabet, Prism Shape, Gold Finish, M 1604, 1900s, 4 In.	1320
Apple, Cast Iron, Kyser & Rex, M 1621, 5¼ x 3 In.	554
Bank Building, Book Keeper's Magic Bank, Tin, Painted, 6¼ x 5 In.	3383
Bank Building, Chicago Bank, Cast Iron, John Harper, M 1067, 1893, 6 x 5½ In.	3900
Bank Building, Columbia, Cast Iron, Kenton, M 1070, 5 In.	275
Bank Building, Home Savings Bank, Cast Iron, Dog, Finial, J. & E. Stevens, M 1237, 6 In.	123
Bank Building, Presto Bank, Cast Iron, Kyser & Rex, 3¾ x 4½ In.	349
Bank Building, Tower Bank, Cast Iron, Painted, Combination Lock, Kyser & Rex, M 1198, 7 In.	390
Baseball Player, Gold Uniform, Red Stockings, Red Hat, Bat, In Hands, A.C. Williams, M 18, 6 In.	210
Buffalo, Tail Twists To Remove, Cast Iron, Semimechanical, 9¾ x 5¾ In.	840
Bull, Cast, White Painted, 6 x 11 In.	123
Cannon, Marked U.S., Shoots Penny, Hits Castle, Dreadnught Marked Spain, 1898, 8½ In.	1440
City, Cast Iron, Yellow Chimney, Butterfly Trap, M 1101, 7 x 4½ In.	1800
Devil, 2 Faces, Red, Cast Iron, A.C. Williams, M 31, 4½ In.	720
Dog, Mottled Green & Brown Glaze, Coleslaw Fur, Geo. Wagner, Penn., c.1860, 6 In.	1190
Dog, Spitz, Grey Iron Casting Co., M 409, 4½ x 4¼ In.	175
Doghouse, Bulldog, White, Ring-Hanger Collar, White Bead Eyes, 1900s, 7 x 10 In.	2125
Economy Accumulates Wealth, Cast Iron, Nickeled, Beehive Top, 7 x 7 In.	738
Eiffel Tower, Cast Iron, Sydenham & McOustra, M 1074, 9 x 5½ In.	1046
Elephant With Chariot, Cast Iron, Paint, Hubley, M 467, 8¼ In.	450
Freezer, North Pole Bank, Ice Cream, Nickel Plated, Grey Iron Casting, M 1371, 1922-28, 4 In.	212
Gas Pump, Fire Chief, Nickel Plated, Silver Nozzle, 15 x 5½ In.	96
Globe, Coin Slot, Paper, Pedestal, Cast Iron, 4¼ In.	360

Baccarat, Figurine, Madonna, Robed, Cross For Face, Marked, 1900s, 7 In.
$365

Leland Little Auctions

Bank, Mechanical, Acrobat, Gymnast Kicks Clown, Cast Iron, J. & E. Stevens, c.1890, 5 x 7 In.
$2,520

Cowan's Auctions

Bank, Mechanical, Bulldog, Glass Eyes, Tail Trigger, J. & E. Stevens, c.1875, 8 x 6½ In.
$1,440

Thomaston Place Auction Galleries

Bank, Mechanical, Elephant, Howdah, Man Pops Out, Cast Iron, c.1885, 5 ½ In.
$575

Theriault's

Bank, Mechanical, Lion, Monkey, Yellow, Green, Cast Iron, 9 ½ x 9 In.
$676

Cottone Auctions

Bank, Mechanical, Magician, Lowers Arms, Hat Covers Coin, J. & E. Stevens, c.1910, 8 x 7 In.
$1,920

Cowan's Auctions

Bank, Mechanical, Monkey & Parrot, Tin, Saalheimer & Strauss, Germany, 1930s, 6 x 4 ½ In.
$246

Cowan's Auctions

Bank, Mechanical, Novelty Bank, Door Opens, Teller, Iron, J. & E. Stevens, c.1890, 7 x 5 In.
$570

Cowan's Auctions

Bank, Mechanical, Rabbit, Cabbage, Coin Slot, Ears Lift, Cast Iron, Kilgore, c.1910, 2 x 4 In.
$390

Cowan's Auctions

Bank, Mechanical, Uncle Sam, Coin Falls Into Bag, Beard Moves, 1886, 11 ½ x 5 In.
$870

Thomaston Place Auction Galleries

Barber, Chair, Horse Head, Yellow Enamel, Leather Seat, Emil J. Paidar, c.1910, 43 x 21 In.
$3,600

Cowan's Auctions

Gollywog, Brass, Oxidation, M 87, England, 5¾ In.	60
Graf Zeppelin, Silvered, Cast Iron, A.C. Williams, M 1428, 6¾ In.	200
Grandfather Clock, Cast Iron, Japanned, M 1543, 7 x 4 In.	3075
Indian Family, Cast Iron, J.M. Harper, M 224, 4 x 5 In.	660

Mechanical banks were first made about 1870. Any bank with moving parts is considered mechanical. The metal banks made before World War I are the most desirable. Copies and new designs of mechanical banks have been made in metal or plastic since the 1920s. The condition of the paint on the old banks is important. Worn paint can lower a price by 90 percent.

Mechanical, 3 Football Players, Cast Iron, Painted, J. & E. Stevens, 1800s, 6 x 7½ In.	3600
Mechanical, Acrobat, Gymnast Kicks Clown, Cast Iron, J. & E. Stevens, c.1890, 5 x 7 In. . . *illus*	2520
Mechanical, Artillery, Soldier, Cannon, Fort Wall, Cast Iron, J. & E. Stevens, 8 x 6 In.	1169
Mechanical, Artillery, Union Soldier With Cannon, J. & E. Stevens, c.1892	540
Mechanical, Bank Building, Panorama, Coin Changes Scene, J. & E. Stevens, 7 x 4½ In.	1815
Mechanical, Bear & Tree Stump, Cast Iron, Judd, 5 In.	400
Mechanical, Betsy Ross & Flag, Cast Iron, 11 In.	677
Mechanical, Boy Robbing Bird's Nest, Tree, Cast Iron, J. & E. Stevens, 6 x 8 In.	4920
Mechanical, Boy Scout Camp, Boy Raises Flag, Cast Iron, J. & E. Stevens, 9¾ In.	1968
Mechanical, Bulldog, Glass Eyes, Tail Trigger, J. & E. Stevens, c.1875, 8 x 6½ In. .... *illus*	1440
Mechanical, Darktown Battery, 3 Black Baseball Players, J. & E. Stevens, 7 x 10 In.	2125
Mechanical, Drumming Polichinelle, Tin Penny Drum, Lithographed Paper, 1860, 18 In.	3450
Mechanical, Elephant, Howdah, Man Pops Out, Cast Iron, c.1885, 5½ In. .... *illus*	575
Mechanical, French Cigarette Vending, Tin Lithograph, c.1920, 6 In.	360
Mechanical, Frog On Lattice, Cast Iron, Red, White, Blue, Eyes Roll, J. & E. Stevens, 4 In.	960
Mechanical, Joe Socko, Boxers, Box, c.1937, 3½ In.	420
Mechanical, Jonah & Whale, Cast Iron, Painted, Shepard Hardware, 1800s, 10½ In.	1440
Mechanical, Leprechaun, Sitting, Cast Iron, J. & E. Stevens, Painted, 8¼ x 8½ In.	1620
Mechanical, Lion, Monkey, Yellow, Green, Cast Iron, 9½ x 9 In. .... *illus*	676
Mechanical, Magician Bank, Cast Iron, Red Table, Yellow Stairs, J. & E. Stevens, 8½ In.	6150
Mechanical, Magician, Lowers Arms, Hat Covers Coin, J. & E. Stevens, c.1910, 8 x 7 In. .... *illus*	1920
Mechanical, Monkey & Parrot, Tin, Saalheimer & Strauss, Germany, 1930s, 6 x 4 In. .... *illus*	246
Mechanical, Mosque, Gorilla, Tray On Head, Cast Iron, Gold Finish, Judd, 9 x 5¾ In.	615
Mechanical, Novelty Bank, Door Opens, Teller, Iron, J. & E. Stevens, c.1890, 7 x 5 In. ..... *illus*	570
Mechanical, Organ Grinder & Monkey, Cast Iron, Painted, Hubley, 8¾ x 7¾ In.	1046
Mechanical, Organ Grinder, Monkey, Crank, Cast Iron, Kyser & Rex, 6 x 4 In.	861
Mechanical, Owl, Head Turns, Cast Iron, Painted, J. & E. Stevens, 7¾ In.	1107
Mechanical, Penny Pineapple, Commemorates Hawaii As State, Colorful, c.1960	420
Mechanical, Piano, Windup, Plays Music, Cast Iron, E.M. Roche, 8 x 6 In.	523
Mechanical, Rabbit, Cabbage, Coin Slot, Ears Lift, Cast Iron, Kilgore, c.1910, 2 x 4 In. .... *illus*	390
Mechanical, Rooster, Crows, Moves Head, Cast Iron, Kyser & Rex, c.1880, 6¼ In.	395
Mechanical, Speaking Dog, Wags Tail, Cast Iron, Shepard Hardware, 7½ In.	1080
Mechanical, Squirrel & Tree Stump, Press Lever, Mechanical Novelty Works, c.1890, 4 x 7 In.	1475
Mechanical, Tammany, Seated Man, Cast Iron, Painted, J. & E. Stevens Co., 1800s, 6 In.	175
Mechanical, Tammany, Seated Man, Head Moves, J. & E. Stevens, 6 x 4 In.	840
Mechanical, Trick Dog, Jumps Through Hoop, Cast Iron, Paint, Hubley, 8½ x 7 In.	469
Mechanical, Uncle Sam, Coin Falls Into Bag, Beard Moves, 1886, 11½ x 5 In. .... *illus*	870
Mechanical, Uncle Sam, Eagle, Arm Lowers, Drops Coin In Bag, Cast Iron, Paint, c.1910	175
Mechanical, Zoo, Monkey, Lion & Bear In Windows, Cast Iron, Painted, Kyser & Rex, 4 In.	1353
National, Brass, 2 Glass Panels, Square Box Form, c.1900, 6¼ In.	138
Pay Phone, Pressed Steel, Sturco Toy Co., 4 x 3¾ In.	188
Pig, Seated, Bow, Shimer Toy Co., M 606, 3 x 5 In.	153
Policeman, Standing, Double Breasted Uniform, Arcade, M 182, 5½ In.	483
Rabbit, Green Base, Kyser & Rex, Embossed 1884, 2½ In.	450
Safe, Fidelity Trust, Cast Iron, Clock Face & Hands, J. Barton Smith, M 903, 6½ x 6 In.	480
Safe, Padlock, Key, 4 Reserves, Courting Couples, Green, Black, Stencils, 8¾ x 11 In.	1026
Safe, Royal Safe Deposit, Cast Iron, Combination Lock, M 671, 6 x 5¼ In.	215
Safety Deposit, Double Combination Dial, Ornate Molding, Keyless Lock Co., 5¾ In.	90
Songbird On Stump, Cast Iron, A.C. Williams, M 664, 4¾ In.	240
Steamboat, Gold Paint, Cast Iron, A.C. Williams, M 1459, 2¼ x 7¾ In.	300
Street Clock, Cast Iron, Red & Gold Paint, A.C. Williams, M 1548, 6 In.	461

Barometer, Banjo, Gilt, Carved, Paper Face, Tassels, Germany Specialwerk, c.1950, 36 x 14 In.
$354

Leland Little Auctions

Basket, Splint, Woven, Oak, Double Wrapped Rim, Bentwood Handle, 9 x 12 x 10 In.
$30

Hess Auction Group

Basket, Splint, Woven, Rib, White Oak, Shelton Sisters, c.1900, 6 x 4 In.
$2,457

Jeffrey S. Evans

Basket, Splint, Woven, Stamped Decoration, c.1900, 8½ x 12 In. **$94**

Garth's Auctioneers & Appraisers

Battersea, Box, Motto, This Box I Intend A Gift For My Friend, Pink, Dots, Oval, 2⅛ In. **$258**

Bunch Auctions

Battersea, Case, Scent Bottle, Cork Stopper, Flowers, Pink Ground, 3½ In. **$80**

Bunch Auctions

TIP

Stains can be removed from woven baskets with a diluted solution of hydrogen peroxide.

Taxi, Yellow Cab, Cast Iron, Black & Orange Paint, Arcade, M 1493, 7¾ In.	330
Uncle Sam, Hand Out, Platform Base, Eagle, Cast Iron, Paint, 1800s, 5 x 11 In.	1800

BARBER collectibles range from the popular red and white striped pole that used to be found in front of every shop to the small scissors and tools of the trade. Barber chairs are wanted, especially the older models with elaborate iron trim.

Basin, Porcelain, Landscape, Figures, Chinese Export, c.1765, 13¼ In.	1875
Chair, Horse Head, Yellow Enamel, Leather Seat, Emil J. Paidar, c.1910, 43 x 21 In. *illus*	3600
Chair, Koken, Round Seat, Footed, 46¾ In.	412
Pole, Multicolor, Painted, Wood, 43 x 9 In.	177
Pole, Red, White, Cannonball Finial, Double Turned Post, Central Ball, 88 In.	188
Pole, Turned Wood, Paint, White, Red Stripes, Ball Finial, Stepped Base, c.1880, 72 In.	1275
Pole, Wooden, Painted, Red, White, c.1875, 23 In.	240

BAROMETERS are used to forecast the weather. Antique barometers with elaborate wooden cases and brass trim are the most desirable. Mercury column barometers are also popular with collectors. It is difficult to find someone to repair a broken one, so be sure your barometer is in working condition.

Banjo, Ebonized, Parcel Gilt, Acanthus, 38½ In.	375
Banjo, Gilt, Carved, Paper Face, Tassels, Germany Specialwerk, c.1950, 36 x 14 In. *illus*	354
Banjo, Selsi, Mahogany Case, Rosette & Conch Shell Marquetry Inlay, 1900s, 32 x 9 x 2 In.	540
Banjo, Thermometer, Scroll, Vanetti & Benzzoni, England, 41 x 10 In.	264
Cerulty & Son, Stick, Mahogany, Inlay, Signed, c.1800, 38½ In.	225
Stick, Gothic Walnut, Ripple Carved Front, Black Incised Silver Dial Plate, Mercury, 38 In.	1029
Stick, Timby's, Rosewood, Beaded Case, Mercury Tube, Label, Patent 1857, 37 In.	100
Thermometer, Fornelli, Regency, Mahogany, Brass Spheres, Lotus Bezels, Sheffield, 44 In.	500
Thermometer, Hygrometer, Fruitwood Cased Barometrum, Brass Backplate, Hanger, 1700s, 39 x 6 In.	960
Viardot Opticien, Giltwood, Basket & Tassel Carved, Thermometer Neck, France, 37 In.	896
Wheel, Inlaid Mahogany, Silvered Dial, Masonic Symbols, Hydrometer, 47 x 15 In.	121
Wheel, Thermometer, Mahogany Frame, Inlaid Highlights, 1900, 38 In.	85

BASALT is a special type of ceramic invented by Josiah Wedgwood in the eighteenth century. It is a fine-grained, unglazed stoneware. Some pieces are listed in that section. The most common type is black, but many other colors were made. It was made by many factories. Some pieces are listed in the Wedgwood section.

Bust, Robert Burns, Jacket, Scarf, c.1840, 7½ In.	1425
Figurine, Psyche, Butterfly Wings, L. Hjorth & Eneret, Marked, Denmark, c.1850, 15 x 4 In.	875
Jardiniere, Gods & Goddesses, Scrolled Grapevines, Lion Mask Ring Handles, 5 x 7 In.	295
Loving Cup, Charles Dickens, Bas-Relief Bust, Characters, 11½ x 8½ In.	175
Vase, Cherub, Playing Harp, Oval, 3¾ In.	102

BASEBALL *collectibles are in the Sports category, except for baseball cards, which are listed under Baseball in the Card category.*

BASKETS of all types are popular with collectors. American Indian, Japanese, African, Nantucket, Shaker, and many other kinds of baskets may be found in other sections. Of course, baskets are still being made, so a collector must learn to judge the age and style of a basket to determine its value. Also see Purse.

Acorn, Ash, Twine Stringholder, 5½ In.	29
Berry, Splint, Oak, Square, Arched Handle, Appalachia, 1890s, 11 x 8 In.	198
Egg, Oak, Splint, Bentwood Handle, Bentwood Taped Rim, c.1800, 5 x 7 In.	70
Eskimo, Lid, Stripped, Woven Baleen, Polar Bear, Walrus, Herbert Koonuk, 1900s, 2 x 4 In.	500
Eskimo, Lid, Walrus Ivory Figure, 2 Polar Bears, 1900s, 5 In.	900
Eskimo, Lid, Walrus Ivory Figure, 2 Seals Resting On Heart, 1900s, 4 In.	480
Fruit, Hexagonal, Woven Splint, Double Bentwood, 5¼ x 15½ In.	413
Hamper, Wicker, Hinged Lid, Gesso Roses, Wood Feet, c.1905, 25 x 14 In.	275
Higgins, Swing Handle, Round, 11 x 8 In.	35

Ikebana, Oval Base, Burled Wisteria Handle, Meiji Period, 15 In.	344
Ikebana, Split Bamboo, Entwined Splint Handle, 16 In.	510
Ikebana, Split Bamboo, Hourglass, Openwork, Flower Shape, 16 In.	960
Ikebana, Split Bamboo, Red, Rope Handle, 23 x 15 In.	840
Nantucket, Oval, Stationary Handles, Al Brown, 6 x 13 In.	960
Nantucket, Oval, Swing Handle, Yellow & Green, 9 x 16½ In.	153
Nantucket, Round, Swing Handle, Richard Swain, 8 x 11¾ In.	1320
Nantucket, Round, Swing Handle, Walnut, 5¼ x 8½ In.	510
Oyster, Wire Frame, Chain-Link Design, Turned Wood Handles, France, 1930s, 8 x 19 In.	215
Picnic, Solid Top, Sidney Gage, Marked TK Hass Manchester B & MRR, 12 x 7 x 7 In.	174
Skep, Bee, Coil, Rye Straw, Openwork Handle, 16 x 15½ In.	247
Splint, Woven, Oak, Double Wrapped Rim, Bentwood Handle, 9 x 12 x 10 In. *illus*	30
Splint, Woven, Original Color, Stamped Decorations, 1800s-1900s, 8½ x 12 In.	94
Splint, Woven, Rib, White Oak, Shelton Sisters, c.1900, 6 x 4 In. *illus*	2457
Splint, Woven, Stamped Decoration, c.1900, 8½ x 12 In. *illus*	94
Twig, Bent, Mortised, Wicker, Vieth, 12 x 8¼ In.	181
Wicker, Plaques, Butterfly, Faded, Color, 6¾ To 12 In.	136

BATCHELDER products are made from California clay. Ernest Batchelder established a tile studio in Pasadena, California, in 1909. He went into partnership with Frederick Brown in 1912 and the company became Batchelder and Brown. In 1920 he built a larger factory with a new partner. The Batchelder-Wilson Company made all types of architectural tiles, garden pots, and bookends. The plant closed in 1932. In 1936 Batchelder opened Batchelder Ceramics, also in Pasadena, and made bowls, vases, and earthenware pots. He retired in 1951 and died in 1957. Pieces are marked *Batchelder Pasadena* or *Batchelder Los Angeles*.

BATCHELDER
LOS ANGELES

Bookend, Tile Inset, Brown, Pea Pods, 3¼ x 3¼ In.	900
Tile, Castle, Turrets, Trees, Blue, Brown, 11¾ x 5¾ In.	393

BATMAN and Robin are characters from a comic strip by Bob Kane that started in 1939. In 1966, the characters became part of a popular television series. There have been radio and movie serials that featured the pair. The first full-length movie was made in 1989.

Book, Son Of The Demon, 1st Edition, Mike Barr, Jerry Bingham, Hardcover, 1987	48
Costume, Helmet & Cape, Plastic, Vinyl, Blue, Black, Ideal, Box, 1966	225
PEZ Dispenser, Batman, Box, 1985	10
Toy, Batmobile, Die Cast, Figures, Box, Corgi Toys, c.1966, 5½ In.	245

BATTERSEA enamels, which are enamels painted on copper, were made in the Battersea district of London from about 1750 to 1756. Many similar enamels are mistakenly called Battersea.

Box, Courting Couple, Lid, 18th Century, 2 x 4 In.	455
Box, Motto, This Box I Intend A Gift For My Friend, Pink, Dots, Oval, 2⅛ In. *illus*	258
Case, Scent Bottle, Cork Stopper, Flowers, Pink Ground, 3½ In. *illus*	80

BAUER pottery is a California-made ware. J.A. Bauer bought Paducah Pottery in Paducah, Kentucky, in 1885. He moved the pottery to Los Angeles, California, in 1910. The company made art pottery after 1912 and introduced dinnerware marked *Bauer* in 1930. The factory went out of business in 1962 and the molds were destroyed. Since 1998, a new company, Bauer Pottery Company of Los Angeles, has been making Bauer pottery using molds made from original Bauer pieces. The pottery is now made in Highland, California. Pieces are marked *Bauer Pottery Company of Los Angeles*. Original pieces of Bauer pottery are listed here. See also the Russel Wright category.

Candleholder, Orange, Matt Carlton, 4 x 2½ In.	40
Monterey Moderne, Baker, Solid, Oval, Speckled	20
Monterey Moderne, Casserole, Solid, Coppertone, Metal Holder	20
Monterey Moderne, Serving Bowl, Solid, Speckled, Round, 13 In.	80

Bauer Ringware

Bauer Ringware pattern, very popular today, can be dated from the mark. "Bauer" or "Bauer Los Angeles" were the earliest. Pieces marked "Bauer Made in USA" or "Bauer USA" were made in the mid-1930s.

Bauer, Ring, Pitcher, Blue, 1930s, 4⅜ x 5 In.
$45

Ruby Lane

Bauer, Ring, Pitcher, Yellow, Ice Lip, c.1940, 7¼ In.
$120

Replacements, Ltd.

Bavaria, Vase, Laughing Jackasses, Kookaburras, Blue, Green, 2 Square Handles, 3¼ In.
$30

Woody Auction

B

Beatles, Lunch Box, Thermos, Portraits, Embossed, 1965, 8 x 7 In.
$1,169

Morphy Auctions

Beatles, Postcard, McCartney, Starr, Harrison, Lennon, Blue Jackets, Color Photo, Early 1960s
$22

Ruby Lane

Beehive, Plate, Melitta, Woman, Standing, Blue & Gold Border, K. Weh, Royal Vienna, 9½ In.
$150

Cowan's Auctions

Bell, Hotel, Cast Iron, Elf Legs, 3 x 5½ x 6 In.
$342

AntiqueAdvertising.com

Monterey Moderne, Teapot, Solid, Speckled, Pink, 2 Cup		42
Monterey, Casserole, Lid, Beige, Speckled, 1½ Qt.		30
Monterey, Casserole, Yellow, Qt.		10
Monterey, Serving Bowl, Turquoise, 13 In.		80
Ring, Carafe, Lid, Turquoise, Wooden Handle, Marked		85
Ring, Pitcher, Blue, 1930s, 4⅜ x 5 In.	*illus*	45
Ring, Pitcher, Yellow, Ice Lip, c.1940, 7¼ In.	*illus*	120
Ring, Plate, Hand Painted Cowboy On House, 11 In.		145
Vase, Ruffled, Blue, Matt Carlton, 7¾ In.		175

BAVARIA is a region in Europe where many types of porcelain were made. In the nineteenth century, the mark often included the word *Bavaria*. After 1871, the words *Bavaria, Germany*, were used. Listed here are pieces that include the name *Bavaria* in some form, but major porcelain makers, such as Rosenthal, are listed in their own categories.

Celery Dish, Open Handles, Blue Flowers, 13 In.		100
Charger, Round, Marked, Classical Scene, Black Border, Gold Brocade Trim, 14 In.		60
Salt & Pepper, Pink Roses, Twisted, 2½ In.		25
Sugar, Lid, Autumn Colored Leaves, Gold Trim, c.1900		45
Toothpick Holder, Cobalt Blue, Gilt, Fireworks, Oval, 2¾ In.		32
Vase, Laughing Jackasses, Kookaburras, Blue, Green, 2 Square Handles, 3¼ In.	*illus*	30

BEADED BAGS *are included in the Purse category.*

BEATLES collectors search for any items picturing the four members of the famous music group or any of their recordings. Because these items are so new, the condition is very important and top prices are paid only for items in mint condition. The Beatles first appeared on American network television in 1964. The group disbanded in 1971. Ringo Starr and Paul McCartney are still performing. John Lennon died in 1980. George Harrison died in 2001.

Cake Decoration, Photo, Green Heart, Plastic, Pointed Spike, 1966, 3 In., 3 Piece		20
Compact, Powder Puff, Beatles, 3 In. Diam.		275
Doll, Cloth, Felt Face & Hands, Cardboard Guitar, Official Mascot Doll, 29 In.		175
Doll, John, George, Paul, Ringo, Playing Instruments, Plastic, Box, 3 In., Set of 4		110
Lunch Box, Thermos, Portraits, Embossed, 1965, 8 x 7 In.	*illus*	1169
Pillow, Faces, Autographs, Nordic House, c.1964, 12 x 12 In.		120
Playing Cards, Portraits, Gemaco, Box, 1970s		30
Postcard, McCartney, Starr, Harrison, Lennon, Blue Jackets, Color Photo, Early 1960s	*illus*	22
Record, Let It Be, 33⅓ RPM, 1970		24
Suspenders, Clip, Help, Black, Teal, Purple, Yellow, Y-Back, 1980s		39
Ticket Stub, Forest Hills Concert, Tour Booklet, 1964		1000

BEEHIVE, Austria, or Beehive, Vienna, are terms used in English-speaking countries to refer to the many types of decorated porcelain bearing a mark that looks like a beehive. The mark is actually a shield, viewed upside down. It was first used in 1744 by the Royal Porcelain Manufactory of Vienna. The firm made what collectors call Royal Vienna porcelains until it closed in 1864. Many other German, Austrian, and Japanese factories have reproduced Royal Vienna wares, complete with the original shield or beehive mark. This listing includes the expensive, original Royal Vienna porcelains and many other types of beehive porcelain. The Royal Vienna pieces include that name in the description.

Imperial and Royal Porcelain
Manufactory
Vienna, Austria
1749–1827

Bourdois & Bloch
Paris, France
c.1900

Waechtersbach Earthenware
Factory
Schlierbach, Hesse, Germany
1921–1928

Bowl, Allegorical Scene, Women Around Fountain, Continental, 1800s, 3 ¼ x 9 ¾ In.	60
Bowl, Lid, 2 Handles, Red, 4 Medallion Scenes, Venus & Adonis, Signed, 4 ¾ x 7 ½ In.	150
Charger, Love Lighter Than Butterfly, Red, Winged Putti, F. Lezleb, Royal Vienna, 14 In.	2205
Figurine, Monkey, Embracing, Glazed, Perched, Brown Base, Vienna, 1900s, 14 x 6 ½ x 5 In.	813
Jardiniere, Porcelain, Lobed Bowl, Cobalt Blue Body, Gilt Highlights, Mark, 8 ¾ x 9 In.	182
Plaque, Diana In Bath, Red, Cream, Pink & Blue Border, Gold Highlights, 18 In.	1560
Plate, Hand Painted, Geometric Border, Titled Grechisch Idylle, 2 Women, Greek Vase, 9 ½ In.	545
Plate, Melitta, Woman, Standing, Blue & Gold Border, K. Weh, Royal Vienna, 9 ½ In. ...... *illus*	150
Plate, Nude Woman Portrait, Hand Painted, Signed Weigel, Royal Vienna, 1900s, 9 ½ In.	1375
Plate, Nude Woman, Enameled, Marked Im Bade, Wagner, Royal Vienna, 1900s, 9 In.	2400
Plate, Nude Woman, Hand Painted, Burgundy, Marked Loreley, Royal Vienna, 1900s, 9 ½ In.	1063
Teapot, Red, Figures Dancing, Gilt Bronze Dolphin Mount Handle, Royal Vienna, 8 In.	438
Tray, Blue, Cream & Maroon Borders, Classic Painted Scene, Oval, Marked, 18 In.	120
Tray, Scalloped Rim, Open Side Handle, Red Background, Gilt Filigree, 1 ¾ x 17 x 15 In.	273
Tray, Scalloped Rim, Open Side Handle, Red, Gilt Filigree, 17 x 15 In.	273
Tureen, Lid, Women, Parcel Gilt, Compressed Pear Shape, Reserves, Green, 13 x 11 In.	544
Urn, Cobalt Blue, Wide Base, Gilt, Enamel Filigree, Man, Monk, Woman, 21 x 12 In.	847
Urn, Cupid, Women, Red Background, Enamel Highlights, Panels, 16 x 6 ½ In.	968
Urn, Gilt, Women, Courtyard, Putti, Wine, 17 ¾ x 11 In.	96
Urn, Lid, Love, Nymphs, Cupid, Light Pink, Handles, Pinched Waist Foot, 19 ½ x 11 In.	937
Urn, Lid, Turned Finial, Animals In Garden, Border, Round Base, Royal Vienna, 15 x 12 x 8 In., Pair	1513
Urn, Painted Scene, 3 Fates, 4 Winged Putti, Square Base, Royal Vienna, 26 x 12 x 9 In.	5445
Urn, Purple, Figures Reserves, Signed Rinaldo & Almida, 18 ¼ In.	720
Vase, Double Handle, Nude Woman, Cherub, Burgundy, Marked, Royal Vienna, 1900s, 8 In.	270
Vase, Woman Portrait, Burgundy, Gilt Decoration, Echo Markings, Royal Vienna, 1900s, 11 In.	1125
Vase, Woman Portrait, Flowers, Blue Slip, Marked Erbluth, Royal Vienna, 1900s, 5 In.	531
Vase, Women, Dancing, Robes, Togas, Landscape, 7 ¼ In.	72

BEER BOTTLES *are listed in the Bottle category under Beer.*

BEER CANS are a twentieth-century idea. Beer was sold in kegs or returnable bottles until 1934. The first patent for a can was issued to the American Can Company in September of that year, and Gotfried Kruger Brewing Company, Newark, New Jersey, was the first to use the can. The cone-top can was first made in 1935, the aluminum pop-top in 1962. Collectors should look for cans in good condition, with no dents or rust. Serious collectors prefer cans that have been opened from the bottom.

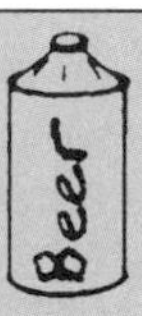

83 Beer, Pull Top, Beldo & Willmarth, Evanston, Illinois, Late 1960s, 12 Oz.	1250
Aero Club Pale Select, Cone Top, East Idaho Brewing, Pocatello, Early 1950s, 12 Oz.	500
American Dry Extra Premium Lager, Flat Top, 5 Star Brewing, N.Y., Late 1950s, 12 Oz.	45
A-Treat Birch, Pull Top, A-Treat Bottling Co., Allentown, Pa., 1970, 12 Oz.	200
Beverwyck Irish Brand Cream Ale, Cone Top, Albany, N.Y., Late 1940s, 12 Oz.	250
Bock Beer, Flat Top, Goat Head, Red, Black, Gold, Metropolis Brewery, 1958	300
Brown Derby Lager Beer, Flat Top, Red Hat, White, Gold, Atlantic Brewing Co.	25
Bull Dog Ale, Flat Top, Red, Green, Grace Brothers Co., 1958	35
Carling A-1, Pull Top, Carling Brewing Co., Phoenix, Arizona, 1967, 12 Oz.	150
Chief Oshkosh Beer, Cone Top, Metallic, Oshkosh Brewing Co.	300
Drewrys Ale, Flat Top, Canada's Pride Brand, South Bend, Ind., Early 1940s, 12 Oz.	400
Eastside Beer, Flat Top, Eagle, Los Angeles Brewing, 1950	45
Gablinger's Beer, Forrest Brewing Co.	25
Gold Medal Beer, Cone Top, Stegmaier Brewing Co.	250
Keglined Badger, Flat Top, Whitewater Brewing Co., Wisconsin, 1936, 12 Oz.	5000
Old Ranger Premium, Pull Top, Hornell, Trenton, New Jersey, Target Image, 1965	550
Weber Waukesha, Cone Top, Waukesha, Wisconsin, Early 1950s, 12 Oz.	375

BELL collectors collect all types of bells. Favorites include glass bells, figural bells, school bells, and cowbells. Bells have been made of porcelain, china, or metal through the centuries.

Bronze, Battle, Bands, Handle, Japan, 10 In.	500

Bell, Tower, Bronze, Bracket Mount, Iron, Warner & Sons, Ltd., England, 11 x 13 ¾ In.
$1,020

Thomaston Place Auction Galleries

Belleek, Basket, Twig, Openwork Rim, Flowers, Shamrocks, Double Handle, Irish, 2 ¾ x 8 In.
$300

Thomaston Place Auction Galleries

Belleek, Bowl, Woven Strands, Applied Pink & Yellow Roses, Handles, Ireland, 11 In.
$138

Bunch Auctions

Belleek Baskets
Irish Belleek collectors can date the "woven" baskets and bowls by looking closely at the strands of clay in the basket's weave. Each strip in the weave is made of several strands of clay. Baskets woven with clay made of four strands date from about 1900. Fewer strands were used on newer baskets. Look at the bottom of a bowl or basket and count the strands.

Bennington, Crock, Bird, J. & E. Norton, Stoneware, 1800s, 3 Gal., 16½ In.
$1,558

Copake Auctiona

Bennington, Cuspidor, Acorns, Brown, Mottled, 9 In.
$36

Rich Penn Auctions

Bennington, Pitcher, Hound Handle, Rockingham Glaze, Hunt Scene, Grapevines, 1800s, 8 In.
$330

Garth's Auctioneers & Appraisers

Bronze, Cylindrical, Repeating Sets Of Panels, Lotus Blossoms, Dragon Hanger, 1600s, 17 x 9 In...	240
Cast Iron, Turtle, Moving Head, Brown, Black, 3½ x 2½ In.	256
Gong, Brass, Wrought Iron, Relief Portrait, Roland A. Ronceveux, Scrolled Support, 32 x 31 In.	475
Gong, Dinner, Etched Flowers, Burl Wood Mallet, India, 1950s, 6¾ x 8½ In.	47
Gong, Quarter Circle, Hole Near Arc, Brass, Harry Bertoia, c.1950, 6½ x 9 In.	5310
Gong, Silver Deposit, Thai Nakon, Bone, Tusks, Wood Stand, Base, Thailand, 1900s, 9 x 11 x 5 In..	469
Hotel, Black Marble Base, Levered Striker, 4¼ x 2¾ In.	212
Hotel, Brass, Wall Hung, 8½ x 8 In.	18
Hotel, Cast Iron, Elf Legs, 3 x 5½ x 6 In. *illus*	342
Hotel, Iron, Snail, Button, Clockwork, Mechanical, 2½ x 4⅜ In.	247
Metal, Bear, Bell Raised Like Umbrella, Levered Button, Goldtone Base, 8 x 3¾ In.	718
Plantation, Metal, Yoke Support, Chamfered Post, Cross Base, West Indies, 1800s, 65 x 14 In.	384
Sleigh, 24 Brass Bells, Incised, Leather Strap, 100 In.	106
Tower, Bronze, Bracket Mount, Iron, Warner & Sons, Ltd., England, 11 x 13¾ In. *illus*	1020

BELLEEK china was made in Ireland, other European countries, and the United States. The glaze is creamy yellow and appears wet. The first Belleek was made in 1857 in the village of Belleek, County Fermanagh, in what is now Northern Ireland. In 1884 the name of the company became the Belleek Pottery Works Company Ltd. The mark changed through the years. The first mark, black, dates from 1863 to 1891. The second mark, black, dates from 1891 to 1926 and includes the words *Co. Fermanagh, Ireland.* The third mark, black, dates from 1926 to 1946 and has the words *Deanta in Eireann.* The fourth mark, same as the third mark but green, dates from 1946 to 1955. The fifth mark (second green mark) dates from 1955 to 1965 and has an *R* in a circle added in the upper right. The sixth mark (third green mark) dates from 1965 to 1981 and the words *Co. Fermanagh* have been omitted. The seventh mark, gold, was used from 1981 to 1992 and omits the words *Deanta in Eireann.* The eighth mark, used from 1993 to 1996, is similar to the second mark but is printed in blue. The ninth mark, blue, includes the words *Est. 1857*, and the words *Co. Fermanagh Ireland* are omitted. The tenth mark, black, is similar to the ninth mark but includes the words *Millennium 2000* and *Ireland.* It was used only in 2000. The eleventh mark, similar to the millennium mark but green, was introduced in 2001. The twelfth mark, black, is similar to the eleventh mark but has a banner above the mark with the words *Celebrating 150 Years.* It was used in 2007. The thirteenth trademark, used from 2008 to 2010, is similar to the twelfth but is brown and has no banner. The fourteenth mark, the Classic Belleek trademark, is similar to the twelfth but includes Belleek's website address. The Belleek Living trademark was introduced in 2010 and is used on items from that giftware line. All pieces listed here are Irish Belleek. The word *Belleek* is now used only on pieces made in Ireland even though earlier pieces from other countries were sometimes marked *Belleek.* These early pieces are listed in this book by manufacturer, such as Ceramic Art Co., Lenox, Ott & Brewer, and Willets.

Belleek Pottery Co.
1863–1891

Ceramic Art Co.
1894–1906

Willets Manufacturing Co.
1879–1912+

Basket, Blue Rope & Floral Highlights & Naturalistic Loop Handles, 1900, 5½ x 9 In.	78
Basket, Parian Ware, Double Twig Handle, Oval, Flowers & Shamrocks, 2¾ x 8 x 6 In.	300
Basket, Twig, Openwork Rim, Flowers, Shamrocks, Double Handle, Irish, 2¾ x 8 In. *illus*	300
Bowl, Woven Strands, Applied Pink & Yellow Roses, Handles, Ireland, 11 In. *illus*	138
Figure, Erin, Ireland, Standing, Draped Urn, Harp, Celtic Cross, 3rd Mark, Black, 1926-46, 17 In.	984
Tankard, Cream Background, Woman Watching Artist, Grapes & Leaves Reverse Gold Trim, 14 In.	360
Tankard, Gilt, Yellow Roses, Filigree, 14½ x 8½ In.	346
Vase, Trumpet, Gilt, Orange Roses, Red, Pale Green, 15¼ x 4¾ In.	72
Vase, Twist Fluting, Applied Roses, Green Leaves, Cream, 2¾ In.	30

BENNINGTON ware was the product of two factories working in Bennington, Vermont. Both the Norton Company and Lyman Fenton & Company were out of business by 1896. The wares include brown and yellow mottled pottery, Parian, scroddled ware, stoneware, graniteware, yellowware, and Staffordshire-type vases. The name is also a generic term for mottled brownware of the type made in Bennington.

Crock, Bird, J. & E. Norton, Stoneware, 1800s, 3 Gal., 16½ In.	*illus*	1558
Crock, Cobalt Blue, Flowers, Leaves, E. & L.P. Norton, 11½ In., 2 Gal.		265
Cuspidor, Acorns, Brown, Mottled, 9 In.	*illus*	36
Jug, Hound Handle, Hunt Scene, Marked Vance Eco, 1900s, 13 In.		236
Jug, L. Norton & Son, Flowers, Tooled Spout, Stamped, 1830s, Gal., 11 x 7½ In.		600
Pitcher, Hound Handle, Rockingham Glaze, Hunt Scene, Grapevines, 1800s, 8 In.	*illus*	330
Trivet, Brown Glaze, David Gill, 8 In.		113
Vase, Stag, Tree Stump, Coleslaw Grass, Flint Enamel, 1850s, 11 x 12 In.	*illus*	2400

BERLIN, a German porcelain factory, was started in 1751 by Wilhelm Kaspar Wegely. In 1763, the factory was taken over by Frederick the Great and became the Royal Berlin Porcelain Manufactory. It is still in operation today. Pieces have been marked in a variety of ways.

Box, Lid, Gilt, Roses, Flowers, Garland, White Ground, Bronze Casing, 1700s, 1½ x 3 In.		1265
Cup & Saucer, Multicolor Ducks, Petal Shape, Brown & Gold, Marked, 1800s, 2¼ x 5 In.		2500
Group, Gilt, Woman, Men, Sedan, 18th Century Costume, Flowers, c.1900, 9 x 9¾ In.	*illus*	747
Plaque, Marriage, Sword Stamp, Hand Painted, c.1850, 16 x 13 In.		813
Vase, Painted, Multicolor Flowers, Royal Berlin, c.1900, 6½ x 15¼ In.	*illus*	580
Vase, Woman, Pink Dress, Leaf Scrolls, Palmettes, Gold Ground, Swan Handles, 17 In.		1140

BESWICK started making pottery in Staffordshire, England, in 1894. The pottery became John Beswick Ltd. in 1936. The company became part of Royal Doulton Tableware, Ltd. in 1969. Production ceased in 2002 and the John Beswick brand was bought by Dartington Crystal in 2004. Figurines, vases, and other items are being made and use the name Beswick. Beatrix Potter figures were made from 1948 until 2002. They shouldn't be confused with Bunnykins, which were made by Royal Doulton.

Basket, Vertical Leaf, Continuous Loop Handle, Blue, Green, No. 819, 11 x 10 In.		75
Figurine, Cat, Persian, Seated, Looking Up, c.1970, 8½ In.	*illus*	110
Figurine, Cat, Seated, Looking Up, Gray, White, No. 1030, 6¼ In.		125
Figurine, Cat, Siamese, Ceramic, Blue Eyes, 1900s		24
Figurine, Dog, Collie, No. 1814, 3¼ x 4½ x 1½ In.		78
Figurine, Dog, Foxhound, No. 2264, 3 x 3¾ In.		95
Figurine, Dog, Pinscher, Annastock Lance, No. 2299, 5¾ x 6½ x 3 In.		98
Figurine, Horse, Shire Foal, Gray Gloss, No. 1053, 1962, 4½ In.		40
Figurine, Mr. Benjamin Bunny, Beatrix Potter, No. BP-3B, 4 In.		150
Figurine, Rabbit, Scratching Ear, No. 824, 2 In.		18
Jug, Blue, No. 137, 4½ In.		39
Plaque, Mallard Duck, No. 596/1, 10 In.		69
Teapot, Peggotty, Lid, No. 1116, 1940s, 6 x 8 In.		65
Vase, Orange, Lime, 6¾ x 3 In.		55
Vase, Pinched, Urn Shape, Ring, Green, No. 347, 1930s, 4½ In.		49
Vase, Ship On Stormy Sea, Peach, Mottled Turquoise, No. 1083, 1940s, 7 In.		65
Vase, Wood Effect, Bulbous, No. 1657, c.1952, 11 In.		110

BETTY BOOP, the cartoon figure, first appeared on the screen in 1930. Her face was modeled after the famous singer Helen Kane and her body after Mae West. In 1935, a comic strip was started. Her dog's was named Pudgy. Although the Betty Boop cartoons ended by 1938, there was a revival of interest in the Betty Boop image in the 1980s and new pieces are being made.

Blanket, Yellow Ruffled Edge, 15 x 11 In.		120
Doll, Celluloid, Jointed Head & Arms, Heart On Dress, Japan, 1930s, 8 In.	*illus*	1298

Bennington, Vase, Stag, Tree Stump, Coleslaw Grass, Flint Enamel, 1850s, 11 x 12 In.
$2,400

Garth's Auctioneers & Appraisers

Berlin, Group, Gilt, Woman, Men, Sedan, 18th Century Costume, Flowers, c.1900, 9 x 9¾ In.
$747

Bunch Auctions

Berlin, Vase, Painted, Multicolor Flowers, Royal Berlin, c.1900, 6½ x 15¼ In.
$580

Ruby Lane

Beswick, Figurine, Cat, Persian, Seated, Looking Up, c.1970, 8½ In. $110

Ruby Lane

Betty Boop, Doll, Celluloid, Jointed Head & Arms, Heart On Dress, Japan, 1930s, 8 In. $1,298

Hake's Americana & Collectibles

Betty Boop, Figurine, Dress, Composition, Fleischer Studios, 1931, 14 In. $2,500

Ruby Lane

Doll, Composition, Wood Arms & Legs, Fleischer, Label, c.1920, 11 In.	595
Doll, Wood, Jointed, Cameo Doll Co., 1930s, 12 In.	475
Figurine, Dress, Composition, Fleischer Studios, 1931, 14 In. *illus*	2500
Figurine, Plaster, Gold Halter Dress, c.1930, 13½ In.	150
Wall Pocket, Betty Walking Bimbo, Porcelain, 1930s	85
Watch, Red Leather Band, Hearts As Numbers, Bright Ideas Unlimited, 9 In.	30
Watch, Tin, Cameo, String Band, Japan, 1930s, 1½ x 1 In.	25

BICYCLES were invented in 1839. The first manufactured bicycle was made in 1861. Special ladies' bicycles were made after 1874. The modern safety bicycle was not produced until 1885. Collectors search for all types of bicycles and tricycles. Bicycle-related items are also listed here.

Higgins, Boy's, Purple, Leather Seat, Spokes, Light, Chain Guard, Carrier Rake, c.1950	855
Lantern, Solar, Carbide, Missing Reservoir Cap, Mounting Hardware	20
M.D. Stebbings, Pneumatic, Chilion Wood Frame, Woman's, c.1898, 23 In.	7605
Schwinn, Black Phantom, Bell, Rear Saddlebags, 1950s	1112
Schwinn, Panther, Balloon Tires, Delta Rocket Ray Front Light, c.1953	1287
Schwinn, Phantom, Black, Red, Chrome, Bendix Brake, Persons Balloon Seat, 1950s *illus*	1652
Sears, Spaceliner, Allstate Safety Tread Tires, c.1965	936
Tricycle, Fairy, Tiller, Leather Seat, Red, Wood Handle, Worthington Co., c.1900, 39 x 55 In.	275
Tricycle, Haywood-Wakefield, Wood, Paint, Shaped Plank Seat, 1800s, 19 x 22 In.	315
Velocipede, Rear Level Pedal Drive, Pinstriping, Morse & Morton, c.1870, 65 x 47 In.	21060

BING & GRONDAHL is a famous Danish factory making fine porcelains from 1853 to the present. Underglaze blue decoration was started in 1886. The annual Christmas plate series was introduced in 1895. Dinnerware, stoneware, and other ceramics are still being made today. The figurines remain popular. The firm has used the initials *B & G* and a stylized castle as part of the mark since 1898. The company became part of Royal Copenhagen in 1987.

B. & G.	B&G KJØBENHAVN DANMARK B&G	COPENHAGEN PORCELAIN BING & GRONDAHL B&G
Bing & Grondahl 1895+	Bing & Grondahl 1915+	Bing & Grondahl 1983+

Bell, Christmas, 1982, Christmas Tree, 3 In.	32
Bowl, Oval, Shallow, Raised Circular Foot, Hennin Koppel, 5 x 18 In.	375
Cake Plate, Dolphin Handles, Violets & Berries, 10 In.	75
Cup & Saucer, Flowers, Garland, Blue, Demitasse	19
Figurine, Boy & Girl, Children Reading, Porcelain, c.1949, 4 x 4 In. *illus*	165
Figurine, Cat, Sitting, Gray, 4¾ In. *illus*	60
Figurine, Dog, Pekingese, 2 In.	250
Figurine, Mother Love, Ingeberg Irminger, Porcelain, Marked, 11 In. *illus*	485
Group, Boy With Dog, 5 x 3½ In.	125
Group, Children Reading, 4 x 4 x 4 In.	69
Group, First Kiss, 7½ In.	30
Plaque, Cherub Picking Fruit, Cupid, 6 x 4 In.	199
Plate, Centennial Anniversary, Towers Of Copenhagen, 1895-1995, 12¾ In.	125
Plate, Christmas, 1921, Pigeons In The Castle Court, 7¼ In.	45
Plate, Christmas, 1943, The Ribe Cathedral, 7 In.	85
Plate, Christmas, 1969, Arrival Of Christmas Guests, 7⅛ In.	10
Plate, Christmas, 1974, Christmas In The Village, 7 In.	25
Plate, Easter, 1910, Mary Magdalene By The Grave, 7⅜ In.	55
Plate, Easter, 1911, Angel Flew Down From Heaven, 7⅜ In.	55
Plate, Mother's Day, 1972, Mare & Foal, 6½ In.	15
Plate, Mother's Day, 1986, Elephant & Calf, 5¾ In.	15
Sculpture, Monkey, Watches Turtle, Dahl Jensen, 13½ x 16 In.	1375
Vase, Stick Neck, Apple Blossom, No. 230-5143, 5 In.	28

BINOCULARS of all types are wanted by collectors. Those made in the eighteenth and nineteenth centuries are favored by serious collectors. The small, attractive binoculars called opera glasses are listed in their own category.

Aitchison & Co., Aluminum, Collapsible, 5 x 4 ½ In.	406
King Optical Co., Monocular, Brass, Travel, Telescope, Swivel Lens, 2 Hinged Covers, 4 x 2 In..	182
Lawrence & Mayo, Lynx, Brass, Compass, c.1910, 4 x 1 ¾ In. .... *illus*	325

BIRDCAGES are collected for use as homes for pet birds and as decorative objects of folk art. Elaborate wooden cages of the past centuries can still be found. The brass or wicker cages of the 1930s are popular with bird owners.

Bamboo, Domed, Hexagonal Tiers, Tassels, Porcelain Feeders, c.1900, 25 x 15 In......	2400
Metal, Domed Cylinder, S-Scroll Feet, Black, Perch, 2 Feed Holders, 30 x 15 In.	73
Metal, Painted, Regency Style, Pagoda Tops, Bamboo Bases, Pair, 1900s, 82 ½ x 15 ½ In........	2750
Metal, White, Domed, Barrel Roof, Stand, 36 x 19 In.......................................	117
Metal, Wrought Iron, Architectural, Gray, Floral, 1900s, 71 In........................	240
Sheet Metal, House Shape, 40 x 42 In...	234
Tin, Flowers, Arched, Ring Handle, 15 x 12 In...	72
Twigs, Birch Bark, Painted Details, Tin Cage, Adirondack, c.1910, 74 x 19 In. .... *illus*	530
Wire, Cone Shape, 14 In...	70
Wire, Steamboat Shape, 3 Decks, Plants, Windows, Flag, Red, White, Blue, c.1875, 25 x 26 In..	785
Wirework, House, Turrets, Green, White, 31 ¼ x 33 ¼ In...............................	120
Wood, Business Office, H R, Carved, 2 Wood Binds, Scalloped Arcades, 16 ½ x 32 In.	1210
Wood, Wire, Domed, Platform Base, Wire Fence, Glass Feeders, c.1900, 20 x 14 In.	240

BISQUE is an unglazed baked porcelain. Finished bisque has a slightly sandy texture with a dull finish. Some of it may be decorated with various colors. Bisque gained favor during the late Victorian era when thousands of bisque figurines were made. It is still being made. Additional bisque items may be listed under the factory name.

Bust, Contesse Dubary, Swept Back Hair, Off The Shoulder Attire, 27 x 16 In...........	1792
Centerpiece, Putti, Flowers, Butterflies, White, Collingwood & Greatbach, 14 x 17 In.	75
Centerpiece, Seated Nudes, Empire, Parcel Gilt, 10 ¾ x 4 ¾ In.	4500
Figurine, Bird, Goshawk, Kaiser, Bavaria Germany, 11 ½ In................................ *illus*	106
Figurine, Diving Woman, Continental, 1900s, 15 In..	125
Figurine, Farmer, Collecting Vegetables, Basket, Hat, Boots, 27 In.....................	110
Figurine, Piano Baby, Young Child Wearing Bonnet, Pulling Socks Off, Pink & White, 9 ½ In.	210
Figurine, Young Women, 18th Century Dress, Holding Mask, Architectural Base, 1800s, 22 In..	144
Group, Young Man & Woman, Walking Under Umbrella, Germany, 22 In...................	180
Pitcher, Grapevine, Pink & White Stripes, 13 ¾ In..	42

BLACK memorabilia has become an important area of collecting since the 1970s. The best material dates from past centuries, but many recent items are also of interest. F & F is the mark used on plastic made by Fiedler & Fiedler Mold & Die Works, Inc. in the 1930s and 1940s. Objects that picture a black person may also be listed in this book under Advertising, Sign; Bank; Bottle Opener; Cookie Jar; Doll; Salt & Pepper; Sheet Music; Toy; etc.

Bell, Aunt Jemima, Kerchief, Rings, 4 ¼ In.	25
Box, Sample, Aunt Jemima Pancake Flour, Miniature, 4 Oz., 1919, 3 x 3 In.................	210
Bust, Woman, Found Objects, Sheet Metal, Red, Yellow, Earrings, 30 x 23 In...............	270
Cookie Jars are listed in the Cookie Jar category.	
Doll, African Dancer, Felt, Shoebutton Eyes, Red Lips, Reed Skirt, Lenci, Italy, 1920, 16 In.	4600
Doll, Automaton, Man Strums Banjo, Papier-Mache, Crossed Legs, Flirty Eyes, Germany, 16 In.	1495
Doll, Bisque Head, Intaglio Eyes, Sculpted Hair, Bent Limb Baby Body, Heubach, 11 In.............	1093
Doll, Boy, Bisque Socket Head, Glass Eyes, Sculpted Curls, Wide Smile, Heubach, 11 In.............	575
Doll, Cloth, Black Cotton, Oil Painted, Stitched Features, Bead Earrings, Yarn Hair, 20 In........	403
Doll, Composition Head, Cardboard Torso, Creeping, Clockwork, Ives, 11 In............................	1020
Doll, Folk Art, Velvet, Sateen, Embroidered, Applique Eyes, Silk Lips, Yarn Hair, c.1910, 21 In...	230
Doll, Leo Moss, Black, Composition Head, Glass Eyes, Kid Body, Short Hair, 1911, 22 In. .. *illus*	2857
Doll, Leo Moss, Papier-Mache, Socket Head, Sculpted Curls, Glass Eyes, 19 In. .... *illus*	8050

Bicycle, Schwinn, Phantom, Black, Red, Chrome, Bendix Brake, Persons Balloon Seat, 1950s
$1,652

Burchard Galleries

TIP
Don't store ceramic dishes or figurines for long periods of time in old newspaper wrappings. The ink can make indelible stains on china.

Bing & Grondahl, Figurine, Boy & Girl, Children Reading, Porcelain, c.1949, 4 x 4 In.
$165

Ruby Lane

Bing & Grondahl, Figurine, Cat, Sitting, Gray, 4 ¾ In.
$60

Replacements, Ltd.

Bing & Grondahl, Figurine, Mother Love, Ingebirg Irminger, Porcelain, Marked, 11 In.
$485

Ruby Lane

Binoculars, Lawrence & Mayo, Lynx, Brass, Compass, c.1910, 4 x 1 ¾ In.
$325

Ruby Lane

Birdcage, Twigs, Birch Bark, Painted Details, Tin Cage, Adirondack, c.1910, 74 x 19 In.
$530

Garth's Auctioneers & Appraisers

Bisque, Figurine, Bird, Goshawk, Kaiser, Bavaria Germany, 11 ½ In.
$106

Hess Auction Group

Black, Doll, Leo Moss, Black, Composition Head, Glass Eyes, Kid Body, Short Hair, 1911, 22 In.
$2,857

DuMouchelles

Black, Doll, Leo Moss, Papier-Mache, Socket Head, Sculpted Curls, Glass Eyes, 19 In.
$8,050

Theriault's

Black, Slave Tag, Servant, Copper, Diamond, Cut Corners, Charleston, Lafar, 1812, 2 ½ In.
$3,120

Brunk Auctions

Blenko, Lampshade, Chimney Shape, Wayne Husted, c.1955, 9 ½ In.
$55

Ruby Lane

Boch Freres, Vase, Crows, Oval, Glazed, Charles Catteau, Stamped, 11 x 6 In.
$1,875

Rago Arts and Auction Center

Doll, Mammy, Red, Black, White Patterned Handkerchiefs, Handmade, 1920s, 17 In		295
Doll, Young Girl, Blackamoor, Floral Dress, Waving, New Orleans, 1900s, 8 ½ In		6
Figure, Mammy, Holding Wood Basket, Tan Blouse, Red Skirt, Red Bandanna, 6 ¾ x 7 ¼ In		37
Figurine, Fisherman, Bucket, Fish, Shirt, Red, Pants, White, Cap, Wood, 16 In		238
Jewelry, Stickpin, Bust, Man's Head, Deep Red Stone, Carved, 14K Gold Mount, Box, ¾ In		500
Slave Tag, Servant, Copper, Diamond, Cut Corners, Charleston, Lafar, 1812, 2 ½ In	*illus*	3120
Toys are listed in the Toy category.		
Vase, Utopian, Boy With Floppy Hat, Owens, 8 In		354

BLENKO GLASS COMPANY is the 1930s successor to several glassworks founded by William John Blenko in Milton, West Virginia. In 1933, his son, William H. Blenko Sr., took charge. The company made tablewares and vases in classical shapes. In the late 1940s it hired talented designers and made innovative pieces. The company made a line of reproductions for Colonial Williamsburg. It is still in business and is best known today for its decorative wares and stained glass.

BLENKO HANDCRAFT

Decanter, Amberina, Ball Stopper, 1960s, 7 ½ x 4 In		45
Decanter, Amethyst, Stopper, Signed, 1952, 21 ¾ In		187
Decanter, Blue, Stopper, Wayne Husted, 1959, 15 ½ In		378
Decanter, Orange, 14 ½ In		65
Jug, Chartreuse, Air Bubbles, Applied Handle, Pontil, c.1948, 11 In		140
Lampshade, Chimney Shape, Wayne Husted, c.1955, 9 ½ In	*illus*	55
Pitcher, Anderson, No. 976, c.1962, 17 In		168
Pitcher, Orange, Miniature, Crackle Glass, 3 ½ In		10
Punch Bowl, 10 Cups, Ruby, Label, c.1950		175
Vase, Amberina, c.1964, 8 In		60
Vase, Amethyst Glass, Wayne Husted, Original Sticker, 24 ½ x 5 ½ In		281
Vase, Bubble, Raindrop, Square Cylinder, 13 x 2 ½ x 3 In		250
Vase, Optic, Sea Green, Pontil, 1950, 11 ½ x 10 In		129
Vase, Orbit, Blown Smoke Glass, 1950s, 7 In		146
Vase, Tangerine, Crackle Bell, Crimp Top, No. 388, 1950s, 8 ½ In		75

BLOWN GLASS, *see Glass-Blown category.*

BLUE GLASS, *see Cobalt Blue category.*

BLUE ONION, *see Onion category.*

BLUE WILLOW, *see Willow category.*

BOCH FRERES factory was founded in 1841 in La Louviere in eastern Belgium. The pottery wares resemble the work of Villeroy & Boch. The factory closed in 1985. M.R.L. Boch took over the production of tableware but went bankrupt in 1988. Le Hodey took over Boch Freres in 1989, using the name Royal Boch Manufacture S.A. It went bankrupt in 2009.

BOCH FRERES KERAMIS MADE IN BELGIUM

Box, La Louviere Enameled Art Deco, Signed Under Base, 5 x 6 ½ x 6 ½ In		34
Vase, Art Deco, Blue Enamel, Crackle Glaze, Charles Catteau, 9 x 5 ½ In		452
Vase, Art Deco, Gold Collar, Handles, Turquoise Interior, Enamel, Signed, 7 ½ x 5 ¾ In		181
Vase, Art Deco, Gold Handles, Turquoise Interior, Enamel, Signed, 8 ¾ x 5 In		90
Vase, Crows, Oval, Glazed, Charles Catteau, Stamped, 11 x 6 In	*illus*	1875
Vase, Flowers, Cobalt Blue Ground, Marked, Impressed 1885, 9 ¾ In	*illus*	250
Vase, Geometric Designs, Brown, Black, Beige, Glazed, Gres Keramis, 1928, 12 x 15 In		3250
Vase, Keramis, Flowers, Art Deco, 11 In		246
Vase, Penguins, Black, Green, Crackled, Keramis, 1927, 9 x 9 In		1875
Vase, Perseus & The Gorgons, Glazed, Gilt, Keramis, 1936, 13 x 9 In		875
Vase, Stylized Boats, Birds, Glazed, Stamped, Signed, 13 ½ x 8 In	*illus*	1125

BOEHM is the collector's name for the porcelains of Edward Marshall Boehm. In 1953 the Osso China Company was reorganized as Edward Marshall Boehm Inc. In the early days of the factory, dishes were made, but the elaborate and lifelike bird figurines are the best-known ware. Edward

---

Boch Freres, Vase, Flowers, Cobalt Blue Ground, Marked, Impressed 1885, 9 ¾ In.
$250

Neal Auction Co.

Boch Freres, Vase, Stylized Boats, Birds, Glazed, Stamped, Signed, 13 ½ x 8 In.
$1,125

Rago Arts and Auction Center

Boehm, Northern Parula Warbler, Flowers, Leaves, 15 ½ x 10 ¼ In.
$424

Leland Little Auctions

Bone, Box, Sewing, Lid, Prisoner Of War, Hunting Scene, Divided Interior, 1800s, 3 x 8 x 7 In.
$1,088

Neal Auction Co.

Bone Dish, Butterflies, Flowers, Crescent Shape, Gold Trim, Japan, c.1950, 6¾ In.
$18

Ruby Lane

Bookends, Cat, Brass, Walter Von Nessen, Chase Brass & Copper Co., 1930s, 7¼ x 4 In.
$1,000

Rago Arts and Auction Center

Bookends, Horse, Balking, Brown Over Orange Matte Glaze, Marked, Auburn, 9⅝ x 11½ In.
$944

Humler & Nolan

Marshall Boehm, the founder, died in 1969, but the firm continued to design and produce porcelain. The Museum of American Porcelain Art bought the assets, including the molds and trademarks, in 2015. The museum, expected to open in 2018, is located in South Euclid, Ohio, a suburb of Cleveland. The Boehm Showroom in Trenton, New Jersey, has exclusive use of the molds and trademarks. It also does restoration work and has some retired figures for sale.

Boehm Porcelain, LLC
1952–1954

Boehm Porcelain, LLC
1959–1970

Boehm Porcelain, LLC
1971+

Giraffes, Mother, Child, 29½ x 19½ In.		625
New Generation Eagle, 1993, 15 x 11 In.		250
Northern Parula Warbler, Flowers, Leaves, 15½ x 10¼ In.	illus	424

BOHEMIAN GLASS, *see Glass-Bohemian*

 BONE includes those articles made of bone not listed elsewhere in this book.

Box, Sewing, Lid, Prisoner Of War, Hunting Scene, Divided Interior, 1800s, 3 x 8 x 7 In...	illus	1088
Figurine, Anthurium, Small Pot, Carving, Japan, 1900s, 10 In.		344
Figurine, Cricket, Eggplant Vine, Carving, Japan, 1900s, 10 In.		780
Figurine, Female Figure, Basket, Carving, Africa, 1900s, 12 In.		180
Figurine, Guanyin, Carved, Bird Head Dress, Chinese, 1800s		660
Figurine, Hunchback Of Notre Dame, Carving, Character, France, 1900s		180
Figurine, Mythical Beast, Carved, Facing Upward, Without Stand, Japan, 1900s, 4¼ In.		406
Frame, Leaf Form Applique, Carved Cherubs, Beveled Mirror, Napoleonic, 3½ x 20 In.		3900
Game, Prisoner-Of-War, Napoleonic, 26 Non-Matching Bone Dominos, 6½ x 1¼ In.		960
Spatula, Chavin Cupsinique, Carved, Jaguar, Snake Design, 7 x 1½ In.		895

 BONE DISHES were considered a necessary part of a table setting for the Victorian table. The crescent-shaped dish was kept at the edge of the dinner plate so the bones removed from the fish could be stored away from the uneaten food. Some bone dishes were made in more fanciful shapes and many resemble fish.

Blue Onion Pattern, Blue Danube, c.1960, 6⅝ x 3⅛ In.		25
Butterflies, Flowers, Crescent Shape, Gold Trim, Japan, c.1950, 6¾ In.	illus	18
House, Stream, Bridge, Brown & White, Transferware, Royal Crownford, England, 6¾ In.		12

 BOOKENDS have probably been used since books became inexpensive. Early libraries kept books in cupboards, not on open shelves. By the 1870s bookends appeared, especially homemade fret-carved wooden examples. Most bookends listed in this book date from the twentieth century. Bookends are also listed in other categories by manufacturer or material. All bookends listed here are pairs.

Balking Horse, Brown & Orange Matte Glaze, Marked, Auburn, 10 x 11½ In.		945
Big Rig Truck, Bronze, Hammered, Molded, Arched Top, Flared Base, 1930s, 6 x 6 In.		405
Buffalo, Bronze, Standing, Base, Paul Herzel, Pompeian Bronze Works, 1920, 5 x 6¾ x 2 In.		295
Cat, Brass, Walter Von Nessen, Chase Brass & Copper Co., 1930s, 7¼ x 4 In.	illus	1000
Dog, Scottish Terrier, Cast Iron, Bradley & Hubbard, 5 x 3 x 2 In.		225
Eagle, Federal Shield, Head In Profile, Metal, 4¼ In., Pair		60
Fish Leaping, Bronze, E.T. Hurley, Signed, c.1925, 6 In.		2360
Hiawatha, Cast Iron, Male, Female, Busts, Quote, 1920, 6¼ x 5¾ In., Pair		140
Horse, Balking, Brown Over Orange Matte Glaze, Marked, Auburn, 9⅝ x 11½ In.	illus	944
Johnny Appleseed, Bronze, Plaque, Molded Figure, Hammered, 1920s, 6 x 4 In.		420
Lovebirds, Silvered Bronze, H. Vandaele, 3⅞ x 2⅝ In.		1000
Man, Seated, Bronze, 7¼ In.		113

Mice, Oak, Carved, Robert Mouseman Thompson, England, 1900, 6 x 4 x 3½ In. .... *illus*	750
Pelican, Art Deco, Gray Green Crystalline Glaze, Guerin Pottery, 5 x 6 In. .... *illus*	501
Pony Express Rider, Silver Plated, Metal, Marked H.A.M.N., 5½ x 6 x 3 In.	488
Rebecca At The Well, Semigloss Gray Glaze, Water In Green, Impressed Logo, 7 x 5½ In.	250
Right Triangle Shape Steel, Forged, Albert Paley, 14½ x 4¼ In., Pair	4375

BOOKMARKS were originally made of parchment, cloth, or leather. Soon woven silk ribbon, thin cardboard, celluloid, wood, silver, tortoiseshell, and metals were used. Examples made before 1850 are scarce, but there are many to be found dating before 1920.

Brass, Enameled, Shepherd's Hook, Butterfly, 5⅝ In.	11
Brass, Reverse Crystal, Cow Jumped Over The Moon, 2¼ In.	49
Celluloid, Die Cut, Triangular Top, Purple Lilies, Victorian, 5¼ x 1½ In.	14
Mother-Of-Pearl, Anchor, Mirror, c.1800, 2¾ x 1 In. .... *illus*	384
Silk, Red, Shepherdess & Lamb Drawing, 12 In.	42
Sterling Silver, Butterfly, James Avery, 2⅛ In.	35
Sterling Silver, Eagle Head Finial, Tiffany & Co., 3¼ In.	115
Sterling Silver, Greek Masks, Comedy & Tragedy, 2¾ x 1¼ In.	58
Sterling Silver, Interlocking Circles, Punched, c.1950, 2¾ In.	95

BOSSONS character wall masks (heads), plaques, figurines, and other decorative pieces were made by W.H. Bossons, Limited, of Congleton, England. The company was founded in 1946 and closed in 1996. Dates shown are the date the item was introduced.

BOSSONS

Wall Mask, Man, Green Hat, Split Mustache, 6 x 5 In.	18
Wall Mask, Man, Hat, Dog, Multicolor, 9½ x 9 In.	30
Wall Mask, Man, Raccoon Hat, 7 x 5 In.	18
Wall Mask, Man, Red Turban, Blue Shirt, Yellow Big Cat, 8½ x 9½ In. .... *illus*	24
Wall Mask, Man, Striped Turban, Gray Beard, 7½ x 5 In.	18

BOSTON & SANDWICH CO. *pieces may be found in the Sandwich Glass category.*

BOTTLE collecting has become a major American hobby. There are several general categories of bottles, such as historic flasks, bitters, household, and figural. ABM means the bottle was made by an automatic bottle machine after 1903. Pyro is the shortened form of the word *pyroglaze*, an enameled lettering used on bottles after the mid-1930s. This form of decoration is also called ACL or applied color label. For more prices, go to kovels.com. Shapes of bottles often indicate the age of the bottle.

Calabash flask	Teakettle ink	Case gin bottle
1840-1870	1830-1885	1650-1920

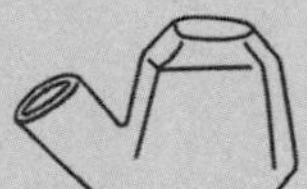

Avon started in 1886 as the California Perfume Company. It was not until 1929 that the name Avon was used. In 1939, it became Avon Products, Inc. Avon has made many figural bottles filled with cosmetic products. Ceramic, plastic, and glass bottles were made in limited editions from 1965 to 1980. There was a limited-edition bottle collecting frenzy and prices rose. By 2018 the bottle prices were back to a very low level.

Avon, Car, 1965 Corvette Stingray, Green, Contents, Box, 1970s	13
Avon, Car, Porsche, 1968, Amber, Wild Country After Shave, Box, 2 Oz.	16
Avon, Dog, St. Bernard, Avon Spicy After Shave, Amber Glass, 5 Oz.	10
Avon, Gas Pump, Remember When, Wild Country After Shave, Red, 1976-77, 4 Oz., 9½ In.	8
Avon, Hammer, On The Mark Everest After Shave, Amber Glass Handle, 2½ Oz., 8½ In.	10
Avon, Heavenly Angel, Candid Cologne, Box, 1980s, 1 Oz.	6
Avon, Little Miss Muffet, Topaze Cologne, Milk Glass, 1978-80, 2 Oz.	5
Avon, Merry Mouse, Milk Glass, Zany Cologne, Box, 1979, ¾ Oz.	11
Avon, Old Fashion Boot, Pincushion Top, Moonwind Cologne, Blue, Box, 1970s, 5¼ In.	12
Avon, Pheasant, Oland Aftershave Lotion, 1970s, 12 x 7 In.	9

Bookends, Mice, Oak, Carved, Robert Mouseman Thompson, England, 1900, 6 x 4 x 3½ In.
$750

Rago Arts and Auction Center

Bookends, Pelican, Art Deco, Gray Green Crystalline Glaze, Guerin Pottery, 5 x 6 In.
$501

Humler & Nolan

Bookmark, Mother-Of-Pearl, Anchor, Mirror, c.1800, 2¾ x 1 In.
$384

Ruby Lane

Bossons, Wall Mask, Man, Red Turban, Blue Shirt, Yellow Big Cat, 8½ x 9½ In.
$24

Martin Auction Co.

B

Bottle, Bitters, Dr. Flint's Quaker, Aqua, 4 Panels, Applied Mouth, Label, Contents, c.1880, 9 ½ In.
$3,738

Bottle, Bitters, Ear Of Corn, National, Patent 1867, Collar Mouth, Yellow Amber, 12 In.
$527

Bottle, Bitters, Pig, Berkshire, Amann & Co., Cincinnati, Olive Amber, 1870s, 10 In.
$2,808

Bottle, Bitters, S.T. Drake's, Plantation, 6 Log Cabin, Patented 1862, Yellow Amber, 10 In.
$152

Bottle, Bitters, Simon's Centennial, Bust, Washington, Green Aqua, Ring Mouth, 1876-80, 9 ⅞ In.
$748

Bottle, Bitters, Star, Wait's Liver & Kidney, Label, Amber, Tooled Lip, c.1895, 9 In.
$380

Bottle, Cologne, 6-Panel, Light Blue Opalescent, Hexagonal, Stopper, c.1855, 7 x 5 In.
$526

Bottle, Flask, Cornucopia, Olive Green, Keen-Marlboro Street Glassworks, c.1835, 6¾ In.
$175

Bottle, Flask, Cornucopia, Urn, Teal Blue, Sheared Tooled Lip, Open Pontil, c.1843, Pt.
$380

B

Avon, Upside Down, Flower Blossom, Clear, Gold Tone Plastic Cap, 1970s, 3 In.	10
Barber, Amber, Hobnail, 8¼ In.	20
Barber, Cranberry Opalescent, 8 In.	113
Barber, Cranberry Opalescent, Stripes, Stick Neck, 6¾ In.	70
Barber, Cut Glass, Green Cut To Clear, Honeycomb, Crosscut, Silver Rim & Stopper, 7¾ In.	150
Barber, Milk Glass, Courting Couples, Flower Wreaths, Pair	297

Beam bottles were made to hold Kentucky Straight Bourbon, made by the James B. Beam Distilling Company. The Beam series of ceramic bottles began in 1953.

Beam, Black Hills, Mt. Rushmore, Regal China, 1969, 4/5 Qt.	12
Beam, BPOE, Benevolent Order Of Elks, Centennial 1868-1968, Round, Star, Handle, 11 In.	23
Beam, Genie Bottle Style, Aqua Blue, Swirl Pattern, Cork Stopper, Regal China, 1966, 13 In.	18
Beam, Kentucky Derby, 100th, Churchill Downs, 1974, 4/5 Qt.	28
Beam, Las Vegas, Hoover Dam, Lake Mead, Attractions, Regal China, 1970s, 12 x 6 In.	20
Beam, Pony Express, Man On Horseback, St. Joseph, Mo., Sacramento, Calif., Regal China	40
Beer, Dr. Cronk, Cobalt Blue, 12-Sided, Sloping Collar, 1845-60, 9⅝ In.	1265
Beer, G. Van Benschoten Brown Stout, Slug Plate, Teal, Blob Top, c.1850, 7 In.	345
Beer, Jacob Schuster, Danville, Pa., Slug Plate, Brown Stout, Green, 7¼ In.	288
Beer, Long's Champagne, Cincinnati, Ohio, Yellow Amber, 10-Sided, Double Collar, 9 In.	690
Beer, P.L. Brewing Co., Danville, Pa., Yellow Amber, Tooled Loop Seal Mouth, 7 In.	173
Bininger, A.M. & Co., Old Dominion Wheat Tonic, Grass Green, 1860-70, 9¾ In.	1093
Bininger, A.M. & Co., Old Dominion Wheat Tonic, Olive Yellow, 1860-65, 9¾ In.	518
Bininger, A.M., No. 375 Broadway N.Y., Strawberry Puce, Sloping Collar, 9¾ In.	1265
Bininger, A.M., No. 375 Broadway N.Y., Topaz, Sloping Collar, 1860-70, 9¾ In.	489
Bininger, Bininger's Travelers Guide, Amber, Teardrop Flask, Double Collar, 6¼ In.	575
Bitters, American Life, P.E. Iler, Omaha, Neb., Cabin, Amber, Tapered Collar, 9¼ In.	4025
Bitters, Aromatic Orange Stomach, Semi-Cabin, Orange Amber, Sloping Collar, 9 In.	1495
Bitters, Baker's Orange Grove, Semi-Cabin, Yellow Apricot, c.1870, 9½ In.	1035
Bitters, Bancroft's, D.W. Bancroft, Marshfield, Vt., Aqua, c.1875, 9 In.	1035
Bitters, Berkshire, Amann & Co., Cincinnati, O., Figural, Pig, Tobacco Amber, 10 In.	3163
Bitters, Bourbon Whiskey, Barrel, Strawberry Puce, Flattened Collar, c.1870, 9½ In.	489
Bitters, Bourbon Whiskey, Barrel, Topaz Puce, Flattened Collar, 9¼ In.	460
Bitters, Brown's Celebrated Indian Herb, Indian Princess, Chocolate Amber, 12 In.	1955
Bitters, C.C. Doty Genuine Vermont, Yellow Amber, Rounded Shoulders, Label, 8⅜ In.	863
Bitters, Carlsbader, Crown, Anchor, 2 Indented Bands, Sloping Collar, c.1890, 10¼ In.	690
Bitters, Doctor Fisch's, W.H. Ware, Patented 1866, Fish, Golden Amber, c.1870, 11½ In.	403
Bitters, Dr Bull's Superior Stomach, St. Louis, Amber, Arched Sides, 1875-85, 9 In.	242
Bitters, Dr. C.W. Roback's Stomach, Cincinnati, O., Barrel, Yellow Olive Amber, 9½ In.	3450
Bitters, Dr. Flint's Quaker, Aqua, 4 Panels, Applied Mouth, Label, Contents, c.1880, 9½ In. *illus*	3738
Bitters, Dr. Flint's Quaker, Providence, R.I., Aqua, Applied Mouth, Label, 9¼ In.	863
Bitters, Dr. J. Hostetter's Stomach, Dark Olive, Arched Sides, 1860-70, 9⅞ In.	230
Bitters, Dr. Planett's, Aqua, Swirls, Tapered Collar, 9⅞ In.	374
Bitters, Drake's Plantation, 6 Log, Apricot Puce, Sloping Collar, 9⅞ In.	518
Bitters, Drake's Plantation, 6 Log, Cherry Puce, Sloping Collar, c.1870, 10 In.	253
Bitters, Drake's Plantation, 6 Log, Shaded Citron, Sloping Collar, 9¾ In.	3738
Bitters, Drake's Plantation, 6 Log, Yellow Amber, Sloping Collar, 9⅞ In.	748
Bitters, Drake's Plantation, 6 Log, Yellow Olive, Arabesque, Patented 1862, Cabin, 10 In.	863
Bitters, Ear Of Corn, National, Patent 1867, Collar Mouth, Yellow Amber, 12 In. *illus*	527
Bitters, Figural, Pig, Suffolk, Philbrook & Tucker, Boston, Amber, 9½ In.	460
Bitters, Foster's Tonic, Blue Aqua, Double Collar, Iron Pontil, 1850-60, 8⅛ In.	3163
Bitters, Greeley's Bourbon, Barrel, Smoky Olive Topaz, Flattened Collar, c.1870, 9 In.	575
Bitters, H.L. Mishler's Keystone, Solvent Remedy, Antidyspeptic, Yellow Amber, 9½ In.	4905
Bitters, Hall's, E.E. Hall, New Haven, Established 1842, Barrel, Golden Amber, 9¼ In.	138
Bitters, Holtzermann's Patent Stomach, Cabin, Amber, Sloping Collar, Label, 9⅞ In.	1265
Bitters, J.C. & Co., Pineapple, Amber, Double Collar, 1865-75, 8⅝ In.	863
Bitters, Jackson's Aromatic Life, Yellow Green, Indented Panels, Sloping Collar, 9 In.	3450
Bitters, John Root's, 1834, Buffalo, N.Y., Semi-Cabin, Amethyst Tint, Tooled Lip, 10⅛ In.	748
Bitters, Jones Universal Stomach, Williamsport, Penn., Amber, Double Collar, 9⅛ In.	480
Bitters, Kelly's Old Cabin, Patented 1863, Cabin, Deep Amber, 9½ In.	3450
Bitters, Kimball's Jaundice, Troy, N.H., Yellow Olive, Sloping Collar, Label, c.1850, 7 In.	1955

Bottle, Flask, Eagle In Flight, Anchor, Smooth Base, Double Collar, Yellow, Olive, c.1860, Pt.
$4,095

Glass Works Auctions

Bottle, Gemel, Blown, Pale Teal, Rough Pontil, c.1825, 9¼ x 3½ In.
$93

Jeffrey S. Evans

Bottle, Ink, Pressed Glass, Blue Green Whitish Flecks, 16 Vertical Column Shape, c.1835, 1⅝ In.
$246

Glass Works Auctions

Bottle, Medicine, Worlds Hair Restorer, Pink Amethyst, Double Collar, c.1870, 7 In.
$644

Glass Works Auctions

Bottle, Seal, Natichitoches Gegrundet, 1811, Label, Green, Louisiana, 1800s, 9 ½ In.
$854

Neal Auction Co.

Bitters, Morning Inceptum, 5-Point Star, Yellow Amber, 3-Sided, c.1872, 12 ⅝ In.	288
Bitters, N.K. Brown, Iron & Quinine, Burlington, Vt., Yellow Amber, Tooled Lip, 8 ⅜ In.	863
Bitters, National, Ear Of Corn, Amber Shaded To Yellow, 1867-75, 12 ½ In.	345
Bitters, Old Homestead Wild Cherry, Cabin, Golden Yellow, Sloping Collar, 9 ¾ In.	489
Bitters, Pig, Berkshire, Amann & Co., Cincinnati, Olive Amber, 1870s, 10 In. _illus_	2808
Bitters, S.T. Drake's, Plantation, 6 Log, Patented 1862, Yellow Amber, 10 In. _illus_	152
Bitters, Simon's Centennial, Bust, Washington, Green Aqua, Ring Mouth, 1876-80, 9 ⅞ In. _illus_	748
Bitters, Simon's Centennial, Bust, Washington, Aqua, Striations, 10 In.	644
Bitters, Sol Frank's Panacea, Golden Amber, Lighthouse, Double Collar, c.1870, 10 In.	4313
Bitters, Solomons' Strengthening & Invigorating, Savannah, Georgia, Blue, 9 ⅝ In.	2223
Bitters, Star, Wait's Liver & Kidney, Label, Amber, Tooled Lip, c.1895, 9 In. _illus_	380
Bitters, Tellers Herb, 1834, Yellow Amber, Indented Panels, Double Collar, 10 In.	805
Bitters, Wild Cherry, H.P. Herb, Cherry Tree, Cabin, 7Up Green, Tooled Lip, 8 ¾ In.	5750
Bitters, William Allen's Congress, Semi-Cabin, Green, Indented Panels, 10 ¼ In.	1495
Bitters, William Allen's Congress, Semi-Cabin, Blue Green, Sloping Collar, 10 ⅜ In.	1955
Coca-Cola bottles are listed in the Coca-Cola category.	
Cologne, 6 Panel, Light Blue Opalescent, Hexagonal, Stopper, c.1855, 7 x 5 In. _illus_	526
Cologne, Bead & Rib Pattern, Cobalt Blue, Cylindrical Neck, Tooled Lip, c.1870, 5 ¾ In.	489
Cologne, Blue, Palmette & Scroll, Pinched Waist, Inward Rolled Lip, Flared Base, 5 ¾ In.	1170
Cologne, Bunker Hill Monument, Deep Cobalt Blue, Tooled Lip, 1865-80, 12 In.	633
Cologne, Hermes Head, Robin's-Egg Blue Opalescent, Trophy, Outward Rolled Lip, 6 ½ In.	978
Cologne, Overlay, Cobalt Cut To Clear Spots, Bulbous, Tapered, Stopper, Pontil, c.1855, 5 In.	207
Cologne, Vertical Ribs, Flowers, Lavender Blue, 6-Sided, Bulbous Center, Rolled Lip, 9 In.	575
Cosmetic, Dr. Tebbetts' Physiological Hair Regenerator, Pink Amethyst, 7 ⅝ In.	978
Cosmetic, G.A.P. Mason Alpine Hair Balm, Providence, R.I., Olive, Indented Panels, 7 In.	8625
Cosmetic, Professor Mott's Magic Hair Invigorator, 25 Cents, Aqua, Pontil, 6 ⅜ In.	460
Cure, Frog Pond, Chill & Fever, Amber, Indented Panels, Tooled Lip, c.1890, 7 ⅛ In.	403
Cure, Kluttz's Chill, Kluttz & Co., Salisbury, N.C., Aqua, Tooled Lip, c.1880, 6 In.	690
Cure, Mead & Carrington's Fever & Ague, Aqua, Tapered Collar, 1840-60, 6 ⅝ In.	1955
Cure, Simon's Hepatic Compound Of Liver, Pelzer & King, Charleston, Amber, 9 ⅜ In.	1265
Cure, Warner's Safe Diabetes, Safe, Rochester, N.Y., Slug Plate, Amber, 9 ½ In.	460
Decanter, Deep Olive Yellow, Spiral Ribs, Diamond Band, Flared Lip, 3-Piece Mold, Pt.	2925
Demijohn, Aqua Blue, Bubbles, Dip Mold, Sloping Collar, 1840-60, 11 In.	2875
Demijohn, Olive Topaz, Sloping Collar, Iron Pontil, 12 ¼ In.	920
Demijohn, Sapphire Blue, Sloping Collar, c.1870, 12 ¼ In.	2760
Figural, Milk Pail, Boston, Mass, Turquoise, Tin Lid, Swing Handle, Pt.	242
Figural, Pig, Duffy Crescent Saloon, Louisville, Rooster On Crescent Moon, Amber, 7 ½ In.	1380
Figural, Pig, Good Old Bourbon In A Hog's, Finger Pointing, Amber, 6 ¼ In.	460
Figural, Pineapple, Golden Yellow Amber, Double Collar, Pontil, c.1870, 8 ⅝ In.	460
Figural, Waiter, Frosted, Black Frosted Head Closure, 1890-1910, 14 In.	150
Flask, Book, Flint Enamel Glaze, Stamped Hoo Doo Bible, Mark, Fenton's 1849, 1849-58, 6 In.	840
Flask, Cactus, Engraved, Profile, Silver Mine, Hallet Kilbourn, 7 ½ x 5 ½ In.	3025
Flask, Cannon, A Little More Grape, Blue Green, Sheared, Taylor, Pt.	546
Flask, Chestnut, 24 Swirled Ribs, Aqua, Flattened, Applied Lip, Pontil, 8 ¼ In.	863
Flask, Chestnut, 24 Swirled Ribs, Red Amber, Sheared, Pontil, Zanesville, 5 ½ In.	257
Flask, Chestnut, Oval, Slender Neck, c.1800, 9 In.	71
Flask, Chestnut, Yellow Olive Green, Outward Rolled Lip, Pontil, 8 ⅜ In.	345
Flask, Corn For The World, Orange Amber, Red Tones, Double Collar, Qt.	2223
Flask, Cornucopia & Urn, Light Emerald Green, Sheared, Pontil, ½ Pt.	546
Flask, Cornucopia, Olive Green, Keen-Marlboro Street Glassworks, c.1835, 6 ¾ In. _illus_	175
Flask, Cornucopia, Urn, Teal Blue, Sheared Tooled Lip, Open Pontil, c.1843, Pt. _illus_	380
Flask, Diamond Pattern, Citrine, 1800s, 5 ¾ In.	960
Flask, Double Eagle, Cornflower Blue, Double Collar, 1860-70, Qt.	546
Flask, Double Eagle, Forest Green, Sheared, Pontil, Stoddard, Pt.	878
Flask, Double Eagle, Moonstone, Amethyst Tone, Sheared, Pt.	3163
Flask, Double Eagle, Pale Apple Green, Sheared Mouth, Pt.	1610
Flask, Double Eagle, Yellow Amber, Ring Mouth, Pt.	489
Flask, Double Eagle, Yellow Olive, Sheared, Pontil, Qt.	702
Flask, Double Masonic, Light Blue Green, Tooled Lip, Pontil, ½ Pt.	460
Flask, Eagle & Cornucopia, Aqua, Sheared, ½ Pt.	690

Flask, Eagle & Cornucopia, Blue Aqua, Pontil, ½ Pt.	345
Flask, Eagle & Grapes, Amber, Pontil, Sheared Mouth, Qt.	633
Flask, Eagle & Grapes, Yellow Olive, Amber Tone, Sheared, Pontil, Qt.	7020
Flask, Eagle & Lyre, Deep Aqua, Ribbed Sides, Sheared, Pontil, Pt.	3218
Flask, Eagle & Masonic Arch, Smoky Sapphire, Tapered, Rolled Lip, Pt.	978
Flask, Eagle & Stag, Coffin & Hay, Aqua, Side Ribs, Pontil, ½ Pt.	431
Flask, Eagle & Tree, Green Aqua, Ribbed Sides, Pontil, Sheared Mouth, Qt.	1150
Flask, Eagle & Willington, Blue Green, Sloping Collar, Pt.	2645
Flask, Eagle & Willington, Shaded Orange To Blood Amber, Qt.	1170
Flask, Eagle In Flight, Anchor, Smooth Base, Double Collar, Yellow, Olive, c.1860, Pt. *illus*	4095
Flask, Eagle, Concentric Rings, Light Green, Sheared, Pontil, Qt.	5850
Flask, Flag & Stoddard, Yellow Amber, Olive Tone, Sheared, Pontil, Pt.	17550
Flask, Flora Temple, Blue Aqua, Mouth Ring, Pt.	1404
Flask, For Pike's Peak, Prospector & Eagle, Aqua, Sheared, ½ Pt.	345
Flask, For Pike's Peak, Prospector, Hunter, Yellow Olive, Pt.	2574
Flask, Franklin & Dyott, Aqua, Sheared Mouth, Qt.	431
Flask, Horse, Yellow Olive, Globular, Flattened, Ring Mouth, Pt.	2106
Flask, Horseman & Hound, Deep Claret, Sheared, Pontil, Pt.	4388
Flask, Jackson & Eagle, Light Green, Pontil, Pt.	3163
Flask, Jenny Lind & Glasshouse, Calabash, Sapphire Blue, 9¾ In.	3163
Flask, Jenny Lind & Glasshouse, Calabash, Shaded Olive, Applied Lip, Qt.	2070
Flask, Jenny Lind & Lyre, Blue Aqua, Sheared & Tooled Lip, Pt.	748
Flask, Jenny Lind & Lyre, Deep Aqua, Sheared Mouth, Pontil, Qt.	936
Flask, Jenny Lind, Calabash, Pale Green, Double Collar, Qt.	219
Flask, Kossuth & Frigate, Calabash, Yellow Olive, Sloping Collar, Qt.	24150
Flask, Kossuth, Bridgeton & Sloop, Light Blue Green, Pt.	556
Flask, Kossuth, Bust & Tree, Golden Yellow, Sloping Collar, Qt.	556
Flask, Lafayette & Eagle, Aqua, Sheared Mouth, Pt.	460
Flask, Lafayette & Liberty Cap, Yellow Amber, Olive Tone, ½ Pt.	1053
Flask, Masonic & Eagle, Light Green, Pontil, Sheared Mouth, Pt.	489
Flask, Masonic & Eagle, Olive Green, Sheared Mouth, ½ Pt.	345
Flask, Masonic & Eagle, Pink Tint, Sheared Mouth, Tooled Lip, Pt.	1093
Flask, Masonic Arch & Eagle, Clear, Tooled Lip, Keene, Pt.	3803
Flask, Mediterranean, Green, Globular, Flared, Cylindrical Neck, 25 In.	2700
Flask, Pitkin Type, 16 Broken Ribs, Swirled To Right, Emerald Green, Half Post, 6¾ In.	489
Flask, Pitkin Type, 16 Broken Ribs, Swirled To Right, Emerald Green, Sheared, Pontil, 5¾ In.	431
Flask, Pitkin Type, 24 Ribs, Swirled To Right, Emerald Green, Sheared Mouth, Half Post, 7 In.	1265
Flask, Pitkin Type, 30 Broken Ribs, Swirled To Right, Aqua, Half Post, 1815-35, 6⅝ In.	489
Flask, Pitkin Type, 35 Broken Ribs, Blue Green, Sheared Mouth, Half Post, 1820-30, 6 In.	575
Flask, Pitkin Type, 36 Broken Ribs, Swirled To Left, Yellow Olive, 1790-1830, 7 In.	2415
Flask, Pitkin Type, 36 Broken Ribs, Swirled To Right, Yellow Olive, Half Post, 4¾ In.	1265
Flask, Scroll, Aqua Blue, Sheared Mouth, ½ Pt.	460
Flask, Scroll, Blue Aqua, Pinched Waist, Sheared Mouth, Qt.	546
Flask, Scroll, McCarty & Torreyson, Aqua, Shaped, Iron Pontil, Pt.	2070
Flask, Scroll, McCarty & Torreyson, Aqua, Shaped, Qt.	3163
Flask, Scroll, Sage Green, Applied Mouth Ring, Pontil, 1845-60, Pt.	2340
Flask, Scroll, Sapphire Blue, Applied Mouth Ring, Iron Pontil, Qt.	5265
Flask, Sheaf Of Wheat & Westford, Shaded Amber, Sheared, ½ Pt.	1404
Flask, Sheaf Of Wheat, Calabash, Smoky Aqua, Amber Striations, Qt.	3218
Flask, Sheaf Of Wheat, Farm Tools, Dove, Amber, Sheared, ½ Pt.	1170
Flask, Sheets & Duffy, Kensington, Blue Aqua, Strapside, Ring Mouth, Qt.	207
Flask, Soldier & Sunflower, Calabash, Blue Green, Sloping Collar	978
Flask, Spring Garden & Anchor, Olive Yellow, Applied Collar, Pt.	1150
Flask, Stiegel Type, Diamond Daisy Over Flutes, Amethyst, Sheared, Pontil, Pocket, 5 In.	4680
Flask, Success To The Railroad, Horse Pulling Cart, Yellow Olive, Pt.	575
Flask, Summer & Winter Tree, Shaded Blue Green, Double Collar, Qt.	805
Flask, Summer & Winter, Golden Yellow, Amber Tone, Double Collar, Qt.	1521
Flask, Sunburst, Aqua Blue, Vertical Ribs, Sheared Mouth, ½ Pt.	242
Flask, Sunburst, Clear Green, Horizontal Ribs On Sides, Pt.	690
Flask, Sunburst, Clear, Sheared, Pontil, ½ Pt.	690

Bottle, Shaker, Cough Cure, Aqua, Label, Claurice Baker Extract Co., c.1890, 5⅜ In.
$149

Glass Works Auctions

Bottle, Shaker, Mixed Pickles, E.D. Pettengill Co., Patd. Jany 11th 1898, 7¼ In.
$632

Glass Works Auctions

BOTTLE

Bottle, Shaker, Pepper Relish, E.D. Pettengill & Co., Aqua, Label, c.1890, 5⅜ In.
$431

Glass Works Auctions

Bottle, Shaker, Syrup, Canterbury, N.H., Aqua, Applied Collar, Open Pontil, c.1850, 7 In.
$1,035

Glass Works Auctions

Bottle, Snuff, Red Jasper, Overlay, Figural Landscape, White Ground, Stopper, 2¾ In. .
$100

Eldred's Auctioneers and Appraisers

Flask, Sunburst, Moss Green, Horizontal Ribs, Sheared Mouth, Pt.	4600
Flask, Sunburst, Old Amber, Horizontal Ribs, Sheared Mouth, ½ Pt.	1840
Flask, Sunburst, Yellow Green, Tapered, Sheared Mouth, Pontil, Pt.	2430
Flask, Sunburst, Yellow Olive, Horizontal Ribs, Tapered, ½ Pt.	920
Flask, Taylor & Fells Point Monument, Pink Amethyst, Sheared, Pt.	17250
Flask, Traveler's Companion & Star, Yellow Green, Double Collar, Pt.	6435
Flask, Union, Clasped Hands & Eagle, Calabash, Citron, Double Collar	1035
Flask, Union, Clasped Hands & Eagle, Golden Yellow, Ring Mouth, ½ Pt.	690
Flask, Union, Clasped Hands & Wreath, Aqua, Ring Mouth, ½ Pt.	242
Flask, Washington & Bridgeton, Aqua, Pontil, Sheared & Tooled Lip, Qt.	374
Flask, Washington & Eagle, Pale Apple Green, Pontil, Pt.	460
Flask, Washington & Fells Point Monument, Light Pink Amethyst, Pt.	805
Flask, Washington & Jackson, Deep Grass Green, Pontil, Pt.	1610
Flask, Washington & Jackson, Yellow Amber, Olive Tone, Pontil, Pt.	316
Flask, Washington & Monument, Aqua, Tooled Lip, Pontil, Pt.	431
Flask, Washington & Taylor Never Surrenders, Emerald Green, Sheared, Qt.	1265
Flask, Washington & Taylor Never Surrenders, Pink Puce, Pontil, Qt.	6325
Flask, Washington & Taylor, Clear, Amethyst Tint, Pontil, Pt.	633
Flask, Washington & Taylor, Deep Sapphire Blue, Sloping Collar, Qt.	4888
Flask, Washington & Tree, Calabash, Aqua, Double Collar, Qt.	161
Flask, Washington, Father Of His Country, Golden, Puce Striations, Qt.	11115
Flask, Washington, Father Of His Country, Shaded Blue Green, Pt.	1404
Flask, Will You Take A Drink, Duck, Pale Aqua, Strapside, ½ Pt.	748
Food, Dabler's Flavors, Vanilla Caramel, Paper Label, 1920s, 8 Oz.	15
Food, Dorlon & Shaffer Pickled Oysters, Fulton Market, N.Y., Aqua, 5⅞ In.	316
Food, Pettengill's Pure Horse Radish, Blue Aqua, Stepped Sides, Swollen Neck, 6 In.	173
Food, Warsaw Salt Co., Monogram, Choice Table, Amber, Square, Screw Lid, c.1900, 6 In.	196
Fruit Jar, A. Stone & Co., Philada, Aqua, Threaded Closure, Pt.	920
Fruit Jar, Ball Mason, Script, Yellow Amber, ABM Lip, Screw Cap, 1910-20, Pt.	374
Fruit Jar, Cornflower Blue, Petaled Shoulders, Square Collar Mouth, 1845-60, 10¼ In.	1053
Fruit Jar, E.C. Flaccus Co., Trademark, Stag's Head, Yellow, Rayed Milk Glass Lid, Pt.	1150
Fruit Jar, Eagle, Aqua, Glass Lid, Iron Yoke Closure, 1870-80, Pt.	1265
Fruit Jar, Eureka, 7, Pat'd Dec 27th, 1864, Aqua, Ground Lip, Metal Cap, Pt.	184
Fruit Jar, F & J Bodine, Philada, Aqua, Ground Lip, Tin Lid, Pt.	1035
Fruit Jar, Flaccus Bros., Steers Head, Green, Metal Band, Milk Glass Lid, c.1910, Pt.	546
Fruit Jar, Flaccus Bros., Steers Head, Milk Glass, Ground Lip, Matching Cap, Pt.	242
Fruit Jar, Flaccus Bros., Steers Head, Straw Yellow, Metal Band, Milk Glass Lid, Pt.	805
Fruit Jar, Gilberds, 5-Point Star, Aqua, Stepped Glass Lid, Wire Closure, c.1885, Pt.	1265
Fruit Jar, Haines's Improved, March 1st 1870, Aqua, Glass Lid, Wire Clamp, Qt.	127
Fruit Jar, Hilton's, Pat. Mar. 10th 1868, Blue Aqua, Original Glass Lid, Wire Clamp, Qt.	460
Fruit Jar, Howe Jar, Scranton, Pa., Aqua, Domed Glass Lid, Wire Closure, c.1890, Pt.	184
Fruit Jar, John M. Moore & Co., Script, Aqua, Glass Lid, Iron Yoke Clamp, 1861-70, Pt.	4888
Fruit Jar, Ladies Favorite, Woman Holding Jar, Wm. L. Haller, Carlisle, Pa., Aqua, Pt.	10350
Fruit Jar, Lafayette, Script, Patented Sept. 2, 1884, Aug. 4, 1885, Glass Stopper, Clamp, Pt.	345
Fruit Jar, Mason, Amber, Screw On Zinc Lid, 1880-95, Pt.	374
Fruit Jar, Mason, Light Blue Green, ABM Lip, Screw-On Lid, 1915-25, Pt.	81
Fruit Jar, Mason's Keystone, Patent, Nov. 30th, 1858, Light Topaz, Zinc Lid, Pt.	403
Fruit Jar, Mason's Patent, Nov. 30th 1858, Maltese Cross, Straw Yellow, Pt.	518
Fruit Jar, Mason's Patent, Nov. 30th 1858, Yellow Olive, Milk Glass Lined Zinc Lid, Pt.	546
Fruit Jar, Mason's Patent, Nov. 30th 1858, Yellow, Amber Tone, Midget Pt.	2415
Fruit Jar, Mason's, SCCo, Monogram, Patent Nov. 30th 1858, Yellow, Amber Striations, Pt.	978
Fruit Jar, MGMCo, Monogram, Clear, Zinc Screw-On Lid, 1890-95, Qt.	161
Fruit Jar, Millville Atmospheric Fruit Jar, Aqua, Domed Glass Lid, Iron Yoke Clamp, Pt.	230
Fruit Jar, Moore's Patent, Dec 3d 1861, Aqua, Glass Lid, Iron Yoke Clamp, Pt.	431
Fruit Jar, Newman's, Patent Dec. 20th 1859, Clear, Tin Cap, c.1860, Qt.	805
Fruit Jar, Petal, Grass Green, 10 Shoulder Panels, Qt.	1495
Fruit Jar, Protector, Aqua, 6-Sided, Indented Panels, Wire Closure, c.1875, Pt.	374
Fruit Jar, Safety, Golden Amber, Glass Lid, Wire Clamp, 1891-96, Pt.	173
Fruit Jar, Safety, Valve Patd May 21 1895 HC, Triangle, Lime Green, Metal Clamp, Pt.	242
Fruit Jar, Salem Jar, Aqua, Threaded Glass Stopper, 1871-79, Qt.	489

Fruit Jar, Tillyer, Blue Aqua, Embossed Glass Lid, Wire Closure, Qt.	138
Fruit Jar, Trademark Lightning, Putnam 109, Yellow, Wire Closure, Pt.	242
Fruit Jar, Western Pride, Patented June 22, 1875, Aqua, Glass Lid, Metal Clamp, Qt.	230
Fruit Jar, Winslow Jar, Aqua, Olive Striation, Glass Lid, Wire Closure, 1870-85, Pt.	374
Gemel, Blown, Pale Teal, Rough Pontil, c.1825, 9 1/4 x 3 1/2 In.. illus	93
Gin, Charles' London Cordial, Old Amber, Bubbles, Case, 1845-60, 8 1/4 In.............................	2760
Gin, Charles' London Cordial, Yellow Grass Green, Sloping Collar, 1855-65, 8 In....................	489
Gin, Fairchild's Excelsior, Aqua, Sloping Collar, 9 5/8 In.	92
Gin, Fairchild's Excelsior, Yellow Green, Case, Sloping Collar, 9 1/2 In.................................	316
Gin, London Jockey Club House, Horse & Rider, Olive, Square, Iron Pontil, c.1860, 9 1/2 In.......	7480
Gin, R.E. Messenger & Co., London, Cordial, Olive, Case, Double Collar, 8 In.......................	316
Gin, Yellow Olive, Square, Tapered, Case, Flared Rim, Pontil, 11 In.	1287
Household, Osborn's Liquid Polish, Yellow Olive, Bubbles, Inward Rolled Lip, 3 3/4 In.............	690
Ink, 12-Sided, Green, Amber Striations & Swirls, Outward Rolled Lip, c.1860, 2 In.................	546
Ink, Chas. Straker & Sons, Teakettle, Redware, Brown Glaze, Smooth Sides, 3 In.	219
Ink, College Inn, Inside Pennant, Pottery, Brown Glaze, 1875-95, 2 3/4 In............................	805
Ink, Cone, Green, Outward Rolled Lip, 1840-60, 2 5/8 In...	316
Ink, Cone, Yellow Olive Amber, Pontil, Sheared Mouth, Tooled Lip, 2 1/4 In........................	288
Ink, Geometric, Dark Yellow Olive, Tooled Disc Mouth, Pontil, 1815-35, 1 5/8 In..................	316
Ink, Igloo, Cobalt Blue, Smooth Base, Ground Lip, 1865-80, 2 In...................................	863
Ink, J. & I. E. M., Igloo, Citron, Paneled Base With Letters, 1875-90, 1 3/4 In......................	920
Ink, J. & I. E. M., Igloo, Teal, Paneled Base, Tooled Lip, c.1805, 1 5/8 In...........................	1150
Ink, Pitkin Type, 36 Ribs, Swirled To Left, Forest Green, Disc Mouth, Pontil, 1790-1820, 1 5/8 In.	230
Ink, Pitkin Type, Swirled, Cone, Yellow, Olive, Pontil, c.1800, 2 In.	2378
Ink, Pressed Glass, Blue Green Whitish Flecks, 16 Vertical Column Shape, c.1835, 1 5/8 In. illus	246
Ink, R.F., Black Amethyst, Round Base, Cylindrical Top, Inward Rolled Lip, 2 1/4 In.............	242
Ink, Teakettle, 8 Concave Sides, Cobalt Blue, Brass Neck Ring, c.1885, 2 In.........................	431
Ink, Teakettle, 8-Sided, Amethyst, Brass Neck Ring, 1875-90, 2 In..................................	288
Ink, Teakettle, 8-Sided, Cobalt Blue, Pinched Waist, Brass Neck Ring, c.1880, 2 1/8 In.	633
Ink, Teakettle, 8-Sided, Turquoise, Ground Lip, c.1880, 2 In.	863
Ink, Teakettle, Amber, Sloping Side, c.1885, 2 3/8 x 4 1/4 In.	288
Ink, Teakettle, Birds Nest, Clambroth, Sheared Mouth, Pontil, Neck Ring, c.1880, 2 3/4 In.	431
Ink, Umbrella, 8-Sided, Amethyst Tint, Inward Rolled Lip, 1840-60, 2 1/2 In.	374
Ink, Umbrella, 8-Sided, Deep Old Amber, Sheared Mouth, Tooled Lip, 2 1/2 In.....................	374
Ink, Wolverhampton, G.G.M., Patent, Pottery, Dark Brown Glaze, England, 3 In.	265
Medicine, Apothecary, Hyalite, Aqua Cerassor, Black Glass, Bohemia, c.1925, 9 In.	82
Medicine, Bartine's Lotion, Light Cobalt Blue, Sloping Collar, 1840-60, 6 1/4 In...................	6325
Medicine, By A.A. Cooley, Hartford, Con., Olive Green, Oval, Sheared, Pontil, 4 1/2 In.	431
Medicine, C. Brinkerhoff's Health Restorative, $1.00, Yellow Amber, Pontil, 7 3/8 In.............	805
Medicine, David Rahm, Catawissa, Aqua, Arched Sides, Inward Rolled Lip, 4 1/2 In.	546
Medicine, Delmonico's Syrup Pectoral, New York, Aqua, Rolled Lip, Pontil, c.1850, 7 In.	288
Medicine, Dr. Crook's Wine Of Tar, Citron, Sloping Collar, c.1875, 8 7/8 In.......................	207
Medicine, Dr. E.D. Hayes, Vegetable Humor Syrup, Aqua, Panels, Pontil, c.1850, 7 1/2 In.......	805
Medicine, Dr. Eaton's Infantile Cordial, Church & Dupont, Aqua, Paneled, 5 1/8 In.	374
Medicine, Dr. Ham's Aromatic Invigorating Spirit, Iron Pontil, Aqua, c.1850, 8 In...............	199
Medicine, Dr. Ira Warren's Blood & Bile Purifier, Aqua, Panels, Sloping Collar, 9 In.	1093
Medicine, Dr. J. Clawson Kelley's Antiseptic Detergent, New York, Aqua, 9 In....................	748
Medicine, Dr. Markley's Family Medicines, Lancaster, Pa., Blue Aqua, Double Collar, 8 In.	1093
Medicine, Dr. Wilson's Horse Ointment, Blue Green, Cylindrical, Rolled Rim, 4 x 3 In.	7020
Medicine, Dunn's Liniment, Indented Panels, Pontil, Sloping Collar, c.1850, 5 5/8 In..............	633
Medicine, Elixir Gentian Compd., J.W. Von Nieda & Co., Amber, Double Collar, 11 In..........	316
Medicine, H. Lake's Indian Specific, Aqua, Panel, Tapering Neck, Rolled Rim, 8 3/4 In.	431
Medicine, Hamptons V. Tincture, Mortimer & Mowbray, Balto., Grass Green, 6 1/2 In..........	2530
Medicine, L.A. Page's Horse Liniment, Buffalo, N.Y., Blue Aqua, Sloping Collar, 6 In.	936
Medicine, Mortimore's Rheumatic Compound & Blood Purifier, Green, Double Collar, 7 In. ...	4025
Medicine, Moses Dame's Wine Of The Woods, Aqua, Squared Lip, c.1870, 8 In.	316
Medicine, Myers' Rock Rose, New Haven, Aqua, Sloping Collar, c.1850, 9 In.	1265
Medicine, Nubian, Tea For The Liver, Man & Hat, Yellow Amber, 8 1/4 In.	276
Medicine, S.M. Beebe's Horse Liniment, Green, Rectangular, Beveled Corners, 5 3/8 In.............	11115

Bottle, Soda, F. Sherwood, Bridgeport, New Haven, Teal Blue, Blob Mouth, Iron Pontil, c.1850, 6 3/8 In.
$644

Glass Works Auctions

Bottle, Soda, J. & W. Coles, Superior Soda & Mineral Water, Sapphire Blue, c.1850, 7 1/2 In.
$633

Glass Works Auctions

Bottle, Soda, T.W. Gillett, New Haven, 6-Pointed Star, Cobalt Blue, Blob Mouth, Iron Pontil, c.1850, 7 In.

$644

Glass Works Auctions

Bottle, Soda, T.W. Gillett, New Haven, Cobalt Blue, 8-Sided, Iron Pontil, c.1850, 7½ In.

$862

Glass Works Auctions

Bottle, Whiskey, A.M. Binnger & Co, N.Y., Cannon, Amber, Sheared Tooled Lip, c.1868, 12½ In.

$995

Glass Works Auctions

Medicine, S.M. Kier Petroleum, Pittsburgh, Sapphire Blue, Sloping Collar, 6⅜ In.	1093
Medicine, Shaker Syrup, D. Miller & C., Aqua, 8-Sided, Sloping Collar, c.1850, 7⅜ In.	253
Medicine, Smith's Green Mountain Renovator, East Georgia, Vt., Old Amber, 7⅛ In.	2415 to 5463
Medicine, Swaim's Panacea, Philada., Olive Green, Rounded, Indented Panels, 8 In.	288
Medicine, Tilden & Co., New Lebanon, N.Y., Olive, Indented Panels, c.1850, 7 In.	2875
Medicine, Vaughn's Vegetable Lithontriptic Mixture, Buffalo, Blue Aqua, 8¼ In.	316
Medicine, Worlds Hair Restorer, Pink Amethyst, Double Collar, c.1870, 7 In. _illus_	644
Milk, Borden's, Logo, Quality Milk, Amber, Square, Qt.	30
Milk, Colvert's Milk, Hobnail Top, Medallion, ⅓ Qt.	77
Milk, Hendrick's, Don't Run Out, Get More Milk For The Weekend, ½ Gal.	25
Milk, Hunter's Dairy, Ashland, PA, Red Pyro, Qt.	35
Milk, Portland Milk Producers, Irradiated, Vitamin D, 1935, Qt.	80
Milk, Romney Dairy, Pyro Glaze, Try Our Chocolate Drink, 1940s, ½ Pt.	18
Milk, Valley View Dairy, Red Pyro, Baby, Yours To Love, 1930s, Qt.	32
Milk, Village Farm Dairy, War Bond, War Plane, Truck, Dairy Scenes, Red Text, 1 Qt.	33
Mineral Water, Aetna Mineral Spouting Spring, Monogram, AE, Saratoga, N.Y., Aqua, Pt.	5750
Mineral Water, B. Bennett, Williamsport, Pa., Slug Plate, Blue Green, Blob Top, 7¼ In.	690
Mineral Water, Bethesda Spring Water, Saratoga Springs, N.Y., Aqua, Qt.	1725
Mineral Water, Coon & Spencer's Nectarian, N.Y., Blue, 8-Sided, Blob Top, 8 In.	3163
Mineral Water, Darien Mineral Springs, Darien Center, N.Y., Aqua, Double Collar, Pt.	230
Mineral Water, Deep Rock Spring, Oswego, N.Y., Trade Mark, Monogram, Aqua, Pt.	242
Mineral Water, G.W. Weston & Co., Saratoga, N.Y., Deep Olive Green, Double Collar, Qt.	316
Mineral Water, Hamilton & Church Excelsior, Slug Plate, Teal, 8-Sided, Blob Top, 7¼ In.	1150
Mineral Water, Hulshizer & Co., Premium, Slug Plate, Blue Green, 8-Sided, Blob Top, 8 In.	575
Mineral Water, John Volpert, Minersville, Pa., Emerald Green, Blob Top, 7⅜ In.	460
Mineral Water, Magnetic Spring, Henniker, N.H., Yellow Amber, Sloping Collar, Qt.	242
Mineral Water, Middletown Healing Springs, A.W. Gray & Son, Vt., Green, Qt.	460
Mineral Water, Oak Orchard, Acid Springs, Alabama, Genessee Co., N.Y., Blue Green, Qt.	431
Mineral Water, Pavilion & United States Spring Co., Raised US, Blue Green, Pt.	5750
Mineral Water, Pavilion & United States Spring Co., Saratoga, N.Y., Blue Green, Pt.	173
Mineral Water, Rockbridge Alum Water, King, Aqua, Rounded Shoulders, Tooled Lip, 10¼ In.	690
Mineral Water, Siderite Springs, Manchester Conn., Emerald Green, Double Collar, Pt.	2530
Mineral Water, Wm. Betz & Co., Pittsbg., Blue Aqua, 10-Sided, Sloping Collar, 7⅞ In.	460
Nursing, Baby Feeder, Etched Biberon Limande Robert, Cork, Ivory Cap, 9 In.	70
Nursing, Blown, Etched Aus Liebe, Leafy Branches, Pewter Mount & Nipple, 7 In.	188
Nursing, Blown, Flask Shape, Indented Body, Pewter Cap, Tube, Nipple, 1886, 5 In.	76
Nursing, Blown, Pewter Mount, Vent Hole, Long Tube, c.1850, 7 In.	153
Perfume bottles are listed in the Perfume Bottle category.	
Pickle, Cathedral, 6-Sided, Teal, Outward Rolled Lip, 13 In.	748
Pickle, Cathedral, 8 Arched Sides, Blue Green, Rolled Collar, Pontil, 13¾ In.	435
Pickle, Cathedral, Light Blue Green, Square, Beveled Corners, Rolled Collar, 11½ In.	702
Pickle, Cloverleaf, 8 Lobes, Amber, Rolled Collar, 7⅞ In.	1404
Poison, Cobalt Blue, Slanted Shoulder, Pontil, c.1850, 7 In.	100
Poison, Embalming Fluid, Steriol, Undertaker Supply Of Chicago, Paper Label, 1930s, 8 In.	145
Poison, Embossed Not To Be Taken, Cobalt Blue, Coffin, 3½ x 1¼ In.	69
Poison, Hobnail, Olive Green, Flask, Sheared Mouth, Tooled Lip, 1845-60, 5 In.	431
Poison, Ribbed Panels, Emerald Green, c.1880, 2⅛ In.	89
Sarsaparilla, Cookes, Cobalt Blue, Cylindrical, Rounded Shoulder, Sloping Collar, 8 In.	5463
Sarsaparilla, Dr. M.C. Parker's, Blue Green, Case, Sloping Collar, c.1865, 9⅜ In.	633
Sarsaparilla, Dr. Martin's Compound Syrup Of Snake Root, Aqua, 8¾ In.	4973
Sarsaparilla, Dr. Townsend's, Albany, N.Y., Emerald Green, Sloping Collar, Pontil, 9½ In.	460
Sarsaparilla, Dr. Townsend's, Albany, Grass Green, Sloping Collar, c.1855, 8¼ In.	207
Sarsaparilla, Dr. Townsend's, Albany, N.Y., Olive Amber, Sloping Collar, c.1850, 9¾ In.	460
Sarsaparilla, Dr. Wynkoop's Katharismic Honduras, Cobalt Blue, c.1850, 9¼ In.	10925
Sarsaparilla, Georges, Comstock & BR-N.Y., Aqua, Tapered Collar, Pontil, 9½ In.	1840
Sarsaparilla, Shaker's, Prepared By United Society, Shaker Village, O., Aqua, 5¼ In.	920
Scent, Blue Green, 20 Ribs, Swirled To Right, Sheared Mouth, 3⅜ In.	150
Scent, Blue Jasper, Octagonal, White Classical Figure, Leaf Borders, 1700s, 4 In.	185
Scent, Imperial Perfumed Salts, Lavender, McCormick & Co., Bee, Green, Crown Stopper, 2 In.	403

Scent, Ruby Red, Silver Plate, Tubular, Hinged Lid, Screw Cap, Engraved, 1880	215
Seal, F Trott, 1798, Wine, Dark Olive Amber, String Lip, 9 x 4 ½ In.	2457
Seal, Fox Over TL, Monogram, Wine, Black Glass, Old Amber, 1780-1800, 10 In.	1840
Seal, I.L.M. Smith Wine Merchant Baltimore, Deep Yellow Olive, Lip, c.1810, 10 In.	1380
Seal, John Colby Fynone 1882, Deep Olive Amber, Double Collar, Wax Seal, 11 In.	748
Seal, Jon Mason Boston, Wine, Deep Olive Amber, Cylindrical, Magnum, 13 In.	3163
Seal, Joseph Peabody, Wine, Deep Olive Amber, Sloping Collar, 10 ½ In.	489
Seal, L. Lewis, 1823, Wine, Olive Green, Cylindrical, Double Collar, 11 In.	1035
Seal, Natichitoches Gegrundet, 1811, Label, Green, Louisiana, 1800s, 9 ½ In. *illus*	854
Seal, P.G. & Old Bristol Porter Co., Wine, Deep Olive, Cylindrical, England, 8 ⅝ In.	152
Seal, R.H.C., 1815, Wine, Olive Amber, Pontil, England, 11 ¼ In.	374
Seal, Sir Will Strickland Bart., 1809, Wine, Olive Green, Shaped Neck, England, 9 ⅜ In.	460
Seal, Wine, W.V.Z., Stylized Bee, Dark Olive Green, Sheared, Applied String Lip, 11 In.	2415
Shaker, Cough Cure, Aqua, Label, Clarice Baker Extract Co., c.1890, 5 ⅜ In. *illus*	149
Shaker, Horse Radish, Shaker Man, Rolled Lip, Label, 5 ¼ In.	633
Shaker, Mixed Pickles, E.D. Pettengill Co., Patd. Jany 11th 1898, 7 ¼ In. *illus*	632
Shaker, Pepper Relish, E.D. Pettengill & Co., Aqua, Label, c.1890, 5 ⅜ In. *illus*	431
Shaker, Pickle, E.D. Pettengill Co., Clear, Fluted Shoulder, Tooled Lip, Label, c.1900, 11 In.	545
Shaker, Syrup, Canterbury, N.H., Aqua, Applied Collar, Open Pontil, c.1850, 7 In. *illus*	1035
Snuff, Agate, Chalcedony, Pilgrim Flask Form, Handles, Stopper, 2 In.	108
Snuff, Agate, Chalcedony, Urn Shape, Butterfly Handles, Pierced Oval Foot, 2 In.	480
Snuff, Agate, Chalcedony, Urn Shape, Relief Bat, Bamboo, Gray Ground, 2 ¼ In.	156
Snuff, Agate, Moss, Oval, Melon Ribbing, Stopper, 2 In.	125
Snuff, Bone, 2 Birds, 3 Figures In Erotic Activity, China, 1900s, 2 ⅔ In.	132
Snuff, Bone, Carved, Lotus Leaf, Immortals, Clouds, Ball Finial, Japan, c.1900, 4 ¼ In.	120
Snuff, Cloisonne, Butterflies, Prunus, Blue Ground, Stopper, Chinese, 3 In.	92
Snuff, Cloisonne, Silver, Gilt, Crown, Cabochon Garnet, Pan-Slavic, c.1860, 3 x 2 In.	778
Snuff, Glass, Aqua, Pear Shape, Crane, Tree, 1800-50, 2 ¾ In.	1440
Snuff, Glass, Overlay, Butterfly, Flower, Calligraphy, Black On Clear, 2 ¼ In.	540
Snuff, Glass, Overlay, Snowflake, Blue Characters On White, Jade Stopper, 2 ½ In.	96
Snuff, Glass, Spangle, Yellow, Red Stopper, 1700s, 1 ½ In.	660
Snuff, Glass, Sunburst, Yellow Olive, Ribbed Sides, Sheared Mouth, Pontil, c.1820, 6 ⅞ In.	3803
Snuff, Glass, Yellow, Oval, Relief Dragon Carving, Stopper, 2 In.	100
Snuff, J.J. Mapes, No. 61 Front St., N-York, Olive, Tombstone Shape, Flared Rim, 4 ⅜ In.	403
Snuff, Jade, Celadon, Rectangular, Jade Stopper, c.1925, 3 In.	937
Snuff, Jade, Spinach, Figures, Pavilions, Pine Trees, Stopper, 3 ½ In.	375
Snuff, Jade, Spinach, Zoomorphic Ringed Mask, Hombre, Stopper, Chinese, 1700s, 2 ¾ In.	1125
Snuff, Lapis Lazuli, Squat, Chinese, 1900, 1 ¾ In.	360
Snuff, Milk Glass, 2 Blue Birds, Standing On Red Heart, Tapered, Bohemian, 1700s, 3 In.	125
Snuff, Overlay, Red Pahua, Clear Ground, 3 ½ In.	360
Snuff, Peking Glass, Turtle, White Opal, Cobalt Coiled Snake, Gilt Stopper, 3 In.	375
Snuff, Pink Quartz, Oval, Cotton-Like Matrix, Stopper, 2 In.	469
Snuff, Porcelain, Famille Rose, White, Boys In Landscape, Agate Stopper, 3 In.	128
Snuff, Porcelain, Figure Carrying Lantern, Chinese Blue Glaze, Swollen Shoulder, 3 In.	256
Snuff, Porcelain, Kidney Bean Shape, Yellow, Glass Stopper, 2 In.	540
Snuff, Pottery, Red, Buff Ground, Bulbous, 2 ¾ In.	128
Snuff, Red Jasper, Overlay, Figural Landscape, White Ground, Stopper, 2 ¾ In. *illus*	100
Snuff, Reverse Painted, Foo Lions, Scholars, Courtyard, Calligraphy, Chinese, 1800s, 2 ½ In.	1188
Soda, 7Up, Girl, Swimsuit, Green, Logo, 8 In.	15
Soda, A.W. Rapp's Improved, R, New York, Green, Sloping Collar, 7 ¼ In.	920
Soda, Catawba Club Beverages, 8 ½ In.	120
Soda, Charles Clark, Charleston, S.C., Yellow Olive, Blob Top, 7 ⅜ In.	748
Soda, Crystal Palace Premium, W. Eagle, New York, Teal, Blob Top, 7 ¼ In.	1265
Soda, Drink Tom's, Flavored Soft, 1950s, 8 ¾ x 2 ½ In.	45
Soda, E.Y. Cronk, Root Beer, Monogram, EYC, Blue, Lightning Closure, 7 ⅝ In.	690
Soda, F. Sherwood, Bridgeport, New Haven, Teal Blue, Blob Mouth, Iron Pontil, c.1850, 6 ⅜ In. *illus*	644
Soda, Frostie, Old Fashioned Root Beer, Woman, Silhouette, 1950s, 12 Oz.	9
Soda, Gardner & Brown, Torpedo, Yellow Green, Sloping Collar, 8 ¾ In.	978
Soda, Geo. Eagle, Blue Aqua, Diagonal Rib Panel, Sloping Collar, 7 In.	1150
Soda, Howell & Smith, Buffalo, Blue Green, Blob Top, 6 ¾ In.	288

Bottle, Wine, Black Glass, Onion Shape, Olive Green, Sheard Lip, Pontil, c.1700, 5 ⅝ In.
$644

Glass Works Auctions

Bottle Opener, Donkey, Cast Iron, Brown, Black, Original Paint, Marked, c.1950, 3 x 3 In.
$85

Ruby Lane

Bottle Opener, Lion, Open Mouth, Brass, 7 In.
$510

Milestone Auctions

Bottle Opener, Parrot, Perched On Stand, Cast Iron, Red, Yellow, Black, 1900s, 5 1/2 x 1 3/4 In.
$90

Ruby Lane

Bottle Stopper, Wood, Carved, Folk Art, Germany, 9 x 3 1/2 In.
$45

Ruby Lane

Box, Candle, Tin, Dome Hasp, Folded, Solder Joints, Painted, Hinged Lid, 1800s, 9 x 12 In.
$325

Hess Auction Group

Soda, J. & W. Coles, Superior Soda & Mineral Water, Sapphire Blue, c.1850, 7 1/2 In............ *illus*	633
Soda, J.J. Sprenger, Holidaysburgh, Pa., Cobalt Blue, Blob Top, 7 1/2 In.	1840
Soda, J.T. Brown, Chemist, Boston, Torpedo, Blue, Blob Top, c.1860, 8 3/4 In.	1265
Soda, J.W. Harris, New Haven, Conn., Cobalt Blue, 8-Sided, Blob Top, Pontil, 8 In.	690
Soda, Knicker Bocker, N.Y., Cobalt Blue, 10-Sided, Sloping Collar, 7 1/2 In.	748
Soda, Mackinney & Roberts, Beverage, Embossed M & R, 1800s, 9 1/2 In.	38
Soda, Orange Crush, Amber Brown, 1960s, 10 Oz.	9
Soda, Root Beer Syrup, Enameled Porcelain, Metal Cap, 12 3/4 x 3 3/8 In.	153
Soda, Seymour & Co., Buffalo, N.Y., Cobalt Blue, Blob Top, 7 1/4 In.	480
Soda, Smile, Swollen Top, Patent, 1922, 6 1/2 x 1 3/4 In.	35
Soda, Squirt, Green Swirl, Little Squirt Logo, 1970s, 10 Oz.	17
Soda, Sun Rise Beverages, 1960s, 10 Oz.	10
Soda, T.W. Gillett, New Haven, 6-Pointed Star, Cobalt Blue, Blob Mouth, Iron Pontil, c.1850, 7 In.. *illus*	644
Soda, T.W. Gillett, New Haven, Cobalt Blue, 8-Sided, Iron Pontil, c.1850, 7 1/2 In. .... *illus*	862
Soda, Taylor's Best, Cobalt Blue, Cucumber Form, Sloping Collar, 8 1/4 In.	3450
Soda, W. Eagle, New York, Premium, Cobalt Blue, 8-Sided, Blob Top, 7 In.	242
Soda, W. Eagle, Vestry, Varick & Canal Sts., Light Blue Green, Blob Top, 7 3/8 In.	219
Soda, Wm. Russell, Balt., Yellow Green, Torpedo, Sloping Collar, 8 7/8 In.	863
Syrup, Display, Howel's, Orange-Julep, Glass, Enameled Label, 12 3/8 x 3 1/4 In.	604
Syrup, Ferro-Phos, Display, Drink Ferro-Phos, Glass Of Beverage, Glass, Enameled Label, 12 x 3 In.	777
Syrup, Ferro-Phos, Drink The Favorite Beverage, 5 Cents, Aluminum Cap, 11 1/2 x 3 3/8 In.	776
Target Ball, 7 Horizontal Rings, Root Beer Amber, Sheared, c.1880, 2 3/8 In.	242
Target Ball, Bogardus, Pat'd April 10 1877, Diamond, Amber, Band, Sheared, 2 3/8 In.	265
Target Ball, Bogardus, Pat'd April 10 1877, Diamond, Cobalt Blue, Center Band, 2 3/8 In.	748
Target Ball, Bogardus, Pat'd April 10 1877, Diamond, Shaded Light Olive, Band, 2 3/8 In.	748
Target Ball, C. Newman, Diamond, Amber, Center Band, Sheared Mouth, c.1890, 2 3/8 In.	748
Target Ball, For Hockey's Patent Trap, Diamond, Light Grass Green, Sheared Lip, 2 3/8 In.	489
Target Ball, For Hockey's Patent, Diamond, Light Vaseline, Sheared Lip, 2 3/8 In.	460
Target Ball, Glashutten Dr. A. Frank, Charlottenburg, Diamond, Yellow Olive, 2 3/8 In.	173
Target Ball, Gurd & Son, 185 Dundas Street, London, Amber, Center Band, Sheared, 2 3/8 In.	575
Target Ball, Ira Paine's Filled, Pat, Oct. 23 1877, Yellow Amber, Sheared, 2 3/8 In.	374
Target Ball, Man Shooting, In Circle, Diamond, Amethyst, Striations, Sheared, 2 3/8 In.	633
Target Ball, Man Shooting, In Circle, Diamond, Grass Green, Sheared Lip, 2 3/8 In.	374
Target Ball, Stars & Bars, Embossed, Yellow Amber, Sheared, c.1890, 2 5/8 In.	1035
Target Ball, W.W. Greener St. Mary's Works, Diamond, Pink Amethyst, Band, 2 3/8 In.	690
Utility, Shaft & Globe, Light Green, Applied String Lip, Miniature, 3 3/8 x 2 1/2 In.	2106
Whiskey, A.M. Binnger & Co, N.Y., Cannon, Amber, Sheared Tooled Lip, c.1868, 12 1/2 In. *illus*	995
Whiskey, Casper's, Made By Honest North Carolina People, Cobalt Blue, Lady's Leg, Qt.	527
Whiskey, Chas. D. Myers & Co., Wilmington N.C., Amber, Flask, Double Collar, 6 In.	920
Whiskey, Elephant, Golden Amber, Flattened Chestnut Flask, Handle, 6 In.	878
Whiskey, Jno. H. Kuch, Wilmington, N.C., Strapside Flask, 1885-1900, 1/2 Pt.	374
Whiskey, Mohawk Pure Rye, Patented Feb 9 1868, Indian Princess, 12 1/4 In.	4025
Whiskey, Seal, Thos. McKoy Groceries & Liquors, Yellow Amber, Double Collar, Qt.	1265
Whiskey, Spirits, 30 Ribs, Swirled To Left, Grass Green, Straight-Sided, String Lip, 5 3/8 In.	5175
Whiskey, Star, New York, W.B. Crowell, Seal, Amber, Applied Spout & Handle, 8 1/4 In.	1725
Whiskey, T.J. Dunbar & Co. Cordial Schnapps, Schiedam, Olive, Double Collar, 9 3/4 In.	855
Whiskey, Turner Brothers, New York, Barrel, Cherry Puce, Flattened Lip, 10 In.	633
Whiskey, Van Brunt's Aromatic Schnapps, Schiedam, Grass Green, Sloping Collar, 10 In.	489
Whiskey, Voldner's, Aromatic Schnapps, Schiedam, Yellow Olive, Sloping Collar, Case, 10 In.	863
Whiskey, W. Genaust, Wilmington, N.C., Yellow Amber, Strapside, Double Collar, 7 1/2 In.	489
Whiskey, Wharton's, 1850, Chestnut Grove, Blue Aqua, Teardrop Flask, 6 1/2 In.	518
Wine, Black Glass, Onion Shape, Olive Green, Sheard Lip, Pontil, c.1700, 5 5/8 In. .... *illus*	644
Wine, Carolina Wine & Liquor Store, Asheville, N.C., Anchor, Aqua, Strapside, 1/2 Pt.	489
Wine, Kidney, Deep Olive Green, Germany, 1740-70, 7 3/8 In.	374
Wine, Mallet, Olive Amber, Cloverleaf Pontil, Sheared Mouth, String Lip, c.1750, 8 In.	184
Wine, Olive Green, Wicker Covered, Sheared Mouth, c.1779, 10 In.	2587
Wine, Onion, Deep Olive Green, String Lip, England, c.1685, 6 x 3 1/4 In.	3738
Wine, Onion, Embossed Seal, Lion, Olive, Pontil, c.1700, 5 In.	3845
Wine, Onion, Olive Amber, Blue Gray Tones, Threaded Neck, Handle, c.1725, 6 1/4 In.	9200
Wine, Onion, Olive Amber, Blue Opaline Tones, Applied String Lip, c.1710, 6 x 5 3/4 In.	1265
Wine, Onion, Yellow Olive, Squat, String Lip, Pontil, 6 x 5 In.	633

B

Wine, Sake, Porcelain, Sword, Helmet, Flag, Cherry Blossoms, Oval, Japanese Military.............	149
Wine, Sake, Pottery, Brown Glaze, Cream Calligraphy, 10 ½ In..	60
Wine, Shaft & Globe, Dark Green, Rampant Lion, String Lip, Pontil, 1655-60, 9 ½ In.	9775
Wine, Shaft & Globe, Yellow Olive, Squat, String Lip, 6 ½ In.	2070
Wine, Shaft & Globe, Yellow Olive, String Lip, England, 1650-60, 9 ¼ In.	4888
Zanesville, 24 Ribs, Swirled To Left, Yellow Amber, Olive Tone, Globular, 9 In.	1955
Zanesville, 24 Ribs, Swirled To Right, Light Apple Green, Globular, 1815-35, 7 ¾ In.	920
Zanesville, 24 Swirled Ribs, Light Honey Amber, Globular, 1800s, 7 ¼ In.	1200
Zanesville, 24 Swirled Ribs, Light Olive Green, Globular, 1800s, 8 In..	4080
Zanesville, 24 Swirled Ribs, Pale Olive, Globular, Long Neck, 1800s, 7 ½ In.	3960
Zanesville, 24 Swirled Ribs, Reddish Amber, Globular, Long Neck, 1800s, 8 In.	1140
Zanesville, 24 Tightly Swirled Ribs, Golden Amber, Globular, Long Neck, 1800s, 8 In.............	1800

BOTTLE CAPS for milk bottles are the printed cardboard caps used since the 1920s. Crown caps, used after 1892 on soda bottles, are also popular collectibles. Unusual mottoes, graphics, and caps from bottlers that are out of business bring the highest prices.

Crown, Bud Light Beer, Logo, c.1990......................................	50
Crown, D.G. Yuengling, Cream On Brown..	90
Crown, Koehler's, Red On Silver, Metallic	125
Crown, Yan Jing Beer, Red & White, Beijing, China..	4
Paper, Cedarside Dairy, Waterloo, Iowa, Pasteurized, Red, Yellow, 1 ⅜ In......................	3
Paper, Dalecrest Dairy Farm, Stockport, Ohio, Blue On White..............................	12

BOTTLE OPENERS are needed to open many bottles. As soon as the commercial bottle was invented, the opener to be used with the new types of closures became a necessity. Many types of bottle openers can be found, most dating from the twentieth century. Collectors prize advertising and comic openers.

Brass, Golf Ball, 5 In.	45
Brass, Golf Club, 6 ½ In.	28
Brass, Lincoln Cathedral, 1950s, 5 ⅝ In.................................	45
Cast Iron, Drunk Man, Street Sign, Skyline Drive, Virginia, 4 In.	25
Cast Iron, Sailboat, 7 ½ x 3 ¼ In.	12
Cast Iron, Seal, Flippers Out, 2 ½ x 5 In.	12
Donkey, Cast Iron, Brown, Black, Original Paint, Marked, c.1950, 3 x 3 In. ....*illus*	85
Iron, Spanish Woman, Blue Dress, Red Fan, Red Shoes, 9 In.	17
Lion, Open Mouth, Brass, 7 In. ....*illus*	510
Parrot, Perched On Stand, Cast Iron, Red, Yellow, Black, 1900s, 5 ½ x 1 ¾ In...........*illus*	90
Silver Plate, Figural, Crab, Onyx Eyes, 5 x 6 ½ In.	295
Sterling Silver, Cactus Pattern, Georg Jensen..............................	140
Teakwood, Stainless, Japan, c.1950, 6 In.	12

BOTTLE STOPPERS are made of glass, metal, plastic, and wood. Decorative and figural stoppers are used to replace the original cork stoppers and are collected today.

Bronze, Pig Head, Sailor Hat, c.1915, 2 In.	350
Silver Plate, Chimney Sweep, 2 ¼ In...	38
Sterling Silver, Fox, c.1875, 2 In...	420
Wood, Carved, Folk Art, Germany, 9 x 3 ½ In. ....*illus*	45
Wood, Dachshund, Black Forest, Glass Eyes, c.1920, 2 ½ In.	76
Wood, Man Wearing Hat, Woman With Scarf, Anri, 5 x 1 ¾ In.	40
Wood, Man, On Beer Barrel, Tipping Hat, 5 ½ In.	14
Wood, Man, Tam-O'-Shanter, Reddish Hair & Beard, 2 ⅝ In.	19
Wood, Victorian Wallpaper Design, Painted, 3 ½ x 2 In........................	28

BOXES of all kinds are collected. They were made of wood, metal, tortoiseshell, embroidery, or other material. Additional boxes may be listed in other sections, such as Advertising, Battersea, Ivory, Shaker, Tinware, and various Porcelain categories. Tea Caddies are listed in their own category.

Box, Cigarette, Hinged Lid, Shagreen, Birch, Adjustable Divider, London, c.1930, 7 x 4 In.
$427

Neal Auction Co.

Box, Knife, Georgian, Serpentine Front, Mahogany, Inlay, Fitted Interior, c.1800, 14 x 11 In.
$1,080

Brunk Auctions

Box, Knife, Mahogany, Brass Mounts, Felt Lined, England, c.1790, 14 x 8 x 10 In.
$240

Cowan's Auctions

Box, Pipe, Softwood, Blue Paint, Cutouts, Drawer, Clay Pipe, Wall, Pa., 1800s, 18 In.
$265

Hess Auction Group

Box, Ribbon, Wallpaper, Flowers & Leaves, Oval, 1800s, 2 x 4⅝ x 3⅜ In.
$413

Hess Auction Group

Box, Rosewood, Lift Top, Raised Dragon & Cloud Design, Metal Mount & Lock, c.1910, 6 x 14 In.
$150

Eldred's Auctioneers and Appraisers

6-Board, Red, Green, Black, Gold Diamond, Brass Bail Handle, 1800s, 4 x 9 In.	1200
Ballot, Lift Lid, Walnut, Handle, c.1910, 6 x 16 In.	359
Bentwood, Multicolor Floral, Blue Ground, Children Playing Transfer, c.1825, 7 x 18 In.	224
Bible, Oak, Hinged Writing Slope, Lock Plate, Arched Arcaded Apron, Ball Finials, Stand, 33½ x 24 In.	968
Book Shape, Wood, Eve In The Garden, Woman, Floral Wreath, 1800s, 6 x 4¾ In.	450
Bride's, Wood, Painted, Birds, Stylized Flowers, Black Ground, France, c.1900, 8 x 11 In.	360
Bronze, Ashanti, Sacred, Square, Plaquettes Of Mudfish & Human Mask, 1800s, 7 x 7½ x 7 In.	2160
Bronze, Garlands, Mother-Of-Pearl, Woman's Portrait, Padded Silk Interior, France, 4 x 3 In.	625
Bronze, Openwork, Zodiac, Cedar Lined, Red, Oscar Bach, c.1920, 4 x 7 In.	202
Candle, Oak, Slide Lid, c.1810, 7 x 10 In.	356
Candle, Tin, Dome Hasp, Folded, Solder Joints, Painted, Hinged Lid, 1800s, 9 x 12 In. ..... *illus*	325
Casket, Kingwood, Slightly Curved, Lateral Handles, French Regency, 16 x 26 x 19 In.	2000
Cigarette, Hinged Lid, Shagreen, Birch, Adjustable Divider, London, c.1930, 7 x 4 In. ...... *illus*	427
Cigarette, Lid, Shagreen, Light Purple, Birch Interior, Divider, London, c.1930, 2 x 8 x 4 In.	448
Desk, Red, Keyhole, Hinged Top, 24 x 24½ In.	70
Document, Brass Tacks, Bail Handle, Escutcheon, James Roche Trunk Maker, c.1810, 5 x 14 In.	438
Document, Dome Lid, Softwood, Green Paint, c.1810, 4¼ x 9¾ In.	70
Document, Inlay, Wood, 1900s, 15 x 9 In.	46
Document, Mother-Of-Pearl, Inlay, Cranes, Landscape, Flowers, Vines, 15½ x 11¾ In.	363
Document, Pine, Old Red Stain, Black Stenciled Lettering, 1880, 17 x 33 x 18 In.	96
Document, Softwood, Feather Paint, c.1800, 5¼ x 11¼ In.	153
Document, Tooled Leather, Brass Tacks, Painted Sides, Initials G W, 7 x 14 In.	129
Dome Lid, Dovetailed Case, Grain Decoration, Panel On Lid, House, 1800s, 8½ x 18 x 11 In.	960
Dresser, Bolivian Rosewood, White Ash Stripe, Turned Wood, Jerry Patrasso, 2½ x 3⅞ In.	260
Dresser, Coffin Shape, Leaves, Copper, Wood, John Pearson, 1901, 18½ x 1½ In.	2000
Dresser, Coffin Shape, Regency Boulle, Ebony, Rosewood, Mother-Of-Pearl, 6 x 13 In.	295
Dresser, Ebony, Bird's-Eye Maple, Stripes, Philip Weber, 1½ x 6¼ In.	260
Dresser, Fruitwood, Satinwood, Geometric Star Designs, 1800s, 4 x 11 In.	132
Dresser, Gilt, Coffin Shape, Green Jewels, Sevres Style, 2 x 4¼ In.	343
Dresser, Glass, Pink, Cut To Clear, Hinged Lid, France, c.1880, 5 x 4 In.	640
Dresser, Opaline Glass, Diamond, Quilted, Coffin Shape, Gilt Hinge, White, 3⅝ x 5 In.	281
Dresser, Porcelain, Blue, Bronze Mount, Gilt, Flowers, Landscapes, Sevres Style, 6 x 9½ In.	150
Hat, Lacquered Cardboard, Flip Lid, Lined, Side Latches, Handle, France, c.1905, 10 x 18 In.	920
Hat, Wallpaper, Lid, Oval, Flowers, Leaves, Scrolls, 9¼ x 13 In.	118
Hide Covered, Nail Head Decoration, Lock, 5 x 10 In.	75
Jewelry, Burl, Brass Trim, Glass Buttons, Victorian, 11½ x 3½ In.	244
Jewelry, Cobalt Blue, White Flowers, Casket Shape, Hinged Lid, Silver Plate Frame, Victorian, 9 x 6 In.	180
Jewelry, Coffin Shape, Walnut, Relief Game Birds, Leaves, Pokerwork Ground, 8 x 14 In.	375
Knife, George III, Fruitwood, Mahogany Inlay, Sloped, Shaped, 14½ x 8 In.	500
Knife, Georgian, Serpentine Front, Mahogany, Inlay, Fitted Interior, c.1800, 14 x 11 In. .. *illus*	1080
Knife, Mahogany Veneer, Shaped Front, Inlaid Trim, Shell Patera, 1700s-1800s, 15 x 12 In.	510
Knife, Mahogany, Brass Mounts, Felt Lined, England, c.1790, 14 x 8 x 10 In. ...... *illus*	240
Knife, Walnut, Inlaid, Shaped Handle, Heart Cutouts, Divided, 5 x 11 In.	360
Lift Lid, Walnut, Inlaid Scrollwork, Pierced Iron Hardware, Bun Feet, 11 x 15 In.	4500
Pantry, Round, Bentwood, Flowers, Text, Varnish, Scandinavia, 6½ x 17 In.	290
Pantry, Round, Bentwood, Laced Fingers, Flowers, Scroll, Inscription, Scandanavia, 6 x 13 In.	420
Pine, Yellow, Hinged Lid, Yellow, Date Inside 1915, Molded Trim, 6¼ x 22 x 13 In.	113
Pipe, Heart Cutout, Drawer, Old Spanish Brown Stain, Signed, 1800s, 5½ x 5½ x 23 In.	240
Pipe, Softwood, Blue Paint, Cutouts, Drawer, Clay Pipe, Wall, Pa., 1800s, 18 In. .... *illus*	265
Pipe, Tiger Maple, Shaped Top, Drawer, Shell Carved, 16½ In.	480
Porcelain, Green, Cut Glass, Flowers, 2 Bronze Handles, Wood Base, 4 x 4 x 3 In.	649
Razor, Slide Lid, Pine, Leather Strap, Dovetailed, Painted, 1800s, 2 x 11 In.	1202
Ribbon, Wallpaper, Flowers & Leaves, Oval, 1800s, 2 x 4⅝ x 3⅜ In. .... *illus*	413
Rosewood, Lift Top, Raised Dragon & Cloud Design, Metal Mount & Lock, c.1910, 6 x 14 In. .. *illus*	150
Salt, Mixed Wood, Wall, Painted, Katie Frieher, Anno Domini 1797, 16 x 11 x 9 In. .... *illus*	443
Salt, Mixed Wood, Lower Drawer, Hanging Eyelet, 16½ x 10 In.	383
Sculpture, Brick, Robert Arneson, Interior Brick, Painted Earthenware, 1969, 3 x 9 x 5 In.	2375
Stepped Lid, Inlaid, Geometric, Parquetry, Fabric Lined, Mirror, 1800s, 7½ x 11 x 7 In.	431
Storage, Slide Lid, Paint Decorated, c.1820, 3½ x 6½ In.	153

Storage, Slide Lid, Softwood, Blue Paint, c.1810, 14 x 28 In.	472
Tantalus, Stack Of 4 Books, Multicolor, 6¾ In.	163
Tobacco, 2 Hinged Lids, Beaded Edges, Green Felt, English Oak, 1930s, 6 x 12 x 9¼ In.	96
Treasure, Pine, Archaic Stylized Metal Hinges, Lock, Working Key, 1900, 18 x 19 x 19 In.	54
Trinket, Bentwood, Oval, Bird, Tulips, Continental, 1800s, 6 x 17 In.	175
Trinket, Bentwood, Oval, Continental, 1800s, 4¼ In.	113
Trinket, Bentwood, Oval, Flowers, Angels, Decoupage, 1800s, 4¼ x 14¼ In.	125
Trinket, Bronze, Nude, Woman, Reclining, Sleeping, 5½ x 6 In.	1180
Trinket, Faux Tortoiseshell, Copper Lid, Embossed Scene, Siege De La Bastille, 2 x 3 In.	870
Trinket, Heart Shape, Gilt Metal, Graziella Lichel, Porcelain Plaque, Marked, 1900s, 1 x 3 x 3 In.	120
Trinket, Multicolor, Bronze, Jewels, Stylized Flowers, Jay Strongwater, 1 x 3 In.	148
Trinket, Red, Green, Floral, Leafy Designs, Sweden, 1800s, 4½ In.	300
Vanity, Silver, Miniature Portrait, Oval, Nude Woman, 3½ x 2¾ In.	300
Vanity, Silver, Oval, Repousse, Figures, Garden Party, 3¾ x 7¾ In.	900
Wallpaper, Blue & White Leaves, Brown Ground, 1800s, 3 x 4¼ In.	613
Writing, Slant Front, Hinged Top, Quillwork, 4¾ x 14⅛ In.	1875

BOY SCOUT collectibles include any material related to scouting, including patches, manuals, and uniforms. The Boy Scout movement in the United States started in 1910. The first Jamboree was held in 1937. Girl Scout items are listed under their own heading.

Canteen, Aluminum, Canvas Carrying Case, c.1950, 7½ In.	*illus*	39
Match Holder, Cylindrical, Gold Plated, 3½ In.		109
Pin, Lapel, Logo, Green Enamel, Sterling Silver, 1960s		33

BRADLEY & HUBBARD is a name found on many metal objects. Walter Hubbard and his brother-in-law, Nathaniel Lyman Bradley, started making cast iron clocks, tables, frames, andirons, bookends, doorstops, lamps, chandeliers, sconces, and sewing birds in 1854 in Meriden, Connecticut. The company became Bradley & Hubbard Manufacturing Company in 1875. Charles Parker Company bought the firm in 1940. There is no mention of Bradley & Hubbard after the 1950s. Bradley & Hubbard items may be found in other sections that include metal.

Frame, Open Leaves, Shell Finial, Brass, 12 x 8 In.		55
Lamp, 8 Bent Panels, Arts & Crafts Filigree, White, Yellow, Green When Lit, 24 x 8 In.		164
Lamp, Bronze, Lotus Petal Base, 8-Panel Top, Latticework Frame, 1910, 18 x 13 In.		900
Lamp, Caramel Slag, Glass Panels, Metal Frame & Base, 1900s, 22 x 16 In.	*illus*	570
Lamp, Electric, 3-Light, Domed Shade, Slag Glass, Eucalyptus, c.1910, 22 x 22½ In.		875
Lamp, Gold Decorated Cast Iron, Double Handled Base, Single Socket, 29 x 6½ In.		354
Lamp, Hanging, Brass Frame & Font, Crystal Prisms, Cranberry, 1800s, 30 x 10 In.		450
Lamp, Hanging, Nickel Plated Brass Font, Embossed Swirl, Leafy Decoration, 1890, 34 In.		84
Lamp, Octagonal, Bent, Slag Glass Shade, Metal Overlays, Verde Green Finish, 1905, 19 In.		968
Lamp, Oil, Woman, Bicycle, Victorian, 10 In. Shade, Floor, 57½ In.		1295
Lamp, Parlor, Oil, Cast White Metal Base, Pierced, Pink Cased Shade, c.1870, 20 In.	*illus*	94
Lamp, Silvertone Floral Cover, Marble Shaft, Embossed Brass Base, Electrified, 28 x 7 In.		118
Lamp, Slag Glass, Paneled Shade, Filigree, White, Yellow, Green, Metal Base, 7½ x 18 In.		590
Letter Holder, Hunt Scene, Dogs, Deer, Marked, 9 x 5 In.		150
Pen Tray, Iron, Indian Chief Heads, Connecting Necklace, c.1920, 11 x 2 In.		200

BRASS has been used for decorative pieces and useful tablewares since ancient times. It is an alloy of copper, zinc, and other metals. Additional brass items may be found under Bell, Candlestick, Tool, or Trivet.

Alms Dish, Nuremburg, Petal Form, 2 Surrounding Rings, Gothic Inscription, 1500s, 17 In.	360
Bed Warmer, Hinge, Pierced, Engraved, Turned Wooden Handle, c.1780, 42 In.	105
Bed Warmer, Pan, Floral Leaf, Diamond, Pierced, Socket, England, c.1830, 12 x 32 In.	40
Bed Warmer, Punched Decoration, Turned Wooden Handle, Green Paint, 1800s, 45 In.	38
Belt Plate, Colonial Artillery, Crown Over Crossed, Cannon Ball Pyramid Below, 1700, 3 x 3 In.	94
Bowl, Oak Lion's Head, Ring Handles, 6¾ x 9½ In.	88
Bowl, Ornate Indo-Persian Repousse, Ceremonial, Carved, Mongoose Stand, 5 x 5 x 3 In.	30

Box, Salt, Mixed Wood, Wall, Painted, Katie Frieher, Anno Domini 1797, 16 x 11 x 9 In.
$443

Hess Auction Group

Boy Scout, Canteen, Aluminum, Canvas Carrying Case, c.1950, 7½ In.
$39

Ruby Lane

Bradley & Hubbard, Lamp, Caramel Slag, Glass Panels, Metal Frame & Base, 1900s, 22 x 16 In.
$570

Garth's Auctioneers & Appraisers

Bradley & Hubbard, Lamp, Parlor, Oil, Cast White Metal Base, Pierced, Pink Cased Shade, c.1870, 20 In.
$94

Garth's Auctioneers & Appraisers

Brass, Statue, Woman, Standing, Classically Dressed, Bouquet, Ram's Head Torchiere, 14 1/2 In.
$389

Leland Little Auctions

Brass, Urn, Lions, Masks, Scrollwork, Paw Feet, Gilt, 43 1/2 x 27 1/2 In.
$3,068

Burchard Galleries

Bride's Basket, Blue Cased, Flowers, Frosted Ruffled Rim, Silver-Plated Frame, Acme, 12 In.
$98

Rich Penn Auctions

Bronze, Censer, Lid, 4 Sections, Phoenix, Fish, Dragons, Lion Masks, Chinese, 19 x 16 In.
$14,400

Brunk Auctions

Bronze, Censer, Square, Panels Of Chinese Dragon, Elephant, Handles, Xuande Mark, 3 x 5 In.
$244

Neal Auction Co.

Bronze, Gong, Hammered, Arched Rosewood Stand, Tibet, 21 In.
$250

Eldred's Auctioneers and Appraisers

Bronze, Sculpture, Barker, James, Otter & Pup Nestled In Seagrass, 10 1/4 In.
$563

Eldred's Auctioneers and Appraisers

Box, 4 Copper Character Medallions To Corners, Serpentine Jade, Etched, 1900, 1 x 4 In.	31
Box, Lid, Repousse, Lockable, Merlot Color, Velveteen, Continental, 1800s-1900s, 1½ x 3¾ x 3 In.	192
Box, Lion's Head, Rectangular, Loose Ring Handles, 1800s, 6½ In.	168
Box, Planter, Snake, Ormolu Handles & Trim, Ball Feet, French Marquetry, 8 x 16 x 10 In.	563
Box, Quartersawn Oak, Double Pigeonhole Compartment, c.1890, 10 x 13 x 8¾ In.	342
Bucket, Iron Rod Handle, Wired Rim, Hanger, Copper Rivets, 1870, 14 x 9⅜ In.	40
Cannon, 6 Pounder, Wood Base, Model, 9¼ x 23¾ In.	264
Charger, Egyptian, Repousse, Old Busch Groves, Leaves, 1900s, 28 In.	90
Cigarette Box, Lid, Floral Jade Disc, Cedar, Medallion, Engraved Flowers, 6 x 3½ x 2½ In.	53
Coffeepot, Wood Handle & Finial Knop, Bearing Three Indistinct Marks, 1770, 9⅜ In.	5625
Cross, Rods, Enamel Center, Frappe James, 1959, 14 x 9½ In.	88
Crucifix, Figures, Relief, Enamel, Cyrillic Inscription, Russia, 6¾ In.	120
Drinking Horn, Griffin Pedestal, Cherubs, Animal Heads, Relief, 26 In.	950
Figure, Cheetah, Copper, Regal Pose, Sergio Bustamante, 1900s, 19 In.	300
Frame, Sunburst, 4 Corners, 7½ x 6 In.	406
Ginger Jar, Cloisonne, Black & White, Peonies, Black Geometric Background, 1900, Pair	88
Jewelry Box, Glass, Enamel, Green, Emerald Glass Panel, 2½ x 5 In.	100
Jewelry Box, Rosewood, Key, Jugendstil, Erhard & Sohne, 9½ x 4½ In.	2875
Mailbox, Centered With Applique Brass Tree, Newcomb College, c.1925, 11½ x 9 In.	1464
Pail, Swing Handle, Oval Mouth, H.W. Hayden, c.1875, 7½ In.	48
Pitcher, Chromed, Rectangular, Sloped Top, Handle, Revere Copper & Brass Co., Stamped, 1930s, 12 In.	1190
Plaque, Bismarck, Helmet, Relief, 18 In. Diam.	325
Plaque, Kaiser Wilhelm I, Helmet, 18 In. Diam.	325
Roasting Jack, Clockwork Spring, English Shield Of Arms Case, Iron Wheel, c.1875, 6 x 14 In.	110
Scissors, Style Of Carl Aubock, 25½ In.	288
Sculpture, Benin, Bamun, Cow, West Africa, 21 In.	156
Sculpture, Pagoda, Bells, Tiered, 49 In.	3932
Sculpture, Parrot, Nickel, Etched, Arch Hanger, Sergio Bustamante, 1900s, 45 In.	531
Sculpture, Reindeer, Horn, Upward, 4 Legs, 1900s, 42 In.	540
Sculpture, Ribbon, In Loop, Russell Secrest, c.1970, 15 x 10 In.	1121
Sculpture, Solid, Old Man Of The Sea, Hands In Pockets, Weathered Face, 14 x 6 x 4½ In.	120
Smoking Stand, Demilune Rack, Canister, Lid, Circular, Green Painted Base, 1800s, 10 In.	123
Smoking Tray, 3 Graduated Containers, Figural Scenes, Beaded, Trumpet Feet, 5¾ x 8 In.	277
Spyglass, Leather Covered, Single Extension, Mahogany Case, 1800, 20 In.	615
Statue, Woman, Standing, Classically Dressed, Bouquet, Ram's Head Torchiere, 14½ In. illus	389
Surveyor's Transit, E Whiton Maker, 3 Liquid Levels, Compass, 1800s, 12 x 15 x 7½ In.	1625
Tazza, Round Form, Straight-Sided, Tall Pedestal Foot, 1900, 4 x 9¼ In.	37
Tray, Hammered, Etched, Geometric, Floral, Persia, 20 x 20 x 1 In.	41
Tray, Pierced Carved Handle, Triangle, Star Design, 1800, 3½ x 12 x 17 In.	168
Tray, Tabletop, Large, Silver Inlay, Raised Flat Rim, Kufic Inscription, Turkey, 1853, 27 In.	1320
Urn, Baroque Style, Inverted Pear Shape, Angel Head Mounts, Continental, c.1875, 21½ In. Pair	625
Urn, Lions, Masks, Scrollwork, Paw Feet, Gilt, 43½ x 27½ In. illus	3068
Urn, Silvered, Putti, K Base, Lioness, Reclining Bacchus, 15¾ x 8 In.	1080

BRASTOFF, *see Sascha Brastoff category.*

BREAD PLATE, *see various silver categories, porcelain factories, and pressed glass patterns.*

BRIDE'S BOWLS OR BASKETS were usually one-of-a-kind novelties made in American and European glass factories. They were especially popular about 1880 when the decorated basket was often given as a wedding gift. Cut glass baskets were popular after 1890. All bride's bowls lost favor about 1905. Bride's bowls and baskets may also be found in other glass sections. Check the index at the back of the book.

Amber Glass, Rolled Rim, Tricornered, Gilt Frame, Cherub, Moser Style, 10 x 11 In.	210
Amberina, Ruffled Edge, Dewdrop Design, Silver Plated, Winged Maiden, Meriden, 1800s, 9 x 4 In.	1150
Blue Cased, Flowers, Frosted Ruffled Rim, Silver-Plated Frame, Acme, 12 In. illus	98
Cobalt Blue Glass, Ruffled Square, White Exterior, Flowers, Silver Plated Frame, 8½ x 12 In.	300
Cranberry Cased, Mother-Of-Pearl, Herringbone, Ruffled, Silver Tripod, Putti, 14 In.	3383
Cranberry Glass, Enamel Branch, Blossom & Bird, Silver Plate, Conquistadors, 11 x 8½ In.	120

Bronze, Sculpture, Barye, Alfred, Dog, Hat & Gloves, Signed, A. Barye Fils, c.1850, 6½ In.
$1,140

Brunk Auctions

Bronze, Sculpture, Chiparus, Antinea, Silver, Gold Patina, Marble Base, c.1925, 27 In.
$14,750

Cottone Auctions

Bronze, Sculpture, Chiparus, Dancing Woman, Painted, Marble Base, Signed, 16 In.
$15,996

James D. Julia Auctioneers

Bronze, Sculpture, Frishmuth, Harriet Whitney, Extase, Nude Woman, Arms Over Head, 1920, 19¾ In.
$14,760

Cowan's Auctions

Bronze, Sculpture, Kalish, Max, Steel Rougher, 1926, 13½ In.
$12,300

Cowan's Auctions

Bronze, Sculpture, Moigniez, Jules, Dog, Bird, Signed, 29 x 42 In.
$2,928

Neal Auction Co.

Cranberry Glass, Engraved Flowers, Gold Stencil Highlights, Rogers, 12 x 12 In.	540
Cranberry Opalescent, Diamond Quilted, Silver Plated Scroll Frame, 11 In.	156
Cranberry Opalescent Glass, Narrow Ruffle, Silver Plated Frame, 8¼ x 8¼ In.	157
Cranberry Opalescent Glass, Silver Plated Frame, 14½ x 10 In.	272
Green & White Glass, Ribbed & Ruffled, Floral Highlights, Cherub, Silver Plated Frame, 11 x 11 In.	420
Lavender, White Flowers, Gold Leaves, Twisted Brass Holder, 11 x 9 In.	74
Peachblow, Melon Ribbed, Blossoms & Branches, Silver Plated Frame, Webb, 12 x 10 In.	1320
Pink & White Glass, Shell Shape, Silver Plated Frame, 8 x 10 In.	180
Pink Ruffled Glass, White Exterior, Enamel Floral Decor, Silver Plated Frame, Aurora, 13 x 13 In.	210
Red Glass, Ruffled Bowl, Enamel Flowers, Silver Plated Frame, 13 x 13 In.	300
Satin Glass, Lavender, White, Ruffled, Blossoms & Orange Leaf, Gilt Metal Frame, 15 x 17 In.	330
White Cased, Flowers, Pink Inside, Crimped Rim, Silver Plated Frame	240
White Cased, Pink, Pears, Amber Ruffled Rim, 2-Tier Silver Plated Frame, 12 In.	212

 BRISTOL glass was made in Bristol, England, after the 1700s. The Bristol glass most often seen today is a Victorian, lightweight opaque glass that is often blue. Some of the glass was decorated with enamels.

Vase, Gilded Rims, Elongated Bottle Shape, Multicolor Tropical Birds, 1800s, 22 In.	369
Vase, White, Enameled Band, Beaded Swags, Tulip Neck, Coiled Serpent, 14 x 4 In., Pair	458

BRITANNIA, *see Pewter category.*

BRONZE is an alloy of copper, tin, and other metals. It is used to make figurines, lamps, and other decorative objects. Bronze lamps are listed in the Lamp category. Pieces listed here date from the eighteenth, nineteenth, and twentieth centuries. Shown here are marks by three well-known makers of bronzes.

POMPEIAN BRONZE COMPANY

Armor Bronze Corp. c.1919–c.1926, 1934–1948	Bradley and Hubbard Mfg. Co. 1875–c.1940	Pompeian Bronze Co. Undated

Basket, Figural Lid, Lady Of The Evening, Sitting, Concealed Derriere, 7 x 6 In.		1125
Blotter, Dog, Onyx, 4½ x 6¼ In.		225
Bowl, Erte, Fruit Of Life, Turbaned Woman, 1985, 8½ x 10 In.		960
Bowl, Lily Pad Shape, Frog On Rim, Japan, 3¼ x 7 In.		120
Bowl, Louis XVI, Artichoke Shape, Teal, Gilt Bronze Base, France, c.1900, 9¼ In.		1168
Bust, French, D.C., Ralph Waldo Emerson, 17½ In.		1250
Bust, Holden, Harold, Chiricahua, Wood Base, Signed, 1991, 13¾ In.		360
Bust, Old Man, Vietnam, c.1940, 9 x 9 In.		325
Bust, Villanis, Emmanuel, La Sibylle, Woman, Jeweled Crown, Robes, 27 x 19 In.		2205
Bust, Woman, Wearing Hat, Victorian, 16 In.		303
Censer, Double Dragon Handles, 3-Footed, 5½ x 7½ In.		300
Censer, Lid, 4 Sections, Phoenix, Fish, Dragons, Lion Masks, Chinese, 19 x 16 In.	*illus*	14400
Censer, Silver Inlay Decoration, Elephant Head Tripod Stand, Japan, 1800s, 7¼ x 7 In.		600
Censer, Silver Inlay, Effigy Handles, Chinese, 1800s		413
Censer, Square, Panels Of Chinese Dragon, Elephant, Handles, Xuande Mark, 3 x 5 In.	*illus*	244
Centerpiece, Nude, Sitting, Flanked By Dancers, Rouge Marble Base, Signed Matti, 18 x 21 In.		2205
Drum, Sunburst, Concentric Bands, Geometric Patterns, 26 In.		1071
Ewer, Gilt, Angels, Scrolling Filigree, Handles, Pieced, Griffins, 22¼ x 8 In., Pair		1575
Gong, Hammered, Arched Rosewood Stand, Tibet, 21 In.	*illus*	250
Incense Burner, Bird, Meiji, Japan, 5 x 5 In., Pair		246
Jar, Dome Lid, Basket Form, Knot Form Handles, Grasshopper, Leaves, Japan, 1900s, 13 x 8 In.		938
Jardiniere, Bamboo, Cherry Blossoms, Japan, 8 x 10 In.		343
Jardiniere, Cylindrical, Leafy Scroll Border, 3-Footed, Knees, 10 x 8¾ In.		3438
Jardiniere, Dragons, Entwined, 13 In.		4500

Jardiniere, Putti, Reclining Nude, Wavy Rim, Grapevine, A. Kinsburger, 15 1/4 x 15 1/2 In..........	1890
Jardiniere, Silvered, Gadrooned Sides, Greek Key Band, Lion Handles, Paw Feet, 19 In.	813
Jewelry Box, Coffin Shape, Enamel, Filigree, Angels, Putti, 6 x 8 In................	630
Mirror, Hand, Molded, Cranes, 9 x 3 1/2 In.	50
Paper Clip, Figural Dog's Head, Greyhound, Glass Eyes, Austria, c.1900, 5 x 2 In.	725
Planter, Hydrangeas, Birds, Leaves, Butterflies, Incised, Multicolor, 1900s, 7 x 11 In.	241
Plaque, Abstract, Bright Colors, Etched, Patinated, Philip LaVerne, 65 1/4 x 24 3/4 In.	4687
Plaque, Cerebus, Rooster, Round, Baskin, Leonard, 1969, 6 1/2 In.	375
Plaque, Chinese Warriors, Traditional Robes, Philip & Kevin LaVerne, 65 x 24 in...........	10000
Plaque, Horse Head, Inscribed Nick On Edge, Oval, Continental, 1900s, 17 In.	225
Plaque, Nude With Macaw, Art Deco, Octagonal, Delannoy, Maurice, 2 1/2 In.	24
Plaque, Putti, Musical Instruments, 2 3/4 In.	246
Plate, Classical Nudes, Leaves, Benches, 17 In.	58
Sculpture, 2 Cranes, Turtle, 14 x 12 1/2 In.	956
Sculpture, 2 Herons, Mother & Child, Lily Pad Shape Base, Verdigris, 15 1/2 In.	605
Sculpture, Angel Embracing Child, Polished, France, c.1875, 13 1/2 In.	1000
Sculpture, Angel, Wings, Draped Robe, Rockwork Base, c.1920, 53 x 38 In.	3000
Sculpture, Asian Water Buffalo, Standing Bull, Head Down, c.1950, 8 x 15 In.	96
Sculpture, Atlas, Kneeling, Supports Moss Covered Globe, On Shoulders, 1900s, 30 x 17 In.	937
Sculpture, Barker, James, Otter & Pup Nestled In Seagrass, 10 1/4 In. .... *illus*	563
Sculpture, Barye, Alfred, Arab, On Horseback, Galloping, 1800s, 25 x 28 1/2 In.	1250
Sculpture, Barye, Alfred, Dog, Hat & Gloves, Signed, A. Barye Fils, c.1850, 6 1/2 In. .... *illus*	1140
Sculpture, Bear, Seated, Pink Marble Platform, 4 3/4 x 6 x 4 In.	720
Sculpture, Bergman, Franz, Running Man, Cold Paint, Geschutzt, Marked, 9 In................	399
Sculpture, Bergman, Monkey, Tray, Cold Paint, Marked, 4 1/8 x 4 1/2 x 3 1/4 In.	720
Sculpture, Beszedes, Laszlo, Hungarian Man, Cold Paint, Marble Stand, Signed, 16 In.	240
Sculpture, Buffalo Skull, Green Cold Paint, Skull, Horns, 1 3/4 x 5 1/2 In.............	184
Sculpture, Butterfly Dancer, Gilt, Enamel, Octagonal Base, Louis, Chalon, c.1900, 16 x 6 In...	10925
Sculpture, Camel, Lying Down, Bedouin Rider, 2 Parts, France, 1900s, 19 In.	1000
Sculpture, Chiparus, Antinea, Silver, Gold Patina, Marble Base, c.1925, 27 In. .... *illus*	14750
Sculpture, Chiparus, Dancing Woman, Painted, Marble Base, Signed, 16 In. .... *illus*	15996
Sculpture, Crab, Raised Pincers, Protruding Eyes, Japan, Graduating Sizes, 1 To 6 In., 4 Piece.	1000
Sculpture, Dahlberg, C., Wild Men, Wild Cattle, Cowboy On Horse, Chasing Bull, 1994, 28 In.	1200
Sculpture, Dakon, Stephan, Sashaying Woman, Painted, Marble Base, c.1930, 5 1/2 In.	295
Sculpture, Dante, Oval Marble Base, 7 1/2 x 7 1/2 In.	492
Sculpture, Eagle, Soaring, Patina, Cold Paint, Rocky Base, 1900s, 70 x 58 In................	2750
Sculpture, Elephant, Trunk Up, Standing, 11 5/8 x 10 1/4 In.	200
Sculpture, Elk, Calling, Patina, Signed, Cartier, Thomas, 17 In.	847
Sculpture, Eros, Carrying Dolphin & Swan, c.1900, 25 1/2 x 10 x 23 In., Pair..........	2000
Sculpture, Erte, Wedding, Couple, Holding Hands, 1980s, 16 1/2 x 18 In.	2812
Sculpture, Erte, Wisdom, Woman, Egyptian Eagle In Hand, 1980s, 16 x 13 In.	2375
Sculpture, Etienne-Martin, Stacked Blocks, Gouges, 15 1/2 x 16 In.................	6875
Sculpture, Fernandez, Armand, Venus Off Shore, Nude Female Torso Split By Propellers, 15 1/2 In.	4687
Sculpture, Foo Dog, Openwork Flower Ball, 9 x 11 In.................	192
Sculpture, Fraser, J.E., Indian Princess, Buffalo Nickel, 1921, 6 x 8 1/2 x 6 In.................	350
Sculpture, Fremiet, Emmanuel, Snake Charmer, 16 3/4 In.	3500
Sculpture, Frid, Misha, Male & Female With Harp, 24 x 20 In.	205
Sculpture, Frid, Misha, Male Playing Flute, Female Listens, Seated On Rock, 1991, 22 In.	205
Sculpture, Frishmuth, Harriet Whitney, Extase, Nude Woman, Arms Over Head, 1920, 19 3/4 In. .. *illus*	14760
Sculpture, Gabbrielli, Donatello, Child, Turtle, Copper Fitting, For Fountain, 14 x 8 1/2 In.	750
Sculpture, Ganapati Ganesh, On Throne, 13 x 12 x 6 1/2 In.	1920
Sculpture, Good, J. Willis, Horse, Saddle, c.1870, 15 1/2 In..........................	2400
Sculpture, Gross, Chaim, Mother, Daughter, Swings From Arms, Black Marble Base, 12 In.....	1320
Sculpture, Guillot, Anatole, Rebecca At The Well, Holding Jug, Ruins, Palm Tree, 31 x 14 In...	2835
Sculpture, Head Of Buddha, Peaceful Face, Eyes Cast Downward, Thailand, c.1920, 8 In.	1375
Sculpture, Holden, Harold, Green Broke, Wood Base, 1981, 20 In................	738
Sculpture, Holden, Harold, Samson, Horse, Wood Base, Signed, 1991, 13 3/4 In.	430
Sculpture, Kalish, Max, Steel Rougher, 1926, 13 1/2 In. .... *illus*	12300
Sculpture, Kauba, Carl, Chief White Cloud, Brown, Gold Patina, Green Marble Base, 21 x 10 In.	678

Bronze, Sculpture, Rug Seller, Cold Painted, Stamped, Austria, 8 x 6 In. $488

Bronze, Sculpture, Schmidt, Julius, Abstract, Nooks, Crannies, 1964, 13 In. $8,255

Bronze, Sculpture, Vanderveen, Loet, Roaring Lion, Polished, Incised, Signed, 21 x 23 In.
$4,000

New Orleans Auction Galleries

TIP
Worcestershire sauce is a good brass polish.

Bronze, Urn, Thunder Pattern, Bird Handles, Chinese Export, 12 In.
$2,125

Freeman's Auctioneers & Appraisers

Brownies, Candleholder, Smoking Set, Brownie, 3 Barrels, Majolica, 1895, 8 In.
$200

Theriault's

Sculpture, Kieff, Antonio, Flame, Abstract Torch, Marble Base, Canada, 1985, 21 ¼ x 5 In.	1000
Sculpture, Kieff, Antonio, Flowing, Twisting, Looping Strand, Marble Base, Canada, 31 x 9 x 7 In.	2250
Sculpture, Kubera, God Of Wealth, Gilt, Sino Tibetan, 11 In.	1321
Sculpture, Man On Horse, Wood Base, Signed, 1996, 13 x 14 In.	780
Sculpture, Mene, Pierre Jules, Dog, Tied To Post, Pulling At Lead, France, 9 ⅛ x 12 ⅝ In.	1080
Sculpture, Mice Hauling Egg, Red Marble Base, Signed, Valton, Charles, 1851-1918, 4 ¼ x 4 ¼ x 2 ¾ In.	600
Sculpture, Mohr, Larry, Planks, Dark Brown, 20 ½ x 15 In.	922
Sculpture, Moigniez, Jules, Dog, Bird, Signed, 29 x 42 In. *illus*	2928
Sculpture, Monk, Holding Stein, Signed, F. Julland 86, 7 ¾ In.	120
Sculpture, Monument, Case, Salesman's Sample, Parker Co., 21 ½ x 8 ¾ In.	833
Sculpture, Nude, Dancing, Leg Up, Arms Out, Black, Polished, 16 ½ In.	480
Sculpture, Osborne, Leo, Blackhawk, 1993, 25 x 10 In.	567
Sculpture, Paladino, Mimmo, Unicorn, Brutalist Style, 10 x 6 In.	3125
Sculpture, Pappas, John, Woman, Leaning, Against Post, 16 x 7 In.	413
Sculpture, Pappas, John, Woman, Nude, Reclining, Chair, 1970, 14 x 10 In.	649
Sculpture, Parakeet, On Perch, Glass Dome, Vienna, c.1900, 7 In.	443
Sculpture, Pautrot, F., Les Chats, Cats, Patina, Signed, 1868, 8 In.	1188
Sculpture, Pina, Alfredo, Reclining Nude, Drapery, Gilt, Italy, 7 x 21 In.	1375
Sculpture, Renaissance Soldier, Throwing Dice, Signed, Russia, 1800s, 9 x 12 In.	2160
Sculpture, Rhino, Standing, Hinged Lid On Back, Chinese, 14 ¾ In.	275
Sculpture, Rug Seller, Cold Painted, Stamped, Austria, 8 x 6 In. *illus*	488
Sculpture, Samurai, Fighting Tiger, Spears, In Mouth, 23 ½ x 17 ½ In.	504
Sculpture, Schmidt, Julius, Abstract, Nooks, Crannies, 1964, 13 In. *illus*	8255
Sculpture, Schreyvogel, Charles, Last Drop, Horse, Man, Kneels, Gives Water, Bowl, c.1903, 12 x 18 In.	2750
Sculpture, Sheep Grazing, Alphonso, Arson, 6 x 9 In.	1062
Sculpture, Titled, Shalako Maiden, Girl, Large Katsina Doll, Water Jar, 1993, 6 x 5 x 12 In.	130
Sculpture, Valton, Charles, Lion, Prowling, Post, 18 ½ In.	1375
Sculpture, Vanderveen, Loet, Roaring Lion, Polished, Incised, Signed, 21 x 23 In. *illus*	4000
Sculpture, Woman Partially Nude Reclining, Recamier, France, 15 ½ x 29 ½ In.	2700
Sculpture, Woman, Nude, Sleeping, Crossed Legs, 1982, 15 x 14 In.	1298
Sign, Relief, Tavern Scene, 1906, 11 x 8 In.	120
Tazza, Moigniez, Jules, Bird Of Prey Support, France, 10 ½ In.	600
Tray, Bonsai Cultivation, Rectilinear, Wave Design Sides & Feet, Signed, 5 ¾ x 24 x 15 In.	1920
Tray, Enamel, Mirror Inset, Courting Couples, Leaves, Scrolls, Multicolor, 15 x 9 ½ In.	250
Urn, Birds, Branches, Persimmon Trees, Wooden Prayer Tablet, 30 ½ In.	295
Urn, Campana Form, Scrollwork, Lotus Base, Rampant Lion Handles, 27 In., Pair	1750
Urn, Relief Decoration, Pear Shape Body, Fox Head At Handle Base, Seal Mark, 8 ¼ x 4 ¼ In.	120
Urn, Thunder Pattern, Bird Handles, Chinese Export, 12 In. *illus*	2125
Vase, Flared Scalloped Rim, Tigers, Deer, Landscape, Round Foot, Japan, 21 ½ x 13 In.	1440
Vase, Fuchs, E., Climbing Child, Flowers, Art Nouveau, Marked, c.1900, 16 ½ In., Pair	1375
Vase, Giambaldi, Art Nouveau, Nude, Standing, Tree Trunk, Metal Liner, 10 x 5 ¾ In.	562
Vase, Inlay, Dragon, Japan, 11 ¾ In.	600
Vase, Moreau, Francois & Lois, Nude Woman, Winged, Flowers, 19 x 11 ½ In.	2000
Vase, Noboru, Nogawa, Inlay, Rooster, 1900s, 4 ¼ In.	383
Vase, Stick, Fuchs, E., Relief Filigree, Flying Birds, Putti, Climbing Fence, 16 ¾ In., Pair	1890
Vase, Yellow, Green Tint, Flowers & Leaves, Nouveau, Marked H. Sibeud, 12 In.	590

 BROWNIES were first drawn in 1883 by Palmer Cox (1840–1924). They are characterized by large round eyes, downturned mouths, and skinny legs. Toys, books, dinnerware, and other objects were made with the Brownies as part of the design.

Basket, Bonbon, Chocolates, Engraved, Ruffled Rim, Swing Handle, Footed, 5 x 6 ¼ In.	36
Blotter, Brownie Figure, Silver Plate, Unmarked, 2 x 4 ¾ In.	210
Candleholder, Smoking Set, Brownie, 3 Barrels, Majolica, 1895, 8 In. *illus*	200
Candy Container, Policeman, Papier-Mache, Removable Head, Germany, c.1895, 10 In. *illus*	1300
Candy Container, Uncle Sam, Papier-Mache, Nodder, Spring, Germany, 1890, 6 In. *illus*	1600
Clock, Figural, 8 Brownies, Cast Metal, Bronze Finish, Roman Numerals, c.1900, 7 In. *illus*	850
Figurine, Uncle Sam, Papier-Mache, Nodder, Long Legs, Germany, c.1895, 12 In. *illus*	1400
Napkin Ring, Standing, Embossed, Silver Plate, 1 ½ In.	180

BRUSH-MCCOY, *see Brush category and related pieces in McCoy category.*

BRUSH POTTERY was started in 1925. George Brush first worked in 1901 in Zanesville, Ohio. He started his own pottery in 1907, but it burned to the ground soon after. In 1909 he became manager of the J.W. McCoy Pottery. In 1911, Brush and J.W. McCoy formed the Brush-McCoy Pottery Co. After a series of name changes, the company became The Brush Pottery in 1925. It closed in 1982. Old Brush was marked with impressed letters or a palette-shaped mark. Reproduction pieces are being made. They are marked in raised letters or with a raised mark. Collectors favor the figural cookie jars made by this company. Because there was a company named Brush-McCoy, there is great confusion between Brush and Nelson McCoy pieces. Most collectors today refer to Brush pottery as Brush-McCoy. See McCoy category for more information.

Bank, Pig, Brown Speckled Glaze, Tan Sponge Daubs, 1930s, 5½ x 2¾ In.	65
Ginger Jar, Brown, Gold, Ivory, Onyx Glaze, c.1930, 7 In.	39
Jardiniere, McCoy, Tulips, Ribbed, Burgundy Gloss, c.1925, 4 x 3½ In.	45
Pitcher, Nurock, Brown, Yellow, 7¼ x 6 In.	120
Planter, Girl Holding Basket & Flowers, Bonnet, Ribbons, Blond, 8 x 9½ In.	18
Vase, Blue Onyx, Oval, Footed, c.1924, 6¼ In.	40
Vase, Cobalt Blue, Marbleized, Marked, Brush McCoy, 1924, 6¼ In. .... *illus*	40
Vase, Trojan Horse Head, Black Gloss, c.1950, 10 In.	89

BUCK ROGERS was the first American science fiction comic strip. It started in 1929 and continued until 1967. Buck has also appeared in comic books, movies, and, in the 1980s, a television series. Any memorabilia connected with the character Buck Rogers is collectible.

Space Gun, Metal, 25th Century, Daisy Mfg. Co., 1930s, 10 In.	285
Toy, Rocket Ship, Tin Lithograph, Louis Marx, Windup, 1927, 12 In.	1095
Toy, Spaceship, Orange, Yellow Wings, Sparking Action, Clockwork, Marx, 12 In.	450

BUFFALO POTTERY was made in Buffalo, New York, after 1902. The company was established by the Larkin Company, famous manufacturers of soap. The wares are marked with a picture of a buffalo and the date of manufacture. Deldare ware is the most famous pottery made at the factory. It has either a khaki-colored or green background with hand-painted transfer designs. The company reorganized in 1956 and was renamed Buffalo China before being bought by Oneida Silver Company.

Buffalo Pottery 1907	Deldare ware 1909	Emerald Deldare 1912

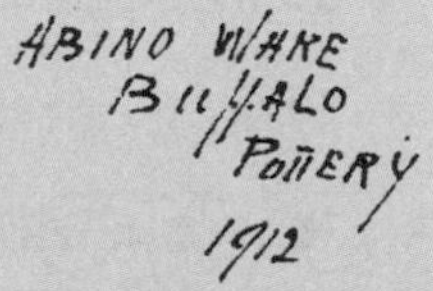

BUFFALO POTTERY

Bone Dish, Pagoda, Trees, Blue & White, 6½ x 3½ In.	75
Candleholder, Shield, Men Talking, 1909, 6⅞ In.	293
Pitcher, Rip Van Winkle, Brown Transfer, 1906, 5⅞ In.	94
Pitcher, Sperm Whaling, The Capture, Ship Niger, New Bedford, Brown, White, 7 In. ...... *illus*	480
Plate, Bread & Butter, Cream Background, Brown Scroll Design On Rim, 6¼ In.	5
Platter, Waldorf Lunch Anniversary, Couples Dancing, 1915, 12 In.	468

BUFFALO POTTERY DELDARE

Candle Shield, Handle, Emerald, 7 In. .... *illus*	649
Candlestick, B. Willon, 8⅞ In.	175
Humidor, There Was An Old Sailor & He Had A Wooden Leg, 7 In.	152
Humidor, Ye Lion Inn, Signed, M. Gryhardt, 1909, 7 In. .... *illus*	472
Match Holder, Bands, Leaves, Flowers, 3½ x 6 In. .... *illus*	413
Plate, Dr. Syntax, Misfortune At Tulip Hall, 8⅜ In.	163

Brownies, Candy Container, Policeman, Papier-Mache, Removable Head, Germany, c.1895, 10 In.
$1,300

Theriault's

Brownies, Candy Container, Uncle Sam, Papier-Mache, Nodder, Spring, Germany, 1890, 6 In.
$1,600

Theriault's

This is an edited listing of current prices. Visit **Kovels.com** to check thousands of prices from previous years and sign up for free information on trends, tips, reproductions, marks, and more.

Brownies, Clock, Figural, 8 Brownies, Cast Metal, Bronze Finish, Roman Numerals, c.1900, 7 In. $850

Theriault's

Brownies, Figurine, Uncle Sam, Papier-Mache, Nodder, Long Legs, Germany, c.1895, 12 In. $1,400

Theriault's

Plate, Peacock, Emerald, 12 In. .... *illus* 2242

BUNNYKINS, *see Royal Doulton category.*

BURMESE GLASS was developed by Frederick Shirley at the Mt. Washington Glass Works in New Bedford, Massachusetts, in 1885. It is a two-toned glass, shading from peach to yellow. Some pieces have a pattern mold design. A few Burmese pieces were decorated with pictures or applied glass flowers of colored Burmese glass. Other factories made similar glass also called Burmese. Burmese glass was made by Mt. Washington until about 1895, by Gunderson until the 1950s, and by Webb until about 1900. Fenton made Burmese glass after 1970. Related items may be listed in the Fenton category, the Gundersen category, and under Webb Burmese.

Bride's Basket, Ruffled Rim, Spider Mums, Silver Plated Frame, Marked, 15 x 10 In. 242
Cologne Bottle, Butterfly, Flowers, Blue, Pink, Yellow, Silver Screw-Off Lid, Webb & Sons, 5 In. 600
Fairy Lamp, Ruffled Base, Clear Clark Insert, Matching Shade, Ivy, 5¾ x 6½ In. 660
Jar, Lid, Acorn & Branch, Silver Plated Lid & Bail, Mt. Washington, 5¾ In. 150
Lamp, Ruffled Base, 2 Clear Clark Inserts, Decorated Shade, 6 x 7½ In. 360
Pitcher, Enameled Pink Rose, Stems, Leaves, 9 In. .... *illus* 1452
Sugar Shaker, Egg Shape, Leaf Design, Mt. Washington, 4¼ In. 150
Syrup, Spider Mums, Yellow, White, Blue, Silver Plated Spout, 6 In. 665
Vase, Bud, Figural, Squirrel & Palm Fronds, Silver Plated Stand, Meriden, Victorian, 9½ In. .. 120
Vase, Fish, Net, Seaweed, High Shoulder, Pink To Green, 7¼ x 6 In. .... *illus* 3750
Vase, Gourd Shape, Tricolor Gold Enamel Branch & Blossoms, Mt. Washington, 12 In. 780
Vase, Quatrefoil Top, Leaves, Polished & Ground Pontil, 1800s, 2¾ In. .... *illus* 188
Vase, Square, Shaped Rim, Herons, Flowers, Spattered Gilt, 6½ x 4½ In. 16380
Vase, Trumpet, Round Base, c.1875, 23½ In. 625
Vase, Trumpet, Yellow & Tan, Mt. Washington, 7 In. Diameter Base, 25 In. 720

BUSTER BROWN, the comic strip, first appeared in color in 1902. Buster and his dog, Tige, remained a popular comic and soon became even more famous as the emblem for a shoe company, a textile firm, and other companies. The strip was discontinued in 1920. Buster Brown sponsored a radio show from 1943 to 1955 and a TV show from 1950 to 1956. The Buster Brown characters are still used by Brown Shoe Company, Buster Brown Apparel, Inc., and Gateway Hosiery.

Sign, Buster & Tige, Celluloid Over Masonite, Easel Back, Beveled, 14 x 14 In. .... *illus* 448
Toy, Army Scout Plane, Buster Brown Logo On Top Wing, Steelcraft, c.1920, 22 In. Wing 450
Toy, Seesaw, Tige, Ramp, Ball, Clockwork, Germany, 10 In. 660

BUTTER CHIPS, or butter pats, were small individual dishes for butter. They were the height of fashion from 1880 to 1910. Earlier as well as later examples are known.

Brown Leaf Design, Transferware, 3⅛ In. 7
Majolica, Daisy, Pink, George Jones, 3 In. 169
Majolica, Swan On Lake, Cream Basket Weave Border, Green Center, 3 In. 145
Moss Green Flowers, Gilt, Scalloped Edge, Transferware, 1800s, 3 In., 6 Piece 60

BUTTER MOLDS *are listed in the Kitchen category under Mold, Butter.*

BUTTON collecting has been popular since the nineteenth century. Buttons have been used on clothing throughout the centuries, and there are millions of styles. Gold, silver, or precious stones were used for the best buttons, but most were made of natural materials, like bone or shell, or from inexpensive metals. Only a few types favored by collectors are listed for comparison.

Brass Colored Metal, Cherub, Brick Wall Background, 1¹⁄₁₆ In. 26
Brass, Hand Painted, Enamel Cherub, Green, Rococo Shape, c.1890, 1⅛ In. .... *illus* 95
Celluloid, Imitation Wood, Loop Shank, 1930s, 1⁷⁄₁₆ In. 10

B

Brush, Vase, Cobalt Blue, Marbleized, Marked, Brush McCoy, 1924, 6¼ In.
$40

Ruby Lane

Buffalo Pottery, Pitcher, Sperm Whaling, The Capture, Ship Niger, New Bedford, Brown, White, c.1910, 7 In.
$480

Eldred's Auctioneers and Appraisers

Buffalo Pottery Deldare, Candle Shield, Handle, Emerald, 7 In.
$649

Cottone Auctions

Buffalo Pottery Deldare, Humidor, Ye Lion Inn, Signed, M. Gryhardt, 1909, 7 In.
$472

Hess Auction Group

Buffalo Pottery Deldare, Match Holder, Bands, Leaves, Flowers, 3½ x 6 In.
$413

Cottone Auctions

Buffalo Pottery Deldare, Plate, Peacock, Emerald, 12 In.
$2,242

Cottone Auctions

Burmese, Pitcher, Enameled Pink Rose, Stems, Leaves, 9 In.
$1,452

James D. Julia Auctioneers

Burmese, Vase, Quatrefoil Top, Leaves, Polished & Ground Pontil, 1800s, 2¾ In.
$188

Garth's Auctioneers & Appraisers

Burmese, Vase, Fish, Net, Seaweed, High Shoulder, Pink To Green, 7¼ x 6 In.
$3,750

Woody Auction

BUTTON

Buster Brown, Sign, Buster & Tige, Celluloid Over Masonite, Easel Back, Beveled, 14 x 14 In.
$448

AUTHORIZED
BUSTER BROWN
DEALER

Button, Brass, Hand Painted, Enamel Cherub, Green, Rococo Shape, c.1890, 1⅛ In.
$95

Ruby Lane

TIP
A heavy odor from smoke or mildew lowers the value of a collection of paper.

Buttonhook, Sterling Silver, Polished Steel, Floral, Scroll Pattern, c.1910, 8¾ In.
$95

Ruby Lane

Celluloid, Pinwheel, Triad Design, Sawtooth Edge, Orange, c.1930, 1¼ In.	7
Fabric, Embroidered Silk, Yellow, Gold, Geometric Design, 1½ In.	9
Glass, Black, Flower, Victorian, ⅞ In.	12
Metal, Brass Color, Pears, Dark Patina, 1½ In.	32
Mother-Of-Pearl, Leaves, Carved, 1½ In.	18
Plastic, Yellow, Hobart No. 76, Colt Manufacturing Co., 1930s, 1⅜ In.	11
Steel, Pierced, Cut, Georgian, 18th Century, 1 1/16 In.	74

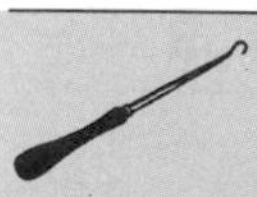

BUTTONHOOKS have been a popular collectible in England for many years and are now gaining the attention of American collectors. The buttonhooks were made to help fasten the many buttons of the old-fashioned high-button shoes and other items of apparel.

Sterling Silver, Art Nouveau, Poppies, Bows, Adie & Lovekin, c.1905, 6½ In.	71
Sterling Silver, Arts & Crafts, Monogram, 14th Century Pattern, Shreve, c.1915, 8 In.	195
Sterling Silver, Asymmetrical Baroque Scroll, c.1890, 7 In.	95
Sterling Silver, Polished Steel, Floral, Scroll Pattern, c.1910, 8¾ In. .... *illus*	95
Sterling Silver, Red, Banded Agate, c.1900	103
Sterling Silver, Repousse, Victorian, 4 In.	65

BYBEE POTTERY of Bybee, Kentucky, was started by Webster Cornelison. The company claims it started in 1809, although sales records were not kept until 1845. The pottery is still operated by members of the sixth generation of the Cornelison family. The handmade stoneware pottery is sold at the factory. Various marks were used, including the name *Bybee*, the name *Cornelison*, or the initials *BB*. Not all pieces are marked. A mark shaped like the state of Kentucky with the words *Genuine Bybee* and similar marks were also used by a different company, Bybee Pottery Company of Lexington, Kentucky. It was a distributor of various pottery lines from 1922 to 1929.

Vase, 3 Handles, Caramel Glaze, Tan Over Brown, Crystallization, Marked, 1927, 7⅝ In. *illus*	208
Vase, Chalice Shape, Handles, Light Blue High Glaze, Crystalized, Marked, 8 In.	189

CALENDARS made to hang on the wall or to be displayed on a desk top have been popular since the last quarter of the nineteenth century. Many were printed with advertising as part of the artwork and were given away as premiums. Calendars illustrated by famous artists or with guns, gunpowder, or Coca-Cola advertising are most prized.

1893, Walter A. Wood, Mowing & Reaping Machine, 9 x 7½ In.	271
1899, Antikamnia, Comical Skeleton, Quack Medicine, Textured Paper, 10 x 7 In.	920
1900, Oakes Manufacturing Co., Bright Dreams, Children, Embossed .... *illus*	75
1900, Sweet Rest, Children, Germany, 6½ x 8½ In. .... *illus*	39
1901, Dr. Daniel's Veterinary Medicines, Equestrian Couple, Gate, 14⅜ x 20 In.	1064
1902, Briggs Brewing Co., Scroll, Leaves, Landscape, 13¾ x 11 In.	247
1905, Dr. Daniel's Veterinary, Snowbound, Illustrator Rene Quentin, Full Pad, 19 x 24⅝ In.	424
1905, Laflin & Rand Powder Co., Hunters In Canoe, Dec. Page, 15 x 29 In.	10370
1906, Gibson Girls, 13 Pages, 12 x 15 In.	115
1908, Marlin Firearms Co., Duck Hunters, G.M. Arnott Artist, 15 x 24 In.	2318
1911, Gold Miners, Lithographed, Milwaukee Harvesting Machines, Oct., 13 x 23 In.	420
1913, Buffalo Fertilizer Works, Eagle, Aerial View Of Farmland, River, Frame, 26 x 18 In.	1782
1913, Dutch Boy Paints, Lewis White Lead, Dutch Boy Painter, 42 x 18 In.	210
1913, John Deere Plow Co., White Silhouette, Cardboard, Full Pad, 20 x 9¾ In.	3795
1913, Peterbreidt, Brewing, Dutch Boy & Girl, Triangular, Hanging, 12 x 12 In.	230
1917, Pratt's Veterinary, Boy, Hens, Eggs, Full Pad, 12 x 7⅜ In.	306
1918, Ford, Early Cars, Farm, Farmhouse, Couple, Woman, Climbs In Car, 26⅞ x 21⅜ In.	920
1926, Snuff Tobacco, Crowing Rooster, Pure Snuff, Useful, 17 x 9 In.	495
1927, Winchester Firearms, Hunter On Snowshoes, Frank Stick Artist, Nov. Page, 15 x 26 In.	522
1929, Edison Mazda, Golden Hours, Maxfield Parrish, Full Pad, 19⅛ x 8½ In.	236
1929, Edison Mazda, Trees, Cardboard, 20 x 9⅜ In.	306
1929, Mutual Insurance Co., Peaceful Country, Roll-Down, Green, 39½ x 16 In.	69
1938, Hercules Gunpowder, The Alchemist, N.C. Wyeth, Full Pad, 30¼ x 13 In.	140

1941, Bending Bros., Pin-Up Girl, Bathing, Cardboard Lithograph, Earl Moran, 10 x 5 In.	15
1942, Hercules Gunpowder, Primal Chemist, N.C. Wyeth, Full Pad, 30 1/4 x 13 In.	141
1944, Sabin Coal Co., Thy Rocks & Rills, Brown & Bigelow, 16 1/2 x 11 1/2 In.	129
1955, Mutual Insurance Co., Peaceful Country, Roll-Down, Brown & Bigelow, 33 1/4 x 16 In.	69
1963, Edison Mazda, Solitude, Girl, Sunlit Canyon, Maxfield Parrish, 20 x 9 1/2 In.	265
Merchants Gargling Oil Liniment, Veterinary Medicine, Horse, 14 x 10 7/8 In.	224

CALENDAR PLATES were popular in the United States as advertising giveaways from 1906 to 1929. Since then, a few plates have been made every year. A calendar and the name of a store, a picture of flowers, a girl, or a scene were featured on the plate.

1909, Roses, Buds, Leaves, 8 1/4 In.	22
1910, 4 Seasons, Homer Laughlin, 9 In.	30
1910, Carnations, Philips J. Kemmeter, Gen. Mdse., 9 1/4 In.	25
1910, Monk, Pouring Beer, Steubenville	17
1912, Owl, On Book, Wooded Scene, 8 In.	95
1915, Panama Canal, Decal, Allendale Home Bakery, Gold Rim, 6 3/8 In.	38
1976, 200th Anniversary, Red, White, Blue, Eagle, Flag, Banner, Motto, 9 In.	22
1978, God Bless Our House, Village, Brown, Alfred Meakin, 9 In.	15
1978, Samurai Warriors, Wedgwood, 10 In.	24
1980, Scrolls, Wreath, Blue & White, Currier & Ives, 10 In.	14
1984, Zodiac Sign, Farm Scene, God Bless This House, Royal Staffordshire, 8 3/4 In. *illus*	25
1996, Blue, Roman Figures, Outdoor Scene, Spode, 10 3/8 In. *illus*	10

CAMARK POTTERY started out as Camden Art Tile and Pottery Company in Camden, Arkansas. Jack Carnes founded the firm in 1926 in association with John Lessell, Stephen Sebaugh, and the Camden Chamber of Commerce. Many types of glazes and wares were made. The company was bought by Mary Daniel in the early 1960s. Production ended in 1983.

Cornucopia, Green, No. 820, 7 3/4 In.	58
Ewer, Robin's-Egg Blue, Foil Label, c.1940, 5 In.	22
Figurine, Dog, Pointer, Blue Glaze, Paper Sticker, 2 1/2 x 4 1/2 In.	30
Lamp Base, Luster Scenic, Hubbell Socket, Cast Hole On Foot, Brass Cap, Ohio, 1926, 14 In.	600
Plaque, Horse Head, Paper Label, 1930s, 7 1/2 In.	145
Vase, Black, Ribbed, Pinched Rim, c.1925, 6 1/4 In.	49
Vase, Wide Mouth Top, Ribbed, Green & Blue Glaze, c.1930, 5 1/4 x 3 1/4 In. *illus*	99

CAMBRIDGE GLASS COMPANY was founded in 1901 in Cambridge, Ohio. The company closed in 1954, reopened briefly, and closed again in 1958. The firm made all types of glass. Its early wares included heavy pressed glass with the mark *Near Cut*. Later wares included Crown Tuscan, etched stemware, and clear and colored glass. The firm used a *C* in a triangle mark after 1920.

NEAR - CUT
Cambridge Glass Co.
c.1906–c.1920

Cambridge Glass Co.
c.1937

TUSCAN
Cambridge Glass Co.
1936–1954

Caprice, Bowl, Moonlight Blue, Curved, Footed, 5 In.	26
Caprice, Cake Plate, Moonlight Blue, Footed, 11 1/2 In.	39
Caprice, Dish, Moonlight Blue, Beaded Rim, Handles, 3 x 8 In.	28
Caprice, Ice Bucket, Moonlight Blue, Tongs, 6 x 5 3/8 In.	247
Caprice, Pitcher, Juice, 32 Oz.	95
Caprice, Pitcher, Tilted Ball Shape, Ice Lip, 6 1/2 x 3 1/2 In.	95
Caprice, Salt Cellar, Moonlight Blue, 4-Footed, 2 x 1 In.	18
Caprice, Tumbler, Iced Tea, 12 Oz.	50
Carmen, Mug, Ruby, 4 1/4 In.	55
Cascade, Sugar & Creamer	20

Bybee, Vase, 3 Handles, Caramel Glaze, Tan Over Brown, Crystallization, Marked, 1927, 7 5/8 In.
$208

Humler & Nolan

Calendar Paper, 1900, Oakes Manufacturing Co., Bright Dreams, Children, Embossed
$75

Ruby Lane

Calendar Paper, 1900, Sweet Rest, Children, Germany, 6 1/2 x 8 1/2 In.
$39

Ruby Lane

Cambridge Glass— After 1958
Cambridge Glass Company went out of business in 1958 and the molds were sold to the Imperial Glass Company and later to other glass factories. Many pieces have been reproduced.

Calendar Plate, 1984, Zodiac Sign, Farm Scene, God Bless This House, Royal Staffordshire, 8¾ In. $25

Ruby Lane

Calendar Plate, 1996, Blue, Roman Figures, Outdoor Scene, Spode, 10⅜ In. $10

Ruby Lane

Use paper plates between your china plates to help prevent chipping

Camark, Vase, Wide Mouth Top, Ribbed, Green & Blue Glaze, c.1930, 5¼ x 3¼ In. $99

Ruby Lane

Chantilly, Cake Plate, Handles, 13½ x 10½ In.	45
Chantilly, Serving Bowl, 3 x 8 In.	17
Chantilly, Syrup, Straight-Sided, Silver Rim & Handle, 4⅝ In.	155
Cherub, Dish, Ritz Blue, Lid, Divided, 3 Sections, Gilt Metal Base, 6 x 7 In.	180
Crown Tuscan, Bowl, Figural, Nude & Seashell Design, 9½ x 11 In.	72
Crown Tuscan, Dish, 3 Sections, 6½ In.	24
Crown Tuscan, Platter, Pink, 14½ In.	55
Crown Tuscan, Relish, 3 Sections, Scalloped Edge, Handles, 7¾ In.	32
Decagon, Candleholder, Amber, 3½ In., Pair	45
Decagon, Cup & Saucer, Emerald Green, 2¾ In.	12
Diane, Pitcher, 7⅝ x 8 In.	225
Draped Lady, Flower Frog, Rolled Rim, Acid Cut Scroll Design, 1920s, 14 x 14 In.	84
Florentine, Sugar & Creamer, Pink.	75
Keyhole, Candleholder, 3-Light, 1920s, 6¼ x 8 In., Pair	68
Keyhole, Plate, Yellow, Double Handled, 1930s, 6¾ In.	18
Marjorie, Biscuit Jar, Squat, 8¾ In.	95
Moderne, Bowl, Squared Pulled Edge Tips, Paneled, Yellow, 10¼ In.	40
Near Cut, Plate, 8½ In.	21
Near Cut, Vase, Snowflake, c.1910, 6 In.	40
Pristine, Cornucopia, Moonlight Blue, c.1940, 8 In.	40
Rose Point, Bowl, 9 In.	40
Rose Point, Celery Dish, 3 Sections, Tab Handles, Footed, 12 x 7 In.	50
Rose Point, Coaster, 3½ In. Diam.	60
Rose Point, Compote, Ruffled Rim, 4 In.	28
Rose Point, Decanter, Stopper, 11¼ In.	121
Rose Point, Goblet, 8⅜ In.	41
Square, Relish, 2 Sections, 6½ In.	21
Stradivari, Cocktail Glass, Moonlight Blue, 5¼ In.	28
Swan, Candy Dish, Emerald Green, Open Back, c.1928, 6 In.	135
Vase, Bud, Green Matte Glaze, Impressed Oakwood Bottom, 6½ In.	70
Wheat Sheaf, Compote, 6 In.	45
Wheat Sheaf, Compote, c.1910, 4½ In.	45
Wildflower, Bonbon, Rippled, Scalloped Edge, Handles, 3¾ x 7½ In.	45
Wildflower, Butter, Cover, Open Handles, 7 In.	145
Wildflower, Fruit Cocktail, Gold Trim, 4½ Oz.	30

CAMBRIDGE POTTERY was made in Cambridge, Ohio, from about 1895 until World War I. The factory made brown-glazed decorated artwares with a variety of marks, including an acorn, the name *Cambridge*, the name *Oakwood*, and the name *Terrhea*.

Ewer, Oakwood Glaze, No. 216, 10¾ In.	72
Pitcher, Standard Glaze, No. 102, 5½ In.	125
Planter, Palms, 5 x 3 In.	145
Vase, Squat, Pansies, 2½ x 2⅝ In.	68

CAMEO GLASS was made in much the same manner as a cameo in jewelry. Parts of the top layer of glass were cut away to reveal a different colored glass beneath. The most famous cameo glass was made during the nineteenth century. Signed cameo glass pieces by famous makers are listed under the glasswork's name, such as Daum, Galle, Legras, Mt. Joye, Webb, and more. Others, signed or unsigned, are listed here. These marks were used by three cameo glass manufacturers.

Albert Dammouse	Ernest–Baptiste Léveillé	François–Eugène Rousseau
1892+	c.1869–c.1900	1855–1885

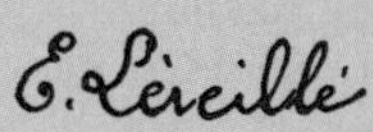

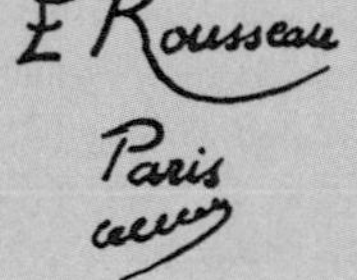

Bowl, Asymmetrical Form, Gold Gilt Rim, Relief Gold Fishes, Seaweed, 8 x 11 In.	100

Jar, Azure Flowers, Olive Green Flowers, Brown Leaves, Honey Satin, 1900, 6½ In.	1046
Lamp, Domed Shade, Eagles Flight, Mountainous, Landscape Base, 1900, 9 In.	1353
Lamp, Domed Shade, Rose Ground, Red, Leaves, Conforming Base, 1900, 14 x 6¾ In.	5228
Lamp, Domed Shade, Water Iris, Dragonflies, 1900, 16 x 7¾ In.	369
Perfume Bottle, Citron Ground, White Cameo, Flowers, Sterling Silver Cap, 1900, 7 In.	800
Perfume Bottle, Red, White, Bottle Form, Swan's Head, Sterling Silver Stopper, c.1900, 6 In.	5228
Powder Box, Circular, Flowers, Burgundy, Shaded Rose, Satin, c.1920, 1920, 2¼ x 4 In.	431
Scent Bottle, Clear, Central Panel, Cameo Flowers, Round, Silver Lid, England, 6 In.	2420
Vase, Azure, Olive Green, Flowers, Shaded Satin, Amber Ground, 1900, 11 In.	1353
Vase, Blue Body, Jasmine Decoration, Accented Butterfly, Banding At Neck, Base, 1900, 9 In.	738
Vase, Blue To Clear, Stick Neck, Birds, Flowers, Branches, 10 x 5½ In., Pair	1122
Vase, Bottle, Amber, Brown, Poppies, 1914-36, 6¾ In.	492
Vase, Bottle, Flowers, Burgundy, Satin Ground, 6¾ In.	923
Vase, Bridge, Mountains, Trees, Arsall, France, 4¼ x 3 In.	200
Vase, Bud, Flowers, Butterfly, Carved, Red & White, c.1900, 2¾ x 3½ In.	750
Vase, Burgundy Flowers, Etched To Shaded, Rust Ground, Pedestal Base, 1900, 9⅜ In.	369
Vase, Double White, Blue Glass, Passion Flower, Double Band At Foot, 1900, 8¾ In.	461
Vase, Fire Polished, Acid Etched, Lotus Blossoms, Leafy Tendrils, 1800s, 26 In.	6150
Vase, Flowers & Tendrils, Enamel Decoration, Slender Waist, France, 12 x 3¼ In.	170
Vase, Flowers, Flared Rim, White Cameo Flowers, Swirling Shades, Burgun & Schverer, 6 In.	6352
Vase, Gilt, Flowers, Leaves, Green To Frosted, Flared Rim, Honesdale, c.1907, 14 x 4 In. ... *illus*	760
Vase, Gourd Shape, White Cameo Flowers, Red Body, Polished Pontil, 1900, 8 In.	461
Vase, Green Glass, Cameo Leaves, Iridescent Ground, E. Michel, Signed, 14 In.	484
Vase, Green Leaves, Flowers, White, Signed Arsall, 12 x 5 In.	312
Vase, Honey Satin Ground, Green Ferns, 1900, 19 In.	308
Vase, Iris, Amethyst To Clear, Cressiere, France, 6 In.	234
Vase, Mottled Orange, Cream Body, Dark Rust Floral, Decoration, Charder, 1920, 16 In.	492
Vase, Mythological, Man & Woman Around Tree, Caramel Color, Burgun & Schverer, 12 In.	6292
Vase, Narrow Mouth, Cylindrical, Etched, Purple Wisteria, Shaded Pink, 1900, 7 In.	431
Vase, Narrow Mouth, Cylindrical, Red, Leaves, Berries, Shaded Yellow, Satin, 1900, 7 In.	984
Vase, Orange, Fish, Underwater Vegetation, Trapped Bubbles, Green Base, 1900, 30 In.	8918
Vase, Overlaid, Acid Etched, Landscape, Trees, Water, Birds, Satin Ground, 1900, 8⅛ In.	738
Vase, Pillow Form, Brown Wisteria, Honey Color, Satin Ground, 1900, 13 In.	615
Vase, Purple Flowers, Green Stems, Arsall, 1900s, 13 x 4¼ In.	311
Vase, Rooks, Branch, Trees, Fire Polished, Red To Yellow To Blue To Green, France, 11 x 4 In.	2691
Vase, Snowdrops, Leaves, Wheel Carved, Gold Highlights, Burgun & Schverer, 5 In. ... *illus*	2360
Vase, Trees, Pathways, Mottled Salmon & Cream Background, Lamartine, 10¾ In.	968
Vase, Trumpet, Red Orchid, Yellow Shaded To White Ground, 1918-33, 5⅞ In.	523
Vase, White Sunflower, Mint Green Shaded To Honey, 1900, 4½ In.	308

CAMPAIGN *memorabilia are listed in the Political category.*

CAMPBELL KIDS were first used as part of an advertisement for the Campbell Soup Company in 1904. The kids were created by Grace Drayton, a popular illustrator of the day. The kids were used in magazine and newspaper ads until about 1951. They were presented again in 1966; and in 1983, they were redesigned with a slimmer, more contemporary appearance.

Book, Campbell Kids At Home, Rand McNally & Co.	19
Bowl, Lithograph Transfer, Kids In Field, G.G. Drayton, 1920s, 7½ In.	30
Doll, Porcelain, Auburn Hair, Jointed Arms & Legs, Glass Eyes, Patricia Loveless, 10 In.	65
Mug, Kids, Occupational, M'm M'm Good, Westwood, 1997, 3⅜ In.	12
Spoon Rest, Kids, Apron, Hat, Red Trim, Ceramic, 1950s, 4 In., Pair	29
Spoon, Silver Plate, Boy, Girl, International Silver, 1960s, 6 In., 2 Piece	42

CANDELABRUM refers to a candleholder with more than one arm to hold many candles; a candlestick is designed to hold one candle. The eccentricity of the English language makes the plural of candelabrum into candelabra.

2-Light, 3 Cups, Old Sheffield Plate, Sunburst Mark, 1800s, 18 x 18 In., Pair	250

Cameo Glass, Vase, Gilt, Flowers, Leaves, Green To Frosted, Flared Rim, Honesdale, c.1907, 14 x 4 In.
$760

Jeffrey S. Evans

Cameo Glass, Vase, Snowdrops, Leaves, Wheel Carved, Gold Highlights, Burgun & Schverer, 5 In.
$2,360

Humler & Nolan

Candelabrum, 2-Light, Silver, Jade, Pierced, Julius Rappoport, 11 ¼ x 8 In., Pair
$5,670

Fontaine's Auction Gallery

Candlestick, Altar, Giltwood, Carved, Baroque Style, Acanthus Leaves, c.1800, 29 ½ In., Pair
$1,625

New Orleans Auction Galleries

Candlestick, Bronze, Groundhog, Rowfant Club, Laurence Isard, 2003, 8 x 4 ¾ In.
$720

Cowan's Auctions

Candlestick, Bronze, Regency Style, Gilt, Lion Legs, 1900s, 13 x 5 In., Pair
$875

Neal Auction Co.

Candlestick, Nickel Plated, 24 Interlocking Triangular Holders, 2 Dishes, Nagel, Stoffi, Germany, 1960
$688

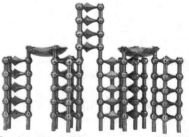

Rago Arts and Auction Center

2-Light, Amphitrite Figural, 1800s, 14 x 9 ¾ In.	4375
2-Light, Copper, Hammered, Square Columns, Secessionist, Germany, 12 x 7 In.	188
2-Light, Foo Dog, Pedestal, Leaves, 12 ⅜ In., Pair	6250
2-Light, George III, Pressed, Cut Glass, Pendants, 30 x 21 In., Pair	625
2-Light, Silver Plate, Stand, Stylized Bobeche, English Hallmark, 1900s, 18 In.	60
2-Light, Silver, Jade, Pierced, Julius Rappoport, 11 ¼ x 8 In., Pair *illus*	5670
3-Light, 4 Cups, Acanthus, Swag, Bead Decoration, Odiot French Silver, 1800s, 19 x 12 x 11 In. Pair.	8750
3-Light, Art Nouveau, Bronze, Gilt, Swirling Arms, Tree Shape, 11 x 10 In., Pair	425
3-Light, Empire, Bronze, Gilt, Nike Holding Cornucopia, Lyre, Black, France, 1800s, 19 ½ In., Pair.	2640
3-Light, Giltwood, Tole, Urn, Roses, 1800s, 18 ¼ In., Pair	2000
3-Light, Louis XV, Amethyst Cut, Pressed Glass, c.1900, 21 x 14 In., Pair	1125
3-Light, Ormolu Mount, Green Glaze, Garlands, 19 ½ x 15 ½ In., Pair	625
3-Light, Satin Glass, Pink, Hanging Chain, Brass Fittings, 12 x 19 In.	210
3-Light, Sconce, Knopped Stem, Weighted Foot, 1966-67, 16 In.	185
3-Light, Scrolling, Urn, Beaded Base, 19 ¾ x 12 In.	750
4-Light, 5 Cups, Silver, Scroll, Floral Decoration, Weighted Base, c.1950, 21 x 21 x 16 In., Pair	2125
4-Light, Art Nouveau, Silver, Ed Wollenweber, Germany, 16 ½ In.	4500
4-Light, Silver On Copper, 4 Candle Cups, Gadrooned Border, 1800s, 22 x 18 In.	51
4-Light, Silver Plate, Column, Acanthus, Griffins, Lion Masks, Camels, Drapes, 21 ½ In., Pair	2750
4-Light, Silver Plate, Georgian, Corinthian Twist Support, Swags, 25 In., Pair	400
4-Light, Silver Plate, Vase Shape Support, Swans, 13 ½ x 10 In.	150
4-Light, Trumpet Shape, Marble, Brass, Silver, 12 x 15 In.	875
5-Light, Articulated, Alvaro Cianfanelli, Italy, 1950, 3 ½ x 18 ¾ In.	343
5-Light, Bronze, Marble, Flowers, Putti, Bas Relief Panels, Paw Feet, 31 x 16 In., Pair	826
5-Light, Bronze, Putti, Fish, Flowers, Branches, Ormolu, Onyx, 26 In.	840
5-Light, Crystal, Swirling Designs, Large Discs, Candle Prickets, 1800s, 12 In., Pair	2125
5-Light, Figural, Young Boy, Girl, Floral Decoration, Tripod Base, c.1850, 19 In.	85
5-Light, Woman, Holds Up Candle Cups, Rams Head, Hoof, 43 x 13 In.	288
6-Light, Napoleon III, Putti, Fruiting Basket, Roses, Lilies, Daisies, Mums, 17 ½ In., Pair	1063
7-Light, Brass, Acanthus Draped Scrolling, Baroque Style, 1900, 22 x 9 ½ In.	87
7-Light, Clustered Columns, Scrolling Tripod Base, Stepped Base, 28 ½ In.	937
8-Light, Verdigris Copper, Steeple Finial, Swan-Neck Stems, Conical Candle Cups, 43 x 25 In.	1800
12-Light, Brass, Stylized Triangle Shape, After Bruno Paul Anderson Foundry, 16 x 27 ½ In.	562
Girandole, Bronze, Crystal, Cut Spire, 4 Tiers, Garlands, Drops, 25 x 8 ¾ In., Pair	600
Louis XV Style, Gilt Bronze, 6 Candle Arms, Ribbon, Bellflower, 1800s, 25 In.	600
Silver, Guerci, Bulbous Stem, 4 Scroll Arms, Fluted Bell Nozzle, 1900s, 17 x 12 In. Pair	2375

CANDLESTICKS were made of brass, pewter, glass, sterling silver, plated silver, and all types of pottery and porcelain. The earliest candlesticks, dating from the sixteenth century, held the candle on a pricket (sharp pointed spike). These lost favor because in times of strife the large church candlesticks with prickets became formidable weapons, so the socket was mandated. Candlesticks changed in style through the centuries, and designs range from Classical to Rococo to Art Nouveau to Art Deco.

Acanthus Collar, Ring Turned Stem, Engraved Monogram, France, 10 In., Pair	531
Altar, Gilt Bronze, Restauration Style, Oval Portraits At Base, Angels, France, c.1875, 70 x 24 In.	1125
Altar, Giltwood, Carved, Baroque Style, Acanthus Leaves, c.1800, 29 ½ In., Pair *illus*	1625
Altar, Gothic, Ormolu, Arches, Saints, Buttresses, 30 ¾ x 7 In., Pair	2000
Aluminum, Abstract, Smoothed, Stretched, Denis Wagner, 1970s, 15 ½ x 18 ½ In.	625
Bocage, Pair Of Cherubs, Quivers, Knees, 1800s, 7 ½ In.	180
Brass, Lobed Candle Cups, Leaves, Turned Stem, Dish Shape Base, 7 x 5 ¼ In., Pair	47
Brass, Rectangular Octagonal Base, Push-Up, 1900s, 8 x 3 ½ x 3 In.	90
Brass, Silver Plated, Sliced Cutouts, 8 ½ x 6 ½ In., Pair	625
Brass, Tapered, Spread Foot, Lambda, Arts & Crafts, Robert Jarvie, 6 In., Pair	1375
Brass, Trumpet, Mid-Drip Ring, Corded Stem, England, 1600s, 5 ½ In.	2000
Brass, Turned Stem, Scalloped, Push-Up Ejection Mechanism, England, 1700s, 7 ¾ In.	120
Brass, Turned Stem, Triangle, Animal Form Feet, Spain, 1690, 10 In.	390
Bronze, Gilt, Blue, Stepped Base, 18 ¼ In., Pair	7500
Bronze, Groundhog, Rowfant Club, Laurence Isard, 2003, 8 x 4 ¾ In. *illus*	720
Bronze, Louis XVI Style, Flower & Lizard Design, Lion Leg Base, Pair, c.1890, 12 In.	795

> **TIP**
> *Always support the arm of a candelabrum when putting in the candles.*

Candlestick, Silver, Octagonal Base, Reeded Post, Urn Sockets, Engraved, England, 12 In., Pair
$660

Brunk Auctions

Candlestick, Snuffer, Silver, Gadroon Border, Marked, P & W Bateman, England, 1809, 4 x 6 x 5 In.
$900

Brunk Auctions

Candlesticks

The seventeenth-century brass candlestick had a square base and fluted column. In the 1700s, a smaller candlestick base was made because it took up less space on the gaming table. In the eighteenth century, candlesticks had hexagonal or ornamented bases, and candelabra were used to give more light. In the nineteenth century, candlesticks became larger and more ornate. By the 1850s, oil lamps replaced the candle as a main source of illumination.

CANDLESTICK

Candy Container, Belsnickle, White Coat, Golden Crown, Composition, Feather Tree, Germany, 19 In.
$16,800

Bertoia Auctions

Candy Container, Child, On Snowball, Bisque, Cotton Batting, Glass Eyes, Heubach, Germany, 7 In.
$420

Bertoia Auctions

Bronze, Malachite, Gilt Bronze, Neoclassical Style, c.1850, 10 x 3 In.	813
Bronze, Multiple Sections, Removable Cups, Candle Pricks, Chinese, 28 In., Pair	120
Bronze, Patinated, Swags, Greek Key, Ferdinand Barbedienne, c.1870, 10¾ In., Pair	1250
Bronze, Regency Style, Gilt, Lion Legs, 1900s, 13 x 5 In., Pair .... *illus*	875
Bronze, Running Figure, Arm Up, Holds Trophy, Gilt, 14 In.	688
Bronze, Seahorse, E.T. Hurley, Signed, c.1925, 11 In., Pair	885
Chamber, Cut Glass, Strawberry Diamond, Hobstar Base, Clear Blank, 5 In.	1140
Chamber, Removable Snuffer, Urn Shape, Sconce, George III, England, 1801-02, 4 In.	185
Cobra, Brass, Candle Cup From Head, 11 In., Pair	70
Column, Brass, Round Stepped Bases, Applied Handles, 1800s, 13 In., Pair	240
Copper, Hammered, Cylindrical Stem, Domed Foot, 2 Shaped Handles, 10 In., Pair	275
Gilt Bronze, Engine Turned, c.1935, 8½ In., Pair	500
Gilt Bronze, Swirled Fluting, Swags Of Laurel, Christofle, Marked, France, c.1875, 11 In., Pair	1875
Iron, Walnut, Courting, Spiral, Fingertip Carrier, Candle Raiser, 1780, 3¾ x 7½ In.	170
Marble, Louis XVI Shape, Carved, Ormolu, Gilt Bronze Mounts, 1800s, 9 In., Pair	554
Nickel Plated, 24 Interlocking Triangular Holders, 2 Dishes, Nagel, Stoffi, Germany, 1960.. *illus*	688
Ormolu, Louis XVI, Seated Putti, Urn Shape Candle Cup, Round Base, c.1900, 7 In., Pair	1250
Pewter, Shou Character, Square Base, Pricket, Chinese, c.1880, 10½ In., Pair	625
Porcelain, Tree, Flower Strewn, Woodsman, Sled, Wife, Sitzendorf, c.1875, 15 x 8½ In.	125
Pottery, Blackamoor, Holding Cornucopia, Tin Glazed, Multicolor, 25 In., Pair	688
Ruby Glass, Cut To Clear, 12¼ In.	66
Silver Plate, Brass, Skyscraper, Post Shape Handles, Louis Rice, 1920s, 8 x 3¾ In.	3625
Silver Plate, Georgian, Shaped Base, Towle, 11¾ In., Pair	120
Silver, 7 Amethyst Spheres, Cylindrical, Stepped Foot, 9⅜ In.	2125
Silver, Fluted, Scrolling, George IV, Sheffield, Marked, c.1824, 8 x 4½ In., 4 Piece	3125
Silver, Knopped Cylinder, Chased, Repousse, Flowers, Leaves, Russia, 14 x 5 In., Pair	875
Silver, Knopped Stem, Shaped Foot, c.1915, 10½ In., 4 Piece	2101
Silver, Octagonal Base, Reeded Post, Urn Sockets, Engraved, England, 12 In., Pair .... *illus*	660
Silver, Oval Base, Urn Sockets & Post, Thomas Bradbury & Sons Ltd., England, 1924, 12 In., Pair..	780
Silver, Repousse, Floral Design, Removable Bobeches, 11½ In., Pair	875
Silver, Urn Shape, Sconce, Knopped Stem, Square Foot, 1762-63, 8½ In.	369
Slag Glass, Patinated Copper Overlay, Trapezoidal, Green, 5 x 5 In., Pair	812
Snuffer, Silver, Gadroon Border, Marked, P & W Bateman, England, 1809, 4 x 6 x 5 In. .. *illus*	900
Stone, Blue John, Mottled Red, 8-Sided Base, Cabochons, Bronze Fittings, 7 In., Pair	3250
Walnut, Pricket, Graduated Ball & Bobbin, Leaf Trim, 3 Large Bun Feet, 65 In., Pair	2500
Wood, Glass Shade, Painted, Green, Gilt, Flaring Rims, 1800s, 18 x 7 In.	492

CANDLEWICK GLASS *items may be listed in the Imperial Glass and Pressed Glass categories.*

CANDY CONTAINERS have been popular since the late Victorian era. Collectors have long favored the glass containers, but now all types, including tin and papier-mache, are collected. Probably the earliest glass container sold commercially was the Liberty Bell made in 1876 for sale at the Centennial Exposition. Thousands of designs were made until the cost became too high in the 1960s. By the late 1970s, reproductions were being made and sold without the candy. Containers listed here are glass unless otherwise described. A Belsnickle is a nineteenth-century figure of Father Christmas. Some candy containers may be listed in Toy or in other categories.

Basket, Plastic, Yellow, Basket Weave, Bunnies, Rosbro, 6 x 4 In.	29
Belsnickle, On Large Snowball, White Robe, Germany, 20 In.	7200
Belsnickle, Wearing Pink Robe, Gold Sprinkle, Tree Sprig, Germany, 9 In.	600
Belsnickle, White Coat, Golden Crown, Composition, Feather Tree, Germany, 19 In. .... *illus*	16800
Cat, Black, Removable Head, Hollow Body, Unmarked, Germany, 8½ x 11 In.	791
Child, On Snowball, Bisque, Cotton Batting, Glass Eyes, Heubach, Germany, 7 In. .... *illus*	420
Doll, Mary Had A Little Lamb, Bisque, Glass Eyes, Silk Dress, Germany, c.1900, 9 In.	690
Doll, Woman, Bisque Bust & Arms, Painted, Blond Mohair, Hat, Cone Bottom, 13 In.	2300
Father Christmas, Cardboard, Composition, Red Robe, Fur Beard, Germany, 13 In. ...... *illus*	1328
George Washington, On Horseback, Spotted, Figural, 10½ x 8½ In.	1552
Hen House, Chicken, Cardboard, Loofah, Cotton Batting, Wire, Felt, c.1915, 3¼ In.	117
Little Bo Peep, On Sheep, Glass Eyes, Says Baa, Heubach, 15 In.	3300

Pencil, Wood, Cardboard, Dark Brown, 1900, 5½ In.	*illus*	100
Pumpkin Head, Papier-Mache, Winking Eye, Smile, Teeth, Germany, c.1920, 2½ x 4 In.		450
Pumpkin Man, Jack-O'-Lantern Head, Composition, Germany, 7½ In.	*illus*	708
Pumpkin Man, Painted Face, Green, Candy Box, Black, Germany, 6¼ x 3 In.		158
Rooster, Composition, Multicolor, 7½ In.	*illus*	180
Santa Claus, Colorless, Glass, 5¼ In.		75
Santa Claus, Standing, Laughing, 11½ In.		760
Santa Claus, Standing, Rabbit Fur Beard, Red Felt Robe, Antique, Germany, 9½ In.		560
Santa, Eating Walnut, Wood, Mechanical, Germany, 7 In.		1560
Skier, Bisque Head, Skis, Red Hat, Scarf, 9 In.		438
Stork, Papier-Mache, Wood Beak, Spun Cotton, Cardboard, White, 9⅜ In.		81
Stove, Ruby Glass, c.1925, 4 In.		93
Tin, Lid, Paint, Flowers, Landscape, Mother's Day Poem, Paper, c.1900, 3 x 9 In.		125
Train, Plastic, Clear, 4 x 2 In.		15

CANES and walking sticks were used by every well-dressed man in the nineteenth century, but by World War I the style had changed. Today canes are used by few but the infirm. Collectors prize old canes made with special features, like hidden swords, whiskey flasks, or risqué pictures seen through peepholes. Examples with solid gold heads or made from exotic materials are among the higher-priced canes. See also Scrimshaw.

Alligator, Stippled Carved Shaft, Brass Tip, 1920s, 35 In.		202
Bone, Horse Heads, Outstretched Necks, Engraved J. Jay Nestrell, c.1860, 37 In.	*illus*	1110
Bone, Relief Grape Design, Wood Shaft, Engraved Band, Inscribed, 1800s, 35 In.		120
Butternut, Relief, Eagle, American Shield, Square, Compass, Fraternal Symbols, 34 In.		1080
Dog Head, Greyhound, Carved Bone, Silver Collar, Mounted On Wood, Metal Tip, 1800s, 36 x 4¾ In.		120
Glass, Clear, White, Cranberry, Blue & Amethyst Swirl Spirals, Victorian, 36 In.		72
Ivory, Ball Handle, Mother-Of-Pearl At Top, 1800s, 34 In.		192
Ivory, Elephant, Ball Handle, Diamond, Geometric, Strong Inlays, 1800s, 36 In.		360
Ivory, Elephant, Eagle Perched, Shield At Front, 1800s, 35 In.		240
Ivory, Mushroom, Mother-Of-Pearl, Baleen Band, 1800s, 33 In.		168
Ivory, Spiral Turned Handle, Hardwood Shaft, 2 Diamond Inlays, 1800s, 38 In.		300
Ivory, Whale, Ball Turned Handle, Whalebone Shaft, 1800s, 33 In.		330
Ivory, Whale, Face, Hardwood Shaft, 1800s, 34 In.		204
Ivory, Whalebone Handle, Walrus Ivory, Island Wood Banding At Top, 1900s, 32 In.		216
Parasol, Ivory, Field Workers, Leaves, Flowers, Continental, 11½ In.		688
Parrot, Carved, Painted, 34½ In.		501
Presentation, Carved, Humans, Horses, Steer, Hog, Birds, c.1800		590
Shillelagh, Irish Bata, Anglophone, Blackthorn, 35 In.		94
Sword, Bamboo Style Handle, 35 In.		203
Sword, Engraved Silver Handle By S.E. Sweetland To WHP, 36 x ½ In.		336
Tortoiseshell, Inlaid Narwhal, Twisted Body, Rosewood Knob, c.1875, 37 In.		2375
Walking Stick, Antique Revolver Handle, Mahogany Shaft, Brass Collar, 36 x ½ In.		671
Walking Stick, Antler Handle, Dog's Head, Wood Shaft, c.1910, 35½ In.		390
Watch, Paper Dial, Roman Hour Numerals, Long Turned Wood Shaft, Silver Marks, 34 In.		968
Whalebone, Carved Hand Grasping Shaft, Hardwood Shaft, c.1850, 33½ In.		313
Whalebone, Eagle's Head, 3 Whalebone Bands, Mid 1800s, 33½ In.		900
Whalebone, Shell Inlay, Hardwood Shaft, c.1850, 38 In.		900
Whaleman, Whale Ivory, Octagonal Form, 1800s, 36 In.		1080
Whaleman, Whalebone Handle, Island Wood, Whalebone Banding, 1800s, 32 In.		240
Whaleman, Whale's Tooth Handle, Whalebone Shaft, 1800s, 33 In.		300
Wood, Berry, Vine Design, Thorns, 1800s, 34 In.		120
Wood, Bone Handle, Button Sleeve, Belt At Base, 1800s, 36 In.		180
Wood, Carved, Handle, Woman & Man, Seated In Chair, Red Paint Traces, c.1910, 35½ In.		120
Wood, Clenched Fist, Holding Baton, 1800s, 36 In.		168
Wood, Ebony Shaft, Leaves, Pineapple, Rope Twist Design, 1800s, 36 In.		240
Wood, Ebony, Bone End, Rings, Rope Twist Design, 1800s, 35 In.		192
Wood, Fox Head, Brass Tack Eyes, 1900s, 40 In.		168
Wood, Human Head, Legs Carved, Snakes, 1800s, 35 In.		144
Wood, Soldier's Boot, Brass Wirework, 1862, 36 In.		420

Candy Container, Father Christmas, Cardboard, Composition, Red Robe, Fur Beard, Germany, 13 In.
$1,328

Bertoia Auctions

Candy Container, Pencil, Wood, Cardboard, Dark Brown, 1900, 5½ In.
$100

Ruby Lane

Candy Container, Pumpkin Man, Jack-O'-Lantern Head, Composition, Germany, 7½ In.
$708

Hess Auction Group

Candy Container, Rooster, Composition, Multicolor, 7 ½ In.
$180

Bertoia Auctions

Cane, Bone, Horse Heads, Outstretched Necks, Engraved J. Jay Nestrell, c.1860, 37 In.
$1,110

Milestone Auctions

Canton, Cider Jug, Replaced Lid, Blue & White, Landscape, 11 In.
$265

Hess Auction Group

CANTON CHINA is blue-and-white ware made near the city of Canton, in China, from about 1795 to the early 1900s. It is hand decorated with a landscape, building, bridge, and trees. There is never a person on the bridge. The "rain and cloud" border was used. It is similar to Nanking ware, which is listed in this book in its own category.

Cider Jug, Replaced Lid, Blue & White, Landscape, 11 In.	*illus*	265
Dish, Shrimp, Landscape, Porcelain, c.1900, 10 In.	*illus*	312
Platter, Fishing Boats, Houses, Octagonal, 1800s, 16 In.		173
Platter, Houses, Trees, Clouds, Men, 15 In.		120
Platter, Landscape Decoration, 1900, 15 In.		390
Platter, Landscape, Bridge, Octagonal, 15 ¾ In.		390
Platter, Landscape, Bridge, Octagonal, 17 ½ In.		360
Platter, Landscape, c.1800, 18 In.		345
Platter, Well & Tree, 1800s, 13 ¾ x 17 In.		214
Punch Bowl, House, Trees, 1800s, 6 ½ x 16 In.		366

CAPO-DI-MONTE porcelain was first made in Naples, Italy, from 1743 to 1759. The factory moved near Madrid, Spain, and operated there from 1771 until 1821. The Ginori factory of Doccia, Italy, acquired the molds and began using the crown and *N* mark. In 1896 the Doccia factory combined with Societa Ceramica Richard of Milan. It eventually became the modern-day firm known as Richard Ginori, often referred to as Ginori or Capo-di-Monte. This company also used the crown and *N* mark. Richard Ginori was purchased by Gucci in 2013. The Capo-di-Monte mark is still being used. "Capodimonte-style" porcelain is being made today by several manufacturers in Italy, sometimes with a factory name or mark. The Capo-di-Monte mark and name are also used on cheaper porcelain made in the style of Capo-di-Monte.

Box, House Form, Neoclassical Figures, Bronze Finials & Feet, 13 x 13 In.	2000
Centerpiece, Conch, Red Coral, Shells, Pedestal, c.1880, 7 In.	234
Figurine, Satyr, Blanc-De-Chine, Hand Flute, 8 x 3 In.	125
Group, Couple, Woman Stands Over Man, Glazed Biscuit Porcelain, 9 x 5 ½ In.	100
Group, Courting Couple, Musical Instruments, Luigi Zortea, Italy, 8 x 7 In.	22
Urn, People, Classic Clothes, Garlands, Bouquets, Porcelain, 1800s, 9 ½ In., Pair	175
Vase, Gilt, People On Skis, Richard Ginori, 1930s, 7 ¼ x 7 In.	1375

CAPTAIN MARVEL was introduced in February 1940 in Whiz comic books. An orphan named Billy Batson met the wizard, Shazam, and whenever he said the magic word he was transformed into a superhero. A movie serial was released in 1940. The comic was discontinued in 1954. A second Captain Marvel appeared in 1966, a third in 1967. Only the original was transformed by shouting "Shazam."

Puzzle, Rides Engine Of Doom, Box, 1941	185
Toy, Car, Racing, Clockwork, Box, Automatic Toy Co., 4 In., 4 Piece	330
Toy, Figurine, On Card, Super Powers Collection, Shazam, Red, 7 x 9 ¼ In.	187
Toy, Statuette, Plastic, Multicolor, Box, R.W. Kerr Co., 1946, 6 ½ In.	344

CAPTAIN MIDNIGHT began as a network radio show in September 1940. The first comic book appeared in July 1941. Captain Midnight was really the aviator Captain Albright, who was to defeat the Nazis. A movie serial was made in 1942 and a comic strip was published for a short time. The comic book version of Captain Midnight ended his career in 1948. Radio premiums are the prized collector memorabilia today.

Badge, Decoder, Pinback, Premium, 1940s, 1 ¾ x 2 ¼ In.	*illus*	70
Badge, Flight Commander, Pinback, Brass, 1942, 1 ½ x 1 In.		50
Comic Book, King Of Villains, No. 14 Mile High Pedigree, 1943		432
Membership Spinner Coin, Gilded Metal, 1940, 1 ¼ In.		7
Mug, Ovaltine, The Heart Of A Hearty Breakfast, Red, Premium, Box, 3 In.		42
Ring, Secret Compartment, Red Stone, Metal Band, Aztec Designs, c.1946		132

CARAMEL SLAG, *see Imperial Glass category.*

Canton, Dish, Shrimp, Landscape, Porcelain, c.1900, 10 In.
$312

Captain Midnight, Badge, Decoder, Pinback, Premium, 1940s, 1¾ x 2¼ In.
$70

Carlton Ware, Vase, Fantasia, 2 Exotic Birds, Flying, Magical Landscape, England, 7 In.
$413

CARDS listed here include advertising cards (often called trade cards), baseball cards, playing cards, and others. Color photographs were rare in the nineteenth century, so companies gave away colorful cards with pictures of children, flowers, products, or related scenes that promoted the company name. These were often collected and stored in albums. Baseball cards also date from the nineteenth century, when they were used by tobacco companies as giveaways. Gum cards were started in 1933, but it was not until after World War II that the bubble gum cards favored today were produced. Today over 1,000 cards are issued each year by the gum companies. Related items may be found in the Christmas, Halloween, Movie, Paper, and Postcard categories.

Advertising, Bankrupt Sale, Fine Clothing, Black Man Playing Cello, Caricature, 1890s, 3 x 1¾ In.	10
Baseball, Al Kaline, Detroit Tigers, Topps, No. 201, 1954	10000
Baseball, Babe Ruth, No. 32, U.S. Caramel, 1932	1999
Baseball, Ernie Banks, Chicago Cubs, Topps, No. 80, 1954	130
Baseball, Hank Aaron, Milwaukee Braves, Topps, No. 170, 1965	1500
Baseball, Joe Collins, Yankees, Topps, No. 202, 1952	600
Baseball, Mickey Mantle, New York Yankees, Bowman, 1955	200
Baseball, Sandy Koufax, Brooklyn Dodgers, Topps, No. 123, 1955	110
Baseball, Satchel Paige, St. Louis Browns, Topps, No. 220, 1953	64
Baseball, Ted Williams, Boston, Bowman, No. 66, 1954	360
Football, Charles Trippi, Chicago Cardinals, Bowman, No. 60, 1954	40
Football, Joe Montana, Rookie, San Francisco 49ers, Topps, No. 216, 1981	99
Greeting, Valentine, Boy & Girl, Victorian Clothing, Umbrella, Die Cut, 4 x 2 In.	22
Greeting, Valentine, Flapper Girl, Dog, Moving, Louis Katz, 1921, 8 x 4 In.	18
Greeting, Valentine, Puppies, Heart Shape, Dog House, Red Flowers, 5 x 9 In., 1915	25
Playing, Babes In Woods, Theatrical, George H. Walker & Co., c.1893, Full Deck	500
Playing, Edison Mazda, Egypt, 1922 Calendar Girl, On Front, Full Deck, 3⅞ x 2¾ In.	47
Playing, Edison Mazda, Waterfalls, 1932 Calendar Girl, On Front, 3⅞ x 2¾ In.	35
Playing, Faro, Empire Card Co., Marked, c.1880, Full Deck	150
Playing, Green Club No Revoke, Different Color Suits, Hanzel Card Co., 1923, 52	100
Playing, Steamboat, Watermelon Joker, Russell & Morgan, 1883, Full Deck	150

CARDER, *see Aurene and Steuben categories.*

CARLTON WARE was made at the Carlton Works of Stoke-on-Trent, England, beginning about 1890. The firm traded as Wiltshaw & Robinson until 1957. It was renamed Carlton Ware Ltd. in 1958. The company went bankrupt in 1995, but the name is still in use.

Bowl, Butterflies, Blue, Gilt, Marked, c.1900, 4¾ x 9 In.	65
Jug, Oval, Golfers, Caddie, Swing Lid, 6 In.	210
Vase, Fantasia, 2 Exotic Birds, Flying, Magical Landscape, England, 7 In. .... *illus*	413
Vase, Flared, Cameo, Girls Dancing, Orange Luster, Black Ground, c.1925, 4¾ In.	125

CARNIVAL GLASS was an inexpensive, iridescent pressed glass made from about 1907 to about 1925. More than 1,000 different patterns are known. Carnival glass is currently being reproduced. Here are three marks used by companies that have made 20th-century glass.

Imperial
1910–1924

Northwood Glass Co.
1910–1918

Cambridge Glass Co.
1901–1954, 1955–1958

Acorn Burrs, Butter, Cover, Amethyst, Northwood, 6 x 7 In.	301
Acorn Burrs, Punch Bowl, Marigold, Northwood, Marked, c.1900, 10¾ x 11 In.	450
Apple Blossom, Bowl, Nut, Marigold, 2 x 5 In.	25
Apple Blossom, Bowl, Ruffled, Marigold, 7 In.	40
Beaded Shell, Mug, Blue	128
Bellaire, Toothpick Holder, Marigold, c.1960	23

Carnival Glass, Marigold, Punch Bowl, Acorn Burrs, Northwood, Marked, c. 1900, 10¾ x 11 In.

$450

Ruby Lane

> **TIP**
> To clean carnival glass, try using a mixture of ½ cup ammonia and ⅛ cup white vinegar.

Carousel, Horse, Galloping, Carved, Painted, Mounted On Roller Base, 63 x 48 In.

$2,714

Hess Auction Group

Carousel, Horse, Jumper, White, Brown Saddle, Horsehair Tail, 63 x 60 In.

$960

Susanin's Auctioneers & Appraisers

Broken Arches, Creamer, Footed, Marigold, Imperial	26
Cherry & Cable, Tumbler, Marigold	60
Cherry & Lattice, Tumbler, Amethyst, 4 In.	34
Coin Dot, Bowl, Green, 3-In-1 Edge, 9 In.	48
Columns & Rings, Dish, Hat Shape, Marigold, 2 x 6 In.	55
Diamond & Fan, Candle Lamp, Marigold, 1970s, 8 In.	40
Diamond Point, Candle Lamp, Amber, 7 x 7 In.	22
Diamond Rings, Bowl, Marigold, Ruffled, 9 In.	30
Double Stem Rose, Bowl, Domed Foot, Ruffled Edge, Amethyst, Dugan, 8 x 4 In.	150
Dragon & Lotus, Bowl, Iridescent Finish, Ruffled Rim, 1900s, 2 x 9 In.	60
Dragon & Lotus, Bowl, Spatula Foot, Green Iridescent, 9 In.	189
Dragon & Lotus, Plate, Cobalt Blue, Bowl, 8 In.	42
Fine Rib, Vase, Ruffled Edge, Green, Northwood, 7 In.	89
Fish Scale & Beads, Berry Bowl, Marigold, Ruffled, 2 x 6 In.	40
Floral & Grape, Vase, Jack-In-The-Pulpit, Marigold, Dugan, 3 x 5 In.	25
Fruits & Flowers, Plate, Green, 7 In.	101
Good Luck, Bowl, Piecrust Edge, Marigold, Northwood, 8¾ In.	125
Good Luck, Plate, Purple, Basketweave, 9 In.	46
Grape & Cable, Compote, Amethyst, Northwood, 4½ x 6½ In.	75
Grape & Cable, Plate, Green, Northwood, 9 In.	100
Grapevine Lattice, Plate, Ruffled, Dugan-White, 7 In.	48
Greek Key, Bowl, Domed & Rayed Foot, Green, 4 x 6 In.	65
Harvest Grape, Sugar & Creamer, Tray, Blue	30
Holly, Bowl, Ruffled, Amethyst, Fenton, 8¼ In.	40
Holly, Plate, White, Fenton, 1905, 9¾ In.	65
Lattice & Grape, Tumbler, Royal Blue, 4⅛ In.	35
Marigold, Punch Bowl, Acorn Burrs, Northwood, Marked, c. 1900, 10¾ x 11 In. *illus*	450
Nippon, Bowl, Ice Blue, Northwood, 9 In.	150
Open Rose, Plate, Amber, 9 In.	145
Orange Tree, Plate, Blue, 9 In.	54
Orange Tree, Rose Bowl, Twig Feet, Marigold, 5 x 4 In.	60
Paneled Dandelion, Tumbler, Marigold	21
Pansy, Bowl, Ruffled Edge, Green	43
Pansy, Relish, Ruffled, Oval, Green, 9 x 5 In.	45
Pansy, Sugar, Open, Purple, Handles, 3 x 6 In.	40
Panther, Berry Bowl, Butterfly, Crimped Rim, 3 Ball & Claw Feet, 1900s, 4 x 9 In.	48
Peacock At The Fountain, Spooner, Marigold, 4 In.	34 to 49
Peacock At The Fountain, Tumbler, Pumpkin Marigold, 4 In.	32
Peacocks & Grapes, Bowl, 3 Tab Feet, Panels, Green, 3 x 7 In.	90
Piggy Bank, Ohio Oil Co., Marigold, c.1960, 3 x 4 x 2 In.	28
Pine Cone, Plate, Crimped Edge, Blue, 6 In.	68
Rays & Ribbons, Ruffled, Scalloped Edge, Amethyst, 9½ In.	65
Ribbon Edge, Bowl, Amethyst, Fenton, 7¾ In.	60
Rose Garden, Vase, Blue, Iridescent, Boat Shape, Scalloped Edge, 9¾ In.	225
Rose Show, Plate, Emerald Green, Northwood, c.1905, 9½ In.	700
Rustic, Vase, Marigold, 9 In.	42
Sable Arch, Bell, Teal Green, 6¼ In.	60
Sailboats, Plate, Blue, 6 In.	145
Seacoast, Pin Tray, Green, 5¼ x 4 In.	185
Stag & Holly, Bowl, Ruffled Rim, Iridescent Amethyst, 1900s, 4¼ x 11 In.	120
Star Medallion, Pitcher, Marigold, 1930s, 6 In.	35
Star Of David, Bowl, Ruffled, Amethyst, 9 x 2¾ In.	100
Stippled Rays, Bowl, Crimped, Trefoil, Green, 10 x 3 In.	64
Thistle & Thorn, Bowl, Marigold, 4-Footed, 1920s, 5½ x 4 In.	25
Three Fruits, Plate, Marigold, Basketweave, 9 In.	21
Tree Trunk, Vase, Amethyst, 10½ In.	90
Wishbone, Console, Green, Purple, Beaded Crimped Edge, 8½ In.	277
Wreath Of Roses, Bonbon, Marigold, Stemmed Foot, Handles, Fenton, 9 In.	20
Zippered Heart, Sauce Bowl, Ruffled Edge, Purple	54

CAROUSEL or merry-go-round figures were first carved in the United States in 1867 by Gustav Dentzel. Collectors discovered the charm of the hand-carved figures in the 1970s, and they were soon classed as folk art. Most desirable are the figures other than horses, such as pigs, camels, lions, or dogs. A stander has all four feet on the carousel platform; a prancer has both front feet in the air and both back feet on the platform; a jumper has all four feet in the air and usually moves up and down. Both old and new animals are collected.

Cat, Prancer, Blue & Red Saddle Blanket, Tail Up, Wood, Glass Eyes, 41 x 43 In.	1000
Clown Head, Wood, Carved, Paint, Smiling, Conical Hat, Pompom, c.1880, 13 In. High	2300
Dog, Pouncing, Saddle, Painted, 29 x 60 In.	9075
Horse, Galloping, Carved, Painted, Mounted On Roller Base, 63 x 48 In. .... *illus*	2714
Horse, Jumper, Blue & White Pelt, Red Bridle, Allen Herschell, 1902, 31 x 9 In.	531
Horse, Jumper, Brass Pole, Iron, Caramel, Red, White, Blue Saddle, c.1900, 48 x 44 x 12 In.	2160
Horse, Jumper, Carved Wood, Original Paint, c.1900, 51 x 35 In. .... *illus*	3400
Horse, Jumper, Middle Row, Fish Scale Armor On Blanket, Tein & Goldstein, 1908, 52 x 49 In.	9075
Horse, Jumper, White, Brown Saddle, Horsehair Tail, 63 x 60 In. .... *illus*	960
Horse, Prancer, Bronze, Patinated, Cold Painted, 71 In.	1000
Horse, Prancer, Horsehair Tail, Brown, White Socks, Armitage Herschell, c.1925, 47 x 15 In.	1125
Horse, Prancer, Horsehair Tail, Leather Tack, Beige, Spots, Armitage Herschell, 46 x 13 In.	1560
Horse, Prancer, Painted, Spotted, Applied Tin & Nailhead Accents, 56 In.	384
Horse, Prancer, Purple, Black Saddle, Cast Metal, 48 x 38 In.	205
Horse, Prancer, White, Lavender Bridle, Red Saddle, Horsehair, 58½ x 59 In.	480
Horse, Stander, Stargazer, Glass Eyes, Carved Tail, Bedroll Saddle, Charles Carmel, 76 x 76 x 16 In.	4200
Horse, Stander, White, Wood Carved, Furling Mane, Brass Stand, 1900s, 57 x 45 In.	840
Lion, Full Mane, Stander, Bared Teeth, 45 x 50 In.	687
Moose, Prancer, Carved Sea Life, Rectangular Platform, Robert Holden, 63 In.	3000
Pig, Jumper, Tan, Glass Eyes, Red Saddle Blanket, 39 x 50 In.	937
Rabbit, Jumper, Green Saddle Blankets, Gold Rope, Glass Eyes, 61 x 44 In.	1250

CARRIAGE means several things, so this category lists baby carriages, buggies for adults, horse-drawn sleighs, and even strollers. Doll-sized carriages are listed in the Toy category.

Baby, Black, Oilcloth Hood, Rubber Tires, Effanbee Dy-Dee, 1930s, 22 x 33 x 26 In.	1299
Baby, Stroller Carriage, Hood, Wicker, Metal, Wood Wheels, c.1890, 20 x 36 In. .... *illus*	495
Baby, Walnut Color Wicker, Turned Wood Handle, Wrought Iron Frame, 1880s, 37 x 20 x 39 In.	950
Baby, Wicker, Metal Frame, Wood Spoke Wheels, Basket, c.1890, 20 x 36 x 45 In.	421
Baby, Wicker, Wing Design, Hood, Honey Pattern Upholstery, 32 x 16 In.	295
Buggy, Rattan, Wood, Metal Frame & Wheels, 29 x 16 x 29 In.	273
Buggy, Steel, Wood, Wicker, Spoke Wheels, Brake, Hedstrom Union Co., 37 x 21 x 44 In.	45
Sleigh, 1-Horse Open, White Paint, Upholstered Seat, Sweden, c.1870, 90 x 39 x 42 In.	2200
Sleigh, 1-Horse, Single Runner, Wooden, Velvet Seat, c.1900, 48 x 74 In.	600
Stroller, Wicker Stick & Ball, White Paint, Umbrella, c.1900, 33½ In.	275

CASH REGISTERS were invented in 1884 because an eye on the cash was a necessity in stores of the nineteenth century, too. John and James Ritty invented a large model that resembled a clock and kept a record of the dollars and cents exchanged in the store. John Patterson improved the cash register with a paper roll to record the money. By the early 1900s, elaborate brass registers were made. More modern types were made after 1920. Cash registers made by National Cash Register Company are most often collected.

National, Brass, Cast Fleur-De-Lis, White Marble Panel, HC Sheetz, 17 x 21 In.	594
National, Candy Store, Cast Brass, Copper Plate Trim, 1900s, 20 x 9 x 15 In. .... *illus*	660
National, Dolphin Style Case, Brass, Marble Shelf, Wood Trim, Model 332, 17 x 17 x 16 In.	325
National, Haussner Stag Bar, Brass, Oak, Pointing Hand, Multicolor Keys, 22½ x 20 In.	615
National, Inlaid Wood, Marble Shelf, Receipt Cage	1220
National, Ionic Pattern, Nickel Plated, Cast Iron, Restored	976
National, Model 311, Crest, Relief Filigree Decorated Sides, Dolphin Figures, 21 x 10 x 16 In.	726
National, Model 313, Nickel, White Marble Shelf, 1915, 21 x 10 x 16 In.	885

Carriage, Baby, Stroller Carriage, Hood, Wicker, Metal, Wood Wheels, c.1890, 20 x 36 In.
$495

Ruby Lane

Cash Register, National, Candy Store, Cast Brass, Copper Plate Trim, 1900s, 20 x 9 x 15 In.
$660

Garth's Auctioneers & Appraisers

Cash Register, National, Model 349-22, Wide Base, 2 Drawers, c.1915, 18 x 27 In.
$330

Rich Penn Auctions

TIP
Clean brass with commercial brass polish. Wear white cotton gloves. The gloves make the difference.

CASH REGISTER

Cash Register, Visible Bank, National, Metal, Glass, No Key, 1900s, 6¼ x 6¾ In. $180

Garth's Auctioneers & Appraisers

Castor, Pickle, Satin Glass, Pink, Quilted, Plated Frame, 10½ In. $149

Bunch Auctions

Caughley, Plate, Temple, Landscape, Blue, White, Gilt, 7½ In. $150

Ruby Lane

National, Model 349-22, Wide Base, 2 Drawers, c.1915, 18 x 27 In. .... *illus*	330
National, Model 442, Ornate Brass Finish, Crank Machine, Time Printer, 1897, 24 x 20 x 17 In.	1080
Visible Bank, National, Metal, Glass, No Key, 1900s, 6¼ x 6¾ In. .... *illus*	180

CASTOR JARS for pickles are glass jars about six inches in height, held in special metal holders. They became a popular dinner table accessory about 1890. Each jar had a top that was usually silver or silver plate. The frame, also of a silver metal, had a handle that arched above the jar and a hook that held a pair of tongs. The glass jar was often painted. By 1900, the pickle castor was out of fashion. Many examples found today have reproduced glass jars in old holders. Additional pickle castors may be found in the various Glass categories.

Pickle, Acid Cut Panel, Silver Plate, Child Finial, Middletown Silver Plate Frame, 11 In.	240
Pickle, Apricot & Yellow, Gold Highlights & Flowers, Forbes Silver Plate Frame, 11 In.	180
Pickle, Blue, Coin Spot, Enamel Branch, Fruit, Silver Plate Frame, 13 In.	630
Pickle, Blue, Egg Shape, Flowers, Silver Plate Frame, 9¾ In.	300
Pickle, Broken Column, Ruby Stain, 1891, 11¾ In.	200
Pickle, Cobalt Blue, White Flowers, Meriden Silver Plate Frame, 13 In.	180
Pickle, Cranberry Coin Spot, Bird, Blossom, Branch, Barbour Silver Plate Frame, 12 In...........	540
Pickle, Cranberry Coin Spot, Branch, Rogers Smith Silver Plate Frame, 11 In....................	270
Pickle, Cranberry Coin Spot, Flowers, Derby Silver Plate Frame, 2 Tongs, 11 In.	1800
Pickle, Cranberry Diamond Quilted, Butterfly, Blossom, Hood Barkentin, Silver Plate, 14 In. ..	1560
Pickle, Cranberry Glass, Diamond Quilted, Slide Lid, Rogers Silver Plate Frame, 11 In.	120
Pickle, Engraved, 3-Footed, Riverside Glass Works, 8 In..	93
Pickle, Frosted, Embossed, Bird & Flowers, Reed & Barton Silver Plate Frame, 16 In...............	300
Pickle, Glass, Blue, Melon Ribbed, Controlled Bubble, Silver Plate Frame, 9½ In.	270
Pickle, Glass, Green, Enamel, Gold Stencil, Silver Plate Lid, Tongs, 9¾ In.	300
Pickle, Glass, Watermelon, Pearl Diamond Quilted, Reed & Barton Silver Plate Frame, 8¾ In.	420
Pickle, Glass, Yellow Cased, White Swirl Design, Gold Branch, Silver Plate Frame, 12 In.........	210
Pickle, Green, Mary Gregory Scene, Rockford Silver Plate Frame, 12 In.........................	180
Pickle, Ice Blue Opalescent, Coralene Butterfly, Flowers, Silver Plate Frame, Tongs, 10 In.	840
Pickle, Metal Mount, Wheel, Rosettes, 10¾ x 5½ In.	45
Pickle, Peach, Enamel Blossom, Branch, Reed & Barton Silver Plate Frame, 9¾ In.................	540
Pickle, Pink Opalescent, Hobnail Insert, Meriden, Silver Plate Frame, 12 In.	240
Pickle, Rubina, Coin Spot, Coralene Flowers, Derby Silver Plate Frame, 6¾ In.........	480
Pickle, Ruby Glass, Cased Deep Insert, Flowers, Silver Plate Frame, Victorian, 9 In.	108
Pickle, Ruby Glass, Stained, Broken Column, Triple Plate Stand, US Glass Co., c.1891, 10 In....	187
Pickle, Satin Glass, Pink, Quilted, Plated Frame, 10½ In......................... *illus*	149
Pickle, Smoky, Enamel Berry Branch, Tufts Silver Plate Frame, 2 Handles, 8½ In.	330
Pickle, Vaseline, Cranberry, Leaf Mold, Tufts Silver Plate Frame, Victorian, 6¼ In.	480
Pickle, White Nailsea, Cranberry Threaded, Set, Silver Plate Frame, 11 In.	1800
Pickle, White Opal Ware, Blue Floral, Silver Plate Frame, 2 Tongs, 12 In.	330

CASTOR SETS holding just salt and pepper castors were used in the seventeenth century. The sugar castor, mustard pot, spice dredger (shaker), bottles for vinegar and oil, and other spice holders became popular by the eighteenth century. These sets were usually made of sterling silver with glass bottles. The American Victorian castor set, the type most collected today, was made of silver plated Britannia metal. Colored glass bottles were introduced after the Civil War. The sets were out of fashion by World War I. Be careful when buying sets with colored bottles; many are reproductions. Other castor sets may be listed in various porcelain and glass categories in this book.

3 Bottles, Blue Glass, Stand, Center Handle, Greensburg Glass Co., 1891, 9⅜ In.	2106
3 Bottles, Center Handle, Greensburg Glass Co., c.1891, 9 In.	263
4 Bottle, King's Crown, Excelsior, Ruby Stained, Adams & Co., 9½ In.	128

CATALOGS are listed in the Paper category.

CAUGHLEY porcelain was made in England from 1772 to 1814. Caughley porcelains are very similar in appearance to those made at the Worcester factory. See the Salopian category for related items.

Bowl, Flowers, Blue, Pink, Orange Stars On Band, c.1820, 4 x 9 In.	108
Jug, Birds, Fruit, Scroll Handle, Blue, White Ground, 5¾ In.	269
Jug, Vignettes, Men, Fishing, River, Landscape, Blue, White, 1700s	196
Plate, Temple, Landscape, Blue, White, Gilt, 7½ In. .... *illus*	150
Waste Bowl, Flowers, Leaves, Blue, White, c.1785, 4¾ In.	1200

CAULDON Limited worked in Staffordshire, Great Britain, and went through many name changes. John Ridgway made porcelain at Cauldon Place, Hanley, until 1855. The firm of John Ridgway, Bates and Co. of Cauldon Place worked from 1856 to 1859. It became Bates, Brown-Westhead, Moore and Co. from 1859 to 1862. Brown-Westhead, Moore and Co. worked from 1862 to 1904. About 1890, this firm started using the words *Cauldon* or *Cauldon Ware* as part of the mark. Cauldon Ltd. worked from 1905 to 1920, Cauldon Potteries from 1920 to 1962. Related items may be found in the Indian Tree category.

Mustache Cup, Rose Sprays, Gilt Trim, 4½ x 2⅜ In.	144
Plate, Baltimore Oriole, Flowers, Pink, White, Ironstone, Henry Pausch, 9 In. .... *illus*	25
Vase, Stick Neck, 10 In.	311

CELADON is the name of a velvet-textured green-gray glaze used by Chinese, Japanese, Korean, and other factories. This section includes pieces covered with celadon glaze with or without added decoration.

Bowl, Carved Exterior, Grooves, Wave Band Interior, 3¾ x 11⅜ In. .... *illus*	183
Bowl, Crosshatched, 3-Footed, Chinese, 10¼ x 7 In.	1936
Bowl, Deep Rim, Chinese, 4¼ In.	450
Bowl, Flared Mouth, Bisque Base, Glazed Center, Chinese, 2 x 7 In.	400
Bowl, Flared Rim, Round Foot, 6 In.	63
Bowl, Pinched Rim, 4 Upturned Edges, Porcelain, Japan, 2½ x 6⅜ In.	65
Brush Washer, Jade, With Chilong, Oval Dish, Finely Carved, Qing Dynasty, 2 x 4 In.	3120
Brush Washer, Ormolu Mount, Female Mask, 2¾ x 5 In.	8125
Cachepot, Porcelain, Globular Form, 2 Legs, Leaf Pattern, Chinese, c.1950, 5½ x 9 In.	688
Censer, Cylinder, Lattice, 3-Footed, 5½ In.	780
Censer, Glaze, Molded, 8 Buddhist Objects, 3-Footed, Yongzheng, Chinese, 2 x 8 In.	625
Censer, Impressed Lotus Blossom, Claw Feet, 12 x 3¾ In.	3953
Censer, Incised Flower Band, Footed, 5½ x 6½ In.	406
Censer, Tripod, Fitted Silver Lid, Jungin, Copy, 1920, 3 x 3 In.	295
Charger, Fluted, Leaf Shape Rim, 18½ In.	10285
Dish, Carved Decoration, Glazed, Ceramic, Engraved, Japan, 1960, 2 x 6 In.	250
Dish, Curved Sides, Rim, Flowers, 1600s, 15½ In.	687
Dish, Flower Heads, Leaves, Vines, Longquan, Chinese, 10¼ In.	660
Dish, Incised Flowers, Korea, 7½ In.	330
Dish, Lobed Rim, Bat Design, Encircling Shou Character, 1900, 10¼ In.	123
Elephant, Glazed Porcelain, Carved, Peonies, Tassels, Japan, 1950, 10 x 7 In.	495
Jar, Funerary, Dome Lid, Stoneware, Gourd Finial, Song Dynasty, 10½ In.	1625
Jar, Lid, Floral Bouquet, Lotus Bud Knob, Chinese, 1900, 13 In.	123
Jar, Porcelain, Carved, Chrysanthemum, Leaves, Plants, Leaf Tip Borders, Chinese, 12 In. *illus*	732
Lamp Base, Grecian Figures, Pate-Sur-Pate, Bronze Base, J. Hinks & Sons, c. 1875, 26 In., Pair . *illus*	500
Pendant, Rectangular Plaque, Sage Seated, Pair Of Cranes, Pine Tree, 4 Characters, 2¼ x 1⅝ In. .	554
Plate, Porcelain, Glazed, Ito Shirozaemo, Mount Fuji, Colored Background, 1900s, 1 x 8 In. ...	75
Plate, Ribbed, Wide Rim, 2 x 11 In.	826
Plate, Twin Fish, Footed, Chinese, 6½ In.	500
Saucer, Song Style Ru Kiln, Brush Washer, Porcelain, Chinese, 1 x 5¾ In.	625
Teapot, Porcelain Tetsubin, Tanuki Spout, Legs, Tails, Handle, 1900s, 3 x 5 In.	60
Vase, 6-Sided, Dome Lid, Deity, Chinese, Yongzheng, Marked, c.1925, 9 x 5 In., Pair	688
Vase, Allover Peony Design, Underglaze Blue, Mark On Base, Chinese, 8¼ In.	111
Vase, Bottle, Crackle Glaze, Chinese Ge Style, Green, Stand, 1800s, 15 In.	320
Vase, Incised Flowerheads, Basket Weave, Overall Crackle, Oval, Chinese, 9 In.	488
Vase, Korean Style, White Slip, Inlay, Cranes, Gyokudo Tezuka, 1900s, 8 x 4 In.	195
Vase, Korean Style, White Slip, Inlay, Cranes, Tall, Gyokudo Tezuka, 1940, 12 x 5 In.	398

Cauldon, Plate, Baltimore Oriole, Flowers, Pink, White, Ironstone, Henry Pausch, 9 In.
$25

Ruby Lane

Collect Cats & Dogs
Looking for a different kind of collection? Save cat and dog feeding bowls that speak for themselves with animal pictures or words. Because they are all low round bowls they look best on the floor or a very low shelf or even on the stairs, at the edge of each step.

Celadon, Bowl, Carved Exterior, Grooves, Wave Band Interior, 3¾ x 11⅜ In.
$183

Neal Auction Co.

Celadon, Jar, Porcelain, Carved, Chrysanthemum, Leaves, Plants, Leaf Tip Borders, Chinese, 12 In.
$732

Neal Auction Co.

Celadon, Lamp Base, Grecian Figures, Pate-Sur-Pate, Bronze Base, J. Hinks & Sons, c.1875, 26 In., Pair
$500

New Orleans Auction Galleries

Celluloid, Hair Comb, Art Nouveau Swirls, 3 Teeth, c.1880, 3 x 3 In.
$55

Ruby Lane

Vase, Lid, Finial, Incised, Rounded Midsection, Fluted Neck, 13 In.	590
Vase, Trumpet, Stoneware, Incised Lattice Design, Ming Dynasty, 15 In.	1320
Water Dropper, Double Walled, Dragon, Cloud, 1900-50, 3½ In.	84

CELLULOID is a trademark for a plastic developed in 1868 by John W. Hyatt. Celluloid Manufacturing Company, the Celluloid Novelty Company, Celluloid Fancy Goods Company, and American Xylonite Company all used celluloid to make jewelry, games, sewing equipment, false teeth, and piano keys. The name *celluloid* was often used to identify any similar plastic. Celluloid toys are listed under Toy.

Button, George Vanderbilt Cup Race, Green Car, 5 Flags, 1¾ In.	72
Dresser Box, Portraits, Women, Pink Flowers, Green Ground, Octagonal, 14 x 14½ In.	250
Figurine, Clamshell, Diorama, House, Tree, Children, River, Windmill, Japan	10
Hair Comb, Art Nouveau Swirls, 3 Teeth, c.1880, 3 x 3 In. *illus*	55
Photo Album, Little Red Riding Hood, Floral Highlights, Clasp, Vintage Pictures, 11 x 8½ In.	108
Photo Album, Victorian, Winter Village Scene, Inset Medallion, 2 Children Ice Skating, 9 x 12 In.	108
Photo Album, Victorian, Young Blond Woman, Portrait, Cream Border, 10 x 8½ In.	72
Photo Album, Victorian, Young Woman Holding Red Roses, Portrait, 11 x 8½ In.	84
Photo Album, Victorian, Young Woman, Portrait, Holly Border, 12 x 9¼ In.	120
Photo Album, Young Girl Carrying Flowers, Woman On Bench, Victorian, 11 x 8½ In.	72
Pin, Sailing Ship, C Clasp, 1¾ In.	26
Pin, Winchester Junior Rifle Corps, Crossed Rifles, 1920s, ¾ In.	35
Rattle, Felix The Cat, Pink Umbrella, Black, White, Red Smile, 4¾ In.	250

CELS are listed in this book in the Animation Art category.

CERAMIC ART COMPANY of Trenton, New Jersey, was established in 1889 by Jonathan Coxon and Walter Scott and was an early producer of American belleek porcelain. It became Lenox, Inc. in 1906. Do not confuse this ware with the pottery made by the Ceramic Arts Studio of Madison, Wisconsin.

Bowl, Shooting Star, Gold, Blue, Cream Ground, Pink, c.1920, 8½ x 4 In.	345
Cider Jug, Apples, Beaded Handle, 1894-1906, 6 x 7 In.	96
Cider Jug, Cider, Grapes, Beaded Handle, 1894-1906, 6 In.	96
Figure, Green, Glazed, Elaborate Headdress, Han Style, 8½ In.	885
Mug, Hand Painted, Grapes, Leaves, Luster Gold, c.1894, 5 x 4 In. *illus*	225
Mug, Hunting Dogs, Gold Handle, Gold Trim Bottom, 1906, 5 x 5 In.	135
Vase, Floral Motif, Gray, Preach, Marked, Blackmore, c.1915, 10 x 4½ In.	525

CERAMIC ARTS STUDIO was founded about 1940 in Madison, Wisconsin, by Lawrence Rabbitt and Ruben Sand. Their most popular products were molded figurines. The pottery closed in 1955. Do not confuse these products with those of the Ceramic Art Co. of Trenton, New Jersey.

Bell, Figural, Woman, Ruffled Dress, Flowered Purse, Black Hair, 5½ In.	43
Candleholder, Double, Flowered Blouse, Scarf, Blond, c.1948, 5 x 5 In.	85
Figurine, Cat, Sitting, Blue Bow, 3 In.	17
Figurine, Donkey, Flower Saddle, c.1949, 4¾ In.	58
Figurine, Lamb, Flower Collar, Tilted Head, c.1952, 3 x 2½ In.	30
Figurine, Little Boy Blue, Lying Down, Legs Crossed, Hat, Horn, 5 x 2¼ In.	29
Figurine, Little Miss Muffet, Sitting On Tuffet, Blond Hair, 4 x 2 x 2 In.	20
Fruit, Blue Pale Fuchsia, Glazed, Franco Mari, 1900s, 8¾ x 12 x 12 In.	38
Head Vase, Becky, Hat, Braids, Striped Shirt, 5½ In.	59
Head Vase, Lotus, High Gloss, Marked, c.1940, 8 x 4¼ In. *illus*	119
Head Vase, Manchu, Hat, Pink Cheeks, Beard, 7½ x 5 x 3 In.	119
Salt & Pepper, Dog & Cat, Plaid, Polka Dot, Blues, Pinks, 3 In.	35
Salt & Pepper, Pigs, Tutu, Shorts, 1950s, 3¼ In.	12
Shelf Sitter, Boy, Playing Harmonica, Blue Shirt, 4½ x 2½ In.	22

CHALKWARE is really plaster of Paris decorated with watercolors. One type was molded from Staffordshire and other porcelain models and painted and sold as inexpensive decorations in the nineteenth century. This type is collected today. Figures of plaster, made from about 1910 to 1940 for use as prizes at carnivals, are also known as chalkware. Kewpie dolls made of chalkware will be found in the Kewpie category.

Bank, Cat, Coin, 2-Part Mold, Mustache, Eyebrows, Pink, Red, Mouth, 1800s, 6 ½ In.	135
Bust, Demeter, Plaster, Roman Goddess, Agriculture, 1900s, 5 ½ x 3 ½ x 10 In.	7
Bust, Shakespeare, Portrait, Continental, 1900s, 15 In.	96
Figurine, Birth Of Venus, Enameled, Stamped, France, 1900s, 24 In.	44
Figurine, Black Elephants, Painted Ivory, Colored Tusks, Green Verdigris, 1920, 2 ¼ x 4 ¼ In.	50
Figurine, Boy Scout, Hand Decorated, Removable Walking Stick, 1993, 7 ½ In.	185
Figurine, Cat, Kittens, Seated, 7 ½ In.	188
Figurine, Cat, Seated, Painted, Oval Base, c.1840, 6 In. .... *illus*	240
Figurine, Cat, Seated, Striped, Black & White, Red Ribbon, Round Plinth, 15 ¾ In.	6655
Figurine, Dog, Seated, Curly Hair, Black Ears, 1800s, 5 ½ In.	397
Figurine, Dog, Standing, Curly Hair, Black Ears, 1800s, 7 ½ In.	549
Figurine, Poodle, Pink Ears, 7 ¼ In.	212
Figurine, Rooster, Hollow Molded, Painted, Pennsylvania, 1800s, 6 ½ In. .... *illus*	189
Figurine, Squirrel, Tan, Black Spots, 1800s, 6 ⅜ In.	854
Figurine, Woman, Orange, Brown, Shawl, Gray Stripes, Purple Skirt, HN 1759, 1936, 8 In.	89
Group, Lovebirds, Yellow, Red Highlighting, 1800s, 6 In.	671
Match Holder, Man's Face, 1800s, 2 ¼ x 3 In.	95
Pitcher, Robin's-Egg Blue, Tiny Pink Rose, Green, Etruria Mellor, 1800s, 10 x 9 x 11 In.	30
Plaque, Embossed, Appeal To Great Spirit, 6 ½ x 9 In.	31
Plaque, German Shepherd, Leather Collar, Buckle Design, Glaze Finish, 1960-70s, 9 ½ x 31 In.	37
Sculpture, Fruit, Box Of Dates, Red, Orange, Green, Brown, 14 x 13 In.	117
Sculpture, Oranges, Figs, Multicolor, 14 x 13 In.	117
Stringholder, Figural, Chef's Head, Hanging Hook, Hand Painted, 1950s	150
Sugar, Bisque Cherub Lid, Scrolling Crossed Sweeps, Continental, 1900s	19
Tray, Genre Scene, Blue, White, Architectural, Figures, 1800s, 8 ¼ x 5 ¾ In.	90

CHARLIE CHAPLIN, the famous comedian, actor, and filmmaker, lived from 1889 to 1977. He made his first movie in 1913. He did the movie *The Tramp* in 1915. The character of the Tramp has remained famous, and in the 1980s appeared in a series of television commercials for computers. Dolls, candy containers, and all sorts of memorabilia with the image of Charlie's Tramp are collected. Pieces are being made even today.

Automaton, Charlie, Whistler, Spring Driven, Swiveling, Head, Wood, 14 x 4 ¼ In.	2057
Toy, Charlie, Flocked Face, Windup, Schuco, Box, c.1910, 6 ½ In. .... *illus*	1080

CHARLIE MCCARTHY was the ventriloquist's dummy used by Edgar Bergen from the 1930s. He was famous for his work in radio, movies, and television. The act was retired in the 1970s. Mortimer Snerd, another Bergen dummy, is also listed here.

Charm, Sterling Silver, Signed, E.B., ⅞ In.	28
Paper Doll, Trench Coat, Jacket, Ascot, Top Hat, 1930s, 15 In.	100
Pencil Sharpener, Bakelite, Decal, Butterscotch, 1 In. Diam.	54
Pin, Charlie, Bust, Figural, Celluloid, c.1938, 1 ⅛ In.	25
Toy, Charlie, Tin Lithograph, Windup, Marx, 8 In.	325
Toy, Charlie, Walker, Clockwork, Top Hat, Black Tux, Tin Lithograph, Marx, 8 In.	270

CHELSEA porcelain was made in the Chelsea area of London from about 1745 to 1769. Some pieces made from 1770 to 1784 are called Chelsea Derby and may include the letter *D* for *Derby* in the mark. Ceramic designs were borrowed from the Meissen models of the day. Pieces were made of soft paste. The gold anchor was used as the mark, but it has been copied by many other factories. Recent copies of Chelsea have been made from the original molds. Do not confuse Chelsea porcelain with Chelsea Grape, a white pottery with luster grape decoration. Chelsea Keramic is listed in the Dedham category.

Adderley, Soup, Dish, White, Blue Grape Sprigs, 1900, 9 In.	45

Ceramic Art Co., Mug, Hand Painted, Grapes, Leaves, Luster Gold, c.1894, 5 x 4 In.
$225

Ruby Lane

Ceramic Arts Studio, Head Vase, Lotus, High Gloss, Marked, c.1940, 8 x 4 ¼ In.
$119

Ruby Lane

Chalkware, Figurine, Cat, Seated, Painted, Oval Base, c.1840, 6 In.
$240

Cowan's Auctions

Chalkware, Figurine, Rooster, Hollow Molded, Painted, Pennsylvania, 1800s, 6½ In.
$189

Hess Auction Group

Charlie Chaplin, Toy, Charlie, Flocked Face, Windup, Schuco, Box, c.1910, 6½ In.
$1,080

Cowan's Auctions

Chelsea, Bocage, Male, Female, Scrolled Base, England, 1800s, 11½ In., Pair
$180

Brunk Auctions

Bocage, Male, Female, Scrolled Base, England, 1800s, 11½ In., Pair .... *illus*	180
Figurine, Goat, Horned, Seated, Brown, Grass, 5 x 3 In.	300

CHELSEA GRAPE pattern was made before 1840. A small bunch of grapes in a raised design, colored with purple or blue luster, is on the border of the white plate. Most of the pieces are unmarked. The pattern is sometimes called Aynsley or Grandmother. Chelsea Sprig is similar but has a sprig of flowers instead of the bunch of grapes. Chelsea Thistle has a raised thistle pattern. Do not confuse these Chelsea patterns with Chelsea Keramic Art Works, which can be found in the Dedham category, or with Chelsea porcelain, the preceding category.

Dish, Grapes, Flowers, Shaped Rim, Molded, Green Grape Leaves, 1800s, 10 In.	420

CHELSEA SPRIG is similar to Chelsea Grape, a pattern made before 1840, but has a sprig of flowers instead of the bunch of grapes. Chelsea Thistle has a raised thistle pattern. Do not confuse these Chelsea patterns with Chelsea Keramic Art Works, which can be found in the Dedham category, or with Chelsea porcelain.

Cake Plate, Hexagon Shape, Hand Painted, Flowers, Pink, Green, Brown, c.1870, 9 In.	71

CHINESE EXPORT porcelain comprises the many kinds of porcelain made in China for export to America and Europe in the eighteenth, nineteenth, and twentieth centuries. Other pieces may be listed in this book under Canton, Celadon, Nanking, Rose Canton, Rose Mandarin, and Rose Medallion.

Board Box, Game, Folding, Gilt, Backgammon Inside, 1800s, 19 x 19 In.	200
Bowl, Cobalt Blue, Stars, Arched Detail, 2 Armorial Shields, 1800, 6 x 14 In.	1169
Bowl, Decorated, Enameled Flowers, Turquoise Ground, Cloud Design, 2⅝ x 5⅝ In.	277
Bowl, Famille Rose, Bird & Butterfly Panels, Gilt Key Borders, c.1850, 16 In. .... *illus*	375
Bowl, Famille Rose, Figural Scenes, Floral Spray, Birds, 1700s, 6 x 14 In.	2520
Bowl, Famille Rose, Flowers, Leaves, 1800s, 8¾ In.	94
Bowl, Famille Rose, Marked, Qianlong Nian Zhi, Carved Wood Stand, 1970, 10 x 10 x 4¾ In. ..	118
Bowl, Fish, Famille Rose, Birds, Flowers, Interior Fish, Crabs, c.1910, 23 In., Pair	2250
Bowl, Flowers, Silver Trim, 1900s, 6 In	108
Bowl, Huntsman, Galloping Horse, 4 Hunting Scenes, 1765, 11 In.	1875
Bowl, Imperial Yellow, 4 Kanji Reserves, Light Green Scroll, 10½ In.	125
Cachepot, Famille Rose, Animal Mask Handles, 8¼ x 9¾ In.	366
Canister, Urn Form, Chrysanthemums, Chased Ground, Luen Wo, 1900, 5⅜ In.	615
Charger, Decorated, Green Background, Garden Design, Peonies, 19 In.	424
Charger, Famille Rose, Central Medallion, Trees, Peonies, c.1900, 15½ In.	531
Charger, Famille Rose, Figures, Birds, Flowers, Butterflies, Vines, Paw Feet, 5¼ x 16¾ In.	976
Charger, Flowers, Central Fan, Blue, White, c.1960, 14 In.	650
Cider Jug, Floral Sprays, Barrel Form, Loop Handle, Monogram, c.1850, 9 x 8 In.	750
Coffeepot, Lighthouse Shape, Fitzhugh, Flowers, Butterflies, Blue, White, 10 In.	450
Coffeepot, Square, Plum Flower, Panel, Faux-Bois Stem, Bamboo Handle, 7 In.	6765
Cooler, Wine, Famille Rose, Flower Sprays, Sprigs, Handles, 6 x 8 In.	375
Dish, Armorial, Arms Of Wearg Impaling Montague & Monthermer, c.1720, 15¼ In.	1250
Dish, Armorial, Burrell Impaling Raymond, Prunus Branches, 15½ In.	8750
Dish, Famille Rose, Fruit & Flowers, Daoguang, Marked, c.1840, 7½ In.	95
Dish, Famille Rose, Radiating Petals, Roses, Pink, Green, 1800s, 11 In.	125
Dish, Famille Verte, Phoenix, Flowers, Fish, Sea Creatures, 1700s, 9⅜ In., Pair	1664
Dish, Hot Water, Lid, Sepia, Sacred Bird, Butterfly, Gilt Artichoke Finial, c.1835, 14 In.	1000
Figurine, Elephant, Glazed, Famille Rose, Ruyi Border, Curled Trunk, c.1850, 7½ x 10 In.	1063
Figurine, Famille Rose, Phoenixes, Perched On Pierced Rockwork, 24 In., Pair	3250
Figurine, Guanyin, White, Multicolor Decorations, 1900s	272
Figurine, Silver & Enamel Peacock, Teak Stand, Colorful Design, 7¼ x 5 In.	1080
Fishbowl, Equestrians, Pink Band, Rim, 1900s, 25¼ In.	1080
Jar, Dome Lid, Famille Rose, Painted Insects, Flowers, Phoenix, Swollen, 26¾ In.	813
Jar, Famille Rose, White Reserve, Roses, Yellow & Green Shoulders, 24½ In., Pair	4000
Jar, Gilt Silver, Turquoise, Jade Highlights, 3-Legged Teak Stand, Dragon Handles, 8 x 6 In.	240
Jar, Lid, Famille Rose, Flowers, 8 Dragons, 18 x 11 In. .... *illus*	4800

Chinese Export, Bowl, Famille Rose, Bird & Butterfly Panels, Gilt Key Borders, c.1850, 16 In.
$375

Eldred's Auctioneers and Appraisers

Chinese Export, Jar, Lid, Famille Rose, Flowers, 8 Dragons, 18 x 11 In.
$4,800

Brunk Auctions

Chinese Export, Plate, Famille Rose, Pagoda, Bats, Flower Border, 1800s, 9 ½ In.
$287

Bunch Auctions

Chinese Export, Teapot, Figural, Crane Nestled In Lotus Leaf, Bud Lid, Fish In Beak, c.1800, 5 x 8 In.
$800

Brunk Auctions

Chinese Export, Tureen, Figural, Frog, Yellow, Green, Finial, Foo Dogs, Butterflies, c.1890, 7 x 10 In.
$450

Cowan's Auctions

Chinese Export, Tureen, Lid, Orange Fitzhugh, Flower Head Knop, Openwork Handles, c.1800, 15 x 10 In.
$2,160

Thomaston Place Auction Galleries

Chinese Export, Tureen, Phoenix, Garden, Finial, Boar's Head Handles, 1800s, 8½ In.
$660

Brunk Auctions

Chinese Export, Vase, Famille Rose, Bands, Birds, Flowers, Elephant Head Handles, 1800s, 14¾ In.
$2,400

Michann's Auctions

Chintz, Summertime, Dish, Divided, Floral, Royal Winton, Marked, 10 x 11 In.
$265

Ruby Lane

Time or Money
According to a study, spending money in a way that saves time makes people happier than spending money on things. (Bottomline Personal)

Jardiniere, Dragon, Ocean Wave, Blue, White, 1900s, 18 x 22 In.	950
Jardiniere, Famille Rose, Birds On Branches, Rectangular, 7 x 13 x 8 In., Pair	2176
Jardiniere, Famille Rose, Children, Garden, Floral Band, Metal Mount, Key Pattern, 14 x 16 In.	625
Jug, Lid, Flowers, Fruit Finial, 1900, 9½ In.	156
Jug, Pear Shape, Loop Handle, Painted, Gilt Vine, Cartouches, Flowers, 1850, 15 In.	875
Lamp, Ginger Jar, Multicolor, Light Gray, Butterflies, Chrysanthemums, 30 x 9 x 9 In.	83
Lantern, Famille Rose, Seated Cats, Wild Roses, Rockery, 10¼ In.	188
Mug, Strap Handle, Cobalt Blue, Painted, Gilt, 1800s-1900s, 5½ x 4¼ In., Pair	7800
Planter, Peach Tree, 1900s, 26 In.	85
Plaque, Goats, Stream, Calligraphy, 23 x 14½ In.	344
Plate, Armorial, Scalloped Edges, Floral Sprays, Gilt, Family Crest, 1700s, 9¾ In.	1800
Plate, European Fisherman, Pink, c.1790, 9 In.	300
Plate, Famille Rose, Pagoda, Bats, Flower Border, 1800s, 9½ In. *illus*	287
Plate, Hexagonal Armorial, Gilt Cross, Ram's Head Emblem, Chain Detail, 1700s, 8½ In., Pair	960
Plate, Oval, Barbed Rim, Lions, Crown, Decorated Flower Sprays, 1700s, 19 In.	1625
Plate, Painted, Arms Of Sandilands, Flowers, Blue, Gilding, 1735, 9 In.	2500
Plate, Painted, Arms Of Van Herzeele, Decorated Grisaille, Gilding, 1740, 9 In.	2125
Plate, Pronk Arbor, 12 Reserves, Fruit, Flowers, People, c.1738, 9 In.	3750
Plate, Pseudo Tobacco Leaf, Oval Shape, Rounded Sides, Flowers, Color & Gilt, 10 In.	938
Plate, Women & Flowers, Famille Rose, Pair, Marked, c.1900, 9½ In.	1200
Platter, Blue Fitzhugh, Armorial, Arms Of Hill Dawe, c.1790, 11¾ In., Pair	2125
Platter, Blue Fitzhugh, Oval, Floral Motifs, Central Pagoda, 1800s, 3 x 18 x 13 In.	900
Platter, Rectangular, Blue, White, Flower Sprays, Diaper Border, 1800s, 15⅝ In.	250
Platter, Tobacco Leaf, Red Flowers, Cobalt Blue Leaves, c.1875, 11¾ In.	2928
Punch Bowl, Famille Rose, Center Medallion, Men On Terraces, Flared, Broad Rim, 6 x 19 In.	750
Punch Bowl, Famille Rose, Flowers, Birds, Panels, Interior Scenes, 6⅝ x 13 In.	400
Punch Bowl, Famille Rose, Peonies, Roses, Orange, Purple, White, c.1750, 15½ In.	2125
Punch Bowl, Famille Rose, People, Courtyard, Lake, Hills, 11½ In.	1815
Sauceboat, Blue, White, Floral, Pair, c.1750, 10 x 4 In.	375
Saucer, Diaper Border, Birds, Flowers & Figures, Blue Floral Ground, 1880, 13 In.	3125
Saucer, Famille Rose, Ruby Ground, Mountains, Marked, 1800s, 4 In., Pair	625
Tankard, Figures In Battle, Medallion, Dragon Handle, Monogram, 1800s, 6 In.	2460
Teapot, Crane Shape, Turquoise Mottled, Glaze, Lotus, Fish In Its Beak, 1800, 5¼ x 8 x 4 In.	800
Teapot, Cylindrical, Lid, Gilt, Masted Ship, Flying American Flag, c.1750, 6 In.	3600
Teapot, Figural, Crane Nestled In Lotus Leaf, Bud Lid, Fish In Beak, c.1800, 5 x 8 In. *illus*	800
Teapot, Gilt, Round Reserves, Birds, 5½ x 8½ In.	106
Tureen, Duck Lid, Vegetable, Porcelain, Hand Painted, 1900s, 7 x 9 x 8 In.	671
Tureen, Figural, Frog, Yellow, Green, Finial, Foo Dogs, Butterflies, c.1890, 7 x 10 In. *illus*	450
Tureen, Lid, Orange Fitzhugh, Flower Head Knop, Openwork Handles, c.1800, 15 x 10 In. *illus*	2160
Tureen, Lid, People, Flowers, Double Boar Handles, Multicolor, 8¾ x 12 In.	480
Tureen, Lid, Stand, Famille Rose, Gilt, Figure, Palms, 1735-96, 15⅝ In.	2375
Tureen, Oval, Orange Fitzhugh, Gilded Handles, Porcelain, 1790-1810, 11 x 15 x 10 In.	2160
Tureen, Phoenix, Garden, Finial, Boar's Head Handles, 1800s, 8½ In. *illus*	660
Tureen, Rabbit Lid, Famille Verte, Plants, Insects, Marked, c.1890, 9 x 14 In.	2180
Vase, 6-Sided, Mandarin, Multicolor, Faux Bois Panels, Courtyard Scene, 1800, 12 x 5¾ In., Pair.	5313
Vase, Beaker Shape, Flared Rim, Cobalt Blue, Gilt, 1800, 10 x 5½ In., Pair	308
Vase, Bottle, Blue Fitzhugh, Foo Dogs, 13 In.	750
Vase, Double Gourd, Blue, White, Flowers, Leaves, 20¼ In., Pair	4375
Vase, Famille Noir, Cylindrical Top, Landscape, Scholars, Generals, 17 In.	535
Vase, Famille Noire, Beasts, Rockery, Cresting Waves, 10½ In.	211
Vase, Famille Rose, Bands, Birds, Flowers, Elephant Head Handles, 1800s, 14¾ In. *illus*	2400
Vase, Famille Rose, Chrysanthemums, Rock, Cricket, 9¼ In.	1416
Vase, Famille Rose, Moon, Dragon Form Handles, 1700s, 18 x 12 x 3¾ In.	1020
Vase, Famille Rose, Rectangular, Dragon Head Handles, Bats, Peaches, Cobalt, 18 x¾ x 7 In.	600
Vase, Famille Verte, Globular, Long Neck, Phoenix, Rockwork, Handles, 9½ In.	1220
Vase, Fan Shape, Fluted, Oval, Serpentine Rim, Court, Scrolls, Flowers, 7 x 12 In.	147
Vase, Flower Bands, Stiff Leaves, Zoomorphic Handles, 10 In.	252
Vase, Green Ivy, Elephant, Figures, Horse, Crane, Fish, Red Ground, 18½ In.	246
Vase, Hu Form, Flame Glaze, Red, Purple, Blue & White, Marked, 12 x 6⅞ x 5¾ In.	2760
Vase, Mallet Form, Decorated, Songbird Perched, Yuanwen Wuguo Zhizhai, 6⅛ In.	584

Vase, Man, Rides Deer, Antlers, Blue, White, 12½ In.	181
Vase, Numerous Figures, Various Pursuits, 1900s, 13 In.	3998
Vase, River, Boats, Orange, Green, c.1970, 22 In.	6875
Vase, White, Oval, 6 Blue Incised Panels, Decorated, Different Tree, 6¾ In.	234

CHINTZ is the name of a group of china patterns featuring an overall design of flowers and leaves. The design became popular with English makers about 1928. A few pieces are still being made. The best known are designs by Royal Winton, James Kent Ltd., Crown Ducal, and Shelley. Crown Ducal and Shelley are listed in their own sections.

Atlas China Co.
c.1934–1939

Old Foley/James Kent
c.1955

Royal Winton MADE IN ENGLAND

Royal Winton
c.1951+

Cheese Keeper, Ivory, Flowers, Gilt Trim, Scalloped Dish, Dome Lid, Ball Finial, 4 x 7 In.	50
Cranstone, Pitcher, Grimwades, Dutch Shape, 4¼ In.	55
Hazel, Platter, Royal Winton, 12 In.	155
Heather, Jug, Lord Nelson, 4½ In.	165
Julia, Plate, Scalloped Edge, Gilt, Royal Winton, 10 In.	61
Rosalynde, Platter, James Kent, 12 x 6 In.	200
Rosebud, Platter, Pointed Rim, Oval, 11 In.	58
Summertime, Berry Bowl, Royal Winton, 4¼ x 4¼ In.	45
Summertime, Butter, Cover, Royal Winton, 6 x 4 In.	200
Summertime, Dish, Divided, Floral, Royal Winton, Marked, 10 x 11 In. .... *illus*	265
Violet, Snack Set, Tray, Cup, Lefton, 1950s	40

CHOCOLATE GLASS, sometimes mistakenly called caramel slag, was made by the Indiana Tumbler and Goblet Company of Greentown, Indiana, from 1900 to 1903. It was also made at other National Glass Company factories. Fenton Art Glass Co. made chocolate glass from about 1907 to 1915. More recent pieces have been made by Imperial and others.

Dish, Lid, Bird On Nest, 4¾ x 5½ In.	240
Dish, Lid, Rabbit, 5 x 10 In.	220
Dolphin, Dish, Lid, Beaded Rim, c.1902, 4½ In.	50
Figurine, Bicentennial Eagle, Fenton, 3 x 3 In.	25
Geneva, Cruet, Pressed Facet Stopper, McKee Glass Co., c.1902, 6¾ In.	475
Geneva, Syrup, McKee Glass Co., 1902, 6 In.	225
Rabbit, Dish, Lid, 4¼ x 5½ In.	225 to 325
Vase, Marked, Fenton, 10 x 5½ In.	520

CHRISTMAS PLATES *that are limited edition are listed in the Collector Plate category or in the correct factory listing.*

CHRISTMAS collectibles include not only Christmas trees and ornaments listed below, but also Santa Claus figures, special dishes, and even games and wrapping paper. A Belsnickle is a nineteenth-century figure of Father Christmas. A kugel is an early, heavy ornament made of thick blown glass, lined with zinc or lead, and often covered with colored wax. Christmas cards are listed in this section under Greeting Card. Christmas collectibles may also be listed in the Candy Container category. Christmas trees are listed in the section that follows.

Belsnickle, Brown Coat, Ermine, Feather Tree Sprig, Composition, 5½ In. .... *illus*	3300
Blotter, Holly Berries, Celluloid, Kingans Logo, 3 x 8 In.	35
Box, Razor Blades, Santa Claus Theme, Round Shaving, 1920s-1930s, 4 x 7 In.	30
Candy Containers are listed in the Candy Container category.	
Cookie Jar, Drummers Drumming, Around Christmas Tree, Fitz & Floyd, 18½ x 13¾ In.	244
Dish, Lid, Chimney, Santa Claus, Green, Transparent, c.1900, 5½ x 3¼ In.	234

Christmas
Vintage Shiny Brite ornaments sold for about $20 in 2018. The old boxes are also collected and reused for storage each year.

Christmas, Belsnickle, Brown Coat, Ermine, Feather Tree Sprig, Composition, 5½ In.
$3,300

Bertoia Auctions

Christmas, Mold, Santa Claus, Cast Iron, Griswold, 12¼ In.
$189

Hess Auction Group

This is an edited listing of current prices. Visit **Kovels.com** to check thousands of prices from previous years and sign up for free information on trends, tips, reproductions, marks, and more.

Christmas, Mold, Santa Claus, Tin, 20 In.
$1,140

Bertoia Auctions

Christmas, Reindeer, Nodding, Windup, Felt Saddle, Fur Over Composition, Germany, 17 In.
$3,600

Bertoia Auctions

Christmas, Toy, Santa Claus, Riding Elephant, Carrying Tree, Papier-Mache, 7¼ In.
$517

Bunch Auctions

Christmas, Toy, Santa Claus, Riding Wicker Bicycle, Red Robe, Rabbit Fur Beard, 9 x 10 In.
$1,920

Bertoia Auctions

Christmas Tree, Feather, 3 Tiers, Stenciled Base, Germany, 15 In.
$180

Bertoia Auctions

Christmas Tree, Ornament, Andy Gump, Gold Iridescent, Red Lips, Red Hat, 1900-30, 2¾ In.
$126

Bunch Auctions

Christmas Tree, Ornament, Angel, Die Cut, Dresden, 8 In.
$65

Ruby Lane

Christmas Tree, Ornament, Clown, Cello, Glass, West Germany, 4¾ In.
$54

Ruby Lane

Christmas Tree, Ornament, Icicle, Spun Cotton Wool, Germany, 4½ In.
$40

Ruby Lane

C

TIP
Dust glass Christmas ornaments with a feather duster.

Christmas Tree, Ornament, Halibut, Gold, Dresden, 1900-30, 5 x 3 In.
$115

Bunch Auctions

Christmas Tree, Ornament, Kugel, Bunch Of Grapes, Golden Amber, 5 In.
$390

Bertoia Auctions

Christmas Tree, Ornament, Kugel, Cluster Of Grapes, Glass, Amber, Baroque Cap, 6 In.
$442

Hess Auction Group

Christmas Tree, Ornament, Kugel, Egg Shape, Glass, Green, 5 Leaf Cap, Germany, 3 ¼ In.
$265

Hess Auction Group

Christmas Tree, Ornament, Mushroom, Clip-On, Glass, Metal, 6 In.
$52

Ruby Lane

Christmas Tree, Ornament, Pickle, Glass, Green, 4 ½ In.
$13

Ruby Lane

Christmas Tree, Ornament, Santa Claus, Holding Christmas Tree, Red Coat, c.1890, 5 In.
$18

Eldred's Auctioneers and Appraisers

Christmas Tree, Stand, Picket Fence, Gates, Arched Holder, Wood, Painted, c.1875, 15 ¾ x 15 ¾ In.
$420

Garth's Auctioneers & Appraisers

Chrome, Figure, Stylized Dancer, Black Metal Base, Ronson, 12 x 7¼ In. $375

Fontaine's Auction Gallery

Cinnabar, Box, Lid, Black, Red, Carved, Fruit, Flowers, Leaves, Round, 2¾ x 7 In. $2,806

Neal Auction Co.

Civil War, Cannon, Model 1841 Mountain Howitzer, 12 Pounder, Bronze, Cyrus Alger, 1853, 37 In. $69,000

James D. Julia Auctioneers

Dish, Lid, Santa Claus, Sleigh, c.1900, 4½ x 3½ In.	187
Display, Santa Claus In Auto, Vintage, Germany, 28 In.	2700
Greeting Card, Annie Oakley, Little Sure Shot, Folding, Christmas In East & West, 1891, 5 x 4 In.	480
Greeting Card, Mandrake, Top Hat, Gloves, Santa Claus Outfit, 1939, 8 x 10 In.	75
Greeting Card, Metallic Silver, Red, Tree, Harvey Comic, Santa Claus, Little Lota, 1950s, 5 x 7 In.	25
Greeting Card, White, Green Text, Pogo, Albert, Grundune, Children, 1961, 4¼ x 5⅜ In.	75
House, Seated Santa Claus, Cardboard, Loofah Tree, Glitter, Japan, c.1930, 7½ In.	46
Mold, Santa Claus, Cast Iron, Griswold, 12¼ In. .... *illus*	189
Mold, Santa Claus, Tin, 20 In. .... *illus*	1140
Mug, Santa Claus, Holly Leaves, Berries, Ruby, Arcoroc, France, 3⅞ x 3 In.	27
Nodder, Christkindl, White Frock, Red Felt Robe, Germany, 36 In.	3900
Plate, Couple, Gold, Blue, Round Corners, Bjorn Wiinblad, 12 x 12 In.	200
Reindeer, Nodding, Windup, Felt Saddle, Fur Over Composition, Germany, 17 In. .... *illus*	3600
Rudolph, Mold, Chocolate, Tin, 5 x 5 In.	423
Santa Claus, Mold, Chocolate, Tin, 9½ x 4½ In.	79
Santa Claus, Sign, Reindeer, Die Cut, Embossed, 1890s, 12 x 18¾ In.	23
Santa Claus, Sign, With Sack, Tree, Toys, William Gray Dry Goods, 15⅜ x 10½ In.	517
Sign, Cat In The Hat, Merry Christmas To All, 52½ In.	175
Sign, Santa Claus, Standing, Fingering Beard, 53½ In.	58
Stickpin, Green, Holly Leaf, Short Hanger, Dark Gold Bell, Red, 1905	24
Toy, Santa Claus, Die Cut, Red, White, Green, Sears Belt, Ventriloquist, 1948, 6¾ x 13 In.	35
Toy, Santa Claus, Riding Elephant, Carrying Tree, Papier-Mache, 7¼ In. .... *illus*	517
Toy, Santa Claus, Riding Wicker Bicycle, Red Robe, Rabbit Fur Beard, 9 x 10 In. .... *illus*	1920
Toy, Santa Claus, Sleigh, Reindeer, Red, Black, Kyser & Rex, 12½ In.	2160

CHRISTMAS TREES made of feathers and Christmas tree decorations of all types are popular with collectors. The first decorated Christmas tree in America is claimed by many states, including Pennsylvania (1747), Massachusetts (1832), Illinois (1833), Ohio (1838), and Iowa (1845). The first glass ornaments were imported from Germany about 1860. Paper and tinsel ornaments were made in Dresden, Germany, from about 1880 to 1940. Manufacturers in the United States were making ornaments in the early 1870s. Electric lights were first used on a Christmas tree in 1882. Character light bulbs became popular in the 1920s, bubble lights in the 1940s, twinkle bulbs in the 1950s, plastic bulbs by 1955. In this book a Christmas light is a holder for a candle used on the tree. Other forms of lighting include light bulbs. Other Christmas collectibles are listed in the preceding section.

Feather, 3 Tiers, Stenciled Base, Germany, 15 In. .... *illus*	180
Ornament, Andy Gump, Gold Iridescent, Red Lips, Red Hat, 1900-30, 2¾ In. .... *illus*	126
Ornament, Angel, Die Cut, Dresden, 8 In. .... *illus*	65
Ornament, Clown, Cello, Glass, West Germany, 4¾ In. .... *illus*	54
Ornament, Dog, Pug, Tan & Brown, Curly Tail, Dresden, 3 In.	360
Ornament, Dresden, Crowing Rooster, Colorful, Marked E.M., c.1900, 4 In.	94
Ornament, Halibut, Gold, Dresden, 1900-30, 5 x 3 In. .... *illus*	115
Ornament, Icicle, Spun Cotton Wool, Germany, 4½ In. .... *illus*	40
Ornament, Kugel, Bunch Of Grapes, Golden Amber, 5 In. .... *illus*	390
Ornament, Kugel, Cluster Of Grapes, Glass, Amber, Baroque Cap, 6 In. .... *illus*	442
Ornament, Kugel, Egg Shape, Glass, Green, 5-Leaf Cap, Germany, 3¼ In. .... *illus*	265
Ornament, Kugel, Glass Ball, Cobalt Blue, Germany, 4½ In.	177
Ornament, Mushroom, Clip-On, Glass, Metal, 6 In. .... *illus*	52
Ornament, Pickle, Glass, Green, 4½ In. .... *illus*	13
Ornament, Santa Claus, Holding Christmas Tree, Red Coat, c.1890, 5 In. .... *illus*	18
Stand, Bust, Santa, Concrete, 11 In.	175
Stand, Cast Iron, Santa Claus In Red Robe, Germany, 9½ x 9½ In.	900
Stand, Musical, Cylinder, Pressed Tin, Green Hilly Base, Rotates, 14 In.	7480
Stand, Picket Fence, Gates, Arched Holder, Wood, Painted, c.1875, 15¾ x 15¾ In. .... *illus*	420

CHROME items in the Art Deco style became popular in the 1930s. Collectors are most interested in high-style pieces made by the Connecticut firms of Chase Brass & Copper Co., Manning-Bowman & Co., and others.

C

Chandelier, 20-Light, Atomic Orb, Faceted Balls, 20 Lights, 1900s, 36 x 21 In.	1750
Cocktail Shaker, Stepped Tray, Manhattan, N. Bel Geddes, Revere, 1930s, 14-In. Tray	875
Figure, Dog, Mack, Bulldog, Hood Ornament, Canine, 1900s	25
Figure, Stylized Dancer, Black Metal Base, Ronson, 12 x 7¼ In. *illus*	375
Martini Shaker, Flared, Red Bakelite Handle, Art Deco, 1930, 13 x 7½ In.	68
Sculpture, Raindrops, Metal, Artisan House, Curtis Jere, 1900s, 37 x 24 x 8 In.	2520

CIGAR STORE FIGURES of carved wood or cast iron were used as advertisements in front of the Victorian cigar store. The carved figures are now collected as folk art. They range in size from counter type, about three feet, to over eight feet high.

Indian Maiden, Yellow Dress, Green Stripe, Moccasins, Rifle, Wood, 1800s, 56½ In.	11115
Indian, Brave, Rifle, Yellow Top, Square Base, 56½ In.	11115
Indian, Chief With Rifle, Wood, c.1970, 85 In.	9760
Indian, Utica Club Cigars, Chalkware Figure, 17 In.	1445
Man, Bust, Black, Blue Jacket, Red Bowtie, Handful Of Cigars, 29 x 19½ In.	5748

CINNABAR is a vermilion or red lacquer. Pieces are made with tens to hundreds of thicknesses of the lacquer that is later carved. Most cinnabar was made in the Orient.

Bowl, Lacquer, Dragon, Carved Traditional Detail, Chinese, 3 x 6½ In.	30
Box, Boy, Man, Walking, Garden, Trees, Rocks, Chinese, 5½ x 3¾ In.	115
Box, Flattened Pumpkin Shape, Stem Handle, Flowers, 6½ x 3¼ In.	115
Box, Lid, Black, Red, Carved, Fruit, Flowers, Leaves, Round, 2¾ x 7 In. *illus*	2806
Box, Lid, Circular, Red Relief Design, Battling Warriors, 1800s, 12 In.	4800
Box, Panels, Cranes, Rockery, Peaches, Butterflies, Leaves, Green Ground, 10¼ In.	813
Charger, Dragons, Ruyi Heads, Cines, 15 In.	4000
Figure, Horse Head, Patterned Skin, Turquoise Beads, Windblown Mane, Open Mouth, 15 In.	1188
Jar, Lid, Figures, Pavilions, Pine Trees, Mountains, 10½ In.	1500
Jardiniere, Hexagonal, Deer, Cartouche, 11 x 13 In.	480
Tray, Figures In Landscape, Clouds, Mountains, Upturned Sides, Scrolls, 2 x 15 In.	1220
Tray, Figures In Landscape, Diapering, Square, Bracket Feet, Chinese, 2 x 14 In.	3172
Vase, Black On Red, Floral Cartouches, Rouleau Form, Pair, c.1900, 9 In.	156
Vase, Cream, Carved Flowers, Red Medallion, Brass Rim, Pinched Neck, 10 In., Pair	188
Vase, Panels, Playful Foo Dogs, 15 In.	1000
Vase, Temple Jar Shape, Landscape, Lotus, 1900s, 8 In.	360

CIVIL WAR mementos are important collectors' items. Most of the pieces are military items used from 1861 to 1865. Be sure to avoid any explosive munitions.

Badge, Clover Shape, 2nd Corps. Insignia, 1st Minnesota Volunteers, With Stick, Pin, 2 x ½ In.	1476
Badge, Confederate, D.A. Ayers, 2nd S. Carolina, Artillery, 2 Parts, Panel & Shield, 4 In.	1680
Broadside, Laboring Men Of New York, No Riots, Democratic Working Man, 1863, 11 x 18 In.	6600
Broadside, Political, Friends Of The Government, Philadelphia, Pa., Frame, 9½ x 12 In.	1800
Broadside, Recruitment, 1st Battalion Maine Sharpshooters, 1864, 11 x 16 In.	500
Broadside, Recruitment, Harris' Light Cavalry, Plattsburg, N.Y., 14 x 20 In.	3120
Broadside, Recruitment, U.S. Army, 15th Infantry, Unmarried Men, 11 x 16 In.	780
Broadside, Reward, Female Runaway, Slave, 27 x 21 In.	10800
Broadside, U.S. Grant, Horseback, Excursion Tickets, NY West Shore Railway, 16 x 22 In.	1080
Cane, Ferrule, Silver & Wood Handle, Horses, Flowers, Andersonville Prison Stockade, 35 In.	510
Cane, General W.H. Noble, High Relief Wood, Silver Engraved Cap, 37 In.	615
Cannon, Model 1841 Mountain Howitzer, 12 Pounder, Bronze, Cyrus Alger, 1853, 37 In. *illus*	69000
Canteen, Painted, Bull's-Eye, J. Ruth CO, G., 1861-65, 17th Penn. Cavalry *illus*	369
Canteen, Tin, Drum, Iron Dipped, Convex Sides, Spout, 3 Sling Loops, 5¾ x 1½ In.	558
Canteen, Veteran's, Painted Farm Scene, Back Painted Gold, 1860s *illus*	338
Carte De Viste, U.S. Grant *illus*	488
Drum, William Kilbourn, Red Rim, Tension Rope, Leather Adjustment Tab, 1858-63, 14 x 16 In.	840
Game, Lithograph, Maze, Hand Colored, Running Blockade, Charles Magnus, c.1861, 24 x 20 In.	3240
I.D. Tag, Gideon Dutcher, 37th Massachusetts Infantry, Sterling Silver, 1 x 1¾ In.	1200

C

Civil War, Canteen, Painted, Bull's-Eye, J. Ruth CO, G., 1861-65, 17th Penn. Cavalry
$369

Skinner, Inc.

Civil War, Canteen, Veteran's, Painted Farm Scene, Back Painted Gold, 1860s
$338

Skinner, Inc.

Civil War, Carte De Viste, U.S. Grant
$488

Blackwell Auctions

Civil War, Medal, Veteran's, Ladder Bars, Star, Wm H. Hall, May 11 61, Mass. Inft'y, 5 In.
$492

Skinner, Inc.

Civil War, Plate, Pickett's Charge, Lee, Hancock, Longstreet, Meade, Edwin Bennett Pottery, 9¾ x 13 In.
$480

Cowan's Auctions

Civil War, Trivet, Reunion, Heart Shape Handle, CSA Letters, Iron, 1922
$96

Milestone Auctions

Clarice Cliff, Jug, Delica, Flowers, Dots, Snake Handle, Multicolor Drip Glaze, 5¾ x 5¾ In.
$375

Ruby Lane

I.D. Tag, Prisoner Of War, Paper, Sgt. Oliver Lighthall, 115th New York Volunteers, 2 x 3 In.		615
Medal, Veteran's, Ladder Bars, Star, Wm H. Hall, May 11 61, Mass. Inft'y, 5 In. .... *illus*		492
Mirror, Cast Iron, Oval Frame, Eagle Above, Shield Below, Draped Flags, 1862, 19 x 11 In.		390
Musket, Colt, Percussion, .54 Caliber, Bayonet, Lock Plate Stamped 1863, 40-In. Barrel		840
Plate, Pickett's Charge, Lee, Hancock, Longstreet, Meade, Edwin Bennett Pottery, 9¾ x 13 In. *illus*		480
Poster, General Lee & Army Have Surrendered, Albany, New York, 1865, 21 x 28 In.		3240
Trivet, Reunion, Heart Shape Handle, CSA Letters, Iron, 1922 .... *illus*		96

CKAW, *see Dedham category.*

CLARICE CLIFF was a designer who worked in several English factories, including A.J. Wilkinson Ltd., Wilkinson's Royal Staffordshire Pottery, Newport Pottery, and Foley Pottery after the 1920s. She is best known for her brightly colored Art Deco designs, including the Bizarre line. She died in 1972. Reproductions have been made by Wedgwood.

Bizarre, Bowl, Applique Idyll Daffodil, 13 In.	2500
Bizarre, Sugar Basin, Applique Idyll, 1932, 4½ In.	1200
Bizarre, Vase, Pink Flowers, Magenta Outline, Blue Ground, 4¼ x 8 In.	617
Fantasque, Pitcher, Sunrise Athens Shape, Marked, 6¾ In.	1200
Harvest, Basket, Arched Handle, Marked, 1940s, 9 In.	575
Jug, Delica, Flowers, Dots, Snake Handle, Multicolor Drip Glaze, 5¾ x 5¾ In. .... *illus*	375
Jug, Large Flowers, Red, Yellow, Purple, Marked On Base, 1932-33, 11 In.	277
Jug, Lotus Shape, Abstract, Geometric Shapes, Blue, Orange, Green, Purple, 1928-30, 11 In.	584
Jug, Tree, Curving Black Trunk, Blue Stylized, Leaves, Orange, Yellow, Green, 1934, 12 In.	492
Rhodanthe, Teapot, Lynton Shape, Marked, 1930s, 19 In.	360

CLEWELL was made in limited quantities by Charles Walter Clewell of Canton, Ohio, from 1902 to 1955. Pottery was covered with a thin coating of bronze, then treated to make the bronze turn different colors. Pieces covered with copper, brass, or silver were also made. Mr. Clewell's secret formula for blue patinated bronze was burned when he died in 1965.

Mug, Copper Clad, Rivets, 1908, 4½ x 5 In.	36
Vase, Acid Threaded Surface, Copper & Bronze, Striated Decoration, 9 x 10 x 7⅞ In.	570
Vase, Copper Clad, Brown Neck, Green Base, 3½ x 7¼ In.	162
Vase, Copper Clad, Handles, 5¼ x 7 In.	300
Vase, Copper Clad, High Shoulders, 10½ x 7⅞ In. .... *illus*	570
Vase, Copper Clad, Incised Zigzag Band, 4½ x 3¾ In.	180
Vase, Copper Clad, Turquoise, 2 Handles, Engraved, 6⅜ In.	1003

CLIFTON POTTERY was founded by William Long in Newark, New Jersey, in 1905. He worked there until 1909 making lines that included Crystal Patina and Clifton Indian Ware. Clifton Pottery made art pottery until 1911 and then concentrated on wall and floor tile. By 1914, the name had been changed to Clifton Porcelain and Tile Company. Another firm, Chesapeake Pottery, sold majolica marked *Clifton Ware.*

Jug, Tan, Black, Overlapping Geometric Open Diamonds, 4½ In.	22
Vase, Tan, Brown, Black Outlines, Swirl, Indian Ware, 1910-20, 7 x 10 In.	139
Vase, Turquoise, Squat, Matte, Signed, 3 x 2 In	139

CLOCKS of all types have always been popular with collectors. The eighteenth-century tall case, or grandfather's, clock was designed to house a works with a long pendulum. The name on the clock is usually the maker but sometimes it is a merchant or other craftsman. In 1816, Eli Terry patented a new, smaller works for a clock, and the case became smaller. The clock could be kept on a shelf instead of on the floor. By 1840, coiled springs were used and even smaller clocks were made. Battery-powered electric clocks were made in the 1870s. A garniture set can include a clock and other objects displayed on a mantel.

8-Day, Ship Bell Strike, Brass, Ship's Wheel Design, Silver Dial, Chelsea, 5 In.	1560
Advertising, Drink Vernors, Yellow, Red, Model 18040, Case, Pam Clock Co., c.1957, 20 In.	1740
Advertising, Hester Batteries, Double Bubble, Battery On Dial, Light-Up, 4 x 15 In.	1093

C

Advertising, Oldsmobile Service, Metal, Plastic, Glass, 5 x 16 In.	1783
Advertising, Whistle, Golden Orange, Soda Bottle, Elf, 23 x 23 In.	1035
Advertising, White Owl Cigars On Panel, Oak, Shaped Skirt, 38 x 16 In.	600
Animated, Bollard, Silvered & Bronze, Thermometer, Barometer, Compass, 1800s, 20 In. *illus*	9440
Annular Dial, Louis XVI, Gilt Bronze, Marble, Columns, Swags, Torch, Quiver, France, 1700s, 15 In.	2500
Annular Dial, Louis XVI, Gilt Bronze, Urn Shape, Pinecone Finial, 18 In.	2500
Annular Dial, Silver, Cobalt Blue Enamel, Urn Shape, 7 Onyx Portrait Medallions, 7 In.	3025
Annular Dial, Terrestrial Globe, Ebonized Wood, 4 Posts, Engraved Brass Plate, 11 x 8¾ In.	545
Ansonia, 2 Women, Art & Commerce, 8-Day Time & Strike, Gong, 1890s, 20 x 25 In. *illus*	1045
Ansonia, Accomac, Porcelain, Leafy Case, Enameled Dial, 1800-1900, 12 In.	36
Ansonia, Fountain, Porcelain, Beveled Crystal, Roman Numerals, 22 x 14 In.	787
Ansonia, Gold Decorated Case, Applied Accents, Open Escapement, 13 x 7 x 4 In.	118
Ansonia, Porcelain, Brass, Glass, Purple, Flowers, Blue, Yellow, c.1890, 17¾ x 9 In. *illus*	1386
Ansonia, Radical, Porcelain, Open Escapement, Glass Door, 14 x 11 In.	201
Ansonia, Regulator, Brass, Painted Porcelain Face, Open Escapement, 10 x 6 In.	72
Ansonia, Regulator, Crystal, Green Marble Base & Top, Pillars, Gilt Metal Trim, 6 x 12 In.	600
Ansonia, Shelf, 2-Tone Metal Case, Open Escapement, 15 x 11 In.	120
Ansonia, Skeleton, Mahogany, Brass Chapter Ring, Pendulum, 36 x 16 In.	484
Ansonia, Swing, 2 Women, Huntress & Fisher, 8-Day Movement, c.1900, 25 In. *illus*	3480
Ansonia, Swing, Figure, Arcadia, 8-Day Movement, c.1905, 31½ In. *illus*	6150
Banjo, E. Taber, Alarm, Iron Dial, Blued Steel Hands, Weight Driven, 34 x 9¾ In.	3328
Banjo, E.O. Stennes, Girandole, Painted Metal Dial, Gilt Trim, Weymouth, Mass., 45 x 12 In.	6655
Banjo, Federal Style, Mahogany, Reverse Painted, Masted Ships, Eagle Finial, c.1950, 32 In.	538
Banjo, Foster Campos, Girandole, Pierced Hands, Painted Metal Dial, Black Numbers, 46 In.	3025
Banjo, Gilt & Creme, Round Dial, Eglomise Panel, Winged Figures, 1800s, 45 In.	630
Banjo, J.J. Beals & Co., Iron Dial, Roman Numerals, Moon Hands, Weight Driven, 35 x 10 In.	605
Banjo, Lyre Front, Painted Metal Dial, Roman Numerals, Brass Bezel, American, 41 In.	1089
Banjo, Mahogany, Arched Top, Turned Finial, Metal Dial, Roman Numerals, 33 x 11 In.	303
Banjo, Mahogany, Gilt, Patriotic Theme, Eagle Finial, Original Pendulum, 1925, 42 x 10 In.	2160
Banjo, Mahogany, Painted Metal Dial, Roman Numerals, Inset Throat Panel, 40 x 11 In.	273
Banjo, Mahogany, Painted Metal Dial, Roman Numerals, Weight Driven, American, 1900s, 32 x 10 In.	605
Banjo, Mahogany, Roman Numerals, Brass Pendulum, 1900s, 29 x 12 In.	510
Banjo, R. Tosely, Painted Glass Panels, Black & Gold, Metal Dial, Roman Numerals, 33 x 11 In.	212
Banjo, Reverse Painted Panel, Aurora, Brass, Giltwood, Roman Numerals, 39¾ x 10 In.	1230
Banjo, S. Willard, Mahogany Veneer, Gilt Rope Twist & Drops, Marked Dial, c.1820, 40 In.	960
Biedermeier, Shelf, Temple, Onyx Columns, Urn Top, Dolphins, Enamel Dial, 1800s, 23 x 11 In.	738
Biedermeier, Shelf, Temple, White Onyx Columns, Ebonized Dial, Eagle, Putti, 1800s, 23 x 13 In.	677
Black Forest, Cuckoo, Carved, Oak Leaves, Roman Numerals, c.1900, 17½ x 13 In. *illus*	665
Black Forest, Regulator, Wall, Pierced, Carved, Porcelain Dial, Miniature, 15 x 7 In.	726
Blinking Eye, Blackamore, Animated, Playing Street Organ, Porcelain Dial, 18 x 13 In.	4840
Bracket, Brass, Red Boulle Inlay, Bronze Warrior Figure, Flower Finials, 44 x 24 x 10 In.	5445
Bracket, Caldwell, J.E., Chinese Chippendale, Mahogany, Gilt Tombstone Dial, 1880, 29 x 15 In.	4500
Bracket, Daft, Thomas, Mahogany, Bronze, Scroll Feet, Marked, 1788, 23 x 14 x 8 In.	8845
Bracket, Hepplewhite, Mahogany, Pillar & Scroll, Painted Dial, Weight Driven, 29 x 16 In.	240
Bracket, Regency, Ebonized, Brass Inlay, Arched, Leaves, Ball Feet, J. Howden, Edinburgh, 20 In.	625
Bracket, Rosewood, Gothic Arch, Silvered Dial, Roman Numerals, 1 Fusee, 10 x 7 In.	2299
Bracket, Triple Fusee, Silvered Dial, Brass Backplate, Applied Filigree Spandrel, 19 x 12 In.	2723
Bracket, Winterhalder & Hofmeier, Silvered Dial, Blued Hands, Brass Backplate, 28 x 17 In.	1936
Bracket, Winterhalder & Hofmeier, Silvered Dial, Brass Plate, Gilt Filigree Spandrel, 19 x 12 In.	484
Brillie, Electric, Oak, Glass, Marble Back, Enamel Dial, Roman Numerals, 1930s, 18 x 13 In.	484
Bristol, Shelf, Wood, Round, Rectangular Base, 14¾ In.	117
Carriage, Aesthetic, Champleve, Black Roman Numerals, Sub Alarm Dial, 6 x 4 In.	5143
Carriage, Bourdin, Grande Sonnerie, Porcelain Dial, Spring Driven, Alarm, 6½ x 4 In.	5143
Carriage, Brass, Beveled Glass, Chime, 5 x 3¾ In.	720
Carriage, Brass, Engraved Dial, Hour Repeater, Strike Mechanism, 7 x 4 In.	484
Carriage, Brass, Gilt, Oval, Porcelain Dial, Sub Alarm, Lever Escapement, 6 x 5 x 4 In.	726
Carriage, Brass, Gilt, Roman Numerals, 2 Sub Dials, Calendar, Spring Driven, 6½ x 4 In.	1029
Carriage, Brass, Polished, Thermometer, Rhinestone Bezel, Hinged Handle, 6¾ x 5 x 3½ In.	787
Carriage, Brass, Silvered Filigree, Hour Repeater, Porcelain Dial, Sub Alarm Dial, 7 x 4 In.	424
Carriage, Caldwell, J.E., Gilt, Porcelain Dial, Hour Repeater, Roman Numerals, 5 x 4 In.	1452

Clewell, Vase, Copper Clad, High Shoulders, 10½ x 7⅞ In.
$570

Thomaston Place Auction Galleries

Clock, Animated, Bollard, Silvered & Bronze, Thermometer, Barometer, Compass, 1800s, 20 In.
$9,440

Cottone Auctions

Clock, Ansonia, 2 Women, Art & Commerce, 8-Day Time & Strike, Gong, 1890s, 20 x 25 In.
$1,045

Cowan's Auctions

Clock, Ansonia, Porcelain, Brass, Glass, Purple, Flowers, Blue, Yellow, c.1890, 17 ¾ x 9 In.
$1,386

Morphy Auctions

Clock, Ansonia, Swing, 2 Women, Huntress & Fisher, 8-Day Movement, c.1900, 25 In.
$3,480

Cowan's Auctions

Clock, Ansonia, Swing, Figure, Arcadia, 8-Day Movement, c.1905, 31 ½ In.
$6,150

Cowan's Auctions

Clock, Black Forest, Cuckoo, Carved, Oak Leaves, Roman Numerals, c.1900, 17 ½ x 13 In.
$665

James D. Julia Auctioneers

Clock, Castle, Wendell, Model, Lunar Eclipse, Bronze, Patina, 1990, 23 x 6 In.
$5,313

Rago Arts and Auction Center

Clock, Hermle, Queensway, Shelf, Wood, Triple Key Wind, 29 ¾ x 10 ½ In.
$288

Morphy Auctions

TIP
An original, old stained clock dial is more valuable than a new repainted dial.

Carriage, Drocourt, Rococo, Bronze, Gilt, Blue, Pink, Putti, Cornucopia, 9½ x 5½ In.	9680
Carriage, Enamel, Gilt, Flowers, Scrolls, Bronze, France, c.1950, 6½ x 3 In.	2750
Carriage, Jacot Henri, Brass, Gilt, Porcelain Dial, Lever Escapement, Gong, France, 6¼ x 4 In.	908
Carriage, Porcelain Dial, Hour Repeater, Spring Driven, Platform Lever Escapement, 7 x 5 In.	3933
Carriage, Porcelain Dial, Platform Lever Escapement, Gilt Brass Back, 6¾ x 4¾ In.	1150
Carriage, Rococo Figural, Hour Repeater, Gilt Bronze Case, Porcelain Dial, Coiled Gong, 9½ x 6 In.	8773
Cartel, Louis XIV Style, Bronze, Pinecones, Oak Leaf Swags, France, c.1875, 25 x 13 In.	625
Cartel, Louis XV Style, Gilt Bronze, Putti Masks, Urn, Bellflower Finial, 1800s, 48 In.	2640
Cartel, Louis XV Style, Wood, Red Paint, Flower Accents, Gilt Mounts, 12½ x 6½ In.	480
Cartier, Engraved Brass Dial, Porcelain Insets, Roman Numerals, 9½ x 6 In.	666
Castle, Wendell, Model, Lunar Eclipse, Bronze, Patina, 1990, 23 x 6 In. .... *illus*	5313
Chelsea, Desk, Filigree, Silvered Dial, 9½ x 9 x 3½ In.	1089
Chelsea, Ship's Bell, Tambour No. 3, Copper Bronze, Bowed Silver Dial, Ball Feet, c.1917, 10 In.	984
Chelsea, Ship Strike, Brass, 1900s, 5½ In.	270
Cole, James, Mirror, Concave Metal Dish, Roman Numerals, Brass Rosettes, 29 x 14 In.	605
Crystal Ball, World Time, Celluloid Dial, 6 Sub Dials, 8-Day, Swill Lever, Pin Pallet, 5 In.	484
Cuckoo, Wood, Bones, Voodoo, Marked Poppo On Face, 1900s	24
Dunning, J.N., Gallery, Mahogany, Round Dial, Hinged Door, Roman Numerals, c.1830, 37 In..	4250
Dwarf, Brass, Roman Numeral, Glazed Waist Door, Chimes, Bracket Feet, 49 In.	185
Eureka, Electric, 1000-Day, Roman Numerals, Spade Hands, Gilt Brass Bezel, 11 x 7 In.	1936
Eureka, Electric, Glass Dome, Porcelain Dial, Brass Bezel, Magnetic Plate, 1906, 15 x 8 In.	1815
Eureka, Regulator, Crystal, Oak, Beveled Glass, Porcelain Dial, Roman Numeral, 14 x 8 In. ...	1815
Farcot, Porcelain Dial, Musical Putti, Platform Lever Escapement, Marble Base, 6½ x 7 In.....	545
Farcot, Porcelain Dial, Stylized Roman Numerals, Strike Mechanism, 16 x 5¾ In................	968
Farmer, Edward, Shelf, Chinoiserie, Jade, 2 Vases, Scrolls, Gilt Openwork, c.1925, 7 x 6 In.	8750
Fehrenbach, Black Slate, Classical Form, Marbleized Columns, Brass Trim, 1800s, 13 x 14 In..	125
Figural, Elephant, Seated, On Barrel, Scrolled Legs, Rocaille Base, 1800s, 22 x 16 In.	2829
Figural, Putto, Shell, Frog, Bird, Louis XVI Style, Bronze, Gilt, Patinated, c.1790, 11 In.	1625
French, Diorama, Store Fronts, Bail Handle, Provincial, 1800s, 18 x 23 In................................	336
French, Garniture Set, Agate, Marble, Beehive Form, 13 x 12 In., 3 Piece....................	205
French, Gilt Bronze, Guilloche Panels, Erato With Bird & Cherub, Laurel Swags, 21 In.	1063
French, Gilt Bronze, Pagoda Top, Swags, Leaves, Medallions, Serpent Handle, 8¾ In.	1750
French, Gilt, Patinated Bronze, Atlas Holding Glass Dial, Swan Neck, 1810, 4 x 7½ In.	2375
French, Mixed Wood, Shaped, Ebonized, Inlaid, Delzers Fils, Saint-Flour, c.1900, 19 x 20 In. ..	96
G. Rohde, Electric, Zebrawood, Celluloid, Chrome, Herman Miller Label, 1935, 5 x 10 In.	563
George Nelson, Electric, Desk, Pill, Walnut, Turned, Stained, Enameled Metal, Quartz, c.1954, 7 x 6 In.	1125
Gilbert, Crystal Regulator, Porcelain Dial, Onyx Top, Brocot Escapement, 14 x 9 x 5¼ In.	424
Gilt Bronze, Mounted Blanc De Chine, Soft Paste, Buddha & Tole Base, 1800s, 13 x 12 In.	938
Gravity, Sawtooth, Wood, Carved, Acanthus Crest, Gadrooned, Round Face, Brass Rod, 27 In.	138
Gustav Becker, Regulator, Silvered Brass Dial & Bezel, Roman Numerals, Vienna, 62 x 20 In.	545
Hermle, Queensway, Shelf, Wood, Triple Key Wind, 29¾ x 10½ In. .... *illus*	288
Herschede, Silvered Dial, Incised Numerals, Spring Driven, Lever Escapement, 15 x 30 In.	182
Howard Miller, Asterisk, Yellow, Battery, G. Nelson, 1900s, 10 In.	270
Howard Miller, Spike, G. Nelson, 1900s, 19 In.	660 to 840
Howard Miller, Walnut, Enamel, Round, Concave, Model 2203, G. Nelson, 1900s, 11 In.	438
Howard, E., Marble Face, Wood, Gallery, Roman Numerals, Anchor Escapement, 35 x 54 In. ..	5143
Howard, E., Regulator, Metal Dial, Anchor Escapement, Ebonized Pendulum, 33 x 15 In........	3630
Howard, E., Regulator, Metal Dial, Roman Numerals, Moon Hands, 38 x 13 In.	7865
Howard, E., Regulator, Painted Metal Dial, Blued Spade Hands, Marked, 42 x 21 In.	4538
Howard, E., Regulator, Pendulum, Painted Metal Dial, Roman Numerals, 35 x 18 In.	3933
Howard, E., Regulator, Wall, Painted Metal Dial, Anchor Escapement, 32 x 16 In.....................	1513
Howard, E., Yacht Wheelhouse, Oak, Round, Painted Zinc Dial, Roman Numerals, 8-In. Dial.	1694
Imperial, Regulator, Painted Metal Dial, Sub Seconds, Electric Movement, 42 x 19 In...............	242
Ingraham, 2 Paper Dials, Roman Numerals, Perpetual Calendar, 22 x 13 x 5½ In.................	726
Ithaca, Calendar, Double Dial, Walnut & Ebony, Beveled Glass, Pendulum, Key, 19 x 10 In.	1920
Japy Freres, 2-Tone Gilt, Patinated, Erato Holding Lyre, Spring Driven, 19 x 28 x 8 In.	3933
Japy Freres, Cartel, Oak, Carved, Lion's Head, Grapes, c.1885, 26 x 19 In. .... *illus*	313
Japy Freres, Crystal Regulator, Champleve Bezel, Brass Dial, Roman Numerals, 15 x 9 In.	2178
Japy Freres, Figural, Native Princess, Gilt Bronze, Napoleon III, c.1850, 16 x 14 In. .... *illus*	4270
Japy Freres, Porcelain Dial, Roman Numerals, Spring Driven, Pendulum, 1890s, 35 x 13 In...	726

Clock, Japy Freres, Cartel, Oak, Carved, Lion's Head, Grapes, c.1885, 26 x 19 In. $313

New Orleans Auction Galleries

Clock, Japy Freres, Figural, Native Princess, Gilt Bronze, Napoleon III, c.1850, 16 x 14 In. $4,270

Neal Auction Co.

Clock, Japy Freres, Shelf, Blue Opaline Glass, Porcelain Dial, 1800s, 12 x 7 In. $427

Neal Auction Co.

Clock, Knox, Archibald, Liberty & Co., Magnus, Silver, Enamel, Cymric, 1903, 6 x 4 In.

$43,750

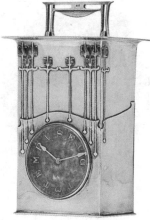

Rago Arts and Auction Center

Clock, Knox, Archibald, Liberty & Co., Pewter, Enamel, Copper, Tudric, c.1905, 8 x 5 ½ In.

$3,250

Rago Arts and Auction Center

Clock, Shelf, Empire, Figural, Woman, Standing, Porcelain Face, Urn, Anchor, c.1810, 17 x 13 In.

$660

Cowan's Auctions

Japy Freres, Portico, Leafy, Porcelain Dial, Roman Numerals, France, 19 x 9 ½ x 5 ¼ In.	146
Japy Freres, Regulator, Crystal, Shelf, France, 11 ¾ In.	138
Japy Freres, Shelf, Blue Opaline Glass, Porcelain Dial, 1800s, 12 x 7 In. .... *illus*	427
Japy Freres, Shelf, Bronze, Cast, Black, Shakespeare, Seated, 16 x 20 In.	383
Japy Freres, Shelf, Sphinx, Metal Dial, Enamel Numerals, Urn, 19 x 14 x 8 In.	666
Jugendstil, Wrought Iron, Cylindrical, Brass Roman Numerals, Pendulum, Key, 8 x 13 In.	108
Junghans, Westminster Chime, Brass Pendulum, Silvered Dial, Black Hands, 20 x 14 In.	1029
Knox, Liberty & Co., Archibald, Magnus, Silver, Enamel, Cymric, 1903, 6 x 4 In. .... *illus*	43750
Knox, Liberty & Co., Archibald, Pewter, Enamel, Copper, Tudric, c.1905, 8 x 5 ½ In. ...... *illus*	3250
LeCoultre, Atmos, Brass, Glass, Chapter Ring, Torsion Pendulum, c.1990, 9 ½ x 8 ¼ In.	840
Lyre, Girandole, Metal Dial, Roman Numerals, Weight Driven, 47 x 15 In.	4235
Lyre, Mahogany, Carved, Leaves, Eagle Finial, Painted Dial, Brass Movement, 42 x 11 In.	4800
Marble, White Alabaster Dial, Brass Ring, Figural Bird, Slate Base, 13 x 30 x 9 In.	236
Marti Et Cie, Regulator, Gilt Bronze Putto, Columns, Silvered Dial, Glass Panels, 21 In.	1625
Mystery, Jefferson, Golden Hour, Glass Face, Floating Hands, Electric, 9 x 7 ½ In.	96
Mystery, Junghans, Swinging Arm, Boy, Spelter, Vintage Garments, Gridiron Pendulum, 16 In.	1089
Mystery, Junghans, Swinging Arm, Spelter Figure, Gridiron Pendulum, Gilt Brass Ribbon, 14 In.	484
Mystery, Lyre, Bronze Ormolu, Urns, Swags, Cobalt Blue Porcelain, Jeweled Bezel, 24 x 10 In.	6353
Mystery, Mermaid, Gilt, Rotating Counterweight, Silvered Ring, Marble Base, Devon, 10 x 8 In.	666
Mystery, Portico, 4 Columns, Bronze Dore, Inverted Gridiron Pendulum, 20 x 9 ½ In.	5143
Mystery, Swinging Arm, Glaneuse, Holding Pendulum, Porcelain Dial, Roman Numerals, 27 In.	1513
Mystery, Swinging Arm, Idylls Of Spring, Spelter Figure, Tree Trunks, Rouge Marble, 28 In.	5143
Mystery, Woman, Spelter, Spring Garments, Holds Torsion Pendulum, Nest, 28 x 11 In.	6050
New Haven, Steeple, Mahogany, 1800s, 18 ¾ In.	50
Novelty, Silver, Enamel, Scenic Story Panels, Domed Base, Eagle Finial, 8 ½ x 3 In.	3630
Overglaze, Children, Wolf, Leaves, 1800, 11 In.	492
Portico, Architectural, Porcelain Dial, Spiral Columns, Marquetry Base, 1800s, 8 x 17 In.	156
Portico, Ebonized Case, Abalone & Gilt, Onyx Columns, Flowers, 1800s, 25 In.	313
Portico, Empire Style, Mahogany, Gilt Bronze Columns, Fan & Pendulum Dial, 19 In.	3250
Portico, Mahogany, Fire Gilt Ormolu Mounts, 8-Day Time & Strike, 1800s, 19 x 10 In.	660
Portico, Napoleon III, Ebonized, Brass Columns, Bell, c.1810, 18 x 10 In.	244
Portico, Neoclassical, White, Silvered Dial, Roman Numerals, France, 21 ¾ x 11 x 6 In.	146
Portico, Rose Marble, Gilt, Chain, Suspended Sun King Pendulum, 1900, 13 x 7 ½ In.	339
Pyramid, Slate Case, Marble, Cast Bird, Silvered Diamond, 11 x 16 x 4 ¼ In.	295
Regulator, Black Metal Dial, Gold Painted Roman Numerals, Anchor Escapement, 46 x 16 In.	7260
Regulator, Calendar, Exposed Brocot Escapement, Gridiron Pendulum, Steel Bell, 15 x 9 In.	1815
Regulator, Crystal, Gold Dore Filigree Case, Black Numbers, Mercurial Pendulum, 14 x 8 In.	182
Regulator, Crystal, Marble, Brass, 2 Porcelain Dials, Calendar, Open Moon Hour, 17 x 10 In.	7260
Regulator, Onyx, 2 Columns, Silvered Dial, Sweep Seconds Hand, Electric, 9 ¾ x 6 In.	4840
Regulator, Oval, Brass, Porcelain Dial, Roman Numerals, Jeweled Pallets, French, 19 x 8 In.	605
Regulator, Pinwheel, Porcelain Dial, Roman Numerals, Brass Bezel, Iron Dust Box, 96 x 27 In.	1634
Regulator, Pinwheel, Wall, Jewelers, Walnut, Brass, Porcelain Dial, Moon Hands, 92 x 26 In.	5748
Regulator, Porcelain Dial, Roman Hour Numerals, Brass Bezel, Vienna, Horseshoe Hallmark, 53 x 18 In.	3328
Regulator, Vienna, Wall, Gold Dial, Pendulum, Decals, Cherubs, 3-Weight, 52 x 18 In.	960
Regulator, Wag-On-Wall, Walnut, Marked GB, Germany, 40 x 16 In.	240
Regulator, Wall, Burl Walnut, 2-Weight, Pendulum, Key, 49 x 17 In.	330
Regulator, Wall, Rectangular, Angular Cornice, Glass Over Face & Pendulum, 1900s, 55 x 18 In.	120
Regulator, Walnut, 3-Weight, Striking Gong, c.1900, 53 x 16 In.	384
Regulator, Walnut, Carved, Porcelain Dial, Glass Door, c.1870, 92 x 34 In.	3660
Self-Winding Co., Gallery, No. 10, Oak, Painted Metal Dial, Spring Driven, 1884, 33 x 20 In.	605
Seth Thomas, Bank, Oak, Scrolled Brackets, Painted Dial, c.1895, 30 x 43 In.	1952
Seth Thomas, Lincoln, No. 16, Lyre, Paper Dial, Roman Numerals, Weight Driven, 28 x 17 In.	363
Seth Thomas, Mahogany, 30 Wooden Weights, Reverse Painted Panel, 1820, 30 x 14 In.	450
Seth Thomas, Porcelain Dial, Roman Numerals, Brass Bezel, Beveled Crystal, 16 x 22 In.	363
Seth Thomas, Regulator, Crystal, Brass, Gold Wash, Porcelain Dial, Mercury Pendulum, 1910, 12 In.	110
Seth Thomas, Regulator, School, Drop Box, Open Case, Pendulum, Key, 23 x 15 In.	84
Seth Thomas, Rosewood, 2 Gilt Columns, Eglomise Panel, Rose, 2 Glazed Doors, 32 x 19 In.	300
Seth Thomas, Shelf, Double Dial, Painted Metal, Spade Hands, Silvered Bezel, 1875, 32 x 16 In.	1392
Seth Thomas, Shelf, Walnut, Arched Cornice, Brass Bell, 3 Finials, Southern Calendar, 31 In.	767
Seth Thomas, Wall, Gallery, Santa Fe Railway System, Oak, Round, Hinged, Beveled Glass, 25 In.	900

Clock, Shelf, French Restauration, Sailor, Gilt Bronze, Suspension Movement, c.1835, 17 In.
$500

New Orleans Auction Galleries

Clock, Shelf, Liberty & Co., Pewter, Copper, Enamel, Stamped, Tudric, c.1910, 7 x 4 In.
$1,375

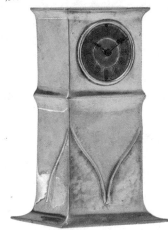

Rago Arts and Auction Center

Clock, Shelf, Louis Philippe, Gilt Bronze, Figural, Sultana, Leaves, Scrolls, c.1835, 21 x 16 In.
$1,000

New Orleans Auction Galleries

Clock, Tall Case, Aaron Willard, Mahogany, 3 Brass Finials, Boston, c.1790, 98 In.
$9,450

Leslie Hindman Auctioneers

Clock, Tall Case, Foster Campos, Grandmother, Maple, Pembroke, Mass., 1900s, 60 x 13 In.
$630

Leslie Hindman Auctioneers

Clock, Tall Case, G. Oves, Federal, Cherry, Tiger Maple, 8-Day, Lebanon, Pa., 96 In.
$5,015

Hess Auction Group

Clock, Tall Case, Herschede, Mahogany, Gilt & Silvered Dial, Moon Dial, 9 Tubes, c.1910, 101 In.
$4,500

Cowan's Auctions

83

Clock, Tall Case, Joshua Wilder, Mahogany, Painted Ship, Hingham, Mass., c.1810, 88 In.
$10,710

Leslie Hindman Auctioneers

Clock, Tall Case, S. Mulliken, Chippendale, Arched Hood, Brass Dial, 8-Day, Pendulum, 83 In.
$3,900

Brunk Auctions

Shelf, 2 Male Figures, Oval Base, Spring Driven Movement, 1800s, 14 x 7¾ x 4¾ In.	480
Shelf, Acanthus, Enameled, Arabic & Roman Numerals, France, 1800s, 33 x 23 x 11 In.	5938
Shelf, Alabaster, Gilt Bronze, Neoclassical Table Form, Columns, France, 13 x 7½ In.	720
Shelf, Alabaster, Ormolu, White Enamel Dial, Time Only Movement, 1880, 11 x 7¼ In.	540
Shelf, Animated Cupid, Porcelain Dial, Roman Numerals, Strike Mechanism, France, 18 x 11 In.	2420
Shelf, Art Deco, Onyx, Granite, Marble, Geometric, Continental, 1900s, 8¼ x 17 In.	60
Shelf, Black Copper Finish, Granite Top, Brass Works, 8-Day, Roman Style, 11 x 18 In.	120
Shelf, Brass, Pierced Case, Porcelain Chapter Ring, 1800, 16 In.	234
Shelf, Bronze, Gilt, Acanthus, Leafy Scrolls Over All, Urn Finial, 1900s, 29 x 16 x 9 In.	4920
Shelf, Bronze, Gilt, Blue Porcelain, Dial With Calendar, France, 1820, 14 x 6 In.	4375
Shelf, Bronze, Gilt, Farmer, Horse, c.1890, 15 x 16 In.	671
Shelf, Bronze, Gilt, Sailor, Anchor, Paddles, Barrel Feet, Paris, c.1810, 14 x 12 x 4 In.	12500
Shelf, Bust, Algerian Gypsy Woman, Winged Crown, Coins, Time Is Money, Spelter, 26 x 15 In.	1260
Shelf, Cathedral, Gothic Spires, Pierced Steeple, Gilt & Silvered Bronze, c.1830, 24 In.	1750
Shelf, Champleve Decoration, Porcelain Dial, Arabic 5-Minute Markers, Brass Bezel, 9 In.	787
Shelf, Chariot, Goat Pulled, Cherubs, Bronze, Gilt, Pink Band, 20 In.	10455
Shelf, Corchia & De Harak, Aurora, Aluminum, Tubular, Rotating Filters, 8¼ x 5¼ In.	146
Shelf, Empire Style, Patinated Metal, Gilt Mask, Torches, Owls, Pinecone Finial, 19 In.	938
Shelf, Empire, Figural, Woman, Standing, Porcelain Face, Urn, Anchor, c.1810, 17 x 13 In. *illus*	660
Shelf, Empire, Marble, Ormolu, Bronze Cylinder Movement, Urns, Pendulum, 16 In.	276
Shelf, Empire, Silk Thread, Silvered Dial, Animated Cupid Figure, France, 17 x 7 In.	1573
Shelf, Enameled Features, Bronze Base, Stepped Foot, Rounded Top, Tiffany & Co., 10 In.	9075
Shelf, Farmer Couple, Gilt Metal, Cylindrical Dial, White Onyx Base, 1900s, 11 In.	150
Shelf, Federal Style, Mahogany, Carved Crest, Brass Finials, Wood Pendulum, Mass., 37 x 14 In.	726
Shelf, Figural, Cleopatra, Art Nouveau, Marked, Goldscheider, 24 x 10 x 26 In.	842
Shelf, French Restauration, Sailor, Gilt Bronze, Suspension Movement, c.1835, 17 In. *illus*	500
Shelf, Lepine, J., Calendar, Brass, Columns, Glass, Porcelain Dial, 2 Engraved Sub Dials, 15 In.	1573
Shelf, Liberty & Co., Pewter, Copper, Enamel, Stamped, Tudric, c.1910, 7 x 4 In. *illus*	1375
Shelf, Louis Philippe, Bronze, Patinated & Gilt, c.1830, 16 x 9½ In.	1500
Shelf, Louis Philippe, Gilt Bronze, Figural, Sultana, Leaves, Scrolls, c.1835, 21 x 16 In. *illus*	1000
Shelf, Lyre, Marble, Bronze, Porcelain Dial, Calendar Ring, Pinwheel Escapement, 21 x 9 In.	3630
Shelf, Lyre, Marble, Rhinestone Bezel, Black Numbers, France, 17 In.	1210
Shelf, Mahogany Veneer, Reverse Painted, Painted Dial, Paw Feet, 1830, 28 x 17 In.	281
Shelf, Mahogany, Porcelain Dial, Silvered Bezel, Battery Operated, 1902, 17 x 12 x 7¾ In.	3328
Shelf, Marble, Black Slate Case, Silvered Dial, Battery Operated, 15 x 15 x 4 In.	354
Shelf, Marble, Brass Ormolu Mount, Filigree Finials, Garland, Porcelain Dial, 17 x 8 In.	303
Shelf, Marble, Bronze, Woman, Playing Lute, Rouge Plinth Base, Lion's Head, 20¾ In.	3465
Shelf, Marble, Eagle, Serpent, c.1850, 13 x 15¾ In.	390
Shelf, Marble, Woman, Ball, Black Slate Case, France, 15 x 15 x 4 In.	146
Shelf, Movado, Spinning, Brushed Aluminum, 6¼ x 3¼ x 1¼ In.	30
Shelf, Munger & Benedict, Painted Metal Dial, Acanthus Columns, Weight Driven, 38 x 22 In.	847
Shelf, Porcelain, Enameled Scene & Beading, Domed Top, Corner Finials, France, 13 In.	363
Shelf, Porcelain, Floral Case, Roman Numerals, 8-Day Time & Strike, 17 In.	246
Shelf, Rectangular, Geometric Design, Marble, Silver Dial, 17 x 19 x 4¾ In.	531
Shelf, Reverse Painted, Andrew Jackson, Rectangular, 25 In.	81
Shelf, Rococo, Exotic Wood, Putti, Scrolls, Lion Mask Handles, Paw Feet, Germany, c.1850, 13 In.	100
Shelf, Slate, Leafy Scroll, Stone Decoration, Inscribed, James Rankin, c.1890, 13 In.	238
Shelf, Tower, Pagoda Finial, Metal, Porcelain Dial, Soldier Nods, Woman Waves, 1850s, 10 In.	345
Shelf, Winged Cupid Figure, Porcelain Dial, Roman Numerals, Convex Crystal, 20 x 19 In.	5445
Shelf, Wood, Peaked, Carved, Pillars, Brass Dial, Finial, Musical Alarm, Germany, c.1880	1800
Silver Gilt, Enamel, Jeweled Elephant, Oval Base, Marked R, 1800, 9¼ In.	6150
Skeleton, Brass Dial, Incised Roman Numerals, Single Chain Fusee, 19 x 14 In.	787
Skeleton, Brass, Silvered Chapter Ring, Wood Base, Glass Dome, France, c.1885, 16 In.	1125
Skeleton, Brass, Wood Base, Silvered Dial, Striking Alarm, Pendulum, Key, 12 In.	1020
Skeleton, Great Wheel, 10 Spokes, Brass, Alabaster, Beaded, Porcelain Ring Dial, 12 x 8 In.	2057
Skeleton, LeCoultre, Brass, Fluted Frosted Glass, 12 Pyramids For Numerals, 8 x 6½ In.	575
Skeleton, Triple Dial, Silk Thread Suspension, Brocot Escapement, Roman Numerals, 10 In.	1331
Skeleton, Water Wheel, Glass Dial, Rosewood Base, Graham Deadbeat Escapement, 18 x 18 In.	908
Spelter, Figural Woman, 4 Brass Feet, Diamond Shaped Dial, 18 x 19 x 4 In.	413
Square, Cream, Matte, Silver, Gold Case, Caliber Cut Rubies, 1935	6250

Stone Dial, Deer, Marble Base, Plaque, 1958, 11 x 27 x 4 In.	413
Tall Case, Aaron Willard, Mahogany, 3 Brass Finials, Boston, c.1790, 98 In. .... *illus*	9450
Tall Case, Arched Cornice, Figural Scenes, Architectural Elements, 1800s, 84 x 20 In.	800
Tall Case, B. & W. Morice, Mahogany, Painted Iron Dial, 2 Sub Dials, 8-Day, London, 84 In. ...	605
Tall Case, Bronze Mounted, Figural Man's Head, Glass Panel, Pendulum, 28 x 11 In.	545
Tall Case, Cherry, Pine, Fretwork Bonnet, 30-Hour, Columns, New England, c.1785, 85 In.	660
Tall Case, Cherry, Tombstone Door, Moon Dial, 8-Day, c.1810, 83 x 16 In.	761
Tall Case, Chippendale, Walnut, Brass Works, Pennsylvania, 1700, 94 In.	2903
Tall Case, Columns, Brass Spandrels, Roman Numerals, Hour Strike Movement, 1800, 89 In.	369
Tall Case, Comtoise, Brass Works, 8-Day Movement, France, 1998, 92 In.	246
Tall Case, Fluted, Calendar Sub Dial, Wooden Movement, 1825, 92 In.	615
Tall Case, Foster Campos, Grandmother, Maple, Pembroke, Mass., 1900s, 60 x 13 In. .... *illus*	630
Tall Case, G. Oves, Federal, Cherry, Tiger Maple, 8-Day, Lebanon, Pa., 96 In. .... *illus*	5015
Tall Case, Gazo, Rancho Bernardo, Oak, Medallion, Gilt Dial, Pendulum, 3-Weight, 1900s, 84 In..	500
Tall Case, George Hoff, Walnut, Arched Panel Door, Side Lights, Moon Phase, 1800, 97 In.	5000
Tall Case, Georgian, Mahogany, Fluted Columns, Arched Brass Dial, Canada, 1800s, 91 In.	4200
Tall Case, Georgian, Mahogany, Inlaid Fan, Shell, Brass Face, Cherubs, Crowns, c.1790, 90 In..	600
Tall Case, Gooseneck, Eagle Finial, Tombstone Glass Door, Painted Face, 91 x 20 x 11 In.	240
Tall Case, Hepplewhite, Cherry, Bonnet, Columns, Goosenecks, Tombstone Door, Red, 1800s, 86 In.	330
Tall Case, Hepplewhite, Cherry, Painted Dial, Moon Phase, c.1820, 92 x 19 In.	7500
Tall Case, Hermle, Scroll Pediment, Eagle, Gilt, Moon Phase, 3-Weight, Germany, 1900s, 90 In.	240
Tall Case, Herschede, Cherry, Serpentine Bonnet, Silvered Brass Dial, Moon Dial, c.1950, 87 In.	420
Tall Case, Herschede, Mahogany, Fluted Pilasters, Arched Pediment, Moon Dial, 1900s, 82 x 15 In..	600
Tall Case, Herschede, Mahogany, Gilt & Silvered Dial, Moon Dial, 9 Tubes, c.1910, 101 In. *illus*	4500
Tall Case, Herschede, Silvered Dial, Beveled Glass Door, Deadbeat Escapement, 99 x 26 In......	1634
Tall Case, J. Cotton, Oak, Red Lacquer, Chinoiserie, Portraits, King & Queen, England, 98 In.	3125
Tall Case, James, Webb, Mahogany, Brass, Calendar Window, Bracket Base, 85 x 25 x 9 In.......	413
Tall Case, Joshua Wilder, Mahogany, Painted Ship, Hingham, Mass., c.1810, 88 In. .... *illus*	10710
Tall Case, Mahogany, Brass Gear Time, Wood Dial, Flowers, Inset Medallion, 96 x 18 In.	354
Tall Case, Mahogany, Columns, Urn Finials, Painted Dials, Moon Phase, 1815, 22 x 11 In.	7200
Tall Case, Mahogany, Inlaid, Gilt Trim, Engraved, Brass Dial, Musical, England, 1700s, 93 In..	3600
Tall Case, Mahogany, Scrolled Pediment, Brass Finials, 8-Day, England, c.1800, 98 In.	480
Tall Case, Mahogany, Ship, Brass Works, Embossed Pendulum, Horse, Don Cossack, 1800s, 88 In....	466
Tall Case, Majestic, Model 20, Wood, Turned, Finials, Radio, Chimes On Hour, 1931, 68 x 19 In.....	360
Tall Case, Morbier, Pine, Brass Repousse Flowers, Children, Roman Numerals, 1800s, 57 In...	406
Tall Case, Oak, Carved, Calendar Dial, Striking Gong, c.1880, 99 x 21 In.	671
Tall Case, Painted, Arched Top, Ornamental Frieze, Baroque Style, American, c.1900, 92 In. ..	1125
Tall Case, Pediment, Brass Finial, Door, Eglomise Frieze, Roman Numerals, 87 x 22 In...........	492
Tall Case, Riley Whiting, Grain Painted, Red, Arched Bonnet, Cutout Feet, 1800s, 85 x 17 In...	960
Tall Case, S. Mulliken, Chippendale, Arched Hood, Brass Dial, 8-Day, Pendulum, 83 In.. *illus*	3900
Tall Case, Solomon Parke, Tiger Maple, Arched Calendar, Painted Metal Dial, 1790, 93 x 22 In.	4235
Tall Case, Synchronome, Oak, Metal Dial, Steel Pendulum, Electric Movement, 50 x 10 In......	1210
Tall Case, Synchronome, Silvered Metal Bezel & Dial, Roman Numerals, 50 x 10 In................	2057
Tall Case, T. Snow, Oak, Mahogany, Painted Dial, Farm Scene, Flowers, Bradford, c.1810, 95 In.	875
Tall Case, Tobey, Oak, Mask Crest, Bagpipers, Tavern Scene, Tiffany & Co. Dial, 102 In............	12100
Tall Case, W. Young, Nottingham, Federal, Oak, Painted Dial & Moon Phases, 92 In.	531
Tall Case, Wag-On-Wall, Cherry, Walnut, Beaded Door, Turned Feet, 1840, 88 x 19 x 11 In.	360
Tall Case, Walnut Veneer, Stepped Pediment, Arched Glazed Bonnet, Pilasters, 1800s, 87 In. ..	1046
Tall Case, Walnut, Brass, Iron Dial, Ball & Eagle, Turned Columns, c.1810, 91 x 19 In.	2340
Tall Case, Walnut, Mahogany, Ship In Landscape, Bracket Feet, c.1790, 99 x 21 In....................	28160
Tall Case, Walnut, Stepped Cornice, Arched Glazed Bonnet, Pilasters, 1700s, 23 x 11 In.	1599
Tall Case, Wm. Lister, George III, Oak, Brass Dial, Moon Phase, Signed, c.1800, 85 x 19 In.	610
Tavern, Mahogany, Painted Metal Dial, Roman Numeral, Spade Hands, Weight Driven, 36 x 14 In..	756
Telechron, Wall, Master, Type B, Oak, Metal Dial, Electric Movement, Tubular Bob, 35 x 17 In.	666
Terry, Eli, Pillar & Scroll, Painted Wood Dial, Blued Hands, Brass Pendulum Bob, 31 x 18 In. .	484
Terry, Eli, Regulator, Wall, Painted Metal Dial, Brass Plates, 33 x 15 x 4 In.	484
Terry, Henry, Mahogany, Stenciled, Reverse Painted, Wooden Works, 8-Day, c.1830, 35 In. *illus*	300

Tiffany clocks that are part of desk sets made by Louis Comfort Tiffany are listed in the Tiffany category. Clocks sold by the store Tiffany & Co. are listed here.

Clock, Terry, Henry, Mahogany, Stenciled, Reverse Painted, Wooden Works, 8-Day, c.1830, 35 In. $300

Clock, Wall, Napoleon III, Bronze Mounted, Gong, Inlay, Portrait, Louis XIV, c.1870, 54 In. $3,200

Clock, Water, Queen Anne, Brass, Oak
Supports, Tyme Flyes, Exeter, Anno Dom
1710, 29 x 9 In.
$360

Cloisonne, Jardiniere, Banners,
Dragons, Birds, Black, Blue, Pink,
9 x 14 In.
$650

Cloisonne, Smoking Tray, Rosewood,
3 Compartments, Foo Dog Finials,
13 x 13 In.
$192

Vincenti Et Cie, Lyre, Marble, Bronze Sunburst Mask, Beads, Enamel Dial, France, 17 In.	1063
Wall, Brass On Leather, Round Case, Metal Dial, Open Escapement, 1800s, 9 In.	96
Wall, Cornice Top, Rectangular, Glass Pane Door, Pendulum, 1900s, 30 x 11 In.	36
Wall, F. Weinberg, Dancer, Enameled Steel Wire, Black Dial, Electric, 1950s, 27 x 23 In.	1750
Wall, Napoleon III, Bronze Mounted, Gong, Inlay, Portrait, Louis XIV, c.1870, 54 In. *illus*	3200
Wall, Round, Pendulum, Short Post, 1900s, 21 In.	23
Wall, W. Potts, Round Dial, Roman Numerals, Pendulum, Leeds, England, 1800s	88
Water, Queen Anne, Brass, Oak Supports, Tyme Flyes, Exeter, Anno Dom 1710, 29 x 9 In. *illus*	360
Waterbury, Saranac, Wall, Walnut, Carved, Glass Door, Cranes, Gridiron Pendulum, 29 x 15 In.	242
Welch & Co., Regulator, Wall, Calendar, Walnut, Scrolls, 34½ x 14¾ In.	242
Welch, E.N., Shelf, Mahogany, Octagonal, Stencils, Coil Chime, 18 x 11 In.	240
Windmill, Animated, Conical, 4 Blades, Silvered Dial, Spring Driven, France, 19 x 6½ In.	5445

 CLOISONNE enamel was developed during the tenth century. A glass enamel was applied between small ribbons of metal on a metal base. Most cloisonne is Chinese or Japanese. Pieces marked *China* were made after 1900.

Bowl, Dome Lid, Blue Background, Red, Yellow, Dragons, Phoenix, Jade Shou Symbol, Chinese, 8 In.	908
Bowl, Swatow, Red, Underglaze Blue Design, Chinese, 3⅝ x 8 In.	308
Box, Brass, Enamel, Blue, Spiral, 1900s	72
Cachepot, Bronze, Lotus, Rockery, Bird, Diaper Ground, 10½ In.	125
Censer, Archaic Taoist Masks, Loop Handles, 3 Tapered Legs, Blue, Multicolor, 20¼ x 17½ In.	1210
Censer, Globe, 3 Lion-Head Feet, Decorated, Clouds, 1900, 4⅝ x 5⅛ In.	431
Censer, Ming Style Cauldron Form, Arched Handle, Squat Belly, Coarse Interior, 1700s, 4½ x 6¾ In.	2340
Censer, Oval, Tripod Base, Loop Handles, 4-Character Qianlong Mark On Base, 5 In.	660
Charger, 4 Dragons, Imperial Palace, Black Ground, 18 In.	218
Charger, Bronze, Peacock, Hen, Rockery, Lotus, Stand, 30¼ In.	438
Cricket Cage, Gourd Form, Chrysanthemums On Blue Ground, Cover, Horn Finial, c.1925, 5 In.	330
Egg, Silver Plated Stand, 4 In.	431
Ewer, Duck Shape, Standing, Beak Up, Chinese, 7½ In.	660
Figurine, Dragon, Turtle, Green Back, Purple Body, Multicolor Head, 1900s, 10 x 14 In.	59
Figurine, Horse, Gilt Metal, Teakwood Stand, Parade Dress, Box, Chinese, 8 x 7 In.	540
Figurine, Qilin, Mythological Horned Horse, Fire Tail, Removable Head, 6½ x 7 In.	118
Jar, Egg Shape, Gilded Silver, Red, Colorful Floral Background, Chinese, 4 In.	60
Jardiniere, Banners, Dragons, Birds, Black, Blue, Pink, 9 x 14 In. *illus*	650
Jardiniere, Bronze, Goldfish, Foo Dog Handles, Multicolor, 15½ In.	219
Jardiniere, Bronze, Playful Horse, Foo Dog Handles, Multicolor, 15½ In.	219
Jardiniere, Lotus Shape, Aquatic Decorated Base, Birds, Lily Pads, 1900s, 17 x 20 In.	2520
Planter, Wire Jade Tree, Amber Carved, Floral, Filigree Decoration, Chinese, 19 x 14 In.	424
Plaque, Perched Owl, Red, Blue, Wood Frame, J. Trippetti, 6 x 6 In.	343
Plate, Bamboo, Chrysanthemums, Butterfly, Turquoise, Japan, 1890, 11 x 11 x 1¼ In.	59
Plate, Bamboo, Chrysanthemums, Cranes, Japan, 1890, 11 x 11 x 1¼ In.	71
Rooster, Bronze, Openwork, Over Oval Box, 8½ In., Pair	688
Sake Pot, Handle, Spout, 3 Short Feet, Cherry Flowers, Petals, White, Pendant Lappets, 3¹⁄₁₆ In.	250
Smoking Tray, Rosewood, 3 Compartments, Foo Dog Finials, 13 x 13 In. *illus*	192
Smoking Tray, Rosewood, 3 Covered Compartments, Lighter, Dog Finials, c.1900, 2 x 13 In.	200
Snuff Bottle, Double Gourd, Shape, Scrolling Vine Design, Chinese, 1900, 2½ In.	277
Stirrups, Pahua Design, Yellow Ground, Inscribed, 1800s, 8 In.	120
Tray, Hen, Rooster, Chick, Pale Blue Ground, Flower Border, Japan, 11½ In.	720
Tray, Mallard Drake, In Flight, Full Moon, Gourd Seal, Flower Border, Japan, 11½ In.	1920
Umbrella Stand, Plum Blossoms, Chrysanthemums, Peonies, Black Enamel, 24 x 9¾ In.	460
Urn, Lid, Dark Green, Enamel Decorated, Goldstone Background, Phoenixes, Japan, 13 x 7 In.	666
Vase, Birds, Maple Branches, Cherry Blossoms, Chrysanthemums, Black, Japan, 10 In.	1210
Vase, Bronze, Scrolls, Blue Bands, Flowers, Red, 15¼ In.	188
Vase, Cherry Blossoms, Prunus Tree, Sky, Black Ground, c.1925, 48 In.	650
Vase, Chrysanthemums, Celadon Ground, Artist's Seal, Late 19th Century, 7½ In.	390
Vase, Dove, Branch, Flowers, Leaves, Japan, 9¾ In.	1573
Vase, Dragon, Bulbous Body, Long Neck, Gray Ground, Japan, 11 In.	180
Vase, Enamel, Black Background, 5 White Flying Cranes, Silver, Japan, 8½ In.	605
Vase, Fish, Flowers, Wireless Enamel, Dark Blue To Purple, Aichi Hayashi Saku, 10 x 6 In.	8750

C

Vase, Flowers, Red Ground, Pair, 1900s, 7 In.	156
Vase, Iznik Style, Twin Elephant Head Handles, Red Leaves, Blue, Green, Black Enamels, 9 In.	350
Vase, Landscape, Cranes, Water, Cherry Blossoms, 13 x 6 ½ In., Pair	175
Vase, Leaves, Fruit, Green, Orange Enamel, Red, Plum Blossoms, Chrysanthemums, 18 x 11 In.	9500
Vase, Lid, Leaves, Bronze Color, Japan, 1900s, 7 In.	42
Vase, Lobed, Butterflies, Dragon, Phoenix, Crane, Flowers, Diaper, Brown, Blue, 12 x 30 In.	260
Vase, Miniature, Home Shrines, Flowers On Black Background, Scrolling Wires, 2 ¾ In.	135
Vase, Slender Neck, Peony, Bush, Buds, 2 Butterflies, Blooms, Dark Blue Background, 6 In.	225
Vase, Sosuke Style, Scenes From Watanabe Seitei's Woodblock Prints, 9 ½ In. _illus_	688
Vase, Turquoise, Bamboo, Roses, Lilies, Round Base, Tall Neck, Japan, 23 In.	563
Vide Poche, Stylized Shell, Serpentine, Tray, Floral, Enamel, Bronze, 1900s, 1 x 8 x 7 ¾ In.	277

CLOTHING of all types is listed in this category. Dresses, hats, shoes, underwear, and more are found here. Other textiles are to be found in the Coverlet, Movie, Quilt, Textile, and World War I and II categories.

Christian Dior	Norman Norell	Arnold Scaasi
1947–present	1958–1972	1956–2015

Belt, 18K Gold, Diamond Peridot, Italian Leather, Judith Ripka, 1980s, 39 x 1 In.	7500
Belt, Black, Lambskin Leather, Chained, CC Logo, Chanel, Italy, 30 In.	400
Belt, Gold, Metal, Intertwined Chain, Yellow Leather, CC Logo, Chanel, 31 In.	280
Belt, Leather, Black, Gucci, Golden Square Buckle, Logo, Italy, 34 In.	120
Bloomers, Cotton, Florettes, Daisy Lace Trim, Drawstring Waist, Woman's, c.1890	485
Boots, Black, Silver, Leather, Flat, CC Logo, Chanel, Italy, Size 37.5	600
Boots, Cowboy, Layered Leather, Let'er Buck, Hearts, Woman's, 1950s, Size 7-8	6710
Boots, Leather, Embroidered, Navruz Festival, Uzbekistan, 16 In.	48
Capelet, Sable, Cowl Collar, Bias Pelts, Petal Hem, 3-Hook Closure, 1950s, 14 ½ In.	1500
Chaps, Buffalo, Wooly, Collins Prescott, Child's, 1930s-40s, 31 In. _illus_	1610
Chaps, White Wooly, Hamley	2196
Cloak, Cadet Store, Black, Wool Fabric, Red, 1915, 40 In.	118
Coat, Black Saga Mink, Band Collar, Puff Sleeves, 3 Hooks, 1980s, Size 8-10, 45 In.	750
Coat, Black, Shawl, Collar, 2 Side Slash Pockets, Pelt Cuff, 52 In.	366
Coat, Buffalo Hide, Shawl Collar, Full-Length, Authentic Frontiersman	732
Coat, Cashmere & Wool, Green, Hermes, France, Size 38	2350
Coat, Crushed Velvet, Floral Pattern, Long Jacket, Le Chateau, Canada, Woman's, 32 In.	84
Coat, Crystal Fox Trims, Slash Pockets, Horizontal Pelt Cuffs, Guard Hairs, 48 x 21 In.	838
Coat, Era Ultra Soft Fur, Sheared Muskrat, Pockets, Stand-Up Collar, Black, Woman's, 1920s, 36 In.	54
Coat, Full-Length Bear Skin, Tanned & Manufactured By National Fur, Shawl Collar	610
Coat, Full-Length, Mink, 2 Outside Pockets, 1 Inside Open Pocket	300
Coat, Full-Length, Persian Lamb, Brown, Buchara, Greece	1000
Coat, Mink, Azurine, Notched Collar, Buttons, Cream, Belle Jacob, 44 In. _illus_	254
Coat, Mink, Dark Brown, 2 Outside Pockets, Blackglama	360
Coat, Mink, Shawl Collar, Taupe Satin Lining, Hook Closure, Lunaraine, 1970s, Size 6	625
Coat, Mink, Short, Tie Closures, Label, Furs By Cahn, Nashville, 1900s, 23 In.	840
Coat, Mohair, Fox Collar, White, Raglan Sleeves, Mayfair Of Calif., 1960s, Size 8, 46 In.	625
Coat, Persian Lamb, Sable Edges, Princess Hem, Satin Lining, 42 In.	938
Coat, Sable, Vertical Pelts, Notched Collar, Cuffs, Petal Hem, Self-Tie, Size 12, 47 In.	2250
Coat, Short, Silver Fox, Shawl Collar, Hook Closure, Dolman Sleeves, Silk Lined, 1980s, Size 12 _illus_	625
Coat, Stroller, Brown Mink, Notched Collar, Flared Sleeves, Hooks, 1960s, 30 In.	2750
Coat, Tweed, No Collar, Green, Wool, Chanel, France, Size 40	1640
Costume, Patriotic, U.S. Flag, 1876 Centennial, Wool, Boy's, c. 1890, 23 In. Long _illus_	984
Dress, Capped Sleeve, Ruched Center Seam, Silk Blend, Multicolor, Celine, Size 40	113
Dress, Navy, V-Neck, Sailor Collar, Self-Tie Belt, Flowered Hem, Jean Paul Gaultier, Size S	101
Dress, Pink, Silk, Sleeveless, Mock Neck, Box Jacket, Vera Maxwell, c.1975	195
Dress, Ruffled Hem & Bust, Ribbon Tie Straps, Self-Tie Belt, Green, Dolce & Gabbana, Size 38	441

Cloisonne, Vase, Sosuke Style, Scenes From Watanabe Seitei's Woodblock Prints, 9 ½ In.
$688

Eldred's Auctioneers and Appraisers

Clothing, Chaps, Buffalo, Wooly, Collins Prescott, Child's, 1930s, 31 In.
$1,610

Allard Auctions

Clothing, Coat, Mink, Azurine, Notched Collar, Buttons, Cream, Belle Jacob, 44 In.
$254

DuMouchelles

Clothing, Coat, Short, Silver Fox, Shawl Collar, Hook Closure, Dolman Sleeves, Silk Lined, 1980s, Size 12
$625

C

New Orleans Auction Galleries

Christening Gowns

The first time a child was seen in public was for the christening ceremony. The baby was dressed up and introduced to the neighbors. By the eighteenth century, christening gowns were white. Many were embroidered, and most had matching bonnets. The expensive gowns were often used for more than one child and then handed down. Many have names and dates embroidered on the inside.

Clothing, Costume, Patriotic U.S. Flag, 1876 Centennial, Wool, Boy's, c.1890, 23 In. Long
$984

Cowan's Auctions

Dress, Sarff Zumpano, Wrap, A Line, Applique, Silk, Giraffe, Flowers, Olive Green, Size 12 .. *illus*	250
Dress, Silk Jersey Bibliotheque, Orange, Hermes, France, Size 38	890
Dress, Spaghetti Straps, Empire Waist, Bows, Side Zipper, Chiffon, Christian Dior	214
Dress, V Neck, Navy, Polka Dot, Back Zipper, Matching Buckle, Oscar De La Renta, Size 4	139
Gloves, Black, Cashmere, CC Logo, Chanel, Multicolor, Silver Glitters, 10 In.	500
Gloves, Black, Sellier Leather, Cashmere, Hermes, Gold Buttons, France, 6 ½ In.	430
Gloves, Fingerless, Beige, Tweed, Leather, Chanel, CC Logo, Size 7 ½ In.	770
Gloves, Fingerless, Black, Leather, Chanel, CC Logo, Size 8	800
Hat, Bicorner, Gold, Metal Case, British Officer, England, 1800s-1900s, 17 In.	132
Hat, Blue, Red, Tin, Star, Party Mao, 10 x 7 ½ In.	35
Hat, Cap, Ostrich Leather, Brown, Hermes, Paris, Size 58	200
Hat, Chanel, Cashmere, Silk, Wool, CC Logo, Navy Blue, Small	400
Hat, Cowboy, Felt, Stetson, Hamley & Co., Pendleton, Oregon, Cast Iron Stand, Size 7 ½ In.	730
Hat, Straw, Navy Blue, Hermes, Italy	390
Jacket, Autumn Haze, Brown, Mink, 2 Side Slash Pockets, Velvet, Silk, 32 In.	177
Jacket, Black, Gray Trim Classic, 4 Pockets, Cashmere, Coco Chanel, Italy, Size 42	700
Jacket, Fur, Gray, Linda Richards, Medium, Fits Size 2-6	550
Jacket, Leather, Biker Style, Black, Collar, Fringed Sleeves, Woman's, Size Medium, 1900	44
Jacket, Leather, Bull, Suede, Beadwork To Shoulders, Fringe, Men's, Size Large, 1900	44
Jacket, Leather, Earthtone, Tassel Fringe Lapel & Lower Body, Silver Buttons, Woman's, 1900 .	56
Jacket, Leather, Riding Style, Rope Perimeter, Tassels, Faux Bone Beadwork, 1900	163
Jacket, Nutria Stroller, Tapered Waist, Belled Sleeves, Shawl Collar, 2 Pockets, 29 x 20 In.	224
Jacket, Pockets, Leather Button, Bright Orange, Satin Lining, 1970	180
Jacket, Silk, Embroidered, Gold-Plated Coin Hooks, Chinese, 1900s, 40 x 60 In. .... *illus*	1680
Jacket, Suede, Navy, Cropped, Scalloped Hem, Front Buttons, Side Pockets, Chloe	300
Jacket, Swing, Fur, Mink, Autumn Haze, c.1950, 27 In.	214
Jacket, Tweed, Antique Rose, Chain Loop Button, Chanel, 1997, Size 34	1180
Jumpsuit, Short, Pleats, Silk, Ivory Color, Red Trim, CC Button, Chanel, France, Size 40	830
Prison Uniform, Striped Shirt, Pants, Metal Buttons Stamped N.C. Prison, c.1925, Man's	1000
Robe, Silk, Embroidered, Cherry Blossoms, Blue Damask, Forbidden Stitch, c.1900, 36 In.	660
Robe, Silk, Embroidered, Gold Threadwork, Flowers, Cream Ground, Gilt Buttons, 1880s	390
Robe, Warrior's, Peking Opera, Metallic Thread, Embroidered, c.1910, 58 In.	509
Sash, Beaded, Panel, Animal, Yoruba People, Nigeria, 52 x 7 ¼ In.	31
Scarf, Brown, Leopard Pattern, Louis Vuitton, Cashmere, Silk, France, 72 x 35 In.	398
Scarf, Mink, Champagne, Black Stripes, Tubular, 7 x 100 In.	938
Scarf, Monogram, Brown, Christian Dior, Silk, 30 x 30 In.	160
Scarf, Red, White, Silk, Huge CC Logo, Chanel, Italy, 34 x 33 In.	500
Scarf, Silk, Cashmere, Fuchsia Pink, Louis Vuitton, France, 53 x 73 In.	650
Scarf, Silk, Central Park, Laurence Bourthoumieux, Hermes, 36 x 36 In.	405
Scarf, Silk, Equateur, Parrots, Leopards, Robert Dallet, Box, 36 x 36 In.	313
Scarf, Silk, Les Folies Du Ciel, Hot Air Balloons, Dirigibles, Rope Twist Border, Hermes, 36 x 36 In.	281
Scarf, Silk, Pink, Nautical, Waves, Seashells, Circle, Parures Oceanes, Hermes, 36 x 36 In.	200
Scarf, Silk, Rayon, Pink, Gray, Beaded Fringe, Emilio Pucci, 67 x 12 In.	101
Scarf, Silk, Yellow, Black Stripes, Gold Coats Of Arms, Hermes, 36 x 36 In.	225
Shawl, Wool, Machine Woven, Hand Stitched Border, Scotland, 1800s, 126 x 55 In.	1063
Shirt, Western, Dark Rodeo Design, c.1950, 36-In. Bust, Woman's	183
Shoes, Chanel, Sandal, Chained Strap, Tan, Gold, Cork Platform, CC Logo, Italy, Size 37	430
Shoes, Leather & Wood, Brass & Iron Tacks, Brass Buckles, 1700s, 5 ½ In., Child's .... *illus*	295
Shoes, Worn By Blinko The Clown, Leather .... *illus*	510
Stole, Mink, Evening, Lined, Chocolate Silk, Hand Knotted Fringe, Nutria, 1920, 42 x 20 In. ...	118
Sundress, Cotton, Spaghetti Straps, Back Zipper, Logo Design, Chanel	284
Top, Cashmere & Silk, Beige, Hermes, France, Size Small	600
Top, Short Sleeves, Cotton Knit, Stripes, Black & Taupe, Chanel, Italy, Size 40	230
Tunic, Chief's, Green, 8 Knives Pattern, Yoruba People, Nigeria, 45 x 87 In.	120
Tunic, Nazca, Camelid, Red, Blue, Brown & Cream, Geometric Patterns, 22 x 21 In.	2100
Tunic, Nazca, Wool, Camelid, Zoomorphic, Dangling Tassel, 33 x 26 In.	1800
Uniform, Guard, Bearskin Busby, Ceremonial Tunic, Leather Belt, England, 1950s	360
Vest, Brain Tanned, Elkhide Back, Beaded, Floral Sign, Starburst, 1920s, 20 x 19 In.	600
Vest, Floral, Light Blue, Cut Beads, Velvet, Calico, 1900s, 21 x 19 In.	1500
Vest, Leather, Bold Geometric Design, Front Panels, Fringe, Patina, 1900	450

Vest, Rabbit Fur, Beige, Chanel, France, 1997, Size 38.. 1050

COALPORT ware was made by the Coalport Porcelain Works of England beginning about 1795. Early pieces were unmarked. About 1810–25 the pieces were marked with the name *Coalport* in various forms. Later pieces also had the name *John Rose* in the mark. The crown mark was used with variations beginning in 1881. The date 1750 is printed in some marks, but it is not the date the factory started. Coalport was bought by Wedgwood in 1967. Coalport porcelain is no longer being produced. Some pieces are listed in this book under Indian Tree.

| Coalport Porcelain Manufactory 1820 | Coalport Porcelain Manufactory c.1881 | Coalport Porcelain Manufactory 1960 |

Bowl, Entwined Handles, Flower Cartouches, Gilt, Green, 4¾ x 12 In. 218
Platter, Delicate, Blue, Green, Sprig Pattern, 1983, 16 x 21 x 3 In. 83
Platter, Drainer, Imari, Peonies, Gilt, Vines, Fish Scale Medallions, c.1810, 22 In. .... *illus* 780
Urn, Roses, Cobalt Blue, White Panels, Pink Roses, Latticework, 9½ x 7¼ In. 302

COBALT BLUE glass was made using oxide of cobalt. The characteristic bright dark blue identifies it for the collector. Most cobalt glass found today was made after the Civil War. There was renewed interest in the dark blue glass in the late 1930s and glass dinnerware was made.

Atomizer, Clear, Star & Bar Design, Square, 9 In... 180
Cruet, Cut To Clear, Stopper, 8 In.. 156
Flask, Decorated Moon, Rectangular Base, Greek Key Design, Leaves, Flowers, 13 x 9 In. 246
Sugar, Blown, Galleried Rim, Knop Finial, Trumpet Foot, c.1830, 8 x 4⅝ In. .... *illus* 1755
Vase, Stick Neck, Homegaard Gulvase, 1960s, 14½ In. 35

COCA-COLA was first served in 1886 in Atlanta, Georgia. It was advertised through signs, newspaper ads, coupons, bottles, trays, calendars, and even lamps and clocks. Collectors want anything with the word *Coca-Cola*, including a few rare products, like gum wrappers and cigar bands. The famous trademark was patented in 1893, the *Coke* mark in 1945. Many modern items and reproductions are being made.

Banner, Howdy Pardner, Masonite, Wood, 105 x 15 In. 1368
Bottle Opener, Drink Coca-Cola, Mounted, Brown & Starr, Pat. April 21, 1925.................... 69
Bottle, Syrup, Backbar, White Lettering, Aluminum Cap, 1920s, 12 x 3½ In. 525
Cooler, Airline, Metal, Side Mount, Bottle Opener, Red, 1950, 14½ x 18½ In. 200
Cooler, Couch, Upholstered, White Leather, Tufted, Red, Coca-Cola Buttons, 33 x 70 x 24 In. .. 1920
Cooler, Model GBV-50, 10 Cent Slider Vending Machine, Enamel, Decals, 38 x 30 x 18 In. 1200
Mannequin, Waitress, Gray, 1950s Style Dress, Apron, Brown Wig & Glasses, 68 x 20 In.......... 450
Menu Board, Drink Coca-Cola In Bottles, Menu Items, Coke Button, Masonite, 1945, 35 x 17 In. .. 575
Refrigerator, Drink Coca-Cola, Model CA-2-B16, Monitor Top, Red, G.E., 1934, 64 x 28 x 25 In. .. 2040
Sign, Girl, White Feather Hat, Green Border, Paper On Wood, 26 x 37 In. 48
Sign, Santa Claus, Things Go Better With Coke, Season's Greetings, 1900s, 56 x 40 In. .... *illus* 48
Thermometer, Girl Drinking, Silhouette, Delicious, Refreshing, 1939, 16 x 7 In. 422
Thermometer, Tin, Bottle Shape, Logo In Center, Coke On Neck, Robertson, 16 x 5 In............ 144
Tip Tray, 1903, Hilda Clark, Delicious, Refreshing, Round, Lithograph, 4 In.............. *illus* 780
Tip Tray, 1909, Exhibition Girl, Blue Dress, Summer Night Scene, 6¼ x 4½ In. 271
Tip Tray, 1914, Betty, White Hat, Pink Scarf, 6⅛ x 4⅜ In. 141
Toy, Truck, Yellow Cab, Stake Body, Decals, Wheels, Tin Lithograph, Marx, 19 In............. 210
Tray, 1938, Girl In Yellow Hat, Seated, Drink Coca-Cola, Gold Trim, 13 x 10 In. 324

Clothing, Dress, Sarff Zumpano, Wrap, A-Line, Applique, Silk, Giraffe, Flowers, Olive Green, Size 12
$250

Kaminski Auctions

Clothing, Jacket, Silk, Embroidered, Gold-Plated Coin Hooks, Chinese, 1900s, 40 x 60 In.
$1,680

Cowan's Auctions

Clothing, Shoes, Leather & Wood, Brass & Iron Tacks, Brass Buckles, 1700s, 5½ In., Child's
$295

Hess Auction Group

Clothing, Shoes, Worn By Blinko The Clown, Leather
$510

Freedom Auction Company

Coalport, Platter, Drainer, Imari, Peonies, Gilt, Vines, Fish Scale Medallions, c.1810, 22 In.
$780

Brunk Auctions

Cobalt Blue, Sugar, Blown, Galleried Rim, Knop Finial, Trumpet Foot, c.1830, 8 x 4⅝ In.
$1,755

Jeffrey S. Evans

COFFEE MILLS are also called coffee grinders, although there is a difference in the way each grinds the coffee. Large floor-standing or counter-model coffee mills were used in the nineteenth-century country store. Small home mills were first made about 1894. They lost favor by the 1930s. The renewed interest in fresh-ground coffee has produced many modern electric mills, hand mills, and grinders. Reproductions of the old styles are being made.

Arcade, Upper Jar, Lid, Crank, Wall Mount, 19 x 5 In.	143
Box, Drawer, Band Inlay, Thumb Molded Edge, Brass Hopper, Iron Handle, c.1830, 6 In.	163
Bronson-Walton Co., Old Glory Theodore Roosevelt, Cleveland, Ohio, 10½ In. *illus*	265
Enterprise, 2 Wheels, Crank, 1873, 10¾ In.	577
Enterprise, Cast Iron, Original Drawer, Black, Pinstriping, Crank Handle, 5 x 5 x 11 In.	180
Enterprise, No. 2, 2 Wheels, Red & Blue Paint, 12½ x 10 In. *illus*	600
Enterprise, No. 3, Embossed Wheels, Stencils, Wood Drawer, Eagle Finials, 15 In.	420
Enterprise, No. 216, Cast Iron, Eagle Finial, Tin Pan, 1898, 69 x 26 In.	4235
Enterprise, Red, 2 Wheels, Cast Iron Drawer, Wood Base, 14 x 10 In.	423
Enterprise, Red, White, Blue, Painted, Iron, Liberty Shield Decal, 1800s, 13 In.	390
Enterprise, Urn Shape Receptacle, 2 Wheels, Red, Cast Iron, 21 In.	338
Landers, Frary & Clark, Decals, Stencils, Drawer, Cast Iron, 12 In.	1920
Landers, Frary & Clark, No. 11, Crank Arm, Wood Base, Cast Iron Drawer, 12 x 7 In. *illus*	295
Landers, Frary & Clark, Universal No. 2, 2 Wheels, Cast Iron, Green Paint, 12½ In. *illus*	501
Mahogany, Ogee Veneer, Drawer, Brass, Molded Knob, Sandwich Glass, c.1890, 6 x 6 x 11 In.	85
Red Paint, Wood Base, Drawer & Knob, 1800s, 21 x 20 x 21 In.	300
Smokestack Hopper, Pierced Decorated, Spoked Wheels, Lane Brothers, 40 x 20 x 29 In.	2420
Swift Mill, Lane Brothers, No. 12, 2 Wheels, Cast Iron, Painted, New York, 14 In. *illus*	354

COIN SPOT is a glass pattern that was named by collectors for the spots resembling coins, which are part of the glass. Colored, clear, and opalescent glass was made with the spots. Many companies used the design in the 1870–90 period. It is so popular that reproductions are still being made.

Syrup, Lid, Green Opalescent, Applied Green Handle, c.1900, 6 In. *illus*	58

COIN-OPERATED MACHINES of all types are collected. The vending machine is an ancient invention dating back to 200 B.C., when holy water was dispensed from a coin-operated vase. Smokers in seventeenth-century England could buy tobacco from a coin-operated box. It was not until after the Civil War that the technology made modern coin-operated games and vending machines plentiful. Slot machines, arcade games, and dispensers are all collected.

Arcade, A.B.T., Billiard, The Churchill, Stained Wood, Felt, 1928, 34 x 27 x 47 In.	3998
Arcade, American Machine & Foundry, American Indy Racing, Steering Wheel, 1967, 61 x 36 In.	1680
Arcade, Bally, Hill Climb, Motorized Bike, Handlebar Grip, 1972, 74 x 27 x 44 In.	9375
Arcade, Bally, Horse Racing, Electro-Mechanical, Coin Dispenser, 1941, 69 x 26 x 60 In.	400
Arcade, Bally, Hot Rods, Racing, Shooting, Electro-Mechanical, 1949, 67 x 27 x 54 In.	480
Arcade, Bally, Marksman, Shooting, Fox, Rabbits, Farmland, 1961, 72 x 25 In.	9000
Arcade, Bally, Road Runner, Racing, Holographic Imaging, 1971, 71 x 28 In.	4613
Arcade, Baseball, Countertop, Green Cabinet, 10 x 15 x 27 In.	300
Arcade, Casino Golf, Oak Housing, Electro-Mechanical, 2-Tone Paint, 52 x 25 In.	3900
Arcade, Chester-Pollard, Play Football, Scoring Chits, 1926, 72 x 44 x 20 In.	4480
Arcade, Chicago Coin, All American Basketball, Shuffle Alley, Platform, 1967, 73 x 31 In.	2214
Arcade, Chicago Coin, Baseball, Batter Up, Moving Lights, 1958, 75 x 60 In.	4200
Arcade, Chicago Coin, Baseball, Shuffle, Animated Scoreboard, 1940, 65 x 97 In.	2160
Arcade, Chicago Coin, Goalee Hockey, Figure, Handles, 1945, 64 x 45 In.	1800
Arcade, Chicago Coin, Long Range Rifle Gallery, Wood Cabinet, 1961, 70 x 28 In.	1140
Arcade, Chicago Coin, Pistol, Shoot For Fun, Bubble Head Cabinet, 1947, 78 x 40 In.	3998
Arcade, Cragg, Gypsy Card Reader, Spooky Looking, 1942, 71 x 21 In.	6765
Arcade, Exhibit Supply Co., Love Tester, Measure Sex Appeal, Oak, c.1930, 83 In.	3300
Arcade, Exhibit Supply Co., Six Shooter, Dale Pistol, 10 Cent, 1950s, 75 x 25 In.	3300
Arcade, Exhibit Supply, Dale Gun Patrol, Shooting, World War II Theme, 1951, 75 x 25 In.	3000

C

Arcade, Exhibit Supply, Rotary Merchandiser, Digger, Crane Game, 1930s, 47 x 30 In.	660
Arcade, Exhibit Supply, Viewer, 2 Barrels, Man & Woman, 1956, 70 x 46 In.	4612
Arcade, Games Inc., Hole In One Golf, Aqua, Orange Speckles, 1957, 67 x 28 In.	492
Arcade, Genco, Baseball Hi-Fly, Skill Holes, Slots, 1956, 70 x 25 In.	6150
Arcade, Genco, Baseball Pool, Billiards Style, Illuminated, 1956, 50 x 35 x 66 In.	600
Arcade, Genco, Big Top Rifle, Wood, Carnival, Clowns, 1954, 74 x 32 In.	1560
Arcade, Genco, Davy Crocket, Shooting Rifle, Moving Target, 1956, 67 x 24 In.	922
Arcade, Genco, Sky Gunner, Shooting, Realistic Recoil Mechanism, 1953, 81 x 24 In.	4800
Arcade, Genco, Wild West, Shooting, Criss Cross Match, 1955, 75 x 31 In.	2400
Arcade, Haydon Mfg., Pussy, Shooting, Faux Brick Cabinet, Painted, 1930, 67 x 22 In.	1845
Arcade, Haydon, Clown Shooter, Original Face, Pistol A.B.T., 1920s, 68 x 23 In.	984
Arcade, Hunter, Shooting, Navy Blue, Metal Duck, Win Gumball, 18 x 9¼ In.	615
Arcade, International Mutoscope, Atomic Bomber, Viewfinder, Knobs, 1946, 86 x 24 In.	5227
Arcade, International Mutoscope, Drive Mobile, Drive Yourself, Road Test, 1941, 80 x 32 In.	4200
Arcade, International Mutoscope, Hockey, Oak, Glass, 1940, 37 x 22 x 41 In.	1560
Arcade, International Mutoscope, Sky Fighter, War Theme, 1940, 94 In.	6765
Arcade, Irving Kaye, Stanley Cup, Hockey, Wood Housing, 1960s, 35 x 84 In.	338
Arcade, License Bureau, For Amusement, Card Dispenser, Wood, Plastic, 77 x 22 In.	660
Arcade, Midway, Deluxe Shooting, Circus Theme, Retro Graphics, 1961, 64 x 25 x 67 In.	8400
Arcade, Midway, Monster Gun, Shooting, Moving & Glowing Targets, 1967, 63 x 24 In.	1440
Arcade, Midway, Twin Pirate Gun, Timed, Shooting, 1974, 72 x 30 x 35 In.	7380
Arcade, Midway, Winner, Car Race, Animated Scoreboard, 1964, 59 x 27 x 52 In.	6600
Arcade, Munves, Baseball, Bat-A-Ball, Turquoise Cabinet, 71 x 15 In.	1440
Arcade, Munves, Bike Race, 2 Players, Circular Track, 2 Wheels, 1940s, 72 x 28 In.	4305
Arcade, National Novelty, K.O. Fighters, Boxing, Interactive, 1928, 64 x 41 In.	3600
Arcade, Norwat, Miniature Steam Shovel, Crane, Oak, Aluminum, 1930s, 71 x 20 In.	4200
Arcade, Scientific Machine Corp., Basketball, Dark Green Housing, 1950s, 82 x 24 In.	720
Arcade, Scientific, Pitch 'Em & Bat 'Em, Baseball, Wood Case, 1948, 77 x 26 In.	3690
Arcade, Seeburg, Coon Hunt, Shooting, Target Cabinet, 1954, 70 x 31 x 18 In.	8400
Arcade, Sega, Lunar Rescue, Space, Explorer Car, Wood, Steel, Joystick, 1973, 74 x 30 In.	8750
Arcade, Shooting Game, Mechanical, Aluminum Hardware, Oak Case, 1930s, 17 x 10 In.	2280
Arcade, Stoner, Turf Champs, Horse Racing, Electro-Mechanical, 1936, 43 x 25 x 45 In.	3600
Arcade, United Derby, Derby Roll, Horse Race, 10 Balls, Oak Case, 1955, 73 x 25 x 81 In.	3300
Arcade, United, Carnival Gun, Shooting Game, Targets, Wood Cabinet, 1954, 73 x 44 In.	1200
Arcade, United, DeLuxe Jungle Gun, Shooting Stationary Targets, 1954, 74 x 31 In.	1875
Arcade, United, Hockey, Mechanical, Stenciled, Black Grip, 1950, 38 x 27 x 46 In.	600
Arcade, United, Midget Alley Bowling, Oak, Green Speckled Cabinet, 1958, 70 x 73 In.	3998
Arcade, United, Pirate Gun, Shooting, Wood, 1956, 71 x 29 x 38 In.	1800
Arcade, United, Sky Raider, 2 Fire Cannons, Real Gunfire Sounds, 62 x 26 In.	3600
Arcade, Viewing, Rosenfield, Sultan's Favorite, Drop Card, Oak, Gold Castings, 1906, 77 In.	1680
Arcade, W.D. Bartlett, Crane, Digger, 1931, 34 x 26 In.	3600
Arcade, Willams, Road Racer, Steering Wheel, Reaction Indicator, 1962, 69 x 24 In.	8750
Arcade, Williams Baseball, Box Score, Wood, Glass, Skill Holes, 1947, 63 x 70 In.	1353
Arcade, Williams Baseball, Double Header Shuffle Alley, Running Men, 1950, 68 x 97 In.	8610
Arcade, Williams, Be A Sidewalk Engineer, Bulldozer, Aqua Blue Cabinet, 1955, 54 x 49 In.	5625
Arcade, Williams, Touchdown, Football, Backbox Animation, 1965, 72 x 25 x 47 In.	3900
Dispenser, Cigarettes, Figural, Woman's Face, San Francisco Alfred Dunhills, 1940-50, 6¼ x 7¼ In.	210
Fortune Teller, Erickson, Ask Swami, Napkin, Dispenser, Cards, 1950s, 9 x 7½ In.	320
Fortune Teller, Exhibit Supply, Astrology, Astrologer, Fortune Cards, 1930, 85 x 26 In.	3600
Fortune Teller, Exhibit Supply, Cupid's Post Office, Oak, Cupid, Mailman, 1920s, 88 x 30 In.	5100
Fortune Teller, Exhibit Supply, Palmistry, Oak Cabinet, 2 Coin Slides, c.1930, 85 x 20 In.	4500
Fortune Teller, Exhibit Supply, Smiling Sam Vodoo Man, Animated, 1939, 78 x 22 In.	8400
Fortune Teller, Exhibit Supply, True Love Letter Post Office, 2 Coin Slides, 1920s, 78 x 20 In.	720
Fortune Teller, Genco, Gypsy Grandma, 10 Cent, Canopy, Pedestal, 1956-57, 77½ In.	4235
Fortune Teller, Himebaugh, Your Fortune Told By Astrology, Colonial Style, Oak, 70 x 47 In.	2880
Fortune Teller, Marvin & Casler, Palm Reader, Oak, Nickel Plated, 1905, 65 x 28 In.	4613
Fortune Teller, Munves, Human Analysis, Grip, Dispenses, Characteristics, 63 x 22 In.	1440
Fortune Teller, Munves, Mystic Pen, Aqua Cabinet, 1930s, 69 x 20 In.	2700
Gumball, 1 Cent, Garden City Novelty Co., c.1936, 12 x 9 In. .... illus	480
Home Billiardette, Pool Table, 4 Cue Sticks, 1931, 42 x 35 x 24 In.	4305

Coca-Cola, Sign, Santa Claus, Things Go Better With Coke, Season's Greetings, 1900s, 56 x 40 In.
$48

Garth's Auctioneers & Appraisers

Coca-Cola, Tip Tray, 1903, Hilda Clark, Delicious, Refreshing, Round, Lithograph, 4 In.
$780

Rich Penn Auctions

Coffee Mill, Bronson-Walton Co., Old Glory Theodore Roosevelt, Cleveland, Ohio, 10½ In.
$265

Hess Auction Group

Coffee Mill, Enterprise, No. 2, 2 Wheels, Red & Blue Paint, 12 ½ x 10 In.
$600

Woody Auction

Coffee Mill, Landers, Frary & Clark, No. 11, Crank Arm, Wood Base, Cast Iron Drawer, 12 x 7 In.
$295

Hess Auction Group

Coffee Mill, Landers, Frary & Clark, Universal No. 2, 2 Wheels, Cast Iron, Green Paint, 12 ½ In.
$501

Hess Auction Group

Home Billiardette, Pool Table, 5 Cent, Wood, Nickel Plated Trim, Ball, Cue, 1931, 36 x 27 In.	4095
Music Box, H.G. Vossen, Orchestrion, Oak Case, Mirrors, Glass Panel, c.1910, 94 x 55 In. *illus*	1200
Pinball, Atlas Indicator, Tango, Playing Card Theme, 1932, 38 x 15 In.	390
Pinball, Bally, Baseball, Double Header, Animated Scoreboard, 1956, 71 x 57 In.	384
Pinball, Bally, Heavy Hitter, Baseball, Animated Backbox, 1947, 55 x 38 In.	2280
Pinball, Bally, Signal, Stool Pigeon Style Ball Tilt System, Electro-Mechanical, 1934, 42 x 20 In.	369
Pinball, Chicago Coin, Bowling, King Pin, Animated Pins, 1951, 71 x 29 In.	2160
Pinball, Chicago Coin, Super Par Golf, Illuminated Back, 1965, 70 x 25 x 57 In.	6600
Pinball, Data East, Phantom Of The Opera, Electronic Marquee, 1990, 74 x 31 In.	2040
Pinball, Exhibit Supply, Samba, Dancers, Wood Cabinet, 1948, 62 x 25 In.	330
Pinball, Exhibit Supply, Short Stop, Baseball, Brass Plaque, 1940, 63 x 25 In.	960
Pinball, Genco, Golden Nugget, Showgirls, Wooden Console, 1953, 64 x 24 In.	840
Pinball, Genco, Jumpin Jack, Carnival, Vertial, Flipper, 6 Balls, Bell, 68 x 24 In.	300
Pinball, Gottlieb, Big Hit Baseball, Lighted Display, 2 Flippers, 1977, 69 x 26 In.	840
Pinball, Gottlieb, Buffalo Bill, Western Theme, 1950, 64 x 25 x 55 In.	2767
Pinball, Gottlieb, Diamond Lill, 5 Cent, Roy Parker Artwork, 1954, 61 x 25 In.	1071
Pinball, Gottlieb, Fire Queen, Fierce Woman, Lights, 1977, 63 x 28 In.	533
Pinball, Gottlieb, Guys, Dolls, Wood Rails, 1953, 67 x 25 In.	570
Pinball, Gottlieb, Hawaiian Beauty, Tropical Graphics, 1954, 65 x 54 In.	3465
Pinball, Gottlieb, Jack 'N Jill, Back Glass Animation, 1948, 68 x 26 In.	431
Pinball, Gottlieb, Roto Pool, Billiard, Electro-Mechanical, 1958, 66 x 23 In.	900
Pinball, Gottlieb, Sunshine Baseball, Hidden Payout Door, 1936, 53 x 25 In.	3000
Pinball, J.H. Keeney, Stepper-Upper, Horse Racing Theme, 1938, 67 x 26 In.	1320
Pinball, Jennings Sportsman, Woodland Landscape, Hunter, 1934, 42 x 22 In.	799
Pinball, Rock-Ola, World Series, Mechanical, Superior Housing, 1934, 49 x 19 In.	2280
Pinball, Rock-Ola, World's Fair Jigsaw Puzzle, Animated, 10 Steel Balls, 1933, 49 x 18 In.	4920
Pinball, United, Steeple Chase, Horse Racing, 1950s, 69 x 25 In.	900
Pinball, Western, Center Smash, College Football, Green, Black, 1936, 56 x 28 In.	9600
Pinball, Williams, Dealer Choice, Cards Theme, 4 Players, 70 x 30 In.	484
Pinball, Williams, Tim-Buc-Tu, Playing Cards, Saloon Theme, Single Player, 1956, 66 x 25 In.	270
Pinball, Williams, Turf Champ, Horse Racing, Race Track, 1958, 66 x 25 x 63 In.	320
Pinball, Wood Rail Platform, Electro-Mechanical, Back Glass Animation, 1937, 52 x 22 In.	600
Player Piano, Walnut, Stained Glass, Brass Coin Slot, Paper Roll Action, 1912	300
Skill, Allied Leisure, Monte Carlo, Driving, Dodging, Steering Wheel, 1973, 48 x 28 In.	2000
Skill, Caille Bros., Hygienic Exerciser, Lung Tester, Cast Iron, Marble, 1900s, 72 x 17 In.	2700
Skill, Chicago Coin, TV-Baseball, Pitcher Control Feature, 1966, 71 x 25 In.	1476
Skill, Pace, Whiz Ball, 1 Cent, Keys, c.1930, 17 x 10 In.	504
Skill, R.W. McKenney, Hi-Li, Basque, Wood Cabinet, 1932, 26 x 27 x 10 In.	2040
Skill, Science Machine, Totalizer, Basketball, 5 Cent, 21 x 13 In.	363
Slot, Art Deco, 1 Cent, Yellow, Multicolor Trim, c.1935, 21 x 12 In. *illus*	4250
Slot, Buckley, Bonanza, 5 Cent, Red, Coin Decoration, 26 x 16 In.	360
Slot, Burnham, Gum, Cast Iron, Side Dispenser, 4-Footed, 26 x 17 In.	6765
Slot, Caille Bros., Ben Hur, Gaming Wheel, Play Nickels, 1908, 22 x 16 In.	3900
Slot, Caille Bros., Naked Lady, Aluminum, 3-Reel, 1925-31, 22 x 16 In.	1920
Slot, Caille Bros., Superior Jackpot, Side Mint Vender, 3-Reel Strips, 1929, 26 x 15 In.	1680
Slot, Groetchen, Columbia, 25 Cent, Blue, Green, Silver Stripes, c.1936, 18 ½ x 15 In.	409
Slot, Groetchen, Columbia, Aluminum, Black Matte, 1930, 18 x 15 In.	540
Slot, Jennings, Chief, Brown & Gold Paint, Chief's Head Relief, c.1940, 58 x 20 In.	813
Slot, Jennings, Ciga-Rola, Spin Reels, Cigarettes, 1937-39, 60 x 19 In.	4500
Slot, Jennings, Mints Of Quality, 3-Reel Strips, Elves, 1925, 24 x 15 In.	1920
Slot, Jennings, Sun Chief, 10 Cent, Tic Tac Toe, Chief Bust, Sun Ray, c.1950, 28 In.	936
Slot, Jennings, Sun Chief, 25 Cent, 27 ½ In.	650
Slot, Mills High Top, 25 Slot, Red, Black, Yellow Stripes, 26 x 16 In. *illus*	826
Slot, Mills, 10 Cent, Tan & Red Paint, Bells, Key, c.1950, 26 x 16 In.	720
Slot, Mills, Black Beauty, Metal, 25 Cent, 1800s, 26 x 16 In	732
Slot, Mills, Blue Bell, 10 Cent, Key, c.1950, 27 x 16 In.	792
Slot, Mills, Blue Bell, 5 Cent, Blue & Red, c.1950	480
Slot, Mills, Bursting Cherry, Diamond Bell, 10 Cent, Cash Box, c.1937, 26 In.	1232
Slot, Mills, Chevron Q.T., Oak, Aluminum, Orange, Bent Coin Release, 1938, 19 x 12 In.	1230
Slot, Mills, Hightop, Dark Red, 26 x 16 In.	826

Slot, Mills, Iowa Novelty, Aluminum, Side Mint Vendor, Gooseneck Bell, 1926, 24 x 19 In.	6875
Slot, Mills, O.K., Gum Vendor, Oak Cabinet, Gooseneck Receiver, 1912, 57 x 15 In.	9225
Slot, Mills, Q.T., Aluminum, Matte Black Finish, 1934, 18 x 13 In.	1020
Slot, Mills, Roman Head, White, Blue, Aluminum Casting, 1932, 26 x 16 In.	1800
Slot, Mills, Sweetheart, 5 Cent, Gold Glitter Paint, c.1950, 19 x 13 In.	720
Slot, Mills, Thunderbird, 5 Cent, Metal, 1900s, 26 x 16 In.	1464
Slot, Mills, War Eagle, 25 Cent, Wood Cabinet, Marble Top, 1931, 24 x 14 In.	1125
Slot, Novelty, 7 Way, Multi-Bell, Chrome Detail, Jackpot Bank, 1936, 26 x 17 In.	2560
Slot, Super Mog Mog, Pachislot, Keys, Japan, 1990, 32 x 19 x 16 In.	30
Slot, Watling, Rol-A-Top, 5 Cent, Red, Yellow, Gilt, Cornucopia, Coins, 1925, 26 x 16 In.	2340
Slot, Watling, Treasury, Eagle, Coins, Yellow, 3-Reel, Aluminum, 1935, 24 x 16 In.	2700
Stereoscope, Drop Card Viewer, Red, Blue, Metal Cabinet, Marquee Card, 1940s, 60 x 16 In.	1140
Stereoscope, Mills, Drop Card Viewer, 1 Cent, Oak Cabinet, 1905, 73 x 20 In.	6150
Strength Tester, Caille Bros., Grip, Lung, Oak Cabinet, 1904-05, 64 x 20 In.	2700
Strength Tester, Caille Bros., Tug-Of-War, Mickey Finn, Metal, 1904, 59 x 22 In.	9000
Strength Tester, Exhibit Supply Co., Electric Energizer, Oak, Knight Dragon, c.1928, 78 In.	4500
Strength Tester, Exhibit Supply, Pull Tiger's Tail, Oak Cabinet, 1928, 64 x 30 In.	5100
Strength Tester, Hercules, Grip, Squeeze, Golden Oak Cabinet, 1929-33, 90 x 21 In.	8400
Strength Tester, Mills, Iron Plate, Lift, Metal Bezel, Coppertone Finish, 67 x 22 x 27 In.	6655
Strength Tester, Mills, Owl, Lift Bar, Wood, Metal Foot Plate, 1905, 66 x 21 In.	5400
Strength Tester, Punching Bag, Oak, Decorative Castings, 1910, 79 x 29 In.	6000
Trade Stimulator, A.B.T., Wagon Wheels, 5 Cent, 3-Reel, Wood, Painted, 6 x 11 In.	192
Trade Stimulator, Games Of Nevada, Winner, Horse Race, Betting Option, 1974, 61 x 47 In. ...	7380
Trade Stimulator, Gumball, Daval, Bell Slide, 5-Reel, c.1938	1245
Trade Stimulator, Marvel, Baseball, Pinball Type, Skill, Reverse Painted, Glass Panel, 19 x 13 In. .	726
Trade Stimulator, Mills, Wizard Fortune Teller, Cast Aluminum, 1919, 19 x 14 In.	1320
Trade Stimulator, Paupa & Hochriem, Pilot, Nautical Scenes, 6 Way Coin Head, 1906, 15 x 12 In.	9600
Trade Stimulator, Rock-Ola, Five Jacks, Coin Flip, Wood, Metal, 1930, 21 x 18 In.	1680
Vending, Advance Machine, Matchbook, 1 Cent, Iron Base, Cylindrical Dome, 1916, 17 x 7 In. ...	688
Vending, Automatic Clerk, Gum, Mansfield's Choice Pepsin, Glass, Clockwork, Bells, 1902, 16 x 7 In.	1140
Vending, Buy Blades, 10 Cent, 4-Way Coin Head, Countertop, 1940s, 19 x 13 In.	360
Vending, C. Cretors, Popcorn Popper, Peanut Roaster, Earn More, 1910s, 69 x 31 In.	4200
Vending, Cigaromat, Fresh Cigars, Green, Red Pinstripes, 1950s, 59 x 20 In.	5228
Vending, Condoms, Poon-Tang, Red Paint, Female Devil, 1950s, 34 x 4 In.	1386
Vending, Daval American, Gumball, Eagle, Flowers, 1 Cent, Key, c.1933, 12 x 9 In.	344
Vending, Groetchen, Sparks, Gumball, 1 Cent, Reels Of Cigarette Logos, c.1940, 13 In.	180
Vending, Hot Dog, 5 Cent, Dachshund, Woman, Beach Scene, Shadowbox, 32 In.	1080
Vending, Hot Popcorn, Robot, Arms Hold Cups, Orville Redenbacher, c.1970............................	875
Vending, Jennings, Mints, 3-Reel Strips, 4 Mint Columns, 1925, 25 x 18 In.	1800
Vending, L. Steiner Mfg., Postcards, 25 Cent, Steel, Blue, Red, White Lettering, 1950s, 20 x 16 In.	400
Vending, Northwestern, Matches, Cigar Cutter, 1 Cent, Cast Iron, c.1920, 13 x 6 In.	2525
Vending, Pace, 4 Column Front Vender, Aluminum, Art Deco Surface, 1935, 24 x 17 In.	1320
Vending, Peanuts, Cast Iron, Pierced Decorated Trap Door, Glass Globe, 17 In.	363
Vending, Peanuts, Smilin' Sam From Alabam', Black Paint, Stand, 1931, 44 x 17 In.	8400
Vending, R.D. Simpson, Candy, Nuts, Gum, Chrome Base, 1927, 13 x 9 In.	600
Vending, R.D. Simpson, Columbus Model, Candy, Nuts, Gum, Chrome, Glass, 1927, 15 In.	480
Vending, Stoner, Univendor, Candy, Art Deco, Coin Mechanism, 1931, 71 x 30 In.	5700
Vending, Victor, Gumball, Pinball Game, Wood, 1940s, 15 x 9 x 20 In.....................................	338
Vending, Victor, Gumball, Topper DeLuxe, 1 Cent, Lion's Club Plate, 44 In.	108
Vending, Wilbur, Chocolate, 5 Cent, Wall Mount, Steel, Orange Paint, 34 x 45 In......................	1150
Viewing, International Mutoscope, Babe Ruth, Black, Green, Card Reel, 1920, 65 x 29 In.	4500
Viewing, International Mutoscope, Silver Gloves Boxing, Pistol Control, Red Cabinet, 1948, 67 x 26 In..	9600

COLLECTOR PLATES are modern plates produced in limited editions. Some may be found listed under the factory name, such as Bing & Grondahl, Royal Copenhagen, Royal Doulton, and Wedgwood.

Bradford Exchange, The Marking Tree, Native Americans On Horseback, 1993, 8¼ In.	39
Knowles, Dalmatian Puppies Sitting On Fire Hose, We've Been Spotted, 8½ In. .... *illus*	10
Pickard, Ruby Throated Hummingbird & Lilies, 6½ In.	39

Coffee Mill, Swift Mill, Lane Brothers, No. 12, 2 Wheels, Cast Iron, Painted, New York, 14 In.
$354

Hess Auction Group

Coin Spot, Syrup, Lid, Green Opalescent, Applied Green Handle, c.1900, 6 In.
$58

Jeffrey S. Evans

Coin-Operated, Gumball, 1 Cent, Garden City Novelty Co., c.1936, 12 x 9 In.
$480

Rich Penn Auctions

Coin-Operated, Music Box, H.G. Vossen, Orchestrion, Oak Case, Mirrors, Glass Panel, c.1910, 94 x 55 In. $1,200

Cowan's Auctions

Coin-Operated, Slot, Art Deco, 1 Cent, Yellow, Multicolor Trim, c.1935, 21 x 12 In. $4,250

Heritage Auctions

Coin-Operated, Slot, Mills High Top, 25 Slot, Red, Black, Yellow Stripes, 26 x 16 In. $826

Burchard Galleries

Royal Copenhagen, Christmas, 1956, Blue, White, Denmark, 7 1/4 In.	95

COMIC ART, or cartoon art, includes original art for comic strips, magazine covers, book pages, and even printed strips. The first daily comic strip was printed in 1907. The paintings on celluloid used for movie cartoons are listed in this book under Animation Art.

Illustration, Pogo Comic Strip, 2 Panels, Blue, Black, Signed, Walt Kelly, Frame, 1968, 26 x 20 In.	396
Illustration, Pogo Comic Strip, 3 Panels, Blue, Black Ink, Walt Kelly, 1967, 5 1/2 x 19 In.	452
Sketch, For Better Or For Worse, Frame, Lynn Johnston, 1947, 5 1/4 x 7 1/4 In.	28
Strip, Blondie, Cookie, Signed, Chic Young, July 6, 1948, 4 Panels, 1 Shown, 6 x 19 In. .... *illus*	344
Strip, Captain & The Kids, Multiple Panel, India Ink, Rudolph Dirks, 1947, 15 x 23 In.	650

COMMEMORATIVE items have been made to honor members of royalty and those of great national fame. World's Fairs and important historical events are also remembered with commemorative pieces. Related collectibles are listed in the Coronation and World's Fair categories.

Charm, J. Geils Band, Madison Sq. Garden, Many Thanks, Keith, Greg, Carl, 14K Gold, 1971 ...	215
Medal, Military, Semper Paratus, Enamel, Monogram, Tiger's Head, 1833, 2 In. .... *illus*	98
Pitcher, Washington Light Infantry, Confederate, Flag, Obelisk, Wedgwood, 1800s, 8 1/4 In.	3360
Plaque, Train, No. 1 Engine, Bulmer's Stone, Copper, Oak, 1909, 11 x 5 In. ...... *illus*	160
Plate, George V & Queen Mary, Roses, Blue & White, 1911, 10 1/2 In.	275
Plate, Queen Elizabeth 85th Birthday, Seated, Gold Trim, 1985	20
Watch Fob, Victoria Diamond Jubilee, Pendant, Brass, 1897, 1 1/8 In.	35

COMPACTS hold face powder. A woman did not powder her face in public until after World War I. By 1920, the beauty parlor, permanent waves, and cosmetics had become acceptable. A few companies sold cake face powder in a box with a mirror and a pad or puff. Soon the compact was designed by jewelers and made of gold, silver, and precious materials. Cosmetic companies began to sell powder in attractive compacts of less valuable metal or plastic. Collectors today search for Art Deco designs, famous brands, compacts from World's Fairs or political events, and unusual examples. Many were made with companion lipsticks and other fittings.

Cartouche, Woman, Father, City Walk, Canal, Green Borders, Leaves, Square, 3 1/4 In.	281
M. Buccellati, Brushed Silver, Square, Canted Corners, Jade Cabochon, 3 In.	563
Silvertone Metal, Paint, Couple, Tree, Mirror, Powder Puff, Hinged Lid, c.1930, 3 In	15
Tiffany & Co., Blue Guilloche, 18K Gold, Lozenge Pattern, Diamond Latch, 3 x 2 In.	3000

CONSOLIDATED LAMP AND GLASS COMPANY of Coraopolis, Pennsylvania, was founded in 1894. The company made lamps, tablewares, and art glass. Collectors are particularly interested in the wares made after 1925, including black satin glass, Cosmos (listed in its own category in this book), Martele (which resembled Lalique), Ruba Rombic (1928–1932 Art Deco line), and colored glasswares. Some Consolidated pieces are very similar to those made by the Phoenix Glass Company. The colors are sometimes different. Consolidated made Martele glass in blue, crystal, green, pink, white, or custard glass with added fired-on color or a satin finish. The company closed for the final time in 1967.

Ashtray, Santa Maria, Green Wash	275
Charger, Dancing Nymph, Blue, 17 In.	1375
Toothpick Holder, Crisscross, Cranberry Opalescent, c.1894, 2 3/8 In. .... *illus*	163
Vase, Catalonian, Green, 8 In.	53
Vase, Dancing Nymph, Tan, White Ground, 11 1/2 In.	156
Vase, Lovebirds, Teal, Brown Leaves, White, 10 1/2 In.	125

CONTEMPORARY GLASS, *see Glass-Contemporary.*

COOKBOOKS are collected for various reasons. Some are wanted for the recipes, some for investment, and some as examples of advertising. Cookbooks and recipe pamphlets are included in this category.

A Bride's Very First Cookbook, Potpourri Press, Cardboard Stock, 48 Pages, 1966	48
ABC Of Casseroles, Peter Pauper Press, Hardcover, 61 Pages, 1954, 7 1/2 x 4 1/2 In.	10
Better Homes & Gardens Barbecue Book, 162 Pages, 1956	14
Betty Crocker, Red Pie Cover, 5-Ring Binder, Golden Press, 1970s	55
Betty Crocker's Picture Cookbook, First Edition, Red & White Cover, c.1950 ...... *illus*	250
Campbell's Great American Cookbook, 340 Pages, 1984, 10 x 8 In.	28
Houston Junior League, Hardcover, 432 Pages, 1968	18
It's A Picnic, Nancy Fair McIntyre, Viking Press, 145 Pages, 1969, 9 x 5 In.	12
Jewish Cook Book, Mildred Grossberg Bellin, Bloch Publishing, N.Y., Red Cover, 1946	45
Pillsbury, Best Of The Bake-Off Collection, 1000 Recipes, 608 Pages, 1959, 7 x 9 In.	30
Psi Iota Xi Sorority, 1930s, 7 3/4 x 5 In.	25
Snake, Rattle & Ro Tel, Crazy Sam Enterprises, Knapp Sherrill Co., Spiral Bound, 1986.	34
Someone's In The Kitchen With Dinah, Doubleday & Co., 180 Pages, 1971, 9 x 6 In.	20
Watkins, Spiral Bound, 192 Pages, Copyright 1936	25
White House, Saalfield Publishing, 609 Pages, 1923, 9 x 7 In.	60

COOKIE JARS with brightly painted designs or amusing figural shapes became popular in the mid-1930s. Many companies made them and collectors search for cookie jars either by design or by maker's name. Listed here are examples by the less common makers. Major factories are listed under their own names in other categories of the book, such as Abingdon, Brush, Hull, McCoy, Metlox, Red Wing, and Shawnee. See also the Disneyana category. These are marks of three cookie jar manufacturers.

Brush Pottery Co.	TWIN-WINTON ©	FITZ AND FLOYD, INC. ©MCMLXXX FF
1925–1982	Twin Winton Ceramics 1946–1977	Fitz and Floyd Enterprises LLC 1960–1980

Betsy Ross, Standing, Sewing Flag, 9 x 5 1/2 In.	34
Car, Coupe, Yellow, Black Wheelhouse & Fender, Pottery, 6 1/2 x 13 In. .... *illus*	36
Convertible, Driven By Irish Wolfhounds, 1950s, 8 1/4 In.	90
Cookie Roundup, Cowboy, Chaps, Lasso, 10 1/2 x 8 1/2 In.	72
Dog, White Terrier, Blue Tooth Bandage, USA, 11 1/2 In.	28
Happy Clown, Holding Belly, Lopsided Grin, USA, c.1950, 11 1/2 In.	85
Holy Devil Halo Boy, Smiling, Freckles, Halo, DeForest Of California, 1950s, 12 In.	275
Oscar The Grouch, California Originals, 11 1/2 In.	95
Owl, Large Green Eyes, Cap, Treasure Craft, 1960s, 11 1/2 In.	58
Pig, Off-White, Brown Eyes & Hooves, Fitz & Floyd, 1976, 10 1/2 In.	103
Racoon, Flower Bouquet, Fitz & Floyd, 9 1/2 In.	24
Raggedy Ann, Sitting, On Barrel, California Originals, 13 In.	125
Rooster & Chicken, Barnyard, Brown, Painted, Tapered, Lid, Ceramic, 1930s, 12 In.	610
School Bus, Yellow, Blue, Children, 6 x 11 3/4 In.	12
Strawberry, Red, Sears, USA, 1950s, 7 x 7 1/2 In.	60
Whimsical Teddy Bear, Policeman Uniform, Twin Winton, USA, 1950s, 11 In.	75

COORS dinnerware was made by the Coors Porcelain Company of Golden, Colorado, a company founded with the help of the Coors Brewing Company. Its founder, John Herold, started the Herold China and Pottery Company in 1910 on the site of a glassworks owned by Adolph Coors, the founder of the Coors brewery. The company began making art pottery using clay from nearby mines. Adolph Coors Company bought Herold China and Pottery Company in 1914. Chemical porcelains were made beginning in 1915. The company name was changed to Coors Porcelain Company in 1920, when Herold left. Several lines of dinnerware were made in the 1920s and 1930s. Marks on dinnerware and cookware made by Coors include Rosebud, Glencoe Thermo-Porcelain, Colorado, and other names. Coors stopped making nonessential wares at the start of World War II. After the war, the pottery made ovenware, teapots, vases, and a general line of pottery, but no dinnerware—except for special orders. In 1986 Coors Porcelain became Coors Ceramics. The com-

Collector Plate, Knowles, Dalmatian Puppies Sitting On Fire Hose, We've Been Spotted, 8 1/2 In.
$10

Ruby Lane

Comic Art, Strip, Blondie, Cookie, Chic Young, July 6, 1948, Signed, 4 Panels, 1 Shown, 6 x 19 In.
$344

Hake's Americana & Collectibles

Commemorative, Medal, Military, Semper Paratus, Enamel, Monogram, Tiger's Head, 1833, 2 In.
$98

Skinner, Inc.

Commemorative, Plaque, Train, No. 1 Engine, Bulmer's Stone, Copper, Oak, 1909, 11 x 5 In.
$160

Ruby Lane

Consolidated Glass, Toothpick Holder, Crisscross, Cranberry Opalescent, c.1894, 2 ⅜ In.
$163

Jeffrey S. Evans

Cookbook, Betty Crocker's Picture Cookbook, First Edition, Red & White Cover, c.1950
$250

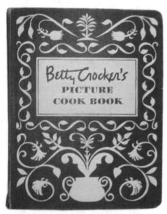

Betty Crocker's
PICTURE
COOK BOOK

Ruby Lane

TIP

Be sure to take any labels off your glass and save them. The acid in the labels will permanently etch the glass.

Cookie Jar, Car, Coupe, Yellow, Black Wheelhouse & Fender, Pottery, 6 ½ x 13 In.
$36

Martin Auction Co.

---

pany is still in business making industrial porcelain. For more prices, go to kovels.com.

Coors Porcelain Co. 1920s	Coors Porcelain Co. 1934–1942	Coors Porcelain Co. 1934–1942

Beer Tray, Logo, Red & White, c.1978, 13 ¼ x 13 ¼ x 1 ¾ In. .... *illus*	24
Bowl, Batter, Handle, Lip, Rosebud, Rose, 8 In.	50
Bowl, Vegetable, Lid, Round, Rosebud, Rose	198
Bowl, Vegetable, Round, Rosebud, Blue, 9 In.	64
Cup & Saucer, Rosebud, Blue	46
Cup & Saucer, Rosebud, Rose	55
Custard Cup, Rosebud, Rose, 3 ¾ x 2 ½ In., 4 Piece	65
Plate, Cake, Rosebud, Blue, 11 In.	47
Plate, Dessert, Rosebud, Yellow, 7 In.	16
Plate, Luncheon, Rosebud, Blue, 9 ¼ In.	32
Plate, Luncheon, Rosebud, Orange, 9 ¼ In.	32
Platter, Oval, Rosebud, Green, 13 In.	109
Salt & Pepper, Wheat Pattern, Cream, Gold, 4 In.	30
Vase, Green To Purple Matte Glaze, Handles, Art Deco, c.1930, 7 ½ In.	70
Vase, Urn Shape, Handles, Blue, 10 In.	35

 COPELAND pieces listed here are those that have a mark including the word *Copeland* used between 1847 and 1976. Marks include *Copeland Spode* and *Copeland & Garrett*. See also Copeland Spode, Royal Worcester, and Spode.

Bust, Hop Queen, Hops & Leaves In Hair, Parian Ware, Joseph Durham, 12 x 7 In.	250
Figurine, Egeria, Seminude, J.H. Foley R.A, 1800s, 28 ½ In. .... *illus*	768
Invalid Feeder, Half Cover, Handle, Tower, Blue & White Transfer Decoration, 3 x 7 ¼ In.	236

 COPELAND SPODE appears on some pieces of nineteenth-century English porcelain. Josiah Spode established a pottery at Stoke-on-Trent, England, in 1770. In 1833, the firm was purchased by William Copeland and Thomas Garrett and the mark was changed. In 1847, Copeland became the sole owner and the mark changed again. W.T. Copeland & Sons continued until a 1976 merger when it became Royal Worcester Spode. The company was bought by the Portmeirion Group in 2009. Pieces are listed in this book under the name that appears in the mark. Copeland, Royal Worcester, and Spode have separate listings.

Bottle, Feeding, Ironstone, Blue & White Transfer, River, Tower, 7 In.	460
Jug, Pilgrims, Blue, White, 1907, 9 ½ x 9 In. .... *illus*	150

COPPER has been used to make utilitarian items, such as teakettles and cooking pans, since the days of the early American colonists. Copper became a popular metal with the Arts & Crafts makers of the early 1900s, and decorative pieces, like desk sets, were made. Copper pieces may also be found in Arts & Crafts, Bradley & Hubbard, Kitchen, Roycroft, and other categories.

Chase Brass and Copper Co., Inc. 1930s	Craftsman Workshop Mark of Gustav Stickley c.1900–1915	Potter Studio c.1900–1929

Ashtray, Hammered, Incised, Anvil Symbol On Bottom, Craftsman, 1920s, 5¾ In.	60
Bed Warmer, Engraved Pan, Hinged Lid, Maple Handle, 1800s, 43 In. *illus*	70
Begging Bowl, Hammered, Incurved, Pierced, Islamic Calligraphy, 1800s, 12 x 5 In.	1280
Bowl, Footed, Engraved Dragon Design, Edo Period, Japan, 9 In.	360
Box, Enameled, Outdoor Scene On Top, Hand Hammered, 7 x 4 In.	767
Box, Enameled, Silver, Cat, Piano, William Spratling, 1900s, 1¼ x 8½ x 4 In.	120
Casserole, Lid, Raised Fleur-De-Lis, Coat Of Arms, Dolphins, 7 x 14½ In.	144
Chocolate Pot, Pear Shape, Turned Wood Handle, Splay Feet, Lid, France, 1700s, 8 In.	1025
Cistern, Water, Cylindrical, Patina, Handles, Spigot, Wood Finial, c.1925, 22 In.	120
Cuspidor, Turtle, Spring Loaded Head, Press To Raise Shell, Tin Pan, 5 x 13 In. *illus*	847
Dish, Scene, 2 Figures On Rafts, Moonlit Sky, Japan, c.1900, 12½ In. *illus*	2723
Escargot Pan, Round, Molded, 10 Bubble Trays, Rolled Rim, France, c.1910, 16 In.	190
Figurine, Acrobat, Circular Pedestal Base, 1919, 25 In.	354
Frame, Repousse, Flowers, Squared Corners, Arts & Crafts, England, 10½ x 14 In.	422
Frame, Shaped, Repousse Flowers, Arts & Crafts, England, 9 x 10½ In.	468
Jardiniere, Hammered, Fluted Bulbous Body, Circular Collar Foot, 1800s, 10 x 18 x 16 In.	311
Jardiniere, Hammered, Handles, Iron, Wrought, c.1905, 19 x 20 In.	5312
Jug, Harvest, Tapering Rim, Loop Handle, 1800s, Gal., 11 In.	120
Jug, Harvest, Wide Spout, W.R. Loftus Limited, Loop Handle, 1800s, ½ Pt., 4½ In.	81
Kettle, Apple Butter, No. 10, Iron Bail Handle, Crimped Seam Tabs, 22 x 32 In.	500
Kettle, Swing Handle, Swan Neck Spout, Impressed J. Elbert, 1800s, 10½ In.	183
Lampshade, Mica, Metal Frame, Glass Beads, 1900s	113
Letter Rack, Butterfly Shape, Relief, 3 x 4 In.	295
Mask, Conquistador, Human Face, Painted, Spain, Late 1800s, 17 In.	48
Measure, Chas G. Schenk, Bail Handle, Brass Plate, 1892, 4⅞ x 11 x 16 In. *illus*	120
Molds are listed in the Kitchen category.	
Pot, Lid, Cabochons, Handles, Hammered, Patina, Brass, WMF, Germany, c.1910, 11 x 15 In.	3750
Sculpture, Bust, Bishop Saint Figure, Glass Jewels, Gothic Style, Germany, 4⅜ In.	1500
Sculpture, Hanging, Hand Woven Wire, D'Lisa Creager, 54 x 32 In. *illus*	5937
Sculpture, Wire, Hand Woven, Dripping Shape, Hanging, D'Lisa Creager, 83 x 16 In.	11250
Sculpture, Wire, Hand Woven, Droplet Shapes, Hanging, D'Lisa Creager, 40 x 28 In.	10625
Teapot, Lotus Leaf Shape, Crab On Lid, Double Bail Handle, Stamped, c.1900, 6½ In. *illus*	132
Tray, Hammered, Mexican Man, Donkey, Anvil Symbol, Craftsman, c.1915, 18 x 6 In.	185
Tray, Oval, Handles, Gustav Stickley, 23½ x 11 In.	1125
Tub, Lid, Turned Handle, 16 x 25 In.	50
Vase, Art Nouveau, Sterling Silver, Stand, Gorham, Marked, 4 x 3 In.	177
Vase, Basket Shape, Handle, Hammered, Russia, 20 In.	363
Vase, Bud, Buttressed, Hammered, Nickel Accent, Karl Kipp, Roycroft, Marked, c.1906, 8 x 4 In.	4375
Warming Pan, Wooden Handle, Patina, Victorian, England, 1870, 10 x 10 x 46 In.	30

COPPER LUSTER items are listed in the Luster category.

 CORALENE glass was made by firing many small colored beads on the outside of glassware. It was made in many patterns in the United States and Europe in the 1880s. Reproductions are made today. Coralene-decorated Japanese pottery is listed in the Japanese Coralene category.

Sculpture, Blossoming Vertical Branches, Female Figure, Wood Base, Chinese, 1900s, 6 In.	375
Vase, Gilt, Ruffled Mouth, Blue Flowers, Yellow To Red Ground, 7½ x 5 In.	500
Vase, White Flowers, Leaves, Tapered, Blue, Yellow, Pink, 11 x 5 In.	2812
Vase, Wide, Squat, Beige Flowers, Pea Green Ground, 8 x 6 In.	93

CORDEY CHINA COMPANY was founded by Boleslaw Cybis in 1942 in Trenton, New Jersey. The firm produced gift shop items. In 1969 it was acquired by the Lightron Corp. and operated as the Schiller Cordey Co., manufacturers of lamps. About 1950 Boleslaw Cybis began making Cybis porcelains, which are listed in the Cybis category in this book.

Bust, Girl, Blond Ringlets, Hat, Holding Bouquet, 7 In.	125
Figurine, Girl Carrying Roses & Pitcher, Flowered Skirt, 10½ In.	95
Figurine, Woman, Victorian Blue Dress, Blue Flowers In Hair, c.1940, 14 In.	149

Coors, Beer Tray, Logo, Red & White, c.1978, 13¼ x 13¼ x 1¾ In.
$24
Ruby Lane

Copeland, Figuine, Egeria, Seminude, J.H. Foley R.A, 1800s, 28½ In.
$768

Neal Auction Co.

Copeland Spode, Jug, Pilgrims, Blue, White, 1907, 9½ x 9 In.
$150

Myers Auction Gallery

97

Copper, Bed Warmer, Engraved Pan, Hinged Lid, Maple Handle, 1800s, 43 In.
$70

Copper, Measure, Chas G. Schenk, Bail Handle, Brass Plate, 1892, 4⅞ x 11 x 16 In.
$120

Corkscrew, Accordion, Brass, Winchester, 3½ x 5½ In.
$24

Garth's Auctioneers & Appraisers

Copper, Sculpture, Hanging, Hand Woven Wire, D'Lisa Creager, 54 x 32 In.
$5,937

Martin Auction Co.

Corkscrew, Lady's Leg, Pink & White Stockings, Graef Schmidt, Marked, c.1910, 2⅝ x 1¼ In.
$485

Hess Auction Group

Copper, Cuspidor, Turtle, Spring Loaded Head, Press To Raise Shell, Tin Pan, 5 x 13 In.
$847

James D. Julia Auctioneers

Copper, Dish, Scene, 2 Figures On Rafts, Moonlit Sky, Japan, c.1900, 12½ In.
$2,723

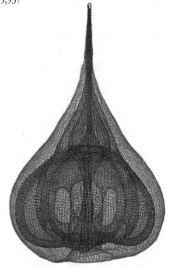

Rago Arts and Auction Center

Copper, Teapot, Lotus Leaf Shape, Crab On Lid, Double Bail Handle, Stamped, c.1900, 6½ In.
$132

Ruby Lane

Coronation, Bike Fender, Decorative, George V, Elizabeth, Celluloid, 12 In.
$180

James D. Julia Auctioneers

Eldred's Auctioneers and Appraisers

Milestone Auctions

CORKSCREWS have been needed since the first bottle was sealed with a cork, probably in the seventeenth century. Today collectors search for the early, unusual patented examples or the figural corkscrews of recent years.

Accordion, Brass, Winchester, 3 ½ x 5 ½ In.	*illus*	24
Bell Shape, Metal, Marked, H. Baker & Co., W. Germany, 5 ¼ In.		39
Bird, Burl, Chrome Screw, 7 ¼ In.		25
Grapevine Root, France, 6 ½ In.		24
Lady's Leg, Pink & White Stockings, Graef Schmidt, Marked, c.1910, 2 ⅝ x 1 ¼ In.	*illus*	485
Stag Horn, 3 ⅞ x 4 ⅜ In.		35
Wood, Turned Handle, W. Germany, 5 ½ In.		19

CORONATION souvenirs have been made since the 1800s. Pottery, glass, tin, silver, and paper objects with a picture of the monarchs and date have been sold at many coronations. The pieces that mention King Edward VIII, the king who was never crowned, are not rare; collectors should be sure to check values before buying. Related pieces are found in the Commemorative category.

Ashtray, George VI, Queen Elizabeth, Profiles, Red, Blue Enamel, Silver Plate, 1937, 4 x 4 In.	148
Beaker, George V, Queen Mary, Images, Transfer, Tapered, Royal Doulton, 1911, 4 In.	45
Bike Fender, Decorative, George V, Elizabeth, Celluloid, 12 In. .... *illus*	180
Bottle, Feeding, Queen Victoria, Stoneware, Salt Glaze, Brampton, 1837, 7 ¾ In.	914
Bowl, King George VI, God Save The King, Crown, Scalloped Rim, Glass, Painted, 1937, 10 In.	55
Cup & Saucer, Queen Elizabeth II, Portrait, Gilt Trim, 1953	25
Cup, Queen Victoria, Portrait, Tin Glaze, Porcelain Enamel, Diamond Jubilee, 3 In.	95
Door Knocker, Queen Elizabeth II, Brass, Coat Of Arms, Lion, Unicorn, 1953, 3 x 2 In.	30
Handkerchief, Queen Elizabeth, Carriage, Children, British Flags, Cotton, 9 x 9 In.	30
Jar, Lid, Queen Elizabeth II, Cream, Gold Trim, Royal Crest On Back, 5 x 3 In. .... *illus*	60
Jug, Queen Victoria Coronation, Blue, White, Portrait, Ruffled Rim, 1837, 8 In.	410
Pin, Edward VII, Cutout Silhouette In Enamel Circle, Leaves, Sterling, 1902, 2 In.	95
Pitcher, Queen Elizabeth II, Portrait, Johnson Brothers, Rosedawn, 1953, 5 x 4 In.	60
Plate, Queen Alexandra, Portrait, Flags, Leaf Border, Wedgwood, 1902, 9 In.	40
Sign, Queen Elizabeth, Prince Philip, Portrait, Flags & Crown, Cardboard, 1953, 27 x 19 In.	360
Spoon, George VI, Queen Elizabeth, Coat Of Arms, 1937, 4 In.	22
Tankard, Edward VIII, Glass, Engraved Crown & ER VIII, c.1937, 5 ½ In.	156
Tin, Queen Elizabeth II, Duke Of Edinburgh, Fox's Glacier Mints, 1953, 5 x 4 x 3 In.	30

COSMOS is a pressed milk glass pattern with colored flowers made from 1894 to 1915 by the Consolidated Lamp and Glass Company. Tablewares and lamps were made in this pattern. A few pieces were also made of clear glass with painted decorations. Other glass patterns are listed under Consolidated Lamp and also in various glass categories. In later years, Cosmos was also made by the Westmoreland Glass Company.

Butter, Cover, Flowers, Quilted Diamond Ground, Victorian, 5 ¾ x 8 In.	*illus*	83
Condiment Set, 3 Bottles, Metal Lids, 8 x 6 In.		36
Lamp, Oil, Strawberries, Flowers, 7 x 8 ½ In.		43
Salt & Pepper, 3 ¾ x 2 ½ In., Pair		18
Sugar, Lid, Yellow, Pink, Blue, White Ground, 6 x 5 In.		30
Syrup, Dome Lid, Handle, 6 ½ x 4 In.		24

COVERLETS were made of linen or wool during the nineteenth century. Most of the coverlets date from 1800 to the 1880s. There was a revival of hand weaving in the 1920s and new coverlets, especially geometric patterns, were made. The earliest coverlets were made on narrow looms, so two woven strips were joined together and a seam can be found. The weave structures of coverlets can include summer and winter, double weave, overshot, and others. Jacquard coverlets have elaborate pictorial patterns that are made on a special loom or with the use of a special attachment. Makers often wove a personal message in the corner. Quilts are listed in this book in their own category.

Coronation, Jar, Lid, Queen Elizabeth II, Cream, Gold Trim, Royal Crest On Back, 5 x 3 In.
$60

Ruby Lane

Cosmos, Butter, Cover, Flowers, Quilted Diamond Ground, Victorian, 5 ¾ x 8 In.
$83

Hess Auction Group

Coverlet, Double Weave, Navy Wool, Cotton, Great Seal, U.S., Stars, Grapevine Border, Fringe, 105 x 79 In.
$1,320

Cowan's Auctions

Coverlet, Jacquard, 4 Color, Signed, H. Stager, Mount Joy, Lancaster Co., Pa., c.1850, 76 x 81 In.
$177

Hess Auction Group

Coverlet, Jacquard, Agriculture & Manufactures, July 4, 1836, C. Lounsburry, 76 x 100 In.
$475

Hess Auction Group

Coverlet, Jacquard, Red, Green, Cream, Black, J. Witmer, Lancaster Cty., c.1850, 2 Panel, 74 x 93 In.
$475

Hess Auction Group

John Henry Meily (1817–1884) 1842–1850s	Matthew Rattray (1796–1872) 1822–1872	Samuel Stinger (c.1801–1879) 1838–1879

Double Weave, Navy Wool, Cotton, Great Seal, U.S., Stars, Grapevine Border, Fringe, 105 x 79 In. . *illus*	1320
Flowers, Red, Ivory, Woven, Inscribed Corners, Rose Of Alendale, c.1850, 74 x 90 In.	405
Jacquard, 4 Color, Signed, H. Stager, Mount Joy, Lancaster Co., Pa., c.1850, 76 x 81 In. *illus*	177
Jacquard, Agriculture & Manufactures, July 4, 1836, C. Lounsburry, 76 x 100 In. *illus*	475
Jacquard, Blue, Red, Green, Yellow, Wool, Cotton, Bird, Tree, Flower, Joseph Devler, 1837, 40 x 37 In.	700
Jacquard, Blue, White, Wool, Cotton, Center Seam, 3 Sides, Top Edge Bound, 1840, 90 x 84 In.	250
Jacquard, Blue, White, Wool, Cotton, Fringe, Center Seam, Eagle Block, 1860, 86 x 76 In.	325
Jacquard, Central Flower Medallion, Spread Wing Eagles, Fruit, Leaves, 84 x 86 In.	643
Jacquard, Central Star, Flowers, Fish Scale, Feather, Fringe, 3 Sides, 1800s, 83 x 84 In.	995
Jacquard, Flower Medallions, Corner Blocks, House, c.1844, 76 x 80 In.	128
Jacquard, Flowers, Vine Border, Fringe, Singed, Peter Liecey, 78 x 96 In.	325
Jacquard, Masonic, Blue, Natural, Agriculture & Manufactures, Ruth Vincent, 1829, 76 x 97 In.	590
Jacquard, Red, Black, White, Cotton, Wool, Central Medallion, Urns, c.1850, 84 x 84 In.	38
Jacquard, Red, Blue, Wool, Flowers, Star Motifs, Rolled Top Hem, Fringes, 1850, 82 x 76 In.	160
Jacquard, Red, Green, Cream, Black, J. Witmer, Lancaster Cty., c.1850, 2 Panel, 74 x 93 In. *illus*	475
Jacquard, Red, Green, Cream, Blue, Flowers, Geometric, Vine Border, Schnee, Penna, 86 x 90 In. .	287
Jacquard, Red, White, Central Star Medallion, Peacock Border, c.1825, 78 x 88 In.	188
Jacquard, Sunbursts, Flowers, Flower Border, 2 Panel, E. Ettinger, Pa., 1838, 70 x 90 In.	256
Jacquard, Wool, Blue, Red, Yellow, Star, Geometric, White Cotton, Wool, 1840, 80 x 100 In.	120
Masonic, Blue & Neutral, Eagle Border, Compass, Motto, July 4, 1829, 76 x 95 In.	500
Overshot, Black, Red, Linen Warp, Wool Weft, Border Decoration, 85 x 100 ½ In.	380
Overshot, Blocks, Split Strips, Stars, Fringe, 1800s, 82 x 95 In.	128
Overshot, Blue, Natural, Border Design, Linen Warp, Wool Weft, 2 Panels, 71 x 80 ¼ In.	70
Overshot, Cream, Green, Blue, White, Block Pattern, 76 x 86 In.	300
Overshot, Navy, Hemmed Edges, Wide Border, 1800s, 73 x 100 In.	117
Overshot, Red, Black, White, Geometric, Crossnore School, 1925, 75 x 95 In.	140
Overshot, Red, Dark Blue, Natural, Linen Warp, Wool Weft, Fringe, 2 Panels, 75 x 92 In.	322

COWAN POTTERY made art pottery and wares for florists. Guy Cowan made pottery in Rocky River, Ohio, a suburb of Cleveland, from 1913 to 1931. A stylized mark with the word *Cowan* was used on most pieces. A commercial, mass-produced line was marked *Lakeware*. Collectors today search for the Art Deco pieces by Guy Cowan, Viktor Schreckengost, Waylande Gregory, or Thelma Frazier Winter.

Bowl, Jazz, Glazed, Viktor Schreckengost, c.1931, 8 ¼ x 13 ¾ In. *illus*	15000
Figurines, Russian Peasants, Balalaika Player & Dancer, Alexander Blazys, c.1927, 11 In., Pair *illus*	300
Sculpture, Head, Woman, Bobbed Hair, White, Art Deco, Waylande Gregory, 1930s, 16 In.	1080
Vase, Volcanic-Like Glaze, Black Over April Green Flambe, Marked, Impressed Logo, 7 x 11 In.	100

CRACKER JACK, the molasses-flavored popcorn mixture, was first made in 1896 in Chicago, Illinois. A prize was added to each box in 1912. Collectors search for the old boxes, toys, and advertising materials. Many of the toys are unmarked. New toys are usually paper, older toys are tin, paper, or plastic.

Doll, Boy, Sailor Suit, Package, 1980, 12 x 5 In. *illus*	30
Toy, Toonerville Trolley, Tin Lithograph, Germany, Copyright 1922, 2 In. *illus*	106

CRACKLE GLASS was originally made by the Venetians, but most of the wares found today were made since the 1800s. The glass was heated, cooled, and refired so that many small lines appeared inside the glass. Most was made from about 1930 to 1980, although some is made today. The glass is found in many colors, but collectors today pay the highest prices for amberina, cranberry, or ruby red. Cobalt blue is also popular. More crackle glass may be listed in those categories in this book.

Vase, Orange Latticework, 9 x 3¾ In. 180

CRANBERRY GLASS is an almost transparent yellow-red glass. It resembles the color of cranberry juice. The glass has been made in Europe and America since the Civil War. It is still being made, and reproductions can fool the unwary. Related glass items may be listed in other categories, such as Rubina Verde.

Beaker, Cased, Bohemian, 7-Sided, 6 Optic Medallions, Engraving, Stag, 4½ In. 120
Bowl, Opalescent, 9½ In. 48
Bowl, Pedestal, Cherub, Flowers, Draped Woman, Handles, 17¾ x 11½ In. 2250
Celery Vase, Cut To Clear, Hourglass Stem, 7½ In. .... *illus* 2700
Epergne, 4 Traditional Lilies, Stems, Clear Glass Rigaree, 22 In. 1140
Ewer, Crackle, Pulled Verde Glass Handle, Bulbous Base, Tapering Neck, Kralik, 8¼ In. 34
Jewelry Box, Gold & White Enamel Bird & Flowers, Gilt Metal Fittings, Round, 4½ x 3¼ In. ... 270
Liquor Dispenser, Figural, 2-Wheel Metal Cart, Moser Keg, Stopper, Metal Spigot, 8 x 12 In. .. 600
Muffineer, 12-Sided, Silver Plated Lid, 5¼ In. 24
Vase, Bronze Mounted Rim, Trumpeted, 3 Figural Putti Heads, Decorated Platform, 18 x 8 In. 91
Vase, Gilt, Enamel, Flowers, Dots, Acanthus, 7½ In. 45
Vase, Ruffled Rim, Hobnails, 4½ x 5½ In. 36
Vase, Silver Overlay, Tulip, Flared Mouth, Clear Glass Foot, Floral, Monogram, 1900, 12 In. 1200
Vase, Sterling Silver Overlay, Oval, Trumpeted Rim, Roses, Calla Lilies, 14 x 6 In. 2723
Water Set, Pitcher, Inverted Coin Spot, Ruffled Top, Clear Handle, 6 Tumblers, 7 Piece 61
Wineglass, Webb Rock Crystal & Cut Stem Pattern, Scalloped Base, Signed W. Fritsche, 6 In... 13200

CREAMWARE, or queensware, was developed by Josiah Wedgwood about 1765. It is a cream-colored earthenware that has been copied by many factories. Similar wares may be listed under Pearlware and Wedgwood.

Basket, Tray, Openwork, Scalloped, 10¼ In. 200
Bough Pot, Shaped, Oval, Winged Mythical Animal, 10 In. 125
Coffeepot, Flowers, Blue Transfer, Copeland & Garrett, 1800s, 5 In. 60
Jug, Bulbous Shape, 3 Black Transfer Prints, Symbols, Verses, 1800, 11 In. 461
Jug, Bulbous Shape, Multicolor Enameled, Liverpool Type, 1817, 9 In. 308
Jug, Enameled Black, Masonic Symbols, Farmers, Spout In Cartouche, 1817, 8⅛ In. 277
Jug, Marbleized, Brown Neck, Strap Handle, c.1810, 5¼ In. .... *illus* 523
Mug, Undecorated, Raised Banding, Handle On Molded Foot, 1800s, 5¾ In. 93
Teapot, Oval, Floral Finial, Double Entwined Handle, Reeded Spout, Multicolor, 1770, 5 In. 584
Teapot, Painted, Leafy Clusters Of Cherries, 1770-80, 6 In. 500
Teapot, Painted, Woman Standing, Gadrooned & Beaded Borders, 1765-75, 5³⁄₁₆ In. 125
Vase, 2 Female Faces, Leaves, Hexagonal Base, Lakin & Poole, 6 In. 660
Vase, Flower Frog Lid, Green Band, Swag, Portrait Oval, 8⅝ In., Pair 1169

CREIL, France, had a faience factory as early as 1794. The company merged with a factory in Montereau in 1819. It made stoneware, mocha ware, and soft paste porcelain. The name *Creil* appears as part of the mark on many pieces. The Creil factory closed in 1895.

Foot Tub, Gilt, Courting Couple, Cobalt, Lavender, Porcelain, 9¾ x 22¼ In. .... *illus* 620
Plate, Lobster, Blue Edge, Felix Bracquemond, 1867, 5⅝ In. 108
Tray, Caesar Pardoning Marcellus, Reticulated, 1808-18, 13¾ x 9½ In. 360
Tray, Reticulated, Grisaille Transfer, Pardoning Marcellus, c.1808, 14 In. 384

CROWN DUCAL is the name used on some pieces of porcelain made by A.G. Richardson and Co., Ltd., of Tunstall and Cobridge, England. The name has been used since 1916. Crown Ducal is a well-known maker of chintz pattern dishes. The company was bought by Wedgwood in 1974.

Teapot, Crown Ducal, 4 In. 225

Cowan, Bowl, Jazz, Glazed, Viktor Schreckengost, c.1931, 8¼ x 13¾ In. $15,000

Rago Arts and Auction Center

Cowan, Figurines, Russian Peasants, Balalaika Player & Dancer, Alexander Blazys, c.1927, 11 In., Pair $300

Cowan's Auctions

TIP
Rub white toothpaste on crayon marks on the wall to remove the marks.

Cracker Jack, Doll, Boy, Sailor Suit, Package, 1980, 12 x 5 In. $30

Ruby Lane

Cracker Jack, Toy, Toonerville Trolley, Tin Lithograph, Germany, Copyright 1922, 2 In.
$106

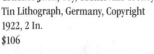

Hess Auction Group

Cranberry Glass, Celery Vase, Cut To Clear, Hourglass Stem, 7 ½ In.
$2,700

Woody Auction

Creamware, Jug, Marbleized, Brown Neck, Strap Handle, c.1810, 5 ¼ In.
$523

Skinner, Inc.

 CROWN MILANO glass was made by the Mt. Washington Glass Works about 1890. It was a plain biscuit color with a satin finish decorated with flowers and often had large gold scrolls. Not all pieces are marked.

Biscuit Jar, Cream, Blue, Pink Hobnail, Sea Life, Jewel Highlights, Silver Plate Lid, 6 x 7 In.	780
Biscuit Jar, Repousse Crab, Melon Ribbed, Applied Berries, Red, Purple, 6 x 8 In. .... *illus*	258
Ewer, Handles, Ball Shape, Cream & Taupe Tones, Enamel Acorn & Leaves, Marked, 5 ¾ In. ...	540
Rose Bowl, Tapestry, Red Flowers, Yellow Leaves, Opaque White Ground, 4 In.	263
Sweetmeat, Hand Decorated, Fall Color Holly Leaves, Silver Cover, Marked, 3 x 6 In.	266
Sweetmeat, Yellow, Orange, Molded Diamond Texture, Jewel, Silver Plate Lid, Bail, 3 ¾ x 6 In. ..	720
Vase, Thistle, Twist Neck, 2 Handles, Cream Tones, 12 In..........	1200
Vase, Trumpet, Colonial Ware, White, Colorful Flowers & Applied Punte, Marked, 10 In.	210

CROWN TUSCAN *pattern is included in the Cambridge glass category.*

 CRUETS of glass or porcelain were made to hold vinegar, oil, and other condiments. They were especially popular during Victorian times and have been made in a variety of styles since the eighteenth century. Additional cruets may be found in the Castor Set category and also in various glass categories.

Amber Paneled Glass, Blue Rope Handle, Faceted Stopper, Pontil, c.1910, 7 ⅝ x 3 ¼ In. *illus*	150
Cranberry Glass, Gilt, Viola, Leaves, Cone Stopper, 6 ½ In.	12
Cranberry Opalescent, Coin Spot, Stopper, 6 ½ x 4 In.	48
Cranberry Opalescent, Hobnail, Ribbed Handle, 7 ¼ In.	120
Cut Glass, Russian, Cranberry Cut To Clear, 5 ¾ In.........	360
Rose To White Glass, Faceted Amber Stopper, Twisted Handle, Thomas Webb, c.1895, 6 ¾ x 3 In... *illus*	595
Slag Glass, Purple, Diamond Quilted, Stopper, 7 x 3 In.	22 to 30

 CT GERMANY was first part of a mark used by a company in Altwasser, Germany (now part of Walbrzych, Poland), in 1845. The initials stand for C. Tielsch, a partner in the firm. The Hutschenreuther firm took over the company in 1918 and continued to use the *CT* until 1952.

Plate, Luncheon, Fish, Pink Rose Border, Gold Trim, 8 ½ In.	64
Platter, Fish, Pink Rose Border, Gold Trim, 21 ½ x 9 In.	199
Relish, Yellow Flowers, Purple Shaped & Pierced Border, c.1910, 13 ¼ x 8 ½ In.........	42
Tray, 2 Sections, Applied Handle, Yellow Flowers, Ruffled Rim, 10 x 4 In.........	95

 CURRIER & IVES made the famous American lithographs marked with their name from 1857 to 1907. The mark used on the print included the street address in New York City, and it is possible to date the year of the original issue from this information. Earlier prints were made by N. Currier and use that name from 1835 to 1847. Many reprints of the Currier or Currier & Ives prints have been made. Some collectors buy the insurance calendars that were based on the old prints. The words *large, small,* or *medium folio* refer to size. The original print sizes were very small (up to about 7 x 9 in.), small (8 ⅘ x 12 ⅘ in.), medium (9 x 14 in. to 14 x 20 in.), and large (larger than 14 x 20 in.). Other prints are probably later copies. Other prints by Currier & Ives may be listed in Card, Advertising and in the Sheet Music category. Currier & Ives dinnerware patterns may be found in the Adams or Dinnerware categories.

Across The Continent, Town, Train, River, c.1868, 22 x 30 In.	2834
Battle At Cedar Mountain, Soldiers Attacking, 1862, 8 ¾ x 12 ¾ In.	526
Bombardment & Capture Of Fredericksburg VA, Dec. 1862, 13 x 16 In.........	298
Farmer's Home-Harvest, Frame, 24 ½ x 30 ½ In. .... *illus*	250
Little Daisy, Girl, Flowers, 15 ½ x 11 ⅝ In.........	250
My Little White Kitties, Playing Dominoes, 1850s, 9 ⅞ x 14 In.........	115
The Happy Home, Family On Sofa, 1840s, 10 x 14 In.	95
The Lexington Of 1861, Fighting In Street, 13 x 10 In., Frame, 21 x 18 In.........	350

C

CUSTARD GLASS is a slightly yellow opaque glass. It was made in England in the 1880s and was first made in the United States in the 1890s. It has been reproduced. Additional pieces may be found in the Cambridge, Fenton, and Heisey categories. Custard glass is called *Ivorina Verde* by Heisey and other companies.

Biscuit Barrel, Woman, Walking Dog, Child, 9 x 5 In.	42
Maize is its own category in this book.	
Vase, Beading, Sibley Ill, Red Lettering, 6 x 3 In.	24

CUT GLASS has been made since ancient times, but the large majority of the pieces now for sale date from the American Brilliant period of glass design, 1875 to 1915. These pieces have elaborate geometric designs with a deep miter cut. Modern cut glass with a similar appearance is being made in England, Ireland, Poland, the Czech Republic, and Slovakia. Chips and scratches are often difficult to notice but lower the value dramatically. A signature on the glass adds significantly to the value. Other cut glass pieces are listed under factory names, like Hawkes, Libbey, and Sinclaire.

Banana Bowl, Hobstar, Strawberry Diamond, Cane & Fan, 4 x 9 In.	63
Basket, Flower, Russian, Persian Buttons, Hoare, 8 x 11 In.	1440
Basket, Hobstar Chain & Star Motif, 4¼ x 6¼ In.	180
Basket, Thousand Eye, Strawberry Diamond Border, Hobstar Center, Twist Handle, 5 x 6¼ In..	360
Bottle, Whiskey, Pinwheel, Hobstar, Crossed Bar & Fan Design, 13½ In.	330
Bowl, 3 Facet Cut Hobstars, Prisms, Flat Bottom, Gibbs, Kelley & Co., 1899, 4 x 10 In.	600
Bowl, Comet, J. Hoare, Signed, 2 x 9 In.	150
Bowl, Diamond Cut, Gilt, Bronze Base, Sphinx Supports, c.1900, 6 x 7 In.	1188
Bowl, Engraved, Strawberry, Silver Reticulated Border, Dominick & Haff, 2¼ x 13 In.	240
Bowl, Epergne, Wire Frame, Bright, Thistle, Roses, 10 x 9½ In.	125
Bowl, Geometric Pattern Hobstars, Strawberry Diamond, Fan Cut, 8¾ x 14 In.	480
Bowl, Geometric, Pattern, Early 1900s, 3¾ x 8 In. *illus*	252
Bowl, Hobstar & Cane Border, 6-Point Hobstar Center, 3 x 7 In.	50
Bowl, Hobstar Center, Concave Pillar & Zipper, Gorham Silver Rim, 3¼ x 8¾ In.	540
Bowl, Hobstar, Cane, Silver Rim, Scrolling Flowers, Redlich & Co., 4¼ x 7 In.	1560
Bowl, Hobstar, Divided Diamonds, Stars, Rayed Starts, 4 x 9 In.	23
Bowl, Hobstar, Flared Fans, Notched Miters, Strawberry Diamond, 3⅝ x 9 In.	23
Bowl, Hobstar, Prism & Fan, Embossed Sterling Rim, Shreve, Crump & Low, 5¾ x 11 In.	360
Bowl, Marquis, Signed, J. Hoare, 2¾ x 10 In.	125
Bowl, Oxford, Flared, J. Hoare, 3 x 12 In.	400
Bowl, Royal Pattern, Hunt, 3 x 8 In.	90
Bowl, Silver Mounts, Silver Rim, Embossed Leafy Scroll Rim, Shreve & Co., 4 x 10 In.	615
Bowl, Sparkler Pattern, Signed, J. Hoare, 1½ x 7 In.	100
Bowl, Strawberry Diamond, Rainbow, 4⅞ In.	420
Bread Tray, Folded, Marquise, Signed J. Hoare, 2½ x 12 x 5½ In.	210
Bread Tray, Princeton, Empire, 11 x 7 In.	175
Butter, Cover, Crosscut, Hoare, 4 In.	307
Butter, Eminent, Clark, 1908, 6 x 8 In.	108
Candlestick, Flower & Leaf, 10 In., Pair	110
Candlestick, Hobstar, Diamond & Fan, Cup Holder, Facet Ring, Scalloped Foot, 9¾ In.	330
Candlestick, Lexington, 8 Spear Prisms, Petal Foot, Dorflinger, 9¼ In. *illus*	360
Carafe, Flowers & Ribbons, Cork Topped, Acorn, Gilt Metal Mounted, Germany, 1700s, 11 In. .	4000
Carafe, Hobstar, Strawberry Diamond, Cane & Vesica, Mandarin, Dorflinger, 8 In.	210
Carafe, Water, Brunswick, Signed, Hawkes, 7 In.	175
Celery Tray, Arabian II, Signed, Egginton, 11 In.	480
Celery Tray, Sultana, Dorflinger, 12 x 5 In.	175
Cheese & Cracker Server, Silver, Rim, Engraved Flowers & Butterflies Motif, 2½ x 12 In.	360
Cheese Dish, Saxonia Pattern, Empire, 7 x 9½ In.	180
Claret Jug, Bulbous Body, Silver, Intaglio Flowers, Mechanical Lid, J.C. Edington, 12 x 6 In.	1392
Claret Jug, Spiral Cut, Rope Twist Handle, Silver Neck & Lid, France, c.1900, 10 In., Pair	1375
Claret Jug, Swirled Tusk, Hobstar, Bar & Fan Motif, Gorham Silver Spout & Handle, 9¼ In.	2700
Cologne Bottle, Rainbow Shading, Vesica, Diamond & Star, Faceted Stopper, 6¼ In,	720
Cologne Bottle, Richelieu Pattern, J. Hoare, Embossed Gorham Silver Floral Stopper, 6 In.	780

Creil, Foot Tub, Gilt, Courting Couple, Cobalt, Lavender, Porcelain, 9¾ x 22¼ In.
$620

Ahlers & Ogletree Auction Gallery

Crown Milano, Biscuit Jar, Repousse Crab, Melon Ribbed, Applied Berries, Red, Purple, 6 x 8 In.
$258

Blackwell Auctions

Cruet, Amber Paneled Body, Blue Rope Handle, Faceted Stopper, Pontil, c.1910, 7⅝ x 3¼ In.
$150

Ruby Lane

SELECTED CUT GLASS MARKS WITH DATES USED

J.D. Bergen & Co.
1885–1922
Meriden, Conn.

Tuthill Cut Glass Co.
1902–1923
Middletown, N.Y.

Pairpoint Corporation
1880–1938
New Bedford, Mass.

Libbey Glass Co.
1888–1925
Toledo, Ohio

C. Dorflinger & Sons
1852–1921
White Mills, Pa.

T.B. Clark and Co.
1884–1930
Honesdale, Pa.

Majestic Cut Glass Co.
1900–1916
Elmira, N.Y.

Wright Rich Cut Glass Co.
1904–1915
Anderson, Ind.

T.G. Hawkes & Co.
1880–1962
Corning, N.Y.

H.C. Fry Glass Co.
1901–1934
Rochester, Pa.

H.P. Sinclaire & Co.
1905–1929
Corning, N.Y.

House of Birks
c.1894–1907+
Montreal, Quebec, Canada

Laurel Cut Glass Co.
1903–1920
Jarmyn, Pa.

J. Hoare & Co.
1868–1921
Corning, N.Y.

L. Strauss & Sons
c. 1894–1917
New York, N.Y.

Compote, Clear, Green Border, Flute Pattern, Rayed Base, 8 x 6 In.	180
Compote, Hobstar, Strawberry Diamond, Cane & Star, Notched Stem, Scalloped Hobstar Foot, 10 x 6 In.	180
Compote, Jelly, Hobstar, Cane, Strawberry Diamond, Teardrop Notched Stem, Hobstar Base, 9 x 6 In.	150
Compote, Rainbow, Ruffled, Silver Mica Highlights, Pedestal, Clear Textured Foot, 4 x 5 In.	108
Cruet, Hobstar, Vesica, Strawberry Diamond & Fan Design, Cut Stopper, 7¾ In.	180
Cup, Gilt & Painted, Hunting Scene, Germany, 1700s, 3 In.	1375
Cup, Strawberry Diamond & Star, Triple Notched Handles, Silver Rim, 3½ In.	480
Decanter, Basket Weave, 10 In.	960
Decanter, Cane, Rayed Base, Clear Blank, Fitted Lapidary Stopper, 11 In.	30
Decanter, Creswick, Egginton, 14¼ In.	300
Decanter, Essex, Monogram, Shield Shape, Hobstar Base, Dorflinger, 11 In.	660
Decanter, Handle, Pyramidal Bottle, Waterlily & Blossom, Silver Stopper, Theodore B. Starr, 12 In.	780
Decanter, Hob Diamond, Pedestal, Rayed Foot, Clear Blank, Dorflinger, 13 In.	600
Decanter, Wheat & Swirl, Sterling Silver Stopper, J. Hoare, 13¼ In.	1700
Decanter, Wine, Engraved, Porron, Tapering Spout, Fan Pattern, 1800s, 10 x 10 In. *illus*	185
Dish, Boat Shape, Russian, Star Cut Buttons, Clear Blank, 3 x 14 x 4 In.	780
Dish, Primrose, Oval, Tuthill, 2¾ x 7 In.	225
Dresser Box, Odolet, Square, Silver Fittings, C.F. Monroe, 5 x 8 In.	1440
Epergne, Pedestal, Hobstar, Vesica, Strawberry Diamond Motif, Cut Base, 10 x 8 In.	1020
Ewer, Pinwheels, Fans, Diamond, Notched Handle, 14 x 7 x 4½ In.	137
Finger Bowl, Crystal City Pattern, J. Hoare, 3 x 4⅞ In.	1680
Goblet, Water, Croesus Pattern, J. Hoare, 6 In.	150
Hair Receiver, Lotus, Hobstar Base & Lid, Egginton, 3¼ x 4 In.	96
Humidor, Harvard, Hobstar Lid, Ray Base, 8¾ In.	180
Ice Bucket, Tab Handle, Pluto, J. Hoare, 5½ x 6 In.	150
Ice Cream Tray, Tab Handle, Hobstar, Vesica, Nailhead & Strawberry Diamond, Star & Fan	180
Ice Tub, Alhambra, Meriden, 4 x 6¼ In.	720
Ice Tub, Flashed Hobstar, Fan & Feathered Leaf, Clear, Base, 5½ x 7 In.	36
Ice Tub, Tab Handles, Arbutus, Hobstar Base, 5¾ x 7¼ In.	350
Jar, Hobstar, Block, Feather & Fan Motif, Square Base, Prism Lid, 6¼ In.	180
Jug, Hobstar, Vesica & Fan, Notched Handle, Rayed Base, 9 In.	123
Jug, Strawberry Diamond, Star, Punte & Crossed Bar, Oval, Silver Plate Spout & Handle, England, 9 In.	36
Lamp, Banquet, Whale Oil, Pressed & Cut Foot, Hollow Stem, 2 Burners, 1800s, 12 In.	3600
Lamp, Whale Oil, Brass Candlestick, Frosted Shade, Double Burner, 1800s, 15 In. *illus*	344
Loving Cup, 3 Handles, Crosscut & Strawberry Diamond, Fan, Hobstar Base, 6 In.	270
Loving Cup, Russian & Pillar, Gorham Silver Floral Handles, Flashed Hobstar Base, 7 x 9 In.	2760
Paperweight, Hobstar, Strawberry Diamond, Cane & Fan Motif, 3¾ x 2¼ In.	1200
Pitcher, Engraved, Lions In Jungle, Standing Over Kill Scene, Monogram, 8 In.	1560
Pitcher, Hobstar, Nailhead Diamond, Arch, Prism & Fan, Notched Handle, Pedestal Base, Russia, 10 In.	420
Pitcher, Water, Bulging Columns, Triple Notched Handles, Silver Spout, 9 In.	240
Pitcher, Water, Carolyn, Triple Notched Handle, J. Hoare, 7½ In.	300
Plate, Expanding Star, 7 In.	600
Plate, Hobstar, Cane & Strawberry Diamond, Gorham Silver Border, 10 In.	300
Plate, Manhattan, Clark, 7½ In.	25
Plate, Parisian, Dorflinger, 7¼ In.	60
Plate, Prima Donna, Clark, 9 In.	120
Plate, Snowflake & Holly, Sinclaire, 6⅞ In.	840
Plate, Trellis, Hoare, 7⅛ In.	840
Punch Bowl, 2 Parts, Hobstar, Cane, Strawberry Diamond, 11 x 10 In.	420
Punch Bowl, Stand, Arabian, Egginton, 12⅛ x 14½ In.	10200
Punch Set, Montrose, Green Cut To Clear, Dorflinger, 15-In. Bowl, 13 Piece *illus*	114000
Rum Jug, Fredericka, Triple Notched Handle, Pattern Cut Stopper, W.C. Anderson, 8¼ In.	330
Salt Dip, Marlboro, Hobstar Base, Dorflinger, Master, 3½ In.	180
Spooner, Hobstar, Nailhead & Strawberry Diamond, Vesica, Prism & Fan, Triple Notched Handles, 5 In.	150
Sugar Shaker, Strawberry & Nailhead Diamond, Hobstar & Prism, Silver Top, Wilcox, 4 In.	330
Tankard, Hobstar, Cane, Strawberry Diamond & Fan, Triple Notched Handle, Ray Base, 12 In.	12
Tankard, Hobstars, Strawberry Diamond, Star & Fan, Gorham Silver Spout & Collar 17 In.	96
Tankard, Prism Body, 3 Notched Handles, Silver Spout, Amethyst Jewels, Monogram, Marked, 12 In.	270
Tankard, Russian Pattern, Star Buttons, 11 In.	720
Tazza, Harvard, Scalloped & Rolled Rim, Hobstar Base, 9 x 7½ In.	96

Cruet, Rose To White, Faceted Amber Stopper, Twisted Handle, Thomas Webb, c.1895, 6¾ x 3 In.
$595

Ruby Lane

Currier & Ives, Farmer's Home-Harvest, Frame, 24½ x 30½ In.
$250

Garth's Auctioneers & Appraisers

Cut Glass, Bowl, Geometric, Pattern, Early 1900s, 3¾ x 8 In.
$252

Garth's Auctioneers & Appraisers

TIP
Is it cut or pressed glass? Feel the edges of the design of the glass. Cut glass has sharp edges; pressed-glass designs are molded into the glass.

Cut Glass, Candlestick, Lexington, 8 Spear Prisms, Petal Foot, Dorflinger, 9 ¼ In.

$360

Brunk Auctions

Cut Glass, Decanter, Wine, Engraved, Porron, Tapering Spout, Fan Pattern, 1800s, 10 x 10 In.

$185

Brunk Auctions

Cut Glass, Lamp, Whale Oil, Brass Candlestick, Frosted Shade, Double Burner, 1800s, 15 In.

$344

Garth's Auctioneers & Appraisers

Tazza, Vesica, Crosscut Diamond, Prism & Fan, Hobstar Foot, Clear Blank, 9 x 9 In.	360
Teapot, Alberta, Hawkes, 6 x 9 In. .... *illus*	1560
Tobacco Jar, Ball's-Eye & Prism, Hobstar Base, Silver, Stag Horn Handles, Finial, 7 ¼ x 9 ½ In.	2280
Tray, Hiawatha, Sinclaire, 14 ¾ In.	799
Tray, Round, Bristol Rose, Clear Blank, Full Teeth, Mt. Washington, 11 In.	600
Tray, Venetian, Round, Straus, 10 ¾ In.	80
Tumbler, Andrew Jackson, A & J, Sunbursts, Star, Sulphide, c.1825, 3 x 3 In.	11700
Tumbler, Thistle, Gold Leafy Band, St. Louis Cristal, France, 4 In., 12 Piece	1476
Tumble-Up, Carafe, Tumbler, Hollow Diamond, Dorflinger, 2 Piece	2640
Vase, Hobstar, Strawberry Diamond & Fan, 16 In.	150
Vase, Modified Wheat, Russian Scalloped Foot, J. Hoare, 10 In.	570
Vase, Pinched Waist, Prism Body, Hobstar, Strawberry Diamond & Fan Top, 9 ½ In.	270
Vase, Tall Baluster Shape, Molded, Diamond Panels, 8-Point Stars, 17 In.	666
Vase, Trumpet, Hobstar, Crosscut Diamond & Concave Pillar, 10 In.	90
Wine Rinser, 2 Spouts, Ridged Cuts, Faceted Panels, 1800s, 3 ¾ x 4 ¾ In.	74
Wine, Cranberry, Clear, Crosscut Diamond & Fan, 4 ¾ In.	120
Wine, Parisian, Scalloped, Hobstar Base, Dorflinger, 4 ½ In.	300

CYBIS **CYBIS** porcelain is a twentieth-century product. Boleslaw Cybis came to the United States from Poland in 1939. He started making porcelains in Long Island, New York, in 1940. He moved to Trenton, New Jersey, in 1942 as one of the founders of Cordey China Co. and started his own company, Cybis Porcelains, about 1950. The firm is still working. See also Cordey.

Bust, Clown, Funny Face, Orange Paint, Blue Puff Balls, Ruffled Collars, 8 In.	54
Bust, Madonna, Bird Perched On Wrist, 10 In.	72
Figurine, American White Buffalo, Wood Base, 13 ½ x 18 In.	1080
Figurine, Columbia, Bisque, White Dress, Blue Cape, Eagle, Shield, c.1976, 16 x 7 In. .... *illus*	63
Group, Bears, Mother, Cubs, 18 ½ In.	522

CZECHOSLOVAKIA is a popular term with collectors. The name, first used as a mark after the country was formed in 1918, appears on glass and porcelain and other decorative items. Although Czechoslovakia split into Slovakia and the Czech Republic on January 1, 1993, the name continues to be used in some trademarks.

CZECHOSLOVAKIA GLASS

Atomizer, Clear, Painted Red Panels, White Enamel Decoration, Marked, 7 In.	72
Lamp, Glass Marble, Crystal, Incision Work, Brass Finial, Harp, 1900s	42
Vase, Yellow, Pink, Pinched Mouth, 12 ¼ In.	70

CZECHOSLOVAKIA POTTERY

Bowl, Centerpiece, 3 Figural Putti Holding, Ivory High Glaze, Ink Stamp, 8 x 14 In.	120
Pitcher, Grapes, Pears, Leaves, Ditmar Urbach, 8 In.	65
Pitcher, Portrait, Blue Stars, Cream Ground, 9 In.	62
Vase, Stylized Flowers, Red, Green, Cream, Blue, Scallop Trim, Reticulated Base, 8 ½ In.	135

DANIEL BOONE, a pre–Revolutionary War folk hero, was a surveyor, trapper, and frontiersman. A television series, which ran from 1964 to 1970, was based on his life and starred Fess Parker. All types of Daniel Boone memorabilia are collected.

Doll, Traditional Hat & Outfit, Madame Alexander, 8 In.	48
Lunch Box, Fighting Indians, Metal, 1950s	75
Match Safe, Head Shape, Hinged, Brass, 29th Natl. Encpt, Louisville, c.1895, 3 In.	985
Spoon, Old Kentucky Home, Horse, Whiskey Barrel, Sterling Silver, 5 ¾ In.	46

 D'ARGENTAL is a mark used in France by the Compagnie des Cristalleries de St. Louis. The firm made multilayered, acid-cut cameo glass in the late nineteenth and twentieth centuries. D'Argental is the French name for the city of Munzthal, home of the glassworks. Later the company made enameled etched glass.

Bowl, Lily Pond, Orange, Purple, 6 ½ x 3 ¼ In.	357

Vase, Flowers, Vines, Brown, Amber, 4 x 7 In.	200
Vase, Orchid, Deep Red Flowers, Leaves, Stems, Yellow Ground, Signed, 13 ½ In.	847
Vase, Scenic, Lake Como, Red, Brown, Yellow Ground, Signed, 21 ½ In.	1815
Vase, Squat Disc, Maroon, Green, c.1925, 4 In.	687
Vase, Virginia Creeper, Purple, White, 3 x 8 In.	200

DAUM, a glassworks in Nancy, France, was started by Jean Daum in 1875. The company, now called *Cristalleries de Nancy*, is still working. The *Daum Nancy* mark has been used in many variations. The name of the city and the artist are usually both included. The term *martele* is used to describe applied decorations that are carved or etched in the cameo process.

Daum 1890	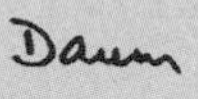 Daum 1960–1971	 Daum 1960–1971

Bowl, Enamel Decorated, Orchid, Leaves, Cameo, Signed, 3 ½ In.	1331
Ceiling Light, Electric, 3-Light, Grapevines, Gold, Green, Orange, 24 x 14 In.	3000
Chandelier, 6-Light, Iron, Grapes, Cream, Gold Speckled Shades, France, 35 x 22 In.	6875
Cologne Bottle, Winter Scene, Orange, Yellow, Brown, Signed, 5 In.	2420
Figurine, Elephant, Trunk Up, Amber, Brown, 8 ½ x 9 In.	1168
Figurine, Eve, Long Hair, Apple, Rocky Ground, Amber, Rose Pink, 16 ¾ In.	2875
Figurine, Horse Head, France, Signed, 9 In.	145
Figurine, Parrot, On Perch, Blue, Green, Pate-De-Verre, 11 ¼ In. *illus*	550
Group, Horse, 4 Riders, Amber, Purple, Brass Swords, C. Poincignon, 12 x 12 In. *illus*	1989
Inkwell, Dome Lid, Flowers, White Ground, Square Body, Cameo, Signed, 2 x 3 In.	2420
Jar, Lid, Opalescent, Enameled Flowers, Leaves, Cameo, Gilt Glass Stopper, 3 In. *illus*	2723
Lamp, 3 Colors, Carved Scene, Frosted White, Green & Red, Lake, Trees, Cameo, 18 x 9 ½ In.	3600
Lamp, Mountainous Landscape, Brass Washed Metal, c.1900, 18 x 13 In.	1000
Lamp, Table, Grapevine, Vines, Leaves, Metal Collar Base, Cameo, Signed, 14 ½ In.	6050
Lamp, Winter Scene, Trees, Yellow & Orange Sky, Cameo, Shade 5 ½ In., Lamp 12 ¾ In.	9619
Open Salt, Winter Scene, Yellow, Cameo, 1 ¼ x 2 In.	1170
Perfume Bottle, Green Etched, Iris, Leaves, Gilt Accents, Cameo, 1910, 7 ½ In.	492
Pitcher, Nightshade, White To Yellow, Etched, Gilt, Internal Decoration, France, 5 x 5 In.	3750
Pitcher, Red, Yellow, White, Green, Pink, Applied Insects, Handle, Signed, 7 In.	2420
Pitcher, Water, Leaf, Vine, Molded Red Snail, c. 1925, 7 ½ In.	687
Scent Bottle, Flask, Flowers, Stems, Red, Green, Frosted Ground, Silver Cap & Shot Glass, Cameo, 6 In.	3025
Sconce, Glass, Clear Frost, Bird On Shade, Cameo, Shade 6 In., 9 In.	1210
Sculpture, Electre, Woman Encased In Green Wave, Pate-De-Verre, Olivier Brice, 15 In.	1187
Vase, 2 Handles, Frosted Background, Enameled Violets, 4 ¼ x 8 In.	420
Vase, Acid Etched, Winter Scene, Snow, Square, Rounded Corners, 3 x 3 x 2 ¾ In.	1808
Vase, Amethyst, Platinum, Green, Hanging Leaves, Cameo, Marked, 8 In.	2242
Vase, Autumn, Trees, Lake, Etched, Enamel, Signed, France, 9 ¼ In.	8125
Vase, Berry, Chalice Form, Tree Branches, Yellow To Maroon Ground, Cameo, Signed, 9 ½ In.	3509
Vase, Blackberry, Mottled Tan, Cream, Green Leaves, Iridescent Ground, Cameo, Signed, 17 In.	4537
Vase, Bleeding Heart, Enamel, Heart Plants, Leaves, Stems, Cameo, Signed, 27 ½ In.	9680
Vase, Blue Cornflowers, Gold Highlights, Flared Neck, Cameo, Marked, 7 ½ In.	3658
Vase, Blue Glass Interior, Gilt Bronze, Teardrops, Lacrima, Andre Dubreuil, c.1990, 17 x 8 ½ In.	1250
Vase, Bottle Shape, Winter Scene, Trees, Yellow & Orange Ground, Signed, 6 In.	1694
Vase, Bulbous Body, Cylindrical Neck, Opalescent & Yellow, 4 ¾ In.	544
Vase, Carved, Leaves, Red Poppy Flower, Cameo, Signed, 6 In.	5445
Vase, Carved, Tobacco Flower, Red, Brown, Yellow Ground, Wide Mouth, Signed, 3 In.	3025
Vase, Carved, Tobacco Flowers, Dark Red, Squat, Mottled Orange Ground, Cameo, Footed, 7 In.	1089
Vase, Coreopsis, Internally Decorated, Bulbous Foot, 6 ⅝ x 2 In. *illus*	1062
Vase, Cylindrical, Impressionistic, Pine Trees, Orange To Blue Sky, Birds, Signed, Cameo, 12 ½ In.	7260
Vase, Daffodil, Pate-De-Verre, Yellow, Green, 9 ¾ x 7 ¾ In.	1375
Vase, Daffodils, Egg Shape, Irregular Rim, White, Green Base, Round, France, c.1920, 7 x 4 In.	7500
Vase, Enamel, Flowers, Stems, Autumn Colors, Yellow Ground, Cameo, Signed, 5 In.	2662
Vase, Enameled Winter Tree Scene, Yellow & Orange Sky, Oval Base, Cameo, Signed, 14 ½ In.	7865

Cut Glass, Punch Set, Montrose, Green Cut To Clear, Dorflinger, 15-In. Bowl, 13 Piece
$114,000

Brunk Auctions

TIP
Put a silver spoon in a glass before pouring in hot water. It will absorb heat and keep the glass from cracking.

Cut Glass, Teapot, Alberta, Hawkes, 6 x 9 In.
$1,560

Brunk Auctions

Daum, Figurine, Parrot, On Perch, Blue, Green, Pate-De-Verre, 11 ¼ In.
$550

Woody Auction

DAUM

Daum, Group, Horse, 4 Riders, Amber, Purple, Brass Swords, C. Poincignon, 12 x 12 In.
$1,989

Forsythes' Auctions

Daum, Jar, Lid, Opalescent, Enameled Flowers, Leaves, Cameo, Gilt Glass Stopper, 3 In.
$2,723

James D. Julia Auctioneers

Daum, Vase, Coreopsis, Internally Decorated, Bulbous Foot, 6 5/8 x 2 In.
$1,062

Rago Arts and Auction Center

Daum, Vase, Farm Scene, Trees, Farm House, Blue Sky, Enamel, Cameo, Signed, 10 In.
$10,890

James D. Julia Auctioneers

Daum, Vase, Gourd, Multicolor, Textured, Applied Wrapping Handle, Signed, 11 1/2 In.
$3,025

James D. Julia Auctioneers

Daum, Vase, Mold Blown, Green Leaves, White Shaded To Orange To Blue, Signed, 9 1/2 In.
$2,420

James D. Julia Auctioneers

Daum, Vase, Mushrooms, Etched, Enameled Inside, Handles, Signed, c.1900, 6 x 6 1/2 In.
$9,375

Rago Arts and Auction Center

De Morgan, Vase, Stylized Leaves, Flowers, Red, Cream, Copper Highlights, 17 1/2 In.
$1,815

James D. Julia Auctioneers

De Vez, Vase, Sailboats, Shore, Trees, Blue, Yellow, Green, Cameo, 4 3/8 x 3 7/8 In.
$409

Jeffrey S. Evans

Vase, Enameled, Flowers, Stems, Scrolling, Gilded Band, Cameo, Signed, 4 In.	2238
Vase, Farm Scene, Trees, Farm House, Blue Sky, Enamel, Cameo, Signed, 10 In. *illus*	10890
Vase, Figures, Burgundy, Gilded Highlights, 2 Fires, Cameo, Signed, 5¾ In.	2000
Vase, Fuchsia, Purple, Pink, Green Leaves, Etched, Internal Decoration, c.1920, 4¾ x 2¼ In..	1625
Vase, Gourd, Multicolor, Textured, Applied Wrapping Handle, Signed, 11½ In. *illus*	3025
Vase, Green, Foil Inclusions, Internal Decoration, France, 1920s, 11¼ x 6 In.	937
Vase, Internal Decoration, Stick, Mottled Yellow & Red, Signed, 13½ In.	303
Vase, Iris, Violet Rim, Yellow Body, Pate-De-Verre, 11 In.	514
Vase, Magnolias, Green, Orange White, Shouldered, Cameo, Signed, 8 In.	4537
Vase, Mold Blown, Green Leaves, White Shaded To Orange To Blue, Signed, 9½ In. *illus*	2420
Vase, Mold Blown, Village, Trees, Sunset, France, 1900s, 11¼ x 4 In.	5937
Vase, Mushrooms, Etched, Enameled Inside, Handles, Signed, c.1900, 6 x 6½ In. *illus*	9375
Vase, Orchids, Pate-De-Verre, Violet, 12½ x 9½ In.	1875
Vase, Padded & Carved Floral, Green, Blue, Yellow, Brown, Enameled, 4 In.	2662
Vase, Pillow, Internal Decoration, Bulbous, Flat, Orange, Yellow, Frosted Ground, 7 x 4½ In. .	424
Vase, Pinecone, Trees, Lake, Cream, Tans, Cameo, 9¼ x 2¼ In.	2000
Vase, Purple, Beige Ground, Berries On Thorns, Flaring Shape, Cameo, Marked, 12 In.	5900
Vase, Round, Flared Rim, Purple, Tiger Lily Blossoms, Cameo, 12¼ x 9¾ In.	4537
Vase, Ruffled Mouth, Dark Purple, Brown, Gilt Highlights, Flowers, 4½ x 4¾ In.	625
Vase, Sprig Leaves, Branches, Flower Blossom, Cameo, 11½ In.	6050
Vase, Tall Trees, Pink & Purple Field, Mottled, 4¾ x 2¾ In.	3437
Vase, Thorns, Brown Leaves, Green Mottled Ground, Footed, Collar, 6 In.	1056
Vase, Trees, Shrubs, Red, Yellow, Flared Rim, Green Base, Internal Decoration, Cameo, 10 x 4 In...	1125
Vase, Tulips, Orange, Green, Gilded, Gilded Foot, Cameo, Signed, 4 In.	1331
Vase, Tulips, Striated Green & Yellow Flowers, Blue Ground, Cameo, Signed, 16 In.	5445
Vase, Violet Grapes & Vines Yellow, Orange, Green Ground, Cameo, Signed, 15 In.	2057
Vase, Yellow Ground, Red Flowers, Cameo, Signed, 14 In.	1815

DAVY CROCKETT, the American frontiersman, was born in 1786 and died in 1836. The historical character gained new fame in 1954 when the Walt Disney television show ran a series of episodes featuring Fess Parker as Davy Crockett. Coonskin caps and buckskins became popular and hundreds of different Davy Crockett items were made.

Lamp, Covered Wagon, Cactus, Wood, Plastic Shade, Box, Cactus Crafts, 1955, 4 x 5 x 5½ In..	150
Sign, Get Up Soda, Hey Kids!, Get Your Davy Crockett Hat, Only 25 Cents, 1950s, 17 x 11 In.	59

DE MORGAN art pottery was made in England by William De Morgan from the 1860s to 1907. He is best known for his luster-glazed Moorish-inspired pieces. The pottery used a variety of marks.

Ewer, Footed, Flowers, Blue Ground, 9 In.	723
Tile, Flowing Leaves, Green, 6 x 6 In.	850
Tile, Seated Boar, Blue & White, 1880s, 6 x 6 In.	950
Tile, Yellow Flowers, Leaves, 1890s, 5 x 5 In.	168
Vase, Globular, Flowers, Blue, c.1890, 7½ In.	1234
Vase, Stylized Leaves, Flowers, Red, Cream, Copper Highlights, 17½ In. *illus*	1815

DE VEZ was a signature used on cameo glass after 1910. E. S. Monot founded the glass company near Paris in 1851. The company changed names many times. Mt. Joye, another glass by this factory, is listed in its own category.

Biscuit Jar, Tricolor, Peach To Aqua, Venetian Boaters, Sailors, City, Columns, 7 x 4¼ In.	1404
Vase, Harbor, Sailboat, Teal, Leaves, White Ground, Cameo, 3 x 6¼ In.	406
Vase, Lake, Mountain, Pale Blue, Dark Blue Background, 3¼ In.	527
Vase, Pink Mountains, Green Trees, Cameo, 3 x 6¼ In.	325
Vase, Sailboats, Shore, Trees, Blue, Yellow, Green, Cameo, 4⅜ x 3⅞ In. *illus*	409
Vase, Straight Neck, Purple, Sailboats, Cameo, 3¼ x 8 In.	260
Vase, Trees, Pond, Pink, Green, 2½ x 5¾ In	390
Vase, Violets, Pale Yellow Ground, Cameo, 4½ x 10½ In.	175

D

Decoy, Canada Goose, Black, Gray & White Paint, Glass Eyes, 1900s, 13 x 21 x 9¼ In.
$210

Garth's Auctioneers & Appraisers

Decoy, Canada Goose, Black, Tan, Cream, Wood, Havre De Grace, Maryland, 24 In.
$1,320

Thomaston Place Auction Galleries

Decoy, Canada Goose, Original Paint, Glass Eyes, Salmon, Red Ground, Frank Resop, 20 In.
$9,000

Garth's Auctioneers & Appraisers

Decoy, Fish, Rainbow Trout, Carved, Push-Pin Eyes, Tin Fins, Lead Weight, 10⅜ In.
$70

Hess Auction Group

109

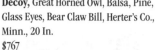

Decoy, Great Horned Owl, Balsa, Pine, Glass Eyes, Bear Claw Bill, Herter's Co., Minn., 20 In.
$767

Hess Auction Group

Decoy, Merganser, Brush Head, Painted, Wood, Iron Weight, 20 In.
$177

Copake Auction

DECORATED TUMBLERS *may be listed by maker or design or in Advertising, Coca-Cola, Pepsi-Cola, Sports, and other categories.*

 DECOYS are carved or turned wooden copies of birds, fish, or animals. The decoy was placed in the water or propped on the shore to lure flying birds to the pond for hunters. Some decoys are handmade; some are commercial products. Today there is a group of artists making modern decoys for display, not for use in a pond. Many sell for high prices.

Black Duck, Circular Wooden Base, Martin D. Collins Decoys, c.1975, 13 ½ In.	438
Black Duck, Gus Wilson, Rocking Head, Weight Attached By Chain, 1920s, 18 In.	1920
Bluebill Hen, Wood, Metal, William Porterfield, Holtwood, Pa., 1970, 12 x 5 ¾ x 12 In.	71
Bluebill, John Roth, Wisconsin, Original Paint & Glass Eyes, 1930, 16 In.	390
Brant, Hollow Carved, Attributed To Jess Birdsall	108
Bufflehead, Painted, Tack Eyes, M. Hancock, Virginia, c.1960, 11 In., Pair	420
Canada Goose, Black, Gray & White Paint, Glass Eyes, 1900s, 13 x 21 x 9 ¼ In. *illus*	210
Canada Goose, Black, Tan, Cream, Wood, Havre De Grace, Maryland, 24 In. *illus*	1320
Canada Goose, Canvas Cover, Painted, George Boyd, Seabrook, New Hampshire, c.1925, 26 In.	1000
Canada Goose, Carved, Painted, Signed On Base, Tom Taber, 1979, 12 x 23 x 8 ¼ In.	254
Canada Goose, Glass Eyes, Mason Decoy Factory, c.1910, 20 In.	420
Canada Goose, Original Paint, Glass Eyes, Salmon, Red Ground, Frank Resop, 20 In. *illus*	9000
Canvasback Drake, Glass Eyes, Original Paint, Branded E.K Sanders, 14 In.	300
Canvasback, Original Paint, Glass Eyes, John Roth, Wisconsin, Signed In Pencil, 19 In.	150
Canvasback, Typed Label On Underside, Original Paint, Glass Eyes, Frank Strey, Wisconsin, 19 In.	531
Coot, Original Paint, Glass Eyes, Owner's Initial On Bottom, Gust Gus Nelow, 15 In.	390
Crow, Glass Eyes, Applied Wings, Metal Legs, Black, 17 x 5 ½ In.	108
Dove, Preening, Glass Eyes, Carved Detailed Wing, Marked Gibian, 10 ½ In.	687
Drake, Glass Eyes, Red, Cream, Brown, Mason Decoy Factory, c.1910, 14 ½ In.	480
Duck, Anthony Elmer Crowell, Original Paint, Inked Stamp On Bottom, 1 ¾ In.	2000
Eagle, Glass Eyes, Carved Feathers, 6 x 8 In.	156
Fish, Rainbow Trout, Carved, Push-Pin Eyes, Tin Fins, Lead Weight, 10 ⅜ In. *illus*	70
Fish, Suckerfish, Wood, Painted, Tin Fins, Folk Art, Oscar Peterson, c.1925, 7 In.	165
Goldeneye Drake, Glass Eyes, Stevens Factory, 1900-50, 14 ¾ In.	840
Goldeneye, Common, Turned Head, Hollow Body, Branded, Whitney, 16 In.	120
Goose, Slat, Marked Pequaw-Honk Club, A. Elmer Crowell, c.1925, 42 In.	812
Great Horned Owl, Balsa, Pine, Glass Eyes, Bear Claw Bill, Herter's Co., Minn., 20 In. *illus*	767
Hen, Tack Eyes, Head Turned To Right, 1940, 17 In.	144
Mallard Drake, Hand Carved, Primitive Style Wood Sculpture, Signed, Chris Boone, 15 x 5 x 8 In.	248
Merganser Drake, Painted, Miles Hancock, 1940-50, 15 ½ In.	240
Merganser, Brush Head, Painted, Wood, Iron Weight, 20 In. *illus*	177
Pintail Hen, Glass Eyes, Mason Decoy Factory, c.1910, 17 In.	1080
Pintail Hen, Original Paint, Red Sticker KHN, Eddie Granier, c.1950, 17 In.	1920
Shorebird, Black-Belly Plover, On Later Stand, 1900s, 11 In.	240
Shorebird, Robin Snipe, Glass Eyes, Gibian Carved On Bottom, 9 ½ In. *illus*	660
Swan, Chesapeake Bay Style, Glass Eyes, 1900s, 29 In.	270
Swan, John Cannon Waterfield, Yellow Pine, Lead Weighted Base, 1800s, 26 x 28 x 11 In.	4800
Swan, White, 30 x 19 In.	204
Teal Hen, Blue, Driftwood, Basswood, Delaware, William Veasay, 1970, 14 x 11 In.	248
Turtle, Duck Hunting, Single Piece, Yellow Pine, Raised Head, Carved Eyes, 1800s, 22 In.	1320
Wood Duck Drake, Glass Eyes, Scratch Feather Paint Detail, c.1925, 12 In. *illus*	1440

 DEDHAM POTTERY was started in 1895. Chelsea Keramic Art Works was established in 1872 in Chelsea, Massachusetts, by members of the Robertson family. The factory closed in 1889 and was reorganized as the Chelsea Pottery U.S. in 1891. The firm used the marks *CKAW* and *CPUS*. It became the Dedham Pottery of Dedham, Massachusetts. The factory closed in 1943. It was famous for its crackleware dishes, which picture blue outlines of animals, flowers, and other natural motifs. Pottery by Chelsea Keramic Art Works and Dedham Pottery is listed here.

Duck, Plate, Blue, White, 1898-1928, 8 ⅜ In.	123
Night & Morning, Pitcher, Rooster, Owl, Blue Ink Stamp, 5 In. *illus*	200

Rabbit, Flower Frog, Blue & White, 6 x 4 ¼ In.	575
Rabbit, Plate, Blue & White, 8 ½ In.	29
Rabbit, Salt & Pepper, Blue & White, 3 ½ In.	149
Snow Tree, Plate, Blue & White, 8 ½ In.	345
Turkey, Plate, Dinner, Blue & White, 10 In.	175
Vase, Shouldered, Marbled Glaze, 8 x 4 In.	1526
Vase, Tan & Blue Drip Glaze, Hugh Cornwall Robertson, 8 x 4 ½ In. *illus*	840

DEGUE is a signature acid etched on pieces of French glass made by the Cristalleries de Compiegne beginning about 1925. Cameo, mold blown, and smooth glass with contrasting colored rims are the types most often found. The factory closed in 1939.

Vase, Art Deco, Mottled Red Glass, Black Geometric Design, Cameo, Signed, 15 In.	1089
Vase, Art Deco, Pink, Body Sculpted In Flower Heads, Serrated Leaves, 8 x 5 ¾ In.	177
Vase, Boston Ivy, Purple To Red To Orange, Cameo, France, 6 ¼ x 16 In.	650

DELATTE glass is a French cameo glass made by Andre Delatte. It was first made in Nancy, France, in 1921. Lighting fixtures and opaque glassware in imitation of Bohemian opaline were made.

Vase, Art Deco, Blown Out, Iron Mount, Mottled Pink, Red, Mica Flecks, 5 ¾ x 3 ¼ In.	113
Vase, Cattleya Orchid, Small Mouth, Purple To Blue, 5 x 8 ¼ In.	275
Vase, Gloriosa Lily, Purple, Pink Ground, 3 ½ x 8 In.	325
Vase, Orchid, Purple Cut To Pale Yellow, Mottled, 6 ½ x 18 In.	750

DELDARE, *see Buffalo Pottery Deldare.*

DELFT is a special type of tin-glazed pottery. Early delft was made in Holland and England during the seventeenth century. It was usually decorated with blue on a white surface, but some was polychrome, decorated with green, yellow, and other colors. Most delftware pieces were dishes needed for everyday living. Figures were made from about 1750 to 1800 and are rare. Although the soft tin-glazed pottery was well-known, it was not named delft until after 1840, when it was named for the city in Holland where much of it was made. Porcelain became more popular because it was more durable, and Holland gradually stopped making the old delft. In 1876 De Porceleyne Fles factory in Delft introduced a porcelain ware that was decorated with blue and white scenes of Holland that reminded many of old delft. It became popular with the Dutch and tourists. By 1990 all of the blue and white porcelain with Dutch scenes was made in Asia, although it was marked *Delft*. Only one Dutch company remains that makes the traditional old-style delft with blue on white or with colored decorations. Most of the pieces sold today were made after 1891, and the name *Holland* usually appears with the Delft factory marks. The word *Delft* appears alone on some inexpensive twentieth- and twenty-first-century pottery from Asia and Germany that is also listed here.

Birdcage, Blue, White, Illustrations, Birds Of Paradise, Animals, Porcelain, Holland, 1900s, 16 x 11 In.	1800
Bowl, Flowers, Stars, Red, Green, Flower Spray Interior, c.1740, 7 x 11 ¾ In. *illus*	1792
Bowl, Pavilions, Rocky View, Decorated Diaperwork, Blue Dots, 1770-85, 10 In.	625
Bowl, Town Scene, Fisherman, Cobalt Blue Underglaze, 1700s, 13 In.	313
Bowl, Underplate, Flowers, Scalloped Rim, Dutch, Late 1800s, 16 In. *illus*	2500
Charger, Archer, Hunter, Deer, Lambeth, England, 1700s, 14 In.	570
Charger, Hand Decorated, Blue Floral & Rock Design, Yellow Edge, Rim Flakes, 1700s, 13 In.	270
Charger, Hexagonal, Stork, Leafy Design, Earthenware, 15 ½ In.	159
Charger, Horse, Rider, Trees, Flower, Vine Border, Blue, Green, Yellow, Initialed IDM, c.1750, 13 ¾ In.	660
Charger, Painted Rim, Scrolled Cartouche Flanked, Griffins, 1600s, 15 In.	5000
Charger, Painted, Couple Flanking, Blue Dash Border, 1690-1710, 13 In.	4375
Charger, Windmill, Tree, Horse, Rider, 16 In.	110
Clock, 8-Day Time & Strike Movement, Pendulum & Key, 10 x 8 x 4 ¼ In.	132
Clock, Miniature, Tall Case Shape, Windmill & Boats, 1900, 4 ¾ x 3 ¼ In.	960
Console, Blue, White, Birds, Flowers, Landscape, Porcelain, Holland, 1700s, 8 x 12 In.	780
Ginger Jar, Lid, Birds In Garden Cartouche, Dutch, 1700s, 12 In., Pair *illus*	938

Decoy, Shorebird, Robin Snipe, Glass Eyes, Gibian Carved On Bottom, 9 ½ In. $660

Eldred's Auctioneers and Appraisers

Decoy, Wood Duck Drake, Glass Eyes, Scratch Feather Paint Detail, c.1925, 12 In. $1,440

Eldred's Auctioneers and Appraisers

Dedham, Night & Morning, Pitcher, Rooster, Owl, Blue Ink Stamp, 5 In. $200

Hess Auction Group

Dedham, Vase, Tan & Blue Drip Glaze, Hugh Cornwall Robertson, 8 x 4½ In. $840

Thomaston Place Auction Galleries

Dogwood Depression Glass

Dogwood is decorated with a flower that has been given many names. Collectors have called this pattern Apple Blossom, B Pattern, Magnolia, or Wildrose. It was made from 1930 to 1934 by Macbeth-Evans Glass Company. It is found in Cremax, Crystal, Green, Monax, Pink, and Yellow. Some Pink pieces are trimmed with gold. Some pieces were made with such thin walls that the factory redesigned the molds to make the pieces thicker.

Delft, Bowl, Flowers, Stars, Red, Green, Flower Spray Interior, c.1740, 7 x 11¾ In. $1,792

Neal Auction Co.

Jar, Blue, Man Smoking Pipe, Sailing Ships, Marked Manilla, 3 Bells, 1700s, 10 In.	500
Jar, Lid, Blue & White, Bulbous, 1800s, 18 In.	2125
Jar, Lid, Blue & White, Octagonal, c.1800, 22 In., Pair	458
Jar, Lid, Hexagonal, Lion Finial, Floral Sprigs, Bouquets, Marked, 19 x 10 In., Pair	2125
Pilgrim Flask, Figures, Leaves, Pierced, 4 Handles, Footed, Dutch, 1900s, 9 In. ... *illus*	500
Plaque, Square, Blue, White, Rounded Corners, 2 Ducks In Pond, Holland, 1700s, 9 x 9 In.	531
Plate, Portraits, William & Mary, Painted, 1690, 8⅝ In.	5185
Plate, Stag In Landscape, Red, Blue Green, Diamond Border, 1700s, 8½ In.	256
Puzzle Jug, Flowers, Scrolls, Verse, Pierced Neck, England, c.1750, 7¼ In. ... *illus*	1170
Stein, Portrait, Man Drinking Wine, Bulbous, Pewter Lid, Footed, 5 Liter, 17¾ In. ... *illus*	600
Tulipiere, Peacock Decoration, 5 Holders, Footed, Marked, DePauw, 1700s, 8 In. ... *illus*	1500
Vase, Blue, White, Collar, Flowers, Animals, Birds, Insects, Porcelain, Holland, 1700s, 13 In.	390
Vase, Tulip, Courting Couple, Village Landscape, Heart Shape, 5 Openings, Footed, 9 x 7 In.	366
Water Jug, Blue, White, Bulbous, Double Handle, Hunting, Camels, Snakes, 1800s, 11 x 7 In.	375

 DENTAL cabinets, chairs, equipment, and other related items are listed here. Other objects may be found in the Medical category.

Chair, Adjustable Headrest, Attached Lamp, Swivel Seat, Metal, Ford R.R., 1900s, 44 x 20 x 26 In.	575
Dental Chart, Pull-Down, Human Dentition, Linen, Hagemann, 1960s, 67 x 47 In.	525
Instrument, English Key, Extracting Tool, Astra Co., 18th Century, 4½ x 3½ In.	125
Spittoon, Stainless Steel, Hole In Bottom, c.1930, 12 x 3½ In.	300
Tin, Dr. Tepper's Gum Lyke, Artificial Gum Material, Litho, Industrial Rubber Corp., 6 x 3 In. ... *illus*	118
Tin, Floss, Nylon, Blue White, Curity, Bauer & Black, 1⅛ In.	18
Trubyte Tooth Vitality Scale, False Teeth, Fan Shape, Maroon Plastic, Dentist Supply Co.	35

DENVER is part of the mark on an American art pottery. William Long of Steubenville, Ohio, founded the Lonhuda Pottery Company in 1892. In 1900 he moved to Denver, Colorado, and organized the Denver China and Pottery Company. This pottery, which used the mark *Denver*, worked until 1905, when Long moved to New Jersey and founded the Clifton Pottery. Long also worked for Weller Pottery, Roseville Pottery, and American Encaustic Tiling Company. Do not confuse this pottery with the Denver White Pottery, which worked from 1894 to 1955 in Denver.

Vase, Nasturtiums, Embossed, Green Matte Glaze, Ink Stamp Logo, 1903, 5⅛ In.	3540

DEPRESSION GLASS is an inexpensive glass that was manufactured in large quantities during the 1920s and early 1930s. It was made in many colors and patterns by dozens of factories in the United States. Most patterns were also made in clear glass, which the factories called *crystal*. If no color is listed here, it is clear. The name *Depression glass* is a modern one and also refers to machine-made glass of the 1940s through 1970s. Sets missing a few pieces can be completed through the help of a matching service.

Baltic Royal Ruby, Sherbet, Anchor Hocking, 6½ In.	13
Baltic Royal Ruby, Tumbler, Anchor Hocking, 4½ In.	10
Blue Mayfair, Candy Dish, Footed, Lid, Hocking Glass, 1930s, 6 In. ... *illus*	225
Cameo, Sherbet, Green, 3 In.	26
Charm, Bowl, Fruit, Green, 4¾ In.	8
Charm, Plate, Luncheon, Ruby, 8¼ In.	15
Charm, Platter, 11 In.	45
Cherry Blossom, Cake Plate, Green, 1930s, 10¼ In.	35
Cherry Blossom, Saucer, Pink, Child's, 4 In.	11
Colonial, Bowl, Vegetable, Green Border, Blue & Red Flower, Green Leaves, 9¼ In.	24
Colony, Dish, Hazel Atlas, 9½ In.	12
Colony, Serving Bowl, Hazel Atlas, 10¾ In.	24
Crackle, Bowl, Orange, 7 x 3 In.	25
Crisscross, Loaf Pan, Refrigerator Dish, Hazel Atlas, 8½ x 4 x 3 In.	25
Crystal Happenings, Egg Relish Dish, 11 In.	21
Diamond Block, Jug, 16 Oz.	32
Diamond Point Amber, Candleholder, Indiana Glass	18

Delft, Bowl, Underplate, Flowers, Scalloped Rim, Dutch, Late 1800s, 16 In.
$2,500

Freeman's Auctioneers & Appraisers

Delft, Ginger Jar, Lid, Birds In Garden Cartouche, Dutch, 1700s, 12 In.,
Pair
$938

Freeman's Auctioneers & Appraisers

Delft, Pilgrim Flask, Figures, Leaves, Pierced, 4 Handles, Footed, Dutch,
1900s, 9 In.
$500

Freeman's Auctioneers & Appraisers

Delft, Puzzle Jug, Flowers, Scrolls, Verse, Pierced Neck, England, c.1750,
7 ¼ In.
$1,170

Freeman's Auctioneers & Appraisers

Delft, Stein, Portrait, Man Drinking Wine, Bulbous, Pewter Lid, Footed,
5 Liter, 17 ¾ In.
$600

The Stein Auction Company

Delft, Tulipiere, Peacock Decoration, 5 Holders, Footed, Marked,
DePauw, 1700s, 8 In.
$1,500

Freeman's Auctioneers & Appraisers

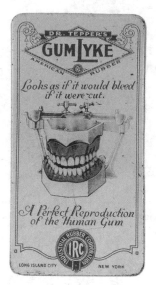

Dental, Tin, Dr. Tepper's Gum Lyke, Artificial Gum Material, Litho, Industrial Rubber Corp., 6 x 3 In.
$118

Depression Glass, Blue Mayfair, Candy Dish, Footed, Lid, Hocking Glass, 1930s, 6 In.
$225

Diamond Point Crystal, Compote, Lid, Indiana Glass, 11½ In.		25
Diamond Point Crystal, Wine, Indiana Glass, 5¼ In.		10
Diamond Quilted, Creamer, Pink		21
Dogwood, Bowl, Pink, 3½ x 9¾ In.		45
Dogwood, Cake Plate, Pink, Fluted Edge, 13 In.		124
Dogwood, Pitcher, Smooth Handle, MacBeth-Evans, 80 Oz., 8 x 8 In.		45
Dogwood, Tumblers, MacBeth-Evans, 4 x 3 In., 8 Piece		124
Floragold, Bowl, Dessert, Jeannette Glass, 5½ In.		16
Floragold, Bowl, Jeannette Glass, 9½ In.		21
Floral, Cup, Green		21
Hellenic Green, Bowl, Fruit, Jeannette Glass, 2⅜ In.		12
Hellenic Green, Bowl, Salad, Stand, Jeannette Glass, 8¾ In.		22
Hellenic Green, Ice Bucket, Jeannette Glass, 5 In.		20
Laurel, Goblet, Iced Tea, Anchor Hocking, 7 In.		10
Laurel, Goblet, Water, Anchor Hocking, 5½ In.		7
Laurel, Sherbet, Anchor Hocking, 3½ In.		8
Madrid, Bowl, Fruit, Amber, Federal Glass, 5 In.		8
Madrid, Bowl, Vegetable, Federal Glass, 10 In.		15
Madrid, Sugar, Federal Glass		12
Miss America, Berry Bowl, 6¼ In.		9
Miss America, Bowl, Oval, Anchor Hocking, 1935-38, 8 In.		25
Miss America, Cake Plate, Pink, Footed, 1930s, 12 In.		50
Miss America, Celery Dish, Anchor Hocking, 1935-38		11
Miss America, Plate, 10¼ In.		14
Miss America, Plate, Salad, 8½ In.		8
Miss America, Plate, Salad, Anchor Hocking, 1935-38, 8½ In.		8
Miss America, Relish, 4 Sections, Anchor Hocking, 1935-38, 9 In.		8
Miss America, Relish, 5 Sections, Anchor Hocking, 1935-38, 12 In.		25
Miss America, Relish, Anchor Hocking, 1935-38, 12 In.		21
Miss America, Salt Cellar		30
Moroccan Amethyst, Bowl, Hazel Atlas, 6 In.		11
Moroccan Amethyst, Bowl, Oval, Handles, Hazel Atlas, 7¾ In.		14
Park Avenue, Ashtray		10
Park Avenue, Cup		5
Pioneer Line, Plate, Smoke, Federal Glass, 11⅜ In.		10
Pitcher, Water, Opaque Blue, Enamel Leaf & Blossoms, Ribbed Handle, Rigaree, 8 In.		30
Rosemary, Bowl, Fruit, 5 In.		5
Sierra, Pinwheel, Dinner Plate, Pink, Jeannette, c.1932, 8¾ In.	*illus*	15
Soreno, Butter, Cover, Green		10
Sweetheart, Pitcher, Pink Dogwood, MacBeth-Evans, 8 x 8 In.		28
Windsor, Cake Stand, Clear, Federal Glass, 4½ x 11 In.		32
Windsor, Pitcher, Clear, Federal Glass, 5⅝ In.		20
Windsor, Tray, Clear, Federal Glass, 8⅜ In.		15
Windsor, Torte Plate, Jeannette Glass, 13⅝ In.		32

DERBY has been marked on porcelain made in the city of Derby, England, since about 1748. The original Derby factory closed in 1848, but others opened there and continued to produce quality porcelain. The Crown Derby mark began appearing on Derby wares in the 1770s.

Bowl, Scalloped, Urn, Flowers, Musical Instruments, Oval, c.1780, 12½ x 9¾ In.	*illus*	129
Figurine, Grotesque Punches, Dwarfs, Waistcoats, Playing Mandolin, Violin, 8 In., Pair		1037
Teapot, Warming Stand, 11½ In.		121
Toothpick Holder, Silver Plate, Chick & Wishbone, Engraved Best Wishes, Victorian, 2¼ x 3½ In.		30
Toothpick Holder, Silver Plate, Young Boy Holding Stick, Standing Near Bucket, Tufts, 2¾ x 3 In.		108

DICK TRACY, the comic strip, started in 1931. Tracy was also the hero of movies from 1937 to 1947 and again in 1990, and starred in a radio series in the 1940s and a television series in the 1950s. Memorabilia from all these activities are collected.

Book, Dick Tracy & The Bicycle Gang, Better Little Book No. 144, 3 x 4 ½ In.	28
Book, Pop-Up, Capture Of Boris Arson, Pleasure Books, 1935, 9 ¼ x 8 In.	495
Key Ring, Goldstone, Enamel, Yellow, Blue, Acrylic, Gift Creations, 1990, 1 ½ In.	5
Ring, Good Luck, Compartments, Relief Portrait, Brass, Adjustable, 1938	130
Toy, Police Squad, Tin, Green, Windup, 1949, 12 x 4 In.	100

DICKENS WARE *pieces are listed in the Royal Doulton and Weller categories.*

DINNERWARE used in the United States from the 1930s through the 1950s is listed here. Most was made in potteries in southern Ohio, West Virginia, and California. A few patterns were made in Japan, England, and other countries. Dishes were sold in gift shops and department stores, or were given away as premiums. Many of these patterns are listed in this book in their own categories, such as Autumn Leaf, Azalea, Coors, Fiesta, Franciscan, Hall, Harker, Harlequin, Red Wing, Riviera, Russel Wright, Vernon Kilns, Watt, and Willow. For more prices, go to kovels.com. Sets missing a few pieces can be completed through the help of a matching service. Three examples of dated dinnerware marks are shown here.

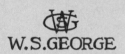

W.S. George Pottery Co. Late 1930s–1940	Royal China Co. 1950s+	Salem China Co. 1940s–1960

Al Fresco, Bowl, Cereal, Misty Gray, Brusche, 6 In.	10
Al Fresco, Chop Plate, Olive Green, Glossy, Brusche, 13 In.	45
Al Fresco, Plate, Bread & Butter, Yellow, Speckled Pottery, Glossy, Brusche, 6 In.	8
Al Fresco, Saucer, Pale Green, Speckled Pottery, Glossy, Brusche	3
Apple Blossom, Platter, Johnson Brothers, 12 In.	32
Apple Trio, Bowl, Fruit, Blue Ridge, 5 ⅜ In.	12
Apple Trio, Plate, Bread & Butter, Blue Ridge, 6 ¼ In.	11
Apple Trio, Plate, Salad, 3 Red Apples, Green Border, Colonial, Blue Ridge, 9 In.	12
Apple Trio, Plate, Salad, Blue Ridge, 8 ⅜ In.	12
Big Apple, Creamer, Brown Stems, Veins, Green Edge, Blue Ridge	15
Bird Of Paradise, Mug, Fitz & Floyd, 3 ¾ In.	25
Bird Of Paradise, Plate, Salad, Fitz & Floyd, 7 ½ In.	20
Blue Bonnet, Chop Plate, Harmony House, 12 ½ In.	32
Bramble, Creamer, Green Ivy-Like Leaves, Thorny Brown Stems, Blue Ridge	7
Bramble, Plate, Dinner, Green Ivy-Like Leaves, Thorny Brown Stems, Blue Ridge, 10 ⅛ In.	12
California Farmhouse, Saucer, White, Yellow Border, Brock	3
California Wild Flower, Bowl, Vegetable, Pink Trim, Cream Background, Brock, 9 In.	25
California Wild Flower, Soup, Dish, Gray Trim, Cream Background, Brock, 7 In.	15
California Wild Flower, Soup, Dish, Pink Trim, Cream Background, Brock, 7 In.	15
Carol's Roses, Chop Plate, Colonial, Pink, Yellow, Red Roses, Blue Ridge, 12 In.	65
Castleton, Cup & Saucer, Flair, Gray On Cream, Pink Flower, Platinum Trim, Blue Ridge	25
Chanticleer, Cup, Fanciful Rooster, Russet Trim, Brock	6
Chanticleer, Plate, Bread & Butter, Fanciful Rooster, Russet Trim, Brock, 7 In.	5
Cheerio, Chop Plate, 2-Tone, Yellow & Brown Flowers, Leaves, Skyline, Blue Ridge, 13 In.	24
Contempo, Platter, Beige Matte, Brusche, 13 In.	30
Country Fair, Plate, Salad, Pear, Cherries, Colonial, Green Trim, Blue Ridge, 9 In.	12
Country Road, Sugar, Lid, Yellow, Daisy-Like Flowers, Green & Brown Leaves, Blue Ridge	21
Country Sage, Bowl, Cereal, Homer Laughlin, 6 ¼ In.	5
Country Sage, Bowl, Vegetable, Lid, Homer Laughlin	25
County Sage, Butter, Cover, Homer Laughlin	18
Crab Apple, Saucer, Green Leaves, Red Trim, Colonial, Blue Ridge	4
Dairy Maid, Cup & Saucer, Crooksville	21
Dairy Maid, Plate, Dinner, Crooksville, 10 ¼ In.	15
Dazzle, Plate, Bread & Butter, Flowers, Yellow, Brown, Solid Green, Blue Ridge, 6 In.	8
Desert Sand, Plate, Dinner, Johnson Brothers, 10 ½ In.	16

Depression Glass, Sierra, Pinwheel, Dinner Plate, Pink, Jeannette, c.1932, 8 ¾ In.
$15

Ruby Lane

Derby, Bowl, Scalloped, Urn, Flowers, Musical Instruments, Oval, c.1780, 12 ½ x 9 ¾ In.
$129

Strawser Auction Group

TIP
Coffee or tea stains can be removed from a cup by scrubbing with salt on a sponge.

Dinnerware, Old Country Roses, Bowl, Lid, Royal Albert, 2 ⅞ In.
$80

Replacements, Ltd.

Dionne Quintuplets, Doll, Composition, Original Outfits, Wood Scooter, 1930s, 5 Babies
$1,295

Ruby Lane

Dirk Van Erp, Lamp, Copper, Hammered, Mica Shade, 2 Sockets, Closed Windmill Stamp, c.1912, 16 In.
$13,750

Rago Arts and Auction Center

TIP
Ketchup is a good emergency copper cleaner.

Dirk Van Erp, Vase, Copper, Hammered, Tapered Shoulder, c.1920, 8 ⅛ x 5 ¼ In.
$1,679

Ruby Lane

Fleur Orientale, Bowl, Fruit, Fitz & Floyd, 5 ⅜ In.	9
Fleur Orientale, Plate, Dinner, Fitz & Floyd, 10 ½ In.	25
Frageria, Plate, Green Rim, Red Strawberries, Blue Ridge, 10 ¼ In.	14
French Peasant, Soup, Dish, Blue Ridge, 8 ½ In.	32
Golden Heron, Mug, Fitz & Floyd, 4 In.	32
Golden Heron, Plate, Dinner, Fitz & Floyd, 10 ¼ In.	25
Golden Wheat, Bowl, Fruit, Edwin M. Knowles, 5 ⅜ In.	7
Golden Wheat, Plate, Dinner, Edwin M. Knowles, 10 ¼ In.	10
Golden Wheat, Soup, Dish, Edwin M. Knowles, 7 ⅝ In.	11
Greenbrier, Casserole, Lid, Paden City	55
Greenbrier, Chop Plate, Dell Green, Paden City, 12 ¾ In.	62
Harvest Time, Gravy Boat, Iroquois	20
Harvest Time, Platter, Iroquois, 12 In.	20
Harvest Time, Sugar, Lid, Iroquois	12
Harvest, Plate, Piecrust Shape, Green Border, Cherries, Grapes, Pear, Blue Ridge, 9 ⅜ In.	12
Hawaiian Fruit, Plate, Square, Blue Ridge, 8 In.	25
Hawaiian Fruit, Platter, Round, Blue Ridge, 14 In.	55
Hawaiian, Creamer, Fruit, Single Brown Line Trim, Pineapple, Pear, Plum, Blue Ridge	15
Hawaiian, Platter, Fruit, Oval, Single Brown Line Trim, Pineapple, Pear, Plum, Blue Ridge, 14 In.	40
Hibiscus, Cup & Saucer, Salem	28
Honolulu, Plate, Cherries, Green Border, Multicolor Leaves, Blue Ridge, 8 ¼ In.	12
Hostess, Cup, Edwin M. Knowles	12
Hostess, Plate, Bread & Butter, Edwin M. Knowles, 6 ⅛ In.	10
King Edward, Soup, Dish, Underplate, Cream, Gold Trim, Red Laurel, Castleton	21
Lazy Daisy, Bowl, Vegetable, Split, Taylor, Smith & Taylor, 10 ¼ In.	20
Lazy Daisy, Coffeepot, Lid, Taylor, Smith & Taylor, 8 ½ In.	45
Lazy Daisy, Creamer, Iroquois	12
Margaret Rose, Soup, Dish, Rim, Johnson Brothers, 8 In.	36
Marmora, Plate, City & River Scenes, Blue Transfer, William Ridgway & Co., 1840s, 10 In.	30
Melody, Bowl, Cereal, Square, Johnson Brothers, 6 In.	9
Moselle, Plate, Bread & Butter, Blue & Gold, Radford, 6 ¼ In.	8
Mountain Ivy, Saucer, White, Ring Of Purple, Gray Berries, 2-Tone Green Leaves, Blue Ridge	4
Naturewood, Plate, Buffet, Pfaltzgraff, 9 ¾ In.	14
Naturewood, Server, Square, Serenity Green, Pfaltzgraff, 8 ½ In.	21
Naturewood, Spoon Rest, Serenity Green, Pfaltzgraff	8
Old Country Roses, Bowl, Lid, Royal Albert, 2 ⅞ In. *illus*	80
Peony, Plate, Salad, Blue, Scalloped Edge, Booths, 8 In.	21
Quaker Apple, Creamer, Green Rim, Leaves, Blue Ridge	35
Red Apple, Plate, Dinner, Red Border, Colonial, Blue Ridge, 10 ¼ In.	22
Red Poinsettia, Cup & Saucer, Gray Center, 2-Tone Green Leaves, Blue Ridge	12
Regency, Plate, Salad, Johnson Brothers, 8 In.	15
Rehobeth, Plate, Salad, Pink & Blue Flowers, Leaves, Thin Brown Line Edge, Blue Ridge	12
Rondelet, Plate, Salad, Peach, Fitz & Floyd, 7 ½ In.	12
Rosalee, Plate, Dinner, Paden City, 9 ⅞ In.	15
Rustic Plaid, Bowl, Vegetable, Cream, Brown Sponge, Brown & Green Stripes, Blue Ridge, 9 In.	35
San Marino, Soup, Cream, Handles, Flintridge	14
South Pacific, Plate, Dinner, Green, Yellow Fruit, Dark Green Leaves, Brock, 11 In.	21
Spring Hill Tulip, Bowl, Vegetable, Colonial, Yellow & Brown Tulips, Oval, Blue Ridge, 9 ⅜ In.	22
Spring Rose, Cup & Saucer, Flared, Homer Laughlin	7 to 14
Sweet Pea, Plate, Salad, White, Pink Border, Colonial, Blue & Pink Flowers, Blue Ridge, 7 In.	12
The Gatineau, Sugar, Ribbed, Open, Radford, 2 ½ In.	37
Tick Tack, Plate, Dinner, Piecrust, Apple, Pear, Green Cross-Stitch, Blue Ridge, 9 In.	25
Trinidad, Plate, Dessert, Radford, 7 In.	8
Trinidad, Saucer, Radford	12
Trotter, Creamer, Crooksville	13
Trotter, Cup & Saucer, Crooksville	23
Victorian Rust, Plate, Bread & Butter, Radford, 6 In.	13
Victorian Rust, Plate, Dinner, Radford, 10 ¼ In.	46
Victorian Rust, Plate, Salad, Radford, 7 In.	27

Violet, Fluted, Chop Plate, Radford, 13 In.	43
Violet, Fluted, Plate, Bread & Butter, Radford, 6 In.	10
Violet, Scalloped, Butter, Cover, Radford	109
Violet, Scalloped, Cup & Saucer, Footed, Radford...................................	34
Violet, Scalloped, Platter, Oval, Radford, 13 In.	68
Whirlygig, Plate, Dinner, Piecrust, Green Trim, 2-Tone Flower, Green Leaves, Blue Ridge, 11 In.	20
Whole Wheat, Bowl, Vegetable, Mikasa, 9¾ In.	25
Whole Wheat, Shaker, Pepper, Mikasa, 5 Hole	15
Wild Cherry No. 3, Bowl, Green Brush Marks, Brown, Green Leaves, Red Cherries, Blue Ridge, 10 In. ..	25
Wild Strawberry, Saucer, Blue Ridge	10
Winterwood, Mug, Tall, Pfaltzgraff, 5⅜ In.	13
Winterwood, Tray, Pfaltzgraff, 9¼ In.	16
Yellow Daisy, Sugar & Creamer, Brown Centers, Dark Green Leaves, Blue Ridge	50
Yorktown, Sugar, Lid, Edwin Knowles...	67
Yorktowne, Bread Basket, Pfaltzgraff, 12½ In.	12
Yorktowne, Casserole, Lid, Individual, Pfaltzgraff	10
Yorktowne, Cup, Custard, Pfaltzgraff, 2¾ In.	3
Yorktowne, Honey Pot, Pfaltzgraff	12
Yorktowne, Salt & Pepper, Pfaltzgraff...	23

DIONNE QUINTUPLETS were born in Canada on May 28, 1934. The publicity about their birth and their special status as wards of the Canadian government made them famous throughout the world. Visitors could watch the girls play; reporters interviewed the girls and the staff. Thousands of special dolls and souvenirs were made picturing the quints at different ages. Emilie died in 1954, Marie in 1970, Yvonne in 2001. Annette and Cecile still live in Canada.

Book, We're Two Years Old, Girls On Cover, Whitman Co., 1936........................	13
Bowl, Porcelain, Red Band, Marie In Highchair, c.1935, 5½ In.	40
Doll, Composition, Original Outfits, Wood Scooter, 1930s, 5 Babies.......... *illus*	1295
Doll, On Scooter, Rompers, Hats, Alexander, 1930s, 8 In.	1195
Plate, Souvenir, Tab Handles, Girls In Highchairs, Maple Leaf, 12 In.	115
Postcard, Girls, Dr. Dafoe, Sitting On Curb, World Copyright N.E.A., 1936	24
Spoon, Silver Plate, Carlton, 1930s, 5 Piece...	55

DIRK VAN ERP was born in 1860 and died in 1933. He opened his own studio in 1908 in Oakland, California. He moved his studio to San Francisco in 1909 and the studio remained under the direction of his son until 1977. Van Erp made hammered copper accessories, including vases, desk sets, bookends, candlesticks, jardinieres, and trays, but he is best known for his lamps. The hammered copper lamps often had shades with mica panels.

Andirons, Large Ball, Wide Set Feet, Copper, Hammered, Wrought Iron, 16 x 13 In.	10000
Basket, Canoe Shape, Handle, Fixed, Pierced, Copper, Hammered, 7½ x 11 In.........	1375
Ice Bucket, Copper, Hammered, Tapered, Flared, Dome Lid, Loop Finial, 12 x 8 In..........	2000
Inkwell, 2 Wells, Hinged Lids, Copper, Hammered, Glass Inserts, Tray, 2¾ In. Wells, 12 In.	1120
Lamp, Copper, Hammered, Mica Shade, 2 Sockets, Closed Windmill Stamp, c.1912, 16 In. *illus*	13750
Lamp, Electric, Hanging, 1-Light, Bean Pot, Copper, Hammered, Mica, 1915-29, 10 x 11 In.	5312
Pitcher, Copper, Hammered, Tin Interior, c.1912, 10½ x 8½ In............................	687
Vase, Copper, Hammered, Tapered Shoulder, c.1920, 8⅛ x 5¼ In. .... *illus*	1679

DISNEYANA is a collectors' term. Walt Disney and his company introduced many comic characters to the world. Mickey Mouse first appeared in the short film "Steamboat Willie" in 1928. Collectors search for examples of the work of the Disney Studios and the many commercial products modeled after his characters, including Mickey Mouse and Donald Duck, and recent films, like *Beauty and the Beast* and *The Little Mermaid*.

Bank, Donald Duck, Figural, Donald Holding Coin, Porcelain, Paint, 1940s, 6 In.....................	60
Bank, Mickey Mouse, Tin, Mechanical, Saalheimer & Strauss, Germany, 7 In.	9600
Box, Mickey Mouse, Lithograph, Hoffmann, 1930s, 8¼ x 10 x 7 In.	375
Candy Jar, Ludwig Von Drake, Lolly Pops For Boys & Girls, Peak Lid, 1961, 9 In......................	345

D

Cel, Best Looking at You
Thinking of buying an original animation cel from a cartoon or Disney movie? The best show a character with eyes open, looking at you.

Disneyana, Comb, Mickey Mouse, Fabric Over Cardboard Case, American Hard Rubber Co., 1930s, 5 In.
$195

Hake's Americana & Collectibles

Disneyana, Comic Book, Donald Duck, Cardboard, 10 Cents, K.K. Publications, Whitman, 1938, 80 Pages
$8,437

Hake's Americana & Collectibles

Disneyana, Lawn Ornament, Mickey Mouse, Wood, Yellow, Black, Red, White, c.1935, 27 In.
$595

Ruby Lane

Disneyana, Lunch Box, Mickey Mouse, Donald Duck, Nephews, Pluto, Metal, Adco Liberty Mfg., 1954
$519

Hake's Americana & Collectibles

Cel, see Animation Art category.

Comb, Mickey Mouse, Fabric Over Cardboard Case, American Hard Rubber Co., 1930s, 5 In. *illus*	195
Comic Book, Donald Duck, Cardboard, 10 Cents, K.K. Publications, Whitman, 1938, 80 Pages *illus*	8437
Figurine, Mickey Mouse, Red Pants, Green Shoes, Bisque, 1930s, 1 ½ In.	3
Figurine, Pinocchio, Red Shorts, Blue Bowtie, Feather In Hat, c.1946, 3 x 3 ¼ x 6 ¼ In.	175
Key Fob, Walt Disney World, Skull, Crossbones Logo, Brass, Keychain, 1970s, 1 ⅜ In.	15
Lawn Ornament, Mickey Mouse, Wood, Yellow, Black, Red, White, c.1935, 27 In. *illus*	595
Lunch Box, Mickey Mouse, Donald Duck, Nephews, Pluto, Metal, Adco Liberty Mfg., 1954 *illus*	519
Map, United States, Mickey Mouse, Travel Club, Mills Bakery, 1938, 16 x 24 In.	395
Pencil Sharpener, Cinderella, Decal, Scalloped, Gray, 1950s, 1 ⅛ In.	50
Pencil Sharpener, Mickey Mouse, Holding Pencil, Red, Green Pencil, Round, 1930s, 1 In.	85
Pin, Donald Duck, Ax, Hose, Fire Prevention Week, Oct. 9-15, Hancock School, 1990s, 2 In.	20
Pin, Mickey Mouse, Red Pants, Allentown, Philadelphia, 1930s, 1 ¼ In.	75
Record, Mickey Mouse Club, How To Be A Mouseketeer, Walt Disney, 36 Songs, 1962	240
Toy, Donald Duck, Handcar, Donald, Dog House, Pluto, Clockwork, Lionel, 11 In.	300
Toy, Jiminy Cricket, Hopper, Tuxedo, Top Hat, Umbrella, Linemar, Japan, 6 In.	300
Toy, Mickey Mouse Choo-Choo, Train, Wood, Metal, Push Pull, Fisher-Price, c.1938 *illus*	154
Toy, Mickey Mouse, Band, Piano, Violinist, 9 In.	1020
Toy, Mickey Mouse, Ferris Wheel, Donald Duck, 6 Cars, Chien Co., 17 In.	210
Toy, Mickey Mouse, Handcar, Mickey, Minnie, O Gauge, Red, Lionel, 9 In.	390
Toy, Mickey Mouse, Jazz Drummer, Orange Drum, Easel Back, Chein, 1935, 6 ½ In.	660
Toy, Mickey Mouse, Riding Toy, Rocker Base, Wood, Iron Rods, Marked, 1930s, 23 x 35 x 10 In.	72
Toy, Pinocchio, Acrobat, Monstro The Whale, Marx, 11 In.	210
Toy, Pinocchio, Doll, Composition Head, Torso, Jointed Wood Limbs, Ideal Novelty Co., c.1940, 11 In.	120
Toy, Pinocchio, Doll, Composition, Wood, Jointed, Red, Box, 10 In. *illus*	210
Toy, Pinocchio, Red Overalls, Hat, Blue Bow, Tin Lithograph, Windup, 8 ½ In.	180
Wristwatch, Donald Duck, Deluxe, Tag, Ingersoll, Box, 1947, 3 ½ x 4 ¾ In. *illus*	701

DOCTOR, *see Dental and Medical categories.*

 DOLL entries are listed by marks printed or incised on the doll, if possible. If there are no marks, the doll is listed by the name of the subject or country or maker. Notice that Barbie is listed under Mattel. G.I. Joe figures are listed in the Toy section. Eskimo dolls are listed in the Eskimo section and Indian dolls are listed in the Indian section. Doll clothes and accessories are listed at the end of this section. The twentieth-century clothes listed here are in mint condition.

A.M., 410, Girl, Toddler, Bisque Head, Glass Eyes, Retractable Teeth, 18 In.	748
A.M., 1894, Nun, Bisque Socket Head, Glass Sleep Eyes, Jointed, Habit, c.1895, 20 In. *illus*	399
A.M., Bisque Head, Glass Eyes, Toddler, Antique Costume, c.1910, 13 In.	2280
A.M., Bisque Head, Painted Face, Blond Wig, Mariner Costume, c.1910, 16 In.	5016
A.M., Smiling Girl, Blue Eyes, Red Wig, Composition Body, White Dress, 1890-1920, 30 In.	100
Abby Cady, Cloth, Folk Art, Painted Face, Blue Dress & Bonnet, 1900s, 25 In.	3192
Advertising, Red Riding Hood Shoes, Cloth, Text On Back, 11 ¼ x 4 ⅜ In. *illus*	94
Alexander dolls are listed in this category under Madame Alexander.	
Alice Couturier, Bisque, Swivel Head, Mohair Wig, Boutique Label, France, c.1870, 13 In.	3420
Armand Marseille dolls are listed in this category under A.M.	
Arranbee, Nancy Lee, Composition, Green Sleep Eyes, Human Hair, Jointed, Gown, 18 In.	230
Automaton, Catalan Dancer, Bisque Head, Papier-Mache, Wood Cabinet, 80 x 37 ½ In.	5322
Automaton, Chinese Tea Server, Bisque, Glass Eyes, Mohair, Wood Tea Set, L. Lambert, 19 In.	6325
Automaton, Clown, Traditional Costume, Gold Bells, Ringling Brothers, 1950s, 68 x 15 In.	5440
Automaton, Dandy Smoker, Black, Papier-Mache Head, Marbled Wood Cabinet, 1935, 37 x 18 In.	8056
Automaton, Figure, Man, Whistling, Key Wind, Head Turns, Painted, Germany, 13 ½ In. *illus*	384
Automaton, Girl At Piano, Bisque, Mohair, Papier-Mache, Hands & Head Move, c.1884, 21 In.	9775
Automaton, Girl With Surprise Basket, Lifts Lid, Bird, Sniffs Flowers, L. Lambert, France, 20 In.	4888
Automaton, Lady With Mandolin, Bisque, Carton Body, Strums, Roullet Et Decamps, 20 In.	4600
Automaton, Piano Player, Wooden Cabinet, 8 Tracks, Gear Mechanism, 68 x 26 x 20 In.	9000
Automaton, Polichinelle, Strikes Tin Drum, Kicks, Papier-Mache, Wood, Cloth, c.1860, 18 In.	3450
Automaton, Professor & Dunce, Bisque, Wood, Heads Turn, Books Lift, Roullet Et Decamps...	11500

Automaton, Saucy Jester With Mandolin, Papier-Mache, Wood, L. Lambert, c.1890, 20 In.	9200
Automaton, Spanish Dancer With Tambourine, Carton Body, L. Lambert, 1890, 21 In.	5175
Babyland Rag, Muslin, Cafe-Au-Lait Complexion, Painted, Gown, Bonnet, Baby, 14 In.	633
Bahr & Proschild, 2 Faces, Bisque, Smile, Scowl, Glass Eyes, 2 Teeth, Bent-Limb Baby, 9 In.	460
Barbie dolls are listed in this category under Mattel, Barbie.	
Barrois, Bisque Head, Swivel Neck, Kid Body, Period Costume, c.1860, 18 In.	4560
Barrois, Bisque Swivel Head, Enamel Eyes, Mohair Wig, Dowel Joints, Skirt, Jacket, c.1860, 18 In.	4560
Bergmann dolls are also in this category under Simon & Halbig.	
Black dolls are also included in the Black category.	
Bru Jne, Bisque, Blue Paperweight Eyes, Original Wig, Bebe, 17 In.	6600
Bru Jne, Bisque, Smiling, Swivel Head, Mohair Wig, Gusset-Jointed, c.1872, 18 In.	2964
Bru Jne, Girl, Golden Era, Bisque Swivel Head, Kid Edged Bisque Shoulder Plate, c.1884, 19 In.	19950
Buffalo Bill Cody, Plaster Head, Arms & Feet, Cotton Outfit, Felt Hat, 12 In.	360
Bye-Lo Baby, Wax Dome Head, Eyes Closed, Cloth Body, Grace Putnam, c.1922, 18 In.	1150
Cabbage Patch Kids, Vinyl Head, Brown Yarn Hair, Cloth Body, Box, 1984, 16 In.	50
Cage, Wood, Carved Head, Articulated Arms & Hands, Openwork Skirt, 60 x 37 In.	3000
Catterfelder Puppenfabrick, 200, Boy, Bisque, Painted, Jointed Composition & Wood, 20 In.	2990
Chase, Girl, Stockinet, Pressed & Oil Painted, Blond Bob, Stitch-Jointed, Dress, 1920, 16 In.	2185
Chase, Little Nell, Stockinet, Oil Painted, Blond Braids, Stitch-Jointed, c.1910, 15 In.	1495
Chase, Stockinet, Pressed & Painted Features, Impasto Curls, Stitch-Jointed, 1900, 16 In.	575
Chase, Woman, Stockinet, Black Complexion, Oil Painted, Fleecy Hair, Dress, Apron, 26 In.	3680
Cloth, Chinese, Oil Paint Face, Human Hair, Muslin Body, Farmer's Clothes, c.1910, 19 In. *illus*	171
Cloth, Down Home Girl, Hand Sewn, Straw Stuffed, 1870-80, 21 In.	765
Cloth, Drawn Face, Cotton Stuffed, Red Calico Skirt, 1890s, 23 In.	695
Cloth, Flat Face, Painted Features & Curls, Stuffed Muslin, Stitch-Jointed, 1880s, 20 In.	288
Cloth, Homespun, Stitched Head, Oil Painted Features, Dress, Shoes, American Folk Art, 28 In.	1265
Cloth, Miss Chitty, Stitched On Shoulder Head, Oil Painted, Homespun Dress, c.1875, 17 In.	2415
Cloth, Paraffin Head, Glass Eyes, Blond Hair, Red Gingham Dress, Hat, 30 In.	71
Cloth, Raggedy Ann, Stitch-Jointed, Original Dress & Pinafore, Volland, c.1920, 16 In.	1083
D. Heizer, Catherine The Great, Cloth Over Wire, Padded, Gown, Gems, 1934, 10 In.	2875
D. Heizer, Empress Eugenie Of France, White Ruffled Dress, Marked, 10 In.	3420
D. Heizer, Marie Antoinette, Cloth Over Wire, Padded, Gown, Bonnet, Feathers, Gems, 10 In.	4600
D. Heizer, Victoria & Albert, Cloth Over Wire, Padded, Costumes, Jewels, 1936, 9 In., Pair	2990
Dehors, Fashion, Bisque Swivel Head, Tilts, Blond Mohair, Kid, Gusset-Jointed, Gown, 14 In.	3220
Door Of Hope, Bride, Wood, Painted, Chignon, Comb, Cloth Body, Red Silk Tunic, Beads, 12 In.	1380
Door Of Hope, Buddhist Priest, Wood Socket Head, Painted, Cloth Body, Linen Kimono, 12 In.	575
Door Of Hope, Farmer, Carved Head, Woven Straw Over Blue Denim Suit, c.1920, 13 In.	969
Door Of Hope, Manchu Matron, Wood, Painted, Cloth Body, Silk Kimono, Pants, 1920s, 11 In.	2415
Door Of Hope, Modern Bride, Wood, Cloth Body, Flowers In Hair, Kimono, c.1925, 11 In. *illus*	2352
Effanbee, Anne Shirley, Composition, American Children, D. Cochran, c.1938, 20 In. *illus*	1344
Eliza, Wax Shoulder Head, Blue Glass Eyes, Brunette Tendrils, Stuffed Cloth, 1882, 24 In.	2530
F. Schmidt, 1295, Boy, Bisque, Sleep Eyes, Brunette Fleece Wig, Composition, Wood, 16 In.	748
Farnell, King George VI, Cloth Head, Velvet Tunic, Crown, England, c.1937, 16 In.	1140
Fashion, Bisque, Rosy Cheeks, Aqua Silk Dress, Blond Braids, F.G., 18 In.	1020
Fashion, Cobalt Blue Eyes, Strawberry Blond, Underwear & Boots, 1800, 16 In.	780
Fashion, M'lle. Frou-Frou, Boston, Bisque, Trousseau, Trunk, 1870s, 21 In.	8625
Fashion, Peaches & Cream Complexion, Gray Eyes, Blond Mohair, Silk Outfit, 18 In.	1080
French, Bisque, Peaches & Cream, Brown Paperweight Eyes, Human Hair Wig, Kid Body, 21 In.	699
French, Bisque, Straight Wrist, Wood Body, Large Amber Eyes, Satin Dress, Child, 23 In.	1353
French, Brown Paperweight Eyes, Rosy Cheeks, Wood Body, Ivory Wool Outfit, Bebe, 17 In.	2286
French, Porcelain, Painted Detail, Wire Lever Eyes, White Flowered Dress, Hat, Marked Brevete, 17 In.	3306
Frozen Charlotte, Porcelain, Black, Sculpted & Painted Features, Boy, Girl, Germany, 5 In., Pair	690
G.I. Joe figures are listed in the Toy category.	
Gaultier, Bisque Head, Plump Cheeks, Glass Paperweight Eyes, Ringlets, Ball-Jointed, 20 In.	4025
Gebruder Heubach dolls may also be listed in this category under Heubach.	
Gebruder Heubach, Boy, Laughing, Bisque Socket Head, Composition, Ball Joints, c.1910, 28 In.	1710
German, 2 Heads, Topsyturvy, Bisque, Black, White, Skirt Flips, c.1885, 12 In.	748
German, 3 Faces, Bisque, Black Crying, Brown Smiling, White Sleeping, Brass Knob, 14 In.	1725
German, Baby Stuart, Bisque, Glass Sleep Eyes, Removable Bisque Cap, Jointed, 17 In.	1265

Disneyana, Toy, Mickey Mouse Choo-Choo, Train, Wood, Metal, Push Pull, Fisher-Price, c.1938
$154

Rich Penn Auctions

Disneyana, Toy, Pinocchio, Doll, Composition, Wood, Jointed, Red, Box, 10 In.
$210

Rich Penn Auctions

Disneyana, Wristwatch, Donald Duck, Deluxe, Tag, Ingersoll, Box, 1947, 3½ x 4¾ In.
$701

Hake's Americana & Collectibles

SELECTED DOLL MARKS WITH DATES USED

Effanbee Doll Co.
1922+
New York, N.Y.

Lenci
1922+
Turin, Italy

Hertwig & Co.
1864–c.1940
Katzhütte, Thüringia, Germany

Kämmer & Rheinhardt
1886–1932
Waltershausen, Thüringia, Germany

J.D. Kestner Jr.
1805–1938
Waltershausen, Thüringia, Germany

Ideal Novelty & Toy Co.
1961
New York, N.Y.

L.A. & S.

Louis Amberg & Son
1909–1930
Cincinnati, Ohio; New York, N.Y.

BRU. J^NE R
11

Bru Jne. & Cie
c.1879–1899
Paris, France

Armand Marseille
c.1920
Köppelsdorf, Thüringia, Germany

DÉPOSE
TÊTE JUMEAU

Maison Jumeau
1886–1899
Paris, France

Bähr & Pröschild
1871–1930s
Ohrdruf, Thüringia, Germany

DÉPOSE
S.F.B.J.

S.F.B.J. (Société Française de Fabrication de
Bébés & Jouets)
1905–1950+
Paris and Montreuil-sous-Bois, France

ALBEGO
10
Made in Germany

Alt. Beck & Gottschalck
1930–1940
Nauendorf, Thuringia, Germany

Schoenau & Hoffmeister
1901–c.1953
Sonneberg, Thuringia, Germany

Gebruder Heubach
1840–1938
Lichte, Thuringia, Germany

German, Bisque Socket Head, Glass Eyes, Mohair, Stuffed, Chanticleer Costume, 1915, 14 In. .		575
German, Bisque Swivel Head & Limbs, Sculpted Curls, Cobalt Glass Eyes, Muslin, c.1875, 11 In.		863
German, Bisque, Bathing Beauty, Diver, Mohair Wig, Silk & Ribbon Clothing, 4¾ In.		300
German, Bisque, Google Eyes, Brown Hair, 5 In. .... *illus*		825
German, Bisque, Kid, Painted, Sculpted Curls, Trousseau, Wood Box, c.1880, 21 In.		1265
German, Bisque, Lady, Blond Sculpted Hair, Tulle Gown, c.1880, 10 In.		513
German, Blue Sleep Eyes, Blond Wig, Pierced Ears, Open Mouth, Kid Body, 1910, 23 In.		120
German, Boy, Bisque Head, Glass Eyes, Sculpted Windblown Hair, Jointed, Wool Suit, 28 In.		4140
German, Boy, Girl, Composition, Blond Mohair, Jointed, Folk Costumes, c.1925, 8 In., Pair		288
German, Gentleman, Porcelain, Painted, Sculpted Feathered Hair, Muslin, Silk, c.1870, 13 In.		575
German, Girl, Bisque Head, Blond Wig, Glass Eyes, Wood Ball Joints, White Dress & Cap, 28 In.		153
German, Grape Lady, Porcelain, Sculpted Hair, Snood & Berries, Muslin Body, c.1870, 11 In.		633
German, Indian Woman, Bisque Socket Head, Mohair Wig, Teeth, Papier-Mache, c.1900, 17 In. ..... *illus*		288
German, Lady, Papier-Mache, Muslin Beaded Gown, Attributed To Muller, c.1850, 17 In.		1596
German, Lady, Porcelain Head, Black Painted Hair, Stitch-Jointed, Brevete, c.1850, 14 In.		1824
German, Lady, Porcelain, Black Sculpted Looping Braids, Muslin Body, c.1850, 21 In.		6038
German, Newborn Baby, Bisque Dome Head, Flanged Neck, Glass Eyes, Muslin, 8 In., Pair		230
German, Penny Wooden, Bedpost Shape Head, Painted, Jointed, Silk Gown, c.1890, 11 In.		575
German, Porcelain Shoulder Head, Painted, Brown Hair, Kid Body, Dress, c.1840, 33 In.		1840
German, Porcelain Shoulder Head, Painted, Sculpted Waves, Plump Muslin & Kid Body, 23 In.		403
German, Queen Louise, Bisque Head, Composition Body, Accessories, 1900s, 27 In.		84
German, Staatdamen, High Society Lady, Wax, Glass Eyes, Mohair Wig, Gown, Boots, 18 In.		575
German, Wax Over Papier-Mache, Blue Glass Eyes, Blond Mohair Braids, Gold Costume, 18 In.		518
German, Wax, Woman, Spinning Wheel, Flowers, Glass Dome, 1850s, 8½ In.		209
Gre-Poir, Cloth, Painted, Side-Glancing Eyes, Mohair Curls, 1930s, 18 In.		755
Half Dolls are listed in the Pincushion Doll category.		
Handwerck, Bisque Head, Leather, Blue Eyes, China Hand, Marked, Horseshoe, 1872-1902, 20 In.		50
Hartmann, Man, Bisque, Glass Eyes, Mohair Wig & Mustache, Greek Folk Costume, 16 In.		403
Hertel Schwab, 165, Jubilee Googly, Bisque, Glass Eyes, Mohair Bob, Jointed, Toddler, 19 In.		4025
Hertel Schwab, 2 Faces, Bisque, Smile, Scowl, Sleep Eyes, Bent-Limb Baby Body, 19 In.		460
Hertel Schwab, Blue Glass Googly Eyes, Watermelon Smile, Rosy Cheeks, Child, 15 In.		2700
Heubach, see also Gebruder Heubach.		
Heubach, 6971, Bisque Socket Head, Glass Sleep Eyes, Laughing, Ball-Jointed, Chld, 18 In.		1380
Heubach, 7550, Bisque, Glass Sleep Eyes, Mohair, Jointed Composition, c.1912, Child, 13 In.		633
Heubach, 7847, Bisque, Glass Sleep Eyes, Human Hair, Composition & Wood, Dress, 19 In.		1265
Heubach, Boy, Bisque Head, Intaglio Eyes, Impish Smile, Molded Hair, Bent-Limb Baby, 12 In.		805
Heubach, Molded Hair, Blue Eyes, Kid Body, Black Velvet Outfit, 1910, 10 In.		84
Indian dolls are listed in the Indian category.		
J. Beecher, Missionary Rag Baby, Stuffed Stockinet, Stitched & Painted, c.1890, 24 In.		2070
J.D.K. dolls are also listed in this category under Kestner.		
Japanese, Ichimatsu, Papier-Mache, Gofun Finish, Painted, Muslin Arms & Legs, 1930s, 21 In.		978
Jenny Lind, China Head, Leather Arms, Cloth Body, 30 In.		165
Joanny, Bisque Head, Glass Eyes, Blond Mohair, Composition & Wood, Bebe, c.1888, 20 In.		6038
Jumeau, Bisque, Brown Eyes, Molded Mouth, Brown Silk Dress, Bebe, 17 In.		1143
Jumeau, Bisque, Young Girl, Swivel Head, Gusset-Jointed, Day Dress, c.1878, 14 In.		1368
Jumeau, Brown Eyes, Open Mouth, Upper Teeth, Wood Body, Blue Silk Dress, Lace, Bonnet, 21 In.		1524
Jumeau, Brown Glass Sleep Eyes, Open Mouth, Blond Long Tail Wig, Underwear, 1907, 29 In.		923
Jumeau, Child, Light Blue Gray Eyes, Black Eyeliner, Aqua Earrings, Silk Outfit, 1950s, 18 In.		3175
Jumeau, Fashion, Gray Blue Paperweight Eyes, Dress & Chemise, Antique Wig, Bebe, 15 In.		510
K * R, 101, Peter, Bisque Socket Head, Painted Eyes, Pouty Lips, Tyrolean Costume, 15 In.		6038
K * R, 114, Hans, Bisque, Brown Glass Eyes, Jointed Composition & Wood, Velvet, 21 In.		4600
K * R, 117, Mein Liebling, Bisque Head, Brown Glass Eyes, Mohair, Composition, Wood, 15 In.		3220
K * R, 117, Mein Liebling, Boy, Bisque, Blue Glass Eyes, Mohair Bob, Ball-Jointed, Suit, 17 In.		4600
K * R, 117n, Baby Darling, Bisque Head, Flirty Glass Eyes, 4 Teeth, Mohair Wig, Box, 25 In.		1495
K * R, 117n, Bisque Head, Flirty Glass Eyes, 4 Teeth, Human Hair, Ball-Jointed, Child, 28 In.		805
K * R, 117x, Flapper, Bisque, Glass Eyes, Dimples, 4 Teeth, Mohair Bob, Jointed, 14 In.		863
K * R, 124, Moritz, Bisque Head, Upturned Nose, Flirty Eyes, Composition, Wood, Jointed, 16 In.		9775
K * R, 126, Bisque Head, Sleep Eyes, 2 Teeth, Mohair Bob, Starfish Hands, Toddler, 9 In.		1093
K * R, 128, Bisque Head, Composition Body, 1900s, 15 In.		88

Doll, A.M., 1894, Nun, Bisque Socket Head, Glass Sleep Eyes, Jointed, Habit, c.1895, 20 In.
$399

Theriault's

Doll, Advertising, Red Riding Hood Shoes, Cloth, Text On Back, 11¼ x 4⅜ In.
$94

DOLL

Doll, Automaton, Figure, Man, Whistling, Key Wind, Head Turns, Painted, Germany, 13 ½ In.
$384

Hess Auction Group

Doll, Cloth, Chinese, Oil Paint Face, Human Hair, Muslin Body, Farmer's Clothes, c.1910, 19 In.
$171

Theriault's

Doll, Door Of Hope, Modern Bride, Wood, Cloth Body, Flowers In Hair, Kimono, c.1925, 11 In.
$2,352

Theriault's

Doll, Effanbee, Anne Shirley, Composition, American Children, D. Cochran, c.1938, 20 In.
$1,344

Theriault's

Doll, German, Bisque, Google Eyes, Brown Hair, 5 In.
$825

DuMouchelles

Doll, German, Indian Woman, Bisque Socket Head, Mohair Wig, Teeth, Papier-Mache, c.1900, 17 In.
$288

Theriault's

D

K * R, 131, Boy, Bisque Head, Googly Glass Eyes, Impish Smile, Mohair, Jointed, Toddler, 15 In..	5750
K * R, Boy, Blue Glass Eyes, Blond Mohair, Open Mouth, Black Velvet Suit, Shoes, Socks, 1900s, 20 In..	450
K * R, Flirty Eyes, Dirty Blond Mohair Wig, Older Outfit, Leather Shoes, Marked, 20 In............	445
K * R, Marie, Bisque Socket Head, Painted, Blond Mohair Braids, Jointed Composition, 7 In. ...	863
K * R, Young Boy, Bisque Socket Head, Ball-Jointed, Gentleman's Suit, c.1912, 20 In.	3705
Kathe Kruse, Boy, Socket Head, Blond Human Hair, Cloth Body, Jointed, c.1935, 21 In.... *illus*	863
Kathe Kruse, Du Mein, Stockinet, Pressed & Painted, Bent-Limb Baby, c.1925, 20 In.	1495
Kathe Kruse, Ilse, Cloth, Oil Painted, Jointed Hips, Marked, c.1925, 16 In.	6840
Kathe Kruse, Trudy, Cloth, Painted, Pouty, Brown Hair, Jointed, Dress, Hat, 1945, Box, 14 In..	863
Kestner, Baby Jean, Bisque Dome Head, Sleep Eyes, 2 Teeth, Bent-Limb Baby, c.1914, 14 In.	690
Kestner, Bisque Head, Plump Cheeks, Blue Glass Sleep Eyes, Blond Mohair, Child, 14 In.	1840
Kestner, Bisque Head, Sleep Eyes, Closed Mouth, Mohair Wig, Ball-Jointed, c.1885, 29 In.	2850
Kestner, Bisque Socket Head, Composition, Wooden Ball Joints, Mariner Costume, c.1882, 16 In....	2166
Kestner, Bisque, Blue Eyes, Human Hair, Lace Dress, Bonnet, Leather Shoes, 1900, Child, 16 In.	1500
Kestner, Bisque, Kid Edged Body, Peg-Jointed, Glass Eyes, Mohair Wig, Silk, c.1880, 6 In.........	1093
Kestner, Chinese Child, Bisque Socket Head, Black Mohair Wig, Composition Body, c.1912, 16 In.... *illus*	2990
Kestner, Gibson Girl, Bisque Shoulder Head, Marked, c.1910, 21 In.	1083
Kestner, Pale Bisque, Brown Glass Sleep Eyes, Silk & Lace Outfit, Boots, Child, 16 In...............	1270
Kewpie dolls are listed in the Kewpie category.	
Kley & Hahn, 531, Boy, Bisque Dome Head, Painted, Jointed Composition & Wood, Suit, 23 In..	1150
Kley & Hahn, Bisque Socket Head, Glass Eyes, Mohair Wig, Ball-Jointed, c.1912, 18 In.	2394
Kling, Bisque Shoulder Head, Dresden Rose & Ruffles, Sculpted Curls, Muslin, Kid, 24 In.	2185
KPM, German, Lady, Porcelain Shoulder Head, Angular Face, Sculpted Chignon, Dress, Bonnet, 20 In.	2760
KPM, Woman, Porcelain Head & Limbs, Sculpted Hair, Muslin Body, c.1850, 15 In. .... *illus*	3220
KPM, Woman, Porcelain Shoulder Head, Painted, Muslin, Leather, Stitch-Jointed, 20 In. *illus*	3640
Lady, Bisque, Muslin, Painted, Sculpted Brown Curls, Blue Bead Coronet, Germany, 17 In.	575
Lenci, 148/6, Felt, Swivel Head, Painted Features, Brunette Mohair Ringlets, Organdy, 16 In. ..	575
Lenci, 900A, Felt, Painted, Side-Glancing Eyes, Jointed, Floppy Legs, Ruffled Dress, 1927, 14 In..	460
Lenci, Child, Felt, Swivel Head, Painted Features, c.1927, 12 In..	798
Lenci, Dutch Boy, Wooden Shoes, Pressed & Painted Facial Features, Swivel Head, c.1933, 9 In..	570
Lenci, Felt Painted Face, Mohair, Jointed Arms, Legs, Dress, Shoes, Hat, 1930s, 22 In.	300
Lenci, Felt, Painted, O-Shape Mouth, Auburn Mohair Wig, Red Coat, Holding Piglet, 9 In.	288
Lenci, Felt, Swivel Head, Pressed & Painted Features, Orange Coat & Hat, c.1927, 12 In.............	798
Lenci, Flapper & White Poodle, Felt, Gish Face, Painted, Mohair Bob, Sateen Legs, 24 In.	1265
Lenci, Girl, Felt, Painted, Blond Mohair Curls, Turquoise Dress & Cloche, 12 In.........................	518
Lenci, Josephine Baker, Felt, Danse Banane Costume, Bananas, Leaves, Bracelets, 18 In.	6038
Lenci, Kiki, Cloth, Painted, Brown Eyes, Blond Wig, Organdy Dress, Bow, 1936, 14 In................	7763
Lenci, Pouting Boy, Felt, Side-Glancing Eyes, Brunette Mohair, Tyrolean Costume, 17 In.	805
Lenci, Sailor, Pipe, Felt, Swivel Head, Googly Eyes, Brunette Bob, Costume, Cap, c.1933, 9 In..	460
Lenci, School Boy, Felt, Pressed, Painted, Side-Glancing Eyes, Sweater, Shorts, Shoes, 17 In.....	1093
Lenci, Felt, Swivel Head, Blond Mohair Wig, Jointed, Wedding Dress, c.1932, 17 In............ *illus*	1495
Leo Moss, Lady, Papier-Mache Shoulder Head, Brown Complexion, Sculpted Curls, 28 In........	7188
Lucy Peck, Wax Shoulder Head, Blue Lever Sleep Eyes, Painted, Human Hair, England, 20 In.	2875
Lulie, Bisque Shoulder Head, Painted, Sculpted Bob, 2 Teeth, Dress, 1955, 8 In.	345
M. Wellington, Cloth, Stockinet, Stitched & Oil Painted, Plump Face, Toddler, c.1883, 24 In.	4370
Madame Alexander, Susie Q, Bobby Q, Cloth, Googly Eyes, Rosy Cheeks, Wool Hair, 15 In., Pair ...	863
Madame Paderewski, Cloth, Seamed Face, Fleecy Hair, Jointed, Polish Relief Fund, 15 In. .... *illus*	2280
Mama Mehitibal & Twins, Rubber Shoulder Head, Painted, Cloth, c.1860, 13-16 In., 3 Piece	2990
Margot Of Italy, Felt, Side-Glancing Eyes, Blond Mohair Wig, Box, 1920s, 20 In. .... *illus*	748
Marionette, Camphor Wood, Carved, Silk Embroidered Clothing, Qing Dynasty, Chinese, 30 In. ...	24
Martha Thompson, Bisque, Gray Paperweight Eyes, Blond, Pinned Curls, Blue Silk Outfit, 15 In.	840
Mary Branca, Queen Elizabeth I, Clay Composition, Velvet, Marked, c.1950, 14 In.	741
Mary Branca, Queen Victoria, Composition, Cloth, White Stiffened Wig, c.1950, 11 In.	345
Mattel, Barbie, Fashion Luncheon, Titian Bubble Cut, Blue Eyes, Outfit No. 1656, 1961	385
Mattel, Barbie, No. 1, Pink Skin Tone, Brunette, Signed, Ruth Handler, Box, 1959, 11 In.	6200
Mignonette, Bisque, Blond, Peg-Jointed, Lace Gown, Box, Accessories, c.1882, 5 In.	1596
Milliner's Model, Papier-Mache Shoulder Head, Painted, Sculpted Hair, Germany, c.1860, 34 In..	978
Nina B. Albritton, Cloth, Shaped Head, Stuffed, Painted, Antique Dress, c.1915, 21 In.	7125
Paper dolls are listed in their own category.	

D

Doll, Kathe Kruse, Boy, Socket Head, Blond Human Hair, Cloth Body, Jointed, c.1935, 21 In.
$863

Theriault's

Doll, Kestner, Chinese Child, Bisque Socket Head, Black Mohair Wig, Composition Body, c.1912, 16 In.
$2,990

Theriault's

Doll, KPM, Woman, Porcelain Head & Limbs, Sculpted Hair, Muslin Body, c.1850, 15 In.
$3,220

Theriault's

Doll, KPM, Woman, Porcelain Shoulder Head, Painted, Muslin, Leather, Stitch-Jointed, 20 In.
$3,640

Theriault's

"Special" Dolls
Dolls exported to the United States in the late 1800s and early 1900s were often given special marks. In Germany, dolls for the U.S. market were marked "Special," while dolls for the German market were marked "Spezial."

Papier-Mache, Lady, Shoulder Head, Painted, Human Hair Curls, Kid Body, c.1825, 19 In.	5750
Papier-Mache, Lady, Shoulder Head, Sculpted Ringlets, Kid & Wood, Germany, c.1840, 18 In.	2760
Papier-Mache, Shoulder Head, Cloth Body, Leather Arms & Hands, Calico Dress, c.1865, 11 In.	345
Papier-Mache, Woman, Shoulder Head, Sculpted Coronet, Kid & Wood, Germany, c.1840, 17 In.	1380
Pincushion dolls are listed in their own category.	
Raggedy Ann, Cloth, Yarn Hair, Shoebutton Eyes, Painted Face, Volland, c.1920, 16 In.	950
Raynal, Felt, Pressed & Painted, Side-Glancing Eyes, Brunette Mohair Bob, c.1935, 13 In.	863
Rohmer, Fashion, Bisque Swivel Head, Blond Lamb's Wool Wig, Kid Body, Jointed, 1857, 17 In.	4140
Rohmer, Porcelain Swivel Head & Limbs, Gusset-Jointed, Taffeta Costume, c.1860, 18 In.	9120
S & H dolls are listed here as Simon & Halbig.	
S.F.B.J., 235, Boy, Bisque, Glass Eyes, Smile, Flocked Hair, Jointed Composition, Suit, 17 In.	1093
S.F.B.J., 251, Bisque, Sleep Eyes, Human Hair, 2 Teeth, Bent-Limb Baby, Basket, Layette, 8 In.	1265
S.F.B.J., 301, Bisque Head, Composition Body, Brown Eyes, Brown Wig, Dress, 35 In.	325
S.F.B.J., Bluette, Bisque Socket Head, Blue Sleep Eyes, Teeth, Jointed Arms, Legs, 12 In. .... *illus*	825
Schlaggenwald, Lady, Porcelain, Painted, Human Hair, Sloping Shoulders, Dress, Bonnet, 17 In.	3680
Schlaggenwald, Porcelain, Painted, Human Hair Wig, Muslin, Porcelain Limbs, Gown, 18 In.	1495
Schmidt, Wendy, Bisque Socket Head, Brown Glass Eyes, Mohair, Composition, Wood, 7 In.	1840
Schoenhut, 301, Wood, Intaglio Eyes, Blond Mohair Bob, Jointed, c.1912, Child, 16 In.	1150
Schoenhut, Girl, Wood, Painted Face, Carved Hair, Jointed Body, 14 ½ In.	625
Schoenhut, Schnickel-Fritz, Carved Hair, Teeth, Jointed, Painted Eyes, c.1911, 15 In. ...... *illus*	3556
Schoenhut, Wood, Brown Intaglio Eyes, Brunette Mohair, Spring-Jointed, Dress, c.1912, 16 In.	1150
Schoenhut, Wood, Intaglio Eyes, Brunette Mohair Bob, Jointed, Dress, Boots, Bow, 19 In.	920
Schoenhut, Wood, Oil Painted, Blond Mohair Bob, Spring-Jointed, Dress, Shoes, 19 In.	575
Schoenhut, Wood, Socket Head, Plaid Dress, Laced Shoes, c.1912, 14 In.	627
Shirley Temple dolls are included in the Shirley Temple category.	
Simon & Halbig, 939, Bisque Head, Glass Eyes, Human Hair, Composition, Wood, Child, 25 In.	863
Simon & Halbig, 949, Bisque Head, Sleep Eyes, Open Mouth Teeth, Mohair Wig, Child, 25 In.	863
Simon & Halbig, 1078, Bisque Head, Composition Body, Blue Eyes, White Dress, c.1890, 35 In.	425
Simon & Halbig, 1079, Bisque Head, Brown Wig, Blue Eyes, Composition Body, c.1890, 22 In.	130
Simon & Halbig, 1159, Bride, Bisque, Glass Eyes, 4 Teeth, Human Hair, Satin Gown, Veil, 20 In.	2645
Simon & Halbig, 1199, Asian Child, Bisque, Amber Tint, Brown Eyes, Teeth, Brocade, 14 In.	1610
Simon & Halbig, 1469, Flapper, Bisque, Heart Shape Face, Glass Eyes, Beaded Dress, 14 In.	4600
Simon & Halbig, 1489, Erika, Bisque Head, Chubby, Glass Sleep Eyes, Teeth, Mohair Bob, 21 In.	2300
Simon & Halbig, Bisque, Brown Glass Sleep Eyes, Cotton Outfit, Black Stockings, Child, 6 In.	123
Simon & Halbig, Bisque, Socket Head, Glass Eyes, Wooden Ball Joints, c.1910, Child, 20 In.	2964
Simon & Halbig, Lady, Bisque Swivel Head, Sculpted Braids, Bow, Glass Eyes, Suit, 13 In.	1380
Simon & Halbig, Oily Bisque, Square Teeth, Dark Brown Glass Sleep Eyes, Silk Shoes, Child, 23 In.	889
Soldier, Porcelain, Painted, Stitch-Jointed Cloth, Civil War Union, Uniform, c.1860, 24 In.	1035
Sonneberg, Bisque, Auburn Human Hair, Composition & Wood, Original Silk, Child, 15 In. ...	2430
Sonneberg, Bisque Socket Head, Glass Eyes, Mohair, Composition, Wood, Bebe, 11 In.	1610
Steiff, Mecki & Micki, Vinyl Head, Hedgehog Features, Mohair Torso, Clothes, 32 In., Pair	2760
Steiner, Bisque Head, Sleep Eyes, Blond Mohair, Jointed Composition, Play Suit, Bebe, 10 In.	6670
Steiner, Bisque Socket Head, Blue Glass Eyes, Blond Mohair, Jointed Composition, Bebe, 17 In.	3910
Steiner, Blue Eyes, Straight Wristed, Aqua Silk Shoes, Older Handmade Dress, Bebe, 17 In.	2074
Steiner, Gigoteur, Bisque Head, Dress, Carton Torso, Arms Wave, Cries Mama, Bebe, 17 In.	3220
Steiner, Living Eye, Bisque Flanged Head, Googly Eyes, Impish Grin, Muslin, 12 In.	748
Thuillier, Bebe, Bisque, Glass Paperweight Eyes, Auburn Mohair, Composition, Wood, 13 In.	6613
Topsyturvy, Pink, Green, Orange, Black Cotton, Geometric Pattern Dress, 1930s, 12 In.	325
Vogue, Toddles, Boy, Girl, Composition, Painted Features, Matching Dress & Suit, 8 In., Pair...	403
Walking, Bisque Head, Painted, Carton Torso, Skirt Hides Mechanism, Morrison, 1860s, 10 In.	633
Walking, Little Girl, Bisque, Legs Move, Metal Carriage, Mignonette, Vichy, Paris, 12 In.	4255
Wax Over Gesso, Fashionable Lady, Painted, Glass Eyes, Wood Block Torso, c.1870, 18 In. *illus*	392
Wax Over Papier-Mache, Cropped Curls, Hairband, Muslin, Wood, Pantaloons, Child, 6 In.	288
Wax, Cloth, Glass Eyes, Kid Leather Arms, Original Gown, Headdress, 1800s, 20 ½ x 9 In.	200
Wax, Girl, Shoulder Head, Bead Eyes, Painted Hair, Stuffed Cloth Body, 1860, Miniature, 5 In.	690
Wax, Girl, Shoulder Head, Blue Glass Eyes, Tendrils, Stuffed Muslin, Dress, Cape, Hood, 18 In.	1265
Wax, Princess Victoria, Blue Glass Eyes, Stuffed Cloth Body, Ball Gown, Pierotti, 15 In.	1840
Wax, Shoulder Head, Glass Eyes, Brunette Mohair, Muslin, Silk Gown, England, c.1875, 22 In.	1495
Wood, Gentleman, Painted, Inset Eyes, Brown Mohair, Velvet & Silk Suit, c.1790, 19 In.	21275
Wood, Lady, Painted Over Gesso, Flaxen Wig, Cloth Body, England, c.1820, 9 In.	2415

D

Doll, Lenci, Felt, Swivel Head, Blond Mohair Wig, Jointed, Wedding Dress, c.1932, 17 In. $1,495

Doll, Margot Of Italy, Felt, Side-Glancing Eyes, Blond Mohair Wig, Box, 1920s, 20 In. $748

Doll, Schoenhut, Schnickel-Fritz, Carved Hair, Teeth, Jointed, Painted Eyes, c.1911, 15 In. $3,556

Theriault's

Theriault's

Doll, S.F.B.J. Bluette, Bisque Socket Head, Blue Sleep Eyes, Teeth, Jointed Arms, Legs, 12 In. $825

DuMouchelles

Doll, Wax Over Gesso, Fashionable Lady, Painted, Glass Eyes, Wood Block Torso, c.1870, 18 In. $392

Doll, Madame Paderewski, Cloth, Seamed Face, Fleecy Hair, Jointed, Polish Relief Fund, 15 In. $2,280

Theriault's

DuMouchelles

Theriault's

125

Doll Clothes, Dress, Wedding, Silk, Ivory, Lace, Bustled Train, c.1870, For 16-In. Doll
$795

Ruby Lane

Doorstop, Dog, Boxer, Standing, Cast Iron, Painted, 1800s, 10 x 9¾ In.
$112

Neal Auction Co.

Doorstop, Fruit Bowl, Flowers, Multicolor Paint, Cast Iron, Marked, Hubley 456, 7 In.
$180

Bertoia Auctions

DOLL CLOTHES

Barbie, Pink Ball Gown, Red Coat, No. 933	95
Barbie, Red Flare Coat, Hat, Gloves, Purse, No. 939	35
Barbie, Scuba-Do, No. 1788	30
Barbie, Zebra Swimsuit, Cat's Eye Sunglasses	45
Beach Hat & Purse, Straw, Felt Dots, 1950s, For 10 In. Doll	45
Boots, Black Kidskin, Tan Leather, Wood Heels, Fits Huret Fashion, c.1850, 2½ In.	920
Boots, Spurs, Red, 1950s, 2 In.	28
Coat, Skirt, Muff, Burgundy Wool, Black Velvet, Gray Lamb's Wool, Fashion, 13 In.	460
Dress, Cotton, Mauve & Cream Checks, Cap Sleeves, Velvet Bonnet, Fashion, 12 In.	633
Dress, Wedding, Silk, Ivory, Lace, Bustled Train, c.1870, For 16-In. Doll........ *illus*	795
Ginnette, Bunting & Bonnet, White, Pink Satin Lining, Dynel, c.1957	26
Gown, Bronze Silk, Flowers, Velvet Bands, Pouf Sleeves, Lace, Fashion, c.1865, 13 In.	345
Gown, Cotton, White, 2-Tier Skirt, Rickrack, Drawstring Waist, Fashion, 13 In.	1150
Gown, Infant's, Purple, Checkered, Bonnet, France, 1860s, 12 In.	627
Gown, Lady's, Muslin, Flowers, Green, Brown, Pagoda Sleeves, Overlay Edges, 14 In.	805
Gown, Muslin, Floral Transfer Pattern, Pagoda Sleeves, c.1850, 14 In.	798
Jacket & Skirt, Black & White Pique, Soutache, Striped, Coat, Braid, Fashion, c.1870	1035
Lingerie, Aqua Blue Silk, White Cotton, Matching Lace, Jumeau, c.1890, 14 In.	350
Polka Dot Shirt, Red Shorts, Red Bow, Ginny, Vogue Dolls Inc.	45

DONALD DUCK *items are included in the Disneyana category.*

DOORSTOPS have been made in all types of designs. The vast majority of the doorstops sold today are cast iron and were made from about 1890 to 1930. Most of them are shaped like people, animals, flowers, or ships. Reproductions and newly designed examples are sold in gift shops. These are three marks used by doorstop makers.

Bradley & Hubbard
Manufacturing Co.
1854–1940

HUBLEY

Hubley Manufacturing Co.
1894–1965

WILTON PRODUCTS INC
WRIGHTSVILLE
PA.

Wilton Products, Inc.
c.1935–1989

---

3 Geese, White, Cast Iron, Marked, Hubley, 8 In.	270
Anne Hathaway Cottage, Flowers, Cast Iron, Hubley, 6½ In.	270
Aunt Jemima, Red Dress, White Apron, Cast Iron, 9 In.	497
Bathing Beauties, Art Deco, Cast Iron, Anne Fish, Hubley, 11 x 5 In.	368
Bugler Boy, Soldier, Blowing Bugle, Rifle, Hat, Brown, Cast Iron, 12⅛ In.	3900
Cape Cod Cottage, Climbing Flowers, Trees, Cast Iron, Hubley, 5⅝ In.	180
Cat, Licking Paw, Black & White, Marked, Sculptured Metal Studios, 11 In.	9600
Cockatoo, On Stump, Red, Orange, Blue & Green Tail, 8¼ In.	660
Colonial Woman, Pink Frock, Cream Skirt, 10½ In.	90
Dog, Boxer, Standing, Cast Iron, Painted, 1800s, 10 x 9¾ In. .... *illus*	112
Dog, French Bulldog, Black & White, Cast Iron, Hubley, 8 x 6½ In.	204
Dog, King Charles Spaniel, Sitting, Wavy Fur, 6 x 4 In.	420
Elephant, Cast Iron, Original Paint, Bradley & Hubbard, 1900s, 9½ x 2¾ In.	780
Flamingo, Pink, Standing, Reeds, Green, Hubley, 10½ In.	900
Fruit Bowl, Flowers, Multicolor Paint, Cast Iron, Marked, Hubley 456, 7 In. .... *illus*	180
Golfer, Putting, Early Attire, Grassy Putting Green, Hubley, 8½ In. .... *illus*	540
Highland Lighthouse, Buildings, Grass, 8⅛ In.	1440
Horse & Jockey, White Horse, Resting Jockey, Blue Vest, 14¼ In.	1921
Jonquils, Blowing In Breeze, Yellow, Orange, Cast Iron, Hubley, 7 In.	360
Kittens In Basket, 2 Cream, 1 Black, Green Base, Rosenstein, 1932, 6¾ x 10 In.	660
Koala Bear, Black, Yellow Outline, Orange Ears, Cast Iron, Taylor Cook, 5¾ In.	660
Little Red Riding Hood, Holding Basket, Wolf, Cast Iron, Paint, c.1900, 8 x 6 In.	600
Lobster, Red, Cast Iron, 12½ x 6½ In. .... *illus*	2700

Mammy, Hand On Hips, Smiling, Green Dress, Blue Apron, Red Shawl, Cast Iron, 1930s, 8¾ In.		55
Mammy, Hands On Hips, Double Wedge Back, Orange Dress, Iron, Litco		270
Naughty Puss, Girl, Cat, Claws In Dress, Cast Iron, H.L. Judd, 1920s, 9 In.		995
Owl, Standing On Books, Painted, Eastern Specialty Mfg. Co., 9¼ In.	*illus*	660
Parrot, Standing, Rocky Base, Old Repaint, Cast Iron, 1920, 7½ In.		168
Pelican, Standing, 2-Sided, Cast Iron, Marked, Spencer, Guilford, Conn., 15 x 4 In.	*illus*	5100
Poinsettia, Red, Green, Stenciled Pot, Cast Iron, 9¾ In.		840
Poppy Basket, Black Basket, Red Poppies, Art Deco Style, Cast Iron, 10½ In.		540
Punch & Judy, Full Figure, Cast Iron, 12½ In.		106
Rabbit, Garden, Picket Fence, Cast Iron, 1900, 6¾ x 8¼ In.		172
Rabbit, Sitting, 2-Sided, Part Of Series Of 4, Spencer, Guilford, 12 In.	*illus*	5400
Rhumba Dancer, Full Figure, Ruffled Dress, Head Scarf, Orange, Green, Cast Iron, 11 In.		1320
Rose Basket, Cast Iron, Hubley, 11 In.		83
Skunk, Full Figure, Painted, Tail Up, 6 x 8 In.	*illus*	780
Squirrel, Cast Iron, Seated On Log, Eating Acorn, Bradley & Hubbard, 1900s, 11 x 9¾ In.		660
Twin Kittens, Green Base, Grace Drayton, Hubley, 7½ x 5½ In.		147
West Wind, Girl Walking In Breeze, Flowers, Rubber Knobs, Judd, 18 In.	*illus*	4800

DOULTON was founded about 1858 in Lambeth, England. A second factory was opened in Burslem, England, by 1871. The name *Royal Doulton* appeared on the company's wares after 1902 and is listed in the Royal Doulton category in this book. Other Doulton ware is listed here. Doulton's Lambeth factory closed about 1956.

Doulton and Co.	Doulton and Co.	Doulton and Co.
1869–1877	1880–1912, 1923	1885–1902

Bowl, Flowers, Glazed, Stoneware, Lambeth, 7½ x 10 In.		219
Cup, 3 Handles, Dog Reserve, Glazed, Stoneware, Lambeth, 6 x 7 x 7 In.		813
Cup, Cylindrical, Raised Tavern, 3 Hunting Dogs, Stoneware, Lambeth, 1890, 7 In.		219
Cup, Mouse, Stoneware, George Tinworth, 4½ x 4 In.		375
Flagon, Goats, Incised, Sgraffito, Lambeth, 1868, 9¾ x 4½ In.		407
Group, Lambeth, Monkeys Embracing, Mother, Baby, Stoneware, 1800s, 6 x 5 In.		407
Jug, Blue, White, Designs, Stoneware, Lambeth, 1880, 9 In.		75
Jug, Designs, Silver Rim, Glazed, Stoneware, Lambeth, 9 x 5 x 6 In.		250
Jug, Silver Rim, Oriental, Multiple Dragons, Stoneware, Lambeth, 1885, 7¾ x 5 x 9½ In.		313
Mug, Glazed, Oars, Rowers, Stoneware, Lambeth, 9 x 7 x 5 In.		219
Pitcher, Leaves, Glazed, Raised Decoration, Lambeth, 7 x 7 x 5 In.		688
Plate, Gilt, Leafy Scrolls, Light Purple Flowers, 9⅛ In.		12
Urn, Indian Pattern, Panels, Flowers, Elephant Masks, Faience, c.1890, 17 x 20 In.	*illus*	2375
Urn, Stoneware, Enameled Birds & Branches, Cobalt Blue Base, 2 Handles, c.1880, 5½ In.		175
Vase, 2 Rabbits, Full Moon, Landscape, Glazed, Hand Decorated, 4⅞ In.		120
Vase, Art Nouveau, Glazed, Incised Decoration, Lambeth, 1902, 14 x 5 In.		344
Vase, Flowers, Architectural Patterns, Stoneware, Lambeth, 1884, 10½ x 4 x 4 In.		250
Vase, Glazed, 2 Neck Handles, Stoneware, Lambeth, 9 x 5½ In.		250
Vase, Incised Horse, Blue Chalice Band, Blue Scrolls, Lambeth, H. Barlow, 11½ In., Pair		671
Vase, Water Lilies, Glazed, Lambeth, 12 x 4½ In.		438
Vase, Windblown, Treescape, Mottled Orange, Purple Ground, 1910-33, 11 In.		738

DRESDEN and Meissen porcelain are often confused. Porcelains were made in the town of Meissen, Germany, beginning about 1706. The town of Dresden, Germany, has been home to many decorating studios since the early 1700s. Blanks were obtained from Meissen and other porcelain factories. Some say porcelain was also made in Dresden in the early years. Decorations on Dresden are often similar to Meissen, and marks were copied. Some of the earliest books on marks confused Dresden and Meissen, and that has remained a problem ever since. The Meissen "AR" mark and crossed swords mark are among the most forged marks on porcelain. Meissen pieces are listed

D

Doorstop, Golfer, Putting, Early Attire, Grassy Putting Green, Hubley, 8½ In. $540

Bertoia Auctions

Doorstop, Lobster, Red, Cast Iron, 12½ x 6½ In. $2,700

Bertoia Auctions

Doorstop, Owl, Standing On Books, Painted, Eastern Specialty Mfg. Co., 9 ¼ In.

$660

Bertoia Auctions

TIP

Loud dogs and nosy neighbors are good security.

Doorstop, Pelican, Standing, 2-Sided, Cast Iron, Marked, Spencer, Guilford, Conn., 15 x 4 In.

$5,100

Bertoia Auctions

---

in this book under Meissen. German porcelain marked "Dresden" is listed here. Irish Dresden and Dresden made in East Liverpool, Ohio, are not included in this section. These three marks say "Dresden" although none were used by a factory called Dresden.

Karl Richard Klemm
c.1891–1914

Ambrosius Lamm
c.1887+

Carl Thieme / Saxon Porcelain Manufactory
c.1903

Figurine, Ballerina, Arm Raised, Ruffled Skirt, Signed, Porcelain, Volkstedt, 1800s-1900s, 13 In...	219
Figurine, Parakeet, Red, 3 In.	360
Group, Courting Couple, Sedan Carriage, Multicolor, 9 ¼ x 6 ¼ In.	132
Group, Courting Couple, Table, Flowers, Frankenthal, 5 ½ x 5 ¼ In.	11
Group, Musicians, Full Skirts, Knickers, 11 x 19 In.	717
Nodder, Man, Seated, Flowered Robe, Purple Ruffle, Hinged Tongue, 8 ½ x 8 In.	593
Urn, Base, Figural Handles, Applied Flowers, Putto, 20 In.	400
Vase, 4 Panels, Couples Courting, Flowers, Gilt, Hand Painted, 1900s, 11 In. .... *illus*	375
Vase, Maiden Floating In Clouds, Gilt, George Heufel Co., 7 x 4 In. .... *illus*	550
Vase, Portrait, Napoleon, Flowers, 6 ¼ In.	281

DUNCAN & MILLER is a term used by collectors when referring to glass made by the George A. Duncan and Sons Company or the Duncan and Miller Glass Company. These companies worked from 1893 to 1955, when the use of the name *Duncan* was discontinued and the firm became part of the United States Glass Company. Early patterns may be listed under Pressed Glass.

Canterbury, Vase, Pink Opalescent, Ruffled Rim, 3 ¾ x 5 ¾ In.	68
Dogwood, Cigarette Box, White Opalescent, 5 x 4 In.	175
First Love, Candlestick, 2-Light, c.1930, 6 x 4 In., Pair	70
Gold Band Of Tulips, Vase, c.1940, 12 x 3 In.	75
Late Block, Syrup, Ruby Stained, c.1890, 6 ¼ In.	292
Lily Of The Valley, Goblet, 8 Oz., 6 ¾ In.	32
Sandwich, Plate, Dessert, 7 In.	12
Scalloped Six Point, Toothpick Holder, 2 ½ In.	20
Snail, Banana Stand, c.1890, 6 x 9 ½ In.	58
Snail, Cheese Dish, c.1890, 6 ⅛ In.	128
Snail, Compote, c.1890, 13 In.	81
Snail, Sugar, Lid, c.1890, 5 ½ In.	93
Swag Block, Open Salt, Amber Stained, c.1891, 8 ⅛ In.	58
Tavern, Basket, Scalloped Edge, 11 ¼ x 7 ¼ In.	40
Whitney, Centerpiece, Silver Overlay, 11 ½ x 3 ¾ In.	45

DURAND art glass was made from 1924 to 1931. The Vineland Flint Glass Works was established by Victor Durand and Victor Durand Jr. in 1897. In 1924 Martin Bach Jr. and other artisans from the Quezal glassworks joined them at the Vineland, New Jersey, plant to make Durand art glass. They called their gold iridescent glass Gold Luster.

Jar, Amber, Rosette, Applied Green Leaves, Iridescent Gold Highlights, 7 ¼ In.	790
Lamp, Electric, Trumpet Shape, Pinched Rim, Threaded Glass, Spelter Base, 15 ¾ In., Pair.....	1008
Lamp, Gilt Metal Mounts, Gold Iridescent Vase Shape, Body, Threaded Glass, 12 x 26 In..........	480
Lamp, Iridescent, Feather Design, Cast Metal Base, Single Socket, 48 In.	531
Rose Bowl, King Tut, Iridescent Gold, Green, Oval, c.1920, 4 In.	527
Vase, Blue, Gold, Iridescent, Urn Shape, Marked, 8 In.	325
Vase, Blue Iridescent, Oval, Shouldered, Flared Rim, 8 ¼ x 6 ½ In. .... *illus*	500
Vase, Cluthra, Beehive Shape, Mottled Aqua, Kimble, 1924-31, 6 ¼ In. .... *illus*	140
Vase, Cluthra, Blue, Green, White, Footed, 11 ½ In.	498
Vase, Emerald Green, Feather Decoration, Polished Pontil, 1925, 9 ½ x 4 ¼ In.	396

Vase, Flared Rim, Luster Body, Polished Pontil, Blue, Iridescent, 1924-31, 12 In.	923
Vase, Gold Iridescent, Cylindrical, Flared Rims, Silver, Engraved Signature, Durand 1968, 6 x 4 In.	396
Vase, Gold Iridescent, Pulled Feather, Threading, Signed, Polished Pontil, 1900s, 7¾ In. *illus*	420
Vase, Gold Iridescent, Signed, Shape No. 1710, 8¼ x 7½ In.	424
Vase, King Tut, Green & Gold Iridescent, Fluted Mouth, 1924-31, 14 x 5¼ In. *illus*	1287
Vase, Ribbed, Crackle, Blue To Clear, c.1924, 8 In.	1404
Vase, Topaz Crackle, Textured, Squat, Marked, 7 x 8½ In.	1121
Vase, Trumpet, Amethyst, Optic Ribbed, Applied Round Foot, 1924-31, 15½ x 5⅜ In. *illus*	555
Vase, Yellow Ground, White, Orange Mottled, Urn Shape, Marked, 9 In.	177

DURANT KILNS was founded by Jean Durant Rice in 1910 in Bedford Village, New York. He hired Leon Volkmar to oversee production. The pottery made both tableware and artware. Rice died in 1919, leaving Leon Volkmar to run the business. After 1930 the name Durant Kilns was changed and only the Volkmar mark was used. See the Volkmar category.

Bowl, Flared, Volcanic Turquoise Glaze, Marked, c.1915, 5 x 15 In.	177
Vase, Green Matte Glaze, Bulbous, Volkmar, c.1900, 18 In.	1532
Vase, Shouldered, Turquoise, Volkmar, c.1917, 8 In.	450

ELVIS PRESLEY, the well-known singer, lived from 1935 to 1977. He became famous by 1956. Elvis appeared on television, starred in 27 movies, and performed in Las Vegas. Memorabilia from any of the Presley shows, his records, and even memorials made after his death are collected.

Album, Separate Ways, Vinyl Record, Pickwick Label, 1972, 33 RPM	5
Button, Portrait, Las Vegas, Filliforms, 1970, 3⅜ In.	20
Lithograph, Black & White, Corniche, Young Elvis, Holding Guitar, c.1950, 27 x 19 In.	550
Photo, Black & White, 1950s, 27½ x 19½ In.	550
Photo, Elvis, On Bull, Stay Away Joe, 1968, 8 x 10 In.	75
Plate, Studio Session, Playing Guitar, Delphi, 8 In.	15
Record, Elvis For Everyone, RCA, 1965	95
Record, Good Rockin' Tonight, Limited Edition, Red, Vinyl, 45 RPM, 1986 *illus*	14
Record, Pot Luck With Elvis, RCA, 1960s	16
Stickpin, Goldtone, Portrait, 1950s, 2¾ In.	65

ENAMELS listed here are made of glass particles and other materials heated and fused to metal. In the eighteenth and nineteenth centuries, workmen from Russia, France, England, and other countries made small boxes and table pieces of enamel on metal. One form of English enamel is called *Battersea* and is listed under that name. There was a revival of interest in artist-made enameling in the 1930s and a new style evolved. There is now a recently renewed interest in the artistic enameled plaques, vases, ashtrays, and jewelry. Enamels made since the 1930s are usually on copper or steel, although silver was often used for jewelry. Graniteware, the factory-made household pieces made of tin or iron, is a separate category in this book. Enameled metal kitchen pieces may be included in the Kitchen category. Cloisonne is a special type of enamel using wire dividers and is listed in its own category. Descriptions of antique glass and ceramics often use the term *enamel* to describe paint, not the glass-based enamels listed here. Marks used by three important enamelists are shown here.

Lilyan Bachrach	Kenneth Bates	Edward Winter
1955–2015	1920s–1994	1932–1976

Bowl, Copper, 4 Evangelists, Pulled Pewter Edge, Karl Drerup, 10 In.	1187
Bowl, Copper, African Hunters, Lion, Karl Drerup, 2 x 10 In. *illus*	1375
Bowl, Copper, Dragon, Pulled Pewter Edge, Karl Drerup, 10 In. *illus*	1187
Bowl, Fruit, Electric Age, Metal, Laminate, N. Du Pasquier, Memphis, 1984, 14 In. *illus*	4063

Doorstop, Rabbit, Sitting, 2-Sided, Part Of Series Of 4, Spencer, Guilford, 12 In.
$5,400

Bertoia Auctions

Doorstop, Skunk, Full Figure, Painted, Tail Up, 6 x 8 In.
$780

Bertoia Auctions

Doorstop, West Wind, Girl Walking In Breeze, Flowers, Rubber Knobs, Judd, 18 In.
$4,800

Bertoia Auctions

Doulton, Urn, Indian Pattern, Panels, Flowers, Elephant Masks, Faience, c.1890, 17 x 20 In.
$2,375

Neal Auction Co.

Dresden, Vase, 4 Panels, Couples Courting, Flowers, Gilt, Hand Painted, 1900s, 11 In.
$375

Ruby Lane

Dresden, Vase, Maiden Floating In Clouds, Gilt, George Heufel Co., 7 x 4 In.
$550

Ruby Lane

Durand, Vase, Blue Iridescent, Oval, Shouldered, Flared Rim, 8 1/4 x 6 1/2 In. .
$500

Fontaine's Auction Gallery

Durand, Vase, Cluthra, Beehive Shape, Mottled Aqua, Kimble, 1924-31, 6 1/4 In.
$140

Jeffrey S. Evans

Durand, Vase, Gold Iridescent, Pulled Feather, Threading, Signed, Polished Pontil, 1900s, 7 3/4 In.
$420

Garth's Auctioneers & Appraisers

Durand, Vase, King Tut, Green & Gold Iridescent, Fluted Mouth, 1924-31, 14 x 5 1/4 In.
$1,287

Jeffrey S. Evans

Durand, Vase, Trumpet, Amethyst, Optic Ribbed, Applied Round Foot, 1924-31, 15 1/2 x 5 3/8 In.
$555

Jeffrey S. Evans

Bowl, Lobed Square, Raised Round Foot, Gilt Rim, Pomegranate, Bat Mark, Chinese, 3 x 6 ½ In.	123
Bowl, Ship, Warriors, Nude, Copper, Karl Drerup, 11 ½ In. .... *illus*	1187
Box, Hinged Collars, Cuffs, Blue, White Floral, Gilt Metal Feet, Braided Rope Mold, 6 ¼ x 7 ½ In.	420
Cigarette Case, Flowers, Blue, White, Cabochon Clasp, Russia, 1894, 3 x 3 ½ In.	1091
Cigarette Case, Portrait, Ivan Khlebnikov, Russia, 1888, 4 ½ In.	6000
Crucifix, Brass, Relief Figural, Cyrillic, Russia, 1800, 7 In.	120
Panel, 3 Tiles, Men, Birds & Goats, Metal, Frame, Karl Drerup, 20 ½ x 6 ½ In. .... *illus*	2250
Pill Box, 2 Impressionistic Birds, 1 ¾ x 1 ¼ x 1 In.	48
Plaque, Calligraphic Cliffs, Copper, On Board, Signed, William Harper, 1966, 8 ¾ x 16 ½ In. *illus*	545
Plaque, Farming Scene, Metal, Frame, Karl Drerup, 9 ⅜ x 9 ⅜ In.	1750
Plaque, Shapes, Black, Yellow, Light Blue, White, Copper, Kurt Lewy, Belgium, 4 ½ x 3 ¼ In....	1250
Plaque, Tropical Rhythms, Copper, Frame, Signed Kenneth F. Bates, 9 x 9 In. .... *illus*	1815
Plate, Fish, Copper, Foil Backed, Signed, RIMI, 11 ¼ x 13 In. .... *illus*	173
Sculpture, Aluminum, Signed & Numbered, Dorothy Gillespie, 12 ½ x 11 ½ x 7 ½ In. .... *illus*	750

ERPHILA is a mark found on Czechoslovakian and other pottery and porcelain made after 1920. This mark was used on items imported by Ebeling & Reuss, Philadelphia, a giftware firm that was founded in 1866 and out of business sometime after 2002. The mark is a combination of the letters *E* and *R* (Ebeling & Reuss) and the first letters of the city, Phila(delphia). Many whimsical figural pitchers and creamers, figurines, platters, and other giftwares carry this mark.

Dresser Box, Doll, Masquerade Ball, Jester Outfit, Blue, 5 ¾ x 4 ½ In.	27
Dresser Box, Doll, Pink, Madame Pompadour, 1920s, 6 ¼ In.	90
Figurine, Dutch Boy, Sitting, Hands In Pocket, 5 In.	20
Figurine, Sparrow, Gray, Taupe Brown, 3 ½ x 3 In.	45
Pitcher, Rooster, Red, Black Yellow, Geometric Designs, 9 In...	275
Teapot, Dog, Begging, Brown, Black, c.1947, 8 ½ In.	75
Teapot, Rabbit, Seated, Paw Spout, Tail Handle, 7 ½ In.	53

ES GERMANY porcelain was made at the factory of Erdmann Schlegelmilch from 1861 to 1937 in Suhl, Germany. The porcelain, marked *ES Germany* or *ES Suhl*, was sold decorated or undecorated. Other pieces were made at a factory in Saxony, Prussia, and are marked *ES Prussia*. Reinhold Schlegelmilch also made porcelain. There is no connection between the two factories. Porcelain made by Reinhold Schlegelmilch is listed in this book under RS Germany, RS Poland, RS Prussia, RS Silesia, RS Suhl, and RS Tillowitz.

Egg Holder, 6 Wells, Scalloped Rim, Gold, Royal Saxe, 1900s, 9 In.................................... *illus*	139
Watering Can, Red Flowers, Leaves, c.1918, 6 ½ x 9 In.	55

ESKIMO artifacts of all types are collected. Carvings of whale or walrus teeth are listed under Scrimshaw. Baskets are in the Basket category. All other types of Eskimo art are listed here. In Canada and some other areas, the term *Inuit* is used instead of Eskimo. It is illegal to sell some whale parts that are used to made decorative items. The law has changed several times, so check the legality before you buy or sell.

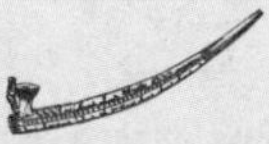

Boat, Umiak, Greenland, Narrow Stern, Bow Boards, Gunwales, Model, 1950s, 39 ¾ In.	480
Bowl, Beaver Shape, Effigy Potlatch, Carved Wood, Abalone Eyes, J.C. Koosher, 1800s, 15 ½ In.	2400
Box, Hinged Lid, Stamped Starburst, Top Inlaid, Turquoise, Angled Fylfot Cross, 1930s-1940s, 1 x 2 ½ In.	110
Doll, Composition Face, Leather, Fur, Textile, Alaska, 16 In.	36
Figurine, Woman, Kneeling, Black, Inuit, 1984, 5 In.	150
Goggles, Caribou Hoof, Triangular, Slits, Leather Straps, Inuit, 1900s, 1 ⅜ x 5 ¼ In.	125
Goggles, Integral Visor, Wood, Red Stain, Hide Ties, 1900s, 1 ⅝ x 6 ½ x 3 ¾ In........................	1560
Goggles, Thin Slit, Bone, Carved, Human & Walrus Shapes, 1900s, 5 ¼ x 2 ¼ In.....................	1500
Group, 3 Walruses, On Ice Floe, Ivory, Mounted On Whale Baleen, 1970s, 7 x 4 ½ x 3 In...........	110
Group, Polar Bear, Cub, Walrus Ivory, 3 ¾ In.	240
Knife, Ivory, Octagonal, Turned Tapered Handle, Inset Blade, 1800s, 19 In.	510
Mask, Human Face, Whalebone, c.1950, 9 x 7 ½ In.. *illus*	748
Moccasins, Sealskin, Smoked Moosehide, Fur, Beads, Alaska, c.1925, 11 ½ In.................. *illus*	209
Model, Kayak, Greenland, Cedar, Bas Relief, Multicolor, c.1900, 24 ½ In.	390

Elvis Presley, Record, Good Rockin' Tonight, Limited Edition, Red, Vinyl, 45 RPM, 1986
$14

Ruby Lane

Twentieth-Century Enamels
Enameling is not a new art. The basic techniques used today were discovered by the sixteenth century. Arts & Crafts artists used enamel, but sparingly, in the early 1900s. Copper trays had a few enamel leaves and copper-covered bowls were made with metal tops with an enameled circle set in a bezel. In the 1920s and '30s, Boston artists, including Elizabeth Copeland, Katharine Pratt, and Gertrude Twichell, made enameled clock faces and jewelry. By the 1950s, the new midcentury style of enamels had spread nationwide.

Enamel, Bowl, Copper, African Hunters, Lion, Karl Drerup, 2 x 10 In.
$1,375

Rago Arts and Auction Center

This is an edited listing of current prices. Visit **Kovels.com** to check thousands of prices from previous years and sign up for free information on trends, tips, reproductions, marks, and more.

Enamel, Bowl, Copper, Dragon, Pulled Pewter Edge, Karl Drerup, 10 In. $1,187

Rago Arts and Auction Center

Enamel, Bowl, Fruit, Electric Age, Metal, Laminate, N. Du Pasquier, Memphis, 1984, 14 In. $4,063

Rago Arts and Auction Center

Enamel, Bowl, Ship, Warriors, Nude, Copper, Karl Drerup, 11½ In. $1,187

Rago Arts and Auction Center

Expensive Easter Eggs

Faberge made 50 Imperial Easter Eggs. Some Imperial eggs are still missing: 1886, Hen egg with Sapphire Pendant; 1888, Cherub egg with Chariot; 1889, Necessaire egg; 1896, Alexander III egg; 1897, Mauve Enamel egg; 1902, Empire Nephrite egg; 1903, Royal Danish Jubilee egg; and 1909, Alexander II Commemorative egg.

Model, Kayak, Greenland, Wood, Sealskin, Harpoon Mounted, 15¼ In.	180
Tool, Bone, Sharpened Wedge, Inked, Scrimshaw Caribou, 1900s, 5½ In.	110
Tooth, Masked Figure, Orca, Rich Brown Patina, 1900s, 4½ In.	540
Totem Pole, 7 Figures, Inked Details, Bone Base, 1920s, 11 In.	325
Toy, Fidget, Holes, Walrus Ivory, Stepped, Pinholes, 3 In.	360
Tusk, 2 Cameramen Taking Photos, 4 Men Playing Percussion Instruments, 1900s, 11 In.	900
Tusk, 5 Horizontal Scenes, Human Figures, 1800s, 2¾ x 3½ In.	270
Tusk, Walrus, Face, 3 Fierce Dogs, Engraved, 1900, 7 In.	120

ETLING
FRANCE

ETLING glass pieces are very similar in design to those made by Lalique and Phoenix. They were made in France for Etling, a retail shop. They date from the 1920s and 1930s.

Bust, Female, Blue Robe Draped Over Her Head, Long Braided Hair, Inscribed, 16 x 8½ x 8 In.	363

 ФАБЕРЖЕ КФ

FABERGE was a firm of jewelers and goldsmiths founded in St. Petersburg, Russia, in 1842, by Gustav Faberge. Peter Carl Faberge, his son, was jeweler to the Russian Imperial Court from about 1870 to 1917. The rare Imperial Easter eggs, jewelry, and decorative items are very expensive today.

Bell, Bowenite, Square, Neoclassical, Garnets, White Enamel, Gold Laurel, Red, 1900s, 2¼ In.	2000
Egg, Music Box, Holly, Silver, Ruby Enamel, Gold Case, Vermeil Crown, Limited Edition, 1986, 6 In.	1251
Letter Opener, Nephrite Jade, 14K Yellow Gold, Dore, Cyrillic Mark, 1896-1908, 8 In.	4800
Snuffbox, 18K Yellow Gold, Red Guilloche Enamel, Gem Set Square, Cyrillic Mark, Perchin, 1895	7800

 FAIENCE refers to tin-glazed earthenware, especially the wares made in France, Germany, and Scandinavia. It is also correct to say that faience is the same as majolica or Delft, although usually the term refers only to the tin-glazed pottery of the three regions mentioned.

Charger, Hunter, Tulip & Flowerhead Border, Yellows & Greens, 17 In.	214
Jar, Lid, Tree Peonies, Red, White, Leaves, Yellow Ground, John Bennet, 1882, 15½ x 12 In.	7500
Jardiniere, Flowers, Pierced Insert, 5 Scrolled Feet, 1800s, 13½ In. .... *illus*	270
Letter Holder, Blue, Flower Sprays, 3 Sections, Montagnon, 5¾ x 10 In.	63
Platter, Peasant Girl, Mule, House, Trail, Blue Border, France, 16¼ x 23½ In.	141
Tile, Owl, Cuerda Seca, Frame, Stamped, Hartford, Ct., c.1910, 9½ In. .... *illus*	2250
Tureen, Soup, Lid, Blue Flowers, Lemon Knop, 10 In.	500
Vase, Cherry Blossoms, Faux Lapis Ground, Gilt, Faience Mfg. Co., c.1890, 9 x 6 In. .... *illus*	625

 FAIRINGS are small souvenir boxes and figurines that were sold at country fairs during the nineteenth century. Most were made in Germany. Reproductions of fairings are being made, especially of the famous *Twelve Months after Marriage* series.

Box, Mirror, Lute, Horn, Multicolor, 1800s, 6 x 4 In.	77
Box, Piano, Sheet Music, Landscape Picture, Staffordshire, 3 x 2 x 4 In.	155
Box, Sewing, Embossed Thimble, Scissors, Needles, Buttons, H & G, 2 In.	63
Dresser Box, Mirror, Pocket Watch, Ring, Jars, Conta Boehme, 2 x 3 x 4 In.	85
Trinket Box, Cloth Draped, Pocket Watch, Book, Gilt, Conta Boehme	45
Trinket Box, Hand, Gold Band On Wrist, 2½ In.	28
Trinket Box, Oval, Scrolling, Blue Accents, Staffordshire, 2 x 3¾ In.	18

FAIRYLAND LUSTER *pieces are included in the Wedgwood category.*

FAMILLE ROSE, *see Chinese Export category.*

FANS have been used for cooling since the days of the ancients. By the eighteenth century, the fan was an accessory for the lady of fashion and very elaborate and expensive fans were made. Sticks were made of ivory or wood, set with jewels or carved. The fans were made of painted silk or paper. Inexpensive paper fans printed with advertising were giveaways in the late nineteenth and early twentieth centuries. Electric fans were introduced in 1882.

Advertising, Pabst Brewing Co., 5 Women, Building, Wood, Cardboard, Round, 15⅜ x 10 In.	212

Enamel, Panel, 3 Tiles, Men, Birds & Goats, Metal, Frame, Karl Drerup, 20 ½ x 6 ½ In. $2,250

Rago°Arts and Auction Center

Enamel, Plaque, Tropical Rhythms, Copper, Frame, Signed Kenneth F. Bates, 9 x 9 In. $1,815

Rachel Davis Fine Arts

Enamel, Plate, Fish, Copper, Foil Backed, Signed, RIMI, 11 ¼ x 13 In. $173

Uniques & Antiques

Enamel, Sculpture, Aluminum, Signed & Numbered, Dorothy Gillespie, 12 ½ x 11 ½ x 7 ½ In. $750

Rago Arts and Auction Center

ES Germany, Egg Holder, 6 Walls, Scalloped Rim, Gold, Royal Saxe, 1900s, 9 In. $139

Ruby Lane

Enamel, Plaque, Calligraphic Cliffs, Copper, On Board, Signed, William Harper, 1966, 8 ¾ x 16 ½ In $545

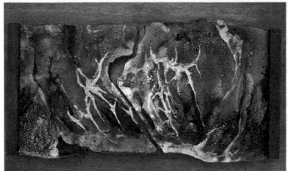

Rachel Davis Fine Arts

TIP
To remove an unwanted gummed price sticker, try heating it with a hair dryer. The glue will melt a bit, and it will be easier to peel off the sticker.

FAN

Eskimo, Mask, Human Face, Whalebone, c.1950, 9 x 7 1/2 In. $748

Allard Auctions

Eskimo Moccasins, Sealskin, Smoked Moosehide, Fur, Beads, Alaska, c.1925, 11 1/2 In. $209

Cowan's Auctions

Faience, Jardiniere, Flowers, Pierced Insert, 5 Scrolled Feet, 1800s, 13 1/2 In. $270

Cowan's Auctions

Faience, Tile, Owl, Cuerda Seca, Frame, Stamped, Hartford, Ct., c.1910, 9 1/2 In. $2,250

Rago Arts and Auction Center

Bamboo, Paper, Folding, Wasps, Flowers, Blue, Cream Ground, c.1900, 12 1/2 In.	1320
Electric, Ceiling Fixture, Single Socket, Stenciled Black Filigree, Glass Shade, 42 x 26 In.	4840
Electric, Emerson, Oscillating, North Wind, 14 x 11 1/2 In.	77
Electric, Eskimo, 3 Blades, 18 x 25 In. *illus*	147
Electric, Hunter Zephair, 4 Blades, Black, 21 x 18 In.	99
Electric, Robbins & Myers, 4 Blades, Oscillating, c.1910, 20 1/2 x 17 1/2 In. *illus*	47
Electric, Westinghouse, 4 Blades, Brass Wire Housing, Old Black Paint, Cast Iron Base, c.1935, 20 In.	240
Mother-Of-Pearl, Folding, Silver Gilt, Gold Peacock, Dancers, Musicians, Victorian, Box, 12 1/2 In. *illus*	1968
Mother-Of-Pearl, Sticks, Folding, Silver Gilt Overlay, Women, Landscape, 10 1/2 x 20 In.	75
Plastic, Airbrush Painted, Hawaiian Scenes, Hong Kong, c.1960, 6 In.	7

FAST FOOD COLLECTIBLES *may be included in several categories, such as Advertising, Coca-Cola, Toy, etc.*

FEDERZEICHNUNG, *see Loetz category.*

FENTON ART GLASS COMPANY was founded in 1905 in Martins Ferry, Ohio, by Frank L. Fenton and his brother, John W. Fenton. They painted decorations on glass blanks made by other manufacturers. In 1907 they opened a factory in Williamstown, West Virginia, and began making glass. The company stopped making art glass in 2011 and assets were sold. A new division of the company makes handcrafted glass beads and other jewelry. Copies are being made from leased original Fenton molds by an unrelated company, Fenton's Collectibles. The copies are marked with the Fenton mark and Fenton's Collectibles mark. Fenton is noted for early carnival glass produced between 1907 and 1920. Some of these pieces are listed in the Carnival Glass category. Many other types of glass were also made. Spanish Lace in this section refers to the pattern made by Fenton.

Fenton Art Glass Co. 1970–1975	Fenton Art Glass Co. 1980s	Fenton Art Glass Co. 1983+

Amberina, Bowl, Fruit, 8 1/4 In.	75
Captive Rose, Bowl, Royal Blue Base, c.1910, 8 In.	75
Coinspot, Pitcher, Cranberry, Clear Applied Twisted Handle, 7 x 5 In.	61
Crystal Crest, Cake Plate, 4 x 11 In.	45
Daisy & Button, Sugar & Creamer, Milk Glass	44
Daisy & Button, Top Hat, Milk Glass, 3 3/4 In.	12
Figurine, Bird Of Happiness, Cobalt Blue, Floral Motif, Signed, 1980s, 6 x 4 1/2 In. *illus*	69
Figurine, Bird, Bright Crystal Color, Lavender, Green Floral Decoration, 1997, 2 1/2 x 4 In.	45
Figurine, Bird, Cameo, Chocolate Roses, 4 In.	29
Figurine, Butterfly, Blue, Yellow, Green, On Stand, 1990, 4 1/2 x 3 1/4 In.	45
Figurine, Butterfly, Olive Green, On Stand, 1990, 4 1/2 In.	30
Figurine, Cat, French Opalescent, 3 3/4 In.	25
Figurine, Cat, Sitting, Hand Painted, Flowers, 3 1/2 In.	65
Figurine, Donkey, Pink, Embossed Logo, 5 x 5 In.	39
Figurine, Elephant, Trunk Up, Ruby Amberina, 3 1/2 In.	30
Figurine, Mouse, Frosted Asters, Blue Satin, 3 In.	29
Figurine, Puppy, Flowers, 1990	65
Goblet, Priscilla Green, 6 1/8 In.	34
Hobnail, Bowl, Colonial Green, Candle, Footed, 3 5/8 x 6 1/2 In.	24
Hobnail, Butter, Cover, Milk Glass	28
Hobnail, Compote, Milk Glass, Ruffled, 6 1/2 x 9 1/2 In.	72
Hobnail, Jug, Milk Glass, 9 x 7 In.	67
Hobnail, Pitcher, Pink Pearl, Iridescent, 5 1/2 In.	35
Hobnail, Planter, Milk Glass, Footed, 4 x 4 x 3 In.	30
Hobnail, Shoe, Victorian, Cobalt Blue, 2 x 5 In.	15
Hobnail, Slipper, Cat, Cobalt Blue, 2 1/2 x 5 1/2 In.	22

Hobnail, Toothpick Holder, Amber, 3 In.	25
Hobnail, Top Hat, Opalescent Blue	22
Jug, Handle, Silver Crest, White, Clear Fluted Rim, 8 In. *illus*	56
Lily Of The Valley, Bell, Opalescent Blue, 1970s, 5¼ In.	17
Lotus, Serving Bowl, Ruby Red, 8½ x 2½ In.	24
Mosaic, Vase, Threaded, Urn, c.1925, 8 In.	2600
Opalescent Swirl, Pitcher, Ruffled Rim, Flowers, 7 x 5 In. *illus*	48
Peach Crest, Vase, Melon Lobed, Double Crimpled Ruffle, 5½ x 3 x 3 In.	19
Satin, Bowl, Green, Crimped, 10¼ In.	40
Silver Crest, Bowl, Low, Red, 1930s, 10 In.	1500
Spiral Optic, Decanter, c.1934, 11 In.	450
Spiral Optic, Vase, Pinched, Cranberry, 8 In.	89
Swirl, Bell, Light Blue, 6¾ In.	25
Thumbprint Amber, Bowl, Ruffled, 2¼ x 7¾ In.	15
Thumbprint, Compote, Ruffled, 6 x 18 In.	18
Vase, Embossed Rose, Ruffled Mouth, Yellow Over White Cased Glass, 8 In.	55
Vase, Fan, Orange, Yellow, Brown, White, Vasa Murrhina, 7 x 7½ In.	49
Vase, Mosaic, Threaded, Multicolored, 1925, 8 x 2½ In. *illus*	2600

FIESTA, the colorful dinnerware, was introduced in 1936 by the Homer Laughlin China Co., redesigned in 1969, and withdrawn in 1973. It was reissued again in 1986 in different colors and is still being made. New colors, including some that are similar to old colors, have been introduced. One new color is introduced in March every year. The simple design was characterized by a band of concentric circles beginning at the rim. Cups had full-circle handles until 1969, when partial-circle handles were made. Harlequin and Riviera were related wares. For more prices, go to kovels.com.

Fiesta 1936–1970	Fiesta Kitchen Kraft 1939–c.1943	Fiesta Casual 1962–c.1968

Apricot, Platter, 11½ In.	25
Apricot, Sauceboat	35 to 48
Black, Pitcher, Miniature, 3¼ In.	25
Chartreuse, Pitcher, Water, Disc	325
Cobalt Blue, Nappy, 4¾ In.	30
Cobalt Blue, Pitcher, Carafe, Lid, Marked, 10 x 6 In. *illus*	175
Cobalt Blue, Plate, Dinner, 10 In.	13
Cobalt Blue, Salt & Pepper	16
Gray, Casserole, Lid, Footed	295
Gray, Pitcher, Miniature, 3¼ In.	62
Gray, Pitcher, Water, Disc, 7½ In.	200
Gray, Plate, Dinner, 10¼ In.	25
Gray, Platter, 12½ In.	60
Green, Casserole, Lid *illus*	86
Ivory, Chop Plate, 15 In.	60
Light Green, Jug, 2 Pt.	80
Light Green, Pitcher, Disc, 7½ In.	110
Light Green, Shaker, Ball, Foot, 2½ In.	12
Light Green, Teapot, Lid, 8 Cup, 7 In.	195
Medium Green, Bowl, 6¼ In.	30
Medium Green, Cup, Loop Handle, 2¾ In.	49
Medium Green, Mixing Bowl, No. 4	149
Medium Green, Plate, Dinner, 9 In.	40
Periwinkle, Bowl, 8⅜ In.	16

Faience, Vase, Cherry Blossoms, Faux Lapis Ground, Gilt, Faience Mfg. Co., c.1890, 9 x 6 In.
$625

Rago Arts and Auction Center

Fan, Electric, Eskimo, 3 Blades, 18 x 25 In.
$147

Copake Auction

Fan, Electric, Robbins & Myers, 4 Blades, Oscillating, c.1910, 20½ x 17½ In.
$47

Hess Auction Group

Fan, Mother-Of-Pearl, Folding, Silver Gilt, Gold Peacock, Dancers, Musicians, Victorian, Box, 12 ½ In.
$1,968

Morphy Auctions

Fenton, Figurine, Bird Of Happiness, Cobalt Blue, Floral Motif, Signed, 1980s, 6 x 4 ½ In.
$69

Ruby Lane

Fenton, Jug, Handle, Silver Crest, White, Clear Fluted Rim, 8 In.
$56

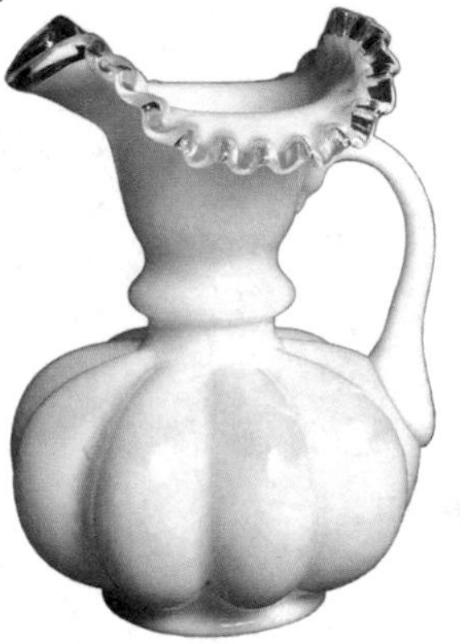

Replacements, Ltd.

Fenton, Opalescent Swirl, Pitcher, Ruffled Rim, Flowers, 7 x 5 In.
$48

Martin Auction Co.

Periwinkle, Mug, Ring Handle, 3 ½ In.		7
Red, Bowl, Fruit, 4 ¾ In.		30
Red, Bowl, Fruit, 5 ½ In.		25
Red, Cup & Saucer		19
Red, Mixing Bowl, No. 1		325
Red, Pitcher, Carafe, 9 ¼ In.		285
Red, Tumbler, Juice, 3 ½ In.		65
Rose, Eggcup		54
Shamrock, Casserole, Lid, 9 ¼ In.		40
Shamrock, Cup & Saucer		10
Shamrock, Plate, Dinner, 10 ½ In.		10
Turquoise, Mixing Bowl, No. 3		49
Turquoise, Soup, Dish, 8 ½ In.		39
Turquoise, Tumbler, Water, Disc		75
Yellow, Mixing Bowl, No. 2		160
Yellow, Plate, Dinner, 10 In.		24
Yellow, Saucer		8

FINCH, *see Kay Finch category.*

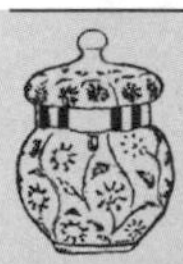

FINDLAY ONYX AND FLORADINE are two similar types of glass made by Dalzell, Gilmore and Leighton Co. of Findlay, Ohio, about 1889. Onyx is a patented yellowish white opaque glass with raised silver daisy decorations. A few rare pieces were made of rose, amber, orange, or purple glass. Floradine is made of cranberry-colored glass with an opalescent white raised floral pattern and a satin finish. The same molds were used for both types of glass.

Creamer, Floradine, Raspberry, Opal White Flowers, Opaque Handle, 4 ½ In.		298
Creamer, Onyx, Ivory, Platinum Flowers, Colorless Applied Handle, 4 ½ In.		40
Shaker, Sugar, Onyx, White Opaline, Daisies, Ribbed, 5 ½ x 3 ¼ In.		376
Spooner, Floradine, Raspberry, White Flowers, 4 ½ In.		350
Spooner, Onyx, Platinum Flowers, 4 ¼ x 2 ½ In.		120
Tumbler, Onyx, Platinum Flowers, Barrel Shape, Polished Rim, 3 ½ In.		140

FIREFIGHTING equipment of all types is collected, from fire marks to uniforms to toy fire trucks. It is said that every little boy wanted to be a fireman or a train engineer 75 years ago and the collectors today reflect this interest.

Alarm Box, Aluminum, Red, White Pull Lever, Gamewell, Newton, Mass., No. 674, 17 In.		192
Bucket, Green Ground, Mercury & Stephen B. Ives, 1800s, 13 In.		2640
Bucket, Leather, Dog, Wings, Multicolor, Strap, England, 10 x 13 In.		250
Bucket, Leather, Inscribed J. Miller No. 1, Red, 1800s, 13 In.		1500
Bucket, Leather, Inscribed Willard Smith, Black, 1800s, 12 In.		200
Bucket, Leather, Red, Sandwich 8 Fire Brigade, c.1850, 11 ¼ x 16 In.	*illus*	819
Bucket, Leather, Spread Wing Eagle, Mechanic Fire Society, Red, Black Rim, 12 ½ In.	*illus*	7200
Bucket, Leather, USS Hartford, Anchor At Center, 1861-2-3-4, 11 In.		1440
Extinguisher, Nickel, Turn Valve Cap, Glass Front Cabinet, Boka Mfg., 1946, 3 ½ x 7 ½ x 2 ¼ In.		30
Fire Mark, Water Wagon, Red Black Ground, Round, Iron, Cast, F.I. Co., 1900s, 12 In.		92
Hydrant, Cast Iron, L-90A Product, Model 1452, Rensselaer Valve Mfg., 1945, 42 x 18 In.		90
Lantern, Parade, What The Foreman Says Goes, Marching Man, Black, Red, 19 ½ In.		936
Sign, Hat Shape, Veteran Firemen's Association New York City, 20 x 32 In.		5445
Trumpet, Tin, Folded Seam, 17 In.		198

FIREPLACES were used to cook food and to heat the American home in past centuries. Many types of tools and equipment were used. Andirons held the logs in place, firebacks reflected the heat into the room, and tongs were used to move either fuel or food. Many types of spits and roasting jacks were made and may be listed in the Kitchen category.

Andirons, Aluminum, Cube, Spheres, Stacked, Glass, Art Deco, 13 ¼ In.		1500

Andirons, Brass, Aesthetic Revival, Pierced Blossom, Scrollwork, c.1890, 19 In................. *illus*	701
Andirons, Bronze, Beaux-Arts Style, Scrolled Feet, Flame Finials, c.1925, 32 x 12 ½ In............	1125
Andirons, Cast Iron, Cat, Perched, Scrolls, 17 x 16 In., Pair	105
Andirons, Cast Iron, Figural, Massosoit, Full Body, Black Paint, c.1890, 19 x 18 In. .... *illus*	1452
Andirons, Cast Iron, George Washington, 14 x 18 In...	468
Andirons, Cast Iron, Hessian Soldiers, Marching, Yellow Pants, Red Jackets, 19 ½ x 19 In........	321
Andirons, Cast Iron, Louis XV, Scrolls, Gilt, 9 In..	125
Andirons, Cast Iron, Owl Form, Glass Eyes, 13 x 8 x 18 In..	549
Andirons, Cast Iron, Pheasant, 13 ½ x 26 In.. *illus*	3240
Bellows, Carved Griffin Handles, Filigree Trim, Brass Nozzle, Incised Back, 17 x 8 x 1 ½ In.....	242
Bellows, Turtleback, Whaleboats, Whales, Brown, Yellow, c.1825, 19 In........................... *illus*	200
Bellows, Wood, Box Shape, Rectangular Body, Turned Handle, Brass Trim, Nozzle, 25 In........	62
Chenets, Andirons, Bronze, Laming Urn, Leaves, Winged Mask, Cattails, 15 ½ In.	500
Chenets, Andirons, Cast Iron, Putti, Molded, Scrolled, Gilt, Urn, Oak Leaf Garlands, 19 x 25 In.	3900
Coal Scuttle, Lift Lid, Metal, Mother-Of-Pearl, Brass Hardware, 16 ½ x 10 ½ In. .... *illus*	120
Coal Scuttle, Tin, Black Lacquered, Birds, Landscape Panel, 21 ½ x 14 ½ In............................	363
Fender, Black Painted Decorative Wire, Brass Finials, Paw Feet, 1800s, 14 x 51 x 17 In.	480
Fender, Brass, Wirework, George III, Urn Finials, c.1810, 17 x 60 x 20 In.	549
Fender, Bronze, Dog, Mastiff, Gilt Filigree Mounts, Empire, 11 x 13 x 5 ¾ In.............................	1815
Fender, Bronze, Regency, Serpentine, Pierced Sides, Flowers, Leaves, c.1835, 9 x 67 In.............	855
Fender, Cage Shape, Domed, Semicircle, Wire, Iron, Wrought, 26 ½ x 26 ½ In. .... *illus*	184
Fender, Gilt, Bronze, Empire, Griffins, 11 ¾ x 46 In..	281
Fender, Gilt, Bronze, Lion's Mask, Scrolls, Mahogany Base, Padded Tufted Top, 107 In.	1375
Fender, Iron, Twisted Shaft Spindles, Ball Finials, Red Paint, 10 x 42 x 13 In. .... *illus*	590
Fire Back, Cast Iron, Raised Relief, Woman, Harp, Cattails, Moon, c.1890, 25 x 20 In.............	1100
Grate, Brass, Iron, Serpentine Top, Relief Carved, Tombstone Cartouche, 1800s, 28 x 25 x 14 In.	492
Hearth Broom, Wood Handle, Straw, 33 In..	350
Hearth Hook, Carp, Wood, Bamboo Pole, Iron, Japan, 86 In.	252
Holder, Firewood, U Shape, Wrought Iron Framework, Paddle Form Feet, 1900, 15 x 24 In.	48
Insert, Federal, Iron, Brass, Leaf & Rosette, Signed, S. Thompson, 34 x 35 ½ In............... *illus*	1722
Log Bin, Brass, Repousse, Slant Lid, Tavern, Hunting, Trophies, Stag, Bail Handles, 27 x 33 In... *illus*	438
Log Bin, Copper, Oval, Straight Sides, Handles, 1800s, 14 x 27 In.	31
Log Bin, Copper, Oval, Straight Sides, Wood Handles, c.1900, 13 ½ x 28 In.............................	94
Log Cradle, Metal, Scroll, Black, Rectangular, 21 ½ x 27 In..	72
Mantel is listed in the Architectural category.	
Screens are also listed in Furniture.	
Screen, Brass, Wirework, 1800s, 30 x 48 In.	1220
Screen, Brass, Wirework, Serpentine, Repeating Circles, Finials, 1830s, 15 x 47 In....................	450
Screen, Edgar Brandt, Wrought Iron, France, 1920s, 36 x 30 ½ In. .... *illus*	8750
Screen, Embroidered, Bouquet, Cherry, Walnut, Oval, Tripod Saber Legs, 1800s, 55 In............	120
Screen, Needlework Panel, Central Red Flower & Leaves, Iron, Gold Leaf, c.1865, 39 In.	1025
Screen, Needlework Panel, Flowers, Twisted Cast Iron Frame, Oval, 4 Legs, Huret, France, 39 In.	2280
Screen, Stained Glass, Ellipses, Columns, Brown, Green Red, 1900s, 33 x 21 In........................	82
Screen, Wrought Iron, Scrolls, Circles, 36 In..	175
Tongs, Ember, Scrolled Handle, Ornaments, Cast Iron, 1700s-1800s, 19 In.................. *illus*	660
Tool Set, Brass, Iron, Faceted Handles, Tongs, Shovel, Poker, Stand, 1800s, 38 In., 4 Piece.. *illus*	488

FISCHER porcelain was made in Herend, Hungary. The wares are sometimes referred to as Herend porcelain. The pottery was originally founded in Herend in 1826 and was bought by Moritz Fischer in 1839. Fischer made replacement pieces for German and Far Eastern dinnerware and later began making its own dinnerware patterns. Figurines were made beginning in the 1870s. The company was nationalized in 1948. Martin's Herend Imports, Inc., began importing Herend china into the United States in 1957. The company was privatized in 1993 and is now in business as Herend.

MF

Coffeepot, Rothschild Bird, Butterflies, Gilt, Rose Finial, 1900s, 10 ½ In.....................................	192
Group, 2 Giraffes, Marked Herend Underside Of Foot, 7 ½ x 5 x 3 ½ In.	559
Jardiniere, Black, White, Green, Flowers, Dolphin Handles, 1900, 8 x 11 x 9 In.........................	615
Vase, Musicians Carrying Instruments Through Snow & Green, Yellow Ducks, 19 In.................	550

F

Fenton, Vase, Mosaic, Threaded, Multicolored, 1925, 8 x 2 ½ In.
$2,600

Ruby Lane

Fiesta, Cobalt Blue, Pitcher, Carafe, Lid, Marked, 10 x 6 In.
$175

Ruby Lane

Fiesta, Green, Casserole, Lid
$86

Strawser Auction Group

Firefighting, Bucket, Leather, Red, Sandwich 8 Fire Brigade, c.1850, 11 ¼ x 16 In.
$819

Jeffrey S. Evans

Firefighting, Bucket, Leather, Spread
Wing Eagle, Mechanic Fire Society, Red,
Black Rim, 12 ½ In.
$7,200

Eldred's Auctioneers and Appraisers

Fireplace, Andirons, Brass, Aesthetic
Revival, Pierced Blossom, Scrollwork,
c.1890, 19 In.
$701

Neal Auction Co.

Fireplace, Andirons, Cast Iron, Figural,
Massosoit, Full Body, Black Paint,
c.1890,
19 x 18 In.
$1,452

James D. Julia Auctioneers

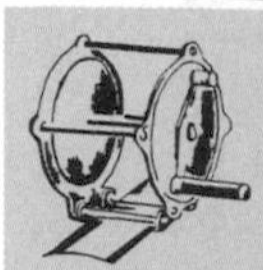

FISHING reels of brass or nickel were made in the United States by 1810. Bamboo
fly rods were sold by 1860, often marked with the maker's name. Lures made of
metal, or metal and wood, were made in the nineteenth century. Plastic lures were
made by the 1930s. All fishing material is collected today, and even equipment of
the past 30 years is of interest if in good condition with original box.

Creel, Split Willow, Brown Leather Trim, 16 x 9 ½ In.	342
Creel, Wicker, Leather Straps, Slide Tab, Patent Number, c.1935, 15 x 10 In.	42
Rod, Halibut, Wood, Copper Reel, Mathews Conveyer Co., c.1910, 39 In.	365
Tin, Rainbow Quality Silkworm Gut Leader, Green, Lithograph, 1 ⅛ x 3 ½ In.	212

FLAGS *are included in the Textile category.*

FLASH GORDON appeared in the Sunday comics in 1934. The daily strip started in
1940. The hero was also in comic books from 1930 to 1970, in books from 1936, in
movies from 1938, on the radio in the 1930s and 1940s, and on television from 1953
to 1954. All sorts of memorabilia are collected, but the ray guns and rocket ships are
the most popular.

Book, Caverns Of Mongo, Alex Raymond, Grosset & Dunlap, 7 x 5 In., 219 Pages	395
Book, Pop-Up, Tournament Of Death, Pleasure Books, 1935, 20 Pages, 9 x 8 In.	285
Toy, Rocket Fighter Ship, Red, Yellow Wings, Clockwork, Marx, 12 In.	300

FLORENCE CERAMICS were made in Pasadena, California, from World War II
to 1977. Florence Ward created many colorful figurines, boxes, candleholders, and
other items for the gift shop trade. Each piece was marked with an ink stamp that
included the name *Florence Ceramics Co.* The company was sold in 1964 and although the name
remained the same, the products were very different. Mugs, cups, and trays were made.

Basket, Floraline Pattern, Gilt Trim, Footed, 9 In.		22
Figurine, Charmaine, Green Dress & Green Bonnet, Lace Parasol, c.1954, 8 ½ In.	*illus*	65
Figurine, Elaine, White, Gold Trim, Green Bonnet & Mittens, 6 In.		28
Figurine, Rose Marie, Lace Accents, Flowers, 7 In.		75

FLOW BLUE was made in England and other countries about 1830 to 1900. The dishes were
printed with designs using a cobalt blue coloring. The color flowed from the design to the white
body so that the finished piece has a smeared blue design. The dishes were usually made of ironstone china. More Flow Blue may be found under the name of the manufacturer. These three
marks are found on flow blue dishes.

W.H. Grindley & Co. (Ltd.) c.1880–1891	Johnson Brothers c.1913+	Wood & Son(s) (Ltd.) 1891–1907

Bowl, Vegetable, Chappoo, Lid, Ironstone, 7 ¾ x 13 ¼ In.		141
Cheese Dish, Tray, Gilt, Top Handle, 9 ½ x 7 In.		60
Pitcher, Shell & Palm Tree, c.1850, 7 x 8 ¼ In.		73
Platter, Belmont Pattern, Oval, 14 x 19 In.		198
Platter, Dark Blue, Gray Floral Borders, Nude Kneeling Potter Mark, Ivory, 1886, 15 x 18 In.		95
Platter, Pagoda, Bushes, 14 ¼ x 18 ¼ In.		88
Platter, Trees, Rocks, J. & G. Alcock, 14 x 18 In.		275
Teapot, Landscape, Buildings, Scinde Pattern, Blue, White, 4 x 5 In.	*illus*	720
Teapot, Troy Pattern, 8 ½ x 9 In.		77
Tureen, Lid, John Maddock & Sons, 8 ¼ x 7 ½ In.		72

FLYING PHOENIX, *see Phoenix Bird category.*

Fireplace, Andirons, Cast Iron, Pheasant, 13 ½ x 26 In.
$3,240

Cowan's Auctions

Fireplace, Bellows, Turtleback, Whaleboats, Whales, Brown, Yellow, c.1825, 19 In.
$200

Eldred's Auctioneers and Appraisers

Fireplace, Coal Scuttle, Lift Lid, Metal, Mother-Of-Pearl, Brass Hardware, 16 ½ x 10 ½ In.
$120

Cowan's Auctions

Fireplace, Fender, Cage Shape, Domed, Semicircle, Wire, Iron, Wrought, 26 ½ x 26 ½ In.
$184

Bunch Auctions

Fireplace, Fender, Iron, Twisted Shaft Spindles, Ball Finials, Red Paint, 10 x 42 x 13 In.
$590

Hess Auction Group

Fireplace, Insert, Federal, Iron, Brass, Leaf & Rosette, Signed, S. Thompson, 34 x 35 ½ In.
$1,722

Brunk Auctions

Fireplace, Log Bin, Brass, Repousse, Slant Lid, Tavern, Hunting, Trophies, Stag, Bail Handles, 27 x 33 In.
$438

Neal Auction Co.

Fireplace, Screen, Edgar Brandt, Wrought Iron, France, 1920s, 36 x 30½ In.
$8,750

Rago Arts and Auction Center

Fireplace, Tongs, Ember, Scrolled Handle, Ornaments, Cast Iron, 1700s-1800s, 19 In.
$660

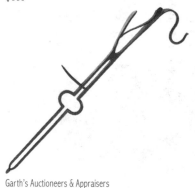

Garth's Auctioneers & Appraisers

Fireplace, Tool Set, Brass, Iron, Faceted Handles, Tongs, Shovel, Poker, Stand, 1800s, 38 In., 4 Piece
$488

Neal Auction Co.

Florence Ceramics, Figurine, Charmaine, Green Dress & Green Bonnet, Lace Parasol, c.1954, 8½ In.
$65

Ruby Lane

Flow Blue, Teapot, Landscape, Buildings, Scinde Pattern, Blue, White, 4 x 5 In.
$720

Strawser Auction Group

Folk Art, Cage, Squirrel, Tin, Wood, Old Salmon, Lime & Red Paint, Penn., 1800s, 16 x 31 In.
$236

Hess Auction Group

Folk Art, Mailbox Holder, Wood, Painted, Uncle Sam, 18 x 56 In.
$319

Copake Auction

FOLK ART is also listed in many categories of this book under the actual name of the object. See categories such as Box, Cigar Store Figure, Paper, Weather Vane, Wooden, etc.

Alligator, Wood, Carved, Red Glass Eyes, Nail Teeth, Articulated Jaw, c.1900, 21 x 5 In.	610
Bench, Ransford Naugler, Nova Scotia, 20 x 9 ½ x 27 In.	43
Bird Tree, 3 Birds, Parrots, Green, Orange, Pedestal, Signed D&D, Daniel Strawser, 1995, 10 x 17 In.	230
Bird Tree, 6 Birds, Octagon Pedestal, Carved, Painted, Wired, Signed D&BS, 1975, 10 x 18 In.	230
Bird Tree, Blue Jays, c.1900, 19 In.	305
Bird Tree, Yellow Finches, Tree Limb, 1800s, 6 x 7 ½ In.	976
Broom, Serpentine Handle, Numerous Incised Lines, Natural Bristles Bound, 1800, 19 In.	2880
Bust, Caesar, Laurel Leaf Crown, Carved, c.1840, 5 ¼ In.	47
Bust, Man, Root Head, Trace Black Paint, 7 ½ In.	60
Bust, Soldier, Tricorner Hat, High Collar, Epaulets, 36 ½ x 29 x 4 In.	1982
Cage, Squirrel, Tin, Wood, Old Salmon, Lime & Red Paint, Penn., 1800s, 16 x 31 In. ...... *illus*	236
Cat, Seated, Blue, White, Holding Fish, Curved Whiskers, 1983, 8 x 11 x 4 ½ In.	475
Cup, Saffron, Strawberries, Blue Ground, Joseph Lehn, 2 ⅞ In.	6710
Dog, Hound, Spotted, White, Carrying Brown Boot, Wood, Lonnie & Taylor Money, 13 x 18 In.	49
Dog, Jumping, Catching Stick, Floppy Ears, Wood, R. Minshew, 68 In.	270
Eagle, Wood, Carved, Multicolor Paint, David Ludwig, York Co., Pa., 5 ½ In.	531
Fireman's Head, Red Nose, Steel, 23 x 32 In.	263
Horse, Prancing, Braces, On Back, Tin, Silhouette, Cutout, 27 x 36 In.	300
Key Holder, Wood, Black Paint, Hand Painted Eyes, Smiling Lips, 1920s-30s, 8 ¾ In.	80
Lion, Coiled Attacking Snake, Multicolor, Wood, 9 ¼ x 18 In.	2420
Mailbox Holder, Wood, Painted, Uncle Sam, 18 x 56 In. *illus*	319
Man, Bearded, Carrying Canoe, Log, 7 ¾ In.	63
Man, Fish, Donald Boudreau, Nova Scotia, 69 In.	1966
Man, Suit, Tie, Pistol, African American, 51 In.	600
Mask, Ceremonial Dance, Carved, Paint, Gracejo, Smiling, Mexico, 1940s, 10 x 7 In.	2000
Parrot, Wood, Green, 13 x 4 In.	108
Peg Rack, Hills, Peaks, Green, 3 Pegs, 1800s, 20 x 7 In.	234
Penny Mat, Diamond Shape, 3 Part Felt Pieces, Concentric Circles, Stitching, 19 x 14 In.	47
Plaque, Man, Seated, Cup, Red Horse, Tree, Wood, Frame, 11 ¾ In.	819
Rooster, Carved, Salmon, Brown Wings, Green Body, Deco-Tex Carver, 10 ¼ In.	8850
Rooster, Schimmel Type, Fantail, Softwood, Unpainted, 1870, 4 ½ x 1 x 5 In.	180
Rug, American Military Helicopter, Bomber Motifs, Mineral Dyes, 62 x 38 In.	750
Stand, Smoking, Silhouettes, Jiggs & Maggie, Wood, Painted, 2-Sided, 23 In. .... *illus*	826
Statue Of Liberty, Wood, Stylized, Old Green Paint, c.1940, 59 In.	600
Uncle Sam, Silhouette, Wood, Painted, 36 In.	767
Watch Hutch, Abalone, Bone Inlay, Mahogany, Flower, Heart, 6 ¼ x 5 ¼ In.	968
Whale, Tail Up, Gray, Brown, Mottled, 43 In.	625
Whirligig, Dancing Old Salt, Pine, Painted, Tin Hat Brim, Pivoting Arms, 1900s, 22 x 10 x 8 In.	360
Whirligig, Doughboy, Uniform, Stars & Stripes Paddles, Painted, Pine Base, c.1915, 30 In. *illus*	7380
Whirligig, Happy Jack, Wooden, Painted, c.1900, 12 ½ In.	312
Whirligig, Indian Boy, Tunic, Notched Collar, Gray, c.1900, 11 x 8 In. *illus*	600
Whirligig, Man, Carved, Painted Wood, Gray Tunic, Dark Red, Brown, 1900, 11 x 8 x 1 ¾ In.	600
Whirligig, Man, Hat, Paddle Arms, 18 ¼ In. *illus*	283
Whirligig, Multiple Paddles, Tin Blades, Revolving Post, 1900-50, 24 x 28 In.	450
Whirligig, Postman, Carved Face, Top Hat, White, Blue, Arrow, 1920-40, 42 x 10 x 45 In.	260
Whirligig, Sailor, Hat, Carved, Painted, Red & Black Paddles, Mounted On Stand, 1800s, 16 ½ In. *illus*	216
Whirligig, Soldier, Wood, 18 ½ In.	248
Whirligig, Wood Craft, Metal Attachments, Churning Woman, 18 x 9 ⅝ x 12 In.	120
Woman, Arms Tight At Sides, Thick Eyebrows, c.1920, 8 In.	23
Woman, Hardwood, Varnished, Wearing Dress, 2 Sections, Coin Slot, W. Virginia, c.1930, 31 x 11 x 7 In.	1140
Woman, On Horse, Red Shirt, Green Skirt, Articulated, c.1900, 9 x 8 ¼ In.	46

FOOT WARMERS solved the problem of cold feet in past generations. Some warmers held charcoal, others held hot water. Pottery, tin, and soapstone were the favored materials to conduct the heat. The warmer was kept under the feet, then the legs and feet were tucked into a blanket, providing welcome warmth in a cold carriage or church.

Walnut, Tin, Pierced Heart, Wire Bail Handle, Penn., 1800s, 6 ½ x 9 In. *illus*	189

Folk Art, Stand, Smoking, Silhouettes, Jiggs & Maggie, Wood, Painted, 2-Sided, 23 In.
$826

Hess Auction Group

Folk Art, Whirligig, Doughboy, Uniform, Stars & Stripes Paddles, Painted, Pine Base, c.1915, 30 In.
$7,380

Skinner, Inc.

F

Folk Art, Whirligig, Indian Boy, Tunic, Notched Collar, Gray, c.1900, 11 x 8 In. $600

Thomaston Place Auction Galleries

Folk Art, Whirligig, Man, Hat, Paddle Arms, 18¼ In. $283

Copake Auction

Folk Art Is Hot
Folk art is still a hot collectible, but folk art can be "younger," items made into the early 1900s.

Wood, Turned Posts, Heart Punched Tin Decoration On Door, 1900s, 9 x 8 In. 70

FOOTBALL *collectibles may be found in the Card and the Sports categories.*

FOSTORIA glass was made in Fostoria, Ohio, from 1887 to 1891. The factory was moved to Moundsville, West Virginia, and most of the glass seen in shops today is a twentieth-century product. The company was sold in 1983; new items will be easily identifiable, according to the owner, Lancaster Colony Corporation. Additional Fostoria items may be listed in the Milk Glass category.

Argus, Juice, Green, 2⅞ In.	7
Baroque, Candlestick, Cornucopia, 4 x 4½ In.	30
Candlestick, Cornucopia, Baroque Shape, Clear, 4 x 4½ In., Pair	30
Century, Sugar, Pink, 4 In.	15
Classic Gold, Sherbet, 4¾ In.	11
Colony, Vase, Clear, Swirl Shape, Flared Rim, Fluted Foot, c.1935, 14 In. .... *illus*	225
Georgian, Sherbet, 5¼ In.	18
Glamour, Sherbet, Green, 5 In.	10
Glamour, Tumbler, Iced Tea, Green, 6½ In.	16
Heirloom, Bowl, Blue, Opalescent, Oblong Shape, 1950s, 14 x 8 In. .... *illus*	90
Jamestown, Butter, Cover, Amber, ¼ Lb.	37
Jamestown, Plate, Luncheon, Blue, 8¼ In.	26
Jamestown, Tumbler, Iced Tea, Blue, 6 In.	16
Mayfair, Relish, 5 Sections, 13¼ In.	45
Moonstone, Goblet, Blue, 6 In.	8
Sheraton, Tumbler, Iced Tea, 6½ In.	21
Simplicity, Cordial, 3⅞ In.	10
Simplicity, Goblet, 7½ In.	26

FOVAL, *see Fry category.*

FRAMES *are included in the Furniture category under Frame.*

FRANCISCAN is a trademark that appears on pottery. Gladding, McBean and Company started in 1875. The company grew and acquired other potteries. It made sewer pipes, floor tiles, dinnerware, and art pottery with a variety of trademarks. It began using the trade name *Franciscan* in 1934. In 1936, dinnerware and art pottery were sold under the name Franciscan Ware. The company made china and cream-colored, decorated earthenware. Desert Rose, Apple, El Patio, and Coronado were best sellers. The company became Interpace Corporation and in 1979 was purchased by Josiah Wedgwood & Sons. The plant closed in 1984, but production of a few patterns shifted to China and Thailand. For more prices, go to kovels.com.

Gladding, McBean & Co. 1934–1963	Gladding, McBean & Co. c.1940	International Pipe and Ceramics 1963+

Acacia, Chop Plate, 13 In.	78
Amapola, Bowl, Vegetable, 9⅜ In.	20
Amapola, Casserole, 14¾ In.	32
Amapola, Creamer	10
Amapola, Cup & Saucer	8
Amapola, Plate, Bread & Butter, 6¾ In.	5
Antigua, Bowl, Vegetable, Divided, 11 In.	25
Antigua, Plate, Bread & Butter, 6⅛ In.	3
Antigua, Plate, Dinner, 10⅜ In.	10

Folk Art, Whirligig, Sailor, Hat, Carved, Painted, Red & Black Paddles, Mounted On Stand, 1800s, 16 ½ In.
$216

Eldred's Auctioneers and Appraisers

Foot Warmer, Walnut, Tin, Pierced Heart, Wire Bail Handle, Penn., 1800s, 6 ½ x 9 In.
$189

Hess Auction Group

Fostoria, Colony, Vase, Clear, Swirl Shape, Flared Rim, Fluted Foot, c.1935, 14 In.
$225

Ruby Lane

Fostoria, Heirloom, Bowl, Blue, Opalescent, Oblong Shape, 1950's, 14 x 8 In.
$90

Ruby Lane

Franciscan, Desert Rose, Gravy Boat, Underplate, Cream, Pink, Green, c.1940, 9 x 6 In.
$25

Ruby Lane

Franciscan, Spice, Coffeepot, Cream Ground, Flowering Plant, 1961-65, 10 ½ In.
$45

Ruby Lane

Franciscan, Starburst, Creamer, Marked, 1950's, 4 x 3 In.
$23

Ruby Lane

Frankart, Lamp, Figural, Nude Woman, Black, Replaced Frosted Glass Shade, 1928, 10 ½ In.
$750

Ruby Lane

TIP
Need a quick measurement at an antiques show? A penny is ¾ inch in diameter; a dollar bill is almost 6 inches long.

Frankart, Smoking Stand, Nude Women, Globe, Green, Mottled, 21¾ x 7½ In.
$2,360

Burchard Galleries

Fraternal, Masonic, Jug, Pink Luster, Transfer, Sunderland, 9 x 3½ In.
$130

Hess Auction Group

Fraternal, Masonic, Mug, Creamware Transfer, c.1810, 3¼ In.
$212

Hess Auction Group

Antique Green, Plate, Bread & Butter, 6¼ In.		12
Apple, Creamer		21
Apple, Plate, Dinner		16
Arcadia, Cup & Saucer		10
Arcadia, Plate, Bread & Butter, 6⅜ In.		7
Arcadia, Platter, 16 In.		80
Autumn, Bowl, Vegetable, 9¼ In.		31
Autumn, Butter, Cover		23
Autumn, Casserole, Lid		50
Autumn, Creamer		13
Autumn, Gravy Boat, Attached Underplate		20
Autumn, Plate, Bread & Butter, 6½ In.		4
Autumn, Plate, Dinner, 10½ In.		20
Autumn, Salt & Pepper		18
Beverly, Cup & Saucer, After Dinner		21
Beverly, Platter, 14 In.		78
Beverly, Salt & Pepper		44
Bird 'N Hand, Creamer		15
Bird 'N Hand, Cup & Saucer		6
Bird 'N Hand, Plate, Salad, 8¼ In.		12
Blanc, Bowl, Vegetable, 10¾ In.		21
Blue Dawn, Plate, Dinner, 10¾ In.		15
Blue Dawn, Plate, Salad		10
Blueberry, Bowl, Fruit, 5¼ In.		8
Bountiful, Bowl, Cereal, 6 In.		15
Bountiful, Cup & Saucer		11
Bountiful, Plate, Dinner, 10⅝ In.		33
Cafe Royal, Bowl, Vegetable, Divided, 11 In.		40
Cafe Royal, Butter, Cover		30
Cafe Royal, Compote, 6 In.		64
Cafe Royal, Cup & Saucer		6
Cafe Royal, Gravy Boat, Underplate		25
Cafe Royal, Plate, Dinner, 10⅝ In.		24
Cafe Royal, Salt & Pepper, 2⅝ In.		28
Cameo, Cup & Saucer		8
Cameo, Plate, Salad, 8⅜ In.		7
Chestnut Weave, Plate, Dinner, 10⅝ In.		24
Cloud Nine, Sugar, Lid		18
Corinthian, Plate, Dinner, 10¾ In.		45
Desert Rose, Berry Bowl, c.1940, 5 In.		8
Desert Rose, Gravy Boat, Underplate, Cream, Pink, Green, c.1940, 9 x 6 In.	*illus*	25
October, Platter, 14 In.		74
Poppy, Chop Plate, 12 In.		98
Spice, Coffeepot, Cream Ground, Flowering Plant, 1961-65, 10½ In.	*illus*	45
Starburst, Creamer, Marked, 1950's, 4 x 3 In.	*illus*	23
Starburst, Mustard Jar, c.1953, 3½ In.		52

FRANKART INC., New York, New York, mass-produced nude "dancing lady" lamps, ashtrays, and other decorative Art Deco items in the 1920s and 1930s. They were made of white lead composition and spray-painted. *Frankart Inc.* and the patent number and year were stamped on the base.

Bookends, Dog, Scottish Terrier, 5 x 5 In.		72
Bust, Woman, Flower Headband, Metal, Bronze Tones, Marked, c.1925, 6½ x 5 In.		110
Figurine, Cat, Seated, Cast Metal, 8½ In.		84
Lamp, Double Nude, Green, Art Deco		330
Lamp, Figural, Nude Woman, Black, Replaced Frosted Glass Shade, 1928, 10½ In.	*illus*	750
Smoking Stand, Nude Woman, Ankles Crossed, Arms Up, Round Pan, 1920, 23¾ In.		600
Smoking Stand, Nude Women, Globe, Green, Mottled, 21¾ x 7½ In.	*illus*	2360

FRANKOMA POTTERY was originally known as The Frank Potteries when John F. Frank opened shop in 1933. The name "Frankoma," a combination of his last name and the last three letters of Oklahoma, was used beginning in 1934. The factory moved to Sapulpa, Oklahoma, in 1938. Early wares were made from a light cream-colored clay from Ada, Oklahoma, but in 1956 the company switched to a red clay from Sapulpa. The firm made dinnerware, utilitarian and decorative kitchenwares, figurines, flowerpots, and limited edition and commemorative pieces. John Frank died in 1973 and his daughter, Joniece, inherited the business. Frankoma went bankrupt in 1990. The pottery operated under various owners for a few years and was bought by Joe Ragosta in 2008. It closed in 2010. The buildings, assets, name, and molds were sold at an auction in 2011.

Bowl, Flower Frog, Ivory Matte Glaze, Marked, 1935, 3 x 11 In.	94
Figurine, Water Carrier, Nude, Woman, Green, Signed, 12 In.	192
Trivet, Bicentennial Liberty Bell, 6 ¼ In. Diam.	24

FRATERNAL objects that are related to the many different fraternal organizations in the United States are listed in this category. The Elks, Masons, Odd Fellows, and others are included. Also included are service organizations, like the American Legion, Kiwanis, and Lions Club. Furniture is listed in the Furniture category. Shaving mugs decorated with fraternal crests are included in the Shaving Mug category.

Eastern Star, Pin, Past Matron, Enamel, Pearl, Diamond	69
Eastern Star, Sign, Light-Up, Pentagram, Wood Case, Paint, Multicolor, 41 x 45 In.	285
Elks, Watch Fob, Elk Tooth, Bronze, Logo, 1940s, 1 ¼ In.	90
Masonic, Jug, Pink Luster, Transfer, Sunderland, 9 x 3 ½ In.	*illus* 130
Masonic, Jug, Symbols, Overglaze, Multicolor Enamel, Bulbous, Staffordshire, 1830, 9 ¼ In.	277
Masonic, Letter Opener, Sterling Silver, Camel, A.A.O.N.M.S., 1900s	36
Masonic, Mug, Creamware Transfer, c.1810, 3 ¼ In.	*illus* 212
Masonic, Paperweight, Initials, Presentation, 3 ⅝ In.	50
Masonic, Pitcher, Symbols, Verse, Black Transfer, Presentation, James Albert, c.1800, 8 In.	415
Masonic, Plaque, Round, Applied Brass Compass & Square, c.1900, 5 ½ In.	*illus* 187
Masonic, Print, Masonic Tie, Fraternity Fine Art Co., Boston, Frame, 1888, 29 x 23 In.	*illus* 130
Masonic, Relish, Logo, Green Stripe Border, Mayer China, c.1925, 5 x 11 In.	75
Odd Fellows, Sugar, Lid, Canted Corners, Burgundy & Green, Mayer China, 1920s, 4 x 4 In.	50

FRY GLASS was made by the H.C. Fry Glass Company of Rochester, Pennsylvania. The company, founded in 1901, first made cut glass and other types of fine glasswares. In 1922 it patented a heat-resistant glass called Pearl Ovenglass. For two years, 1926–1927, the company made Fry Foval, an opal ware decorated with colored trim. Reproductions of this glass have been made. Depression glass patterns made by Fry may be listed in the Depression Glass category. Some pieces of cut glass may also be included in the Cut Glass category.

Basket, Trojan Pattern, Triple Notched Handle, Signed, 5 ½ x 5 In.	150
Bowl, Petal Foot, Clear Swirl, Green, 10 In.	295
Pitcher, Crackle Glass, Applied Green Handle, 1900-50, 10 ¾ In.	108

FRY FOVAL

Bowl, Jade Color, Opaque Foot, Sterling Silver Flower & Leaf Rim, 10 x 3 In.	225
Cup & Saucer, Blue Handle, Stippled Center	50
Grill Plate, Opalescent, 10 ½ In.	35
Sugar & Creamer, White Opalescent, Cobalt Blue Opaque Handles	90

FULPER POTTERY COMPANY was incorporated in 1899 in Flemington, New Jersey. It made art pottery from 1909 to 1929. The firm had been making bottles, jugs, and housewares since 1805. Vasekraft is a line of art pottery with glazes similar to Chinese art pottery that was introduced in 1909. Doll heads were made about 1928. The firm became Stangl Pottery in 1929. Stangl Pottery is listed in its own category in this book.

Bookends, Liberty Bell, Green Matte, Pair, Marked, 7 In.	177

Fraternal, Masonic, Plaque, Round, Applied Brass Compass & Square, c.1900, 5 ½ In.
$187

Jeffrey S. Evans

Fraternal, Masonic, Print, Masonic Tie, Fraternity Fine Art Co., Boston, Frame, 1888, 29 x 23 In.
$130

Hess Auction Group

Fulper, Lamp, Leaded Glass, Glazed Earthenware, Vasekraft, c.1911, 18 ½ x 14 ¼ In.
$6,875

Heritage Auctions

FULPER

Fulper, Vase, Green, Leopard Skin Crystalline Glaze, Incised Racetrack Mark, c.1920, 17 In.
$812

Rago Arts and Auction Center

Fulper, Vase, Mission Matte Glaze, Brown, Columns, Vasekraft, 12¼ x 5 In.
$6,250

Rago Arts and Auction Center

Furniture, Armoire, French Provincial, Fruitwood, 2 Panels, Molded Cornice, 1800s, 82 x 42 In.
$594

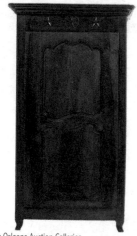

New Orleans Auction Galleries

Bookends, Sleepy Reader, Mottled Green Glaze, Man, Open Book In Lap, 1900s, 6 x 5 x 6 In. ..	480
Bookends, Triangular, Aztec Faces, Green, Blue, 6 x 2¾ In., Pair	531
Bowl, Scalloped, Iron Stand, Seahorse Design, 1900s, 15-In. Bowl, 32 x 20 In. Stand	240
Candle Lamp, Arts & Crafts, Hooded, Deep Blue Crystalline Glaze, 3 Glass Inserts, 10 In.	1000
Candle Shield, Arts & Crafts, Deep Blue Crystalline Glaze, 3 Glass Inserts, Mark, 11 In.	1180
Flower Frog, Woman In Canoe, Brown, Blue, Green, High Glazes, Mark, 4 x 7½ In.	94
Jug, Cobalt Blue, Bird, Branch, 3 Gal., 15¾ In.	472
Jug, Cobalt Blue, Flowers, Stoneware, 4 Gal., 16½ In.	188
Jug, Cobalt Blue, Leaves, Stoneware, 2 Gal., 13½ In.	224
Lamp Base, 2 Handles, Cream & Tan Glaze, Dripping, Hole In Base, Mark, 11 x 11 In.	1080
Lamp Base, Multicolor Flambe, Vasekraft, c.1908, 22 x 9 In.	815
Lamp, Leaded Glass Shade, Flambe Glaze, Vasekraft, 1909, 16 x 22 In.	7500
Lamp, Leaded Glass, Glazed Earthenware, Vasekraft, c.1911, 18½ x 14¼ In. *illus*	6875
Lamp, Mushroom Shade, Green & Tan Glaze, Slag Glass Inserts, Spread Base, 14 In.	3500
Lamp, Parrot, Porcelain, Lighted Base, Signed, 1930, 9 x 6½ x 9¼ In.	826
Vase, 2 Handles, Mauve Glaze, Lavender & Green Tones, Mark, 11 x 11 In.	360
Vase, Brown & Black Flambe, Over Mustard Matte, 1910s-20s, 10½ x 7 In.	625
Vase, Buttress, Cucumber Crystalline Glaze, Ink Stamp Mark, 8¼ In.	170
Vase, Cattail, Verte Antique Glaze, 1910s, 12¾ x 4¾ In.	4687
Vase, Dark Purple, High Shoulders, Double Handles, 7 x 7 In.	117
Vase, Famille Rose Matte Glaze, Dripped, Dark Blue & Black Glaze, 7½ In.	720
Vase, Gloppy Green, White Glaze, 2 Handles, Mark, 11 In.	177
Vase, Green, Brown Glaze, Marked, 8 In.	325
Vase, Green, Leopard Skin Crystalline Glaze, Incised Racetrack Mark, c.1920, 17 In. *illus*	812
Vase, Handles, Cucumber Crystalline Glaze, Die Stamp Mark, Logo, 12 In.	150
Vase, Ivory Glaze, Mustard Ground, Bulbous, Squat, Mark, 8 x 10 In.	1180
Vase, Lid, Aqua Crystalline & Gray Glaze, Mark, 17 In.	413
Vase, Mahogany Color, Ivory Flambe, Black Ground, Mark, 7 x½ In.	236
Vase, Mission Matte Glaze, Brown, Columns, Vasekraft, 12¼ x 5 In. *illus*	6250
Vase, Monumental, Crystalline Aqua & Gray Green Glaze, 16 In.	350
Vase, Oval, Blue, Gray, Tan Glaze, Mark, 5 x½ In.	266
Vase, Purple & Pink Flambe Glaze, c.1915, 16 x 7½ In.	187

FURNITURE of all types is listed in this category. Examples dating from the seventeenth century to the 2000s are included. Prices for furniture vary in different parts of the country. Oak furniture is most expensive in the West; large pieces over eight feet high are sold for the most money in the South, where high ceilings are found in the old homes. Condition is very important when determining prices. These are NOT average prices but rather reports of unique sales. If the description includes the word *style*, the piece resembles the old furniture style but was made at a later time. It is not a period piece. Small chests that sat on a table or dresser are also included here. Garden furniture is listed in the Garden Furnishings category. Related items may be found in the Architectural, Brass, and Store categories.

Armchairs are listed under Chair in this category.

Armoire, Crown Molded, 2 Paneled Doors, 4 Drawers, France, 1900	746
Armoire, Federal Style, Mahogany, Flush Doors, Reeded Legs, Louisiana, c.1810, 84 x 56 In.	7625
Armoire, French Provincial, Cream Paint, 2 3-Panel Doors, Block Feet, 1880s, 84 In.	1125
Armoire, French Provincial, Fruitwood, 2 Panels, Molded Cornice, 1800s, 82 x 42 In. *illus*	594
Armoire, Henry II, Oak, Carved Crown, Panel Doors, Leaves, Scrolls, 179 x 44 In.	593
Armoire, Louis XV Style, Fruitwood, Carved, Cherub, Mirrors, c.1910, 105 x 64 In. *illus*	1952
Armoire, Louis XVI Style, Paneled Doors, Inlay, Mirrors, Ormolu, c.1910, 106 x 82 In. *illus*	580
Armoire, Louisiana, Mahogany, Scalloped Doors, Shaped Apron, c.1810, 81 x 53 x 20 In.	1830
Armoire, Pine, Grain Painted, Carved, Fitted Interior, Continental, 1800s, 76 In. *illus*	600
Armoire, Tropical Hardwood, Paneled Doors, c.1810, 77 x 56 x 23 In.	1952
Bar Cart, Chrome Frame, Laminate Shelves, Red, 30 x 18 In.	96
Bar Cart, Franziksa Hosken, Chrome Steel, Birch Plywood, Casters, 27 x 40 In.	1875
Barstool, Aalto, Birch, Low Back, Disc Seat, Finland, 27½ In., Pair *illus*	400
Bed, American Rococo, Rosewood, Carved Headboard, New York, c.1875, 70 x 59 In.	2500
Bed, Art Deco, Eric Bagge, Walnut, Rosewood, Mercier Freres, France, 1920, 55 x 81 In.	1500
Bed, Canopy, Antebellum, Wood, Barley Twist, c.1850, 108 x 108 In.	747

Bed, Cherry, Rope, Scrolled Headboard, Turned Post, c.1810, 48 x 48 x 83 In.	160
Bed, Federal, Walnut, Arched Canopy, Spindle Rails, Child's, 1800s, 63 x 30 In.	240
Bed, Four-Poster, Adirondack, Birch Logs, Bentwood Branches, 78 x 85 x 78 In.	360
Bed, Four-Poster, Log, Double Rails, American Rustic, c.1950, 78 x 74 x 63 In.	125
Bed, Four-Poster, Low, Maple, Scrolled Headboard, Turned Legs, c.1820, 89 x 73 x 52 In.	5490
Bed, Four-Poster, Mahogany, Federal, Headboard, Original Finish, c.1810, 83 x 79 In.	152
Bed, Four-Poster, Mahogany, Palm Carved Arched Headboard, Jamaica, c.1800, 86 x 80 In.	4270
Bed, Four-Poster, Pencil Posts, Maple, Canopy, Eldred Wheeler, 1900s, 86 x 64 In. *illus*	875
Bed, Four-Poster, Rosewood, Paneled Headboard, Shell Crest, c.1875, 102 x 68 In.	7375
Bed, Four-Poster, Sheraton, Tester Top, Blue Paint, 83 ½ x 51 ½ x 78 In.	1400
Bed, Half-Tester, Walnut, Pierced Crest, Scrolled Leaves, Panels, 1800s, 93 x 45 In.	600
Bed, Jean Prouve, Enameled Steel, Mahogany, Upholstered, 1950s, 36 x 77 In.	5625
Bed, Parcel Gilt, 2 Drawers, Top Compartment, Calligraphic Painting, Chinese, 87 x 89 In.	2160
Bed, Reeded Posts, Scrolling Panel Headboard, Twin, 1900s, 82 x 38 In.	660
Bed, Renaissance Revival, Gilt, Incised, Ebonized, Porcelain Plaque, c.1890, 87 x 80 In. *illus*	2560
Bed, Shaker, Maple, Pine, Arched Headboard, Red, Tapered Legs, 31 x 79 In.	390
Bed, Wedding, Lacquered, Canopy, Gallery, Shelf, Drawers, Sino-Indonesian, 94 In. *illus*	313
Bench, Alligator, Cast Bronze, Patinated, Judy Kensley McKie, 1992, 16 x 67 In.	46875
Bench, Black Forest, Standing Bears, Incised, Flowers, Leaves, 26 x 34 In.	4000
Bench, Black, Stenciled Floral Decoration, Upturning Rest For Reverse Seating, 1800s, 72 In.	270
Bench, Blue, Figures, Heart, Flower, Panels, Peter Hunt, 46 ½ x 18 ½ In.	96
Bench, Bootjack, Mortised Construction, 72 In.	127
Bench, Bronze, X Shape Base, Seated Men Standards, Bench On Necks, Italy, 21 x 27 In.	1020
Bench, Burl, Upholstered, Figured Walnut Skirt, 1800s, 20 x 47 ½ In.	1625
Bench, Chippendale Style, Mahogany, Needlework Top, Brass Tacks, 6 Legs, 17 x 45 In.	1230
Bench, G. Nakashima, Walnut, Hickory, Rosewood, Conoid, 1976, 32 x 87 x 38 In.	33750
Bench, Gossip, Mahogany, Upholstered, Sleigh Back, Table, Lyre, c.1945, 32 x 37 In.	520
Bench, Jacobean, Flowers, Scrolls, Ring Turned Stretchers, c.1900, 19 x 22 In.	4250
Bench, M. Levin, Nymph, Shaped Seat, Conjoined By Splines, 18 ½ x 23 In.	2016
Bench, Piano, Wendell Castle, Laminated Cherry, Adjustable, Signed, 1963, 19 x 19 In.	20000
Bench, Pine, 3 Stepped Shelves, Gray Paint, Over Red, c.1850, 37 x 41 ½ In.	780
Bench, Pine, Painted, Brown, Yellow, Red Stencil Decoration, 1800s, 15 x 60 In.	168
Bench, Pine, Turned Legs, Rolled Backrests, 29 x 55 In.	320
Bench, Poul Kjaerholm, PK80, Lacquered Wood Slab, Cushion, Chrome Legs, c.1957, 72 In.	3250
Bench, Shaker, Pine, 4 Diagonal Braces, Rosehead Nails, Half Round Arched Sides, 13 x 53 In.	480
Bench, Softwood, Yellow Paint, Mortised Legs, Pa., 1800s, 19 x 86 x 12 In. *illus*	106
Bench, Window, Regency, Lucite, Scroll Arms, Legs, Charles Jones, 1970s, 27 x 44 In. *illus*	360
Bookcase, Arts & Crafts, Mahogany, Leaded Glass, Painted, England, c.1905, 66 x 45 In. *illus*	3375
Bookcase, Bonnet Top, Gothic Revival, Mullioned Glass Doors, Drawers, Blind Doors, 94 x 45 In.	188
Bookcase, Ettore Sottsass, Carlton, Laminated Wood, Metal Label, Memphis, 78 x 75 In. *illus*	26250
Bookcase, Federal, Desk, Mahogany, Glazed Doors, Inlay, Butler's Case, c.1810, 106 In. *illus*	5400
Bookcase, Frankl, Skyscraper, Mahogany, Lacquer, c.1928, 71 x 34 In. *illus*	22500
Bookcase, Georgian Style, Mahogany, Inlay, Glazed Doors, Drawer, c.1890, 88 x 32 In. *illus*	813
Bookcase, Herts Bros., Revolving, Oak, Drawers, Brass, c.1880, 54 In., Pair *illus*	3750
Bookcase, Lincoln Desk, Walnut, 4 Turned Legs, 1900, 72 x 41 x 19 In.	170
Bookcase, Mahogany, Adjustable Shelves, 2 Half Drawers, 3 Full Length Drawers, 1800s, 88 x 43 In.	354
Bookcase, Mahogany, Breakfront, Bellflower Carved, Ogee Bracket Feet, 101 x 83 In.	4880
Bookcase, Oak, Stickley, 4 Shelves, c.1925, 42 x 20 In.	813
Bookcase, Regency, Mahogany, Glass Doors, Inlay, Pullout Board, 1800s, 91 x 47 In. *illus*	1200
Bookcase, Richard Lauret, Chrome Steel Bars, 1970s, 67 ½ x 54 In.	5625
Bookcase, Secretary, Louis XV Style, Cream Paint, Chinoiserie, 86 x 43 In.	2500
Bookcase, Secretary, Mahogany, 2 Drawers, Flared Cornice, Shelf, c.1840, 79 x 51 In.	366
Bookcase, Victorian, Mahogany, Carved, Mirrors, Shelves, Drop Front, 1800s, 73 x 66 In. *illus*	1476
Bookcase, Walnut, Carved, Clock, Theodolite & Sextant, c.1860, 72 x 75 In.	1952
Bookrack, Oak, Trough Shape, Arched Ends, Pooh & Piglet Cutouts, c.1940, 8 x 20 In.	80
Breakfront, 2 Parts, Fretwork Glass Doors, Over Doors, Baker, c.1950, 91 x 96 In. *illus*	2040
Breakfront, Aesthetic Revival, Oak, Carved, Relief, Herter Brothers, c.1890, 90 In. *illus*	7680
Breakfront, Mahogany, Protruding Section, Mullioned Doors, England, c.1810, 80 x 50 In. *illus*	600
Buffet, Drawer, Bowtie Inlay, Handles, 80 x 26 x 15 In., 1930s.	500
Buffet, French Provincial, Fruitwood, Canted Corners, Drawers, Doors, c.1850, 42 x 60 In. *illus*	1500

Furniture, Armoire, Louis XV Style, Fruitwood, Carved, Cherub, Mirrors, c.1910, 105 x 64 In.
$1,952

New Orleans Auction Galleries

The Bed Is A Status Symbol
In the seventeenth and eighteenth centuries the bed was a status symbol. The head of the house and his wife used the bed, which had curtains that gave privacy. Others often slept in one room on small mats on the floor.

Furniture, Armoire, Louis XVI Style, Paneled Doors, Inlay, Mirrors, Ormolu, c.1910, 106 x 82 In.
$580

New Orleans Auction Galleries

This is an edited listing of current prices. Visit **Kovels.com** to check thousands of prices from previous years and sign up for free information on trends, tips, reproductions, marks, and more.

F

FURNITURE

Furniture, Armoire, Pine, Grain Painted, Carved, Fitted Interior, Continental, 1800s, 76 In.
$600

Cowan's Auctions

Furniture, Bar, Stool, Aalto, Birch, Low Back, Disc Seat, Finland, 27 ½ In., Pair
$400

Palm Beach Modern Auctions

Furniture, Bed, Four-Poster, Pencil Posts, Maple, Canopy, Eldred Wheeler, 1900s, 86 x 64 In.
$875

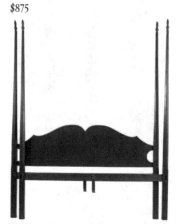

Eldred's Auctioneers and Appraisers

Buffet, Henry II Style, Painted, Leaf Accents, Doors, Drawers, 2 Parts, c.1910, 106 x 70 In. .. *illus*	1500
Bureau, Dutch Oak, Slant Front, 2 Short Over 2 Long Drawers, Inlaid Floral, 1800s, 37 x 33 In.	1250
Bureau, Linen Press, Mahogany, 4 Drawers, Molded Beam, Turned Shaft, 1800s, 71 x 37 In.... *illus*	390
Bureau, Sheraton, Bowfront, Mahogany, Veneer, Rope-Turned Columns, c.1820, 44 x 41 In....	360
Cabinet, 2 Doors, Cherry, Square Base, 84 x 42 x 20 In.	283
Cabinet, 2 Drawers, Lacquered Surfaces, Leafy Design, 1800s, 23 x 17 In.	120
Cabinet, Bar, Art Deco, Parchment, Fruitwood, Side Doors, Mirror, c.1930, 38 x 45 In. .... *illus*	896
Cabinet, Bar, Parzinger, Mahogany, Illuminated, Brass, Mirror, Glass, Doors, 1960s, 74 x 66 In.	12500
Cabinet, Biedermeier, Square Maple, Canted Corners, Cock Beaded Drawer, 1900, 29 x 15 x 13 In..	311
Cabinet, Borge Mogensen, Teak, Brass, 4 Doors, P. Lauritsen & Sons, 1950s, 35 x 54 In... *illus*	2250
Cabinet, Brass, Arched Cornice, Rectangular Case, Glazed Door, 1900, 33 x 26 In.	902
Cabinet, Carved, Lacquer, 6 Sections, Doors, Scenes, Chinese, c.1925, 87 x 48 In............. *illus*	1875
Cabinet, Collector's, Aesthetic Revival, Walnut, Carved Owls, 3 Glazed Doors, 67 In.	3250
Cabinet, Console, Leininger, Maple Veneer, Drawers, String Inlay, Glass Top, c.1950, 37 x 94 In.	600
Cabinet, Corner, Bowed Front, Doors, Painted Scene, Shelves, Continental, 1700s, 36 x 24 In. .*illus*	375
Cabinet, Corner, Walnut, Carved, Jesters, Arched Glass Door, 1800s, 106 x 55 In.	4850
Cabinet, Display Cases, Electric, Elongated Rectangular Doors, 1900s, 78 x 32 In., Pair	120
Cabinet, Display, Blue, Satin Lined, Upholstered Interior, Cross Banded, Cast Brass, 48 x 24 In.	218
Cabinet, Display, French Louis, Veneer, Gilt Brass, Crossbanded, Inlay, 64 ½ x 28 In.	281
Cabinet, Display, J. Hoffmann, Beech, Fruitwood, Glass, J. & J. Kohn, c.1910, 77 x 32 In. . *illus*	8750
Cabinet, Elm, Brass Mounts, Chinese, 64 ½ x 43 In. *illus*	212
Cabinet, Filing, Oak, 3 Rows, 3 Columns, Letter Size, c.1925, 43 x 49 ½ In.	500
Cabinet, Filing, Oak, 8 Drawers, Label Slots, Brass Pulls, Library Bureau, c.1900, 52 x 33 In. ..	4000
Cabinet, Folio, Mixed Wood, Molded, 6 Drawers, Base, c.1910, 27 x 42 In. *illus*	576
Cabinet, Frankl, Mahogany, Brass Handles & Feet, 3 Drawers, 1940s, 38 x 62 In.	3250
Cabinet, G. Nakashima, Hanging, Walnut, 1957, 15 x 57 In.	15000
Cabinet, G. Nakashima, Hanging, Walnut, 1965, 15 x 68 x 15 In.	16250
Cabinet, G. Nakashima, Hanging, Walnut, Pandanus Cloth, 1963, 18 x 84 x 16 In.	40625
Cabinet, G. Nakashima, Triple Sliding Door, Walnut, 1963, 32 x 84 x 22 In.	26250
Cabinet, George III Style, Mahogany, 2 Doors Over Drawer, Oval Burl Panels, 32 x 22 In.	813
Cabinet, Gio Ponti, Walnut, Enameled Wood, Glass, 3 Doors, Boxy, 1950s, 63 ½ x 70 In.	9375
Cabinet, Hanging, Sponged, Heart Below Arched Cornice, Gottshall, Marked W.J.G. 79, 14 In.	130
Cabinet, Herter Bros., Renaissance Revival, 3 Parts, Carved, Gilt, c.1870, 51 x 70 In. .... *illus*	14640
Cabinet, Illuminated, Messy Bookshelf, Lacquer, Mahogany, Gilt Metal, Aldo Tura, 52 x 34 In..	4687
Cabinet, J. Hoffmann, Beech, Fruitwood, Pine, Nickeled Brass, 1900s, 77 x 31 x 18 In., Pair	8750
Cabinet, Library, Wood, 120 Catalog Drawers, Pullout Shelves, c.1910, 72 x 40 In.	4000
Cabinet, Linen, Neoclassical Style, Painted, 4 Doors, Shelves, Italy, 1900s, 84 x 52 In.	300
Cabinet, Mahogany, Neoclassical, 2 Cupboard Doors, Inlay, Leaf Vines, c.1850, 69 x 44 In.	1375
Cabinet, McCobb, Aluminum Frame & Handles, Walnut Drawers, 1960s, 34 x 36 In.	1375
Cabinet, Medals, Georgian, Fruitwood, 10 Drawers, Lined, H-Stretcher, c.1900, 23 x 27 In. *illus*	800
Cabinet, Modern, Plate Rack, Glass Doors, 40 x 65 x 12 In.	125
Cabinet, Molded Cornice, Glass Door Fretwork, Center Drawer, Floral Garland, 72 x 42 x 13 In.	413
Cabinet, Music, Mahogany, Painted Rural Scene, France, 41 ½ x 21 ½ In.	118
Cabinet, Music, Majorelle, Inlaid River Scene, Shelf, Drawer, Slots, c.1900, 56 x 32 In. ..... *illus*	2000
Cabinet, Oak, Carved, Blocked Frieze, Molded Top, Bracket Feet, c.1890, 33 x 59 In.	1586
Cabinet, Oak, Carved, Religious Figure, Door, Lower Shelf, Belgium, 1800s, 51 x 21 In. .. *illus*	189
Cabinet, Oak, Glass Panels & Shelves, Gargoyle, Cherub, Flowers, 67 x 50 In. .... *illus*	1298
Cabinet, P. Evans, Cityscape, Chrome Steel, Rectangles, Squares, 4 Drawers, 4 Doors, 32 x 90 In..	8750
Cabinet, P. Evans, Custom Double, Chrome, Chrome Steel, Rosewood, 1970s, 33 x 180 x 23 In..	12500
Cabinet, P. Evans, Deep Relief, Patinated, Multicolor, Cleft Slate, 1970, 32 x 97 x 22 In.	50000
Cabinet, P. Evans, Directional, Patchwork, Mixed Metals, Steel, 1970s, 80 x 36 In. .... *illus*	17500
Cabinet, P. Evans, Patchwork, Copper, Bronze, Cleft Slate, Laminate, 1970s, 26 x 60 x 20 In....	7500
Cabinet, P. Evans, Sculpture Front, Torch Cut, 23K Gold Leaf, Painted, 1968, 30 x 75 x 24 In. .	137500
Cabinet, P. Evans, Steel, Sculptural, Torch Cut, Welded, Painted, 1968, 24 x 15 In........... *illus*	15000
Cabinet, P. Evans, Wall, Welded, Enameled Steel & Bronze, 1960s, 36 x 24 x 13 In.	12500
Cabinet, P. Evans, Wavy Front, Welded, Multicolor, Cleft Slate, Gold Leaf, 1971, 21 x 49 In.	43750
Cabinet, P. Evans, Welded, Enameled Steel, Bronze, Slate, 1960s, 32 x 96 x 21 In.	26250
Cabinet, Perriand, Mahogany, Laminate, Enameled Steel, Sliding Doors, 4 Drawers, 28 x 62 In....	8750
Cabinet, Pine Board, Green, Slant Front, Shallow, Horizontal, 38 x 36 x 8 In.	283

Furniture, Bed, Renaissance Revival, Gilt, Incised, Ebonized, Porcelain Plaque, c.1890, 87 x 80 In.
$2,560

Neal Auction Co.

Furniture, Bed, Wedding, Lacquered, Canopy, Gallery, Shelf, Drawers, Sino-Indonesian, 94 In.
$313

Freeman's Auctioneers & Appraisers

Furniture, Bench, Softwood, Yellow Paint, Mortised Legs, Pa., 1800s, 19 x 86 x 12 In.
$106

Hess Auction Group

Furniture, Bench, Window, Regency, Lucite, Scroll Arms, Legs, Charles Jones, 1970s, 27 x 44 In.
$360

Brunk Auctions

Twin Beds
Twin beds were designed by Thomas Sheraton in England in the eighteenth century. They did not become popular or even acceptable until the twentieth century. The Hays Code covering morals in movies ruled in 1934 that married couples could only be pictured in twin beds about a foot apart. It became stylish.

Furniture, Bookcase, Arts & Crafts, Mahogany, Leaded Glass, Painted, England, c.1905, 66 x 45 In.
$3,375

Rago Arts and Auction Center

Furniture, Bookcase, Federal, Desk, Mahogany, Glazed Doors, Inlay, Butler's Case, c.1810, 106 In.
$5,400

Brunk Auctions

Furniture, Bookcase, Ettore Sottsass, Carlton, Laminated Wood, Metal Label, Memphis, 78 x 75 In.
$26,250

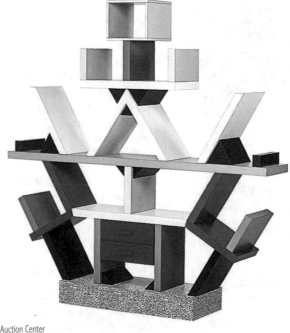

Rago Arts and Auction Center

Furniture, Bookcase, Frankl,
Skyscraper, Mahogany, Lacquer, c.1928,
71 x 34 In.
$22,500

Neal Auction Co.

Furniture, Bookcase, Georgian Style,
Mahogany, Inlay, Glazed Doors, Drawer,
c.1890, 88 x 32 In.
$813

New Orleans Auction Galleries

Cabinet, Print, Hamilton, Steel, Aluminum Handles, 10 Drawers, 2 Sections, 36 x 47 In.	156
Cabinet, R.M. Stevens, Rosewood, Nickeled Brass, Long Pulls, 3 Doors, 2 Drawers, 56 x 67 In..	1250
Cabinet, Revolving, 8-Sided, Marquee, 72 Drawers, Pumpkin Colored, 33 x 21 In.	1978
Cabinet, Rosewood, Inlay, Drawers, Columns, Mirrored Door, c.1880, 54 x 23 In., Pair ... *illus*	9000
Cabinet, Shaped Marble, Glossy Marquetry, 2 Drawers, Gilt Metal Mounts, 1900, 30 x 25 In., Pair.	89
Cabinet, Sideboard, Rounded Corners, 2 Glass Doors, 3 Drawers, 6 Legs, 1800s, 90 x 74 x 25 In.	767
Cabinet, Softwood, 11 Drawers, Mushroom Pulls, 1800s, 29 ½ x 45 x 17 ½ In.	1100
Cabinet, Spice, 13 Drawers, Bird's-Eye Maple, Ribbed Glass Knobs, 23 ½ x 12 In.	121
Cabinet, Vitrine, Louis XV, Gallery, Shelf, Courting Couple, Landscapes, Electrified, 58 x 28 In.	1125
Cabinet, Wall, Pine, Red Paint, Glazed Door, 1800s, 34 x 20 In.	300
Cabinet, Walnut, 12 Drawers, Tambour Door, 39 x 25 x 20 In.	649
Cabinet, Walnut, Arched Shell Crest, Raised Panel Doors, S-Scroll Feet, c.1910, 85 x 54 x 21 In.	3965
Cabinet, Wine, Maitland-Smith, Pedimented, Scrollwork, Acanthus Leaf Crest, 91 x 40 ½ In...	2700
Cabinet, Wine, Renaissance Revival, Walnut, Marble, Twist Columns, 1800s, 47 x 20 In.	2250
Cabinet, Wood, Carved, Glass, Mirror, 4 Drawers, Ring Handles, 2 Doors, 33 x 76 In.	2875
Candlestand, Cherry, Cut Corners, Vase Shape Pedestal, Arched Legs, 1800s, 29 In.	120
Candlestand, Cherry, Pedestal, 3 Cabriole Legs, Snake Feet, 1700s, 26 In.	180
Candlestand, Chippendale, Cherry, Square Top, Padded Feet, c.1901, 26 x 18 In.	187
Candlestand, Chippendale, Mahogany, Tilt Top, Birdcage, Ball & Claw Feet, c.1775, 27 x 23 In.	938
Candlestand, Curly Maple, Dish Top, Tripod Base, 25 x 14 In.	480
Candlestand, Federal, Mahogany, Tilt Top, Rectangular, Canted Corners, c.1800, 30 In. *illus*	720
Candlestand, Gray Marble Top, Beveled Edge, 27 x 18 In.	900
Candlestand, Mahogany, Dish Top, Slipper Feet, Arched Legs, Chippendale, 25 x 20 In.	640
Candlestand, Mahogany, Walnut, Parker Black Portsmouth, 1900s, 27 x 14 In.	60
Candlestand, Maple, Circular Top, Vase Shape Pedestal, Padded Feet, 1800s, 26 In.	204
Candlestand, Maple, Red Paint, 8-Sided Top, Pedestal, 3 Spider Legs, 1800s, 26 In.	96
Candlestand, Maple, Tiger Maple, Circular Top, Turned Pedestal, Snake Feet, 1800s, 25 In. ...	156
Candlestand, Mixed Wood, Adjustable, Turned Shaft, 43 In. *illus*	1180
Candlestand, Oak, Extension Arm, Elbow Jointed, Block Base, 29 In.	1770
Candlestand, Painted, Circular Top, Cabriole Legs, 1700s, 28 In.	60
Candlestand, Papier-Mache, Tilt Top, Gilt, Mother-Of-Pearl Inlay, 1800s, 27 x 22 In. ..... *illus*	185
Candlestand, Pine, 8-Sided Top, Red Stained Tripod Base, Turned Pedestal, 1800s, 25 In.	120
Candlestand, Pine, Ash, X Base, Adjustable, Pegged Mortise & Tenon, 36 x 15 In.	2420
Candlestand, Pine, Birch, Square Top, Red Stained Finish, Square Legs, 1900s, 22 In.	144
Candlestand, Porringer Cut Corners, Pedestal, Padded Feet, 27x 18 In.	144
Candlestand, Queen Anne, Cherry, Tray Top, Pad Feet, Drawer, c.1780, 26 x 16 In.	1945
Candlestand, Rosewood, Marble Top, Barley Twist Legs, Bracket Feet, c.1850, 34 x 16 In.	6222
Canterbury, Mahogany, Brass Gallery, c.1890, 25 x 18 In. *illus*	500
Canterbury, Steel Tubes, Bronze Fittings, Artichoke Finials, Casters, c.1975, 21 x 18 In.	750
Canterbury, Wood Slats, Knopped Tops, Brass Casters, c.1925, 19 x 19 ¾ In.	259
Cart, Pine, Walnut Stain, Brass, Border Trim, 1950, 33 x 13 In.	108
Cassone, Fruitwood, Painted, Venetian Canal Scene Front, Bracket Feet, 1700s, 24 ½ x 65 In..	1250
Cassone, Walnut, Dovetailed, Iron Hardware, 24 x 62 In.	1416
Cellarette, Federal, Poplar, Pine, Drawer, Inlaid Escutcheon, Hinged Lid, c.1820, 36 x 20 In...	8400
Cellarette, Mahogany, Carved, Inset Panels, Brass Mounted, Fitted Interior, 1800s, 31 x 27 In..	1952
Cellarette, Sarcophagus Shape, Hinged Lid, Paw Feet, Shaped Sides, 1800s, 26 x 20 x 20 In....	5612
Cellarette, Sheraton, Banded Mahogany, Satinwood, Bellflowers, Children, c.1840, 21 ⅜ x 22 In.	550
Cellarette, Stand, Federal, Walnut, Dovetailed, c.1800, 37 x 19 In.	23600
Chair & Ottoman, Eames, Rosewood Frame, Tan Leather Padding, Herman Miller, 1976, 32 In.	576
Chair Commode, George III, Mahogany, Vase Shape Splat, Padded Arms, c.1785, 36 In.. *illus*	427
Chair Set, Aalto, Garden, Pine, c.1938, 35 ½ In., 4.	10000
Chair Set, Bootjack Splat, Paint Decorated, Stamped, Ebersol, 33 In., 4 .... *illus*	236
Chair Set, Crest Rail, 2 Slats, Turned, Shaped, Stenciled, Rush Seat, Hitchcock, 33 In., 6	688
Chair Set, G. Nakashima, Captain's, Walnut, 1974, 29 x 24 In., 8	10625
Chair Set, G. Nakashima, Cone Shape, Walnut, Hickory, 1966, 36 x 20 In., 6	21250
Chair Set, G. Nakashima, Walnut, Grass Seats, 1963, 28 x 23 x 20 In., 6.	11875
Chair Set, Gondola Shape, Arched Crest, Vase Shape Splat, Saber Legs, 34 In., 6	688
Chair Set, Hepplewhite, Mahogany, Shieldback, Prince Of Wales Plumes, 38 In., 8	1625
Chair Set, Painted Crest Rails, Splats, Plank Bottom, Incised C Lolley, c.1835, 32 In., 6... *illus*	960
Chair Set, Rohlfs, Tall Back, Padded Seat, Buffalo, N.Y., 1900s, 53 In., 4 .... *illus*	6250

F

Furniture, Bookcase, Herts Bros., Revolving, Oak, Drawers, Brass, c.1880, 54 In., Pair
$3,750

Naudeau's Auction Gallery

Furniture, Bookcase, Regency, Mahogany, Glass Doors, Inlay, Pullout Board, 1800s, 91 x 47 In.
$1,200

Cowan's Auctions

Furniture, Bookcase, Victorian, Mahogany, Carved, Mirrors, Shelves, Drop Front, 1800s, 73 x 66 In.
$1,476

Cowan's Auctions

Furniture, Breakfront, 2 Parts, Fretwork Glass Doors, Over Doors, Baker, c.1950, 91 x 96 In.
$2,040

Cowan's Auctions

Furniture, Breakfront, Aesthetic Revival, Oak, Carved, Relief, Herter Brothers, c.1890, 90 In.
$7,680

Neal Auction Co.

Furniture, Breakfront, Mahogany, Protruding Section, Mullioned Doors, England, c.1810, 80 x 50 In.
$600

Eldred's Auctioneers and Appraisers

Furniture, Buffet, French Provincial, Fruitwood, Canted Corners, Drawers, Doors, c.1850, 42 x 60 In.
$1,500

New Orleans Auction Galleries

A Dovetail Substitute

Dovetails that held drawers and other parts of wooden furniture together were hand cut in the eighteenth century. With the abundance of new tools and the availability of electricity and other power sources in the nineteenth century, inventors improved many products. In 1867, Charles Knapp invented a substitute for the dovetail joint: a scallop and peg joint. The "pegs" went into a hole in the center of each scallop cut into the side of the drawer front. Knapp invented a machine to cut all the pieces.

Furniture, Buffet, Henry II Style, Painted, Leaf Accents, Doors, Drawers, 2 Parts, c.1910, 106 x 70 In.
$1,500

New Orleans Auction Galleries

Furniture, Bureau, Linen Press, Mahogany, 4 Drawers, Molded Beam, Turned Shaft, 1800s, 71 x 37 In.
$390

Eldred's Auctioneers and Appraisers

Furniture, Cabinet, Bar, Art Deco, Parchment, Fruitwood, Side Doors, Mirror, c.1930, 38 x 45 In.
$896

Neal Auction Co.

Furniture, Cabinet, Borge Mogensen, Teak, Brass, 4 Doors, P. Lauritsen & Sons, 1950s, 35 x 54 In.
$2,250

Rago Arts and Auction Center

Furniture, Cabinet, Carved, Lacquer, 6 Sections, Doors, Scenes, Chinese, c.1925, 87 x 48 In.
$1,875

New Orleans Auction Galleries

Furniture, Cabinet, Corner, Bowed Front, Doors, Painted Scene, Shelves, Continental, 1700s, 36 x 24 In.
$375

New Orleans Auction Galleries

Furniture, Cabinet, Display, J. Hoffmann, Beech, Fruitwood, Glass, J. & J. Kohn, c.1910, 77 x 32 In.
$8,750

Rago Arts and Auction Center

Furniture, Cabinet, Elm, Brass Mounts, Chinese, 64 ½ x 43 In.
$212

Hess Auction Group

Furniture, Cabinet, Folio, Mixed Wood, Molded, 6 Drawers, Base, c.1910, 27 x 42 In.
$576

Neal Auction Co.

Furniture, Cabinet, Herter Bros., Renaissance Revival, 3 Parts, Carved, Gilt, c.1870, 51 x 70 In.
$14,640

Neal Auction Co.

Revival Furniture

In the years following World War I (1914–18), Americans turned to different revival styles of furniture that sparked memories of the past. Almost every old style—from Windsor chairs, Chippendale chests, and wing chairs to bulky, William and Mary dining room sets and Empire pieces—was slightly changed and marketed to the general public at reasonable prices.

Furniture, Cabinet, Medals, Georgian, Fruitwood, 10 Drawers, Lined, H-Stretcher, c.1900, 23 x 27 In.
$800

Brunk Auctions

Furniture, Cabinet, Music, Majorelle, Inlaid River Scene, Shelf, Drawer, Slots, c.1900, 56 x 32 In.
$2,000

Rago Arts and Auction Center

Furniture, Cabinet, Oak, Carved, Religious Figure, Door, Lower Shelf, Belgium, 1800s, 51 x 21 In.
$189

Hess Auction Group

Furniture, Cabinet, Oak, Glass Panels & Shelves, Gargoyle, Cherub, Flowers, 67 x 50 In.
$1,298

Hess Auction Group

F

Furniture, Cabinet, P. Evans, Directional, Patchwork, Mixed Metals, Steel, 1970s, 80 x 36 In. $17,500

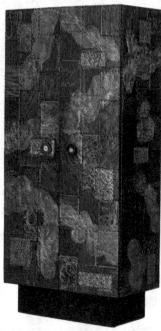

Rago Arts and Auction Center

Furniture, Cabinet, P. Evans, Steel, Sculptural, Torch Cut, Welded, Painted, 1968, 24 x 15 In. $15,000

Rago Arts and Auction Center

TIP

Veneered furniture should not be placed near steam radiators, open windows, or groups of potted plants. The veneer will eventually "bubble" from the moisture.

Chair Set, Thonet, Bentwood, Upholstered Seat & Back, 33 In., 4	755
Chair Set, Tove & Edvard Kindt-Larsen, Lounge, Teak, Vinyl, 1950s, 30 x 30 x 31 In., 4	2875
Chair Set, Walnut, Laminated, Shaped Back, Dish Seat, Cherner, 1958, 32 In., 4	1125
Chair Set, Wegner, Oak, Teak, Paper Cord, C. Hansen & Son, 1960s, 30 In., 8	3000
Chair Set, Wegner, Sculptured Teak, Vinyl, Johannes Hansen, 1960s, 30 In., 6	8750
Chair, 3-Slat Back, Pewter Inlay, Arms, Liberty & Co., England, c.1910, 47 In. *illus*	812
Chair, Acadian, Ladder Back, Acorn Finials, Scroll Arms, Hide Seat, Green, c.1830, 34 x 20 In.	976
Chair, Acadian, Painted, Turned Finials, Shaped Slats, Rush Seat, Child's, c.1810, 22 x 14 In. .	1220
Chair, Adirondack, Birch Frame, Bentwood Back, Continuous Arm, 36 In.	156
Chair, Anglo-Colonial, Bamboo, Shaped Crest, Rush Splat, Arms, c.1910, 41 In., Pair *illus*	4750
Chair, Antler Frame, Moose & Elk, Upholstered Seat, Victorian, 39 x 43 In.	688
Chair, Art Deco, Ebonized, Lattice Back, Faux Bamboo Legs, 33 In., Pair	478
Chair, Art Nouveau, Boudoir, Woman's, Carved, Blue Over-Upholstered, 35 x 24½ In.	3630
Chair, Balloon Back, Papier-Mache, Gilt, Mother-Of-Pearl Inlay, 1800s, 35 In. *illus*	360
Chair, Bamboo, Cane Seat, Tapestry Upholstered Cushion, Arms, Chinese, 29 In. *illus*	720
Chair, Baronial Style, Mahogany, Pierced Splat, Padded Seat, Arms, c.1890, 60 In., Pair *illus*	1125
Chair, Baroque, Giltwood, Padded Seat & Back, Swags & Scrolling, Italy, 1800s, 51 In.	1188
Chair, Bentwood Frame, Tufted Black Leather Upholstery, 31 x 26 x 33 In.	177
Chair, Bergere, Louis XV Style, Fruitwood, Cabriole Legs, Closed Arms, c.1790, 37 In., Pair	795
Chair, Bergere, Neoclassical, Marble, Nose, Mouth, Chin, Neck, Black, Closed Arms, 28 x 31 In.	7040
Chair, Bergere, Walnut, Paneled Crest, Reeded Legs, Eagle Head, Closed Arms, 1800s, 37 x 26 In. .	2318
Chair, Bird's-Eye Maple, Spanish Feet, 1750, 39 In.	120
Chair, Birthing, Wood, Carved, Vinyl Seat, Plank Splat, Cutout Crest, c.1880, 30 In.	160
Chair, Black Forest, Standing Bear Back Splat & Legs, Scroll Arms, 25 x 14 In. *illus*	584
Chair, Block Molded Legs, H-Stretcher Base, 1780, 17 In.	360
Chair, Bruno Rey, Oak Frames, Stylized Flower Shapes, 20½ x 21¾ In., Pair	1586
Chair, C. Pollock, Outer Shell, Black Upholstery, Knoll, c.1975, Pair *illus*	192
Chair, Campaign, Iron, Folding, Brass Arms, Finials, Cushion, Italy, 34 x 27 In. *illus*	1722
Chair, Campeche, Mahogany, Stallion's Head Crest, Brass Nailhead Trim, Leather, c.1830, 40 In. .	1586
Chair, Campeche, Oak, Carved, Embossed Leather, Incised Arms, Mexico, c.1890, 33 x 31 In. *illus*	976
Chair, Cappellini, Thinking Man's, Enameled Steel, Green, c.1986, 29 x 26 In.	1000
Chair, Captain's, D.R. Dimes, Maple, Windsor Style, 1900s, 17½ In.	281
Chair, Carved, Shaped Top Rail, Scroll Arm, Legs, Off-White Upholstery, 31 x 32 In.	177
Chair, Chippendale Style, Carved Back, Upholstered Bench Seat, 40 x 53 In.	177
Chair, Chippendale Style, Mahogany, Pierced, Blind Fret Carving, 1900, 17 x 18 In.	192
Chair, Chippendale, Mahogany, Carved, Crest Rail, Arms, c.1785, 37 x 23 In.	9360
Chair, Chippendale, Mahogany, Pierced Carved Splat, Trapezoid Seat, H-Stretcher, 36 In.	125
Chair, Chippendale, Mahogany, Pierced Splat, Needlepoint Seat, 39 In. *illus*	165
Chair, Chippendale, Mahogany, Upholstered, Shaped Crest, Scroll Arms, c.1800, 45 In.	2040
Chair, Chrome Frame, Modern, c.1950, 29 In., Pair	531
Chair, Cockfighting, Mahogany, Easel-Back Platform, Leather Upholstery, c.1865, 32 In. *illus*	1875
Chair, Corner, George III Style, Oak, Carved Crest, Face, Flowers, Pierced Slats, 1800s, 31 In. ..	435
Chair, Corner, Maple, Necessary, Black Paint, Slip Seat, c.1780, 30 x 16 In.	293
Chair, Corner, Walnut, Upholstered Seat, 1790, 32 In.	360
Chair, Denis Wagner, Cast Aluminum, Sculptural, 3 Legs, 1970s, 33 x 30 In.	2125
Chair, Directoire, Cast Iron, Brass Finials, Curule Legs, Arms, 42 x 21 In.	244
Chair, Dirk Jan Rol, Lounge, Janine Abraham, Bamboo, Rattan, 1950s, 33 x 31 x 28 In.	3375
Chair, Duncan Phyfe Style, Curule, Mahogany, 32 In.	597
Chair, E&T Kindt-Larsen, Cherry, Upholstered, High Arms, Cross Bars, 1950s, 28 In.	1875
Chair, Eames, DKR-1, Fiberglass, Enameled Steel, Herman Miller, 31 x 22 In. *illus*	313
Chair, Eames, Lounge, Ottoman, Leather, Rosewood, 16 x 31 x 32 x 30 In.	2375
Chair, Eames, Lounge, Ottoman, Veneer, Leather, Herman Miller, c.1975, Chair 32 x 32 In.	4250
Chair, Eames, Molded Fiberglass, Black Leather, Walnut Dowel, Steel Wire, 1953, 31 x 25 In.	1187
Chair, Eames, Time Life, Aluminum, Black Leather, Casters, Herman Miller, 27 In.	500
Chair, Easy, Anglo-Indian, Hardwood, Carved, Pierced, Closed Arms, c.1875, 35 In. *illus*	1750
Chair, Egyptian Revival, Parcel Gilt, 31¾ In.	2250
Chair, Egyptian Revival, Parcel Gilt, Bone, Mother-Of-Pearl, Paw Feet, 43 x 24 In.	1664
Chair, Egyptian Revival, Parcel Gilt, Cedar, Arms, 30½ In.	1375
Chair, Erich Dieckmann, Walnut, Striped Cushion, 1930s, 30½ x 21½ x 23 In.	1062
Chair, Esherick, Hickory, Cherry, Saddle Leather, Carved Signature, 1957, 31 x 18 x 19 In.	5625

Furniture, Cabinet, Rosewood, Inlay, Drawers, Columns, Mirrored Door, c.1880, 54 x 23 In., Pair
$9,000

Naudeau's Auction Gallery

Furniture, Candlestand, Mixed Wood, Adjustable, Turned Shaft, 43 In.
$1,180

Hess Auction Group

Furniture, Candlestand, Federal, Mahogany, Tilt Top, Rectangular, Canted Corners, c.1800, 30 In.
$720

Eldred's Auctioneers and Appraisers

Furniture, Candlestand, Papier-Mache, Tilt Top, Gilt, Mother-Of-Pearl Inlay, 1800s, 27 x 22 In.
$185

Cowan's Auctions

Furniture, Canterbury, Mahogany, Brass Gallery, c.1890, 25 x 18 In.
$500

New Orleans Auction Galleries

Furniture, Chair Commode, George III, Mahogany, Vase Shape Splat, Padded Arms, c.1785, 36 In.
$427

New Orleans Auction Galleries

Furniture, Chair Set, Bootjack Splat, Paint Decorated, Stamped, Ebersol, 33 In., 4
$236

Hess Auction Group

FURNITURE

Furniture, Chair Set, Painted Crest Rails, Splats, Plank Bottom, Incised C Lolley, c.1835, 32 In., 6
$960

Garth's Auctioneers & Appraisers

Furniture, Chair, 3-Slat Back, Pewter Inlay, Arms, Liberty & Co., England, c.1910, 47 In.
$812

Rago Arts and Auction Center

Furniture, Chair, Balloon Back, Papier-Mache, Gilt, Mother-Of-Pearl Inlay, 1800s, 35 In.
$360

Cowan's Auctions

Furniture, Chair Set, Rohlfs, Tall Back, Padded Seat, Buffalo, N.Y., 1900s, 53 In., 4
$6,250

Rago Arts and Auction Center

TIP
If you have an old chair that wobbles, try this: Save a wine bottle cork. Cut across the cork to make a disc. Put it under the short leg that causes the wobble. It may take several tries to get the cork disc just the right size.

Furniture, Chair, Anglo-Colonial, Bamboo, Shaped Crest, Rush Splat, Arms, c.1910, 41 In., Pair
$4,750

New Orleans Auction Galleries

Furniture, Chair, Bamboo, Cane Seat, Tapestry Upholstered Cushion, Arms, Chinese, 29 In.
$720

Brunk Auctions

Chair, F. & U. Campana, Favela, Pine, Birch Plywood Frame, Arms, 2000s, 30 x 26 In. ..... *illus* — 5313

Chair, F. Myers, Anodized Aluminum, Bent Sheets, Slightly Reclined, 1971, 42 ½ x 33 In. .... — 4375

Chair, Fauteuil, Louis VI, Upholstered, Domed Back, Cabriole Legs, Arms, 1880s, 36 In. .... — 938

Chair, Fauteuil, Louis XV, Walnut, Carved, Upholstered, Scroll Arms, Hoof Feet, c.1820, 43 In. — 1342

Chair, Fireside, Kindt-Larsen, Cherry, Vinyl, Gustav Bertelsen & Co., 1950s, 28 ½ In. .... *illus* — 2750

Chair, G. Nakashima, Lounge, Cherry, White Webbing, Armrest, 1958, 27 x 66 x 32 In. .... — 37500

Chair, G. Nakashima, Lounge, Walnut, Hickory, Arms, 1965, 33 x 33 x 29 In. .... — 7500

Chair, G. Nakashima, Lounge, Walnut, Plaid Cushion, 1966, 30 ½ x 24 In. .... — 4687

Chair, G. Nakashima, Walnut, Upholstered, 1971, 31 x 24 In. .... — 5937

Chair, G. Stickley, Cube, Oak, Leather Cushion, No. 328, Box Mark, 31 x 24 In. .... — 3750

Chair, G. Stickley, Morris, Drop Arm, Slatted, c.1908, 40 x 33 In. .... — 3250

Chair, G. Stickley, Morris, Leather Cushion, Decal Label, c.1908, 39 ½ x 31 ½ In. .... *illus* — 2000

Chair, Galle, Art Nouveau, Mahogany, Carved, Inlay, Iris, Upholstered, Signed, 39 In. ..... *illus* — 1000

Chair, Gaming, Rohlfs, Wood, Shaped Seat, 1 Arm Support, Triangle Base, 1900, 29 ½ In. ...... — 1750

Chair, Gehry, Ottoman, Red Beaver, 1987, 31 x 33 In. .... — 4750

Chair, Gehry, Wiggle, Corrugated Cardboard, Masonite, Germany, 2000, 34 x 14 ½ In., Pair ... — 3000

Chair, Gondola, Parcel Gilt, Velvet Upholstery, Egg Shape, Trapdoor Compartment, 31 In. .... — 1875

Chair, Gothic Revival, Swivel, Fitted Cushion, Carved, 52 In. .... — 497

Chair, Guglielmo Ulrich, Lounge, Upholstered, Enameled Wood, 1940s, 32 x 41 x 39 In. .... — 5000

Chair, H. Bertoia, Bird, Ottoman, Knoll International, c.1952, 38 ½ x 38 In. .... — 1188

Chair, H. Bertoia, Diamond, Chrome, Blue Upholstery, Knoll, Pair, c.1950, 34 x 27 In. .... — 1300

Chair, H. Bertoia, Diamond, Enameled Steel, Knoll Assoc., 33 x 28 In. .... *illus* — 281

Chair, Hugo Franca, Pequi Wood, Rope, Sculptural, Saddle Seat, Split Wood Back, 58 x 21 In. — 4687

Chair, Ice Cream Parlor, Kohn-Mundus, Bentwood, Stencil, c.1880, 34 In. .... — 1005

Chair, J. Hoffmann, Adjustable, Bent Beech, Steel, Suede, c.1905, 42 x 27 In. .... — 10000

Chair, J. Hoffmann, Ebonized Beech, Paper Labels, Ink Stamp, Arms, 1900s, 36 In., Pair .... — 4376

Chair, Japanese, Figural Carved Dragons, Shaped Arms, Bone Eyes, 30 In. .... — 267

Chair, Jeanneret, Birch, Zinc Plated, Webbing, Upholstered, 1950s, 30 x 23 In., Pair .... — 4063

Chair, Jeanneret, Student, Teak, Cane, Modified X Frame Sides, Writing Table, 31 x 24 In. .... — 2250

Chair, Jeanneret, Teak, Cane, Upholstered, Stenciled Markings, 1950s, 32 x 20 x 24 In. .... — 6875

Chair, John Risley, Luger Mfg., Iron, Welded, Male & Female Outlines, Raymor, 54 In., Pair *illus* — 1230

Chair, Knoll, Womb, Red, Orange, Cloth, Black Metal Legs, 35 x 38 x 33 In .... — 885

Chair, Ladder Back, Arched Slats, Green Paint, Rush Seat, Pa., c.1800, 43 In. .... *illus* — 413

Chair, Ladder Back, Black Paint, 4 Horizontal Splats, Turned Front Stretcher, 1700, 43 In. .... — 270

Chair, Le Corbusier, Chrome, Leather, 29 ½ x 24 In. .... — 250

Chair, Le Corbusier, Lounge, Chrome Steel, Leather, Stamped, Cassina, c.1970, 24 x 39 In. *illus* — 875

Chair, Le Corbusier, Lounge, Teak, Woven Wicker, Upholstered, 1960s, 31 In., Pair.................. — 3250

Chair, Library, William IV, Mechanical, Mahogany, Upholstered, Arms, c.1835, 51 In. ..... *illus* — 3000

Chair, Lounge, Bamboo, Rattan, Round, Enameled Iron, 1950s, 32 ½ In., Pair .... *illus* — 3375

Chair, Lounge, Barrel, Art Deco, Enameled Wood, Upholstered, France, 1920s, 32 x 29 In., Pair — 2375

Chair, Lounge, Curved Arms & Legs, Silver Leaf, Lamb's Wool Upholstery, 1950s, 30 In. .... — 2200

Chair, M. Ballendate, Concept 902, Red Polyurethane, Chrome, Splayed Leg, Italy, 33 In. .... — 254

Chair, Mahogany, Barrel Back, Molded Legs, Silk Upholstery, 1800s, 46 In. .... — 1982

Chair, Mahogany, Shaped Crests, Flower Vase Carving, Arms, 1800s, 39 In., Pair .... — 1560

Chair, Mahogany, Tapered Legs, H-Stretcher Base, 1790, 44 In. .... — 300

Chair, McCobb, Symmetric Group, High Back, Walnut, Upholstered, 1950s, 28 In., Pair .... — 1875

Chair, Memphis, De Lucchi, Enameled Steel, Disc Back, Lacquered Wood, Rubber, 35 x 26 In. *illus* 554

Chair, Moravian, Walnut, Shaped Back, Crescent Moon Shape Cutout, 34 ½ In., Pair...... *illus* — 700

Chair, Morris, Oak, Folding Back, Square Drop Seat, Slatted Legs, c.1900, 39 x 30 In. .... — 488

Chair, Oak, Barley, Cane back, Leafy Scroll, Upholstered Seat, 47 x 24 x 27 In .... — 118

Chair, Ottoman, Eames, Label, Herman Miller, c.1973 .... *illus* — 2520

Chair, Ottoman, Old Hickory, Adirondack Style, Varnished, Leather Cushions, 37-In. Chair..... — 390

Chair, P. Evans, Bronze, Composite, Upholstered, Arm, 1970s, 27 x 26 x 20 In........................... — 33750

Chair, Painted, Lovers, Barrel Style Seat, Floral, Stretchers, Vernis Martin, 30 x 23 x 20 In. ...... — 118

Chair, Patio, Tropitan, Rattan Saucer, Iron Frame, Cushions, c.1945, 30 x 28 In., Pair............. — 1350

Chair, Philippe Starck, Bubble Club, Molded Plastic, Kartell, 2001, 40 x 29 In., Pair........ *illus* — 750

Chair, Phyllis Morris, Faux Bamboo, Enameled Metal, Upholstered, 34 In., Pair .... *illus* — 677

Chair, Pierced Crest, Solid Splat, Scrolling Arms, Ball & Claw Feet, 1900s.................................. — 169

Chair, Pierre Patout, Stained, Lacquered Wood, Upholstered, 1930s, 36 x 23 x 21 In., Pair....... — 3625

Chair, Poul Jensen, Lounge, Upholstered, Label, 1960s, 28 x 30 x 33 In., Pair............................ — 6875

Furniture, Chair, Baronial Style, Mahogany, Pierced Splat, Padded Seat, Arms, c.1890, 60 In., Pair
$1,125

New Orleans Auction Galleries

Furniture, Chair, Black Forest, Standing Bear Back Splat & Legs, Scroll Arms, 25 x 14 In.
$584

Leland Little Auctions

Furniture, Chair, C. Pollock, Outer Shell, Black Upholstery, Knoll, c.1975, Pair
$192

Selkirk Auctioneers & Appraisers

Furniture, Chair, Campaign, Iron, Folding, Brass Arms, Finials, Cushion, Italy, 34 x 27 In.
$1,722

Cowan's Auctions

Furniture, Chair, Campeche, Oak, Carved, Embossed Leather, Incised Arms, Mexico, c.1890, 33 x 31 In.
$976

Neal Auction Co.

Furniture, Chair, Chippendale, Mahogany, Pierced Splat, Needlepoint Seat, 39 In.
$165

Hess Auction Group

Chair, Pyrography Decorated, Keyhole Back, 4 Turned Legs, 1910, 29 x 17 In.	147
Chair, Queen Anne Style, Baluster Shape Splat, Cabriole Legs, Dutch, 1800s, 45 In., Pair *illus*	369
Chair, Queen Anne, Raked Back, Cabriole Legs, Side Stretchers, 45 ½ x 15 In.	6050
Chair, Racket, Vestergaard-Jensen, Teak, Brass, Microfiber, Decal, 1950s, 46 x 29 In. *illus*	11875
Chair, Risom, Lounge, Original Upholstery, Knoll, 1940s, 32 x 29 x 29 In.	3673
Chair, Robsjohn-Gibbings, Lounge, Walnut, Upholstered, 1950s, 32 ½ In., Pair *illus*	8750
Chair, Rococo Revival, Rosewood, Carved, Scrolled Stiles, Upholstered, 38 ½ In. *illus*	3355
Chair, Rococo, Laminated Rosewood, Bird, Flower Cluster, Arms, 48 x 26 x 29 In.	3660
Chair, Rosewood, Carved, Dragons, Shaped Seat, Arms, Chinese, 1800, 43 In. *illus*	610
Chair, Sausage-Turned Stiles, 4 Graduated Slats, 1700s, 17 In.	168
Chair, Scissor Lounge, Birch, Zinc Plated Metal, Webbing, 1950s, 28 x 22 In.	1625
Chair, Shaker, Maple, Brown, 3 Slats, Club Cutouts, Rush Seat, c.1850, 41 x 16 in.	480
Chair, Single Piece, Brown Leather Tacked, Hardwood Frame, Rectangular Feet, 30 x 18 In.	338
Chair, Spanish Foot, Rush Seat, Old Red Surface, Queen Anne, New England, 42 In.	211
Chair, Stainless Steel Frame, Angular, Leather Sling Seat, 33 In.	688
Chair, Swivel, Norguet, Rive Droite, Brushed Steel, Upholstered, Arms, E. Pucci, 28 In. *illus*	1875
Chair, T. Pedersen Frederica, Stingray, Chrome Steel, Polypropylene, 35 ½ x 48 In.	1750
Chair, Tub, Neoclassical, Mahogany, Carved, Greek Key, 3-Panel Back, Italy, c.1835, 28 In. *illus*	3750
Chair, Tufted Burnt Orange Leather, Cantilevered Bent Plywood, 1900, 36 x 26 x 34 In.	246
Chair, V. Kagan, Lounge, Ottoman, Walnut, Dreyfuss, 1950s, 34 In. & 15 x 20 In. *illus*	20000
Chair, V. Kagan, Lounge, Walnut, Wool, Retractable Footrest, Kagan-Dreyfuss, 1950s, 39 In. *illus*	6875
Chair, V. Kagan, Swivel, Sculpted Walnut, Leather, Arms, 1950s, 35 x 27 In., Pair	10000
Chair, V. Panton, Plastic, Fehlbaum & Co. For Herman Miller, 1967, 32 x 23 In. *illus*	438
Chair, Walnut, Balloon Back, Needlepoint, Floral Carved, Crest, c.1810, 52 x 29 In.	123
Chair, Walnut, Carved, Trapezoid Slip Seat, George III, 1800s, 38 x 23 x 23 In.	549
Chair, Walnut, Yoke Crest Rail, Vase Shape Splat, Slip Seat, Cabriole Legs, 1750, 40 In.	720
Chair, Walter Lamb, Lounge, Bronze Frame, Woven Rope Seat & Back, c.1950, 31 In. *illus*	1920
Chair, Wegner, Valet, Oak, Teak, Johannes Hansen, Branded Mark, 1960s, 37 In. *illus*	10625
Chair, Wendell Castle, Molar, Gel-Coated Fiberglass, Rubber, 1960s, 26 x 38 x 32 In., Pair	1875
Chair, William & Mary, Oak, Carved, Pierced Crest & Splat, Cabriole Legs, c.1700, 50 In.	125
Chair, Windsor, Bow Back, 7 Spindles, Shaped Saddle Seat, 1800s, 17 In.	108
Chair, Windsor, Bow Back, Old Red Paint, 38 In.	316
Chair, Windsor, Fanback, Mixed Wood, Saddle Seat, Continuous Arm, 1800s, 46 In.	450
Chair, Windsor, Nutting, Maple, 37 ½ In.	216
Chair, Windsor, Pine, Writing Arm, Painted, 1800s, 35 In.	900
Chair, Windsor, Sack Back, Kittinger, Black Paint, Knuckle Arm, 40 In.	281
Chair, Windsor, Sack Back, Paddle Grip Arms, Carved Saddle Seat, Painted, N.Y., c.1790, 36 In.	1695
Chair, Windsor, Sack Back, Turned Legs & Stretcher, Saddle Seat, 1780s, 37 x 23 In.	210
Chair, Windsor, Spindle Back, Writing Arm, Drawer Under Seat, New Haven, c.1790, 29 In. *illus*	11250
Chair, Windsor, Turned Legs & Stretcher, Saddle Seat, Continuous Arm, 1780s, 38 x 22 In.	300
Chair, Wing, Chippendale Style, Hunting Design Upholstery, 4 Legs, Carved Knees, 1900, 45 In.	240
Chair, Wing, Chippendale Style, Mahogany, Upholstered, Outscrolled Arms, 1900s, 38 In.	125
Chair, Wing, Federal, Walnut, Tapered Back, Flared Wings, Scrolled Arms, 43 x 26 x 19 In.	1830
Chair, Wing, Mahogany Carved, Leather, Brass Nailhead Trim, Claw Feet, Child's, 30 In.	739
Chair, Wood, 3 Carved Splats, Square Legs, Chinese, c.1900, 29 In., Pair *illus*	750
Chair, Wormley, Janus, Model 5609, Stained Mahogany, Upholstered, 1960s, 30 In.	1125
Chair, Rocker, is listed under Rocker in this category.	
Chaise Longue, Louis XV, Fruitwood, Arched Back, Upholstered, 1700s, 41 ½ x 64 In.	2375
Chest, 4 Drawers, Painted, Mahantango Valley, Pa., c.1830, 51 x 41 In. *illus*	5310
Chest, American Federal, Cherry, 4 Graduated Drawers, Flared Feet, c.1825, 38 x 39 In.	500
Chest, American Federal, Cherry, 6 Graduated Drawers, 52 ½ x 38 In.	236
Chest, American Federal, Hepplewhite Style, Tiger Maple, 2 Over 3 Drawers, c.1825, 38 x 45 In.	750
Chest, Birch, Maple, Dentil Molded Cornice, 6 Drawers, Brass Bail Handles, 1790, 59 In.	960
Chest, Blanket, 6-Board, Dovetailed, Turned Feet, c.1925, 26 x 50 In.	420
Chest, Blanket, Carved, Walnut, Poplar, Dovetail, Turnip Feet, 22 ¾ x 42 In.	1210
Chest, Blanket, Dovetailed, Interior Compartment, Lid, Pencil Drawings, 38 x 18 x 17 In.	41
Chest, Blanket, Grain & Sponge, Hinged Top, 2 Drawers, Bracket Feet, c.1820, 42 x 44 In.	625
Chest, Blanket, Grain Painted, Feathered, J. Rupp, Hanover, Pa., 1860s, 24 x 44 In. *illus*	708
Chest, Blanket, Hepplewhite, Lid, Dovetailed, Drawers, Till, Stylized Tulip, Pa., 28 x 51 In. *illus*	2950
Chest, Blanket, J. Palmer, Red Paint, Flower Vases, Pa., c.1875, 23 x 39 In. *illus*	9440

Furniture, Chair, Cockfighting, Mahogany, Easel-Back Platform, Leather Upholstery, c.1865, 32 In.
$1,875

New Orleans Auction Galleries

Furniture, Chair, Eames, DKR-1, Fiberglass, Enameled Steel, Herman Miller, 31 x 22 In.
$313

Wright

Furniture, Chair, Easy, Anglo-Indian, Hardwood, Carved, Pierced, Closed Arms, c.1875, 35 In.
$1,750

New Orleans Auction Galleries

Furniture, Chair, F. & U. Campana, Favela, Pine, Birch Plywood Frame, Arms, 2000s, 30 x 26 In.
$5,313

Rago Arts and Auction Center

Furniture, Chair, Fireside, Kindt-Larsen, Cherry, Vinyl, Gustav Bertelsen & Co., 1950s, 28 1/2 In.
$2,750

Rago Arts and Auction Center

Furniture, Chair, G. Stickley, Morris, Leather Cushion, Decal Label, c.1908, 39 1/2 x 31 1/2 In.
$2,000

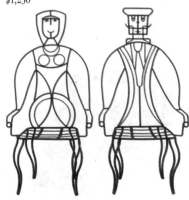

Rago Arts and Auction Center

Furniture, Chair, Galle, Art Nouveau, Mahogany, Carved, Inlay, Iris, Upholstered, Signed, 39 In.
$1,000

Rago Arts and Auction Center

Furniture, Chair, H. Bertoia, Diamond, Enameled Steel, Knoll Assoc., 33 x 28 In.
$281

Wright

Furniture, Chair, John Risley, Luger Mfg., Iron, Welded, Male & Female Outlines, Raymor, 54 In., Pair
$1,230

Palm Beach Modern Auctions

F

FURNITURE

Furniture, Chair, Ladder Back, Arched Slats, Green Paint, Rush Seat, Pa., c.1800, 43 In.
$413

Hess Auction Group

Furniture, Chair, Le Corbusier, Lounge, Chrome Steel, Leather, Stamped, Cassina, c.1970, 24 x 39 In.
$875

Rago Arts and Auction Center

Furniture, Chair, Library, William IV, Mechanical, Mahogany, Upholstered, Arms, c.1835, 51 In.
$3,000

New Orleans Auction Galleries

Chest, Blanket, Lift Top, Pine, Later Red Wash, Floral Cartouches, 1800, 24 x 48 In.	96
Chest, Blanket, M. Warwood, Poplar, Red Flame Graining, Pa., 27 x 40 In.	330
Chest, Blanket, Pine, 3 Drawers, Red, 1-Board Top, c.1840, 37½ x 42 In.	7800
Chest, Blanket, Pine, Dovetailed, Grain Painted, Turned Feet, Pa., c.1825, 44 x 22 In.	270
Chest, Blanket, Pine, Grain Painted, Fitted, Till, New England, Miniature, c.1825, 7 x 12 In.. *illus*	2118
Chest, Blanket, Pine, Lift Top, Painted, Drawers, Iron Hinges, Brass Pulls, c.1810, 38 x 39 In. .	470
Chest, Blanket, Pine, Red Paint, Interior Till, Bootjack Ends, Drawer, Refinished, 32 x 38 In...	120
Chest, Blanket, Pine, Red Paint, Snipe Hinges, Ditty Box Interior, 1800s, 25 In.	192
Chest, Blanket, Pine, Sponge Graining, Square Nails, Drawer, Molding, c.1850, 43 In. ... *illus*	1250
Chest, Blanket, Pine, Tombstone Panels, Whirligig Flowers, Iron Strap Hinges, 49 In.	2040
Chest, Blanket, Rosewood, Carved, Figures, Exotic Bird, Asia, Miniature, 21 x 31 x 17 In.. *illus*	200
Chest, Blanket, Softwood, Arched Panels, Putty, 1800s, 22 x 51½ x 23½ In.	2900
Chest, Blanket, Softwood, Molded Lid, Sponged, Turned Feet, 24½ x 43½ x 22 In.	800
Chest, Blanket, Yellow Pine, Poplar, Circles, Stylized Plant Stalks, 26 x 43 In.	7800
Chest, Bombe, Faux Tortoiseshell, Ebonized Trim, 3 Drawers, Paw Feet, 30 x 36 In.	2375
Chest, Campaign, Mahogany, Walnut, Drawers, 2 Sections, England, 1800s, 43 x 39 In.. *illus*	1560
Chest, Campaign, Tropical Hardwood, 7-Drawers, Turned Feet, Base Molding, c.1810, 36 x 39 In..	1952
Chest, Cherry, Southern, 4-Drawers, Shaped Base, Federal, c.1820, 38 x 39 x 20 In.	1342
Chest, Chippendale Style Chest, 2 Small Drawers, 2 Long Drawers, 1900, 36 x 41 In.	240
Chest, Chippendale, Mahogany, Bowfront Silver, 3 Drawers, Gadrooned Top, 33 x 39 In.	854
Chest, Chippendale, Maple, Pine, 4 Drawers, Oval Brasses, Ogee Bracket, 1700s, 35 x 38 In.	600
Chest, Chippendale, Pine, 4 Drawers, Dovetailed, Shaped Bracket Feet, 36 x 40 In.	1020
Chest, Chippendale, Serpentine, 4 Drawers, Ball & Claw Feet, 34 x 42 In.	3933
Chest, Coin, Ton-Kwe, Wood, Metal Mounts, Korea, 1800s, 29½ In. *illus*	531
Chest, Cookie-Corner Top, Star Punched, Flower, Leafy Design, 1810, 41 x 45 In.	480
Chest, Dower, Chippendale, Shell Carved, 3 Lipped Drawers, Ball & Claw, 48 x 22 In.	726
Chest, Dower, Lid, Strap Hinges, Till, Dovetailed, Berks County, c.1800, 25 x 53 In. .. *illus*	10500
Chest, Drawer, Neoclassical, Mahogany, Brass Inlay, Signed, New York, 1800s, 48 x 23 x 62 In.	807
Chest, Dressing, Maple, Faux Bamboo, Mirror, 3 Drawers, Turned Feet, c.1910, 81 x 43 In.	1539
Chest, Dressing, Rosewood, Marble, Mirror, 2 Shelves, Carved, American, c.1850, 91 x 45 In.	6710
Chest, Drop Front, Mahogany, Leather Writing, 4 Short Drawers & 2 Long, 1800s, 42 x 41 In...	472
Chest, Empire, Cherry, Burl Mahogany Veneer, American, 44 x 43 In. *illus*	71
Chest, Empire, Cherry, Overhanging Drawer, Miniature, c.1835, 21 x 21 In. *illus*	360
Chest, Federal, Walnut, Inlay, Carved Molded Edge, Southern, Miniature, 30 x 24 In. *illus*	2160
Chest, G. Nakashima, Walnut, 4 Drawers, Slot Handles, Board Supports, 1958, 32 x 42 In.	9375
Chest, G. Stickley, Oak, Drawers, Red Decal, Part Label, c.1907, 48 x 40 In. *illus*	10000
Chest, Georgian Style, Walnut Veneer, Ribbon Inlay, 2 Over 3 Drawers, 1900, 32 x 30 In.	300
Chest, Golden Oak, Pressed Mold Decorations, Brass Hardware, 1900s, 56 x 43 In.	390
Chest, Hepplewhite, Cherry, 3 Over 2 Drawers, 5 Graduated Drawers, c.1820, 60 x 43 In.	900
Chest, Jacobean Style, 5 Drawers, Black Paint, Yellow Gold Stenciled, 1900s, 38 x 39 In.	510
Chest, Koa Wood, Exposed Dovetails, Asymmetrical Handles, 20 x 42 In.	4800
Chest, License Plate Designed Drawers, Wood, Metal Sides, Ornate Knob, 32 x 33 In.	92
Chest, Lift Top, False Single Drawer, Early French, 46 x 24 x 28 In.	170
Chest, Linen Press, Chippendale, Walnut, Screw Press, Drawers, c.1790, 66 x 37 In. *illus*	1280
Chest, Lingerie, French Provincial, Fruitwood, Leather, 5 Drop Front Drawers, 64 x 22 In.	1188
Chest, Mahogany Veneer, Fruitwood Inlay, 5 Long Drawers, 1900s, 46 x 40 In.	720
Chest, Molded Top, 2 Over 3 Drawers, Turned Feet, Miniature, 1800, 12 x 14 In.	240
Chest, Mule, Pine, Grain Painted, Lift Top Over 2 Drawers, Double Cutout Feet, 40 x 43 In.	660
Chest, Oak, 6-Board, Heart Shape Wrought Iron Strap Hinges, 25 x 40 In.	2420
Chest, Oak, Chest, Allover Paneled, Horizontal Hinged Top, 1900s, 30 x 50 In.	300
Chest, Pine, Blue Paint, Interior, Lidded Till, 1800, 14 x 43 x 15 In.	270
Chest, Pine, Grain Painted, Iron Hinges, Circular Wood Pulls, Bootjack Ends, 1790, 38 In.	300
Chest, R. Parzinger, White, Studded, Drawer, Door, Wood, Metal, 17 x 20 In.	4750
Chest, Shaker, Pine, 7 Drawers, Dovetailed, Quarter Round Molding, 47 x 39 In.	8400
Chest, Sheraton, Cherry, 2 Short Drawers Above 4 Long Drawers, c.1835, 51 x 44 In. ... *illus*	423
Chest, Sheraton, Mahogany, 4 Drawers, Turret-Form Corners, Rope-Turned Posts, 1815, 44 x 39 In.	204
Chest, Sheraton, Stiles, Drawer, Cherry, 1900, 48 x 42 x 21 In.	283
Chest, Spanish Colonial, Walnut, Carved, Painted, Religious Figures, 1800s, 22 x 46 In.. *illus*	540
Chest, Storage, Yellow, Green Diamonds, Circles, Red, Blue, Yellow, 24 x 18 In.	272
Chest, Sugar, Cherry, Hinged Lid, Shaped Skirt, Drawer, Tennessee, 32 x 29 In.	3900

Furniture, Chair, Lounge, Bamboo, Rattan, Round, Enameled Iron, 1950s, 32 ½ In., Pair
$3,375

Rago Arts and Auction Center

Furniture, Chair, Memphis, De Lucchi, Enameled Steel, Disc Back, Lacquered Wood, Rubber, 35 x 26 In.
$554

Palm Beach Modern Auctions

Furniture, Chair, Moravian, Walnut, Shaped Back, Crescent Moon Shape Cutout, 34 ½ In., Pair
$700

Hess Auction Group

Furniture, Chair, Ottoman, Eames, Label, Herman Miller, c.1973
$2,520

Selkirk Auctioneers & Appraisers

Furniture, Chair, Philippe Starck, Bubble Club, Molded Plastic, Kartell, 2001, 40 x 29 In., Pair
$750

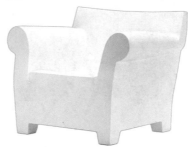

Wright

Furniture, Chair, Phyllis Morris, Faux Bamboo, Enameled Metal, Upholstered, 34 In., Pair
$677

Palm Beach Modern Auctions

Furniture, Chair, Queen Anne Style, Baluster Shape Splat, Cabriole Legs, Dutch, 1800s, 45 In., Pair
$369

Cowan's Auctions

Furniture, Chair, Racket, Vestergaard-Jensen, Teak, Brass, Microfiber, Decal, 1950s, 46 x 29 In.
$11,875

Rago Arts and Auction Center

Furniture, Chair, Robsjohn-Gibbings, Lounge, Walnut, Upholstered, 1950s, 32 ½ In., Pair
$8,750

Rago Arts and Auction Center

FURNITURE

Furniture, Chair, Rococo Revival, Rosewood, Carved, Scrolled Stiles, Upholstered, 38 ½ In.
$3,355

Neal Auction Co.

Furniture, Chair, Rosewood, Carved, Dragons, Shaped Seat, Arms, Chinese, 1800, 43 In.
$610

Neal Auction Co.

Furniture, Chair, Swivel, Norguet, Rive Droite, Brushed Steel, Upholstered, Arms, E. Pucci, 28 In.
$1,875

Rago Arts and Auction Center

Furniture, Chair, Tub, Neoclassical, Mahogany, Carved, Greek Key, 3-Panel Back, Italy, c.1835, 28 In.
$3,750

New Orleans Auction Galleries

Furniture, Chair, V. Kagan, Lounge, Ottoman, Walnut, Dreyfuss, 1950s, 34 In. & 15 x 20 In.
$20,000

Rago Arts and Auction Center

Furniture, Chair, V. Kagan, Lounge, Walnut, Wool, Retractable Footrest, Kagan-Dreyfuss, 1950s, 39 In.
$6,875

Rago Arts and Auction Center

> **TIP**
> Never pick up a chair by
> the arms. Pick it up under
> the seat. The arms could
> loosen or crack.

Furniture, Chair, V. Panton, Plastic, Fehlbaum & Co. For Herman Miller, 1967, 32 x 23 In.
$438

Wright

Furniture, Chair, Walter Lamb, Lounge, Bronze Frame, Woven Rope Seat & Back, c.1950, 31 In.
$1,920

Eldred's Auctioneers and Appraisers

Furniture, Chair, Wegner, Valet, Oak, Teak, Johannes Hansen, Branded Mark, 1960s, 37 In.
$10,625

Rago Arts and Auction Center

Furniture, Chair, Windsor, Spindle Back, Writing Arm, Drawer Under Seat, New Haven, c.1790, 29 In.
$11,250

Eldred's Auctioneers and Appraisers

Furniture, Chair, Wood, 3 Carved Splats, Square Legs, Chinese, c.1900, 29 In., Pair
$750

Freeman's Auctioneers & Appraisers

Furniture, Chest, 4 Drawers, Painted, Mahantango Valley, Pa., c.1830, 51 x 41 In.
$5,310

Hess Auction Group

Furniture, Chest, Blanket, Grain Painted, Feathered, J. Rupp, Hanover, Pa., 1860s, 24 x 44 In.
$708

Hess Auction Group

Furniture, Chest, Blanket, Hepplewhite, Lid, Dovetailed, Drawers, Till, Stylized Tulip, Pa., 28 x 51 In.
$2,950

Hess Auction Group

Furniture, Chest, Blanket, J. Palmer, Red Paint, Flower Vases, Pa., c.1875, 23 x 39 In.
$9,440

Hess Auction Group

Furniture, Chest, Blanket, Pine, Grain Painted, Fitted, Till, New England, c.1825, Miniature, 7 x 12 In.
$2,118

James D. Julia Auctioneers

FURNITURE

Furniture, Chest, Blanket, Pine, Sponge Graining, Square Nails, Drawer, Molding, c.1850, 43 In.
$1,250

Garth's Auctioneers & Appraisers

Furniture, Chest, Blanket, Rosewood, Carved, Figures, Exotic Bird, Asia, Miniature, 21 x 31 x 17 In.
$71

Hess Auction Group

Furniture, Chest, Campaign, Mahogany, Walnut, Drawers, 2 Sections, England, 1800s, 43 x 39 In.
$1,560

Cowan's Auctions

Furniture, Chest, Coin, Ton-Kwe, Wood, Metal Mounts, Korea, 1800s, 29 ½ In.
$531

Freeman's Auctioneers & Appraisers

Furniture, Chest, Dower, Lid, Strap Hinges, Till, Dovetailed, Berks County, c.1800, 25 x 53 In.
$10,500

Hess Auction Group

Furniture, Chest, Empire, Cherry, Burl Mahogany Veneer, American, 44 x 43 In.
$71

Hess Auction Group

Furniture, Chest, Empire, Cherry, Overhanging Drawer, Miniature, c.1835, 21 x 21 In.
$360

Garth's Auctioneers & Appraisers

Furniture, Chest, Federal, Walnut, Inlay, Carved Molded Edge, Southern, Miniature, 30 x 24 In.
$2,160

Brunk Auctions

F

Chest, Sugar, Federal, Cherry, Maple, Walnut, Lift Top, Drawer, Tennessee, 26 x 20 In.		540
Chest, Tiger Maple, 2 Over 3 Drawers, Inlay, Ohio, 1800s, Miniature, 12 x 13 In. .... *illus*		1080
Chest, Walnut Veneer, Maple, Inlay, 11 Drawers, Cabriole Legs, Pad Feet, c.1740, 71 In.. *illus*		2706
Chest, Walnut, Molded Lid, Secret Compartment, Engraved Lock, 24 x 54 x 24 In.		2000
Chest, Wedding, Pine, Lift Top, Dovetailed, Blue Paint, Side Till, Signed, 1898, 49 x 26 In. *illus*		480
Chest, Wood, Leather Wrapped, Stylized Inca Motifs, Brass Studs, 9 x 6½ x 6½ In.		125
Chest-On-Chest, George III, 7 Drawers, Mahogany, Bracket Feet, 76 x 44 In.		3250
Chest-On-Chest, Georgian, Mahogany, Drawers, Brass Pulls, Inlay, 1700s, 75 x 42 In. ... *illus*		390
Chiffonier, Regency, Rosewood, Brass Grill Doors, Pleated Silk, c.1820, 49 x 53 In.		3725
Chifforobe, 2 Drawers, 2 Cupboard Doors, 2 Lower Drawers, Short Turned Legs, 1900s, 59 x 40 In.		132
China Cabinet, Hepplewhite Style, Cherry, Inlay, Muncie, Pa., c.1940, 81 x 37½ In.		177
Clothespress, Paneled Doors, 4 Drawers, Campaign Style Brasses, 40 x 48 In.		726
Coat Hook, Fontana Arte, Patinated Brass, Glass, 1960, 10 x 9 x 8½ In.		1625
Coat Rack, Turned Mahogany Post, Flame Finial, 8 Coat Hooks, Acanthus Column, 79 x 22 x 22 In.		605
Coffer, Walnut, Fruitwood, Paneled Front, Shield Center, Paw Feet, c.1675, 22 x 16 In.		1000
Column, Marble, Lobed, Leafy Corinthian Capitals, Italy, 62 In., Pair		2250
Commode, Bombe, Fruitwood, Marble Top, Drawers, Scroll Inlay, Italy, 1800s, 37 x 57 In. .*illus*		1125
Commode, George III, Mahogany, Inlay, Gallery, Doors, Drawer, 1700s, 32 x 20 In. .... *illus*		397
Commode, Harlequin, Checkerboard, Black, White, Serpentine, 2 Drawers, Cabriole, 33 x 39 In., Pair.		1664
Commode, Hepplewhite, Mahogany, Drawer, Doors, c.1810, 42 x 55 In. .... *illus*		11400
Commode, Louis XV Style, Painted Flowers & Birds, Shaped Marble Top, 32 x 30 In.		1750
Commode, Louis XV-XVI Style, Marble Top, Inlaid Drawer, Cabriolet Legs, c.1950, 34 x 52 In ..		1125
Commode, Louis XVI, Cherry, Cookie Corner Top, 3 Frieze Drawers, 2 Deep Drawers, 36 x 45 In.		738
Commode, Louis XVI, Gilt, Bronze Mount, Green Marble Top, 2 Frieze Drawers, 39½ x 59 In.		1375
Commode, Louis XVI, Mahogany, Metal Mount, 3 Drawers, 32½ x 32 In.		1375
Commode, Mahogany, Inlaid Front, Lattice, Wreath, Marble Top, 1780s, 28 x 38 In., Pair		5000
Commode, Neoclassical Style, Parcel Gilt, Distressed, Reverse Painted Panel, 34 x 42 In.		915
Commode, Provincial Regence, Fruitwood, Bombe Case, 3 Drawers, Scroll Toes, c.1775, 34 x 52 In.		1375
Commode, Provincial Regence, Oak, Drawers, Carved Apron, Legs, 1700s, 37 x 49 In...... *illus*		875
Commode, Regence, Bronze, Gilt, Parquet, 3 Drawers, 34 x 52 In.		5000
Commode, Regency Style, Painted, Marble Top, 3 Drawers, Shaped Legs, 1700s, 34 x 48 In.		1000
Commode, Rococo Revival Style, Painted, Drawers, Marble Top, Italy, 36 x 32 In., Pair... *illus*		750
Commode, Venetian, Painted, 3 Drawers, Serpentine Marble Top, Scalloped Apron, 34 x 47 In..		488
Commode, Walnut Veneer, Burl Medallion, 2 Drawers, Italy, 1800, 35 x 50 x 21½ In.		900
Commode, Walnut, Fruitwood, 3 Drawers, Inlaid Veneer, Italy, c.1790, 33 x 49 In. .... *illus*		5000
Commode, Walnut, Marble Top, 4 Drawers, c.1810, 40 x 51 In.		750
Console, Mirror Back, Arched Crest, Parcel Gilt Bird, Marble Top Base, 31 x 30 In.		2640
Cradle, Georgian, Oak, Copper, Canopy, Posts, Rocker, Scotland, 1800s, 41 x 45 In.		1200
Cradle, Gothic Designs, Oak, Rectangular, Continental, c.1850, 60 x 46 In.		875
Cradle, Spindles, Traces Of Black, Red Paint, c.1825, 14 x 35 In.		120
Credenza, B. Kjaer, Rosewood, Oak, 2 Sliding Doors, 3 Drawers, Denmark, 1960s, 31 x 81 In..		2125
Credenza, Walnut, Glazed Doors, Shaped Top, Open Shelves, c.1860, 40 x 90 In............... *illus*		1125
Cupboard, 2 Doors, 2 Interior Shelves, Single Drawer, 76 x 45 x 15 In.		266
Cupboard, Applied Molding, 2 Doors, Vertical Iron Rods, 1800s, 68 x 36 x 13 In.		390
Cupboard, Barrel Corner, Inverted, Carved, Shell, Butterfly, Single Door, 35 x 17 x 34 In.		597
Cupboard, Bonnetiere, Henry II, Stepped Crown, Spindled Frieze, Leaves, Flowers, 78 x 34 In.		300
Cupboard, Bonnetiere, Louis XIV, Stepped Crown, 3-Panel Door, Drawer, Block Feet, 86 x 28 In.		400
Cupboard, Bonnetiere, Walnut, Plated Metal Accents, Inlay, Multiple Shelves, 86 x 43 x 25 In.		688
Cupboard, Carved, Leaves, Arched Fretwork, Shelves, 1800s, 94 x 58 x 24 In.		472
Cupboard, Corner, Chippendale, Walnut, Glass & Paneled Doors, c.1790, 90 x 47 In........ *illus*		3360
Cupboard, Corner, Federal, Cherry, 2 Sections, 87 x 54 In. .... *illus*		502
Cupboard, Corner, Mahogany, Molded Cornice, Shelf, Blue Green Paint, 1800s, 35 x 21 x 20 In.		500
Cupboard, Corner, Maple, 2 Parts, Glass Doors, Shelves, Drawers, Pa., c.1840, 83 x 49 In. *illus*		900
Cupboard, Corner, Oak, Pine, Old Gray Alligatored Paint, Doors, 82 x 33 In.		900
Cupboard, Corner, Walnut, 4 Burl Doors, Tombstone Arch, 81 x 49 In.		907
Cupboard, Hanging, Door, Glass Pane, Yellow, Sponge Paint, Bail Handle, 10¼ x 15 In.. *illus*		125
Cupboard, Jacobean, Oak, Masks, Paneled Door, Drawer, Leaves, Capitals, 50 x 50¼ In.		4250
Cupboard, Jelly, Blue Paint, 4 Interior Shelves, Bracket Base, c.1850, 58½ x 37 In........... *illus*		813
Cupboard, Mahogany, 4 Doors Flanked, Alternate Column-Form Inlay, 1808, 43 x 38 In.		540
Cupboard, Pantry, Wood, Paint, 2 Sections, Panel Door, Molded Crest, 1850, 84 x 33 In...........		1500

Furniture, Chest, G. Stickley, Oak, Drawers, Red Decal, Part Label, c.1907, 48 x 40 In.
$10,000

Rago Arts and Auction Center

Furniture, Chest, Linen Press, Chippendale, Walnut, Screw Press, Drawers, c.1790, 66 x 37 In.
$1,280

Neal Auction Co.

Furniture, Chest, Sheraton, Cherry, 2 Short Drawers Above 4 Long Drawers, c.1835, 51 x 44 In.
$423

James D. Julia Auctioneers

FURNITURE

Furniture, Chest, Spanish Colonial, Walnut, Carved, Painted, Religious Figures, 1800s, 22 x 46 In.
$540

Cowan's Auctions

Furniture, Chest, Tiger Maple, 2 Over 3 Drawers, Inlay, Ohio, Miniature, 1800s, 12 x 13 In.
$1,080

Cowan's Auctions

Furniture, Chest, Walnut Veneer, Maple, Inlay, 11 Drawers, Cabriole Legs, Pad Feet, c.1740, 71 In.
$2,706

Skinner, Inc.

Furniture, Chest, Wedding, Pine, Lift Top, Dovetailed, Blue Paint, Side Till, Signed, 1898, 49 x 26 In.
$480

Cowan's Auctions

Furniture, Chest-On-Chest, Georgian, Mahogany, Drawers, Brass Pulls, Inlay, 1700s, 75 x 42 In.
$390

Cowan's Auctions

Furniture, Commode, Bombe, Fruitwood, Marble Top, Drawers, Scroll Inlay, Italy, 1800s, 37 x 57 In.
$1,125

New Orleans Auction Galleries

Furniture, Commode, George III, Mahogany, Inlay, Gallery, Doors, Drawer, 1700s, 32 x 20 In.
$397

New Orleans Auction Galleries

Furniture, Commode, Hepplewhite, Mahogany, Drawer, Doors, c.1810, 42 x 55 In.
$11,400

Eldred's Auctioneers and Appraisers

Furniture, Commode, Provincial Regence, Oak, Drawers, Carved Apron, Legs, 1700s, 37 x 49 In.
$875

New Orleans Auction Galleries

Cupboard, Pennsylvania Dutch Federal, Walnut, 2 Parts, 85 x 56 In.	1534
Cupboard, Pewter, Pine, Painted, Peg & Groove, Open Shelves, Door, 1800s, 87 x 33 In. . *illus*	2280
Cupboard, Pewter, Pine, Shelves, Drawers, Door, Washington Courthouse, c.1825, 75 In. *illus*	1200
Cupboard, Pine, Brown Stain, Paneled Door, Interior Shelves, Painted, 1800s, 42 x 30 In.	300
Cupboard, Pine, Green Paint, Wood Pulls, 2-Shelf Interior, 1840, 39 x 42 In.	720
Cupboard, Pine, Inset Panel Door, Porcelain Handle, 29 x 18 In.	1920
Cupboard, Red Paint, 2 Paneled Upper Doors, 3 Drawers, 1900s, 70 x 44 In.	360
Cupboard, Shaker, Hanging, Fold-Out Desk, Cherry, Pine, 37 ½ x 18 In.	1000
Cupboard, Shaker, Hanging, Poplar, Pine, Fall Front Work Surface, 26 x 26 ½ In.	840
Cupboard, Softwood, Blue Over Red, Interior Shelves, 67 ½ x 47 ½ In.	708
Cupboard, Step Back, 4 Doors, Scalloped Cornice, Flower Panels, Mongolia, c.1880, 63 x 81 In.	600
Cupboard, Step Back, Pine, 2 Sections, 2 Glazed Doors, Shelf, Pa., c.1825, 84 In.	960
Cupboard, Step Back, Pine, Poplar, Red Paint, Open Shelves Over Door, 71 x 39 In.	875
Cupboard, Storage, Pine, 2 Doors, Shelves, Painted, c.1850, 70 x 47 In. *illus*	182
Cupboard, Walnut, Flour Bin, Lift Top & Sliding Panel, c.1900, 62 x 37 x 21 In.	510
Cupboard, Wood, Paint, First Aid, White, Red, Door, Shaped Crest, 1800s, 72 x 36 In.	800
Daybed, Arched, Circular Tapered Legs, Upholstered, Bolster Cushion, 1900, 29 x 54 In.	591
Daybed, Baroque, Gilt, Masks, Acanthus, 8-Footed, Continental, c.1880, 33 ½ x 95 In.	6875
Daybed, Frank Lloyd Wright, From Wingspread, 17 x 78 In.	3625
Daybed, Jean Prouve, Enameled Steel, Mahogany, Black Upholstery, c.1950, 24 x 36 In.	5625
Daybed, Mahogany, Cylindrical Crests, Paneled Foot & Headboard, 33 x 71 x 27 In.	2074
Daybed, Poul Kjaerholm, Matte Chrome Steel, Wood, Rubber, Tufted, F. Hansen, 12 x 76 In.	5938
Desk, 2 Drawers, Matte Chrome Steel, Enameled Wood, Glass Top, 1970s, 30 x 54 In.	5625
Desk, 4 Drawers, Molded Edge, Casters, England, 1800, 33 x 23 x 25 In.	900
Desk, Baroque Revival, Rosewood, Celluloid, Abalone Inlay, Putti, Birds, Griffins, 42 x 55 In.	1210
Desk, Chair, A. Rosen, Rosewood, Removable Glass Shelves, 58 In., Chair 38 In. *illus*	1968
Desk, Chippendale, Embossed Gilt Leather, Gadroon, Openwork Corbels, 29 x 38 x 21 In.	207
Desk, Clerk's, Mahogany, Slant Front, Slatted Shelf, 3 Frieze Drawers, England, 55 x 72 In.	3000
Desk, Edwardian, Painted, Compartments, Slots, Drawers, Leather Insert, Carlton House, 36 x 41 In.	625
Desk, Fitted Interior, Star Inlay, Prospect Door, Diamond Shape, 1800s, 47 x 40 x 22 In.	1750
Desk, French Style, 2 Drawers, Nailed, Iron Pulls, Molded Edge, Cabriole Legs, 30 x 68 In.	420
Desk, G. Nakashima, Double Pedestal, Walnut, Signed, 1969, 29 x 60 x 30 In.	18750
Desk, G. Nakashima, Walnut, 2-Sided, Wall Mounted, 2 Drawers, 29 x 72 ½ In.	5625
Desk, Galle, Art Nouveau, Poppy Design, Side Drawers, 38 x 31 x 19 In. *illus*	236
Desk, Gilt, Acanthus, Stretcher, Shaped Top, Shell, 2 Dovetailed Drawers, 29 ½ x 56 In.	720
Desk, Hepplewhite, Mahogany, Fold-Out Top, Drawers, Pigeonholes, c.1800, 42 x 42 In.	390
Desk, Lift Top, Rosewood, Brass, Compartmented Interior, 1800, Miniature, 6 x 18 x 10 In.	96
Desk, Maple, Burl, Satinwood Veneer Inlay, 1900s, 40 x 30 In.	192
Desk, Maple, Fitted Interior, 4 Drawers, Brass Bail Pulls, 1790, 43 In.	390
Desk, Maple, Mother-Of-Pearl Inlay, Frieze Drawers, Block Legs, 1950s, 32 x 63 In.	4900
Desk, Maple, Satinwood Veneer, Inlay, 3 Drawers, Tapered Legs, 1900s, 40 x 30 In.	192
Desk, On Frame, Chestnut, Slant Front, Fitted Interior, Drawers, 1700s, 40 x 31 In. *illus*	118
Desk, Orin Raphael, 6 Drawers, Dividers, Pullouts, 30 x 56 x 32 In.	122
Desk, Overseer's, Mixed Wood, Slant Front, Plain Frieze, Pegged Legs, c.1810, 41 x 30 In.	1586
Desk, Oxbow, Chippendale, Mahogany, 6 Drawers, 44 x 42 In.	1089
Desk, Partners, Pedestals, Georgian Style, Mahogany, Tooled Leather, 50 x 72 In. *illus*	732
Desk, Partners, R.J. Horner, Pedestals, Mahogany, Winged Griffin, Serpentine Front, 30 x 56 In.	10080
Desk, Plantation, Mahogany, Scalloped Paneled Front, 2 Drawers, 62 x 36 x 24 In.	976
Desk, Rectangular Case, Hinged Lid, Leather Surface, Drawers, Animals, 1900, 38 x 42 In.	86
Desk, Roll Top, Rosewood, Leafy Crest, Shelves, Glazed Doors, Cabriole Legs, c.1840, 101 x 48 In.	2440
Desk, Roll Top, Walnut, 2 Pedestal, Indianapolis Cabinet Co., 53 x 60 In. *illus*	960
Desk, Slant Front, Chippendale, Inlay, 4 Graduated Drawers, c.1775, 42 x 40 In.	1320
Desk, Slant Front, Chippendale, Maple, Chestnut, Fitted, Rhode Island, c.1780, 39 x 36 In.	840
Desk, Slant Front, Walnut, Leaf & Flower Inlay, Block Feet, Continental, 1800s, 40 x 35 In.	540
Desk, Standing, Figured Walnut, Slant Front, Drawer, Virginia, c.1825, 48 x 41 In.	600
Desk, Stepped Back, Removable, France, 47 x 33 x 42 In.	140
Desk, Trustee, Shaker, Pine, Red, 4 Inset Doors, Shelves, Drawers, c.1850, 72 x 40 In.	6600
Desk, Vargueno, Oak, Leather, Double Doors, Pierced Bronze Escutcheons, 59 x 26 ½ In.	553
Desk, Victorian, Drop Front, Oak, Needlepoint Clad, Twist Carved Legs, 53 x 36 In.	1197

F

Furniture, Commode, Rococo Revival Style, Painted, Drawers, Marble Top, Italy, 36 x 32 In., Pair
$750

New Orleans Auction Galleries

Furniture, Commode, Walnut, Fruitwood, 3 Drawers, Inlaid Veneer, Italy, c.1790, 33 x 49 In.
$5,000

New Orleans Auction Galleries

Furniture, Credenza, Walnut, Glazed Doors, Shaped Top, Open Shelves, c.1860, 40 x 90 In.
$1,125

New Orleans Auction Galleries

TIP
Don't ship furniture from a hot to a cold climate or a wet to a dry climate, if it can be avoided. The wood will expand or contract, causing cracks and other damage.

FURNITURE

Furniture, Cupboard, Corner, Chippendale, Walnut, Glass & Paneled Doors, c.1790, 90 x 47 In.
$3,360

Brunk Auctions

Furniture, Cupboard, Corner, Federal, Cherry, 2 Sections, 87 x 54 In.
$502

Hess Auction Group

Furniture, Cupboard, Corner, Maple, 2 Parts, Glass Doors, Shelves, Drawers, Pa., c.1840, 83 x 49 In.
$900

Eldred's Auctioneers and Appraisers

Furniture, Cupboard, Hanging, Door, Glass Pane, Yellow, Sponge Paint, Bail Handle, 10 1/4 x 15 In.
$125

Eldred's Auctioneers and Appraisers

Furniture, Cupboard, Jelly, Blue Paint, 4 Interior Shelves, Bracket Base, c.1850, 58 1/2 x 37 In.
$813

Eldred's Auctioneers and Appraisers

Furniture, Cupboard, Pewter, Pine, Painted, Peg & Groove, Open Shelves, Door, 1800s, 87 x 33 In.
$2,280

Cowan's Auctions

Furniture, Cupboard, Pewter, Pine, Shelves, Drawers, Door, Washington Courthouse, c.1825, 75 In.
$1,200

Garth's Auctioneers & Appraisers

F

168

Furniture, Cupboard, Storage, Pine, 2 Doors, Shelves, Painted, c.1850, 70 x 47 In. $182

James D. Julia Auctioneers

Furniture, Desk, Chair, A. Rosen, Rosewood, 2 Removable Glass Shelves, 58 In., Chair, 38 In. $1,968

Palm Beach Modern Auctions

Furniture, Desk, Galle, Art Nouveau, Poppy Design, Side Drawers, 38 x 31 x 19 In. $236

Burchard Galleries

Furniture, Desk, On Frame, Chestnut, Slant Front, Fitted Interior, Drawers, 1700s, 40 x 31 In. $118

Hess Auction Group

Furniture, Desk, Partners, Pedestals, Georgian Style, Mahogany, Tooled Leather, 50 x 72 In. $732

Neal Auction Co.

Furniture, Desk, Roll Top, Walnut, 2 Pedestal, Indianapolis Cabinet Co., 53 x 60 In. $960

Furniture, Desk, Wooton, Aesthetic Revival, Walnut, Bird's-Eye Maple Panels, c.1875, 70 x 43 In. $9,075

James D. Julia Auctioneers

Brunk Auctions

Furniture, Desk, Wooton, Walnut, Eastlake Style, Barreled Doors, Fitted Interior, 1800s, 70 x 44 In.
$6,765

Cowan's Auctions

Furniture, Dinette Set, Russel Wright, Drop Leaf, 2 Chairs, Conant Ball, c.1950, 3 Piece
$225

Selkirk Auctioneers & Appraisers

Furniture, Dinner Gong, G. Stickley, Oak, Stand, Red Decal, c.1902, 36 x 31 In.
$5,625

Rago Arts and Auction Center

Furniture, Dresser, Frankl, Station Wagon, Mahogany, Leather, Johnson, 1940s, 32 x 66 In.
$1,250

Rago Arts and Auction Center

Furniture, Dumbwaiter, George III, Mahogany, Round Tiers, Turned, Splayed Legs, c.1785, 46 In.
$625

New Orleans Auction Galleries

Furniture, Etagere, Charles Tisch, Rosewood, Inlay, Doors, Open Shelves, Mirrors, 1800s, 54 In.
$875

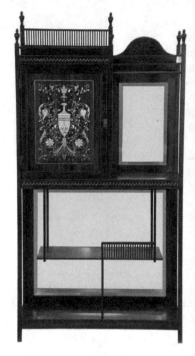

Naudeau's Auction Gallery

Furniture, Etagere, Chrome Frame, Glass Shelves, Brass Corners, X-Stretchers, 72 x 30 In.
$1,375

New Orleans Auction Galleries

Desk, Walnut, Satinwood Veneer, 8 Drawers Over 3 Drawers, Demilune, 1900, 35 x 54 In.	270
Desk, Wegner, Andreas Tuck, Teak, Brass, 1960s, 28 x 81 x 36 In.	8125
Desk, Wooton, Aesthetic Revival, Walnut, Bird's-Eye Maple Panels, c.1875, 70 x 43 In. ..... *illus*	9075
Desk, Wooton, Walnut, Eastlake Style, Barreled Doors, Fitted Interior, 1800s, 70 x 44 In. *illus*	6765
Desk, Zebra Wood, Leather Top, Diagonal Back Shelf, Glass, 29 x 64 x 36 In.	354
Dinette Set, Russel Wright, Drop Leaf, 2 Chairs, Conant Ball, c.1950, 3 Piece .... *illus*	225
Dining Set, Gehry, Table Maple, Glass Top, 4 Chairs, Marked, 1997, Chair 33 ½ In., 5 Piece	4063
Dinner Gong, G. Stickley, Oak, Stand, Red Decal, c.1902, 36 x 31 In. .... *illus*	5625
Display Case, Beveled Glass, Elephant Ivory, Reeded Bun Feet, Drawer, 1800, 8 x 22 x 12 In....	1680
Dresser, Arne Vodder, 2 Banks Of 4 Drawers, Sibast, 1960s, 32 x 78 x 19 In.	6875
Dresser, Frankl, Station Wagon, Mahogany, Leather, Johnson, 1940s, 32 x 66 In. .... *illus*	1250
Dresser, G. Stickley, 9 Drawers, Turned Knobs, c.1907, 50 x 36 In.	4375
Dresser, George III, 2 Drawers, Cupboard Door, 3 Drawers, 1800s, 40 ½ x 79 In.	875
Dresser, R.J. Horner, Rococo Revival, Mahogany, Beveled Mirror, Frieze, c.1890, 78 x 41 In.	365
Dresser, Shaker, Pine, 5 Graduated Drawers, Walnut Pulls, Mass., 1848, 42 ½ x 36 In.	8400
Dresser, Welsh, 3 Drawers, Reeded Edges, Cup Hooks, Molded Cornice, 73 x 60 In.	360
Dry Sink, Blue, Door, Panels, Shelf, Swag Base, 34 x 33 ½ In.	450
Dry Sink, Light Blue, Door, Knob, 1900s, 48 x 16 In.	180
Dry Sink, Pine, Back Shelf, Left-Hand Drawer, 2 Paneled Cupboard Doors, 1800s, 52 In.	168
Dry Sink, Pine, Gallery Back, Side Shelf & Drawer Over Well, 2 Doors, 39 x 40 In.	2375
Dumbwaiter, George III, Mahogany, Round Tiers, Turned, Splayed Legs, c.1785, 46 In... *illus*	625
Easel, Baroque, Giltwood, Carved Phoenix Birds, Floral Swags, Winged Masks, 86 In.	2250
Easel, Stained Beech, Bent Canes, 3 Legs, Metal, Austria, c.1906, 66 ½ x 23 ½ In.	1250
Etagere, 3 Tiers, Mahogany, Base Drawer, Fluted Baluster, Turned Feet, Casters, 46 x 27 x 16 In. .	896
Etagere, Charles Tisch, Rosewood, Inlay, Doors, Open Shelves, Mirrors, 1800s, 54 In. ..... *illus*	875
Etagere, Chrome Frame, Glass Shelves, Brass Corners, X-Stretchers, 72 x 30 In. .... *illus*	1375
Etagere, Walnut, Marble Top, Molded Shield Crest, Leaves, Oak Branches, 94 x 51 In.	1331
Footstool, Dmitri Omersa, Pig, Floppy Ears, Leather Eyes, Metal Feet, 1900s, 17 x 25 x 12 In...	468
Footstool, Ebonized Bamboo, Gilt, Flared Legs, Upholstered Top, c.1890, 15 x 19 In. .... *illus*	355
Footstool, Hinged Lid, Neoclassical, Mahogany, Open Interior, Upholstered, 1800s, 18 x 16 In.	1125
Footstool, Louis XVI, Oval, Brass Tacks, Fluted Legs, 6 ½ x 14 ½ In.	1089
Footstool, Neoclassical, Pickled Mahogany, Scrolled Base, Leather Cushion, 15 In., Pair.........	1625
Footstool, Pig, Leather, 12 x 18 In.	720
Footstool, Queen Anne Style, Mahogany, Carved, Cabriole Legs, False Fur, c.1900, 19 x 26 In. .	246
Frame, Giltwood, Leaves, Gadroon, 69 x 100 In.	2125
Frame, Louis XIII, Giltwood, Carved, Acanthus Scroll, Garlands, 1600s, 67 x 97 In. .... *illus*	3000
Frame, Louis XIV, Giltwood Molding, Carved, Shell Cartouches, c.1900, 58 x 69 In.......... *illus*	900
Frame, Repousse Peacocks, Half Sun, Leaves, Silver-Plated Copper, Art Nouveau, 6 ½ x 9 In. *illus*	195
Hall Stand, Art Deco, Mirror, Drip Pan, Leaves, Tendrils, 74 x 33 In.	358
Hall Stand, Iron, Mirror, 75 ½ x 28 In..	544
Hall Tree, Black Forest Style, Carved Bear In Tree, Standing Bear, 1900s, 79 x 21 In.	720
Highboy, Queen Anne, Cherry, Cove-Molded Cornice, 10 Drawers, 72 x 35 In.	1815
Highboy, Queen Anne, Walnut, Drawers, Fan Carved, Cabriole Legs, 1700s, 73 x 38 In..... *illus*	2880
Highboy, William & Mary, Oak, Cornice Over 3 Drawers, Lower 3-Drawer Section, 1700s, 62 x 41 In.	875
Highchair, Limbert, Oak, Leather Seat, Tacks, Tray On Pin Hinge, 35 x 18 In.	250
Highchair, Spindle Back, Original Paint, Pennsylvania, 35 In............................. *illus*	75
Humidor, Mahogany, Doghouse, Lift Roof, Cigar Storage, Bun Feet, 1800s, 8 x 10 In..............	280
Humidor, Marble Top, Inlay, 1 Drawer, 1 Door, Open Cabinet, Short Feet, 32 x 19 In.	1440
Kneeler, Prie-Dieu, Bobbin-Turned Cruciform Back Splat, Top Shape Feet, Armrest, 34 x 18 In. .	200
Lap Desk, Burl, Slant Front, c.1800, 9 ¼ x 21 ½ In...	708
Lap Desk, Curly Maple, Bone Inlay, Lid, Eagle, Figures, Divided Interior, c.1840, 18 x 10 In. *illus*	210
Lap Desk, Rosewood Veneer, Inlaid Quatrefoil, Eagle, Brass, Fitted Interior, 1800, 5 x 14 x 10 In.	84
Lap Desk, Wood, Inlaid, Thistle, Geometric, Leather, Box, 17 x 11 x 5 In.	59
Lectern, Eagle Form, Outstretched Wings, The Bible Rests, Fully Detailed, 67 x 25 x 24 In.	3000
Lectern, Eagle, Perched, Wings Out, Head Down, Roughhewn Base, 38 In.	423
Letter Box, Mahogany, Fruitwood Veneer, Slant Front, Pull-Out Desk, Fitted Interior, 12 x 16 In.	281
Library Steps, 4 Risers, Spiral, Mahogany, 1900s, 59 In...	375
Library Steps, Ladder, Collapsing, Wood, Brown Leather, Brass Tacking, Cuffs, 91 In.............	1920
Library Steps, Mahogany, Folding, England, c.1875, 94 ½ x 12 ½ In...............................	3750

Furniture, Footstool, Ebonized Bamboo, Gilt, Flared Legs, Upholstered Top, c.1890, 15 x 19 In.
$355

Neal Auction Co.

Furniture, Frame, Louis XIII, Giltwood, Carved, Acanthus Scroll, Garlands, 1600s, 67 x 97 In.
$3,000

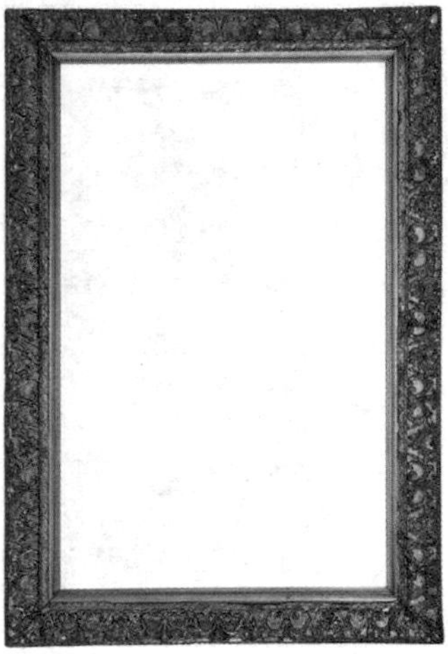

Brunk Auctions

Furniture, Frame, Louis XIV, Giltwood Molding, Carved, Shell Cartouches, c.1900, 58 x 69 In.
$900

Brunk Auctions

F

FURNITURE

Furniture, Frame, Repousse Peacocks, Half Sun, Leaves, Silver-Plated Copper, Art Nouveau, 6 ½ x 9 In.
$195

Treadway Gallery

Furniture, Highboy, Queen Anne, Walnut, Drawers, Fan Carved, Cabriole Legs, 1700s, 73 x 38 In.
$2,880

Cowan's Auctions

Furniture, Highchair, Spindle Back, Original Paint, Pennsylvania, 35 In.
$75

Hess Auction Group

T I P

Don't lock furniture with antique locks. If they stick, it is almost impossible to open the door or drawer without damaging the wood.

Furniture, Lap Desk, Curly Maple, Bone Inlay, Lid, Eagle, Figures, Divided Interior, c.1840, 18 x 10 In.
$210

Garth's Auctioneers & Appraisers

Furniture, Library Steps, Mahogany, Turned Post, Leather Treads, Brass Finial, England, 60 In.
$625

Neal Auction Co.

Furniture, Love Seat, Wormley, Mahogany, Mohair, Dunbar, 1960s, 31 x 48 In.
$1,375

Rago Arts and Auction Center

Furniture, Mirror, Brass Frame, Embossed, 48 x 29 In.
$295

Hess Auction Group

Furniture, Mirror, Bronze, Art Nouveau, Woman, Painted, Marble Base, Moreau, c.1910, 20 In.
$300

Cowan's Auctions

Library Steps, Mahogany, Spiral, Turned Tapered Support, Brass Finial, 1900s, 63 x 19 In.....	550
Library Steps, Mahogany, Turned Post, Leather Treads, Brass Finial, England, 60 In..... *illus*	625
Love Seat, Wormley, Mahogany, Mohair, Dunbar, 1960s, 31 x 48 In. .... *illus*	1375
Mirror, Baroque, Giltwood, Oak Leaves, Scrollwork, Pierced, c.1885, 36 x 29 In.	1750
Mirror, Black Forest, Antlers, Oval, c.1920, 40 x 24 In.	2000
Mirror, Bradley & Hubbard, Pierced Crest, Impressed Frame, Round, Brass, Easel Back, 17 In..	625
Mirror, Brass Frame, Embossed, 48 x 29 In. .... *illus*	295
Mirror, Brass, Beveled, Cherub Design, Easel Back, 9 x 11 In.	108
Mirror, Brass, Silvered, Rococo Style, Indian, Wood, 42 x 43 In.	125
Mirror, Brass, Yellow, Raw Finish, Square, Unbeveled Pane, 1900s	138
Mirror, Bronze, Art Nouveau, Woman, Painted, Marble Base, Moreau, c.1910, 20 In. .... *illus*	300
Mirror, Burl, Live Edge, 25 x 50 In.	125
Mirror, Carved, Giltwood, Pediment, Scrolling Foliage, 1800, 44 x 28 In.	300
Mirror, Carved, Wood, Gilt, 40 x 31 x 30 x 24 In.	343
Mirror, Cheval, Aesthetic Revival, Maple, Faux Bamboo, c.1890, 66 x 35 In. .... *illus*	640
Mirror, Cheval, Georgian, Mahogany, Oval, Saber Legs, Beveled, 64 x 24 In.	192
Mirror, Circular, Brass, Frame, Turnable, 1900s, 16 In.	72
Mirror, Convex, Parcel Giltwood, Dolphins, Ebonized Eagle & Beading, 51 In., Pair	8750
Mirror, Cushion, Giltwood, Rococo Design, Crest Decorated, France, c.1875, 54 x 34 In.	938
Mirror, Dressing, G. Stickley, c.1903, 69 x 28 In.	10000
Mirror, Elongated, Hexagonal, Roses, Leaves, Oval, Wrought Iron, 1920	365
Mirror, Federal, Carved, Gilt, Convex, Round, Eagle, Scrolling Leaf Tips, 43 x 24 In.	1875
Mirror, Federal, Giltwood, Molded, Acorn Drop Finials, Signed, TH Tisdale, 46 x 26 In.... *illus*	540
Mirror, Federal, Giltwood, Reverse Painted Panel, Columns, c.1835, 48 x 28 In. .... *illus*	420
Mirror, Figural, Bird, Dragon Decoration, 1800s, 28 In.	108
Mirror, Figures, Dragon, Bronze, Japan, 5 In.	450
Mirror, Frame, Multiple Levels Of Classic Laurel & Acanthus, 1800s, 36 x 29 In.	396
Mirror, French Rococo, Giltwood, Flowers & Rocaille Work, c.1900, 30 x 26 In., Pair	938
Mirror, Giltwood, Aesthetic, Oval, Cane Design, Flowers, Fruit, Branches, c.1890, 43 x 34 In. ..	512
Mirror, Giltwood, Bowknot Crest, Floral Garland, Molded Surround, 78 x 41 In.	1098
Mirror, Giltwood, Carved, Leafy, Rococo, c.1820, 60 x 41 In.	2880
Mirror, Giltwood, Girandole Bull's-Eye, Eagle, Scrolling Acanthus, 1800s	2375
Mirror, Giltwood, Girandole, Ebonized, Carved, Candelabra, Cherubs, Louis XVI, 44 x 36 In...	384
Mirror, Giltwood, Marble, Flower Basket Crest, Finials, Bilboa, Spain, c.1900, 27 x 12 In. *illus*	1800
Mirror, Giltwood, Molded, Grapes, Leaves, Pierced Vines, c.1915, 61 x 33 In...................... *illus*	2500
Mirror, Giltwood, Original Gilt Surface, 38 x 31 In...	610
Mirror, Giltwood, Parcel Ebonized, Carved, Female Mask, Sphinxes, c.1890, 67 x 28 In............	1875
Mirror, Giltwood, Pier, Pendants, Mother & Child Frieze, Columns, c.1810, 47 x 32 x 6 In.	854
Mirror, Giltwood, Pierced Rocaille, Canopy Crest, Scrolls, Flowerheads, 48 In., Pair...............	3000
Mirror, Giltwood, Spilt Baluster, Acanthus Corners, c.1930, 53 x 28 In.	976
Mirror, Giltwood, Square Corners, France, 56 x 31 In.	938
Mirror, Hepplewhite, Giltwood, Gesso, Phoenixes, Flowers, Urn, Ribbon, Putti, Swags, 54 x 26 In.	1512
Mirror, Italian, Venetian, Cartouche Shape, Carved, Gesso, Giltwood, Painted, 1900s, 28 x 16 In..	136
Mirror, J. Mozer, Soul Window, Kevlar Reinforced, Resin, 33 x 36 In...	2000
Mirror, Joints, Glass Strapwork, Frame, Octagonal, Venetian Style, Italy, 1900s, 43 x 31 In.	1875
Mirror, Leafy Scroll, Gadroon Designs, Faux Burl Stiles, 84 x 65 x 12 In.	266
Mirror, Louis XIV Style, Giltwood, Shell, Bellflower, Pierced, Segmented Plates, 53 In.	1250
Mirror, Louis XVI Style, Cream Paint, Giltwood, Wreath, Swags, Egg & Dart Trim, 55 In..........	1375
Mirror, Mahogany, Giltwood, Phoenix Figure, Chippendale, Ginsburg & Levy, c.1775, 44 x 23 In..	585
Mirror, Maitland-Smith Design, Ornate, Frame, Pair, 39 x 20 In.	265
Mirror, Napoleon III, Giltwood, Branches & Lattice Frame, c.1890, 48 x 38 In. .... *illus*	1500
Mirror, Napoleonic, Prisoner-Of-War, Bone Appliques, Cherubs, Lions, c.1810, 31 In. ...... *illus*	3900
Mirror, Oak, Adjustable, Pittsburgh Plate Glass Co., Chicago, Floor, c.1910, 75 x 28 In............	1100
Mirror, Ornate Silver, Floral, Fancy, Bevel, 10 x 10 x 1 ½ In.	83
Mirror, Oval, Brass, Beveled, Floral & Lattice Design, Cherubs, Easel Back, 1900, 13 x 17 In....	48
Mirror, Oval, Venetian Glass Frame, 2-Tone, 42 x 22 In.	1553
Mirror, Painted, Giltwood, 57 x 29 x 30 x 20 In.	937
Mirror, Palm Trees, Sun, Cut Mirror Sections, 48 x 31 In.	118
Mirror, Patinated & Polished Brass, Black, Gold, Karl Springer, 1980s, 60 x 41 In.	3250
Mirror, Pier, Arched Top, Minerva Head, Raised Panels, Rosettes, c.1870, 93 x 34 In..............	750

Furniture, Mirror, Cheval, Aesthetic Revival, Maple, Faux Bamboo, c.1890, 66 x 35 In.
$640

Neal Auction Co.

Furniture, Mirror, Federal, Giltwood, Molded, Acorn Drop Finials, Signed, TH Tisdale, 46 x 26 In.
$540

Cowan's Auctions

TIP
Don't retouch gold leaf picture frames or other gold trim with anything but real gold leaf.

Furniture, Mirror, Federal, Giltwood, Reverse Painted Panel, Columns, c.1835, 48 x 28 In. $420

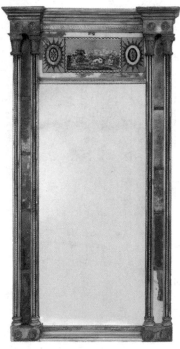

Eldred's Auctioneers and Appraisers

Furniture, Mirror, Giltwood, Marble, Flower Basket Crest, Finials, Bilboa, Spain, c.1900, 27 x 12 In. $1,800

Cowan's Auctions

Furniture, Mirror, Giltwood, Molded, Grapes, Leaves, Pierced Vines, c.1915, 61 x 33 In. $2,500

New Orleans Auction Galleries

Furniture, Mirror, Napoleon III, Giltwood, Branches & Lattice Frame, c.1890, 48 x 38 In. $1,500

Neal Auction Co.

Furniture, Mirror, Napoleonic, Prisoner-Of-War, Bone Appliques, Cherubs, Lions, c.1810, 31 In. $3,900

Eldred's Auctioneers and Appraisers

Furniture, Mirror, Regency, Convex, Giltwood, Eagle Crest, Leaves, Ribbon Molding, 44 x 30 In. $2,400

Eldred's Auctioneers and Appraisers

Furniture, Mirror, Shaving, Hardwood, Mother-Of-Pearl Inlay, Lions, Chinese, 1900s, 28 x 19 In. $720

Cowan's Auctions

F

Mirror, Pier, Cream Paint, Gilt Classical Figures, Egg & Dart Molding, 66 x 39 In.	2125
Mirror, Red Lacquer Surround, Giltwood, Scrollwork, c.1930, England, 64 x 30 In.	2000
Mirror, Regency, Convex, Giltwood, Eagle Crest, Leaves, Ribbon Molding, 44 x 30 In. *illus*	2400
Mirror, Reverse Painted, Riverscape, 1800s, 35 x 21 In.	120
Mirror, Rococo Revival, Giltwood, Carved, Molded Oval Frame, Peace Trophee, c.1850, 36 x 37 In.	488
Mirror, Rococo Style, Leafy Scroll Crest, Grapevine Side Trim, 72 x 29 x 9 In.	177
Mirror, Shaving, Hardwood, Mother-Of-Pearl Inlay, Lions, Chinese, 1900s, 28 x 19 In. *illus*	720
Mirror, Tabernacle, Federal, Giltwood, Grape Leaf Tablet, Rope Twist Columns, 56 x 31 In.	750
Mirror, Trifold, Oak Frame, Carved Legs On Casters, 1800s, 67 x 27 x 24 In.	1180
Mirror, Vanity, Oval, Floral, Figural Highlights, Porcelain, 1900	47
Ottoman, Tufted, Blue Upholstery, Silk Fringe, Casters, Round, 16 x 39 In.	437
Overmantel Mirror, see Architectural category.	
Pedestal, Composition, Molded, Inset Panels, Basket Of Flowers, 1900s, 35 x 19 In. *illus*	275
Pedestal, Empire, Mahogany, Ram's Head Masks, 36 x 24 In.	1750
Pedestal, Marble, Tapered Ring-Turned Column, Round Top, 1800, 42 In., 3 Piece	225
Pedestal, Neoclassical Style, Kingwood, Marble Top, Inlay, Block Feet, 49 x 12 In., Pair	563
Pedestal, Neoclassical, Mirror, 50 ½ In., Pair	281
Pedestal, Tapered, Stepped Square Top, Bronze Leaf & Ribbon Mounts, 36 x 15 In.	254
Pie Safe, Butterscotch Over Blue Paint, Punched Tin Panels, Urns, 1800s, 64 In. *illus*	3304
Pie Safe, Country Store, Oak, Glass Sides, 3 Shelves, Square, 32 x 22 ½ In. *illus*	236
Pie Safe, Pine, Grain Painted, 2 Doors, Screen Panels, 53 x 50 In.	1440
Pie Safe, Pine, John Evans, Blue, Punched Tin Panels, Interior, Long Drawer, c.1850, 57 x 39 In.	1750
Pie Safe, Punched Tin Panels, 2 Doors, Drawer, Scalloped Apron, Yellow, 52 x 40 In.	960
Pie Safe, Walnut, Star Punched Tin Panels, Dovetailed Drawer, c.1850, 46 x 52 In. *illus*	1320
Play Pen, Wood, Folding Floor, Slatted, Built-In Ball Toy, Casters, c.1950, 27 x 38 In.	325
Podium, Eagle, Oak, Turned Sphere, Column, To The Glory Of God, 61 ¾ x 19 In.	1008
Rack, Baking, 3 Shelves, S-Scroll, 48 ¾ x 15 ¾ In.	117
Rack, Baking, 4 Shelves, Marble Tray, S-Scroll, 4 Trays, 77 x 54 In.	128
Rack, Baking, Iron, Brass Accents, 3 Tiers, Scrolled Crest, Black, France, 80 x 42 In.	600
Rack, Kimono, Engraved, Grass, 62 x 72 In.	420
Rack, Plate, Rohlfs, Cutouts, Dark Brown Wood, 1902, 54 ¾ x 35 ¾ In.	5937
Rack, Quilt, Oak, Mortised, Pegged, 35 ½ x 41 In.	33
Rack, Wine Board, Primitive Style, Tapered Holes, 1900s, 58 x 38 In.	330
Recamier, Empire, Mahogany, Giltwood, Portugal, c.1810, 36 ¾ x 90 In. *illus*	6875
Recamier, Regency, Rosewood, Partial Back, Outscrolled Arm, c.1835, 33 x 80 In. *illus*	1625
Rocker, 2-Slat Back, Shaped Armrests, Painted, Child's, c.1850, 21 x 12 In.	105
Rocker, Art Deco, Tubular, Slat Steel, Bicycle Wheel Rockers, 1920, 31 ½ In.	140
Rocker, Bentwood Twig, Plank Seat, 37 x 22 In.	108
Rocker, Bentwood, Woven Seat, 1900s	58
Rocker, Black Paint, Ocher Striping, Birdcage Crest Rail, Raised Comb, 1800s, 15 In.	240
Rocker, Canada Goose, Glass Eyes, Painted, C.M. Cunningham, Dover, Ma., 1900s, 23 x 36 In.	72
Rocker, Chrome, Scrolls, Upholstered Seat, 40 ½ In.	117
Rocker, Eames, Molded Plastic, Yellow, 1950s, 27 x 25 In.	1500
Rocker, G. Nakashima, Lounge, Walnut, Hickory, Single Arm, 1978, 35 x 31 In. *illus*	6875
Rocker, Oak Slat, 48 x 24 In.	88
Rocker, Platform, Wicker, Braided Arms, Arched Legs, 47 x 27 In.	244
Rocker, Pressed Back, Cat, Kitten, Victorian, 29 In.	99
Rocker, Ralph Rapson, Ash Frame, Canvas Webbing, Inscribed C S Knoll, 1945, 27 x 29 In. *illus*	1375
Rocker, Shaker, Acorn Finials, Mushroom-Capped Arms, Rush Seat, Child's, 1800s, 16 In.	144
Rocker, Shaker, Maple, Birch, Tall Finials, 5 Slats, Rush Seat, c.1860, 47 x 16 ½ In.	6600
Rocker, V. Kagan, E. Wilson, Embroidered, Wool, Walnut, Leather, 1960s-80s, 39 In. *illus*	11875
Rocker, V. Kagan, Sculpted Oak, 1970s, 41 x 33 In.	6250
Rocker, V. Kagan, Wood, Sculpted, Enameled, White, 1970s, 39 x 32 ½ In.	3750
Rocker, Walter Lamb, Bronze, Nylon Rope, Arms, Brown Jordan, 1950s, 32 x 22 In. *illus*	1875
Rocker, Windsor, Comb Back, Walnut, Pine, Writing Arm, Painted, 1800s, 43 In. *illus*	270
Screens are also listed in the Architectural and Fireplace categories.	
Screen, 3-Panel, Folding, Butterflies, Flamingos, Herons, c.1950, 65 x 60 In.	510
Screen, 3-Panel, Garden Scene, William Oden Waller, 69 x 29 In.	1920
Screen, 3-Panel, Landscape, Branches, Blooms, Scalloped Top, George Parker, 62 x 79 In. *illus*	584
Screen, 3-Panel, Teak, Waisted Fabric Panels, 60 x 60 In.	3750

Furniture, Pedestal, Composition, Molded, Inset Panels, Basket Of Flowers, 1900s, 35 x 19 In.
$275

New Orleans Auction Galleries

Get What You Pay For
Be sure you get what you pay for. Many designers created handmade pieces, then had the designs mass-produced. If the furniture was very popular, it was often copied. Copies are worth much less than original works.

Furniture, Pie Safe, Butterscotch Over Blue Paint, Punched Tin Panels, Urns, 1800s, 64 In.
$3,304

Hess Auction Group

Furniture, Pie Safe, Country Store, Oak, Glass Sides, 3 Shelves, Square, 32 x 22 ½ In.
$236

Hess Auction Group

Furniture, Pie Safe, Walnut, Star Punched Tin Panels, Dovetailed Drawer, c.1850, 46 x 52 In.
$1,320

Garth's Auctioneers & Appraisers

Golden Oak

Golden oak is Victorian, Mission, and Art Deco. The Golden Oak period (1880–1920) is named for the wood that was most popular for furniture at the time. Walnut was used when Victorian-style furniture was first made, but it became harder to find. The most available wood was oak. Cabinetmakers began to use "quarter cut" oak, which made a board with attractive graining patterns. The oak was given a light golden finish as well as darker finishes. The furniture was made not only of oak, but also had parts of ash, beech, maple, and hickory.

Screen, 4-Panel, Forest, Deer, Stream, Oil, Varnished Silver Leaf, 72 x 64 In.	1920
Screen, 6-Panel, Wood, Inset Porcelain Tiles, Famille Verte, 75 x 90 In.	13310
Screen, 8-Panel, Black Lacquer, Figures In Landscapes, 84 x 128 In. _illus_	130
Screen, 8-Panel, Porcelain, Wood, Figural & Flowers, 1800s, 31 x 50 In.	570
Screen, Cinnabar, Black Lacquer, Garden Scene, 2-Sided, Chinese Characters, Stand, 29 In.	7500
Screen, Dressing, Majorelle, Carved, Silk Fabric On Panels, Art Nouveau, 66 x 53 In.	2057
Screen, Table Plaque, House, River, Mountains, 2 Seals On Bottom, 1900, 10 ⅞ x 7 ½ In.	677
Secretary, Drop Front, Inlay, 3 Drawers, Continental, 40 x 20 x 57 In.	878
Secretary, Federal, Roll Top, Inlay, Eagle, Glazed Doors, Shelves, Drawers, c.1815, 44 x 40 In. _illus_	1045
Secretary, French Provincial, Fruitwood, Drop Front, Fitted Interior, 26 x 20 In.	938
Secretary, George III, Drop Front, Mahogany, Broken-Arch Top, 1900s, 88 In.	1020
Secretary, Louis XV Style, Kingwood, Bombe, Fitted, Marble, Drawers, c.1910, 59 In. _illus_	1063
Secretary, Mahogany, Drawer Over Drop Front, Lower Drawers, c.1875, 56 x 39 In. _illus_	688
Secretary, Mitchell & Rammelsberg, Gothic Revival, Fold-Out, c.1850, 105 In. _illus_	1320
Secretary, Sheraton, Mahogany, Glass & Paneled Doors, Drawers, Shelves, 1820, 78 x 41 In.	1140
Server, Chinese Style, Sliding Top, Over Drawer, Cupboard Doors, 1900, 32 x 38 In.	91
Server, Corner, Biedermeier, 3 Tiers, Bowfront Shelves, Column, Saber Legs, c.1900, 59 In.	180
Server, Empire Style, Mahogany, Marble Top, Doors, Gilt Bronze, c. 1885, 40 x 92 In. _illus_	1875
Settee, Adam Style, Satinwood, Caned Back, Arms & Seat, Painted Designs, 1800s, 34 In. _illus_	1250
Settee, Belter, Rococo Revival, Serpentine, Rosalie With Grapes, c.1855, 42 x 67 In.	2250
Settee, Black Forest, Walnut, Boar Hunt, Animal Pelt, Arms, c.1890, 58 x 67 In. _illus_	2400
Settee, G. Nakashima, Walnut, Arms, 1965, 31 x 35 In.	5938
Settee, G. Nakashima, Walnut, Plaid Cushion, 1965, 30 ½ x 59 ¾ In.	8750
Settee, Hitchcock Chair Co., Double Back, Lyre Supports, Rush Seat, 34 ½ x 18 In.	1452
Settee, Louis XV, Cherry, Serpentine Back, Cushions, Reeded Arms, Cabriole Legs, 34 ½ x 55 In.	184
Settee, Majorelle, Mahogany, Carved, Curved Back, France, c.1900, 30 x 54 In.	937
Settee, Meridienne, Mahogany, Cane Seat & Back, Arm, West Indies, 1800s, 83 In. _illus_	2432
Settee, Sheraton, Mahogany, 3 Shieldback, Scroll Arms, Tapered Legs, c.1890, 55 x 38 In.	365
Settee, Windsor, Double Back, Spindles, Bamboo Turnings, Arms, c.1810, 34 x 4 In.	2280
Settle, George III, Oak, Paneled Back, Plank Seat, Open Arms, c.1890, 41 x 59 In.	688
Settle, Poplar, Green Paint, Stenciled, 3 Shaped Splats, Plank Seat, Arms, Pa., 1800s, 78 In. _illus_	738
Shelf, A. Hovmand-Olsen, Teak, Laminate, Brass, Denmark, 1960s, 8 ½ x 59 In.	2500
Shelf, Black Forest, Grapevines, Clusters, Triangular, Bracket, 24 x 20 ½ In.	812
Shelf, Hanging, Georgian, Mahogany, Arched Pediment, 3 Shelves, 1900s, 48 x 30 In., Pair	1235
Shelf, Hanging, Pine, Whale End, Smoked Decoration, 4 Shelves, c.1870, 32 In.	438
Shelf, Mahogany, Mystical Dragon, Continental, 21 x 12 In.	150
Shelf, Mirror, Phillip Lloyd Powell, Shaped Wood, Grain, Giltwood, Walnut, 72 x 17 In.	8750
Shelf, Parade Horse, Carved, Wood, Bracket, 8 x 7 ½ In., Pair	90
Shelf, Poplar, Fretwork, Nudes, Arrows, Leaves, Pinwheels, Flowers, c.1939, 41 x 22 In. _illus_	292
Shelf, Shaped Top, Corinthian Style Backboard, Carved, Bracket, 19 ½ x 22 In.	250
Shelf, Wall, Display, Grain Painted, Hourglass Elements, Scalloped Crest, 25 x 29 In.	90
Shelf, Wall, Walnut, Stag, Antlers, Shaped Brackets, Leaves, c.1880, 15 ¼ x 15 In.	93
Shelf, Wall, Wood, Curtains & Woman's Health, Nude Woman & Cherub, 44 x 26 In.	968
Sideboard, B. Rohne, Kanji Script, Bronze, Etched, Patinated, Enameled, c.1981, 30 x 78 In.	4375
Sideboard, D. Pabst, Mahogany, Hooded Top, Shelves, c.1880, 104 x 74 In. _illus_	11875
Sideboard, D. Pabst, Walnut, Gallery Top, Mirror, Marble, Drawers, c.1880, 104 x 75 In. _illus_	10200
Sideboard, Empire, Tiger Maple, Stepped Top, Drawers, Paneled Doors, 1800s, 63 x 74 In. _illus_	1045
Sideboard, Federal, Inlay, Dovetailed Drawers, Doors, c.1800, 39 x 73 x 27 In. _illus_	16800
Sideboard, Federal, Mahogany, Figured Birch, 4 Drawers, 2 Doors, 42 x 48 In.	938
Sideboard, Federal, Mahogany, Inlay, 2 Drawers, Crossbanded Arched Apron, 41 x 73 In.	1936
Sideboard, G. Stickley, Oak, Iron Hinges, 2 Doors, 4 Drawers, 8 Legs, 49 x 69 In.	8750
Sideboard, Glass, Inset Marble, Drawer, 2 Doors, Side Cabinets, 78 x 74 x 19 In.	708
Sideboard, Hepplewhite Style, Mahogany, Divided Drawer, Shelf, 1800s, 37 x 69 In.	354
Sideboard, Limbert, Oak, Cutout Gallery, Metal Label, c.1910, 43 x 57 In. _illus_	4062
Sideboard, Limbert, Oak, Drawers, Doors, Mirror, Shelf, Branded, c.1908, 58 x 60 In. _illus_	4063
Sideboard, Louis XVI, Mahogany, Ormolu Mount, Marble Top, 1900s, 40 x 98 ½ In.	861
Sideboard, Mahogany, Bowfront, 1-Drawer, Spade Feet, c.1820, 36 x 49 In.	320
Sideboard, Mahogany, Shaped Top, 3 Drawers, 4 Cupboard Doors, 1800s, 39 In.	2400
Sideboard, Mahogany, Shaped Top, Frieze Drawer, Side Cabinets, c.1790, 39 x 66 In.	2048
Sideboard, Marble, Beveled Glass, Carved Supports, Mirror, 75 x 57 In.	708

Furniture, Recamier, Empire, Mahogany, Giltwood, Portugal, c.1810, 36¾ x 90 In.
$6,875

Heritage Auctions

Furniture, Recamier, Regency, Rosewood, Partial Back, Outscrolled Arm, c.1835, 33 x 80 In.
$1,625

New Orleans Auction Galleries

Furniture, Rocker, G. Nakashima, Lounge, Walnut, Hickory, Single Arm, 1978, 35 x 31 In.
$6,875

Rago Arts and Auction Center

Furniture, Rocker, Ralph Rapson, Ash Frame, Canvas Webbing, Inscribed C S Knoll, 1945, 27 x 29 In.
$1,375

Los Angeles Modern Auctions

Furniture, Rocker, V. Kagan, E. Wilson, Embroidered, Wool, Walnut, Leather, 1960s-80s, 39 In.
$11,875

Rago Arts and Auction Center

Furniture, Rocker, Walter Lamb, Bronze, Nylon Rope, Arms, Brown Jordan, 1950s, 32 x 22 In.
$1,875

Rago Arts and Auction Center

Furniture, Rocker, Windsor, Comb Back, Walnut, Pine, Writing Arm, Painted, 1800s, 43 In.
$270

Cowan's Auctions

Furniture, Screen, 3-Panel, Landscape, Branches, Blooms, Scalloped Top, George Parker, 62 x 79 In.
$584

Cowan's Auctions

Furniture, Screen, 8-Panel, Black Lacquer, Figures In Landscapes, 84 x 128 In.
$130

Hess Auction Group

F

FURNITURE

Furniture, Secretary, Federal, Roll Top, Inlay, Eagle, Glazed Doors, Shelves, Drawers, c.1815, 44 x 40 In.
$1,045

Cowan's Auctions

Furniture, Secretary, Louis XV Style, Kingwood, Bombe, Fitted, Marble, Drawers, c.1910, 59 In.
$1,063

New Orleans Auction Galleriesa

Furniture, Secretary, Mahogany, Drawer Over Drop Front, Lower Drawers, c.1875, 56 x 39 In.
$688

New Orleans Auction Galleries

Furniture, Secretary, Mitchell & Rammelsberg, Gothic Revival, Fold-Out, c.1850, 105 In.
$1,320

Cowan's Auctions

Sideboard, Pine, Contemporary, Central Drawer, 2 Drawers On Each Side, 42 x 38 In.	192
Sideboard, Roycroft, Oak, Copper, 3 Drawers Over 3 Drawers, 2 Doors, 46 x 66 In.	11000
Sideboard, Serpentine, Mahogany, 2 Drawers, Bellflower Pendants, Cuffs, c.1890, 39 x 71 In.	1812
Sideboard, Sheraton, Maple, Walnut, Carved, Gallery, Dovetailed, c.1825, 50 x 67 In. *illus*	1560
Sofa, Berger, Peduzzi-Riva, U. DeSede, Leather, 12 Sections, c.1970, Section 29 x 26 In.	6875
Sofa, Biedermeier, Walnut, Crest Rail, Inlay, Out-Curved Arms, Upholstered, c.1830, 36 x 93 In.	2420
Sofa, Chesterfield, Leather, Tufted, Rolled Arms, Brown, Bun Feet, 81 In.	437
Sofa, Chippendale Style, Mahogany, Upholstered, 83 In.	140
Sofa, Chromcraft, Plastic, Blue Upholstery, 27 x 80 x 30 In.	1000
Sofa, Confidante, Upholstered, Tassels, 2 Seats, 66 ½ In.	1000
Sofa, Florence Knoll, Chrome Steel, Rectangular Bench, Post Legs, 1960s, 30 x 91 In.	1250
Sofa, Frits Henningsen, Oak, Upholstered, 1940s, 32 x 73 x 28 In.	6876
Sofa, Hancock & Moore, Hand Antiqued, Chestnut Brown, Leather, 87 x 29 x 22 In.	4602
Sofa, Hancock & Moore, Triple Seat, Serpentine, Cordovan Leather, 1900s, 36 x 86 In.	750
Sofa, Hans Hollein, Mitzi, Burl, Upholstered, Poltronova, c.1981, 38 x 80 In. *illus*	2625
Sofa, Karl Springer, Walnut, Leather, Upholstered, 1980s, 27 x 72 In. *illus*	13750
Sofa, Knoll, Cream Upholstery, Chrome Legs, c.1950, 32 x 90 In. *illus*	938
Sofa, Louis XV Style, Carved Crest, Painted, Closed Arms, c.1900, 42 ½ x 88 In. *illus*	1000
Sofa, Louis XV, Silvered Wood, Cabriole Legs, 40 x 71 In.	313
Sofa, Mahogany, Carved, Molded Seat Rail, Turned Legs, Casters, Yellow, c.1820, 36 x 72 x 24 In.	896
Sofa, Padded & Scalloped Back, White, Cabriole Legs, Ball & Claw Feet, c.1910, 36 x 85 In.	2125
Sofa, Rococo, Laminated Rosewood, Bird Pattern, c.1850, 49 x 73 x 28 In.	11590
Sofa, S. Karpen Bros., Peacock Crest, Cherub, Lions, Serpentine Apron, Tufted, 49 x 76 In.	7560
Sofa, Shells, Shaped Back, Rope Trim, Netted Seat, New Brunswick, c.1825, 35 In.	4613
Sofa, Sheraton, Mahogany, Inlay, Curved Back, Turned & Reeded Legs, c.1800, 35 x 72 In. *illus*	780
Sofa, Southern Classical, Mahogany, Dolphin, Scroll Arms, Stylized Fish Skirt, 30 x 91 In.	6600
Sofa, Teak, Jeanneret, Upholstered, Camel Color, Black Trim, c.1950, 32 x 71 In.	26250
Sofa, Walnut, Curved Crest Rail, Carved Arms, Scrolled Feet, 1800s, 37 x 88 x 30 In.	366
Spice Cabinet, Mahogany, Oak, Door, 12 Drawers, Dovetailed, Brass Handle, 11 x 8¾ In.	410
Stand, Basin, Copper Bowl, Brass Studded, Gray Paint, Cast Iron, 1900s, 20¾ x 16 In.	234
Stand, Bedside, Carved Backsplash, Rouge Marble, 3 Drawers, 1800, 39 x 17 In.	68
Stand, Box, Gun, Inlay, X-Shape Stretcher, 23 x 19¾ In.	640
Stand, Cherry, Mother-Of-Pearl Inlay, 3 Tiers, Morocco, c.1890, 40 x 16 In.	1100
Stand, Corner, Aesthetic Revival, Bamboo, Scrolls, 4 Lacquered Shelves, 75 x 27 In.	900
Stand, Drawer, Maple, Turned Legs, 1800s, 28 x 21 In.	156
Stand, Drop Leaf, Drawer, Pine, Tiger Maple, Brass, Turned Legs, 1800s, 29 In.	240
Stand, Drop Leaf, Sheraton, Mahogany, Drawer, Bird's-Eye Maple, Reeded Legs, 1810, 28 x 17 In.	192
Stand, Eames, Eiffel Tower, Enamel, Black, 19 x 24 ½ In.	2500
Stand, Empire, Mahogany, Paneled & Dovetailed Drawers, Brass Pulls, c.1850, 29 x 24 In.	120
Stand, Federal, Drop Leaf, Mahogany, 3 Drawers, Writing Surface, Brasses, c.1810, 28 x 18 In.	549
Stand, Fern, Brass, Swirled Marble, Scroll Design, Green, Brown, 30 x 14 In.	150
Stand, Fern, Wood, Figured, Old Scandinavian Woman, 37 x 12 In.	210
Stand, G. Stickley, Oak, 2 Over 1 Drawers, Branded, Label, c.1912, 22 x 17 In. *illus*	1500
Stand, G. Stickley, Somno, Drawer, Shelf Under Drawer, Red Decal, c.1902, 34 x 20 In. *illus*	5000
Stand, Hepplewhite, Cherry, Mahogany, Drawer, Tapered, Country, 1900s, 29 x 22 x 20 In.	227
Stand, Louis Philippe, Frieze Drawer, Door, Plinth Base, Bracket Feet, c.1880, 29 x 15 In.	154
Stand, Magazine, Louis XV, Blue, Cream, Stretcher Shelf, Cabriole Legs, 25 x 23 In.	750
Stand, Magazine, Rectangular, Canvas Sling, Danish Hardwood, 1968, 18 x 17 x 17 In.	123
Stand, Magazine, Robsjohn-Gibbings, Mahogany, X-Shape, Tray Top, 1954, 22 x 29 In.	469
Stand, Mahogany, Tiger Maple, 2 Drawers, Ring-Turned Legs, 28 ½ x 17 ½ In.	605
Stand, Music, Metal, Iron, Scrolls, Painted, Outdoor, 51 ½ In., Pair	64
Stand, Music, William IV, Mahogany, 2-Sided, 2 Brass Candle Arms, c.1850, 47 In.	1250
Stand, Onyx, Green, Brass, 3 Tiers, Turned Onyx Legs, 30 In.	693
Stand, Pan, Copper, Hammered, 1800s, 29 x 23 In.	2760
Stand, Plant, Art Nouveau, Maple, Chip Carved, Shelf, Dolphin, Shell, c.1910, 36 In. *illus*	375
Stand, Plant, Gilt, Birds, Flowers, 4 Pierced Trestle Legs, 33 ¼ x 25 In.	200
Stand, Plant, Michael Hurwits, 7 Roses, Carved, Painted, Cherry, Mosaic, 1990s, 40 x 15 In., Pair.	4688
Stand, Plant, Wrought Iron, 4 Tiers, Demilune, Twisted Supports, Painted, c.1900, 46 x 68 In.	480
Stand, Rococo Style, Italian Gilt, Painted, 25 x 19 In.	375

Furniture, Server, Empire Style, Mahogany, Marble Top, Doors, Gilt Bronze, c.1885, 40 x 92 In.
$1,875

New Orleans Auction Galleries

Roll-Top Patent
The first American patent for a horizontal tambour roll-top desk was issued in 1850 to Abner Cutler. The Cutler desk became the best-known commercial desk in the United States in the late nineteenth century.

F

Furniture, Settee, Adam Style, Satinwood, Caned Back, Arms & Seat, Painted Designs, 1800s, 34 In.
$1,250

Neal Auction Co.

Furniture, Settee, Black Forest, Walnut, Boar Hunt, Animal Pelt, Arms, c.1890, 58 x 67 In.
$2,400

Brunk Auctions

Furniture, Settee, Meridienne, Mahogany, Cane Seat & Back, Arm, West Indies, 1800s, 83 In.
$2,432

Neal Auction Co.

Furniture, Settle, Poplar, Green Paint, Stenciled, 3 Shaped Splats, Plank Seat, Arms, Pa., 1800s, 78 In.
$738

Cowan's Auctions

Furniture, Shelf, Poplar, Fretwork, Nudes, Arrows, Leaves, Pinwheels, Flowers, c.1939, 41 x 22 In.
$292

Jeffrey S. Evans

Furniture, Sideboard, D. Pabst, Mahogany, Hooded Top, Shelves, c.1880, 104 x 74 In.
$11,875

Naudeau's Auction Gallery

Furniture, Sideboard, D. Pabst, Walnut, Gallery Top, Mirror, Marble, Drawers, c.1880, 104 x 75 In.
$10,200

Naudeau's Auction Gallery

Furniture, Sideboard, Empire, Tiger Maple, Stepped Top, Drawers, Paneled Doors, 1800s, 63 x 74 In.
$1,045

Cowan's Auctions

F

Stand, Shaker, Cherry, Pine, Drawer, Varnish, Red Stain, Cherry Pull, c.1840, 26 x 25 In.	1000
Stand, Shaped Top, Separator, Lower Drawer, 2 x 25 x 17 In.	118
Stand, Shaving, Gothic Revival, Rosewood, Mirror, Spiral-Twists, Drawer, c.1850, 71 x 19 In.	940
Stand, Shaving, Walnut, Carved, Eastlake, Victorian, 75 In.	165
Stand, Sheraton, Mahogany, Bird's-Eye Maple Veneer, Reeded Legs, 28 ½ x 17 ¼ In. *illus*	4800
Stand, Smoking, Arts & Crafts, Hinged Lid, Quartersawn Top, Copper Lined, 30 x 28 In.	847
Stand, Smoking, Figural, Butler, Painted, 2-Sided, 41 ½ In. *illus*	59
Stand, Smoking, Iron, Cast, Parrot, Pail, 31 ½ In.	125
Stand, Tiers, 4 Shelves, Iron, Small, Pyramidal, Ash, 1900s, 25 x 12 In.	255
Stand, Tray, Victorian, Mahogany, 2-Board, Hinged, Front Load, c.1850, 48 x 32 In.	1255
Stand, Turned Leg Dresser, Cookie Corner Top, 1800s, 18 x 18 x 28 In.	562
Stand, Victorian, Brass, Marble Top, Ornate, 31 x 15 ½ In.	165
Stand, Walnut, Circular Frame, 4 Monopodial Supports, Carved Human Heads, 1900s, 22 x 20 In.	181
Stand, Wood, Turned, Spool, Pin Cup Final, 8 ⅝ In.	354
Stool, E. Saarinen, Tulip, Enameled Aluminum, Upholstered Seat, Knoll, 1970s, 18 x 16 In.	250
Stool, Empire Style, Chinoiserie Upholstery, 13 x 17 In.	96
Stool, English Arts & Crafts, Oak, Triangular, Incised Supports, c.1910, 18 x 16 In. *illus*	192
Stool, Esherick, Cotton, Ash Wood, Signed, Dated, 1966, 26 x 17 x 17 In.	4688
Stool, Esherick, Figured Walnut, Hickory, Convex Seat, 3 Legs, 1960, 15 x 13 ½ In.	4687
Stool, Fruitwood, Grotto Taste, Shell Seat Back, Adjustable, 3 Legs, Paw Feet, 1800s, 25 In.	813
Stool, G. Siegel, Bent Beech, Upholstered, 1900s, 20 x 18 In., Pair	1188
Stool, George III, Mahogany, Serpentine Rail, Turned Tapered Legs, 18 x 20 In.	671
Stool, Giltwood, Louis XV Style, Padded Top, Floral Carved Apron, c.1850, 17 x 22 In., Pair	1750
Stool, Jordan Mozer, Hudson, Magnesium Aluminum Alloy, Mohair, 1998, 47 x 19 x 26 In., Pair	6875
Stool, Mahogany, Concave, Splayed Legs, Stretcher, Upholstered, 17 ½ x 18 In.	1875
Stool, Mahogany, Square Tapered Splayed Legs, Leather Upholstery, 1800s, 17 ½ In.	132
Stool, Milking, Red Paint, Mortised Leg, Pennsylvania, 1800s, 17 ½ x 16 ½ In.	59
Stool, Perriand, Enameled Wood, Original Paperwork, 1940s, 11 x 13 In.	5313
Stool, Philip Arctander Style, Faux Fur Upholstery, Wood Legs, 18 x 14 In., Pair *illus*	2337
Stool, Rectangular, X-Curule Frame, Paneled Legs, Upholstered Seat, 1900, 18 x 24 x 17 In.	124
Stool, Regency Style, Padded Seat, Round, 3 Women's Laced Boot Legs, 20 x 15 In., Pair	1875
Stool, Venetian, Blackamoor, Crouching Figure, Padded Top, Italy, c.1790, 22 x 19 In. *illus*	3250
Stool, Windsor, Blue Over Original Red Paint, c.1800, 11 ½ In.	265
Storage Unit, Eames, Drawers, Open Shelves, Sliding Panels, Herman Miller, 1950, 58 x 47 In. *illus*	11250
Table, 3 Columns, Pedestal, 9-Sided Top, Ball & Claw Feet, 29 x 42 In.	625
Table, 4 Stacked Books, Top One Hinged, Bottom 3 Are Drawers, Gilt, 20 x 21 In.	688
Table, A. Pearsall, Bronzed Resin Over Wood, Laminate, Drum Shape, c.1965, 19 x 24 In.	1188
Table, Ado Chale, Coffee, Resin, Brass, Enameled Steel, Bone, c.1980, 13 ½ x 38 In.	13750
Table, Aesthetic Revival, Ebonized, Carved Sunflowers, Vine, Shelf, 29 x 48 In.	1250
Table, Alabaster, Oval, Gilt Brass, Twist Turned Legs, Ball & Claw Feet, 1900s, 34 x 32 x 20 In.	896
Table, Aldo Tura, Game, Chess, Stained & Lacquered Parchment, Wood, 1960s, 29 x 31 In.	2500
Table, Altar, Hardwood, Cylindrical Legs, Chinese, 40 ½ x 17 ½ In.	544
Table, Altar, Lacquer, Red, 5 Drawers, 34 x 72 ½ In.	250
Table, Art Nouveau, Rectangular, Peacock Center, 4 Cylindrical Legs, 29 x 41 x 31 In.	1210
Table, Baker Furniture, Nesting, Lacquer, Scenes, Lyre Shape Legs, 1800s, 27, 19, 12 In., 3 Piece	185
Table, Barker's, Cast Iron, Pendant, Frieze, C-Scroll Legs, c.1820, 29 x 43 x 29 In.	1220
Table, Baroque, Walnut, Dovetailed Drawers, Teardrop Pulls, Scalloped Skirt, 1700s, 39 x 23 In.	1800
Table, Bench, Mixed Wood, Red, Baton Supports, Square Seat, Arched, 29 x 46 In.	2242
Table, Butler's, Mahogany, 4 Hinged Drop Leaves, Square Legs, Kittinger, 25 x 52 x 37 In. *illus*	59
Table, Card, Federal Style, Mahogany, Carved Pedestal, Reverse Arch Legs, 1900, 30 x 37 In.	72
Table, Card, Federal, Inlay, Tapered Legs, Demilune, 1900s, 30 x 36 x 18 In.	113
Table, Card, Hepplewhite, Mahogany, Sapwood String Inlay, Tapered Legs, c.1825, 30 x 37 In.	240
Table, Card, Hepplewhite, Mahogany, String Inlay, Tapered Legs, c.1825, 30 x 37 In.	240
Table, Card, Mahogany, Brass Trim, Inlay, Reeded Legs, Felt Top, Demilune, 29 x 43 In.	312
Table, Card, Mahogany, Molded Edge, Tapered Legs, String Inlay, 1800, 29 x 36 In.	360
Table, Card, Mahogany, String Inlay, Flowers, 1800, 29 x 36 In.	570
Table, Card, Sheraton, Mahogany, Shaped Top, Reeded Legs, c.1815, 29 ½ x 35 ½ In. *illus*	240
Table, Center, Aesthetic Revival, Walnut, Marble Top, Carved Owls, Paw Feet, 1880s, 30 x 45 In.	9760
Table, Center, American Rococo, Rosewood, Carved, Marble Top, c.1855, 29 x 41 In. *illus*	21960

Furniture, Sideboard, Federal, Inlay, Dovetailed Drawers, Doors, c.1800, 39 x 73 x 27 In.
$16,800

Brunk Auctions

Furniture, Sideboard, Limbert, Oak, Cutout Gallery, Metal Label, c.1910, 43 x 57 In.
$4,062

Rago Arts and Auction Center

Furniture, Sideboard, Limbert, Oak, Drawers, Doors, Mirror, Shelf, Branded, c.1908, 58 x 60 In.
$4,063

Rago Arts and Auction Center

Furniture, Sideboard, Sheraton, Maple, Walnut, Carved, Gallery, Dovetailed, c.1825, 50 x 67 In.
$1,560

Garth's Auctioneers & Appraisers

Furniture, Sofa, Hans Hollein, Mitzi, Burl, Upholstered, Poltronova, c.1981, 38 x 80 In.
$2,625

Rago Arts and Auction Center

Furniture, Sofa, Karl Springer, Walnut, Leather, Upholstered, 1980s, 27 x 72 In.
$13,750

Rago Arts and Auction Center

Furniture, Sofa, Knoll, Cream Upholstery, Chrome Legs, c.1950, 32 x 90 In.
$938

Selkirk Auctioneers & Appraisers

Furniture, Sofa, Louis XV Style, Carved Crest, Painted, Closed Arms, c.1900, 42 ½ x 88 In.
$1,000

New Orleans Auction Galleries

Furniture, Sofa, Sheraton, Mahogany, Inlay, Curved Back, Turned & Reeded Legs, c.1800, 35 x 72 In.
$780

Cowan's Auctions

Furniture, Stand, G. Stickley, Oak, 2 Over 1 Drawers, Branded, Label, c.1912, 22 x 17 In.
$1,500

Rago Arts and Auction Center

Furniture, Stand, G. Stickley, Somno, Drawer, Shelf Under Drawer, Red Decal, c.1902, 34 x 20 In.
$5,000

Rago Arts and Auction Center

Furniture, Stand, Plant, Art Nouveau, Maple, Chip Carved, Shelf, Dolphin, Shell, c.1910, 36 In.
$375

Neal Auction Co.

Table, Center, Guerson, Circular Flange, Marble, 6-Point Star, Palmettes, 27 x 30 In.		591
Table, Center, Jacobean, Oak, Recessed Frieze, Scrolls, Leaves, Turned Supports, 32 x 58 In.		500
Table, Center, Mahogany, Carved, Marble Top, Scrolled Legs, Frieze, 1800s, 29 x 37 x 31 In.		1152
Table, Center, Mahogany, Marble Top, Narrow Frieze, Melon Feet, c.1805, 29 x 38 x 38 In.		1098
Table, Center, Mahogany, Slate Top, Hocked Legs, Paw Feet, 1900s, 30 x 30 In.		2304
Table, Center, Marble, Lion Supports, Paw Feet, Circular Top, 29 x 35 In.		896
Table, Center, Neoclassical, Tilt Top, Classical Figures, Italy, c.1820, 30 x 50 In.		625
Table, Center, Rosewood, Carved, Marble Top, S-Scroll Legs, Lobed Finial, c.1850, 30 x 47 In.		1220
Table, Center, Scalloped Edges, Carved Aprons, Cabriole Legs, Stretchers, 30 ½ x 46 In.		937
Table, Cherry, Mirror, 2 Half Drawers, Turned Legs, 1820, 39 x 41 In.		360
Table, Chippendale, Drop Leaf, Mahogany, Swing Leg, Ball & Claw Feet, 1700s, 22 x 47 In. *illus*		960
Table, Coffee, Adrian Pearsall, Walnut Base, Glass Top, Craft Associates, c.1960, 16 x 50 In. *illus*		1500
Table, Coffee, Brass, Tapered, Fluted Legs, Stretchers, Glass Top, 16 ½ x 54 In.		600
Table, Coffee, Bronze, Bamboo Design, Mirror Top, X-Stretcher, 18 x 28 x 28 In.		854
Table, Coffee, Bronze, Shagreen, Bamboo, Hairpin Legs, c.1980, 12 ½ x 47 In.		1250
Table, Coffee, Cherry, Stack, Laminated, Cone Shape Pedestals, 65 x 39 In.		3287
Table, Coffee, Glass Top, Rocket On Stretcher, Gold Washed Metal, Russia, 1960s, 21 x 43 In.		5625
Table, Coffee, Illuminating Sculptural, Insect, Brass, Agate, 1970s, 15 ¼ x 48 x 32 In.		2250
Table, Coffee, Lacquer, Geometric Shapes, Style Of Fernand Dresse, France, 1970s, 16 x 39 In.		2375
Table, Coffee, Laminate, Chrome Steel, 4 Trapezoid Tables Lift Up & Out, Black, 15 x 59 In.		6250
Table, Coffee, Louis XV, Marble Top, Rectangular, Carved, 1900s, 18 x 51 In.		307
Table, Console, Brushed Chrome Steel, Sandblasted, 36 x 62 In.		3750
Table, Console, Cockrell, Steel, Zigzags, Cookie Cutter Shape, Signed, 84, 32 x 36 In.		256
Table, Console, Fruitwood, Frieze, Square Tapered Legs, Louis Philippe, c.1860, 32 x 41 In.		406
Table, Console, Iron, Acanthus, Crossed Branches, Bellflower Swags, Glass Top, 37 x 93 ½ In.		2125
Table, Console, J. Wade Beam, T-Shape, Stainless Steel, Reverse Painted Glass, 29 ½ x 72 In.		4062
Table, Console, Louis XV, Serpentine, C-Scrolls, Flower Garlands, 32 ½ x 27 In., Pair		4000
Table, Console, Maple, Cast Stone, Demilune Top, Scroll Leaf Legs, 3-Footed, 30 x 36 In., Pair		625
Table, Console, R. Subes, Marble, Nickeled Steel, 3 Scrolls, 34 ½ x 65 In.		7500
Table, Console, Walnut, Carved, Molded Top, Scrolled Toes, 1900s, 32 x 29 x 19 In.		1408
Table, D. Deskey, Coffee, Aluminum, Walnut, Oak, 6 Legs, 16 ½ x 67 In.		750
Table, Dining, Diamond Pattern, Veneer Inlay, Shaped Legs, Brass End Caps, 30 x 76 x 37 In.		236
Table, Dining, Drop Leaf, Mahogany, Swivel Top, 2 Parts, Quervelle, c.1810, 30 x 90 x 46 In.		1000
Table, Dining, Georgian, Walnut, Foldover Console, Leafy Carving, c.1910, 31 x 60 In.		813
Table, Dining, Mahogany, 3 Parts, Drop Leaf, Plan Frieze, c.1820, 29 x 98 x 52 In.		2560
Table, Dining, Mahogany Veneer, Pad Feet, Double Pedestal, 29 ½ x 73 In.		250
Table, Dining, Oak, Carved Frieze, Round, Griffin Legs, Blocked Feet, Casters, 30 x 60 In.		3965
Table, Dining, Round, Marquetry, Yin, Yang, 6 Legs, 30 x 53 ¾ In.		1122
Table, Dressing, Carved, Acanthus, Beveled Mirror, Drawers, Lion's Head Ring Pulls, 1800s		537
Table, Dressing, Charles X, Mahogany, Marble Top, Mirror, Swan Stretchers, c.1815, 59 x 34 In.		670
Table, Dressing, Mahogany, Marble Top, Dolphin Supports, 12-Sided Mirror, 59 In.		969
Table, Dressing, Queen Anne Style, 1 Drawer, Mahogany, Oval Mirror, 51 x 37 ¾ In.		281
Table, Drop Leaf, Burl, Pedestal, 4-Footed, Italy, 29 x 33 In.		288
Table, Drop Leaf, Chippendale, Mahogany, Arcaded Frieze, 26 x 32 In.		1513
Table, Drop Leaf, Mahogany, Frieze Drawer, Brass Paw Feet, 1800s, 29 x 39 x 24 In.		1920
Table, Drop Leaf, Mahogany, Reeded Legs, 1800, 29 x 48 x 17 In.		192
Table, Drop Leaf, Neoclassical, Figured Mahogany, Philadelphia, 1820, 40 In.		1000
Table, Drop Leaf, Oak, Drawer, Stretcher Base, 1800, 17 x 46 x 16 In.		144
Table, Drop Leaf, Oak, Gateleg, Rope-Twist Legs, Bun Feet, 1800s, 28 x 33 In. *illus*		240
Table, Drop Leaf, Queen Anne, Marquetry, Flowers, Cornucopia, Butterflies, 28 x 41 In.		4235
Table, Drop Leaf, Rosewood, Molded, 2 Drawers, c.1850, 30 x 22 x 20 In.		488
Table, Drop Leaf, Sheraton, Flame Birch, Black, Red, Turned Legs, 29 x 36 In.		450
Table, Drop Leaf, Sheraton, Maple, Dovetailed Drawer, c.1835, 29 x 59 In. Open *illus*		563
Table, Eames, Molded, Plywood, Herman Miller, 15 In.		316
Table, Elaborate, Inlay, Chariot, 32 x 32 x 22 In.		188
Table, Empire, Walnut, 4 Drawers, Fluted Legs, Stretcher Shelf, Round, 27 ½ x 23 ½ In.		738
Table, Esherick, Side, Mahogany, Cherry, Carved W.E. 60, 1960, 22 x 23 ½ x 22 In. *illus*		7500
Table, Farm, Hepplewhite, Walnut, Apron, Drawer, Tapered Legs, Pa., c.1775, 30 x 60 In.		385
Table, Farm, Oak, Carved, Overhang Top, Drawer, Block Legs, c.1810, 29 x 70 In.		4000

Coat Racks

Coat racks are an ignored furniture form. The oak coat rack once favored by offices can still be found in antiques shops. Less common but more unusual are the coat racks designed by Eames, Sottsass, and other twentieth-century designers. These often look more like sculpture than furniture.

Furniture, Stand, Sheraton, Mahogany, Bird's-Eye Maple Veneer, Reeded Legs, 28 ½ x 17 ¼ In.
$4,800

Eldred's Auctioneers and Appraisers

Furniture, Stand, Smoking, Figural, Butler, Painted, 2-Sided, 41 ½ In.
$59

Hess Auction Group

FURNITURE

Furniture, Stool, English Arts & Crafts, Oak, Triangular, Incised Supports, c.1910, 18 x 16 In.
$192

Neal Auction Co.

Furniture, Stool, Philip Arctander Style, Faux Fur Upholstery, Wood Legs, 18 x 14 In., Pair
$2,337

Palm Beach Modern Auctions

Furniture, Stool, Venetian, Blackamoor, Crouching Figure, Padded Top, Italy, c.1790, 22 x 19 In.
$3,250

New Orleans Auction Galleries

Furniture, Storage Unit, Eames, Drawers, Open Shelves, Sliding Panels, Herman Miller, 1950, 58 x 47 In.
$11,250

Los Angeles Modern Auctions

Furniture, Table, Butler's, Mahogany, 4 Hinged Drop Leaves, Square Legs, Kittinger, 25 x 52 x 37 In.
$59

Hess Auction Group

Furniture, Table, Card, Sheraton, Mahogany, Shaped Top, Reeded Legs, c.1815, 29 ½ x 35 ½ In.
$240

Garth's Auctioneers & Appraisers

Furniture, Table, Center, American Rococo, Rosewood, Carved, Marble Top, c.1855, 29 x 41 In.
$21,960

Neal Auction Co.

Furniture, Table, Chippendale, Drop Leaf, Mahogany, Swing Leg, Ball & Claw Feet, 1700s, 22 x 47 In.
$960

Cowan's Auctions

Furniture, Table, Coffee, Adrian Pearsall, Walnut Base, Glass Top, Craft Associates, c.1960, 16 x 50 In.
$1,500

Los Angeles Modern Auctions

Furniture, Table, Drop Leaf, Oak, Gateleg, Rope-Twist Legs, Bun Feet, 1800s, 28 x 33 In.
$240

Cowan's Auctions

F

Table, Federal, Cherry, Inlay, Drawer, 2 Knobs, Tennessee, 29 x 31 In.	360
Table, Federal, Maple, Overhanging Top, Drawer, New England, c.1815, 28 x 18 In. .... *illus*	545
Table, Finn Juhl, Niels Vodder, Dining, Teak, Extension, c.1950, 28 x 78 In.	20000
Table, Fontana Arte, Side, Brass, Mirror, Glass, 1950s 17 ½ x 28 In.	3125
Table, Fornasetti, Balloons, Lacquered & Ebonized Wood, Round, 17 x 19 In.	2500
Table, Fornasetti, Zeus & Hera, Lacquered Metal, Wood, Brass, Round, 19 x 24 In.	1750
Table, Frankl, Coffee, Greek Key, Lacquered Wood, Johnson Co., 1950s, 15 x 45 In.	625
Table, French Provincial, Fruitwood, 2 Frieze Drawers, c.1850, 29 x 53 In.	1625
Table, French Provincial, Fruitwood, Marble Top, Beverage Holders, Drawer, c.1775, 27 x 19 In.	1188
Table, Fruitwood, 2-Board Top, Iron Stretchers, 1700s, 31 x 83 In. .... *illus*	793
Table, G. Crespi, Rotating, Round Tiers, White Lacquer, Italy, 1970s, 16 ½ x 29 ½ In.	8125
Table, G. Nakashima, Coffee, Slab, Walnut, Rosewood Butterfly, 1969, 15 x 75 x 40 In.	33750
Table, G. Nakashima, Coffee, Walnut, Rosewood Butterfly, 1969, 14 x 75 In.	33750
Table, G. Nakashima, Dining, Boat Shape, Turned Leg, Rosewood, 1958, 29 x 84 x 40 In.	33750
Table, G. Nakashima, Dining, Cone Shape, Book-Matched, Walnut, Rosewood, 1966, 29 x 96 x 50 In.	40625
Table, G. Nakashima, Dining, Trestle, Walnut, 1963, 29 x 60 x 41 In.	3750
Table, G. Nakashima, Side, Cross Legged, Walnut, 1964, 21 x 27 x 27 ½ In.	11875
Table, G. Nakashima, Side, Figured English Walnut, Rosewood, 1973, 54 In.	23750
Table, G. Nakashima, Side, Walnut, Natural Slab Top, 1963, 21 x 26 In. .... *illus*	9375
Table, G. Nakashima, Walnut, Trestle, 1963, 29 x 60 x 41 In.	3750
Table, G. Stickley, Director's, Trapezoid-Shape Supports, Big Pegs, c.1907, 29 x 84 In.	8750
Table, G. Stickley, Library, Oak, 6 Drawers, c.1912, 30 x 66 x 36 In. .... *illus*	1875
Table, Galle, 2 Tiers, Rosewood, Walnut, Mahogany, Cabriole Legs, 30 ½ x 31 ½ In.	2662
Table, Galle, Nesting, Oak, Inlaid Landscape, Boats, Marked, Largest 28 In., 4 Piece	1875
Table, Galle, Side, Heart Shape, Walnut, Fruitwood Inlay, Shelf, France, c.1900, 31 x 22 In.	1750
Table, Galle, Side, Rectangular, 2 Tiers, Turret Corners, Molded Edge, 30 x 28 x 16 In.	2057
Table, Game, Accordion Action, Walnut, Needlework, 28 x 28 In.	2250
Table, Game, Backgammon, Cabriole Legs, 28 ⅞ x 29 ¾ In.	375
Table, Game, Cabriole Legs, Inlaid Top, Gaming Board, 30 x 15 x 31 In.	625
Table, Game, Federal, Mahogany, Carved, Foldover, Spiral-Turned Legs, c.1800 .... *illus*	896
Table, Game, Federal, Mahogany, Foldover Top, Conforming Frieze, c.1810, 29 x 36 In.	488
Table, Game, Federal, Mahogany, Foldover, Seymour School, Boston, c.1825, 28 x 38 In.	688
Table, Game, Folding, Checkers, c.1900, 24 In.	82
Table, Game, Georgian Style, Mahogany, Double Foldover, Baize Interior, 30 x 29 x 14 In.	1230
Table, Game, Louis Philippe, Burl, Veneer, Foldover Top, Leather, 31 x 17 ½ In.	1440
Table, Game, Louis XV, Cherry, Inlay, Green, Cookie Corner, Hoof Feet, 28 ½ x 32 ½ In.	400
Table, Game, Mahogany, Felt Top, Card Drawers, Inlaid Counters, c.1940, 30 x 36 In.	1165
Table, Game, Mahogany, Foldover Top, Frieze, Maple Panel, c.1810, 28 x 34 In.	375
Table, Game, Neoclassical, 36 Game Squares, Painted Surface, Italian, 17 ½ x 53 ½ In.	7500
Table, Game, Queen Anne, Burl Veneers, Carved, Leather, Drawer, 1700s, 29 x 28 In.	480
Table, Game, Queen Anne, Mahogany, Handkerchief, Foldover, Chip Cups, 1700s, 29 x 36 In.... *illus*	2337
Table, Game, Queen Anne, Shell Carved, Burl Veneers, Leather, 1700s, 29 x 28 In.	480
Table, Game, Sheraton, Bird's-Eye Maple, Mahogany, String Inlay, Reeded Legs, 30 x 36 In.	484
Table, Game, Swivel Top, Brass Frieze, Gilt, Paw Feet, Casters, c.1815, 29 x 36 x 18 In.	1200
Table, Game, Walnut, Parquetry, Medallion, Foldover, 31 ½ x 38 ¼ In.	500
Table, Garry Bennett, Rain, Mixed Wood, Carved, Stain & Paint, 29 x 89 In...................... *illus*	4687
Table, Garry Knox Bennett, Mixed Hardwood, Carved, Stained, Painted, Wood, 29 x 89 x 36 In.	4688
Table, Georges Mathias, Polished, Brushed Brass, Pyrite, 1980s, 14 x 23 In., Pair	6875
Table, Georges Mathias, Side, Polished Brass, Geometric Shape, c.1980, 13 ½ x 23 In., Pair	6875
Table, Gothic Style, Leafy Acanthus Design, Casters, 5 Leaves, 70 x 46 In.	270
Table, H. Probber, 3 Corner, Travertine Top, 21 x 23 In.	112
Table, Hardwood, Porcelain, Circular Top, Carved Skirt, Rose Medallion, 1900, 31 x 22 In.	2640
Table, Harvest, Pine, Oak, Tapered Legs, 4-Board Top, Drawers, Breadboard, 29 x 78 ½ In.	180
Table, Harvest, Pine, Single-Board Top, Conforming Apron, Drawer, 28 x 84 ½ In.	6352
Table, Hepplewhite, American Country, Walnut, Overhanging Board, Black Paint, 27 x 36 In.	938
Table, Herb Seigel, Oak, Walnut, glass top, 48 x 48 x 18 In.	219
Table, Humidor, Green Marble, Drawer, Porcelain Line, Cabriole Legs, 1800, 36 x 17 In.	80
Table, I. Noguchi, Dining, Round Laminate, Spokes, Black Base, Knoll, c.1955, 29 x 48 In.	500
Table, I. Vose, Game, Mahogany, Hinged Top, Green Interior, Paw Feet, Boston, c.1825, 29 x 32 In.	360

Furniture, Table, Drop Leaf, Sheraton, Maple, Dovetailed Drawer, c.1835, 29 x 59 In. Open
$563

Garth's Auctioneers & Appraisers

Furniture, Table, Esherick, Side, Mahogany, Cherry, Carved W.E. 60, 1960, 22 x 23 ½ x 22 In.
$7,500

Rago Arts and Auction Center

Furniture, Table, Federal, Maple, Overhanging Top, Drawer, New England, c.1815, 28 x 18 In.
$545

James D. Julia Auctioneers

Furniture, Table, Fruitwood, 2-Board Top, Iron Stretchers, 1700s, 31 x 83 In.
$793

New Orleans Auction Galleries

Furniture, Table, G. Nakashima, Side, Walnut, Natural Slab Top, 1963, 21 x 26 In.
$9,375

Rago Arts and Auction Center

Furniture, Table, G. Stickley, Library, Oak, 6 Drawers, c.1912, 30 x 66 x 36 In.
$1,875

Rago Arts and Auction Center

Furniture, Table, Game, Federal, Mahogany, Carved, Foldover, Spiral-Turned Legs, c.1800, 28 x 29 In.
$896

Neal Auction Co.

Furniture, Table, Game, Queen Anne, Mahogany, Handkerchief, Foldover, Chip Cups, 1700s, 29 x 36 In.
$2,337

Brunk Auctions

Table, Indian Rustic Style, Hardwood, Teak, Double Frustum, 1900s, 20 In.	300
Table, J. Adnet, Enameled Iron, Leather, Brass, Glass, 1950s, 23 x 29 In.	5000
Table, J. Bearden, Side, Steel, Mottled, Mossy, Green, Cave Shape Opening, Gilt, 21 x 24 In.	3125
Table, Jules Leleu, Game, Macassar, Ebony, Brass, 1940s, 29 x 31 In.	5313
Table, Keal John, Side, Walnut, 2 Doors, Brutalist Glass, Copper Handle, 19 x 27 x 27 In.	188
Table, Kittinger, Walnut, Double Pedestal, Vase Shape, 1900, 30 x 79 x 48 x 19 In.	360
Table, Knoll Assoc., Round Marble Top, Brushed Steel Base, 1960s, 29 x 78 In.	2375
Table, Lacquer, Brown, Pierced Skirt, Painted, Floral, Chinese, 1900s, 33 x 52 x 16 In., Pair	480
Table, Lane, Wood, Chrome, Whimsical Style, 24 x 19 x 19 In.	100
Table, Le Strutture Temano, Pastel Tubes, Glass Top, Italy, 1979, 45 x 19 ¾ In.	4687
Table, Library, Regency, Rosewood, Banded, Frieze Drawers, Splayed Legs, 29 x 54 In.	2500
Table, Limbert, Library, Oak, Oval Top & Shelf, Branded, c.1905, 29 ½ x 48 In. *illus*	5312
Table, Limbert, Oak, Round Top, Stretcher, Square Cutouts, No. 148, 29 In.	1600
Table, Louis XV, Fruitwood, Oak, 2 Leaf Drawers, Cabriole Legs, c.1900, 31 x 39 In.	1188
Table, Louis XV, Silver-Plated Brass, Onyx Top, Leafy Design, 30 x 21 In.	875
Table, Louis XVI, Porcelain, Paint Decorated, Scene, Surrounded Plaques, 1800, 21 x 31 In.	8610
Table, M. Nakashima, Walnut, Rosewood, Live Edge, Trapezoid End, Post End, 1993, 20 x 42 In.	10000
Table, M. Taylor, Round, Grain, Brass Shoes, 16 ¼ x 51 In.	1045
Table, Mahjong, Mahogany, Octagonal, Folding Base, 4 Drawers, Stool, c.1875, 31 ½ In.	138
Table, Mahogany, Brass, Banded Tilt Top, Saber Legs, Paw Feet, c.1810, 28 x 49 In.	2176
Table, Mahogany, Burl Accents, Single Dovetailed Drawer, Turned Legs, 1800s, 27 x 20 In.	180
Table, Mahogany, Drop Leaf, Frieze Drawer, Button Feet, Tapered Legs, c.1810, 28 x 38 In.	512
Table, Mahogany, Lobed, Leafy, Columnar Support, Carved Scrolling Legs, 1930, 29 ½ x 29 In.	90
Table, Mahogany, Rope-Turned Legs, Brass Casters, 1800s, 29 In.	300
Table, Mahogany, Tilt Top, Piecrust, Birdcage, Carved, Ball & Claw Feet, 45 In.	562
Table, Maitland-Smith, 3 Stacked Books, Side Drawers, Turned Feet, 16 x 35 In.	915
Table, Maitland-Smith, Coffee, Marble, Brass, Metal Label, 15 ½ x 40 In.	625
Table, Maitland-Smith, Venetian Style, Painted, Drawer Over Door, Tag, 29 x 26 In., Pair *illus*	813
Table, Majorelle, Art Nouveau, Walnut, 5 Leaves, 29 x 132 In. Fully Extended	3025
Table, Maple, Drawer, Turned Legs, 1900s, 26 x 36 In.	156
Table, Maple, Satinwood Inlay, Checkerboard Top, Acanthus Leaf-Carved Legs, 1900s, 29 In.	216
Table, McCobb, Coffee, 3 Drawers, Caned Shelf, Aluminum Edge, Signed, 16 x 20 x 60 In.	396
Table, McCobb, Linear Group, Calvin, Walnut, Brushed Steel, 18 x 18 x 26 In.	226
Table, Meeks, Pier, Neoclassical, Mahogany, Marble Top, Mirror, c.1840, 36 x 40 In. *illus*	1830
Table, Neoclassical, Mahogany, Lift Top, Red Paper Lining, Trestle Base, 31 x 24 In.	1875
Table, Nesting, Dunbar, Mahogany, Leather, Trapezoid Top, c.1950, 22 x 25 In., 3 Piece *illus*	531
Table, Oak, Marble, Scalloped Frieze, Molded Cabriole Legs, 34 x 23 x 18 In.	653
Table, Oval, Walnut, Pedestal, Brass Capped, 1800, 29 x 48 x 40 In.	1020
Table, P. Evans, Chess, Coffee, Welded, Patinated, Multicolor Steel, Glass, 1970s, 16 x 45 In.	7500
Table, P. Evans, Coffee, Cityscape, Bronze, Steel, Walnut Burl, Glass, 1970s, 16 x 42 in.	2500
Table, P. Evans, Coffee, Glass Top, Round, Base, 3-D Triangles, Bronze, Steel, 16 x 42 In.	1375
Table, P. Evans, Coffee, Glass Top, Square, Base, Checkered Laid Bars, Torch Cut, 16 x 44 In.	1000
Table, P. Evans, Coffee, Glass Top, Steel Welded, Signed, 1967, 18 x 42 In.	1999
Table, P. Evans, Dining, Bronze, Steel, Walnut, Glass Top, Cityscape, c.1970, 16 x 42 In.	2500
Table, P. Evans, Dining, Cityscape, Walnut Burl, 1970s, 30 x 60 x 40 In.	2375
Table, P. Evans, Dining, Cityscape, Walnut Burl, Steel, Glass, Rectangles, 1970s, 29 ½ x 48 In.	8750
Table, P. Evans, Dining, Directional, Mixed Metal, Glass, 1971, 84 x 44 In. *illus*	7995
Table, P. Evans, Dining, Glass Top, Welded, Steel, Bronze Base, 1969, 28 ½ x 68 ½ In.	22500
Table, P. Evans, Sculptured Metal, Welded, Patinated Steel, Bronze, Glass, 1969, 30 x 96 x 48 In.	22500
Table, P. Guth, Beech, Rosewood, Marquetry, Flowers, Trees, Tiers, France, c.1900, 52 x 21 In.	937
Table, Pembroke, Figured Mahogany, Shaped Leaves, Drawer, Rococo Pull, 28 x 20 In.	1560
Table, Pembroke, Frieze Drawer, Reeded Tapered Legs, 1800s, 28 x 35 x 22 In.	854
Table, Pembroke, Hepplewhite, Mahogany, Oak, Inlaid Skirt, 29 ½ x 19 In.	150
Table, Pembroke, Mahogany, Scalloped Skirt, Square Legs, 1700s, 28 x 21 In.	480
Table, Pembroke, Mahogany, Spiral Legs, Casters, Federal, c.1810, 29 x 36 In.	244
Table, Pesce, Waffle, Resin, Enameled Steel, 2000s, 28 x 53 In. *illus*	3500
Table, Philip & Kelvin LaVerne, Coffee, Chan, Bronze, Pewter, 1960s, 17 x 36 In. *illus*	4688
Table, Phillip Lloyd Powell, Coffee, Stacked, Carved Walnut, Slate Top, c.1960, 19 x 43 In.	18750
Table, Picnic, Fir, 6-Board, Bench Seats, Log Stretchers, Deerwood, c.1935, 30 x 72 In.	995
Table, Pier, Mahogany Carved, Marble Top, Ogee Frieze, Mirror Back, c.1820, 38 x 36 x 18 In.	512

F

Furniture, Table, Garry Bennett, Rain, Mixed Wood, Carved, Stain & Paint, 29 x 89 In.
$4,687

Rago Arts and Auction Center

Table Measures

When buying a dining room table, remember you need at least 24 inches for each person. It is better to allow 30 inches. So a 10-foot-long table could seat four on the side comfortably, five if you don't mind close quarters. You need an extra foot at the ends to seat an extra person there. Watch out for the apron or top. Antique tables were 27 to 28 inches from the floor. Today the table is 29 to 30 inches tall. Try sitting on a dining room chair with your legs under the table before you buy.

Furniture, Table, Limbert, Library, Oak, Oval Top & Shelf, Branded, c.1905, 29 ½ x 48 In.
$5,312

Rago Arts and Auction Center

Furniture, Table, Maitland-Smith, Venetian Style, Painted, Drawer Over Door, Tag, 29 x 26 In., Pair
$813

New Orleans Auction Galleries

Furniture, Table, Meeks, Pier, Neoclassical, Mahogany, Marble Top, Mirror, c.1840, 36 x 40 In.
$1,830

Neal Auction Co.

Furniture, Table, Nesting, Dunbar, Mahogany, Leather, Trapezoid Top, c.1950, 22 x 25 In., 3 Piece
$531

Cottone Auctions

Furniture, Table, P. Evans, Dining, Directional, Mixed Metal, Glass, 1971, 84 x 44 In.
$7,995

Palm Beach Modern Auctions

Furniture, Table, Pesce, Waffle, Resin, Enameled Steel, 2000s, 28 x 53 In.
$3,500

Rago Arts and Auction Center

Furniture, Table, Philip & Kelvin LaVerne, Coffee, Chan, Bronze, Pewter, 1960s, 17 x 36 In.
$4,688

Rago Arts and Auction Center

Furniture, Table, Pier, Neoclassical, Mahogany, Marble Top, Drawer, Mirror, 1800s, 36 x 50 In.
$1,312

Neal Auction Co.

F

Furniture, Table, Serving, George III, Mahogany, Fluted & Fan Inlay, c.1790, 33 x 53 In.
$4,613

Brunk Auctions

Furniture, Table, Sewing, Hardwood, Paint Decorated, Lift Top, Cabriole Legs, 1800s, 32 x 17 In.
$450

Cowan's Auctions

TIP

Rearrange lamps, figurines, vases, and other knickknacks on tabletops. If you don't, sunlight will fade the exposed wood, which will become lighter than the covered sections.

Table, Pier, Neoclassical, Mahogany, Marble Top, Drawer, Mirror, 1800s, 36 x 50 in. .... *illus*	1312
Table, Pietra Dura, Marble Inlaid Top, Metal Base, Black Paint, Italy, 25 x 53 In.	960
Table, Pine, Red Paint, Turned Legs, 1800s, 30 In.	240
Table, Pine, Woods, Breadboard Ends, Brown Stain, 1900s, 30 x 70 In.	1200
Table, Plateau, Onyx, Brass, Enamel, Drawer, Turned Brass Legs, 4¾ x 6¾ In.	504
Table, Polished, Etched Brass, Agate, Enameled Steel, 1980s, 15 x 46 x 23 In.	5938
Table, Provincial, Fruitwood, Inlaid Flowers, Drawer, Barley Twist Legs, 30 x 20 In.	2250
Table, Quatrefoil Form, Inset Marble Top, Pierced, Shaped Skirt, Carved Legs, 20 x 20 x 20 In.	443
Table, Queen Anne Style, Japanned, Gilt Chinoiserie, Marble Top, 31 x 24 x 18 In.	369
Table, Queen Anne, Drop Leaf, Walnut, Shaped Frieze, Cabriole Legs, c.1820, 27 x 12 In.	1375
Table, R. Subes, Console, Nickeled Steel, Marble, Unmarked, 34 x 65 x 18 In.	7500
Table, Regency, Mahogany, Rounded Rectangle, Splayed Legs, 29 x 38 In.	1625
Table, Regency, Veneer, Burl, Ebonized, Pedestal, Leather, False Drawers, 29 x 32 In.	1200
Table, Rosewood, Burl, Round Top, 2 Drawers, Brass Cuffs, c.1910, 30 x 36 In.	500
Table, Round Glass Top, Gilt Flower Shape Base, 1900, 17 x 19 In.	83
Table, Round Marble Top, Wood, Carved, Fluted, Tapered Legs, 24 x 31 In.	118
Table, Rounded Corners, Baluster Pedestal, Caster Feet, Custom Pads, 1900, 28 x 54 x 38 In. ..	861
Table, Roycroft, Console, Chestnut, 30 x 84 x 20 In.	3750
Table, Rudi Stern, Coffee, Neon, Concentric Circles, Square Base, Glass, 1976, 15 x 40 In.	2000
Table, Secretary, Rosewood, Mahogany, Leather, Brass, Art Deco, 1930s, 51 x 24 In.	2000
Table, Serving, George III, Mahogany, Fluted & Fan Inlay, c.1790, 33 x 53 In. .... *illus*	4613
Table, Sewing, Black Lacquer, Gilt Chinoiserie, Trestle Base, 27 x 25 In.	492
Table, Sewing, Hardwood, Paint Decorated, Lift Top, Cabriole Legs, 1800s, 32 x 17 In. ...... *illus*	450
Table, Sewing, Mahogany, Satinwood, Pullout Basket, Drawer, 2 Knobs, c.1920, 30 x 21 In.	256
Table, Sewing, Shaker, Pine, 12 Drawers, Sewing Surface, Upper Drawer Section, c.1845, 39 x 26 In.	10200
Table, Sewing, Walnut, Serpentine, Silk Basket, Ceramic Casters, 1800s, 28 x 22 In.	1400
Table, Sheraton, Demilune, Mahogany, Turned Legs, 1800, 28 x 44 x 19 In.	360
Table, Sheraton, Softwood, Farm, Red Painted, Pennsylvania, 30 x 43½ In.	325
Table, Side, Acadian, Cypress, Frieze Drawer, Square Legs, c.1810, 27 x 29 In.	1952
Table, Side, Art Nouveau, Marquetry, Daffodils, 2 Tiers, France, c.1900, 30 x 28 In.	937
Table, Side, Arts & Crafts, Round, Hairpin Legs, 4 Rectangular Feet, c.1925, 29¾ x 19½ In.....	1875
Table, Side, Burl Acacia, Round, Figural Maiden Legs, Draping French Ribbons, 1920s, 29 x 28 In...	904
Table, Side, Glass Top, Round, Aluminum Base, Rubber, American Industrial, 18 x 24 In.	1250
Table, Side, Glass, Lucite, 5 Alternating Height Central Supports, 29 x 8½ In.	187
Table, Side, Round Glass Top, Palm Tree Base, Multicolor, 24 x 26 In., Pair	1750
Table, Side, Round, Human Legs, Pink Skirt, Shoes, 35 x 24 In.	234
Table, Side, Skyscraper, Enamel, Silvered Wood, Chrome Metal, Silvered Glass, 23 x 14 In.	4062
Table, Side, Tree Roots, c.1908, 35 x 24 x 25 In.	1625
Table, Side, Walnut, Carved, Tray Top, Paneled Doors, Flared Feet, c.1810, 20 x 19 x 11 In........	305
Table, Southern Painted, Scrubbed Top, Plain Apron, Square Legs, c.1820, 39 x 21 In.	1287
Table, Tabouret, Chippendale, Marble Top, Carved Gilt Frame, 17 x 20 x 18 In.	923
Table, Tavern, Maple, Drawer, Lower Shelf, Turned Legs, 1900s, 26 x 36 In.	156
Table, Tavern, Maple, Pine, Breadboard Top, Brown, Circular Wood Pull, 1800s, 27 In............	360
Table, Tavern, Queen Anne, Pine, Round Top, Maple Base, 35 In.	360
Table, Tavern, William & Mary, Walnut, Drawer, Dovetailed, Scalloped Skirt, c.1750, 26 x 37 In.	295
Table, Tea, George III, Tilt Top, Mahogany, Circular Top, Snake Feet, c.1800, 28 x 37 In...........	813
Table, Tea, Mahogany, Turned Pedestal, Cabriole Legs, Ball & Claw Feet, 1780, 29 In.	192
Table, Tea, Tray Top, Painted, Flowers, Nautical Harbor, Bamboo Legs, c.1830, 26 x 19 In........	480
Table, Thomas Brooks, Dining, Walnut, Carved Frieze, Molded, Pedestal, 30 x 47 In...............	1280
Table, Tiger Maple, 2 Rectangular Leaves, Square Tapered Legs, 1800s, 27 x 14 In.	720
Table, Tilt Top, Mahogany, Floral Carved Legs, Ball Feet, Irish Style, 1900, 29 x 31 In.	390
Table, Tilt Top, Queen Anne, Birdcage, Tripod Base, Cabriole Legs, Snake Feet, 29 x 24 In.	540
Table, Tilt Top, Walnut, Birdcage, 3 Scrolled Legs, England, 1700, 29 x 27 In.	360
Table, Victorian, Walnut, Carved, Flower Reserve, Trestle Base, c.1860, 60 x 36 In............ *illus*	17690
Table, Victorian, Walnut, Parlor, Marble Top, Ornate Base, 30½ x 35½ In.	354
Table, W. McArthur, Side, Tiers, Wood, Aluminum, Lacquer, c.1928, 20 x 12 In. .... *illus*	3500
Table, W. Von Nessen, Side, Aluminum, Enameled Steel, 1930s, 18½ x 18 In. .... *illus*	6875
Table, Wake, Oak, Drop Leaf, Gateleg Support, Block Feet, England, 28 x 87 In.........................	625
Table, Walnut, Banded Top, Narrow Frieze, Melon Feet, c.1820, 28 x 47 In.	2048

Furniture, Table, Victorian, Walnut, Carved, Flower Reserve, Trestle Base, c.1860, 60 x 36 In.
$17,690

Neal Auction Co.

Furniture, Table, W. McArthur, Side, Tiers, Wood, Aluminum, Lacquer, c.1928, 20 x 12 In.
$3,500

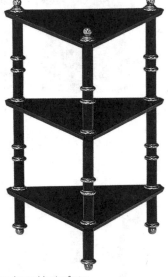

Rago Arts and Auction Center

Furniture, Table, W. Von Nessen, Side, Aluminum, Enameled Steel, 1930s, 18 1/2 x 18 In.
$6,875

Rago Arts and Auction Center

Furniture, Table, Wormley, Console, Carved Shell, Model 3050, Dunbar, 30 x 30 In.
$2,944

Palm Beach Modern Auctions

Furniture, Tabouret, Rosewood, Marble Top, Openwork, Ball & Claw Feet, c.1910, 19 x 17 In.
$300

Eldred's Auctioneers and Appraisers

Furniture, Tray, On Stand, Wood, Box Stretcher, Cabriole Legs, Scroll Feet, Chinese, 14 In.
$423

Freeman's Auctioneers & Appraisers

Furniture, Umbrella Stand, Black Forest, Carved, Bear, Copper Tray, c.1890, 45 x 16 In.
$3,840

F

Neal Auction Co.

Furniture, Umbrella Stand, G. Stickley, Oak, Copper Base, Pan, Red Decal, c.1904, 27 x 12 In.
$11,250

Rago Arts and Auction Center

FURNITURE

Furniture, Vanity, P. Evans, Cityscape, Brass, Mirror, Shelf, Bench, Mirror 70 x 20 In.
$3,375

Rago Arts and Auction Center

Furniture, Vitrine, Louis XV-XVI Style, Mahogany, Marble Top, Brass, Mirror, c.1910, 63 In.
$1,250

New Orleans Auction Galleries

Furniture, Vitrine, Robert Mitchell, Gilt, Painted, Glass Panes, Door, Scenes, 1800s, 70 x 34 In.
$720

Cowan's Auctions

Furniture, Washstand, Tiger Maple, 2 Tiers, Turned Legs, Drawer, Dovetailed, 1800s, 33 x 20 In.
$1,045

Cowan's Auctions

Furniture, Washstand, Walnut, Backsplash, 2 Drawers, Turned Legs, Shelf, 1800s, 36 x 37 In.
$144

Eldred's Auctioneers and Appraisers

Furniture, Wastebasket, G. Stickley, Wood Slats, Craftsman Label, 1912-16, 14 In.
$3,750

Rago Arts and Auction Center

Furniture, Window Seat, Chippendale, Mahogany, Carved, Outscrolled Arms, c.1780, 29 x 39 In.
$1,140

Eldred's Auctioneers and Appraisers

Furniture, Window Seat, Federal, Mahogany, Scroll Arms, Needlepoint Upholstery, 42 In.
$472

Hess Auction Group

Table, Walnut, Shaped Frieze, Drawer, Turned Legs, H-Stretcher, c.1810, 26 x 35 In.	610
Table, Walnut, Square Fluted, Carved Tapered Legs, 1810, 27 ¾ x 17 ¾ In.	132
Table, Walnut, Wide Skirt, Round, Child's, 1900s, 19 x 24 In	136
Table, Walter Lamb, Bronze Frame, Plexiglas Top, Brown-Jordan, c.1950, 17 x 23 In., Pair.......	1080
Table, Weiman, Tea, Chippendale Style, Mahogany, Openwork Gallery, Tripod Base, 30 x 32 In.	305
Table, Wendell Castle, Coffee, Bright Promises II, Bubinga Veneer, Fiberglass, 16 ½ x 56 In.	8750
Table, Wendell Castle, Molar Swivel, Gel-Coated Fiberglass, Rubber, 1960s, 22 x 38 x 33 In......	2625
Table, Wendell Castle, Molar, Gel-Coated Fiberglass, Rubber, 1960s, 28 x 57 x 48 In.	2500
Table, William & Mary, Mahogany, Trumpet Legs, Carved, Drawer, 1800s, 28 x 41 In.	1750
Table, Work, Mahogany, Lift Top, 2 Drawers, Maple Stiles, 1800s, 31 x 20 x 16 In.	488
Table, Wormley, Console, Carved Shell, Model 3050, Dunbar, 30 x 30 In. .... *illus*	2944
Table, Wormley, Sheaf Of Wheat, Marble, Stained Ash Base, Dunbar, 21 x 27 In.	813
Table, Wormley, Sheaf Of Wheat, Travertine Top, Brass, Wood, 1950s, 25 ½ x 27 In.	344
Table, Writing, Empire, Mahogany, Leather Top, Dovetailed Drawers, Escutcheons, 28 x 39 In. ...	1080
Table, Writing, Late Georgian Style, Mahogany, 3 Drawers, Tooled Leather Top, 29 x 61 x 31 In.	2750
Tabouret, Baroque, Giltwood, Marble Top, 3 Carved Legs, Paw Feet, Italian, c.1925, 21 x 20 In..	1063
Tabouret, G. Stickley, Round, Stretcher, c.1902, 22 x 24 In..	4375
Tabouret, Rosewood, Marble Top, Openwork, Ball & Claw Feet, c.1910, 19 x 17 In. .... *illus*	300
Tea Cart, Brass, Glass, Oval Top, Splayed Gallery, 3 Tiers Rotate Out, 29 x 30 In.	1063
Tea Cart, Mahogany, 3 Shelves, 2 Drawers, 1800s, 42 x 47 In...	1220
Tea Cart, Metamorphic, Renaissance Revival, Walnut, 3 Shelves, Trestle, 43 x 32 In.	512
Tray, On Stand, Wood, Box Stretcher, Cabriole Legs, Scroll Feet, Chinese, 14 In. .... *illus*	423
Umbrella Stand, Black Forest, Carved, Bear, Copper Tray, c.1890, 45 x 16 In. .... *illus*	3840
Umbrella Stand, Black Forest, Mother Bear, Holding Tree Limbs, Bear, 76 x 28 In.	3125
Umbrella Stand, Brass-Bound Oak Cask, Barrel Shape, 1800, 26 x 12 x 10 ½ In.	330
Umbrella Stand, G. Stickley, Oak Slats, Iron Riveted Hoops, Tapered, 24 x 10 In.	2000
Umbrella Stand, G. Stickley, Oak, Copper Base, Pan, Red Decal, c.1904, 27 x 12 In......... *illus*	11250
Umbrella Stand, Iron, Scroll Decoration, Molded Drip Pan, Cast, Wrought, 26 x 17 In.	549
Umbrella Stand, Walnut, Carved, Brass Handles, Gilt, Bun Feet, 46 x 13 In.	2688
Vanity, P. Evans, Cityscape, Brass, Mirror, Shelf, Bench, Mirror 70 x 20 In. .... *illus*	3375
Vitrine, George III, Mahogany, Glazed, Mullions, Shelves, 3 Doors, 83 x 71 In.	3250
Vitrine, Glass, Painted Wood, Hinged Top, Sloping Sides, Cabriole Legs, Italy, 32 x 35 In.	2500
Vitrine, Louis XV-XVI Style, Mahogany, Marble Top, Brass, Mirror, c.1910, 63 In.............. *illus*	1250
Vitrine, Mahogany, Demilune, Painted, Putti, Curved Glass Door, Ormolu, 61 In.....................	813
Vitrine, Robert Mitchell, Gilt, Painted, Glass Panes, Door, Scenes, 1800s, 70 x 34 In. .... *illus*	720
Wagon, Coaster, Wood, Box, Green, Tin Rims, Iron Undercarriage, 1900s, 16 x 36 x 16 In.	193
Wall Unit, P. Evans, Sculptured Metal, Bronze, Composite, Glass, Enamel, 1969, 78 x 86 In.....	8750
Washstand, Tiger Maple, 2 Tiers, Turned Legs, Drawer, Dovetailed, 1800s, 33 x 20 In. ..... *illus*	1045
Washstand, Walnut, Backsplash, 2 Drawers, Turned Legs, Shelf, 1800s, 36 x 37 In. .... *illus*	144
Washstand, Walnut, Corner, Triangular Shelves, Splayed Legs, 1800s, 39 x 21 In.	300
Wastebasket, G. Stickley, Wood Slats, Craftsman Label, 1912-16, 14 In............................ *illus*	3750
Window Seat, Chippendale, Mahogany, Carved, Outscrolled Arms, c.1780, 29 x 39 In. ..... *illus*	1140
Window Seat, Federal, Mahogany, Scroll Arms, Needlepoint Upholstery, 42 In................. *illus*	472
Wine Cage, Flat Disc, Door, Casters, Wrought Iron, 72 x 25 In.	209

G. ARGY-ROUSSEAU is the impressed mark used on a variety of glass objects in the Art Deco style. Gabriel Argy-Rousseau, born in 1885, was a French glass artist. In 1921, he formed a partnership that made pate-de-verre and other glass. The partnership ended in 1931 and he opened his own studio. He worked until 1952 and died in 1953.

Bowl, Ceres Pattern, Alternating Panels, Orange & Yellow Brown, Signed, 3 In.	4235
Jar, Lid, Roses, Lavender, Blue, Frosted, Pate-De-Verre, Signed, 3 x 3 ½ In. .... *illus*	2478
Pendant, Butterfly, Blue, Yellow, Brown, Pate-De-Verre, 2 ⅛ In.	878
Powder Box, Lid, Honesty Pattern, Stylized Leaves, Signed, 3 ¼ x 3 ¾ In......................... *illus*	1936
Vase, Frosty Ground, Purple, Snowberries, Pate-De-Verre, Signed, 4 In.	3540
Vase, Green Mask Surrounded By Grape Leaves, Cream Color, 3 ⅞ In.	1512
Vase, Lilac, Green Ground, Berries, Leaves, Pate-De-Verre, Signed, 4 In.	3422
Vase, Orchid Blue, Brown, Palm Fronds, Leaves, Deco, Signed, 3 In.	2950
Vase, Purple, Green Leaves, White, Pate-De-Verre, c.1925, 6 In.	5312

G. Argy-Rousseau, Jar, Lid, Roses, Lavender, Blue, Frosted, Pate-De-Verre, Signed, 3 x 3 ½ In.
$2,478

Humler & Nolan

G

G. Argy-Rousseau, Powder Box, Lid, Honesty Pattern, Stylized Leaves, Signed, 3 ¼ x 3 ¾ In.
$1,936

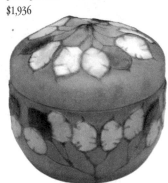

James D. Julia Auctioneers

Galle, Vase, Passion Flower, Blue, Yellow, Acid Etched, Cameo, Signed, 17 x 11 In.
$10,000

Rago Arts and Auction Center

This is an edited listing of current prices. Visit **Kovels.com** to check thousands of prices from previous years and sign up for free information on trends, tips, reproductions, marks, and more.

GALLE

Galle, Vase, Poppies, Shaded Red, White Ground, Footed, Cameo, 24¾ In.
$11,250

Rago Arts and Auction Center

Galle Pottery, Figurine, Dog, Seated, Flowers, Kimono, Cat Locket, Faience, c.1890, 12 x 9 In.
$1,750

Rago Arts and Auction Center

Galle Pottery, Wall Pocket, Fish Swimming, Bird Flying, Waves, Clouds, Stamped, Majorelle, 13 In.
$5,143

James D. Julia Auctioneers

GALLE was a designer who made glass, pottery, furniture, and other Art Nouveau items. Emile Galle founded his factory in France in 1874. After Galle's death in 1904, the firm continued to make glass and furniture until 1931. The *Galle* signature was used as a mark, but it was often hidden in the design of the object. Galle cameo and other types of glass are listed here. Pottery is in the next section. His furniture is listed in the Furniture category.

Beaker, Gilt, Enamel, Applied Decoration, Banded, Acid Etched, c.1900, 6½ In.	2812
Bowl, Orchids, Grasshopper, Purple, Red, White, Tulip Shape, France, c.1900, 6¾ x 8 In.	8125
Bowl, Red Roses, Buds, Leaves, Frosted Yellow Ground, Boat Shape, Cameo, Signed, 13 In.	3630
Jar, Lid, Dragons, Flowers, Red, Frosted Yellow Side Panels, Squared, Cameo, Signed, 7 In.	9075
Lamp, Base, Cone Shape, Bronze Collar, Flowers, Leaves, Blue, Cameo, Signed, 11 In.	363
Night-Light, Amber Leaves, Yellow Ground, Single Socket, Bronze Cap, Cameo, Signed, 5 In.	3630
Perfume Bottle, Goddess Of Destiny, Enamel, 6 In.	5700
Sconce, Pink, Frosted, Blossoms, Cameo, Brass Mount, Signed, 10 x 7½ In.	2714
Vase, Acid Etched Red Flowers, Yellow-Amber Ground, Flattened, c. 1900, 5¾ x 4½ In.	904
Vase, Amber, Brown, Etched, Flowers, Narrow, Cameo, 1914-36, 9 In.	861
Vase, Amethyst Stems, Leaves, Flowers, White Ground, Tapered, Cameo, Signed, 10 In.	907
Vase, Azure & Brown Flowers, Shaded Blue & Yellow Ground, Cameo, 1900, 10 In.	1046
Vase, Banjo, Flowers, Leaves, Purple Cut To Amber, Cameo, 8¾ x 2¾ In.	875
Vase, Banjo, Purple Flowers, Stems, Leaves, Pink Ground, Cameo, Signed, 6½ In.	544
Vase, Beetle, Branches, Leaves, Green, Brown, Cameo, 14¼ In.	6050
Vase, Blown-Out, Cherries, Green Leaves, Peach Ground, Bulbous, Signed, 10½ In.	11192
Vase, Blown-Out, Crocus, Red, Flowers, Stems, Yellow Ground, Baluster, Signed, 8 In.	1452
Vase, Blown-Out, Flowers, Purple, Blue, Shouldered, Frosted Yellow, Cameo, Signed, 11½ In.	4840
Vase, Blown-Out, Fuchsia, Blue Flowers, Leaves, Yellow Ground, Signed, 11½ In.	6050
Vase, Blown-Out, Rhododendron, Red, Green, Frosted Amber Ground, Squat, Signed, 10½ In.	18150
Vase, Blue Stems, Leaves, Frosted Yellow Ground, Squat, Cameo, Signed, 4½ x 8½ In.	4235
Vase, Brown Leaves & Buds, Green Ground, Fire Polished, Low, Oval, Signed, 3 x 10 In.	1375
Vase, Brown Trees, Lake, Canoe, Shaded Yellow Green Ground, Cameo, 1900, 13 x 4½ In.	2034
Vase, Bud, Clematis, Brown, Cameo, c.1925, 19½ x 6½ In.	1000
Vase, Carved, Flowers, Frosted Pink & Green, Carved Flowers, Cameo, Signed, 4 In.	540
Vase, Cherry Blossoms, White Ground, Shouldered, Signed, 15 In.	5445
Vase, Daffodil, Green, Yellow, Frosted Ground, Slender, Waisted, Cameo, Signed, 22 In.	1331
Vase, Dragonfly, Water Lilies, Stick Neck, Green, Acid Etched, c.1920, 12½ x 5½ In.	3000
Vase, Fisherman With Large Fish, Light Blue, Opalescent, Rounded, Cameo, 6 In.	11495
Vase, Flowers, Olive Green, Light Green Ground, Swollen Base, Tapered, Cameo, Signed, 8 In.	726
Vase, Flowers, Tapered, Purple Burgundy, Dish Base, Cameo, 4½ x 3¼ In.	377
Vase, Fuchsia, Saffron, Teardrop Form, Flared Rim, Cameo, 10 In.	545
Vase, Fuchsia, Stems, Leaves, Yellow Ground, Footed, Flared Lip, Cameo, Signed, 9 In.	2420
Vase, Hydrangea, Bulbous, Tapered, Frosted Ground, Cameo, 6 In.	484
Vase, Intaglio Leaves, Cylindrical, Swollen, Gilt, Cream Ground, Signed, 13 In.	6050
Vase, Iris, Blue Purple, Yellow Ground, Acid Etched, Cameo, 14 x 3¾ In.	2812
Vase, Iris, Lavender, Cream Ground, Fire Polished, Shouldered, Cameo, Signed, 5 In.	242
Vase, Irises, Stems, Leaves, Purple & Cream Ground, Spread Foot, Cameo, Signed, 16½ In.	1210
Vase, Landscape, Pink, Green, Purple, Cameo, 10½ x 3 In.	472
Vase, Leafy Vine, Red Over Citron Ground, Cameo, Signed, 8 In.	2242
Vase, Nasturtium, Green, Gilt, Etched Mark, 1900, 3 x 3¾ In.	1046
Vase, Oak Leaves, Amber, Green, Frosted Pink & White Ground, Swollen, Cameo, Signed, 13 In.	3327
Vase, Olive Green, Frosted Ground, Stick Neck, Cameo, Signed, 2 In.	826
Vase, Orange Spider Mums, Pink Ground, Tapered, Spread Foot, Cameo, Signed, 12 In.	2057
Vase, Passion Flower, Blue, Yellow, Acid Etched, Cameo, Signed, 17 x 11 In. .... *illus*	10000
Vase, Pinecone, Pine Branches, Acid Etched, Tan, White, Cameo, 13 x 5¼ In.	1500
Vase, Poppies, Shaded Red, White Ground, Footed, Cameo, 24¾ In. .... *illus*	11250
Vase, Purple Flowers, Leaves, Stems, White Satin Ground, Cameo, 1900, 5½ x 2¼ In.	300
Vase, Purple Flowers, Leaves, White, Long Neck, Cameo, 5¼ x 2¾ In.	250
Vase, Purple Mountains, Amber Trees, Short Neck, Tapered, Cameo, 5½ x 3¼ In.	630
Vase, Red Flower, Leaves, Stems, Bulbous, Slender Neck, Cameo, 1900, 12 x 3¾ In.	678
Vase, Red Lilies, Pale Green Ground, Tapered, Cameo, 10½ x 3 In.	11107
Vase, Red Poppy, Funnel Neck, Cameo, Signed, 1900, 20 In.	861
Vase, Roses, Acid Etched, Cameo, 14½ x 4 In.	1375

G

Vase, Scenic Mountains, Blue & Green, Purple Trees, Boat Shape, Cameo, Signed, 7 1/2 x 5 1/2 In.	2178
Vase, Scenic, Riverside, Trumpet Rim, Frosted Ground, Cameo, 9 3/4 In.	908
Vase, Scenic, Trees, Lake, Square Corset Form, Cameo, 10 In.	120
Vase, Seaweed, Orange, Yellow, Green, Acid Etched, Fire Polished, Cameo, c.1900, 9 x 4 In.	9375
Vase, Stars, Columbines, Orange, Red, Beige, Acid Etched, Foil Inclusions, c.1900, 12 x 6 In.	7500
Vase, Stick, Green Leaves, Purple Flowers, Cream Ground, Bulbous Foot, Cameo, Signed, 23 In.	1936
Vase, Sycamore, Orange Highlights, Swollen Base, Cameo, Signed, 18 x 2 In.	968
Vase, Water Lilies, White Shaded To Yellow, Purple Leaves, c.1920, 8 x 4 1/4 In.	812
Vase, Water Lily, Pink, Gray, Brown, 6 3/4 x 4 In.	413

GALLE POTTERY was made by Emile Galle, the famous French designer, after 1874. The pieces were marked with the initials *E. G.* impressed, *Em. Galle Faiencerie de Nancy,* or a version of his signature. Galle is best known for his glass, listed above.

Bowl, Crackle Glaze, 3-Footed, Carved Wooden Lid, 1900s, 11 x 4 3/4 x 12 In.	156
Bowl, Flowers, Dolphin Heads On Each Side, Brown Glaze, Handle, 9 3/4 x 14 In.	968
Bowl, Reticulated, Glazed, 10 x 7 3/4 In.	130
Box, Fleur-De-Lis, White, Violas, Leaves, Gilt, 3 1/2 x 10 1/2 In.	250
Figurine, Cat, Blue Hearts, Yellow, Faience, Signed E. Galle, 7 1/2 x 5 In.	1560
Figurine, Dog, Seated, Flowers, Kimono, Cat Locket, Faience, c.1890, 12 x 9 In. .... *illus*	1750
Vase, Earth Tone Glazes, 4 Overlapping Leaves Shape, Marked, 9 x 7 In.	1180
Vase, Folded Leaves, Flower Stalks, Green, Red, Yellow, 9 x 7 In.	1200
Wall Pocket, Fish Swimming, Bird Flying, Waves, Clouds, Stamped, Majorelle, 13 In. ..... *illus*	5143

GAME collectors like all types of games. Of special interest are any board games or card games. Transogram and other company names are included in the description when known. Other games may be found listed under Card, Toy, or the name of the character or celebrity featured in the game. Gameboards without the game pieces are listed in the Gameboard category.

Bagatelle, Table Top, Mahogany, Folding Case, England, 1800s, 41 1/2 x 20 In.	688
Box, Cribbage, Dominoes, Dice, Bone, Napoleonic, Prisoner-Of-War, Sliding Top, c.1810, 8 In... *illus*	600
Box, Mahogany, Inlaid Brass, Monogram, 110 Mother-Of-Pearl Counters, France, 12 x 9 In.	113
Checkers, Chess, Plastic, Oilcloth Board, Red Cross Set, P.O.W.s, Box, 1940s, 13 x 13 In.	50
Chess Set, Civil War Pieces, Polystone, Walnut & Maple Veneer Board, 13 x 19 x 2 In.	71
Chess Set, Malachite, Alabaster, Missing Piece, 1975	88
Chess Set, Medieval Chessmen, Inlaid Gray & Briar Veneer Wood, 18 x 18 x 2 In.	139
Cribbage, Light & Dark Wood Fans, Diamond Inlays, Moon, Arrow, 1800s, 14 x 5 1/2 In. .. *illus*	540
Flivver, Yellow, 4 Die Cut Buses, Milton Bradley, 16 1/2 In.	180
Fortune Telling, Boys & Girls, Here's Your Fate, Spinner, Whitney, 1920s	205
Horse Racing, Jeu De Course, Spring Operated, 2 Rings, 4 Jockeys, J&P France, 1910, 13 x 6 In.	480
Mahjong, 164 Black Based Tiles, 5 Multicolor Trays, Alligator Leather Case, 1900s	813
Mahjong, Bakelite Tiles, Brass Holder, Red, Yellow, Green, Blue, Faux Alligator Case, 19 x 9 In.	120
Mahjong, Bone Tiles, Art Decor, Wooden Case, Black, Dragon, Chinese, 1900s	96
Mahjong, Bone Tiles, Wooden Case, Lacquered, 3 Drawers, A.L. Reed Co., 1900s	132
Mahjong, Faux Ivory Tiles, 5-Drawer Case, Etched, Art Deco, Chinese, 1900s	100
Mahjong, Ivory, Veneer, Wooden Box, 1900s, 5 1/2 x 3 In.	36
Mahjong, Tiles, Dice, Pushers, Posts, Alligator Case	96
Monopoly, Wooden Houses, Hotels, Cards, Waddingtons, Great Britian, 1940s	75
Old Maid, Cards, Color Illustrations, Box, Instructions, 17 Pairs, c.1880	125
Pinball, 3 Ring Circus, Wood Case, Glass Top, Metal Balls, 31 x 16 x 9 1/2 In.	540
Puzzle, 3 Scenes, Families, Seasons, Trees, Jannin Of Paris, Box, c.1855, 12 x 9 In. .... *illus*	345
Puzzle, Fire Engine Picture, Fire Wagon, 3 Horses, McLoughlin Bros., Box, 18 In. .... *illus*	120
Puzzle, Fire Engine Scroll, 3 Cardboard Pictures, McLoughlin Bros., Box, 11 x 17 In. ...... *illus*	177
Roulette Wheel, Gilt Stenciled Numbers, Chrome Plated Spindle, Brass Rim, 9 x 34 In.	2723
Roulette Wheel, Stainless Steel, Plastic Base, France, c.1960, 4 x 18 In.	156
Shooting, Whirli Bird, Metal Frame, Tabletop, Tin Lithograph, 1950s, 13 x 6 In.	20 to 30
Spider & The Fly, Discs, Red, Blue, Waverly Toy Works, c.1889, 4 x 4 In.	78
Wheel Of Chance, 4 Spokes, Plate, White, Black, Red Stenciled Numbers, c.1920, 36 x 1 x 1 In.	140
Wheel Of Chance, Painted Red, Mustard Yellow, Black, 1900s, 63 In. .... *illus*	480

Game, Box, Cribbage, Dominoes, Dice, Bone, Napoleonic, Prisoner-Of-War, Sliding Top, c.1810, 8 In.
$600

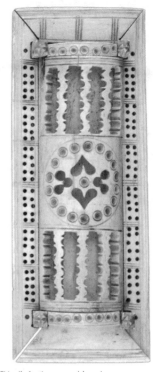

Eldred's Auctioneers and Appraisers

Game, Cribbage, Light & Dark Wood Fans, Diamond Inlays, Moon, Arrow, 1800s, 14 1/2 x 5 1/2 In.
$540

Eldred's Auctioneers and Appraisers

TIP
Missing part of a jigsaw puzzle? Make a color photocopy of the picture of the puzzle on the box. Enlarge or shrink the copy to exactly the size of the puzzle. Then cut it to make the missing piece. It will be an almost perfect match.

G

Game, Puzzle, 3 Scenes, Families, Seasons, Trees, Jannin Of Paris, Box, c.1855, 12 x 9 In.
$345

Theriault's

Game, Puzzle, Fire Engine Picture, Fire Wagon, 3 Horses, McLoughlin Bros., Box, 18 In.
$120

Bertoia Auctions

Game, Puzzle, Fire Engine Scroll, 3 Cardboard Pictures, McLoughlin Bros., Box, 11 x 17 In.
$177

AntiqueAdvertising.com

TIP

It is not just ivory mahjong tiles that are wanted; collectors also like Bakelite tiles. Newer, plastic tiles are not selling well.

Wheel Of Chance, Painted, Marked, Fair Supply Co., 23 In. .... *illus*	425
Wheel Of Chance, Yellow, Green Stand, 21 1/2 x 6 In.	497
Ya-Lo, Football Card Game, Offensive Cards, Defensive Cards, 17 x 10 In.	23

GAME PLATES are plates of any make decorated with pictures of birds, animals, or fish. The game plates usually came in sets consisting of 12 dishes and a serving platter. These sets were most popular during the 1880s.

Birds, Oval Platter, 12 Plates, Gilt Scroll Edge, Porcelain, Coronet, c.1915, 13 Piece	815
Deer, Tree, Tall Grass, G. Demartine & Co., Gold Trim, 8 In.	125
Duck, In Flight, Over Pond, Gilt Trim, Limoges, c.1900, 8 3/4 In.	145
Fish, Flower Border, Green Trim, Victoria, Angel, Austria, 8 In., 12 Piece	1000
Mallard, Sunset Landscape, Ribbed, Gilt, Cauldon, 19th Century, 8 3/4 In.	170
Pheasant, Tall Grass, O. & E.G. Royal Austria, c.1910, 12 In.	45
Quail In Flight, Marshland, Oval, Scalloped Edge, Haviland, c.1890, 18 x 13 x 2 In.	295

GAMEBOARD collectors look for just the board without the game pieces. The boards are collected as folk art or decorations. Gameboards that are part of a complete game are listed in the Game category.

Automobile, Car Names, Red, Blue, Orange, Octagonal, Wood, 1940s, 23 x 33 In.	396
Checkers, Black & Red, Silver-Painted Lines, Molded Edge, Square, c.1900, 16 1/2 In. ...... *illus*	6765
Checkers, Black Squares, Natural Pine, c.1875, 17 x 20 In.	150
Checkers, Black, White, Green, Painted, 2-Sided, 1800s, 12 x 14 1/2 In.	312
Checkers, Black, White, Various Advertising, 21 1/2 x 21 1/2 In.	105
Checkers, Dark & Light Stain, c.1920, 12 3/4 x 12 1/2 In.	113
Checkers, Glass, Wood Frame, Painted, Red, Gilt, c.1840, 19 x 19 In.	140
Checkers, Nine Men's Morris, 2-Sided, c.1890, 13 1/4 x 13 1/4 In.	480
Checkers, Oak & Black Squares, Molded Edge, c.1920, 18 1/2 x 24 In.	93
Checkers, Old Gray Overpaint, Signed Duco, 1900s, 21 x 21 In. .... *illus*	438
Checkers, Pine Barrel Top, Green & Cream, 1800s, 19 In.	81
Checkers, Pine, Painted, Black & Yellow, c.1925, 19 x 29 In.	406
Checkers, Pine, Red & Black, Green Frame, c.1890, 16 x 16 In.	140
Checkers, Red, Black, Geometric Curves, 27 1/4 x 17 1/4 In.	390
Checkers, Red, White, Wood, 31 x 19 1/2 In.	360
Checkers, Walnut & Maple, Molded Frame Edge, 14 1/2 In.	177
Checkers, Wood, Red & Black Paint, Yellow Back, c.1890, 24 x 15 3/4 In. .... *illus*	330
Checkers, Wood, Red & Black, 20 1/2 x 28 In.	82
Checkers, Wood, Red & White Squares, Green Border, H. Gable's, c.1925, 19 x 19	228
Checkers, Yellow, Green, c.1950, 17 3/4 x 17 In.	88
Chess, Inlaid, Burl Walnut, Masonic Symbols, Wide Frame, 1899s, 22 1/4 In.	153
Chess, Inlay, Light & Dark Squares, Game Piece Trays, Triangles, 1900s, 28 x 18 In. .... *illus*	147
Chess, Wood, Marquetry, Ebony, Bone, 1900s, 13 In.	156
Chinese Checkers, Cream, Green, Red, Tan, Circle, 6-Point Star, 26 x 26 In.	70
Dart, Hunter & Horse, Cork, Hanging Rope, Signed, Mermade, 1960s, 23 x 17 In.	195
Parcheesi, Checkers, 2-Sided, Red, Green, Yellow, 1800s, 18 1/4 x 18 1/2 In.	175
Parcheesi, Checkers, Pink Border, Red & Green Squares, 18 x 18 In.	5142
Parcheesi, Circles, Diamonds, Green, Light Blue, 25 x 19 In.	251
Parcheesi, Pine, Orange & Green Paint, Made By GKS, Dec. 30, 1898, 17 In.	540
Parcheesi, Pine, Red, Pink, Black, Yellow, White, c.1940, 16 x 16 In.	388
Parcheesi, Red, Green, Paint, c.1920, 20 1/2 x 20 1/2 In. .... *illus*	649

GARDEN FURNISHINGS have been popular for centuries. The stone or metal statues, urns and fountains, sundials, small figurines, and wire, iron, or rustic furniture are included in this category. Many of the metal pieces have been made continuously for years.

Aquarium, Steel Frame, Metal Rose Swags, Glass, c.1905, 15 x 20 In.	515
Arbor, Shelves, S-Scrolls, Arched, 96 x 72 In., 3 Piece	224
Arbor, Metal, Lattice Work, Decoration, 85 1/2 x 58 1/2 In., 3 Piece	96
Bench, 8 Women, Holding Hands, Wrought Iron, Welded, 30 x 60 In.	512
Bench, Arched Back, Medallion, Classical Maiden, Pierced Vines, Cast Iron, 74 In., Pair	3500

Game, Wheel Of Chance, Painted Red, Mustard Yellow, Black, 1900s, 63 In.
$480

Eldred's Auctioneers and Appraisers

Game, Wheel Of Chance, Painted, Marked, Fair Supply Co., 23 In.
$425

Copake Auction

Gameboard, Checkers, Black & Red, Silver Painted Lines, Molded Edge, Square, c.1900, 16½ In.
$6,765

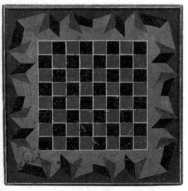

Skinner, Inc.

A Bit of Game History

Checkers, called "droughts" in England, appears to have been familiar to Egyptians in the first few centuries B.C. The game reached Europe sometime between the twelfth and sixteenth century.

Chess may or may not have developed from checkers, but it was being played in India in the sixth century. By the year 1000, it had spread to Europe.

Parcheesi is the national game of India, where it was invented in the sixth century. From there it spread throughout the world. A "cross and circle game," it is also known as parchisi, derived from the Indian word *pacis*, which means 25. Selchow & Righter trademarked the game as Parcheesi in 1874.

Gameboard, Checkers, Old Gray Overpaint, Signed Duco, 1900s, 21 x 21 In.
$438

Garth's Auctioneers & Appraisers

Gameboard, Checkers, Wood, Red & Black Paint, Yellow Back, c.1890, 24 x 15¾ In.
$330

Eldred's Auctioneers and Appraisers

Gameboard, Chess, Inlay, Light & Dark Squares, Game Piece Trays, Triangles, 1900s, 28 x 18 In.
$147

Copake Auction

Gameboard, Parcheesi, Red, Green, Paint, c.1920, 20½ x 20½ In.
$649

Copake Auction

GARDEN

Garden, Chair, Gothic Pattern, Cast Iron, Pierced, Scroll Arms, Carron Design, 1800s, 35 In., Pair
$3,000

Neal Auction Co.

Garden, Seat, Rosewood, Barrel Shape, Inset Porcelain, Butterflies, Chinese, 1800, 12 In.
$300

Eldred's Auctioneers and Appraisers

Garden, Seat, White On Blue, Porcelain, Drum Shape, Birds, Flowers, 1800s, 18 In., Pair
$600

Eldred's Auctioneers and Appraisers

Garden, Settee, Rococo Revival, Cast Iron, Fleur-De-Lis, Vines, Scroll Arms, 1800s, 33 x 40 In.
$1,500

Neal Auction Co.

TIP

Outdoor stonework and statues, even if made of granite, can be damaged by acid rain, frost, and plants like ivy. Put garden statues on stands to keep the moisture from the grass away from the statue. Wash with a hose and a soft brush.

Garden, Sundial, Tombstone Shape, Engraved Pewter Gnomon, Por Jesus Bal, 1822, 19 x 13 In.
$1,188

Garth's Auctioneers & Appraisers

Gaudy Dutch, Pitcher, Carnation, Soft Paste, 5 In.
$472

Hess Auction Group

Gaudy Dutch, Plate, Carnation, Green & Yellow Leaves, 8⅜ In.
$200

Hess Auction Group

Bench, Black Forest, Pierced, Figural Bear Ends, Carved Wood, 1900s, 38 x 67 In......	2640
Bench, Branches, Leaves, Vine, Slatted Seat, Branch Legs, 30 x 50 ¼ In......	1830
Bench, Cast Iron, Leaves & Berries On Back, Griffin-Form Legs, c.1925, 30 x 43 In.....	938
Bench, Cast Iron, Serpentine Crest, Horseshoe Back, Gothic, 1810, 35 x 44 In......	1024
Bench, Gothic Style, Cast Iron, Honeycomb Pattern Seat, 1900s, 34 x 56 In., Pair	2125
Bench, Grotto, Mecca, Clamshell Seats, Italy, 37 ¼ x 57 In.....	6875
Bench, Iron, Strap, White, 48 In......	175
Bench, Man, Woman, Seated, Flat, John Kennedy, 50 x 42 In......	4375
Bench, Overlapping Arches, Iron, 36 In......	480
Bench, Repeating Arches, Leaves, White, 35 x 45 In......	2460
Birdbath, Baboon, Sitting, Bowl On Head, Stepped Base, White Glaze, Terra-Cotta, 1900s, 22 In.	240
Birdbath, Circular Basin, 2 Resting Doves, Leaf Base, Cast Iron, 1900s, 33 x 22 In.	438
Birdhouse, Building, 3 Tiers, Tower, Yellow, Red Trim, 1900s, 45 In.	146
Birdhouse, English Cottage, 2 Porches, Bay Windows, Black Roof, Miller Iron Works, 11 x 14 In.	1560
Cart, 3 Tiers, 2 Wheels, Scrolls, Hearts, Metal, 60 x 67 In.	155
Chair Set, Regency Style, Folding, Welded, Interlaced Back, Black Paint, 1900s, 34 In., 4	1080
Chair, Gothic Pattern, Cast Iron, Pierced, Scrolled Arms, Carron Design, 1800s, 35 In., Pair *illus*	3000
Chaise Longue, Richard Schultz, Wire, Square Foot, Disc Wheel, Knoll Assoc., 1963 29 x 72 In.	715
Chiminea, Fireplace, Grapes, Vines, Terra-Cotta, 42 ¼ x 22 In.	36
Dining Set, Patio, Iron, Scroll Design, Round Top, 4 Chairs, Fabric Seat Covers, 1960s	955
Figure, Buddha, Concrete, 1800s, 44 x 17 In......	62
Figure, Diana, With Quiver & Bow, Terra-Cotta, 1900s, 51 x 15 In.	1125
Figure, Griffin, On Molded Plinths, Wings Spread, Cast Stone, England, c.1900s, 33 x 18 In.....	2250
Figure, Lion, Seated, Molded Stone, Raised Base, England, c.1900, 24 x 10 ½ In., Pair	1063
Figure, Lion, Seated, On Globe, Doric Column, Bronze, Cast Iron, 48 x 14 In., Pair......	1100
Figure, Lion, Seated, Shield, Curly Mane, Stone, 47 In., Pair	9375
Figure, Woman, Stone, Classically Dressed, Cup, Basket Of Grapes, Leaves, 64 In......	625
Finial, Ball, Cement, 13 ¾ x 12 ¼ In., Pair......	72
Fountain, Brass, Bronze, Copper, Discs On Spikes, Silas Seandel, 1960s, 72 x 48 In.	4062
Fountain, Classical Water Carrier, Female, Shell, Dolphins, Weathered Patina, 94 In., Pair.....	8125
Fountain, Stork, Wings Out, Beak Up, Flowers, Paint, Spelter, 42 x 42 In......	3135
Fountain, Water Carrier, Maiden, Seated, Holding Jug, Patinated, 30 In......	750
Fountain, Woman, Bathing, Urn, Leaves, Bird, Dolphins, Mathurin Moreau, Iron, 52 x 21 In.	1200
Gnome, White Beard, Red Hat & Shoes, Yellow Apron, Iron, Continental, 1800s, 29 In......	960
Hitching Post, Horse Head, Colonial Column Features, Cast Iron, 1800s, 44 x 6 x 6 ½ In.	923
Jar, Black Paint, Iron, Egg & Dart Rim, Floral Sides, Victorian, 30 x 22 In......	510
Jardiniere, Bentwood, Urn Shape, Basket Weave, Turned Pedestal, 33 x 23 In., Pair......	786
Lavabo, Hand Forged, Ornamental, Wall Rack, Large Pan, Hanger, c.1700, 54 x 18 x 19 In.	300
Lawn Jockey, Black, Cast Iron Base, Mounted, 37 x 10 x 12 In.	360
Lid, Wood, Octagonal, Signed, Chinese, 1800s, 17 In.	270
Mailbox, Cube, Man, On Horseback, Pedestal, Square Foot, Cast Iron, 45 x 15 In.	200
Ornament, Armillary Sphere, Tripod Base, 41 ½ x 27 In......	134
Ornament, Dog Barking, Cast Iron, Black Paint, 37 x 33 In......	60
Ornament, Stork, White, Cast Iron, 42-In. Wing Span, 42 In. Tall	3355
Ornament, Urn Shape, Fruit, Flowers, Cast Stone, c.1950, 16 ½ x 9 In., Pair	913
Patio Set, Iron & Wire, Table, 4 Chairs, Round Table, 28 ½ x 48 In., 5 Piece......	200
Plant Stand, see also Furniture, Stand, Plant	
Planter, Adam, Eve, Garden, Concrete, Rectangular, 8 x 32 In., Pair......	247
Planter, Apostles, Aggregate Stone, Square Base, 19 ½ x 20 In.	253
Planter, Iron, Wirework, Semicircle, 47 ½ x 31 In.	120
Planter, Sheet Metal, Tapered Square, Ring Handles, Ball Feet, 44 x 32 In., Pair......	1750
Planter, Urn, Metal, Acanthus Bands, Rolled Rim, Figural Handles, 20 x 16 In......	384
Planter, Zinc, Rectangular, Ring Handle, 19 ¾ x 19 ¾ In., Pair......	343
Seat, Rosewood, Barrel Shape, Inset Porcelain, Butterflies, Chinese, 1800, 12 In............. *illus*	300
Seat, White On Blue, Porcelain, Drum Shape, Birds, Flowers, 1800s, 18 In., Pair .... *illus*	600
Settee, Rococo Revival, Cast Iron, Fleur-De-Lis, Vines, Scroll Arms, 1800s, 33 x 40 In. ..... *illus*	1500
Settee, Shaped, Teak, Upholstered Cushion, 34 ½ x 67 In.	275
Sprinkler, Alligator, Green, 1930s, 11 x 6 In......	204
Sprinkler, Alligator, Heart Shape Sprayer, 8 ½ In......	330

Gaudy Dutch, Plate, No Name Pattern, Flowers, Leaves, Blue, Orange, Green, 8 ¾ In.
$11,210

Hess Auction Group

G

Gaudy Dutch, Plate, Single Rose, 10 In.
$472

Hess Auction Group

Gaudy Dutch, Plate, Sunflower, 7 ½ In.
$236

Hess Auction Group

TIP
Save your broken dishes, vases, and other decorative china to make mosaic stepping stones or tabletops for your garden. Chipped vases can still be used for flowers or turned upside down to make toad homes.

Gene Autry, Costume, Vest, Chaps, Double Holster, Rubber Galoshes, Child's
$72

Rich Penn Auctions

Gene Autry, Poster, Hills Of Utah, Gene's A Doctor On Horseback!, c.1956, 41½ x 27½ In.
$72

Rich Penn Auctions

Sprinkler, Cowboy, Lasso, Red Bandanna, Aluminum, 1950s, 30 x 13 In.	1430
Sprinkler, Duck, Mallard, White, Standing On Half Shell, Iron, Bradley & Hubbard, 13 In.	660
Sprinkler, Figural, Duck, Cast Iron, Angled Spouts, Top Of Head, c.1920s, 6 x 13 In.	200
Sprinkler, Frog, Seated, On Ball, Red Zigzag, 10 In.	780
Sprinkler, Turtle, Head Raised, 3-Prong, Cast Iron, 8 x 12 x 6½ In.	360
Stake, Marker, Cast Iron, Embossed 14, Quatrefoil Shape, Victorian, 1800s, 14 In.	45
Sundial, Astrological, Horoscope Signs, Cast Metal, 30 x 28 In.	1026
Sundial, Count Only Sunny Hours, Virginia Metal, Iron, Brass, 1940s, 10 In. Diam.	875
Sundial, Tombstone Shape, Engraved Pewter Gnomon, Por Jesus Bal, 1822, 19 x 13 In. .. *illus*	1188
Table, Cast Iron, Paint, Round, Openwork Scroll, Cabriole Legs, 1800s, 25 x 39 In.	995
Table, Iron, Aluminum, Round Glass Top, Swan Shape Support, Square Base, 30½ x 36 In. ...	480
Topiary, Graduated, White, Spiral, Fleur-De-Lis Finials, 3 Piece	64
Trellis, Arched Window, Painted, Metal, 74 x 30 In.	448
Trellis, Arched, Picket Fence, White, Model, c.1920, 16 x 18 In.	88
Urn, Bands, Terra-Cotta, 39 x 32 In., Pair	600
Urn, Basket Weave, Stepped Round Foot, 18 x 13½ In., Pair	205
Urn, Concrete, Raised Flowers, Ram's Head, 26 x 20 In., Pair	540
Urn, Iron, Classical Figures, Lions' Heads, 24 x 36 In.	175
Urn, Seated Putti, Ram's Head, Gadrooned, 27½ In., Pair	625
Wheelbarrow, Wood, Red, Black, Stencil, Tin Hubcaps, Strap Iron, Dan Patch, 1920-40s, 39 x 16 x 15 In.	60

GAUDY DUTCH pottery was made in England for the American market from about 1810 to 1820. It is a white earthenware with Imari-style decorations of red, blue, green, yellow, and black. Only sixteen patterns of Gaudy Dutch were made: Butterfly, Carnation, Dahlia, Double Rose, Dove, Grape, Leaf, Oyster, Primrose, Single Rose, Strawflower, Sunflower, Urn, War Bonnet, Zinnia, and No Name. Other similar wares are called Gaudy Ironstone and Gaudy Welsh.

 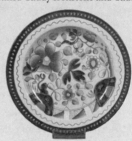 

Grape pattern	Single Rose pattern	War Bonnet pattern
1810–1820	1810–1820	1810–1820

Coffeepot, Red Flowers, Blue Bands, 1800s, 11½ In.	2318
Creamer, Red Flowers, Blue Leaves, 1800s, 4¼ In.	549
Creamer, Single Rose, Helmet Shape, 5 In.	1062
Pitcher, Carnation, Soft Paste, 5 In. *illus*	472
Plate, Butterfly, 6½ In.	501
Plate, Carnation, Green & Yellow Leaves, 8⅜ In. *illus*	200
Plate, Dove, Green, Yellow Leaves, 8⅜ In.	106
Plate, Dove, Red Flowers, Leaves, 1800s, 9¾ In.	275
Plate, No Name Pattern, Flowers, Leaves, Blue, Orange, Green, 8¾ In. *illus*	11210
Plate, Single Rose, 10 In. *illus*	472
Plate, Sunflower, 7½ In. *illus*	236
Waste Bowl, Primrose, 3 x 6 In.	560

 GAUDY WELSH is an Imari-decorated earthenware with red, blue, green, and gold decorations. Most Gaudy Welsh was made in England for the American market. It was made from 1820 to about 1860.

Pitcher, Red Orange, Green Dragon Handle, 1800s, 10 In.	120
Tureen, Porcelain, Lid, Orange, Blue Flowers, 1800s	96
Vegetable, Dome Lid, Flowers, Multicolor, 10 x 9 In.	70

GENE AUTRY was born in 1907. He began his career as the "Singing Cowboy" in 1928. His first movie appearance was in 1934, his last in 1958. His likeness and that of the Wonder Horse, Champion, were used on toys, books, lunch boxes, and advertisements.

Costume, Vest, Chaps, Double Holster, Rubber Galoshes, Child's	*illus*	72
Poster, Hills Of Utah, Gene's A Doctor On Horseback!, c.1956, 41 ½ x 27 ½ In.	*illus*	72

GIBSON GIRL black-and-blue decorated plates were made in the early 1900s. Twenty-four different 10 ½-inch plates were made by the Royal Doulton pottery at Lambeth, England. These pictured scenes from the book *A Widow and Her Friends* by Charles Dana Gibson. Another set of twelve 9-inch plates featuring pictures of the heads of Gibson Girls had all-blue decoration. Many other items also pictured the famous Gibson Girl.

Belt Buckle, Sterling Silver, Art Nouveau, 3 ½ x 1 ½ In.		295
Photo, Black Plastic Frame, Hat, Cape, 6 In.		30
Plate, A Quiet Dinner With Dr. Bottles, 1900, 10 ¼ In.	*illus*	85
Plate, Message For The Outside World, 10 ½ In.		115
Plate, Miss Babbles Brings A Copy, 10 ½ In.		69
Plate, Mr. Waddles Arrives Late, 10 ½ In.		95
Plate, She Finds Some Consolation, 10 ½ In.		120
Plate, She Goes To The Fancy Dress Ball, 10 ½ In.		98
Plate, She Looks For Relief From Some Of The Old Ones, 10 ½ In.		125
Plate, They Go Fishing, 10 ½ In.		95
Postcard, Hands In Muff, Dog Pointing, Winter Scene		15
Stickpin, Enamel, Gold Plated, 2 ½ In.		15
Tin, Cigarette, Navy Dress, Rings Of Smoke, Lithograph, c.1900, 4 ¼ x 3 In.		42

GILLINDER pressed glass was first made by William T. Gillinder of Philadelphia in 1863. The company had a working factory on the grounds at the Centennial and made small, marked pieces of glass for sale as souvenirs. They made a variety of decorative glass pieces and tablewares. The company was out of business by the early 1930s.

GILLINDER

Compote, Oval, Frosted, c.1879, 11 ¾ x 5 ½ In.	210
Pitcher, Milk, Westward Ho, c.1879, 7 ½ In.	321

GIRL SCOUT collectors search for anything pertaining to the Girl Scouts, including uniforms, publications, and old cookie boxes. The Girl Scout movement started in 1912, two years after the Boy Scouts. It began under Juliette Gordon Low of Savannah, Georgia. The first Girl Scout cookies were sold in 1928.

Charm, Silver, Heart, Amber Guilloche, 1930s, ⅝ x ⅝ In.		65
Charm, Silver, Senior Roundup, Mountain, Trees, 1962, ¹¹⁄₁₆ In.		35
Cup, Telescoping, Embossed Emblem, 2 ½ In.		18
Doll, Brownie, Painted Brown Eyes, Dark Brown Hair, Terri Lee, c.1950, 16 In.	*illus*	200
Jumper, Elastic Stretch Belt, Felt Hat, Yellow Bow Tie Pin, Sash, c.1958, Size 10		95
Pin, Brownie, Brass, Dancing Pixie, c.1940, 1 ¼ x 1 ⅜ In.	*illus*	20
Sewing Kit, Green Vinyl Case, Insignia, Thread, Needles, 1960s, 4 x 2 In.		20

GLASS factories that are well known are listed in this book under the factory name. This category lists pieces made by less well-known factories. Additional pieces of glass are listed in this book under the type of glass, in the categories Glass-Art, Glass-Blown, Glass-Bohemian, Glass-Contemporary, Glass-Midcentury, Glass-Venetian, and under the factory name.

Candle Lamp, Green Feathered, Brass Holder & Shade, Favrile, Marked, 12 ½ In.	944
Cocktail Shaker, Vintage, Chrome Top, Strainer, Modern Design, 9 ¾ x 4 x 4 In.	224
Decanter Set, Cranberry, Gold Trim, Flower, c.1925, 11 ½ In., 11 Piece	110
Dresser Box, Casket Shape, Gilt Bronze Mounts, c.1900, 10 x 7 In.	1995
Pitcher, Ruffled Rim, Cranberry, Pink, Diamond Quilted, Floral, Ribbed Frosted Handle, 8 ½ x 7 ¾ In.	118

Gibson Girl, Plate, A Quiet Dinner With Dr. Bottles, 1900, 10 ¼ In.
$85

Ruby Lane

Girl Scout, Doll, Brownie, Painted Brown Eyes, Dark Brown Hair, Terri Lee, c.1950, 16 In.
$200

G

Ruby Lane

Girl Scout, Pin, Brownie, Brass, Dancing Pixie, c.1940, 1 ¼ x 1 ⅜ In.
$20

Ruby Lane

GLASS

Glass-Art, Basket, Blue Cut To Gray, Winged Griffins, Leaves, 1800s, 8 In. $420

Garth's Auctioneers & Appraisers

Glass-Art, Compote, Lid, Cobalt, Cut Scalloped Rim, Paneled Body & Lid, 13 In. $500

Garth's Auctioneers & Appraisers

Glass-Art, Sculpture, Picasso, Stylized Face, Mustache, Long Hair, Green Glass, Murano, 9 In. $6,050

James D. Julia Auctioneers

GLASS-ART. Art glass means any of the many forms of glassware made during the late nineteenth or early twentieth century. These wares were expensive when they were first made and production was limited. Art glass is not the typical commercial glass that was made in large quantities, and most of the art glass was produced by hand methods. Later twentieth-century glass is listed under Glass-Contemporary, Glass-Midcentury, or Glass-Venetian. Even more art glass may be found in categories such as Burmese, Cameo Glass, Tiffany, and other factory names.

Item	Price
Basket, Blue Cut To Gray, Winged Griffins, Leaves, 1800s, 8 In. .... *illus*	420
Biscuit Jar, White Satin, Pink Flowers, Melon Ribbed, Silver Plate Lid & Bail, 6½ In.	60
Bottle, Brown, Gilt, Leaf, Stopper, 1900s	60
Bowl, Amethyst Swirl, Iridescent Design, Loetz Style, 4 x 11 In.	180
Bowl, Cherry Blossoms, Red, Pale Green, Enamel, Gilt, Wheel Carved, 4¼ x 7 In.	5937
Bowl, Clear, Molded, Etched, Hexagonal, Gilt Edge, c.1925, 8 x 10 In.	500
Bowl, Green Opalescent, Gilt Metal Frame, Cherub, 14 x 11 In.	84
Bowl, Green, Clear, Enamel Flowers, Oval, Moser Style, 2¾ x 7 In.	60
Bowl, Relief Decorated, Raised, Flared Rim, Circular Foot, 1928-31, 3¾ x 7¼ In.	400
Box, Cobalt Blue, White Enamel, Gold Trim, Round, Hinged, Lid, Gilt Metal Feet, 3¾ x 4½ In. ..	150
Box, Hinged Lid, Blue, Gold Enamel Flowers, Apples, Round, Gilt Metal Feet, 5½ x 5 In.	270
Box, Lid, Blown-Out, Gold Plate, 1900, 5 x 7 In.	492
Box, Square, Blue, Iridescent, Green Oil Spot, Hinged, Brass Lid, Engraved Holly, 2 x 3 In.	150
Candle Lamp, Gold Iridescent, Twisted Base, Ruffled Shade, Gorham Mounts, 14 In.	720
Caviar Server, Blue, Pedestal, Underplate, Gilt, Leaves, 5 x 5 x 6½ In.	53
Chalice, Opaque White, Cobalt Blue Applied Handle, Pedestal, 8 In.	72
Compote, Greco Roman Image, Frosted, Green, 5½ x 11½ In.	59
Compote, Lid, Cobalt, Cut Scalloped Rim, Paneled Body & Lid, 13 In. .... *illus*	500
Cruet, Enamel Dragonfly & Blossom, Amber Ribbed Handle & Stopper, 7¼ In.	120
Cup & Saucer, Clear, Floral Garland, Gold Stencil Highlights, 3-Footed	60
Dresser Box, Hinged Lid, Blue Iridescent, Gold Swirl, Round, 3¼ x 5½ In.	330
Epergne, 3 Opalescent, Bowls, Enamel Flowers, Ruffled, Gilt Metal Stand, 25 x 21 In.	960
Epergne, Cranberry Shaded, Clear Ruffled Bowl, 3 Trumpet Vases, Rigaree, 20 In.	210
Epergne, Lily, Pink, White, Enamel, 2 Pedestals, 15 In.	180
Jar, Green, Gilt, Daisies In Gilt, Melon Shape, Silver Plate, 1800, 8½ In.	185
Kaleidoscope, Stained, Triangle, Color Wheel, Ruth Elizabeth Green, 1900s, 55 In.	600
Pitcher, Blown, Mace, Janusz Pozniak, 11 In.	219
Pitcher, Verde D'Gris Shaded To Terra-Cotta, Bulbous, Signed, George De Feure, 7¼ x 7 In. ...	283
Salt, Cranberry Glass, Clear Petal Rim, Silver Plate Frame, 1¾ x 2½ In.	108
Sculpture, Fish, 3 Brightly Colored, Transparent, Green Reeds, 6 x 8½ In.	221
Sculpture, Picasso, Stylized Face, Mustache, Long Hair, Green Glass, Murano, 9 In. .... *illus*	6050
Seal, Citron, Gilt Silver, Mount, 4 Cavaliers, Cabochons, Case, c.1890, 4 In.	2125
Shaker, Jellyfish, Granulare, Richard Marquis, Zanfirico, 2016, 9 x 5 In.	2375
Sugar, Pedestal Victorian, Pink Opaque, Meriden, Silver Plate Stand, 7 x 7 In.	150
Sweetmeat, Zipper Mold, Pink, White, Gold Enamel Flowers, Turtle Lid, 4 x 4½ In.	420
Syrup, Hinged Lid, Acid Cut Ground, Enamel Flowers, Silver Plate Rim & Spout, 7 In.	120
Tazza, Blue Aurene, Pedestal Base, 1912, 3⅝ x 11 In.	615
Tray, Leaf Shape, Emerald Green, Enamel, Moser Style, 11 In.	120
Tumbler, Flowers, 2 Butterflies, Transparent Amber, Gilt Rim, 1910, 3⅞ In.	123
Vase, Amber Shaded To Dusty Rose, 3 Gray Medallions, Bulbous, Slender Neck, 8 In.	1512
Vase, Bag Shape, Yellow Shaded, Amethyst Flowers, Gold Stencil, 6¼ In.	180
Vase, Black Flowers, Branches, Opaque White Ground, Acid Cut, 6¼ x 7½ In.	136
Vase, Blue Luster Heart & Vine, White Ground, Orange Interior, 1920s, 8⅝ x 4½ In.	330
Vase, Bronze Gold, Salt Glaze, Pear Form, Mark Peisner, 1969, 3 In.	118
Vase, Caramel & Green Cased Swirl, 1800s, 6½ In. .... *illus*	625
Vase, Carved, Pillow, Deep Blue Iridescent, Polished, 13 x 6 x 11 In.	94
Vase, Chintz, Stripes, Blue & Green, Tinted Ground, D. Nash, 1920, 10 In.	308
Vase, Cranberry, Flowers, Acid Etched, Egg Shape, Footed, Threaded Rim, 7 In.	240
Vase, Cypriot, Mandarin, Red, Blue Iridescent Lava Drip, Charles Lotton, 6¼ x 3¾ In.	480
Vase, Enamel Flowers, Leaves, Branches, Cream, Pink Interior, Ruffled Rim, 8 x 8½ In.	295
Vase, Etched, Water Plants, Azure, Purple, Amber, Yellow, Gray Frosted Ground, 1900, 12 In.	1968

Vase, Figures, Dogs, Signed, Marcel Goupy, 1920s, 10 x 7 In................................ *illus*	6250
Vase, Glass, Ribbed Body, Rainbow Of Hues, Gold & White Leafy Scroll Collar, 8 x 5 ½ x 3 ½ In.	443
Vase, Green Iridescent, Waisted, Bulbous Base, Pierced Gunmetal Collar, 8 x 5 In.	57
Vase, Greyhounds, Black, White, Red, Green, Enameled, 1920s, 10 x 7 In.	8750
Vase, Harvest Moon, Blue Over Red Cased, Rick Satava, 8 x 6 In................................	480
Vase, Heart, Iridescent, 4 ½ In.	4920
Vase, Honey Brown, White Overlay, Flower Heads, Acanthus Leaves, 1890-1900, 3 ¾ In.	1230
Vase, Iridescent, Seafoam Green, Salmon Ground, Bulbous, Carlson Studio, 6 x 3 ¾ In.	90
Vase, Latticinio, Trailing Orange & Yellow, Cream Ground, Wide Mouth, 1978, 7 ⅝ In.	1968
Vase, Leaves, Etched, Bulbous, 1896, 14 x 15 In.	82
Vase, Light Gold Shaded To Dark Gold, 10 x 3 ¾ In.	124
Vase, Lilies, Buds, Leaves, 12 Ribs, 8 Prunts, Copper Wheel Engraved, 1900-30, 14 x 7 ⅝ In.	50
Vase, Multicolor, Free Form Iridescent Swirls, 1900s, 12 x 32 x 26 In.	660
Vase, Opaque Blue, Bird, Blossom, Figural Owl, Silver Plate Stand, Victorian, 11 In.	300
Vase, Periwinkle Blue, Etched, Leaves, Vines, Signed, Marny, 5 ¾ x 2 ½ In........................	51
Vase, Petal, Rosebuds, Bulbous, Red, White Cameo Band, 1900, 3 ½ In.	308
Vase, Pink & White Stripes, Notched Yellow Threaded Swirl Overlay, 8 ¼ In.	96
Vase, Poppies, Shaded Green, Textured, Gilt Rim, Silver Base, 1895-1920, 5 In.	523
Vase, Red Cypriote, Caramel, Gold Iridescent, Caramel, 1900, 9 In.	5535
Vase, Red Leaves, Etched Berries, Orange Ground, Shaped Neck, Pillow Form, 1900, 6 In........	984
Vase, Red Leaves, Vines, Etching Green, Gilt Trim, 1800, 9 In.	1353
Vase, Relief Flowers, Leaves, Butterflies, Ivory Ground, 1887-1900, 8 In.........................	338
Vase, Rubina Opalescent Shaded To Vaseline, Pedestal, Clear Glass Foot, 12 In.	180
Vase, Ships, Waterscape, Shaded Honey, Azure Satin Ground, 1900, 15 In.	369
Vase, Smoky Quartz, Blue Rigaree, Fish & Birds, 3 Legs, Signed, August Jean, 20 In., Pair	1210
Vase, Tropical Flowers, Leaves, Lizard, Mouse, Beetle, Simulated Jade, c.1890, 6 ½ In.	3444
Vase, Trumpet, Clear Swirled Rigaree, Square Top, Pulled Petal Feet, 9 ½ In.	150
Vase, Trumpet, Green & Gold Pulled Feather, Gold Iridescent Interior, Lundberg, 13 x 6 In......	203
Vase, Trumpet, Iridescent, Gold Texture, Lundberg Studios, 041286, 12 x 5 ¾ In.	147
Vase, Trumpet, Pale Yellow, Brass Foot, Acanthus, 47 ¼ In..	750
Vase, White Iridescent Crackle, 3 Tadpoles, Green Trim, Loetz Style, 4 x 5 ½ In.	150
Vase, White, Flowers, Blue Ground, Cameo, Prussia, 1900, 6 ⅞ In.................................	615
Vase, White, Green, Honeycomb, Ruffled Black Rim, Foil Sticker, 8 ¾ x 4 In........................	28
Vase, Yellow Flowers, Green Leaves, Mottled Ground, Oval, 1920-60, 4 ¾ In........................	1353
Vase, Yellow Satin, 4 Dimpled Sides, Enameled Flowers, 7 In.	18

GLASS-BLOWN. Blown glass was formed by forcing air through a rod into molten glass. Early glass and some forms of art glass were hand blown. Other types of glass were molded or pressed.

Bottle, Yellow Olive Amber, Globular, Pinched Neck, Rolled Collar, c.1830, 5 In.	761
Box, Liuli, Gold, Silver Leaf, Kyohei Fujita, Square, 7 In.	4688
Candlestick, Molded, Clear, 5-Step Quatrefoil Base, c.1850, 11 In., Pair..........................	510
Charger, Brushed Metal Stand, Lino Tagliapietra, Murano, 1985, 18 In..........................	3500
Compote, Amethyst Overlay, Coaching Scene, Trees, Country Inn, 1800s, 9 ½ In. .... *illus*	300
Decanter, Dog Shape, Ears, Tail, 4 Loop Legs, Silver-Mounted Cork, 1900s, 6 ¾ x 10 ¾ In........	197
Dish, Aqua, Flared, Ribs, 3-Piece Mold, Mt. Vernon Glass Works, c.1830, 2 x 5 In.	5850
Flask, Yellow, Black, Dante Marioni, 1992, 28 x 11 x 8 In.	4063
Goblet, Dante Marioni, 1995-97, 9 x 4 In., 4 Piece...	1875
Jar, Shaded Yellow Olive Green, Flared Mouth, 1820-40, 7 x 6 In.	936
Pear, Colored Crushed Powders, 1949, 24 In.	1500
Pitcher, Aqua, Baluster, Strap Handle, Double Knob, Circular Base, South Jersey, 1830, 7 ¼ In..	1250
Pitcher, Colorless, Flared Neck, Pinched Spout, 1800s...	165
Plate, Mandala Series, Murrine, Latticinio, Canes, Richard Ritter, 1990, 3 x 12 In.	1875
Rolling Pin, Orange, Translucent, Open End, 1900s, 20 In.	56
Sculpture, Blue Dot, Frosted, Laura De Santillana, 9 x 9 x 2 In.	8750
Sculpture, Discuss Thrower, Livio Seguso, 21 x 10 x 4 In.	1500
Sculpture, Dog, Sandblasted, Richard Jolley, 2008, 9 x 7 In...	2375
Sculpture, Triolet Series, Sandblasted, Murrine, Latticinio, Canes, Richard Ritter, 1990, 9 x 11 In.	1875

Glass-Art, Vase, Caramel & Green Cased Swirl, 1800s, 6 ½ In.
$625

G

Glass-Art, Vase, Figures, Dogs, Signed, Marcel Goupy, 1920s, 10 x 7 In.
$6,250

Glass-Blown, Compote, Amethyst Overlay, Coaching Scene, Trees, Country Inn, 1800s, 9 ½ In.
$300

Glass-Blown, Sugar, Lid, Round, Red & White Looping, 1800s, 6¾ In. $690

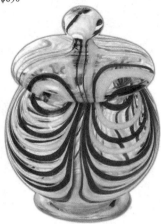

Garth's Auctioneers & Appraisers

Glass-Bohemian, Compote, Green To White, Rolled Rim, 10 Reserves, c.1885, 5⅜ x 7¾ In. $263

Jeffrey S. Evans

Glass-Bohemian, Goblet, Spa, Amber Cut To Clear, Etched, 1800s, 6¼ In. $160

Neal Auction Co.

Shade, Hurricane, Berries, Stars, Banded Rim, 1800s, 25 In., Pair	2640
Sugar, Lid, Round, Red & White Looping, 1800s, 6¾ In. .... *illus*	690
Tumbler, Orange Amber, Bubbles, Tooled Rim, Pontil, Stoddard, c.1855, 4¾ In.	345
Vase, Brown, Transparent, Flared Mouth, 12¼ In.	469
Vase, Devil Horn, Blue, Yellow, 1900s, 14 In.	60
Vase, Green Iridescent, Pulled Feather, Ruffled Neck, 6 x 6 In.	1125
Vase, Green, Purple, Yellow, Dimpled, Teardrop Rolled In Mouth, 8 x 5 In.	1875
Vase, Swirled, Purple Iridescent, Squat, Flared Neck & Rim, 1960-90, 3½ x 4½ In.	60
Witch's Ball, Cranberry, Raised White Twisted Ribs, Metal Rim, c.1880, 5 In.	490

GLASS-BOHEMIAN. Bohemian glass is an ornate overlay or flashed glass made during the Victorian era. It has been reproduced in Bohemia, which is now a part of the Czech Republic. Glass made from 1875 to 1900 is preferred by collectors.

Adolf Beckert
c.1914–1920s

Gräflich Schaffgotsch'sche
Josephinenhutte
c.1890

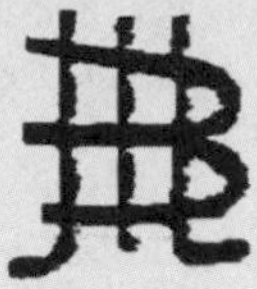

J. & L. Lobmeyr
1860+

Bowl, Dome Lid, Satin, Frosted Amethyst Threading, Bulbous Base, Kralik, 4½ x 5 In.	45
Bowl, Gilt, Enameled, Fluted, Scalloped, 1900s, 12 x 12 x 5¾ In.	53
Bowl, Grape Clusters, Leaves & Vines, Amber, Polished Rim, c.1900, 7½ In.	45
Bowl, Iridescent Murrine, Scalloped, Fluted, Lobed, Kralik, 4¾ x 8 In.	152
Bowl, Stand, Purple, Flowers, Leaves, Vines, Scalloped, Kralik, c.1925, 10¼ In.	437
Box, Lid, Amber Overlay Windows, Gold Stencil Highlights, 10-Sided, 4¼ x 4 In.	72
Butter, Cover, Overlay Panels, Cobalt Cut To Clear, Round, Scalloped Edge, 7 In.	427
Carafe, Cut, Etched, 2 Women In Field, 4 Panels, 1800s, 8⅜ x 4 In.	1440
Chalice, Lid, Emerald Green Cased Lid & Bowl, Enamel Courting Scene, Garland, 11 In.	240
Chalice, Medallions, Ruby Overlay, Engraved Flowers, Gold Stencils, 10 In.	84
Cologne Bottle, Cranberry Overlay, Oval & Square Windows, Enamel Highlights, 8-Sided, 7 In.	84
Compote, Green To White, Rolled Rim, 10 Reserves, c.1885, 5⅜ x 7¾ In. .... *illus*	263
Cup, Cased, Cranberry, 3 Diamond Point Windows, Gold Stencils, Pedestal, 5¼ In.	96
Decanter, White & Cranberry, Stopper, 8 In.	84
Ewer, Amethyst Iridescent Veining, Triangular, Ruffled Rim, Pallme-Koenig, 16 x 6½ In.	323
Garniture, Urns, Round Box, White Overlay, Cut To Red, Flowers, c.1875, 3 Piece	156
Goblet, Spa, Amber Cut To Clear, Etched, 1800s, 6¼ In. .... *illus*	160
Ice Bucket, Flowers, Castles, Etched, 7½ x 6½ In.	150
Jug, Claret, Female Mask, Etched, Engraved, Neoclassical, 1800s, 12 x 6 In. .... *illus*	1440
Tankard, Eagle, Wreath, Gold Stars, Liberti, Barrel Shape, 5 In.	185
Vase, Blue, Green, Art Nouveau, Glass, 1900s, 16 x 7 In.	1625
Vase, Buttercups, Butterflies, Dark Green, Stick Neck, c.1900, 16 x 5 In.	593
Vase, Cream & Orange Cased, Exotic Birds, Flowers, Crimped & Folded Rim, 7¼ In.	70
Vase, Enamel Flowers, Gold Leaves, 18 In.	177
Vase, Flower Shape, Blue Flash, Pulled Openwork Rim, Kralik, 11 In. .... *illus*	265
Vase, Flower, Gilt, Multicolor, Romania, 1900s, 13 x 8½ In.	42
Vase, Gold Cut To Clear, Sage Green, Tapered, 14 x 5½ In., Pair	241
Vase, Green, Raised Gilt Scroll, Lattice, Reserves, Leaves, 18⅝ x 5¾ In.	129
Vase, Intaglio Cut, Green To Clear, Flowers, Squared, 5⅞ x 2 In.	222
Vase, Iridescent Glaze, Metal Art Nouveau Mount, Kralik, 21 In. .... *illus*	1000
Vase, Iridescent, Female, Diaphanous Dress, Rose Blossoms, Flared Rim, 1900, 7¾ x 6 In.	197
Vase, Leaves, Green, Copper Overlay, Metal Mount, 4½ x 3 In.	150
Vase, Maroon, Aventurine, Swirls, Rindskopf, 9 In.	236
Vase, Opaque Yellow, Enamel Bird, Branch, Blossom Dots, Harrach, 10 In.	210
Vase, Portraits In Reserves, Emerald Cut To Calcite, 18½ In., Pair	1600
Vase, Red, Yellow, Undulating Bands, Battuto Surface, D.V. Adriano, 1945, 10 In.	344
Vase, Ruby Overlay, Flowers Alternate With Dots, White Ground, 8¾ x 7 In.	90

Vase, Scroll Rim, White Cut, Grapevine Designs, 22 x 8 In.	236
Vase, Tapered, Undulating Rim, Green, Iridescent, Kralik, Austrian, 6 ½ In.	102
Vase, Vladimir Jelinek, 12 x 7 x 4 In.	938
Vase, White Opal Iridescent, Spiral Neck, Melon Rib Base, Kralik, Austria, 9 ½ In.	57
Vase, Yellow, Orange Iridescent, Mottled, Art Nouveau, 9 ¼ In.	437
Vase, Yellow, Pink, Marbled, Half Twist Body, Rindskopf, 13 In.	266
Wine, Rhine, Green Cut To Clear, Enamel Flowers, Scalloped Base, 8 ¼ In.	150

GLASS-CONTEMPORARY includes pieces by glass artists working after 1970. Many of these pieces are free-form, one-of-a-kind sculptures. Paperweights by contemporary artists are listed in the Paperweight category. Earlier studio glass may be found listed under Glass-Midcentury or Glass-Venetian.

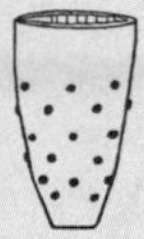

Basket, Citron, Orange Lip Wrap, Dale Chihuly, 1992, 10 x 19 x 14 In.	4688
Basket, Persian, Blue, Red, Red Lip Wrap, Dale Chihuly, 1989, 19 x 33 x 18 In.	6250
Basket, Soft Cylinder, Asymmetrical, Dale Chihuly, 1987, 15 x 10 In.	11250
Bottle, Blue Iridescent, Looping, Stopper, Signed, Lundberg, 1977, 9 x 4 ½ In.	181
Bottle, Genie, Cobalt, Purple & Gold Iridescent, Marked, Lotton, 1989, 13 In.	472
Bottle, Platinum Decoration, Blue Iridescent, Charles Lotton, 1977, 5 ¾ x 2 ¼ In.	283
Bowl, Carp, Seaweed, Green, Purple, Acid Etched, Foil Inclusions, Cameo, 9 ¾ x 7 In.	1062
Bowl, Cityscape, Acid Etched, Painted, Jay Musler, 1985, 9 x 18 In.	10000
Bowl, Filet-De-Verre, Fused Threads, Mary Zynsky, 7 ½ x 14 In.	4062
Bowl, Macchia, Red, Yellow, Black Lip Wrap, Dale Chihuly, 8 x 9 x 7 In.	1875
Bowl, Medusa, Tapio Wirkkala, Venini, 1960s, 4 x 11 In.	1250
Bowl, Portrait, Woman, Openwork Hair, Red, Charlie Miner, c.1990, 14 x 17 In.	2625
Bowl, Red, Dark Red Spots, Black Lip, Blown, 7 ¾ x 8 ½ In.	2500
Bowl, Red, Yellow Lozenges, Ribbons, Dale Chihuly, 1984, 10 ½ x 13 ½ In.	11250
Bowl, Veloce, Filet-De-Verre, Fused, Threaded, Fan Shape, Toots Zynsky, 1992, 7 x 14 In.	15000
Charger, Abstract, Multicolor Canes, Signed W.S. Hunting, 19 ¾ In.	138
Decanter, Label, Mihai Topescu, 22 x 11 In.	42
Goblet, Face, Hair, Chin Resting In Hand, Gilt Inclusions, 12 ½ In.	60
Plaque, Field, Flowers, Woods, Panels, Steven Stelz, 24 x 19 In.	2722
Plaque, Wildflowers, Majestic Trees, Framed Panels, Steven Stelz, 22 x 24 In.	2178
Plaque, Wildflowers, Trees, Signed, Steven Stelz, 22 ½ x 31 In.	1936
Sculpture, Blue, Amber, Egg Shape, Stand, Peter Vanderlaan, 13 x 17 In.	351
Sculpture, Botanical, Cloistered Glass, Prickly Pear, Blossoms, Paul Stankard, 6 In.	6050
Sculpture, Botanical, Dried Flowers, Seeds, P. Stankard, 1989, 5 x 3 In. *illus*	6050
Sculpture, Botanical, Lady's Slipper, Green Leaves, Signed, Stankard, 5 x 3 In.	4840
Sculpture, Buddha, Gold, Headdress, Blue Ground, Melissa Ayotte, 2007, 3 x 3 ⅜ In.	484
Sculpture, Butterflies, Laminated, Painted, Bohumil Elias, 4 x 20 In.	3500
Sculpture, Cocoon, Cased, Patinated Iron, Steve Tobin, Vistosi, 1991, 76 x 13 In.	1625
Sculpture, Orb, Cantilevered, Blue, Purple, Peter Vanderlaan, 13 x 17 In.	351
Sculpture, Piccolo, Pink, Gold Foil, Gold Handles, Blown, Dale Chihuly, 9 x 8 In.	8750
Sculpture, Pilchuck Aerial, Evergreen, Blown, Dale Chihuly, 1996, 6 x 7 x 8 In.	813
Sculpture, Putti, Swan, Gilt, Dale Chihuly, 1995, 7 x 5 In.	3750
Sculpture, Pyramid, Granite Bottom, Metal Wire, William Carlson, 1987, 10 x 9 x 5 In.	2625
Sculpture, Relax Series, Dino Rosin, 29 x 10 ½ In.	2000
Sculpture, Seaform, Red, Black Lip Wrap, Dale Chihuly, 1998, 7 x 11 In., 2 Piece	4688
Sculpture, Shockwave, Blown, Cut, Sandblasted, Iridized, Concetta Mason, 25 x 16 In.	2500
Sculpture, Sphere, Internal Color, Blue, Trapped Bubbles, 1990, 5 ¼ x 5 ½ In.	185
Sculpture, Triolet Series, Blown, Murrine, Latticinio, Canes, R. Ritter, c.1990, 8 x 10 ½ In.	1875
Sculpture, Universal Harmony, Blown, Cut, Sandblasted, Enamel, Concetta Mason, 22 x 15 In.	1750
Sculpture, XO, Cast, Signed, Steven Weinberg, 780204, 7 x 7 In.	2750
Shell, Flat Panel, Undulating Edges, Pistil Form Inside, Dale Chihuly, 1941, 29 x 23 In.	8750
Teapot, Crazy Quilt, Murrine, Pink, Blue, White, Richard Marquis, 5 ¾ x 5 ½ In.	3125
Vase, Aqua, Purple, Brown, Small Mouth, Dominick Labino, 5 ½ x 5 ½ In.	371
Vase, Blown, Multicolor, Applied Ringlet Strips, Foil Inclusions, Chihuly, 19 x 10 In.	9375
Vase, Blown, Signed, Vladimir Jelinek, Czech Republic, 11 x 7 In.	937
Vase, Blue Iridescent, Pulled Feather, Dragonflies, Cattails, Orient & Flume, 1975, 5 ¾ x 3 In.	215
Vase, Blue, Gold Feather Band, Miniature, Marked, Orient & Flume, 1975, 3 In.	212

Glass-Bohemian, Jug, Claret, Female Mask, Etched, Engraved, Neoclassical, 1800s, 12 x 6 In. $1,440

Brunk Auctions

Glass-Bohemian, Vase, Flower Shape, Blue Flash, Pulled Openwork Rim, Kralik, 11 In. $265

Humler & Nolan

Glass-Bohemian, Vase, Iridescent Glaze, Metal Art Nouveau Mount, Kralik, 21 In.
$1,000

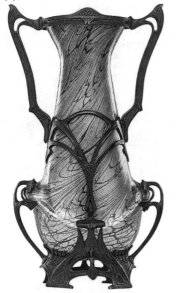

Rago Arts and Auction Center

Glass-Contemporary, Sculpture, Botanical, Dried Flowers, Seeds, P. Stankard, 1989, 5 x 3 In.
$6,050

James D. Julia Auctioneers

Vase, Blue, Iridescent, Orient & Flume, 1984, 6 In.	120
Vase, Cylinder, Blanket, Amber, Dale Chihuly, 1976, 11 x 7 ½ In.	10000
Vase, Etched, Joel Philip Myers, 1981, 9 x 5 In.	4375
Vase, Gold Iridescent, Green, Pink, Orient & Flume, 6 ⅛ In.	222
Vase, Incalmo, Yellow, Blue, Signed, Sonja Blomdahl, 1996, 15 x 11 In.	6875
Vase, Inlaid Flowers, Orient & Flume, 1976, 5 x 5 In.	136
Vase, Inlaid, Zipper, Pulled Feather, Aubergine Rim, Orient & Flume, 1977, 8 ¾ x 2 ¾ In.	203
Vase, Iridescent Gold, Blue, Lundberg Studios, 1900s, 7 ¼ In. .... *illus*	240
Vase, King Tut Decoration, Red, Blue, Charles Lotton, 3 ¾ x 2 ¾ In.	283
Vase, King Tut, Blue Silver, White Ground, Marked, Lotton, 2003, 9 ½ In.	531
Vase, Multicolor Iridescent, Feathering, Lundberg, 1999, 12 In.	212
Vase, Multiflora, Signed, Charles Lotton, 6 x 4 ¼ In.	203
Vase, Opal, Silver Blue Webbing, Leaves & Vines, Charles Lotton, 1974, 9 In.	590
Vase, Papillion, Studio, Engraved Signature, Aaron Slater, 4 ¾ x 4 ¼ In.	147
Vase, Poppies, Blue, Purple, Acid Etched, Cameo, Jonathan Harris, 9 ¾ x 5 ½ In.	687
Vase, Pulled Feather, Batwing, Purple, Green, Peach, Orient & Flume, 1976, 6 x 4 In.	158
Vase, Rainbow Iridescent, Wide Shoulders, Orient & Flume, 9 x 8 In.	1700
Vase, Shard, Blue, Gray, Snowy, William Morris, c.1983, 13 x 13 In.	5000
Vase, Soft Cylinder, Blown, Dale Chihuly, 1987, 14 ½ x 10 In. .... *illus*	11250
Vase, Stylized Sticks, Leaves, Etched, Bulbous, 4 x 15 In.	177
Vase, Trumpet, Fluted, Blue Aurene, Lundberg Studios, 12 ¾ In.	141
Vase, Yellow, Blue Feather, Magenta Highlights, Satava, 1979, 8 ½ In.	201
Wine, Teapot Base, Richard Marquis, 1988, 10 ¼ x 3 ½ In.	1875

GLASS-CUT, *see Cut Glass category.*

GLASS-DEPRESSION, *see Depression Glass category.*

GLASS-MIDCENTURY refers to art glass made from the 1940s to the early 1970s. Some glass factories, such as Baccarat or Orrefors, are listed under their own categories. Earlier glass may be listed in the Glass-Art and Glass-Contemporary categories. Italian glass may be found in Glass-Venetian.

Dish, Line Cut, Molded, Brown Crystals, Tapio Wirkkala, Finland, c.1950, 9 ½ In.	375
Sculpture, Suomi-Finland Series, Blue, Lavender, Marvin Lipofsky, 10 x 11 In.	2375
Sculpture, Suomi-Finland Series, Red, Lavender, Marvin Lipofsky, 9 ½ x 14 ½ In.	3250

GLASS-PRESSED, *see Pressed Glass category.*

GLASS-VENETIAN. Venetian glass has been made near Venice, Italy, since the thirteenth century. Thin, colored glass with applied decoration is favored, although many other types have been made. Collectors have recently become interested in the Art Deco and 1950s designs. Glass was made on the Venetian island of Murano from 1291. The output dwindled in the late seventeenth century but began to flourish again in the 1850s. Some of the old techniques of glassmaking were revived, and firms today make traditional designs and original modern glass. Since 1981, the name *Murano* may be used only on glass made on Murano Island. Other pieces of Italian glass may be found in the Glass-Contemporary and Glass-Midcentury categories of this book.

Aquarium, 6 Fish, Turquoise Band, Reed, Multicolor, 11 ½ x 12 In.	1573
Bird, Millefiori Eyes, Red, Blue Ground, Vistosi Murano, 1960s, 6 ¾ x 8 ¼ x 4 In.	7200
Bowl, Blown, Gold Foil Inclusions, Lino Tagliapietra, 1976, 3 x 7 ¼ In.	625
Bowl, Blown, Mosaic, Barovier & Toso, 1960s, 6 x 7 In. .... *illus*	2125
Bowl, Medusa, Spirals, T. Wirkkala, Venini, Murano, Marked, c.1960, 4 x 11 In.	1250
Charger, Blown, Brushed Metal Stand, Signed, Lino Tagliapietra, Murano, 1985, 18 In.	3500
Compote, Green, Pedestal Base, 3 White Swans, 7 ¾ x 6 ¾ In., Pair	206
Figurine, Bird, Blown, Copper Feet, Alessandro Pianon, Vistosi, 1960s, 9 ½ In. .... *illus*	5313
Figurine, Clown, Black Shoes, Blue & Yellow Robe, 12 x 8 In.	108
Mirror, Wall, Etched Leafy Scrolls, Beveled Edge Panel, 1900, 35 x 27 In.	192
Paperweight, Multicolor Twisted Ribbons, Gold Aventurine, Crowned, Murano, 3 ½ x 4 ¾ In.	102

G

Glass-Contemporary, Vase, Iridescent Gold, Blue, Lundberg Studios, 1900s, 7 ¼ In. $240

Glass-Contemporary, Vase, Soft Cylinder, Blown, Dale Chihuly, 1987, 14 ½ x 10 In. $11,250

TIP

Glass becomes cloudy if not kept completely dry when not in use. That is why decanters and vases often discolor.

Glass-Venetian, Bowl, Blown, Mosaic, Barovier & Toso, 1960s, 6 x 7 In. $2,125

Glass-Venetian, Figurine, Bird, Blown, Copper Feet, Alessandro Pianon, Vistosi, 1960s, 9 ½ In. $5,313

Glass-Venetian, Vase, Antares, 3 Stacked Beakers, Michele De Lucchi, Murano, 1983, 19 x 13 In. $938

Venetian Glass

The glass-blowing traditions of Venice were revitalized in the 1850s. It is said that 80 percent of the Venetian glass made from 1855 to 1914 was purchased by Americans traveling in Italy.

Glass-Venetian, Vase, Bolle, Bottle, Pink, Green, Yellow Band, Tapio Wirkkala, 1984, 19 In.
$2,714

Cottone Auctions

Gonder, Vase, Peacock, Wine Brown, Drip Glaze, 1950s, 11½ x 11 In.
$68

Ruby Lane

Graniteware, Coffeepot, Green & White Swirl, Black Trim, 9¾ In.
$266

Hess Auction Group

Sculpture, Conch Shell, Blown & Iridized, Inclusions, Lino Tagliapietra, 4 x 9 In.	1625
Sculpture, Discus Thrower, Blown, Signed, Livio Seguso, Murano, 21 x 10 In.	1500
Sculpture, Fish, Free-Form, Fused Canes, Blue, Green, Pink, Clear Fins, 1900s, 15 x 17 In.	180
Sculpture, Ribbed, Vase Shape, Blown, Lino Tagliapietra, 1995, 16 x 14 In.	10000
Sculpture, Stylized Couple, Loop, Entwined Ends, Signed, R. Austro, Italy, 1900s, 23 In.	188
Vase, Half White Speckled, Half Clear, Yellow Band, L. Tagliapietra, 1985, 15 x 6 In.	937
Vase, Anse Volante, Green Iridescent, Handles, Giorgio Ferro, Murano, c.1950, 8 x 8½ In.	2125
Vase, Antares, 3 Stacked Beakers, Michele De Lucchi, Murano, 1983, 19 x 13 In. *illus*	938
Vase, Blown, Lines, Marbled Green, Yellow, Blue, Lino Tagliapietra, 1992, 9½ x 9 In.	5000
Vase, Bolle, Bottle, Pink, Green, Yellow Band, Tapio Wirkkala, 1984, 19 In. *illus*	2714
Vase, Canne, White, Gray Green, 2 Openings, Lino Tagliapietra, 1996, 7½ x 5 In.	2500
Vase, Green Ground, Egg Shape, White & Yellow Splotches, 1900s, Murano, 20¾ In.	135
Vase, Incamiciato, Iridescent, Squat, Fulvio Bianconi, 5 x 5½ In.	375
Vase, Interior Murrines, Opalescent Ground, Bulbous, Italy, 11 x 11 In.	1210
Vase, Mauve, Gold Threading, Murano, c.1975, 15½ x 11 In., Pair	1250
Vase, Orange Swirl, Free-Form, Folded Rim, Murano, c.1960, 9 x 9 In.	145
Vase, Pezzato, Tessere, Opaque Orange, Yellow, Red, Fulvio Bianconi, 1950s, 8¾ In.	10000
Vase, Pueblo, Torpedo Shape, Caramel Bands, Stripes, 1986, 13 x 4¾ In.	4062
Vase, Rainbow, Round, Lino Tagliapietra, 1990, 10¼ x 9 In.	1000
Vase, Red, Purple, Stripes, Flame Shape, Massimiliano Schiavon, 22 x 10½ In.	1207
Vase, Red, Teardrop Shape, Carved, Polished, Small Mouth, 7 x 5 In.	7500
Vase, Ruby Cut To Clear Etched, Rococo Flowers, Oval Leafy Medallions, 8 x 5 In.	177
Vase, Sidone, Tapered, Wide Mouth, Ercole Barovier, Murano, c.1950, 7 x 5 In.	6250
Vase, Sidone, Tessere, Ercole Barovier, 1950s, 8 x 5 x 4 In.	6250
Vase, Stripes, Green, White, Round, Ribbed, Yoichi Ohira, 6 x 5¼ In.	6250
Vase, Yellow, Applied Drips, Relief Alligators, Drip Feet, Cylindrical, 12 x 7 In., Pair	276

GLASSES for the eyes, or spectacles, were mentioned in a manuscript in 1289 and have been used ever since. The first eyeglasses with rigid side pieces were made in London in 1727. Bifocals were invented by Benjamin Franklin in 1785. Lorgnettes were popular in late Victorian times. Opera Glasses are listed in the Opera Glass category.

14K Gold, Wire Frame, Ball Ends	153
Lorgnette, Art Nouveau, Sterling Silver, Gilt, Spectacles Handles, 5¼ In.	106
Lorgnette, Platinum, Diamonds, Openwork Handle, Tiffany & Co., 28-In. Link Chain	2040
Mod Style, Blue, Purple, Round, Case, Emilio Pucci, France, 6½ x 5½ In.	118
Ox Horn Frame, Metal Bridge, Forehead Pad, Chinese, 1800s	123

GOEBEL is the mark used by W. Goebel Porzellanfabrik of Oeslau, Germany, now Rodental, Germany. The company was founded by Franz Detleff Goebel and his son, William Goebel, in 1871. It was known as F&W Goebel. Slates, slate pencils, and marbles were made. Soon the company began making porcelain tableware and figurines. Hummel figurines were first made by Goebel in 1935. Since 2009 they have been made by another company. Goebel is still in business. Old pieces marked *Goebel Hummel* are listed under Hummel in this book.

Candleholder, Angel, Blond, Wings, Red Hat, Dress, 1980s, 4 In.	20
Creamer, Elephant, Seated, Raised Trunk, Orange, Black Eyes, Feet, c.1940, 5 In.	50
Figurine, Bird, Ringed Prover, On Branch, 2 x 2 In.	25
Figurine, Dog, Boxer, Black, Tan, c.1968, 7 x 7 x 2 In.	53
Figurine, Dog, Welsh Corgi, Brown, Cream, 5 x 6 x 2 In.	89
Group, Rabbit, Bunny, Brown, c.1975, 4 x 5¾ In.	18
Ornament, Clown, Red Cheeks & Buttons, Black Shoes, Hat, Box, 1983, 4 In.	15
Plate, Owls, On Branch, Brown, Cobalt Blue Ground, 1980, 10¼ In.	38
Salt & Pepper, Friar Monks, Brown	17
Wall Plaque, Angel, Sacrart, c.1960, 4¾ x 3¾ In., Pair	125

GOLDSCHEIDER was founded by Friedrich Goldscheider in Vienna in 1885. The family left Vienna in 1938 and the factory was taken over by the Germans. Goldscheider started factories in England and in Trenton, New Jersey. It made figurines and other ceramics. The New Jersey factory started in 1940 as Goldscheider–U.S.A. In 1941 it became Goldscheider–Everlast Corporation. From 1947 to 1953 it was Goldcrest Ceramics Corporation. In 1950 the Vienna plant was returned to Mr. Goldscheider but it closed in 1953. The Trenton, New Jersey, business, called Goldscheider of Vienna, is a wholesale importer.

Bust, Woman, Black Hair, Orange Jewelry, Marked, Terra-Cotta, 12 ½ x 7 In.	240
Bust, Woman, White Hair, Orange Hat, Marked, Terra-Cotta, 11 x 7 In.	228
Figurine, Scheherazade, Blue Veil, Water Jug On Head, Joseph Lorenzl, 23 In.	2714
Figurine, Woman, Holding Umbrella, Wolfhound, Oval Base, 1920-37, 13 In.	800
Vase, Alligator, Bronze, 7 x 8 In.	1375

GOLF, see Sports category.

GONDER CERAMIC ARTS, INC., was opened by Lawton Gonder in 1941 in Zanesville, Ohio. Gonder made high-grade pottery decorated with flambe, drip, gold crackle, and Chinese crackle glazes. The factory closed in 1957. From 1946 to 1954, Gonder also operated the Elgee Pottery, which made ceramic lamp bases.

Figurine, Panther, Lying Down, Glossy Brown Glaze, 7 x 18 In.	24
Vase, Ewer Shape, Green & Brown Glaze, Bulbous, Squat, Elongated Handle & Spout, 8 In.	45
Vase, Peacock, Wine Brown, Drip Glaze, 1950s, 11 ½ x 11 In. ....*illus*	68
Vase, Shell Shape, Light Purple, Round Foot, 12 x 8 In.	9

GOOFUS GLASS was made from about 1900 to 1930 by many American factories. It was originally painted gold, red, green, bronze, pink, purple, or other bright colors. Colors were cold painted or sprayed on, not fired on, and were not permanent. Many pieces are found today with flaking paint, and this lowers the value. Both goofus glass and carnival glass were sold at carnivals, but carnival glass colors are fired on and don't flake off.

Bowl, Green Birds, Red Berries, Center Glower, Yellow Ground, 10 In.	12
Charger, Red Roses, 8 Petal Sections, Gold Ground, 11 ½ In.	8
Dish, Opalescent, Ruffled Wide Rim, Round Foot, Multicolor, 3 ¾ x 8 ½ In.	18
Figurine, British Tank, Man Of Ross Crest, 4 ½ x 2 ½ In.	112
Figurine, Bull Dog, Coat Of Arms, Hastings & St. Leonards, 2 ¼ In.	50
Vase, Teignmouth Crest, Red, Cylindrical, 2 In.	18
Vase, Wakefield Crest, Blue, Gold, Bulbous, 1 ½ In.	15

GOUDA, Holland, has been a pottery center since the seventeenth century. Two firms, the Zenith pottery, established in 1749, and the Zuid-Hollandsche pottery, made the colorful art pottery marked *Gouda* from 1898 to about 1964. Other factories that made "Gouda" style pottery include Regina (1898–1979), Schoonhoven (1920–present), Ivora (1630–1965), Goedewaagen (1610–1779), Dirk Goedewaagen (1779–1982), and Royal Goedewaagen (1983–present). Many pieces featured Art Nouveau or Art Deco designs. Pattern names in Dutch are often included in the mark.

Gouda / Plateelbakkerij Zenith 1915	Gouda / Kon. Hollandsche Pijpen–en Aardewekfabriek Goedewaagen 1923–1928	Gouda / Zuid–Holland Platteelbakkerij 1926+

Charger, Abstract Decoration, Green, Terra-Cotta & Gold, Hanging Wire, 1920-21, 13 In.	156
Vase, Flowers, Leaves, Green, Blue, Ivory, Handles, c.1906, 10 In.	298
Vase, Flowers, Leaves, Red, Gold, Cobalt Blue, White, 5 In.	50
Vase, Squat Body, Finches, Butterflies, Yellow Poppies, Rosenberg Style, Handles, 9 x 7 In.	1300

Graniteware, Cream Can, Black, White, 7 ¼ x 4 ¼ In.
$42

Martin Auction Co.

Grueby, Vase, Melon Ribbed, Spherical, Green Matte, Black Accents, 1900, 9 ½ In.
$9,600

Eldred's Auctioneers and Appraisers

Grueby, Vase, Overlapping Leaves, Curdled Green Glaze, Wilhelmina Post, c.1905, 11 In.
$5,625

Rago Arts and Auction Center

Grueby, Vase, Squat, Flowers, Green, Yellow, Ruth Erickson, Incised RE, c.1905, 4 x 5¾ In.
$3,250

Rago Arts and Auction Center

Grueby, Vase, Yellow Irises, Green Matte Glaze, W. Post, Faience Stamp, c.1900, 12½ In.
$5,312

Rago Arts and Auction Center

Gustavsberg, Vase, Squares, Wilhelm Kage, Farsta, Incised, 1950s, 13 x 9 In.
$3,625

Rago Arts and Auction Center

GRANITEWARE is enameled tin or iron used to make kitchenware since the 1870s. Earlier graniteware was green or turquoise blue, with white spatters. The later ware was gray with white spatters. Reproductions are being made in all colors.

Geuder, Paeschke & Frey Co.
1905–c.1972

Iron Clad Manufacturing Co.
1888–1913

Lalance & Grosjean
Manufacturing Co.
1877–1955

Basin, 2 Handles, Chrysotile, Agateware, Blue, 1890, 19 x 6¼ In.		110
Coffeepot, Green & White Swirl, Black Trim, 9¾ In.	*illus*	266
Cream Can, Black, White, 7¼ x 4¼ In.	*illus*	42
Mug, Retro Red, White Kitchen, Glossy Trim, 4 x 2⅝ In.		8

 GREENTOWN glass was made by the Indiana Tumbler and Goblet Company of Greentown, Indiana, from 1894 to 1903. In 1899, the factory became part of National Glass Company. A variety of pressed glass was made. Additional pieces may be found in other categories, such as Chocolate Glass, Holly Amber, Milk Glass, and Pressed Glass.

Cord Drapery, Butter, Lid, Amber, 6¼ In.	225
Cord Drapery, Pitcher, Cobalt Blue, 8½ In.	350
Dewey, Condiment Tray, Nile Green, 1½ x 8½ In.	250
Dewey, Cruet, Nile Green, c.1898, 5¾ In.	650
Dewey, Sugar, Lid, Nile Green, c.1898, 4¾ In.	275
Holly Amber, Compote, Jelly, Beaded Rim, Golden Agate, 6 In.	850
Holly Amber, Cruet, Beaded Rim, Golden Agate, 6¼ In.	1400
Holly Amber, Tumbler, Beaded Rim, Golden Agate, 3½ In.	1300
Teardrop & Tassel, Pitcher, Amber, 1900-03, 8½ In.	250
Teardrop & Tassel, Pitcher, Cobalt Blue, 1900-03, 8⅞ In.	140

 GRUEBY FAIENCE COMPANY of Boston, Massachusetts, was founded in 1894 by William H. Grueby. Grueby Pottery Company was incorporated in 1907. In 1909, Grueby Faience went bankrupt. Then William Grueby founded the Grueby Faience and Tile Company. Grueby Pottery closed about 1911. The tile company worked until 1920. Garden statuary, art pottery, and architectural tiles were made until 1920. The company developed a green matte glaze that was so popular it was copied by many other factories making a less expensive type of pottery. This eventually led to the financial problems of the pottery. Cuerda seca and cuenca are techniques explained in the Tile category. The company name was often used as the mark, and slight changes in the form help date a piece.

Tile, 3-Set Tableau, Galleon Ship Center, Seagulls & Waves Each Sides, 8 x 8 In.		3000
Tile, Ship, Masts, Flanked By Sea Gulls, Marked, Frame, 1900s, 8 x 8 In., 3 Piece		3540
Tile, Yellow Tulip, Green Ground, Tiffany Bronze Frame, 6 x 6 In.		4838
Trivet, The Pines, Oak Frame, c.1925, 6 x 6 In.		3000
Vase, 3-Petal Flowers, Matte Green Glaze, 13 x 9½ In.		4100
Vase, Buds, Green, Wilhelmina Post, c.1905, 4 x 3½ In.		4375
Vase, Carved Irises, 2 Colors, 1905, 12¼ x 8½ In.		6250
Vase, Curdled Tan Matte Glaze, Bulbous, Flared Rim, 5 x 4 In.		594
Vase, Flower Buds, Leaves, Lobed, Green, White Edges, c.1902, 8¼ x 5½ In.		937
Vase, Flower Buds, Leaves, Shaped Mouth, Green, 1906, 8 x 4 In.		1062
Vase, Gourd, Green Leathery Glaze, Impressed Logo, 3 In.		350
Vase, Green Matte Glaze, Elongated, Marked, 9½ In.		2360
Vase, Green Matte Glaze, Tapered, Swollen Petal Rim, 7 x 4 In.		3250
Vase, Melon Ribbed, Spherical, Green Matte, Black Accents, 1900, 9½ In.	*illus*	9600
Vase, Overlapping Leaves, Curdled Green Glaze, Wilhelmina Post, c.1905, 11 In.	*illus*	5625

Vase, Side Ribbed, Green Matte Leather Glaze, Impressed Logo, Incised Monogram, 9 ½ In.	2000
Vase, Squat, Curdled Green Matte Glaze, Impressed Bottom Circular Logo, 3 x 6 ¼ In.	350
Vase, Squat, Flowers, Green, Yellow, Ruth Erickson, Incised RE, c.1905, 4 x 5 ¾ In. .... *illus*	3250
Vase, Squat, Leaves, Round, Faience Stamp, c.1902, 4 ½ x 9 ½ In.	2500
Vase, Stylized Leaves, Green Matte, 1905, 5 ½ x 3 ½ In.	937
Vase, Yellow Irises, Green Matte Glaze, W. Post, Faience Stamp, c.1900, 12 ½ In. .... *illus*	5312

GUN. *Only toy guns are listed in this book. See Toy category.*

GUSTAVSBERG ceramics factory was founded in 1827 near Stockholm, Sweden. It is best known to collectors for its twentieth-century artwares, especially Argenta, a green stoneware with silver inlay. The company broke up and was sold in the 1990s but the name is still being used.

Gustavsberg	Gustavsberg	Gustavsberg
1839–1860	1940–1970	1970–1990s

Bowl, Green & White Bands, Twirled Ribbons, Dots, 6 x 10 In.	187
Figurine, Elephant, Lisa Larson, 4 ¾ x 6 ¾ In.	500
Plaque, Leaf Or Cut Seed, Yellow, Brown, Signed Lisa Larson, 8 ¾ x 8 ¾ In.	125
Vase, Squares, Wilhelm Kage, Farsta, Incised, 1950s, 13 x 9 In. .... *illus*	3625
Vase, Surrea, Applied Vine, White, Stoneware, W. Kage, Sweden, c.1950, 13 ¼ x 5 ¾ In.	188
Vase, Tapered, Glazed, Wilhelm Kage Gustavsberg, 8 x 5 In.	2000

HAEGER POTTERIES, INC., Dundee, Illinois, started making commercial artwares in 1914. Early pieces were marked with the name *Haeger* written over an *H*. About 1938, the mark *Royal Haeger* was used in honor of Royal Hickman, a designer at the factory. The firm closed in 2016. See also the Royal Hickman category.

Bowl, Green, Footed, 4 ½ x 14 In.	48
Bust, Stylized, Green, R. Rush, 1947, 12 In.	60
Ewer, Yellow, Shape No. 408, Handle, Marked, c.1955, 19 In. .... *illus*	98
Figurine, Dog, Russian Wolfhound, Standing, Sticker, 7 x 12 In.	235
Vase, Brown, Orange, Burnt Orange, Earth Wrap, Snakeskin Texture, 1970s, 11 ½ In. ...... *illus*	42

HALF-DOLL, *see Pincushion Doll category.*

HALL CHINA COMPANY started in East Liverpool, Ohio, in 1903. The firm made many types of wares. Collectors search for the Hall teapots made from the 1920s to the 1950s. The dinnerware of the same period, especially Autumn Leaf pattern, is popular. The Hall China Company merged with Homer Laughlin China Company in 2010. Autumn Leaf pattern dishes are listed in their own category in this book.

Andrew, Creamer, 4 ¼ In.	22
Arizona, Cup & Saucer, Footed	10
Arizona, Gravy Boat	66
Blue Garden, Casserole, Lid, Round, 8 In.	48
Bouquet, Cup & Saucer, Footed	10
Bouquet, Plate, Dinner, 11 In.	29
Bouquet, Teapot, Lid, 4 Cup, 4 ⅝ In.	186
Cameo Rose, Platter, Oval, 11 In.	35
Caprice, Casserole, Lid, Oval, 2 Qt.	62
Caprice, Gray Boat	33
Caprice, Platter, Oval, 15 In.	43
Century Fern, Cup & Saucer	20
Century, Relish, 4 Sections, 8 ½ In.	48
Flamingo, Coffeepot, Lid, 8 Cup, 6 ½ In.	60
Frost Flowers, Bowl, Vegetable, Square, 8 In.	18
Frost Flowers, Cup & Saucer, Footed	7

Haeger, Ewer, Yellow, Shape No. 408, Handle, Marked, c.1955, 19 In.
$98

Ruby Lane

Haeger, Vase, Brown, Orange, Burnt Orange, Earth Wrap, Snakeskin Texture, 1970s, 11 ½ In.
$42

Ruby Lane

Hall, Teapot, Maroon, Gold, High Gloss, 6 Cup, Los Angeles Shape, 1930s, 9 x 6 In.
$45

Ruby Lane

Halloween, Jack-O'-Lantern, Papier-Mache, Surprised, White Teeth, Wire Hanger, 9 1/2 In.
$128

Jeffrey S. Evans

Halloween, Postcard, Little Girl, Witch, Black Cat, Pumpkin, Frances Brundage, No. 120, 1910
$75

Ruby Lane

Golden Glo, Casserole, Lid, Basket Weave	95
Harlequin, Platter, 17 In.	82
Heather Rose, Bowl, Cereal, Lugged, 7 3/8 In.	14
Heather Rose, Cup & Saucer, Footed	9
Heather Rose, Plate, Dinner, 10 In.	8
Modern Ivory, Teapot, Lid, 6 Cup	64
Mt. Vernon, Plate, Bread & Butter, 6 In.	6
Mt. Vernon, Serving Bowl, Footed, 10 3/4 In.	26
Mt. Vernon, Soup, Dish, 7 In.	8
Mulberry, Platter, Oval, 17 In.	47
Orange Poppy, Sugar & Creamer	90
Pinecone, Celery, 11 x 5 In.	33
Pinecone, Cup & Saucer, Footed	24
Red Poppy, Casserole, Lid, 1 1/2 Qt.	42
Rose Parade, Casserole, Lid, Tab Handles	45
Rose Parade, Sugar & Creamer	200
Rose Parade, Teapot, 6 Cup	64
Rose White, Sugar Shaker	14
Royal Rose, Salt & Pepper	41
Serenade, Bowl, Dessert, 5 1/2 In.	8
Serenade, Gravy Boat	20
Serenade, Platter, Oval, 13 In.	41
Teapot, Aladdin Lamp, Lid, Yellow, 6 5/8 x 10 3/4 In.	65
Teapot, Lid, Santi-Grid, Chinese Red, White, Art Deco, 1940s, 5 1/2 x 4 1/2 In.	38
Teapot, London Shape, Hand Painted, 10 1/2 In.	199
Teapot, Maroon, Gold, High Gloss, 6 Cup, Los Angeles Shape, 1930s, 9 x 6 In. *illus*	45
Tomorrow's Classic, Bowl, Cereal, 6 In.	12

 HALLOWEEN is an ancient holiday that has changed in the last 200 years. The jack-o'-lantern, witches on broomsticks, and orange decorations seem to be twentieth-century creations. Collectors started to become serious about collecting Halloween-related items in the late 1970s. Old costumes and papier-mache decorations, now replaced by plastic, are in demand.

Automaton, Witch, In Pumpkin, 24 x 36 In.	976
Bucket, Jack-O'-Lantern, Plastic, Orange, Black, Strap Handle, c.1968, 11 x 8 In.	18
Decoration, Scary Butler, Black Suit, Ratty Hair, Tray, Fangs, Composition, Life Size	82
Horn, Flying Witch, Yellow Plastic Mouth Piece, Tin, US Metal, 1950s, 12 x 2 1/2 In.	65
Jack-O'-Lantern, Papier-Mache, Surprised, White Teeth, Wire Hanger, 9 1/2 In. *illus*	128
Mold, Chocolate, Tin, Devil, 5 1/2 In.	214
Mold, Chocolate, Tin, Owl, 4 1/2 x 4 In.	101
Mold, Chocolate, Tin, Pumpkin, 3 x 3 1/2 In.	113
Mold, Chocolate, Tin, Witch, 5 1/2 In.	124
Postcard, Little Girl, Witch, Black Cat, Pumpkin, Frances Brundage, No. 120, 1910 *illus*	75

 HAMPSHIRE pottery was made in Keene, New Hampshire, between 1871 and 1923. Hampshire developed a line of colored glazed wares as early as 1883, including a Royal Worcester–type pink, olive green, blue, and mahogany. Pieces are marked with the printed mark or the impressed name *Hampshire Pottery* or *J.S.T. & Co., Keene, N.H.* (James Scollay Taft). Many pieces were marked with city names and sold as souvenirs.

Lamp, Green Matte Base, Original Fittings, Copper Shade, Bird, 1870s-1920s, 13 x 4 In.	420
Lamp, Handel Mosserine Shade, Green Glaze, Water Lily Base, Marked, 22 1/2 In.	2006
Vase, Molded Flowers, Blue Matte Glaze, Bulbous, Tapered Neck, Marked, 6 In.	200
Vase, Relief Leaves, Green Matte Glaze, c.1920, 7 1/4 In. *illus*	369
Vase, Urn Shape, Surround Of Leaf Blades, Green, Incised, 7 In.	502
Vase, Wide Angle Handles, Support, Green Matte Glaze, Round Foot, 8 x 5 1/2 In.	94
Wall Pocket, Green Matte Glaze, Twin Water Lily Buds Between Leaf Pods, 7 1/4 x 5 1/4 In.	160

HANDBAG, *see Purse category.*

HANDEL glass was made by Philip Handel working in Meriden, Connecticut, from 1885 and in New York City from 1893 to 1933. The firm made art glass and other types of lamps. Handel shades were made not only of leaded glass in a style reminiscent of Tiffany but also of reverse painted glass. Handel also made vases and other glass objects.

Chandelier, Teroma Glass Globe, Painted Woodland Scene, Henry Bedigie	1413
Lamp Base, Marble Platform, 3 Scrolling Legs & Light Clusters, Faux Candle Casing, 60 In.	605
Lamp, 1-Light, Bronzed Spelter Lily Pad Base, Green & White, 1910, 18 x 11 In.	960
Lamp, 2-Light, Frosted, Pink Carnation & Leaves, Gold Trim, 19 x 12 In.	660
Lamp, 2-Light, Painted Shade, Aquarium, Underwater Scene Of Fish, Signed, 14 1/2 In.	60500
Lamp, 2-Light, Patinated Cast Metal, Stained Glass Apple Blossom Garlands, 20 In.	1180
Lamp, 3-Light, Leaded, Geometric, 12-Sided Shade, Green Slag Glass, Signed, 24 In.	2420
Lamp, 3-Light, Opal Glass, Domed Shade, Satin Background, Blue Border, 24 In.	2057
Lamp, 3-Light, Patinated Mixed Cast Metal, Composite Base, Ball Fixture, 71 x 18 In.	1888
Lamp, 4-Light, Leaded, Slag Glass, 12-Panel Shade, Bronze Base, 1900s, 25 x 21 In.	3960
Lamp, 4-Light, Reddish Brown Base, Flower, Gooseneck Sockets, 65 In.	2420
Lamp, 4-Light, Slag, Glass, Sunset, Tropical Scene, Heat Cap, 24 In.	2420
Lamp, Apple Blossom Shade, Pink, Green, Patinated Base, Marked, c.1925, 22 x 16 In.	1750
Lamp, Art & Crafts, Green, Red, Patinated Metal, c.1910, 19 x 12 In.	2000
Lamp, Bronze, Glass Shade, Daffodils, Leaves, Light Ground, Signed, 24 In.	3630
Lamp, Bungalow Style, Painted Metal, Green, Slag Glass, c.1920, 22 x 15 In.	1125
Lamp, Domed Shade, Birds Of Paradise, Glazed Pottery & Metal Base, c.1924, 24 In. *illus*	6250
Lamp, Domed Shade, Evergreen Tree Tops, Trunk Base, Green To Salmon Ground, 24 x 18 In.	3900
Lamp, Domed Shade, Greek Ruins, Patinated Metal Base, c.1914, 23 x 18 In. *illus*	3750
Lamp, Domed Shade, Underwater Scene, Fish, Plants, Mermaid Base, Signed, 15 In. *illus*	36300
Lamp, Enamel, Egg Shape, Pink Iridescent Interior, Crackled Exterior, 6 1/2 In.	847
Lamp, Hanging, 3-Light, 8-Panel Shade, Vine Overlays, Caramel Slag Glass, 24 In.	847
Lamp, Hanging, Blue Macaw, Globe, Patinated Metal Fittings, c.1922, 28 x 10 In. *illus*	2375
Lamp, Hanging, Globe, Fall Trees, Birds, Gold Iridescent Ground, Signed, 30 1/2 In.	2420
Lamp, Hexagonal Opal Glass Printed Shade, Green Mosserine Finish, Signed, 15 x 6 x 13 In.	908
Lamp, Mosserine, Matte Finish, Shades 14 In. Diameter, Lamp 23 1/2 In.	1694
Lamp, Octagonal, Reverse Painted, Blackberries, Leaves, Orange Yellow Ground, 22 In.	2178
Lamp, Painted Metal, Glass, Shade, Autumn Landscape, c.1920, 11 x 10 In.	875
Lamp, Painted Pheasant Shade, Multicolor, 3-Footed, 1910-20s, 59 1/2 x 18 In.	5625
Lamp, Painted Pine Forest Shade, Classical Base, Patinated Metal, Slag Glass, c.1915, 65 In.	4687
Lamp, Pine Tree, Domed Shade, Yellow, Acid Etched, 6 Panels, Bronze Tree Trunk, 22 x 15 In.	3300
Lamp, Red, Yellow Flowers, Leaves, Pewter Base Finish, Marked, 15 In.	1936
Lamp, Ribbed Panels, Leaves, Brown Cattail Shade 19 1/2 In., Lamp 22 1/2 In.	4537
Lamp, Shade, Cone Shape, Chrysanthemum, Signed, 3 Sockets, 25 In.	2420
Lamp, Shade, Cone Shape, Sunset Venetian Harbor, Spelter Base, 14 In.	908
Lamp, Shade, Seascape, Bronze Baluster Base, Spread Foot, 24 In.	8125
Lamp, Slag Glass, Sunset Landscape, Palm Trees, Lake, Metal Base, 19 3/4 In.	3750
Lamp, Slag Glass, Sunset, Pines, Overlap, Bronzed Metal, 24 3/4 In.	5000
Lamp, Sunset Pines, Slag Glass, Bronzed Metal, Signed, 10 x 7 In.	1700
Sconce, 1-Light, Flower, Leaves, Slag Glass Shade, Green, Orange, 1910s-20s, 15 x 6 In., Pair	2125
Shade, 6 Panels, Sunset Glass, Metal Overlay, 7 In. Diam.	665
Vase, Autumn, Meadow, Trees, Waisted, Teroma, Marked G. Lockrow, 10 1/2 In.	1180
Vase, Autumn, Mountains, Shouldered, Footed, Teroma, Marked J. Bailey, 10 In.	1062

HARDWARE, *see Architectural category.*

HARKER POTTERY COMPANY was incorporated in 1890 in East Liverpool, Ohio. The Harker family had been making pottery in the area since 1840. The company made many types of pottery but by the Civil War was making quantities of yellowware from native clays. It also made Rockingham-type brown-glazed pottery and whiteware. The plant was moved to Chester, West Virginia, in 1931. Dinnerware was made and sold nationally. In 1971 the company was sold to Jeannette Glass Company, and all operations ceased in 1972. For more prices, go to kovels.com.

Hampshire, Vase, Relief Leaves, Green Matte Glaze, c.1920, 7 1/4 In.
$369

Leland Little Auctions

Handel, Lamp, Domed Shade, Birds Of Paradise, Glazed Pottery & Metal Base, c.1924, 24 In.
$6,250

Rago Arts and Auction Center

Handel, Lamp, Domed Shade, Greek Ruins, Patinated Metal Base, c.1914, 23 x 18 In.
$3,750

Rago Arts and Auction Center

Handel, Lamp, Domed Shade, Underwater Scene, Fish, Plants, Mermaid Base, Signed, 15 In. $36,300

Handel, Lamp, Hanging, Blue Macaw, Globe, Patinated Metal Fittings, c.1922, 28 x 10 In. $2,375

Harker, Jug, Pirate, Earring, Green Glaze, Braid Handle, 1960s, 4 3/8 In. $30

Cake Plate, Square, Scalloped, Handle, 1940s, 12 In.	15
Cameoware, Plate, 7 1/4 In.	10
Jug, Pirate, Earring, Green Glaze, Braid Handle, 1960s, 4 3/8 In. ..... *illus*	30
Mallow, Cake Server, 9 1/4 In.	15
Skyscraper, Salt & Pepper Shakers, 4 1/4 In.	15

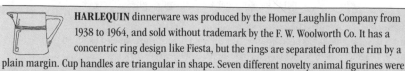

HARLEQUIN dinnerware was produced by the Homer Laughlin Company from 1938 to 1964, and sold without trademark by the F. W. Woolworth Co. It has a concentric ring design like Fiesta, but the rings are separated from the rim by a plain margin. Cup handles are triangular in shape. Seven different novelty animal figurines were introduced in 1939. For more prices, go to kovels.com.

Blue, Double Eggcup, 3 3/4 In.	29
Rose, Bowl, Rolled Rim, 6 1/4 In.	10
Rose, Teapot, 1950s, 4 7/8 In.	85
Spruce Green, Platter, Oval, 11 x 9 In.	55
Spruce Green, Sauceboat, 3 x 8 1/2 In.	65

HATPIN collectors search for pins popular from 1860 to 1920. The long pin, often over four inches, was used to hold the hat in place on the hair. The tops of the pins were made of all materials, from solid gold and real gemstones to ceramics and glass. Be careful to buy original hatpins and not recent pieces made by altering old buttons.

Amethyst, 14K Yellow Gold, Bulb Shape Bezel, c.1910, 4 1/2 x 3/4 In.	330
Clear Dome, Dog Head, Terrier, Glass, Metal, 4 x 3/4 In.	30
Gilt Metal, Talon, 2 x 11 1/2 In. ..... *illus*	60

HATPIN HOLDERS were needed when hatpins were fashionable from 1860 to 1920. The large, heavy hat required special long-shanked pins to hold it in place. The hatpin holder resembles a large saltshaker, but it often has no opening at the bottom as a shaker does. Hatpin holders were made of all types of ceramics and metal. Look for other pieces under the names of specific manufacturers.

Brass, Boy On Horse ..... *illus*	3750
Carnival Glass, Grape & Cable Pattern ..... *illus*	90
Cloisonne, Birds & Branches ..... *illus*	5400
Glass, Crown Milano, Enamel Decoration, Mt. Washington, 2 1/2 x 5 1/4 In.	147
Porcelain, 2-Sided, Gentlemen's Faces, Smiling, Scowling, Sculpted Curls, 1860, 4 In.	230

HAVILAND china has been made in Limoges, France, since 1842. David Haviland had a shop in New York City and opened a porcelain company in Limoges, France. Haviland was the first company to both manufacture and decorate porcelain. Pieces are marked *H & Co., Haviland & Co.,* or *Theodore Haviland.* It is possible to match existing sets of dishes through dealers who specialize in Haviland china. Other factories worked in the town of Limoges making a similar chinaware. These porcelains are listed in this book under Limoges.

HAVILAND&Cᵒ Limoges	**Théo Haviland Limoges FRANCE**	**Haviland France**
Haviland and Co. 1876–1878; 1889–1931	Theodore Haviland 1893–early 1900s	Haviland and Co. c. 1894–1931

Ramekin, Underplate, Rose Petals, Gilt Trim, c.1900	25
Vase, Gilt Rim, Decoration, Thistle Border, Rose-Colored Ground, 1895-1920, 9 3/8 In.	1599
Vase, Man Reading Under Tree, Oval, Marked, c.1885, 10 1/2 x 7 In. ..... *illus*	2250
Vase, Young Woman & Tree Scene, Lake Background, Signed, France, 3 1/2 In.	420

HAVILAND POTTERY began in 1872, when Charles Haviland decided to make art pottery. He worked with the famous artists of the day and made pottery with slip glazed decorations. Production stopped in 1885. Haviland Pottery is marked with the letters *H & Co.* The Haviland name is better known today for its porcelain.

HAVILAND & Co
Limoges

Haviland and Co.
1875–1882

H & Co
L

Haviland and Co.
1875–1882

C F H
G D M
FRANCE

Charles Field Haviland
1891+

Vase, Red Bleeding Hearts, Green Leaves, Mottled Gold Ground, c.1895, 4 5/8 In. 3198

HAWKES cut glass was made by T. G. Hawkes & Company of Corning, New York, founded in 1880. The firm cut glass blanks made at other glassworks until 1962. Many pieces are marked with the trademark, a trefoil ring enclosing a fleur-de-lis and two hawks. Cut glass by other manufacturers is listed under either the factory name or in the general Cut Glass category.

Bottle, Whiskey, Chrysanthemum, Cut Strap Handle & Stopper, 8 1/2 In.	560
Bowl, Fruit, Olympia, 2 3/4 x 16 5/8 In.	1680
Bowl, Napoleon, 2 3/4 x 10 In.	200
Bowl, Top Hat Shape, Flared Rim, 3 5/8 x 10 In.	266
Candlestick, Russian, Swirl Pillar Stem, 11 3/4 In., Pair	1800
Carafe, Water, Chrysanthemum, Cut Ring Neck, Heavy Blank, 9 1/2 In.	900
Celery Tray, Modified Lattice & Rosette, Marked, 11 x 5 3/4 In.	1140
Cheese & Cracker Server, Hobstar, Strawberry & Crosscut Diamond, Stand, 4 x 11 In.	540
Cologne Bottle, Teutonic, Stopper Marked, Hobstar Base, 7 1/4 In.	330
Cologne Bottle, Venetian, Silver Stopper, Bailey Banks & Biddle Monogram, 6 1/2 In.	240
Decanter, Brunswick, Bowling Pin Shape, Cut Stopper, 14 1/2 In.	840
Decanter, Handle, Chrysanthemum, Triple Notched, 12 In.	330
Decanter, Liqueur, Chrysanthemum, Embossed Silver Flip Lid, Attached Chain, 9 1/2 In.	720
Dish, Divided, 2 Handles, Princess, Marked, Clear, 3 x 8 x 12 In.	270
Dish, Shell, Alternating Pillar, Strawberry Diamond, Clear Blank, 6 1/4 In.	300
Jar, Smelling Salts, Gladys, Embossed Silver Flip Top, Glass Stopper, 3 1/4 In.	240
Jug, Handle, Grecian, Crosshatch Band Neck, Scalloped Ray Cut Foot, 8 In.	330
Jug, Whiskey, Marquis Cut, Hobstar Band, Fans, Panel Cut Neck, Stopper, 15 x 3 3/4 In.	210
Ladle, Teutonic Handle, Gorham Silver Dipper, 17 In.	360
Lamp, Water, Pedestal Globe, Engraved, School Of Fish Scene, Mica Shade, 12 In.	420
Martini Pitcher, Stirrer, Flying Duck Scene, Signed J. Sidot, 11 In.	120
Plate, Russian, Pillar, Canterbury Buttons, 9 1/4 In.	720
Punch Bowl, Stand, 8 Cups, Queens, 15 x 15 In., 10 Piece	11400
Punch Bowl, Stand, Crosscut Diamond, Fan, Cranberry Cut To Clear, 13 3/4 In.	1920
Punch Bowl, Teutonic Pattern, Signed, 11 x 13 In.	1440
Sauceboat, Devonshire, Triple Notched Handle, Hobstar Base, Signed, 4 3/4 x 6 3/4 In.	420
Tankard, Aberdeen, Clear Tusk Highlights, Triple Notched Handle, 11 In.	540
Teapot, Alberta, 6 x 9 In.	1560
Tray, Constellation, 12 In.	3250
Tray, Round, Pueblo, Signed, 8 In.	28800
Tumbler, Iced Tea, Crosshatched, Multisided Stems, 7 In.	83
Vase, Blue Transparent, Engraved Flowers, 1900-20, 11 In.	246
Vase, Cherry Blossoms, Blue Glass Painted Ground, Gilt, Acid Stamped, 13 In. .... *illus*	147
Vase, Intaglio, Crystal, Carved, Oriental Scene, Palm Trees, Pagoda, Marked, 12 In.	242
Vase, Pedestal, Bismark, Marked, 10 In.	100
Vase, Queens, Cylindrical, 14 3/4 In.	780

HEAD VASES, generally showing a woman from the shoulders up, were used by florists primarily in the 1950s and 1960s. Made in a variety of sizes and often decorated with imitation jewelry and other lifelike accessories, the vases were manufactured in Japan and the U.S.A. Less elaborate examples were made as early as the 1930s. Religious

Hatpin, Gilt Metal, Talon, 2 x 11 1/2 In.
$60

Mike Clum Auctions, Inc.

Hatpin Holder, Brass, Boy On Horse
$3,750

Mike Clum Auctions, Inc.

Hatpin Holder, Carnival Glass, Grape & Cable Pattern
$90

Mike Clum Auctions, Inc.

H

Hatpin Holder, Cloisonne, Birds &
Branches
$5,400

Mike Clum Auctions, Inc.

Haviland, Vase, Man Reading Under
Tree, Oval, Marked, c.1885, 10½ x 7 In.
$2,250

Rago Arts and Auction Center

The Haviland Family
Pieces marked "Johann Haviland" were made in Germany
from 1907 to 1924. They are
not the famous French Haviland china made by Theo-
dore Haviland Company or
Haviland & Company. These
are marked with variations of
the name *Theodore Haviland*
or *Haviland.*

themes, babies, and animals are also common subjects. Other head vases are listed under manufacturers' names and can be located through the index in the back of this book.

African Woman, Bowl On Head, 1950s, 5½ x 4⅜ In. .... *illus*	85
Snow Lady, Cape & Hood, Cream, Gold, Long Eyelashes, Rubens, 1963, 6 In. .... *illus*	75
Woman, Pearls, Red Hat, Yellow Brim, Napco, 4¾ In.	17
Women, Hat, Applied Flowers On Brim, Earrings, 5 In.	54
Women, Pink Hat, White Bow, Long Eyelashes, Collar, Napco, 4¾ In.	18
Women, White Hat, Red Brim, Blond Hair, Napco, 6 In.	60

 HEINTZ ART METAL SHOP used the letters *HAMS* in a diamond as a mark. In 1902,
Otto Heintz designed and manufactured copper items with colored enamel decorations under the name Art Crafts Shop. He took over the Arts & Crafts Company in
Buffalo, New York, in 1903. By 1906 it had become the Heintz Art Metal Shop. It
remained in business until 1930. The company made ashtrays, bookends, boxes, bowls, desk sets,
vases, trophies, and smoking sets. The best-known pieces are made of copper, brass, and bronze
with silver overlay. Similar pieces were made by Smith Metal Arts and were marked *Silver Crest.*
Some pieces by both companies are unmarked.

Candlestick, Flower Form, Bobeche, Sterling On Bronze Stamped Marking, 14 x 5⅞ In.	354
Lamp, 1-Light, Flowers, Sterling On Bronze, 6¼ x 12 In.	1534
Lamp, Candlestick Shape Base, Sterling On Bronze, Cattail Design, 10 x 8¾ In.	1534
Lamp, Patinated Bronze, Sterling On Bronze, Verdigris, Flowers, 1920, 15 x 12 In.	1920
Lamp, Sterling On Bronze, Lily, Verdigris, 12 x 11 In.	1320

HEISEY glass was made from 1896 to 1957 in Newark, Ohio, by A. H. Heisey and Co., Inc. The
Imperial Glass Company of Bellaire, Ohio, bought some of the molds and the rights to the trademark. Some Heisey patterns have been made by Imperial since 1960. After 1968, they stopped
using the *H* trademark. Heisey used romantic names for colors, such as Sahara. Do not confuse
color and pattern names. The Custard Glass and Ruby Glass categories may also include some
Heisey pieces.

Heisey
1900–1957

Heisey
Paper label

Heisey
Paper label

Animal, Dog, Scottie	103
Animal, Goose, Wings Up	109
Banded Flute, Nappy, 4½ In.	45
Bead Panel & Sunburst, Butter, Ruby Stained, c.1897, 6 In.	163
Candy Dish, Paneled, Footed, Gold Leaf, Lid, 10¼ x 4 In.	68
Continental, Compote, 8½ In.	25
Coronation, Tumbler, Old Fashioned, Gold Band, 8 Oz.	50
Crystolite, Centerpiece, 11 In.	100
Double Rib & Panel, Basket, 6 In.	20
Greek Key, Jelly, Footed, 5 In.	35
Greek Key, Jug, Qt.	70
Greek Key, Tankard, 3 Pt.	120
Greek Key, Tankard, Pt.	65
Ice Bucket, Ormolu Frame, Rectangular, Canted Corners, Laurel Rails, 10 x 8½ x 5 In.	467
Ipswich, Sugar & Creamer	15
Ipswich, Tumbler, 8 Oz.	50
Ipswich, Tumbler, 10 Oz.	75
Jar, Gilt Metal Jeweled Lid, 3 x 4½ In.	108
Kalonyal, Celery Dish, 11 In.	25
Lariat, Sugar & Creamer, Tray, 3 Piece	25

H

Locket On Chain, Tumbler, Gilt, c.1896-1904, 3¾ In.	198
Moongleam, Cruet, 2 Oz.	40
Old Sandwich, Bowe, Console, Sahara, 4 x 11 In.	105
Orchid Etch, Bowl, Scalloped, 1940s, 12 x 4 In. *illus*	49
Pineapple & Fan, Vase, Trumpet, 12 In.	50
Pinwheel & Fan, Basket, 6 In.	100
Pinwheel & Fan, Nappy, 8 In.	280
Plantation, Compote, 5 x 7 In.	65
Plantation, Sugar & Creamer	22
Prince Of Wales, Toothpick Holder, Plumes	58
Priscilla, Toothpick Holder	25
Provincial, Tumbler, Footed, 8 Oz.	70
Puritan, Jug, Squat, Pt.	25
Puritan, Jug, Squat, Qt.	25
Puritan, Tankard, 3 Pt.	90
Ridgeleigh, Decanter	175
Ridgeleigh, Plate, 10½ In.	320
Sunburst, Pitcher, ½ Gal.	90
Town & Country, Nappy, 6 In.	50
Tudor, Vase, 8½ In.	55

HEREND, *see Fischer category.*

HEUBACH is the collector's name for Gebruder Heubach, a firm working in Lichten, Germany, from 1840 to 1925. It is best known for bisque dolls and doll heads, the principal products. The company also manufactured bisque figurines, including piano babies, beginning in the 1880s, and glazed figurines in the 1900s. Piano Babies are listed in their own category. Dolls are included in the Doll category under Gebruder Heubach and Heubach. Another factory, Ernst Heubach, working in Koppelsdorf, Germany, also made porcelain and dolls. These will also be found in the Doll category under Heubach Koppelsdorf.

Candy Container, Snowball Shape, Child, Sitting, White Cotton Suit, 9¼ In. *illus*	862
Vase, 2 Cherubs, Teasing Lobster In Ocean, Luster Glaze, Impressed Logo, 6¾ In.	50

HISTORIC BLUE, *see factory names, such as Adams, Ridgway, and Staffordshire.*

HOBNAIL glass is a style of glass with bumps all over. Dozens of hobnail patterns and variants have been made. Clear, colored, and opalescent hobnail have been made and are being reproduced. Other pieces of hobnail may also be listed in the Duncan & Miller and Fenton categories.

Banana Boat, Footed, Milk Glass, 9 x 12 In.	72
Lamp, Hanging Electric, Brass, 2-Tone Conical Shade, Clear Frosted Top, 10 x 7 x 8¼ In.	152

HOLLY AMBER, or golden agate, glass was made by the Indiana Tumbler and Goblet Company of Greentown, Indiana, from January 1, 1903, to June 13, 1903. It is a pressed glass pattern featuring holly leaves in the amber-shaded glass. The glass was made with shadings that range from creamy opalescent to brown-amber.

Sugar, Lid, 6 In.	945
Toothpick Holder	980

HOLT-HOWARD was an importer that started working in New York City in 1949 and moved to Stamford, Connecticut, in 1955. The company sold many types of table accessories, such as condiment jars, decanters, spoon holders, and saltshakers. Its figural pieces have a cartoon-like quality. The company was bought out by General Housewares Corporation in 1968. Holt-Howard pieces are often marked with the name and the year or *HH* and the year stamped in black. The *HH* mark was used until 1974. The company also used a black and silver paper label. Holt-Howard production ceased in 1990 and the remainder of the company was sold to Kay Dee Designs. In 2002, Grant Holt and John Howard started Grant-

Hawkes, Vase, Cherry Blossoms, Blue Glass Painted Ground, Gilt, Acid Stamped, 13 In.
$147

Leland Little Auctions

Head Vase, African Woman, Bowl On Head, 1950s, 5½ x 4⅜ In.
$85

Ruby Lane

Head Vase, Snow Lady, Cape & Hood, Cream, Gold, Long Eyelashes, Rubens, 1963, 6 In.
$75

Ruby Lane

H

Heisey, Orchid Etch, Bowl, Scalloped, 1940s, 12 x 4 In.
$49

Ruby Lane

Heubach, Candy Container, Snowball Shape, Child, Sitting, White Cotton Suit, 9¼ In.
$862

Bunch Auctions

Holt-Howard, Figurine, Asian Girl, Blue Dress, Oriental Pattern Stamps, 1959, 5½ In.
$64

Ruby Lane

Howard Associates and made a new piece, a retro pixie cookie jar marked *GHA* that sold from a mail-order catalog. Other retro pixie pieces were made until 2006.

Candleholder, Baby Fawn, Mother Mary, Foil Sticker, 5 x 3½ In.	32
Candleholder, Noel, Wreath, Santa Claus, c.1959, 4 x 9 In.	74
Coffeepot, Coq Rouge, Red Rooster, Electric, c.1962, 8½ In.	95
Cookie Jar, Pixie Ware, Winking, Orange Stripes, 11 x 8 In.	165
Cream Crock, Pixie Ware, Aqua Stripes, 2¾ x 3¾ In.	25
Figurine, Asian Girl, Blue Dress, Oriental Pattern Stamps, 1959, 5½ In. .... *illus*	64
Figurine, Japanese Girl, Blue Dress, 1959, 5½ In.	64
Jar, French Dressing, 4¼ In.	40
Jar, Mustard, Rooster, 4 x 3 In.	28
Jar, Pixie Ware, Ketchup, 4 In.	95
Jar, Pixie Ware, Mustard, Frowning	90
Pitcher, Santa, Winking, 7 In.	24
Salt & Pepper, Christmas Birds, Holly, Bow On Heads, Green, c.1950, 3 In.	72
Salt & Pepper, Cozy Kittens, Large Eyes, 1961	45

HOPALONG CASSIDY was a character in a series of 28 books written by Clarence E. Mulford, first published in 1907. Movies and television shows were made based on the character. The best-known actor playing Hopalong Cassidy was William Lawrence Boyd. His first movie appearance was in 1919, but the first Hopalong Cassidy film was not made until 1934. Sixty-six films were made. In 1948, William Boyd purchased the television rights to the movies, then later made 52 new programs. In the 1950s, Hopalong Cassidy and his horse, named Topper, were seen in comics, records, toys, and other products. Boyd died in 1972.

Book, Hopalong Cassidy & The Bar 20 Cowboy, Little Golden Book, 1952	18
Book, Pop-Up, Hopalong Cassidy Lends A Helping Hand, Bonnie Book, 20 Pages, 1950s	49
Box, Display, Portrait, Chocolate Coconut Candy, 5 Cents, Die Cut, c.1950, 9 x 5 x 8 In.	375
Card, Gun Shape, Portrait, Happy Birthday, Buzza-Cardozo, 8 x 3 In.	195
Doll, Hopalong, Vinyl Head & Hands, Stuffed Body, Scarf, Pin, Hat, 1950s, 23 In.	279
Game, Board, Hopalong Wearing Badge, Milton Bradley, c.1950, 18 x 18 In.	32
Hair Clip, Hopalong Portrait, Initials, Metal, 2 In.	48
Invitation, Boy & Girl, Western Wear, Howdy Pard, 3 x 4 In.	18
Lamp, Aladdin, White Glass, Ribbed, Paper Shade, William Boyd Ltd., 17 In. .... *illus*	240
Shirt, Rayon, Embroidered Cassidy & Topper, Brown, Child's	55
Skirt, Cotton, Black, Fringe, Hoppy On Pockets, Size 14	72
Thermos, Hopalong, Horse, Yellow, Aladdin, c.1950, 6 x 3¾ In.	75
Toy, Hopalong, Ranger Rider, Lasso, Tin Lithograph, Marx, Windup, 9½ x 11¼ In.	395
Toy, Shooting Gallery, Box, Red, Yellow, Automatic Toy Co. .... *illus*	150
Tumbler, Milk Glass, Hopalong Fixing Wagon Wheel, 1940s, 4 In.	35
Wristwatch, Saddle Shape Display, 1950s	235

HORN was used to make many types of boxes, furniture inlays, jewelry, and whimsies. The Endangered Species Act makes it illegal to sell many of these pieces.

Cup, Buffalo, Quilled, Tied-On Rawhide Lid, 1900s, 7¼ x 11 x 4 In.	160
Drinking Horn, Continental, Brass Mounted, Medieval, Ball & Claw Feet, 13 x 15 In.	4750

Howard Pierce

HOWARD PIERCE began working in Southern California in 1936. In 1945, he opened a pottery in Claremont. He moved to Joshua Tree in 1968 and continued making pottery until 1991. His contemporary-looking figurines are popular with collectors. Though most pieces are marked with his name, smaller items from his sets often were not marked.

Figurine, Goose, Long Neck, Cream To Brown, 7 In.	15
Figurine, Mouse, Big Ears, Brown, Gray, c.1950, 4 x 2 In.	95
Figurine, Road Runner, 9 x 4 In.	35
Figurine, Siamese Cat, Stylized, Raised Ears, 1950s, 8 In.	115

HOWDY DOODY and Buffalo Bob were the main characters in a children's series televised from 1947 to 1960. Howdy was a redheaded puppet. The series became popular with college students in the late 1970s when Buffalo Bob began to lecture on campuses.

Bib, Toddler, Fabric Piping, Tie Cord, Princess Summerfall Winterspring, 1950s, 11 x 13 In.....	60
Doll, Composition Head, Hands, Stuffed Body, 1940s, 22 In.	77
Marionette, Original Production, Scott Brinker.............................. *illus*	16250
Night-Light, Howdy Doody, Seated, 7 In................................	120
Toy, Band, Bob Smith At Piano, Howdy Doody Dancing, Tin Lithograph, Unique Art, 5 In........	480
Toy, Howdy Doody, Pop-Up, Plastic, Wood, Konner Products, 1950s, 6 In.	76
Toy, Marionette, Howdy Doody, Plaid Shirt, Blue Jeans, 17 In..........	36

HULL pottery was made in Crooksville, Ohio, from 1905. Addis E. Hull bought the Acme Pottery Company and started making ceramic wares. In 1917, A. E. Hull Pottery began making art pottery as well as the commercial wares. For a short time, 1921 to 1929, the firm also sold pottery imported from Europe. The dinnerware of the 1940s (including the Little Red Riding Hood line), the matte wares of the 1940s, and the high gloss artwares of the 1950s are all popular with collectors. The firm officially closed in March 1986.

Hull Pottery
c.1915

A.E. HULL
U.S.A.

Hull Pottery
1930s

Hull Pottery
c.1950

Basket Weave, Planter, Green & Brown, 6 In.	65
Bluebird, Sugar, Lid, 9 In.	89
Brown Drip, Bowl, Fruit, 5 3/8 In.	7
Brown Drip, Plate, Bread & Butter, 6 3/4 In.	5
Brown Drip, Plate, Dinner, 10 1/2 In.	8
Brown Drip, Platter, Meat, 14 In.	18
Brown Drip, Salt & Pepper, Mushroom	12
Flowers, Vase, Pale Pink To Blue, Yellow & Pink Flowers, Double Handles, 12 1/2 In.	20
Flowers, Vase, Pink Neck, Yellow Body, Flowers On Green Leaves, Handles, 10 3/4 In.	36
Flowers, Vase, Pink To Cream, Pink & Yellow Flowers, Scalloped Mouth, 8 1/2 In..........	30
Iris, Vase, Pink & Blue, Marked, 7 1/8 In.	39
Magnolia, Bowl, Pink & Yellow Roses, Rounded Corners, Handles, 12 3/4 In...........	18
Rosella, Ewer, Wild Roses, Pink, Green Leaves, Marked, c.1946, 6 1/2 x 4 1/2 In. .... *illus*	70
Tuscany, Basket, Moon, 11 x 10 In.......................	36
Wildflower, Vase, Cornucopia, Marked, 6 3/8 In.	65
Woodland, Cornucopia, Cream Base, Green & Pink Flowers, High Gloss, 1950, 11 In....... *illus*	50

HUMMEL figurines, based on the drawings of the nun M.I. Hummel (Berta Hummel), were made by the W. Goebel Porzellanfabrik of Oeslau, Germany, now Rodental, Germany. They were first made in 1935. The *Crown* mark was used from 1935 to 1949. The company added the *bee* marks in 1950. The *full bee*, with variations, was used from 1950 to 1959; *stylized bee*, 1957 to 1972; *three line mark,* 1964 to 1972; *last bee*, sometimes called *vee over gee*, 1972 to 1979. In 1979 the V bee symbol was removed from the mark. *U.S. Zone* was part of the mark from 1946 to 1948; *W. Germany* was part of the mark from 1960 to 1990. The Goebel *W. Germany* mark, called the *missing bee* mark, was used from 1979 to 1990; *Goebel, Germany*, with the crown and *WG*, originally called the *new mark*, was used from 1991 through part of 1999. A new version of the bee mark with the word *Goebel* was used from 1999 to 2008. A special *Year 2000* backstamp was also introduced. Porcelain figures inspired by Berta Hummel's drawings were introduced in 1997. These are marked *BH* followed by a number. They were made in the Far East, not Germany. Goebel discontinued making Hummel figurines in 2008 and Manufaktur Rodental took over the factory in Germany and began making new Hummel figurines. Hummel figurines made by Rodental are marked with a yellow and black bee on the edge of an oval line surrounding the words *Original M.I. Hummel Germany.* The words *Manufaktur Rodental* are printed beneath the oval. Manufaktur Rodental was sold in 2013 and new owners, Hummel Manufaktur GmbH, have taken over,

Hopalong Cassidy, Lamp, Aladdin, White Glass, Ribbed, Paper Shade, William Boyd Ltd., 17 In.
$240

Rich Penn Auctions

Hopalong Cassidy, Toy, Shooting Gallery, Box, Red, Yellow, Automatic Toy Co.
$150

Rich Penn Auctions

Howdy Doody, Marionette, Original Production, Scott Brinker
$16,250

Pook & Pook

Hull, Rosella, Ewer, Wild Roses, Pink, Green Leaves, Marked, c.1946, 6½ x 4½ In.
$70

Ruby Lane

but the figurines continue to be made in the factory in Rodental. Hummel Manufaktur GmbH, is the new company. Other decorative items and plates that feature Hummel drawings have been made by Schmid Brothers, Inc., since 1971.

Hummel
1935–1949

Hummel
1950–1959

Hummel
2009–present

Figurine, Adventure Bound, Vee Over Bee, 1972-79, 7 x 8 In. .... *illus*	540
Figurine, Madonna With Halo, No. 45 Pastel Colors, Blue Robe, Stars, Small Bee Mark, 11 In.	47
Figurine, Virgin Mary Praying Madonna, Orange Peach Robe, Stylized Bee, 960, 11 In.	49

HUTSCHENREUTHER PORCELAIN FACTORY was founded by Carolus Magnus in Hohenburg, Bavaria, in 1814. A second factory was established in Selb, Germany, in 1857. The company made fine quality porcelain dinnerware and figurines. The mark changed through the years, but the name and the lion insignia appear in most versions. Hutschenreuther became part of the Rosenthal division of the Waterford Wedgwood Group in 2000. Rosenthal became part of the Arcturus Group in 2009.

Figurine, Nude Woman On Horse, Impressed K. Tutter, 12¼ In.	153
Figurine, Nude Woman, Gold Sphere, Bisque, Art Deco, Signed, 1900s, 8 In.	390
Figurine, Nude, Sitting, Holding Flowers, Deer, 8 x 8 In.	525
Figurine, Young Woman, Nude, Feeding Doe, 9½ x 12 In. .... *illus*	312
Group, Nude Child, Riding Bucking Colt, Karl Tutter, 8 x 8 In.	148
Group, Nude, Riding Stallion, Karl Tutter, 12½ x 10 In.	124
Plate, Gold & White Alternating Bands, Flower Basket, 10¼ In.	12

ICONS, special, revered pictures of Jesus, Mary, or a saint, are usually Russian or Byzantine. The small icons collected today are made of wood and tin or precious metals. Many modern copies have been made in the old style and are being sold to tourists in Russia and Europe and at shops in the United States. Rare, old icons have sold for over $50,000. The riza is the metal cover protecting the icon. It is often made of silver or gold.

Ascension Of Christ, Relief, Silver Plate, 4 Disciples, Russia, c.1925, 12 x 10 In.	688
Christ Pantocrator, Silver Gilt, Open Book, Hand Up, Halo, Russia, 12⅜ x 10½ In.	2000
Christ, Silver, Enamel, Open Book, Ivan Khlebnikov, Russia, 1908-17, 7 x 5⅝ In.	1400
Mother & Child, Painted Faces, Brass Overlay, Walnut Shadowbox, 13¾ x 11¾ In.	242
Panel, Matthew, Mark, Luke, John, Embroidered, Gold, Silver, Thread, c.1800, 12 x 9 In., 4 Panels	2500
St. George, Dragon, Princess In Background, Etched Riza, 1800s, 11 x 8½ In.	190
St. John The Evangelist, Painted Wood Panel, Tempera, Greek Orthodox, 1800s, 14 x 13 In..	813
Virgin & Child, Marble Relief, Carved, Gilt Wood Frame, Renaissance Style, Italy, 31 x 9 In. ...	7500
Virgin Mary & Dove, Copper, Mounted To Wood, Punched Copper Border, Spain, 12 x 9 In. ...	288
Virgin Mary, Child, Halos, Flower Border, Brass Over Wood, 12¼ x 10¼ In. .... *illus*	350
Virgin Of Hodigitria, Child, Blue Halos, Silver Oklad, Russia, 1896-1908, 5⅜ x 4½ In.	700

IMARI porcelain was made in Japan and China beginning in the seventeenth century. In the eighteenth century and later, it was copied by porcelain factories in Germany, France, England, and the United States. It was especially popular in the nineteenth century and is still being made. Imari is characteristically decorated with stylized bamboo, floral, and geometric designs in orange, red, green, and blue. The name comes from the Japanese port of Imari, which exported the ware made nearby in a factory at Arita. Imari is now a general term for any pattern of this type.

Bowl, Bird & Flower Scroll Design, Brocade Ground, 1800s, 8 In.	344
Bowl, Brown Bird, Orange Red Flowers, Blue Leaves, c.1730, 10½ In.	425
Bowl, Flowers, Scalloped Rim, Symbols Of Good Fortune, c.1900, 6½ In. .... *illus*	313

H

Bowl, Lotus Shape, Gilt Over Glaze Design, Edo Period, 1700s-1800s, 6 x 6 x 1 ¾ In.	41
Bowl, Ruffled Edge, Paneled, Multicolor, Gilt, Japan, 1800, 4 x 7 ½ In.............................. *illus*	96
Bowl, Storks, Tree, Temple, Blue, Red, Japan, 9 ⅝ x 3 ¾ In.	124
Cachepot, 8-Sided, Panels, Peonies, Birds, Pinched & Flared Rim, Japan, 9 x 14 In.	1188
Chamber Pot, Chrysanthemum Medallion, Trees, Cranes, Flared Lip, Handle, Chinese, 8 In..	750
Charger, 9 Wedges, Scalloped Edge, 18 In...	330
Charger, Blue, Copper Red, Gilt, Garden, Bird, Flowering Branch, Flower Borders, 14 In. *illus*	1875
Charger, Central Cartouche, Monk, Large Belly, Boy, 16 In....................................	144
Charger, Chrysanthemums, Japan, 1900, 12 In.	96
Charger, Chrysanthemums, Water Lilies, Water, Platform, Chinese, 14 In...................... *illus*	247
Charger, Cobalt Blue Branch, Butterfly, Cricket, Orange Leafy Rim, Chinese, c.1750, 17 In.	188
Charger, Cranes, Sages, Landscape, Central Cartouche, Blue Lion, 16 In........................	60
Charger, Figures, Vase, Tree, Multicolor, Gilt, Octagonal, 17 In..............................	123
Charger, Floral Center, Passionflower Border, Chinese, 13 In.................................	72
Charger, Imari, Cranes, Flowering Cherry Tree, Chrysanthemums, Japan, 1800s, 16 In..........	168
Charger, Peacock, Flowers, Waves, Mt. Fuji, Red, Blue, 18 In................................	264
Charger, Porcelain, Dragon, Oversize, Multicolor Enameled Banding, 1900s, 18 In.	240
Charger, Scalloped Rim, Lions, Birds In Shaped Roundels, Flowers, Japan, 17 In...............	172
Charger, Scalloped, Geometric, Flowers, Japan, 1900s, 12 In.	236
Charger, Women, Flowering Landscape, Shaped Panels, 1900s, 21 In.	598
Charger, Women, Landscape, Cherry Blossoms, Flowers, Iron Red, Leaves, Cobalt Blue, 16 In. *illus*	480
Dish, Dragon & Phoenix Panels, Broad Leafy Lip, c.1875, 7 In., 10 Plates.....................	750
Dish, Gilt Lotus Flowers, Green Ground, Red & Blue Highlights, c.1925, 9 In.	216
Dish, Lotus Flowers, Green Ground, Japan, 1900s, 9 In.......................................	216
Dish, Shell Shape, Shellfish, Seagrasses, Japan, 8 ¾ In......................................	216
Fish Platter, Double, Cartouches, Flowers, Children, Songbirds, 16 ¾ In......................	270
Fish Platter, Fish Scale, Wave, Fish Shape, Blue, White, 17 In.	840
Jardiniere, Pedestal, Wide Flat Top Rim, Red, Blue, Gold, Filigree, Japan, 36 In..............	968
Platter, Scalloped Rim, Center Well, Phoenix, Flower Reserves, 15 ½ In.	126
Punch Bowl, Scalloped Rim, Blue & Red, Flowers & Mons, 1800s, 6 ¾ x 14 In..................	600
Serving Dish, Hexagonal, Flower Basket Center, Orange, Blue, White, Japan, Late 1800s, 13 In.	72
Tea Caddy, Square, Floral Cartouches, Blue Ground, Marked, 1800s, 4 ½ In.	390
Umbrella Stand, Cylinder, Blue & Rust, Flowers, Asian, 1900s, 24 x 8 ½ In.................... *illus*	180
Umbrella Stand, Stylized Phoenix, Clouds, Blossoms, Cylindrical, Ribbed, Japan, 22 x 9 In...	635
Urn, Dome Lid, Cartouches, Butterflies, Leaves, c.1850, 23 In., Pair.........................	1750
Vase, Bamboo Shape, Relief Tiger, Flowers, Grasses, 12 ½ In.	132
Vase, Orange, Blue, Green, Gilt, Floral, Phoenixes & Woman In Garden, 18 In., Pair.............	240
Vase, Raised Figural Panels, Multicolor Phoenix, 23 x 10 In.................................	360
Vase, Temple Style, Geisha In Wisteria, 1 Cartouche, Japan, 30 x 12 In.	1020
Vase, Trumpet Shape, Petal Edge, Samurai, Geisha, Wisteria, Pine, Birds, c.1900, 30 In.. *illus*	1063

IMPERIAL GLASS CORPORATION was founded in Bellaire, Ohio, in 1901. It became a subsidiary of Lenox, Inc., in 1973 and was sold to Arthur R. Lorch in 1981. It was sold again in 1982, and went bankrupt in 1984. In 1985, the molds and some assets were sold. The Imperial glass preferred by the collector is freehand art glass, carnival glass, slag glass, stretch glass, and other top-quality tablewares. Tablewares and animals are listed here. The others may be found in the appropriate sections.

Imperial Glass
1911–1932

Imperial Glass
1913–1920s

Imperial Glass
1977–1981

Amelia, Celery Dish, Loop Handles, 10 ¾ In...	22
Amelia, Pitcher, Lip, 18 Oz., 5 In.	20
Animal, Woodchuck, Caramel Slag	60
Beaded Block, Sugar & Creamer, Footed	52
Bellaire, Toothpick Holder, Marigold, 2 ½ In.	23

Hull, Woodland, Cornucopia, Cream Base, Green & Pink Flowers, High Gloss, 1950, 11 In.
$50

Ruby Lane

Hummel, Figurine, Adventure Bound, Vee Over Bee, 1972-79, 7 x 8 In.
$540

Woody Auction

Hutschenreuther, Figurine, Young Woman, Nude, Feeding Doe, 9 ½ x 12 In.
$312

Fox Auctions

Icon, Virgin Mary, Child, Halos, Flower Border, Brass Over Wood, 12 ¼ x 10 ¼ In.
$350

Woody Auction

Imari, Bowl, Flowers, Scalloped Rim, Symbols Of Good Fortune, c.1900, 6 ½ In.
$313

Eldred's Auctioneers and Appraisers

Imari, Bowl, Ruffled Edge, Paneled, Multicolor, Gilt, Japan, 1800, 4 x 7 ½ In.
$96

Eldred's Auctioneers and Appraisers

Imari, Charger, Blue, Copper Red, Gilt, Garden, Bird, Flowering Branch, Flower Borders, 14 In.
$1,875

New Orleans Auction Galleries

Imari, Charger, Chrysanthemums, Water Lilies, Water, Platform, Chinese, 14 In.
$247

Leland Little Auctions

Imari, Charger, Women, Landscape, Cherry Blossoms, Flowers, Iron Red, Leaves, Cobalt Blue, 16 In.
$480

Leland Little Auctions

Imari, Umbrella Stand, Cylinder, Blue & Rust, Flowers, Asian, 1900s, 24 x 8 ½ In.
$180

Garth's Auctioneers & Appraisers

Imari, Vase, Trumpet Shape, Petal Edge, Samurai & Geisha, Wisteria, Pine, Birds, c.1900, 30 In.
$1,063

Eldred's Auctioneers and Appraisers

Indian, Apron, Anishinaabe, Bandolier, Cotton, Flowers, Beads, Fringe, c.1880, 21 x 11 ½ In.
$400

Cowan's Auctions

Indian, Bag, Buffalo Bladder, Buckskin, Quilled Rawhide, Sinew, c.1950, 18 x 8 In.
$345

Allard Auctions

Candlewick, Butter, Cover, ¼ Lb.	45
Candlewick, Compote, 4 In.	15
Candlewick, Relish, 4 Sections, 9½ In.	15
Candlewick, Salt & Pepper	15
Candlewick, Sugar & Creamer	21
Candlewick, Vase, Crimped, 8 In.	90
Chroma, Tumbler, Iced Tea, Amethyst, 5½ In.	25
Early American Hobnail, Tumbler, Ruby, 10 Oz., 3⅞ In.	21
Embossed Rose, Vase, Amethyst, 6 In.	35
Luster Rose, Bowl, Scalloped Rim, 3-Footed, Blue, 7 In.	74
Molly, Tray, Handles, Pink, 12¾ In.	27
Old Williamsburg, Goblet, Amber, 6½ In.	12
Simplicity, Goblet, 6 In.	25
Star Medallion, Pitcher, 5½ In.	23
Vase, Cylindrical, Gold Luster, Flared Rim, Footed, 11 In.	77
Vintage Grape, Goblet, 5⅜ In.	28

INDIAN art from North and South America has attracted the collector for many years. Each tribe has its own distinctive designs and techniques. Baskets, jewelry, pottery, and leatherwork are of greatest collector interest. Eskimo art is listed under Eskimo in this book.

Apron, Anishinaabe, Bandolier, Cotton, Flowers, Beads, Fringe, c.1880, 21 x 11½ In.	*illus*	400
Bag, Buffalo Bladder, Buckskin, Quilled Rawhide, Sinew, c.1950, 18 x 8 In.	*illus*	345
Bag, Chippewa, Bandolier, Cloth Silk Edge, Beaded, Multicolor Flowers, c.1900, 43 x 13 In.		520
Bag, Iroquois, Buckskin, Quilled, Smoked, Beads, 8½ x 8 In.		4235
Bag, Ute, Beaded, Ceremonial Dancer, Leather, 1950s, 11 x 20 In.		68
Bandolier Bag, Anishinaabe, Red & Navy Stroud, Beaded Flowers, c.1875, 43 x 11 In.		2040
Basket, Abenaki, Carrying, Flat Weave, D-Shape Handle, c.1900, 12 x 23 x 13 In.	*illus*	423
Basket, Attu, Lid, Embroidered Pattern, c.1910, 6¼ x 6 In.	*illus*	780
Basket, Chemehuevi, Oval, Diamond Shapes, c.1900, 2½ x 5 x 9 In.		300
Basket, Coil, Pima, Geometric Pattern, 1½ x 4 In.		375
Basket, Elk, Bears, Birds, Pine Trees, c.1925, 9 x 15 In.		6600
Basket, Hat, Yurok, Geometric Designs, Checkered Slashes, c.1900, 3½ x 7 In.		800
Basket, Lid, Modoc, Bear Grass, Twined, 6 x 6 In.		181
Basket, Market, Cherokee, White Oak, Lock Handle, c.1920, 10 x 12 x 8½ In.		180
Basket, Paiute, Beaded, Bowl Shape, Single Rod, Multicolor, c.1950, 4 x 6 In.	*illus*	288
Basket, Papago, Yei Symbols, Turtle Figure On Lid, c.1910, 5½ x 6½ In.	*illus*	173
Basket, Pima, Akimel O'Odham, Storage, Figures, c.1900, 9¼ x 10½ In.	*illus*	461
Basket, Pomo, Fine Weave, Flat Disc, Feathers, Quail Top Knots, c.1950, 3¼ In.	*illus*	230
Basket, Pomo, Single Rod Bowl, Geometric, Shell Disc Beads, Knot Feathers, 1900s, 3½ x 5½ In.		650
Basket, Salish, Lid, Cedar Bark, Woven, Overlapping Designs, Handles, c.1910, 17 x 12 In.	*illus*	184
Basket, Tlingit, Cylindrical, Imbricated, Key-Type Geometric, 1900s, 4 x 5½ In.		425
Basket, Tlingit, Spruce Root, Tapered, Conical, Black, Brown, Tan, Cream, 2¾ In.		360
Belt Buckle, Navajo, Radiating Design, Turquoise Stone, Loloma Style Bezel, Silver, 3½ x 3 In.		425
Boots, Flagstaff, Wrapped, Moccasins, Molded Rawhide, 1960s, 9 In.		375
Bow, Plains, Double Nocked, Sinew String, 19th Century, 14 Arrows, 49 In.		3240
Bowl, Apache, Basket, Coiled, Willow, Devil's Claw, 10 x 2¼ In.		1350
Bowl, Hopi, Pottery, Multicolor, Avian, Hopis, Fannie Nampeyo, 1900s, 2½ x 5 In.		325
Bowl, Maricopa, Pottery, Red, Polished, Black, Pendant, Wave Design, 5½ x 9 In.		159
Bowl, Northwest Coast, Carved, Frog Shape, c.1900, 10 x 4 In.		1245
Bowl, Santo Domingo, Geometric & Scalloped Design, c.1960, 8 x 12 In.		225
Bowl, Santo Domingo, Pottery, Black Line Drawings, White Slip, Red Base, 3 x 7 In.		215
Bowl, Zuni, Pottery, Deer Figures, Orange Swirls, c.1910, 3½ x 9 In.	*illus*	431
Box, Mi'kmaq, Quilled, Birchbark, c.1950, 4 x 6 In.		360
Bracelet, Navajo, 3 Bands, Silver, 3 Turquoise Cabochons, Rope Bezels, 6 In.	*illus*	489
Bracelet, Navajo, Cuff, Coral, Silver, 6½ In.		900
Bracelet, Navajo, Cuff, Silver, Center Stone Framed By Smaller Stones		427
Bracelet, Zuni, Silver, Turquoise, Jet, Coral, Oyster, Sylvester Nache, 6½ In.		375
Cap, Haudenosaunee, Beadwork, Squirrels, Flowers, c.1900, 7 x 10½ In.	*illus*	360

Indian, Basket, Abenaki, Carrying, Flat Weave, D-Shape Handle, c.1900, 12 x 23 x 13 In.
$423

James D. Julia Auctioneers

Indian, Basket, Attu, Lid, Embroidered Pattern, c.1910, 6¼ x 6 In.
$780

Cowan's Auctions

Indian, Basket, Paiute, Beaded, Bowl Shape, Single Rod, Multicolor, c.1950, 4 x 6 In.
$288

Allard Auctions

Indian, Basket, Papago, Yei Symbols, Turtle Figure On Lid, c.1910, 5½ x 6½ In.
$173

Allard Auctions

INDIAN

Indian, Basket, Pima, Akimel O'Odham, Storage, Figures, c.1900, 9 ¼ x 10 ½ In.
$461

Cowan's Auctions

Indian, Basket, Pomo, Fine Weave, Flat Disc, Feathers, Quail Top Knots, c.1950, 3 ¼ In.
$230

Allard Auctions

Indian, Basket, Salish, Lid, Cedar Bark, Woven, Overlapping Designs, Handles, c.1910, 17 x 12 In.
$184

Allard Auctions

Indian, Bowl, Zuni, Pottery, Deer Figures, Orange Swirls, c.1910, 3 ½ x 9 In.
$431

Allard Auctions

Indian, Bracelet, Navajo, 3 Bands, Silver, 3 Turquoise Cabochons, Rope Bezels, 6 In.
$489

Allard Auctions

Indian, Cap, Haudenosaunee, Beadwork, Squirrels, Flowers, c.1900, 7 x 10 ½ In.
$360

Cowan's Auctions

Indian, Doll, Cheyenne, Sally Stands Tall, Buckskin, Beaded, Dress, Late 1900s, 17 In.
$690

Allard Auctions

Indian, Doll, Skookum, Woman, Papoose, Robe, Buckskin Moccasins, c.1910, 33 In.
$173

Allard Auctions

Indian, Figure, Owl, Zuni, Pottery, Painted, c.1935, 9 In.
$720

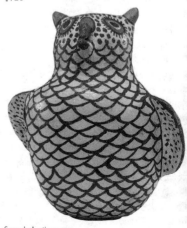

Cowan's Auctions

Club, Crow, Double-Pointed Head, Beaded Handle, Quilled Suspensions, 1900s	150
Club, Sioux, Double-Pointed Stone Head, Rawhide Wrapped Shaft, Beaded, 1800s	500
Cradle, Sioux, Beaded, Red, White Heart, Green, Brass Bells, Ribbons, Beaded Fringe, c.1875..	14400
Dish, Santa Clara Pueblo, Bird Shape, Signed Julie Martinez, 3 x 7 In.	83
Doll, Cheyenne, Sally Stands Tall, Buckskin, Beaded, Dress, Late 1900s, 17 In. .... *illus*	690
Doll, Skookum, Woman, Papoose, Robe, Buckskin Moccasins, c.1910, 33 In. .... *illus*	173
Figure, Owl, Zuni, Pottery, Painted, c.1935, 9 In. .... *illus*	720
Flask, Whiskey, Paiute, Glass, Beaded, Valero Star, c.1910, 7 In. .... *illus*	150
Game Sticks, Anishinaabe, Wood, Inked Numbers, c.1900, 9 In., 20 Piece	330
Gloves, Crow, Gauntler, Buckskin, Flat & Contour Beaded Flowers, c.1950, 18 In.	550
Jar, Casas Grande, Pottery, Teardrop Shape, Line Drawings, Brown, Buff Slip, 1800s, 6 x 7 In..	124
Jar, Jemez Pueblo, Black, Red Clay, Feathers, Mountains, 1993, 6 3/8 x 8 1/2 In.	175
Jar, Nampeyo, Migration Pattern, Multicolor, Adelle Nampeyo, 1900s, 5 x 5 In.	180
Katsina, Hopi, Cheveyo, Black Ogre, Cottonwood, Painted, 1940, 15 x 6 In.	424
Katsina, Hopi, Comanche Warrior, Carved, Painted, Cottonwood, Hopi Pueblo, 1900s, 10 x 5 In.	90
Katsina, Hopi, Kokopelli, Carved, Painted, Cottonwood, 1900s, 9 x 5 In.	124
Katsina, Hopi, Mud Head, Carved, Painted Cottonwood Figure, Koyemsi, 1960, 10 x 5 1/2 In.	79
Katsina, Hopi, Polik Mana, c.1900, 12 In.	2760
Katsina, Zuni, Warrior, Carved, Painted Cottonwood Figure, 1960, 15 x 6 1/2 In.	537
Leggings, Yakima, Red Wool, Gold Cotton Cuff Box, Trim, Ribbon Accents, c.1935, 29 In. *illus*	115
Mask, Iroquois, Copper Clad Eyes, Wood, Horsehair, Signed, c.1970, 12 In.	288
Mask, Northwest Coast, Carved, Paint, Cedar Hook Bird Nose, Inlaid Abalone, 1970s, 11 x 9 In..	275
Medicine, Bag, Navajo, Eagle, Federal Shield, Leather, Brass Beaded Thong Drops, 1900, 7 x 6 In.	79
Moccasins, Arapaho, Beaded Hide, White, Green Blue, Sinew Sewn, 14 x 10 In.	4800
Moccasins, Cree, Buckskin, High Top, Beaded, Sunflowers, Leather, c.1930, 9 In. .... *illus*	345
Moccasins, Northern Plains, Buckskin, Beaded, Cross, Flags On Soles, Child's, c.1950, 7 In. *illus*	259
Necklace, Pendant, Hopi, Ear Of Corn, 14K Gold Choker, Charles Supplee, 17 1/2 In.	6600
Necklace, Venetian Glass, Skunk Trade Beads, Red, White Dots, Single Strand, c.1890, 24 In. ... *illus*	138
Necklace, Zuni, Heishi & Turquoise Nuggets, 3 Strands, c.1925, 28 In.	6150
Olla, Acoma, Geometric Design, Tapering Sides, Convex Base, 1900s, 5 3/4 x 6 3/4 In.	283
Olla, Acoma, Lolita Concha, Traditional Avian Design, Signed, 1940, 9 1/2 x 9 1/4 In.	1469
Olla, Western Apache, Humans, Zigzag, Ladder Elements, c.1925, 18 x 20 In.	3600
Olla, Zuni, Stylized Rainbirds, Geometric Elements, c.1875, 8 x 12 In.	3690
Pendant, Pueblo, Cross, Silver Dragonfly, Turquoise Stone, 1970s, 4 In.	200
Picnic Basket, Winnebago, Hand Woven, Fitted Lid, Carved Handles, 1800s, 9 x 14 In.	135
Pipe Tomahawk, Chippewa, Anishinaabe, File Branded Handle, Forged Blade, c.1875, 21 In..	4800
Pipe Tomahawk, Great Lakes, Ash Handle, Spontoon, c.1875, 16 3/4 In.	5700
Pipe, Chippewa, Effigy, Catlinite, 2 Figures, Inlaid Bead Eyes, Curved Horse, 1900s, 3 1/2 x 8 In..	500
Pipe, Sioux, Carved, Painted Stem, Catlinite Bowl, Buffalo, Sheep Elk, Quillwork, c.1875, 29 In.	4200
Pot, Hopi, Orange Interior, 2 Abstract Bird, Beige Background	50
Pot, Pueblo, Clay, Free-Form, Painted Horses, Marked Russell Sanchez, 1989, 9 x 8 1/2 In.	660
Rattle, Pueblo, Rattle, Gourd, Geometric Designs, 20th Century, 11 In.	1920
Ring, Navajo, Sterling Silver, Coral, Green Turquoise, Leaf Pattern, Size 14.	61
Rug, Navajo, 2 Gray Hills, Central Medallion, Bessie Many Goats, 52 1/2 x 81 In.	605
Rug, Navajo, Diamonds, Sawtooth Edges, Dark Brown, Red, Ivory, Gray, 44 x 70 In.	270
Rug, Navajo, Figures, Dancing, Holding Cornstalks, Kilts, Black Ground, c.1920, 65 x 45 In.	1573
Rug, Navajo, Germantown Eye Dazzler, Fringe Ends, c.1890, 56 x 36 In. .... *illus*	150
Rug, Navajo, Navajoland, Passenger Train, Tractors, Cecilia Curley, 1900s, 23 x 22 In.	250
Rug, Navajo, Postcard, Woven Message, Serrated Border, c.1910, 39 x 43 In. .... *illus*	6325
Rug, Navajo, Storm Design, Red, Black, Gray, White, Betty Bahe, 70 x 104 In.	1440
Rug, Navajo, Wool, Diamonds, Dark Red, Gray, Black, White Border, 1990s, 37 x 29 In.	160
Rug, Navajo, Wool, Gray, Black, White, Burgundy, Gray Stepped Border, 1990s, 48 x 38 In.	275
Rug, Navajo, Yei Figure, Cornstalks, 1980s, 36 x 36 In.	400
Rug, Navajo, Yei Figure, Turquoise Accents, Sawtooth Edges, 1900s, 40 x 28 In.	200
Rug, Navajo, Yei Figure, With Cornstalks, Geometrics Above & Below, c.1920, 76 x 53 In.	2640
Saddle, Blanket, Great Lakes, Wool, Beaded, American Flags, c.1975, 54 x 40 In. .... *illus*	900
Saddle, Blanket, Navajo, Colored Birds, Squash Blossoms, c.1925, 50 x 35 In.	1320
Seed Pot, Taos Pueblo, Hand Painted Kokopeli, Magical Flute, Frame, 1994, 4 3/4 x 5 1/2 In.	325
Sheath, Knife, Anishinaabe, Loom Beaded, c.1875, 12 In.	1320
Shirt, Seminole, Cotton, Patchwork, Machine Sewn, Boy's, c.1910, Chest 34 In. .... *illus*	1440

Indian, Flask, Whiskey, Paiute, Glass, Beaded, Valero Star, c.1910, 7 In. $150

Allard Auctions

Indian, Leggings, Yakima, Red Wool, Gold Cotton Cuff Box, Trim, Ribbon Accents, c.1935, 29 In. $115

Allard Auctions

Indian, Moccasins, Cree, Buckskin, High Top, Beaded, Sunflowers, Leather, c.1930, 9 In.
$345

Allard Auctions

Indian, Moccasins, Northern Plains, Buckskin, Beaded, Cross, Flags On Soles, Child's, c.1950, 7 In.
$259

Allard Auctions

Indian, Necklace, Venetian Glass, Skunk Trade Beads, Red, White Dots, Single Strand, c.1890, 24 In.
$138

Allard Auctions

Indian, Rug, Navajo, Germantown Eye Dazzler, Fringe Ends, c.1890, 56 x 36 In.
$150

Allard Auctions

Indian, Rug, Navajo, Postcard, Woven Message, Serrated Border, c.1910, 39 x 43 In.
$6,325

Allard Auctions

Indian, Saddle, Blanket, Great Lakes, Wool, Beaded, American Flags, c.1975, 54 x 40 In.
$900

Cowan's Auctions

Indian, Shirt, Seminole, Cotton, Patchwork, Machine Sewn, Boy's, c.1910, Chest 34 In.
$1,440

Cowan's Auctions

Indian, Tobacco Bag, Sioux, Hide, Beaded Hourglass Design, c.1900, 31 In.
$1,080

Cowan's Auctions

Spoon, Haida, Horn, Black Horn, Totemic Handle, 1900s, 6 ½ x 2 In.	425
Tobacco Bag, Sioux, Hide, Beaded Hourglass Design, c.1900, 31 In................................. *illus*	1080
Top Hat, Sioux, Beaver, Quillwork Band, U.S. Cavalry Insignia, 1800s	4575
Totem Pole, Northwest Coast, Walrus Ivory, Shaman, Frog, Eagle, c.1940, 10 ½ In. .... *illus*	600
Tray, Cherokee, River Cane, Walnut & Bloodroot Dyes, Rectangular, 4 x 15 x 11 In.	360
Trousers, Santee Sioux, Buckskin, Quilled Flower Figures, Pockets, Cuffs, c.1900, 42 In.	425
Vase, Santa Clara Pueblo, Carved Serpent, Signed Pablita, 5 In..	106
Vase, Santa Clara, Glenda Naranjo, Pottery, Red Glaze, Signed Under Base, 3 ¼ x 4 ½ In.	124
Vase, Tarahumara, Pottery, Oval, In Iron Stand, 20 x 14 In...	45
Vest, Anishinaabe, Velvet, Printed Cotton, Beads, c.1935, Chest 38 In. .... *illus*	984
Vest, Plateau, Aqua, Cotton, Beads, c.1910, Chest 38 In. .... *illus*	1169
Vest, Sioux, Beaded, Upside Down American Flag, Geometric Designs, c.1975, 20 x 18 In.	4200
Weaving, Navajo, Serrated Diamonds, Fringe, Germantown, c.1890, 50 ½ In x 35 In............ *illus*	1476
Weaving, Navajo, Tree Of Life, Black, Red, Feathers & Birds, Wool, 82 x 44 In..........................	2147

INDIAN TREE is a china pattern that was popular during the last half of the nineteenth century. It was copied from earlier Indian textile patterns that were very similar. The pattern includes the crooked branch of a tree and a partial landscape with exotic flowers and leaves. Green, blue, pink, and orange were the favored colors used in the design. Coalport, Spode, Johnson Brothers, and other firms made this pottery.

Butter Pat, Shenango China & Hartford Railroad, 3 ⅜ In.	36
Coffeepot, Rust, Scalloped Rim, Coalport, 8 In..	203
Cup & Saucer, Footed, Gilt Trim, Tuscan, England...	25
Cup & Saucer, Pink & Rose, J.G. Meakin	40
Plate, Luncheon, Pullman Co., 7 ½ In...	59
Platter, Oval, Scalloped Edge, Rust, Coalport, 12 In.	98
Platter, Pink, Syracuse China Co., 14 x 10 In.	35

INKSTANDS were made to be placed on a desk. They held some type of container for ink, and possibly a sander, a pen tray, a pen, a holder for pounce, and even a candle to melt the sealing wax. Inkstands date to the eighteenth century and have been made of silver, copper, ceramics, and glass. Additional inkstands may be found in these and other related categories.

Black Forest, Rooster, Hen, Nesting Bird Inkwells, High Relief, 9 ½ x 16 In................................	1187
Brass, Gilt, William Shakespeare Bust, Applied Scroll, Classical Masks, 2 Pots, 3 x 17 In.	129
Brass, Scalloped Base, Candle Socket, Bell Hook, 4 Removable Accessories, 1800s, 7 x 9 In......	360
Bronze, Flowers, Filigree, Bird's Nest Penholder, Mouse, Stealing Eggs, 2 Inkwells, 11 x 9 In. ..	1088
Bronze, Onyx, Enamel, Opaline Glass Pot, Front Pen Rack, Ball Feet, France, 1800s, 3 x 8 In .	153
Girl, Seated, Boy On Knee, Encrier, Floral, Turquoise, 1800, 6 x 9 ½ In................................	89
Glass, Brass Collar, Lid, Square, Scalloped Design, Pen Stand, 6 ½ x 2 ¼ In...................... *illus*	125
Porcelain, Dual Wells, White China Set, Painted Gold Highlights, Wax Seal Space, 6 x 7 ½ In.	175
Shell, Scroll Rim, Silver, 2 Glass Inserts, George V, 1914-15, 12 In.	369
Silver Plate, Copper Roll, Double Inkwell Bottles, Lidded Well, Side Handle, 1800s, 4 x 9 x 4 In.	336
Silver Plate, Pen Rest, Lid, Compartment, Beaver, Engraved, 1800, 9 ⅜ In.	523
Spelter, Duck Family, 2 Ducklings, Cut Glass, 7 ¼ x 6 ½ x 4 ½ In.	53
Stoneware, 2 Wells, Carved, Birds, Vines, Cobalt Blue Highlights, 1800s, 2 x 5 ¾ In................	519
Stoneware, 2 Wells, Incised, Leaves, Squares, Rosettes, c.1825, 2 x 6 ½ In. .... *illus*	276
Walnut, Brass Mount, Candle Insets, Applied Handle, Paw Feet, 2 ½ x 10 In.	300
Wood, Figural, Black Forest, 2 Foxes, Lamb, Lizard, Snail, Glass Ink Pot, Pen Tray, 12 In.........	972

INKWELLS, of course, held ink. Ready-made ink was first made about 1836 and was sold in bottles. The desk inkwell had a narrow hole so the pen would not slip inside. Inkwells were made of many materials, such as pottery, glass, pewter, and silver. Look in these categories for more listings of inkwells.

Brass, Mayflower, Tall Ship, Textured Base, Removable Ink Pot, 1920s, 5 x 5 In.	280
Brass, Stag Head, Trees, Germany, 4 ⅝ x 4 ⅞ In.	95
Brass, Stamp Box, Green Verdigris Patina, Art Deco, 2 ¼ x 6 ½ x 4 In.	311

Indian, Totem Pole, Northwest Coast, Walrus Ivory, Shaman, Frog, Eagle, c.1940, 10 ½ In.
$600

Cowan's Auctions

Indian, Vest, Anishinaabe, Velvet, Printed Cotton, Beads, c.1935, Chest 38 In.
$984

Cowan's Auctions

Indian, Vest, Plateau, Aqua, Cotton, Beads, c.1910, Chest 38 In.
$1,169

Cowan's Auctions

Indian, Weaving, Navajo, Serrated Diamonds, Fringe, Germantown, c.1890, 50 1/2 x 35 In.
$1,476

Cowan's Auctions

Bronze, Demilune, Ivy-Covered Tree Stump, Charles Louchet, France, 4 x 8 In.	247
Bronze, Dog, Seated, Wearing Bonnet, Cape, Bow, Brass Pot, 7 In.	224
Bronze, Running Coin, 3 Dolphin, Raised Shell, Disc Feet, Empire, 4 In.	163
Cubist Patchwork, Copper, Sterling, Squat Horn Shape, Yamanaka, 3 1/4 x 5 In.	562
Cut Glass, Silver, Ebonized Wood, Center Nib, Brush Dish, Napoleon III, 1800s, 8 In.	447
Cut Glass, Swirled Tusk, Strawberry Diamond & Star Design, Sterling Flip Lid, 6 x 4 In.	850
Glass, Acorn Squash Shape, Hinged Lid, Brass Claw Feet, Spinach Jade, 3 1/2 x 3 In.	875
Glass, Amethyst, Iridescent, Textured Design, Flip Lid, Loetz Style, 3 1/4 x 3 1/2 In.	420
Glass, Cat, Chair, Blue Opaque, c.1885, 4 1/2 In.	321
Glass, Cranberry, Iridescent, Metal Overlay, Loetz Style, 3 x 3 In.	360
Glass, Cranberry, Pulled Feather, Ball Shape, Removable Base, Flip Lid, Loetz Style, 3 x 5 In.	300
Glass, Eagle, Round Reticulated, Swirled Ribs, 1800s, 9 1/2 x 9 In. *illus*	300
Glass, Green, Iridescent, Gilt Metal, Floral Band, Loetz Style, 3 x 3 In.	180
Glass, Green, Iridescent, Ribbed, 4 Pulled Handles, Brass Lid, Mythological Design, 3 3/4 x 4 In.	330
Glass, Green, Iridescent, Silver Overlay Water Lily Design, 2 3/4 x 3 1/4 In.	330
Glass, Green, Iridescent Body, Purple Textured Threaded, Loetz Style, 2 3/4 x 2 1/2 In.	360
Glass, Melon Ribbed, Gold Iridescent, Lava Design, Loetz Style, 3 x 3 1/2 In.	270
Glass, Round Melon Ribbed, Gold Iridescent, Lava Design, Loetz Style, 2 1/4 x 4 In.	330
Glass, Square, Blown Ridges, Gold Iridescent, Lava Design, Loetz Style, 4 1/4 x 3 1/2 In.	300
Glass, Square, Green Iridescent, Gilt Metal Floral Band, Lion Head Lid, Loetz Style, 3 x 4 3/4 In.	540
Glass, Square, Amethyst, Iridescent, Threaded Design, Gilt Metal, Floral Base, 3 x 3 1/4 In.	540
Glass, Square, Cobalt Blue, Iridescent, Peacock Tail, Loetz Style, 1 3/4 x 2 3/4 In.	360
Glass, White, Iridescent, Threaded Purple Iridescent Design, Loetz Style, 2 1/2 x 4 1/2 In.	210
Iron, Figural, Blacksmith, Anvil, Victorian, Signed, 3 In. *illus*	127
Jade, Red Salmon Coral, Round, Silver Mounts, Branches, Carved, 5 x 5 In.	2750
Marble, Glass Containers, Bronze Hinges, Geometric Shape, Art Deco, 12 In.	135
Metal, Deer Head, Antlers, Silver Tone, Glass Insert, 1920s, 6 x 6 In.	58
Plated Amberina, New England Glass, Cast Iron Lid, Ground & Polished Pontil, 1870	720
Porcelain, Maiden & Bird, Scrolled Tray, Gold, Green & Blue Glaze, Ernst Wahliss, 4 x 8 In.	605
Pottery, Green Glaze, Paul Revere, Signed SEG, Monogram Base, 2 1/2 x 4 In.	130
Silver, Cut Glass Body, Hobnail Wheel, Engraved, Bulbous Top, English Hallmarks, 1927, 4 In.	506
Silver, Engraved Flowers, Leafy Garland, Ornate Interlaced Monogram, Gorham, 4 7/8 In.	297
Silver, Gadrooned Edges, Neoclassical Features, Flame Finials, Paw Feet, 1800s, 5 x 11 x 7 In.	1950
Square Well, Flip Lid, Set On Brass Base, Embossed Woman's Head, 2 1/2 x 6 In.	108
Square, Loetz, Red Threaded Overlay, Bronze Flip Lid, Reticulated Floral Base, 5 3/4 x 9 In.	160
Tole, Black, Sphere, Garlands, Finial, Masks, Footed, 9 1/2 In.	200
Wood, Bear, Black Forest, Stylized Tree Stumps, Glass Inserts, 9 x 4 In.	175
Wood, Dog Reclining, Black Forest, Barrel Shape, Pen Tray, 1910, 8 x 3 x 5 In.	314
Wood, Glass, Log Cabin Shape, Storage, Black Forest, Germany, c.1887, 7 x 12 In.	2000
Wood, Hand Painted, Flowers, Black Background, Wood, 9 1/2 x 4 1/2 In.	58

INSULATORS of glass or pottery have been made for use on telegraph or telephone poles since 1844. Thousands of styles of insulators have been made. Most common are those of clear or aqua glass; most desirable are the threadless types made from 1850 to 1870. CD numbers are Consolidated Design numbers used by collectors to indicate shape.

Beehive, Threadless, Olive Amber, Thames Glass Works, New London, 3 In.	3510
CD 102, C.G.I. Co., Lemon Lime Yellow	495
CD 106.2, PSSA No. 9, Light Sage Green, Flat Top	275
CD 113, Hemingray, Ice Aqua, Solid Pour	358
CD 128, Hemingray, Milky White Opalescent	220
CD 139, Brookfield, Combination Safety, Pat. Appld For, Blue Aqua, c.1909	11110
CD 158.9, Boston Bottle Works, Screw Top, Aqua	4510
CD 162, McLaughlin, No. 19, Swirled Red, Red & Blue, 1970s	1045
CD 176, Whitall Tatum Co., No. 12, Mushroom, Straw	8580
Glass, Green To Black, Threadless, Egg Style, Medial Rings, Flat Top, c.1860, 4 1/2 x 3 In. *illus*	498
Hemingray, No. 42, Aqua Green, Beaded, 4 In.	35
Hemingray, No. 45, Clear, 4 In.	40

IRISH BELLEEK, *see Belleek category.*

IRON is a metal that has been used by man since prehistoric times. It is a popular metal for tools and decorative items like doorstops that need as much weight as possible. Items are listed here or under other appropriate headings, such as Bookends, Doorstop, Kitchen, Match Holder, or Tool. The tool that is used for ironing clothes, an iron, is listed in the Kitchen category under Iron and Sadiron.

Ashtray, Oval, Hammered, Molded Catfish Center, Wavy Rim, c.1900, 7 x 5 In.	330
Boot Scraper, Acanthus, Tray, Scalloped, Oval, 7¾ x 9¼ In.	165
Boot Scraper, Cross, Acanthus, Cast Iron, Signed Carron, 9 x 14 In. .... *illus*	184
Boot Scraper, Dog, Dachshund, Cast Iron	70
Boot Scraper, Gargoyle & Dolphin, Scalloped Edge Trough, 11¾ In. .... *illus*	41
Boot Scraper, Unicorn, Figural, Reclining, 24 In.	633
Bootjack, Naughty Nellie, Painted, Reproduction, 10 In.	42
Bowl, Edge, Scalloped, Branch, Stamped, Japan, 1900s	48
Branding Iron, Letter W, On Rod, 20th Century, 27 x 4 x 3½ In.	96
Censer, Auspicious Symbols, Leafy Rim, Relief Carving, Geometric Patterns, 1800s	120
Chalice, Spiked Helmet Form Lid, Flared Rim Bowl, Gold Ivy & Swags, Persia, 9½ x 4½ In.	1560
Deer Skinner, Stamped, John Balliet, Lewisburg, Pa., No. 564, Patd. Jan. 7, 1880, 20 In. *illus*	83
Figure, Cat Head, Blue Paint, On Stand, c.1890, 11 In.	12567
Figure, Cat, Wrought, 18 In.	84
Figure, Deer, Iron, Buck, 8-Point Antlers, Standing Figure, J.W. Fiske, 62 x 47 x 15 In.	4235
Figure, Dog, Retriever, 1900 Style, Seated, 37 x 16 In., Pair	2250
Figure, Guanyin, Crossed Legs, Lotus Leaf, Pagoda, Unsigned, 1800s, 19 x 13 x 8 In.	484
Figure, Mermaid, Braids, Abstract, Flat, G. Bien-Aime, 20¼ x 18¾ In.	187
Figure, Silhouette, Stamped, Square Plinth, Ernest Trova, 1900s	600
Horse Tether, Round, St. Louis 20-MAC-CASH, Cast, 6¾ In.	285
Kettle, Sugar, Flared Rim, 22 x 53½ In.	2562
Letter Box, U.S. Mail, Red, White & Blue Paint, Orr, Painter & Co., Reading, Pa., 15 In.	372
Plaque, Eagle, Cluster Of Arrows, Olive Branch, Shield, Wings Out, 14 x 32 In.	484
Safe, Iron Over Wood, Key Entry, Swivel Wheels, Hobnail Case, c.1835, 30 x 23 In. .... *illus*	4480
Sign, Horse Shape, Black, Equine, Pennsylvania, 18 x ¼ In.	150
Slave Collar, Black, Bells, Hinged, Lock, Hand Forged, 1850s	4612
Stand, Viking Ship, Quadruped Base, 1900s, 32 In. .... *illus*	96
Stove, Parlor Ball, Drying Rack, Rare, Chamberlain & Douglas, Patented	120
Stringholder, Cast, Hinged Flange, Patent Date On Band, 6½ x 5 In.	50
Strong Box, Lid, Hinged, Bail Handles, Model, 1900-50, 7¼ x 9½ In.	313
Strong Box, Silvered, Leaves, Birds, Panels, Footed, Key, Germany, 4½ x 7 In.	2340
Target, Shooting Gallery, Row Of Birds, Carnival, 26 x 4 In. .... *illus*	248
Target, Shooting Gallery, Soldier, Gun, Mounted, 7 In. .... *illus*	248
Windmill Weight, Bull, Old, Nebraska, 1900-15, 18 x 24 In.	425
Windmill Weight, Horse, Dempster Mill Mfg. Co., 17½ x 17 In.	497
Windmill Weight, Horseshoe, c.1900, 13 In.	351
Windmill Weight, Rooster, White, Red Comb, Elgin Wind Power & Pump Co., 19½ In.	1800
Windmill Weight, Spear, Custom Stand, Original, 1890-1915, 24 x 9½ In.	460
Windmill Weight, Star, U.S. Wind Engine & Pump Co., Ill., 14 In. .... *illus*	900

IRONSTONE china was first made in 1813. It gained its greatest popularity during the mid-nineteenth century. The heavy, durable, off-white pottery was made in white or was decorated with any of hundreds of patterns. Much flow blue pottery was made of ironstone. Some of the decorations were raised. Many pieces of ironstone are unmarked, but some English and American factories included the word *Ironstone* in their marks. Additional pieces may be listed in other categories, such as Chelsea Grape, Chelsea Sprig, Flow Blue, Gaudy Ironstone, Mason's Ironstone, Moss Rose, Staffordshire, and Tea Leaf Ironstone. These three marks were used by companies that made ironstone.

TJ & J Mayer's
1842–1855

W. Baker & Co. (Ltd.)
1893+

Wood & Son(s) (Ltd.)
1910+

Bottle Feeder, Blue & White Transfer, Flowers, Branches, Swags, 6½ In.	259

Inkstand, Glass, Brass Collar, Lid, Square, Scalloped Design, Pen Stand, 6½ x 2¼ In.
$125

Ruby Lane

Inkstand, Stoneware, 2 Wells, Incised, Leaves, Squares, Rosettes, c.1825, 2 x 6½ In.
$276

Cottone Auctions

Inkwell, Glass, Eagle, Round Reticulated, Swirled Ribs, 1800s, 9½ x 9 In.
$300

Brunk Auctions

Inkwell, Iron, Figural, Blacksmith, Anvil, Victorian, Signed, 3 In.
$127

Copake Auction

insulator, Glass, Green To Black, Threadless, Egg Style, Medial Rings, Flat Top, c.1860, 4½ x 3 In.
$498

Jeffrey S. Evans

Iron, Boot Scraper, Cross, Acanthus, Cast Iron, Signed Carron, 9 x 14 In.
$184

Leland Little Auctions

Iron, Boot Scraper, Gargoyle & Dolphin, Scalloped Edge Trough, 11¾ In.
$41

Hess Auction Group

Iron, Deer Skinner, Stamped, John Balliet, Lewisburg, Pa., No. 564, Patd. Jan. 7, 1880, 20 In.
$83

Hess Auction Group

Pitcher, Lake, Blue Transferware, 11½ In. 134
Plate, Blue Spatter, Tulip, 8⅜ In. 35
Platter, Blue, Light Blue, Willow Pattern, 1800s, 17 x 22 x 3 In. 94
Platter, Mulberry, Strawberry Pattern, Octagonal, Scalloped Corners, 13 x 16 In. 295

Ispanky

ISPANKY figurines were designed by Laszlo Ispanky, who began his American career as a designer for Cybis Porcelains. He was born in Hungary and came to the United States in 1956. In 1966 he went into business with George Utley in Trenton, New Jersey. Isplanky made limited edition figurines marked with his name and Utley Porcelain Ltd. The company became Ispanky Porcelains Ltd. in 1968 and moved to Pennington, New Jersey. Ispanky worked for Goebel of North America beginning in 1976. He worked in stone, wood, or metal, as well as porcelain. He died in 2010.

Bust, Madonna, With Bird, c.1959, 11½ x 7½ In. 195
Figurine, Cinderella, Washing Floor, Signed, c.1960, 12 x 8 In. 496
Figurine, Girl, On Chair, Long Hair, 7 x 4 In. 150
Figurine, Girl, Seated On Rock, Blonde Braids, Hat, Flowers On Lap, 1960s, 8 In. 250
Figurine, Winter, Yellow Dress, Blue Cape, c.1983, 9 In. 60
Vase, Seminude, Long Braid, Flower Cables, 1 x 6 x 6 In. 125

IVORY from the tusk of an elephant is thought by many to be the only true ivory. To most collectors, the term *ivory* also includes such natural materials as walrus, hippopotamus, or whale teeth or tusks, and some of the vegetable materials that are of similar texture and density. Other ivory items may be found in the Scrimshaw and Netsuke categories. Collectors should be aware of the recent laws limiting the buying and selling of elephant ivory and scrimshaw.

Box, Hinged Door, 3 Drawers, Dragons, Waves, 1900s, 4¾ x 3¾ In. .... *illus* 1200
Card Case, Figures, Terraces, Pine Trees, Leaves, 4¼ In. 563
Carving, Colored Sculpture, Bok Choy Cabbage, Floral Blossoms Cluster, 1900s, 6 In. 1320
Carving, Tabletop, Chinese, Miniature Screen, Rosewood, Bas Relief Panels, 1800s, 9 x 15 In. 1440
Figurine, Deity, 4 Arms, Standing On Lotus Blossom, India, 1800s, 5 In. 80
Figurine, Fisherman, Children, Net, Distracted By Frogs, 12½ In. 900
Figurine, Lotus Plant, Chinese, 1800s, 2 In. 590
Figurine, Man & His Dog, Man, Dog, Japanese Travelers, 1 In. 490
Figurine, Standing Buddha, Arms Up, Holding Balls, 8 In. 976
Figurine, Standing Lohan, Head Turned Right, Censer In Hands, Refined Portrait, 1700s, 11 In. 1800
Group, Mountains, Sea Dragon, Figures, Pavilions, Clouds, Pines, 18½ In. 4250
Pie Crimper, Walrus Bone, Unicorn Shape, Inlaid Ebony Eyes, Nostrils, c.1850, 7 In. .... *illus* 3600
Plaque, Venus, Attended By Cherub, Continental, c.1850, 3¾ x 5 In. 390
Seal, Tortoise, Blue Eyes, Square Platform, Chinese, 1800s, 2¾ In. 600
Teether, Whistle, Twist Carved, c.1825, 4½ In. 165
Thread Dispenser, Pincushion, Walrus, Carved, Mounting Clamp, 1800s, 2 x 2 In. .... *illus* 240

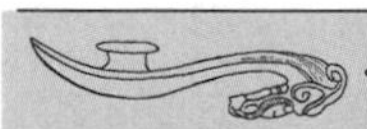

JADE is the name for two different minerals, nephrite and jadeite. Nephrite is the mineral used for most early Oriental carvings. Jade is a very tough stone that is found in many colors from dark green to pale lavender. Jade carvings are still being made in the old styles, so collectors must be careful not to be fooled by recent pieces. Jade jewelry is found in this book under Jewelry.

Basin, Spinach, 4 Lobes, Bats, Dragonflies, Geometric Patterns, Footed, 3¾ x 9½ In. 469
Belt Buckle, Dragon, Interlocking, 2 Symmetrical Carvings, Chinese, 1800s, 4¼ x 1½ In. 3500
Belt Buckle, Dragon, Interlocking, Incised Hook, 2 Pierced Carvings, 1900s, 1½ x 4¼ In. 93
Belt Buckle, Dragon, Relief, 4 In. 937
Belt Buckle, Fruit, Vine, Spinach Green, 2¾ In. 510
Belt Hanger, 9 Seed Shape Bosses, 2 Columns, Green, 1700s, 2¾ In. 510
Belt Hanger, Celadon, Rectangular, Openwork, Dragon & Pearl Carving, 3 In. 438
Bowl, Handles, Spinach Green, 4 Ruyi Shape Feet, Loose Ring Handles, c.1850, 8 In. 813
Bowl, Lotus, 8 Petals, Buddhist Emblem, Perforated, 5⅜ In. 7500
Bowl, White, Lotus Shape, Flower, Ring Handle, 1 x 4 In. 4500

Iron, Safe, Iron Over Wood, Key Entry, Swivel Wheels, Hobnail Case, c.1835, 30 x 23 In.
$4,480

Iron, Target, Shooting Gallery, Row Of Birds, Carnival, 26 x 4 In.
$248

Copake Auction

Neal Auction Co.

Iron, Stand, Viking Ship, Quadruped Base, 1900s, 32 In.
$96

Iron, Target, Shooting Gallery, Soldier, Gun, Mounted, 7 In.
$248

Iron, Windmill Weight, Star, U.S. Wind Engine & Pump Co., Ill., 14 In.
$900

Copake Auction

Rich Penn Auctions

> ### TIP
> You can tell a piece of jade by the feel.
> It will be cold, even in warm weather.

Ivory, Box, Hinged Door, 3 Drawers, Dragons, Waves, 1900s, 4 ¾ x 3 ¾ In.
$1,200

Eldred's Auctioneers and Appraisers

Ivory, Pie Crimper, Walrus Bone, Unicorn Shape, Inlaid Ebony Eyes, Nostrils, c.1850, 7 In.
$3,600

Eldred's Auctioneers and Appraisers

Eldred's Auctioneers and Appraisers

Ivory, Thread Dispenser, Pincushion, Walrus, Carved, Mounting Clamp, 1800s, 2 x 2 In.
$240

TIP
To test a piece of jade to see if it is real, use a small penknife. Rub the tip of the knife across the bottom of the piece until there is a mark. A white line means the knife scratched the stone and it is not jade. A black line means the stone scratched the blade and it is probably jade.

Jade, Disc, Exotic Birds, Flowers, Leaves, Relief, Wood Stand, 5¾ In.
$330

Bowl, White, Peach Shape, 1½ x 3½ In.	2640
Box, Lid, Ormolu Mounted, Rooster Finial, Bronze, Nicholas Haydon 1900s, 3 x 7 x 5⅜ In.	480
Brush Holder, Oval, Daoist, Relief Figures, Celadon, Stone, Gray, Russet, 1900, 4⅞ x 5 In.	677
Brush Washer, Carved, Monkey Resting On Edge Of 2 Peaches, Double, 2 x 3 In.	150
Brush Washer, Green, Ruyi Shape, Fungus & Bat Carving, 6 In.	500
Carving, Yellow, Bat & Double Gourd Design, 3 In.	200
Censer, Carved, Green, Foo Dogs, 4 Dragon Faces, Rings, Side Handles, Chinese, 7 x 7 x 4 In.	242
Censer, Silver Filigree, Turquoise, Coral, Celadon Cup, Finial, Multicolor, 6½ x 7 In.	2375
Chime, 2 Opposing Coiled Dragons, Knotted Silk Tassel, Hardwood Stand, 7½ x 5¼ In.	4750
Disc, Exotic Birds, Flowers, Leaves, Relief, Wood Stand, 5¾ In. *illus*	330
Dog, Laying Front Paws Together, Bulging Eyes, Ears, 1700s, 2⅜ In.	420
Effigy, Man Squatting, Carving, Central America, 1400s, 8 In.	570
Ewer, Lid, Lotus Blossoms, Meandering Leaf Stems, Leafy Finial, 7½ In.	12500
Ewer, Nephrite, Silver Filigree Mounts, Faces, Beaded Rows, Cloud, Dragon, Tibet, 7 In.	10300
Fan, Pierced, 2 Battling Dragons, Scrolled Handle, Lu Symbol, Bats, Clouds, 12½ In.	2000
Figural, Buddha Head, Mottled Orange, Brown, Dark Green, 8¼ x 3¼ x 3¼ In.	472
Figurine, Birds & Roses, Carved Serpentine, 7½ x 6¾ x 3 In.	118
Figurine, Elephant, Emerald Green, 1990, 3½ x 2½ In.	475
Figurine, Horse, Lying On Side, Hind Leg Touches Head, Russet Inclusions, 4 x 6 In.	625
Figurine, Man, Seated, Praying Hands, Arch, 8 x 4 In.	717
Figurine, Man, White, 1 Hand Up, 1 Hand Holds Cup, Pale Celadon, 6¾ In.	2500
Figurine, Woman, Branch, Blossom, In Robe, Chinese, 1900s, 9¼ In.	60
Girdle Hook, Bird, Green, 3¼ In.	390
Gourd, Double, Carved, Leaves, 2 Attached Stems, Chinese, 2½ x 1⅜ In. *illus*	720
Lotus Cup, Pods, Flowers, Toad, Phoenix, Wood Stand, 5¼ In.	3750
Mirror, White, Carved, Celadon Jade Handle, Silver Mounts, Chinese, 10¼ In.	1875
Monkey, Seated, Holding Peach, Carved Fern In Verso, Chinese, 2⅝ In.	123
Pendant, Bat, Carved, Coins, Ruyi Fungus, Multicolor Stone, Brownish, 1¾ x 1½ In.	100
Pendant, Celadon, Oval, Carved Flowers, Flower Border, 1900s, 3 In.	200
Pendant, Celadon, Russet, Shield Shape, Relief Dragon Design, 3½ In.	500
Pendant, Hardstone Carving, Han Dragon, Mystical Beast, Green	200
Pendant, Kylin, Scrolls 1 Side, 2 Gourds, Multicolor Stone, 1¾ x 1 x ¼ In.	60
Pendant, White, 2 Bean Pods, c.1800, 3 In.	360
Plaque, 2-Sided, Carved, White Gray, Birds In A Flower Landscape, Wood Stand, 6 In.	150
Plaque, Carved, Figures In Landscape, Calligraphy On Reverse, 2 In.	120
Plaque, Celadon, Fish In Underwater Seascape, Plants, Reticulated, Chinese, 2½ x 2 In.	720
Plaque, Dragon, Writhing, Bat, Bird, Flowers, Leaves, Pierced, Pale Green, 2⅞ In. *illus*	900
Scepter Mirror, Silver, Cloisonne, Dimensions, Showing Light Signs Of Age, 8 x 3 In.	250
Scepter, Cross Shape, Bats, Flowers, Peonies, Dragons, Calligraphy, Wood, 21 In.	5100
Scepter, Ruyi, Cloud Shape Head, 2 Bats, Serpentine Handle, Chinese, 1¾ x 9 x 3 In.	545
Scholar's Boulder, Attendant, Path, Overhanging Branches, Black, Gray, 5 In.	605
Sculpture, Dragon Boat, Jadeite, Sails, Waves Stand, 41 x 41½ In.	480
Seal, Family, Lozenge Shape, Hollow Domed Top, Opposing Dragons, 3 x 2 x 1 In.	300
Snuff Bottle, Domed, Stopper, Carved Insect, Translucent Green Fissures, Chinese, 1¾ x 2 In.	221
Toggle, Monkey, Peach Branches, 2 Peaches, Pierced, Carved, China, 1800s-1900s, 2½ In.	312
Tray, Metal Scroll Handles, Footed, 7¾ In.	3750
Tree, Hardstone, In Cloisonne Jardiniere, Agate, Amethyst, Coral, Turquoise, c.1900, 17 In.	600
Tree, Rectangular Jardiniere, Agate Peonies, Pair, c.1925, 19 In.	720
Vase, Dark Green, Pagoda Lid, Hanging Bells, Pierced Cylinder, Dragon Heads, 23 x 13 In.	750
Vase, Flattened Beaker, 4¼ In.	3500
Writer's Coupe, Lotus Pod & Leaf With Cicada, Length 5 In.	1200

JAPANESE WOODBLOCK PRINTS *are listed in this book in the Print category under Japanese.*

JASPERWARE can be made in different ways. Some pieces are made from a solid-colored clay with applied raised designs of a contrasting colored clay. Other pieces are made entirely of one color clay with raised decorations that are glazed with a contrasting color. Additional pieces of jasperware may also be listed in the Wedgwood category or under various art potteries.

Plaque, Ceramic, Mother & Daughter, Marked, 1900s	36

"WHAT'S HOT AND WHAT'S NOT IN ANTIQUES & COLLECTIBLES" AND RECORD PRICES

Prices are a little higher than last year, and many record prices were set as bidders fought for the best of the best, especially the best of collectibles and art made after 1950, and sculpture and pottery made after 2000. (See the end of this section for some of this year's record prices.) There have been changes in the way art and antiques are collected, thanks to the Internet, cell phones, tablets, computers, and other electronic ways to buy and sell. Some changes are caused by lifestyle and changing fashions. Older collectors (now older than 65) wanted collections of good to excellent examples. That was their goal. Now perfect pieces are the goal for many. There is interest in "design," and there are museum exhibits and collectors who display and explain modern teapots, unfamiliar furniture, even vases or corkscrews as good or bad "design." It's a hard term to define since everything is designed by someone. But it seems to say that today there is great design in any category, including painting, sculpture, jewelry, kitchen tools, cars, packaging, advertising, clothing, and more. That has shifted some buyers' attention in the antique and vintage collectors' world to great graphics, unique jewelry, unusual chairs and tables, glass, silver, pottery, and even medical devices. But the most apparent change of interest in the present era is condition. Excellent condition is required to get the top price for many antiques, especially furniture (refinishing), mechanical banks (repaint) and other metal collectibles (amount of original paint and no damage), and bottles, glass, and ceramics (no chips, no cracks, no flaws, perfect paper label, no repairs no matter how old). And there is also an interest in repaired pieces from the 1700s and early 1800s, like stapled export porcelain. "Go-with" and "make-dos" are collecting categories. Buyers want broken goblet stems made into candleholders or damaged eighteenth century porcelain teapots with silver spouts added as replacements. It may be just part of the way being "green" and recycling has influenced our thoughts. We can brag that antiques collectors were the first serious recyclers. On the other hand, this has been another year of the weak "collecting economy" that started in 2008 for the small collectibles like figurines and single plates, popular in the 1960s and '70s.

Many items are repaired or restored before being sold and the only way to know this is to contact a person on the sales staff before the sale and ask. It is often not part of the catalog description. Malls and shops have been closing, but many shows and shops seem to get better prices than they could get ten years ago. Collectors and dealers agree that "good stuff sells" and well-run shows, shops, and sales are doing "OK." Usable furniture in good condition and decorative "smalls" are selling for expected prices. The 1890's oak dining tables that were hard to sell by 2000–2008 are attracting more buyers because of the low prices. The "best" of every type of antique or collectible is in demand. Some auctions get prices that are close to retail. But easy-to-find antiques are at about one-third of retail because the Internet has revealed the large, worldwide supply. Art, including prints, has totally flipped. Norman Rockwell, portraits, and Warhol paintings are selling for millions.

There is still a problem with bids from China. In the past some bidders refused to honor their bids and instead asked for a price reduction—or just didn't pay for or pick up a purchase. Often the sale price is reported online at the time of the auction bid, but there is rarely a public announcement that the bid was not honored. Most auction houses selling expensive art and antiques now require a cash deposit before the sale that will be forfeited if a buyer does not honor a bid.

What's Selling Where

Since 1953, the year our first book was published, the antiques world has gone from one or two antiques shows in a city per year to one almost every week. But with so many new online ways to buy and sell antiques, many shows have been discontinued. Auctions of expensive antiques used to be held in New York, Chicago, and a few other large cities. Small towns had "farm auctions" held outside in a farmhouse yard, or a local auctioneer who sold antiques, tractors, and tools in the barn. There were no malls, no Internet shops, house sales, or auctions. Today many major cities have auction houses that run auctions at their galleries with online access that reaches buyers in every country. And major auctions are also online from London, Paris, Hong Kong, and other major cities. Every day there are dozens of auctions you can watch and place bids on from your computer or phone. And there are several online auction sites that advertise and list the coming auctions, then handle the competing bids in real time. There are also timed auctions, usually for one type of collectibles like bottles, that are online for a specified length of time, about two weeks. That means that many buyers do not even see the real piece, just a picture and a description.

It has become more difficult to sell vintage collections of figurines and small advertising items like tape measures or glass shoes. Pressed glass is priced so low it is now a bargain and selling a bit better. Carnival glass rarities are hitting all-time highs while common pieces are difficult to sell. In 2012, prices leveled for things with international appeal, like Chinese porcelain and ivory, but with the endangered species laws changes at state and national levels, some things just can't legally be sold by any means.

New rules from the U.S. Fish and Wildlife Service went into effect July 6, 2016. Some ivory items, including antiques, have been seized and crushed because some feel allowing anything of ivory to be sold suggests that ivory is valuable and living elephants are being killed for profit. Many EPA laws forbid the sale of parts of endangered species: elephants (ivory), rhinoceros (horns), eagles (feathers), tigers and other cats (skins), and even some types of turtles (shells). There is also pressure to do what is politically correct and this may cause an unexpected legal problem even if it is an historic item. Sales of vintage Ku Klux Klan items and caricatures of black, Irish, Chinese, Indian, and Jewish people on postcards or joke figurines are criticized and result in bad publicity or removal from a sale. Beware of anything that mentions religion in a derogatory manner. Legal auctions of historic antique guns caused controversy and unpleasant publicity and the laws covering guns, ammunition, and even antique firearms are being argued by many government and protest groups.

Hummel, figurine, Adventure Bound Woody Auction

From 2013 to 2015, Chinese bidding slowed down for all but top-quality pieces. From 2008 to 2016, Hummel, Royal Doulton figurines and character jugs, "country furniture" with peeling paint, and "brown furniture" like period Chippendale desks have gone way down in value. And by 2016 the major auction houses led the way by accepting only higher-priced items to sell. Sotheby's and Christie's won't sell antiques or art worth less than thousands of dollars in their important sales. Some advertising auctions want items over $500 or $1,000. Large advertising signs, enameled metal signs, die-cut cardboard advertising, auto-related pieces, even small oil cans and other small tins with great graphics are up but only if in very good to excellent condition. Rock 'n' roll and travel posters still sell well.

Antiques as an Investment?

The economic problems that started in 2008 with the stock market crash and housing bust spread to antiques and collectibles. There is still a saying that if you buy antiques, they go up in value every year and are a good investment. That is only half true. If you buy the right antiques and sell at the right time, they sell for higher prices than you paid, even when you factor in inflation. Consider this: Our first price book (1967) lists a Diamond Dyes cabinet for $50. In 2015 "Evolution of Woman" was $360; "Blond Fairy" was $1,112; and "Washer Woman" with blue background $1,680. This year "Evolution of Woman" is $472 and "Redheaded Fairy" is $430. The cabinets have been so popular there are now fake cabinets in a slightly smaller size and copies of the tin panel from the cabinet door being sold as a vintage sign.

Art as investment is the latest trend for millionaires and billionaires. The prices of very important art have been rising faster than most traditional investments like real estate or stocks and bonds. And the buyer has the added prestige of great taste, sophistication, and bragging rights for owning a one-of-a-kind masterpiece. Highest price for a famous painting this year was $450,312,500 for a painting by Leonardo da Vinci. Quality and works of recognized contemporary artists sell high because collectors consider it an "investment" that will increase in value. Newly popular are works by contemporary studio potters and glass artists that are made in non-traditional shapes. Teapots and vases are not made to be used, but are one-of-a-kind, large, and often colorful sculptures. Tiffany lamps have become so expensive there are now higher prices for other lamps with glass shades, like Handel, Pairpoint, Moe Bridges, and Pittsburgh. Mixed metal furniture by Paul Evans from the 1950s and later is still setting records. Wooden furniture by George Nakashima is popular and expensive and continues to go up in price. And all artist-made wood carvings and bowls are going up in price and selling quickly. Three years ago, a dealer at Design Miami filled his booth with antique Japanese baskets made for flower arrangements. He collected them while visiting Japan and priced them at $10,000 and up. Some were signed, most were not, but he knew how to identify maker and date. They sold immediately. Since then antique baskets of all kinds have gone up in price, including those made

Handel, lamp, underwater scene
James D. Julia Auctioneers

by American Indians and African tribes. Experts can identify the best. During the same years, the Longaberger basket frenzy saw prices go from more than $1,000 for a rare, new limited-edition basket sold in a pyramid scheme to less than $25 for most of the Ohio-made baskets. The company went out of business in 2018. There is more interest and rising prices for TV, radio, space exploration, and computer collectibles. Unique celebrity-related photographs, autographs, clothing, or belongings like baseballs or guitars can start bidding wars if the celebrity is still remembered by the 40-year-old bidder. Vintage watches by Rolex and Patek Philippe are in demand and prices are rising higher, especially for those made soon after 1926, when the first waterproof models were made. Many of those are bought to wear, not just to display. Additions to auctions that started in 2010 are designer purses by makers like Hermès or Chanel that sell for thousands of dollars. Special-edition sneakers made by Nike and other name brands are selling for hundreds to thousands of dollars to "sneakerheads." The birth of the sneakerhead culture in the U.S. came in the 1980s and can be attributed to three major sources: basketball, Michael Jordan's Air Jordan line of shoes in 1985, and hip-hop music. Some are displayed, a few are worn, and many are not really collected but often are bought to use or to re-sell to make a profit.

What's Hot? What's Not?

Of major interest today, and getting high prices, are antique guns and ammunition, the best of modern furniture, and modernist jewelry by artists like Art Smith. Early comic books in excellent condition are selling at high prices and the comics that feature the first appearances of Batman, Superman, Wonder Woman, and other super-heroes or first issues like "Action Comics" No. 1 with the introduction of Superman are selling for even higher thousands of dollars. The original art for the covers of important comic books or magazines are selling as art, not collectibles, and Norman Rockwell's paintings have sold recently for more than $1 million. His prints are selling for hundreds of dollars to those who like the art but have less money. Daniel Boone, Hopalong Cassidy, and even Flintstones items are down, but Betty Boop collectibles are up in price. Advertising posters and packages from stores, gasoline station products, and even road signs are popular. Good graphics bring very high prices.

There are still bargains to be had, some that have been emerging as "collectibles" over the last ten years. Big is still "big." Groups of small figurines or sets of plates are very hard to sell. Large-scale accent pieces like huge crocks, floor vases, centerpieces, bronze sculptures, large posters, and garden statuary attract decorators as well as the owners of large homes. Blue and white, the colors favored in the seventeenth and eighteenth centuries, are back. New is bright yellow. Anything from clothes and glass to ceramics and furniture in the "newest style" between the 1950s and 2010 is hot. They are all going up in price and attracting new, younger buyers. Iron objects like bookends, doorstops, pots and pans, even snow eagles and carnival shooting targets are getting harder to find and sell quickly. But costume jewelry is the most popular item we see selling at shows and online. Prices for pieces marked with important makers' names

Rookwood, vase, turquoise flowers
Rachel Davis Fine Arts

can sell for as much as $1,500 to $2,500. Unmarked pieces of jewelry are bargains when compared to new store prices. A few very popular collectibles of the past, like Roseville and Rookwood pottery, Mexican silver jewelry and almost any clear glass is still down in price for all but the largest and most important pieces.

The meltdown price of sterling silver the last few years made it profitable to destroy many pieces. Hundreds of coin silver items, especially spoons and no-name sterling serving dishes and flatware, disappeared in the meltdown craze. Sterling by well-known companies or designers like Tiffany, Gorham, and Liberty now get top dollar. And very modern unfamiliar shapes make tea and coffee services saleable at high prices. Almost all coin silver spoons and serving pieces that were not destroyed are hard to sell for a little less than meltdown price even if in perfect, useable condition. (Meltdown price in June 2018 was $13.82 per ounce.)

A search engine service noted that lower-priced items and younger searchers for collectibles indicate new audiences for art antiques and collectibles. An interest in female artists is growing perhaps along with the interest in jobs and treatment of women in political discussions. May 2018 was a unique month for antiques and art prices. The major auctions were having blockbuster sales of paintings and sculpture, many pieces estimated at millions of dollars. A Picasso painting sold for $115 million, a Monet picture of water lilies was $20.6 million, and a Modigliani painting of a nude set a record at $157.2 million. Dozens of other pictures went for record prices. But the amazingly high sale prices hid a possible problem. There were many pictures that had just one bid or there was an arranged sale if no one bid high enough. An investor or a group would buy the painting, hoping it would eventually sell for more. The auction house agreed to cut the buyer's premium or do something else that made the price paid lower than the ordinary bid. There may be more interest in middle-priced art because it may go up in price. There are few buyers with the millions of dollars required for the best of the best. Or it might show that new buyers want to find talented new artists that appeal to younger tastes.

RECORD PRICES

CLOCKS & WATCHES

Wristwatch at auction (image 1): $17,752,500 for a Rolex "Paul Newman" Cosmograph Daytona wristwatch, reference No. 6239, stainless steel, off-white dial, tachymeter bezel, 17 jewels, 37-mm diameter, with crocodile "bund-style" strap. Given to Paul Newman by his wife Joanne Woodward and engraved "Drive Carefully, Me." Sold October 27, 2017, by Phillips Auction in association with Bacs & Russo, New York.

FURNITURE

Kentucky furniture (image 2): $498,750 for a Chippendale walnut secretary made in Kentucky for Captain John Cowan, lower section with 4 graduated drawers, drop-front desk opens to 9 secret drawers behind central door that divides 2 sets of 4 pigeonholes and 4 drawers. Top section with broken arched pediment above 2 doors that open to adjustable interior shelves, 1796, 103 x 43 in. Sold October 21, 2017, by Cowan's Auctions, Cincinnati, Ohio.

1.

2.

GLASS

Largest piece of cut glass (image 3): $66,000 for an American Brilliant Cut Glass punch bowl and stand, with ⅝-in. deep cutting, 29 in. tall, 26-in. diameter. rim, weighing about 150 lbs., c.1905. Bought by the Corning Museum of Glass. Sold October 27, 2017, by John McInnis Auctioneers, Amesbury, Massachusetts.

MISCELLANEOUS

Single motorcycle at auction (image 4): $929,000 for a Vincent Black Lightning 998 cc motorcycle, completely original, unrestored, 1 of 30 Black Lightnings made, 1951. The Vincent set an Australian speed record in 1953 when Jack Ehret rode it to an average speed of 141.5 mph. Sold January 25, 2018, by Bonhams, Las Vegas.

3.

Image credits:
1   Phillips
2   Cowan's Auctions
3   John McInnis Auctioneers
4   Bonhams

4.

5.

Camera at auction (image 5): $2,957,304 (€2,400,000) for a Leica O series camera, serial number 122, matching lens cover and original folding finder, original paint and working, 1923. Sold March 10, 2018, by WestLicht Photographica Auction, Vienna, Austria.

An 1860 Lincoln name flag (image 6): $40,124 for an 1860 glazed cotton parade flag emblazoned "For President Abraham Lincoln" and "For Vice President, Hannibal Hamlin," 33 small & large stars scattered in the canton, 8 ½ x 12 ¼ in. Sold July 12, 2017, by Hake's Americana & Collectibles, York, Pennsylvania.

6.

Bass guitar (image 7): $68,750 for a 1961 Fender Precision bass guitar, serial number 60228, with strap, case, and photo archive, owned and played by James Jamerson. Sold June 17, 2017, by Heritage Auctions, Beverly Hills, California.

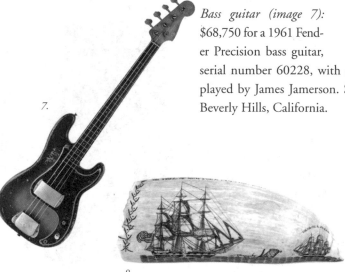

7.

8.

Scrimshaw whale's tooth (image 8): $456,000 for a whale's tooth inscribed "Engraved by Edward Burdett of Nantucket Onboard the Ship William Tell," picturing 3 whaling ships, a whaleboat capturing a whale, a coastal lighthouse and more, each ship with American flag, 1830-1833, 8 in. Sold July 20, 2017, by Eldred's Auctioneers, East Dennis, Massachusetts.

Decorative carving by the maker (image 9): $96,000 for a Black Duck in the standing position by Ira D. Hudson, c.1930, 15 in. long. Sold February 16, 2018, by Copley Fine Art Auctions, Charleston, South Carolina.

Image credits:
5   WestLicht Photographica Auction
6   Hake's Americana & Collectibles
7   Heritage Auctions
8   Eldred's Auctioneers and Appraisers
9   Copley Fine Art Auctions
10   Christie's
11   Heritage Auctions
12   Heritage Auctions
13   Christie's
14   Christie's

9.

PAINTINGS & PRINTS

Leonardo da Vinci painting (image 10): $450,312,500 for the painting "Salvator Mundi" (Saviour of the World), by Leonardo da Vinci, oil on walnut board, framed, c.1500, 26 x 18 in. Sold November 15, 2017, by Christie's, New York.

10.

Frank Frazetta painting (image 11): $1,792,500 for the Frank Frazetta painting "Death Dealer 6," oil on Masonite, 1990, 18 x 30 in. Sold May 12, 2018, by Heritage Auctions, Chicago, Illinois.

Norman Rockwell original study (image 12): $1,680,000 for the 1948 original study for "Tough Call" by Norman Rockwell, oil on paper, framed, signed, and inscribed to "Beans" Reardon. "Saturday Evening Post" cover study, April 23, 1949. Sold August 19, 2018, by Heritage Auctions, Dallas, Texas.

11.

12.

Claude Monet painting (image 13): $84,667,500 for the Claude Monet oil on canvas painting, "Nympheas en Fleur" (Monet's famous water lilies painting), stamped signature, painted c.1914-1917, 63 x 70⅞ in. Sold May 8, 2018, by Christie's, New York. Part of the Rockefeller Collection.

13.

Henri Matisse painting (image 14): $80,750,000 for the Henri Matisse oil on canvas painting, "Odalisque Couchee aux Magnolias," signed lower right, painted in Nice, France, 1923, 23¾ x 31⅞ in. Sold May 8, 2018, by Christie's, New York. Part of the Rockefeller Collection.

14.

15.

PAPER

Titanic letter (image 15): $165,776 for a letter written April 13, 1912, by American businessman and Titanic passenger Oscar Holverson to his mother, written on Titanic notepaper. Holverson died when the Titanic sank but his wife survived; the letter was in his pocket and eventually made its way to his mother. Sold October 21, 2017, by Henry Aldridge & Son Auction, Devizes, England.

Certified copy (image 16): $31,924.90 for an "All Star Comics" No. 8, December 1941-January 1942, featuring the first appearance of Wonder Woman, rated CBCS 2.5 Good+. Sold July 13, 2017, by Hake's Americana & Collectibles, York, Pennsylvania.

16.

Dracula movie poster (image 17): $525,800 for the "Dracula" movie poster (Universal, 1931) style A one sheet, starring Bela Lugosi. One of only two examples of the poster known to exist. Sold November 18, 2017, by Heritage Auctions, Dallas Texas.

17.

Casablanca movie poster (image 18): $478,000 for the only surviving Italian issue movie poster for "Casablanca," (Warner Brothers, 1946), Humphrey Bogart and Ingrid Bergman, 55 ½ x 78 ¼ in. Sold July 30, 2017, by Heritage Auctions, Dallas, Texas.

Marvel Comics Silver or Bronze Age cover (image 19): $478,000 for the original art for "The Amazing Spider-Man #100," drawn by John Romita Sr., presented in "floating heads" style, more than two dozen famous faces surround a full-body image of Spider-Man. Sold February 26, 2018, by Heritage Auctions, Dallas, Texas.

18.

19.

20.

Piece of American comic art (image 20): $717,000 for the original art cover "Fritz the Cat," by Robert Crumb, (Ballantine, 1969). Sold May 18, 2017, by Heritage Auctions, New York.

First edition Harry Potter book (image 21): $140,288 for a first edition of "Harry Pottery and Philosopher's Stone" by J. K. Rowling, inscribed to a friend and her family, dated one month and a day after the book was published on July 27, 1997. Sold November 15, 2017, by Bonhams, London, England.

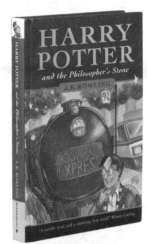

21.

The Far Side comic strip original artwork (image 22): $31,700 for the original artwork for the "The Far Side" daily comic strip dated 10-31-83, signed by cartoonist Gary Larson (Chronicle Features, 1983), ink over graphite on Bristol board, image area 6 ½ x 7 ½ in. Sold May 12, 2018, by Heritage Auctions, Chicago, Illinois

POLITICAL

Political postcard (image 23): $27,500 for the 1920 Jugate postcard with Democratic running mates James M. Cox and Franklin D. Roosevelt, 5 ¼ x 3 ¼ in. Sold February 24, 2018, by Heritage Auctions, Dallas, Texas.

22.

Washington inaugural button (image 24): $225,000 for the earliest artifact, an inaugural button referring to George Washington as the "Father of His Country," copper shell and lead-filled back, stamped bust image of Washington and the words "Pater Patriae," Latin for "Father of the Country," 25 mm (1 in.). Sold February 24, 2018, by Heritage Auctions, Dallas, Texas.

23.

24.

Image credits:
15 Henry Aldridge & Son Auction
16 Hake's Americana & Collectibles
17 Heritage Auctions
18 Heritage Auctions
19 Heritage Auctions
20 Heritage Auctions
21 Bonhams
22 Heritage Auctions
23 Heritage Auctions
24 Heritage Auctions

POTTERY & PORCELAIN

Arequipa pottery (image 25): $93,750 for an Arequipa pottery pot by Frederick H. Rhead with squeezebag decoration of stylized white and pink flowers, long stems with leaves on a teal blue ground, marked, 1912, 6 ¼ x 5 ½ in. Sold January 20, 2018, by Rago Arts and Aucton Center, Lambertville, New Jersey.

25.

Fiesta Maroon coffeepot (image 26): $20,125 for a Maroon coffeepot with handle and round base, thought to be only one known to exist, pre-1973, 10 ½ in. Sold March 17, 2018, by Strawser Auctions, Wolcottville, Indiana.

26.

American face jug (image 27): $100,300 for an American stoneware face harvest jug from Edgefield, South Carolina, 1845-1855, mottled green alkaline glaze, oval shape with arched horizontal handle, tubular pouring spout, applied clay to face, bulging eyes, curved eyebrows, incised hair, and carved teeth. Sold with Stereopticon photograph "The Aesthetic Darkey" from "Aiken and Vicinity," by J.A. Palmer, Aiken, S.C., 1882, pictures an African American boy with an Edgefield face harvest jug made by the same artisan that made this record-price jug. Sold July 22, 2017, by Crocker Farm, Sparks, Maryland.

Chinese ceramics (image 28): $37,700,000 for a Chinese porcelain shallow bowl (brush washer), blue green, Northern Song dynasty (AD 960–1127), 5-in. diam. Sold October 3, 2017, by Sotheby's, Hong Kong.

27.

28.

SPORTS

Jackie Robinson Brooklyn Dodgers rookie "Color Barrier" jersey (image 29): $2,050,000 for the 1947 Jackie Robinson Brooklyn Dodgers game-worn rookie jersey. Sold January 30, 2018, by Heritage Auctions, Dallas, Texas.

Hank Aaron game-used rookie bat (image 30): $132,000 for the 1954 rookie bat used by Hank Aaron, 36 in., 33 oz. Sold February 24, 2018, by Heritage Auctions, Dallas, Texas.

29.

30.

31.

Game-worn shoes (image 31): $190,373 for a pair of Michael Jordan's game-worn and dual-signed Converse shoes from the 1984 Olympics' gold-medal-winning game against Spain. Sold June 11, 2017, SCP Auctions, Laguna Niguel, California.

College basketball jersey (image 32): $264,000 for a Purdue Boilermakers basketball jersey, game worn by No. 13 John Wooden in the early 1930s. Sold May 18, 2018, by Heritage Auctions, Dallas, Texas.

32.

33.

TOYS, DOLLS & BANKS

North American Teddy bear (image 33): $39,000 for a Steiff clown teddy bear, brown-tipped mohair with original nose stitching, glass eyes, original hat & ruff, and caps and buttons with trailing F. Includes baby book showing teddy bear was given in April 1911, 19 in. Sold March 25, 2017, by Bertoia Auctions, New Jersey.

34.

French character doll (image 34): $333,500 for a French doll designed by Antoine Edmund Rochard, bisque swivel head, cobalt blue glass inset eyes, closed mouth, pierced ears, and blond human hair in braids, coronet, kid poupee body, gusset jointed, with antique silk costume, c.1868, 30 in. Sold January 6, 2018, by Theriault's, Annapolis, Maryland.

Luke Skywalker figure (image 35): $50,622 for a "yellow hair" "Star Wars" Luke Skywalker figure, 12 Back-C AFA 95 mint, Kenner, 1978, 3¾ in. Sold November 16, 2017, Hake's Americana & Collectibles, York, Pennsylvania.

35.

Any Star Wars figure (image 36): $76,700 for a "Star Wars" Ben (Obi-Wan) Kenobi, 23 Back-A, AFA 80 NM double telescoping action figure on blister card, Kenner, 1978, 3¾ in. Sold November 16, 2017, by Hake's Americana & Collectibles, York, Pennsylvania.

Prototype Star Wars figure (image 37): $86,383 for the "Star Wars" Boba Fett rocket-firing figure, unpainted, custom case displays prototype figure and rocket separately and L-slot rocket-firing mechanism, Kenner, 1979, 3¾ in. Sold March 15, 2018, by Hake's Americana & Collectibles, York, Pennsylvania.

36.

Image Credits
33 Bertoia Auctions
34 Theriault's
35 Hake's Americana & Collectibles
36 Hake's Americana & Collectibles
37 Hake's Americana & Collectibles

37.

JEWELRY, whether made from gold and precious gems or plastic and colored glass, is popular with collectors. Values are determined by the intrinsic value of the stones and metal and by the skill of the craftsmen and designers. Victorian and older jewelry has been collected since the 1950s. More recent interests are Art Deco and Edwardian styles, Mexican and Danish silver jewelry, and beads of all kinds. Copies of almost all styles are being made. American Indian jewelry is listed in the Indian category. Tiffany jewelry is listed here.

Belt Buckle, Arrowhead Shape, Red Glass Bullet Cabochon, Rhinestones, 1930s, 4 In.	54
Belt Buckle, Brass, Enamel, Green Glass Beads, Marcasite, Czechoslovakia, 1920s, 3 x 1 In.	48
Belt Buckle, Chevron, Jet Stones, Steel, 2¾ In.	62
Belt Buckle, Green Galalith Plastic, Laminated, Rectangular Design, 1930, 2½ x 1 In.	48
Belt Buckle, Knot, Silver Plate, Clear Rhinestones, White Pearls, 1950s, 2 In.	16
Belt, Leather, Tooled, Silver Buckle, Worn By Valentino, Joseff, 36 In. .... *illus*	6250
Bracelet, 13 Charms, Silver, Rhodium Plated, Forstner, 1970, 7¼ x ⅜ In.	90
Bracelet, Bangle, Bakelite, Carved, Tan & Red	23
Bracelet, Bangle, Bakelite, Citrus Orange, Multicolor Dots, Shultz, 1940, 2½ x 1 In.	395
Bracelet, Bangle, Bakelite, Gray, Cream, Black Swirl, White Dots, Shultz, 1940, 2½ In.	348
Bracelet, Bangle, Bakelite, Navy, Cream Dots, Shultz, 1940, ½ x ⅞ In.	388
Bracelet, Bangle, Bakelite, Yellow Swirls, Aqua, Orange & Blue Dots, Shultz, 1940, 2½ In.	228
Bracelet, Bangle, Hinged, Blue & Green Enamel, Red Cabochons, Goldtone, Ciner, 7 x 5 In.	165
Bracelet, Bangle, Silver, Modernist, Nanna Ditzel, Georg Jensen, 8 x 2⅝ In.	365
Bracelet, Bangle, Silver, Oval, Arts Crafts, Marked, FHB, 7¼ In.	165
Bracelet, Bangle, Silver, Repeating Xs, Marked, Kalo Shop, No. 10, 2⅝ In.	250
Bracelet, Copper, Etched, Green Cabochons, Rhinestones, Faux Pearls, Selro, 1950s, 8 In.	159
Bracelet, Cuff, Ammonite, Silver, Applied Collets, Marked, Aaron Rubinstein, 2 In. .... *illus*	330
Bracelet, Cuff, Lion, Enamel, Rubies, Emerald Eyes, 18K Gold, D. Webb, 6¾ In. .... *illus*	37500
Bracelet, Cuff, Relief Scrolls, Silver Plate, Worn By Tony Curtis, Joseff, 3½ In. .... *illus*	2240
Bracelet, Flowers, Glass Beads, Aqua, Rose, Gold & Enamel Leaves, M. Haskell, 1940, 8 In.	698
Bracelet, Glass, Reverse Painted, Horse, Brown, Brass Link Band, 1930s, 7¼ In.	69
Bracelet, Link, Brickwork, Goldtone, Aurora Borealis Rhinestones, Coro, 7 In.	110
Bracelet, Link, Light Blue & Green Rhinestones, Goldtone Metal, Coro, 7 In.	85
Bracelet, Red Bohemian Garnet, 6½ x ⅝ In.	498
Bracelet, Rhinestones, Nanette Leaves, Silver Metal, 1960, 8 In.	59
Bracelet, Scarab, Gemstone, Domed, Goldtone Metal Mount, 1950-60, 5 x 8 In.	145
Bracelet, Seashells, Silver Metal Horn Shapes, Pink Rhinestones, Swarovski, 8 In.	348
Bracelet, Silver, Concho Style, Ropework, Toggle Clasp, Mexico, 1980, 6½ In.	145
Bracelet, Silver, Faux Emerald & Onyx Stones, 1930s, 2 x 7 In.	210
Bracelet, Silver, Purple & Blue Druzy, 6⅝ In.	150
Bracelet, Silver, Rhodium Plated, Clear & Sapphire Blue Austrian Crystals, 1950s, 7 In.	145
Bracelet, Silver, Zigzag Design, Clear Rhinestones, Chain Bottom, 1960s, 6½ x 2 In.	136
Bracelet, Textured Gold, Chain, Narrow, Monet, 1970s, 7½ In.	168
Bracelet, Tiger, Enamel, Diamonds In Eyes & Mouth, 10K Gold, 7 In. .... *illus*	1125
Bracelet, Zebra, 18K Gold, Enamel, Gemstones, Flexible Links, 6¾ In. .... *illus*	3932
Cigarette Case, Gold, Engine Turned, Monogram, EDC, Guards Club, London, c.1946, 5 In.	2160
Clip, Fur, Carnation, Red Enamel, Rhinestone Edge, Gold Vermeil, Coro, 1946, 2½ In.	240
Clip, Fur, Flowers, Pink & Clear Rhinestones, Silver Metal, Eisenberg, 3½ x 1¾ In.	220
Clip, Fur, Rhinestones, Blue & Clear, Unfoiled, Silver Metal, Eisenberg, 1930s, 4½ In.	350
Clip, Jade, Leafy Mount, Oval, Gold Over Silver, J.P. Petterson, Chicago, 2 In.	938
Clip, Stylized Spray, 3-Sided, Diamonds, Ruby Accents, Art Deco, 2 In., Pair	2829
Cuff Links, Amethyst Cabochons, Silver, Square, Beaded Corners, Kalo Shop, ¾ In.	406
Cuff Links, Black, Leather Straps, Anson, 1955-65, ¾ In.	75
Cuff Links, Blue Rivoli Rhinestone, Textured Metal, Dante, 1970s, 1 In.	85
Cuff Links, Buddha, Ruby Red Glass, Goldtone Metal, Swank, 1965-75, 1¼ x 1 In.	155
Cuff Links, Cobalt Enamel Disc, White Rim, 18K Gold, Diamond, Faberge, ¾ In.	2125
Cuff Links, Coins, Pewter & Nickel Silver, Anson, 1940s, 2¹/₁₆ In.	110
Cuff Links, Diamond, Bezel Set, 18K Gold, Marked, Winston, ¾ In.	1440
Cuff Links, Diamonds, Square In Square, 14K White Gold, ½ x ½ In.	2500
Cuff Links, Disc, Reflective Kaleidoscope, Silver Metal, 1970s, 1 In.	45
Cuff Links, Gemstone, Concave Oval Frame, Gold, Etched Lines, Anson, 1940s, 1 In.	75
Cuff Links, Green Jade, Bean Shape, Silver Mount, E. Peretti, Tiffany, ¾ In.	677

Jade, Gourd, Double, Carved, Leaves, 2 Attached Stems, Chinese, 2½ x 1⅜ In. $720

Brunk Auctions

Jade, Plaque, Dragon, Writhing, Bat, Bird, Flowers, Leaves, Pierced, Pale Green, 2⅞ In. $900

Michann's Auctions

Jewelry, Belt, Leather, Tooled, Silver Buckle, Worn By Valentino, Joseff, 36 In. $6,250

Julien's Auctions

This is an edited listing of current prices. Visit **Kovels.com** to check thousands of prices from previous years and sign up for free information on trends, tips, reproductions, marks, and more.

Jewelry, Bracelet, Cuff, Ammonite, Silver, Applied Collets, Marked, Aaron Rubinstein, 2 In.
$330

Cowan's Auctions

Jewelry, Bracelet, Cuff, Lion, Enamel, Rubies, Emerald Eyes, 18K Gold, D. Webb, 6¾ In.
$37,500

New Orleans Auction Galleries

Jewelry, Bracelet, Cuff, Relief Scrolls, Silver Plate, Worn By Tony Curtis, Joseff, 3½ In.
$2,240

Julien's Auctions

Clamper Bracelets

"Clamper" bracelets, hinged plastic bracelets that open to be put around a wrist, were originally made from umbrella handles. Albert Weiss & Company made the first bracelets, sold under the name *Bon Bon*.

Cuff Links, Lapis Lazuli, Diamonds, Alternating, Rectangular White Gold Mount, 1 In.		1750
Cuff Links, Owl's Head, Gold, Diamond Brows, Star Sapphire Eyes, ¾ In.		1063
Cuff Links, Profile In Relief, Roman, Goldtone, 1950s, ½ In.		65
Cuff Links, Quatrefoil, Black Onyx, Diamond Surround, 18K White Gold, ½ In.		1750
Cuff Links, Quilted Design, Oval Tanzanites, Diamonds, 14K White Gold, ¾ In.		1875
Cuff Links, Satin, Silver Metal, Sapphire Blue Crystal, Anson, 1960s, ¾ In.		55
Cuff Links, Shell Form, 18K Gold, Black & Red Enamel, David Webb, ¾ In.		2375
Cuff Links, Tiger's Eye, Oval, Notched 14K Gold Mount, ¾ In.		875
Cuff Links, Trees, Elliptical, Silver Metal, Red & Black Enamel, Anson, 1950s, 1¼ x ½ In.		75
Dress Set, Man's, 14K Gold Disc, Circle Of 10 Diamonds, Larter & Sons, 7 Piece		738
Dress Set, Man's, Disc, Mother-Of-Pearl, Diamond, 14K Gold, Marked, Lindsay, 6 Piece		2250
Dress Set, Man's, Rock Crystal Cabochons, Cushion Shape, 14K Gold, ⅝ In.		1250
Dress Set, Man's, Black Star Sapphire, 14K Gold Scalloped Mount, 5 Piece		875
Earrings, Agate, Ball Drop, Pierced Yellow Gold Mount, Victorian, Scotland, 1½ In.		298
Earrings, Amethyst Rhinestone, Triangular Gold Inset, Art Deco, Givenchy, 1½ In.		85
Earrings, Bees, Diamond Eyes, 22K Gold, Maija Neimanis, Potter Mellen, 1¼ In.	*illus*	2160
Earrings, Black Diamond, Charcoal Gray Rhinestones, Silvertone, 1960s, 1¾ In.		64
Earrings, Cabochons, Jewel Colors, Clear Rhinestones, Clip-On, Ciner, 1 In.		85
Earrings, Checkerboard, Mother-Of-Pearl, Turquoise, 18K Gold, Clip On, MAZ, 1 In.		2280
Earrings, Cluster, Domed, Clear Pave Rhinestones, Goldtone, Clip-On, Ciner, 1 In.		45
Earrings, Cluster, Domed, Green Aurora Rhinestones, Goldtone, 1960s, 1¼ x ¾ In.		38
Earrings, Cluster, Milky, Dark Pink & Red Glass Stones, Hattie Carnegie, 1 In.		65
Earrings, Comma Form, Topaz, Red, Pink, Green & Clear Rhinestones, Hobe, 1940s		115
Earrings, Cultured Pearls, White Luster, Ribbed Gold, Van Dell, 1950s, ⅝ x ⅜ In.		65
Earrings, Dangle, Diamonds, 14K Rose Gold Filigree Mount, 1½ In.	*illus*	5000
Earrings, Dangle, Rhinestones, Pear Shape, Rhodium Plated, Clip-On, Coro, 2 In.		30
Earrings, Dangle, Rhombus, Silver, Clear Rhinestones, 1960, 2 x 1¼ In.		44
Earrings, Dangle, Rose Gold, Round Glass Diamond Beads, 1960s, 1¼ In.		45
Earrings, Flower, Amethyst Austrian Crystal, Faceted, Rolled Gold, 1940s, ¾ In.		45
Earrings, Flower, Gold Filigree, Green, Topaz & Clear Rhinestones, 1940s, 1 In.		39
Earrings, Huggie, Rubies, Diamonds, 14K Gold, ¾ In.	*illus*	750
Earrings, Infinity, Citrine, 2 Entwined Rings, Smooth, Twisted, 18K Gold, D. Yurman, 1 In.		800
Earrings, Jadeite, Marbleized, Thick & Oval Egg Shapes, Polished, Ronci, 1950s, 1 In.		145
Earrings, Moon Face, Venetian Glass, Hammered 19K Gold Mount, E. Locke, ⅝ In.		2000
Earrings, Moonstone, Clear & Red Rhinestones, Silver Over Gold, Trifari, 1940, 1¼ In.		148
Earrings, Palm Tree, Beach, Seashell, Green Metallic Enamel, Silver Sea Gull, 1960s, 1½ In.		35
Earrings, Pendant, 2 Red Tourmalines, Diamonds Surround Lower, 14K White Gold, 2 In.		726
Earrings, Pendant, Crescents, Dangling, 18K Gold, Marked, Greece, Lalaounis, 3 In.		1875
Earrings, Pendant, Flowers, Birds, Turquoise Accents, 14K Gold & Silver, Victorian, 3 In.		363
Earrings, Pendant, Grape Clusters, Iolites, Diamonds, 18K Rose Gold, Studs, 2 In.	*illus*	750
Earrings, Rectangles, Curved, Silver Metal, Aqua & Green Enamel, L. Bott, 1980s, 2 In.		29
Earrings, Rhinestones, Clear & Black, Givenchy, 1 x 1½ In.		65
Earrings, Silver, Post, Modernist, Scandinavian, ½ In.		135
Earrings, Silver, S-Curve, Clear Faceted Stone, Lily Barrack, 2¾ x ½ In.		150
Earrings, Snail Shell, Nacre, 14K Gold, Ruby, Emerald, Sapphire, Clip-On, MAZ, 1 In.		2400
Earrings, Spray, Aurora Borealis Rhinestones, Goldtone Leaves, Round, Clip-On, Coro, 5 In.		25
Earrings, Starburst, Faceted Crystals, Oval & Pear Cut, 1928 Jewelry Co., 1980s, 1¼ In.		60
Earrings, Starfish, Gold, 1980s, ⅝ x 1¼ In.		18
Earrings, Stylized Apple, Deep Pink Rhinestone, Green Enamel Leaves, DeRosa, 1940, 1 In.		115
Hairpin, Celadon Jade, Openwork, Carved Bats, Peaches, 1880s, 11 In.		2750
Hatpins are listed in this book in the Hatpin category.		
Locket, Gold, Engraved Monogram, Shell, Rhinestones, W&H Co., 1920, 1⅛ In.		238
Locket, Silver, Etched Ivy Leaves, Glass, Victorian, 1882, 2 x 1½ In.		348
Locket, Silver, Heart Shape, Scrolling Leaves, Victorian, 1880s, ⅝ x 1 In.		798
Locket, Silver, Rose & Yellow Gold, Victorian, 1880, 1½ In.		998
Locket, Silver, Seed Pearls, Victorian, 1880s, 1¾ x 1½ In.		795
Necklace & Earrings, Peridot Beads, 42 Strands, Gold Sunflower Clasp & Earrings, Asprey		5250
Necklace & Earrings, Rose Petal, 18K Textured Gold, A. Cummings, 1979, 18-In. Necklace		10800
Necklace, 11 Plaques, Puffy Cherry Blossoms, Silver, Kalo Shop, 15¼ In.		750

J

Necklace, 13 Chains, Blue Seed Beads, Hattie Carnegie, 19 In.		325
Necklace, Beads, Red, Goldtone Spacers, 1960, 13 x 3 In.		28
Necklace, Beads, Teardrop, Purple Glass, Intaglio Leaves, Fishel Nessler & Co., 1930s, 16 In.		98
Necklace, Beads, Translucent Green, Yellow, Amethyst, Red, Orange & Pink, c.1925, 18 In.		229
Necklace, Beads, Wood, Agate, Marbled Tan & White, Flowers, 1950s, 37 In.		65
Necklace, Blue Rhinestones, Goldtone, Schoffel Co., Austria, 1930s-60s, 18½ In.		298
Necklace, Cameo, Green, Woman's Head, Fruit, Flowers, Arrow Shape, Chevron Chain, Parlati.		320
Necklace, Choker, Beads, Hippie, Red, Yellow, Navy, Turquoise, Leather Cord, 1970s, 16 In.		45
Necklace, Choker, Brass, Clear Rhinestones, Czechoslovakia, 1930s, 15¼ x ⅝ In.		179
Necklace, Choker, Stained Glass, Gold Over Silver Metal, 1970s, 24 In.		75
Necklace, Collar, Goldtone, Brass, Ruby Red Bezel, Chain End, 1910, 14 x¾ In.		95
Necklace, Collar, Lion, Goldtone, Satin Finish, Anne Klein, 1980s, 17¼ In.		85
Necklace, Collar, Pendulettes, Polished & Satin 18K Gold, Grecian Style, 17 In.	*illus*	6875
Necklace, Collar, Silver, Hammered, Arts & Crafts, Schroth's Jewelers, 15 In.		175
Necklace, Collar, Silver, Repeating Pinched Points, Los Ballesteros, c.1955		960
Necklace, Face, Etched, Oval, Satin Gold, Chain, 1940-50, 18 In.		95
Necklace, Faux Pearl, Flat Bead Spacers, Gold Over Silver, Napier, 1980s, 16 x 1 In.		68
Necklace, Festoon, Brass, Lace-Like Dangling Chains, 1940s, 16 x 3 x 1 In.		310
Necklace, Flowers, Coral, Goldtone, Worn By Vivien Leigh, Joseff, 17 In.	*illus*	53125
Necklace, Flowers, Red Baguettes, Goldtone, Snake Chain, Coro, 1953, 15 x 2 In.		210
Necklace, Gemstones, Agate, Amethyst, Amber, Chunky Oval Beads, 1970s, 24 In.		145
Necklace, Gemstones, Agates, Glossy White, Red Orange, Black, 1960s, 23½ In.		60
Necklace, Lariat, Dress Clip Ends, Faux Diamonds, Worn By Judy Garland, Joseff	*illus*	18750
Necklace, Link, Multistrand, Interwoven Circles, 18K Gold, Marked, Cartier, 17 In.		5500
Necklace, Marcasite, Carnelian, Carved, Gothic, 15 In.		118
Necklace, Mesh, Chain Link, Ties, Elsa Peretti For Tiffany & Co., 52 In.		2000
Necklace, Pearls, 6 Strands, Clear Glass Beads, Hattie Carnegie, 18 In.		165
Necklace, Pendant, Banded Agate, Gemstones, Gray, Orange, Oval, Wire Wrap, 1980s, 28 In.		85
Necklace, Pendant, Black, Rectangular, Chain, Trifari, 1970s, 36 In.		94
Necklace, Pendant, Cameo, Hardstone, Athena, Headdress, Oval Gold Frame, Chain, 14 In.		330
Necklace, Pendant, Diamond, 14K Gold 6-Prong Mount, Curb Link Chain, Jabel, 19 In.		615
Necklace, Pendant, Diamonds, 18K Rose Gold Filigree, Chain, 18 In.	*illus*	3250
Necklace, Pendant, Heart, Dragon & Phoenix, Relief, 22K Gold, Link Chain, 17 In.	*illus*	688
Necklace, Pendant, Opal, 18K Gold Organic Mount, Chain, 1940s, 2-In. Pendant		1476
Necklace, Pendant, Portrait, Tyrolean Boy, Whitby Jet Beads, Carved, Victorian, 1870, 2 In.		595
Necklace, Pendant, Worn By Errol Flynn In Movie, Joseff Of Hollywood, 20 In.	*illus*	3200
Necklace, Snake, Center Medallion, Silvertone, Foldover Clasp, Givenchy, 15½ In.		135
Necklace, Stars, Bohemian Garnet, Rose Cut & Teardrop, Victorian, 1899, 17 In.		998
Necklace, Tassel, Labradorite Beads, Diamonds, Gold, 25 In., 5-In. Tassel	*illus*	750
Necklace, Tiger, Bead, Ivory Enamel Stripes, Amber Cabochon Eyes, Ciner, 1980s, 18 In.		425
Necklace, Wreath, Filigree, Silver, Turquoise, 1920-30, 24 In.		245
Pendant, Cameo, Hardstone, Bust, Woman Looking Down, 14K Gold, Pearl Edge, 1 In.		431
Pendant, Leaves, Figures, Bow Top, 3 Stone Drops, Austro Hungarian, 3¾ In.	*illus*	584
Pendant, Mourning, Prince William, Watercolor On Paper, Gold, 1700, 1⅜ In.	*illus*	35000
Pendant, Mourning, Urn, Mourner, Verse, Ivory, Hairwork, Gold Frame, 1800s, 3 In.	*illus*	12188
Pendant, Mourning, Woven Hair, Seed Pearls, Initials, Gold, Victorian, 3 x 2 In.	*illus*	677
Pendant, Octopus, 18K Gold, Enamel, 14K Gold Necklace, J.P. Miller, 4⅜ In., 16 In.	*illus*	60500
Pendant, Oval Tourmaline, 3 Silver Curves, 14K Gold Bail, 2¾ x 2 In.	*illus*	363
Pendant, Sun, Face In Center, Textured Frame, 18K Gold, Tiffany & Co., 2¾ In.		2375
Pin & Earrings, Brushed Gold, Red, Blue & Green Square Rhinestones, Clip-On, Boucher, 1 In.		85
Pin & Earrings, Maple Leaf, 18K Textured Gold, Diamonds, Tiffany, 2-In. Pin		923
Pin, 2 Leaves, 1 Blue Rhinestone Pave, 1 Smooth Goldtone, Boucher, 3¼ x 1 In.		75
Pin, 3 Flowers, 18K Gold Basket, Blue & White Enamel, Pink Sapphires, UnoAErre		360
Pin, 12 Jade Beads, Multicolor, On 14K Gold Branch, Ming's, Hawaii, 2¼ In.		246
Pin, Abstract, Silver, Gold, Tourmaline, Seed Pearls, Albert Paley, 1971, 7 x 2 In.	*illus*	26250
Pin, Austrian Crystals, Sapphire Blue, Faceted Chatons, Prong Set, 1950s, 1⅜ In.		75
Pin, Autumn, Swirls, Semi-Translucent Red Glass, Goldtone Metal, 1928 Jewelry Co., 3 In.		65
Pin, Bar, Crescent, 23 Sapphires, 29 Diamonds, Flower Center, Victorian, 2 In.		431
Pin, Bee, 13 Malachite Sections, 18K Textured Gold, R. Wander, 1 In.		1920
Pin, Bee, Silver, Rose Cut Diamonds, Rubies, Emerald, Blue Zircon	*illus*	854

Jewelry, Bracelet, Tiger, Enamel, Diamonds In Eyes & Mouth, 10K Gold, 7 In.
$1,125

New Orleans Auction Galleries

Jewelry, Bracelet, Zebra, 18K Gold, Enamel, Gemstones, Flexible Links, 6¾ In.
$3,932

James D. Julia Auctioneers

Remodeled Victorian Jewelry

Authentic Victorian jewelry that has not been "remodeled" is down in price and seems like a good investment. The supply keeps dwindling and the best of the Victorian designs are being copied. Pieces by name designers or sources like Tiffany & Co., Marcus & Co., Lalique, Georg Jensen, Liberty & Co., or any of the famous Arts and Crafts makers are up in value.

Jewelry, Earrings, Bees, Diamond Eyes, 22K Gold, Maija Neimanis, Potter Mellen, 1¼ In.
$2,160

Cowan's Auctions

J

Jewelry, Earrings, Dangle, Diamonds, 14K Rose Gold Filigree Mount, 1 ½ In.
$5,000

Orleans Auction Galleries   New

Jewelry, Earrings, Huggie, Rubies, Diamonds, 14K Gold, ¾ In.
$750

New Orleans Auction Galleries

Jewelry, Earrings, Pendant, Grape Clusters, Iolites, Diamonds, 18K Rose Gold, Studs, 2 In.
$750

New Orleans Auction Galleries

Jewelry, Necklace, Collar, Pendulettes, Polished & Satin 18K Gold, Grecian Style, 17 In.
$6,875

New Orleans Auction Galleries

Jewelry, Necklace, Lariat, Dress Clip Ends, Faux Diamonds, Worn By Judy Garland, Joseff
$18,750

Julien's Auctions

Jewelry, Necklace, Flowers, Coral, Goldtone, Worn By Vivien Leigh, Joseff, 17 In.
$53,125

Julien's Auctions

Jewelry, Necklace, Pendant, Diamonds, 18K Rose Gold Filigree, Chain, 18 In.
$3,250

Jewelry, Necklace, Tassel, Labradorite Beads, Diamonds, Gold, 25 In., 5-In. Tassel
$750

Jewelry, Pendant, Mourning, Prince William, Watercolor On Paper, Gold, 1700, 1 ⅜ In.
$35,000

Freeman's Auctioneers & Appraisers

New Orleans Auction Galleries

Jewelry, Necklace, Pendant, Heart, Dragon & Phoenix, Relief, 22K Gold, Link Chain, 17 In.
$688

New Orleans Auction Galleries

Jewelry, Necklace, Pendant, Worn By Errol Flynn In Movie, Joseff Of Hollywood, 20 In.
$3,200

Julien's Auctions

New Orleans Auction Galleries

Jewelry, Pendant, Leaves, Figures, Bow Top, 3 Stone Drops, Austro Hungarian, 3 ¾ In.
$584

Cowan's Auctions

Jewelry, Pendant, Mourning, Urn, Mourner, Verse, Ivory, Hairwork, Gold Frame, 1800s, 3 In.
$12,188

Freeman's Auctioneers & Appraisers

Jewelry, Pendant, Mourning, Woven Hair, Seed Pearls, Initials, Gold, Victorian, 3 x 2 In.
$677

Cowan's Auctions

J

Jewelry, Pendant, Octopus, 18K Gold, Enamel, 14K Gold Necklace, J.P. Miller, 4 3/8 In., 16 In.
$60,500

Rachel Davis Fine Arts

Jewelry, Pendant, Oval Tourmaline, 3 Silver Curves, 14K Gold Bail, 2 3/4 x 2 In.
$363

James D. Julia Auctioneers

TIP

Never store rhinestone jewelry in a plastic bag. Moisture inside the bag will cause the stones to discolor.

Pin, Bird Of Paradise, Diamonds, Ruby Eyes, Platinum, 18K Gold, c.1910, 2 1/4 In. *illus*	4500
Pin, Blackamoor, Carved Black Coral, Diamonds, Rubies, Silver, 18K Gold, 2 1/2 In. *illus*	1625
Pin, Blue Cabochons, Clear Rhinestones, Brushed Gold, Hattie Carnegie, 2 In.	165
Pin, Blue Marquise Stone, Clear Rhinestones, Rose Gold Vermeil, Coro, 1940s, 3 x 2 In.	145
Pin, Blue Stones, Unfoiled, Goldtone Metal, M. Boucher, 1950s, 2 In.	285
Pin, Bow, Black Onyx, Diamond Knot, White Gold, Platinum, Art Deco, 1930s, 2 1/2 In.	1230
Pin, Bow, Gold, Clear Rhinestone Knot, Red Baguettes, Coro, 1945s, 2 1/2 x 2 In.	150
Pin, Bow, Green Guilloche, Raised Stars, 18K Gold, Engraved Edge, France, 1920s, 1 1/2 In.	660
Pin, Brown Glass Cabochon, Oval, Green & Topaz Rhinestones, Goldtone Flowers, 2 In.	42
Pin, Cameo, Hardstone, Silhouette, Pearl & Peg Border, 14K Gold, Enamel, 1 In. *illus*	540
Pin, Cameo, Lava, Woman, Grapevines, 14K Gold Filigree Mount, 1 3/4 In. *illus*	369
Pin, Cameo, Shell, Medusa Head In Profile, 14K Gold Frame, 4 Knots, 2 1/2 In.	584
Pin, Circle, Gold Leaves, Scarabs, Oval Gemstones, Glossy, Marbleized, Ronci, 1950s, 1 1/4 In.	78
Pin, Circle, Red Rhinestones, Goldtone, DeLizza & Elster, 1960s, 3 In.	159
Pin, Clover, Suspended Watch, Gold, Black Enamel, Pearl, Louis XVI Hands, Swiss, 3 In.	246
Pin, Cluster, Pink & Lavender Stones, Goldtone, Coro, 2 x 4 In.	85
Pin, Copper, Brass, Art Smith, Marked, 3 x 3 x 1/2 In. *illus*	875
Pin, Coral, Angelskin, Thick Gold Braid, Engraved, 1950s, 1 1/4 In.	120
Pin, Diamonds, 2 Synthetic Sapphires, 18K Gold, Platinum, Art Deco, 2 x 1 In. *illus*	1125
Pin, Dog, Brushed Gold, Black Enamel, Clear Rhinestone, Green Cabochon Eye, Ciner, 1 1/2 In.	65
Pin, Dove, 86 Diamonds, Old European, Silver Over Gold, Ruby Eye, c.1890, 2 3/4 In.	2375
Pin, Enamel, Putti Riding Dolphin, Diamonds, Pearls, Limoges, 1 1/2 x 1 In. *illus*	1800
Pin, Fish, Sterling Silver, Green Enamel, John Paul Miller, 1950s *illus*	5750
Pin, Flower In Crescent, Pink Enamel, Diamond, Krementz, 1910, 1 x 3/4 In.	228
Pin, Flower, Blue Enamel, Green Glass Cabochons, Red Rhinestones, Pearls, 1940, 4 In.	168
Pin, Flower, Concave Leaf, Silver Over Gold, Wrapped Stem, Van Dell, 5 x 3 In.	110
Pin, Flower, Fluted Petals, Diamond Center, 18K Gold, Van Cleef & Arpels, 2 In.	8400
Pin, Flower, Red Rhinestones, Goldtone Metal, Givenchy, 4 x 1 3/4 In.	95
Pin, Flower, Rose Gold Vermeil, Green Enamel Leaves, Coro, 1940s, 2 In.	275
Pin, Flowers, Engraved Satin Gold, Victorian Style, 1950s, 1/2 x 7/8 In.	155
Pin, Garden Fence, Diamond, Ruby, Sapphire & Emerald Flowers, 14K Gold, 1 3/4 In. *illus*	923
Pin, Hat, Sombrero, Silver, Marked, Taxco, Mexico, c.1960, 1 In.	28
Pin, Lady Bug, 18K Brushed Gold, 20 Diamonds, Robert Wander, 1 In.	720
Pin, Lady Bug, 18K Gold, 6 Diamonds, 6 Blue Sapphires, 7/8 x 7/8 In. *illus*	540
Pin, Lady Bug, 32 Rubies, Sapphires, Black Onyx Head, 18K Gold, J. Vitau, 1992, 1 In.	1440
Pin, Lapis, Oval, Silver Leafy Heart Shape Mount, Marked, Petterson, 1 1/4 In.	313
Pin, Leaf, Brushed Gold, Amethyst, Rhinestone, Baroque Pearl, Boucher, 2 1/2 In.	185
Pin, Lily Of The Valley, Silver, Marked, Kalo Shop, No. 206, 3 3/8 x 1 In.	469
Pin, Lion, Walking, 18K Gold, Emerald Eyes, Tiffany & Co., 2 3/4 In.	2750
Pin, MacArthur Heart, Bakelite, Red, 1940s *illus*	795
Pin, Micro Mosaic, Hunter & Blunderbuss, Rectangular, G. Barberi, c.1850, 2 In.	1500
Pin, Micro Mosaic, Scarab, Goldtone Metal, Victorian, 2 1/2 In. *illus*	984
Pin, Mourning, Glass, Black Amethyst, Oval, Beaded Edge, Victorian, 1860, 1 3/8 x 1 In.	75
Pin, Open Umbrella, 18K Gold, Tiffany & Co., 2 In.	1090
Pin, Pansy, Enamel, 14K Gold, Seed Pearl Edge, Crane & Theurer, 1 In. *illus*	900
Pin, Parakeet, Perched On Branch, Enamel, 18K Gold, Diamond Eye, Italy *illus*	570
Pin, Peacock, Rhinestones, Pearls, Gold Ropework, 1970s, 1928 Jewelry Co., 2 1/2 In.	75
Pin, Peacock, Rhinestones, Pink, Lavender, Green, Aqua, Clear, Gold, Swarovski, 1990s, 4 In.	248
Pin, Peak, Boomerang, Sterling Silver, Hans Hansen, 1 5/8 x 3 In.	300
Pin, Pink & Dark Blue Cabochons, Goldtone Metal, 1960s, 1 3/4 In.	28
Pin, Pinwheel, Amethysts, Yellow Sapphires, Diamonds, 18K Gold, Tiffany & Co., 3 In.	5400
Pin, Purple, Red & White Cabochons, Crystals, Silver Mount, Chanel, 2 x 2 In.	202
Pin, Rhinestones, Clear & Red, Cutout Sections, Coro, 3 1/2 x 1 1/2 In.	160
Pin, Rhinestones, Clear, Sapphire, Ruby & Emerald, Vermeil, Trifari, 1948, 2 1/4 In.	230
Pin, Rhinestones, Faux Emerald, Peridot, Ruby, Amethyst & Clear, Satin Gold, 1960s, 2 In.	55
Pin, Rhinestones, Tan, Topaz & Green, Oval, Goldtone Mount, Swarovski, 2 x 1 3/4 In.	158
Pin, Rockfish, Faceted Azure Glass Stone, Blue & Pink Enamel, Coro, 1944s, 3 x 2 In.	465
Pin, Rose Gold Over Silver, Coro, Retro, 1940s, 3 1/2 x 2 In.	265
Pin, Sash, Flowers, Amethyst Stones, Goldtone Metal Mount, 1800s, 3 x 2 In.	95
Pin, Shell, Turbo, 2 Rubies, 2 Sapphires, 2 Emeralds, 14K Gold Ropework, MAZ, 2 In.	450

Jewelry, Pin, Abstract, Silver, Gold, Tourmaline, Seed Pearls, Albert Paley, 1971, 7 x 2 In.
$26,250

Rago Arts and Auction Center

Jewelry, Pin, Bee, Silver, Rose Cut Diamonds, Rubies, Emerald, Blue Zircon
$854

Neal Auction Co.

Jewelry, Pin, Bird Of Paradise, Diamonds, Ruby Eyes, Platinum, 18K Gold, c.1910, 2 ¼ In.
$4,500

New Orleans Auction Galleries

Jewelry, Pin, Blackamoor, Carved Black Coral, Diamonds, Rubies, Silver, 18K Gold, 2 ½ In.
$1,625

New Orleans Auction Galleries

Jewelry, Pin, Cameo, Hardstone, Silhouette, Pearl & Peg Border, 14K Gold, Enamel, 1 In.
$540

Cowan's Auctions

Jewelry, Pin, Cameo, Lava, Woman, Grapevines, 14K Gold Filigree Mount, 1 ¾ In.
$369

Cowan's Auctions

Jewelry, Pin, Copper, Brass, Art Smith, Marked, 3 x 3 x ½ In.
$875

Rago Arts and Auction Center

Jewelry, Pin, Diamonds, 2 Synthetic Sapphires, 18K Gold, Platinum, Art Deco, 2 x 1 In.
$1,125

New Orleans Auction Galleries

Jewelry, Pin, Enamel, Putti Riding Dolphin, Diamonds, Pearls, Limoges, 1 ½ x 1 In.
$1,800

Brunk Auctions

J

237

Jewelry, Pin, Fish, Sterling Silver, Green Enamel, John Paul Miller, 1950s
$5,750

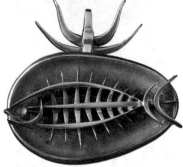

Rachel Davis Fine Arts

Jewelry, Pin, Garden Fence, Diamond, Ruby, Sapphire & Emerald Flowers, 14K Gold, 1 ¾ In.
$923

Cowan's Auctions

Jewelry, Pin, Lady Bug, 18K Gold, 6 Diamonds, 6 Blue Sapphires, ⅞ x ⅞ In.
$540

Brunk Auctions

Jewelry, Pin, MacArthur Heart, Bakelite, Red, 1940s
$795

Morning Glory Jewelry

Jewelry, Pin, Micro Mosaic, Scarab, Goldtone Metal, Victorian, 2 ½ In.
$984

Cowan's Auctions

Jewelry, Pin, Pansy, Enamel, 14K Gold, Seed Pearl Edge, Crane & Theurer, 1 In.
$900

Cowan's Auctions

Jewelry, Pin, Parakeet, Perched On Branch, Enamel, 18K Gold, Diamond Eye, Italy
$570

Cowan's Auctions

Jewelry, Pin, Silver, Loop, Ball Ends, Marked, Art Smith, 2 ¼ x 2 ½ In.
$875

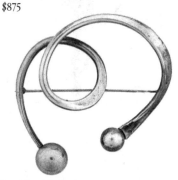

Rago Arts and Auction Center

Jewelry, Pin, Telephone, Silver, Turquoise & Blackstone Dial, Marked, Mexico, 1 ½ In.
$242

James D. Julia Auctioneers

Pin, Shield, Cabochons, Black, Green & Red, Rhinestone Pave, Goldtone, Ciner, 2¾ In.	245
Pin, Silver, Loop, Ball Ends, Marked, Art Smith, 2¼ x 2½ In. .... *illus*	875
Pin, Starburst, Royal Blue Glass Stone Center, Boucher, 2½ In.	265
Pin, Stylized Bow, Silver, Hammered, Industrial Design, J. Petterson, 4 x ¾ In.	100
Pin, Stylized Flower, Leaves, Oval, Silver, J.P. Petterson, Chicago, 2 In.	156
Pin, Sunflower, Silver, Square Ruby Glass Stone, Gold Looped Ribbon, 1940s, 3⅝ x 3 In.	110
Pin, Teardrop, Black Enamel, Black Beads, Satin Gold, 1928 Jewelry Co., 1½ x 4 In.	38
Pin, Telephone, Silver, Turquoise & Blackstone Dial, Marked, Mexico, 1½ In. .... *illus*	242
Pin, Tulip, Poplar, Puffy, Openwork, Round, Scalloped, Silver, Kalo Shop, 2¼ In.	313
Pin, Wreath, Faux Gemstones, Emerald, Aquamarine, Tourmaline, Gold, Van Dell, 1960s, 1¼ In.	55
Ring & Earrings, Hematite Tablet, Intaglio, Centurion's Head, 14K Gold Mount, Wm. Huger..	338
Ring, Angelskin Coral, Carved, Graduated Domes, Separated By 14K Gold Wire, Size 6	363
Ring, Band, 4 Stacked, Diamond X, 18K Tricolor Gold, Enamel, La Nouvelle Bague, Size 4	840
Ring, Bee, On Turquoise, Pearl, Emerald, Diamonds, Rubies, 14K Gold, Size 6½ .... *illus*	2000
Ring, Cameo, Glass, White On Black, Oval Gold Mount, 1940, 1 In.	38
Ring, Carnelian, Intaglio, Goddess Minerva, Oval, 18K Gold Mount, Italy, c.1890	469
Ring, Chrysoprase, Marcasite, Stepped Square Silver Mount, Uncas, 1930, Top ¾ In.	115
Ring, Coin, 1912 Indian Head, Twisted 14K Gold Bezel Mount, Size 6½	369
Ring, Coin, 1960 English Threepence, 14K Gold, 12-Sided Bezel Setting, Size 7¼	369
Ring, Copper, Concave, Oval, Turquoise, Cabochon, 1970s, ⅞ x ¾ In.	34
Ring, Coral Cabochon, Oval, Scalloped Silver Mount, J. Lovato, c.1975, Size 8¼ .... *illus*	1230
Ring, Diamond, 18K Gold, Raised Paisley Band, Jane Bohan, Size 6⅜	338
Ring, Diamond, White Gold, c.1970, Size 7¾	2200
Ring, Dome, 2 Bees On Hive, Sapphires, Diamonds, 14K Gold, Size 7½ .... *illus*	1345
Ring, Dome, Diamond, Ruby, Pierced Gold, 1980, Size 8	580
Ring, Dome, Textured Swirls, 18K Gold, Katy Briscoe, Size 7¾	1625
Ring, Granulated Beads, Between Polished Edges, 19K Gold, E. Locke, Size 7¼	1125
Ring, Infinity, Pinched, 18K Gold, Elsa Peretti, Tiffany & Co., Size 7¼	750
Ring, Monaco Quartz, Faceted, Diamond Corners, 18K Gold Mount, J. Ripka, Size 11	861
Ring, Onyx Cabochon, Silver Mount, 1970s, Size 7	85
Ring, Pietra, Flower Bouquet, Pink Roses, Turquoise, Green Leaves, Gold, 1864, Size 8	698
Ring, Pink Quartz, Yellow & Green Enamel, Etched, Vega Maddux, c.1970, Size 10	598
Ring, Poison, Garnet Cabochon, Locket, Clasp, Gold, Rope Twist, c.1800, Size 10	1040
Ring, Red Murano Glass, Intaglio, Man & Woman, Oval, 22K Gold Mount, Size 6½	2250
Ring, Rhinestones, Etched, Pink, Yellow & Green, Goldtone Metal Mount, 1960s, 1 In.	29
Ring, Sapphire, 2 Diamonds, 14K White Gold, Size 5	2400
Ring, Sapphire, Oval, Diamond Surround, Diamond Shoulders, 14K White Gold, Size 7	484
Ring, Skyscraper, Art Deco, Marcasite, Red Garnet Cabochon, 1920s, Size 6	180
Ring, Sputnik, 18K Gold, 19 Gemstones, H. Stern, Size 9¼	510
Ring, Stylized Woman's Face, 22K Gold, Jean Mahie, 1⅜ In., Size 5½	1440
Ring, Tiger's Eye, Oval, Domed, Gemstone, Gold, Slim Shank, 1950s, Size 5½	145
Ring, Tiger's Eye, Oval, Gemstones, Silver, Beaded, Size 11	75
Ring, Turquoise, Irregular, Imbedded Diamond, Organic Gold Mount, Les Baker, Size 9	308
Ring, Winged Putto, Painted On Porcelain, Silver Mount, J.P. Petterson, Size 5¾	438
Stick Pin, Old European Diamonds, Platinum, Pearl End, 2¾ In.	420

Watches are listed in their own category.

Wristwatches are listed in their own category.

JOHN ROGERS statues were made from 1859 to 1892. The originals were bronze, but the thousands of copies made by the Rogers factory were of painted plaster. Eighty different figures were created. Similar painted plaster figures were produced by some other factories. Rights to the figures were sold in 1893, and the figures were manufactured until about 1895 by the Rogers Statuette Co. Never repaint a Rogers figure because this lowers the value to collectors.

Group, Council Of War, 1868, 24 In.	4275
Group, New York, 1880, 23 In.	740
Group, Rip Van Winkle At Home, 1871, 18 In.	846
Group, Sleepy Hollow, Ichabod Crane, Katrina Van Tassel, 1868, 15 In.	175
Group, Wounded To The Rear One More Shot, 1864, 24 In.	1854

Jewelry, Ring, Bee, On Turquoise, Pearl, Emerald, Diamonds, Rubies, 14K Gold, Size 6½
$2,000

New Orleans Auction Galleries

Jewelry, Ring, Coral Cabochon, Oval, Scalloped Silver Mount, J. Lovato, c.1975, Size 8¼
$1,230

Cowan's Auctions

TIP
Diamonds clean well in club soda.

Jewelry, Ring, Dome, 2 Bees On Hive, Sapphires, Diamonds, 14K Gold, Size 7½
$1,345

New Orleans Auction Galleries

Josef Originals, Figurine, Boy, Bouquet, Serenade, Japan, 5 ¼ x 2 ¾ In. $48

Ruby Lane

Josef Originals, Figurine, Lion, Sad Face, 5 In. $24

Ruby Lane

Judaica, Kiddush Cup, Silver, Flowers, Terfloth & Kuchler, New Orleans, 1859, 9 In. $14,030

Neal Auction Co.

JOSEF ORIGINALS ceramics were designed by Muriel Joseph George. The first pieces were made in California from 1945 to 1962. They were then manufactured in Japan. The company was sold to George Good in 1982 and he continued to make Josef Originals until 1985. The company was sold two more times. The last owner went bankrupt in 2011.

Bell, Wedding Bell, Lavender Dress & Flowers, 3 ½ In.	45
Figurine, Birthday Girl, Age 14, Blond, Sticker, 5 ½ In.	35
Figurine, Birthday Girl, March, Mushroom Shape Dress, Hat, 3 ½ In.	28
Figurine, Boy, Bouquet, Serenade, Japan, 5 ¼ x 2 ¾ In. .... *illus*	48
Figurine, Chinese Girl, Blue Dress, Black Hair, Fan, 4 In.	58
Figurine, Dog, Pekingese, Brown, Tan, 4 ½ In.	24
Figurine, Girl, September, Pink Dress, Flowers, 3 In.	14
Figurine, Kangaroo, Kitten In Pouch, Rocking, Sticker, 5 ¾ In.	18
Figurine, Kittens, Puff & Fluff, Bow, 3 In., 2 Piece	38
Figurine, Lion, Sad Face, 5 In. .... *illus*	24
Figurine, Lion, Sad Face, Paper Label, 5 In.	24
Figurine, Mouse, Holding Ring, Foil Sticker, 2 ¼ In.	11
Figurine, Serenade Boy, Bouquet, Foil Sticker, 5 ¼ In.	48
Planter, Hen, Hat, Sticker, 3 In.	12
Salt & Pepper, Santa & Mrs. Claus, 2 ¾ In. & 3 In.	25
Trinket Box, Nun, Black Habit, Praying, Rosary, 5 In.	76

JUDAICA is any memorabilia that refers to the Jews or the Jewish religion. Interests range from newspaper clippings that mention eighteenth- and nineteenth-century Jewish Americans to religious objects, such as menorahs or spice boxes. Age, condition, and the intrinsic value of the material, as well as the historic and artistic importance, determine the value.

Cloth, Sabbath, Cotton, Embroidered, Colored Silk, Sequins, Fringe, Kurdistan, 1800s, 34 In.	10000
Crown, Torah, Flat, Chased, Leaves, Flower Heads, Gilt Plaque, Knot Design, 1800s, 7 ½ In.	3750
Cup, Laver, Hebrew Inscription, 2 Faceted Scroll Handles, Monster's Heads, Poland, 1865, 6 In.	9375
Dish, Wide Rim, Engraved Crowned Spread Eagle, Lion, Birds & Deer, Plants, 1700s, 14 In.	6250
Kiddush Cup, Silver, Flowers, Terfloth & Kuchler, New Orleans, 1859, 9 In. .... *illus*	14030
Lamp, Sabbath, Pierced Leaves, Inscription, 2 Shelves, Red Faceted Glass Jewel, 1900s, 39 In.	9375
Menorah, Bronze, Silvered, Marble, Moses, Star Of David, Dali, c.1981, 17 x 11 In. .... *illus*	5250
Menorah, Chrome, 9 Removable Arms, Stylized, Illusion Of Steps, Yaacov Agam, 13 x 7 In.	600
Menorah, Golden Gate, Scripture, Swiveling Arms, Dove, Marble Base, F. Meisler, 11 x 15 In.	1375
Menorah, Oil Burning, Laurel Branch, Servant Light, Pal Bell Co., Israel, c.1945, 7 x 8 x 4 In.	307
Menorah, Silver, Desk Shape, Tablets, Embossed Chanukkah In Hebrew, 8 Oil Wells, 8 In.	2000
Plaque, Metal, Spies From Land Of Israel, Inscribed Hebrew, Bezalel, Jerusalem, 5 x 15 In.	2000
Scroll, Esther, Crown Finial, Bezalel Silver Filigree, Jerusalem, c.1915, 7 In.	3000
Talmud, Woodcut Initial Word Panel, Incipits, Intermittent Marginalia, Pen Trails, 14 x 10 In.	6250

JUGTOWN POTTERY refers to pottery made in North Carolina as far back as the 1750s. In 1915, Juliana and Jacques Busbee set up a training and sales organization for what they named Jugtown Pottery. In 1921, they built a shop at Jugtown, North Carolina, and hired Ben Owen as a potter in 1923. The Busbees moved the village store where the pottery was sold to New York City. Juliana Busbee sold the New York store in 1926 and moved into a log cabin near the Jugtown Pottery. The pottery closed in 1959. It reopened in 1960 and is still working near Seagrove, North Carolina.

Bowl, Blue Interior, Marked, 5 ½ In.	42
Bowl, Chinese Blue & Red Glaze, Flared-Out Form, 3 x 9 ½ In.	240
Vase, Chinese Blue & Red Glaze, Asian Bottle Form, Stamped, 9 ⅞ In.	480

JUKEBOXES play records. The first coin-operated phonograph was demonstrated in 1889. In 1906 the Automatic Entertainer appeared, the first coin-operated phonograph to offer several different selections of music. The first electrically powered jukebox was introduced in 1927. Collectors search for jukeboxes of all ages, especially those with flashing lights and unusual design and graphics.

Ami, Model A, Mother Of Plastic, 40 Selections, 78 To 45 RPM, 1946, 69 In.	1294
Rock-Ola, Bubbler, Electronic Song Selector, Kaleidoscopic Bubble Lighting, 60 x 34 x 26 In. .	3520
Rock-Ola, Model 1426, Swirls, Bars, Multicolor, c.1947, 51 x 30 In. .... *illus*	2040
Wurlitzer, Model 71, Wood Veneered Case, Metal Trim Speaker Grill, 1940, 23 x 23 x 19 In......	3751
Wurlitzer, Model 1015 Bubbler, Multi-Sector Phonograph, Walnut Case, 1947, 60 x 30 x 24 In.	6000
Wurlitzer, Model 1080, Colonial, Wood Veneered Case, Serpentine, Speaker, 1947, 59 x 33 In. .	6353
Wurlitzer, Model 2504, High Fidelity Music, Silver, Gold, c.1961, 52 x 34 In. .... *illus*	2700
Wurlitzer, Model 7810, Wagon Wheel, c.1940	1212

KATE GREENAWAY (1846 to 1901, who was a famous illustrator of children's books, drew pictures of children in high-waisted Empire dresses. Her designs appear on china, glass, napkin rings, and other pieces as well as prints and storybooks.

Book, Family Treasury, Derrydale Books, 94 Pages, Hardcover	34
Card Tray, Woman, Silver Plate, James W. Tufts Co., 8 In.	110
Trinket Box, Children In Line Holding Coattails, Hinged, 3⅞ x 3 In.	79
Vase, Bud, Cranberry Glass, Figural Girl, Silver Plate Stand, 7 x 3¾ In.	210

KAY FINCH CERAMICS were made in Corona del Mar, California, from 1935 to 1963. The hand-decorated pieces often depicted whimsical animals and people. Pastel colors were used.

Kay Finch CALIFORNIA

Figurine, Angel, Hands Folded, Blue Wings & Collar, 3⅞ In..	36
Figurine, Angel, Hands Up, Blue Wings, Flower On Skirt, 4½ In.	48
Figurine, Bird, Pink Satin Matte, 4½ In.	41
Figurine, Cat, Ambrosia, Sitting, Pink, Black Eyes, 10 In..	250
Figurine, Cat, Eyes Closed, Head Tilted, 7½ x 6 In...	75
Figurine, Dog, Pekingese, Lying Down, Signed, 13 In..	249
Figurine, Elephant, Peanut, Trunk Up, Raised Foot, Flowers, 1950s...............................	167
Figurine, Owl, Toot, Glazed, Brown, Black, Gold Trim, Burgundy Luster, c.1950, 6 In...... *illus*	39
Figurine, Pig, Sassy, Blond Hair, Flowers, 3½ x 4½ In...	50
Salt & Pepper, Turkey, Taupe Glaze, 3½ In...	45
Vase, Turkey, Taupe Glaze, 10 x 10 In.	115

KAYSERZINN, *see Pewter category.*

KELVA glassware was made by the C. F. Monroe Company of Meriden, Connecticut, about 1904. It is a pale, pastel-painted glass decorated with flowers, designs, or scenes. Kelva resembles Nakara and Wave Crest, two other glasswares made by the same company.

KELVA

Box, Hinged, Green Mottled Background, Pink Floral, White Enamel, 12-Sided, 3¼ x 6 In.	210
Box, Open, Green Mottled, Pink Flowers, Gilt Metal Rim, Marked, 2 x 6½ In.	96
Dresser Box, Lid, Green Mottled, Cream Panels, Pink Flowers, Round, Gilt Metal Feet, 5 x 6 In.	450
Jar, Round, Hinged, Cigars, Pink Mottled Background, Blue Flowers, 5 In.	312
Jewelry Box, Hinged Lid, Blue Mottled, Pink Rose, 6-Sided, 3 x 3¼ In.	210
Jewelry Box, Hinged Lid, Green Mottled, Oak Leaf Lid, Square, 3 x 4 In.	210
Jewelry Box, Hinged Lid, Green Mottled, Pink Flowers, Oval, 3 x 5¼ In.	108
Pin Dish, Marked, Open, Pink Mottled, Blue Flowers, 6-Sided, 1¾ x 4 In.	108
Pin Dish, Open, Mottled Pink, Pale Blue Flowers, Lobed, 1¾ x 4 In. .... *illus*	103
Vase, Pink Tulips, Blue Ground, Shouldered, Scrolled Metal Mounts & Handles, Marked, 12 In.	1770

KENTON HILLS POTTERY in Erlanger, Kentucky, made artwares, including vases and figurines that resembled Rookwood, probably because so many of the original artists and workmen had worked at the Rookwood plant. Kenton Hills opened in 1939 and closed during World War II.

Bookends, Turtle, Green Glaze, Marked, 6 In...	189
Vase, Lamp, Flowers, Trees, Birds, Nude Male & Female, Marked, D. Seyler, 8 In. .... *illus*	142
Vase, Porcelain, 2 Handles, Moresque Details, Blue Glaze, Marked, 6 In...........................	94

Judaica, Menorah, Bronze, Silvered, Marble, Moses, Star Of David, Dali, c.1981, 17 x 11 In. $5,250

Heritage Auctions

Jukebox, Rock-Ola, Model 1426, Swirls, Bars, Multicolor, c.1947, 51 x 30 In. $2,040

K

Rich Penn Auctions

TIP

Before you have a garage or tag sale, check with your insurance agent. If necessary, get short-term liability coverage. Be sure your theft coverage is adequate.

Jukebox, Wurlitzer, Model 2504, High Fidelity Music, Silver, Gold, c.1961, 52 x 34 In.

$2,700

Rich Penn Auctions

Kay Finch, Figurine, Owl, Toot, Glazed, Brown, Black, Gold Trim, Burgundy Luster, c.1950, 6 In.

$39

Ruby Lane

Kay Finch

Kay Finch was a dog-show judge, and her ceramic canine figurines show her understanding of dogs' anatomy. Many of her animals—cats, elephants, monkeys, and pigs —have very human expressions.

Kelva, Pin Dish, Open, Mottled Pink, Pale Blue Flowers, Lobed, 1¾ x 4 In.

$103

Woody Auction

KEW BLAS is the name used by the Union Glass Company of Somerville, Massachusetts. The name refers to an iridescent golden glass made from the 1890s to 1924. The iridescent glass was reminiscent of the Tiffany glass of the period.

Tumbler, Gold Iridescent, Panel Optic, Panels, 1900-30, 3¾ In. .... *illus*	93
Vase, Green & Gold Pulled Feather, Shouldered, Rolled Rim, Tapered, c.1910, 8 In.	354

KEWPIES, designed by Rose O'Neill (1874–1944), were first pictured in the *Ladies' Home Journal.* The figures, which are similar to pixies, were a success, and Kewpie dolls and figurines started appearing in 1911. Kewpie pictures and other items soon followed. Collectors search for all items that picture the little winged people.

Bisque Head, Brown Glass Eyes, Pink Dress, J.D. Kestner, Marked, 1913, 13 In. .... *illus*	13450
Bisque Head, Helmet, Side-Glancing Eyes, Composition, Wood, Handwerck, c.1918, 12 In.	978
Bisque Head, Jointed Arms, Starfish Hands, Blue Wings, Prussian Helmet, c.1912, 5 In.	518
Bisque Head, Painted Face, Jointed, Composition, Marked, O'Neill, Kestner, c.1912, 14 In........	5132
Bisque, Baby, Sitting, Finger In Mouth, 3½ In.	21
Bisque, Crawling, Yellow Ribbon In Hair, 3 x 3 In.	51
Bisque, French Horn, 1½ In.	40
Bisque, Huggers, Blue Wings, Smiling, 5 In.	25
Bisque, Side-Glancing Eyes, Helmet, Wings, Trumpet, 5½ In.	547
Bisque, Sitting, Turkey, 2 In.	365
Bisque, Starfish Fingers, Arms Down, Wrapped In Pink Ribbon, 4½ In.	76
Bisque, Straight Legs, Jointed Arms, Shield Sticker, c.1912, 5½ In.	309
Bisque, Traveler, Suitcase, Umbrella, Blue Wings, Side-Glancing Eyes, c.1913, 3½ In.	250
Bisque, Wings, Side-Glancing Eyes, Open Arms, c.1913, 2 In.	50
Buttonhook, Brass, Steel, 6¼ In.	75
Celluloid, Bride & Groom, Painted Side-Glancing Eyes, 4 In.	65
Chalkware, Frowning Face, 1930s, 12 In.	89
Composition, Movable Arms, Watermelon Smile, Rosy Cheeks, Side-Glancing Eyes, 12 In.	64
Placecard, Sitting, Playing Mandolin, c.1913, 3 x 1¼ x 2¼ In.	275
Plate, Girl & Boy, Cap & Scarf, Socks, Bavaria, 5 In.	22
Salt & Pepper, Arms Down, Gilt Top, Bavaria, 3 In.	20
Salt & Pepper, Crying, Baby, Bisque, Lego, Japan, 3 In.	26
Sand Pail, Kewpie Beach, Castle, Scooties, Tin Lithograph, Rose O'Neill, 1937, 3 x 3 In.	800
Vase, Bud, Flocked Teddy Bear, Marked, Crown, 5¼ In.	695
Vase, Sucking Thumb, Lefton, c.1950, 4 x 3 In.	45

KING'S ROSE, *see Soft Paste category.*

KITCHEN utensils of all types, from eggbeaters to bowls, are collected today. Handmade wooden and metal items, like ladles and apple peelers, were made in the early nineteenth century. Mass-produced pieces, like iron apple peelers and graniteware, were made in the nineteenth century. Also included in this category are utensils used for other household chores, such as laundry and cleaning. Other kitchen wares are listed under manufacturers' names or under Advertising, Iron, Tool, or Wooden.

Berry Scoop, Wood, Triangular Scoop, Handle, Red, 11 x 10 In.	117
Blocking Knife, Shoe Peg, Saddle, Oak, Softwood, Wrought Iron, File, c.1800, 15 x 6 x 2½ In. ..	35
Board, Baking, Spade Shape, 14¾ x 24 In.	175
Board, Cutting, Chestnut, Heart Handle, 21¾ x 11 In.	106
Board, Cutting, Pine, Multiple Boards Joined By 2 Cleats, Original Green Paint, 1856, 29 x 23 In. ..	339
Board, Dough, Softwood, 24 x 17½ In.	35
Bottle Corker, Turned Wood Handle, Cast Iron, France, 26½ x 19 In.	468
Bowl, Wood, Lid, Round, Red, Carved From Solid, 7 x 7 In.	1210
Box, Knife, George III, Mahogany, Ebony Inlay, Shaped, Bowed Front, 14 x 8¾ In., Pair	750
Box, Scouring, Pine, Hinging, Nailed Construction, Gray Paint, 19 x 9 In.	375
Broiler, Electric, Black & Chrome, Bullet Shape, 1960s, 16 In.	120
Broiler, Electric, Chrome, Quik Chef, c.1952, 9 x 13½ In.	129
Broiler, Rotating, Iron, Scrolling, Stylized Heart, 3-Footed, Straight Handle, 1700s, 4¼ In.	702

K

Kenton Hills, Vase, Lamp, Flowers, Trees, Birds, Nude Male & Female, Marked, D. Seyler, 8 In.
$142

Humler & Nolan

Kew Blas, Tumbler, Gold Iridescent, Panel Optic, Panels, 1900-30, 3 ¾ In.
$93

Jeffrey S. Evans

Kewpie, Bisque Head, Brown Glass Eyes, Pink Dress, J.D. Kestner, Marked, 1913, 13 In.
$13,450

Ruby Lane

Iron Pans Smooth

Vintage cast-iron pans were hand-cast in sand, while modern pieces are made by a different method that leaves a rough surface. The old ones bring the highest prices.

Kitchen, Butcher Block, Maple Chopping Block, Tapered Square Legs, c.1910, 30 x 20 x 20 In.
$549

New Orleans Auction Galleries

Kitchen, Butter Stamp, Eagle, Softwood, Half Round, Pennsylvania, 1800s, 3 ½ x 7 In.
$2,242

Hess Auction Group

Kitchen, Butter Stamp, Maple, Carved, Cow, Fence, Tree, 2-Part Construction, 1800s, 4 In.
$295

Hess Auction Group

Kitchen, Butter Stamp, Pineapple, Leaves, Maple, Pennsylvania, 4 ½ In.
$59

Hess Auction Group

Kitchen, Butter Stamp, Wheat, Double Sheaf Design, Handle, Lower, 1800s, 5 ¼ x 3 x 5 In.
$240

Garth's Auctioneers & Appraisers

K

Kitchen, Churn, Iron, Tin, Patented Dec. 18, 1917, Dazey, 25 In.
$94

Hess Auction Group

Kitchen, Cookie Board, Springerle, Pastry, Maple, 12 Panels, Intaglio, Lancaster County, c.1850, 8 In.
$70

Hess Auction Group

Kitchen, Dough Box, Pine, Bootjack Legs, Unattached Lid, Sectioned Interior, 1800s, 31 x 30 In.
$330

Eldred's Auctioneers and Appraisers

Kitchen, Dough Box, Pine, Dovetailed, Canted Sides, 2-Board Top, Footed, c.1850, 26 x 47 In.
$720

Garth's Auctioneers & Appraisers

Kitchen, Dough Box, Softwood, Red Paint, Pennsylvania, 1800s; 11 x 33 x 14 In.
$130

Hess Auction Group

Kitchen, Dough Box, Wood, Red Paint, Dovetailed, Turned Splayed Legs, Pa., c.1790, 29 x 50 In.
$826

Hess Auction Group

Kitchen, Grain Bin, Cherry, Paneled Doors, 3 Drawers, Divided Bin, c.1850, 90 In.
$990

Garth's Auctioneers & Appraisers

TIP
All Pyrex, old or new, is safe to use in the microwave.

Kitchen, Herb Crusher, Iron, Boat Shape Trough, Cutting Wheel, Oak Handle, c.1840, 16 In.
$325

Hess Auction Group

Kitchen, Ice Bucket, Nantucket Basket Style, Lid, Karen Bullock, Cape Cod, 1900s, 10 In.
$469

Eldred's Auctioneers and Appraisers

Kitchen, Mincing Blade, Double, 2 Turned Handles, Cast Iron, c.1850, 9 ½ x 22 In.
$1,000

Eldred's Auctioneers and Appraisers

Kitchen, Mold, Cheese, Heart Shape, Tin, Pierced, Applied Feet, Hanging Ring, Pa., 1800s, 3 ¼ In.
$118

Hess Auction Group

K

Broiler, Rotating, Snake Handle, Star, Iron, 35 In.		117
Butcher Block, Maple Chopping Block, Tapered Square Legs, c.1910, 30 x 20 x 20 In...... *illus*		549
Butter Mold, look under Mold, Butter in this category.		
Butter Paddle, Maple, Shield Shape Bowl, Carved Dog Head, Heart, Cross, 10 ½ In.		536
Butter Stamp, Double Wheat, 4 ½ x 2 ½ In.		169
Butter Stamp, Eagle, Shield, Star, Arrow, 3 ¾ In.		156
Butter Stamp, Eagle, Softwood, Half Round, Pennsylvania, 1800s, 3 ½ x 7 In.................. *illus*		2242
Butter Stamp, Half Round, Eagle, Handle, Pine, 1800s, 3 ½ x 7 In.		793
Butter Stamp, Hardwood, Carved, Stylized Tulip, Sunflower Petal Border, 1800s, 4 ½ x 3 ⅝ In.		265
Butter Stamp, Heart, c.1900, 4 ½ x 3 In.		175
Butter Stamp, Lollipop Shape, 2-Sided, Initialed ZSM, 1800s, 9 In.		732
Butter Stamp, Lollipop Shape, 2-Sided, Tulips, 1816, 8 ¾ In.		2928
Butter Stamp, Lollipop, Hex Symbol, 1800s, 7 ½ In...		292
Butter Stamp, Lollipop, Stock, Walnut, Sprig, 4 Leaves, 1840, 2 ⅞ x 3 ⅞ In.		290
Butter Stamp, Maple, Bird & Floral Carving, 4 ⅝ In...		354
Butter Stamp, Maple, Carved, Cow, Fence, Tree, 2-Part Construction, 1800s, 4 In. .... *illus*		295
Butter Stamp, Pine, Lollipop, Shape Radial Design, 7 ¾ In.		324
Butter Stamp, Pineapple, Leaves, Maple, Pennsylvania, 4 ½ In. .... *illus*		59
Butter Stamp, Round, Eagle, Clutching Arrows, Flanked By Pinwheels, Pine, 5 x 4 ¾ In.		3416
Butter Stamp, Tulip, Burl, Round Case, Lid, Knob Handle, 3 In.................................		330
Butter Stamp, Wheat, Double Sheaf Design, Handle, Lower, 1800s, 5 ¼ x 3 x 5 In. .... *illus*		240
Butter Stamp, Wood, Wheat Design, Half Round, Roped Edge, 7 In.		201
Cake Box, Pine, Bentwood, Nails, Lid, Painted Flowers, Footed, Continental, 1800s, 11 In.		1920
Canister, Lid, Flour, Tin, Bail Handle, Red, Gold Design, c.1890, 31 x 19 In.................		422
Carrier, Utensil, Softwood, Yellow, Heart Cutout Handle, 5 ½ x 15 ¼ In.		165
Cheese Wheel Trolley, Mahogany, Curved, Applied Half Turnings, Casters, 6 ½ x 16 ½ In.		210
Churn, Barrel Shape, Staves, Blue, 24 In..		234
Churn, Dasher Type, 42 In.		117
Churn, Iron, Tin, Patented Dec. 18, 1917, Dazey, 25 In. .... *illus*		94
Churn, Oak, Hickory, Bentwood Hoops, Rosehead Tacks, c.1900, 24 In.		555
Churn, Rectangular, Crank In Front, No. 1 Lightning Churn, 16 x 12 In.		146
Churn, Wood, Metal Bands, Tapered, Iron Hardware, Crank Handle, c.1880		850
Churn, Wood, Yellow, The Lightning, Crank Handle, Cupples Mfg., c.1900, 14 x 12 x 14 In.		170
Coconut Grater, Wood, Rabbit, Iron Spoon, Sawtooth Edge, Thailand, 1960s...........................		1250
Coffee Grinders are listed in the Coffee Mill category.		
Coffee Mills are listed in their own category.		
Cookie Board, Carved Walnut, Tin Border, Mold, German Man, Hat, 1800s, 23 x 8 In.............		840
Cookie Board, Springerle, Pastry, Maple, 12 Panels, Intaglio, Lancaster County, c.1850, 8 In. *illus*		70
Cookie Cutter, Aluminum, Heart, Club, Diamond, Circle, Package, 25 Cents, 1960s, 4 Piece...		10
Cookie Cutter, Mermaid, Tin, 6 In.		68
Cookie Cutter, Mickey Mouse, Tinned Steel, 1930s, 6 ½ x 5 ¼ In.............................		299
Cookie Cutter, Snoopy & Great Halloween Pumpkin, Hallmark, 1974, 6 ½ x 5 ¾ In.		55
Cup, Coconut Shell, Diamonds, Geometric Bands, 1863, 3 ¼ x 2 ½ In.		132
Dough Bowl, Cypress, Rectangular, Angled, Creole, 1800s, 3 ¾ x 33 ½ In.....................		425
Dough Bowl, Wood, Round, 19 ½ x 5 x 2 ¾ In...		66
Dough Box, Handmade, Pine, Patina, c.1800s, 35 ½ x 16 x 13 In...............................		385
Dough Box, Original Paint, Robin's-Egg Blue, Pennsylvania, 16 x 28 x 8 In.		925
Dough Box, Pine, Bootjack Legs, Unattached Lid, Sectioned Interior, 1800s, 31 x 30 In. . *illus*		330
Dough Box, Pine, Dovetailed, Canted Sides, 2-Board Top, Footed, c.1850, 26 x 47 In........ *illus*		720
Dough Box, Proofing, Country Pine, Farmhouse, c.1860s, 43 x 19 x 36 In.		975
Dough Box, Softwood, Red Paint, Pennsylvania, 1800s, 11 x 33 x 14 In. .... *illus*		130
Dough Box, Stand, Turned Legs, Poplar, c.1760, 28 x 54 In.......................................		1367
Dough Box, Walnut, Removable Top, Scalloped Apron, Cabriole Legs, c.1810, 27 x 56 In.		1220
Dough Box, Wood, Red Paint, Dovetailed, Turned Splayed Legs, Pa., c.1790, 29 x 50 In... *illus*		826
Doughnut Cutter, Metal, Wood Handle, 6-Sided, Revolving Wheel Roller, Houpt, 12 In..........		200
Flour Bin, Tin, Glass Window, Hoosier Sellers, 25 ½ In...		130
Flour Sifter, Cornish Ware, T.G. Green, Marked, 1930s, 5 In..................................		130
Flour Sifter, English Brass, Shaker, c.1760, 4 In...		130
Food Chopper, Stainless Steel, 3 Blades, Wood Handle, Foley, Marked.........................		20

Kitchen, Pantry Box, Bentwood, Iron Tacks, Compass, Stars, Checkerboards, c.1850, 4 x 9 In.
$840

Garth's Auctioneers & Appraisers

Kitchen, Peeler, Apple, Mixed Hardwoods, 19th Century, 5 ½ x 9 x 14 In.
$70

Hess Auction Group

Kitchen, Peeler, Apple, Mixed Wood, Wrought Iron, Plank Base, Painted, 1800s, 10 x 14 In.
$236

Hess Auction Group

Kitchen, Rack, Hanging, Roosters, 8 Hooks, 4-Bar Cage, Iron, c.1900, 13 ¾ x 16 ¼ In.
$556

Jeffrey S. Evans

K

Kitchen, Rack, Skewer Set, Diamond Shape, Ram's Horn Style Hooks, 6 Skewers, Iron, 9¾ In.

$409

Jeffrey S. Evans

TIP
Use a Depression glass or plastic knife to cut lettuce. The lettuce won't turn brown.

Kitchen, Roaster, Hearth, Wrought Iron, Swivel Handle, 6 Meat Hooks, Pa., 1800s, 23 x 15 In.

$265

Hess Auction Group

Fork, Flesh, Flowers, Vines, Wrought, Iron, 17½ In.	183
Fork, Flesh, Wrought Iron, Wriggle Work, Fish, Tulip, Thistle, c.1800, 10¼ In.	560
Fork, Flesh, Wrought, Iron, Hanging Hook, 18¼ In.	354
Grain Bin, Cherry, Paneled Doors, 3 Drawers, Divided Bin, c.1850, 90 In. *illus*	990
Griddle, Round, Wrought, Iron, c.1900, 13 x 15 In.	75
Grill, Charcoal, Metal, Wire Basket, Portable, Top Handles, Scroll Feet, 1940s, 12 x 13 In.	75
Herb Crusher, Iron, Boat Shape Trough, Cutting Wheel, Oak Handle, c.1840, 16 In. *illus*	325
Ice Bucket, Nantucket Basket Style, Lid, Karen Bullock, Cape Cod, 1900s, 10 In. *illus*	469
Iron, Coal, Cast, Wood Handle, c.1920	123
Iron, Copper Latch, Javeat P. Led., c.1870	320
Iron, Electric, Copper Base, Bakelite, Sunbeam Ironmaster, Model, A-9, c.1943	50
Iron, Electric, Prilect Universal Electric, England, Plaid Zipper Case, Travel, 1930s	22
Iron, Self-Heating, Peerless, American Specialty Co., 1860-90	220
Iron, Silk, Coal, Brass, Enameled Handle, Dragon Design, Chinese, 4¾ x 2½ x 1 In.	36
Iron, Steam, The Monitor, Black Handle, Pat. Apr 14, 1903, 9 x 3 x 7 In.	30
Kettle, Apple Butter, Copper, Rolled Rim, Iron Bail Handle, 1800s, 11½ In.	128
Kettle, Brass, Wide Cylindrical Neck, Wrought Iron Ring Handles, 12½ x 20 In.	77
Kettle, Sugar, Iron, 1800s, 26 x 55 In.	2318
Knife Box, Dovetailed Constructions, Shaped, 2 Compartments, 15 x 9 In.	263
Match Holders can be found in their own category.	
Match Safes can be found in their own category.	
Measuring Cups, Copper, Brass Handles, 5 Sizes, France, 1950s-60s, 2 x 3½ In., 5 Piece	165
Meat Rack, Hanging, Domed, Circle, 10 Hooks, Iron, 10½ x 13 In.	397
Mincing Blade, Double, 2 Turned Handles, Cast Iron, c.1850, 9½ x 22 In. *illus*	1000
Mixer, Milkshake, Single Serving, Metal, Stainless Steel, Electric, Arnold, 1920s, 18 In.	75
Mixing Bowl, Blue Heaven Atomic, Fire-King	98
Mixing Bowl, Hexagon Optic, Green, Ruffled, 6 In.	23
Mixing Bowl, Tulips, Fire-King, 7¾ x 4¾ In.	30
Mold, Cake, Bunny, Seated, Iron, Griswold, 1900-50, 10 x 11 In.	228
Mold, Cheese, Heart Shape, Tin, Pierced, Applied Feet, Hanging Ring, Pa., 1800s, 3¼ In. *illus*	118
Mold, Marzipan, Heart, Scalloped Shell, Flowers, Anchor, Germany, 11¼ x 9¼ In.	183
Mortar & Pestle, Walnut, Ring Turned, 1700s, 11 In.	60
Mortar & Pestle, Wood, Burl, c.1745, 9 In.	396
Pail, Apple Butter, Brass, Swing Handle, 9 x 13 In.	70
Pantry Box, Bentwood, Iron Tacks, Compass, Stars, Checkerboards, c.1850, 4 x 9 In. *illus*	840
Peeler, Apple, Corer, Cast Iron, Hand Crank, Marked, Rival No. 2, 1889, 15 x 27 In.	600
Peeler, Apple, Mixed Hardwood, 19th Century, 5½ x 9 x 14 In. *illus*	70
Peeler, Apple, Mixed Wood, Wrought Iron, Plank Base, Painted, 1800s, 10 x 14 In. *illus*	236
Peg Rail, German Style, Hooked Pegs, Plate Shelf, 2 Balusters, Red, Green, c.1850, 62 x 5½ x 14 In.	525
Percolator, Aluminum, Glass Knob, Century, Made In U.S.A., 1950s, 7 Cup	25
Pie Crimper, Pastry Wheel, Wood, Turned Handle, Ball Finial, Etched Handle, France, 1960s	15
Pie Crimper, Turned Baluster Handle, Brass, Ball Finial, c.1800, 5 In.	59
Pizza Paddle, Hand Forged Iron, Barley Twist Handle, France, c.1900, 8 x 21 In.	85
Pot, Metal, Straight-Sided, Red, Double Handles, 28½ x 22 In.	234
Rack, Hanging, Roosters, 8 Hooks, 4-Bar Cage, Iron, c.1900, 13¾ x 16¼ In. *illus*	556
Rack, Skewer Set, Diamond Shape, Ram's Horn Style Hooks, 6 Skewers, Iron, 9¾ In. *illus*	409
Reamers are listed in their own category.	
Roaster, Hearth, Wrought Iron, Swivel Handle, 6 Meat Hooks, Pa., 1800s, 23 x 15 In. *illus*	265
Roaster, Meat, Hearth, Tin, 5-Point Star, Door, Grease Spout, Pa., 1800s, 11 x 12 In. *illus*	590
Sadiron, Charles Hyatt, Pat. Aug. 9, 1870	475
Sadiron, Double Ended, Wood Handle, Colebrookdale Iron Co. No. 1, 6½ x 3 In.	100
Sadiron, Double Pointed, Detachable Walnut Handle, Hollow, c.1900, 4 In.	25
Sadiron, Wood Handle, Marked, Asbestos 72-B, c.1900, 6½ In.	29
Salt & Pepper Shakers are listed in their own category.	
Sieve, Tole, Perfection, Flour, Wheat Stalks, 30 In.	105
Skillet, Griswold, No. 4, Slant Logo, Heat Ring	176
Skillet, Hearth, Iron, Wrought, Tripod, Beveled Handle, Hanging Loop, 16½ In.	212
Skimmer, Iron, Flattened Iron, Hanging Hook, Stamped J. Schmidt, 1847, 20 In.	212
Skimmer, Wrought Iron, Brass Bowl, Copper Rivets, Rattail Support, 20 In.	354
Spatula, Wrought Iron, Flattened Handle, Hanging Eyelet, 16½ In.	53

Spice Box, Cherry, Slant Lid, Fitted Interior, Dovetailed, Pa., 1800s, 12 x 10 In.	*illus*	767
Spice Box, Hanging, Mixed Woods, Stencils, 8 Drawers, 16¾ x 11 In.	*illus*	130
Spice Box, Tortoiseshell & Walnut Veneer, 11 Drawers, Footed Base, c. 1775, 13½ x 16 In.		1250
Strainer, Tin, Heart Shape, 3 Punch Shape Circles, 14 x 14 In.		555
Sugar Cutter, Wrought Iron, Scissor Action, Keyhole Handle, 1800s, 12 In., Pair	*illus*	165
Sugar Cutter, Wrought Iron, Scissor Form, 9 In.	*illus*	130
Toaster, Cornstalk, Snakehead Tripod, Loop Handle, Rack, Heart, Iron, 1780, 14 x 16 x 7½ In.		450
Toaster, Hearth, Wrought Iron, Swivel Handle, Triple Rod Racks, 1800s, 20 x 14 In.	*illus*	70
Top-O-Stove Potato Bake, Box, 7 x 4 In.		687
Trammel Hook, Wrought Iron, Twisted, Entwined Loops, Fireplace, 61½ x 3½ In.		110
Trammel, Candleholder, Sawtooth Ratchet, Tin Cup, Adjustable, c.1810, 36 To 56 In.	*illus*	1180
Trencher, Maple, Rectangular, Rounded Ends, Robin's-Egg Blue Exterior, 5 x 20 In.		242
Trivet, see Trivet category.		
Urn, Cutlery, George III, Mahogany, 28½ x 15½ In., Pair		3750
Waffle Iron, Square, 4 Sections, Spring Handle, Pedestal, Griswold, 1908, 15 In.		245

KNIFE collectors usually specialize in a single type. In the 1960s, the United States government passed a law that required knife manufacturers to mark their knives with the country of origin. This seemed to encourage the collectors, and knife collecting became an interest of a large group of people. All types of knives are collected, from top quality twentieth-century examples to old bone- or pearl-handled knives in excellent condition.

Alaskan Skinner, Brown Micarta, Bird's-Head Pommel, 1964-78, 7¼ In.	360
Ax, Brown Micarta, Exotic Hardwood, Smooth White Bone, 13⅞ In.	650
Ax, Marble Safety Axe Co., Molded Handle, c.1903, 10 In.	986
Bowie, Saber Ground Clip Point Blade, Ivory Handle, Brass C-Guard & Pommel, Cooper, 14 In.	1188
Brown Macarta, Brass C-Guard, Brass Pommel, 18 In.	900
Ceremonial, Iron Blade, Wood Carving, Kuba, Democratic Republic Of Congo, 4 x 2 x 17 In.	63
Dagger, Bone, Ceremonial, Stacked Carving, Mythical Figures, Tibet, 1800s	480
Dagger, Mughal, Floral Carved Jade Hilt, Steel Blade, Sheath, 20 In.	1875
Dagger, Mughal, Ram's-Head Rock Crystal Hilt, Gold Decorated Blade, Sheath, 17 In.	938
Dagger, Teak Wood, Steel, Carved Handle, Brass, Sharpened, 1900s, 14 In.	56
Dirk, Flat Ground Spear Point Blade, Black Macarta, Brass Mounts, 17 In.	660
Hardwood, Chancay, Ritual, Scepter, Ancient Patina, Small Monkey Figurine On Top, 11 In.	250
J. Rogers & Sons, Stag Horn, Sheffield, England, Hallmark, Silver & Leather Sheath, 7 In.	1220
Pocket, Brass Handles, 2 Blades, 1910s, 1⅝ x 1⅛ In.	475
Saber Ground Clip Point Blade, Brass Guard, Leather Sheath, Cooper, Aluminum, 15 In.	510
Saber Ground Clip Point Blade, Brass Oval Guard, Aluminum Handled, 13¼ In.	510
Saber Ground Clip Point Blade, Walrus Ivory Handle, Brass Full Guard, Pommel, 9 In.	688

KNOWLES, *Taylor & Knowles items may be found in the KTK and Lotus Ware categories.*

KOSTA, the oldest Swedish glass factory, was founded in 1742. During the 1920s through the 1950s, many pieces of original design were made at the factory. Kosta and Boda merged with Afors in 1964 and created the Afors Group in 1971. In 1976, the name Kosta Boda was adopted. The company merged with Orrefors in 1990 and is still working.

KOSTA

Charger, Sanded Glass, Koi Fish, Black, Amber, Paul Hoff, 12¼ In.	187
Sculpture, Cast Glass, Painted, Wood, Leather, Bertil Vallien, 13 x 12 In. Sq.	6250
Vase, Vicki Lindstrand, Green, Crystal Foot, Signed Under Base, 7¾ x 5½ In.	124

KPM refers to Berlin porcelain, but the same initials were used alone and in combination with other symbols by several German porcelain makers. They include the Konigliche Porzellan Manufaktur of Berlin, initials used in mark, 1823–47; Meissen, 1723–24 only; Krister Porzellan Manufaktur in Waldenburg, after 1831; Kranichfelder Porzellan Manufaktur in Kranichfeld, after 1903; and the Krister Porzellan Manufaktur in Scheibe, after 1838.

K.P.M

Figurine, Ariadne, J.G. Muller, c.1785, 5¼ In.	122
KPM, Lithophane, see also Lithophane category.	

Kitchen, Roaster, Meat, Hearth, Tin, 5-Point Star, Door, Grease Spout, Pa., 1800s, 11 x 12 In.
$590

Hess Auction Group

Kitchen, Spice Box, Cherry, Slant Lid, Fitted Interior, Dovetailed, Pa., 1800s, 12 x 10 In.
$767

Hess Auction Group

Kitchen, Spice Box, Hanging, Mixed Woods, Stencils, 8 Drawers, 16¾ x 11 In.
$130

Hess Auction Group

K

TIP
To be sure your clean iron pan is dry, heat it on a stove burner for a minute.

Kitchen, Sugar Cutter, Wrought Iron, Scissor Action, Keyhole Handle, 1800s, 12 In., Pair
$165

Hess Auction Group

Kitchen, Sugar Cutter, Wrought Iron, Scissor Form, 9 In.
$130

Hess Auction Group

Kitchen, Toaster, Hearth, Wrought Iron, Swivel Handle, Triple Rod Racks, 1800s, 20 x 14 In.
$70

Hess Auction Group

Kitchen, Trammel, Candleholder, Sawtooth Ratchet, Tin Cup, Adjustable, c.1810, 36 To 56 In.
$1,180

Hess Auction Group

Mustache Cup, Carnations, Pink, Orange, 2¾ x 3 In.	18
Painting On Porcelain, Children Reading Book, Giltwood Frame, 1800s, 15 x 17 In.	3690
Plaque, 2 Boys Eating Grapes, 1900s, 11 x 8 In.	1476
Plaque, After The Blind Nydia, Ebonized Frame, 13¼ x 8 In.	2760
Plaque, Brunette Beauty, Multicolor Enamel, 1900s, 9 x 11 In.	738
Plaque, Couple, Doorway, Urn, Classical Robes, 7 x 5 In.	1270
Plaque, La Belle Chocolatiere, Frame, Oval Stamp, Marked, c.1900, 10¾ x 8 In. *illus*	960
Plaque, Mary Magdalene, Painted, Frame, c.1825, 9 x 13 In.	2820
Plaque, Mary, Henry Bucket, Hand Painted, Oval Frame, 1800s, 7¼ x 5 In.	708
Plaque, Monk In Cellar, Frame, 12 x 9 In.	2160
Plaque, Multicolor Decoration, Carved Giltwood Frame, Oval, 1900s, 6¾ x 4⅞ In.	984
Plaque, Multicolor, Carved Giltwood Frame, Maiden With Hat, Oval, 1900s, 11 x 8 In.	2214
Plaque, Nymph, Multicolor Decoration, Giltwood Frame, 1900s, 9¾ x 7¾ In.	3690
Plaque, Peasant Girl, Holding Flowers, Giltwood Frame, 1900s, 13 x 7¾ In.	2952
Plaque, Topless Woman, Giltwood Frame, 9½ x 6¼ In.	3125
Plaque, Topless Woman, Long Hair, Draped Hips, Red Draped Seat, 9 x 6¾ In.	4687
Plaque, William Shakespeare, Oval, Pierced Giltwood Frame, c.1900, 5½ x 4 In.	563
Plaque, Woman, Resting Hand On Chin, Giltwood Frame, 1900s, 9⅜ x 6¼ In.	2337
Plaque, Woman, Wearing Hat, Ruffled Dress, Flowers, Oval, 1900s, 6⅞ x 5 In.	523
Plaque, Woman, Wearing White, Holding Oil Lamp, Veiled, 1900s, 11 x 8½ In.	1046
Plaque, Woman, White Dress, Cherub, Beach, Lake, Porcelain, 9¾ x 7⅜ In.	2750
Platter, Brown, Gray, Gilt, Oval, 17½ In.	101
Urn, Dark Pink, Vignettes, Flowers, Putto, Grape Bunch Knop, Ram's-Head Mask, 18 In.	175
Urn, Lid, Seaside Scene, Molded Gilt Snake, Handles, 1800s, 17 x 19 In., Pair *illus*	720
Vase, Raised Blueberries, Gilt & Green, Baluster, Art Nouveau, Signed, 14 In.	4375

K.T.&K. CHINA **KTK** are the initials of the Knowles, Taylor & Knowles Company of East Liverpool, Ohio, founded by Isaac W. Knowles in 1853. The company made utilitarian wares, hotel china, and dinnerware. It made belleek and the fine bone china known as Lotus Ware from 1891 to 1896. The company merged with American Ceramic Corporation in 1928. It closed in 1934. Lotus Ware is listed in its own category in this book.

Chop Plate, Bouquet, Gold Swag Trim, c.1920	19
Pitcher, Moss Rose, Gold Rim, c.1870, 6½ x 7 In.	75

 KUTANI porcelain was made in Japan after the mid-seventeenth century. Most of the pieces found today are nineteenth century. Collectors often use the term *Kutani* to refer to just the later, colorful pieces decorated with red, gold, and black pictures of warriors, animals, and birds.

Bowl, 3 Phoenix Shape, Cranes, Brocade Mons, 3 x 5 In.	240
Bowl, Fluted Flower Form, Phoenix, Cranes, Green Vine Border, 1800s, 3 x 5 In. *illus*	240
Bowl, Man, Riding Carp, Fan, Flowers, Shaped Edge, 7 In. *illus*	369
Bowl, Short Stem Foot, Outdoor Scene, Peach Festival Crowd, Patterned Band, 2⅞ x 6 In.	123
Bowl, Warmly Colored Tea, Golden Cloud, Pines, Forest, 1926, 5 x 2½ In.	395
Charger, Blooming Flowers, Birds, Round Blue Center, Vase, Blooming Tree, 14⅝ x 2 In.	71
Charger, Children, Scroll, Mountain Landscape, Symbols, Blue, Green, Copper Red, 19 In.	549
Charger, Peacock, Rock, Chrysanthemums, Gilt, Orange, Red, 18 x 2⅝ In.	82
Charger, Peonies, Flying Bird, Mountain, Deer, Temple Gate, Sailboats, 18 x 3 In.	106
Charger, Rust Red, Rooster, Hen, Flower, Songbird, 14 In.	480
Charger, Samurai, Kneeling, Woman Peeks In, Brown Walls, Green Floor, Gilt, 18 x 2⅜ In.	224
Charger, Samurai, Teacher, Lady, Multicolor, Calligraphy, 18¼ x 2 In.	236
Charger, Scholar, Table, Drawing, Rust Red, 15¾ In.	175
Cup, Karatsu Ware, Embodiment, Japan, 1980, 3 x 2 In.	200
Dish, Shoki, Demon Queller Around Skeletons, Brocade Pattern Along Rim, 1800s, 14 In.	510
Figure, Scholar, Blue, White, Bisque, 1900s, 11 In. *illus*	180
Jar, Lid, Relief Dragon Handles, Mythical Beast Finial, Landscape, 13¼ In.	330
Lamp, Gilt, Flared Rim, Men Surrounding, 1900s, 17 In., Pair *illus*	180
Vase, Detailed Pagoda Among Pine Trees, Marked, 1800s, 11 In.	96

Vase, Double Phoenix, Fluted Body, Neck, 10 Facets, Sharkskin, 10 x 5½ In.	106
Vase, Doves, Red Ground, Blue Band, 24½ In., Pair	2000
Vase, Peacocks & Flowers, Red, Gold, Oval, Flared Neck, 1800s, 9 In.	60
Vase, Phoenix, Elephant Head Handles, 14¼ x 12 In.	118
Vase, Slender Neck, Compressed Body, Copper, Red, Gilt, Cartouches, Signed, c.1925, 13 In.	625

L.G. WRIGHT Glass Company of New Martinsville, West Virginia, started selling glassware in 1937. Founder "Si" Wright contracted with Ohio and West Virginia glass factories to reproduce popular pressed glass patterns like Rose & Snow, Baltimore Pear, and Three Face, and opalescent patterns like Daisy & Fern and Swirl. Collectors can tell the difference between the original glasswares and L.G. Wright reproductions because of colors and differences in production techniques. Some L.G. Wright items are marked with an underlined *W* in a circle. Items that were made from old Northwood molds have an altered Northwood mark—an angled line was added to the *N* to make it look like a *W*. Collectors refer to this mark as "the wobbly W." The L.G. Wright factory was closed and the existing molds sold in 1999. Some of the molds are still being used.

Hobnail, Rose Bowl, Ruby, 3 x 4 In.	54
Moon & Stars, Compote, Amber, Flared, 6 x 7 In.	32
Syrup, Lid, Cobalt Blue, White Opalescent Spots, Applied Blue Reeded Handle, 6¼ In. .... *illus*	174

LACQUER is a type of varnish. Collectors are most interested in the Chinese and Japanese lacquer wares made from the Japanese varnish tree. Lacquer wares are made from wood with many coats of lacquer. Sometimes the piece is carved or decorated with ivory or metal inlay.

Basket, Vegetable, Wood, Hand Painted, Foo Dogs, Chinese, 1900s	42
Basket, Wood, Dark Crimson Ground, Black, Gilt Designs, Chinese, 1900s, 26 In.	163
Bowl, Paulownia Design, Red, Brown, Gold, Footed, Japan, 5½ In. .... *illus*	48
Box, Block, Lid, 2 Leafy Plants, Inlaid, Eggshell, Dragonfly, Sprinkled Red, 1985, 6 x 6 x 3 In.	190
Box, Dome, Leather Covered, Gilt, Hardware, 1900s, 5 x 17 x 5 In.	53
Box, Fitted With Small Boxes, Pietra Dura Inlay, Children, On Elephant, Relief, c.1870, 2 x 4 In.	1920
Box, Hinged Panels, Small Compartments, c.1850, 7½ x 17½ In.	48
Box, Inlay, Circular, Daikoku, 7 Boxes Within, Gods Of Good Fortune, 1800s, 4 In. Diam.	1680
Box, Mother-Of-Pearl, Hinged Lid, Gilt Highlights, Red, Paper Lined Interior, 5½ x 11 In.	424
Box, Paste Container, Circular, Wood, Rubbed-In Gold Powders, Protective Layer, 1 x 3⅛ In.	250
Bucket, Red, Banded, Latch, Chinese, 18 In.	250
Cup, Lid, Black, Gold, Brocade, Flower, Vine, Japan, 2¾ In.	216
Cup, Lid, Black, Gold, Paulownia, Chrysanthemum, Japan, 2¾ In.	240
Dish, Black, White Gold Foil, Painted, Stylized Waves, White-Gold Brushed, 1990, 6½ In.	350
Dish, Irregular Pattern Gold Foil, Shell Inlays, 6 x 4⅜ x 9/16 In.	750
Dish, Wood Grain, Protective Layer, Deep Reddish Gloss, ¹³/₁₆ x 8 1/16 In.	300
Figurine, Wood, Deer, Marbled Red & Black Lacquer, Xipi Style, Chinese, 26 x 23 In. ...... *illus*	1220
Kettle, Black, Gold, Flowers, 8 In.	120
Letter Box, Black, Mother-Of-Pearl Inlay, Flowers, 4½ x 9 In.	160
Pitcher, Water, Lid, Red, Angled Semicircle Handle, Wood, 1900s, 15 In. .... *illus*	43
Plate, Dark Brown, Woven, Natural Split Bamboo, Hexagonal, Glossy Gold, 1900s, 6¾ In.	220
Potpourri, Soft Paste Porcelain, Gilt Bronze, Louis XV Style, Rocaille Base, 1800s, 7 x 5 In.	500
Screen, Red, Landscapes & Figures, 6 Panels, Qing Dynasty, 66 x 14 In. Each	840
Shrine, Bifold Door, Gilt, Leaves, Gallery Interior, 35½ x 18½ In.	728
Tea Scoop, Red & Gold, Black & Gold, 1900s, 7 In., 2 Piece	75
Tray, Inland Mother-Of-Pearl, Shinchiku Kinen Yamaguchi, 14 In.	120
Tray, Wood Decorated, Abstract Pattern, Grays, Gold, Silver, Red, Dark Tones, 12 x 10 In.	480
Trinket Box, Magic Flower, Black, Fedoskino, Russia, 1956, 3 x 8¾ In.	152
Vase, Copper, Brass, Silver, Overlapping Squares, Circle, Hammered, Jean Dunand, 5¾ x 4 In.	3000
Vase, Metal, Black, Red, Elongated Triangles, Copper Liner, Dunand, France, 6 x 7 In. ..... *illus*	37500
Vase, Metal, Eggshell, Copper, Cream, Black Cracks, Paul Mergier, 4¾ x 6 In.	1750
Wall Panel, Carved, Cranes, Prunus, Bamboo, Giltwood Frame, Chinese, 32 x 16 In. ...... *illus*	183
Writing Box, Gold Leaf, Flowers, Burmese Shwe-Zawa, 14 x 2¾ x 4½ In.	125

KPM, Plaque, La Belle Chocolatiere, Frame, Oval Stamp, Marked, c.1900, 10¾ x 8 In.
$960

Neal Auction Co.

KPM, Urn, Lid, Seaside Scene, Molded Gilt Snake, Handles, 1800s, 17 x 19 In., Pair
$720

Brunk Auctions

Kutani, Bowl, Fluted Flower Form, Phoenix, Cranes, Green Vine Border, 1800s, 3 x 5 In.
$240

Eldred's Auctioneers and Appraisers

L

LALIQUE

Kutani, Bowl, Man, Riding Carp, Fan, Flowers, Shaped Edge, 7 In.
$369

Leland Little Auctions

Kutani, Figure, Scholar, Blue, White, Bisque, 1900s, 11 In.
$180

Eldred's Auctioneers and Appraisers

Kutani, Lamp, Gilt, Flared Rim, Men Surrounding, 1900s, 17 In., Pair
$180

Brunk Auctions

LADY HEAD VASE, *see Head Vase.*

LALIQUE glass and jewelry were made by Rene Lalique (1860–1945) in Paris, France, between the 1890s and his death in 1945. Beginning in 1921 he had a manufacturing plant in Alsace. The glass was molded, pressed, and engraved in Art Nouveau and Art Deco styles. Most pieces were marked with the signature *R. Lalique*. Lalique glass is still being made. Most pieces made after 1945 bear the mark *Lalique*. After 1978 the registry mark was added and the mark became *Lalique ® France*. In the prices listed here, this is indicated by Lalique (R) France. Some pieces that are advertised as ring dishes or pin dishes were listed as ashtrays in the Lalique factory catalog and are listed as ashtrays here. Names of pieces are given here in French and in English. The Lalique brand was bought by Art & Fragrance, a Swiss company, in 2008. Lalique and Art & Fragrance both became part of the Lalique Group in 2016. Jewelry made by Rene Lalique is listed in the Jewelry category.

R.LALIQUE.FRANCE	LALIQUE FRANCE	*Lalique ® France*
Lalique c.1925–1930s	Lalique 1945–1960	Lalique 1978+

Ashtray, Athena, Frosted, Flower Shape, 3 1/2 x 8 In.	125
Atomizer, Relief Decorated Body, Signed, Gilt Metal Top, Engraved Garland, La Parisien, 6 1/4 In.	303
Bowl, Compiegne, Overlapping Leaves, Frosted, 3 1/2 x 8 In.	236
Bowl, Engraved Swirl Vines, Birds To The Exterior Wall, 11 x 7 1/2 In.	1100
Bowl, Green Wreath, Round Blown Mold, Collie & Terrier, 3 1/4 x 9 1/4 In.	120
Bowl, Nemours, Flower Heads, Shrinking Stylized Rows, 1900s, 4 x 10 In.	431
Bowl, Opalescent Starfish, Frosted, Raised Mark, 1900s, 2 3/4 x 9 1/4 In.	300
Bowl, Pinson, Frosted Foliage & Birds, 3 3/4 x 9 1/4 In.	162
Bowl, Putti, Holding Garland, Figures, Frosted, Molded, Signed, 7 3/4 x 6 1/2 x 3 In.	295
Bowl, Putti, Holding Garland, Molded Body, Signed, 8 1/2 x 12 In.	590
Bowl, Volutes, Spiral Bubbles, Opalescent, Etched R. Lalique, c.1934, 10 In. .... *illus*	248
Candleholder, Mesanges, Birds In Blossom Wreaths, Molded Frosted, 6 x 5 In., Pair	156
Chalice, Frosted Claw Feet Stem, Clear Bowl, Signed, 8 1/2 In.	240
Champagne Cooler, Dancing Nudes, Relief, Frosted Glass, 9 x 10 1/2 In.	183
Chandelier, Monaco Design, Crystal Arms, Floral Top & Bottom, Signed, 36 x 31 In.	3509
Charger, Cote D'Or, Dancing Nude Women, Grapes, 15 3/4 In.	960
Clock, Cinq Hirondelles, 5 Swallows, Clear Glass, Black Enamel, 1920, 6 x 5 1/4 x 2 In.	1750
Clock, Le Jour Et La Nuit, Nude Male & Female, Smoky Topaz, Black Base, 1926, 15 x 12 In.	28750
Decanter, Argos, Square Pedestal, 4 3/4 x 11 In.	260
Decanter, Stopper, Oak Leaf, Foil Lalique Label, 9 x 4 In.	174
Figurine, Aries, Ram's Head, Art Deco, Curled Horns, Frosted, Signed, 6 x 8 In. .... *illus*	726
Figurine, Cat, Seated, Amethyst, Frosted, Signed, R. Lalique, 3 3/4 In. .... *illus*	118
Figurine, Dragon, Amber, 7 3/4 x 11 In.	937
Figurine, Stag, Frosted, Molded, Clear Base, Signed, 10 x 8 3/4 In.	767
Figurine, Swan, Raised Wings, Head Down, Molded, Clear, Frosted, 7 x 14 x 9 In.	1298
Hood Ornament, Eagle Head, Frosted & Clear, Signed, 4 1/4 x 6 x 3 1/4 In.	236
Hood Ornament, Eagle Head, Frosted, Molded, Metal Stand, Etched, 1996, 5 3/4 In. .... *illus*	214
Hood Ornament, Nude Woman, Kneeling, Chrome Base, Marked, 8 In.	5900
Hood Ornament, Saint Christopher, Child On Shoulders, c.1928, 4 1/2 x 4 3/8 In.	625
Lamp, 2-Light, Oriental Style Mounts, Renee Lalique Sophora, 1926, 28 In.	1353
Lamp, Ceiling, 4-Light, Charmes, Electric, Colorless Leaves, Cord Supports, 27 x 13 1/2 In.	1375
Paperweight, Amber, Turtle, Paper Label, Signed, 1900s, 2 x 6 In.	210
Perfume Bottle, Coty Serie, Toilette, Briar Stopper, 5 1/4 x 1 1/4 x 1 1/4 In.	90
Perfume Bottle, Dans La Nuit, Worth Globe, Blue Enamel, Embossed Stars, 5 1/2 x 3 1/2 In.	452
Perfume Bottle, Duncan, Embossed Nude Women, Medallions, Frosted, Rectangular, 1900s, 8 In.	120
Perfume Bottle, Epines, Thistles, Brown Stain, Signed, Molded & Engraved Script, 4 x 3 1/4 In.	480
Perfume Bottle, Hirondelles, Swallows, Frosted, Clear, Sepia Patina, c.1920, 3 1/2 In. .... *illus*	1125
Perfume Bottle, L'Air De Temps, Nina Ricci, Box, 4 In. .... *illus*	130
Ring Holder, Pin Dish, Deux Cygnes, 2 Swans, Frosted, Clear, Etched, 3 3/4 x 3 1/2 In.	47
Vase, Alternating Clear & Frosted Swirl Pattern, 1900s, 10 In.	369
Vase, Bacchantes, Nude Figures, Molded, Frosted, Signed, 1900s, 9 1/2 x 7 1/2 In. ...... *illus*	2125

L.G. Wright, Syrup, Lid, Cobalt Blue, White Opalescent Spots, Applied Blue Reeded Handle, 6¼ In.
$174

Jeffrey S. Evans

Lacquer, Bowl, Paulownia Design, Red, Brown, Gold, Footed, Japan, 5½ In.
$48

Eldred's Auctioneers and Appraisers

Lacquer, Figurine, Wood, Deer, Marbled Red & Black Lacquer, Xipi Style, Chinese, 26 x 23 In.
$1,220

Neal Auction Co.

Lacquer, Pitcher, Water, Lid, Red, Angled Semicircle Handle, Wood, 1900s, 15 In.
$43

Leland Little Auctions

Lacquer, Vase, Metal, Black, Red, Elongated Triangles, Copper Liner, Dunand, France, 6 x 7 In.
$37,500

Rago Arts and Auction Center

Lacquer, Wall Panel, Carved, Cranes, Prunus, Bamboo, Giltwood Frame, Chinese, 32 x 16 In.
$183

Neal Auction Co.

Lalique, Bowl, Volutes, Spiral Bubbles, Opalescent, Etched R. Lalique, c.1934, 10 In.
$248

Hess Auction Group

Lalique, Figurine, Aries, Ram's Head, Art Deco, Curled Horns, Frosted, Signed, 6 x 8 In.
$726

James D. Julia Auctioneers

Lalique, Figurine, Cat, Seated, Amethyst, Frosted, Signed, R. Lalique, 3¾ In.
$118

Hess Auction Group

L

LALIQUE

Lalique, Hood Ornament, Eagle Head, Frosted, Molded, Metal Stand, Etched, 1996, 5¾ In.
$214

Neal Auction Co.

Lalique, Perfume Bottle, Hirondelles, Swallows, Frosted, Clear, Sepia Patina, c.1920, 3½ In.
$1,125

Rago Arts and Auction Center

Lalique, Perfume Bottle, L'Air De Temps, Nina Ricci, Box, 4 In.
$130

Hess Auction Group

Lalique, Vase, Bacchantes, Nude Figures, Molded, Frosted, Signed, 1900s, 9½ x 7½ In.
$2,125

New Orleans Auction Galleries

Lalique, Vase, Damiers, Checkerboard, Frosted, Black Enamel, Etched R. Lalique, 9 x 8½ In.
$3,250

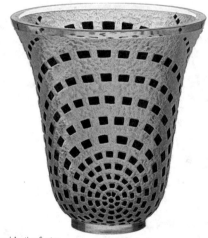

Rago Arts and Auction Center

Lalique, Vase, Mossi, Hobnails, Clear, Frosted, Signed, Lalique France, 1900s, 8½ In.
$590

Brunk Auctions

L

Vase, Bagatelle, Birds, Frosted, Round Mouth & Foot, 6¾ In.	295
Vase, Bud, Clover Heads, Amber, Frosted, Molded, Marked, 5 In.	275
Vase, Ceylan, Parakeets, Branches & Leaves, Frosted Clear Glass, 9½ In.	3327
Vase, Cometes, Comet, Tapers, Frosted, 11 x 11½ In.	2040
Vase, Damiers, Checkerboard, Frosted, Black Enamel, Etched R. Lalique, 9 x 8½ In........ *illus*	3250
Vase, Dampierre, Protruding Birds, Signed Lalique France, 4¾ x 5 In.	342
Vase, Deep Impressed Swirl Design, Black Coloration On Top Of Each Swirl, 8 In.	8470
Vase, Domremy, Thistle, Opalescent, 8½ x 7½ In.	1080
Vase, Domremy, Thistles, Green, Signed, 9 In.	3630
Vase, Druide Mistletoe, Raised Berries, Vines, Green Glass, Spherical, Signed, 7 In.	6655
Vase, Esterel, Oleander Leaves, Globular, Frosted, 1923, 6 x 6½ In.	500
Vase, Ingrid, Frosted Leaves, Clear Ground, Engraved Lalique France, 10½ x 8 In.	813
Vase, Moissac, Overlapping Leaves, Dark Amber, Signed, V-Shape, 5 In.	3630
Vase, Mossi, Hobnails, Clear, Frosted, Signed, Lalique France, 1900s, 8½ In. ...... *illus*	590
Vase, Mures, Blackberries, Frosted, Vines, Thorns, 7⅜ x 8¼ In.	847
Vase, Muscat, Grapes, Vines, Frosted, R. Lalique, France, 6½ In. .... *illus*	1331
Vase, Palestre, Frosted, Clear, Nude Males Posing, France, 1928, 16 x 10 In...........	40625
Vase, Papillon, Butterfly, Black, Marked, 1992, 8½ In. .... *illus*	1440
Vase, Raised Lozenge, Interspersed, Flowering Branches, Renee Lalique, 1927, 5 In.	738
Vase, Saint Cloud, Signature Lalique France On Base, 4½ x 3¾ In.	87
Vase, Satyrs & Leaves, Frosted Glass, Etched, 1900s, 7 x 7½ In., Pair	750
Vase, Sauterelles, Grasshoppers, Clear, Frosted, Grasses, 1912, 10¾ x 9½ In.	2375
Vase, Scrolled Flower Handles, Thorn Branches, 8 x 5¾ In.	363
Vase, Silenes, Clear, Gray Patina, Etched, R. Lalique, 1938, 8 In......... *illus*	2625
Vase, Tortue, Turtle, Tortoiseshell Shape, Textured, Lalique France, 1900s, 11 In........ *illus*	360
Vase, Xian, Dragon, Molded Fish Scales, Clear, Frosted, Signed, Lalique France, 1900s, 8 In.....	180

LAMPS of every type, from the early oil-burning Betty and Phoebe lamps to the recent electric lamps with glass or beaded shades, interest collectors. Fuels used in lamps changed through the years; whale oil (1800–40), camphene (1828), Argand (1830), lard (1833–63), solar (1843–60s), turpentine and alcohol (1840s), gas (1850–79), kerosene (1860), and electricity (1879) are the most common. Early solar or astral lamps burned fat. Modern solar lamps are powered by the sun. Other lamps are listed by manufacturer or type of material.

3 Brass Gingko Leaves, Single Socket, Stems Affixed, Square Base, 76 x 26 x 11 In.	2706
Argand, Brass, Cupid, Psyche, Flower Baskets, Prisms, Honeycomb Shades, 20 In., Pair..........	2125
Betty, Brass, Hinge Lid, Finial, Wrought Iron Hanger, Chain, Peter Derr, 1853, 3 x 3⅞ x 5 In..	1350
Betty, Iron Hook, Hand Wrought Hinge, Wire Wick Pick, H.W. Dietrich, 3 x 3 x 5 In.	85
Betty, Tin, Stand, Pennsylvania, 12 In.............................. *illus*	200
Betty, Trammel, Iron Bracket, Sawtooth, Continental, 1830-90, 4⅜ x 2⅝ x 27 In...................	200
Betty, Wrought Iron, Hanger, Wick Pick, Lead Gallery, 7½ In.	150
Bradley & Hubbard lamps are included in the Bradley & Hubbard category.	
Brass, Cast Marble Base, Embossed Green Glass Shades, 28 x 15 In.	207
Brass, Iron Kettle, Peter Derr, Marked, 1833, 11½ In.	2124
Bronze, Orange Carnival Shade, Bell Shape Yoke, Post, Arts & Crafts, 58 x 8 x 9 In....	840
Camphene, Gilt Bronze, Flowers, 3-Footed, Melon Shape Glass Shade, Prisms, c.1850, 18 In. *illus*	1952
Candlestick, Pricket, Bronze, Elephant, Trunk Up, Entwined Vine, 1900s, 12½ In., Pair........	1250
Ceiling, 5-Light, Brass, Bowl Shape, Pendant Tassel Finial, Single Bell Cased Socket, 32 x 16 In..	726
Ceiling, Enameled, Blue Glass, Bell Lamp Shade, Continental, 7½ x 18 In.	60
Ceiling, Hanging, Rainbow Colored Panels, 3 Tiers, 13½ x 17 In.	117
Chandelier, 1-Light, Counterbalance, Black Ball, Red Shade, A. Lelii, Italy, 1950s, 32 x 65 In..	8125
Chandelier, 3-Light, Bear & Wooden Arms, Center Cluster, Glass Eyes, Single Socket, 31 x 28 In.	3630
Chandelier, 3-Light, Gas & Electric, Brass Fixture, Bent Green, Red Slag Glass, 4 x 7¼ x 4 In.	666
Chandelier, 3-Light, Murano Glass, Pink, Molded Leaves, Drop Finial, 28 In.........	2750
Chandelier, 3-Light, Nickeled Bronze, Frosted, Long Tubes, Germany, 1930s, 48 x 20 In.........	500
Chandelier, 3-Light, Pendants, Chrome, Steel, Enamel, Ornament Shape, 58 x 16 In..............	625
Chandelier, 3-Light, Porcelain, Celadon Glaze, Floral, Gilt, 1900s, 21 x 10 In................	2640
Chandelier, 4-Light, Blown Glass Balls, Naho, Iino, Japan, 24 x 16 In.	4375
Chandelier, 4-Light, Metal, Candle Form Standards, 1900s	36

Lalique, Vase, Muscat, Grapes, Vines, Frosted, R. Lalique, France, 6½ In. $1,331
James D. Julia Auctioneers

Lalique, Vase, Papillon, Butterfly, Black, Marked, 1992, 8½ In. $1,440
Cowan's Auctions

Lalique, Vase, Silenes, Clear, Gray Patina, Etched, R. Lalique, 1938, 8 In. $2,625
Rago Arts and Auction Center

This is an edited listing of current prices. Visit Kovels.com to check thousands of prices from previous years and sign up for free information on trends, tips, reproductions, marks, and more.

Lalique, Vase, Tortue, Turtle, Tortoiseshell Shape, Textured, Lalique France, 1900s, 11 In.
$360

Brunk Auctions

Lamp, Betty, Tin, Stand, Pennsylvania, 12 In.
$200

Hess Auction Group

Lampshade Sizes

A traditional lampshade is 2 to 4 inches wider than the height of the lamp's base. But modern lamps made after the 1940s broke the rules. Designers today are using shades that are of very different proportions to their bases. Some shades are long and thin, some are wide and short, and some have distorted shapes. A new shade in different proportions can update the look of a lamp, but it might look strange in a traditional room.

Chandelier, 4-Light, Tommy Parzinger, Brass, Polished, Frosted Glass, 23 x 21 In.		4687
Chandelier, 4-Light, Wrought Iron, Quatrefoil Ring, Chains, Canopy, 6 ½ x 23 ¾ In.		90
Chandelier, 4-Light, X Shape, Pewter Ring, Stepped Arms, Candleholders Slide, 12 x 28 In.		968
Chandelier, 5-Light, Double Ring, Metal, Glass, Cone, Poul Henningsen, Louis Poulsen, 44 x 26 In.		4063
Chandelier, 5-Light, Hand Cut Crystal Beads, Scroll Arms, 1840s, 43 x 28 In.	*illus*	350
Chandelier, 5-Light, Poul Henningsen, Louis Poulsen, Emperor, Brass, Glass, 1930s, 8 ½ x 24 In.		4688
Chandelier, 5-Light, Regency, Gilt Bronze, Crystals, Wedgwood Plaques, 1800s, 47 In.	*illus*	4500
Chandelier, 6-Light, Bronze, S Shape Arms, Flower Heads, 42 x 27 ½ In.		260
Chandelier, 6-Light, Chrome Plated Brass, Candle Sockets, Pink, Etch, Art Deco, 34 x 33 In.		484
Chandelier, 6-Light, Crown Shape, Rolled Sheet Iron, Piecrust Candlecup, 19 x 24 In.		1210
Chandelier, 6-Light, French Empire Style, Basket Form, Bronze Ring, Cascading Drops, 40 In.		2125
Chandelier, 6-Light, Geometric Star, Mahogany, 38 x 40 In.		406
Chandelier, 6-Light, Gilt Bronze, Cut Glass, Louis XV Style, Faceted Pendant, 1800s, 49 x 28 In.		6250
Chandelier, 6-Light, Gilt Bronze, Empire Style, Yellow, Chains, France, c.1950, 25 x 21		1250
Chandelier, 6-Light, Gilt Bronze, Leafy Scroll, Candle Arms, 3 Chains, c.1890, 20 In.		531
Chandelier, 6-Light, Gilt Metal, Flowers, Basket, 22 x 22 In.		200
Chandelier, 6-Light, Giltwood, Cartouches, Acanthus, S Scroll Arms, c.1900, 25 ¾ x 28 In.		1125
Chandelier, 6-Light, Iron, S-Scrolls, Leaves, Red, Green, Painted, Italy, c.1910, 43 x 33, Pair		1104
Chandelier, 6-Light, Louis Philippe, Gilt, Tole, Hexagonal, Crimped Bobeches, 48 x 29 In.		242
Chandelier, 6-Light, Louis XV, Gilt Tole, Beaded Glass, Cage Shape, 32 ¾ x 24 In.		687
Chandelier, 6-Light, Wrought Iron, Open Basket, C-Scroll Supports, 1900s, 16 x 18 In.		150
Chandelier, 6-Light, Wrought Iron, S-Scroll, 6 Chains, Canopy, 17 x 30 In.		100
Chandelier, 6-Light, Yellow, Green, Balloon, Painted Metal, Louis XVI Style, 1900s, 43 x 17 In.		2125
Chandelier, 7-Light, Alabaster Bowl, Bronze Mount & Chains, Frosted Flame Shades, 40 In.		2500
Chandelier, 8-Light, Bohemian, Amber Glass, Cut Glass Pendants, 33 x 24 In.		625
Chandelier, 8-Light, Brass, Petal Form, Chain, c.1825, 26 In.		510
Chandelier, 8-Light, George III, Molded, Teardrop, Rope, Rosette, Cut, c.1900, 33 In.		10000
Chandelier, 8-Light, Gilt, Metal, Crystal, 1900s, 26 In.		88
Chandelier, 8-Light, Gilt, Steel, Ring, Acanthus, 28 x 26 ½ In.		3000
Chandelier, 8-Light, Gothic, Iron, Candles, Caged Cups, Spears, Chain, 1800s, 20 x 27 In.		1850
Chandelier, 8-Light, Prunus Branches, Patinated Metal, Cameo, Galle, c.1900, 54 x 18 In.		11875
Chandelier, 8-Light, Tole, Yellow, Trumpet Shape Flowers, Green Leaves, 22 x 24 In.		64
Chandelier, 9-Light, Bronze, Gilt, Urn Shape, Swags, Scroll Arms, Bobeches, 32 x 26 In.		1187
Chandelier, 9-Light, Gilt Bronze, Blue Glass, Cut Crystal, Russia, 65 x 35 In.		8125
Chandelier, 9-Light, Gilt Metal, White, Purple Cut Glass, Fleurs-De-Lis, 1700s, 50 x 31 In.		4375
Chandelier, 9-Light, Louis XIV Style, Gilt Bronze, Candlecups, Scrolled Frame, c.1900, 40 x 24 In.		3000
Chandelier, 9-Light, Porcelain, Metal, Bell Shape, Tulip Cups, Metal Leaves, c.1950, 21 In.		1000
Chandelier, 9-Light, Venini, Dripping Pendants, Purple, Chromed Metal, 1960s, 36 x 20 In.		3125
Chandelier, 10-Light, Venetian Style, Brass, Crystal, 27 x 24 In.		240
Chandelier, 12-Light, 2 Tiers, Glass Scroll Corona, Cascades Of Drops, 37 x 28 In.		813
Chandelier, 12-Light, Black Cone Shades, Brass, Style Of Silnovo, 40 x 59 ½ In.		3750
Chandelier, 12-Light, French Empire Style, Prisms, Silver Plate, Wax Candle, 1800s, 31 x 42 In.		421
Chandelier, 12-Light, Giltwood, Scrolls, Leaf, Leaf Bobeches, 45 x 45 In.		1140
Chandelier, 12-Light, Louis XIV Style, Giltwood, Tapered Standard, Leaf Carved, c.1950, 34 x 34		1375
Chandelier, 12-Light, Wood, Iron, Ball, Ring, Reel, S Curve Arms, Dark Green, 17 ½ x 16 In.		4537
Chandelier, 15-Light, Cage, Beaded, Applied Flowers, Prisms, Amethyst, Sweden, 33 In.		2250
Chandelier, 16-Light, Brass, Painted Metal, Spider Style, Oscar Torlasco, 20 x 40 x 40 In.		3250
Chandelier, 18-Light, Bronze, Gilt, Winged Angels, Scroll Arms, 56 x 34 In.		5980
Chandelier, 18-Light, Gilt Bronze, Cage Form, Prisms, c.1910, 38 In.		625
Chandelier, 20-Light, Crystal, Bronze, Drops, Scrolling, Louis XIV Style, c.1950, 52 x 25 In.		2375
Chandelier, 27-Light, Wood, Carved, Bunches, Fruit, Scroll Candle Arms, 1900s, 47 x 39 In.		688
Chandelier, Crystal, Wired, Electricity, Hand Cut, 1840s, 43 In.		351
Chandelier, Duffner & Kimberly, Cone Shape, Red, Green, Brown, Blue, Yellow, Shade 28 In.		9680
Chandelier, French Iron Drying Rack, Glass Bottles, 3 Inverted Tiers, 54 x 29 In.		360
Chandelier, Frosted Glass, Aluminum, Glass Lamp, Art Deco, 22 x 17 x 17 In.		531
Chandelier, Gilt & Silvered Metal, Cut Rock Crystal, Glass, Louis XVI Style, 42 x 32 In.		6250
Chandelier, Gilt Bronze, Louis XV, Flower Swags, Scroll Arms, Candlecups, c.1950, 34 x 23		1375
Chandelier, Giltwood, Forming Clock, Central Stem, Bearded Masks, Italy, 33 x 38 In.		6875
Chandelier, Hexagon, Slag Glass, Green, 10 x 19 ¾ In.		82
Chandelier, Leaded Glass, Water Lilies, Pink, White, Green, 3 Sockets, Steven Stelz, 28 In.		6050
Chandelier, Multicolor With Fold Art Design, Handcrafted, Packing Case, Erzgebirge, 26 In.		390

L

Chandelier, Patinated Decoration, 6 Oil Lamps, Lower Central Finial, 1800s, 36 x 29 In.	....	1080
Chandelier, Patinated Iron Frame, Gothic Influence Crosses, Socket Fixture, 9 x 21 In.	....	295
Chandelier, V. Panton, Waterfall, Mother-Of-Pearl, Laminate, Metal, 1960s, 79 x 39 ½ In.	......	6857
Chandelier, Vermont, Old Gray Paint, Scrolled Tin Arms & Candle Sockets, 1800s, 14 x 22 In.		875
Cylindrical, Bulbous, Enameled Leaves, Gilt, Wood Base, 1897-1931, 17 x 22 In.	....	1968
Desk, Brass, Emeralite Shade, Conical, Swivel Adjustment, 1900s, 15 ½ In.	....	185
Desk, Brass, Enameled Metal, Glass, Fontana Arte, c.1950, 14 x 9 ½ x 9 In.	....	937
Double Burner, Brass, Greek Key Font, Milk Glass Smoke Bells, 1800s, 37 x 37 x 10 In.		563
Eiffel Tower, Patinated Metal, Gothic Influence, 23 x 7 ½ x 7 ½ In.	....	207
Electric, 1-Light, Angelo Lelii, Adjustable, Brass, Enameled, Leather, 1950s, 19 x 14 x 10 In.	.....	6875
Electric, 1-Light, Brass, Enameled Aluminum, Plastic, Philip Johnson, Richard Kelly, 41 x 25 In.	..	7500
Electric, 1-Light, Edgar Brandt, Shade, Wrought Iron, Cast Glass, 1930s, 71 x 18 In.		4375
Electric, 1-Light, Ettore Sottsass, Artemide, Callimaco, Steel, 1982, 79 x 15 In., Pair	....	1875
Electric, 1-Light, Kalmar, Bamboo, Metal, Cellulose Shade, 1950s, 47 x 17 x 26 In.	....	3625
Electric, 1-Light, Paavo Tynell, Taito Oy, Brass, Cane, Linen Shade, 1940s, 60 x 20 In.	....	3250
Electric, 1-Light, Vico Magistretti, Claritas, Aluminum, Brass, 1940s, 51 x 16 x 19 In., Pair	.....	4375
Electric, 2-Light, Blue, Yellow Shade, Enameled Metal, Marble, c.1960, 73 In.	....	1625
Electric, 2-Light, Brass, Enameled Metal, Angelo Lelii, c.1955, 58 x 24 In.	....	4375
Electric, 2-Light, Brass, Green Glass Shades, Beaded Domed Base, 1900s, 22 ½ In.	....	262
Electric, 2-Light, C. Stupell, Quartz Crystal, Wood, Fiberglass Shades, Milk Glass, 37 x 18 In.	. .	2250
Electric, 2-Light, Chocolate Glass Panel Shade, Bronze Finish Spelter, 24 x 18 In.	....	210
Electric, 2-Light, Chromed Steel, Stamped, Stilnovo Italy, 1970s, 25 x 18 In.	.... *illus*	1375
Electric, 2-Light, Fantoni, Ceramic, Paper Shade, Italy, 1950s, 34 ½ In., Pair	.... *illus*	3750
Electric, 2-Light, Filigree, 8 Bent Slag Glass Panels, Brass Base, Bird, Vines, Lattice, 7 x 18 In.		164
Electric, 2-Light, Flowers, Embossed, Pink Glass, Cast Metal Base, 15 x 11 In.	....	177
Electric, 2-Light, G. Nakashima, Walnut, Rosewood, Cedar, Parchment, 1974, 34 x 24 In. *illus*		18750
Electric, 2-Light, Georges Mathias, Brass, Pyrite, 1980s, 35 x 17 x 11 In., Pair	....	3625
Electric, 2-Light, Lightolier, Black, Orange, Painted Metal, Chrome Shades, 58 ½ In.	....	100
Electric, 2-Light, Reverse Painted Shades, Lake Scene Landscape, PLB & G Co., 20 In.	....	484
Electric, 2-Light, Rispal, Mahogany, Brass, Enamel Metal, 2 Shades, 1950, 65 x 21 In.	..... *illus*	5312
Electric, 2-Light, Salem Bros., Domed Shade, Reverse Painted, 10 Pink Orchid Flowers, 7 In.	. .	726
Electric, 2-Light, Slag Glass, Brass, Repeating Windmills, Landscape, 13 In.		236
Electric, 2-Light, Stilnovo, Blue, Yellow, Marble, Perspex, 1950s-60s, 73 x 12 In.	....	1625
Electric, 2-Light, Swans, Obverse Painted, Matte Bold Colored Trees, Bush, Pittsburgh, 22 In.		1029
Electric, 2-Light, Unique Art Glass & Metal Co., Leaded, Domed Shade, Slag Panels, 24 In.	....	908
Electric, 3 Mythical Females, Standard, Flame-Form Finial, 1800, 30 x 23 In.	....	82
Electric, 3-Light, Angelo Lelii, Adjustable, Enameled Brass, 1950s, 62 x 24 In.	.... *illus*	8750
Electric, 3-Light, Angelo Lelii, Arredoluce, Brass, Aluminum, c.1945, 62 x 24 In.	.... *illus*	5000
Electric, 3-Light, Bohemian Glass, Dots, Iridescent, Ludwig Sutterlin, Fritz Heckert, 24 x 17 In.		3250
Electric, 3-Light, Auguste Moreau, Cobalt Blue, Gilt Bronze Basket, Garlands, 1900s, 36 In. *illus*		688
Electric, 3-Light, Brass, Green Onyx, Silk Shade, Brass Finial, c.1935, 29 x 17 In.	....	96
Electric, 3-Light, Dish Shape, Lunaria, Gilt Metal, Round Canopy, 1900, 15 x 22 In.	....	400
Electric, 3-Light, Embossed, Blue Glass, Cast Metal Base, 14 x 11 In.	....	177
Electric, 3-Light, Enamel, Metal, Plastic, 3 Ledges, Cone Shape Shades, 69 ½ x 19 In.	....	2375
Electric, 3-Light, James Leleu, Brass, Glass, Enamel Metal, 1950s, 67 x 26 In.	....	4688
Electric, 3-Light, Mushroom Shape, Myrtlewood, Resin, Copper, Philip Clausen, 77 x 30 In.	...	4687
Electric, 3-Light, Stained Glass, Autumn Leaf Pattern, Bronze Base, Somers, 1990, 30 In.	......	9075
Electric, 3-Light, Stilnovo, Brass, Enamel, Glass, 1950s, 58 In.	....	1250
Electric, 3-Light, Wilkinson, Leaded Shade, Caramel Slag Glass, Brick Geometric, 25 In.	....	2420
Electric, 4-Light, Gilt Bronze, Ringed Stand Ending, 1800s, 57 In.	....	6000
Electric, 4-Light, Wine Dancer, Ruffled Glass Shades, 40 ½ In.	....	82
Electric, 6-Light, Bronze Feet, Marble Base, Restauration, c.1850, 41 ½ x 12 In., Pair	....	625
Electric, 6-Light, Paired Arms, Nickeled Brass, Painted Paper Shade, 1960s, 53 x 17 In., Pair..		9375
Electric, 8 Reverse Painted Bent Glass Panels, Overlay Shade, Landscape, Matching Base, 24 In.		363
Electric, 9 Splayed Chocolate Glass Panels, Pierced Filigree Overlays, Medallion, Fluted, 26 In.		1210
Electric, Acanthus Leaf, Metal, Brown Rub Painted, Black Shade, Lexington Lampcrafters, 24 In.		41
Electric, Acrylic, Brass, Copper, Paper, White Shade, c.1950, 37 x 21 In.	....	1875
Electric, Acrylic, Red, Chromed Steel, Gherpe, Adjustable, Poltronova, 1960s, 15 x 22 x 12 In. .		2875
Electric, Adjustable Ratchet, Maple, Milk Glass Diffuser, Mogul Basket, 1930s, 14 x 14 In.	....	59
Electric, Adjustable, Dragon Holds Shade, Wrought Iron, 70 ½ x 20 In.	....	1625

Lamp, Camphene, Gilt Bronze, Flowers, 3-Footed, Melon Shape Glass Shade, Prisms, c.1850, 18 In.
$1,952

Neal Auction Co.

Lamp, Chandelier, 5-Light, Hand Cut Crystal Beads, Scroll Arms, 1840s, 43 x 28 In.
$350

Copake Auction

Lamp, Chandelier, 5-Light, Regency, Gilt Bronze, Crystals, Wedgwood Plaques, 1800s, 47 In.
$4,500

Cowan's Auctions

LAMP

Lamp, Electric, 2-Light, Chromed Steel, Stamped, Stilnovo Italy, 1970s, 25 x 18 In.
$1,375

Rago Arts and Auction Center

Lamp, Electric, 2-Light, Fantoni, Ceramic, Paper Shade, Italy, 1950s, 34½ In., Pair
$3,750

Rago Arts and Auction Center

Lamp, Electric, 2-Light, G. Nakashima, Walnut, Rosewood, Cedar, Parchment, 1974, 34 x 24 In.
$18,750

Rago Arts and Auction Center

Lamp, Electric, 2-Light, Rispal, Mahogany, Brass, Enamel Metal, 2 Shades, 1950, 65 x 21 In.
$5,312

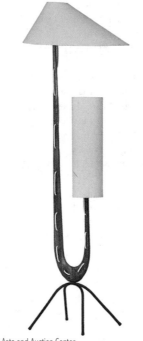

Rago Arts and Auction Center

Lamp, Electric, 3-Light, Angelo Lelii, Adjustable, Enameled Brass, 1950s, 62 x 24 In.
$8,750

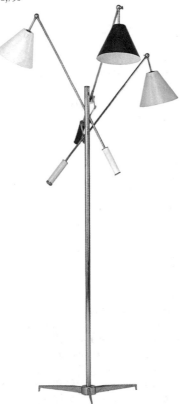

Rago Arts and Auction Center

Lamp, Electric, 3-Light, Angelo Lelii, Arredoluce, Brass, Aluminum, c.1945, 62 x 24 In.
$5,000

Rago Arts and Auction Center

> **TIP**
> *Use a soft-bristle paintbrush to dust lampshades.*

Lamp, Electric, 3-Light, Auguste Moreau, Cobalt Blue, Gilt Bronze Basket, Garlands, 1900s, 36 In.
$688

Brunk Auctions

Electric, Adjustable, Telescoping, Enameled Metal, Brass, Giuseppe Ostuni, 1950s, 56 In.	3750
Electric, Airplane Shape Frame, Chrome Plated Base, Dark Blue, Satin Glass Shade, 7 x 14 In.	605
Electric, Alabaster, Painted Metal, Cloth Shade, 60 x 21 x 21 In.	125
Electric, Arredoluce, Angelo Lelii, Spherical Frosted Glass, Red, White, 10 x 6 In., Pair	1625
Electric, Arredoluce, Marble, Brass, Tole, Acrylic, Adjustable, Angelo Lelii, 1950s, 70 x 14 In.	5625
Electric, Arredoluce, Triennale, Nickeled, Enameled, Aluminum, Marble, Lelii, 1970s, 56½ In.	3500
Electric, Art Nouveau, Bronze, Clambroth Jewels, Chain Switch Socket, 1910, 15 x 10 In.	1680
Electric, Brass Propane Torch Base, Green Cased Glass Shade, c.1920, 19 In.	84
Electric, Brass Washed, Chromed Steel, Lucite, Glass, Linen Shades, c.1935, 20 x 14 In., Pair	937
Electric, Brass, Excelsior, Tripod Paw Feet, Lion Head, Bird Head, Duponi Silk, 7 x 7 x 19 In.	321
Electric, Brass, Palm Tree Shape, Black Square Bases, 69 x 28 In.	3198
Electric, Brass, Piano, Ruby Glass Ball Shade, Adjustable, Ornate, Victorian, 68 In.	1534
Electric, Brass, Rattan, Shell Shape Shade, Paavo Tynell, Taito Oy, Finland, 1940s, 12 x 11 In.	4687
Electric, Bronze Base, 2-Tier Prism Shade, Gold Patina, Art Deco, France, 30 In.	3025
Electric, Bronze Cassolettes, Gilt, Marble, Louis XVI Style, 1810, 13 In., Pair	938
Electric, Bronze Lily Pad Base, 3 Stems, Porcelain Sockets, Art Nouveau, 16 x 13 x 13 In.	666
Electric, Bronze, Birds, Flowers, Trees, Clouds, Dragons, High Relief, 28½ x 13½ In.	1122
Electric, Bronze, Chunk Jewel, Leaded, Flower Shape, Dolphins, 22½ In.	3780
Electric, Bronze, Persian Scene, Seated Woman, Servants, Fan, Carpet, Austria, c.1925, 15 In.	1920
Electric, Cactus, Stacked Green Glass, Italy, 53 x 16½ In.	950
Electric, Cameo, Conch Shell, Mount Vesuvius Scene, Tiered Wood Base, 1970s, 7 In.	500
Electric, Carl Thieme, Porcelain, Flowers, Figures, Germany, c.1895, 52 In. *illus*	923
Electric, Carved Alabaster, Painted Wrought Iron, Art Deco, 1920s, 70 x 24 In.	1250
Electric, Ceiling, Glass, Morning Glories, Medallion, Victorian, 7¼ x 7¼ x 5½ In.	47
Electric, Ceramic, Flowers, Cylindrical, Shade, Brass, 1900s	60
Electric, Ceramic, Gerald Thurston, 3 Ball Yellow, Lightolier, 26½ In.	219
Electric, Chalkware, Dutch Girl, Holds Lid, Amethyst Glass Bowl, c.1920s, 20½ x 15 In.	1375
Electric, Chinese Export, Cockerels, Multicolor, Syrie Maugham, 1900s, 33½ In., Pair	6875
Electric, Chocolate Glass, Pierced Filigree Metal Frame, Red Glass Inserts, 15 x 24 In	236
Electric, Chocolate Glass, Red-Orange Roses, Green Leaves, Vines, 1900s, 14 x 24 In.	108
Electric, Chocolate Glass, White Metal Base, Shade Frame, 12 Panels, 1900s, 21 x 12 In.	469
Electric, Classique, Reverse Painted, Daisies, Butterflies, Metal Base, 22 x 18 In. *illus*	2250
Electric, Cobalt Blue, Cerulean Craquelure Glaze, Signed, Atelier Primavera, 6¼ x 6½ In.	113
Electric, Cut Glass, Vase, Shape, Gilt Bronze, Mahogany Base, Hydrogen, Volta, 1810, 18 x 10 In.	4000
Electric, Decoy, Hen, Feather Decoration, 24 In.	48
Electric, Desk, Bigelow & Kennard, Bronze Base, White, Gold, Iridescent Domed Shade, 16 In.	1694
Electric, Desk, W.D. Teague, Del Giudice, Bakelite, Aluminum, Cellulose, 1939, 11 In. *illus*	256
Electric, Domed Shade, Reverse Painted, Snow-Covered Landscape, Sunset, Jefferson, 14 In.	1029
Electric, Double Gourd, Red Fish, White Ground, Chinese, 1900s, 37 In., Pair	3750
Electric, E. Martinelli, Serpent, Aluminum, Molded Plastic, Label, 19 x 16 In. *illus*	492
Electric, E. Sottass, Chromed Steel, Green, White, Light Tube, Moonlight, 1970s, 74 x 10 In.	3250
Electric, Edgar Brandt, Wrought Iron, Cast Glass, Stamped, 1930s, 71 In. *illus*	4375
Electric, Egg Shape, Veil Of Black Dots, White Daubs, Crackle Glazed, 1930, 21 x 9 In.	124
Electric, Elizabeth Burton, Hammered Copper, Abalone Shell, c.1910, 19 x 12 In *illus*	31250
Electric, Emeralite, Desk, Cased Green Shade, Brass, Marked On Shade, 1900s, 12½ In.	169
Electric, Enameled Iron, Brass, Linen Shade, Adjustable, 1940, 62 x 41 In.	1375
Electric, Flying Tiger Ace, Plated Base, Serpentine Riser, Satin Glass Shade, 15 x 7 x 7 In.	726
Electric, Frederick Cooper, Bronze, Monkey, Rides Elephant, Trunk Up, 29 In.	687
Electric, Gathering Tubes, Sliced Into Oval Shape, 1970s, 30 x 13 In.	8750
Electric, Gilt Metal, Leaves, Milk Glass Globe, 1900s, 42 In.	60
Electric, Glass Art, Leaded Glass, Dome Shade, Flowers, 1900s, 18 In.	144
Electric, Glass Bell, Metal Base, Cooper Luster, Swivel Yolk, 1926, 3¼ x 6 x 6½ In.	125
Electric, Glass Peony, Red, Yellow, Purple, Blue Background, Somers, 36 In.	9680
Electric, Glass, Opalescent, Nude Woman, Seated, Waves, Shell At Back, Footed, 23 x 13 In.	312
Electric, Gorham, Leaded Shade, Slag, Green, White, Grid, Wavy Rim, Spelter, 22¼ In.	1008
Electric, Green, Wash Bottle, Stoneware, Concentric Rings, Ring Handles, 1920, 17 x 15 In.	311
Electric, Greta Von Nessen, Aluminum, Metal, Enameled, Bakelite, 1950s, 14 x 14 In. *illus*	812
Electric, Hebi, Chrome, Adjustable, Hosoe Isao, 1942, 16 x 13 x 13 In.	156
Electric, Iron, Glass, 2 Flower Form Lights, Blown Colored Glass Shades, Leonhardt, 70 In.	600
Electric, Jadeite, Yellow Glass, Alternating, Twisted Stem, Bridge, 60½ In.	224

Lamp, Electric, Carl Thieme, Porcelain, Flowers, Figures, Germany, c.1895, 52 In. $923

Cowan's Auctions

Lamp, Electric, Classique, Reverse Painted, Daisies, Butterflies, Metal Base, 22 x 18 In. $2,250

Rago Arts and Auction Center

Lamp, Electric, Desk, W.D. Teague, Del Giudice, Bakelite, Aluminum, Cellulose, 1939, 11 In.
$256

Neal Auction Co.

Lamp, Electric, E. Martinelli, Serpent, Aluminum, Molded Plastic, Label, 19 x 16 In.
$492

Palm Beach Modern Auctions

Lamp, Electric, Edgar Brandt, Wrought Iron, Cast Glass, Stamped, 1930s, 71 In.
$4,375

Rago Arts and Auction Center

Electric, Jefferson, Painted Poppy, Orange, Yellow, Green Finish Shade, 22 In.	4840
Electric, K. Springer, Chromed Metal, Patina, Lucite Rectangular Shade, 60 In. *illus*	960
Electric, Leaded, Floral, Caramel Slag Geometric, Lion's Head, Long Fluted Stem, 18 In.	1029
Electric, Library, Pull Down, Opalescent, Blue, Coin Dot, Brass Side Arms, 54 x 17 ¼ In.	2268
Electric, Lighthouse, Wooden, Black & White Tower, Yellow Windows, 24 ½ x 15 In.	118
Electric, Lightolier, Painted Metal, Brass Base, 16 ½ In.	250
Electric, Luminaire, Glass, Woman With Gilt Robe, Marble Base, Erte, c.1900, 24 In.	3360
Electric, Lundberg, Iridescent Art Glass, Red, Ribbed, Domed Shade, Shaded Aurene, 15 In.	472
Electric, Marble Base, Beaded, Embroidered Shade, Otto Hafenrichter, 1900s, 12 In.	708
Electric, Massimo Vignelli, Chromed, Brushed Steel, Plexiglas, 1960s, 24 x 16 In., Pair	4063
Electric, Metal Base, Floral Panel Foot, Fluted Shaft, Frosted Amber Glass Shade, 16 x 7 In.	767
Electric, Mission, Oak, Leaded Shade, 74 x 23 In.	1625
Electric, Moderne, Acrylic Base, Finial, 28 ¼ x 8 ½ In.	82
Electric, Moe Bridges, Reverse Painted Shade, Scenic Stream, Meadows, Trees, 20 ½ In.	2420
Electric, Murano Glass, Teardrop Shape, Aqua, 26 ½ In. *illus*	768
Electric, Nude Woman, Knee On Pedestal, Pastel Shade, Chinese, 31 x 20 In.	324
Electric, Oceanic, Michele De Lucchi, Enameled Metal, Memphis, 1981, 29 x 38 In. *illus*	2000
Electric, Opal Glass Shade, Obverse Painted, Stenciled Borders, Cast Iron Base, 26 x 15 In.	273
Electric, Organic Wood Stylized Human, Brass, Paper Shade, Smoky Tunis, 74 x 22 In.	3125
Electric, Original Ruby Glass Shade, Cast Iron Floral Base, 24 In.	366
Electric, Oval Marble Base, Brass, Birds, Crackle Glass Globe Shade, 10 x 15 x 4 ½ In.	177
Electric, P. Fornasetti, Cammei, Red Cameo Faces, Lithographed Metal, 1950s, 15 In.	750
Electric, Painted Cement, Quarry, Beige, White Shade, Sirmos, 30 x 18 In.	937
Electric, Peacock, Standing, Tail Up, Multicolor, Round Foot, 19 x 15 In. *illus*	472
Electric, Pegasus, Marble Base, 12 x 14 x 6 In.	1625
Electric, Pierced Brass, Shaped Circular Base, Leaf, Grapes, Paw Feet, c.1908, 67 x 26 In.	281
Electric, Pierced, 3 Gilt Shore Bird Figures, Marble Base, Inset Perfume Pan, 12 x 6 ½ In.	242
Electric, Plaster, Gold Paint, Green Glass Shade, 20 x 9 In.	344
Electric, Porcelain, Famille Rose, Foo Dog Handles, Gilt Metal Base, 35 In., Pair	1875
Electric, Porcelain, Vase, Brown, Wood Base, Chinese, 1900s	390
Electric, Post, Spelter, Gladiator, With Torch, Cranberry, Hobnail, Globe, Shade, 53 x 15 In.	882
Electric, Pyramid Shade, Caramel Slag, Rippled Cranberry Glass, Cast Brass Paw Feet, 32 In.	152
Electric, R. Wright, Aluminum, Yellow, Wood Knob, Conical Shade, c.1950, 64 In., Pair	438
Electric, Samuel Yellin, Wrought Iron, Patinated, Mica Shade, 61 x 20 In. *illus*	4062
Electric, Sculptural, Perforated Metal, Diagonally Sliced Tubes, 1950s, 25 x 14 In.	1375
Electric, Ship, Mixed Metals, Twisted Brass Shaft, Pierced Base, 71 x 12 In.	325
Electric, Silver Base, Floral Panels, Frosted Glass Shade, Embossed Roses, 16 x 11 In.	649
Electric, Skyscraper, Chrome Plated Base, 3 Standing Dancers, Satin Glass Shade, 12 x 6 ½ In.	1089
Electric, Slag Glass, Stylized Flower Panels, c.1930, 24 x 20 ¼ In.	295
Electric, Staffordshire Spaniel, Gilt Highlights, Black, 1800s, 28 In. *illus*	147
Electric, Stand, Silver, Leaves, 3 Scrolling Supports, Marble, 1900s, 34 In.	120
Electric, Standard, Enamel, Brass Base, Extended Top, 1900s, 59 In.	144
Electric, Student, Plated Brass Base, Greek Key Design, Flowers, 1800s, 21 In. *illus*	175
Electric, Stylized Fish, Italy, c.1950, 42 x 15 In.	687
Electric, Sunset, Reverse & Obverse Painted, Fluted Body, Gold Finish, Black Highlights, 25 In.	1513
Electric, Torchere, Bronze, Courting Couple, Scrolled Base, Stepped Marble Base, 70 x 17 In.	9600
Electric, Torchere, Louis XIV Style, Gilt Bronze, Scrolled Supports, Shade, c.1925, 63 x 17 In.	1750
Electric, Torchere, Milk Glass Bowl Shade, Single Standard, Round Footing, 1900, 66 In.	82
Electric, Tripod, Metallic Glaze, Ka-Kwong Hui, 19 x 8 ½ In.	1750
Electric, Urn Shape, 2 Handles, Multicolor, Scene, Flowers, Square Foot, Porcelain, 1900s, 36 In.	185
Electric, Vase, Mounted As Lamp, Flowers, Delft, Shade, 7 In. *illus*	270
Electric, Walnut, Tole Shade, Table Surface, 4 Legs, 1900s	60
Electric, Wendell Castle, Abstract, 3-Legged, Carved Wood, Copper Shade, 64 x 36 In.	10000
Electric, Wendell Castle, Carved, Multicolor Wood, Patinated Copper, 1993, 31 x 14 x 13 In.	5938
Electric, White Spiderweb, Ivy Banded, Domed, Slag, Chinese Oval Urn, 3 Sockets, 1910, 16 x 16 In.	2640
Electric, White, Cased Glass, Painted Metal, Fontana Arte, 1960s, 31 x 18 ½ In.	1250
Electric, Wilkinson, Overlay Panel, Skewed Pyramidal Platform, Serpentine Arm, 12 x 11 x 10 In.	484
Electric, Willy Daro, Leaf, Gilt Bronze, Gold Washed, 1970s, 19 x 10 x 6 In., Pair	2500
Electric, Winter Scene, Bell Shape Shade, Reverse Painted, Sunset Landscape, Signed, 14 x 14 In.	363
Fairy, Rolled Sides Base, Beaded Candleholder, Red, Green, Brown, Blue, Signed, 6 ½ In.	847

Lamp, Electric, Elizabeth Burton, Hammered
Copper, Abalone Shell, c.1910, 19 x 12 In.
$31,250

Rago Arts and Auction Center

Lamp, Electric, Greta Von Nessen, Aluminum,
Metal, Enameled, Bakelite, 1950s, 14 x 14 In.
$812

Rago Arts and Auction Center

Lamp, Electric, K. Springer, Chromed Metal,
Patina, Lucite Rectangular Shade, 60 In.
$960

Palm Beach Modern Auctions

Lamp, Electric, Murano Glass, Teardrop
Shape, Aqua, 26 ½ In.
$768

Palm Beach Modern Auctions

Lamp, Electric, Oceanic, Michele De Lucchi,
Enameled Metal, Memphis, 1981, 29 x 38 In.
$2,000

Rago Arts and Auction Center

Lamp, Electric, Peacock, Standing, Tail Up,
Multicolor, Round Foot, 19 x 15 In.
$472

Cottone Auctions

Lamp, Electric, Samuel Yellin, Wrought Iron,
Patinated, Mica Shade, 61 x 20 In.
$4,062

Rago Arts and Auction Center

Lamp, Electric, Staffordshire Spaniel, Gilt
Highlights, Black, 1800s, 28 In.
$147

Leland Little Auctions

LAMP

Lamp, Electric, Student, Plated Brass Base, Greek Key Design, Flowers, 1800s, 21 In.
$175

Garth's Auctioneers & Appraisers

Lamp, Electric, Vase, Mounted As Lamp, Flowers, Delft, Shade, 7 In.
$270

Eldred's Auctioneers and Appraisers

Lamp, Fairy, Webb Burmese, Pyramid, Flower Holder, Ivy, Clarke Inserts, 5 x 8 In.
$649

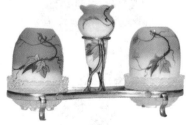

Humler & Nolan

Lamp, Fluid, Figural, Skeleton, Bisque, Miniature, 7 In.
$1,298

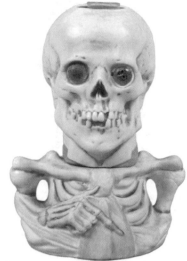

Hess Auction Group

> **TIP**
> When rewiring an old lamp, put a dimmer on the cord to turn the lamp on and off. This will protect the original switch and pull chains. If you must replace any of the parts, save them for the next owner, who may want to restore the lamp.

Lamp, Kerosene, Hanging, Cabin In Winter, Opal, Stamped Brass Frame, Flowers, Prisms, 14 In.
$128

Jeffrey S. Evans

Lamp, Lard, Gilt Bronze, Fruit, Plants, Frosted, Prisms, Starr Fellows, c.1850, 27 In.
$2,750

Neal Auction Co.

Lamp, Oil, Brass, 5 Leaded Colored Glass Inserts, Tulips, Crown-Like Crest, 1800s, 20 x 30 In.
$570

Garth's Auctioneers & Appraisers

Fairy, Webb Burmese, Pyramid, Flower Holder, Ivy, Clarke Inserts, 5 x 8 In. .... *illus*	649
Fairy, Webb Burmese, Ruffled Leaves, Domed Shade, Clarkes Cricklite, 6 In.	1101
Fat, Peter Derr, Copper, Iron, 1844, 6 In.	1708
Fat, Silver Plate, Moth Reflector, 4 Burners, Round Base, Fan Design, 34 1/4 In.	242
Fat, Turned Walnut Stand, 1800s, 13 In.	549
Fluid, Cobalt Blue Glass, Vase Shape, Concave Base, 6 1/2 In.	118
Fluid, Figural, Skeleton, Bisque, Miniature, 7 In. .... *illus*	1298
Fluid, Hobbs, Brockunier & Co., Coin Dot, Cranberry Opalescent, c.1875, 9 5/8 In.	265
Fluid, Pewter, Brass, Chimney, 1850-1900, 17 3/4 In.	1188
Galle, Red Flowers, Leaves, White Satin Ground, Acid-Etched, Cameo, Signed, 6 x 3 1/2 In.	150
Gas, Light, Cold Painted, Solid Cast, Composer, Welsbach, 1800s, 16 In.	219
Gas, Post, Fiske, Verdigris Patina, 6 In.	1027
Gasolier, 3-Light, Spear Prisms, Cascades Of Drops, Crown-Top Shades, Anglo-Irish, 35 In.	2375
Gasolier, 4-Light, Gilt Bronze, Henry Hooper, Graduated Tiers Of Prisms, c.1850, 33 x 27 In....	1000
Gasolier, 6-Light, Brass, Reeded & Scrolled Arms, Leaf-Molded Scroll, c.1885, 36 x 29 In.	815
Gasolier, 12-Light, Brass, Tiers Of Prisms, Drop Cascades, England, c.1880, 40 x 33 In.	6563
Golf, Rupert Nikoll, Adjustable, Enameled, Aluminum, Brass, 1950s, 52 x 12 x 33 In.	4063
Guanyin, Figure With Flowing Robes, On Dragon Stand, Carved Coral, 26 In.	13530
Handel lamps are included in the Handel category.	
Hanging, 1-Light, Flower Form Pebbled Green Glass, Gold Accents, 5 3/4 x 6 In.	118
Hanging, 4-Light, Fixture, Hammered Brass, Central Post, Arts & Crafts, 1900s, 24 x 19 In.	1680
Hanging, 4-Light, Tole, Sand Weighted, 11 In.	93
Hanging, Brass, Counterweight On Chains, Clambroth To Cranberry, Bell Shape, 30 x 7 In.	60
Hanging, Bronze, Psyche Heads, Bow Knots, Pierced, 4 Silk Panels, c.1900, 28 In.	813
Hanging, Coin Spot, Deep Cranberry, Brass Fittings & Chain, 14 In.	330
Hanging, Coraline, Molded, Frosted, 4 Panels, Amber Relief, Griffins, Filigree, 11 x 7 In.	630
Hanging, Cranberry, Diamond Quilt Optic, Domed Shade, 39 In.	1112
Hanging, Cut & Pressed Glass, Thimble Shape, Fronds, Spray, 1900s, 24 x 31 In.	4000
Hanging, Green & White Fronds, Demilune, Spherical Drop, Venetian Glass, 28 x 32 In.	600
Hanging, Hexagonal, Slag Glass, Brass Tassels, Ceiling Mount, 16 In.	35
Hanging, Medallions, Birds, Flowers, Art Deco, 9 x 10 1/2 In.	480
Hanging, P. Henningsen, 5 Tiered Discs, Purple, Blue, White, L. Poulsen, 11 x 19 In.	250
Hanging, Pink Opalescent Hobnail, Domed Shade, Scrolls, Flowers, Charles Parker Co., 46 In. .	936
Hanging, Verdigris Patinated Metal, Caramel Slag Glass Panels, 9 1/2 x 6 x 6 In.	177
Kerosene, 2-Light, Brass, Harp Handle, Opalescent Chimney Shades, 17 3/4 In.	175
Kerosene, Amber Stained Glass, c.1890, 9 In.	105
Kerosene, Blue Pattern Glass Font, Amber Base, 12 In.	60
Kerosene, Cranberry, Clear Skirted Base, Miniature, Marked Hong Kong, 5 In.	12
Kerosene, Cranberry, White Spiraling Threads, 1859, 14 3/4 x 8 1/4 In.	1755
Kerosene, Floral Bouquets, Green Highlights To Base & Globe, 1900, 25 In.	91
Kerosene, Flower, Tapestry, Bulbous Shade, Brass, 1890, 22 In.	1476
Kerosene, Glass, Blue Pattern Font, Amber Base, 14 In.	120
Kerosene, Glass, Pale Blue Satin, Beaded Drape Mold, Miniature, 9 1/4 In.	300
Kerosene, Hanging, 4-Light, Brass, Harp Handle, Medallion, Leaves, Angle Lamp Co., 17 3/4 In..	292
Kerosene, Hanging, Cabin In Winter, Opal, Stamped Brass Frame, Flowers, Prisms, 14 In... *illus*	128
Kerosene, Large, Cranberry Diamond Quilted Shade, Brass Base, 1890s, 17 x 9 In.	150
Kerosene, Majolica, Pokal, Prussian Eagle, Glass Shade, Gold, c.1850, 27 In.	74
Kerosene, Porcelain, Figural, Iris Blossoms, English Mark On Base, 15 In.	330
Kerosene, Skater's, Blue, Perforated Cap, Bail Handle, 11 1/2 x 7 1/8 In.	187
Kerosene, Skater's, Green, Perforated Cap, Bail Handle, Stepped Conical Base, 7 In.	187
Kerosene, Swirl Optic, Cranberry, Brass Frame, Chain, Ceiling Plate, 10 1/2 In.	81
Lard, Gilt Bronze, Fruit, Plants, Frosted, Prisms, Starr Fellows, c.1850, 27 In. .... *illus*	2750
Lily Form, Tapered Body, Carved Wood Base, 29 x 6 1/2 In.	207
National Lead Co., Dutch Boy Painter Figure, Blue Overalls & Cap, 18 x 6 x 5 In.	79
Oak Base, Pyramid Shade, Carved Ship, Adjustable Arm, 7 x 15 x 4 In.	354
Oak Box Base, 2 Caramel Slag Glass Panels, Rectangular, 18 x 22 x 13 In.	826
Oak Frame, Felt Strips, Pebbled Slag Glass, Single Socket Fixture, 4 1/2 x 12 x 29 In.	148
Oil, Arab Woman, Purple & White Burqa, Holds Baskets, Flowers, Porcelain, 1800, 8 x 5 3/4 x 5 3/4 In.	1995
Oil, Bargeware, Rockingham Type Glaze, Teapot Shape, Birds, Flowers, God Bless, 10 In...........	125
Oil, Blanc De Chine, Censer Form, Carved Flowers, Conical Nozzle, Chinese, 3 x 6 1/2 In...........	600

Lamp, Oil, Miner's, Cast Iron, Swing Arm, Twisted Shaft, Hook End, Rooster Finial, 1800s, 25 In.
$177

Hess Auction Group

Lamp, Oil, Wrought Iron, 6-Sided Shade, Glass Panels, Electrified, 62 In.
$570

Fox Auctions

Aladdins Aren't All Old
Many kerosene Aladdin lamps have been reissued since 1974. They are worth much less than old original lamps. The reissues are dated, and the metal collar may be glued on, not attached with brass threads.

LAMP

Lamp, Sconce, 4-Light, Electric, Linked U Shapes, Brushed Steel, Italy, c.1950, 8 x 18 In., Pair
$1,188

Rago Arts and Auction Center

Lamp, Solar, Gilt Bronze, Renaissance Revival, Cut Glass Shade, Frosted, c.1850, 28 In.
$1,586

Neal Auction Co.

Lamp, Solar, Starr Fellows, Gilt Bronze, Frosted & Cut Glass Shade, Marble Base, c.1850, 23 In.
$1,125

Neal Auction Co.

Lamp, Student, Edward Miller, Double, Brass, Glass Shades, Embossed, Electrified, 1800s, 22 x 28 In.
$369

Cowan's Auctions

Lamp, Whale Oil, Blown, Sparking, Button Support, Round Foot, c.1830, 3 ⅞ x 2 ¼ In.
$409

Jeffrey S. Evans

Lamp, Whale Oil, Four Printie Block, Pressed Glass, Blue, Hexagonal, Knop, 1840-50, 11 ¼ x 5 ¼ In.
$351

Jeffrey S. Evans

L

Oil, Blue, Peacock, Feather, Satin Shade, 17½ In.	132
Oil, Brass, 5 Leaded Colored Glass Inserts, Tulips, Crown-Like Crest, 1800s, 20 x 30 In.... *illus*	570
Oil, Brass, White Glass Globe & Chimney, Embossed, 64 In.	420
Oil, Cast Iron, Gothic, Etched Glass Shade, c.1850, 17½ In.	207
Oil, Ceramic, Chimney, Gray, Green Leaves, 18½ In.	112
Oil, Cobalt Blue, Tapered Brass Standard, Etched Shade, c.1850, 29 In., Pair	1188
Oil, Glass, Silver Mount, Oil Tank, Crescent Moon, Crown, Germany, c.1850, 7½ In.	168
Oil, Hanging, Overlay Shade, Folded Rim, Leaves, 1800s, 25 In.	2040
Oil, Miner's, Cast Iron, Swing Arm, Twisted Shaft, Hook End, Rooster Finial, 1800s, 25 In. *illus*	177
Oil, Overlay Glass, Cobalt Blue Over White, Fluted Cut To Clear Column, Ball Shade, 38 In.	1500
Oil, Overlay Glass, White Cut To Peach Font, Flowers, Brass Stand, Marble Base, 25 In., Pair....	1000
Oil, Spout, Saucer Base, Blown Glass Font, Pewter Strap, Roman Numerals, 13 In.	375
Oil, Wrought Iron, 6-Sided Shade, Glass Panels, Electrified, 62 In. *illus*	570
Pairpoint lamps are in the Pairpoint category.	
Patinated Bridge, Figural Griffin & Scrolls, Metal Shaft, Green Onyx Accents, 64 x 15 In.	118
Rope Twist, Carved, Silver Gilded, Italian Baroque, Grapes, Grapevines, 21½ x 6 In., Pair	1063
Scavo Glass, Blown Glass, Nickel Plated Metal, Murano, 1970s, 21 x 21½ In.	875
Sconce, 1-Light, Adam & Eve, Murano, Scavo Glass, Patinated Brass, 1950s, 11½ x 8 In.	3375
Sconce, 1-Light, Gilt, Fiberglass, Crowned Cherubs, 60 x 24 In.	704
Sconce, 1-Light, Globe, Glass, Brass, White, Gray, Massimo Vignelli, Italy, 18½ x 9½ In.	1950
Sconce, 1-Light, Leaf Shape, Gilt Inclusions, Murano, 19 In., Pair	2091
Sconce, 2-Light, Bronze, Gilt, Snakes, Winged Helmet, Scrolling Arms, 15 x 10 In., Pair	307
Sconce, 2-Light, George III, Carved Giltwood, Metal, Bows, Wheat, Swags, Italy, c.1920, 29 In.	840
Sconce, 2-Light, Giltwood, Weapons, Arrows, c.1875, 33 x 13 In., Pair	469
Sconce, 2-Light, Louis XV, Gilt Bronze, Asymmetrical, 14¾ x 13 In., Pair	500
Sconce, 2-Light, Louis XVI, Gilt Metal, Wood, Tassel Back, Ribbon Knot, 25 x 12 In., Pair	312
Sconce, 2-Light, Urn Shape, Satyr, Festoon, Scroll Arms, Gilt Bronze, 21½ In., Pair	1223
Sconce, 2-Light, Wood, Gilt, Scrolling Oak Leaves, Ribbons, Bow, Faceted Cups, 25 In., Pair....	688
Sconce, 3-Light, Electric, Bronze, Gilt, Shield, Leaves, Scroll, 25 x 13 In., Pair	2280
Sconce, 4-Light, Electric, Linked U Shapes, Brushed Steel, Italy, c.1950, 8 x 18 In., Pair .. *illus*	1188
Sconce, 6-Light, Electric, Bronze, Louis XVI, Gilt, Leafy Arms, 31¾ x 17¾ In., Pair	3000
Sconce, Brass, 8-Light, Leafy Stem Decorated To Hold Candles, 1900, 43 In.	204
Sconce, Brass, Glass, Mirrored Back Plate, Double Loop Handle, Half Hexagon, 20 In., Pair	360
Sconce, Candle, Cloisonne, Blue, Flowers, Opalescent Lily Shade, 23 In.	63
Sconce, Candle, Giltwood, Bowknot Backplates, Twisted Arms, Italy, 1900s, 35 x 13 In., Pair...	1000
Sconce, Candle, Large Mirror, Tin Back, Candleholder, Pieced Mirror Reflector, 1900s, 16 In..	330
Sconce, Candle, Rolled, Sheet Metal, Chicken, 13 In.	71
Sconce, Candle, Rolled, Sheet Metal, Face, 17 In.	85
Sconce, Candle, Tin, Relief Heart, Feather Shape Back Panel, Half Round Tray, 5 In., Pair	1586
Sconce, Electric, Metal, Enamel, Brass, Convex Rectangle, Italy, 1950s, 14 x 13 In., Pair	2000
Sconce, Electric, Wall, Metal, Glass, Patinated, Milk Glass, 1900s	63
Sconce, Girandole, Queen Anne, Scroll Arms, 35¾ x 15¾ In.	3000
Sculptural, Glass, Flower Form Lamp, Leaves, Vine, Yellow, Green, Leonhardt, 39 In.	600
Sinumbra, Bronze, Gilt & Patinated, Fluted, Leaves, Frosted & Cut Mushroom Shade, 22 In. ..	2048
Sinumbra, Painted Metal, Black, Gilt Trim, Cut & Frosted Mushroom Shade, c.1830, 27 In.....	256
Slag Glass, Segmented Domed, Floral, Circular Base, c.1905, 24½ In.	125
Solar, Astral, Bronze, Gilt, Globe Shape, Fluted Column, Floral, c.1950, 24 In.	1464
Solar, Bronze, Gilt, Lotus Stem, Squat Frosted Shade, Cut Flowers, 1830s, 28 In.	750
Solar, Gilt Bronze Stand, Rococo Shell, Flowers, Globe Shade, Hooper & Co., c.1850, 29 In.	1750
Solar, Gilt Bronze, Figure With Sword, Floral Cut Shade, Marble Base, c.1850, 21 In.	1586
Solar, Gilt Bronze, Flowers, Fern & Waffle, Marble Base, Cornelius & Co, c.1850, 22 x 9 In.	1952
Solar, Gilt Bronze, Fluted Stem, Cut Glass Shade, Trellis Cut, Hooper, c.1850, 23 In.	1281
Solar, Gilt Bronze, Inverted Pear Font, Dish Base, Cut & Frosted Shade, c.1850, 11 In.	915
Solar, Gilt, Bronze, Leafy Designs, Floral Reserves, c.1850, 24 In.	1920
Solar, Gilt Bronze, Renaissance Revival, Cut Glass Shade, Frosted, c.1850, 28 In.	1586
Solar, Starr Fellows, Gilt Bronze, Frosted & Cut Glass Shade, Marble Base, c.1850, 23 In.. *illus*	1125
Solar, Tin, Brass, Back Reflector, Glass, Embossed, Cornelius Philadelphia, c.1835, 16 In.	1625
Solar, Tin, Brass, Glass, Etched Glass Shade, Starr, Fellows & Co., 1857, 20 In.	1500
Solar, Tin, Brass, Tapered Chimney, Starr, Fellow & Hopper, c.1855, 15 In., Pair	1250
Student, Edward Miller, Double, Brass, Glass Shades, Embossed, Electrified, 1800s, 22 x 28 In. *illus*	369

Lantern, Barn, Candle, Pine Frame, Red Paint, Tin Air Tubes, Iron Handle, 1800s, 10 In.
$1,200

Garth's Auctioneers & Appraisers

L

Lantern, Brass, Hanging Lid, Wall Mounted Frame, 1900s, 23 x 8½ In., Pair
$1,080

Brunk Auctions

Lantern, Candle, Copper, Onion Globe & Removable Socket Base, 1800s, 13 In. $330

Garth's Auctioneers & Appraisers

Lantern, Tin, 3 Glass Panels, Mirror Reflector, Oil Font, Threaded Neck, 1800s, 15 In. $300

Garth's Auctioneers & Appraisers

TIP

Remove small rust spots from old metal with an ink-removing eraser or an old typewriter eraser.

Tiffany lamps are listed in the Tiffany category.

Tole, Chinoiserie, Decorated, Tea Tin, Edwardian, Metal, 1910, 10 x 7 x 19 In.	336
Torchere, Mahogany, Carved, Rope Twist, Ball & Claw Feet, c.1910, 52 x 10 In.	256
Torchere, Tapered Reeded Support, 3 Leaf Scroll Feet, 1900, 68 x 17 In.	430
Tyndale, Mold Blown, Mercury Glass, Frederick Cooper, 39 x 19 In.	63
Wedding, Ripley, Tall White Standard, 2 Blue Fonts, Cut Shades, Clambroth, c.1870, 21 In.	512
Whale Oil, Blown Glass, Brass, Conical Shaped Font, Pipestem Shape Burner, 1800s, 14 In.	281
Whale Oil, Blown Glass, Onion Shape, Cotton Twist Stem, Stepped Base, 9¼ In.	531
Whale Oil, Blown, Sparking, Button Support, Round Foot, c.1830, 3⅞ x 2¼ In. *illus*	409
Whale Oil, Double Bull's Eye, Pewter, Roswell Gleason, Mass., c.1865, 8½ In.	813
Whale Oil, Four Printie Block, Pressed Glass, Blue, Hexagonal, Knop, 1840-50, 11¼ x 5¼ In. *illus*	351
Whale Oil, Silver Plate, Lemon Font, Watson & Son, Sheffield, 10½ In., Pair	120

LAMPSHADE

Cranberry Opalescent, Hobnail, Domed, Rolled Rim, 6 x 13¾ In.	410

LANTERNS are a special type of lighting device. They have a light source, usually a candle, totally hidden inside the walls of the lantern. Light is seen through holes or glass sections.

Barn, Candle, Pine Frame, Red Paint, Tin Air Tubes, Iron Handle, 1800s, 10 In. *illus*	1200
Brass, Caged Case, Arched Top, Turned Wood Handle, Electrified, 1940s, 15 x 6 In.	425
Brass, Carrying Handle, Vented Chimney, Hinged Door, 1939, 16 In.	450
Brass, Hanging Lid, Wall Mounted Frame, 1900s, 23 x 8½ In., Pair *illus*	1080
Brass, Tin Base, Pepper Pot Cap, Chain, Hoop Hanger, Hurricane, 1860-90, 4 x 11 In.	75
Candle, Copper, Onion Globe & Removable Socket Base, 1800s, 13 In. *illus*	330
Candle, Punched Tin, Gold Paint, Conical Top, Hanging Ring, 1800s, 15 In.	130
Candle, Tin, Iron Hog Scraper, 1800s, 8 In.	212
Electric, Copper, Openwork, Globular Shape, Floral Panels, Plinth Base, c.1900, 15 In.	450
Hanging, 6-Light, Glass Panels, Bronze, Hexagonal, Swags, France, c.1950, 57 In.	1250
Hanging, Iron, Sheet Tinned, Green Blown Glass, Bell, Shape, 1800s, 15 In.	2375
Hanging, Punched Tin, Cone Shape, Hinged Door, Wrought Ring Handle, 17 In.	100
Iron, Glass, Bards, Green, 1800s, 12¾ In.	321
Metal, 5-Light, Strapwork, Wood, Louis XV Style, Giltwood Trim, c.1950, 43 x 18 In.	875
Miner's, Brass, Screen Chimney, Carbide, Hughes Bros, c.1920, 2¾ x 8½ In.	110
Tin, 3 Glass Panels, Mirror Reflector, Oil Font, Threaded Neck, 1800s, 15 In. *illus*	300
Tin, American Eagle, Shield, Base, 1800-50, 10½ In.	563
Whale Oil, Cleat Pattern Globe, Tin Base, 1860, 12½ In.	3120
Whale Oil, Tin Base, Etched Flower Shade, 12 In.	300

Le Verre Francais **LE VERRE FRANCAIS** is one of the many types of cameo glass made by the Schneider Glassworks in France. The glass was made by the C. Schneider factory in Epinay-sur-Seine from 1918 to 1933. It is a mottled glass, usually decorated with floral designs, and bears the incised signature *Le Verre Francais*.

Bowl, Green, Purple, White, Geometric Shapes, 7 x 3½ In.	22
Lamp, Electric, Rubaniers, Orange, Frost, Mushroom Shape, Acid Etched, 19 x 18 In.	2875
Lamp, Monnaie Du Pape, Light Green Ground, Vertical Bands, Signed, 10-In. Shade	3630
Lamp, Mushrooms, Leaves, Red, Cream, Brown, Cameo, 7¼ In. *illus*	704
Night-Light, Azurettes, Cobalt Blue Cameo Flowers, Blue Ground, Metal Base, 6 In.	1210
Pitcher, Chenes, Long Spout, Leaves, Purple, Mottled, Orange, White, 12¾ In.	630
Vase, Art Deco Stems, Orange, Blue, Yellow Ground, Shouldered, Marked, 4½ In.	325
Vase, Blue Geometric Water Lilies, Light Blue Mottled Ground, Oval, Signed, 12 In.	4840
Vase, Branches & Blossoms, Violet, Orange, Tile Design, Squat, Signed, 10 x 12 In.	2722
Vase, Dahlias, Bulbous, Tapered Neck, Flared Rim, Purple Over Pink Ground, Signed, 17½ In.	1815
Vase, Dark Violet Cameo Flowers, Orange Ground, Swans, Tapered, Footed, Signed, 33 In.	5445
Vase, Flowers, Yellow, Orange, Blue, 3 x 5½ In.	910
Vase, Lizards, Dragonflies, Mottled Orange, Violet, Yellow Ground, Tapered, Signed, 18 In.	5747
Vase, Red Foxglove, Mottled Glass, Cameo, C. Schneider, 17¾ x 7½ In. *illus*	2340
Vase, Rhododendrons, Dark Violet Flowers, Pink Ground, Footed, Oval, Signed, 12 In., Pair	1210
Vase, Stylized Finch, Violet, Pink Ground, Cameo, Tapered, Signed, 14 In.	3327

Vase, Violet Scarab Beetles, Red Ground, Tapered, Rolled Top Rim, Signed, 15 In. 2420

LEATHER is tanned animal hide and has been used to make decorative and useful objects for centuries. Leather objects must be carefully preserved with proper humidity and oiling or the leather will deteriorate and crack. This damage cannot be repaired.

Backpack, Calf Brown Body, Flap, Pockets, 1930s, 16 x 16 x 7 In.	438
Basket, Applied Leather Handle, Brass Rivets, Pine Bottom, James Livingston, 1880s, 9 x 12 In. *illus*	116
Belt, Tooled, Holster, Flowers, 1900s..	200
Boots, Applique Musical Notes, Black Patent, Labeled, Chelsea Cobbler........................	492
Briefcase, Brown, Fitted Interior, Thailand, 1900s, 18 x 13 x 3 ½ In.	48
Briefcase, Envelope, Gold Clasp, Handles, Louis Vuitton, 10 x 14 In. .... *illus*	450
Briefcase, Gilt Red, Silvery Bronze, 1700s, 12 x 15 In.	188
Briefcase, Light Gray, Dark Gray, Fitted Interior, Thailand, 1900s, 18 x 13 x 3 In.	24
Briefcase, Snakeskin, Python, Combination Lock, Holly Hardwick, 1900s	72
Briefcase, Zippo Grip Label, Monogramed C.O.H., Sienna Suede Interior, 1900, 12 x 20 In.......	86
Bucket, Well Stitched, Strap, Painted, Instituted-1696 Emblem, 1800s, 12 x 11 In.	438
Cuff, Harness, Studded, Brass, Stars, 1930s...	200
Figure, Horse, Standing, 25 ½ x 29 In.	375
Fob, Brass Ring, Thick, Handcrafted, Los Angeles, California, 1 x 4 In..........................	38
Pouch, Tuareg People, Dye, Amulet, Berber Culture, Mali, 18 x 6 In........................	120
Saddlebag, Brown, Pebble Grain, 3 Straps, Duck Liners, Fits McClellan Saddle, 1800s, 20 In. .	1600
Saddlebag, Medical, 2 Bottle Compartments, Brass Fittings, Flap, A.A. Mellier, 1870, 4 x 34 In..	324
Saddlebag, Military, Single, US Logo, 3 Buckle Straps, Single Brass, 1800s, 13 x 12 In.	200
School Bag, Red Ryder Patrol, Red, Tan, Plastic Handle, Western Graphics, 1950s, 14 x 13 In.	4800
Stirrup, Blossom & Leaf Decoration On Toe, Pivotage Hanger, Spain, 1700s-1800s, 9 In.	360
Tobacco Pouch, Suede, Needlework, Dragon, Mt. Fuji, Silver, Japan, 5 ½ In............................	270
Wallet, Dye, Amulet, Berber Culture, Tuareg People, Mali, 12 x 5 In.	120
Wallet, Dye, Amulet, Berber Culture, Tuareg People, Mali, 9 ¾ x 3 ¼ In.	60

LEEDS pottery was made at Leeds, Yorkshire, England, from 1774 to 1878. Most Leeds ware was not marked. Early Leeds pieces had distinctive twisted handles with a greenish glaze on part of the creamy ware. Later ware often had blue borders on the creamy pottery. A Chicago company named Leeds made many Disney-inspired figurines. They are listed in the Disneyana category.

LEEDS POTTERY

Bowl, Blue & White, Oriental Landscape, 4 x 9 ¼ In... *illus*	118
Coffeepot, Flowers, Sprig, Soft Paste, 11 ¾ In.	82
Plate, Blue Feather Edge, American Eagle, Shield In Center, 1800s, 8 ¼ In.	360
Plate, Soup, Blue, Flowers, Berries, Leaves, Embossed Feather Edge, Soft Paste, 10 In. ...... *illus*	472
Platter, Blue Feather Scalloped Edge, Floral Sprays, 1800s, 12 x 16 In. .... *illus*	660
Platter, Pearlware, Feather Edge, Flowers, Leaves, 1800s, 19 x 15 ⅜ In..........................	976
Tureen, Lid, Underplate, Eagle Head Handles, Blue, White, c.1900, 13 ¾ In.	344

LEFTON is a mark found on pottery, porcelain, glass, and other wares imported by the Geo. Zoltan Lefton Company. The company began in 1941. George Lefton died in 1996 and the company was sold in 2001 but the mark *Lefton* is still being used. The company mark has changed through the years, but because marks have been used for long periods of time, they are of little help in dating an object.

Lefton China
1948–1953

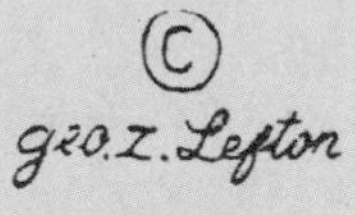

Lefton China
1950–1955

Lefton China
1949–2001

Cookie Jar, Dutch Boy, Blue Pants & Hat, Blond Hair, 9 In.	100
Dish, Holly Christmas Tree, 1970, 7 x 8 In.	10
Pitcher, Hand Painted, Heritage Green, Red Foil Label, Gold Rim, Handle, 7 x 8 ½ In.	12

Le Verre Francais, Lamp, Mushrooms, Leaves, Red, Cream, Brown, Cameo, 7 ¼ In.
$704

Susanin's Auctioneers & Appraisers

Le Verre Francais, Vase, Red Foxglove, Mottled Glass, Cameo, C. Schneider, 17 ¾ x 7 ½ In.
$2,340

L

Treadway Gallery

Leather, Basket, Applied Leather Handle, Brass Rivets, Pine Bottom, James Livingston, 1880s, 9 x 12 In. $116

Leland Little Auctions

Leather, Briefcase, Envelope, Gold Clasp, Handles, Louis Vuitton, 10 x 14 In. $450

Heritage Auctions

TIP

To get a mirror finish on patent leather, rub with a raw onion, then buff with a dry cloth.

Leeds, Bowl, Blue & White, Oriental Landscape, 4 x 9¼ In. $118

Hess Auction Group

Leeds, Plate, Soup, Blue, Flowers, Berries, Leaves, Embossed Feather Edge, Soft Paste, 10 In. $472

Hess Auction Group

LEGRAS was founded in 1864 by Auguste Legras at St. Denis, France. It is best known for cameo glass and enamel-decorated glass with Art Nouveau designs. Legras merged with Pantin in 1920 and became the Verreries et Cristalleries de St. Denis et de Pantin Reunies.

Bowl, Trees On Riverbank, Signed, c.1910, 6 x 12 In. .... *illus*	512
Vase, Art Deco, Etched, Stained Brown Grapevine Band, Yellow Glass, Signed, 1900s, 15 x 7 In.	158
Vase, Bud, Wisteria, Purple, Acid Etched, c.1920, 22 x 6 In.	681
Vase, Cylindrical, Red Branches Of Maple Leaves, White Frost Body, Cameo, Signed, 15 In.	413
Vase, Lake Shore, Path Scene & Leaves, Pink, Blue Background, Cameo, 14½ In.	2117
Vase, Long Neck, Raspberry Vines, Acid Etched, c.1910, 25 x 9 In.	750
Vase, Mottled Blues, Orange, Peacock, Leafy Scroll, Squat, 5½ x 8½ In.	148
Vase, Mountain Landscape, Silhouette, Sheep Herder & Flock, Trees, Oval, Signed, 4 x 5 In.	265
Vase, Red Flowers, Mottled Peach & White Ground, Shouldered, Cameo, Signed, 16 In.	363
Vase, Red Maple Leaves, Crimson Enamel, Frost Textured Body, Marked, Cameo, c.1915, 15 In.	415
Vase, Rubis, Tapered Triangular Shape, Cameo, Acid Etched Signature, 17 x 6½ x 6 In.	1029
Vase, Thistle, Yellow, Orange, Acid Etched, c.1920, 18 x 4 In.	2000
Vase, Trees, Grasses, Purple, White To Amber, Cameo, 13 In.	250
Vase, Vines, Berries, Orange, Acid Etched, 6 x 2¼ In.	750
Vase, Wide Mouth, Reflecting Lake, Spring Leaves, Marmalade Sky, Cameo, 5 x 3½ In.	590

LENOX porcelain is well-known in the United States. Walter Scott Lenox and Jonathan Coxon founded the Ceramic Art Company in Trenton, New Jersey, in 1889. In 1896 Lenox bought out Coxon's interest, and in 1906 the company was renamed Lenox, Inc. The company makes porcelain that is similar to Irish Belleek. In 2009, after a series of mergers, Lenox became part of Clarion Capital Partners. The marks used by the firm have changed through the years, so collectors can date the ceramics. Related pieces may also be listed in the Ceramic Art Co. category.

Bowl, Fluted, Pedestal, 7¾ x 3 In.	10
Bowl, Vegetable, Golden Wreath, Oval, 9½ In.	15
Cake Plate, Flower Bouquet Border, Footed, c.1920, 8 x 4 In.	56
Centerpiece, Fruit, Enamel, Arts & Crafts, c.1920, 9 x 4 In.	525
Clock, Fluted, Battery, 4½ x 4 In.	45
Cross, Lily, 24K Gold, 8¾ x 6½ In.	30
Cup & Saucer, Golden Wreath	9
Figurine, Cat, Playing With Jeweled Ball, 1991, 5 x 2½ In.	20
Figurine, Grasshopper, On Leaf, Acorns, Garden, 3 x 3½ In.	45
Figurine, Princess & Firebird, Matte, 1992, 8½ In.	95
Frame, Flowers, Gadrooned Edge, Embossed, 7¾ x 10 In.	39
Pitcher, Blackberry Vines, Raised, Flowers, 7 In.	32
Plate, Dinner, Alaris, 10½ In.	12
Plate, Dinner, Aristocrat, 10¾ In.	34
Plate, Salad, Alaris, 8 In.	10
Plate, Salad, Aristocrat, 8½ In.	22
Salt & Pepper, Ribbed, Footed, Silver Trim, 5½ In.	40
Tankard, Romeo & Juliet, Bas Relief, Scroll Handle, Gold Neck & Base, 9 In.	59
Vase, Acanthus Leaf, 8½ In.	19
Vase, Gilt, Basket, Flowers, Vine, Blue, Pink, White Ground, Belleek, 7½ In. .... *illus*	72
Vase, Mother's Day, Deer, Gold Trim, 1984, 7½ In.	23
Vase, Octagonal, Gold Trim, 5½ x 3½ In.	35
Vase, Reflective Moon Rising, Cylindrical, Arts & Crafts, Belleek, 11 In.	708
Vase, Rose, Raised, Scalloped Edge, Footed, 4 In.	20
Wine Caddy, Eternal Pattern, Gold Band, 1970s, 13½ x 6 x 3 In.	48

LETTER OPENERS have been used since the eighteenth century. Ivory and silver were favored by the well-to-do. In the late nineteenth century, the letter opener was popular as an advertising giveaway and many were made of metal or celluloid. Brass openers with figural handles were also popular.

L

Item	Price
Acorn Pattern, Sterling Silver, Georg Jensen, 7 ½ In.	225
African Mask, Bone, Carved, 5 ⅞ In. .... *illus*	21
Clown, Birds, Flowers, Brass, 9 In.	210
Cutout Triangles, Tapered Ends, Copper, J.P. Petterson, Chicago, 10 In.	563
Kookabura, Silver Plate, 1940s, 7 In.	143
Lion's Head, Brass, Scimitar-Like Blade, 8 ½ In.	35
Mayan Chief, 2-Sided, Sterling Silver, Peru, c.1950, 7 ½ In. .... *illus*	75
Samurai Warrior, Woman In Traditional Dress, Brass & Copper, c.1880, 9 ½ In.	150
Sassy Snake Handle, Sterling Silver, 8 In.	396

LIBBEY Glass Company has made many types of glass since 1888, including the cut glass and tablewares that are collected today. The stemwares of the 1930s and 1940s are once again in style. The Toledo, Ohio, firm was purchased by Owens-Illinois in 1935 and is still working under the name Libbey Inc. Maize is listed in its own category.

Libbey

Item	Price
Barber Bottle, Colonna Pattern, Gorham Silver Stopper, Signed, 7 ¼ In.	180
Bowl, Columbia Pattern, 4 ¼ x 10 ¼ In.	3750
Bowl, Intaglio Cut, 8-Petal Flowers, Leaves, Vines, 3 ¾ x 8 ½ In. ... *illus*	153
Bowl, Lovebirds, Wisteria, Vines, Leaves, c.1920, 9 x 4 ¼ In. .... *illus*	156
Bowl, Low, Imperial Pattern	80
Carafe, Ellsmere Pattern, 9 In.	200
Celery Tray, Imperial Pattern, Heavy Blank, 11 In.	120
Cider Pitcher, Wedgemere Pattern, Deep Cutting, Outstanding Blank, Cut Handle, 7 In.	9600
Finger Bowl, Aztec Pattern, Original Fire-Polished Rim, 2 ⅛ x 4 ¼ In.	480
Ice Cream Tray, Gloria Pattern, 17 x 10 In.	275
Jug, Harvard Pattern, Cut Handle, 2 Qt., 10 In.	420
Jug, Rum, Flute, Cranberry Cut To Clear, Stopper, 6 ½ In.	480
Nappy, Triangular, Handled, Imperial Pattern, Triple Notched Holder, 7 x 5 ¼ In.	96
Pitcher, Clear, Lavender Blue Threaded Veins, Handle, A.D. Nash, 9 In.	165
Pitcher, Milk, Harvard Pattern, Hobstar Base, 6 ½ In.	180
Plate, Isabella, 9 ⅜ In.	600
Plate, Modified Hobstar Center, Zigzag Border, Signed, 10 In.	210
Punch Bowl, Lenox Pattern, Signed, W.C. Anderson, 5 ¾ x 12 In.	840
Punch Bowl, Scalloped Rim, Spirals, Hobstars, 1896-1906, 7 ½ x 14 In.	1080
Relish, Rolled Rim, 7 ½ In.	210
Rose Bowl, Harvard Pattern, 4 x 5 In.	60
Water Carafe, Marcella Pattern, 9 In.	2040
Water Carafe, Stratford Pattern, Hobstar Base, Deep Cutting, 6 ½ In.	150

LIGHTERS for cigarettes and cigars are collectible. Cigarettes became popular in the late nineteenth century, and with the cigarette came matches and cigarette lighters. All types of lighters are collected, from solid gold to the first disposable lighters. Most examples found were made after 1940. Some lighters may be found in the Jewelry category in this book.

Item	Price
Antler Handle, Silver Ball, Repousse, 9 ½ In.	144
Ants, Butterflies, Beetles, Lacquer, Black, Dunhill, England, 4 x 3 ¼ In.	1125
Black, Gold, Cartier, 3 In.	156
Canister, Brass, Bowers, 3 In.	67
Chrysanthemum, Black, Lacquer, Dunhill, England, 4 x 3 ¼ In.	937
Cigar Cutter, Silver, 4 Cupped Rolling Ball Feet, 3 Cut Slots, Walker & Hall, 3 ¾ x 6 ¼ In.	545
Cigar Store Indian, Cast Iron, 8 x ½ In.	793
Cigar, Moon Face, Kerosene Bowl, Marble Base, 7 ⅞ x 1 ⅝ In.	224
Cigar, Turkish Figure, Hinged Lid, 6 ¾ x 4 In.	184
Dunhill, 14K Yellow Gold, Diamond, White Gold Setting, Art Deco, 2 ½ In.	780
Figural, Conquistador, Spelter, 18 In.	671
Golf Club, Putter, Golf Ball Knob, Cast Metal, Table, 1950s, 4 ½ In.	165
Mums, Green, Ball, Cloisonne, Goldtone, Round Foot, 4 In.	18
Pistol, Flintlock, Walnut Grip, Carved Accents, Candle Socket, Newberry, 1700s, 7 In. ...... *illus*	960
Striker, Rotating Gun Cannon, 4 ¾ x 6 In.	625

Leeds, Platter, Blue Feather Scalloped Edge, Floral Sprays, 1800s, 12 x 16 In.
$660

Garth's Auctioneers & Appraisers

Legras, Bowl, Trees On Riverbank, Signed, c.1910, 6 x 12 In.
$512

Neal Auction Co.

Lenox, Vase, Gilt, Basket, Flowers, Vine, Blue, Pink, White Ground, Belleek, 7 ½ In.
$72

Richard D. Hatch & Associates

L

Letter Opener, African Mask, Bone, Carved, 5 7/8 In.
$21

Ruby Lane

Letter Opener, Mayan Chief, 2-Sided, Sterling Silver, Peru, c.1950, 7 1/2 In.
$75

Ruby Lane

Libbey, Bowl, Intaglio Cut, 8-Petal Flowers, Leaves, Vines, 3 3/4 x 8 1/2 In.
$153

Hess Auction Group

Libbey, Bowl, Lovebirds, Wisteria, Vines, Leaves, c.1920, 9 x 4 1/4 In.
$156

Cordier Auctions

Lighter, Pistol, Flintlock, Walnut Grip, Carved Accents, Candle Socket, Newberry, 1700s, 7 In.
$960

Garth's Auctioneers & Appraisers

Lightning Rod, Mixed Metals, Milk Glass Ball, 4 Stars, Arrow, 67 In.
$360

Rich Penn Auctions

Lightning Rod Ball, White, Stars & Crescent Moon Design, 5 In.
$75

Ruby Lane

Limoges, Vase, Irises, Green Leaves, Pale Green Ground, Double Handles, Gilt, 14 x 8 1/2 In.
$120

Cowan's Auctions

Lindbergh, Bust, Bronze, Don F. Wiegand, 1981, 16 x 22 In.
$8,800

Ruby Lane

L

Table, Chased, Scrolls, Flowers, Howard, 1900, 2 ⅜ In.	246
Woman, Unicorn, Lion, Fruit Trees, Flag, Red Ground, Asprey & Co., 4 x 3 ¼ In.	2125
Zippo, 6-Color Medallion In Front, 100th Anniversary, Borden Company, 1957	290

LIGHTNING RODS AND LIGHTNING ROD BALLS are collected. The glass balls were at the center of the rod that was attached to the roof of a house or barn to avoid lightning damage. The balls were made in many colors and many patterns. Collectors prefer examples made before 1940.

LIGHTNING ROD

Metal, Twisted, Red Glass Ball, 3-Legged Stand, 55 In.	105
Mixed Metals, Milk Glass Ball, 4 Stars, Arrow, 67 In. .... *illus*	360

LIGHTNING ROD BALL

White, Stars & Crescent Moon Design, 5 In. .... *illus*	75

LIMOGES porcelain has been made in Limoges, France, since the mid-nineteenth century. Fine porcelains were made by many factories, including Haviland, Ahrenfeldt, Guerin, Pouyat, Elite, and others. Modern porcelains are being made at Limoges. The word *Limoges* as part of the mark is not an indication of age. Porcelain called "Limoges" was also made by Sebring China in Sebring, Ohio, in the early 1900s. The company changed its name to American Limoges China Company after the Limoges Company in France threatened to sue. American Limoges China Company went out of business in 1955. Haviland, one of the Limoges factories, is listed as a separate category in this book. These three marks are for factories in Limoges, France.

A. Klingenberg
c.1880s–1890s

D & Co.
c.1881–1893

M. Redon
c.1882–1896

Charger, Gilt Rim, Courting Couple, Pink Dress, Garden, 13 ⅝ In.	60
Charger, White Center, Pink Border, Colorful Flowers, Gold Trim Highlights, 12 In.	72
Cider Jug, Grape Decoration, Bernardaud & Co., France, 5 ½ In.	400
Perfume Lamp, Stamped Mark Of LD, Signed In Hand, No Heating Apparatus, 5 ¼ x 5 x 9 In.	113
Plaque, 3 Ducks, Hand Painted, Round, Signed Golsee, 13 In.	108
Plaque, Madonna & Child, Hand Painted, 14 x 9 ½ In.	1078
Plaque, Man & Woman, Seated, On Bench, Marked LRL, 12 In.	96
Plaque, Portrait, Hand Painted, Lavender Dress, Young Woman, Giltwood Frame, 11 x 8 In.	270
Plaque, Woman, Multicolor Decoration, Carved Wood Frame, 1900s, 16 x 12 In.	369
Plate, Charger, Scene, Young Man Courting Woman, Du Bois, 13 In.	108
Platter, Fish, Water, Sky, Jacob Pettit, 1894, 23 x 8 ¾ In.	77
Tankard, Gypsy Dancer, Gilt Trim Highlight, Twisted Branch Handle, 12 x 7 In.	666
Tray, Vanity, Dresser, Hand Painted Peonies, Gilt Rim, White Ware Stamp, Marked, 13 x 9 In.	153
Trinket Box, Zucchini Shape, Metal Fruit Basket Closure, Green Stripes, 5 In.	110
Tureen, Chowder, Flowering Water Lilies, Swimming Fish, 1886, 14 x 8 In.	365
Vase, Irises, Green Leaves, Pale Green Ground, Double Handles, Gilt, 14 x 8 ½ In. .... *illus*	120
Vase, Swollen, Art Deco, Blue, White, Black, Purple, Curved, Signed, Camille Faure, 12 In.	6655
Vase, Tapering Sides, Waisted Neck, Square Mouth, Decorated, Birds, Flowers, Calligraphies, 16 In.	98
Vase, White Shaded, Brown Mottled, Violet, Wildflowers, Green, 1900, 8 In.	3198

LINDBERGH was a national hero. In 1927, Charles Lindbergh, the aviator, became the first man to make a nonstop solo flight across the Atlantic Ocean. In 1932, his son was kidnapped and murdered, and Lindbergh was again the center of public interest. He died in 1974. All types of Lindbergh memorabilia are collected.

Bank, Bust, Flight Cap, Googles Around Neck, Metal, Copper Finish, 1929, 6 In.	195
Bookends, The Aviator, Portrait, Metal, c.1929, 5 ½ x 5 In.	80
Bust, Bronze, Don F. Wiegand, 1981, 16 x 22 In. .... *illus*	8800

Lithophane, Painting, House, Lake, Trees, Multicolor, Brass Stand, Pierced, 1800s, 11 x 5 In.
$297

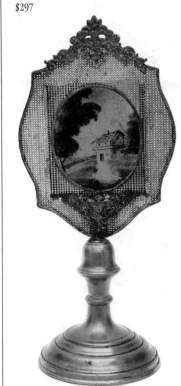

Ruby Lane

L

TIP
Some tea and coffee stains on dishes can be removed by rubbing them with damp baking soda.

Liverpool, Jug, Ship, Success To The George, Captn Frans Waite, Transfer, c.1810, 11 In.
$3,960

Cowan's Auctions

Lladro, Figurine, Boat, Gondolier, Musician, Venetian Serenade, 1983, 13½ x 39¼ In.
$1,062

Burchard Galleries

Lladro, Figurine, Embroiderer, No. 4865, Bordadoro Insular, Salvador Furio, Retired 1994, 11 In.
$354

Burchard Galleries

Lladro, Figurine, Maja, Bust, No. 4668, Busto Maja, Juan Huerta, Retired 1985, 12 In.
$148

Bunch Auctions

Button, King Of The Air, Our Hero, Portrait, Blue On White, 1 In.		22
Photo, Lone Eagle Landing In Canal Zone In France, 1927, 8 x 10 In.		35
Photo, Portrait, 3 x 5 In.		50

LITHOPHANES are porcelain pictures made by casting clay in layers of various thicknesses. When a piece is held to the light, a picture of light and shadow is seen through it. Most lithophanes date from the 1825–75 period. A few are still being made. Many lithophanes sold today were originally panels for lampshades.

Painting, House, Lake, Trees, Multicolor, Brass Stand, Pierced, 1800s, 11 x 5 In.	*illus*	297
Plaque, Fall Scene, Woman, Tree, Metal Frame, c.1855, 5 x 4 In.		201

LIVERPOOL, England, has been the site of many pottery and porcelain factories since the eighteenth century. Color-decorated porcelains, transfer-printed earthenware, stoneware, basalt, figurines, and other wares were made. Sadler and Green made print-decorated wares starting in 1756. Many of the pieces were made for the American market and feature patriotic emblems, such as eagles and flags. Liverpool pitchers are called Liverpool jugs by collectors.

Bowl, Herculaneum, Ship, Peace, Plenty & Independence Vignettes, 6¾ x 13⅞ In.		854
Jug, Farmers Arms, Village Harvest Celebration, 8⅛ In.		708
Jug, Shield, Eagle, Banner, Black Transfer, Pearlware, 8¼ In.		524
Jug, Ship, Success To The George, Captn Frans Waite, Transfer, c.1810, 11 In.	*illus*	3960

LLADRO is a Spanish porcelain. Brothers Juan, Jose, and Vicente Lladro opened a ceramics workshop in Almacera in 1951. They soon began making figurines in a distinctive, elongated style. In 1958 the factory moved to Tabernes Blanques, Spain. The company makes stoneware and porcelain figurines and vases in limited and unlimited editions. Dates given are first and last years of production. Marks since 1977 have the added word *Daisa,* the acronym for the company that holds the intellectual property rights to Lladro figurines.

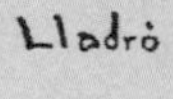

Lladrò	LLADRO ESPANA MADE IN SPAIN	LLADRO HAND MADE IN SPAIN
Lladro 1954	Lladro 1960	Lladro 1965–present

Figurine, Boat, Gondolier, Musician, Venetian Serenade, 1983, 13½ x 39¼ In.	*illus*	1062
Figurine, Dancer, No. 2069, 1977-2000, 17 In.		146
Figurine, Don Quixote, Sitting With Book & Sword, No. 1030, 1969, 14 x 19 In.		325
Figurine, Embroiderer, No. 4865, Bordadoro Insular, Salvador Furio, Retired 1994, 11 In.	*illus*	354
Figurine, Flower Peddler, Boy With Flower Cart, No. 5029, 1979-85, 9¾ In.		125
Figurine, Girl With Little Dog, Bust, Gres, 1970-81, A. Ruiz, 17 In.		605
Figurine, Maja, Bust, No. 4668, Busto Maja, Juan Huerta, Retired 1985, 12 In.	*illus*	148
Figurine, Mermaids Playing, Hair Floating, No. 1349, 1978-83, 16½ In.		598
Figurine, Peace Offering, No. 3559, Original Box, c.1985, 21 x 11 In.		706
Figurine, Puppet Show, Boy, Dog, Cats, No. 5736, Joan Coderch, 1991-96, 6 In.		295
Figurine, Rosalinda, Girl Sitting, Petals, Rose, No. 4836, 1973-83, 8 x 8 x 6 In.		236
Figurine, Sancho Panza, No. 1031, 1970-90, 6 x 11 In.		177
Figurine, Swans Take Flight, No. 5912, Salvador Debon, c.1992, 24 x 24 x 17 In.		708

LOETZ glass was made in many varieties. Johann Loetz bought a glassworks in Klostermuhle, Bohemia (now Klastersky Mlyn, Czech Republic), in 1840. He died in 1848 and his widow ran the company; then in 1879, his grandson took over. Most collectors recognize the iridescent gold glass similar to Tiffany, but many other types were made. The firm closed during World War II.

Box, Hinged, Cranberry, Threaded, Flip Lid, Engraved Holly Berry & Leaf Design, 2¼ x 4¼ In.		120
Chandelier, 4-Light, Bronze, Curving Arms, Flower Form, Glass Shade Holders, 20½ In.		4840

L

Jar, Green, Heavy Gilt Metal Lid, 3 ½ In.	72
Vase, Blue Iridescent, Wavy Rim, Opaque Oil Spot Exterior, 14 In.	1210
Vase, Bronze Holder, Squat, Shouldered, Flaring Neck, 7 Openings, Blue Iridescent, 11 In.	3025
Vase, Bulbous, Pewter Overlay, c.1905, 9 x 6 In.	1000
Vase, Burgundy, Green Striations, Enameled Mums, Shoulder Shape, 12 In.	472
Vase, Candia, Jack-In-The-Pulpit, Iridescent Gold, Bronze Holder, 9 ½ In.	1089
Vase, Creta Rusticana, Pinched Shoulder, Folded Rim, Austria, 6 ½ x 5 ½ In.	68
Vase, Flattened Inverted Teardrop, Flared Rim, Trumpet Base, Flowers, Cameo, 12 In.	2420
Vase, Green, Purple, Gold Iridescent, Ribbed Body, Undulating Rim, Polished Pontil, 8 In.	70
Vase, Honey, Amber, Pewter Mount, Shouldered, Jugendstil, c.1903, 6 In.	1180
Vase, Iridescent, Tapered Body, Flowers, Silver Overlay, 11 x 6 ½ In.	3068
Vase, Oil Spill Iridescent, Flared Neck, 7 x 3 ½ In.	660
Vase, Phanomen, Amethyst Iridescent, Oil Spot, Stepped Neck, Flaring Rim, 14 In.	1331
Vase, Phanomen, Black Bottom, Silver Threads, Iridescent Pulled Bands, c.1900, 4 In.	3932
Vase, Phanomen, Blue, Green, Pulled Feathers, Blown Glass, c.1900, 4 ½ x 5 In.	1875
Vase, Platinum & Blue Iridescent Wavy Bands, Orange, Body, Flowers, Silver Overlay, 10 In.	1694
Vase, Rose Titania, Frosted, Teardrop Shape, 5 ¼ In.	2223
Vase, Rusticana, Pinched, Green, c.1890, 6 In.	95
Vase, Vertical Lines, Silver Overlay, Blown Glass, c.1900, 7 ½ x 5 In. ..... *illus*	5625
Vase, Violetta Pattern, Wide Base, Triangular Rim, Unmarked, 1902, 11 In.	180

LONE RANGER, a fictional character, was introduced on the radio in 1932. Over three thousand shows were produced before the series ended in 1954. In 1938, the first Lone Ranger movie was made. The latest movie was made in 2013. Television shows were started in 1949 and are still seen on some stations. The Lone Ranger appears on many products and was even the name of a restaurant chain from 1971 to 1973.

Badge, Sheriff, 6-Point Star, Portrait, White Metal, 1950, 2 ⅜ In.	125
Belt, Leather, Arrowhead, Tonto, Cartridge, Luster, Embossed, 1940s, 1 ⅛ x 29 In.	125
Safety Rules, 2 Vertical Folds, Signature, Solemn Pledge, 1956, 8 ¼ x 10 In.	95
Toy, Tin, Windup, Silver, Marx, Lasso Spins, c.1938, 8 ½ x 6 In. .... *illus*	389

LONGWY WORKSHOP of Longwy, France, first made ceramic wares in 1798. The workshop is still in business. Most of the ceramic pieces found today are glazed with many colors to resemble cloisonne or other enameled metal. Many pieces were made with stylized figures and Art Deco designs. The factory used a variety of marks.

Longwy Faience Co.
1880–1939

Longwy Faience Co.
1890–1948

Longwy Faience Co.
1951–1948

Bone Dish, Fish Shape, Brown, Tan, 1920s, 8 ¾ x 3 ¾ In., Pair	45
Bowl, Art Deco, Craquelure, Cobalt Blue Rim, Enameled Roundel, Signed, 3 x 10 In.	113
Cigarette Box, Lid, Ashtrays On Each Side, Number Under Base, 1 ½ x 7 In.	68
Vase, Art Deco, Cobalt Blue Carved, Cerulean Crackle Glaze Background, 11 x 9 In.	158
Vase, Atlas, Globe, Maurice-Paul Chevallier, Earthenware, 1930s, 15 x 12 In. .... *illus*	4063
Vase, Cushion Shape, Glazed, 1900, 7 In.	492
Vase, Horses, 2 Handles, Glazed, Rolande Rizzi, c.1910, 22 ¾ In. .... *illus*	1375
Vase, Waisted, Boats, Swans, Flowers, Blue, Multicolor, 8 ½ x 6 ½ In.	62
Wall Pocket, Fawns, Red, Blue, Yellow, Glazed, Marked, c.1910, 18 x 8 In.	531

LOSANTI was made by Mary Louise McLaughlin in Cincinnati, Ohio, about 1899. It was a hard-paste decorative porcelain. She stopped making it in 1906.

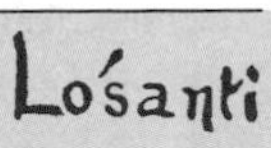

Losanti

Vase, Flowers & Stems In Relief, White Glaze, M.L. McLaughlin, 4 ½ x 3 ½ In.	2800

Loetz, Vase, Vertical Lines, Silver Overlay, Blown Glass, c.1900, 7 ½ x 5 In. $5,625

Rago Arts and Auction Center

Lone Ranger, Toy, Tin, Windup, Silver, Marx, Lasso Spins, c.1938, 8 ½ x 6 In. $389

Ruby Lane

L

Longwy, Vase, Atlas, Globe, Maurice-Paul Chevallier, Earthenware, 1930s, 15 x 12 In. $4,063

Rago Arts and Auction Center

Longwy, Vase, Horses, 2 Handles, Glazed, Rolande Rizzi, c.1910, 22¾ In.
$1,375

Rago Arts and Auction Center

Lotus Ware, Vase, Gilt, Pierced, Reserve, Cherub, Light Blue Neck, Handles, 9¾ x 6 In.
$204

Michann's Auctions

LOTUS WARE was made by the Knowles, Taylor & Knowles Company of East Liverpool, Ohio, from 1890 to 1900. Lotus Ware, a thin porcelain that resembles Belleek, was sometimes decorated outside the factory. Other types of ceramics that were made by the Knowles, Taylor & Knowles Company are listed under KTK.

Teapot, Venice, Flowers, Relief, Ridges, Gold Accents, c.1890, 7 x 4 x 3 In.	399
Vase, Gilt, Pierced, Reserve, Cherub, Light Blue Neck, Handles, 9¾ x 6 In. .... *illus*	204

J.&J.G.LOW **LOW** art tiles were made by the J. and J. G. Low Art Tile Works of Chelsea, Massachusetts, from 1877 to 1902. A variety of art and other tiles were made. Some of the tiles were made by a process called "natural," some were hand-modeled, and some were made mechanically.

Tile, Geometric Design, Arts & Crafts, c.1890, 6 x 6 In.	45
Trinket Box, Stove Tile, Woman Portrait, Neo Classical, Brass, Round, 1880s, 3 In.	225

LOY-NEL-ART, *see McCoy category.*

LUNCH BOXES and lunch pails have been used to carry lunches to school or work since the nineteenth century. Today, most collectors want either early tin tobacco advertising boxes or children's lunch boxes made since the 1930s. These boxes are made of metal or plastic. Vinyl lunch boxes were made from 1959 to 1982. Injection molded plastic lunch boxes were made beginning in 1972. Legend says metal lunch boxes were banned in Florida in 1972 after a group of mothers claimed children were hitting each other with them and getting injured. This is not true. Metal lunch boxes stopped being made in the 1980s because they were more expensive to make than plastic lunch boxes. Boxes listed here include the original Thermos bottle inside the box unless otherwise indicated. Movie, television, and cartoon characters may be found in their own categories. Tobacco tin pails and lunch boxes are listed in the Advertising category.

LUNCH BOX

Bonanza, 6 Series Scenes, Metal, Aladdin, c.1965	145
Campbell's, Dome, Loaf Of Bread, Tomato Soup Thermos, 1968, 9 x 6½ In. .... *illus*	369
Children Playing, Unmarked, Tin Lithograph, 4¼ x 7 x 4¾ In.	45
Deputy Dawg, Vinyl, Sitting Under Tree, No Thermos, c.1961	60
Dr. Seuss, Cat In The Hat, Tin Lithograph, Aladdin, 1970, 7 x 8 In. .... *illus*	92
Fantastic Four, Marvel Super Heroes, Metal, Aladdin, 1976	85
Hershey's, A Kiss For You, Girl & Boy, Metal, Blue, Top Handle, c.1970, 6 x 5 In.	20
Joe Palooka, Cartoon Scenes, Multicolor, Tin Lithograph, Upright Handles, 1948, 4 x 7 In.	180
Knight, On Horse, Castle, Yellow Border, 9 x 6 In. .... *illus*	275
Little Red Riding Hood, Wolf In Bed, Ohio Art, c.1980, 8 x 6 x 3 In.	23
Partridge Family, Metal, Singing, Bus, King-Seely, 1971, 8 x 7 x 4 In.	75
Space Explorer, Colonel Ed McCauley, Original Plastic Cup, Aladdin, 1960	225
Sport Theme, Red, Black, White, Tin, Silverware Tray, Decoware, c.1955, 7¾ x 3⅞ In. .. *illus*	75
Underdog, Villains, Sweet Polly Purebred, Metal, Universal, c.1974	2367
Volkswagen Bus, No Thermos, 11 x 6 In. .... *illus*	1230

LUNCH BOX THERMOS

Plaid, Metal, Butterscotch & Red, Aladdin, Wide Mouth, 6¾ x 3¼ In. .... *illus*	20

LUNEVILLE, a French faience factory, was established about 1730 by Jacques Chambrette. It is best known for its fine biscuit figures and groups and for large faience dogs and lions. The early pieces were unmarked. The firm was acquired by Keller and Guerin and is still working.

Jardiniere, Bird, Flowers, 15 x 20½ In.	800
Sculpture, Lion, Lying Down, Yellow Mane, Tail Over Back, Green Sponge Platform, 17 x 14 In.	3025
Vase, Red, Brown, Honey Ground, Flowers In Bloom, Cameo, Marked, 10 In.	1062

Lunch Box, Campbell's, Dome, Loaf Of Bread, Tomato Soup Thermos, 1968, 9 x 6 ½ In.
$369

Morphy Auctions

TIP

Old, clean cloth diapers are ideal for cleaning metal: very soft and lint free.

Lunch Box, Dr. Seuss, Cat In The Hat, Tin Lithograph, Aladdin, 1970, 7 x 8 In.
$92

Morphy Auctions

Lunch Box, Knight, On Horse, Castle, Yellow Border, 9 x 6 In.
$275

Morphy Auctions

Lunch Box, Sport Theme, Red, Black, White, Tin, Silverware Tray, Decoware, c.1955, 7 ¾ x 3 ⅞ In.
$75

Ruby Lane

Lunch Box, Volkswagen Bus, No Thermos, 11 x 6 In.
$1,230

Morphy Auctions

Collectible Lunch Boxes

Children's vinyl lunch boxes, made from 1959 to 1982, don't sell for as much as metal ones, but they're attracting attention. Many collectors are driven by nostalgia—they want the boxes they carried to school decades ago.

Lunch Box Thermos, Plaid, Metal, Butterscotch & Red, Aladdin, Wide Mouth, 6 ¾ x 3 ¼ In.
$20

Ruby Lane

Lustres, Cranberry Glass, White Overlay, Gilt Trim, Spear Point Prisms, Bohemia, 14 In., Pair
$1,250

New Orleans Auction Galleries

Lustres, Custard Glass, Arched Rim, Knopped Neck, Domed Foot, 12¾ In., Pair
$420

Jeffrey S. Evans

LUSTER glaze was meant to resemble copper, silver, or gold. The term *luster* includes any piece with some luster trim. It has been used since the sixteenth century. Some of the luster found today was made during the nineteenth century. The metallic glazes are applied on pottery. The finished color depends on the combination of the clay color and the glaze. Blue, orange, gold, and pearlized luster decorations were used by Japanese and German firms in the early 1900s. Fairyland Luster was made by Wedgwood in the 1900s. Copies made by modern methods started appearing in 1990. Tea Leaf pieces have their own category.

Fairyland luster is included in the Wedgwood category.
Girandole, Bohemian Overlay Portrait, White Cut To Cranberry Glass, Gilt, 1800s, 11 x 5 In....... 390
Sunderland Luster pieces are in the Sunderland category.

LUSTRES are mantel decorations or pedestal vases with many hanging glass prisms. The name really refers to the prisms, and it is proper to refer to a single glass prism as a lustre. Either spelling, luster or lustre, is correct.

Austrian Glass, Gilt, Prisms, Cut To Emerald, 1800s, 11 In., Pair	350
Bohemian Glass, White Cut To Green, Prisms, Crown Shape, 14 x 7¼ In., Pair......................	412
Bohemian Glass, White Cut To Green, Prisms, Square Reserves, 9½ x 4¾ In., Pair..............	121
Bristol, Pink Opalescent, Gilt, Shamrock, Prisms, 17 In., Pair	150
Cranberry Flash, Cup Shape Top, Clear Prisms, Scalloped Foot, 10 In., Pair	55
Cranberry Glass, White Overlay, Gilt Trim, Spear Point Prisms, Bohemia, 14 In., Pair... *illus*	1250
Custard Glass, Arched Rim, Knopped Neck, Domed Foot, 12¾ In., Pair .... *illus*	420
Emerald Glass, Calcite, Gilt, Crown, Prisms, Electrified, 15 In., Pair	150
Ruby Glass, Painted Flowers, Prisms, Gold Bands, 12½ x 6 In., Pair	415
Women, Flowers, Prisms, 14¼ x 6¾ In., Pair	770

MAJOLICA is a general term for any pottery glazed with an opaque tin enamel that conceals the color of the clay body. It has been made since the fourteenth century. Today's collector is most likely to find Victorian majolica. The heavy, colorful ware is rarely marked. Some famous makers include George Jones & Sons, Ltd.; Griffen, Smith and Hill; Joseph Holdcroft; and Minton. Majolica by Wedgwood is listed in the Wedgwood category. These three marks can be found on majolica items.

George Jones, George Jones
& Sons, Ltd.
1861–1873

Griffen, Smith and Hill
c.1879–1889

Joseph Holdcroft, Sutherland
Pottery
1865–1906

Asparagus Server, Chrysanthemum, Julius Dressler, 10¼ x 17 In.	66
Asparagus Set, Server, Handles, 8 Round Plates, Scalloped, Stalks, c.1905, 9 Piece	960
Cachepot, Cherub Lying In Wheat, 5¾ x 10 In. .... *illus*	142
Charger, Lovers & Putti, Made In Italy, 1900s, 24 In...	54
Charger, Oriental Style, Red, Blue, Green & Gold, Unusual Plate, 1890, 2 x 19 In.	450
Cheese Dish, Lid, Woven Beehive Form, Vine Handle, Blue, Tan, Green, 13 x 13 In.	488
Compote, 3 Dolphin Tails, Dish, Light Blue, Scalloped, 7 x 8½ In..	72
Compote, Man, Doublet, Hose, Gloves, Plumed Hat, Hugo Lonitz, c.1885, 25 In........................	550
Compote, Old Labels, Impressed Mark On Bottom, 1800s, 7 In., Pair .... *illus*	720
Ewer, Underplate, Palissy, Green, Leaf Mat, Lizards, Toad Finial, c.1880, 12 In.	720
Figure, Monkey, Perched On Branch, Unglazed Interior, Base, 9 x 9 x 11 In.	201
Figure, Victorian Woman, Seated On Gilt Metal Wire Chair, Needlepoint Footrest, Italy, 31 In.	300
Game Dish, Gun Dog Lid, 3 Parts, Handles, Paw Feet, 8½ x 14½ In. .... *illus*	2420
Game Dish, Hunting Dog Finial, Running Hare, Handles, Footed, 7 x 12 In.	1586
Garden Seat, Cobalt Blue, Swags, Fruit, Nut, Shells, c.1875, 19½ x 13½ In............................	175
Garden Seat, Elephant On Square Plinth, Pierced Seat Back, 23 x 23 In................................	244

L

Humidor, Figural Dog Lid, Hat, Satchel, Rifle Leaning On Tree Stump, 6 x 6 x 5 In.	210
Jardiniere, Birds, Flowers, Leaves, Pink Interior, George Jones, 1870, 13¾ In.	760
Jardiniere, Multicolor Drip Glaze, Double Handle, Acanthus Leaves, 1900s, 8 x 11 In.	36
Jardiniere, Pedestal, Red, Band Of Leaves, 51 x 19 In.	106
Jardiniere, Stand, Cobalt Blue, Scrolls, 44 x 17½ In.	625
Jardiniere, Swans, Water Lilies, Cattails, Blue, White, Green, 16½ x 18 In.	1625
Pitcher, Quaker Woman, Holding Fan, Multicolor, Minton, 11 In.	93
Pitcher, Serpent Shape Spout, Yellow, Brown, Green, 13 In.	360
Pitcher, Stork, Cattails, Punched Star Ground, Duck's Head Handle, 12 In. ...... *illus*	266
Plaque, Birds, Flowers, Branches, Cattails, 22¼ x 11¼ In.	210
Plaque, Lobster, Aquatic Vegetation, Molded, Palissy Type, Portugal, 11¾ In.	625
Plaque, Man, Brown & Green Outfit, Shields, Saxa Loquuntur, 1900s, 20 x 20 In.	129
Plate, Man, Tavern, Yellow Well, Brown Lip, Scallop Shells, Scrolls, Checkered Ground, 10 In.	24
Stand, Fruit, 5 Tiers, Lions, 2 Peasant Figures, 1800s, 11½ x 12 In. .... *illus*	600
Stand, Multicolor Decorated, Butterfly, Leafy Designs, 1900s, 20 x 11 In.	1416
Sugar, Lid, Bamboo Pattern, Etruscan, 6 In. .... *illus*	30
Syrup, Flowers, White, Blue, Woven Handles, Pewter Lid, 6 In.	54
Table, Birds, Grapevines, Center Cartouche, Baroque Frame, Dart Design, 1900s, 30 x 45 In.	960
Tile, Zanesville, Blue Glaze, Woman Sewing, Children, Marked, 1880s, 13 x 9 In.	1062
Tray, Leaf, Scalloped Yellow Edge, Multicolor, 8 In.	30
Tympanum, Embracing Monks, Molded Arch, Italy, 13 x 27 In.	1750
Urn, Branches, Leaves, Flowers, Multicolor, 17 In.	120
Urn, Grapevines, Musical Instruments, Green, Light Brown, Ram's Head Handles, 15 x 9 In.	80
Urn, Reticulated, Buildings, Flowers, Leaves, Multicolor, St. Clement, 17 x 23 In. ...... *illus*	1000
Vase, Bud, Woman, Carrying Grapes, Man, Seated, Trees, Bench, 20 x 15 In.	220
Vase, Deep Blue Ground, Ribbed Body, Panel, Foliage, Stiff Leaves, 1800s, 37 x 26 In.	431
Vase, Hunter On Horseback, Stag, Continental, 20 x 13 In. .... *illus*	192
Vase, Yellow Bamboo, Cylindrical, Applied Monkeys, Minton, c.1872, 7 In.	2316

MALACHITE is a green stone with unusual layers or rings of darker green shades. It is often polished and used for decorative objects. Most malachite comes from Siberia or Australia.

Box, Napoleon III, Gilt Bronze Mount, Flowers, Signed Tahan Fr. De L'Empereur, 3 x 6 In.	1500
Figure, Standing, Bean Shape Eyes, Conical Hat, Stone Vibrant Colors, 3 x 1¼ In.	685
Tray, Ink, Shaped Edge, Leaves, Chinese, 4½ x 3½ In. .... *illus*	125

MAPS of all types have been collected for centuries. The earliest known printed maps were made in 1478. The first printed street map showed London in 1559. The first road maps for use by drivers of automobiles were made in 1901. Collectors buy maps that were pages of old books, as well as the multifolded road maps popular in this century.

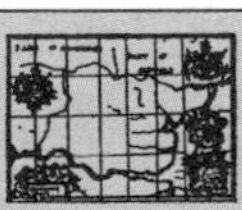

America Septentrionalis, Mermen, California, Jan Jansson, 1641, 20⅛ x 23⅞ In.	3120
Belgium, Netherlands, Limburg, Shield, Cupids, 1662, 5½ x 20 In.	106
Constellations, Northern Sky, Johann Gabriele Doppelmayr, 1730, 19½ x 23 In.	295
Globe, Ancient Zodiac World, Rotating, India, 1900, 33 In.	50
Globe, Brass Meridian, Walnut Cradle Stand, Hammond, c.1933, 12-In. Diam.	458
Globe, Bronzed Base, Paw Feet, G.W. Bacon, England, c.1918, 18-In. Diam., 30 In.	875
Globe, Cardboard, Iron Base, Lions, Paw Feet, Girard & Boitte, c.1875, 25 In.	1305
Globe, Celestial, Brown, Mahogany Stand, Cary, c.1850, 47 In.	2375
Globe, Decorative Stand, Barley Twist Supports, Italy, 1900, 42 x 24 In.	66
Globe, Gilman Joslin, Boston, Cast Iron Tripod Stand, Late 19th Century, 16 x 19 In. ...... *illus*	389
Globe, Hans Wegner, On Stand, Oak, Printed Paper Over Plastic, Brass, 1950s, 40 In.	3000
Globe, Joslin's Celestial, Ebonized Stand, Marked, c.1870, 10 In.	2440
Globe, Light-Up, Explorer Information, Smoked Tabletop Stand, 1986, 12 In.	36
Globe, Lithographed Gores, Brass Half Meridian, Iron Stand, H. Kiepert, Germany, 1888, 36 In.	1280
Globe, Multicolor, Pedestal, 68 In.	3500
Globe, Oak Stand, Hans Wegner, 1950s, 40 In. .... *illus*	3000
Globe, Puzzle, Paper Gores On Bakelite, Iron Stand, Geographical Educator Co., c.1927, 9½ In.	1708
Globe, Replogle, Fitted Stand, World Horizon Series, Interior Light, 1900s, 31 x 16 In.	132
Globe, Stretcher, Turned Legs, 16 x 12 In.	263

Majolica, Cachepot, Cherub Lying In Wheat, 5¾ x 10 In.
$142

Hess Auction Group

Majolica, Compote, Old Labels, Impressed Mark On Bottom, 1800s, 7 In., Pair
$720

Brunk Auctions

Majolica, Game Dish, Gun Dog Lid, 3 Parts, Handles, Paw Feet, 8½ x 14½ In.
$2,420

James D. Julia Auctioneers

M

Majolica, Pitcher, Stork, Cattails, Punched Star Ground, Duck's Head Handle, 12 In.
$266

Hess Auction Group

Majolica, Stand, Fruit, 5 Tiers, Lions, 2 Peasant Figures, 1800s, 11 ½ x 12 In.
$600

Brunk Auctions

Majolica, Sugar, Lid, Bamboo Pattern, Etruscan, 6 In.
$30

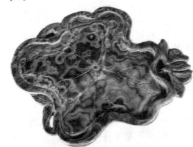

Hess Auction Group

Majolica, Urn, Reticulated, Buildings, Flowers, Leaves, Multicolor, St. Clement, 17 x 23 In.
$1,000

Naudeau's Auction Gallery

Majolica, Vase, Hunter On Horseback, Stag, Continental, 20 x 13 In.
$192

Neal Auction Co.

Malachite, Tray, Ink, Shaped Edge, Leaves, Chinese, 4 ½ x 3 ½ In.
$125

Kaminski Auctions

Map, Globe, Gilman Joslin, Boston, Cast Iron Tripod Stand, Late 19th Century, 16 x 19 In.
$389

Copake Auction

Map, Globe, Oak Stand, Hans Wegner, 1950s, 40 In.
$3,000

Rago Arts and Auction Center

M

Globe, Terrestrial, Rotating, Regency Style, Brass Band, Pedestal Base, 1800s, 41 x 24 In.	3600
Globe, Turned Stand, J.A. Buhler, Germany, 1800s, 11 x 5 ½ In.	605
Globe, Walnut Stand, Stretcher Compass, 44 x 23 In.	2117
Great Lakes, D'Anville, 1775, 19 x 23 In.	510
Louisiana Province, J.B. Homann, Copper Engraving, Hand Colored, c.1720, 19 x 23 In.	6000
Louisiana, Arkansas, Mississippi, Henry Schenck Tanner, 1841, 13 x 11 In.	437
Mexico, Seat Of War, Outlined, U.S. Dragoon Charging At Cannon, 1847, 19 x 24 In.	2760
New Orleans, Insets, Colored, Thomas De Vargas Machuca Lopez, Madrid, 1762, 16 x 16 In.	1750
New Orleans, Norman's Plan, Key References 80 Points, 1845, 24 x 18 In.	1920
New York In North America, Black & White Engraving, Claude Sauthier, 1779, 75 x 57 In.	16800
North & South Carolina, Georgia, Emanuel Bowen, 1747, 16 x 20 In.	720
North & South Carolina, Partially Hand Colored, Johnson, 1866, 27 ½ x 33 ¾ In.	300
North Carolina, Hand Colored, Samuel Lewis, 1795, 18 ½ x 26 In.	780
Plan Of City Of Jefferson, Hand Colored Lithograph, William H. Williams, 1860, 14 ½ x 20 In.	938
Plan Of Yorktown & Gloucester, Lt. John Hills, Black & White Engraved, 1785, 29 x 22 In.	360
Planetarium, Orrery, Sun, Earth, Moon, Metal, Wood, Trippensee Mfg., 30 In.	1750
Southern States, Engraved Pocket, Embossed Cloth Binding, Gilt Letters, 1863, 52 x 39 In.	3250
Southern United States, Carolinas, Georgia, Florida, Cary, 1806, 19 x 21 ½ In.	780
State Of Franklinia, United States, Eastern Section, Hand Colored, Wilkinson, 1783, 11 x 14 In.	420
State Of Sequoyah, Chromolithograph, Vignette, Frame, 1905, 8 x 15 ¾ In.	3500
State Of South Carolina, Lewis, 1795, 16 x 18 In., Pair	600
State Of Texas, Engraved Pocket, Hand Colored, Frame, 1882, 37 x 32 In.	3500
Tokyo, 4 Sections, Multicolor, 1860, 27 ½ x 32 ½ In.	295
Virginia, Black & White Line Engraving, Pieter Van Der Aa, 6 x 9 In., 1707	360
Virginia, Carey & Lee, Engraved, Hand Colored, Geographical Statistical, 1822, 14 x 19 In.	320
West Virginia, Ohio, Engraved Pocket, Embossed Cloth Binding, Gilt Letters, 1865, 32 x 39 In.	2500
World, Hand Colored, Copper Engraving, Gerard Valck, c.1686, 17 x 21 In.	295

MARBLE collectors pay highest prices for glass and sulphide marbles. The game of marbles has been popular since the days of the ancient Romans. American children were able to buy marbles by the mid-eighteenth century. Dutch glazed clay marbles were least expensive. Glazed pottery marbles, attributed to the Bennington potteries in Vermont, were of a better quality. Marbles made of pink marble were also available by the 1830s. Glass marbles seem to have been made later. By 1880, Samuel C. Dyke of South Akron, Ohio, was making clay marbles and The National Onyx Marble Company was making marbles of onyx. The Navarre Glass Marble Company of Navarre, Ohio, and M. B. Mishler of Ravenna, Ohio, made the glass marbles. Ohio remained the center of the marble industry, and the Akron-made Akro Agate brand became nationally known. Other pieces made by Akro Agate are listed in this book in the Akro Agate category. Sulphides are glass marbles with frosted white figures in the center.

Agate, Guinea, One Pitch Line, Cobalt Base, Orange, Blue Spots, ½ In.	*illus*	825
Onionskin, Blue, White, 1 ⅝ In.		80
Peltier, Blue Galaxy, Turquoise, Black Aventurine, Yellow Ribbon, ½ In.	*illus*	1650

MARBLE CARVINGS, such as large or small figurines, groups of people or animals, and architectural decorations, have been a special art form since the time of the ancient Greeks. Reproductions, especially of large Victorian groups, are being made of a mixture using marble dust. These are very difficult to detect, and collectors should be careful. Other carvings are listed under Alabaster.

Abstract Female, Fitted To Brass Spindle, Cylindrical Rotation, Fritz Olsen, 1950s, 4 ¾ x 5 ½ In.		452
Aphrodite, Stature, Venus, Polished Surface, Inscribed, Nude, 22 In.		1936
Bust, Bacchante, White Marble & Gilt Bronze Base, Joseph-Charles Marin, France, 1800s, 10 In.		2375
Bust, Diana, Inscribed, Socle Overall, France, 1893, 18 x 14 In.		1063
Bust, Female Figure, Long Wavy Hair, Pais, Base Shape Corners, 1900s, 15 x 14 x 6 ½ In.		1000
Bust, Giovanni Maria Benzoni, Marble Plinth & Socle, 22 In.	*illus*	4880
Bust, Girl, Lacy Bodice, 1800s, 22 In.		375
Bust, Madame Recamier, Shawl, Head Wrap, c.1875, 24 ½ In.		3250
Bust, Pink, 2 Heads, Signed Flaum, 27 In.		60
Bust, White Head, Red Veins, Torso, Apollo Belvedere, 27 In.		1353

Glass Marbles
Venetian swirl glass marbles, clear glass with ribbons of colored glass, and End of Day glass marbles, with flecks of colored glass, are popular with collectors. An Indian swirl marble sold for $7,700 in 1995. Sulphides, marbles with frosted white figures of animals, flowers, or faces inside, are expensive. A double sulphide marble picturing both a lion and a dog sold in 1987 for $4,200.

Marble, Agate, Guinea, One Pitch Line, Cobalt Base, Orange, Blue Spots, ½ In. $825

Morphy Auctions

Marble, Peltier, Blue Galaxy, Turquoise, Black Aventurine, Yellow Ribbon, ½ In. $1,650

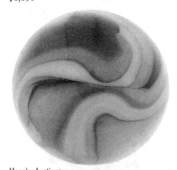

Morphy Auctions

TIP
Don't store old paint rags. They may ignite spontaneously.

M

Marble Carving, Bust, Giovanni Maria Benzoni, Marble Plinth & Socle, 22 In. $4,880

I.M. Chait

Marble Carving, Statue, Dog's Head, Carrara, Italy, 11 x 13 In. $488

Neal Auction Co.

Marble Carving, Urn, Napoleon III, Rouge, Bronze Mounted, Ram's Head Handles, c.1890, 26 In. $1,280

Neal Auction Co.

Bust, Woman, Laurel Leaf Crown, Signed Pugi, 23 x 14 ¼ In.	1875
Bust, Woman, Looks Over Shoulder, 18 ¾ x 10 ¼ In.	312
Bust, Young Girl, Part In Hair, Looking Down, Flowers, 16 In.	352
Figurine, Dog, German Shepherd, Carving, Old Patina, 11 x 15 x 7 ½ In.	285
Font, Octagonal, Central Pillar, 4 Columns, Red Mottled Marble, Round Base, 5 ¾ In.	187
Group, Woman, Seated, Bird, 2 Standing Irish Setter Dogs, 10 x 26 x 5 ½ In.	472
Pedestal, 3 Sections, Rose Carvings, Reeded Column, Octagonal Base, 1900s, 42 x 11 In.	72
Pedestal, Octagonal Top & Base, Column, Acanthus Leaf, Gilt Metal, 56 x 13 In.	207
Pedestal, Revolving Square Top, Fluted, Tapered, Hexagon, 38 ¼ x 14 In.	687
Pedestal, Stepped Round Top, Fluted Column Shaft, Floral Metal, Octagonal Base, 41 x 10 In.	177
Pedestal, Twist Column, Flower Skirt, Octagonal, 40 x 12 In., Pair	383
Pedestal, Twist, Shaft, Stylized Green Key Collar, Round Stepped Base, 39 x 12 In., Pair	495
Pedestal, White, Slender Column, Clipped Corner Square Top & Base, 1900s, 38 x 7 In.	330
Plaque, Portrait, Victorian Woman, 11 x 9 x 1 ½ In.	187
Plaque, Virgin, Child, St. Dominic, High Relief, Signed D. Puech, France, 52 x 34 In.	10000
Plate, Deep Charger, Striated Tan, Gray, 2 Bands Of Relief Carved Islamic Text, 2 ¼ x 17 In.	600
Stand, Iron, Claw Feet, Victorian, 32 x 16 ½ In.	344
Statue, Ariadne, On Panther, After Johann Heinrich Dannecker, 24 x 19 ½ In.	2625
Statue, Boy, Holding A Fish, Kneeling On Rocks, Frog, Flowers, 41 In.	10625
Statue, Children, Peek-A-Boo, c.1880, 24 In.	813
Statue, Cupid & Quiver, France, 1800s, 34 In.	4000
Statue, Diana, Nude, Bow, Quiver, Signed, P. Romanelli, 41 x 16 x 16 In.	5445
Statue, Dog's Head, Carrara, Italy, 11 x 13 In. *illus*	488
Statue, Eagle, Woman, Profile, Open Mouth, Moon, Stars, O. Joe, 26 x 13 ½ In.	630
Statue, Girl, Nude, Reclining, Drape Over Waist, Paw Foot Chair, Tassels, 9 ½ x 11 In.	1799
Statue, Lion, Lucerne, Natural Plinth Base, Dark Verde Alphi, 1900, 3 ½ x 6 ½ x 2 ¼ In.	162
Statue, Lion, Prowling, Muscular, White, Heavy Gray Veining, 14 ½ x 21 In.	1260
Statue, Nude Female, Modernist, 17 In.	236
Statue, Nude Figure, Partially Robed, Standing, Signed, A. Cipriani, 28 In.	1331
Statue, St. Francis, Long Hooded Robe, Dove, Standing, 31 In.	726
Statue, Tiger, Perched, Rocky Outcrop, White, Heavy Black Lines, 21 In.	3009
Statue, Venus, Seated, 1 Knee Up, After Antonio Canova, 1800s, 34 ½ In.	8125
Statue, Venus & Cupid, Terracotta, White, Gilt Bronze Base, French, 15 In.	5250
Statue, Venus De Milo, Nude Top, No Arms, Draped Down Robes, Unsigned, 34 x 10 x 9 In.	2118
Statue, Woman, Barefoot, Doves, Neoclassical, c.1900, 32 x 9 In.	633
Statue, Woman, Bathing, Nude Standing Figure, Leaning, Long Garment, 33 In.	3025
Statue, Woman, Pitcher, Style Of Antiquity, 32 x 8 x 8 In.	1875
Table, Ormolu Mounts, Rams Heads, Cloven Hooves, 22 x 26 x 26 In.	438
Tazza, Mottled Brown, Red & White, Bronze Dore Trim, Putti Stem, c.1885, 13 In.	875
Twisted Loop, White Marble, Black Stand, 2003, 21 ½ x 12 In.	2242
Urn, Lid, Plinth, Derbyshire, Spar, 17 x 5 In.	2562
Urn, Lid, Red, Bronze Mount, Bacchic Masks, Socle Supports, 22 x 6 ¼ In., Pair	275
Urn, Napoleon III, Rouge, Bronze Mounted, Ram's Head Handles, c.1890, 26 In. *illus*	1280
Urn, Potpourri, Ovoid, Bronze Leaf Mounts, Louis XVI Style, France, Pair, c.1900, 18 In.	813
Urn, Ram's Head Base, Rectangular Plinth, Deep Yellow, 1800s, 10 In., Pair	813

MARBLEHEAD POTTERY was founded in 1904 by Dr. J. Hall as a rehabilitative program for the patients of a Marblehead, Massachusetts, sanitarium. Two years later it was separated from the sanitarium and it continued operations until 1936. Many of the pieces were decorated with marine motifs.

Candlestick, Chamber, Blue Matte Glaze, Round Handle, 1900s, 4 x 4 In., Pair	240
Tile, Galleon At Sea, Soft Glazes, Marked With Ship Logo, 6 ½ In.	189
Tile, Landscape, Trees, Reflected In Pond, Olive, Green, c.1908, 6 x 6 In.	12500
Tile, Rampant Lion, Green, Yellow Ground, Square, Wood Frame, 5 In.	550
Tile, Ship, 2-Masted, Sails, Blue, White, 4 ½ x 4 ½ In.	72
Vase, Blue & Green Matte Glazes, Abstract Design, Marked Arthur Baggs, 3 In.	472
Vase, Butterfly, Dark Green Matte Glaze, 4 ½ x 4 In.	1250
Vase, Circles, Blue, Arthur Baggs, Sarah Tutt, 1920s, 4 x 4 ½ In.	2000
Vase, Gray Matte Glaze, Cranes In Deeper Gray, Marked Milner & Tutt, 9 In.	3422

Vase, Round, Mauve Matte Glaze, Marked With Ship Logo, 3 In.		560
Vase, Stylized Chestnut Trees, Light Green Matte Glaze, A. Hennessey, Sarah Tutt, 3 ½ x 4 ¾ In.		3500
Vase, Stylized Clematis, Blue, 1910s, 6 x 4 ¾ In.		1875
Vase, Stylized Clematis, Tan & Brown, Ship Mark, c.1920, 6 ½ x 5 ½ In.	*illus*	3500
Vase, Swollen, Purple Gray Matte Glaze, Marked With Ship Logo, 9 In.		236
Vase, Tan Orange, 5 ½ x 4 ½ In.		687

MARDI GRAS, French for "Fat Tuesday," was first celebrated in seventeenth-century Europe. The first celebration in America was held in Mobile, Alabama, in 1703. The first krewe, a parading or social club, was founded in 1856. Dozens have been formed since. The Mardi Gras Act, which made Fat Tuesday a legal holiday, was passed in Louisiana in 1875. Mardi Gras balls, carnivals, parties, and parades are held from January 6 until the Tuesday before the beginning of Lent. The most famous carnival and parades take place in New Orleans. Parades feature floats, elaborate costumes, masks, and "throws" of strings of beads, cups, doubloons, or small toys. Purple, green, and gold are traditional Mardi Gras colors. Mardi Gras memorabilia ranges from cheap plastic beads to expensive souvenirs from early celebrations.

Crown, King's, Paste Jewels, c.1900	*illus*	960
Dance Card, Oval, Olympians, Harvest & Festival, Krewe, 1907		213
Ducal Badge, Rex, Drama Of The Year, Jeweled Pendant, Red & White Ribbon, 1914		335
Favor, Krewe, Rex, Gilt Loving Cup, Feasts & Fetes, 1903		360
Favor, Letter Opener, Krewe, Rex, 10 ¼ x 1 ⅝ In.		225
Favor, Rex, Silver, Black, Vase, 1917, 5 ⅜ x 5 ⅛ In.		125
Invitation, Ball, Krewe Of Proteus, Myths & Worships Of Chinese, Feb. 16, 1885		305
Invitation, Ball, Krewe Of Proteus, Silver Anniversary, Inspiration Of Proteus, 1906		275
Invitation, Ball, Mistick Krewe Of Comus, Demonology, Snake, Feb. 10, 1891		549
Invitation, Ball, Mistick Krewe Of Comus, Josephus, Feb. 14, 1899		244
Invitation, Ball, Momus, Realms Of Fancy, Charles Briton, 1878, 4 ½ x 7 ⅛ In.		369
Invitation, Ball, Rex, Illustrations From Literature, B.A. Wikstrom, Feb. 6, 1884		366
Invitation, Ball, Rex, Ivanhoe, Striped Robe, F. Appel, Feb. 17, 1885		320
Invitation, Ball, Rex, Pursuit Of Pleasure Theme, Feb. 21st, 1882	*illus*	732
Invitation, Ball, Rex, Rulers Of Ancient Times, Feb. 18th, 1890, Fan Shape	*illus*	406
Invitation, Ball, Twelfth Night Revelers, Kingdom Of Flowers, Charles Briton, 9 x 6 ¾ In.		400
Invitation, Ball, Visions Theme, 1891		305
Parade Bulletin, Krewe Of Proteus, Famous Lovers Of The World, 1915, 28 x 42 In.		553
Parade Bulletin, Krewe Of Proteus, Zoraster, Walle & Co., 1912, 28 x 42 In.		338
Parade Bulletin, Momus, Alice's Adventures In Wonderland, Searcy & Pfaff, 28 x 42 In.		338
Parade Bulletin, Rex, Drama Of The Year, Lithograph, Walle & Co., 1914, 28 x 42 In.		488
Parade Bulletin, Rex, Visions From The Poets, Walle, Mar. 7, 1916, 28 x 42 In.		732
Parade Bulletin, Romantic Legends Theme, Walle & Co. Ltd., 28 x 42 In.		275
Pin, Ball Mask, Rhinestones, Clear Face, Red Lips & Earrings, Mystic Club, 2 In.		64
Pin, Egyptian Head, KOP 1901 On Wide Collar, Krewe Of Proteus, Metal, Enamel		344
Pin, Sunday Sinners, Smiling Pepper, Goldtone Metal, Signed India Stewart, 2001		85

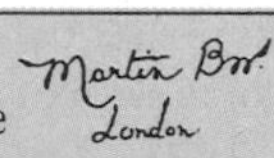

MARTIN BROTHERS of Middlesex, England, made Martinware, a salt-glazed stoneware, between 1873 and 1915. Many figural jugs and vases were made by the four brothers. Of special interest are the fanciful birds, usually made with removable heads. Most pieces have the incised name of the artists plus other information on the bottom.

Martin Bro. London

Pitcher, Leaves, Ball Shape, c.1883, 8 x 5 ¼ In.		750
Vase, Cats, Grooved, Cobalt Blue, Brown, Handles, R.W. Martin, 1883, 9 x 6 In.	*illus*	2750
Vase, Fish, Crab, Seahorses, Green, 1904, 10 ¼ x 4 In.		1875
Vase, Stoneware, Fish, Gray Ground, Brown Decoration, 1800s, 2 ¾ In.		1599

MARY GREGORY is the name used for a type of glass that is easily identified. White figures were painted on clear or colored glass as the decoration. The figures chosen were usually children at play. The first glass known as Mary Gregory was made in about 1870. Similar glass is made even today. The traditional story has been that the glass was made at the Boston & Sandwich Glass Company in

Marblehead, Vase, Stylized Clematis, Tan & Brown, Ship Mark, c.1920, 6 ½ x 5 ½ In. $3,500

Rago Arts and Auction Center

TIP
A tennis ball can be used to rub out scuff marks on vintage linoleum tiles often used in houses before the 1960s.

M

Mardi Gras, Crown, King's, Paste Jewels, c.1900 $960

Neal Auction Co.

Mardi Gras, Invitation, Ball, Rex, Pursuit Of Pleasure Theme, Feb. 21st, 1882 $732

Neal Auction Co.

Mardi Gras, Invitation, Ball, Rex, Rulers Of Ancient Times, Feb. 18th, 1890, Fan Shape
$406

Neal Auction Co.

Martin Brothers, Vase, Cats, Grooved, Cobalt Blue, Brown, Handles, R.W. Martin, 1883, 9 x 6 In.
$2,750

Rago Arts and Auction Center

TIP

For a pollution-free glass cleaner use a mixture of white vinegar and water.

Mary Gregory, Pitcher, Cranberry Glass, Girl, With Bird, Fenton, 9¼ x 7½ In.
$42

Martin Auction Co.

Sandwich, Massachusetts, by a woman named Mary Gregory. Recent research has shown that none was made at Sandwich. In fact, all early Mary Gregory glass was made in Bohemia. Beginning in 1957, the Westmoreland Glass Co. made the first Mary Gregory–type decorations on American glassware. These pieces had simpler designs, less enamel paint, and more modern shapes. France, Italy, Germany, Switzerland, and England, as well as Bohemia, made this glassware. Children standing, not playing, were pictured after the 1950s.

Bell, Amber Cut To Cranberry Glass, Girl, Hills, Fenton, 6 In.	17
Celery Vase, Blue, White, Mottled, Middletown Silver Plated Frame, 6¾ In.	780
Celery Vase, Pink Cased, Mica, Enameled, Silver Plate Stand, Bear Rug Handles, Victorian, 9 In.	1020
Cruet, Gilt, Hills, Tree, Stopper, 6¼ In.	25
Eggnog Bowl, Lid, Cranberry Enameled, 2 Children, In Field Of Flowers, Handle, 8 x 8 In.	420
Jar, Cranberry, Cherub, In Trees, Gilt Metal Base, 4½ In.	180
Pitcher, Cranberry Glass, Girl, With Bird, Fenton, 9¼ x 7½ In. ..... *illus*	42
Toothpick Holder, Cranberry, Girl, Bird, 2½ In.	36
Vase, Green, Girl, Seated On Tree Branch, Pond & Swan, 16 In.	84

MASONIC, *see Fraternal category.*

MASON'S IRONSTONE was made by the English pottery of Charles J. Mason after 1813. Mason, of Lane Delph, was given a patent for this improved earthenware. He usually called it *Mason's Patent Ironstone China*. It resisted chipping and breaking, so it became popular for dinnerware and other table service dishes. Vases and other decorative pieces were also made. The ironstone was decorated with orange, blue, gold, and other colors, often in Japanese-inspired designs. The firm had financial difficulties but the molds and the name *Mason* were used by many owners through the years, including Francis Morley, Taylor Ashworth, George L. Ashworth, and John Shaw. Mason's joined the Wedgwood group in 1973 and the name was used for a few years and then dropped.

Bowl, White Central Reserve, 12 Arches, Coral Flowers, Dark Blue Ground, 10¼ In.	119
Creamer, Vista England, Red, 4½ In.	24
Jar, Decorated Panels, Flowers, Fish, Butterflies, 1830s, 6¾ x 6½ In.	420
Platter, Flowers, Birds, Blue & White Transfer, 21 x 17 In. ..... *illus*	578
Potpourri, Multicolor, Gilt Highlights, Pagoda Form, Tableware, Pierced Lid, 1800s, 8½ x 5 In.	277

MASSIER, a French art pottery, was made by brothers Jerome, Delphin, and Clement Massier in Vallauris and Golfe-Juan, France, in the late nineteenth and early twentieth centuries. It has an iridescent metallic luster glaze that resembles the Weller Sicardo pottery glaze. Most pieces are marked *J. Massier*. Massier may also be listed in the Majolica category.

Figure, Turtle, Streaky Brown & Turquoise Glaze, Marked, c.1890, 12½ x 27 x 21 In.	5313
Plate, Bees, Brown, Green, Yellow, Golfe-Juan, c.1900, 1½ x 12¼ In.	937
Vase, Metallic Drip Glaze, Marked MCM Golfe-Juan, 1900, 5 In.	118
Vase, Round, Urn, Iridescent, Glazed, Leaves, 1900-30, 3 x 4¾ In.	40
Vase, Underwater Scene, Ship, Flaring Handles, Golfe-Juan, c.1900, 12 x 8 In.	2875

MATCH HOLDERS were made to hold the large wooden matches that were used in the nineteenth and twentieth centuries for a variety of purposes. The kitchen stove and the fireplace or furnace had to be lit regularly. One type of match holder was made to hang on the wall, another was designed to be kept on a tabletop. Of special interest today are match holders that have advertisements as part of the design.

Alligator, Mason Regulator Co., 2 x 11½ In.	295
Clark's Clothing House, Badge Shape, 6⅛ x 4½ In.	354
Elephant, Opaline, Blue, 2½ x 4½ In.	22
Fishing Scene, Tin Lithograph, Match Basket, 4⅞ x 3⅜ In.	188
Lighthouse, Cigar Cutter, Ashtray, Brass, Copper, I. Taschner, c.1900, 22 In.	750
Owl, Slag Glass, Brown, Glass Eyes, 3½ In.	22
Oyster Seller, Woman, Bench, Basket Holds Matches, Porcelain, 3¾ x 3½ In. ..... *illus*	189

Pig, Yellow, Black Slip, Striker, Hole For Matches, Yellowware, c.1880, 3 x 5 In. 570
Wagon Train, Indians, Tin Lithograph, 5 x 1½ x 2¾ In. 183

MATCH SAFES were designed to be carried in the pocket. Early matches were made with phosphorus and could ignite unexpectedly. The matches were safely stored in the tightly closed container. Match safes were made in sterling silver, plated silver, or other metals. The English call these "vesta boxes."

Armorial Shield, Silver, Enamel, S. Blanckensee & Sons Ltd, Birmingham, 1904, 2 x 1⅝ In. 180
Bird, Mixed Metal, 3¼ In. 1875
Brass, Egyptian Woman, Flowers, U.S. Capitol, Embossed, 2⅜ In. 38
Brass, Netting, Shells, Embossed, 2½ In. 125
Brass, Oyster Shape, Crab, Starfish, Shrimp, 2¾ In. 225
Buckeye Binder & Mower, Depicts 1900 Equipment 519
Buffalo Printing Ink Works, Relief, Nickel Trim, 1 x 1½ x 2½ In. 336
Cigar Box, Shape, Silver, Sol Habana, Sunburst, Enamel, c.1900, 2 x 1⅛ In. 1599
Cigar Cutter, Sterling Silver, Floral Both Sides, Monogrammed Cartouche, 1900, 2⅜ x 1½ In. ... 180
Farmer's Friend Stacker, Great Color, 1 x ½ x 3 In. 261
Female Golfer, Sterling Silver, Mid Swing, Gold Hat, Scarf, Dress, c.1900, 2⅜ x 1⅞ In. 523
Horse Head, Bridle, Cast Iron, 4 In. .... *illus* 510
Indian, Sterling Silver, Repousse, Portrait, Monogrammed, c.1900, 2 x 1½ In. 400
Iron, Arch, Garland, Leaves, 1871, 4 x 4 In. 46
Maiden In Water, Silver, Art Nouveau, Monogrammed On Upper Lid, 1800, 2 x 1½ In. 400
Man In Canoe, Sterling Silver, Repousse, Rowing, Both Side, c.1900, 2⅜ x 1½ In. 360
Owl Shape, Silver Plate, 2¾ In. 125
Sailing Flag, Silver, Etched, Baker Russell, Chester City, Hall Makers, 1900, 2 x 2 In. 540
Stoneware, Wall Mount, Slab Built, Cobalt Blue Slip, William A. Rodgers, 1877, 5½ x 3½ In. ... 3321
Typewriter, Pot Metal, 3½ x 5 In. .... *illus* 360
White Mountain Co., Silver Plate, Early Wooden Ice Box Shape, 2⅞ x 1⅝ In. 200
Woman's Head, Silver, Repousse, Art Nouveau, F.S. Gilbert, c.1910, 2¾ x 1⅝ In. 135

MATT MORGAN, an English artist, was making pottery in Cincinnati, Ohio, by 1883. His pieces were decorated to resemble Moorish wares. Incised designs and colors were applied to raised panels on the pottery. Shiny or matte glazes were used. The company lasted less than two years.

Vase, Hispano-Moresque Design, Rust Brown Glaze, Marked, 17 In. 189

McCOY pottery was made in Roseville, Ohio. Nelson McCoy and J.W. McCoy established the Nelson McCoy Sanitary and Stoneware Company in Roseville, Ohio, in 1910. The firm made art pottery after 1926. In 1933 it became the Nelson McCoy Pottery Company. Pieces marked *McCoy* were made by the Nelson McCoy Pottery Company. Cookie jars were made from about 1940 until December 1990, when the McCoy factory closed. Since 1991 pottery with the McCoy mark has been made by firms unrelated to the original company. Because there was a company named Brush-McCoy, there is great confusion between Brush and Nelson McCoy pieces. See Brush category for more information.

Brown Drip, Baking Dish, 9 In. 15
Brown Drip, Bowl, Cereal, 6¼ In. 20
Brown Drip, Bowl, Dessert, 6⅝ In. 4
Brown Drip, Mug, 3¾ In. 3
Brown Drip, Plate, Dinner, 10¼ In. 10
Canyon, Bowl, Cereal, 6⅜ In. 10
Canyon, Creamer, 3¾ In. 10
Canyon, Cup, 3½ In. 7
Canyon, Plate, Dinner, 10½ In. 25
Canyon, Plate, Salad, 7½ In. 7
Cookie Jar, Keebler Tree House, 1980s, 9½ x 7½ In. 45
Planter, Turtle, Green, 3¾ x 8 In. 30
Planter, Zebras, Momma & Baby In Field Of Grass, c.1956, 6¾ x 8¼ In. .... *illus* 825

Mason's, Platter, Flowers, Birds, Blue & White Transfer, 21 x 17 In.
$578

Leland Little Auctions

TIP
Do you have a large exposed window? Put up glass shelves and fill them with inexpensive, colorful bottles. A burglar would have to break all of it, with accompanying noise, to get in.

Match Holder, Oyster Seller, Woman, Bench, Basket Holds Matches, Porcelain, 3¾ x 3½ In.
$189

AntiqueAdvertising.com

Match Safe, Horse Head, Bridle, Cast Iron, 4 In.
$510

Bertoia Auctions

McCOY

Match Safe, Typewriter, Pot Metal, 3½ x 5 In.
$360

Bertoia Auctions

McCoy, Planter, Zebras, Momma & Baby In Field Of Grass, c.1956, 6¾ x 8¼ In.
$825

Ruby Lane

McCoy, Vase, Grapes & Leaves, Greens, Tans, Marked, 9¼ x 7⅛ In.
$58

Ruby Lane

Vase, Grapes & Leaves, Greens, Tans, Marked, 9¼ x 7⅛ In. .... *illus*   58

McKEE is a name associated with various glass enterprises in the United States since 1836, including J. & F. McKee (1850), Bryce, McKee & Co. (1850 to 1854), McKee and Brothers (1865), and National Glass Co. (1899). In 1903, the McKee Glass Company was formed in Jeannette, Pennsylvania. It became McKee Division of the Thatcher Glass Co. in 1951 and was bought out by the Jeannette Corporation in 1961. Pressed glass, kitchenwares, and tablewares were produced. Jeannette Corporation closed in the early 1980s. Additional pieces may be included in the Custard Glass and Depression Glass categories.

McKee	PRESCUT	McK
McKee Glass Co. c.1870	McKee Glass Co. c.1904–1935	McKee Glass Co. 1935–1940

Candlestick, Chocolate, Griffin, 7 In. 650
Compote, Dragon, Wafer Construction, 1875, 4⅝ x 8¼ In. 128
Creamer, Barberry, Footed, 5¾ In. 41
Cruet, Chocolate, Sultan, Wild Rose & Bowknot, 7¼ In. 110
Cruet, Naomi, Rib & Bead, Ruby Stained, c.1901, 7 In. 93
Dragon, Berry Bowl, 1 x 4 In. 105
Goblet, Footed, Art Deco, 1922-30s, 8 Oz., 6¼ In. 20
Pitcher, Celtic, Ruby Stained, c.1894, 8⅜ In. 105
Salt & Pepper, Vaseline, Mitered Diamonds, Base, 5¾ In. 70
Salt, Chocolate, Sultan, Wild Rose & Bowknot, 3¼ In. 150
Spooner, Dragon, Scalloped Rim, c.1875, 5 x 3⅜ In. 497
Sugar, Lid, Aztec, Ruby Stained, 1903-27, 6 In. 40
Syrup, Britannic, Ruby Stained, c.1894-1903, 7 In. 275
Syrup, Majestic, Ruby Stained, 6¾ In. 81
Toothpick Holder, Children, Barrel, Peek A Boo, c.1904, 4 In. ...... *illus*   85
Toothpick Holder, Feather, Doric, Amber Stained, c.1896, 2¾ In. 438
Vase, Apollo, Bulbous, 14 In. 55

MECHANICAL BANKS *are listed in the Bank category.*

MEDICAL office furniture, operating tools, microscopes, thermometers, and other paraphernalia used by doctors are included in this category. Veterinary collectibles are also included here. Medicine bottles are listed in the Bottle category. There are related collectibles listed under Dental.

Amputation Kit, Saw, Knife Blades, Tweezers, Ebony Handles, Case, 12½ In. 383
Bag, Doctor's, Leather, Hand Tooled, 17 x 12 In. 684
Bust, Phrenology, Ceramic, Transfer Text, Fowler, 11¾ In. 1711
Bust, Phrenology, Plaster, Paper Labels, Fowler & Wells, 8½ In. 432
Cabinet, Apothecary, 10 Drawers, Cherry, Pine, Poplar, Glass Labels, 2 Doors, 51 x 21 In. 300
Cabinet, Apothecary, 20 Drawers, Nailed, Scratch Beading, c.1875, 21 x 37 In. 600
Cabinet, Apothecary, 20 Drawers, Walnut, Mushroom Knobs, Labels, 39 x 65 In. .... *illus*   3600
Cabinet, Apothecary, 23 Drawers, Softwood, Red, Round Knobs, 22 x 19 In. 826
Cabinet, Apothecary, 28 Drawers, Faded Blue, Pine, Poplar, 1880s, 64 x 38 In. 1464
Cabinet, Apothecary, 32 Drawers, Gold Lettering, 43 In. 660
Cabinet, Apothecary, 36 Drawers, Pine, Porcelain Pulls, Grain Paint, 14 x 48½ In. 1020
Cabinet, Apothecary, 40 Drawers, Pine, Nailed, Porcelain Pulls, 19 x 55 In. 3120
Cabinet, Apothecary, 63 Drawers, Molded Top, 9 Columns, Bracket Feet, 49½ x 73 In. 605
Eye Exam Chart, Wooden, Metal Frame, 2-Sided, E.B. Meyrowitz, 1935, 8 x 6 In. 375
Leech Jar, Creamware, Bands, Petal Shape Handles, Perforated Lid, 9¼ In. 826
Leech Jar, Porcelain, Acanthus Handles, Blue, Tulips, Vines, 9¼ In. 619
Leech Jar, Porcelain, Knob Handles, Perforated Lid, Black Text, 7¾ In. 2714
Leg Splint, Molded Birch Plywood, Evans Product, Charles & Ray Eames, 1943, 42 x 8 x 4 In. 424
Model, Anatomical, Hard Rubber, Painted, Swivel Base, Full Size Multi-Torso, 37 x 17 x 10 In. 600

Sign, Caution, Measles, Black Text, White Ground, 9 ½ x 13 ½ In.	59
Tongs, For Bullet Extraction, Engraved Steel, Bone Handles, Persia, 1800s, 11 In.	600
Wheelchair, Oak, 3 Wheels, Labeled, Wicker Back Seat, Leg Supports, 1900s, 24 x 44 In.	60

MEISSEN is a town in Germany where porcelain has been made since 1710. Any china made in the town can be called Meissen, although the famous Meissen factory made the finest porcelains of the area. The crossed swords mark of the great Meissen factory has been copied by many other firms in Germany and other parts of the world. Pieces of Meissen dinnerware in the Onion pattern are listed in their own category in this book.

Basket, Potpourri, Lid, Oval, Pierced Sides, Flowers, Ribbon Trim, Chestnut Finial, 9 In.	813
Bowl, Undertray, Applied Flowers, Roses, Birds, Leaves, 5 ¼ x 9 In.	5700
Candelabrum, Gilt, Multicolor, 3-Trunk Column, 1800s, 14 x 9 x 6 In., Pair .... *illus*	720
Compote, 2 Handles Basket, Leafy Pedestal Support, 2 Figures, 1800, 12 ¾ In.	92
Compote, 3 Tiers, Reticulated, Figural Finial, Flowers, Insects, 19 In.	461
Dish, Shaped, Chrysanthemum, 2 Leaves, Painted Flowers, Twisted Stem Handle	256
Dresser Box, Oval, Woman, Portrait, Continental, 1800s, 4 ¾ x 2 In.	192
Figurine, Bird, Hand Painted, Black Wings, 1800s, 8 ½ x 11 In.	1020
Figurine, Cockatoo, White, Crossed Swords, c.1925, 14 In.	1000
Figurine, Cupid, Kneeling, Heart On Pillow, Gilt, Crossed Swords Mark, c.1900, 6 ¼ In.	1187
Figurine, Pilgrim, Holding Hat Against Wind, Flowers, 1850-1924, 10 ½ In.	875
Figurine, Venus, 2 Doves, Chariot, Winged Cherub, Blue Crossed Swords Mark, 7 x 6 ½ x 5 ½ In.	1513
Group, Capture Of The Tritons, Nymphs, Nude, Putto, Hauling In Net, 12 ½ x 11 In.	1062
Group, Card Players, Seated Woman & 3 Children, 1800s, 8 ½ x 6 In.	1375
Group, Five Senses, 5 Putti, Allegorical, 6 In.	732
Group, Malabar Musicians, Male & Female, Playing Hurdy-Gurdy, Guitar, 7 x 7 In., Pair	1413
Group, Shepherd With Dog, Shepherdess Holding Crook, c.1800, 11 In., Pair	1000
Group, Sultana, Riding Elephant, Long Robe, Pink & Green Cloak, c.1880, 17 ½ In. .... *illus*	4887
Group, Summer, Girl Playing Mandolin, Boy Sitting, Crossed Swords, c.1890, 6 x 4 ½ In.	427
Group, Woman Peering Into Mirror, Man Regales Her Tales Of His Adventures, 14 x 11 In.	480
Group, Woman With Suitor, Boy, Marked, 1800s, 11 ½ x 8 In.	1000
Plate, Dinner, Kakiemon Style Pine Trees, Birds & Flowers, Gold Rim, 10 ½ In., 12 Piece	688
Plate, Tulip, Rose, Pierced Border, Gold Trim, 9 In., Pair	875
Sconce, 2-Light, Cartouche Form, Courting Scenes, Floral, 1800-1900, 15 x 12 ¾ In., Pair	87
Sweetmeat, Double, Figural, Blue Underglaze, Girl, Cherub, Grinder, 2 Bowls, 7 x 3 ¾ x 6 In.	201
Teapot, Multicolor, Yellow Background, Indian Flowers, Marked, 1740, 3 ¼ In.	3000
Tray, Blue Iris, Rococo Border, White, Handles, 16 x 16 In.	125
Tray, Meat, Gilt, Indian Pink, Flowers, 15 x 9 In.	175
Vase, Gilt, Red Accents, Neuer Ausschnitt, Hallmarked, 4 ¾ x 4 ¾ x 10 In.	94
Vase, Neuer Ausschnitt, Oriental Painting, Flower Ornament, Gold Rim, 5 ½ x 5 ½ x 6 ½ In.	71
Vase, Potpourri, Flower Lids, Cherub, Putto, 11 ½ In., Pair	1375
Vase, Yellow & Pink Flowers, Loving Cup, Double Snake Handles, 20 In.	305

MERRIMAC POTTERY Company was founded by Thomas Nickerson in Newburyport, Massachusetts, in 1902. The company made art pottery, garden pottery, and reproductions of Roman pottery. The pottery burned to the ground in 1908.

Vase, Deep Green Glaze, Tapered, Cylindrical, Flared Rim, c.1900, 12 In.	242
Vase, Green Matte, Squeezebag Decoration, Sinuous Lines, c.1905, 3 ½ x 2 ¾ In.	937
Vase, Leaves, Carved & Applied, Green Crystalline Glaze, c.1905, 4 ½ x 5 In. .... *illus*	3000

METLOX POTTERIES was founded in 1927 in Manhattan Beach, California. Dinnerware was made beginning in 1931. Evan K. Shaw purchased the company in 1946 and expanded the number of patterns. Poppytrail (1946–89) and Vernonware (1958–80) were divisions of Metlox under E.K. Shaw's direction. The factory closed in 1989.

Antique Grape, Bowl, Cereal, 7 In.	16
Antique Grape, Bowl, Vegetable, Round, Divided, 9 In.	77
California Provincial, Cup & Saucer, Vernon, 1960s, Cup 3 ⅝ In.	9
Mayflower, Chop Plate, 12 In.	51

McKee, Toothpick Holder, Children, Barrel, Peek A Boo, c.1904, 4 In.
$85

Ruby Lane

Medical, Cabinet, Apothecary, 20 Drawers, Walnut, Mushroom Knobs, Labels, 39 x 65 In.
$3,600

Thomaston Place Auction Galleries

Meissen, Candelabrum, Gilt, Multicolor, 3-Trunk Column, 1800s, 14 x 9 x 6 In., Pair
$720

M

Brunk Auctions

Meissen, Group, Sultana, Riding Elephant, Long Robe, Pink & Green Cloak, c.1880, 17 ½ In.
$4,887

Bunch Auctions

Merrimac, Vase, Leaves, Carved & Applied, Green Crystalline Glaze, c.1905, 4 ½ x 5 In.
$3,000

Rago Arts and Auction Center

Mettlach, Boot, Figural, 7 x 11 ½ In.
$132

The Stein Auction Company

Mettlach, Punch Bowl, No. 375, Applied Figural Animal Heads, Grapevines, 10 Liter
$630

The Stein Auction Company

Mettlach, Punch Bowl, No. 3088, Noah, Etched, H. Schlitt, Underplate, 6.0 Liter
$264

The Stein Auction Company

M

Organdie, Butter Chip, 2 ½ In.		68
Poppytrail, Relish, Ivy, 2 Sections, Twig Handle, c.1950, 9 In.		32
Provincial Blue, Cup & Saucer		9
Provincial Blue, Plate, Dinner, 10 In.		21
Provincial Rose, Plate, Dinner, 10 In.		28
Red Rooster, Cup & Saucer		28
Vineyard, Saucer		8
Woodland Gold, Teapot, Lid, 5 Cup, 5 In.		54

METTLACH, Germany, is a city where the Villeroy and Boch factories worked. Steins from the firm are marked with the word *Mettlach* or the castle mark. They date from about 1842. *PUG* means painted under glaze. The steins can be dated from the marks on the bottom, which include a date-number code. Other pieces may be listed in the Villeroy & Boch category.

Beaker, No. 2327/1302, American Eagle, Flag, 15 In.		63
Beaker, No. 5045, Figural, Woman, Green Dress, Hands Folded, 8 In.		1050
Boot, Figural, 7 x 11 ½ In.	*illus*	132
Cake Plate, No. 2601, Dancing Figures, Cameo, Blue, White, 6 In.		601
Charger, Etched Stoneware, Roundel, Black Ground, Rust, Buff, Ivory, Pan, 1895, 15 ¼ In.		308
Coaster, Gnomes, 4 In., 5 Piece		132
Jardiniere, No. 2415, Etched, Leaves, Scrolls, 7 In.		360
Lamp, Cylindrical, Shield On 1 Side, 1895, 73 ½ In.		375
Lamp, Monumental Mettlach Beer Stein, Cylindrical, Cavalier On 1 Side, 1895, 73 ½ In.		469
Pitcher, 2 Cherubs, Fish & Ducks, Thea Pattern, Marked, 8 ¾ In.		96
Plaque, Etched, Von Moltke On Horse, Signed, Stocke, 15 In.		325
Plaque, No. 1044/1144, Students & Soldiers Drinking, Schlitt, PUG, 17 In.		850
Plaque, No. 1044/5133, Castle On River, PUG, 18 In.		120
Plaque, No. 1374, Etched, Mosaic, Flowers, 8 ½ In.		138
Plaque, No. 1490, Woman, Feathered Hat, 35 In.		5000
Plaque, No. 1769, Arnold Von Winkelbried Battle Scene, Etched, 14 ½ In.		593
Plaque, No. 2558, Art Nouveau, Flowers, Etched, 15 ½ In.		300
Plaque, No. 3225/1290, Shield, Dresden, 13 x 11 In.		1500
Plaque, No. 7025, Lohengrin, Opera, Mint, Cameo, 15 ½ x 12 In.		688
Punch Bowl, No. 5, Grape Leaves, Cherub Handles, 24 In.		375
Punch Bowl, No. 375, Applied Figural Animal Heads, Grapevines, 10 Liter	*illus*	630
Punch Bowl, No. 3088, Noah, Etched, H. Schlitt, Underplate, 6 Liter	*illus*	264
Stein, Acorn & Leaf Design, Art Nouveau, ½ Liter		160
Stein, Cream Tones, Hunter Holding Hound Back, ½ Liter, 5 x 5 In.		240
Stein, No. 1526, Bowlers, Van Hauten, POG, ½ Liter	*illus*	96
Stein, No. 2036, Character, Owl, Inlaid Lid, ½ Liter		300
Stein, No. 2052, Munich Child, Cherub, Inlaid Lid, Finial, 1895, ¼ Liter, 4 In.		276
Stein, No. 2074, Bird In Cage, Inlaid Lid, ½ Liter		1000
Stein, No. 2639, Blacksmith, Cavalier, Inlaid Lid, ½ Liter		300
Stein, No. 5019/5442, Faience, Cavalier On Barrel, Smoking, Pewter Rim, 1 Liter		960
Stein, Olympic Sports Design, Cameo Relief, Pewter Lid, Thumb Press, 1930s, 8 In.		475
Tray, No. 891, Cupid On Lion, Chromolithograph, Inlaid Stoneware, 13 x 7 In.		564
Vase, Mosaic, Dore, Bronze Mounts, Flowers, 13 ½ In.		625
Vase, No. 2909, Art Nouveau, Etched, Tall Trees, Heart, 14 In.	*illus*	1561
Vase, No. 4127, Luster Glaze, Red, Green, Shouldered, 14 ½ In.		156
Vase, Stoneware, Incised, Poppies, Colorful Painted, 1899, 12 In.		465

MILK GLASS was named for its milky white color. It was first made in England during the 1700s. The height of its popularity in the United States was from 1870 to 1880. It is now correct to refer to some colored glass as blue milk glass, black milk glass, etc. Reproductions of milk glass are being made and sold in many stores. Related pieces may be listed in the Cosmos, Vallerysthal, and Westmoreland categories.

Creamer, Footed, Grape & Leaf, Indiana Glass	12

Dish, Hen On Nest Cover, White, Hazel Atlas, 4 ½ x 3 ½ x 3 ½ In.	12
Fairy Lamp, Pink Flowers, Yellow Flowers, Blue Flowers, 8 In.	84
Jam Jar, Strawberry, Hazel Atlas, c.1936	15
Jar, Enamel Flowers, c.1820, Liter *illus*	420
Lamp, Victoire, Art Deco, Opaque, Car Ornament, 1900s	60
Pitcher, Milk, Orange, Hazel Atlas, 4 In.	17
Pitcher, Pink Neck, White Body, Blue, Pink, Yellow Flowers, 8 ½ In.	54
Salt & Pepper, Gold Top, Grape & Leaf, Indiana Glass	55
Sugar, Dome Lid, Grape Cluster Finial, Turquoise Blue, Grapevines, Footed, 1920s, 6 In.	60
Vase, Opaline, Medallion, 3 Children, Gilt Accents, 4 x 4 x 9 In.	24

MILLEFIORI means, literally, a thousand flowers. Many small pieces of glass resembling flowers are grouped together to form a design. It is a type of glasswork popular in paperweights and some are listed in that category.

Epergne, 4 Trumpet Vases, Ruffled Rims, Italy, 16 ½ x 11 ¾ In. *illus*	625
Ewer, Cobalt Blue, Gold Flecks, Applied Cobalt Handle, Gambaro & Poggi, 13 ½ x 6 ½ In.	342
Knob, Yellow, Green, Red, 1 In.	36

MINTON china was made in the Staffordshire region of England beginning in 1796. The firm became part of the Royal Doulton Tableware Group in 1968, but the wares continued to be marked *Minton*. In 2009 the brand was bought by KPS Capital Partners of New York and became part of WWRD Holdings. The company no longer makes Minton china. Many marks have been used. The word *England* was added in 1891. Minton majolica is listed in this book in the Majolica category.

Minton	 Minton	Minton
c.1822–1836	c.1863–1872	1951–present

Figurine, Sir Henry Havelock, Parian, J.A.P. MacBride, 1858, 14 In. *illus*	250
Ice Bucket, Transfer Roses, Rattan Swing Handle, 10 x 10 In.	100
Jardiniere, Green Background, Pink Rose & Gold Trim Interior Painted, Signed, 7 ½ x 7 ½ In.	180
Plate, Bread & Butter, Golden Diadem, 6 ⅜ In.	22
Plate, Bread & Butter, St. James, 6 ½ In.	37
Plate, Dinner, Golden Diadem, 10 ¾ In.	52
Plate, Dinner, Green Zigzag Rim, 8 Gilt Bands, Tiffany & Co., 10 ⅝ In., 12 Piece	938
Plate, Dinner, Newbury, 10 ¾ In.	42
Plate, Parcel Gilt, Putto, Central Medallion, Turquoise Border, Signed L. Boullemier, 8 ½ In. *illus*	315
Plate, Pate-Sur-Pate, Putti Playing Horn, Pierced Gilt Rim, A. Birks, 9 ¼ In. *illus*	1250
Plate, Salad, Golden Diadem, 8 ¼ In.	28
Plate, White & Ivory, Blue & Gold Trim, England, 1900s, 11 In., 12 Piece	180
Stand, Bamboo, 3 Tiers, Blue Tiles, Pointing Dog, Duck, Hawk, 1800, 31 x 14 x 14 In. *illus*	120
Stand, Blue & White Tile, Brass, Crane, 26 In.	492
Vase, Sevres Style, Gilt Trim, Swirled Blue Fluting, Rose, Leafy Vines, 1860, 16 In.	1599

MIRRORS *are listed in the Furniture category under Mirror.*

MOCHA pottery is an English-made product that was sold in America during the early 1800s. It is a heavy pottery with pale coffee-and-cream coloring. Designs of blue, brown, green, orange, black, or white were added to the pottery and given fanciful names, such as Tree, Snail Trail, or Moss. Mocha designs are sometimes found on pearlware. A few pieces of mocha ware were made in France, the United States, and other countries.

Creamer, 2 Blue Bands, Black Rings, Feathered Spout, Molded Strap, Acanthus, 1845, 4 x 4 ½ In.	70
Mixing Bowl, Green, Seaweed, 7 x 14 In.	188
Mixing Bowl, Seaweed, Band, 12 ¼ In.	144
Mixing Bowl, Wide Blue Band, Gray Putted, Dark Brown Rings, Mocha, 1845, 11 x 5 ⅛ In.	130
Mug, Earthworm, Tan Band, Brown Ring, Tooled Rim, Molded Strap, 1825, 3 ¾ x 4 ⅞ In.	550

Mettlach, Stein, No. 1526, Bowlers, Van Hauten, POG, ½ Liter
$96

Mettlach, Vase, No. 2909, Art Nouveau, Etched, Tall Trees, Heart, 14 In.
$1,561

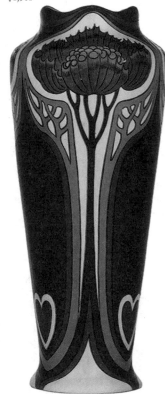

M

Milk Glass, Jar, Enamel Flowers, c.1820, Liter
$420

Fox Auctions

Dating Clues
Words of wisdom from a dealer: "The less writing on the bottom of a vase the older it is." Eighteenth-century pottery and porcelain is unmarked or has a signature or small trademark. By the 1860s, many factories were using number and letter codes to indicate type of clay, molds, and more. The country of origin was used after 1891.

Millefiori, Epergne, 4 Trumpet Vases, Ruffled Rims, Italy, 16½ x 11¾ In.
$625

New Orleans Auction Galleries

Pepper Pot, Earthworm, Light Blue Bands, 4⅝ In.	1003
Pepper Pot, Seaweed, Dome Lid, 4¾ In.	1121
Pepper Pot, Seaweed, Light Blue, Dome Lid, 4¼ In.	767
Pepper Pot, Seaweed, Olive, Black Bands, 9¾ In. .... *illus*	497
Pitcher, Blue Seaweed, Handle, 1800s, 6 In.	142
Pitcher, Cat's-Eye, Barrel Shape, Mint Green Bands, 7 In.	1298
Pitcher, Earthenware, Bands, Pearlware, Blue, Brown, White, Strap Handle, c.1810, 6½ In. *illus*	1045
Pitcher, Earthworm, Yellow, Blue, 7¼ In.	1220
Pitcher, Seaweed, Green Band, Barrel Shape, 5⅞ In.	649
Sugar, Lid, Marbleized Bands, Brown, Blue, Flower Finial, 1800s, 4¼ In.	2196

MONT JOYE, *see Mt. Joye category.*

MOORCROFT pottery was first made in Burslem, England, in 1913. William Moorcroft had managed the art pottery department for James Macintyre & Company of England from 1898 to 1913. The Moorcroft pottery continues today, although William Moorcroft died in 1945. The earlier wares are similar to the modern ones, but color and marking will help indicate the age.

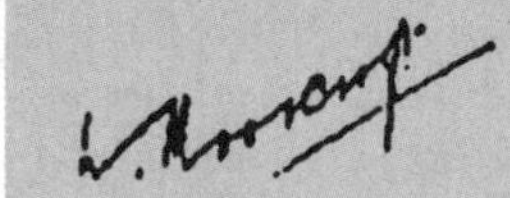

W. Moorcroft Ltd. 1898–c.1905	W. Moorcroft Ltd. 1898–1913	W. Moorcroft Ltd. 1928–1978

Biscuit Jar, Moonlit Blue, Silver Lid, Marked, 7½ In.	2124
Bowl, Pedestal, Hibiscus, Green Hound, Centerpiece, 1897, 10 x 10 x 3 In.	106
Dish, Rose, Yellow, Ground, Footed, Enamel Floral, Peony Branch, 1800s, 14 x 11 x 2¾ In.	130
Pitcher, Milk, Landscape, Blue, Pewter Mount, 1920s, 5¾ x 5¼ In.	1375
Tea Set, Blue, White, Marked, 5 Piece, 10-In. Teapot	2124
Tile, Cherry Blossom, Frame, Square, 8 In.	178
Trinket Box, Bronte Porcelain Enamel, 3½ In.	200
Trinket Box, Otter, Porcelain, Enamel, Marked, 3½ In.	236
Vase, Blackberry, Orange & Green Leaves, 4 In.	423
Vase, Cobalt Blue Ground, Pomegranate Design, Bottle Form, Elongated Neck, 10 x 5 In.	236
Vase, Flambe Glaze, Grape & Vine Designs, 12 x 5½ In.	767
Vase, Grapes, Leaves, Dark Red, 9¼ In.	563
Vase, Moonlit Blue, Marked, 1928, 3 In.	1121
Vase, Mottled Green Ground, Multicolor Pomegranate, Grapes, Cylindrical, 9½ x 3½ In.	2124
Vase, Mottled Green Ground, Multicolor, Grapevine Design, 8¾ x 6½ In.	531
Vase, Mottled Red & Green Ground, Multicolor Freesia, Lilies, 10 x 7 In.	944
Vase, Mustard Yellow & Blue Ground, Multicolor Freesia, Lilies, 10 x 7 In.	708
Vase, Orchid Pattern, Flowers, Cobalt Blue, Background, 1940s, 7½ x 6¼ In.	240
Vase, Orchid, Red Flambe Glaze, Impressed Marks, 11 x 10 In.	1125
Vase, Poppy, Anemone, Signed, Blue, Red, Green, 1920s, 12¼ x 5¾ In.	1187
Vase, Squat, Green & Blue Anemone, 6¼ x 5 In.	354
Vase, Squeezebag, Decoration, Cornflowers, Blues, White, c.1900, 10¾ x 5½ In.	1000
Vase, Trumpet Shape, Flared Foot, Flowers, Pale Green To Navy Blue, 1918, 10½ In. *illus*	300

 MORIAGE is a special type of raised decoration used on some Japanese pottery. Sometimes pieces of clay were shaped by hand and applied to the item; sometimes the clay was squeezed from a tube in the way we apply cake frosting. One type of moriage is called Dragonware by collectors.

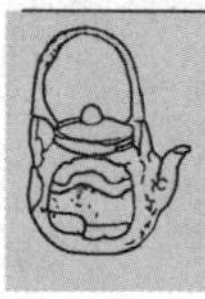

Decanter, Sake, Whistling Bird, Cat, Gold, Bird On Top, Dragonware, 4¼ x 5½ In.	21
Hatpin Holder, Gilt, Round Reserve, Roses, Green, Pink, Nippon, 4½ In.	30
Humidor, Owl, Brown, Gray, Nippon, 6 In.	1053
Jug, Water, Bird, Branch, Tree, Lace Pattern, Double Handles, 8 x 6 In.	750

M

Vase, Black Matte, Gilt, Dragons, Chasing Flaming Pearls, Palm Leaf, 1800s, 8 In.	554
Vase, Cobalt Blue, Flowers, Square, Double Handles On Shoulders, 8½ x 6 In.	125
Vase, Dark Pink Flowers, Pale Green, Fixed Ring Handles, 7½ x 9 In.	406
Vase, Doucai, Black, Chasing Flaming Pearls, Clouds, Flared Rim, Dragonware, 1900s, 18 In.	688
Vase, Famille Verte, Long Neck, Flared Rim, Painted Panels, Dragonware, 20 In.	500
Vase, Feathery Leaves, Spotted Flowers, Cobalt Blue High Handles, 10 x 6½ In.	281
Vase, Flying Geese, Water, Plants, Multicolor, Beaded Handles, 12 x 7 In.	66
Vase, Lotus Flowers, Pods, Japan, 12 x 7 In.	343
Vase, Stick Neck, Pink Rose, Orange, Purple, Flowers, Pale Green, Handles, 9 x 5 In.	62
Vase, Wreath, Flowers, Morimura Brothers, 1890, 6 x 6 x 8¼ In.	59

MOSAIC TILE COMPANY of Zanesville, Ohio, was started by Karl Langerbeck and Herman Mueller in 1894. Many types of plain and ornamental tiles were made until 1959. The company closed in 1967. The company also made some ashtrays, bookends, and related giftwares. Most pieces are marked with the entwined MTC monogram.

Tile, Goose, Rabbit & Chick, Lilac Glaze, Mission Oak Frame, 9⅜ x 20 In., 3 Piece	150
Tile, Square, Airplane & Train, Colorful Matte Glazes, Impressed, Frame, 4⅛ In.	150
Tile, Viking Ship, High Relief, Natural Color Glazes, Black Ground, Marked, 6 In.	118

MOSER glass is made by a Bohemian (Czech) glasshouse founded by Ludwig Moser in 1857. Art Nouveau–type glassware and iridescent glassware were made. The most famous Moser glass is decorated with heavy enameling in gold and bright colors. The firm, Moser Glassworks, is still working in Karlovy Vary, Czech Republic. Few pieces of Moser glass are marked.

Basket, Topaz Amber, Bohemian Cut, Faceted, Tapers, 10½ x 7½ In.	156
Box, Leaf Bands, Raised Enamel, Gilt, Silvered, Brass Ball Feet, Bail Handles, 5 x 6 x 4 In.	1024
Compote, Lid, Gilded, Enameled Blue & Purple Flowers, Tall Stem, 29 In.	3630
Goblet, Green, Grape & Leaf Design, Enamel, Blown, 7½ In. .... *illus*	252
Jewelry Box, Blue Body, Enamel Scallops, Ray Cut Lid, Gilt Metal Feet, 4 In.	120
Lamp, Oil, Enameled Branches, Gray Ground, Lizards, Leaves, Bell Flowers, Chimney, 9¾ In.	1298
Lamp, Oil, Salamander, Smoky Gray Ground, Leaves, Bell Flowers, 10 x 8 In.	246
Pitcher, Art Glass, Blue, Colorful Enamel Leaf, Blossom & Scroll Design, Extended Spout, 9 In.	420
Pitcher, Cranberry, Amber Ground, Enamel, Oak Leaves, Acorn Design, 4½ x 5 In.	590
Pokal, Lid, Green Glass, Enamel Decor, Knight Holding Lance, Maiden Stands Near, 28 In.	1320
Vase, 10-Sided, Cranberry Panels Cut To Clear, Gold Stencil Highlights, 8 In.	210
Vase, Amber, Salamander Design, Florets, Water Driblet At Top, 6½ x 6½ In.	236
Vase, Amethyst, Shaded, Engraved Underwater Sea Life, Gold Trim, 4-Sided, 8¼ In.	720
Vase, Cranberry, Gilt Tendrils, Ruffled Rim, Polished Pontil, 1900s, 7⅜ x 6½ In. .... *illus*	280
Vase, Diamond Shape, Flowers, Birds, Red Beads, Brick Design, Notched Top, 9½ In.	1452
Vase, Gilt, Elephants, Trees, Savannah, Olive Green, 3¾ In.	322
Vase, Intaglio Carved, Padded, Iris Flower, Stems, Leaves, Amethyst Ground, Signed, 4 In.	1210
Vase, Marquetry Tulip, Roses, Red, Green, Wheel Carved Cameo, c.1920, 6½ x 3 In.	1000
Vase, Sapphire, Colorful Enameling & Gold, Insects, Flowers, Stems, Marked, 9½ In.	443

MOSS ROSE china was made by many firms from 1808 to 1900. It has a typical moss rose pictured as the design. The plant is not as popular now as it was in Victorian gardens, so the fuzz-covered bud is unfamiliar to most collectors. The dishes were usually decorated with pink and green flowers.

Tea Set, Teapot, Sugar & Creamer, Waste, 4 Piece..	192

MOTHER-OF-PEARL GLASS, or pearl satin glass, was first made in the 1850s in England and in Massachusetts. It was a special type of mold-blown satin glass with air bubbles in the glass, giving it a pearlized color. It has been reproduced. Mother-of-pearl shell objects are listed under Pearl.

Bowl, Footed, Rainbow Satin, Diamond Quilted, Triangular, 3 Vaseline Glass Feet, 3 x 6 In.....	60
Case, Eyeglasses, Woman, Nude, Seated, Rock, Silk Lined, 2½ x 5½ In.	420
Commode, Mahogany, Ebony, White Marble, Brass, Miniature, 3 Drawers, 1800s, 11 x 14 x 8¾ In..	875

Minton, Figurine, Sir Henry Havelock, Parian, J.A.P. MacBride, 1858, 14 In.
$250

Neal Auction Co.

Minton, Plate, Parcel Gilt, Putto, Central Medallion, Turquoise Border, Signed L. Boullemier, 8½ In.
$315

Clars Auction Gallery

TIP

If you are remodeling or redecorating, think about antiques and collectibles in the work area. A workman will hammer on a wall without worrying about sholves on the other side.

M

Minton, Plate, Pate-Sur-Pate, Putti Playing Horn, Pierced Gilt Rim, A. Birks, 9¼ In. $1,250

Fontaine's Auction Gallery

Minton, Stand, Bamboo, 3 Tiers, Blue Tiles, Pointing Dog, Duck, Hawk, 1800, 31 x 14 x 14 In. $120

Eldred's Auctioneers and Appraisers

Mocha, Pepper Pot, Seaweed, Olive, Black Bands, 9¾ In. $497

Jeffrey S. Evans

Mocha, Pitcher, Earthenware, Bands, Pearlware, Blue, Brown, White, Strap Handle, c.1810, 6½ In. $1,045

Skinner, Inc.

TIP

If you discover a cache of very dirty antiques and you are not dressed in work clothes, make yourself a temporary cover-up from a plastic garbage bag.

Moorcroft, Vase, Trumpet Shape, Flared Foot, Flowers, Pale Green To Navy Blue, 1918, 10½ In. $300

Eldred's Auctioneers and Appraisers

Moser, Goblet, Green, Grape & Leaf Design, Enamel, Blown, 7½ In. $252

Fox Auctions

Moser, Vase, Cranberry, Gilt Tendrils, Ruffled Rim, Polished Pontil, 1900s, 7⅜ x 6½ In. $280

Ruby Lane

Movie, Poster, Forbidden Planet, Walter Pidgeon, Anne Francis, Litho, 24 x 30 In. $762

DuMouchelles

Cruet, Pink Satin, Drape Pattern, Frosted Glass Stopper & Applied Handle, 7 In.	96
Ewer, Diamond Quilted, Apricot Shade, White, Pedestal, Frosted Handle, Rigoree, 12 In.	210
Scissors, Palais Royal, 3¾ In.	100
Vase, Blue Satin, Diamond Quilted, 9 In.	150
Vase, Rainbow Satin, Heavy Blue Coralene Overlay	60

MOTORCYCLES and motorcycle accessories of all types are being collected today. Examples can be found that date back to the early twentieth century. Toy motorcycles are listed in the Toy category.

Lubester, Gas Station, Shell Design, Cast Iron, Chromed Hardware, Yellow, Red, 30 x 12 x 9 In.	369
Lubester, Orange, Black, Metal Cabinet, Hand-Crank Pump, Harley-Davidson, 1930s, 50 x 23 x 10 In..	300
Lubester, Pump, Red Paint, Sheet Metal, Crank Handle, Pennzoil Motor Logo, 40 x 16 x 9½ In..	338
Lubester, Shell-Penn Motor Oil Decal, Red & Yellow Cabinet, Repainted, 58 x 29 x 13 In.	215

MOUNT WASHINGTON, *see Mt. Washington category.*

MOVIE memorabilia of all types are collected. Animation Art, Games, Sheet Music, Toys, and some celebrity items are listed in their own section. A lobby card is usually 11 by 14 inches, but other sizes were also made. A set of lobby cards includes seven scene cards and one title card. An American one sheet, the standard movie poster, is 27 by 41 inches. A three sheet is 40 by 81 inches. A half sheet is 22 by 28 inches. A window card, made of cardboard, is 14 by 22 inches. An insert is 14 by 36 inches. A herald is a promotional item handed out to patrons. Press books, sent to exhibitors to promote a movie, contain ads and lists of what is available for advertising, i.e., posters, lobby cards. Press kits, sent to the media, contain photos and details about the movie, i.e., stars' biographies and interviews.

Button, Walt Disney's Greyfriars Bobby, Picture Of Skye Terrier, 1961, 1¼ In.		25
Fancard, Stan Laurel & Oliver Hardy, Inscribed Hello Lyn, Frame, c.1940, 6 x 4¾ In.		254
Fancard, Wizard Of Oz, Sleepyhead Flowerpot, Munchkin, Margaret Pellegrini, 9½ x 11 In. ..		57
Figurine, Pottery, Laurel & Hardy, On Tricycle Built For 2, Painted, c.1945, 18 x 23 In.		455
Photograph, No Business Like Show Business, Marilyn Monroe Autograph, 1954, 8 x 10 In. ...		720
Poster, Forbidden Planet, Walter Pidgeon, Anne Francis, Litho, 24 x 30 In.	*illus*	762
Poster, H.G. Wells, Time Machine, Rod Taylor, Alan Young, Linen Backed, 1960, 40 x 81 In.		2000
Poster, H.G. Wells, War Of The Worlds, Paramount Pictures, 1953, 22 x 28 In.		18750
Poster, It Came From Outer Space, Richard Carlson, Linen Backed, 1963, 27 x 41 In.		1375
Poster, New Singing Cowboy Star, Jack Randall, 38 x 16 In.	*illus*	85
Poster, Next Neighbors, Musical, Norombega Hall, C. Thayer, 1879, 30 x 14 In.		130
Poster, Shock Punch, Richard Dix, Frances Howard, c.1925, 26 x 41 In.		351
Poster, The Day The Earth Stood Still, Michael Rennie, Patricia Neal, c.1951, 37 x 25 In.	*illus*	698
Poster, The Godfather, Print, Iconic, Advertisement, 1900s		13

MT. JOYE is an enameled cameo glass made in the late nineteenth and twentieth centuries by Saint-Hilaire Touvier de Varraux and Co. of Pantin, France. This same company made De Vez glass. Pieces were usually decorated with enameling. Most pieces are not marked.

Biscuit Jar, Frosted Acid, Enamel Floral, Silver Plated Lid, Handle, 7½ In.	150
Vase, Emerald Green, Silver & Gold Acorn, Oak Leaf Design, 7½ In.	420
Vase, Golden Amber, Fading White Acid, Enamel Floral, 15 In.	960
Vase, Ice Green Acid, Floral Poppy, Gold Highlight, 8¼ In.	330
Vase, Leaves, Gold, Green, Acid Etched, 26 x 9 In.	281
Vase, Twisting, Poppies, Blue, Gilt, France, c.1920, 11¼ x 7 In.	562

MT. WASHINGTON Glass Works started in 1837 in South Boston, Massachusetts. In 1870 the company moved to New Bedford, Massachusetts. Many types of art glass were made there until 1894, when the company merged with Pairpoint Manufacturing Co. Amberina, Burmese, Crown Milano, Cut Glass, Peachblow, and Royal Flemish are each listed in their own category.

Movie, Poster, New Singing Cowboy Star, Jack Randall, 38 x 16 In.
$85

Copake Auction

Movie, Poster, The Day The Earth Stood Still, Michael Rennie, Patricia Neal, c.1951, 37 x 25 In.
$698

M

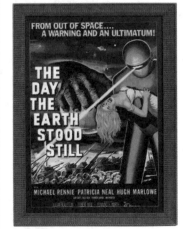

DuMouchelles

TIP
Paper must "breathe." Don't glue it to a backing. It expands and contracts and eventually it will tear.

Mt. Washington, Saltshaker, Baby Chick Head, Pansies, Pink, Yellow, White Ground, 2¼ x 2½ In.
$330

Woody Auction

M

Muller Freres, Vase, Amber Glass, Blue Cameo, Exotic Birds, Flowers, Silver Foil, Textured, 7¼ In.
$545

James D. Julia Auctioneers

Muncie, Vase, Rombic, Green Over Purple, Matte Glaze, Marked, 4⅛ In.
$354

Humler & Nolan

Biscuit Jar, Opal, Pond Lily, Pink, Green, 6 x 7½ In.	693
Bowl, Enfolded Sides, Drip Trim Around Lip, Enameled Flowers, Pink & Yellow Bowl, 6 In.	363
Dresser Box, Square, Hinged, Rose Garland, Bow, Green Background, Floral, 4¾ x 7 In.	210
Muffineer, Lid, Tomato Shape, Yellow Shading, Flowers, c.1875, 3 x 4 In.	59
Pickle Castor, Cranberry Satin, Gold Floral, Set On Pairpoint, Silver Plate, 12 In.	660
Pickle Castor, Glass Insert, Embossed Scrolls, Flowers, Pairpoint Silver Frame, 9 In.	2160
Salt, Cased Cranberry, Spider Mum, c.1880, 2¾ In.	234
Saltshaker, Baby Chick Head, Pansies, Pink, Yellow, White Ground, 2¼ x 2½ In. .... *illus*	330
Vase, Dragon, Horned, Frost, Orange, Red, Star, Leaves, c.1895, 7¾ x 2¾ In.	2457
Vase, Lava, 6 In.	2040
Vase, Lava, Shiny Black, Multicolor Inclusions, Applied Reeded Scroll Handles, 8⅞ x 3½ In.	2691
Vase, Lid, Royal Flemish, Flowers, Multicolor Glass, Double Handles, 1800s, 6¼ x 6 In.	295
Vase, Lily, Peach Blow, Deep Pink, Creamy White, Flaring Lip, Tricorner Top, 9 In.	181

MULLER FRERES, French for Muller Brothers, made cameo and other glass from about 1895 to 1933. Their factory was first located in Luneville, then in nearby Croismare, France. Pieces were usually marked with the company name.

Vase, Amber Glass, Blue Cameo, Exotic Birds, Flowers, Silver Foil, Textured, 7¼ In. .... *illus*	545
Vase, Boar Hunting Scene, Cameo, c.1920, 10 x 9 In.	2875
Vase, Dragonfly, Pond, Landscape, Cameo, c.1900, 7¾ x 3¼ In.	1000
Vase, Green, Orange, Leaves, c.1920, 8½ In.	413
Vase, Shepherds, Tending Flock, Winter, Amethyst To Pale Blue, 5 x 3½ In.	1112
Vase, Trees, Lake, Mountains, Frosted Opalescent Ground, Cameo, Signed, 10½ In.	1815

MUNCIE Clay Products Company was established by Charles Benham in Muncie, Indiana, in 1918. The company made pottery for the florist and giftshop trade. Art pottery was made beginning in 1922. The company closed by 1939. Pieces are marked with the name *Muncie* or just with a system of numbers and letters, like *1A*.

Vase, Rombic, Green Over Purple, Matte Glaze, Marked, 4⅛ In. .... *illus*	354
Vase, White Matte Glaze, Dripped Over Light Blue, Marked, 12 In.	106

MURANO, *see Glass-Venetian category.*

MUSIC boxes and musical instruments are listed here. Phonograph records, jukeboxes, phonographs, and sheet music are listed in other categories in this book.

Accordion, Wood & Metal, Bronze Trim, Manual, M. Hohner, Germany, 1920s	445
Box, Britannia, Smoking Cabinet, Rosewood, Burl Walnut Veneer, Combs, 27 x 16½ In.	1320
Box, Cylinder Rosewood, Drum, Bells, Castanets, 12 Tunes, Swiss, c.1890, 26 x 14 In.	1440
Box, Cylinder, 3 Bells, Wood Case, 10 Tunes, B.H. Abrahams, Swiss, c.1890, 19 In. .... *illus*	600
Box, Cylinder, 8 Tunes, Walnut, Inlaid Flowers, Crossbanded, Bells, Birds, 10 x 21 In.	4375
Box, Cylinder, 39 Teeth In Comb, Transfer Decoration Case, c.1895, 19 In.	503
Box, Cylinder, Comb, 8 Tunes, Tune Card Affixed To Lid, Picard-Lion, 5 x 14 In.	390
Box, Cylinder, Piccolo, Mahogany, Inlaid Case, 8 Tunes, 1880, 27 x 11 x 8 In.	825
Box, Cylinder, Rosewood, Lever Wind, Change-Repeat Switch, c.1900, 5 x 18 In. .... *illus*	854
Box, Cylinder, Silvered, Inlaid, Sublime Harmonie, Mermod Freres, 7 x 24 x 9½ In.	1271
Box, Cylinder, Single Comb, Grain Painted, 8 Tunes, Mermod Freres, Swiss, 1800s, 6 x 17 x 8 In.	281
Box, Cylinder, Zither Attachment, Tune Card, Inlay, 12 Tunes, Mermod Freres, 7 x 26 In.	720
Box, Double Comb, Discs, Walnut Case, Veneer, Acorn Feet, Symphonion, 10 x 16 In.	720
Box, Gilt Metal, Casket, Rectangular, Functional, 1900s	150
Box, Mahogany, Hinged Top, Nude Babies, Garden, Symphonion, 6 x 10⅝ In.	688
Box, Metal Discs, Lacquered, Thorens, Swiss, 1900s, 4 x 12 In.	63
Box, Regina, Folding Coffin Top, Brass Bedplate, Bracket Columns, Lion Feet, 12 x 34 In.	6300
Box, Regina, Oak, Lithograph Panel, Turned Feet, Spring Driven, 9 Discs, 21 x 19 In.	847
Box, Regina, Sublima No. 25, Mahogany, Spindled Gallery, Fluted Corner, 79 x 36 In.	4235
Box, Rosewood, Marquetry, Lever Wind, Sublime Harmonie Tremolo, Swiss, 1890, 8 x 30 In.	1830
Box, Singing Bird On Leaf, Tin, Brass Cage, Ring Handle, Key Wind, 8 In.	1093

Music, Box, Cylinder, 3 Bells, Wood Case, 10 Tunes, B.H. Abrahams, Swiss, c.1890, 19 In. $600

Cowan's Auctions

Music, Box, Cylinder, Rosewood, Lever Wind, Change-Repeat Switch, c.1900, 5 x 18 In. $854

Neal Auction Co.

Music, Box, Singing Bird, Silver, Repousse, Putti, Flowers, Feathered Bird, 4 In. $4,200

Eldred's Auctioneers and Appraisers

TIP
Never hang a stringed instrument by the neck.

Music, Calliaphone, Keyboard, Pipes, Tangley Manufacturing Co., Muscatine, Iowa, 1920s $4,800

Freedom Auction Company

Music, Dulcimer, Sitka Spruce Top, Maple Side, Open Gear Tuners, 1900s, 36 In. $48

Eldred's Auctioneers and Appraisers

Music, Guitar, Acoustic, Martin D28, Hardshell Case $1,966

Copake Auction

Music, Guitar, Electric, Epiphone, Handcrafted, Soft Case, Marked $176

Copake Auction

M

Music, Harp, Browne & Buckwell, Parcel Gilt, Bird's-Eye Maple, Gilt, 45 String, c.1875, 69 In. $2,806

Neal Auction Co.

Music, Harp, Clark Mfg. Co., Lyon & Healy, Irish Designs, Stand, 1900s, 51 ½ In. $1,020

Cowan's Auctions

Music, Harp, Tedeschi & Raffael, Bird's-Eye Maple, 46 Strings, 7 Pedals, c.1900, 70 In. $3,500

New Orleans Auction Galleries

Music, Piano, Baby Grand, H.F. Miller, Ebonized, Player, DVD Player Q.R.S., Bench, 39 x 60 In. $2,196

New Orleans Auction Galleries

Music, Piano, Grand, Steinway & Sons, Ebonized Finish, Pat. 1859 & '72, 1899, 68 x 56 In. $4,425

Cottone Auctions

Box, Singing Bird, 2 Birds, Brass & Wire, France, 1900s, 20½ In.	937
Box, Singing Bird, 2 Birds, Brass Cage, Tole Tree Perch, Clockwork, c.1920, 11 x 5 In.	671
Box, Singing Bird, 2 Birds, Giltwood Cage, Brass, Bun Feet, 20½ In.	3000
Box, Singing Bird, Blue Enamel Flowers, Iridescent Feathers, Moving Beak, Reuge, 2 x 4¾ In.	3250
Box, Singing Bird, Brass Cage, Feathered Birds, Bontems, France, 23 In.	984
Box, Singing Bird, Feathered, Branch, Moving, Chirping, 1890, 12 x 6⅜ In.	341
Box, Singing Bird, Gilt Brass Filigree Case, Feathered Bird, Germany, c.1930, 1¾ In.	1080
Box, Singing Bird, Gilt Brass, Scenic Panels, Signed, E.B., Germany, 1¾ x 4 x 2½ In.	3328
Box, Singing Bird, Silver, Repousse, Putti, Flowers, Feathered Bird, 4 In. .... *illus*	4200
Box, Stand, Cylinder, Burled Veneers, Table, George Baker & Co., 64 x 54 In.	1089
Box, Stand, Cylinders, Silver Comb, Brass, Walnut, Ebonized, Paillard, 13 Tunes, 36 x 40 In. ..	2420
Box, Symphonion, 2 Combs, Musikwerke, 84 Teeth, Walnut Case, Handles, Leipzig, c.1900	1199
Box, Windmill, Gilt Bronze, Enamel, Moving Propellers, Lined Lid, Austria, 1900s, 9 In.	3490
Calliaphone, Keyboard, Pipes, Tangley Manufacturing Co., Muscatine, Iowa, 1920s .... *illus*	4800
Cornet, American, Bell Engraved, Leaf Motif, Birds, Later Case, 1900	308
Drum, African, Animal Hide Surface, Multicolor Band, 3 Legs, 1900s	36
Drum, Cochiti Pueblo, Animal Hide, Painted, New Mexico, 1900s, 5 x 6½ In.	132
Drum, Dark Green, Cream Sides, Brass Tacks, 1800s, 6½ x 12 In.	113
Drum, New Guinea, Hourglass Form, Relief Carving, Lizard Skin Head, Multicolor, 36 x 5 In.....	270
Drum, Wooden, Animal Hide, Carvings, Double Gong, Lizard, Spiders, 45 x 21 In.	200
Drum, Wooden, Snake Skin, Hourglass, West Africa, 12 x 8 In.	120
Dulcimer, Sitka Spruce Top, Maple Side, Open Gear Tuners, 1900s, 36 In. .... *illus*	48
Guitar, Acoustic, Martin D28, Hardshell Case................................. *illus*	1966
Guitar, C. F. Martin, Cedar Top, Mahogany, Ebony Fingerboard, Rosewood Bridge, 1915..........	3894
Guitar, Electric, 4 String, Rosewood Fretboard, Maple, Black, Chromed, 46 x 11 x 2 In.	60
Guitar, Electric, Epiphone, Handcrafted, Soft Case, Marked .... *illus*	176
Guitar, Fender Stratocaster, Electric, Contour Body, 38 In.	6765
Guitar, Fender Telecaster, Electric, Mother-Of-Pearl Pick Guard, Case, 1990s, 38 In.	900
Guitar, Gibson, Nighthawk, Antique Mural Finish, Maple Top, Case, 1995, 38 In.	960
Guitar, Lap, Kay, Steel, Wood, Inlaid Mother-Of-Pearl, 29 Frets, Case, 33 x 10 In.	635
Harp, Browne & Buckwell, Parcel Gilt, Bird's-Eye Maple, Gilt, 45 String, c.1875, 69 In...... *illus*	2806
Harp, Clark Mfg. Co., Lyon & Healy, Irish Designs, Stand, 1900s, 51½ In. .... *illus*	1020
Harp, Kora, Native, Calabash Gourd, Hardwood, African, 49 x 15 x 12 In.	63
Harp, Parcel Gilt, Brass, Leaves, Vines, c.1880, 70 In.	2250
Harp, Tedeschi & Raffael, Bird's-Eye Maple, 46 Strings, 7 Pedals, c.1900, 70 In. .... *illus*	3500
Mandolin, Acoustic, Electric, Rosewood, Maple Neck, Bone Nut & Saddle, Number 707	1250
Mandolin, Collings, 8 String, 28 In.	3444
Mandolin, L. Ricca, Gourd Shape, Inlaid, Brass Mounts, Mother-Of-Pearl Markers, 1900s, 24 In..	84
Mandolin, Maple Body, Ebony Neck, Mother-Of-Pearl Inlay................................	360
Melodeon, S.D. & H.W. Smith, Rosewood, Reticulated Music Stand, 32 x 56 In............	181
Organ, Pump, New England Organ Co., Renaissance Revival, Carved Crest, 79 x 58 In.	726
Organ, Roller, Chautauqua, Oak Case, Stencil, 12 Cobs, 1905, 13 x 18 x 15 In.	450
Organ, Roller, Oak Case, Gold, 49 Cobs, Original Finish, Label, 1900, 18 x 15 x 13 In............	600
Piano, A.C. Bechstein, Marquetry, Bellflower Garlands, Latticework, 60 In.	7500
Piano, Baby Grand, H.F. Miller, Ebonized, Player, DVD Player Q.R.S., Bench, 39 x 60 In... *illus*	2196
Piano, Baby Grand, Lester, Mahogany, Philadelphia, 39½ x 57 In.	118
Piano, Grand, Steinway & Sons, Ebonized Finish, Pat. 1859 & '72, 1899, 68 x 56 In. .... *illus*	4425
Piano, Grand, Steinway & Sons, Model GP-178 PE, Glossy, Square Legs, Bench, 70 In.	3250
Piano, Square, James Henry Houston, Walnut, Inlay, England, c.1827, 33 x 63½ In.	1680
Reed Box, Storage Case, Carved Wood, Slide Lid, Rounded Ends, 1800s, 5 x 1 In.	65
Rhythm, Pounder, Wood Carving, Female Figure, Senufo People, Cote D'Ivoire, 56 x 10 x 8 In..	240
Saxophone, C.G. Conn, Naked Woman, 10M, Engraved Bell, 1946................................	2337
Saxophone, C.G. Conn, Silver, Velvet Case, No. M212908, 1900s................................	192
Saxophone, Selmer Super Balanced Action, Stamped Neck, Cases, S1956........................	9225
Saxophone, Selmer, Mark VI, Stamped Neck, Case................................	9225
Viola, Intermediate, Germany, Bow, Case, 1978, 23 In.	63
Violin, D.A. Hamilton, Case, 4 Bows, Cremona, Tiger Maple, Carved Scrolls, 1926	960
Violin, Maxwell Buffin, 1946, 22¾ In.	250
Xylophone, Carved Wooden Base, 34 x 13½ In..	292

Mustache Cup, Anglo-Japanese Style, Leaves, Tan, Cream, Gold Trim, Saucer, 1880s, 4⅞ In.
$75

Ruby Lane

Nakara, Pin Dish, Open, Orange, Blue Flowers, Gilt Metal Rim, Handles, 1¾ x 5½ In.
$72

Woody Auction

Nanking, Platter, Oval, Cut Corner, Landscape, Bridge, Fences, Flowers, Blue, White, 8 x 11 In.
$200

Eldred's Auctioneers and Appraisers

Nanking, Strainer, Oval, Landscape, Blue, White, Original Strainer, c.1850, 13½ x 16¼ In.
$406

Eldred's Auctioneers and Appraisers

M

This is an edited listing of current prices. Visit **Kovels.com** to check thousands of prices from previous years and sign up for free information on trends, tips, reproductions, marks, and more.

Nanking, Tureen, Underplate, Flowers, Leaves, Blue, White, Double Handles, 7 x 15 In.
$218

Naudeau's Auction Gallery

Napkin Ring, Figural, Silver Plate, Calla Lily With Leaves On Base, c.1885
$210

Ruby Lane

Napkin Ring, Figural, Silver Plate, Cherub, Reining In Stag, G. Weeton, 3 x 4 ½ In.
$150

Woody Auction

Nash, Vase, Golden Iridescent, Molded Prism & Fruit Design, 4 ¼ In.
$702

Jeffrey S. Evans

294

MUSTACHE CUPS were popular from 1850 to 1900 when the large, flowing mustache was in style. A ledge of china or silver held the hair out of the liquid in the cup. This kept the mustache tidy and also kept the mustache wax from melting. Left-handed mustache cups are rare but are being reproduced.

Anglo-Japanese Style, Leaves, Tan, Cream, Gold Trim, Saucer, 1880s, 4 ⅞ In. .... *illus*	75
Bouquets, Gilt Trim & Handle, Nippon, 3 ½ x 4 In.	62
Cobalt Blue & White, Pink Flowers, Gilt Trim, Nippon, 2 ½ In.	65
Flowers, Leaves, Porcelain, 1900s, 3 ¼ x 3 ½ In.	41
Left Handed, Apples, Cherries, Walnuts, Saucer..	490
Pink Flowers, Vines, Beaded, Gilt Handle, 3 x 3 In.	42
Roses, Pastel Pink, Germany, 3 ¾ x 3 ¼ In.	35
Shells, Coral, Majolica, Fish Handle	110
Silver Plate, Chased, Attached Saucer, Art Nouveau, c.1890	125
Silver Plate, Rogers Smith & Co., c.1880	225
Water Lilies, Majolica, Saucer, Samuel Lear	125

NAILSEA glass was made in the Bristol district in England from 1788 to 1873. The name also applies to glass made by many different factories, not just the Nailsea Glass House. Many pieces were made with loopings of either white or colored glass as decoration.

Bottle, Swirl, White, Stick Neck, 1800s, 8 ½ In.	177
Fairy Lamp, 3 Sections, Chartreuse, 5 ½ In.	531
Fairy Lamp, Crimped Rim, Chartreuse, Domed Shade, S. Clark Insert, 3 Parts, c.1900, 5 x 6 In..	470
Finger Lamp, Petal, Stem, Cranberry, Crimped Rim, 9 x 4 ½ In.	1170
Flask, Herringbone, Cranberry, White, c.1875, 7 In.	180
Flask, Twining, White, Clear, 3 x 10 In.	72
Lamp, Electric, Nautilus, Blue, Opalescent, 6-Point Star, 11 ¼ x 6 ⅜ In.	12870
Lamp, Raspberry, Opal Loopings, Satin, Saucer Base, 9 ⅜ x 3 ⅞ In., 3 Piece	5265

NAKARA

NAKARA is a trade name for a white glassware made about 1900 by the C. F. Monroe Company of Meriden, Connecticut. It was decorated in pastel colors. The glass was very similar to another glass, called Wave Crest, made by the company. The company closed in 1916. Boxes for use on a dressing table are the most commonly found Nakara pieces. The mark is not found on every piece.

Dresser Box, Cherubs, Clouds, Amber, Enamel Beads, 2 x 3 In.	302
Dresser Box, Lid, Round, Hinged, Green Tones, Queen Louisa, Pink Floral, Beveled Mirror, 3 x 7¾ In.	780
Dresser Box, Purple Irises, Yellow Ground, Marked, 3 x 6 In.	236
Humidor, Blue, Green Background, Portrait Of Indian Chief, White Enamel, 7 ½ In.	840
Humidor, Cream, Green Tones, English Bulldog, Mug, Pipe, Figural Silver Plated Lid, 6 ¾ In.	270
Jewelry Box, Hinged Lid, 2-Tone, Blue, Pink Flowers, White Enamel, Square, 3 x 4 In.............	180
Jewelry Box, Hinged Lid, 6-Sided, Green, Pink Rose, 3 x 3 ¼ In..	84
Jewelry Box, Hinged Lid, Peach, Yellow, Lavender Flowers, White On Lid, Oval, 3 x 5 ¼ In.......	150
Jewelry Box, Hinged Lid, Pink Tones, Blue Flowers, Square, 3 x 4 In.	210
Jewelry Box, Hinged Lid, Pink, Young Woman, Blue Floral Highlights, Round, 2 ½ x 4 ½ In...	330
Paperweight, 8-Sided, Cobalt Blue & Pink, White Enamel, Gilt Finial, Felt Base.....................	84
Pin Dish, Open, Orange, Blue Flowers, Gilt Metal Rim, Handles, 1 ¾ x 5 ½ In. .... *illus*	72
Ring Box, Hinged Lid, Blue Tones, White Enamel, Round, 1 ¾ x 2 ½ In.	300
Ring Box, Hinged Lid, Peach, Yellow, Courting Scene, Square, 2 ½ x 2 ½ In.	540
Ring Box, Hinged Lid, Pink, Portrait, Young Woman, Round, 2 x 2 ½ In................................	480

NANKING is a type of blue-and-white porcelain made in China from the late 1700s to the early 1900s. It was shipped from the port of Nanking. It is similar to Canton wares listed in that category, but it is of better quality. The blue design was almost the same, a landscape, building, trees, and a bridge. But a person was sometimes on the bridge on a Nanking piece. The "spear and post" border was used, sometimes with gold added. Nanking sells for more than Canton.

Bowl, Cut Corner, Landscape, Blue, White, c.1900, 4 x 9 ½ In.	240

M

Natzler, Vase, Bottle Shape, Turquoise, Gunmetal Glaze, Signed, 11 x 2 In.
$1,875

Rago Arts and Auction Center

Nautical, Bell, Ship's, Tanker Ship, USS Mission De Pala, Brass, 17 In.
$120

Eldred's Auctioneers and Appraisers

Nautical, Bucket, British Royal Navy Deck, Metal, Painted, Handle, HM Dockyard, Chatham, 17 In.
$688

Eldred's Auctioneers and Appraisers

Nautical, Collage, Carnations In Vase, Stamps, Cut, Canceled, Sailor Made, 1954, 12 x 14 In.
$2,400

Rafael Osona Auctions

Nautical, Compass, Ship's, Pine, Gimbal, Slide-Lid Box, Paper Dial, Thaxter & Son, 1800s, 5 x 8 x 8 In.
$125

Garth's Auctioneers & Appraisers

Nautical, Liquor Chest, Ship's, Stand, Camphorwood, Brass, Handles, Bottles, 1800s, 22 x 15 In.
$688

Eldred's Auctioneers and Appraisers

Nautical, Model, Baltimore Clipper, Wood Hull, Mast, String Rigging, Harriet Jane, 1880, 25 x 29 In.
$360

Garth's Auctioneers & Appraisers

Nautical, Model, Gunboat, 18th Century, 1 Mast, Lateen Rig, Plank On Frame, 1900s, 35 In.
$420

Eldred's Auctioneers and Appraisers

N

Nautical, Model, H.M.S. Royal George, Prisoner Of War Carved, c.1790, 22 x 26 In.
$42,000

Nautical, Sailor's Valentine, Shellwork, Heart, Anchor, 8-Sided, Walnut Frame, c.1900, 14 In.
$2,280

Eldred's Auctioneers and Appraisers

Nautical, Spear, Eel, 5 Tines, Serrated Edges, Wood Handle, 26 x 32 In.
$272

Rafael Osona Auctions

Nautical, Model, Steamboat, Portland, Sidewheeler, Wood, Metal, String, Cloth, 1900s, 16 x 36 In.
$840

Garth's Auctioneers & Appraisers

Nautical, Picture, Woolwork, Man-O-War, Sailor Made, Ships, England, 1868, 22 x 30 In.
$19,200

Rafael Osona Auctions

Nautical, Sailor's Valentine, Box, Lid, Shellwork, Glass Frame, Image Of Woman, 1800s, 20 x 17 In.
$277

Cowan's Auctions

Nautical, Sailor's Valentine, Shellwork, Double, Heart, Flowers, Octagonal, Hinged, 1800s, 9¾ In.
$2,160

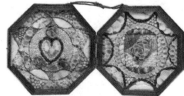

Cowan's Auctions

James D. Julia Auctioneers

N

Platter, Oval, Cut Corner, Landscape, Bridge, Fences, Flowers, Blue, White, 8 x 11 In.	*illus*	200
Platter, Oval, Mazarin, Blue & White Decoration, 17 x 13¾ In.		250
Platter, Perforated Insert, Oval, Landscape, Blue, White, 17½ In.		240
Strainer, Oval, Landscape, Blue, White, Original Strainer, c.1850, 13½ x 16¼ In.	*illus*	406
Tureen, Underplate, Flowers, Leaves, Blue, White, Double Handles, 7 x 15 In.	*illus*	218

NAPKIN RINGS were in fashion from 1869 to about 1900. They were made of silver, porcelain, wood, and other materials. They are still being made today. The most popular rings with collectors are the silver plated figural examples. Small, realistic figures were made to hold the ring. Good and poor reproductions of the more expensive rings are now being made and collectors must be very careful.

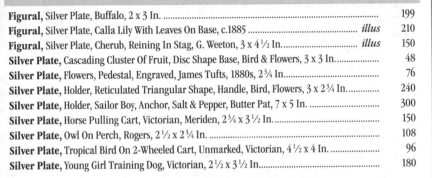

Figural, Silver Plate, Buffalo, 2 x 3 In.		199
Figural, Silver Plate, Calla Lily With Leaves On Base, c.1885	*illus*	210
Figural, Silver Plate, Cherub, Reining In Stag, G. Weeton, 3 x 4½ In.	*illus*	150
Silver Plate, Cascading Cluster Of Fruit, Disc Shape Base, Bird & Flowers, 3 x 3 In.		48
Silver Plate, Flowers, Pedestal, Engraved, James Tufts, 1880s, 2¾ In.		76
Silver Plate, Holder, Reticulated Triangular Shape, Handle, Bird, Flowers, 3 x 2¾ In.		240
Silver Plate, Holder, Sailor Boy, Anchor, Salt & Pepper, Butter Pat, 7 x 5 In.		300
Silver Plate, Horse Pulling Cart, Victorian, Meriden, 2¾ x 3½ In.		150
Silver Plate, Owl On Perch, Rogers, 2½ x 2¾ In.		108
Silver Plate, Tropical Bird On 2-Wheeled Cart, Unmarked, Victorian, 4½ x 4 In.		96
Silver Plate, Young Girl Training Dog, Victorian, 2½ x 3½ In.		180

NASH glass was made in Corona, New York, from about 1928 to 1931. A. Douglas Nash bought the Corona glassworks from Louis C. Tiffany in 1928 and founded the A. Douglas Nash Corporation with support from his father, Arthur J. Nash. Arthur had worked at the Webb factory in England and for the Tiffany Glassworks in Corona.

NASH

Bowl, Iridescent, Favrile, Multicolor, Ribbed Shape, 3 x 7 In.		125
Plate, Wavy Ribbons, Green, Blue, c.1932, 8 In.		420
Vase, Golden Iridescent, Molded Prism & Fruit Design, 4¼ In.	*illus*	702
Vase, Iridescent, Leaves, Flared Foot, c.1928, 4 x 4 In.		338

NATZLER pottery was made by Gertrud Amon and Otto Natzler. They were born in Vienna, met in 1933, and established a studio in 1935. Gertrud threw thin-walled, simple, classical shapes on the wheel, while Otto developed glazes. A few months after Hitler's regime occupied Austria in 1938, they married and fled to the United States. The Natzlers set up a workshop in Los Angeles. After Gertrud's death in 1971, Otto continued creating pieces decorated with his distinctive glazes. Otto died in 2007.

G + O NATZLER

Bowl, Blue Crystalline Glaze, Glazed Earthenware, Gertrud Natzler, 1967, 3 x 5¾ In.		1750
Bowl, Folded, Russet Hare's Fur Glaze, 2½ x 5½ In.		1875
Bowl, Tiger-Eye Glaze, 3 x 9½ In.		625
Bowl, White, Blue, Volcanic Glaze, Straight Walled, 1959, 3¾ x 5¼ In.		5625
Vase, Bottle Shape, Turquoise, Gunmetal Glaze, Signed, 11 x 2 In.	*illus*	1875
Vase, Oxblood, Green, Lavender, Melt Fissures, Bottle Shape, Signed, 10¾ x 3½ In.		8125
Vase, Pinched Back, Straight-Sided, Turquoise, Silver-Black Glaze, 1965, 6 x 5½ In.		2875
Vase, Teardrop, Blue, Mottled, 7¼ x 5½ In.		5312

NAUTICAL antiques are listed in this category. Any of the many objects that were made or used by the seafaring trade, including ship parts, models, and tools, are included. Other pieces may be found listed under Scrimshaw.

Air Pump, Diving, Mark III, Morse Diving Equipment Co., c.1942, 57¾ x 31 In.		2750
Anchor, Iron, Kedge, 36½ x 21 In.		126
Barometer, Stick, Ship's, Mahogany Case, Original Brass Gimbal, G. Agosti, 39½ In.		2400
Bell, Mahogany Mount, Brass Plate Marked Cristobal Colon 1897, Bronze, 7 x 6½ In.		3600
Bell, Ship's, Tanker Ship, USS Mission De Pala, Brass, 17 In.	*illus*	120
Bell, Ship's, Yacht, Arched Mounting Bracket, 12 In.		224

Nautical, Telegraph, Ship's, Brass, Art Deco Style, Twin Plate, Ahead, Astern, 1930s, 44½ In.
$2,400

Eldred's Auctioneers and Appraisers

N

Netsuke, Ivory, Fukurokuju, Dancing, Holding Fly Whisk & Bell, 3⅛ In.
$570

Eldred's Auctioneers and Appraisers

Netsuke, Ivory, Guardian Lion, Resting, Oval Platform, 2 1/8 In.
$300

Eldred's Auctioneers and Appraisers

Netsuke, Ivory, Man, Child, Book, Tea, Tobacco, 1800s, 2 In.
$192

Eldred's Auctioneers and Appraisers

Netsuke, Ivory, Man, Laughing, Riding On Sparrow, 1 3/4 In.
$344

Eldred's Auctioneers and Appraisers

N

Binnacle, Compass, Brass, Iron, Oak, Kelvin & James White, c.1900, 56 x 29 In.	1500
Binnacle, Walnut Pedestal, Hexagonal Brass, Glass Hood, Brass Plaque Mounted, 52 x 25 In.	2125
Binnacle, Walnut, Hexagonal Brass & Glass Hood, Arms, E.S. Ritchie & Sons, 52 1/2 x 25 In.	2040
Blubber Spade, Paddle Shape, Rectangular Shaft, Wrought Iron, 30 In.	330
Blubber Spade, Paddle Shape, Signed W. Johnson, 23 1/2 In.	300
Boat Steps, Mahogany, Rubber Slip Guard, 21 3/4 x 34 In.	192
Bucket, British Royal Navy Deck, Metal, Painted, Handle, HM Dockyard, Chatham, 17 In. *illus*	688
Cannon, Signal, Black, Winchester, 10 Gauge, 17 1/2 In.	780
Chronometer, Model 22, Painted Dial, Black Hour Numbers, Hamilton Watch Co., 1942, 6 x 6 In.	666
Chronometer, Silver Dial, Spring Driven, Single Fusee, Helical Spring, Hinged Lid, 7 x 7 x 7 In.	2420
Clock, Ship's, Brass Bell, Ship's Wheel, 8-Day, Time & Strike, Tin Face, Seth Thomas, 8 In.	490
Clock, Ship's, Brass, Bell, Round, Seth Thomas, c.1910, 6 3/8 In.	120
Clock, Ship's, Chelsea Bell, Commemorative, 13 1/4 x 8 3/4 In.	1560
Collage, Carnations In Vase, Stamps, Cut, Canceled, Sailor Made, 1954, 12 x 14 In. *illus*	2400
Compass, Geomancer, Feng Shui, Pointer, Printed Chart Surrounds, Chinese, 1800s, 5 3/4 In.	450
Compass, Ship's, Gimbal Frame, Wood Case, Wilcox, Crittenden & Co., 1920s, 8 In.	156
Compass, Ship's, Pine, Gimbal, Slide-Lid Box, Paper Dial, Thaxter & Son, 1800s, 5 x 8 x 8 In. *illus*	125
Diving Helmet, Brass, Copper, Round, 18 1/2 In.	108
Diving Helmet, Shoulder Plate, Bronze, Deep Sea, Manufacturer's Tag, 1900s, 19 x 15 x 14 In.	1920
Fid, Whalebone, Shaped, 4 Incised Lines At 1 End, Mid 1800s, 14 1/4 In.	1140
Figurehead, Bust, Admiral Perry, Yellow Vest, Gray Coat, Scrolls, 36 1/2 x 16 1/4 In.	1800
Figurehead, Eagle, Multicolor, Wood, Iron Chain, 41 x 14 x 16 In.	2812
Figurehead, Man, Double-Breasted Waistcoat, Multicolor, 36 In.	2125
Figurehead, Viking, Horned Helmet, Red Cape, 58 x 30 In.	3217
Half-Model, Schooner, 3-Masted, Walnut Satin, Black Background, 1800s, 9 x 42 x 4 In.	1200
Half-Model, Wianno Senior, White, Green Bottom, Mahogany Backboard, c.1950, 22 In.	960
Helm, Yacht, Brass, John Hastie & Co. Ltd., 44 1/2 In.	192
Lantern, Brass, Starboard Lenses, Magnifying Masthead Light, Label, Porter, 1800, 11 In.	216
Lantern, Ship's, Brass, Wire Housing, Red Lens, c.1900, 14 3/4 In.	192
Light, Stern, Fresnel Lens, Copper, Hop Lee & Co., 1900-50, 14 1/2 In.	108
Liquor Chest, Ship's, Stand, Camphorwood, Brass, Handles, Bottles, 1800s, 22 x 15 In. *illus*	688
Masthead Ball, Hudson River Steamer, Pine, 16 In.	420
Model, American Barque, 3-Masted, Mahogany, Case, James A. Wright, 1877, 26 x 35 x 12 In.	780
Model, Baltimore Clipper, Wood Hull, Mast, String Rigging, Harriet Jane, 1880, 25 x 29 In. *illus*	360
Model, Canoe, Birch Bark, Scalloped, Birds, 1900s, 45 In.	875
Model, Canoe, Wood, White, E.M. White, 52 In.	10285
Model, Clipper, Sovereign Of The Seas, 3-Masted, Lifeboat, 38 x 27 1/2 In.	228
Model, Clipper, Sovereign Of The Seas, Wood, String, Paint, Case, c.1950, 18 x 26 In.	240
Model, Gunboat, 18th Century, 1 Mast, Lateen Rig, Plank On Frame, 1900s, 35 In. *illus*	420
Model, H.M.S. Royal George, Prisoner Of War Carved, c.1790, 22 x 26 In. *illus*	42000
Model, Revenue Cutter, String Rigging, Signed Levi Woodbury, 13 1/2 x 17 3/4 In.	150
Model, Schooner, Pride Of Baltimore, Drydock, 2-Masted, Glass Case, 1998, 28 x 35 x 15 In.	1080
Model, Speed Boat, Baby Bootlegger, Mahogany, Bronze, Case, c.1925, 14 1/2 x 45 In.	1750
Model, Steamboat, Portland, Sidewheeler, Wood, Metal, String, Cloth, 1900s, 16 x 36 In. *illus*	840
Model, Tugboat, Edmond J. Moran, 2-Masted, Lifeboat, Mahogany Case, 1900s, 21 x 32 In.	1250
Model, Whaleboat, Nantucket, Line Tubs, Water Cask, Lances, Wood Base, 38 1/2 In., x 52 In.	2625
Octant, Ebony & Brass, Fitted Wood Case, Index Arm, 0-20 Vernier Scale, 1800s, 12 x 10 In.	840
Octant, Ebony, Brass, Case, England, 1800s, 12 In.	531
Paddle, Mermaid's Paddle By Rosebee, Maritime Flags, Ships, Whaleboats, Lighthouse, 64 In.	390
Picture, Woolwork, Man-O-War, Sailor Made, Ships, England, 1868, 22 x 30 In. *illus*	19200
Pond Boat, Wood, Rigging, Cloth Sails, Stand, c.1950, 45 x 36 In.	156
Sailor's Valentine, Box, Lid, Shellwork, Glass Frame, Image Of Woman, 1800s, 20 x 17 In. *illus*	277
Sailor's Valentine, Hexagonal, Flower, Sun Rays, Seed Shells, 6 1/2 x 16 In.	3025
Sailor's Valentine, Octagonal, 2-Sided Shellwork, Heart & Star, Lockable, 1800s, 3 x 12 x 12 In.	4560
Sailor's Valentine, Octagonal, Central Heart, Triangles, Double, 9 1/4 x 18 1/4 In.	2420
Sailor's Valentine, Octagonal, Heart, Clams, Geometric Border, Flower Heads, Double, 3 x 9 In.	3025
Sailor's Valentine, Shells, Central Heart, Anchor, Octagonal Frame, 13 3/4 x 13 3/4 In.	2280
Sailor's Valentine, Shells, Heart & Flower Heads, Think Of Me, Walnut Case, c.1875, 8 1/2 In.	2420

Sailor's Valentine, Shellwork, Double, Heart, Flowers, Octagonal, Hinged, 1800s, 9¾ In. *illus*	2160
Sailor's Valentine, Shellwork, Heart, Anchor, 8-Sided, Walnut Frame, c.1900, 14 In. ...... *illus*	2280
Search Light, Brass, Iron Mount, 1900-50, 24 x 18¼ In.	330
Sextant, Brass, John Bruce & Sons, c.1925, 11 In.	175
Sextant, Ebony Frame, Brass Index Arm, Ivory Degree Scale, Inscribed Capt. Davis, 13 x 15 In.	510
Sextant, Husan, Mahogany Case, Brass Handle, Henry Hughes & Son, 5¼ x 10¼ In..............	192
Sextant, Naval, Metal Frame, Engraved US Navy 1579, 11 In.	228
Ship Model, see Nautical, Model.	
Ship's Wheel, 8-Spoke, Walnut, Central Iron Hub, Outer Ring, Inset Applied Brass Ring, 54 In.	390
Ship's Wheel, Aluminum, Wrapped, Ropework, 1900, 46 In.	120
Ship's Wheel, Pilot House, Wood, Cast Iron & Brass Center, c.1900, 44 In.	200
Sign, Marine Paint, Boat, Figures, Primary Colors, Porcelain, 14 x 24 In..........................	2360
Sign, Quarterboard, Carved, Gilded, Gold Leafing, Lettering, Red Ground, 12 x 52 In.	480
Sign, Schooner, Sara A. Smith, Trailing Vine, Black, Gold, 7½ x 96 In.	363
Spear, Eel, 5 Tines, Serrated Edges, Wood Handle, 26 x 32 In. .... *illus*	272
Sternboard, Carved, Painted, Black & Gold, Eagle Facing Left, Talons, 1900s, 84 x 19 x 5 In. .	9600
Table, Made From Ships Wheel, Beveled Glass Top, Black Enameled Base...............................	900
Telegraph, Blue Face, White Text, Brass, J.W. Ray & Co., England, 47 x 19 In.	2750
Telegraph, Ship's, Brass, Art Deco Style, Twin Plates, Ahead, Astern, 1930s, 44½ In. ...... *illus*	2400
Tiller, Sailboat, Oak, Metal Mounts, Ropework, c.1925, 36½ In.	156
Tool, Whaling, Iron, Combination Blubber Flensing, Hook, Spade Blade, 1800s, 27 In............	1920
Weather Station, 4-Sided, Brass, Tabletop, Clock, Thermometer, Barometer, Hygrometer, 4¾ In.	192

NETSUKES are small ivory, wood, metal, or porcelain pieces used as toggles on the end of the cord that held a Japanese money pouch or inro. The earliest date from the sixteenth century. Many are miniature carved works of art. This category also includes the ojime, the slide or string fastener that was used on the inro cord. There are legal restrictions on the sale of ivory. Check the laws in your state.

Amber, Hotei, Carrying Treasure Sack, 2 In..	132
Bone, Fukurokuju, Holds Fan, 2½ In..	84
Boxwood, Dragonfly, Resting, On Bundle Of Sticks, 3½ In.	1320
Inro, Horn, Flowers, Miao, Chinese, 3½ In.	165
Ivory, 6 Nuts, c.1850, 1¾ In..	192
Ivory, Figure, Carved, Man & Woman In Compromising Position, 1½ x 2 In.	150
Ivory, Fukurokuju, Dancing, Holding Fly Whisk & Bell, 3⅛ In. .... *illus*	570
Ivory, Grazing Horse, Inlaid Eyes, 1700s, 2 In..	330
Ivory, Guardian Lion, Resting, Oval Platform, 2⅛ In.................................... *illus*	300
Ivory, Intercourse, Man, Woman, Robes With Lotus, Signature, 1900s, 1¾ In.	125
Ivory, Man, Carrying Basket, Peaches, Toshimasa, 2¾ In.	840
Ivory, Man, Child, Book, Tea, Tobacco, 1800s, 2 In.................................... *illus*	192
Ivory, Man, Laughing, Riding On Sparrow, 1¾ In.................................... *illus*	344
Ivory, Man, Woman, Child, Bathing Horse, 1½ In.	480
Ivory, Rat, Carved, Onyx Eye, Mother, Litter, Signed, 1900s	188
Ivory, Rat, Chewing On Candle, Inlaid Horn Eyes, 1800s, 2 In........................ *illus*	570
Ivory, Tennin, In Flight, Holding Censer, Hidemasa, c.1850, 1¾ In.	1020
Ivory, Tortoise In Winnowing Basket, Tadatomo, Signed, c.1860, 2 In.	200
Porcelain, Man, Bald, Crouching, 1¾ In.	168
Silver, Puppy With Sandal, c.1925, 2 In.	360
Wood, Carved Boxwood, Roly Poly, Daruma Doll, Signed, 1½ x 1½ In.	71
Wood, Demon, Lowering Grappling Hook, Through Cloud, 1800s, 1¾ In...........................	390
Wood, Man, Laughing, Holding Badger, Transforms Into Teapot, Signed, 2 In....................	240
Wood, Multicolor, Badger Disguised As Priest, Nagamachi Shuzan, Signed, c.1825, 2 In.	600

NEW MARTINSVILLE Glass Manufacturing Company was established in 1901 in New Martinsville, West Virginia. It was bought and renamed the Viking Glass Company in 1944. In 1987 Kenneth Dalzell, former president of Fostoria Glass Company, purchased the factory and renamed it Dalzell-Viking. Production ceased in 1998.

Netsuke, Ivory, Rat, Chewing On Candle, Inlaid Horn Eyes, 1800s, 2 In.
$570

Eldred's Auctioneers and Appraisers

TIP

If you travel when it might snow at your house, have a neighbor run a car up the driveway and make footprints to the door. Untouched drifts in the drive show the house is empty.

N

Newcomb, Bowl, Blue, Incised Flower Rim, Pink & Green, Matte Glaze, Sadie Irvine, 1927, 3 x 9 In.
$1,250

New Orleans Auction Galleries

Newcomb, Candlestick, Black-Eyed Susans, Semimatte Glaze, Sadie Irvine, 1910, 9 x 5 In.
$1,830

Neal Auction Co.

Newcomb, Vase, Blossom, Leaves, Blue, Green, Matte Glaze, Sadie Irvine, 1926, 6½ In.
$2,486

Neal Auction Co.

Newcomb, Vase, Landscape, Oak Trees, Moss, Sunset, Matte Glaze, Sadie Irvine, 1929, 4 x 3 In.
$2,562

Neal Auction Co.

Newcomb, Vase, Moon & Moss, Blue & Green, Matte Glaze, Anna Simpson, 1927, 10¾ x 4½ In.
$7,930

Neal Auction Co.

Addie, Cup & Saucer, Amethyst		25
Carnation, Water Set, Pitcher, 6 Tumblers, Ruby Stained, 7 Piece		128
Heart In Sand, Pitcher, Water, 1914, 8¼ In.		409
Horseshoe Daisy, Pitcher, Clear, Pressed Glass, c.1915, 8 In.		101
Hostmaster, Plate, Luncheon, Red, 8 In.		28
Lorraine, Water Set, Pitcher, 4 Tumblers, c.1912, 5 Piece		70
Oscar, Pitcher, Amethyst		106
Prelude, Cake Plate, 14 In.		77

NEWCOMB POTTERY was founded at Sophie Newcomb College, New Orleans, Louisiana, in 1895. The work continued through the 1940s. Pieces of this art pottery are marked with the printed letters *NC* and often have the incised initials of the artist and potter as well. A date letter code was printed on pieces made from 1901 to 1941. Most pieces have a matte glaze and incised decoration.

Bowl, Blue & Mauve Matte, Marked C.M. Chalaron, 1924, 4 x 6 In.		767
Bowl, Blue, Incised Flower Rim, Pink & Green, Matte Glaze, Sadie Irvine, 1927, 3 x 9 In. *illus*		1250
Bowl, Japanese Plums, Footed, Sadie Irvine, 4 x 7 In.		1979
Bowl, Louisiana Irises, Semimatte Glaze, Alma Mason, 1912, 3 x 8½ In.		1000
Bowl, Matte Glaze, Pink & Green Flowers, Blue Base, Sadie Irvine, 1928, 2¼ x 4½ In.		720
Candlestick, Black-Eyed Susans, Semimatte Glaze, Sadie Irvine, 1910, 9 x 5 In. *illus*		1830
Candlestick, Cherry Blossom, Mauve Matte, Marked S. Irvine, 1919, 7 In.		1062
Charger, Large Oak Tree, Small Pine Tree, Green, Blue Rim, M. LeBlanc, 11 In.		8750
Creamer, Flower Band, Blue, Pink & Green Matte, Marked, J. Meyer, 1924, 4 x 5 In.		938
Lamp, Oil, Olive Green, Brown, Copper Shade, Insert, Electrified, Marked, 7½ x 11½ In.		1062
Pitcher, Daffodils, Blue, Yellow & Green Matte, Marked, A.F. Simpson, 1932, 6½ In.		2500
Pitcher, Flower Buds, Flared Based, Blue, Green, c.1905, 7½ x 5 In.		1875
Plaque, Pine Trees, Henrietta Bailey, Frame, Label, 1915, 10 x 6 In.		2378
Plate, Chrysanthemums, Olive Green, Anna F. Simpson, 1913, 8¾ In.		1187
Vase, Blossom, Leaves, Blue, Green, Matte Glaze, Sadie Irvine, 1926, 6½ In. *illus*		2486
Vase, Blue Glaze Ground, Incised Multicolor Decorated Stylized Flowers, 6¼ x 2¾ In.		1180
Vase, Brown Clay Body, Tapered Neck, Copper Red Glossy Slip Glaze Shoulder, 6½ x 3 In.		767
Vase, Carved, Painted Matte Finish, Spanish Moss, Moon Visible Trees, Irvine, 1928, 7⅞ In.		1900
Vase, Carved, Painted, Irises, Blue Matte, Marked Sadie Irvine, 1911, 12 In.		2124
Vase, Cereus Flowers, Shouldered, Blue, Green, c.1903, 11¾ x 7 In.		5312
Vase, Clover Band, Blue & Green, Swollen Shoulder, H.C. Joor, 1904, 11½ In.		12200
Vase, Cylinder, Blue, Spanish Moss, Moon, 1928, Marked, 8 In.		2242
Vase, Dogwood, Pierced Stand, Cynthia Littlejohn, 1913, 8½ x 4¼ In.		3750
Vase, Flaring, Dogwood Blossoms, Sadie Irvine, 1920, 10 x 4½ In.		2625
Vase, Flowers On Shoulder, White, Yellow Center, Blue, Anna F. Simpson, 1916, 6 x 4 In.		875
Vase, Landscape, Oak Trees, Moss, Sunset, Matte Glaze, Sadie Irvine, 1929, 4 x 3 In. *illus*		2562
Vase, Landscape, Trees, Spanish Moss, Moon, Blue, Anna Simpson, 1924, 10¾ x 4½ In.		6875
Vase, Luster, Drip Glaze Rose, Peach, Green & Tan Shades, Irvine, Monogram, 1931, 8 In.		1500
Vase, Matte, Blue, Green, Pink, Irises, Tapered, Marked, S. Irvine, J. Meyer, 1928, 10 In.		1664
Vase, Moon & Moss Pattern, Blue, Green, Oval, A.F. Simpson, J. Hunt, Marked, 1929, 8½ In.		5000
Vase, Moon & Moss, Blue & Green Matte Glaze, Oval Shape, A.F. Simpson, 1927, 5 In.		1500
Vase, Moon & Moss, Blue & Green, Matte Glaze, Anna Simpson, 1927, 10¾ x 4½ In. *illus*		7930
Vase, Olive Green Shoulders, Yellow, Joseph Meyer, 3¼ x 3½ In.		225
Vase, Oval Shape, Light Ground, Blue Floral, Marked Joseph Meyer, 1902, 7 x 5½ In.		9063
Vase, Pine & Moon, Cabins, Matte Glaze, Green, Blue, Henrietta Bailey, 1925, 16 In.		19456
Vase, Pine Trees, Cinched Waist, Marie De Hoa LeBlanc, 1906, 12 x 4¾ In. *illus*		8125
Vase, Pink Flowers, Green Leaves, Indigo Ground, 8⅝ In.		1708
Vase, Poppy Pods, Henrietta Bailey, 1907, 9¼ x 4 In. *illus*		18750
Vase, Purple Coneflower, Matte Glaze, Green, Blue, Purple, Pink, Yellow, Irvine, 1915, 5 In.		1800
Vase, Relief Pink Flowers, Purple, Sadie Irvine, 1930, 2¼ x 3⅛ In.		400
Vase, Ribbed, White, Joseph Meyer, 3 x 3¼ In.		225
Vase, Round, Trees With Dripping Moss, Blue, Green, Incised, A.F. Simpson, 6 x 9 In.		1062
Vase, Round, Trio Of Mature Leafy Trees Dripping & Spanish Moss, Stamp Marked, 6⅜ In.		900
Vase, Scenic, Live Oaks, Spanish Moss, Anna Francis Simpson, 1916, 4 x 4 In. *illus*		2250
Vase, Seahorses, Turquoise, c.1900, 3¼ x 5 In.		1500

Vase, Separate Stand, Drip Glaze, Rose, Peach, Tan, Marked, 1931, Marked, 8 In.	1770
Vase, Stylized Flowers, On Neck, Shoulders, 2 Handles, 1924, 4 x 5 In.	1125
Vase, Tobacco Plant, Shouldered, Blue White, 6 x 4 In.	2000
Vase, Wild Roses, Blue Ground, Irvine, 1927, 5 3/8 In.	1500

NILOAK POTTERY (*Kaolin* spelled backward) was made at the Hyten Brothers Pottery in Benton, Arkansas, between 1910 and 1947. Although the factory did make cast and molded wares, collectors are most interested in the marbleized art pottery line made of colored swirls of clay. It was called Mission Ware. By 1931 the company made castware, and many of these pieces were marked with the name *Hywood*.

NILOAK	NILOAK POTTERY	NILOAK
Niloak 1910	Niloak c.1910–1920s	Niloak 1930s, 1930s–1947

| Lamp, Marbleized, Original Shade, Brown, Unique Swirl Design, 1900s, 20 x 12 x 8 3/4 In. | 59 |
| Vase, Marbleized, Brown, Blue & Cream Matte Glaze, Oval, Rolled Rim, 6 1/4 x 4 In. | 224 |

NIPPON porcelain was made in Japan from 1891 to 1921. *Nippon* is the Japanese word for "Japan." A few firms continued to use the word *Nippon* on ceramics after 1921 as a part of the company name more than as an identification of the country of origin. More pieces marked *Nippon* will be found in the Dragonware, Moriage, and Noritake categories.

·ORIENTAL·CHINA· ·NIPPON·	HAND PAINTED NIPPON	Hand Painted M NIPPON
Nitto 1890–1921	Nippon 1894–1920	Morimura/Noritake c.1911–1921

Ashtray, 6-Sided Blown Mold, Cigar & Matchbox, Blue Background, 6 In.	48
Ashtray, Brown Tones, Skull Smoking Cigarette Scene, Rare, 5 1/2 In.	480
Ewer, Handled, Green, Large Poppy Flowers, Gold Enamel Highlights, 9 In.	84
Humidor, Green Mark, 6-Sided, Playing Card Decor, 6 1/2 In.	48
Ring Holder, Gold Hand, Flowers, Gold Trim, 1920s, 2 1/2 x 3 1/2 In. .... *illus*	129
Urn, Lid, Gilt, Asters, Green, Flared Foot, 12 1/2 In.	438
Urn, Women, Garden, Flowers, In Reserve, Green, 26 In.	1053
Vase, 2 Handles, Painted Landscape, Gilt, Turquoise, 1900s, 10 In.	30
Vase, Cobalt Blue, Gilt, Beaded, Landscape, 20 In.	1638
Vase, Cylindrical, Flower, Vine, 1920, 12 In. .... *illus*	120
Vase, Fisherman, Family, Wharf, Ginko Leaves, Brown & White Stripe, 1911, 12 3/4 In.	351
Vase, Gilt, Blue, River, Green Riverbank, Mountains, High Angles Handles, 11 x 5 1/2 In.	125
Vase, Gilt, Red, Pink Roses, Green, Cupped & Scalloped Rim, 9 3/4 In.	263
Vase, Gilt, Swans, Riverbank, Double Handles, Footed, 12 x 7 In.	125
Vase, Gilt, Tree, Plain, Mountains, Geometric Band, Tapered, 10 x 6 1/2 In.	62
Vase, Gilt, Wisteria, Angled Handles, Morimura Brothers, 1911-21, 11 5/16 In.	187
Vase, Hand Painted, Gilt, Roses, Ornate, Gold, Multicolor, c.1905, 6 x 7 In. .... *illus*	225
Vase, Squared Lobed Top, 2-Tone Tan Background, Blue Coralene, 1909, 15 In.	1210
Vase, Water, Boat, Cottage, Cobalt Blue, 2 Handles, Angled, 11 x 7 In.	62
Whiskey Jug, Square, Painted Gold Handle, Lake, Palm Tree & Sailboat Scene, Lid, 7 1/4 In.	108

NODDERS, also called nodding figures or pagodas, are figures with heads and hands that are attached to wires. Any slight movement causes the parts to move up and down. They were made in many countries during the eighteenth, nineteenth, and twentieth centuries. A few Art Deco designs are also known. Copies are being made. A more recent type of nodder is made of papier-mache or plastic. These often represent sports figures or comic characters. Sports nodders are listed in the Sports category.

Newcomb, Vase, Pine Trees, Cinched Waist, Marie De Hoa LeBlanc, 1906, 12 x 4 3/4 In.
$8,125

Rago Arts and Auction Center

Newcomb, Vase, Poppy Pods, Henrietta Bailey, 1907, 9 1/4 x 4 In.
$18,750

N

Rago Arts and Auction Center

Newcomb, Vase, Scenic, Live Oaks, Spanish Moss, Anna Francis Simpson, 1916, 4 x 4 In.
$2,250

Rago Arts and Auction Center

Nippon, Ring Holder, Gold Hand, Flowers, Gold Trim, 1920s, 2½ x 3½ In.
$129

Ruby Lane

Nippon, Vase, Cylindrical, Flower, Vine, 1920, 12 In.
$120

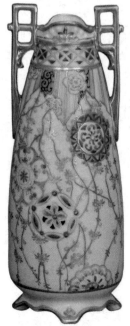

Eldred's Auctioneers and Appraisers

Angel, Bisque, Wings, Holding Branch, c.1900, 3¾ In.	125
Arabian Man, Bisque, Holding Saber, Sitting Crossed Legged, 3 x 2 In.	79
Beatnik, Composition, Glasses, Holding Bowling Pin, 7 In.	28
Boy & Girl, Kissing, Plastic, Red, Blue, Magneto, BGM, W. Germany, 1950s, 3 In.	45
Cat, Papier-Mache, Cobalt Blue, White, Folk Art, 5 In.	41
Dog, Hat, Punch Magazines, Porcelain, 3½ In.	65
Dog, Pug, Cast Metal, Black Paint, c.1910, 2 In.	120
Donkey, Celluloid, Red, Silver Eyes & Teeth, Japan, 4 x 3 In.	25
Dutch Girl, Bisque, Holding Bouquet, 4 In.	49
Gnome, Papier-Mache, Yellow Coat, Green Hat, c.1910, 10 In.	185
Pagod, Man, Head & Hands Move, Gold Pheasant Mark, Continental, c.1900, 10 In. .... *illus*	450

Salt & Pepper Shakers are listed in the Salt & Pepper category.

NORITAKE porcelain was made in Japan after 1904 by Nippon Toki Kaisha. A maple leaf mark was used from 1891 to 1911. The best-known Noritake pieces are marked with the *M* in a wreath for the Morimura Brothers, a New York City distributing company. This mark was used primarily from 1911 to 1921 but was last used in the early 1950s. The *N* mark was used from 1940 to the 1960s, and *N Japan* from 1953 to 1964. Noritake made dinner sets with pattern names. Noritake Azalea is listed in the Azalea category in this book.

Biscuit Jar, Jeweled Pastoral Scene, Raised Gold Enamel Decoration, Green Wreath Mark, 8 x 5¾ In.	113
Bowl, Cereal, Safari, 5⅞ x 2 In.	10
Bowl, Fruit, Safari, 5⅞ x 1½ In.	10
Bowl, September Song, Fruit, 5½ In.	12
Bowl, Vegetable, Blue Haven, 9¾ In.	23
Bowl, Vegetable, Lid, Isabella, 8¼ In.	90
Bowl, Vegetable, Lid, Lorenzo	65
Bowl, Vegetable, Oval, 10⅝ In.	35
Bowl, Vegetable, Palos Verde, 9¾ In.	21
Bowl, Vegetable, Safari, 8½ In.	21
Butter, Cover, Mardi Gras	21
Butter, Up-Sa Daisy, Lid	32
Creamer, Lorenzo	14
Creamer, September Song	14
Cup & Saucer, Miyoshi	12
Cup, Selby	8
Gravy Boat, Up-Sa Daisy	21
Plaque, Collie & Terrier, Round, Blown-Mold, Green Wreath Mark, 10 In.	480
Plaque, Round, Blown-Mold, Horse Head, Black, Green Background, 10 In.	360
Plaque, Round, Blown-Mold, Indian Riding Horse, Green Wreath Mark, 10 In.	300
Plate, Bread & Butter, Safari, 6½ In.	8
Plate, Bread & Butter, September Song, 6⅜ In.	3
Plate, Dinner, Miyoshi, 10⅝ In.	31
Plate, Salad, Miyoshi, 8⅜ In.	12
Platter, Blue Haven, 13¾ In.	20
Platter, Orange County, 13¼ In.	35
Platter, Palos Verde, 13⅜ In.	15
Platter, Palos Verde, 15½ In.	30
Salt & Pepper, Women, Art Deco, Green Hats, c.1900, 2 In.	98
Soup, Dish, Blue Haven, 7½ In.	12
Soup, Dish, Palos Verde, 7½ In.	12
Sugar, Lid, Blue Haven, 2⅝ In.	18
Sugar, Lid, Palos Verde	13
Syrup, Lid, Underplate, Cobalt Blue, Gold, Roses, c.1930, 5 x 4 In. .... *illus*	145
Teapot, Blue Haven, 2⅝ In.	76
Teapot, Lorenzo, 5⅝ In.	65
Vase, Riverside Landscape, Green, Brown, Gold, Blue, c.1910, 9¼ x 3½ In. .... *illus*	229

NORTH DAKOTA SCHOOL OF MINES was established in 1898 at the University of North Dakota. A ceramics course was established in 1910. Students made pieces from the clays found in the region.

N

Although very early pieces were marked *U.N.D.*, most pieces were stamped with the full name of the university. After 1963 pieces were only marked with students' names.

U.N.D.

North Dakota School of Mines
1910–1963

North Dakota School of Mines
c.1913–1963

Dish, Lid, Fluted, Orange Yellow, Signed Lind, 4 x 2½ In.	343
Mug, Burgundy, Carvings, Lion's Head Handle, 6½ x 6 In.	330
Tile, Tennis, Runners Up, Irene McCaffrey, Blue, Green, Yellow, 1934, 6 x 4 In.	1500
Vase, Bentonite, Stylized Wheat, Red, Yellow, F. Huckfield, c.1932, 6¼ x 5 In.	2125
Vase, Buffalo, 5-Panel, Green & Brown Glaze, 6 x 5⅛ In.	1800
Vase, Incised Cowboy, Signed 5 AC Mattson, 3 x 4¼ In.	678
Vase, Red River Ox Cart, Ink Stamp, University Of North Dakota, Grand Forks, 3¼ x 6¾ In.	904
Vase, Rodeo Riders, Turquoise, Julia Mattson, c.1925, 3 x 4⅞ In.	375
Vase, Tall Ships, Brown Matte, Round, H. Rodningen, 1958, 7 x 8 In.	1000
Vase, Tapered, Concentric Rings Encircling Top Opening & Shoulder, Blue Glaze, 2¾ x 4 In.	396
Vase, The Plowman, Bottom Incised, Signed 119 Huck, 5 x 5½ In. *illus*	944
Vase, Wide Shoulder, Tapering Base, Monochrome Glaze, Oxide Flecks, Rings, 8 x 6 In.	413

NORTHWOOD glass was made by one of the glassmaking companies operated by Harry C. Northwood. His first company, Northwood Glass Co., was founded in Martins Ferry, Ohio, in 1887 and moved to Ellwood City, Pennsylvania, in 1892. The company closed in 1896. Later that same year, Harry Northwood opened the Northwood Co. in Indiana, Pennsylvania. Some pieces made at the Northwood Co. are marked "Northwood" in script. The Northwood Co. became part of a consortium called the National Glass Co. in 1899. Harry left National in 1901 to found the H. Northwood Co. in Wheeling, West Virginia. At the Wheeling factory, Harry Northwood and his brother Carl manufactured pressed and blown tableware and novelties in many colors that are collected today as custard, opalescent, goofus, carnival, and stretch glass. Pieces made between 1905 and about 1915 may have an underlined *N* trademark. Harry Northwood died in 1919, and the plant closed in 1925.

Northwood Glass Co.
1902–1910

Northwood Glass Co.
1902–1910

Northwood Glass Co.
1910–c.1915

Bookend, Bear, Seated, Open Mouth, Paws On Books, Opal, Translucent, 9½ x 4¼ In.	200
Butterfly, Candy Dish, Green, Gold Iridescent, Threaded, Ruffled Rim, c.1905, 8 In.	605
Chrysanthemum Sprig, Sugar, Dome Lid, Blue Stain, Gilt, 1899, 6¾ In.	40
Grape & Cable, Hatpin, Amethyst, 3-Footed, c. 1925, 6½ In.	117
Paneled Sprig, Pitcher, Cranberry, Enamel Flowers, 6 In.	30
Pitcher, Ruby To Clear, Leaves, c.1880, 8 In.	93
Royal Oak, Pitcher, Red To Clear, Oak Leaves, 8 In.	93
Stippled Three Fruits, Bowl, Blue, Carnival Glass, 8 In. *illus*	144

NU-ART *see Imperial category.*

NUTCRACKERS of many types have been used through the centuries. At first the nutcracker was probably strong teeth or a hammer. But by the nineteenth century, many elaborate and ingenious types were made. Levers, screws, and hammer adaptations were the most popular. Because nutcrackers are still useful, they are still being made, some in the old styles.

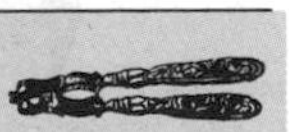

Bear Head, Black Forest, Plier Type Handle, Folk Art, Germany, 7½ In.	116

Nippon, Vase, Hand Painted, Gilt, Roses, Ornate, Gold, Multicolor, c.1905, 6 x 7 In.
$225

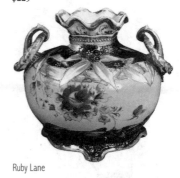

Ruby Lane

Nodder, Pagod, Man, Head & Hands Move, Gold Pheasant Mark, Continental, c.1900, 10 In.
$450

Cowan's Auctions

Noritake, Syrup, Lid, Underplate, Cobalt Blue, Gold, Roses, c.1930, 5 x 4 In.
$145

Ruby Lane

N

North Dakota School of Mines

North Dakota School of Mines pottery was created starting in 1910 to use the North Dakota clay found near the university, located in Grand Forks.

Noritake, Vase, Riverside Landscape, Green, Brown, Gold, Blue, c.1910, 9 1/4 x 3 1/2 In.
$229

Ruby Lane

North Dakota, Vase, The Plowman, Bottom Incised, Signed 119 Huck, 5 x 5 1/2 In.
$944

Soulis Auctions

Northwood, Stippled Three Fruits, Bowl, Blue, Carnival Glass, 8 In.
$144

Richard D. Hatch & Associates

Nutcracker, Dog Head, Wood, Carved, Brienz, c.1915, 7 7/8 In.
$275

Ruby Lane

Nutcracker, Squirrel, Cast Iron, Seated, Tail Up, Rusty, 4 1/2 x 5 1/2 In.
$36

Martin Auction Co.

Occupied Japan, Wall Pocket, Horse Head, Glaze, Chestnut Brown, Black, 1940s, 7 3/8 x 3 5/8 In.
$48

Ruby Lane

Ohr, Pitcher, Squat, Pinched Rim, Indigo, Cutout Handle, Signed, c.1890, 3 x 5 In.
$2,196

Neal Auction Co.

Ohr, Vase, Ocher, Gunmetal & Raspberry Sponged-On Glaze, Crumpled Rim, 3 x 4 1/2 In.
$4,375

Rago Arts and Auction Center

TIP
Quick cure for a leaking flower vase: coat the outside and inside with clear silicone household glue. Coat again if it still leaks.

Chamois Head, Carved, Glass Eyes, c.1880, 8 In.		210
Cherub, Shield, Brass, Victorian, 1800s, 6 3/8 In.		210
Dog Head, Wood, Carved, Brienz, c.1915, 7 7/8 In.	*illus*	275
Dog Head, Wood, Glass Eyes, Germany, c.1920, 9 In.		160
Dog, Brass, c.1900, 5 x 9 In.		89
Dog, Carved, Black Forest, Glass Eyes, 7 1/2 In.		550
Dog, Dachshund, Cast Iron, Wood Base, c.1950, 2 x 7 In.		150
Fisherman, Fish Tail Handle, Wood, 1800s, 8 In.		230
Monkey, Black Forest, Carved, Glass Eyes, Marked, Davos, 8 In.		495
Monkey, Glass Eye, Wood		100
Old Man, Wood, Black Forest, Germany, 8 x 3 x 2 In.		75
Old Man, Wood, Cape, Painted Eyes, c.1900, 8 In.		210
Old Woman, Carved Wood, Fishtail Handle, Mouth Opens & Closes, c.1880, 8 In.		250
Old Woman, Head Scarf, Wood, Germany, c.1890, 9 In.		160
Parrot Head, Silver Plate, c.1950, 6 In.		135
Parrot, Cast Iron, Metal Base, 10 x 6 In.		95
Pirate, Teeth, Wood, Germany, c.1890, 8 In.		140
Rooster, Brass, 1940s, 5 3/4 In.		60
Rooster, Brass, Long Beak, Blue Rhinestone Eyes, Textured Feathering, 6 In.		35
Seminude, Long Hair, Wood, 13 In.		18
Skylab, Silver Plate, Italy, 7 In.		25
Soldier, Wood, Germany, c.1900, 7 1/2 In.		33
Squirrel, Cast Iron, Seated, Tail Up, Rusty, 4 1/2 x 5 1/2 In.	*illus*	36
Squirrel, Holding Nut, Cast Iron, 7 In.		86
Sterling Silver, Crossbar, Webster Co., 6 3/4 In.		75

NYMPHENBURG, *see Royal Nymphenburg.*

OCCUPIED JAPAN was printed on pottery, porcelain, toys, and other goods made during the American occupation of Japan after World War II, from 1947 to 1952. Collectors now search for these pieces. The items were made for export. Ceramic items are listed here. Toys are listed in the Toy category in this book.

Basket, Flowers, Gilt Handle, Woven, 2 In.		21
Salt & Pepper, Bouquet, Gilt Handles, Ball Shape, 2 In.		27
Wall Pocket, Horse Head, Glaze, Chestnut Brown, Black, 1940s, 7 3/8 x 3 5/8 In.	*illus*	48

OFFICE TECHNOLOGY includes office equipment and related products, such as adding machines, calculators, and check-writing machines. Typewriters are in their own category in this book.

Adding Machine, Diera, 9 Digit, Josef Pallweber, Case, 1906	1725
Adding Machine, Left Hand Operation, Wood Base, Lid, Richard Birk, c.1910	6329
Arithnometer, Brass, Wood Case, Crank, 1st Model, Wilgot T. Odhner, 1886	3596
Calculator, Conto, 8 Digit, Spokewheel, Case, Carl Landolt Recenmaschinen, Swiss, 1912	1581
Computer, Apple Macintosh M0001, 1984	574
Computer, Victor 9000 Sirius 1, 5 1/2-In. Floppy Drive, c. 1982	373

OHR pottery was made in Biloxi, Mississippi, from 1883 to 1906 by George E. Ohr, a true eccentric. The pottery was made of very thin clay that was twisted, folded, and dented into odd, graceful shapes. Some pieces were lifelike models of hats, animal heads, or even a potato. Others were decorated with folded clay "snakes." Reproductions and reworked pieces are appearing on the market. These have been reglazed, or snakes and other embellishments have been added.

Bowl, Folded & Pinch Rim, High Gloss Purple Green, Tan Glaze, 3 1/2 x 3 1/4 In.	1080
Dish, Ruffled Rim, Crimped, Greenish Blue Glaze Over Orange Ground, c.1895, 4 In.	2583
Inkwell, Cougar, Inscribed Biloxi, Molded, Blackish Blue Glaze, c.1895, 4 1/2 In.	1476
Inkwell, Federal Shield, Hearts, Green Glaze, Crimpled, Dimpled, c.1895, 6 3/8 x 5 1/2 In.	3198
Mug, Joe Jefferson Metallic Glaze, Inscribed, 3 1/8 In.	400

Ohr, Vase, Ruffled Rim, In-Body Twist, Ocher & Brown Glaze, Stamped, 1895-96, 4 x 5 In.
$5,312

Rago Arts and Auction Center

Onion, Platter, Oval, Meissen, 23 x 17 1/2 In.
$129

Strawser Auction Group

TIP
Repairs on standing figures or pitchers should be made from the bottom up.

Opaline, Bust, George Washington, Centennial, Gillinder & Sons, 1876, 5 3/4 x 3 1/2 In.
$218

Crescent City Auction Gallery

Orphan Annie, Doll, Painted Face & Hair, Red Dress, Freundlich, c.1936, 10 In.
$195

Ruby Lane

Orrefors, Vase, Aquarium, Green Fish & Seaweed, Spherical, Graal, Edvard Hald, 5 1/4 In.
$350

Heritage Auctions

Mug, Wave Pattern, Dark Brown & Ocher Metallic, Incised, 4 In.	767
Pitcher, Ear Handle, Footed, Brown & Ocher Speckled Glaze, c.1896, 7 3/4 x 4 1/2 In.	6875
Pitcher, Rough Gunmetal Glaze, Shaped Handle, Marked, 3 3/8 In.	288
Pitcher, Squat, Pinched Rim, Indigo, Cutout Handle, Signed, c.1890, 3 x 5 In. *illus*	2196
Plaque, Mississippi Sound, Sailboat, American Flag, Fish, Seashells, Crab, 10 1/2 x 10 In.	3997
Vase, Bisque, Bulbous, Ruffled Rim, Zigzag Design, c.1880, 7 In.	1220
Vase, Face, Ruffled Rim, Green, Ocher, Gunmetal Sponged-On Glaze, 5 x 6 In.	2000
Vase, Folded Rim, Ocher, Green, Gunmetal Glaze, 1897-1900, 5 1/2 x 5 1/4 In.	4375
Vase, Folded Rim, Pinched Face, Brown Speckled Glaze, c.1900, 6 1/4 x 4 3/4 In.	5312
Vase, Green Shades Twists & Folds, Black Gunmetal Glaze, Marked, 3 x 4 In.	2596
Vase, Gunmetal Glaze, Green Rim, Impressed, 8 3/8 x 4 1/2 In.	2500
Vase, Gunmetal Matte Glaze, Pinched Waist, Flared Rim, Marked, 6 In.	3904
Vase, Metallic Gray, Dark Green Glazes, Marked, 6 In.	1062
Vase, Ocher, Gunmetal & Raspberry Sponged-On Glaze, Crumpled Rim, 3 x 4 1/2 In. *illus*	4375
Vase, Ruffled Rim, In-Body Twist, Ocher & Brown Glaze, Stamped, 1895-96, 4 x 5 In. *illus*	5312
Vase, Ruffled Shoulder, Indigo & Green Glaze, c.1900, 3 1/2 x 3 1/2 In.	2625
Vase, Scalloped Rim, Dimpled Body, Ocher, Brown, Speckled Glaze, Impressed, 4 3/4 In.	1464
Vase, Squat, Marbleized, c.1905, 3 3/4 x 5 1/2 In.	4687
Vase, Straight Neck, Round Body, Ocher, Raspberry, Speckled Glaze, Impressed, 4 3/4 x 5 1/2 In.	1820

OLD PARIS, *see Paris category.*

OLD SLEEPY EYE, *see Sleepy Eye category.*

ONION PATTERN, originally named bulb pattern, is a white ware decorated with cobalt blue or pink. Although it is commonly associated with Meissen, other companies made the pattern in the late nineteenth and the twentieth centuries. A rare type is called *red bud* because there are added red accents on the blue-and-white dishes.

Clock, Carved Flower Filled, Urn Crest Flanked, Putti, Flowers, Meissen, 1900s, 17 x 10 x 7 In.	1476
Mustache Cup, Blue & White, Fan, Vines, 3 1/8 x 4 3/8 In.	13
Platter, Oval, Meissen, 23 x 17 1/2 In. *illus*	129
Tureen, Lid, Twisted Finial, Shell Pommel Handles, 10 x 11 In.	1125

OPALESCENT GLASS is translucent glass that has the tones of the opal gemstone. It originated in England in the 1870s and is often found in pressed glassware made in Victorian times. Opalescent glass was first made in America in 1897 at the Northwood glassworks in Indiana, Pennsylvania. Some dealers use the terms *opaline* and *opalescent* for any of these translucent wares. More opalescent pieces may be listed in Hobnail, Pressed Glass, and other glass categories.

Adonis, Sugar, Lid, Colorless, Amber, Swirl, Aetna Glass & Manuf. Co., c.1888, 6 1/4 In.	80
Adonis, Syrup, Colorless, Amber, Swirl, Aetna Glass & Manuf. Co., c.1888, 7 In.	100
Compote, White, Blue Cane Twist Rim, 5 1/2 In.	62
Epergne, Trumpet Shape Vases, Diamond Optic, 11 x 10 1/2 In.	60
Goblet, Blown, Blue, Ribbed, Round Foot, 7 3/4 In.	23
Monkey, Spooner, Blue, Rayed Base, c.1890, 5 In.	175
Vase, Fish, Swimming, Jobling, France, 8 5/8 In.	94
Vase, Jack-In-The-Pulpit, 15 x 7 In.	375

OPALINE, or opal glass, was made in white, green, and other colors. The glass had a matte surface and a lack of transparency. It was often gilded or painted. It was a popular mid-nineteenth-century European glassware.

Box, Blue, Gilt Brass Escutcheon, Collar, Filigree, Lock, Key, 5 1/4 x 6 1/2 In.	756
Bust, George Washington, Centennial, Gillinder & Sons, 1876, 5 3/4 x 3 1/2 In. *illus*	218
Tazza, Silver Mount, Egyptian Revival, Caryatids, Ring, Square Base, Claw Feet, 5 x 4 1/4 In.	259

OPERA GLASSES are needed because the stage is a long way from some of the seats at a play or an opera. Mother-of-pearl was a popular decoration on many French glasses.

Enamel, Courting Couples, Red Ground, Mother-Of-Pearl Eye Cups, Brass	448
Enamel, Pink, Butterflies, Blue, Grass, Metal	380
Enamel, Red, Gold Fleur-De-Lis, Mother-Of-Pearl Eye Cups, Telescopic Handle	380

ORPHAN ANNIE first appeared in the comics in 1924. The last strip ran in newspapers on June 13, 2010. The redheaded girl, her dog Sandy, and her friends were on the radio from 1930 to 1942. The first movie based on the strip was produced in 1932. A second movie was produced in 1938. A Broadway musical that opened in 1977, a movie based on the musical and produced in 1982, and a made-for-television movie based on the musical produced in 1999 made Annie popular again, and many toys, dishes, and other memorabilia have been made. A new adaptation of the movie based on the musical opened in 2014.

Badge, Decoder, Star Surrounded By Wreath, 1938, 2 In.	85
Bandanna, Horseshoe & Brand Border, Sandy, Ginger & Joe Corntassel, 1930s, 18 x 18 In.	50
Bank, Dime Register, Metal, Annie & Sandy Sitting, Pat. Pend & Copr., 3 In.	185
Doll, Lithograph Oilcloth, Red Dress, 16 In.	129
Doll, Painted Face & Hair, Red Dress, Freundlich, c.1936, 10 In. .... *illus*	195
Game, Board, Path To Happiness, Parker Brothers, 1981	29
Game, Treasure Hunt, Ovaltine Premium, 1933, 16 ½ x 11 In.	32
Necklace, Annie & Sandy, Raised, Painted Under Glass, Brass Chain, 14 In.	95
Nodder, Bisque, Bell Shape Metal Pull, 1920s, 3 ½ In.	58
Toy, Stove, Pressed Metal, 2 Doors, Handles, Annie & Sandy, Green & Cream, c.1930, 9 x 5 x 8 In.	25

ORREFORS Glassworks, located in the Swedish province of Smaaland, was established in 1898. The company is still making glass for use on the table or as decorations. There is renewed interest in the glass made in the modern styles of the 1940s and 1950s. In 1990, the company merged with Kosta Boda and is still working as Orrefors. Most vases and decorative pieces are signed with the etched name *Orrefors*.

Orrefors

Bowl, Flared, Clear Glass, Signed, Vicke Lindstrom, 18 ½ x 13 In.	190
Vase, Aquarium, Green Fish & Seaweed, Spherical, Graal, Edvard Hald, 5 ¼ In. .... *illus*	350
Vase, Ariel, Stripes, Blue, Gold Vertical, Inscribed, Edvin Ohrstrom, 1952, 2 ¾ x 5 ½ In.	400
Vase, Blue, Art Deco Designs, Graal, Edvard Hald, 3 ½ x 3 ¼ x 2 ½ In. .... *illus*	312
Vase, Camel Oasis, Golden Brown Camels & Palm Trees, Graal, Edvard Hald, 6 In. .... *illus*	1500
Vase, Fish, Green Fish, Seaweed, Graal, Edvard Hald, 6 ⅝ x 5 ½ In.	656
Vase, Fish, Seaweed, Clear Shaded To Green, 8 x 5 In. .... *illus*	281
Vase, Gondolier, Blue, Black, Gold, Graal, Edvin Ohrstrom, 1970, 8 x 5 In.	1000
Vase, Gondolier, Graal, Black Purple, Yellow, 1970, 8 x 5 In.	1000
Vase, Green Apple, Ingeborg Lundin, 1957, 14 ½ x 12 In. .... *illus*	5000
Vase, Woman, Nude, Bathing, Waterfall, Square, Edvin Ohrstom, 1975-99, 8 ⅞ x 5 ¾ In.	35

OVERBECK POTTERY was made by four sisters named Overbeck at a pottery in Cambridge City, Indiana. They started in 1911. They made all types of vases, each one of a kind. Small, hand-modeled figurines are the most popular pieces with today's collectors. The factory continued until 1955, when the last of the four sisters died.

Candlestick, Berries, Leaves, Green, Blue, 1920s, 2 ½ x 3 ¼ In., Pair	750
Figurine, Cockatoo, Perch, Multicolor, 4 ½ In.	325 to 346
Figurine, Granny, Basket Of Apples, 4 ⅛ In.	295 to 315
Vase, Birds, White, Blue, Incised OBK/E/H, Elizabeth & Hannah Overbeck, 6 In. .... *illus*	4062
Vase, Carved Panels, Trees, Brown & Green Matte Glazes, Marked Bottom, 4 In.	1800
Vase, Flowers, Vertical Stripe, Green Matte Glaze, Elizabeth Overbeck, 3 ½ x 4 In.	2142
Vase, Mottled Turquoise, Brown, 6 In.	304
Vase, Trees, Panels, Matte Glaze, Brown, Green, E & H Overbeck, 4 In.	2268
Vase, Vertical Band Of Flowers, Pink & Green, Tan Matte Ground, Bulbous, 4 x 4 In.	2125

OWENS POTTERY was made in Zanesville, Ohio, from 1891 to 1928. The first art pottery was made after 1896. Utopian Ware, Cyrano, Navarre, Feroza, and Henri Deux were made. Pieces were usually marked with a form of the name *Owens*. About 1907, the firm began to make tile and discontinued the art pottery wares.

Orrefors, Vase, Blue, Art Deco Designs, Graal, Edvard Hald, 3 ½ x 3 ¼ x 2 ½ In. $312

Treadway Gallery

Orrefors, Vase, Camel Oasis, Golden Brown Camels & Palm Trees, Graal, Edvard Hald, 6 In. $1,500

Heritage Auctions

O

Orrefors, Vase, Fish, Seaweed, Clear Shaded To Green, 8 x 5 In. $281

Kaminski Auctions

Orrefors, Vase, Green Apple, Ingeborg Lundin, 1957, 14 1/2 x 12 In.
$5,000

Rago Arts and Auction Center

Overbeck, Vase, Birds, White, Blue, Incised OBK/E/H, Elizabeth & Hannah Overbeck, 6 In.
$4,062

Rago Arts and Auction Center

TIP
A vase that has been drilled for a lamp, even if the hole for the wiring is original, is worth 30 to 50 percent of the value of the same vase without a hole.

Oyster Plate, 6 Wells, Landscape, Water, Shores, Boats, Pink Center, Multicolor, 9 In.
$141

Strawser Auction Group

Owens Pottery 1896–1907	Owens Pottery 1896–1907	Owens Pottery 1905+

Humidor, Lid, Gourd Shape, Pink Flowers, Leaves, Gold Highlights, Textured, 7 x 8 In. 200
Jug, Utopian, Indian Painting, Marked M. Stevens, 7 In. 767
Vase, Arts & Crafts, Matte Green, Carved Greek Key, Bulbous, H. Pillsbury, 7 In. 236
Vase, Bottle, Tall, Portrait Of Cat, Marked, 16 In. 325
Vase, Lotus, Fish & Seaweed, Marked C. Chilcote, 12 In. 472
Vase, Matte Utopian, Twist Body, Raspberries On Leaf, Chocolate Brown & Ocher, 13 In. 200
Vase, Opalescent, Exotic Flowers, Black Trim, John Lessell, 13 1/4 In. 212

OYSTER PLATES were popular from the 1880s. Each course at dinner was served in a special dish. The oyster plate had indentations shaped like oysters. Usually six oysters were held on a plate. There is no greater value to a plate with more oysters, although that myth continues to haunt antiques dealers. There are other plates for shellfish, including cockle plates and whelk plates. The appropriately shaped indentations are part of the design of these dishes.

5 Wells, Flower Transfer, Scalloped Edge, Wright Tyndale & Van Roden, Haviland, 9 In. 55
5 Wells, Pale Pink, Flowering Twig, 8 3/4 In. 42
5 Wells, Pink Majolica Style, Made For Port Norris Oyster Co., c.1950, 9 1/4 x 9 1/4 In. 123
5 Wells, Pink, Pale Green Ground, Shaped Border, Gilt, 9 x 9 In. 36
6 Wells, Blue Shells, George Jones, 8 1/2 In. 272
6 Wells, Central Flowers, Pink Ground, Porcelain, 9 In. 36
6 Wells, Gilt, Pale Yellow, Pale Pink, Hexagonal, 9 1/4 In. 72
6 Wells, Gilt, Pink Flowers, Cobalt Rim, 8 1/2 In. 48
6 Wells, Landscape, Water, Shores, Boats, Pink Center, Multicolor, 9 In. .... *illus* 141
6 Wells, Shells, Pale Green Ground, Haviland & Co., 9 In. 514
7 Wells, Blue, Green, Yellow Center, Minton, 9 In. 760

PAINTINGS listed in this book are not works by major artists but rather decorative paintings on ivory, board, or glass that would be of interest to the average collector. Watercolors on paper are listed under Picture. To learn the value of an oil painting by a listed artist, you must contact an expert in that area.

Gouache, Japon Paper, Pencil, Madonna, Erte, Ava Maria, White Robes Kneeling, 10 x 14 In. . 720
Miniature, Man, Black Coat, Brass Case, Frame, 1800s, 3 x 2 1/2 In. .... *illus* 250
Miniature, Woman, Round Rosewood Frame, Signed, c.1810, 3 3/4 In. .... *illus* 94
Miniature, Woman, Voile, Frilled Blue Silk Dress, Black Wood, Brass Roses, 1820s, 5 x 4 In. ... 325
Miniature, Young Child, Blond Hair, Center Part, Oval, Gold Filigree Frame, 2 In. 390
Miniature, Young Woman, Oval, Signed, Beaux, Frame, c.1825, 3 1/2 x 3 In. .... *illus* 94
Oil On Board, Milkweed Pods In Snow, Robert Laessig, 24 x 21 In. .... *illus* 545
Oil On Canvas, 2 Peaches & Fly, Frederick Batcheller, Frame, 8 x 10 In. .... *illus* 1476
Oil On Canvas, 5 Chicks, Slice Watermelon, Ben Austrian, 1870-1921, 7 1/2 x 11 In. .... *illus* 7080
Oil On Canvas, After The Bath, Old Sticker, Klement Olsansky, 30 x 61 In. 660
Oil On Canvas, Continental School, Madonna, Child, Our Lady Of Perpetual Help, 25 x 18 In. *illus* 845
Oil On Canvas, Euclid Beach, Rocket Ships, Shirley Aley Campbell, 1971, 54 x 42 In. .... *illus* 968
Oil On Canvas, Fish Camp By River, 2 Fishermen, John Falter, '42, 24 x 30 In. 11232
Oil On Canvas, Fisherman, Pond, Ducks, Francois Lodewik Van Gulik, Dutch, 29 x 51 In. 840
Oil On Canvas, Grand Junction, Colorado, Landscape, H.R. Bull, Frame, 1800s, 8 x 15 In. 211
Oil On Canvas, Indian, Canoe, Mary E. Locke Chappell Gaylord, 1800s, 20 x 18 In. 491
Oil On Canvas, Interior Scene, Mother, Baby, Giuseppe Magni, 1859-1956, 29 x 22 In. 1123
Oil On Canvas, Landscape, Italian, Peasant Women, Plaque Frame, Domed Glass, 1800s, 3 1/2 In. 475
Oil On Canvas, Modernist Subject, Mirian Holgado, Mexico, 1900s, 39 x 27 In. 737

Oil On Canvas, Mother Mending Dolly, Sunlit Kitchen, Evert Pieters, Dutch, 1916, 35 x 43 In.	3360
Oil On Canvas, Mountain Scene, Landscape, Near Ball Hut, New Zealand, 1800s, 12¾ x 7 In.	399
Oil On Canvas, Near Ste. Anne, Henri Perre, 12 x 16 In.	720
Oil On Canvas, Normandy Village, Les Andelys, A.G. Warshawsky, c.1923, 25 x 32 In....... *illus*	10285
Oil On Canvas, Pirates On Sailing Vessel, Andrew Winter, 1893-1958, 18 x 22 In.	632
Oil On Canvas, Robert Thom, 2 Figures At Bus Stop, 1900s, 22 x 16 In.	386
Oil On Canvas, Schooner In Full Sail, James G. Tyler, 1855-1931, 34 x 26 In.	3200
Oil On Canvas, Snow-Covered Alps, Cabins, Alois Amegger, Austrian, 25 x 36 In.	2880
Oil On Canvas, Spring Woodland, Joachim George Gauthier, Canada, 12 x 14 In.	570
Oil On Canvas, Summer, Lake Masswippi, Helmut Gransow, 22 x 28 In.	660
Oil On Canvas, The Honorable John P. McGoorty, J. Ernest Brierly, 42 x 38 In.	246
Oil On Canvas, Washington Square Park Scene, Dorothy Eisner, 1938, 30 x 40 In.	5616
Oil On Canvas, Winter Scene, Charles Wysocki, Frame, 35 x 47 In.	3690
Oil On Canvas, Woman, Pink Dress, Shawl, Adele Riche, 27 x 21 In.	900
Oil On Masonite, Foot Hill, Sunset, Grandmaison, Orestes Nicholas, Canada, 14 x 18 In.	510
Oil On Masonite, Winter Wind, Dorothy Mary Mould, Canada, 12 x 10 In.	510
Oil On Panel, 3rd Falls, Magpie River, Lawrence Nickle, Canada, 10 x 12 In.	540
Oil On Panel, Ducks, Ducklings, Pond, Constant Artz, Dutch, 12 x 16 In.	1560
Oil On Panel, Kampong Cottage, Flamboyant Tree, Titled 21, Gerald Adolfs, Dutch, 12 x 16 In.	2400
Oil On Panel, Old Log House, West Of Ottawa, Ralph Wallace Burton, Canada, 1979, 11 x 14 In.	600
On Paper, Scroll, Radishes, Calligraphy & Seal Marks, Wu Ch'ang Shih, 43½ x 16 In..... *illus*	6000
Reverse On Glass, 3 Figures, Balcony, River Landscape, Frame, 16 x 22 In. .... *illus*	120

PAIRPOINT Manufacturing Company was founded by Thomas J. Pairpoint in 1880 in New Bedford, Massachusetts. It soon joined with the glassworks nearby and made glass, silver-plated pieces, and lamps. Reverse-painted glass shades and molded shades known as "puffies" were part of the production until the 1930s. The company reorganized and changed its name several times. It became the Pairpoint Glass Company in 1957. The company moved to Sagamore, Massachusetts, in 1970 and now makes luxury glass items. Items listed here are glass or glass and metal. Silver-plated pieces are listed under Silver Plate. Three marks are shown here.

Pairpoint Corp.
1894–1939

Gunderson–Pairpoint Glass
Works
1952–1957

Pairpoint Manufacturing Co.
1972–present

Bottle, Whiskey, Stopper, Octagon Cut, Panels, Rye, 11¾ In.	600
Bowl, Amethyst, English Grape, Engraved, Flared Rim, Applied Foot, 8¾ x 9½ In. .... *illus*	128
Bowl, Ruby Glass, Flared Rim, 5¼ x 11¾ In.	70
Dresser Box, Square, Hinged, Cream Tones, Rose Garland, Woman On Rock, 4 x 7 In.	180
Fairy Lamp, Coralene, Blue & Pink Cornflowers, 7⅞ x 3½ In.	761
Lamp, 2-Light, Carlisle Style Shade, Reverse Painted, Silver Plated Tripod Base, 24 In.	1815
Lamp, 2-Light, Puffy Shade, 6-Sided Base, Venice Pattern, Red, Green, Orange, 22 x 14 In.	1920
Lamp, 3-Light, Directoire, Reverse Painted, Shade, Flowers, Speckled Highlights, 26 In.	2118
Lamp, Bombay Shade, Birds Of Paradise, Green Ground, Reverse Painted, Silver Base, 22 In.	4235
Lamp, Exeter Style Shade, Trumpet, Scenic View, Reverse Painted, 23 In.	1029
Lamp, Hexagonal Shade, Reverse Painted, Tapestry Panels, Floral, Speckled Enamel, 15 x 17 In.	1210
Lamp, Kerosene, Yellow Porcelain Base, Gold Stencil Rampant Lion, Fleur-De-Lis, 23 In.	480
Lamp, Landsdown Style Shade, Reverse Painted, Italian Garden Scene, 28 In.	1513
Lamp, Peacock, Neoclassical, Lions, Snakes, Multicolor, 21 x 17½ In.	1750
Lamp, Puffy San Remo Shade, Green Filigree, Gilt Lined, 24 In.	4235
Lamp, Puffy Shade, Apple Blossom, Bees, Bronze Tree Trunk Base, 25 x 16 In.	21250
Lamp, Puffy Shade, Flowers, 4 Medallions, White Lace Ground, Oxford Shade, 19 In....... *illus*	6253
Lamp, Puffy Shade, Squared Rose, Blue Lattice, Brass Base, 7 x 10 In.	1475
Lamp, Reverse Painted Shade, Ship At Sea, 3 Legs, Shade Signed, Lamp 22 In., Shade 16 In. ...	3932
Lamp, Reverse Painted, Ribbed Shade, Garlands, White Vertical Bands, Signed, 16 In.	2178

Painting, Miniature, Man, Black Coat, Brass Case, Frame, 1800s, 3 x 2½ In. $250

Eldred's Auctioneers and Appraisers

Painting, Miniature, Woman, Round Rosewood Frame, Signed, c.1810, 3¾ In. $94

Hess Auction Group

> **TIP**
> *If possible, hang an oil painting on an inside wall away from direct sunlight.*

P

Painting, Miniature, Young Woman, Oval, Signed, Beaux, Frame, c.1825, 3½ x 3 In. $94

Hess Auction Group

PAIRPOINT

Painting, Oil On Board, Milkweed Pods In Snow, Robert Laessig, 24 x 21 In.
$545

Rachel Davis Fine Arts

Painting, Oil On Canvas, 2 Peaches & Fly, Frederick Batcheller, Frame, 8 x 10 In.
$1,476

Skinner, Inc.

Painting, Oil On Canvas, 5 Chicks, Slice Watermelon, Ben Austrian, 1870-1921, 7½ x 11 In.
$7,080

Copake Auction

Painting, Oil On Canvas, Continental School, Madonna, Child, Our Lady Of Perpetual Help, 25 x 18 In.
$845

Copake Auction

Painting, Oil On Canvas, Euclid Beach, Rocket Ships, Shirley Aley Campbell, 1971, 54 x 42 In.
$968

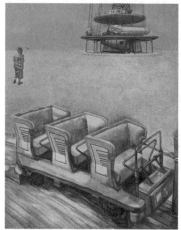

Rachel Davis Fine Arts

Painting, Oil On Canvas, Normandy Village, Les Andelys, A.G. Warshawsky, c.1923, 25 x 32 In.
$10,285

Rachel Davis Fine Arts

Painting, On Paper, Scroll, Radishes, Calligraphy & Seal Marks, Wu Ch'ang Shih, 43½ x 16 In.
$6,000

Eldred's Auctioneers and Appraisers

P

Lamp, Tivoli Linenfold, Frosted Shade, Pink & Yellow Flowers, 24 x 15 In.	1062
Lamp, Vienna Style Shade, Nasturtium, Pastel Background, 2 Hubbell Sockets, 21 In.	1210
Lamp, White, Green Marbling Shade, Roses & Butterflies, Ornate Base, Marked, 22 In.	3894
Puffy Shade, Roses, Pink, Yellow, White, Leafy Ground, Marked, 13 In. Diameter	2722
Toothpick Holder, Silver Plate, Cherub Riding Turtle & Holding Umbrella, 4 x 3 1/2 In.	270

PALMER COX, *Brownies, see Brownies category.*

PAPER collectibles, including almanacs, catalogs, children's books, some greeting cards, stock certificates, and other paper ephemera, are listed here. Paper calendars are listed separately in the Calendar category. Paper items may be found in many other sections, such as Christmas and Movie.

Bookplate, Catharina Eannele, Watercolor, Ink, German Text, Hymnal, 1816, 8 x 5 In. *illus*	600
Bookplate, Magdalena Burkholder, Watercolor, Ink, Bird, Tulip, German Text, 1829, 7 x 5 In. *illus*	1260
Bookplate, Watercolor & Ink On Paper, Colorful Flower, Heart, 7 3/4 x 5 1/2 In.	375
Broadside, Ein Brief Fo Von Gott, King & Baird, Swag Border, German Text, 1860s, 15 x 19 In.	75
Fraktur, Adam Und Eva, Printed Pennsylvania, 1900, 15 1/4 x 12 1/4 In.	70
Fraktur, Birth & Baptism, Tulips, G. Jungmann, Reading, Pa., Frame, 1807, 17 x 20 In. *illus*	944
Fraktur, Daniel, Flowers, Tulips, Red, Yellow, Navy, Brother's Valley, 1806, 7 3/4 x 13 In.	1111
Fraktur, Parrots, Verse, July 30, 1826, George Walters, Watercolor, Ink, 14 x 10 In.	4523
Fraktur, Watercolor, Angels, Verse, 1800s, 7 1/2 x 9 3/4 In. *illus*	1345
Fraktur, Watercolor, Bird, Flower, 1900, 4 1/2 x 3 3/4 In.	637
Fraktur, Watercolor, Flowers, Tulip, Bird, Central Heart, January 1862, 12 1/4 x 10 1/2 In.	7560
Fraktur, Watercolor, Hippocamp & Bird, Lester Breininger, Frame, 1964, 8 x 10 In.	510
Fraktur, Watercolor, Ink, On Paper, Heart, Tulips, Stylized Birds, Pa., 1815, 13 x 8 In. *illus*	256
Indenture, Ink On Vellum, Estate, Casper & Jane Stall, Signed John Potts, 1752, 26 x 15 In.	260
Program, Biggest Rock 'n Roll Show Of '56, Pictures Of Performers, Signatures, 1956, 12 x 9 In.	360
Program, Buffalo Bill's Wild West Programme, Cody & Sampling Of Riders, 1894	300
Scissor Cutting, Award Of Merit, For Spelling, Latticework, Mahogany Frame, 6 x 7 x 3/4 In.	95
Stock Certificate, New York Central Park, 1858, 10 1/2 x 7 In.	240
Stock Certificate, Wells & Fargo, American Express, Signed, Henry Wells, Fargo, Lot Of 5	492

PAPER DOLLS were probably inspired by the pantins, or jumping jacks, made in eighteenth-century Europe. By the 1880s, sheets of printed paper dolls and clothes were being made. The first paper doll books were made in the 1920s. Collectors prefer uncut sheets or books or boxed sets of paper dolls. Prices are about half as much if the pages have been cut.

Cecelia, Kissin Cousin, Dresses, Cardboard, James & Jonathan, Sealed, 1960, 30 In.	125
Girl, Lady Irene, 3 Coats, 3 Hats, Selchow & Richter, 8 1/2 In. *illus*	95
White House, Julia Nixon, Book, Punch Out, Outfits, 6 Pages, 1941, 10 x 14 In.	75

PAPERWEIGHTS must have first appeared along with paper in ancient Egypt. Today's collectors search for every type, from the very expensive French weights of the nineteenth century to the modern artist weights or advertising pieces. The glass tops of the paperweights sometimes have been nicked or scratched, and this type of damage can be removed by polishing. Some serious collectors think this type of repair is an alteration and will not buy a repolished weight; others think it is an acceptable technique of restoration that does not change the value. Printie is the flat or concave surface formed when a paperweight is shaped on a grinding wheel. Baccarat paperweights are listed separately under Baccarat.

Advertising, Dr. Daniels Veterinary Remedies, Don't Gamble, 5 Dice, 1903, 1 3/8 x 3 In.	403
Advertising, George I. Wilber Hops, Hand Blown, Milk Glass, 1 1/2 x 3 In.	283
Advertising, Heisey Glass, Factory Layout, Colorless, Mottled Blue, Amethyst, 3 1/2 x 4 In.	90
Advertising, Yellow Taxicab Service, Early Yellow Cab, Mirror, 3/8 x 3 In.	345
Art Glass, Hexagonal, Flowers, Blue, Clear, 3 In.	238
Art Glass, Lavender Jade, Lion's Head, Carved, 2 In.	750
Ayotte, Rick, Bluebird, Branch, Pink Flowers, 1986, 4 In.	531
Bloch Lucienne, Dog, Green Glass, Takshond, 1940, 5 x 1 1/2 x 1 1/2 In.	53
Bohemian, Glass, Lily, Flower In Pot, Vertical Flutes, 2 15/16 In.	450

Painting, Reverse On Glass, 3 Figures, Balcony, River Landscape, Frame, 16 x 22 In.
$120

Pairpoint, Bowl, Amethyst, English Grape, Engraved, Flared Rim, Applied Foot, 8 3/4 x 9 1/2 In.
$128

Pairpoint, Lamp, Puffy Shade, Flowers, 4 Medallions, White Lace Ground, Oxford Shade, 19 In.
$6,253

P

Paper, Bookplate, Catharina Eannele, Watercolor, Ink, German Text, Hymnal, 1816, 8 x 5 In.
$600

Garth's Auctioneers & Appraisers

Paper, Bookplate, Magdalena Burkholder, Watercolor, Ink, Bird, Tulip, German Text, 1829, 7 x 5 In.
$1,260

Garth's Auctioneers & Appraisers

Protecting Paper
Did you know that the Declaration of Independence is stored at a constant temperature in an inert helium atmosphere? Too bad we can't all afford to protect our paper valuables with helium.

Bronze, Art Nouveau, Bust, Woman In A Bath Holding Book, Reads, 6 In.	246
Bronze, Beast, 2 Smaller Dogs On Its Back, 3 ½ In.	1150
Bronze, Goat, Gilt, 2 ¾ In.	950
Buzzini, Orchid, Clear Glass, 3 ⅛ In.	1200
Caithness, Blue Swirl, Purple Bead, 5 x 3 ¼ In.	40
Ceramic, Block, Grasshopper, Calligraphy, Wooden Box, Japan, 1800s	240
Clichy, Concentric, Opaque Turquoise Ground, 2 ³⁄₁₆ In.	1100
Clichy, Millefiori, Facets, Punty Cuts, Rose Canes, Flower Canes, C-Scrolls, 3 In. ...... *illus*	8715
Clichy, Pink & Green Rose, Signed, 2 ⅝ In.	2500
D'Onofrio, Jim, Southwest Series, Desert Ground, Bowls, Ax, Beaded Necklace, 3 ½ In.	432
D'Onofrio, Jim, Turtle At Water's Edge, Surrounded By Plants, Rocks, Sand, 3 ½ In.	605
Eckstrand, Tropical Fish, Multicolor, 7 ½ x 4 In.	430
Glass, Frit, Rock Of Ages, Translucent Cobalt Blue Ground, 3 ¼ In.	38
Glass, Ruffled Single Cane, Floating Bubbles	80
Glass, Songbird, Resting, Green Vine, Blue Flowers, Art Deco, 1982, 3 In.	308
Grubb, Skull, Horse, Fish, Snake, Rabbit, Cat, Blossom, Richard Marquis, 1999, 3 x 5 In.	875
Howlett, M.P., Frit, Sailboat, Blue Water, Inscribed, 3 ¾ In.	100
Kane, Michael, Frit, Deer, Trees, 3 ⅛ In.	150
Kane, Michael, Frit, Dove, Extended Hand, From A Friend, 3 In.	100
Kaziun, Pale Yellow Crimp Rose, Green Leaves, 2 In.	263
Lundberg, Green, Silver Blue, Butterfly, Gold, Feather, Purple, 1975, 3 x 2 ½ In.	53
Millefiori, 6 Sections, Green Diagonal Bands, 2 ½ In.	36
Millefiori, Flowers, Pink, White, Blue, Murano Glass, 3 x 3 x 3 In.	21
Millefiori, Murano Glass, Flowers In Pink, White, Blue Colors, Original Label, 3 x 3 x 3 In.	24
Millefiori, Pedestal Base, Scotland, 4 ½ In.	250
Millville, Mushroom, White, Spatter, Footed, 3 In.	125
Millville, Pink Crimp Rose, Footed, Jack Choko, 2 ½ In.	164
Millville, Red Crimp Rose, Faceted, Footed, Attributed To Goat Valla, 2 ¾ x 2 ¼ In.	188
Millville, Rose, Pink, Crimp, Faceted, Footed, Harry Caraluzzo, 3 ¼ In.	325
Millville, Rose, Yellow, Crimp, Faceted, Footed, Goat Valla, 2 ⅜ In.	163
Orient & Flume, Spider, Pink Flower, 3 ½ In.	344
Perthshire, Chequer, Multicolor, 2 ¹³⁄₁₆ In.	475
Perthshire, Penguin, Ice Flow, Blue, White, Black, 1975, 3 ⅛ In.	650
Richardson, Colin, Brown, White, Orange Orchids, Leaves, Moss Covered Log, 3 ½ In.	484
Ritter Richard, Face, Blown Glass, Murrine, Signed, 3 x 4 ½ In.	688
Sandwich, Glass, Weed Flowers, Green Stems, Leaves, 1800s, 4 In.	313
Sautner, Flowers, Green, c.1980s, 2 ½ In.	2000
Shaw, Disc, Mountains, Moon, Blue Sea, Crossing Planets, 1990s, 8 ½ x 6 ¼ In.	250
Silver Plate, Figural, Boy Standing By High Wheel Bicycle, Reed & Barton, 3 x 3 In.	84
Simpson, Josh, Planet Series, Overlooking Earth, Multiple Canes, 2 ½ x 5 ½ In.	726
St. Louis, Cherries, Spiral Filigree, Top Printy, 6 Printies, 1975, 3 ⅛ In.	550
St. Louis, Crown Pedestal, Green, White, Pink, Blue Ribbon Cane, Marked SL 1991, Box, 5 In.	484
St. Louis, Mushroom, Blue & White Torsade, 6 Side Printies, 3 ³⁄₁₆ In.	2400
St. Louis, Patterned Millefiori, Canes, Garland, 2 ⅜ In.	550
St. Louis, Pears, Apple, Cherries, Filigree Basket, 2 ¹³⁄₁₆ In.	1800
St. Louis, Stardust Pedestal, Patterned Millefiori Canes, Box, 3 In.	968
St. Louis, Vase, Millefiori, Latticinio, Twisted Cane Rim, 1973, 5 In. .... *illus*	416
Stankard, Paul, Botanical, Flowers, Rectangular, 1988, 6 x 3 ¼ In.	4350
Stankard, Paul, Botanical, Flowers, Root People, Polished, 1990, 5 x 3 x 2 ¾ In.	4063
Stankard, Paul, Flowers, Berry, Word Canes, 2 ½ x 3 In.	2750
Stankard, Paul, Melons, Morning Glories, Bees, Ant, Lampworked Glass, Signed, 3 x 3 In.	2125
Stankard, Paul, Orchid, Green Opaque Ground, 2 ⁵⁄₁₆ In.	1400
Stankard, Paul, Pineland Pickerel, Lampwork, Bee, Flowers, Ant, Roots, Etched, 2 ½ x 3 ½ In.	2299
Tarsitano, Dahlias, Pink, Leaves, 1975-99, 4 In. .... *illus*	1521
Tarsitano, Lifelike Spider, 3 Blue Trumpet Flowers & Leaves, Sandy Ground, Signed Cane, 3 In.	968
Tarsitano, Pears, Green Leaves, Blue Jasper Ground, 1970s, 3 In.	475
Whittemore, Francis, Crimp White Rose, Footed, 2 x 2 ⅜ In.	350
Yellow Wildflower, Bulbous Root, Green Leaves, Colorless, 1973, 3 In.	431
Ysart, Domed, Pink Flowers, Green, White Ground, 3 In.	402

Paper, Fraktur, Birth & Baptism, Tulips, G. Jungmann, Reading, Pa., Frame, 1807, 17 x 20 In.
$944

Hess Auction Group

Paper, Fraktur, Watercolor, Angels, Verse, 1800s, 7½ x 9¾ In.
$1,345

Copake Auction

Paper, Fraktur, Watercolor, Ink, On Paper, Heart, Tulips, Stylized Birds, Pa., 1815, 13 x 8 In.
$256

Neal Auction Co.

Paper Doll, Girl, Lady Irene, 3 Coats, 3 Hats, Selchow & Richter, 8½ In.
$95

Ruby Lane

Paperweight, Clichy, Millefiori, Facets, Punty Cuts, Rose Canes, Flower Canes, C-Scrolls, 3 In.
$8,715

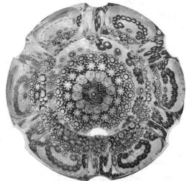

Jeffrey S. Evans

> **TIP**
> *If using a glass shelf to display a paperweight collection, be sure it is strong enough. The ideal size is 18 inches long, 4 inches deep, 1/4 inch thick. Paperweights are very heavy, and collectors tend to add "just one more," which overloads the shelf. Glass will become more brittle and break with age.*

Paperweight, St. Louis, Vase, Millefiori, Latticinio, Twisted Cane Rim, 1973, 5 In.
$416

Susanin's Auctioneers & Appraisers

Paperweight, Tarsitano, Dahlias, Pink, Leaves, 1975-99, 4 In.
$1,521

Jeffrey S. Evans

Papier-Mache, Wig Stand, Figural, Bust, Painted, 1800s, 15 In.
$443

Hess Auction Group

P

313

Parian, Figurine, Cleopatra, 1800s, 15 ½ x 7 x 5 ¾ In.

$438

Neal Auction Co.

Parian, Figurine, Goddess, Diana The Huntress, 9 ½ x 8 ½ In.

$29

Copake Auction

Paris, Cup & Saucer, Gilt, Women, Having Tea, Scroll Handle, Paw Feet, 1800s

$247

Leland Little Auctions

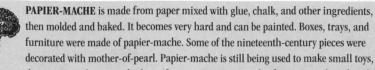

PAPIER-MACHE is made from paper mixed with glue, chalk, and other ingredients, then molded and baked. It becomes very hard and can be painted. Boxes, trays, and furniture were made of papier-mache. Some of the nineteenth-century pieces were decorated with mother-of-pearl. Papier-mache is still being used to make small toys, figures, candy containers, boxes, and other giftwares. Furniture made of papier-mache is listed in the Furniture category.

Box, Figures, In Field, Riffle, c.1890, 4 x 5 In.	311
Easter Bunny, Painted Eyes, Nose, Basket, 11 x 4 In.	29
Easter Egg, Colorful Scene, Sailboat, 1950s, 2 ¾ x 3 ¾ In.	24
Figure, Lion, Jumping, Hind Legs, France, 1890s, 15 x 19 In.	156
Glove Box, Kissing Fairies, Flowers, Scroll, Lid, Art Nouveau, c.1910, 11 x 4 In.	330
Mask, Black Fox, Blackness, Tenses Blank Up, Japan, 9 ½ x 6 x 4 ¾ In.	200
Mask, Figure, Fu Manchu, Conical Hat, Chinese, 1900, 13 x 15 x 14 In.	72
Polar Bear Head, Fiber, Hunt Mount, Mimicking, Signed, Sergio Bustamante, 1900s, 27 x 28 In.	660
Snuffbox, House, Dock, Lake, 1 x 2 ¼ In.	22
Tray, Painted Fruit, Pineapple, Grapes, Gilt, Multicolor, Serpentine, 1800s, 27 x 17 In.	923
Wig Stand, Figural, Bust, Painted, 1800s, 15 In. .... *illus*	443

PARASOL, *see Umbrella category.*

PARIAN is a fine-grained, hard-paste porcelain named for the marble it resembles. It was first made in England in 1846 and gained favor in the United States about 1860. Figures, tea sets, vases, and other items were made of Parian at many English and American factories.

Bust, Apollo Belvedere, England, c.1875, 23 x 18 ½ In.	3000
Clock, Eagle Finial, Woman, 2 Children, Figure, Porcelain Dial, Spring Driven, 16 x 9 x 6 In.	242
Figurine, Cleopatra, 1800s, 15 ½ x 7 x 5 ¾ In. .... *illus*	438
Figurine, Goddess, Diana The Huntress, 9 ½ x 8 ½ In. .... *illus*	29
Figurine, Petrarch, Head Scarf, Holding Up Robes, 1800s, 19 ½ x 7 ½ In.	366
Figurine, Water Carrier, Turban, Jug, Rocks, 10 ¼ x 6 ⅜ In.	90
Group, Venus, Adonis, 2 Classical Figures, Arm In Arm, 1870, 19 In.	492
Vase, Molded Body, Classical Figures, Man Wearing Phrygian Cap, 1800s, 10 In.	185

PARIS, Vieux Paris, or Old Paris, is porcelain ware that is known to have been made in Paris in the eighteenth or early nineteenth century. These porcelains have no identifying mark but can be recognized by the whiteness of the porcelain and the lines and decorations. Gold decoration is often used.

Centerpiece, Bisque, Parcel Gilt, Reticulated, Kneeling Angels, 1800-50, 17 x 15 In.	2750
Centerpiece, Parcel Gilt, Kneeling Angles, Reticulated Bowl, 17 x 15 ¼ In.	2750
Clock, Bisque & Gilt Bronze, Diana Hunting Scene, 1700s, 14 x 11 In.	1500
Compote, Bisque, Parcel Gilt, 2 Tiers, Seated Cherubs, 16 ½ In., Pair	1875
Cup & Saucer, Gilt, Women, Having Tea, Scroll Handle, Paw Feet, 1800s .... *illus*	247
Ferner, Mechanical, Hand Painted, Bird & Flowers, Gold Trim, Flowers, 19 x 9 In.	2700
Figurine, Woman, Turban, Pink Tunic, White Pants, Cushion, 1800s, 9 ½ x 5 ½ In. .... *illus*	270
Goblet, Saucer, Green, Lozenges, Flower Crowns, Bows, Quivers, Leaves, 1785, 4 ¾ In.	6250
Plaque, Moonrise At The Marsh, Black & Gilded Wood Frame, Signed, 18 x 20 In.	1694
Plaque, Portrait, Auguste Jean Jacques Hervieu, Gilt Frame, Inscribed, 1854, 7 In.	1125
Sculpture, Composite, Wood, Metal, Stones, Wall Mounting, Robin Grebe, 1988, 23 x 5 x 7 In.	2625
Stand, Dessert, Anneau D'Or, 3 Tiers, Paw Feet, Feuillet, Signed, 1800s, 12 x 8 In.	397
Tea Set, Teapot, Sugar & Creamer, Cup & Saucer, Tray, Blue, Red, Gilt, White, 6 Piece	275
Teapot, Lid, Cylindrical, Wood Handle, Gilt Metal, Flowers, Marked, 1785, 5 x 5 ½ In.	4000
Urn, Country Scene, Gilt, Mask Handles, Stepped Feet, 19th Century, 13 In., Pair	2040
Urn, Dome Lid, Portrait, Courting Couples, Landscapes, 19 ¾ x 5 ¾ In., Pair	2400
Vase, Cornucopia, Gilt, Pink Flowers, Blue, White, 10 ½ x 9 In., Pair	175
Vase, Gilt, Women, Seated, Fishing, Courting Scenes In Reserve, 17 ½ x 13 In., Pair	457
Vase, Portrait, Shaped Rim, Yellow, Leaves, White, 10 ½ x 7 ¾ In., Pair	88
Vase, Sevres Style, Blue Ground, Cupids, Lovebirds, c.1850, 22 x 8 In., Pair	750
Vase, Stand, Handles, Gilt, Green, Reserves, Landscape, Buildings, 1800s, 9 In., Pair	2750

PATENT MODELS were required as part of a patent application for a United States patent until 1880. In 1926 the stored patent models were sold as a group by the U.S. Patent Office, and individual models started appearing in the marketplace. A model usually has an official tag.

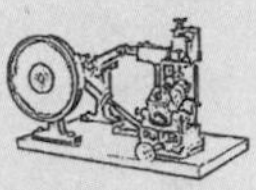

Hot Water Heater, 1900s, 10 In.	480
Truss, Door Hanger, Brass, Wood, Iron, Hanging, 1883, 11 x 18 In.	600
Wagon Brake, Self-Acting, Wood, Brass, Henderson's, c.1868	1230
Washing Machine, Wood, J K Whiteside, Original Card, c.1862, 3 x 4 In. .... *illus*	550

PATE-SUR-PATE means paste on paste. The design was made by painting layers of slip on the ceramic piece until a relief decoration was formed. The method was developed at the Sevres factory in France about 1850. It became even more famous at the English Minton factory about 1870. It has since been used by many potters to make both pottery and porcelain wares.

Dresser Box, Portrait, Round, Silver, Page Freres, France, 1901-05, 1¼ x 5 In. .... *illus*	767
Plaque, Figures, Bird, Blue, 9 x 7¼ In.	92
Plaque, Muse, Holding Cupid's Arrow, Quiver, Trees, Flowers, c.1925, 13½ In.	150
Vase, Angel, Sword, Shield, Cupid, Cafe-Au-Lait, Meissen, 15 In.	8610
Vase, Flowers, Leaves, Brown, Tan, Gold, c.1890, 8½ In.	75
Vase, Gilt, Cupids, Black, 15 In., Pair.	2500

PAUL REVERE POTTERY was made at several locations in and around Boston, Massachusetts, between 1906 and 1942. The pottery was operated as a settlement house program for teenage girls. Many pieces were signed *S.E.G.* for Saturday Evening Girls. The artists concentrated on children's dishes and tiles. Decorations were outlined in black and filled with color.

Bookends, Pink, Curved Panels, Owl On Branch, S.E.G., 4 x 5 In.	1000
Bowl, Stylized Bird Border, Blue & Cream, S. Galner, S.E.G., 2 x 5 In.	219
Bowl, Stylized Daffodil Border, Yellow, F. Levine, S.E.G., 1916, 4 x 10 In.	1875
Cup & Saucer, Lotus Design, Ivory, Blue, Black, Marked, S.E.G.	355
Pitcher, Yellow & Cream Lotus Blossom Border, Taupe, Handle, S.E.G., 9 x 10¼ In.	510
Vase, High Shoulders, Band Of Outlined Trees, Sunset, Blue, S.E.G., 1930, 13½ x 8 In. ..... *illus*	18200

PEACHBLOW glass was made by several factories beginning in the 1880s. New England peachblow is a one-layer glass shading from red to white. Mt. Washington peachblow shades from pink to bluish-white. Hobbs, Brockunier and Company of Wheeling, West Virginia, made Coral glass that it marketed as Peachblow. It shades from yellow to peach and is lined with white glass. Reproductions of all types of peachblow have been made. Related pieces may be listed under Gundersen and Webb Peachblow.

Creamer, Applied Handle, Hobbs, Brockunier & Co., 3¼ In.	293
Cruet, Amber Reeded Handle, Cut Stopper, Ground & Polished Pontil, Hobbs, 1800s, 7 In. .... *illus*	163
Decanter, Rope Twist Handle, Bottle Neck, Amber Stopper, Hobbs, Brockunier & Co., 9 x 5 In.	424
Pitcher, Swirl, Pink To Opal, Applied Handle, Pressed Fan, c.1900, 8¾ In.	70
Vase, Amber Griffin Holder, Deep Red, Yellow, 10 In.	325
Vase, Bud, Opal Cased, Low Bulb Shape, 7¼ In.	94
Vase, Enamel Flowers, Double Gourd Neck, Base, 5 x 4 In.	108
Vase, Morgan, Body, Flared Rim, 5 Figural Griffins, Stepped Bottle Neck, 9¾ In.	968
Vase, Stick, Deep Red, Yellow, 8 In.	354
Vase, Teardrop Shape, Wheeling, 8¼ In.	200

PEANUTS is the title of a comic strip created by cartoonist Charles M. Schulz (1922–2000). The strip, drawn by Schulz from 1950 to 2000, features a group of children, including Charlie Brown and his sister Sally, Lucy Van Pelt and her brother Linus, Peppermint Patty, and Pig Pen, and an imaginative and independent beagle named Snoopy. The Peanuts gang has also been featured in books, television shows, and a Broadway musical. The comic strip is being rerun in some newspapers.

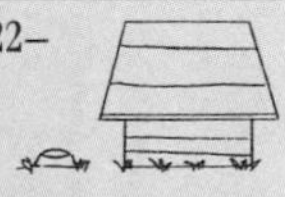

Paris, Figurine, Woman, Turban, Pink Tunic, White Pants, Cushion, 1800s, 9½ x 5½ In.
$270

Myers Auction Gallery

TIP

If you are using glue to fix an antique, work in a room that is about 70ºF. Glue will not work well if it's too hot or too cold.

Patent Model, Washing Machine, Wood, J K Whiteside, Original Card, c.1862, 3 x 4 In.
$550

Ruby Lane

Pate-Sur-Pate, Dresser, Box, Portrait, Round, Silver, Page Freres, France, 1901-05, 1¼ x 5 In.
$767

Alex Cooper Auctioneers

P

PEANUTS

Paul Revere, Vase, High Shoulders, Band Of Outlined Trees, Sunset, Blue, S.E.G., 1930, 13 ½ x 8 In.
$18,200

Rago Arts and Auction Center

Peachblow, Cruet, Amber Reeded Handle, Cut Stopper, Ground & Polished Pontil, Hobbs, 1800s, 7 In.
$163

Garth's Auctioneers & Appraisers

Peanuts, Christmas Ornament, Snoopy, Tennis Racket, 1960s, 2 ¾ In.
$29

Ruby Lane

Pearl, Tea Caddy, Mother-Of-Pearl, Abalone, Compartments, Ball Feet, George III, c.1810, 6 x 9 In.
$1,830

Neal Auction Co.

Pearlware, Mug, Court Figure, Landscape, Pink, Orange, Green, White, 5 In.
$263

Jeffrey S. Evans

Peking Glass, Urn, Lid, Pheasants, Branches, Cut Through Red, Green & Blue, Fish Scale Texture, 6 In.
$375

Fontaine's Auction Gallery

Peking Glass, Vase, Flying Storks, Red, White Ground, 9 ¼ In.
$125

Woody Auction

Peloton, Vase, Ribbed, Tapers, Opaque White, Multicolor Threads, Ruffled Rim, 4 ¾ x 4 In.
$93

Jeffrey S. Evans

Bank, Snoopy, On Doghouse, Red, Plastic, 1966, 4 x 7 In.	9
Book, He's Your Dog Charlie Brown, Hardcover, World Publishing, 1968	48
Christmas Ornament, Snoopy, Tennis Racket, 1960s, 2¾ In. *illus*	29
Cookie Cutter, Linus, Plastic, Green, United Feature Syndicate Inc., 4¾ In.	12
Date Book, Spiral Bound, Monthly Cartoon, Charles Schulz, 1972, 13 x 10 In.	24
Figurine, Woodstock, Typewriter, Ceramic, UFS Inc., 2¾ x 3¾ In.	22
Fishing Rod, Snoopy, Plastic, Zebco, Brunswick Corp., 1982, 33 In.	38
Lunch Box, Thermos, Gang, 1954, 9 x 7 x 4 In.	95
Nodder, Lucy, Blue Dress, Porcelain, 3¾ In.	29
Toy, Cookie Jar, Lucy, Yellow Dress, 12 x 8½ In.	12
Toy, Snoopy, Car, Open, Hoop & Ladder, Seated Driver, Man On Ladder, Dog, 9 In.	600
Toy, Snoopy, Cowboy, Vest, Badge, Hat, Holster, Squeak, Rubber, 1970s, 5½ In.	15

PEARL items listed here are made of the natural mother-of-pearl from shells. Such natural pearl has been used to decorate furniture and small utilitarian objects for centuries. The glassware known as mother-of-pearl is listed by that name. Opera glasses made with natural pearl shell are listed under Opera Glasses.

Basket, Shallow, Oval, Handle, Footed, 3½ x 2¼ In.	18
Tea Caddy, Mother-Of-Pearl, Abalone, Compartments, Ball Feet, George III, c.1810, 6 x 9 In. *illus*	1830

PEARLWARE is an earthenware made by Josiah Wedgwood in 1779. It was copied by other potters in England. Pearlware is only slightly different in color from creamware and for many years collectors have confused the terms. Wedgwood pieces are listed in the Wedgwood category in this book. Most pearlware with mocha designs is listed under Mocha.

Pearl

Coffeepot, Lid, Blue, Serpentine, Hexagon, Snowflake, Floral, c.1815, 11 x 4½ x 6 In.	50
Coffeepot, Tulips, Leaves, Blue Accents, 1800s, 10 x 9½ x 5½ In.	150
Figurine, Andromache Mourning Hector's Ashes, c.1800, 9 In.	795
Figurine, Goat, White Coat, Brown Horns, c.1800, 8¼ In.	549
Mug, Court Figure, Landscape, Pink, Orange, Green, White, 5 In. *illus*	263
Mug, Flowers, Yellow Band, 6 In.	82
Pitcher, Hunter's Dog, Edward Jones Llanfitllin, 7½ In.	177

PEKING GLASS is a Chinese cameo glass first made popular in the eighteenth century. The Chinese have continued to make this layered glass in the old manner, and many new pieces are now available that could confuse the average buyer.

Bowl, Red, Rounded Sides, Carved Relief, Horsemen, Pine Trees, Wood Stand, 6⅛ In.	6875
Box, Circular, Lid Carved In Relief, Stylized Chilong, 2½ In.	2125
Jar, Lid, Blue, 5½ In.	54
Snuff Bottle, Cabbage Shape, Silk Line Presentation Box, 1890-1910, 4½ x 3 x 2 In.	153
Urn, Lid, Pheasants, Branches, Cut Through Red, Green & Blue, Fish Scale Texture, 6 In. *illus*	375
Vase, Cylindrical, Oxblood Over Clear, Gold Flecks, Landscape, Elder & Youth, 9¾ x 4 In.	966
Vase, Flying Storks, Red, White Ground, 9¼ In. *illus*	125
Vase, Hexagonal, Seahorses, Red Cut To Yellow, 9 x 4¼ In.	206
Vase, Imperial Overlay, Glass, Carved Peaches, Butterflies, Dragons, Poetry, 11 x 6 x 6 In.	95
Vase, Lid, Butterscotch, Oval Shape, c.2000, 7 x 5 In.	240
Vase, Octagonal, Red, c.1900, 12 In., Pair	1250
Vase, Pavilion On Rocky Land, Riverside, Red Cased Over Clear, 8 x 4 In.	156
Vase, Waterfall, Trees, Brush, Mountains, Red Cased Over Clear, 9 In.	156

PELOTON glass is a European glass with small threads of colored glass rolled onto the surface of clear or colored glass. It is sometimes called spaghetti, or shredded coconut, glass. Most pieces found today were made in the nineteenth century.

Vase, Ribbed, Ruffled Rim, Opaque White Cased, 3 Peaks, Applied Fan Feet, c.1900, 4 x 3 In.	186
Vase, Ribbed, Tapers, Opaque White, Multicolor Threads, Ruffled Rim, 4¾ x 4 In. *illus*	93

PENS replaced hand-cut quills as writing instruments in 1780, when the first steel pen point was made in England. But it was 100 years before the commercial pen was a

TIP

Pen collectors look for quality workmanship. A gold pen nib is good. The iridium ball fused to some nibs should be intact. The filling system should work or have only a minor problem like a bad ink sac. Replacement sacs are available. Large pens usually bring higher prices than small pens.

Pen, Conway Stewart, Fountain, Dandy, Silver Clip, Medium 18K Gold Nib, London
$151

Leslie Hindman Auctioneers

Pen, Delta, Rollerball, Alfa Romeo, Trofeo Giulietta, Red Resin, Checkered Flag Band
$213

Morton Subastas

Pen, Montblanc, Fountain, 18K Gold Nib, No. 146, c.1970, 5⅝ In.
$475

Ruby Lane

P

Pen, Montgrappa, Fountain, 50th
Anniversary European Union, Blue
Resin, Sapphires
$636

Morton Subastas

Pencil, Mechanical, Parker, Debutante,
Brown, Gold-Filled Trim, Barrel Band,
1939, 11½ In.
$80

Ruby Lane

Pepsi-Cola, Calendar, 1941, Pepsi-Cola
Bottling Co. Of Plymouth, Mass., Glass,
Frame, 24½ x 19½ In.
$1,169

Morphy Auctions

common item. The fountain pen was invented in the 1830s but was not made in quantity until the 1880s. All types of old pens are collected. Float pens that feature small objects floating in a liquid as part of the handle are popular with collectors. Advertising pens are listed in the Advertising section of this book.

Conway Stewart, Fountain, Dandy, Silver Clip, Medium 18K Gold Nib, London	*illus*	151
Delta, Rollerball, Alfa Romeo, Trofeo Giulietta, Red Resin, Checkered Flag Band	*illus*	213
Fox, Gilt Metal, Fluted, 5¼ In.		60
Montblanc, Fountain, 18K Gold Nib, No. 146, c.1970, 5⅝ In.	*illus*	475
Montgrappa, Fountain, 50th Anniversary European Union, Blue Resin, Sapphires	*illus*	636
Plastic, Knurled Knob, Interior Metal, Retracts, Flush, Pocket Clip, 1940s, 4 In.		175
Sheaffer Craftsman, Black & Marbled Green Stripe, Chrome Trim, Fountain, c.1940, 5 In.		63

PENCILS were invented, so it is said, in 1565. The eraser was not added to the pencil until 1858. The automatic pencil was invented in 1863. Collectors today want advertising pencils or automatic pencils of unusual design. Boxes and sharpeners for pencils are also collected. Advertising pencils are listed in the Advertising category. Pencil boxes are listed in the Box category.

Mechanical, Cartier, 14K Gold Telescopic, Ring Bail, 4⅝ In.	306
Mechanical, Cartier, Sketching, 14K Yellow Gold, 4 In.	1499
Mechanical, Celluloid, Eraser, Chatelaine, 1930s, 2⅞ In.	10
Mechanical, Cross, Rolled 10K Gold, Pendant, Box, 3 In.	18
Mechanical, Enamel, Off-White, Pink Flowers, Sterling Silver, Germany, 3¼ In.	129
Mechanical, Marbled Celluloid, Yellow, 1940s	55
Mechanical, Parker, Debutante, Brown Shadow Wave, Gold Filled Trim, 1939, 4½ In.	80
Mechanical, Parker Debutante, Brown, Gold-Filled Trim, Barrel Band, 1939, 11½ In. ... *illus*	80
Mechanical, Silver, Paneled, Engraved, 1900s, 5 In.	68
Mechanical, Tennis Racket Shape, Silver, Sampson Mordan & Co., c.1880	844
Mechanical, Wahl Eversharp, Art Deco, Gold Filled, Greek Key Design	79
Mechanical, Wahl Eversharp, Gold Filled, 1920s, 4 In.	95
Retractable, Sliding Ruler, Sterling Silver, Edward Todd & Co., 12 In.	450
Souvenir, Bullet Shape, Reptile Garden & Monkey Jungle, St. Joseph, Mo., 3 In.	18
Souvenir, Ship, Queen Mary, 1950s, 7 In.	25

PENCIL SHARPENER

Apsco, Giant, Automatic, Yellow, Metal, Celluloid, Mounted	25
Army Tank, Bakelite, Red, 1⅞ x 1 In.	54
Bakelite, Pablo, Decal, Red, Scalloped Edge, c.1930	30
Baker's Chocolate Co., Girl, Cast Iron, 2 In.	25
Clock, Bakelite, Marbleized, Klebes Co., Germany, 1 x 1¼ In.	36
Face, Man, Smiling, Hat, Plaster, c.1970, 1⅝ x 2⅛ In.	7
Ferdinand, Decal, Bakelite, 1 x ¾ In.	50
Globe, Stand, Metal, Tin, Germany, 3⅝ In.	175
Gun, G Man, Transfer, Bakelite, Butterscotch, 1⅝ x 1⅛ In.	54
Heart, Green, Bakelite, Chain, 1950s, 1¼ In.	55
Milk Bottle, Cast Aluminum, 1950s, 1½ In.	20
Scottie Dog, Bakelite, Red, Carved Eyes, 1¾ x 1¼ In.	52
Windmill, Die Cast, 3⅛ In.	7

PEPSI-COLA, the drink and the name, was invented in 1898 but was not trademarked until 1903. The logo was changed from an elaborate script to the modern block letters in 1963. Several different logos have been used. Until 1951, the words *Pepsi* and *Cola* were separated by two dashes. These bottles are called "double dash." In 1951 the modern logo with a single hyphen was introduced. All types of advertising memorabilia are collected, and reproductions are being made.

Pepsi-Cola
1903

Pepsi-Cola
1939–1951

Pepsi-Cola
1965

Advertising Sign, Chalkboard, Have A Pepsi, c.1950, 19½ x 30 In.	125
Advertising Sign, Enamel, Yellow Ground, 1950s, 30 x 55 In.	133
Calendar, 1941, Pepsi-Cola Bottling Co. Of Plymouth, Mass., Glass, Frame, 24½ x 19½ In.....*illus*	1169
Clock, 8-Day, Pepsin Drink, McCrory's 5 & 10 C. Store, Reading, Pa., Ingraham, 36 x 16 x 4 In....*illus*	1089
Clock, Cash Counter, Sticky Pad, Instructions, Original Box, 1970s, 8 x 13 In.	325
Clock, Say Pepsi Please, Metal & Molded Plastic, Light-Up, Square, 16 In. ...*illus*	180
Cooler, Picnic, Drink Pepsi-Cola, Gray & Red, Handle, 1950s, 19 x 19 In.	977
Cooler, White, Bottle Opener, 5 Cent, Embossed, Heintz Co., 1940s, 36 x 32 In. ...*illus*	1200
Sign, Button, Celluloid, 1940-50s, 9 In.	212
Sign, Drink Pepsi-Cola, Blue, Faded Red, Tin, Attached Light Bulbs, 27 In.	90
Sign, Drink Pepsi-Cola, 5 Cents, Double Dash Logo, Tin, 6 x 18 In. ...*illus*	295
Sign, Drive Slow, Tin, 2 Signs Back To Back, Cast Iron Base, Reproduction, 48 x 19 In......*illus*	308
Toy, Horse Drawn Wagon, Cast Iron, Crates & Bottles, 3½ x 8 In.	56
Wall Phone, Vending Machine Shape, 1990, 38 x 20 In.	49

PERFUME BOTTLES are made of cut glass, pressed glass, art glass, silver, metal, enamel, and even plastic or porcelain. Although the small bottle to hold perfume was first made before the time of ancient Egypt, it is the nineteenth- and twentieth-century examples that interest today's collector. DeVilbiss Company has made atomizers of all types since 1888 but no longer makes the perfume bottle tops so popular with collectors. These were made from 1920 to 1968. The glass bottle may be by any of many manufacturers even if the atomizer is marked *DeVilbiss.* The word *factice,* which often appears in ads, refers to large store display bottles. Glass or porcelain examples may be found under the appropriate name such as Lalique, Czechoslovakia, Glass-Bohemian, etc.

Art Glass, 4 Colors, Diagonal Stripes, Latticinio, Purple, Green, Blue, White, c.1875, 5½ In. ...	3125
Atomizer, Silver, Seated Dog, Collar, Hat, 3½ In. ...*illus*	826
Cologne, Iris Design, Silver Hinge Cap, Nouveau, Moser Style, 3½ In.	236
Diamond Cutting, Pyramidal, Rainbow Well, 4½ x 3½ In.	150
Egg Shape, Frosted, Green, Hinged, White Acorn Stopper, Gilt, 5¾ In.	300
Millville, Glass, Mushroom, White, Blue, Spatter, Multicolor, 10 In.	325
Porcelain, Baluster Shape, Embossed Basketry, Purple Monochrome Landscape, 1770, 4 In. ..	438
Porcelain, Baluster Shape, Mythological Figures, Embossed Basketry, Multicolor, 1770, 3¾ In.	438
Silver & Mixed Metal, Applied Brass & Copper Birds, Lizard, Dominick & Haff, 1880, 7½ In.	1599

PETERS & REED POTTERY COMPANY of Zanesville, Ohio, was founded by John D. Peters and Adam Reed in 1897. Chromal, Landsun, Montene, Pereco, and Persian are some of the art lines that were made. The company, which became Zane Pottery in 1920 and Gonder Pottery in 1941, closed in 1957. Peters & Reed pottery was unmarked.

Jardiniere, Tapered, Flowers, Red, Green, Pale Yellow Ground, c.1910, 16 x 13 In., Pair	151
Vase, Chromal Landscape, Teepee & Campfire, Marked, 8⅜ In.	325
Vase, Landscape, Teepee, Campfire, Blue, Brown, Green, 8½ In. ...*illus*	346
Vase, Landsun, Continuous Landscape, Fall Leaves, Fence, 6¼ In.	189

PETRUS REGOUT, *see Maastricht category.*

PEWABIC POTTERY was founded by Mary Chase Perry Stratton in 1903 in Detroit, Michigan. The company made many types of art pottery, including pieces with matte green glaze and an iridescent crystalline glaze. The company continued working until the death of Mary Stratton in 1961. It was reactivated by Michigan State University in 1968.

Bowl, Metallic Glaze, Tan, Horizontal Stepped Lobes, Flared Rim, 3 x 6 In.	313
Pitcher, Blue Metallic Glaze Over Gray, Unmarked, 4¾ x 3¼ In. ...*illus*	325
Pitcher, Cobalt Blue Over White, Metallic Glaze, 4¾ x 3¼ In.	312
Plate, Metallic Glaze, Green & Tan, 3 Incised Apples On Border, 7 In.	250
Vase, Brown Metallic Glaze, High Shoulders, 5½ x 5 In. ...*illus*	975
Vase, Cup Shape, Magenta, Teal, Glazed, 4 x 4¼ In.	375
Vase, Cup Shape, Purple, Tan, Teal, Glazed, Impressed, 4 x 4¼ In.	531
Vase, Gunmetal, Metallic Drip From Rim, Rounded Form, Folded-In Rim, 2 x 3 In.	531

Pepsi-Cola, Clock, 8-Day, Pepsin Drink, McCrory's 5 & 10 C. Store, Reading, Pa., Ingraham, 36 x 16 x 4 In.
$1,089

Fontaine's Auction Gallery

Pepsi-Cola, Clock, Say Pepsi Please, Metal & Molded Plastic, Light-Up, Square, 16 In.
$180

Rich Penn Auctions

Pepsi-Cola, Cooler, White, Bottle Opener, 5 Cent, Embossed, Heintz Co., 1940s, 36 x 32 In.
$1,200

Rich Penn Auctions

Pepsi-Cola, Sign, Drink Pepsi-Cola,
5 Cents, Double Dash Logo, Tin,
6 x 18 In.
$295

Cordier Auctions

Pepsi-Cola, Sign, Drive Slow, Tin,
2 Signs Back To Back, Cast Iron Base,
Reproduction, 48 x 19 In.
$308

Morphy Auctions

P

Perfume Bottle, Atomizer, Silver,
Seated Dog, Collar, Hat, 3 ½ In.
$826

Alex Cooper Auctioneers

Vase, Metallic Glaze, Beehive Shape, Stepped Top, 2 ¼ x 3 In.	813
Vase, Metallic Glaze, Tan, Pink & Green Drip, Rounded Shape, Folded-In Rim, 2 x 2 In.	281
Vase, Metallic Glaze, Turquoise, Purple, Impressed Mark, 5 ½ x 7 ¼ In.	750
Vase, Multicolor Metallic Glaze, Squat Base, Pinched Neck, 4 ¼ x 3 In.	1500
Vase, Pastel Metallic Glaze, Pinched Neck, 12 ¼ In.	2875
Vase, Tan, 5 ½ x 9 In.	562
Vase, Turquoise, Round, 5 ½ x 5 ¾ In.	218

PEWTER is a metal alloy of tin and lead. Some of the pewter made after 1840 has a slightly different composition and is called Britannia metal. This later type of pewter was worked by machine; the earlier pieces were made by hand. In the 1920s pewter came back into fashion and pieces were often marked *Genuine Pewter*. Eighteenth-, nineteenth-, and twentieth-century examples are listed here. Marks used by three pewter workshops are pictured.

Thomas Danforth	Timothy Boardman	William Will
1727–1733	1822–1825	1764–1798

Bookends, Bull Heads, White Metal Finish, 6 ½ x 6 ½ x 5 In.	174
Bowl, Double Handled, Tapered, Hammered, 3-Footed, Stamped Hutton Sheffield, 4 x 8 In.	60
Charger, Engraved Scallops On Rim, Tulips In Center, Crown Touchmark, 1800s, 14 In. *illus*	270
Charger, St. Nicholas, Leaves, Etched, 15 In.	300
Creamer, Bulbous, Flared, Double Scroll Handle, Pedestal, William Will, Penn., c.1780, 4 ½ In.	3750
Flagon, Stacked Discs Finial, Touchmark, Boardman & Co., 1835, 13 ¾ In.	519
Flagon, Woman Shape Handles, Nude, Holding Balls Above Head, Swiss, 1800s, 20 x 12 In.	299
Humidor, Brass, Gold, Metal, Estrid Ericson, Svenski Tenn, 1936, 5 In.	425
Jug, Austen & Son Cork, Marked 1 Gill, Ireland, 1800s, 3 ½ In.	60
Jug, Flowers, Stylized, Woman Handle, Art Nouveau, 14 ¾ In. *illus*	768
Ladle, Soup, Shells, Leaves, Scrolls, c.1850, 13 In.	19
Lamp, Doughnut Shape Font, 3 Burners, Linked Chains, Smoke Bell, 1831, 13 x 22 In.	3750
Lamp, Tripod Base, Ball Feet, 1900s, 30 In.	360
Lamp, Whale Oil, Glass Top, Chamberstick, Reservoir, Roman Numeral, 1800, 5 x 14 In.	270
Measuring Cup, Reinforced Top, Banded, Thomas Warne Mark, Monogram, 1800s, 5 ¾ In.	213
Mold, Candle, 18 Tubes, Metal Wood Frame, H. Biertumpfel, London, 1700s, 19 x 6 In. *illus*	501
Mug, Touchmark, Francis Bassett, Scrolled Handle & Thumb Latch, 7 ¼ In. *illus*	6900
Pitcher, Charles Bentley, Double Banded, Double Scroll, Marked Quart, 1800s, 6 ½ In.	631
Pitcher, Glass Bottom, Banded, Marked Pint, Joseph Morgan, England, 1800s, 5 ¼ In.	601
Pot, Tavern, Horizontal Band, Marked Victoria & Edward VII, England, 1850, 3 ½ In.	601
Tea & Coffee Set, Sugar, Creamer, Tray, Hammered, Tudric, Liberty & Co., c.1920, 5 Piece	500
Tea Set, Arts & Crafts, Hammered, Ring-Based Teapot, Sugar & Creamer, Teapot 8 In.	325
Teapot, Crushed Lapis Handle, Michael Jerry, 5 x 8 In.	875
Teapot, Ebonized Handle, Michael Jerry, 3 ¾ x 7 In.	1250
Teapot, Incised Landscape, Applied Jade Handle, Poem, 6 ½ In.	484
Tray, Repousse, Crown, Dragon, 7 Crosses, 11 In. *illus*	74
Vase, Double Finial, Hinged, Dome Lid, Auricular Handle, Narrow, 1700s, 16 x 11 x 7 ½ In.	492
Vase, Rolled Rim, Tapered Neck, Hammered, Melon-Form Base, Heart Bosses, 9 x 5 In.	420

PHONOGRAPHS, invented by Thomas Edison in 1877, have been made by many firms. This category also includes other items associated with the phonograph. Jukeboxes and Records are listed in their own categories.

Burns-Pollock Electric Mfg., Lamp, Capital, Reproducer, Flip-Up, Shade, 7 Records, 20 In.	2721
Columbia Grafonola, Record Player, Oak Case, Crank, 12 x 16 ¾ In. *illus*	94
Edison, Amberola, Mahogany, Cylinder, 18 x 17 x 22 In. *illus*	265
Edison, Metal, Brass Horn, 3 Wax Cylinders, Hand Crank, Reproducer, c.1905	1100
Edison, Oak Case, 1st Version, Brass, Serial No. C2402, 1900s	1500
Edison, Oak Case, 29 Cylinders, Horn, Original Crank, Reproducer, 1910, 13 x 13 x 9 ¼ In.	475
Edison, Oak Case, Decal, Large Horn, Stand, 1900s	330

Peters & Reed, Vase, Landscape, Teepee, Campfire, Blue, Brown, Green, 8 ½ In. $346

Humler & Nolan

Pewabic, Pitcher, Blue Metallic Glaze Over Gray, Unmarked, 4 ¾ x 3 ¼ In. $325

Treadway Gallery

Pewabic, Vase, Brown Metallic Glaze, High Shoulders, 5 ½ x 5 In. $975

Treadway Gallery

Pewter, Charger, Engraved Scallops On Rim, Tulips In Center, Crown Touchmark, 1800s, 14 In. $270

Garth's Auctioneers & Appraisers

Pewter, Jug, Flowers, Stylized, Woman Handle, Art Nouveau, 14 ¾ In. $768

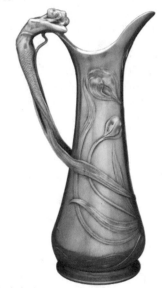

Morphy Auctions

Pewter, Mold, Candle, 18 Tubes, Metal Wood Frame, H. Biertumpfel, London, 1700s, 19 x 6 In. $501

Hess Auction Group

Pewter, Mug, Touchmark, Francis Bassett, Scrolled Handle & Thumb Latch, 7 ¼ In. $6,900

Garth's Auctioneers & Appraisers

Pewter, Tray, Repousse, Crown, Dragon, 7 Crosses, 11 In. $74

Leland Little Auctions

Phonograph, Columbia Grafonola, Record Player, Oak Case, Crank, 12 x 16 ¾ In. $94

P

Hess Auction Group

321

PHONOGRAPH

Phonograph, Edison, Amberola, Mahogany, Cylinder, 18 x 17 x 22 In. $265

Hess Auction Group

Phonograph, Victor, Talking Machine, Victrola, Mahogany, 100 Records, c.1910, 48 x 22 In. $305

Neal Auction Co.

P

Canned Music

Cylinder phonograph records were stored in cardboard containers with top and bottom lids. They resembled food cans. The recorded music had a "tinny" sound when compared with live music. Bandleader John Philip Sousa called the recordings "canned music" and the name stuck. Today *canned music* refers not to the sound quality, but to the soothing recorded music used in elevators, shopping malls, and telephone calls on hold.

Edison, Oak Case, Gem Cylinder, Winding Key, Metal Horn, 1900s	216
Gapford, Model E, Soundbox, Chromed Tone Arm, Tapering Case, Tinplate Panels, 1925	345
Hersteller, Phonolamp, Embroidered Domed Shade, Doors In Base, 1920, 32 In.	2301
Victor, 12-In. Turntable, Triple Spring Motor, Oak Speartip Horn, 1906, 7½ x 16 x 16 In.	1582
Victor, Talking Machine, Victrola, Mahogany, 100 Records, c.1910, 48 x 22 In. .... *illus*	305
Victrola, Boy Blowing Bubbles, Cat, Nursey Model, Horn	65

PHOTOGRAPHY items are listed here. The first photograph was a view from a window in France taken in 1826. The commercially successful photograph started with the daguerreotype introduced in 1839. Today all sorts of photographs and photographic equipment are collected. Albums were popular in Victorian times. Cartes de visite, popular after 1854, were mounted on 2 ½-by-4-inch cardboard. Cabinet cards were introduced in 1866. These were mounted on 4 ¼-by-6 ½-inch cards. Stereo views are listed under Stereo Card. Stereoscopes are listed in their own section.

Album, Victorian Leather Bound, Tooled Cover, Gilt Edged Pages, 1800s, 6 x 5 x 2 In. ...... *illus*	96
Albumen, Mohawk Camp, Mohawk Gold Mining Co., Arizona, 13 x 7 ½ In., c.1892	420
Albumen, Pennsylvania Oil Boom, American Oil Works, J.A. Mather, c.1860, 10 x 13 In.	600
Ambrotype, Boy, Zouave Outfit, Drum, Convex Glass, Half Case, ⅙ Plate	720
Ambrotype, Civil War Veteran, Pennsylvania Governor, Beaver, & Associates, ⅙ Plate	720
Ambrotype, Ruby, Double Armed Cavalryman, ¼ Plate	720
Ambrotype, Union Soldier, Standing, Cartridge Box, Belt Buckle, Musket, ⅙ Plate	780
Ambrotype, White Clay Creek Presbyterian Church, Graveyard, ½ Plate	2160
Cabinet Card, Balloon Jumper, Ink Signed, Studio Of H.H. Campbell	300
Cabinet Card, Calamity Jane, With Repeating Rifle, H.R. Locke, 1895, 6 In.	2829
Cabinet Card, Charles De Rudio, 7th Cavalry, 12 x 14 In.	1168
Cabinet Card, Curley, Custer's Crow Scout, George E. Spencer, c.1893	480
Cabinet Card, Gold Miner, Winter & Pond, Juneau, Alaska, Inscription, c.1890	120
Cabinet Card, Jefferson Davis, Albumen, Signed, Anderson & Co., 1867	1560
Cabinet Card, Lieutenant George Custer, Jose M. Mora, New York, March, 1876	2160
Cabinet Card, Oklahoma Territory, Tecumseh Herald Building, c.1894	360
Cabinet Card, Portrait, Father & Daughter, Black & White, Oval, 1878, 4 x 3 In.	20
Camera, Brownie, Model 2A, Eastman Kodak Co., Box ...... *illus*	180
Camera, Graflex Crown Graphic, Large Format, Kalart Range Finder, 8 ½ x 8 In.	188
Camera, Hasselblad, 500C, Zeiss Planar 80 mm	475
Camera, Hasselblad, 500CM, Carl Zeiss Lens, Hood, Manual, 1973, 4 x 4¾ In. ...... *illus*	952
Camera, Hasselblad, Medium Format, 50 mm Lens, Case, 11 In.	501
Camera, Hasselblad, Medium Format, 80 mm Lens, 4 In.	826
Camera, Spy, Minox B, Leather Case, Box, Germany, 4 In.	123
Carte De Visite, Color Bearer, Kady Brownell, Zouave Uniform, Holding Carbine, Civil War	780
Carte De Visite, Female Doctor, Medical Uniform, Mary Sanborn Cox, Civil War	660
Carte De Visite, George Custer, Oval Brass Frame, 1865	1230
Carte De Visite, George Waring Jr., c.1862	300
Carte De Visite, Man In Buckskins, Metis, Smith & Sons, Brantford, Canada	660
Carte De Visite, U.S. Grant & Staff, Albumen, Civil War, Henszey & Co., c.1865	570
Carte De Visite, White & Black Slaves, New Orleans, Adult, Children, Albumen, 1863 ...... *illus*	1680
Daguerreotype, Captain, Mustache, Wife, Daughter, c.1950, ¼ Plate	2214
Daguerreotype, Carpenter, Work Clothes, Hammer, ⅙ Plate	3690
Daguerreotype, Chemical Laboratory, Half Case, ⅙ Plate	960
Daguerreotype, Indian, Wearing Peace Medal, Case, ⅙ Plate	3000
Daguerreotype, Man Seated, Top Hat, Cigar, Stamped Whitehurst, c.1850, 4 ¼ x 3 ¼ In.	70
Daguerreotype, Man, Dog, Flower Pressed Paper Case, ⅙ Plate	2520
Developer, Kodak, Wood, Stand, Printing Plate, Swivels, 1906, 12 x 8 In.	430
Photograph, Annie Oakley, Shooting Orange From Dog's Head, Pinehurst Golf Club, 8 x 10 In.	615
Photograph, Bathing Girl Revue, Panoramic, Galveston, Texas, 1922, 28 x 10 In.	3900
Photograph, Civil War Soldiers, Hand Colored, 16 x 13 In. ...... *illus*	127
Photograph, H.M.S. Agamemnon, Shore End & Deep Sea, 19 x 22 In.	1264
Photograph, Indian Family, Utes, Jose Remero, 1899, 8 x 6 In. ...... *illus*	99
Photograph, James J. Corbett, With Compliments, Aug. 3rd, 1894, 15 x 11 In. ...... *illus*	597
Photograph, Norfolk Baseball Team, Manager John Phenomenal Smith, c.1900, 21 x 18 In.	110

Photograph, Roy Garrett, Cowboy, With Chaps, Oval, Frame, 17 x 23 In.	238
Photograph, Tattooed Man, Portraits Of Royals, Frame, c.1890, 20 x 23 In. ...... *illus*	420
Photograph, W.I. Stephenson, Round-Up, Panoramic, Black & White, Frame, 30 x 7 In.	153
Photograph, William F. Buffalo Bill Cody, Signed, Inscribed, Albumen, 11 x 16 In. ...... *illus*	2640
Projector, Black Metal, Brass Supports, Glass Picture, Landscapes, 7 x 4 In.	88
Tintype, Bearded Artist, With Easel, Brass Mat, Quarter Panel	510
Tintype, Cavalryman, Corporal, Standing, Cavalry Saber, Camp Backdrop, ¼ Plate	390
Tintype, Family In Horse Drawn Wagon, Whole Plate	492
Tintype, Sergeant Skidmore, Portrait, 3rd & 14th Connecticut, ¼ Plate	102
Tintype, Union Soldier With Musket & Dog, Quarter Plate, Thermoplastic Case	540
Tintype, Union Soldier, Triple Armed, ⅙ Plate, Pressed Paper Case	1440

PICKARD China Company was started in 1893 by Wilder Pickard. Hand-painted designs were used on china purchased from other sources. In the 1930s, the company began to make its own china wares in Chicago, Illinois. The company made a line of limited-edition plates and bowls in the 1970s and 1980s. It now makes many types of porcelains..

Pickard/Edgerton Art Studio 1893–1894   Pickard/Pickard Studios, Inc. 1925–1930   Pickard, Inc. 1938–present

Pitcher, Water, Luster Grape Design, Limoges, Signed, Hessler, c.1930, 12½ In.	215
Vase, Flowers, Blue Bands, Gold Ground, 2 Handles, 8 In. ...... *illus*	224
Vase, Vellum Glaze, Trees, Lake, Gold Handles, Signed, 11 In.	384

PICTURES, silhouettes, and other small decorative objects framed to hang on the wall are listed here. Some other types of pictures are listed in the Print and Painting categories.

Calligraphy, Stag, Ink On Paper, Frame, Spencerian, Frame, 1800s, 13½ x 17½ In.	300
Drawing, Al Hirschfield, Line Drawing Image, Signed Ira Gershwin, 9 x 7¼ In.	79
Gouache On Paper, Cowboy Scene, Illustration, Signed, Morgan Bryan, 21 x 15 In. ...... *illus*	351
Needlework, Embroidery, Regimental, III S.B., Grupp Kaumi, Silk, Frame, Chinese, 22 x 29 In. *illus*	540
Needlework, Fabric, Basket, Flowers & Fruit, Lititz Moravian School, 1820s, 23 x 26 In... *illus*	1652
Needlework, Family Record, Linen, Ermina Drury, Names, Trees, Frame, 1784-1826, 12 x 13 In.	485
Needlework, Flower Basket, Latticework, Chenille, Astilbe, Roses, Tulips, 17 x 20 In.	450
Needlework, George Washington, America's Independence, 16 x 12 In. ...... *illus*	667
Needlework, Hand Woven, Poem, Leaves, House Blessing, Germany, Frame, 1900s, 19 x 17 In.	31
Needlework, Mary Sands, In The Year Of Our Lord, England, 1700s, 18 x 20 In.	211
Needlework, Pastoral, Silk, Woman, Sheep, England, 1800s, 17 x 13 In. ...... *illus*	632
Needlework, Pinks, Snowdrops, Black Ground, Frame, 1800s, 21 x 17 In.	258
Needlework, Silk Thread & Ground, Cottage, Painted Faces, Church, 13 x 16 In. ...... *illus*	30
Needlework, Silk, Eagle, Stars, Stripes, Shield, Flags, Frame, 1800s, 23 x 28 In. ...... *illus*	649
Needlework, Silk, Mary Minor's Embroidery 1810, Shepherdess & Sheep, 17 x 13 In. ...... *illus*	182
Needlework, Wool On Burlap, Crochet Figures, Animals, Birds, Frame, c.1910, 31 x 39 In.	840
Pencil On Paper, Will Rogers, Standing, Cowboy Outfit, Frame, 1940s, 42 x 29 In.	276
Plaque, Portrait, Young Woman, Pink Floral Hair Wreath Scene, Signed, Gilt Wood Frame, 4 x 4 In.	210
Silhouette, Swan Family, 3 Adults, Girl, Signed, Aug. Edouart Fecit Dec. 17th 1840 ...... *illus*	750
Theorem, Applique, Ink, Flowers, Amanda Donohoe, Virginia, Frame, 1849, 10 In.	3900
Theorem, On Velvet, Basket Of Fruit, Bird, Butterfly, Frame, c.1850, 14 x 17 In. ...... *illus*	363
Wall Panel, Hardstone, Antiques & Scholarly Images, Carved Frame, Chinese, 45 x 29 In. *illus*	2000
Watercolor, Blue Ink, Heart, Tulip, New Year 1846, Gilt Frame, 8 x 9 In. ...... *illus*	1140
Watercolor, Clay's Residence, Ashland, Ky., M.E. Warren, Frame, 1847, 8 x 10 In. ...... *illus*	1320
Watercolor, Flowers In Striped Basket, Maple Frame, 13 x 15 In.	630
Watercolor, Indian, Joseph Scheuerle, 1873-1948, 12 x 8 In.	2246
Watercolor, Larry Morez, Hotel Waterloo, 1943, 19 x 14 In.	176
Watercolor, Pen & Ink On Paper, Sphere, Flowers, 2 Birds, Eagle, 1800, 12 x 10 In.	1080

Photography, Album, Victorian Leather Bound, Tooled Cover, Gilt Edged Pages, 1800s, 6 x 5 x 2 In.
$96

Garth's Auctioneers & Appraisers

Photography, Camera, Brownie, Model 2A, Eastman Kodak Co., Box
$180

Weiss Auctions

Photography, Camera, Hasselblad, 500CM, Carl Zeiss Lens, Hood, Manual, 1973, 4 x 4¾ In.
$952

DuMouchelles

PICTURE

Photography, Carte De Visite, White & Black Slaves, New Orleans, Adult, Children, Albumen, 1863
$1,680

Cowan's Auctions

Photography, Photograph, Civil War Soldiers, Hand Colored, 16 x 13 In.
$127

Copake Auction

Photography, Photograph, Indian Family, Utes, Jose Remero, 1899, 8 x 6 In.
$99

Copake Auction

Photography, Photograph, James J. Corbett, With Compliments, Aug. 3rd, 1894, 15 x 11 In.
$597

Copake Auction

Photography, Photograph, Tattooed Man, Portraits Of Royals, Frame, c.1890, 20 x 23 In.
$420

Cowan's Auctions

Photography, Photograph, William F. Buffalo Bill Cody, Signed, Inscribed, Albumen, 11 x 16 In.
$2,640

Cowan's Auctions

Pickard, Vase, Flowers, Blue Bands, Gold Ground, 2 Handles, 8 In.
$224

Morphy Auctions

Picture, Gouache On Paper, Cowboy Scene, Illustration, Signed, Morgan Bryan, 21 x 15 In.
$351

Copake Auction

Picture, Needlework, Embroidery, Regimental, III S.B., Grupp Kaumi, Silk, Frame, Chinese, 22 x 29 In.
$540

The Stein Auction Company

P

PICTURE FRAMES *are listed in this book in the Furniture category under Frame.*

PIERCE*, see Howard Pierce category.*

PILLIN pottery was made by Polia (1909–1992) and William (1910–1985) Pillin, who set up a pottery in Los Angeles in 1948. William shaped, glazed, and fired the clay, and Polia painted the pieces, often with elongated figures of women, children, flowers, birds, fish, and other animals. The company closed in 2014. Pieces are marked with a stylized Pillin signature.

W + P
Pillin

Bowl, Stylized Figure, White Ground, Black Rim, Polia Pillin, 7 1/4 In.	216
Bowl, Women Dancing, Dark Blue, Polia Pillin, 4 1/2 In.	192
Plate, Dancers, Green & White Clothes, Seed Shape, Dark Red, Polia Pillin, 11 In.	540
Vase, Colorful Birds, Yellow Ground, Signed, Polia Pillin, 5 In.	236
Vase, Cylinder, Ballerina, Woman Holding Birds, Signed, Polia Pillin, 10 In.	590
Vase, Cylinder, Ballerina, Woman In White Gown, Birds, Signed, Polia Pillin, 13 1/2 In.	649
Vase, Horse, White Stallion, Woman Rider One Side, Bird Held By Woman Other Side, 7 In.	450
Vase, Man, Woman, White Skirt, Red Bodice, Polia Pillin, 6 In.	240
Vase, Red Volcanic Glaze, Globe Shape, Small Mouth, Polia Pillin, 6 x 6 1/2 In.	2125
Vase, Stick Neck, Horses, Cobalt Blue, Black Ground, Polia Pillin, 10 1/2 In. *illus*	1008
Vase, Stick, Women, Birds, Blue & Purple Bands, Polia Pillin, 6 x 4 In.	218
Vase, Woman, 2 Birds, Marked, 6 In.	236
Vase, Woman, Green Scarf, Birds, Polia Pillin, 5 1/4 In.	192
Vase, Woman, Holding Bird, Marked, 12 In.	590
Vase, Woman, Holding Flowers, Ballerina On Reverse, c.1950, 12 In.	765
Vase, Woman, White Gown, 3 Birds, Ballerina & Tree, 2 Birds, Cylindrical, 13 In.	550
Vase, Yellow & Red Volcanic Glaze, Tube Shape, Small Mouth, Polia Pillin, 14 x 2 1/2 In.	3000

PINCUSHION DOLLS are not really dolls and often were not even pincushions. Some collectors use the term "half-doll." The top half of each doll was made of porcelain. The edge of the half-doll was made with several small holes for thread, and the doll was stitched to a fabric body with a voluminous skirt. The finished figure was used to cover a hot pot of tea, powder box, pincushion, whiskbroom, or lamp. They were made in sizes from less than an inch to over 9 inches high. Most date from the early 1900s to the 1950s. Collectors often find just the porcelain doll without the fabric skirt.

Art Deco Woman, High Collar Shirt, Mauve Dots, Gilt Trim, 5 In.	115
Bisque, Sculpted Braids, Padded Body, Sanitary Commission Fair, 1860s, 11 In.	805
Nude, Dancing Arms, Curls, Head Turned, Dressel & Kister, 5 In.	690
Old Woman, Bisque, Sepia, Gentle Features, Head Scarf, Clasped Arms, Germany, 4 In.	230
Woman, Bird, Bisque, Hip Up, Wig, Bird On Hand, Germany, c.1910, 2 1/2 In.	285
Woman, Butterfly, Nude, Headdress, Dressel & Kister, 6 In.	2760
Woman, Coiled Side Braids, Pink Blouse, Germany, c.1910, 5 In.	288
Woman, Falcon, Nude, Gilt Headdress, Dressel & Kister, 5 1/2 In.	3220
Woman, Fan & Basket Of Dresden Flowers, Gown, Germany, 5 In.	518
Woman, Holding Pitcher, Pouring, Brown Hair, Gold Trim, Dressel & Kister, 5 In.	978
Woman, In Lavender, Ringlets, Purple Bodice, Fan, Dressel & Kister, 4 In.	230
Woman, Of The Court, Curls, Ruffles, Fan, H. Delcourt, 6 In.	633
Woman, Pink Turban, Nude, Dressel & Kister, 5 1/2 In.	518
Woman, Purple Feather & Letter, Nude, Dressel & Kister, 5 In.	230
Young Girl, Clasped Hands, Dresden Flowers, Bohne Sohne, 4 In.	1150

PINK SLAG *pieces are listed in this book in the Slag Glass category.*

PIPES have been popular since tobacco was introduced to Europe by Sir Walter Raleigh. Carved wood, porcelain, ivory, and glass pipes and accessories may be listed here.

Bamboo, Crane, Willow, Japan, 8 1/4 In.	120
Bone, Relief Carving, Poets, Cherry Tree, Mt. Fuji, Cranes, Signed Yoshiyuki, Japan, 8 1/2 In.	720

Picture, Needlework, Fabric, Basket, Flowers & Fruit, Lititz Moravian School, 1820s, 23 x 26 In.
$1,652

Hess Auction Group

Picture, Needlework, George Washington, America's Independence, 16 x 12 In.
$667

Copake Auction

Picture, Needlework, Pastoral, Silk, Woman, Sheep, England, 1800s, 17 x 13 In.
$632

Copake Auction

P

Picture, Needlework, Silk Thread & Ground, Cottage, Painted Faces, Church, 13 x 16 In.
$30

Garth's Auctioneers & Appraisers

Picture, Needlework, Silk, Eagle, Stars, Stripes, Shield, Flags, Frame, 1800s, 23 x 28 In.
$649

Hess Auction Group

Picture, Needlework, Silk, Mary Minor's Embroidery 1810, Shepherdess & Sheep, 17 x 13 In.
$182

James D. Julia Auctioneers

Picture, Silhouette, Swan Family, 3 Adults, Girl, Signed, Aug. Edouart Fecit Dec. 17th 1840
$750

Eldred's Auctioneers and Appraisers

Picture, Theorem, On Velvet, Basket Of Fruit, Bird, Butterfly, Frame, c.1850, 14 x 17 In.
$363

James D. Julia Auctioneers

Picture, Wall Panel, Hardstone, Antiques & Scholarly Images, Carved Frame, Chinese, 45 x 29 In.
$2,000

Neal Auction Co.

Picture, Watercolor, Blue Ink, Heart, Tulip, New Year 1846, Gilt Frame, 8 x 9 In.
$1,140

Garth's Auctioneers & Appraisers

Picture, Watercolor, Clay's Residence, Ashland, Ky., M.E. Warren, Frame, 1847, 8 x 10 In.
$1,320

Eldred's Auctioneers and Appraisers

Pillin, Vase, Stick Neck, Horses, Cobalt Blue, Black Ground, Polia Pillin, 10 ½ In.
$1,008

Clars Auction Gallery

P

Cotton Stone, Folk Art, Civil War, Confederate Soldier, POW, Missouri Prison, Carved, 2 x 2 In.	1046
Filigree, Butterfly, 51 In.	63
Meerschaum, Cheroot, Man, Mustache, Hat, 3 x 2 In. .... *illus*	120
Meerschaum, Yellow, Bakelite Stem, Acorn Head, Dimpled Bowl, 1900s	12
Meerschaum, Young Black Boy, Feather Plume Hat, 5 In.	150
Porcelain, Hunters, Game Landscape, Stag Horn, Hand Painted, 1800s, 22 In.	125
Silver, Bamboo, Dragons, Clouds, Tapered Stem, Small Bowl, Japan, 10 1/4 In.	632
Staghorn, Brass, Bamboo, Sage, Pine Trees, 8 In.	180
Staghorn, Seal, Gourd, Silver Rim, Japan, 7 1/2 In.	156
Walrus Ivory, Carved, Bearded Man's Face, 2-Piece Turned Stem, c.1850, 9 1/4 In. .... *illus*	1560
Wood, Folk Art, Civil War, 151st New York Volunteers, High Relief, Cross, 3 x 2 In.	861

PIRKENHAMMER is a porcelain manufactory started in 1803 by Friedrich Holke and J. G. List. It was located in Bohemia, now Brezova, Czech Republic. The company made tablewares usually decorated with views and flowers. Lithophanes were also made. Manufaktura Pirkenhammer still makes porcelain and ceramic products in the Czech Republic. The mark of the crossed hammers is easy to remember as the Pirkenhammer symbol.

Pirkenhammer
Austria

Ewer, Bulbous Body, Stepped Neck, Gilt Winged Griffin Handle, 10 x 6 In.	182
Plate, Military, Portraits, Eagle, Crown, Flag, Crest, Gilt Rim, 10 In. .... *illus*	184

PISGAH FOREST POTTERY was made in North Carolina beginning in 1926. The pottery was started by Walter B. Stephen, who had been making pottery in that location since 1914. The pottery continued in operation after his death in 1961. The most famous kinds of Pisgah Forest ware are the cameo type with designs made of raised glaze and the turquoise crackle glaze wares.

Pisgah Forest Pottery 1926+	Pisgah Forest Pottery Late 1940s	Pisgah Forest Pottery 1961+

Vase, Blue, Crystalline Glaze, White Clay Body, Logo, 1941, 4 7/8 In.	150
Vase, Blue, Crystalline Glaze, White, Marked, 1941, 5 In.	177
Vase, Bud, Blue, Yellowish Green, Crystalline Pink Glaze, Straight Neck, 4 1/4 In.	313
Vase, Crystalline Glaze, White Shaded To Olive, Silver & Blue, Oval Shape, 8 3/4 In.	540
Vase, Teal Shaded To Aubergine, Swollen Shoulder, Flared Rim, 1929, 12 1/4 In.	554

PLANTERS PEANUTS memorabilia are collected. Planters Nut and Chocolate Company was started in Wilkes-Barre, Pennsylvania, in 1906. The Mr. Peanut figure was adopted as a trademark in 1916. National advertising for Planters Peanuts started in 1918. The company was acquired by Standard Brands, Inc., in 1961. Standard Brands merged with Nabisco in 1981. Nabisco was bought by Kraft Foods in 2000. Kraft merged with H.J. Heinz Company in 2015. Planters brand is now owned by Kraft Heinz. Some of the Mr. Peanut jars and other memorabilia have been reproduced and, of course, new items are being made.

Charm Bracelet, Link, Hook Clasp, Mr. Peanut & Nutshell Charms, Goldtone, 7 In.	50
Container, Figural, Mr. Peanut, Cardboard, Painted, 12 1/2 In.	595
Jar, Glass, Barrel, Mr. Peanut Running, Peanut Finial, Planters Salted Peanuts, 12 x 9 In. *illus*	300
Mug, Plastic, Face, Monocle, Red, 1950s, 3 7/8 In.	16
Nut Spoon, Figural Handle, Pierced, Silver Plate, Carlton, 5 1/4 In.	10
Nut Tray, Mr. Peanut, Cane, Crossed Legs, Die Cast, Gold Plated, USA, 4 x 5 In.	52
Pin Tray, Mr. Peanut, Full Figure, Bisque, Japan, 1920s, 4 x 3 x 2 In.	249
Pin, Mr. Peanut, Trylon & Perisphere, World's Fair, Wood, 1939, 1 7/8 In.	125
Salad Fork & Spoon, Wood, Ceramic, Lefton, Label, 1950s, 9 3/4 In.	145
Salt & Pepper, Plastic, Pink, 3 1/8 In.	20
Stein, Ceramic, Logo, Gold Trim, 1960s, USA, 6 1/4 In.	39
Tin, Salted Peanuts, Mr. Peanut, Pennant, Tin Lithograph, Pocket, 3 1/2 x 2 5/8 x 7/8 In.	2070

Pipe, Meerschaum, Cheroot, Man, Mustache, Hat, 3 x 2 In.
$120

Myers Auction Gallery

Pipe, Walrus, Ivory, Carved, Bearded Man's Face, 2-Piece Turned Stem, c.1850, 9 1/4 In.
$1,560

Eldred's Auctioneers and Appraisers

TIP

To clean the stem and bowl of a collectible briar pipe, dip a pipe cleaner in vodka. Push the pipe cleaner through the stem. Use a dry pipe cleaner for any pipe but a briar pipe.

P

Pirkenhammer, Plate, Military, Portraits, Eagle, Crown, Flag, Crest, Gilt Rim, 10 In.
$184

Bunch Auctions

Planters Peanuts, Jar, Glass, Barrel, Mr. Peanut Running, Peanut Finial, Planters Salted Peanuts, 12 x 9 In. $300

Rich Penn Auctions

Plastic, Sculpture, Pumpkin, Resin, Black, Yellow, Yayoi Kusama, Naoshima, 4 x 3 In. $1,230

Palm Beach Modern Auctions

Plated Amberina, Inkwell, Polished Pontil, Cast Iron Lid, c.1870 $720

Garth's Auctioneers & Appraisers

Tumbler, Clear Glass, Mister Peanut, Yellow, Libbey, 4 5/8 In. 45

 PLASTIC objects of all types are being collected. Some pieces are listed in other categories; gutta-percha cases are listed in the Photography category. Celluloid is in its own category.

Belt Buckle, Duck Head, Yellow, Orange, 2 1/2 x 4 In. 125
Cart, Chrome Base, 2 Tiers, Oval, Wheels, 1970s, 25 x 25 In. 445
Cigarette Case, Catalin, Cream Color, Turntable, Stamped Triggerette, 1900s 42
Crucifix, Blue, Chrome-Like Painted Figure, 1950s, 13 In. 28
Frame, Ivory Color, 3 x 5 In. 8
Mirror, Hand Held, Beveled, Oval, Tortoiseshell-Like, 13 x 4 In. 30
Pitcher, Green, Art Deco, Flip Lid, 1950s, 8 x 7 x 3 In. 22
Pitcher, Kool Aid Man's Face, White, 1980s, 2 Qt., 7 1/2 In. 20
Powder Box, Puff, Hinged, Scalloped, Faux Pearl, Flower, Pink, Menda Co., 1950s, 4 x 3 In. .. 15
Rattle, Rocking Elephant, Pink, Knickerbocker Plastic Co., 4 x 3 In. 14
Salt & Pepper, Orange, Dogwoods, Push Button, Sonette 38
Salt & Pepper, Pear Shape, Yellow & Red, Leaf Shape Tray, Green, 3 3/4 x 6 In. 10
Salt & Pepper, Yellow, Paneled, 2 In. 28
Sculpture, Pumpkin, Resin, Black, Yellow, Yayoi Kusama, Naoshima, 4 x 3 In. .... *illus* 1230
Sculpture, Tower, Multicolor, Plexiglas, Vacuum Formed, Aaronel Gruber, 1918-2011, 74 In. .. 6250
Tissue Box, Hinged, Top Hat, Gloves, Schwarz Brothers, 1950s, 10 x 5 x 2 In. 20
Tray, Red & Gold, Handles, Scroll Design, Italy, 19 x 13 In. 20
Utensil Tray, Red, 4 Compartments, 1960s, 10 x 13 1/2 In. 14

 PLATED AMBERINA was patented June 15, 1886, by Joseph Locke and made by the New England Glass Company. It is similar in color to amberina, but is characterized by a cream colored or chartreuse lining (never white) and small ridges or ribs on the outside.

Creamer, Ribbing, Fuchsia Shading, Amber Glass Handle, 2 In. 3630
Cruet, New England, 6 3/4 In. 150
Inkwell, Polished Pontil, Cast Iron Lid, c.1870 .... *illus* 720
Saltshaker, Cylinder Shape, Hipped Shoulder, Worn Silver Plate Lid, 1800s, 4 In. .... *illus* 2250
Sugar, Ribbed, Deep Fuchsia Shaded To Amber, Handles, 2 In. .... *illus* 7260

 PLIQUE-A-JOUR is an enameling process. The enamel is laid between thin raised metal lines and heated. The finished piece has transparent enamel held between the thin metal wires. It is different from cloisonne because it is translucent.

Bowl, Teakwood Stand, Pink Blossoms, Chinese, 4 1/4 x 6 In. 150
Frame, Scrolls, Yellow, Green, Blue, Oval, Brass Wire, 5 x 3 1/2 In. 1250
Vase, Seed Shape, Flowers, Turquoise Ground, Hardwood Box, Japan, 4 3/4 In. 360

 POLITICAL memorabilia of all types, from buttons to banners, are collected. Items related to presidential candidates are the most popular, but collectors also search for material related to state and local offices. Memorabilia related to social causes, minor political parties, and protest movements are also included here. Many reproductions have been made. A jugate is a button with photographs of both the presidential and vice presidential candidates. In this list a button is round, usually with a straight pin or metal tab to secure it to a shirt. A pin is brass, often figural, sometimes attached to a ribbon.

Badge, Abraham Lincoln, Paper Ribbon, Philadelphia Pa., 1864, 3 x 7 1/2 In. 584
Badge, Bryan, Sepia Toned Real Photo Button Of Young Bryan, Ribbon, 1906, 5 x 1 3/4 In. 208
Badge, Mourning, Abraham Lincoln, Carte De Visite, Black Silk Ribbon, 2 x 8 In. 360
Ballot Box, Mahogany, Drawer, Stenciled, Ward 7, New Eng., 1800s, 5 x 12 In. .... *illus* 125
Ballot, Election, Lincoln, California, 1864, Gold Rush Era Ticket, 7 x 3 In. 1920
Ballot, Electoral College, Grover Cleveland, Thomas Hendricks, 2, 1884, 2 1/2 x 5 In. 180
Ballot, Women's Suffrage, Women Candidates, Presidential Election, New York, 1884 4800
Bandanna, Benjamin Harrison, Levi Morton, Flag, Bust Portraits, c.1888, 23 x 24 1/2 In. 351
Bandanna, Grover Cleveland, Allen Thurman, Federal Eagle, Slogans, c.1892, 22 x 24 1/2 In. .. 263
Bandanna, James Garfield, Chester Arthur, Bust Portraits, Eagles, Shields, c.1880, 18 1/2 x 20 In. .. 234

Bandanna, Teddy Roosevelt, Rough Rider Hat, 1904, 20 x 19½ In.	321
Bandanna, Teddy Roosevelt, Initials In Center Square, Portrait In Border, 19 x 19 In. .... *illus*	144
Bank, William Henry Harrison, Barrel Shape, Hard Cider, Iron, 7 x 5 In.	5700
Bank, William Taft, James Sherman, Cast Iron, Embossed, J.M. Harper, c.1908......................	554
Banner, Win With Willkie For President, Red, Black, White Ground, 25 x 16¼ In.	105
Broadside, Benjamin Butler For President, New York, 1884, 21 x 28 In................................	1800
Bumper Tag, Elect Landon, Uncle Sam, Celluloid, 1936, 5 x 5⅜ In.	410
Button, Alf Landon, Sunflower, Celluloid & Felt, 1936, 2½ In.	138
Button, Alton Parker, Henry Gassaway Davis, 1904, 1¼ In.	339
Button, Ambrose Burnside, 3 Labeled Ribbons, Mounted On Cardboard, c.1915............... *illus*	42
Button, Anti-Vietnam, I'm Part Of The Noisy Majority, US Out Now, 1¾ In.	24
Button, Asks Voters To Open The Doors, 1 In.	25
Button, Bush, Canton, Ohio, Visit, Limited Issue Of 100, 2004, 2¼ In.	35
Button, Carter, Democratic Convention, Lithograph, 1976, 2¼ In.	18
Button, Civilian Conversation Corps, Enamel, Stud, 9/16 In.	56
Button, Franklin Roosevelt, Democratic Rooster Crows, 1936, 1 In.	500
Button, Franklin Roosevelt, First Birthday Ball, 1934, 1 In.	80
Button, Free Angela Davis, Celluloid, 1¾ In.	23
Button, Free Speech Movement, 1 In.	38
Button, Gay Rights Rainbow, 1993, 3½ In.	11
Button, Hoover, National Recovery Act, Celluloid Stud, ⅞ In.	50
Button, Humphrey, Blue, Green, White, Young Citizens Supporting HHH, 1½ In.	10
Button, Irish Politician Died On Hunger, Lord Mayor Of Cork, Macswinney, 1920, 1½ In.	75
Button, John W. Davis, Augustus Owsley Stanley, Cocktail, 1924, ⅞ In.	275
Button, Judge Julius Hoffman, Lightning Rod For Criticism, Celluloid, 1968, 2¼ In.	70
Button, Kennedy, Action Corps., Blue & White, 1½ In.	18
Button, League Of Nations, Celluloid, ¾ In..	21
Button, March On Pentagon, 1960, 2³/₁₆ In.	24
Button, McKinley, Roosevelt, Jugate, Commerce & Industries, 1¼ In................... *illus*	180
Button, National End The War Week, 1977, 1¾ In.	10
Button, Rex Clawson, War On Politics, Celluloid, Pin, Anti LBJ, 2¼ In.	188
Button, St. Louis, Progress Or Decay, Celluloid, ⅞ In.	12
Button, Stop US War In Nicaragua, 1¾ In.	5
Button, Symbols, Eyeball, Moose Head, Female Figures, Ehrman, 1900s, 1¼ In.	15
Button, Theodore Roosevelt, Rough Rider Campaign, Sepia, 1½ In.	546
Button, Two Winners, Theodore Roosevelt, Zig-Zag Gum, Clicker, W&H, 1904, 1¼ In. .... *illus*	1125
Button, USA Minute Women, Anti-Communist Group, 1949, 1½ In.	71
Button, Vietnam, Cambodia, Kent, Augusta, March May 30, SMC, Red Letters, 1967, 1¾ In.	20
Button, Viva Samoza Nicaragua Election, ⅞ In.	10
Button, Warren Harding, Republican, Party Ancestors Campaign Pin, 1920, 2¼ In.	500
Button, Warren Harding, Train Trip, Pacific Coast, Summer, 1923, 1¼ In.........................	420
Button, Wattle Day League S.A., Australia, First Event Celebrated In 1910, 1918, 1¼ In.	65
Button, We Want Debs, Pilgrim Specialty Co., ⅞ In...................................... *illus*	202
Button, William Jennings Bryan, John Kern, 1908, 1¼ In.	345
Button, William O'Dwyer, Portrait, For Mayor, 1945, 3½ In.	139
Button, Willkie Elected President, 1940, 3½ In.	135
Button, Willkie For President In Minneapolis, 1940, 2¼ In..	442
Button, Wilson, I Have Paid My Dollar, Ribbon Border, W&H Back Paper, 1¼ In. .... *illus*	720
Button, Win With Wilson, Seat For Every Pupil, Pioneer Nov. Mfg. Co., New York, ⅞ In.... *illus*	441
Button, Women's Conference, Stylized Peace Dove, 1977, 3 In.	20
Button, Women's Strike For Peace, 1971, 1½ In...	28
Button, Woodrow Wilson, Reading, Inauguration, Pin & Ribbon, 1913	138
Campaign Torch, Eagle, Brass Oil Font, c.1850, 10 In. .... *illus*	1320
Cane, W. McKinley, Tin, Horn Handle, Patriotism Protection Prosperity, c.1896, 33 In.	84
Electoral Ticket, Confederate, Jefferson Davis, Stephens, 4 Uncut, 1860, 7 x 10½ In.	1320
Ferrotype, Abraham Lincoln, Hannibal Hamlin, Campaign, Brass, Doughnut Mount, 1860 ...	660
Figure, Abraham Lincoln, Multicolor Metal, 39 x 19 In.	250
Handbill, Garfield Assassination, Missouri Knights Templar, 1880s..........................	281
Letter, Henry Clay, To Samuel Arnold, Constitutional Law, Signed, 1845, 10 x 8 In.	720
Medal, Andrew McBride, Mayor, Gold, Embossed, Fourth Of July 1913, 1½ In...........................	210

Plated Amberina, Saltshaker, Cylinder Shape, Hipped Shoulder, Worn Silver Plate Lid, 1800s, 4 In.
$2,250

Garth's Auctioneers & Appraisers

Plated Amberina, Sugar, Ribbed, Deep Fuchsia Shaded To Amber, Handles, 2 In.
$7,260

James D. Julia Auctioneers

Campaign Collectibles
You probably won't find anything made before William Henry Harrison's 1840 presidential campaign. It was the first campaign to make a lot of political souvenirs. Brass buttons, bandannas, and dinnerware were made picturing a log cabin and cider casks symbolizing Harrison's false pioneer background (he was from an aristocratic Virginia family).

Political, Ballot Box, Mahogany, Drawer, Stenciled, Ward 7, New Eng., 1800s, 5 x 12 In.
$125

Eldred's Auctioneers and Appraisers

P

POLITICAL

Political, Bandanna, Teddy Roosevelt, Initials In Center Square, Portrait In Border, 19 x 19 In.
$144

Milestone Auctions

Political, Button, Ambrose Burnside, 3 Labeled Ribbons, Mounted On Cardboard, c.1915
$42

Eldred's Auctioneers and Appraisers

Political, Button, McKinley, Roosevelt, Jugate, Commerce & Industries, 1 ¼ In.
$180

Milestone Auctions

Mirror, William Howard Taft, Portrait, Celluloid, Pocket, 1908, 1 ¾ In.	189
Mourning Card, Abraham Lincoln, Black Letters, White Tombstone, 1865, 5 x 3 ½ In.	900
Mug, GOP Elephant, Lavender Glaze, Frankoma, 1983, 4 In.	15
Outfit, Dwight D. Eisenhower, Dress, Parasol, Hat, Stockings, Marked Ike, 1952-56 .... *illus*	240
Parade Torch, Circular Tin Reservoir, Wood Pole In Shape Of Rifle, 1800s, 63 ½ In.	687
Parade Torch, Top Hat Shape, Wood Pole, Tin Reservoir, 48 ½ In.	192
Pass, Member's, John F. Kennedy, House Of Representatives, Signed, 1950, 4 x 2 In.	960
Pencil, Franklin Roosevelt, Garner, Celluloid Over Brass, 1936, 4 ½ In.	75
Pin, John Bell & Edward Everett, Doughnut Shape, Ferrotype, Brass, 1860, 1 ¾ In.	1440
Plaque, Bronze, Teddy Roosevelt, Relief, Fraser Earle, c.1920, 10 x 13 In.	177
Pocket Mirror, Franklin Roosevelt, Sepia Photograph, Flower Border, 2 ¼ In. .... *illus*	1105
Postcard, Theodore Roosevelt, Taft, Patrick Henry, Penciling, 1908	45
Poster, George C. Wallace For Governor, Portrait, Cardboard, 1962, 11 x 14 In.	139
Poster, Hurrah For Tilden & Hendricks, Newspaper Page, Mariposa Gazette, 1876, 18 x 24 In.	600
Poster, Johnson, In Conference With Tommy O'Toole, Photo, 19 x 25 In.	139
Poster, McKinley & Hobart, Campaign Flag Day, Spread Wing Eagle, Canton, 22 x 16 In.	799
Poster, Rhode Island, Democratic Presidential, Hancock, English, Grand Rally, 1880, 24 x 16 In.	60
Poster, Women's Suffrage, Register To Vote, Ratify Suffrage, Rhode Island, 1920, 23 x 17 In., .	1441
Print, Lincoln, Hamlin, Republican Banner Of 1860, Jugate, Frame, 9 ¼ x 13 In. .... *illus*	4413
Ring, John Kennedy, Flasher, JFK, Plastic, 1962	32
Sign, Theodore Roosevelt, Portrait, Fargo Bottling Works, Chromolitho, Frame, 1903, 14 x 22 In.	840
Song Lyrics, Thomas Jefferson, Presidential Campaign, Jefferson & Liberty, c.1800, 13 x 4 In.	300
Songster, Abe Lincoln's Union Wagon, Bust Of Lincoln, c.1864, 4 ½ x 3 In.	480
Sticker, Davis, Bryan, Victory, 1924, 1 ½ In.	212
Ticket, Pennsylvania Congressional Election, Whig Candidates, Snyder, Lieb, 1808, 9 x 11 In..	750
Tray, Bryan, Stevenson, Eagle, Tin Lithograph, Jugate, 13 x 16 In. .... *illus*	293
Tray, Presidents Washington To McKinley, Tin Lithograph, Gettysburg, 12 x 17 In. .... *illus*	363
Uncle Sam, Composite, Red, White, Blue, Hat, 48 In.	480
Uncle Sam, Wood, Carved, Full Length, c.1970, 34 In.	531
Watch Fob, Jimmy Carter, Leaders For A Change, Metal, 1970s, 1 ¾ In.	9
Watch Fob Charm, Anti Cleveland, Nose Thumber, Brass, Mechanical, c.1884, 1 ⁷⁄₁₆ In. . . *illus*	288

POMONA glass is a clear glass with a soft amber border decorated with pale blue or rose-colored flowers and leaves. The colors are very, very pale. The background of the glass is covered with a network of fine lines. It was made from 1885 to 1888 by the New England Glass Company. First grind was made from April 1885 to June 1886. It was made by cutting a wax surface on the glass, then dipping it in acid. Second grind was a less expensive method of acid etching that was developed later.

Toothpick Holder, Art Glass, First Grind, Fish & Coral, 2 ¼ In.	36
Water Set, Pitcher, Tumbler, Frosted, 8 In., 3 Piece	176

PONTYPOOL, *see Tole category.*

POOLE POTTERY was founded by Jesse Carter in 1873 in Poole, England, and has operated under various names since then. The pottery operated as Carter & Co. for several years and established Carter, Stabler & Adams as a subsidiary in 1921. The company specialized in tiles, architectural ceramics, and garden ornaments. Tableware, bookends, candelabra, figures, vases, and other items have also been made. *Poole Pottery Ltd.* became the name in 1963. The company went bankrupt in 2003 but continued under new owners. Poole Pottery became part of Burgess & Leigh Ltd. in 2012. It is still in business, again making pottery in Burslem.

Poole Pottery
1921–1924

Poole Pottery
1924–1950

Poole *handpainted*
Poole Pottery Ltd.
1990–1991

P

Political, Button, Two Winners, Theodore Roosevelt, Zig-Zag Gum, Clicker, W&H, 1904, 1 1/4 In.
$1,125

Political, Button, We Want Debs, Pilgrim Specialty Co., 7/8 In.
$202

Political, Button, Wilson, I Have Paid My Dollar, Ribbon Border, W&H Back Paper, 1 1/4 In.
$720

Political, Button, Win With Wilson, Seat For Every Pupil, Pioneer Nov. Mfg. Co., New York, 7/8 In.
$441

Political, Campaign Torch, Eagle, Brass Oil Font, c.1850, 10 In.
$1,320

Political, Outfit, Dwight D. Eisenhower, Dress, Parasol, Hat, Stockings, Marked Ike, 1952-56
$240

Political, Pocket Mirror, Franklin Roosevelt, Sepia Photograph, Flower Border, 2 1/4 In.
$1,105

Political, Print, Lincoln, Hamlin, Republican Banner Of 1860, Jugate, Frame, 9 1/4 x 13 In.
$4,413

Political, Tray, Bryan, Stevenson, Eagle, Tin Lithograph, Jugate, 13 x 16 In.
$293

Washington Photo a Fake
Think about the world your newly discovered antique lived in when you try to determine age. There are no photographs of George Washington. He died before the camera was invented.

Political, Tray, Presidents, Washington To McKinley, Tin Lithograph, Gettysburg, 12 x 17 In.
$363

Hake's Americana & Collectibles

Political, Watch Fob Charm, Anti Cleveland, Nose Thumber, Brass, Mechanical, c.1884, 1 7/16 In.
$288

Hake's Americana & Collectibles

P

Popeye, Doll, Eugene The Jeep, Composition, Jointed, Wood Tail, Decal, Cameo Doll Co., 1935, 13 In.
$422

Hake's Americana & Collectibles

Pitcher, Gadroon Rim, Floral Handle, Footed Base, Marked Sterling, 9 x 8 1/2 In.	531
Plate, Grapes, Blue, 10 In.	54

POPEYE was introduced to the Thimble Theatre comic strip in 1929. The character became a favorite of readers. In 1932, an animated cartoon featuring Popeye was made by Paramount Studios. The cartoon series continued and became even more popular when it was shown on television starting in the 1950s. The full-length movie with Robin Williams as Popeye was made in 1980. KFS stands for King Features Syndicate, the distributor of the comic strip.

Card, Die Cut, Plastic, Bubble Pipe, Transogram, Blow Bigger, 1950s, 3 3/4 x 6 1/2 In.	75
Doll, Eugene The Jeep, Composition, Jointed, Wood Tail, Decal, Cameo Doll Co., 1935, 13 In. *illus*	422
Figure, The Champ, Boxing Ring, Characters Around Base, Tin Litho, Windup, Marx, 7 x 7 In.	860
Pencil Sharpener, Holding Pencil, Bakelite, Yellow, King Features Syndicate, 1929, 1 3/4 In.	45
Pencil Sharpener, No One Will Miss The Point, Yellow, Green, Tin Lithograph, 1929, 2 3/4 In.	313
Pencil Sharpener, Popeye Walking, Holding Pencil, Plastic, King Features, 1929, 1 3/4 In.	95
Toothbrush Holder, Bisque, Sailor Suit, c.1930, 4 3/4 In.	325
Toy, Bubble Pipe, Popeye's Head, Sailor Hat, Curved Stem, White Plastic, 1950, 6 In.	20
Toy, Motorcycle, Cast Iron, Colorful, Hubley, 8 1/2 In.	2160
Toy, Olive Oyl, Pop-Up, Squeaker, Paper Umbrella, Linemar, Box, 1950s, 7 1/4 In. *illus*	288
Toy, Pistol, Red, Yellow, Tin Lithograph, Marx, 10 In.	300
Toy, Popeye, Airplane, Seated In Cockpit, Monoplane, Windup, Tin Lithograph, 8 1/2 In.	330
Toy, Popeye, Baggage Express, Parrot, In Open Cart, Windup, Multicolor, Marx, 8 In.	1800
Toy, Popeye, Birds, Cages, Tin Litho, Multicolor, Windup, Marx, 8 1/2 x 3 In. *illus*	165
Toy, Popeye, Floor Puncher, Punching Bag, Chein, 6 1/2 In.	780
Toy, Popeye, Roller Skates, Holding Spinach, Mechanical, Tin Lithograph, Linemar, Box, 6 In.	780
Toy, Popeye, Roller Skates, Pipe Bowl, Tin Litho, Multicolor, Linemar, Japan, 6 x 3 In. *illus*	330
Toy, Popeye, Spinach Cart, Cast Figure Of Popeye, 5 1/2 In.	600
Toy, Popeye, Spinning Olive Oyl, On Nose, Clockwork, 9 In.	1680
Toy, Popeye, Tin Lithograph, Windup, Louis Marx, Box, 8 In. Wide	570
Toy, Rowboat, Popeye, At Oars, Open Bench, Pressed Steel, Hoge, 17 In.	510
Toy, Walker, Popeye, Clockwork, Tin Litho, Blue Hat, Red Collar, King Features, c.1932, 6 In.	300

PORCELAIN factories that are well known are listed in this book under the factory name. This category lists pieces made by the less well-known factories. Additional pieces of porcelain are listed in this book in the categories Porcelain-Contemporary, Porcelain-Midcentury, and under the factory name.

2 Ducks In A Pond, Square, Inset Corners, 1800s, 8 3/4 x 8 3/4 In.	87
Basket, Chestnut, Pieced, Applied Swag Garland, Ormolu Mounts, Footed, 5 1/2 x 6 1/2 In.	151
Basket, Gilt, Openwork, Pierced, 4 Paw Feet, France, 1800s, 5 x 13 3/4 In.	240
Bonbon, Raspberries, Scalloped, Gilt, Oscar & Edgar Gutherz, Austria, c.1900, 8 In.	320
Bough Pot, Bombay Chest Shape, Gilt, Pink Swags, Shell Panels, France, 1800s, 8 x 11 x 5 In. *illus*	554
Bowl, Eculle, Gilt, Blue Lapis, Bird, Vicennes, c.1754, 8 In.	1375
Bowl, Flowers, Forest Green, Gilded Accents, Stepped Foot, 1804, 5 1/2 In.	216
Bowl, Gilt, Enamel, Military Scenes, Putto & Dolphin Supports, Sevres Style, 22 x 15 In.	375
Bowl, Painted Flowers, Birds, Reticulated, Royal Berlin, 4 x 12 x 8 In.	113
Box, Lid, Pierced, Lozenge, Rounded, Verte, 1800s, 4 3/4 x 3 x 1 3/4 In.	177
Bust, Bisque, Joseph Haydn, Wood Base, 1800s, 17 In.	1063
Bust, French Nobleman, Hat, Flowers, Wide Lapels, Sitzendorf, c.1900, 10 3/4 x 6 1/2 In.	88
Bust, Marshal Joachim Murat, King Of Naples, Fantasy Costume, c.1775, 4 In.	250
Centerpiece, Bronze Mount, Gilt, Courting Couple, Flowers, Leaves, Blue, 12 1/2 x 15 In.	2074
Centerpiece, Nautilus Shell, Held Up By 3 Cherubs, Applied Floral Highlights, 11 x 17 In.	300
Centerpiece, Oblong, Pink, Pierced, Beaded Mount, Scroll Handles, Putti, 10 1/2 x 15 3/4 In.	1080
Centerpiece, Reticulated Bowl & Base, Flowers, Putti, Potschappel, 15 3/4 In.	123
Charger, Bird, Butterfly, Floral Cartouches, Green, Gilt, Rose Ground, 1800s, 13 In. *illus*	300
Charger, Blue & White, 2 Opposing Phoenix Birds, Field Of Vines & Blossoms, 3 5/8 x 18 In.	660
Charger, Ming Style, Lotus, 2 Dragons, Cobalt Blue, Reign Mark, Jiajing, 1900s, 4 7/8 x 22 In.	554
Charger, Portrait, Woman, Period Dress, Gilt Border, Czechoslovakia, F&M, c.1875, 16 In. *illus*	121
Cider Jug, Original Lid, Dog Finial, Pinched Spout, Landscape Decoration, 1800s, 9 x 6 In.	510

Compote, Courting Couple, Flowers, Bronze, Ormolu, Wreath, Banner, 22 In.	861
Compote, Gilt, Flowers, Columns, Putti, Multicolor, White, Sitzendorf, 19 x 10 In., Pair	605
Compote, Reticulated Basket, Tree-Like Support, Couple, Sitzendorf, 1900s, 16 In.	219
Cup, Chien-Lung, Multicolor Blossoms, Vines On Black Field, Flared Rim, 4 x 3 ⅝ In.	1020
Cup, White Glaze, Red, Blue, Gray, Pale Yellow, Green Overglaze, 3 Roses, 2 x 2 In.	800
Dish, White Glaze, Painted Red, Blue, Gray, Pale, Yellow, Green, Enamel, ⅞ x 4 ¼ In.	800
Dresser Box, Ormolu, Marble Clad Lock, Metal Mounts, Flowers, 5 x 7 x 4 In.	1121
Dresser Box, Red Flowers, Blue Leaves, Green Decoration, Yellow, c. 1830, 2 ½ x 10 In.	336
Dresser Box, Tulips, Grassy Plain, Yellow Ground, Jonas Weber, c. 1850, 2 x 4 In.	4636
Epergne, Cut Glass Bowl, Fruiting Grapevine, 3 Supports, Flowers, Birds, 25 ½ x 16 ½ In.	3000
Epergne, Tobacco Leaf Pattern, Man, Pierced Trays, Vase, Mottahedeh, 17 In.	454
Ewer, White, Pink, Green Tones, Figural Branch, 3 Cherubs, 12 In., Pair	120
Figurine, Ballerina, Gold Shoes, Painted Face, Matte Finish Skin, 1932, 7 In.	149
Figurine, Dog, Spaniel, Lying Down, Black, Brown, Pink, Continental, 1860-1930, 1 x 3 ½ x 6 In.	50
Figurine, Dog, White, Spotted, Blue Coat, Walking, 8 In.	32
Figurine, Falcon, Multicolor Decoration, Naturalistic Tree Stump, 22 x 12 x 8 ½ In.	615
Figurine, Guan Gong, Seated, Throne, Holding Beard, 1900s, 27 ½ In. _illus_	6000
Figurine, Hunter, Deer, Birds, 1900s, 21 x 17 x 10 In.	354
Figurine, Lipizzan, Horse, Rider, Red Coat, Dobrich, Augarten, Austria, 1900s, 13 x 7 x 5 In.	348
Figurine, Monkey, Green, Brown, 1900s, 12 In.	60
Figurine, Reclining Woman, Sculpted Flowers, Art Deco, Signed Kaza, 8 ½ x 12 x 5 ¾ In.	90
Figurine, Tropical Fish, Brown, Flat, Oggetti Mangani, Italy, 15 x 16 In.	343
Flowerpot, Square Box, Multicolor Leaves & Branches, Birds, 1770, 4 ½ x 6 ¾ In.	6000
Ginger Jar, Yellow, Peaches, Butterflies, Flowers, Bronze Lid, c.1800, 9 In.	4100
Group, Hercules & Omphale, Ludwigsburg, 1762, 11 In.	1500
Group, Musician Monkeys, Dancing, Blanc De Chine, Mottahedeh, 1980s, 6 ½ In.	55
Group, Woman & Child, Clothes Whipping In Wind, Italy, 27 In.	360
Group, Woman Standing, Flowers, 2 Putti, Oval Base, 1900, 9 ¾ In.	861
Humidor, Nickel Plated Trim & Fittings, Cork Insulated, Chrome Tag On Door, 6 x 6 x 9 In.	900
Incense Burner, Arhats, Sakyamuni, Theravada Buddhism, Thickly Potted Walls, 1800s, 7 In.	2000
Inkstand, Inkwells, Courting Couple, Landscape, Gilt Bronze Feet, Signed Munger, 7 x 14 ½ In. _illus_	584
Inkstand, Masculine Victorian Desks, Dark Pink, Roses, Pink Flowers, 6 ⅜ x 3 x 3 ¾ In.	298
Jar, Dragon, Flower Design, 1900s, 11 ½ In.	180
Jar, Rolled Rim, Multicolor, Rust Colored, 6 Character Guangxu Markings, 1900s, 13 ¾ In.	86
Jar, Squat, Gilded Silver, Lid, Peacock & Dragon Scene, Blossoms, Chinese, 5 ½ x 5 In.	1080
Jardeniere, Pail Form, Trellis & Flowers, Gilded Rams Head Mounts, 12 x 14 In.	300
Jardiniere, Figures In Landscape, Inverted Pear Shape, Turned-Out Rim, 16 ½ In. _illus_	200
Jug, Pseudo Crest, Fruit Design, 1900s, 12 ¾ In.	156
Letter Box, Cobalt Blue, Leaves, Flowers, 3 Slots, Sevres Style, 5 ½ x 9 In.	437
Lipstick Holder, Woman's Head, Bun, Yellow Polka Dot Bow, Black Hair, 1960s, 7 In.	18
Mustard Pot, Barrel Shape, Embossed Ornamentation, Flowering Branches, 1700s, 3 ¼ In.	1375
Pitcher, Brown-On-White Transfer, Sperm Whaling, Niger, 1900, 6 ½ In.	480
Pitcher, Encrusted Gold, Poppy Flowers, Buds, Wispy Stems, Leaves, 8 x 6 x 5 In.	289
Pitcher, Man Seated, Blue Suit, Black Hat, Spout In Back, 10 In.	58
Plaque, 2 Women In Boat, Gilded Frame, 1900s, 13 x 11 In.	1599
Plaque, Angel, Painted, Carved Giltwood Frame, Oval, 1900s, 9 x 6 ¾ In.	1230
Plaque, Bussende Magdalena, Woman, Reading Book, Dresden-Saxony, 1900s, 4 x 2 ¾ In.	344
Plaque, Cathedral, Renaissance Scene, Signed A. Chaignon, Ebony Frame, 1882, 23 x 15 In.	2700
Plaque, Children Around Tub, Rectangular, Impressed MR, Frame, 1800s-1900s, 13 x 9 ¾ In.	360
Plaque, Cleopatra, Portrait, Hand Painted, Oval, 1900s, 3 x 5 In.	390
Plaque, Couple Running, Painted, Oval, 1900s, 15 x 11 In.	492
Plaque, Daphne, Painted, Carved & Gilded Frame, 5 ¾ x 3 ⅞ In.	369
Plaque, Guardian Angel, Figural Scene, Painted, 1900s, 7 ⅛ x 5 ⅛ In.	615
Plaque, Lorelei, Painted, Pierced Carved Giltwood Frame, 1900s, 9 ⅞ x 7 ⅜ In.	1046
Plaque, Medea, Pierced, Carved Giltwood Frame, 1900s, 7 x 4 ⅞ In.	431
Plaque, Portrait, Marguerite, Wagner, Frame, 1900s, 5 ½ x 4 ¾ In.	200
Plaque, Queen Louisa Of Prussia, Carved Giltwood Frame, Round, Stamped, 1900s, 4 ¼ In.	277
Plaque, Seminude Woman, Landscape, Hand Painted, Frame, Oval, 1900s, 5 x 5 In.	375
Plaque, Woman Holding Flowers, Painted, 1900s, 5 ⅞ x 4 In.	185

Popeye, Toy, Olive Oyl, Pop-Up, Squeaker, Paper Umbrella, Linemar, Box, 1950s, 7 ¼ In.

$288

Hake's Americana & Collectibles

Popeye, Toy, Popeye, Birds, Cages, Tin Litho, Multicolor, Windup, Marx, 8 ½ x 3 In.

$165

Morphy Auctions

P

This is an edited listing of current prices. Visit Kovels.com to check thousands of prices from previous years and sign up for free information on trends, tips, reproductions, marks, and more.

PORCELAIN

Popeye, Toy, Popeye, Roller Skates, Pipe Bowl, Tin Litho, Multicolor, Linemar, Japan, 6 x 3 In.
$330

Morphy Auctions

Porcelain, Bough Pot, Bombay Chest Shape, Gilt, Pink Swags, Shell Panels, France, 1800s, 8 x 11 x 5 In.
$554

Brunk Auctions

Porcelain, Charger, Bird, Butterfly, Floral Cartouches, Green, Gilt, Rose Ground, 1800s, 13 In.
$300

Eldred's Auctioneers and Appraisers

Plaque, Woman With Bird, Gilt Composite Frame, Oval, 1900s, 5 x 4 In.	277
Plaque, Woman, Bare Breasted, Oval, Marked Becky, Gilt Frame, 1900s, 6 x 7¾ In.	390
Plaque, Woman, Holding Fan, Painted, Carved Giltwood Frame, 1900s, 13 x 10 In.	2091
Plaque, Woman, Wearing Large Hat, Painted, Carved Giltwood Frame, 1900s, 5⅞ In.	185
Plaque, Woman, Wearing Laurel, Painted, Giltwood Frame, 1900s, 5⅞ x 3⅞ In.	308
Plaque, Woman, Wearing Red Cap, Painted, Box Style Frame, 1900s, 13 x 11 In.	615
Plaque, Woman, With Blue Ribbon, Painted, Gilded Frame, Oval, 1900s, 5 x 3⅞ In.	308
Plaque, Young Girl, Painted, Pierced Giltwood Frame, 1900s, 6 x 4⅝ In.	615
Plaque, Young Woman, Label, Frame, c.1890, 8¾ x 7 In.	896
Plaque, Young Woman, Playing Harp, Ornate Gilt Wood Frame, Oval, Germany, 4¾ In.	270
Plate, Flowers, Fruits, Dogs, Goats, Golden Rocaille, Purple, Curved Edges, 1825-55, 9¾ In.	4375
Plate, Garden Scene, Blue, White, Scalloped Rim, Marked, Germany, 1700s, 12 In.	108
Plate, Garden Scene, Scalloped Rim, 1800s, 11½ In.	62
Plate, Man With Pipe, Nude Woman, Marked, 1900s, 12 In.	600
Plate, Nymph Flowers, Cobalt Blue Banding, Gilt Highlights, 1900s, 9½ In.	1169
Plate, Serpentine Rim, Blue Band, White Center, Gilt Highlights, Crown, 1900, 9¾ In.	1968
Plate, Woman Portrait, 5 Small Portraits, Hand Painted, Gilt, Green Rim, 1900s, 9½ In.	75
Plate, Young Woman, Hand Painted, Cobalt Blue Rim, 1900s, 7 In.	150
Pot, Barrel Shape, Embossed Ornamental Rings, Flowering Branches, 1730-40, 3¼ In.	1375
Pot, Overglaze Red, Yellow, Green, Persian Blue, 3 Rabbits, 7 x 6 In.	295
Powder Box, Pink & White Stripes, Flapper, Apple On Lid, Germany, 1930, 5 x 3 x 3 In.	90
Punch Bowl, Grapes, Enamel, Gilt, Pedestal, Tressemann & Vogt, c.1900, 7 x 16 In.	975
Sculpture, Female Figure, Sleeping In Chair, Art Deco, 1920, 2¾ x 2¼ x 2¾ In.	80
Stand, Sweetmeat, Blue, White, Female Figure, Acanthus Leaf, Gilt, 1900s, 9 x 9 x 7 In. .. *illus*	120
Tankard, Yellow Roses, Pink Roses, Teal To White, 11¼ In.	72
Teapot, Annette Corcoran, American Bittern, Hand Painted, 1989, 9 x 7 x 4 In.	5625
Teapot, Dome Lid, Chinese Blue, White, Melon Form, Pavilions, 1870, 6½ In.	330
Tile, Classically Dressed Men, Dueling, Signed, France, 12 x 18 In.	840
Tray, 2 Handles, Red, Gilt, Enamel Highlights, Black, Woman In Center, 1896, 13 In.	81
Tureen, Lid, Putto, Fish, Relief, Italy, c.1900, 23¾ In.	2250
Urn, Flowers, Shields, Handles, Carl Thieme, c.1901, 35½ x 14 In., Pair	4250
Urn, Gilt Mount, Bust Handles, Cupids In Reserve, Allegory, Music, Arrows, 21 x 9 In., Pair	5355
Urn, Gilt, Bronze Mount, Courting Couples, Landscape, Pink, Green, 19¼ x 8¾ In.	1800
Urn, Lid, Cherub, Reading, Courting Couple, Flowers, Schierholz, Germany, 16½ In.	313
Urn, Vignettes, Mermaid Handles, Sevres Style, 1800s, 10½ In.	500
Urn, White, Pink, Blue Accents, Painted, Gilt Snake, Germany, 1800s, 17 x 10 In. .... *illus*	720
Urn, Women, Putti, House, Garden, Cobalt Ground, Bronze Mount, Sevres Style, 34 x 15 In.	2160
Vase, 2 Handles, Green, White, Cream Tones, Wildflower, Gold Stencil, Austria, 17 In.	72
Vase, Blue, Gold, Stylized Birds, 7 x 6 In.	200
Vase, Bottle, Mottled Blue Green, Deep Purple Ground, Seal In The Bottom	400
Vase, Boxing Scenes, Burgundy, White, Glazed, 1920s, 10 x 9 In.	3375
Vase, Copper, Red Glaze, Garlic Head Shape, White Crackle Glaze Base, 13 x 18 In.	300
Vase, Dome Lid, Artichoke Knop, Jeweling, Gilt, Garden, Putti, 1900, 30 x 11 In.	984
Vase, Double Gourd, Matte Buff, White Glazed Body, Green Stripes On Tan Ground, 12 In.	275
Vase, Exposition Universalle, Gilt, Flowers, Platinum Ground, Footed, Cactus, 9 x 5 In., Pair	252
Vase, Famille Verte, Elongated Oval, Trumpet Mouth, Figural Medallions, 1800, 23 In.	36
Vase, Figural Scene, Swan Handles, Multicolor, Dome Base, 1800, 19 x 8¼ In.	738
Vase, Fluted, Flower Sprays, Double Handles, c.1754, 5⅛ In.	2125
Vase, Gilt Bronze Mounted, Sevres Style, Raised Gold, Cobalt Blue, Neck, Socle, 1800s, 27 In. ..	554
Vase, Gilt Bronze Mounted, Soft Paste, Baluster Shape, 2 Handles, Knotted, 1800s, 11 x 7½ In..	2750
Vase, Gourd, Nude Woman, Kneeling, Alfred Finot, Joseph & Pierre Mougin, c.1900, 7 x 5 In. ..	875
Vase, Long Neck, Blue Green Band, Deep Purple, 9 In.	400
Vase, Man & Women In Garden, Red Ground, Gold Trim, Tapered, 9 In. .... *illus*	563
Vase, Men, On Horseback, Trees, Reserve, Dark Green, Handles, Russia, 23 x 18 In.	875
Vase, Multicolor Glaze, 2 Handles, Gold Ink Stamp, 6 x 4 In.	40
Vase, Portrait, Woman, Open Robe, Flared Rim, Ivy Leaf Decorations, 23½ x 12 In.	430
Vase, Rouleau Form, Flared Neck, Molded Lip, Dragon, Acanthus Leaf, 1900s, 8 In. .... *illus*	240
Vase, Streaked Red, Brown, Blue, Flaring Ribbed Neck, Footed Base, 10 x 10 x 16 In.	425
Vase, Urn Shape, Flared Mouth, Dragon Form Handles, 1800, 14 x 9 x 7 In.	338
Vase, White, Multicolor, Flared Mouth, Baluster, Battle Scenes, 1900, 31 x 18 In.	523

Vase, Women In Garden, Green, Pink Flowers, Side Panel, Gilt, 1900, 11¾ In., Pair		80
Watch Stand, Penholder, Gilt, Cream, Flowers, Leaves, 9 x 17 In.		225

PORCELAIN-ASIAN includes pieces made in Japan, Korea, and other Asian countries. Asian porcelain is also listed in Canton, Chinese Export, Imari, Japanese Coralene, Moriage, Nanking, Occupied Japan, Porcelain-Chinese, Satsuma, Sumida, and other categories.

Bowl, Bell Shape, Phoenix & Dragon Design, Guangxu, Marked, c.1875, 8 In.		300
Bowl, Blue, While, Waterfalls, Mountains, Japan, 5⅞ x 1½ In.		18
Bowl, Fish, Figures In Garden, Famille Jaune, c.1900, 10¾ x 20 In.	*illus*	250
Bowl, Glaze Enamel Outline, Kakiemon Sakaida, Crisp White, Japan, 3 x 5 In.		165
Bowl, Nabeshima, Pomegranates, Spearhead Border At Foot, Japan, 1900s, 4 x 8 In.	*illus*	120
Charger, Blue, White, Rickshaw, Mums, Signed, Japan, 1900s, 14 x 14 x 1¾ In.		41
Charger, Peacocks, Blue & White Medallions, Landscape, Japan, 1900s, 21 In.		180
Dish, Bamboo Grove, Hirado Decoration, Japan, 1800s, 1 x 7 In.		250
Lamp Base, Blue On Yellow, Double Gourd, Dragons, Pair, c.1900, 24 In.		6600
Plate, Shou & Vine Design, Doucai, Daoguang, Marked, 8 In.		1920
Umbrella Stand, Blue & White, Birds & Flowers, Landscape, 19th Century, 25 In.		360
Umbrella Stand, Lobed, 5 Sections, Central Tapering, Flowers, Japan, Late 1800s, 21 In.	*illus*	369
Vase, Bulbous, 6 Cylindrical Collars, 6 Flanges On Sides, Red Oxide, 13 x 7¾ In.		300
Vase, Bulbous, Rectangular, Square Tops, Handle, Flower, Gilt, 19th Century, 16 In., Pair		1062
Vase, Double Gourd Form, 2 Character Seal Mark On Base, Japan, 1900s, 8¾ In.	*illus*	60
Vase, Gilded Stoneware, Cherry Tree, Full Blossom, Maple, 8 x 7 In.		550
Vase, Gilt, Figures, Dragons, Clouds, High Relief, 8¾ x 4½ In.		1200
Vase, Hexagonal, Enameled Flowers, Branches, Oxblood Over Cream, 17¾ x 9 In.		2040
Vase, Light Turquoise, White Abstract Flowers, Kokyo Kichishin, Japan, 14¼ In.		130
Vase, Peony Flowers, Leaves, Tassels, Pale Blue Speckled Body, Mustard Waves, 18 x 17 In.		3025
Vase, Yellow Glaze, Incised Flowers, 1800s, 8 In.		900

PORCELAIN-CHINESE is listed here. See also Canton, Chinese Export, Imari, Moriage, Nanking, and other categories.

Basin, Pink Rim, Flower Scrolls, Green Interior, Flower Reserves, 15 In.		535
Bowl, Blue & White, Rose Scroll, Lobed, Petal-Barbed Rim, Ming Style, 2 x 14 In.		600
Bowl, Blue, White, Floral Medallion On Bottom, 4 x 12 In.		56
Bowl, Chinese Blue Glaze, Inverted Beehive Form, Lobed, 4 x 9½ In.		1280
Bowl, Cut Corners, Rampant Lion, Swan, Cygnets, 1700s-1800s, 4¾ x 9¾ In.		60
Bowl, Famille Verte, Flared Sides, 4 Paneled Floral Sprays, c.1850, 6 x 12 In.		875
Bowl, Gilt Characters, Coral Ground, Blue Band, 5½ In.		375
Bowl, Lid, Tree, Orange Flowers, 3½ x 4½ In.		5605
Bowl, Mandarin Palette, Familial Scenes, Turquoise, Round Foot, 1700s, 4½ x 10 In.		1800
Bowl, Powder Blue, Flared Sides, Raised Foot, 4 Cartouches, 1800s, 4 x 10 In.		688
Bowl, Sgraffito, 4 Panels, Flower Landscape, Signed, 1800s, 3 x 6 In.		600
Bowl, Turquoise Glaze, Incised Chrysanthemum, Lotus, Peony, 1800s, 4 x 9 In.		256
Bowl, Yellow, Dragons, Flaming Pearls, Chenghua Mark, 3⅜ x 8 In.	*illus*	366
Brush Holder, Cylindrical, Continuous Landscape, Figures, 7½ x 3⅞ In.		185
Brush Rest, Guan Ware, Crackle Glaze, 5 Mountain Form, Unglazed Foot, ¾ x 4 In.	*illus*	250
Brush Washer, Circular, Inverted Rim, Pale Turquoise Glaze, 2½ x 4¼ In.		3390
Brush Washer, Famille Rose, Cylindrical, Flattened Rim, Republic Period, Marked, 4 x 10 In.		2750
Brushpot, Blue, White, 3 Cartouches Of Scholars, Floral Blue, 1900s, 6 x 7 In.		96
Brushpot, Crane, Rockery, Waves, 5¼ In.		189
Charger, Blue, White, Octagonal, 13 In.		62
Charger, Famille Verte, Willow Trees, Birds, Chrysanthemums, Flared Lip, 15 In.		2750
Charger, Figures On Garden Terrace, Flower Head Rim, Diaper Ground, 14 In.		183
Charger, Prunus Branches, Blue & White, Cracked Ice Ground, 11¾ In.		153
Cup, Blue Dragon Roundels, White, 3½ In.		325
Cup, Dragon, Meandering, Commemorating The Dacao, 2¾ In.		1008
Dish, 5 People, Landscape, Crosshatched, Scalloped, Cabriole Legs, 11 x 3 In.		423
Egg, Landscape Scene, Female Figure, Calligraphy To Reverse, Stand, 1900, 2½ In.		88
Figurine, Guanyin, Seated Atop Rocks, Royal Ease, Serene Expression, 1900s, 17 x 9 x 7 In.		300
Flask, Blue & White Moon, Qianlong Mark, Floral Scroll Decoration, 20 x 15 x 5 In.		960

Porcelain, Charger, Portrait, Woman, Period Dress, Gilt Border, Czechoslovakia, F&M, c.1875, 16 In.
$121

James D. Julia Auctioneers

TIP
Either Coca-Cola or Tang can be used to remove stains from porcelain.

Porcelain, Figurine, Guan Gong, Seated, Throne, Holding Beard, 1900s, 27½ In.
$6,000

Eldred's Auctioneers and Appraisers

Porcelain, Inkstand, Inkwells, Courting Couple, Landscape, Gilt Bronze Feet, Signed Munger, 7 x 14½ In.
$584

Cottone Auctions

P

Porcelain, Jardiniere, Figures In Landscape, Inverted Pear Shape, Turned-Out Rim, 16½ In.
$200

Eldred's Auctioneers and Appraisers

Porcelain, Stand, Sweetmeat, Blue, White, Female Figure, Acanthus Leaf, Gilt, 1900s, 9 x 9 x 7 In.
$120

Brunk Auctions

Porcelain, Urn, White, Pink, Blue Accents, Painted, Gilt Snake, Germany, 1800s, 17 x 10 In.
$720

Brunk Auctions

Porcelain, Vase, Rouleau Form, Flared Neck, Molded Lip, Dragon, Acanthus Leaf, 1900s, 8 In.
$240

Eldred's Auctioneers and Appraisers

Porcelain, Vase, Man & Women In Garden, Red Ground, Gold Trim, Tapered, 9 In.
$563

Fontaine's Auction Gallery

Porcelain-Asian, Bowl, Fish, Figures In Garden, Famille Jaune, c.1900, 10¾ x 20 In.
$250

Neal Auction Co.

Porcelain-Asian, Bowl, Nabeshima, Pomegranates, Spearhead Border At Foot, Japan, 1900s, 4 x 8 In.
$120

Eldred's Auctioneers and Appraisers

Porcelain-Asian, Umbrella Stand, Lobed, 5 Sections, Central Tapering, Flowers, Japan, Late 1800s, 21 In.
$369

Brunk Auctions

Porcelain-Asian, Vase, Double Gourd Form, 2 Character Seal Mark On Base, Japan, 1900s, 8¾ In.
$60

Eldred's Auctioneers and Appraisers

Porcelain-Chinese, Bowl, Yellow, Dragons, Flaming Pearls, Chenghua Mark, 3⅜ x 8 In.
$366

Neal Auction Co.

Ginger Jar, Blue & White, Phoenix, Pierced, Carved, Wood Lid, 1800s, 7 1/2 In., Pair	3240
Ginger Jar, Blue Designs, White Background, Double Happiness Characters, 1800s, 8 x 8 x 9 In.	71
Ginger Jar, Multicolor, Family Courtyard Scene, Macau, 1900s, 9 x 9 x 16 In.	95
Jar, Blue & White, Lid, Leaves & Flowers, Unglazed Base, 1800s, 24 x 13 In.	1440
Jar, Dragon, Clouds, Blue, White, 5 3/4 In.	302
Jar, Famille Verte, Flowers, Late Wooden Top, 1662-1722, 7 x 7 3/4 In.	3120
Jar, Famille, Rolled Rim, Oval Body, Enamel, Lotus, Dragonfly, Guangxu, 1800s, 14 x 11 In.	5400
Jar, Lid, Pink Flower, Square Scroll, Green, Blue, Yellow Ground	151
Jar, Lions, Red, Yellow Ground, 3 x 3 1/2 In.	389
Jar, Qilin, Young Child, Cobalt Blue, Underglazed, Double Ring Marking, 1900s, 8 x 5 In.	96
Jar, Temple, Flowers, Branches, Birds, White Ground, 12 1/2 x 9 In.	60
Jardiniere, Clair-De-Lune Glaze, Rectangular, 4 Bracket Feet, c.1900, 3 x 9 In.	192
Jug, Figures, Cobalt Blue Ground, 1800, 11 In.	48
Ornament, Ram, Resting On Platform, Yixing, 1900s, 3 In.	56
Tea Bowl, Imperial Yellow, Incised Dragon Design, Ming, Marked, 4 In., Pair	1000
Teapot, Globular Shape, Floral Knop, Multicolor Enamel, Figures, 1700s, 5 1/2 In.	554
Teapot, Moon Flask Form, Turquoise Glaze, Qilin, Dragon Head Spout, 8 x 8 x 2 In.	300
Tile, Official, Attendants, Children, Grass, Trees, Frame, 15 x 10 In.	2178
Tureen, Carp Shape, Red, 5 x 15 In., 3 Piece	180
Vase, Blanc De Chine, Dragon, Copper Coin, Calligraphy, 1700s, 24 In.	210
Vase, Blue, Animal Handles, Splayed Foot, 7 In.	1200
Vase, Blue, White, 6 Character Kangxi Mark On Base, 12 In.	144
Vase, Blue, White, Crackle Glaze, Leaf, Qianlong, 1900s, 9 In.	63
Vase, Blue, White, People, In Garden, Hexagonal, Animal Handles, 17 In.	563
Vase, Bottle, Peach Bloom, Mottled Copper Red Glaze, Kangxi Mark, 8 In.	732
Vase, Chrysanthemum, Blue, White, 1900s, Stand, 9 x 6 1/2 In. *illus*	9600
Vase, Deep Red Glaze, Bottle Shape, Sang De Boeuf, c.1925, 16 1/2 x 8 In.	688
Vase, Double Gourd, Sgraffito Cranes, Green Clouds, Yellow Ground, 7 3/4 In.	600
Vase, Enamel, Dragon, Yellow, Sgraffito Decoration, Floral, Leafy, 19 x 14 In.	738
Vase, Flambe, Red, Rectangular, Animal Handles, Mock Rings, 9 3/4 In.	250
Vase, Flower, Scrolls, Blue, Red, 6 Character Mark, 1900, 10 1/4 In.	4305
Vase, Hexagonal, Long Neck, People, Landscape, Multicolor, White, 11 1/2 x 3 5/8 In.	200
Vase, Homage Piece, Hand Application, 1900s	108
Vase, Meiping Form, Writhing Green Dragons, Lavender Blossoms, Green Vines, 14 x 8 3/4 In.	840
Vase, Peaches, Bats, Mushrooms, 12 x 7 1/4 In.	2183
Vase, Pink Flowers, White Ground, 31 x 12 In.	88
Vase, Red Orange Foo Dog, Cream Ground, 23 x 11 1/2 In., Pair	657
Vase, Stick Neck, Pear Shape, Brown, 13 In. *illus*	9450
Vase, Stick, Blue, Round Foot, 8 1/2 In.	567
Vase, Tea Dust Glaze, Trumpet Neck, Tapering Foot, 9 3/4 In.	150
Vase, Trumpet, Flambe, Tapers, 13 1/2 In.	153
Vase, Yellow, Brown Design, Birds, Blossoms, Hardwood Stand, c.1950, 29 1/2 In.	2125
Vase, Yellow, Green, Red, Lobed, Fenced Pavilion, 15 1/2 In.	1125

PORCELAIN-CONTEMPORARY lists pieces made by artists working after 1975.

Bowl, Black, Inlay, Schooling Fish, 3 Fish Shape Feet, 2 1/2 x 6 3/4 In.	297
Bowl, Nerikomi, Blue, Brown, Gold Leaf, Thomas Hoadley, 7 x 10 1/2 In.	1750
Figurine, Ballerina, Pensive Woman, Lithe Dancer, 1992	395
Moonpot, Cobalt Blue, Toshiko Takaezu, Small, Rattle, Glazed, 6 x 4 In.	4063
Moonpot, Toshiko Takaezu, Glazed, 5 x 4 1/2 In.	1375
Plate, Opa & Purple Copper Glaze, Incised, Thomas Bezanson, 2 1/2 x 8 7/8 In.	450
Teapot, Adrian Arleo, Mother & Child, Glazed Earthenware, 1994, 10 x 18 x 6 In.	4375
Teapot, Beige, Dark Gray Bottom, Raku Fired, Annette Corcoran, 1983, 3 1/2 In.	153
Teapot, David's Head, Glazed, Gilt, Sergei Isupov, 1994, 10 3/4 x 14 1/2 In. *illus*	2500
Teapot, Kurt Weiser, Night Garden, Melons, Leaves, Sgraffito, Glazed, 1997, 9 x 13 x 3 3/4 In.	6875
Teapot, Kurt Weiser, Portrait, Painted, Base Incised Weiser, 11 x 15 x 5 In.	6875
Teapot, Least Bittern, Painted, White, Yellow, Rust, Black, Annette Corcoran, 1988, 8 3/4 In.	1159
Tureen, Potato Eaters, Black, White, Potato Finial, David Regan, 14 1/2 x 17 1/2 In.	5000
Vase, Black Stripes, Cones, Roseline Delisle, c.1988, 8 x 3 3/4 In.	3540

Porcelain-Chinese, Brush Rest, Guan Ware, Crackle Glaze, 5 Mountain Form, Unglazed Foot, 3/4 x 4 In.
$250

Brunk Auctions

Porcelain-Chinese, Vase, Chrysanthemum, Blue, White, 1900s, Stand, 9 x 6 1/2 In.
$9,600

Myers Auction Gallery

Porcelain-Chinese, Vase, Stick Neck, Pear Shape, Brown, 13 In.
$9,450

Clars Auction Gallery

P

Porcelain-Contemporary, Teapot, David's Head, Glazed, Gilt, Sergei Isupov, 1994, 10¾ x 14½ In. $2,500

Rago Arts and Auction Center

Postcard, Hold-To-Light, The Sculptor's Vision, Woman, Fluted Instrument, 1920 $218

Potter & Potter Auctions

Poster, Exposition Internationale, D'Art De La Ville De Venise, 1907, 25 x 16 In. $211

Copake Auction

Vase, Lotus Flowers, Dragonflies, 5½ x 6¼ In.	2500
Vase, Purple, Chrysanthemum Glaze, Flaring Rim, Brother Thomas Bezanson, 11¾ x 5 In.	5000
Vase, Square, Opal & Purple Copper Glaze, Flat Top, Thomas Bezanson, 6 x 5 In.	1920

PORCELAIN-MIDCENTURY includes pieces made from the 1940s to about 1975.

Girl Seated, Floral Dress, Holding Apple, Books, Lenci, Italy, 1900s, 11 In.	2000
Jesus, Crucifix, Sculpture, Giuseppe Armani, Italy, 1900s	50
Sculpture, Organic Shape, White, Green, Cone Support, c.1965, 4½ x 3 In.	708
Vase, Overglaze, Gold, White, Gilt, Nude Figures, France, c.1960, 12 x 6 In.	2250

 POSTCARDS were first legally permitted in Austria on October 1, 1869. The United States passed postal regulations allowing the card in 1872. Most of the picture postcards collected today date after 1910. The amount of postage can help to date a card. The rates are: 1872 (1 cent), 1917 (2 cents), 1919 (1 cent), 1925 (2 cents), 1928 (1 cent), 1952 (2 cents), 1958 (3 cents), 1963 (4 cents), 1968 (5 cents), 1971 (6 cents), 1973 (8 cents), 1975 (7 cents), 1976 (9 cents), 1978 (10 cents), March 1981 (12 cents), November 1981 (13 cents), 1985 (14 cents), 1988 (15 cents), 1991 (19 cents), 1995 (20 cents), 2001 (21 cents), 2002 (23 cents), 2006 (24 cents), 2007 (26 cents), 2008 (27 cents), 2009 (28 cents), 2011 (29 cents), 2012 (32 cents), 2013 (33 cents), 2014 (34 cents), 2016 (35 cents beginning January 17 and back to 34 cents beginning April 10, 2016), 2018 (35 cents beginning January 21, 2018). While most postcards sell for low prices, a small number bring high prices. Some of these are listed here.

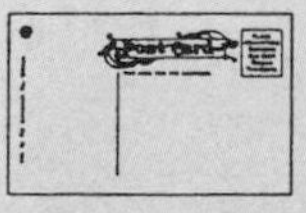

American Indian Soldier, On Harley-Davidson, 3½ x 5½ In., c.1910	180
Bill Hickok, Facsimile, Bowtie, Joppes Mello Milk, Light Handling, 1953, 3½ x 5½ In.	65
Comic, Fat Lady, Donkey, I Ain't The Only Jackass To Support A Woman, Linen Era, 1940s, 6 x 4 In.	5
Comic, Man Catching Cube Of Ice, I Caught Cold, Undivided Back, 1910, 4 x 6 In.	4
Easter Greetings, Embossed, Flowers, Art Deco Border, Postmarked, 1916	5
Great Dane & Chihuahua, Bells On Collars, Raphael Tuck, Oilette Series, c.1910	20
Hold-To-Light, The Sculptor's Vision, Woman, Fluted Instrument, 1920 *illus*	218
Jocular Jinks, Kornelia Kinks Cereal, Black People, Never Mailed, 1907, 6 x 4 In.	25
John Travolta, Photograph, Saturday Night Fever, 5 Pages, Grease, White Suit, 1978, 8 x 11 In.	25
Lone Ranger, Bond Bread Baker, Hole In Bottom, Pencil Notation, 1939, 3½ x 5½ In.	60
Memorial Day, Embossed, Betsy Ross, Making First Flag, c.1905, 3½ x 5½ In.	25
Paul Bunyan, Seated On Stump, Blue Ox, Black Hills, South Dakota, 1950s, 3½ x 5 In.	15
Sanke, 12 Blue Max, Award Winners, Pilots, World War 1, 1917	125
Snowdrops, Peaceful Village Scene, John Winsch, Postmarked 1913	4
Soldiers, Machine Gun In Trenches, World War 1, Nine Fellows, Field Uniforms, Belt-Fed Machine Gun	29
Steve Donovan, Western Marshal, Double Action, Screening, Hole, 1955, 5½ x 8½ In.	40
World's Fair, 1939, New York, Trylon, Perisphere, Linen, Unused	90

 POSTERS have informed the public about news and entertainment events since ancient times. Nineteenth-century advertising and theatrical posters and twentieth-century movie and war posters are of special interest today. The price is determined by the artist, the condition, and the rarity. Other posters may be listed under Movie, Political, and World War I and II.

Circus, Buffalo Bill's Wild West, Sells Floto Circus, Lithographed, 1926, 26 x 38 In.	1920
Circus, J.M. French's Oriental, Monkeys, Lions, Paper Lithograph, 1870s, 29 x 11 In.	431
Concert, Bonnie Dobson, Canadian Folk Singer-Songwriter, Concert Schedule, 1963, 14 x 22 In.	139
Erte Lyric Pera 68, Psychedelic Colors, Swinging Sixties, 1968, 24 x 32 In.	390
Exposition Internationale, D'Art De La Ville De Venise, 1907, 25 x 16 In. *illus*	211
Health, Internationale Hygiene Ausstellung, Dresden, Stars, Large Eye, 1911, 35 x 27 In.	5312
Mother Goose, Lithograph, 1930, 3-Sheet, 40 x 73 In.	630
Music, Mick Jagger, Black Light, Jagger On Stage, 1970, 36 x 24 In. *illus*	90
National Air Races & Aeronautical Expo, Los Angeles, Paper Litho, 1928, 22 x 17 In.	620
Occult, Glows Under Black Light, Love Beads, 1970, 23 x 25 In.	290
Olympic, Winter, Bobsled Team, Lake Placid, N.Y., Color Lithographic, 1932, 40 x 25 In.	250
Olympic, Witold Gordon, III Jeux Olympiques D'Hiver Lake Placid, France, 1932, 42 x 27 In.	3900

P

Panel, Floating In The Lake, Princess Is Attended, Group, Linen Back, 26 x 13 In.	450
Panel, Sailboat Passes, Young Woman, Dog, Stand By The Lake, Linen Back, 12 x 24 In.	350
Panel, Woman Relaxes, Garden, Dog, Roses, Fountain, Linen Back, 12 x 24 In.	290
Passage, Landscape Created, Stone Lithograph, Linen Back, 32 x 15 In.	350
Road Block, Whimsical, Linen Back, George Meunier, 23 x 17 In.	560
Show, Aladdin, Pantomime Theatre, Female With Lamp, England, c.1930, 29 ½ x 39 ½ In.	200
Show, Madame Butterfly, David Belasco, Strobridge Lith. Co., 3 Sheet, 40 x 83 In. .... *illus*	720
Show, Two Bills, Buffalo Bill & Pawnee Bill, Chromolithograph, Frame, 36 x 47 In. .... *illus*	6600
Travel, De Ayer Y De Hoy, Contrasting Old & New Sailing Vessels, Linen Backed, 1920, 12 x 9 In.	95
Travel, Kentucky Derby, Chesapeake & Ohio Railroad, McKnight Kauffer, 1949, 27 x 37 In. *illus*	1320
Wisconsin County Fair, Cowgirl With Horse, Floral, Frame, 1909, 14 ½ x 22 ½ In.	854

POTLIDS are just that, lids for pots. Transfer-printed potlids had their heyday from the 1840s to the early 1900s. The English Staffordshire potteries made ceramic containers with decorative lids for bear's grease, shrimp or meat paste, cold cream, and toothpaste. Printed advertising and pictures of historical events, portraits of famous people, or scenic views were designed in black and white or color. Reproductions have been made.

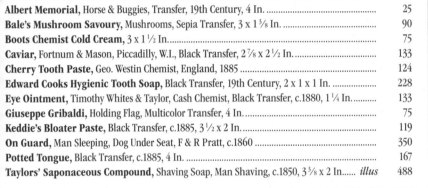

Albert Memorial, Horse & Buggies, Transfer, 19th Century, 4 In.	25
Bale's Mushroom Savoury, Mushrooms, Sepia Transfer, 3 x 1 ⅜ In.	90
Boots Chemist Cold Cream, 3 x 1 ½ In.	75
Caviar, Fortnum & Mason, Piccadilly, W.I., Black Transfer, 2 ⅞ x 2 ½ In.	133
Cherry Tooth Paste, Geo. Westin Chemist, England, 1885	124
Edward Cooks Hygienic Tooth Soap, Black Transfer, 19th Century, 2 x 1 x 1 In.	228
Eye Ointment, Timothy Whites & Taylor, Cash Chemist, Black Transfer, c.1880, 1 ¼ In.	133
Giuseppe Gribaldi, Holding Flag, Multicolor Transfer, 4 In.	75
Keddie's Bloater Paste, Black Transfer, c.1885, 3 ½ x 2 In.	119
On Guard, Man Sleeping, Dog Under Seat, F & R Pratt, c.1860	350
Potted Tongue, Black Transfer, c.1885, 4 In.	167
Taylors' Saponaceous Compound, Shaving Soap, Man Shaving, c.1850, 3 ⅜ x 2 In. ...... *illus*	488

POTTERY and porcelain are different. Pottery is opaque; you can't see through it. Porcelain is translucent. If you hold a porcelain dish in front of a strong light, you will see the light through the dish. Porcelain is colder to the touch. Pottery is softer and easier to break and will stain more easily because it is porous. Porcelain is thinner, lighter, and more durable. Majolica, faience, and stoneware are all pottery. Additional pieces of pottery are listed in this book in the categories Pottery-Art, Pottery-Contemporary, Pottery-Mid-century, and under the factory name. For information about pottery makers and marks, see *Kovels' Dictionary of Marks—Pottery & Porcelain: 1650–1850* and *Kovels' New Dictionary of Marks—Pottery & Porcelain: 1850 to the Present.*

Bough Pot, D Shape, Pierced, 3 Bulb Cups, Engine Turned Dicing, Caneware, 1800s, 6 In.	400
Bowl, Ash Glaze, Fire Color, Foggy Green, Yellow Shizen Yu Glaze, Shell, Japan, 1976, 5 x 5 x 4 In.	550
Bowl, Buff Slip Glaze, Globular, 3 Hollow Rattle Legs, 9 In.	88
Bowl, Gama-Yohen, Textures, Iridescence, Copper, Feather Patterns, 1925, 13 x 7 In.	235
Bowl, Heart, Crimped, Rosettes, Deer, 1800s, 6 ¼ x 5 ½ x 1 In.	150
Bowl, Ironstone, Imari Style Palette, Turner, Marked, c.1805, 5 x 12 In.	480
Bowl, North Georgia, Incised Decoration, 4 ¾ x 12 In.	277
Bowl, Shino Glaze, Light Pink, Gray, Blue, Plum Blossoms, Japan, 35 x 49 In.	300
Bowl, Shoe Shape, Decorated, Landscape Cobalt Blue, Wakoto Yabe, 1900, 3 ⅛ x 4 ¾ In.	615
Bowl, Wheat Color Glaze, Firing Hairlines, Centered Foot, Marked, 2 ¼ x 7 ⅝ In.	2583
Bowl, White Form, Signed Wooden Box, Japanese Robe, Erratic Blue Graffiti, 1946, 14 x 15 x 8 In.	580
Censer, Jun Ware Style, 2 Handles, Tripod Legs, Blue Glaze, Purple, Chinese, 9 ½ x 8 ½ In.	360
Charger, Painted Scene, Man & Woman, Impressed Catalina, 13 ⅝ In. .... *illus*	177
Charger, Rape Of The Sabine Woman Scene, Hand Painted, Oval, 1900s, 27 x 22 In.	1200
Cooler, Blue Banding, White Ground, 1900s, 13 In. .... *illus*	84
Cup, Dragon Skin, Gilded, Beads Glistening, Scales, 3 x 2 ¼ In.	275
Cup, Guinomi, Salt Glaze, Tomobako, Artist's Signature & Seal, 2 ¾ x 3 x 3 In.	200
Cup, Sake Guinomi, Kaki Glaze, Tomobako, Artist's Signature & Seal, 2 ¼ x 2 ½ x 2 ½ In.	200

Poster, Music, Mick Jagger, Black Light, Jagger On Stage, 1970, 36 x 24 In.
$90

Cowan's Auctions

TIP
Excessive humidity will cause mold on paper. Keep the humidity level between 45 and 55 percent.

Poster, Show, Madame Butterfly, David Belasco, Strobridge Lith. Co., 3 Sheet, 40 x 83 In.
$720

Cowan's Auctions

P

Poster, Show, Two Bills, Buffalo Bill & Pawnee Bill, Chromolithograph, Frame, 36 x 47 In.
$6,600

Cowan's Auctions

Poster, Travel, Kentucky Derby, Chesapeake & Ohio Railroad, McKnight Kauffer, 1949, 27 x 37 In.
$1,320

Cowan's Auctions

TIP

Floodlights facing toward the house are better protection than floodlights facing away from the house. Moving figures and shadows can be seen more easily.

Dish, Hot Dog, Dachshund Shape, Sections, Mustard & Relish, 1950s, 7 x 10 In., 3 Piece	60
Figurine, Dog, Great Dane, Seated, White, Black Spots, Collar, Continental, 44 ½ In., Pair	7875
Figurine, Dog, Whippet, Cream, Seated On Yellow Cushion, Tin Glaze, Italy, 24 x 16 In.	793
Figurine, Man, Seated On Lion, Rectangular Base, White Pigment, 1800s, 20 In.	234
Figurine, Monkey, Egg Shape, Applied Dots, Hands Clasped, Brown Glaze, 1800s, 8 ½ x 5 In.	720
Figurine, Uncle Remus, Cast, Signed, Edris Eckhardt, 1936-42, 5 ¾ In. *illus*	968
Figurine, Woman, Standing, Scroll In Left Hand, Right Hand Fist, 15 In.	308
Ginger Jar, Yellow & Pink Opaque, 2 Handles, Removable Lid, England, 7 ¼ In.	210
Group, 2 Children, Wolf, Bird Perched Atop, Overglaze Decoration, 1820, 8 ⅛ In.	4305
Group, 2 Young Male Figures, Arm-In-Arm, Dog By Feet, Overglaze Decoration, 1820, 7 ½ In.	800
Group, Boy & Girl, Standing, Stepped Base, Overglaze Decoration, 1820, 7 ¼ In.	492
Group, Boy, Holding Eggs In Hat, 2 Young Girls Approach, Overglaze Decoration, 1825, 8 ¾ In.	246
Group, Couple, Seated On Bench, Dog At Feet, Leafy Urn, Overglaze Decoration, 1820, 8 ¼ In.	1845
Group, Leaves, Flowers, Birds, 2 Classical Children, Overglaze Decoration, 1810, 10 In.	369
Group, Musicians, Swans, Leaves, Pear Glaze, Overglaze Decoration, 1815, 10 In.	6765
Jar, Canning, Green, Orange Spots, Galena, Script Written One Gal, c.1875, 10 In.	1800
Jar, Canning, Lid, Splotchy Brown, Yellow Runny Spots, Galena, c.1875, 10 ¼ In. *illus*	1500
Jar, Faint Green Glaze, Wooden Lid, Galena, Illinois, c.1865, 12 In.	450
Jar, Group Of Fish, Sculpted Wave, Hook, Clay, Winton & Rose Eugene, 5 ½ x 5 ½ x 6 ½ In.	59
Jar, Multicolor, Stylized Leaves, 1968, 3 ¾ In.	120
Jar, Olive, Oval, Rolled Rim, Continental, 32 ¾ In. *illus*	1098
Jar, Oval, Footed, Tripod Base, Peach Design, Marked, c.1925, 3 ½ In.	144
Jar, Oval, Tripod Base, Lion's-Head Handles, Multicolor Bat, Peach, 1900s, 3 ½ In.	144
Jar, Porcelain Tsubo, Sparrow, Foliage, Vivid Watercolor, 1851-1918, 9 ¾ x 7 In.	137
Jar, Tan, Brown, Geometric Design, Polished, Concave Base, Red, Signed, 1900s, 8 x 6 ½ In.	113
Jar, Teardrop, Brown, Orange, Buff Colored Slip, Line, Drawing, 1900s, 6 ¼ x 7 ¼ In.	125
Jar, Waisted Shape, Cross, Orb Design, 1600s, 9 In.	120
Jardiniere, Floral, Ribbed Body, Marked, 1900s, 12 x 17 In.	300
Jardiniere, Blue, Faience, Nautilus, Seaweed, Stand, Burmantofts, c.1900, 40 In., 2 Piece *illus*	2048
Jug, Salt Glaze, Cobalt Blue, Strap Handle, 17 x 8 In.	147
Lamp, Oil, Saucer, Wheel Made, Pottery, Reddish, Pinched Spout, Base, 5 x 5 ¼ In.	485
Lamp, Sancai Glazed Roof Tile Finial, Wood Stand, Base, Chinese, 1800s, 14 x 28 x 12 In.	330
Mirror Holder, Rabbit Shape, Seated, Ocher, Green, Turquoise, Aubergine, Chinese, 5 ¼ In.	923
Mug, Brown, Green Chinoiserie Landscape, 1700s, 4 ¼ In. *illus*	120
Mug, Dragon, White Metal, 3 Handles, 3 Panels, Marked, 1800s, 4 In.	150
Pitcher, Globular Body, Tall Neck, Trefoil Mouth, Handle, Red Glossy, Gilt, 1883, 9 ½ In.	584
Pitcher, Wine, 2 Shaped Handles, Funnel Neck, Rim Folded Outward, Little Base, 5 x 4 In.	1250
Pitcher, Wine, Biblical, Funnel Shape Neck, 2 Handles, 6 x 4 In.	785
Pitcher, Wine, Phoenician, Burnished Metallic Gray, Funnel Shape Neck, Flat Base, 5 ¾ x 3 In.	750
Plate, Copper Mounted Pottery, Water Lily, 1910, 15 x 7 ⅝ In.	96
Plate, Cranes In Flight, White, Dark, Blue Lines, 1896-1928, 8 ½ In.	2214
Plate, Kinkozan, Gosu Blue, Gilt Border, Flower Cartouche, Japan, 8 ½ In.	390
Roof Tile, Figural, Official Wearing Robe, Standing, Arched Ridge, Glazed, 14 In. *illus*	671
Roof Tile, Figural, Woman, Horse, Turquoise, Yellow, Aubergine Glaze, c.1890, 15 ½ In. *illus*	438
Tankard, Fisherman, Pewter Lid, Footring, 1800s, 11 In. *illus*	120
Tea Bowl, Chawan, Buddhist Symbols, White Slip, Glaze, 6 ½ x 13 In.	1800
Tea Bowl, Chawan, Tea Cup, Shino Ware, White Slip, Red Brown, Ash Glaze, 8 x 13 In.	400
Teapot, 6-Sided, Bamboo Shape Spout, Finial, Raised Leaves, Yixing, c.1890, 5 In. *illus*	2000
Vase, 5-Sided, Angular Handles At Neck, Mottled Green Glaze, 1904, 9 ⅛ In.	8610
Vase, 7 Leaves, Modeled Rising From Base To Lipped Mouth, Green Matte Glaze, 1904, 9 In.	3198
Vase, Black Glaze, Green Dragons, Yellow Clouds, White Water, 8 ¼ In.	375
Vase, Blue Iridescent Glaze, Yellow, Green Crackle, Red Clay, Circular Foot, 4 ½ x 5 ½ In.	308
Vase, Brown To Green, Blue At Base, Pierced Copper, Floral Overlay, 1900, 11 In.	584
Vase, Brownish Green Glaze, Abstract, Handles, Shoji Hamada Style, Japan, 1900s, 24 In.	150
Vase, Central Band Rabbits, Flowers, Intarsia, Printed Mark, 1900, 15 In.	738
Vase, Chrysanthemum, Flowers, Long Neck, Enameled, Japan, 1900s	25
Vase, Cut, Shaped, Angular Form, Linear Decoration, Makoto Yabe, 1900, 29 In.	1845
Vase, Dark Mottled Green Glaze, 1904, 18 ½ In.	6765
Vase, Double Gourd, Celadon Body, Phosphoric Treatment, Double Stamp, 1900s, 8 ½ In.	48
Vase, Flared Rim, Bulbous Base, Speckled, Mottled Glaze, 1900, 6 In.	62

P

Vase, Flared Rim, Cylindrical, Decorated, Poppies, 1930, 6 1/8 In.		185
Vase, Lid, Oval, Cylindrical Neck, Butterflies, Flowers, Relief Cicada Lid, Kyoto, 1800s, 13 In....		406
Vase, Loop Handles, Sunset Lake Scene, Julius Dressler, 18 x 12 x 10 In.		968
Vase, Orchids, Green Ground, Flower On Base, 1896, 11 In.		3321
Vase, Purple, Green Matte Drip Glaze, Ear Handles, National Pottery, 15 1/4 In................ *illus*		142
Vase, Qajar, Flowers, Figures In Relief, Persia, 1900s, 15 In....................................		210
Vase, Round, Sandstone Color, Lion In Center Of Body, 1900s, 3 3/4 In.		6
Vase, Square, Calligraphic Symbols & Flowers, Seto, 1800s, 15 In.		163
Vase, Tapered, Cylinder, Dusty Rose Matte Finish, 1917, 7 1/2 In.		120
Vase, Tokkuri, Salt Glaze, Tomobako, Artist's Signature & Seal, Japan, 5 x 3 3/4 x 3 3/4 In. ...		360
Vase, Tree, Waterscape, Greens, Blues, Artist's Initials On Base, Crazing, 1912, 11 In.........		1599
Vase, Wide Mouth, Broad Leaves, Trailing Buds In Relief, Bottom Glazed, 1900, 5 7/8 In.		615
Water Dropper, Turquoise Glaze, Monkey, Double Gourd Sack, Fly, 1800s, 7 In..................		220

POTTERY-ART. Art pottery was first made in America in Cincinnati, Ohio, during the 1870s. The pieces were hand thrown and hand decorated. The art pottery tradition continued until studio potters began making the more artistic wares about 1930. American, English, and Continental art pottery by less well-known makers is listed here. Most makers listed in *Kovels' American Art Pottery*, such as Arequipa, Ohr, Rookwood, Roseville, and Weller, ae listed in their own categories in this book. More recent pottery is listed under the name of the maker or in another pottery category.

Bowl, Footed, Copper Red On Opalescent White Glaze, Incised On Base Rim, 7 5/8 x 8 5/8 In.......		720
Bowl, Grape Clusters, Salt Glaze, Stoneware, Incised SF, Susan Frackelton, 1890s, 2 x 5 In. *illus*		2000
Bowl, Grapes, Purple, Green, Pink, Cream Ground, Signed, Byrdcliffe, 2 x 5 In. .... *illus*		826
Bowl, Oxblood Glaze, Glazed Stoneware, Ernest Chaplet, Rosary Mark, 1890s, 3 x 14 In.. *illus*		2500
Bowl, Rose, Gray, 3 Tentacles Wrap From Bottom, Marked Majorelle, France, 3 x 7 In...........		266
Candleholder, Cream, Tan Glaze, Peacock Feather Design, Vase Shape, Denbac, 8 In.		384
Charger, Abstract Bull, Wide Eyes, Flaring Nostrils, Jean Cocteau, 1957, 12 5/8 In. .... *illus*		3630
Charger, Dogwood Blossom, Wall Hanging, John Bennett, 1877, 11 1/2 In. .... *illus*		2500
Charger, Enamel, Art Nouveau, Keller & Guerin, Marked Marchuel, 20 1/2 In.		560
Charger, Oval, Jean Cocteau, Stylized Figure, Matte Pottery Ground, Signed, 10 1/2 x 15 In.		3327
Charger, Stylized Black, Red, Blue Enamel Face, White Matte, Jean Cocteau, Signed, 12 In.		3025
Dish, Landscape, Incised Trees, Green Matte, Beige Sky, Blue, Jervis Pottery, 5 x 2 1/2 In.		812
Face Jug, Applied Bulging Eyes, Teeth, Ears, Brown Matte Glaze, W.T.B. Gordy, 7 In.		840
Figurine, 2 Horses, Frolicking, Green Glaze, Rix-Tichacek, Wiener Werkstatte, 6 In...............		938
Figurine, Candle, Kneeling Repose, Turquoise Matte Glaze, Rudolph Lorber, 1925, 6 x 2 3/4 In. ..		118
Figurine, Ceramic, Hippo, Mouth Open, Italy, 1900s, 8 1/4 In.		56
Figurine, Duchess & Alice, Cast Slip, Incised, E. Eckhardt, c.1940, 6 In. .... *illus*		121
Figurine, Elmer Gates, Mojave Indian Storyteller, Redware, Signed, 1900s, 10 x 7 1/2 x 7 3/4 In.		158
Jar, 3 Applied Snakes, Runny Green Glaze, Oval, Rolled Rim, B.B. Craig, N.C., 16 In...............		677
Jar, Carved, Stylized Black Crabs, Winged Insect, J. Edward Barker Studio, Signed, 1938, 6 1/2 x 5 In.		124
Jar, Incised Basket Shape, Fitted Lid, Signed On Foot, J. Edward Barker Studio, 5 1/2 x 8 In........		79
Jardiniere, 6 Panels, Birds, Flowers, Interior Scenes, Koi, 1900s, 18 x 21 In.		156
Jardiniere, Faience, Frederick H. Rhead, Green Glaze, Gilt Accents Handles, Avon, 8 1/4 x 12 In..		254
Pitcher, Art Deco, Crystalline Glaze, Impressed Pierrefonds, France, 4 1/2 In. .... *illus*		236
Pitcher, Light Green, Brown Glaze, Pierrefonds, France, 11 In.		94
Sculpture, Menta Totem, Glazed, Lacquered Wood, E. Sottsass, c.1965, 86 x 19 In. .... *illus*		23750
Tankard, Gray, Cobalt Blue, Charcoal Drip Glaze, Marked, Greber, 8 In.		130
Teapot, Dog, Human Head, Bones, Rusty Wire, Gold Luster, Tom McCanna, 8 5/8 In. .... *illus*		590
Teapot, Folded Lotus Leaf, Flowers, Leaves, 6 1/2 In.		96
Tondo, Glazed Terra-Cotta, 5 Putti Faces, White Figure, Border Fruit, Della Robbia, 11 1/2 In...		75
Urn, Elephant & Antelopes, Blue, Brown, Glazed, 1930s, 12 x 10 In................................		437
Vase, 2 Polar Bears, Climbing Ice, Glazed, Art Deco, Bretby, 9 x 5 In. .... *illus*		708
Vase, 3 Art Nouveau Panels, Blue Glaze, Green, Zark Mark, Ozark Pottery, 9 1/2 In. .... *illus*		1770
Vase, 3 Handles, Relief Scroll Pattern, Green Matte Glaze, Chicago Crucible, 9 x 8 In....... *illus*		885
Vase, Antelopes, Circles, Pink, Gold, Glazed, Gilt, c.1935, 13 x 6 In.		3625
Vase, Applied Cherries, Leaves, Stems, Blue Ground, Limoges Style, CAP Co., 10 In. .... *illus*		325
Vase, Batonnets Et Ondes, Glazed, Signed, TR Lallemant, 1925-33, 7 1/2 In......... *illus*		1875
Vase, Black Bamboo Leaves, Turquoise Glazed Ground, Edmond Lachenal, 1900s, 12 x 9 In....		1080

Potlid, Taylors' Saponaceous Compound, Shaving Soap, Man Shaving, c.1850, 3 3/8 x 2 In.
$488

Glass Works Auctions

Pottery, Charger, Painted Scene, Man & Woman, Impressed Catalina, 13 5/8 In.
$177

Humler & Nolan

Pottery, Cooler, Blue Banding, White Ground, 1900s, 13 In.
$84

Eldred's Auctioneers and Appraisers

Pottery, Figurine, Uncle Remus, Cast, Signed, Edris Eckhardt, 1936-42, 5¾ In. $968

Rachel Davis Fine Arts

Pottery, Jar, Canning, Lid, Splotchy Brown, Yellow Runny Spots, Galena, c.1875, 10¼ In. $1,500

Garth's Auctioneers & Appraisers

342

Vase, Blue, Brown, Metal Leaves, Guerin, Marked E.C. Heights, France, 4 x ½ In., Pair	354
Vase, Bulbous Base, Pomegranates, Berries, Red, Purple, 1928-49, 12 In.	554
Vase, Carved Iris, Etched Design, Awaji, Japan, 9 x 6 In.	34
Vase, Carved Iris, Unusual Design, Awaji, Japan, 10 x 5 ½ In.	57
Vase, Chain Rope Design, America Line, Marked Holland Utrecht, 5 In.	153
Vase, Chantal, 3 Nude Men, Applied, Glazed, Marcello Fantoni, c.1975, 14 x 8 In. *illus*	1000
Vase, Coneflower Blossoms, Stems, Ethel Julia Bouffleur, Iowa State College, c.1923, 11 In. *illus*	23600
Vase, Cream Leaves, Rust Ground, Hylong Pottery, Muscle Shoals, Alabama, 6⅝ In. *illus*	531
Vase, Cylindrical, Band Of Boughs, Pinecones, Green Matte Ground, Incised Mark, 5 x 3 In.	4080
Vase, Deep Blue, Fort Hays Kansas State College, Symbols Around Perimeter, Marked, 6¼ x 7 In.	424
Vase, Dog, Molded, Mottled Orange & Green Matte Glaze, Burley & Winter, 18 In. *illus*	1093
Vase, Dogwood Blossoms, Blue Ground, Signed, John Bennett, 1884, 7½ In. *illus*	2000
Vase, Dolphins & Nude Sea Goddesses, Aventurine Glaze, 1920s, 10 x 9 In.	3250
Vase, Elephants, Black, Cream, Pedestal, Glazed Stoneware, 1935, 62 x 22 In.	31250
Vase, Elongated Form, Titled Iga Hanaire, Yellow Green Glaze, 1948, 9 x 9 In.	299
Vase, Flags & Net Design, America Line, Marked Utrecht, 3 ½ x 5 In.	130
Vase, Flared Collar, White & Blue Glaze, Lizard Handles, Pink Eyes, c.1882, 11 In.	369
Vase, Gazelles, Foliage, Teal, Brown, Purple, Glazed, Gilt, France, c.1930, 14 x 6 In.	4062
Vase, Glazed, Gilt Stoneware, Battle Scene, Green, Blues, Jean Mayodon, c.1940, 14 x 9 In.	4687
Vase, Horses, Pink Drips, Incised Bands, White, Jean Besnard, France, 1930s, 15 ½ x 10 ½ In.	4062
Vase, Incised, Black Glazed Interior, Signed Barker 90, 1938, J. Edward Barker Studio, 9 x 6 In.	130
Vase, Irises, Gray, Valentien Pottery, 1911-14, 8 ½ x 3 In.	1000
Vase, Leaves, Stems, Flowers, Raised, Arabesque, Incised Markham 3366, 10⅜ In. *illus*	2478
Vase, Lid, Double Handle, Flower, Continental, 1900s	84
Vase, Lizard, Tall Neck, Stamped, Edgerton, Wisconsin, Norse, 1900s, 12 x 7 In. *illus*	937
Vase, Medallions Of Nude Figures, Glazed, Earthenware, France, 11 x 6 In.	1500
Vase, Mermaids, Brown, Green, Glazed Earthenware, Marked R B, 1920s, 7 x 5 In.	2250
Vase, Mistletoe, Blue, Green, Incised, William Jervis, c.1910, 6 x 6 In. *illus*	625
Vase, Mottled & Green Drip Glaze, Squat, W.J. Walley, c.1910, 6 x 6 ½ In. *illus*	4062
Vase, Nighttime Landscape, Blue, Signed, Jerome Massier, Marked Vallauris, 7 ½ x 2 ¾ In.	57
Vase, Nude Male Figures, Brown, Cream, Crackle, Glazed Earthenware, 14 x 10 In.	11250
Vase, Nudes, Accordionist, Glazed, Signed, R. Buthaud, c.1928, 12¾ In. *illus*	6875
Vase, Oak Trees, California Faience, Signed, 6 ¼ x 3 ¾ In. *illus*	6875
Vase, Oxblood, Celadon, Gourd Shape, Pierre-Andrien Dalpayrat, Stoneware, France, 1890s, 6 x 4 In.	4687
Vase, Oxblood, Gold, Tendril, Pierre-Andrien Dalpayrat, Stoneware, France, c.1900, 13 x 4 In.	1250
Vase, Oxblood, Turquoise, Pierre-Andrien Dalpayrat, Stoneware, France, c.1900, 11 ½ x 7 In.	5312
Vase, Pillow, Chrysanthemum Flowers, Yellow Brown, 1896, 4¾ x 2 x 3 In.	30
Vase, Red & Moss Crystals Glaze, Stamped, Grand Feu, 1916-18, 12 x 5 In. *illus*	23750
Vase, Round, Stylized Leaves, Violet, Purple, Green Matte Glazes, 1930, 4 ½ In.	984
Vase, Spill, Man, In Stocks, France, c.1875, 5 In.	90
Vase, Squat, Mission Matte Glaze, Grand Feu, 6 ¼ x 3 ½ In.	937
Vase, Tan, Blue Matte, 2 Handles, Marked Logo, Pierrefonds, 10 In.	106
Vase, Thomas Forester & Sons, Yellowware, Vivid Coloring Of Peacock Standing, 1900s, 13 In.	204
Vase, Triangular, Barren Trees, Stream, Evening Sky, Marked, Avon, WP Co., 9 In. *illus*	413
Vase, Tulips, Green, Valentien, San Diego, 1911-14, 5 x 4 In. *illus*	3750
Vase, Water Lily Designs, Hand Carved, Flowed Glazes, Awaji, Japan, 9 ½ x 6 In.	79
Vase, Yellow, Blue, Leaf Design, Marked Logo, Pierrefonds, 8 In.	118
Vase, Yellow, Cream, Gourd Shape, Marked, Mougin, 11 In.	295

POTTERY-CONTEMPORARY lists pieces made by artists working about 1975 and later.

Bottle, Oval, Rust Color, Spiral Lines, Gray Shino Glaze, c.1990, 5¾ In.	160
Bottle, Pilgrim, Iridescent, Rainbow, Beatrice Wood, 1987, 12 ½ x 9 ½ In.	9375
Bottle, Round, Tan Body, Glaze, Spiral Lines, Forming Drops, c.1990, 5 In.	350
Bottle, Shino Ware, Spiral Lines, Orange, Gray, Swirling Lines, c.1990, 5⅜ In.	250
Bowl, Black, Matte, Tapers To Round Foot, Elsa Rady, 6 ½ x 10 In.	708
Bowl, Burnt Orange, Wavy Grooves, Richard Kjaergaard, c.1978, 6 In.	236
Bowl, Dark Clay Body, Glaze, White, Pink, Brown, Black, c.1990, 5 x 3 ¼ In.	575
Bowl, Dark Purple, Light Blue Swirls, Tochiko Takaezu, 7 ½ x 14 In.	1125

Pottery, Jar, Olive, Oval, Rolled Rim, Continental, 32¾ In.
$1,098

Neal Auction Co.

Monteith Bowl
Mr. Monteith was a Scotsman who wore a cloak with a scalloped hem. A large punch bowl with a similar scalloped edge is called a "Monteith bowl." It is usually at least 12 inches in diameter.

Pottery, Jardiniere, Blue, Faience, Nautilus, Seaweed, Stand, Burmantofts, c.1900, 40 In., 2 Piece
$2,048

Neal Auction Co.

Pottery, Mug, Brown, Green Chinoiserie Landscape, 1700s, 4¼ In.
$120

Eldred's Auctioneers and Appraisers

Pottery, Roof Tile, Figural, Official Wearing Robe, Standing, Arched Ridge, Glazed, 14 In.
$671

Neal Auction Co.

Pottery, Roof Tile, Figural, Woman, Horse, Turquoise, Yellow, Aubergine Glaze, c.1890, 15½ In.
$438

Eldred's Auctioneers and Appraisers

Pottery, Tankard, Fisherman, Pewter Lid, Footring, 1800s, 11 In.
$120

Eldred's Auctioneers and Appraisers

P

Pottery, Teapot, 6-Sided, Bamboo Shape
Spout, Finial, Raised Leaves, Yixing, c.1890,
5 In.
$2,000

Pottery, Vase, Purple, Green Matte Drip
Glaze, Ear Handles, National Pottery, 15 ¼ In.
$142

Humler & Nolan

Pottery-Art, Bowl, Grape Clusters, Salt Glaze,
Stoneware, Incised SF, Susan Frackelton,
1890s, 2 x 5 In.
$2,000

Rago Arts and Auction Center

Pottery-Art, Bowl, Grapes, Purple, Green,
Pink, Cream Ground, Signed, Byrdcliffe,
2 x 5 In.
$826

Humler & Nolan

Pottery-Art, Bowl, Oxblood Glaze, Glazed
Stoneware, Ernest Chaplet, Rosary Mark,
1890s, 3 x 14 In.
$2,500

Rago Arts and Auction Center

Pottery-Art, Charger, Abstract Bull, Wide
Eyes, Flaring Nostrils, Jean Cocteau, 1957,
12 ⅝ In.
$3,630

James D. Julia Auctioneers

Pottery-Art, Charger, Dogwood Blossom,
Wall Hanging, John Bennett, 1877, 11 ½ In.
$2,500

Rago Arts and Auction Center

Pottery-Art, Figurine, Duchess & Alice, Cast
Slip, Incised, E. Eckhardt, c.1940, 6 In.
$121

Rachel Davis Fine Arts

Pottery-Art, Pitcher, Art Deco, Crystalline
Glaze, Impressed Pierrefonds, France, 4 ½ In.
$236

Humler & Nolan

Pottery-Art, Sculpture, Menta Totem,
Glazed, Lacquered Wood, E. Sottsass, c.1965,
86 x 19 In.
$23,750

Rago Arts and Auction Center

P

Bowl, Enso Shape Foot, Glaze, Splashes, Dark Clay Body, 4¾ x 3¼ In.	450
Bowl, Folded Iridescent Volcanic, Glazed Earthenware, Beatrice Wood, 2 x 5 x 4 In.....	750
Bowl, Glazed Earthenware, Blue Crystalline, c.1967, 3 x 6 In.	1750
Bowl, Gold Interior, Taped, Painted Exterior, Multicolor, 7 x 7 In.	1475
Bowl, Green Banded, John Ward, 5 x 4¾ In..	5664
Bowl, Green Volcanic Glaze, Cobalt Blue Center, Signed, Beatrice Wood, 1¾ x 6¾ In.	390
Bowl, Irregular Rim, Black Lines, White Ground, Susan Benzle, 3 x 4½ In.	649
Bowl, Landscape Series, Cream, Brown, Raku Fired, Wayne Higby, 1980s, 6¾ x 12¾ In.	3375
Bowl, Millefiori Design, Blue, Cream, 1½ x 2¾ In.	590
Bowl, Straight Sides, Black & White Stripes, Bondil Manz, 3 x 11¼ In.	4720
Bowl, Tan, Cream Bands, Stoneware, Gertrud Vasegaard, c.1980, 4½ x 7 In.	1180
Bowl, Volcanic, Glazed, Folded, Iridescent, Beatrice Wood, 2 x 4½ In. .... *illus*	750
Bowl, White, Black Interior, Dip In Lip, 5 x 4¾ In..	3186
Coupe, Stripes, Green, Brown, Dark Lip, Stoneware, Harrison McIntosh, 4¾ x 6 In.	625
Dish, Lid, Glazed, Wheel Thrown, Kenneth Ferguson, 11 x 12 In.........................	480
Face Jug, Bearded Man, Signed Hy, Georgia Pottery, 2004, 22 x 9¾ In.................	153
Face Jug, Brown Salt Glaze, Handle, Large Eyes, Comical Nose, James Seagraves, 1960, 5 x 5¼ In.	1500
Face Jug, Dark Alkaline Olive, Stone Teeth, Lanier Meaders, 8¼ x 7¼ In.	811
Face Jug, Elf, Signed Hy, Georgia Pottery, 2003, 22 x 9¾ In.	47
Face Jug, Woman, Hood, Georgia Pottery, 2004, 23 x 10 In.	153
Figure, Bear, Sitting On Stump, Eating Honey, Billy Ray Hussey, Stoneware, 7 In.	420
Figure, Elephant, Leaping, Pierced, Teapot, Tom McCanna, 1994, 14 x 15 In.	1200
Figure, Hermit Crab, Snail, Glazed Earthenware, David Gilhooly, 10 x 11 x 6 In.	750
Figurine, Elephant, Dark Blue Matte Glaze, Marked, 5 In., Pair........................	413
Jar, Buttons, Asian Boy Finial, Pagoda Feet, Lynn C. Mattson, 1994, 15 x 5½ In.......	750
Jar, Lid, Blue, Geometric, Pierced, Band, Ka-Kwong Hui, 17½ x 7½ In.	750
Jardiniere, Oval, Wide Mouth, Ridge At Middle, Tan, Black Specks, Karen Karnes, 11½ x 18 In..	3125
Piano Pot, Blue, Black, Tan, Diagonal Stripes, Elizabeth Fritsch, c.1995, 5½ x 9½ In...........	5900
Pillow Pot, Squat, Square Mouth, Black, David Shaner, c.1984, 5 x 10 In.	1652
Plaque, Blue Arrows, Green Lozenge, Pink Reserve, Ka-Kwong Hui, 20 x 16 In..........	468
Plate, Cats, Glazed, Judy Kensley, 1983, 10½ In.	813
Plate, Walking Baby In Diaper, Blue, Pink, Karel Appel, c.1953, 1¾ x 7 In..............	3540
Pot, Lid, Irregular Round, Stoneware, Karen Karnes, 15 x 17 In...........................	6875
Pot, Winged, Black, Colin Pearson, 5½ x 8½ In..	3068
Sculpture, Face In Opening, Wood Base, Signed, Gary Spinosa, 1990, 24 In. .... *illus*	908
Sculpture, Frogs, Devonian Era, Glazed Earthenware, David Gilhooly, 1970, 5 x 14 x 11 In.	750
Sculpture, Frogs, Heart Red & White, Stoneware, David Gilhooly, 7 x 8 x 6 In.	563
Sculpture, Heart, Red & White, Glazed, David Gilhooly, Signed, 6½ x 8 In...............	563
Sculpture, Leg, Roses, Man, Dog, Glazed Hand Decorated Earthenware, Jack Earl, 1993, 23 x 9 x 7 In.	938
Sculpture, Teapot On Stand, Hand Decorated, Earthenware, Jack Earl, 1993, 12 x 12 x 5 In.	1500
Sculpture, Trilobite, Glazed Earthenware, Stoneware, David Gilhooly, 1970, 2 x 14 x 10 In......	313
Tea Bowl, Glazed Stoneware, Brown, Textured, Peter Voulkos, 1997, 5 x 5½ In.........	2750
Teapot, Pipe Shapes, Steven Montgomery, 1989, 6 x 14 In..............................	625
Teapot, Water Tower, Brown, Cream, Green, Daniel Anderson, c.1993, 6 x 10 In.	1298
Vase, Ashanti Lid, Gunmetal, Verdigris Glaze, Stoneware, Robert Turner, 12 x 11 In.	9375
Vase, Blue Over Dark Blue Matte Glaze, Crystalline, Waco Ink Stamp, 6 In. ...... *illus*	130
Vase, Blue, Taupe, Black, Bands, Toshiko Takaezu, c.1998, 7½ x 5 In.................	2832
Vase, Bottle Shape, Alvino Bagni, Raymor Italian Pottery, 1950s, 10½ x 6½ In.	102
Vase, Cityscape, Lidya Buzio, c.1984, 11 x 12 In.	3540
Vase, Coil, Mint Green, Bean Shape, Jacquie Stevens, c.1986, 20 x 16 In...............	354
Vase, Dark Burn Down, Rough Clay, Inclusions, Shiseki, Signed Wood Box, 9 x 5 In.	950
Vase, Faces, Overlap At Eyes, White, Jonathon Adler, 14½ In.	420
Vase, Flat Mouth, Rounded Shoulders, Brown, Green, Karen Karnes, c.1998, 8½ x 10½ In.	1770
Vase, Glazed, Raku Fired, Cream, Dark Brown, Abstract, Paul Soldner, 22¼ x 6 In.	1062
Vase, Glazed, Raku Fired, Pink, Yellow, Cream, Gray, Abstract, Paul Soldner, 19 x 12 In.	4375
Vase, Hand Built, Half Banded, Olive Green, c.1993, 6½ x 5 In........................	10325
Vase, Icarus, Stoneware, Rudy Autio, 1991, 36 x 29 x 20 In..............................	8750
Vase, Le Mie Terre, My Lands, Globe, Gio Ponti, Italy, 1929, 8½ In................... *illus*	5000
Vase, Lid, Rape Of The Sabine Frogs, Glazed, D. Gilhooly, Signed, 1969, 10 x 10 In.	500

Pottery-Art, Teapot, Dog, Human Head, Bones, Rusty Wire, Gold Luster, Tom McCanna, 8⅝ In.
$590

Humler & Nolan

Pottery-Art, Vase, 2 Polar Bears, Climbing Ice, Glazed, Art Deco, Bretby, 9 x 5 In.
$708

Humler & Nolan

Pottery-Art, Vase, 3 Art Nouveau Panels, Blue Glaze, Green, Zark Mark, Ozark Pottery, 9½ In.
$1,770

Humler & Nolan

P

Pottery-Art, Vase, 3 Handles, Relief Scroll Pattern, Green Matte Glaze, Chicago Crucible, 9 x 8 In.
$885

Humler & Nolan

Pottery-Art, Vase, Applied Cherries, Leaves, Stems, Blue Ground, Limoges Style, CAP Co., 10 In.
$325

Humler & Nolan

Pottery-Art, Vase, Batonnets Et Ondes, Glazed, Signed, TR Lallemant, 1925-33, 7 ½ In.
$1,875

Rago Arts and Auction Center

Pottery-Art, Vase, Chantal, 3 Nude Men, Applied, Glazed, Marcello Fantoni, c.1975, 14 x 8 In.
$1,000

Rago Arts and Auction Center

Pottery-Art, Vase, Coneflower Blossoms, Stems, Ethel Julia Bouffleur, Iowa State College, c.1923, 11 In.
$23,600

Humler & Nolan

Pottery-Art, Vase, Cream Leaves, Rust Ground, Hylong Pottery, Muscle Shoals, Alabama, 6 ⅝ In.
$531

Humler & Nolan

Pottery-Art, Vase, Dog, Molded, Mottled Orange & Green Matte Glaze, Burley & Winter, 18 In.
$1,093

Humler & Nolan

Pottery-Art, Vase, Dogwood Blossoms, Blue Ground, Signed, John Bennett, 1884, 7 ½ In.
$2,000

Rago Arts and Auction Center

Vase, Light Blue Matte Glaze, Twin Handles, Waco, Marked, 7 In.	177
Vase, Maquette II, Chunky Strips, Wood Fired, Stoneware, Dimitri Hadzi, 2002, 6 x 3 1/2 In.	3658
Vase, Narrow Mouth, Round, Tan, Vaay, Claude Conover, c.1977, 21 x 18 In.	6785
Vase, Nilo, Ettore Sottsass, Memphis, 1983, 12 x 5 1/2 In. *illus*	384
Vase, Pierced, White, Angela Verdon, 4 x 3 1/2 In.	1003
Vase, Piix, Glazed Stoneware, Engobe, Claude Conover, Signed, 16 1/2 x 15 In.	5313
Vase, Pilgrim Bottle, Cream, Ian Godfrey, c.1985, 6 x 6 1/2 In.	2006
Vase, Raku, Crackle Glaze, Nautilus Shell, Masqueron, Jay Gogin, 1995, 7 1/2 In.	118
Vase, Round, Blue, White, Small Mouth, 9 1/2 x 9 1/2 In.	2242
Vase, Small Mouth, Striped Patches, Black, Brown, Gold, Rick Dillingham, c.1981, 8 1/2 In.	4602
Vase, Square Stoneware, Heavy Ash, Wood Fired Kiln, Owen Rye, 12 In.	338
Vase, Stick, Oxblood Iridescent, Beatrice Wood, 9 1/4 x 4 In.	2875
Vase, Voyager, Female Nudes, Bulging, Stoneware, Rudy Autio, 1991, 30 x 26 x 18 In.	8125

POTTERY-MIDCENTURY includes pieces made from the 1940s to about 1975.

Bowl, Abstract Design, Turquoise, Brown, Maija Grotell, Incised MG, 6 1/2 x 10 In. *illus*	2250
Bowl, Blue Green, Repeating Crowned Loops, Maija Grotell, 6 x 9 In.	812
Bowl, Blue Volcanic Glaze, James Lovera, 3 x 8 In.	1000
Bowl, Farmers, Livestock, Tan, Harrison McIntosh, 1950s, 4 x 7 In.	2750
Bowl, Fish, Purple, Dots, Waylande Gregory, 8 1/2 In.	125
Bowl, Green Drip, Blue Glaze, Gold Color Metal Handle, Titled Hai-Yu Chuki, 7 x 4 In.	380
Bowl, Green Volcanic Glaze, James Lovera, 5 1/2 x 9 3/4 In.	2125
Bowl, Knight, Dragon, Blue, Stoneware, Antonio Prieto, 4 1/2 x 16 3/4 In.	1500
Bowl, Low, Glen Lukens, 1 1/4 x 7 1/2 In. *illus*	938
Bowl, Nudes, Seated, Musicians, Glazed, Incised, Cazaux, c.1960, 4 x 7 In. *illus*	1000
Bowl, Oval, Dark Rim, Translucent Spots, Lucie Rie, 3 1/2 x 7 1/4 In.	9440
Bowl, Oval, Shallow, Dark Rim, Lucie Rie, 5 1/2 In.	3540
Bowl, Pink, Blue, Turquoise, Glen Lukens, 2 1/4 x 12 1/2 In.	937
Bowl, Shallow, 2 Overlapping Faces, Nude, Brown, Blue Gray Glazes, 1959, 10 3/8 In.	738
Brick, River Brick, Earthenware, Acrylic, Robert Arneson, 1969, 5 x 9 x 2 3/4 In. *illus*	3125
Bust, Dress Shirt, Blazer, Laurel Leaves, David Gilhooly, 1970, 19 x 14 In.	3125
Chalice, Double Face, Magical, Tan, Blue, Jim Rumph, 1971, 7 1/2 In.	270
Charger, 3 Stylized Eyes, Green Lines, Circles, Terra-Cotta Ground, Jean Cocteau, 12 1/4 In.	4235
Charger, Dove At Dormer, Glazed, Incised, Signed, Pablo Picasso, 1949, 15 In. *illus*	7500
Charger, Iridescent, Brown, Blue, Beatrice Wood, 12 In.	1500
Charger, Leda & Swan, Earthenware, Edouard Cazaux, 1920s, 3 3/4 x 16 1/2 In.	1125
Dish, Earthtones, Stonelain Pottery, 2 x 13 In.	62
Figurine, Cat On Blue Cushion, Signed, Thelma Frazier Winter, 7 In. *illus*	121
Figurine, Fish Jumping Waves, Figural, Marked, Beato, B. Wood, 4 x 10 In. *illus*	1815
Figurine, Granada, Nude Woman, Signed, Waylande Gregory, 15 In. *illus*	363
Figurine, Mouse, Signed, Thelma Winter, 5 In. *illus*	36
Jar, Black, Red, Striking Avian, Donald Chinana, 1980s, 8 1/2 x 9 1/2 In.	250
Jar, Black, White, Kokopelli Flute, Geometric Forms, Lucy Lewis, 1970s, 4 x 4 1/2 In.	700
Jar, Trophy Shape, Stripes, Handles, Robert Arneson, 1964, 16 x 15 In.	7501
Pitcher, Pablo Picasso, Face, Lines, Handle, Madoura, 10 1/2 In. *illus*	5535
Pitcher, Yan, Pablo Picasso, Limited, 1952, 10 x 4 1/2 In. *illus*	5000
Plaque, Stylized Butterfly, Pink, Green, Ka-Kwong Hui, 16 x 18 1/2 In.	562
Plate, Bouquet Avec Pomme, Apples, Pablo Picasso, Madoura, 1956, 9 3/4 In.	3750
Plate, Fish, Partially Glazed, Pablo Picasso, 1952, 14 x 17 In.	18750
Plate, Flute Player & Goat, Black, White, Pablo Picasso, France, 1956, 10 In.	3625
Plate, Pesci, Fish, Piero Fornasetti, 1955, 10 In., 4 Piece	594
Plate, Ruffled Rim, Blue Grid, Ocher Dip, Concentric Circles, Betty Woodman, 2 x 19 In.	1000
Plate, Swimmers, Seaside, Sea Gulls, Dock, Pablo Picasso, 10 In. *illus*	3360
Plate, Untitled Plate II, Blue, White, Yellow, Roy Lichtenstein, 12 1/4 In.	400
Plate, Yellow Ground, Egg Design, Waylande Gregory, 9 In.	118
Pot, Lid, Landscape, People, Animals, Multicolor, David Gilhooly, 1966, 8 x 14 In.	750
Pot, Moonpot, Rattles, Brown, Cream, Black, Ridges, Incised, Toshiko Takaezu, 21 x 8 In.	4375
Sculpture, Abstract, Matte, Glossy, Maroon, Green, Brown, Robert Arneson, 1964, 8 x 8 In.	6250
Sculpture, Army Of Babar, David Gilhooly, 1966, 11 x 21 In.	937

Pottery-Art, Vase, Leaves, Stems, Flowers, Raised, Arabesque, Incised Markham 3366, 10 3/8 In.
$2,478

Humler & Nolan

Pottery-Art, Vase, Lizard, Tall Neck, Stamped, Edgerton, Wisconsin, Norse, 1900s, 12 x 7 In.
$937

Rago Arts and Auction Center

Art Pottery Fakes

In 2011 art pottery fakes were being sold online by a U.S. company. They are copies, some bad, of Pillin, Natzler, and Ohr pottery. The Ohr pottery fakes have stilt marks on the bottom, something not seen on real Ohr. The Pillin mark is just enough wrong to be noticed. Watch out for them.

P

Pottery-Art, Vase, Mistletoe, Blue, Green, Incised, William Jervis, c.1910, 6 x 6 In.
$625

Rago Arts and Auction Center

Pottery-Art, Vase, Mottled & Green Drip Glaze, Squat, W.J. Walley, c.1910, 6 x 6 ½ In.
$4,062

Rago Arts and Auction Center

Pottery-Art, Vase, Nudes, Accordionist, Glazed, Signed, R. Buthaud, c.1928, 12 ¾ In.
$6,875

Rago Arts and Auction Center

Pottery-Art, Vase, Oak Trees, California Faience, Signed, 6 ¼ x 3 ¾ In.
$6,875

Rago Arts and Auction Center

Pottery-Art, Vase, Red & Moss Crystals Glaze, Stamped, Grand Feu, 1916-18, 12 x 5 In.
$23,750

Rago Arts and Auction Center

Pottery-Art, Vase, Triangular, Barren Trees, Stream, Evening Sky, Marked, Avon, WP Co., 9 In.
$413

Humler & Nolan

Pottery-Art, Vase, Tulips, Green, Valentien, San Diego, 1911-14, 5 x 4 In.
$3,750

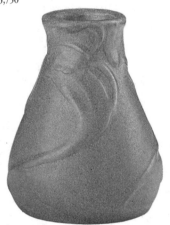

Rago Arts and Auction Center

Pottery-Contemporary, Bowl, Volcanic, Glazed, Folded, Iridescent, Beatrice Wood, 2 x 4 ½ In.
$750

Rago Arts and Auction Center

P

Sculpture, Brick, Finger, Robert Arneson, 5¾ x 8¾ In.	3750
Sculpture, Bricks, Partially Glazed Earthenware, Robert Arneson, 1965, 17¼ x 34 In.	9375
Sculpture, Fire Plug Souvenir, Red, Claes Oldenburg, 1968, 8 x 7¼ In.	8750
Sculpture, Foot, Boot, Hand Built Earthenware, Robert Arneson, 5 x 10½ In.	8750
Sculpture, Garden Pet, Snake, Grass, Rockery, 1967, 5 x 18 In.	6250
Sculpture, Vase Shape, Blue, White, Brown, Stoneware, Robert Arneson, 1964, 13 x 8 In.	3125
Tankard, Light Brown, Blue, Face Decoration, Marked, Madoura, 8 In.	4720
Tea Bowl, Brown, White Plant, Tatsuzo Shimaoka, c.1963, 2½ x 3¾ In.	472
Tea Bowl, Chawan, Oribe Green, Green Glass, Stone Surface, 1959, 6 x 6 x 4 In.	950
Tea Bowl, Glazed, Brown, Footed, Stoneware, Peter Voulkos, 1950s, 4½ x 5½ In.	3250
Tea Set, Teapot, Sugar & Creamer, Manganese, 1950s, 15 Piece, 6 Cups & Saucers	8750
Teapot, Gray, Twisted Spout, Robert Arneson, 1969, 11 x 13 In.	11875
Vase, 3 Turquoise Gouges, Robert Arneson, 10½ x 8½ In.	2500
Vase, Abstract, Blue, Grids, Lines & Dots, Blue Ground, G. Gambone, 5 x 3 In.	531
Vase, Ballet Dancers, Glazed, Earthenware, Cazaux, c.1950, 7 x 6 In.	937
Vase, Blue, Mocha Hare's Fur Glaze, Stoneware, Berndt Friberg, 19½ x 5¼ In.	4375
Vase, Blues, Black, Nude Female Figure, Trees, Glazed, Gilt, 1950s, 14 x 7 In.	1625
Vase, Bottle Shape, Gold Iridescent, Beatrice Wood, 7 x 2½ In.	2000
Vase, Bottle Shape, Iron Glaze, Stoneware, Bernard Leach, 1920, 8 x 5 x 3 In.	2875
Vase, Brick Red, Incised, Shino Glaze, Flat Bottom, Stoneware, Robert Turner, 9½ x 8 In.	3375
Vase, Cavalier & Horse, Blue, Black, Cream, Madoura, P. Picasso, 8½ x 7¼ In.	11250
Vase, Cimil, Signed, Claude Conover, c.1977, 14 x 16 In. illus	7375
Vase, Dancer, Musician, Swirling Background, Glazed Earthenware, 1930s, 13 x 6 In.	1375
Vase, Feelie, Green & Blue Glaze, Rose Cabat, 3 x 3 In.	1625
Vase, Feelie, Green Volcanic Drip Glaze, Rose Cabat, 4¼ x 3 In.	1500
Vase, Feelie, Lavender, Pink, Black, Rose Cabat, 5½ In.	1500
Vase, Feelie, Pink & Purple Glazes, Marked, Cabat, 2⅝ x 2 In. illus	354
Vase, Feelie, Tan, Green, Black, Purple Glaze, Bulbous, Incised, Cabat, 3 x 2½ In.	531
Vase, Geometric, Tomobako, Artist's Signature Seal, Japan, 1970, 11 x 4 x 4 In.	1300
Vase, Green, Red, Copper Glazed, Stoneware, Koyo Yamazaki, 1960, 8 x 8 In.	395
Vase, Hen Subject, Blue, White, Pablo Picasso, France, 1954, 5½ x 6¼ In.	3375
Vase, Incised Decoration, Iron Glaze, Stoneware, Bernard Leach, England, 13 x 6 In.	3625
Vase, Les Vieux Metiers, 8 Occupations, Glazed, c.1930, 13 x 11 In.	1250
Vase, Lid, Animals, Glazed Stoneware, Sgraffito, Wax Resist, Peter Voulkos, 1953, 16 x 7 In.	10625
Vase, Roman Soldiers, Horses, Marcello Fantoni, Italy, 14¾ x 7 In. illus	1375
Vase, Rose, Pale Green, Marked, 3 In.	1298
Vase, Round, Closed Form, Tan, Brown, Toshiko Takaezu, c.1974, 6½ In.	2124
Vase, Round, Stripes, Brown, Purple, Stoneware, Peter Voulkos, 7½ x 6 In.	5937
Vase, Ships, Guido Gambone, C.A.S. Vietri, Italy, After 1937, 10 In. illus	687
Vase, Square, Teal, Black, Red Splatters, Albert Green, 10 x 6½ In.	1062
Vase, UFO Shape, Tan, White, Stripes, Straight Sided Mouth, Claude Conover, 10 x 15 In.	5000
Vase, White, Blue Glaze, Marked, 4 In.	1121
Vase, White, Teal, Antelopes, Glazed Earthenware, c.1935, 16 x 10 In.	5000
Vase, Women Milking Goats, Glazed Earthenware, c.1950, 11 x 7 In.	1375
Vase, Women, Goat, Teal, Gold, Burgundy, Glazes, Gilt, Cazaux, c.1960, 11 x 7 In.	1625
Vase, Young Wood Owl, Pablo Picasso, France, 1952, 10 x 4 In.	5312

POWDER FLASKS AND POWDER HORNS were made to hold the gunpowder used in antique firearms. The early examples were made of horn or wood; later ones were of copper or brass.

POWDER FLASK

Copper, Brass, Stag Head, Oak Leaves, Continental, 1900s, 9¾ In.	270
Leather, Embossed, Hunting Dog, Black, 8 In.	214

POWDER HORN

Carved, Snakes, Dots, Remember, Geometric Shapes, 11 In.	294
Eagle & Indian, Hunting Deer, Bow & Eagle, Carved, Timothy Tansel, 1844, 12 In. illus	3900
Horn, Brass, Arms, Leaves, 2 Hooks, France, 7½ In.	382
Horn, Carved, Mermaid Holding Mirror, Fort, Fish, Hex, Chicken, Isaac Primmer, 1700s, 16 In.	1200
Horn, Siege Of Boston, Carved, Ships, Buildings, Motto, Barnabas Webb, 1776, 13 In. illus	15600
Kentucky Rifleman's Horn, Brass Tacks, Iron Wire Hanger, 16 In.	290

Pottery-Contemporary, Sculpture, Face In Opening, Wood Base, Signed, Gary Spinosa, 1990, 24 In.
$908

Rachel Davis Fine Arts

Pottery-Contemporary, Vase, Blue Over Dark Blue Matte Glaze, Crystalline, Waco Ink Stamp, 6 In.
$130

Humler & Nolan

Pottery-Contemporary, Vase, Le Mie Terre, My Lands, Globe, Gio Ponti, Italy, 1929, 8½ In.
$5,000

Rago Arts and Auction Center

Pottery-Contemporary, Vase, Nilo, Ettore Sottsass, Memphis, 1983, 12 x 5 ½ In.
$384

Neal Auction Co.

Pottery-Midcentury, Bowl, Abstract Design, Turquoise, Brown, Maija Grotell, Incised MG, 6 ½ x 10 In.
$2,250

Rago Arts and Auction Center

Pottery-Midcentury, Bowl, Low, Glen Lukens, 1 ¼ x 7 ½ In.
$938

Rago Arts and Auction Center

Pottery-Midcentury, Bowl, Nudes, Seated, Musicians, Glazed, Incised, Cazaux, c.1960, 4 x 7 In.
$1,000

Rago Arts and Auction Center

Pottery-Midcentury, Brick, River Brick, Earthenware, Acrylic, Robert Arneson, 1969, 5 x 9 x 2¾ In.
$3,125

Rago Arts and Auction Center

Pottery-Midcentury, Charger, Dove At Dormer, Glazed, Incised, Signed, Pablo Picasso, 1949, 15 In.
$7,500

Rago Arts and Auction Center

Pottery-Midcentury, Figurine, Cat On Blue Cushion, Signed, Thelma Frazier Winter, 7 In.
$121

Rachel Davis Fine Arts

Pottery-Midcentury, Figurine, Fish Jumping Waves, Figural, Marked, Beato, B. Wood, 4 x 10 In.
$1,815

Humler & Nolan

Pottery-Midcentury, Figurine, Granada, Nude Woman, Signed, Waylande Gregory, 15 In.
$363

Rachel Davis Fine Arts

P

Royal Crest, Dragon, Engraved, 9¾ In..	2040
Scrimshaw, Animals, Fire-Breathing Dragon, 1800s, 10 In.	2440

PRATT ware means two different things. It was an early Staffordshire pottery, cream colored with colored decorations, made by Felix Pratt during the late eighteenth century. There was also Pratt ware made with transfer designs during the mid-nineteenth century in Fenton, England. Reproductions of the transfer-printed Pratt are being made.

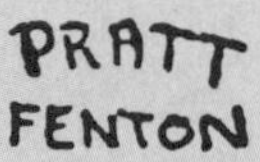

PRATT FENTON

Bough Pot, Flared, Bas-Relief Molded Figures, England, Pair, c.1825, 5 x 6 In.........................	875

PRESSED GLASS, or pattern glass, was first made in the United States in the 1820s after the invention of glass pressing machines. Hundreds of patterns of pressed glass were made in complete table settings. Although the Boston and Sandwich Works was the most famous of the pressed glass factories, there were about sixteen other factories making pressed glass from 1830 to 1850, and still more from 1850 to 1900, when pressed glass reached its greatest popularity. It is now being widely reproduced. The pattern names used in this listing are based on the information in the book *Pressed Glass in America* by John and Elizabeth Welker. There may be pieces of pressed glass listed in this book in other categories, such as Lamp, Ruby Glass, Sandwich Glass, and Souvenir.

12 Diamond, Salt, Blue Green, Double Ogee Form, Petal Foot, 2⅜ In.	1170
Acanthus Leaf, Candlestick, Clear, Master Size, c.1850, Pair, 11 In.	270
Acanthus Leaf, Lamp, Whale Oil, Opaque Green Font, Clambroth Base, c.1850, 12 In., Pair. *illus*	900
Acorn, Shaker, Pink, Hobbs, 2 In.	34
Actress, Cake Stand, Clear, c.1880, 7 x 10 In..	60
Alabama, Butter, Ruby Stain, 6⅛ In...	60
Alabama, Spooner, Ruby Stain, 4½ In.	80
Apollo, Creamer, Amber Stained, Colorless, Frosted, 1891, 7 In.	170
Apollo, Sugar, Lid, Amber Stained, Colorless, Frosted, 1891, 9¼ In.....................	170
Atlas, Pitcher, 52 Oz., 12 In.	101
Barred Oval, Wine, Ruby Stain, Duncan & Sons, c.1891, 6 In.	110
Bellflower, Compote, 5 x 8 In.	45
Big Button, Carafe, Amber Stained, Crystal Glass Co., c.1892, 9¼ In...................	30
Big Button, Pitcher, Ruby Stained, Jug Shape, Applied Handle, c.1892, 7⅝ In........	30
Box-In-Box, Butter, Ruby Stained, c.1900, 6¾ In..	20
Box-In-Box, Pitcher, Water, Ruby Stained & Clear, Riverside, 11¾ In................ *illus*	30
Broken Column, Carafe, Ruby, 8⅜ In..	425
Broken Column, Pitcher, Ruby, c.1892, 8¾ In..	225
Broken Column, Syrup, Ruby, c.1891, 6¼ In.	225
Broken Column, Wine, Ruby, 1891, 4 In.	110 to 120
Cabbage Leaf, Compote, Lid, Rabbit Finial, Riverside, 8 In....................... *illus*	500
Cable, Goblet, 6 In...	41
Candlestick, Column Shape, Yellow, Petal Socles, c.1850, 9 In., Pair...................	188
Candlestick, Opaque Blue, Pebble Socles, Clambroth Base, c.1850, 8½ In., Pair.............. *illus*	192
Celery Vase, Apple Green, A.J. Beatty & Sons, c.1886, 7 In...................................	152
Circle & Ellipse, Vase, Canary Yellow, Hexagonal Base, Pair, c.1850, 7½ In.	200
Daisy & Fern, Syrup, Cranberry Opalescent, Silver Plate Lid, 7 In.........................	72
Diamond Point, Butter, Cover, Ruby, 4 In.	18
Dolphin, Candlestick, Canary Yellow, Petal Socles, c.1850, 10½ In., Pair .... *illus*	313
Elongated Loops, Vase, Canary Yellow, Marble Base, 1800s, 11 In. .... *illus*	75
Holly, Sugar & Creamer..	215
Honeybees, Box, Honeycomb, Etched, Dome Lid, Indiana Glass Co., c.1910, 4 x 6 In.	150
Horn Of Plenty, Vase, Hanging, Emerald Green, Riverside........................... *illus*	23
Inverted Thistle, Plate, Egg, Pink, 11½ In.	39
Loop & Petal, Candlestick, Medium Lavender, Sand Finish, c.1850, 7 In..............	225
Loop & Petal, Candlestick, Vaseline Green, c.1850, 6¾ In., Pair......................... *illus*	240
Loop, Cologne Bottle, Canary Yellow, Stopper, c.1850, 8 In.	175
Lowestoft, Cup & Saucer, Pale Green, Pink Border, Flowers, 1948	28
Palace, Compote, Moon & Stars, 16 x 10 In.	132
Palace, Creamer	52
Petals, Bowl, Cobalt Blue, c.1850, 2½ x 8 In..	1320

PRESSED GLASS

Pottery-Midcentury, Figurine, Mouse, Signed, Thelma Winter, 5 In. $36

Rachel Davis Fine Arts

TIP

When cleaning or repairing antiques, remember less is more.

Pottery-Midcentury, Pitcher, Pablo Picasso, Face, Lines, Handle, Madoura, 10½ In. $5,535

Palm Beach Modern Auctions

This is an edited listing of current prices. Visit **Kovels.com** to check thousands of prices from previous years and sign up for free information on trends, tips, reproductions, marks, and more.

P

PRESSED GLASS

Pottery-Midcentury, Pitcher, Yan, Pablo Picasso, Limited, 1952, 10 x 4½ In.
$5,000

Rago Arts and Auction Center

Pottery-Midcentury, Plate, Swimmers, Seaside, Sea Gulls, Dock, Pablo Picasso, 10 In.
$3,360

Eldred's Auctioneers and Appraisers

Pottery-Midcentury, Vase, Cimil, Signed, Claude Conover, c.1977, 14 x 16 In.
$7,375

Cottone Auctions

Pottery-Midcentury, Vase, Feelie, Pink & Purple Glazes, Marked, Cabat, 2⅝ x 2 In.
$354

Humler & Nolan

> **TIP**
> Don't use any type of tape on porcelain or pottery that has overglaze decorations. Gilding and enamels may pull off when the tape is removed. Antiques shops often tape a lid to a bowl; when you buy, ask the dealer to remove the tape to be sure no damage has been done.

Pottery-Midcentury, Vase, Roman Soldiers, Horses, Marcello Fantoni, Italy, 14¾ x 7 In.
$1,375

Rago Arts and Auction Center

Pottery-Midcentury, Vase, Ships, Guido Gambone, C.A.S. Vietri, Italy, After 1937, 10 In.
$687

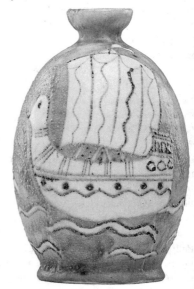

Rago Arts and Auction Center

Pomade Jar, Bear, Blue, c.1850, 4 In.	200
Ribbon, Bowl, Amethyst, c.1850, 2½ x 6 In.	531
Ruby Thumbprint, Cake Stand, Excelsior, Ruby Stained, 5¾ x 9 In.	234
Ruby Thumbprint, Cake Stand, Excelsior, Ruby Stained, 7 x 10¼ In.	163
Ruby Thumbprint, Honey, Excelsior, Ruby Stained, 5¾ x 8 In.	152
Sandwich Star, Spill Holder, Electric Blue, c.1850, 5 In. .... *illus*	300
Spanish American, Pitcher, Clear, c.1898, 9¼ In.	20
Thistle, Compote, 4 In.	13
Tulip, Lamp, Blue Fonts, White Base, c.1925, Pair, 12½ In.	175
Tulip, Vase, Amethyst, c.1850, 10 In. .... *illus*	625
Twisted Loop, Vase, Amethyst, Sugar Bowl Lid Base, c.1850, 9 In.	500
Windows Swirl, Sugar Shaker, Blue Opalescent, Silver Lid, 5 In.	96
X-Ray, Cruet, Clear, Gold Trim, Riverside .... *illus*	23

PRINT, in this listing, means any of many printed images produced on paper by one of the more common methods, such as lithography. The prints listed here are of interest primarily to the antiques collector, not the fine arts collector. Many of these prints were originally part of books. Other prints will be found in the Advertising, Currier & Ives, Movie, and Poster categories.

Audubon bird prints were originally issued as part of books printed from 1826 to 1854. They were issued in two sheet sizes, 26½ inches by 39½ inches and 11 inches by 7 inches. The height of a picture is listed before the width. The quadrupeds were issued in 28-by-22-inch prints. Later editions of the Audubon books were done in many sizes, and reprints of the books in the original sizes were also made. The words *After John James Audubon* appear on all of the prints, including the originals, because the pictures were made as copies of Audubon's original oil paintings. The bird pictures have been so popular they have been copied in myriad sizes using both old and new printing methods. This list includes originals and later copies because Audubon prints of all ages are sold in antiques shops.

Audubon, American Flamingo, Frame, 35 x 26 In.	300
Audubon, Annulated Marmot Squirrel, Lithograph, 7 x 10 In.	100
Audubon, Bewick's Long Tailed Wren, R. Havell, 19 x 12 In. .... *illus*	427
Audubon, Brown Pelican, Havell, 1838, 25 x 37 In.	275
Audubon, Cerulean Warbler, Colored, Engraving, Havell, 1828, 31 x 20 In.	850
Audubon, Children's Warbler, Engraving, J. Whatman, 1835, 38 x 25 In.	400
Audubon, Little Chief Hare, Quadrupeds Of North America, Lithograph, Frame, 14 x 12 In.	350
Audubon, Little Harvest Mouse, 6½ x 10 In.	325
Audubon, Purple Gallinule, Aquatint, Hand Colored, Havell, 1836, 26 x 39 In.	1403
Audubon, Purple Heron, Birds Of America, 28 x 41½ In.	175
Audubon, White Egret, Engraving, Havell, Frame, 26 x 22 In.	80
Calder, Alexander, Lithograph, Joys Of The Neophyte, Sun, Circles, Frame, 1976, 35 x 27 In. . *illus*	4688
Chancellor Livingston Steamer, Lithograph, After A Work By Moses Swett, c.1825, 15 x 11 In.	840
Crimson-Rumped Toucanet, Lithograph, Gould & Richter, Frame, c.1835, 20 x 13 In. . *illus*	540
Currier & Ives prints are listed in the Currier & Ives category.	
Dali, Salvador, Cerises Pierrot, Etching, On Paper, Drypoint, Signed, 1969, 30 x 22 In. ..... *illus*	2304

Icart prints were made by Louis Icart, who worked in Paris from 1907 as an employee of a postcard company. He then started printing magazines and fashion brochures. About 1910 he created a series of etchings of fashionably dressed women, and he continued to make similar etchings until he died in 1950. He is well known as a printmaker, painter, and illustrator. Original etchings are much more expensive than the later photographic copies.

Icart, Ballerina, Sepia Style, Color, 17 x 13 In.	100
Icart, Farewell, Woman, Seated, White Dress, Hat, Blue Ribbon, Etching, Aquatint, 14¾ x 19½ In. .	400
Icart, Geisha On A Bridge, Etching, Color, 26 x 19 In.	275
Icart, Le Panier De Pommes, Color, Etching, Frame, 1920s, 20 x 16 In.	475
Icart, Leda & The Swan, Signed, Frame, 18 x 22 In.	125
Icart, Miss America, Drypoint & Aquatint, Oval, Frame, Signed, 1927, 20 x 15¾ In. .... *illus*	875
Icart, Puppies, Etching, Frame, 1927, 25 x 20 In.	200
Icart, Speed II, 3 Greyhounds, Woman, White Dress, Etching, c.1933, 16 x 26 In.	1125

Powder Horn, Eagle & Indian, Hunting Deer, Bow & Eagle, Carved, Timothy Tansel, 1844, 12 In.
$3,900

Garth's Auctioneers & Appraisers

Powder Horn, Horn, Siege Of Boston, Carved, Ships, Buildings, Motto, Barnabas Webb, 1776, 13 In.
$15,600

Cowan's Auctions

Pressed Glass, Acanthus Leaf, Lamp, Whale Oil, Opaque Green Font, Clambroth Base, c.1850, 12 In., Pair
$900

Eldred's Auctioneers and Appraisers

P

Pressed Glass, Box-In-Box, Pitcher, Water, Ruby Stained & Clear, Riverside, 11¾ In.
$30

Mike Clum Auctions, Inc.

Pressed Glass, Cabbage Leaf, Compote, Lid, Rabbit Finial, Riverside, 8 In.
$500

Mike Clum Auctions, Inc.

Pressed Glass, Candlestick, Opaque Blue, Pebble Socles, Clambroth Base, c.1850, 8½ In., Pair
$192

Eldred's Auctioneers and Appraisers

Pressed Glass, Dolphin, Candlestick, Canary Yellow, Petal Socles, c.1850, 10½ In., Pair
$313

Eldred's Auctioneers and Appraisers

Icart, Winged Victory, Aquatint In Colors, Etching, Frame, Signed, 1918, 21½ x 15 In. ..... *illus*	2000
Icart, Moman Seated Under Trees, Signed, Frame, 27 x 21 In.	125
Icart, Woman, Cat, Carriage, Blue, Green, 16¾ x 19¾ In.	338
Icart, Woman, Red Cap, Holding Vase Near Well, Drypoint Etching, Frame, 24 x 18 In.	275
Icart, Women Playing Music, Frame, c.1925, 35 x 29 In.	200

Jacoulet prints were designed by Paul Jacoulet (1902–1960), a Frenchman who spent most of his life in Japan. He was a master of Japanese woodblock print technique. Subjects included life in Japan, the South Seas, Korea, and China. His prints were sold by subscription and issued in series. Each series had a distinctive seal, such as a sparrow or butterfly. Most Jacoulet prints are approximately 15 x 10 inches.

Jacoulet, Amoureux A Trang, Woodblock, Mandarin Duck Seal, 1935, 15 x 11 In.	475
Jacoulet, Avant L'Audience, Woodblock, 1942, 15 x 11 In.	630
Jacoulet, Bebe Coreen En Costume De Ceremonie, Baby, c.1934, 18 x 14 In.	2280
Jacoulet, Fleurs, Des Iles Lointaines, Water, Flowers, 1940, 14 x 18 In.	2880
Jacoulet, La Confidente, Woman In Costume, Fans, 1942, 18 x 14 In.	5100
Jacoulet, La Confidente, Woodblock, Signed, Frame, 1942, 25 x 21 In.	600
Jacoulet, La Gerbe D'Anthurium, Woman, Flowers, 1951, 18 x 14 In.	3900
Jacoulet, Le Repas Des Mendiants, Beggars Eating, 1938, 19 x 14 In.	2280
Jacoulet, Le Sculpteur De Tokobuei, Sculptor, 1954, 18 x 14 In.	2400
Jacoulet, Le Tresor, Coree, Butterfly Seal, Woodblock, 1940, 18 x 14 In.	1800
Jacoulet, Les Papillons, Mandchoukuo, Woodblock, Boat Seal, Frame, 1939, 20 x 17 In.	425
Jacoulet, Les Petits Voleurs, Man, Sitting On Mountain, 1959, 18 x 14 In.	2040
Jacoulet, Mers Du Sud, Cactus, Signed, 18½ x 14 In.	2500
Jacoulet, Nuit De Neige, Coree, Woodblock, 1939, 15 x 11 In.	1000
Jacoulet, Pecheur De Sawara, Sawara Fisherman, Signed, Woodblock, 18½ x 14 In. .... *illus*	594
Jacoulet, Une Averse A Metalanim, Mandarin Duck Seal, Woodblock, 1935, 15 x 11 In.	500

Japanese woodblock prints are listed as follows: Print, Japanese, name of artist, title or description, type, and size. Dealers use the following terms: *Tate-e* is a vertical composition. *Yoko-e* is a horizontal composition. The words *Aiban* (13 by 9 inches), *Chuban* (10 by 7½ inches), *Hosoban* (13 by 6 inches), *Koban* (7 by 4 inches), *Nagaban* (20 by 9 inches), *Oban* (15 by 10 inches), *Shikishiban* (8 by 9 inches), and *Tanzaku* (15 by 5 inches) denote approximate size. Modern versions of some of these prints have been made. Other woodblock prints that are not Japanese are listed under Print, Woodblock.

Japanese, Eisen, Woman Arranging Flowers, Frame, Oban, Tate-e .... *illus*	120
Japanese, Gekko, Ogata, Fight On Hill, Oban, Tate-e	192
Japanese, Hasui, Kawase, Rain At Kasuga Shrine, Nara, Watanabe D Seal, Oban Tate-e . *illus*	1440
Japanese, Hiroshige, Ferry Boat At Rokugo, Oban, Yoko-e	150
Japanese, Hiroshige, Whale Hunting Off Goto Island, Frame, Oban, Tate-e	375
Japanese, Hokusai, Kasushika, Sunset Over Ryoguku Bridge, Oban, Yoko-e, Frame, 15 x 20 In.	120
Japanese, Koson, Ohara, Goshawk On Snow-Covered Pine, Oban, Tate-e, 22 x 16 In.	360
Japanese, Saito, Kiyoshi, Woman, Pencil Signed, With Seal, Oban, Tate-e, 24 x 18 In.	200
Japanese, Toyokuni III, Man, Woman, Wisteria Screen, Frame, Oban, Diptych .... *illus*	108
Japanese, Toyokuni, 3 Figures Under Cherry Blossoms, Frame, Oban, Yoko-e, 17 x 20 In.	300
Japanese, Toyokuni, Utagawa, Women Preparing For Poetry Reading, Frame, Triptych, 21½ x 36 In. .	180
Japanese, Woodblock, Hiroshige, Ando, Minowa, Kanasugi At Mikawashima, c.1850, 14 x 9 In.	1825
Japanese, Woodblock, Miyajima At Night, Kawase Hasui, 1930s, 5¾ x 3¾ In.	70
Japanese, Woodblock, Nagai Iku, Tama Art, Kappa, Aesthetic, 1950s, 10 x 16 In.	269
Japanese, Yoshida, Toshi, Mount Holly Cross, Vail, Colorado, Oban, Tate-e, 18½ x 27 In.	594
Lopez, Urbano, San Francisco, Lithograph, Pre-Gold Rush, Hills, Buildings, 12 x 10 In... *illus*	480

Nutting prints are popular with collectors. Wallace Nutting is known for his pictures, furniture, and books. Collectors call his pictures Nutting prints although they are actually hand-colored photographs issued from 1900 to 1941. There are over 10,000 different titles. Wallace Nutting furniture is listed in the Furniture category.

Nutting, Canopied Road, Mat, Frame, 12 x 18 In.	68
Nutting, Dell Dale Road, 15 x 13 In.	500
Nutting, Silver Birches, Signed, 1940s, 7 x 8¾ In.	38

P

Pressed Glass, Elongated Loops, Vase, Canary Yellow, Marble Base, 1800s, 11 In. $75

Garth's Auctioneers & Appraisers

Pressed Glass, Horn Of Plenty, Vase, Hanging, Emerald Green, Riverside $23

Mike Clum Auctions, Inc.

Pressed Glass, Loop & Petal, Candlestick, Vaseline Green, c.1850, 6¾ In., Pair $240

Eldred's Auctioneers and Appraisers

Pressed Glass
Pressed glass machines were invented in the 1820s. Molds were made of brass, iron, or other metal. A plunger forced the glass into the mold.
    By the 1840s, American glasshouses were firepolishing their glass. It was reheated after shaping, "melting" the seams a little and smoothing the surface.

Pressed Glass, Sandwich Star, Spill Holder, Electric Blue, c.1850, 5 In. $300

Eldred's Auctioneers and Appraisers

Pressed Glass, Tulip Shape, Vase, Amethyst, c.1850, 10 In. $625

Eldred's Auctioneers and Appraisers

Pressed Glass, X-Ray, Cruet, Clear, Gold Trim, Riverside $23

Mike Clum Auctions, Inc.

Print, Audubon, Bewick's Long Tailed Wren, R. Havell, 19 x 12 In. $427

Neal Auction Co.

TIP
Don't write on the back of a print with either pencil or ink. Eventually the writing will bleed through to the front.

Print, Calder, Alexander, Lithograph, Joys Of The Neophyte, Sun, Circles, Frame, 1976, 35 x 27 In. $4,688

P

Los Angeles Modern Auctions

Print, Crimson-Rumped Toucanet, Lithograph, Gould & Richter, Frame, c.1835, 20 x 13 In.
$540

Brunk Auctions

Print, Dali, Salvador, Cerises Pierrot, Etching, On Paper, Drypoint, Signed, 1969, 30 x 22 In.
$2,304

Neal Auction Co.

Print, Icart, Miss America, Drypoint & Aquatint, Oval, Frame, Signed, 1927, 20 x 15¾ In.
$875

Neal Auction Co.

Nutting, The Swimming Pool, 15½ x 12¼ In.	125
Nutting, Warm Spring Day, 7½ x 12 In.	150
Nutting, Woman, Sitting At Table, Fireplace, Signed Frame, 11¾ x 7¾ In.	125

Parrish prints are wanted by collectors. Maxfield Frederick Parrish was an illustrator who lived from 1870 to 1966. He is best known as a designer of magazine covers, posters, calendars, and advertisements. His prints have been copied in recent years. Some Maxfield Parrish items may be listed in Advertising.

Parrish, Daybreak, Frame, c.1923, 20 x 12 In.	189
Parrish, Dinkey-Bird, Girl On Swing, Castle, Frame, 17 x 12 In.	145
Parrish, Garden Of Allah, 8-Sided Frame, 1920s, 20½ x 11½ In.	248
Parrish, Knave Of Hearts, Wheelbarrow Of Cabbage, Frame, 12½ x 7½ In.	110
Parrish, Peaceful Valley, English Landscape, Frame, c.1940, 17 x 13 In.	130
Rockwell, Doctor & Doll, Stethoscope, Little Girl, Desk, Books, Signed, 29½ x 24 In. ...... *illus*	1800

Woodblock prints that are not in the Japanese tradition are listed here. Most were made in England and the United States during the Arts and Crafts period. Japanese woodblock prints are listed under Print, Japanese.

Woodblock, Baumann, Gustave, Marigolds, Sunny Messengers, Signed, c.1916, 11 x 10 In.. *illus*	2816
Woodblock, Baumann, Gustave, Quiet Corner, Blue, Yellow, Matte, Frame, 7½ x 8½ In.	4375
Woodblock, Rice, William, King Orchid Brazil, Purple, Pink, Green, Blue, c.1925, 9 x 12 In.	2500
Woodblock, Rice, William, Kingfisher, Blue, Green, White, Orange, c.1925, 9 x 12 In.	2500
Woodblock, Rice, William, Old Kauffman Homestead, c.1925, 10½ x 14 In.	1375

PURINTON POTTERY COMPANY was incorporated in Wellsville, Ohio, in 1936. The company moved to Shippenville, Pennsylvania, in 1941 and made a variety of hand-painted ceramic wares. By the 1950s Purinton was making dinnerware, souvenirs, cookie jars, and florist wares. The pottery closed in 1959.

Apple, Chop Plate, 11¾ In.	49
Apple, Pitcher, Red, Yellow, Brown, Green, 1940s, 5½ In.	15
Apple, Salt & Pepper, 2½ In.	15
Fruit, Jug, 5½ In.	26
Mountain Rose, Vase, Basket, Double Spouted, Oval, 6 x 6 x 3 In.	15

PURSES have been recognizable since the eighteenth century, when leather and needlework purses were preferred. Beaded purses became popular in the nineteenth century, went out of style, but are again in use. Mesh purses date from the 1880s and are still being made. How to carry a handkerchief, lipstick, and cell phone is a problem today for every woman, including the Queen of England.

2-Tone Gold, Clutch, Diamond Clasp, Interior Mirror, Cartier, Italy, 3½ x 5 In.	20400
Bagatelle, Empreinte Leather, Hobo, Orange, Braided Handle, Louis Vuitton, 14 x 12 x 5 In.	2001
Beaded, Clutch, Cream Glass, Celery Green, Goldtone, Hobe Frame, 1950, 11 x 7½ In.	1198
Beaded, Glass, Wrist, Flapper, Iridescent Blue, Long Fringe, Tapered Handle, 1920s, 4 x 6 In.	95
Beaded, Gold Thread, Mary Frances, 1900s, 9 x 6½ In.	72
Beaded, Satin, Blue, Pink, White, Double Flap, Chain Strap, Chanel, 10 x 6 In.	7812
Beaded, Satin, Silk Lining, Crocheted, Meshwork, Floral, Mirror, Powder, 1910, 13 x 5½ In.	41
Big Hornback Crocodile, Zippered Envelope Style, Suede Cloth Lining, 14 x 8 x 9½ In.	300
Calfskin, Suede, Tricolor Diamond Flap, Red, Navy Blue, Gray, 2-Way, Celine, 13 x 9 x 2 In.	870
Canvas, Olive Green, Tan Leather, Saddle Stitched, Birkin B40, Hermes, 11 x 16 In. *illus*	7500
Crocodile, Leather, Clutch, Piano, Crisscross, Orange, Bottega Veneta, 5½ x 8 x 2 In.	2330
Damier Vernis, Petrol Blue, Louis Vuitton, Spain, 8⅝ x 6¾ x ¾ In.	498
Dresden Mesh, Silk Screen, Fringe, Silk Lining, Deco Frame, Chain, Whiting & Davis, c.1915, 8 x 5 In.	305
Goldtone, Chain Shoulder Strap, Foldover Cover, Snap, Paloma Picasso, 8 x 6 In.	59
Hard Case, Lion Face, Bejeweled, Marked Bellini Collection, Chinese, 1900s, 6¼ In.	48
Intrecciato, Gold Leather, Hobo, Grommet, Top Zip Closure, Bottega Veneta, 10 x 16 x 2 In.	680
Leather, Backpack, Burgundy, Buckled Shoulder Strap, Cartier, France, 8½ x 11 x 4 In.	650
Leather, Backpack, Louis Vuitton, Soho Damier, Brown, Centenaire Edition, France, 9¾ x 12 x 4 In.	800
Leather, Backpack, Matelasse, Quilted, Black, Chanel, Gold CC Logo, Turn Clasp Closure, 11 x 8 x 3 In.	2500

P

Print, Icart, Winged Victory, Aquatint In Colors, Etching, Frame, Signed, 1918, 21 ½ x 15 In.
$2,000

Rago Arts and Auction Center

Print, Jacoulet, Pecheur De Sawara, Sawara Fisherman, Signed, Woodblock, 18 ½ x 14 In.
$594

Eldred's Auctioneers and Appraisers

Print, Japanese, Eisen, Woman Arranging Flowers, Frame, Oban, Tate-e
$120

Eldred's Auctioneers and Appraisers

Print, Japanese, Hasui, Kawase, Rain At Kasuga Shrine, Nara, Watanabe D Seal, Oban Tate-e
$1,440

Eldred's Auctioneers and Appraisers

Print, Japanese, Toyokuni III, Man, Woman, Wisteria Screen, Frame, Oban, Diptych
$108

Eldred's Auctioneers and Appraisers

Print, Lopez, Urbano, San Francisco, Lithograph, Pre-Gold Rush, Hills, Buildings, 12 x 10 In.
$480

Cowan's Auctions

Print, Rockwell, Doctor & Doll, Stethoscope, Little Girl, Desk, Books, Signed, 29 ½ x 24 In.
$1,800

Eldred's Auctioneers and Appraisers

Print, Woodblock, Baumann, Gustave, Marigolds, Sunny Messengers, Signed, c.1916, 11 x 10 In.
$2,816

Neal Auction Co.

Purse, Canvas, Olive Green, Tan Leather, Saddle Stitched, Birkin B40, Hermes, 11 x 16 In.
$7,500

New Orleans Auction Galleries

P

Pyrex, Casserole, Lid, Crazy Daisy, Divided, Green, White, 1½ Qt.
$25

Etsy

Pyrex, Creamer, Old Town, Blue Band, 2¾ In.
$6

Etsy

Pyrex, Mixing Bowl Set, Nesting, New Dots Pattern, 4 Piece
$200

Etsy

Leather, Backpack, Yellow, Salvatore Ferragamo, Italy, 8½ x 7½ x 4¾ In.	490
Leather, Brown, Quilted, 2 Leather & Gold Straps, Chanel, 6½ x 9½ In.	1320
Leather, Calf, Red, Retourne Kelly, Palladim Hardware, Hermes, 2008, 10 x 8 In.	8125
Leather, Clutch, Britannia Skull Box, Blush, Black, Alexander McQueen, 4 x 6½ x 2 In.	380
Leather, Clutch, Wristlet, Pink, Adjustable Strap, Vitello Daino, Prada, 7½ x 2 x 1½ In.	535
Leather, Coin, U.S. Battleship Maine, Image Of Battleship	49
Leather, Cuir Opera, Black, Louis Vuitton, France, 7½ x 8⅝ x 2⅜ In.	390
Leather, Dark Red, Goldtone Hardware, Hermes, Paris, France, 8½ x 12 In.	1080
Leather, Gucci Satchel, Embossed GC, Brown Tassels, Detachable Shoulder Strap, 13 x 16 In.	330
Leather, Hobo, Soho, Off-White, Single Loop Shoulder Strap, Gucci, 13 x 18½ x 6 In.	850
Leather, Kelly, Blue, Gold Trim, Hermes, 9½ x 12½ In.	1230
Leather, License Plates, Little Earth, Barrel Form, Recycled, 1900s, 8¾ In.	24
Leather, Messenger, Black, Flap, Push-Lock Closure, Adjustable Strap, Tiffany, 15 x 11 x 4¼ In.	630
Leather, Messenger, Flap, Dark Brown, Crossbody Strap, Salvatore Ferragamo, 11 x 10 x 2½ In.	500
Leather, Messenger, Jypsiere, Bordeaux Logo, Front Flap, Swivel Clasp, Hermes, 13 x 11 x 6 In.	7990
Leather, Monogram Canvas, Shoulder Bag, Bel Air, Louis Vuitton, 8¾ x 11¼ In.	826
Leather, Pouchette, Quilted, Silver, Chain Strip, Chanel, 6¼ x 10 In.	1534
Leather, Red, Brown, Dooney & Bourke, 1900s, 9 x 12 In.	38
Leather, Tote Bag, Clear Plastic, Tethered, Louis Vuitton France, 1900s, 13 x 11 In.	252
Leather, Tote, Arion, Brown, Silvertone Hardware, Hermes, 11 x 20 In.	3125
Leather, Tote, Beige, Ivory, Black, Goldtone Zipper, Optional Shoulder Strap, Givenchy, 10 x 9 In.	1320
Leather, Tote, Calfskin, Phantom, Chocolate Brown, Dark Green, Suede Wings, Celine, 12 x 12 In.	1375
Lizard, Pearlized Sand, Foldover, Chain & Leather Strap, Francesca, J. Bolinger, 10 In.	688
Matelasse, Dark Orange, CC Emblem, Chain, Strap, Chanel, 8¾ x 7 x 2¾ In.	1500
Mesh, Coin, 14K Yellow Gold, Cabochon Sapphire, c.1920, 2 In.	1025
Nylon, Quilted, Calfskin Bottom, Hobo, Chanel, Black, Silver Link Chain Handle, 9 x 14 x 4 In.	2301
Patent Leather, Hobo, Roady, Dark Pink, Single Looped Handle, Saint Laurent, 10 x 15 x 6½ In.	500
Pochette Milla, Chain, Pouch, Monogram, Louis Vuitton, France, 3½ x 5⅞ In.	390
Python Skin, Messenger, Taupe, Blue, Round Silhouette, Top Zip Pocket, Chloe Drew, 9½ x 10 x 4 In.	1370
Satin, Aqua, Pink, Rose, Lavender, Goldtone, Filigree Wirework, Hobe Frame, 1950, 11 x 9½ In.	998
Silver, Dance, Floral Cartouche Border, Chain Handle, William B. Kerr, 1900, 4 x 3½ In.	224
Snakeskin, Clutch, Flat Envelope, Green, Off-White, Oscar De La Renta, Grafton, 9 x 13 x 1 In.	370
Suede, Embroidered, Tote, Taupe, Faux Fur Trim, Chanel, 12 x 12½ In.	826
Suede, Leather, Backpack, Brown, Single Strap, Zippered Pocket, Gucci, Italy, 10 x 10 x 2¾ In.	360
Swarovski Crystals, Les Extraordinaires, Black Mink, Feline, Louis Vuitton, 7½ x 8½ In.	4750
Velvet, Clutch, Black, Magnetic Flap Closure, Goldtone Open Handle, Jimmy Choo, 9½ x 2 x 5 In.	290
Wicker, Horse Racing Theme, Felt, Vinyl Cover, Lucite Trim & Handles, Atlas, 1960s, 12 x 8 In.	395

PYREX glass baking dishes were first made in 1915 by the Corning Glass Works. Pyrex dishes are made of a heat-resistant glass that can go from refrigerator or freezer to oven or microwave and are nice enough to put on the table. Clear glass dishes were made first. Pyrex Flameware, for use on a stovetop burner, was made from 1936 to 1979. A set of four mixing bowls, each in a dfferent color (blue, red, green, and yellow), was made beginning in 1947. The first pieces with decorative patterns were made in 1956. After Corning sold its Pyrex brand to World Kitchen LLC in 1998, changes were made to the formula for the glass.

Bowl, Soap, Flamingo, 6¼ In.		9
Butter, Blue, Lid, Snowflake		15
Casserole, Lid, Crazy Daisy, Divided, Green, White, 1½ Qt.	*illus*	25
Creamer, Old Town, Blue Band, 2¾ In.	*illus*	6
Gravy Boat, Butterfly Gold		10
Mixing Bowl Set, Nesting, New Dots Pattern, 4 Piece	*illus*	200
Syrup, Green, Spring Blossom, 4⅛ In.		10
Tub, Butter, Green, Spring Blossom, 5⅝ In.		10

Quezal QUEZAL glass was made from 1901 to 1924 at the Queens, New York, company started by Martin Bach. Other glassware by other firms, such as Loetz, Steuben, and Tiffany, resembles this gold-colored iridescent glass. Martin Bach died in 1921. His son-in-law, Conrad Vahlsing Jr., went to work at the Lustre Art Company about 1920. Bach's son, Martin Bach Jr., worked at the Durand Art Glass division of the Vineland Flint Glass Works after 1924.

Bowl, Green Feather, Gold Trim, Flare Ruffled Trim, Gold Iridescent, 4 x 6½ In		968
Bowl, Iridescent Pulled Feather Design, Calcite Background, Crackle Edge, 3 x 7 In.		726
Ceiling Fixture, 2 Floriform Shades, Gold Iridescent Interior, Calcite Exterior, 9½ x 16 In.		484
Compote, King Tut, Iridescent, Footed, c.1925, 6½ x 6¼ In.	*illus*	287
Lamp, 1-Light, Floriform Shade, Pearlescent Exterior, Green, Gold Pulled Design, 17 In.		484
Lamp, 3-Light, Patinated Brass, Pea Green Domed Glass Base, Iridescent Floriform, 21 x 7½ In.		354
Lamp, Arching Stem, Flaring Lip Shade, Gold Iridescent, 16 In.		3025
Lampshade, Trumpet, Iridescent, Ribbed Sides, c.1925, 5 x 4⅝ In.		1200
Vase, Golden Feathers, Green Leaves, Yellow Ground, Pear Shape, 9 In.		2360
Vase, Heart & Vine, Threaded, Blown & Applied Glass, c.1925, 5¾ x 3¼ In.	*illus*	732
Vase, Iridescent, Gold, Glass, Flared Rim, Pontil Scar, 9⅝ x 4½ In.		325
Vase, Jack-In-The-Pulpit, Iridescent Gold, 15½ x 9¾ In.		800
Vase, Pulled Feather, Bulging Shoulder, Flaring Tricorn Lip, Green, Gold, Signed, 7½ In.		1089
Vase, Pulled Feather, Cream Neck, Green Body, Round Foot, 11 x 4 In.		1875
Vase, Pulled Feather, Floriform, Wavy Rim, Zebra Pattern, Crackle Edge, 7¾ x 6½ In.		847
Vase, Pulled Feather, Iridescent, Wavy Crackle Edge, 5 x 5½ In.		545
Vase, Pulled Feathers, Ruffled Rim, Green, Pink, Brown, c.1905, 7 x 3½ In.		750
Vase, Pulled Feathers, Sweet Pea, Iridescent Gold, Green, 6⅛ x 5½ In.		702
Vase, Pulled Feathers, Sweet Pea, Iridescent Gold, Green, 7¾ x 5½ In.		1989
Vase, Pulled Feathers, Trumpet, Ruffled, Green, Pink, Iridescent, c.1910, 7½ x 5 In.		875
Vase, Silver Overlay, Cylindrical, 10 x 4¼ In.		531

QUILTS have been made since the seventeenth century. Early textiles were very precious and every scrap was saved to be reused. A quilt is a combination of fabrics joined to a filler and a backing by small stitched designs known as quilting. An appliqued quilt has pieces stitched to the top of a large piece of backing fabric. A patchwork, or pieced, quilt is made of many small pieces stitched together. Embroidery can be added to either type.

Amish, Basket Pattern, Pieced Cotton, Black Ground, Crib, Holmes Country, 41 x 32 In.	*illus*	480
Amish, Patchwork, Diamond Pattern, Rayon, Lancaster County, 82 x 84 In.	*illus*	325
Appliqued, Basket Of Flowers, 80 x 89 In.	*illus*	130
Appliqued, Poinsettia, Red, White Background, 5 Pots, 81 x 67 In.		180
Appliqued, Red, Green, Floral, 1800s, 77 x 95 In.	*illus*	246
Appliqued, Star In Diamond, Yellow, Orange & Salmon, 1900s, 80 x 93 In.	*illus*	150
Appliqued, Sunbonnet Sue & Diamond, Zigzag Border, Pink Embroidery Floss, 1930s, 74 x 82 In.		185
Appliqued, Texas Lily, Lily & Rose Flowerbox Swags, c.1860, 91¾ x 71½ In.		625
Appliqued, Tulips, Red & Green, Red Border, Youth, 63 x 72 In.	*illus*	106
Appliqued, Whig Rose, Swag & Tulip Border, Red, White, Blue, 82 x 82 In.		812
Crazy, Patchwork, Embroidered, Figures, Birds, Plants, Owl, Moon, c.1880, 66 x 66 In.		3125
Crazy, Patchwork, Silk, Velvet, Cotton, Caterpillar, Flowers, Hand, 63½ x 76 In.		70
Crazy, Silk, Hand Painted, 1888, 48 x 68 In.		144
Patchwork, Basket Of Flowers, Lehigh County, Pa., 77 x 78 In.		201
Patchwork, Block, 40 Squares, Printed Pattern, Woven Plaid Fabrics, 1860-90, 66 x 78 In.		120
Patchwork, Double Wedding Ring, Pastel & White, 73 x 89 In.		77
Patchwork, Embroidered, 450 Names, Pinwheels, Red, White, Church Women, c.1910, 76 x 92 In.		2550
Patchwork, Flying Birds, Cheddar, Red, Blue, Green, 80 x 88 In.		293
Patchwork, Irish Chain Pattern, Red Ground, Black & White Grid, 88 x 90 In.	*illus*	189
Patchwork, Log Cabin, Blues & White, 80 x 89 In.		66
Patchwork, Log Cabin, Corduroy, Satin, Satin Backing, 70 x 71 In.		819
Patchwork, Log Cabin, Red & White, Rack Included, 1800s, 75 x 75 In.		300
Patchwork, Pastels, Red, Yellow Bars, 66½ x 82½ In.		44
Patchwork, Sawtooth Border, Princess Feathers, 60 x 64 In.		240
Patchwork, Star, 9 Blocks, Cotton, Red, Green, White, Fabrics, Printed, 1870, 71 x 69 In.		200
Patchwork, Star Of Bethlehem, Corner Stars, Half Stars, Multicolor, Calico, 1860, 78½ x 79 In.		750
Patchwork, Wedding Ring, Pink, Multicolor, c.1930s, 70 x 94 In.		146
Patchwork, Yo-Yo, Hand Stitched, Circles, Fabric, 3 Dimensional, 1920, 52 x 66 In.		41
Patchwork, Zigzag, Yellow, White, 70 x 90 In.		380

Quezal, Compote, King Tut, Iridescent, Footed, c.1925, 6½ x 6¼ In.
$287

Brunk Auctions

Quezal, Vase, Heart & Vine, Threaded, Blown & Applied Glass, c.1920, 5¾ x 3¼ In.
$732

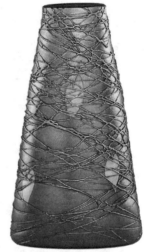

Rago Arts and Auction Center

Quilt, Amish, Basket Pattern, Pieced Cotton, Black Ground, Crib, Holmes Country, 41 x 32 In.
$480

Cowan's Auctions

Quilt, Amish, Patchwork, Diamond Pattern, Rayon, Lancaster County, 82 x 84 In.
$325

Quilt, Appliqued, Star In Diamond, Yellow, Orange & Salmon, 1900s, 80 x 93 In.
$150

Hess Auction Group

Garth's Auctioneers & Appraisers

Quilt, Appliqued, Basket Of Flowers, 80 x 89 In.
$130

Quilt, Appliqued, Tulips, Red & Green, Red Border, Youth, 63 x 72 In.
$106

Hess Auction Group

Hess Auction Group

Quilt, Appliqued, Red, Green, Floral, 1800s, 77 x 95 In.
$246

Quilt, Patchwork, Irish Chain Pattern, Red Ground, Black & White Grid, 88 x 90 In.
$189

Copake Auction

Hess Auction Group

QUIMPER pottery has a long history. Tin-glazed, hand-painted pottery has been made in Quimper, France, since the late seventeenth century. The earliest firm was founded in 1708 by Pierre Bousquet. In 1782, Antoine de la Hubaudiere became the manager of the factory and the factory became known as the HB Factory (for Hubaudiere-Bousquet), de la Hubaudiere, or Grande Maison. Another firm, founded in 1772 by Francois Eloury, was known as Porquier. The third firm, founded by Guillaume Dumaine in 1778, was known as HR or Henriot Quimper. All three firms made similar pottery decorated with designs of Breton peasants and sea and flower motifs. The Eloury (Porquier) and Dumaine (Henriot) firms merged in 1913. Bousquet (HB) merged with the others in 1968. The group was sold to an American holding company in 1984. More changes followed, and in 2011 Jean-Pierre Le Goff became the owner and the name was changed to Henriot-Quimper.

	HR. *Quimper*	*HenRiot Quimper*
Quimper Early 19th century	Quimper c.1886–1926	Quimper 1926+

Bust, Queen, Lace Head Cover, Crown, Cone, Green, Yellow, White, 21 ½ In.		225
Coffee Set, Yellow Fleur-De-Lis, Blue Trim, Lobed Shape, Marked HB, 6-In. Pot, 8 Piece		275
Dish, Lid, Tray, Man, Woman, Field, Bushes, Blue Trim, Henriot, 8 ½ In.		84
Jar, Lid, Yellow Border, Cobalt Blue, Henriot, 4 ½ x 4 ¼ In.		84
Planter, Duck Shape, Yellow, Flowers, Signed, 10 In.		72
Tub, Tree, Blue & Yellow Arabesque Decoration, Marked HB, 1980s, 13 x 13 In.		458
Wall Pocket, Umbrella Shape, Faience, Marked Henriot Quimper 142, 13 In.	*illus*	92

RADFORD pottery was made by Alfred Radford in Broadway, Virginia; Tiffin and Zanesville, Ohio; and Clarksburg, West Virginia, from 1891 until 1912. *RADURA.* Jasperware, Ruko, Thera, Radura, and Velvety Art Ware were made. The jasperware resembles the famous Wedgwood ware of the same name. Another pottery named Radford worked in England and is not included here.

Jardiniere, Pedestal, Majolica, 3 Handles, Birds & Flowers Design, Marked, 41 ½ In.		501
Vase, Radura, 4 Handles, Molded Leaves & Flowers, 10 ⅛ In.	*illus*	439

RADIO broadcast receiving sets were first sold in New York City in 1910. They were used to pick up the experimental broadcasts of the day. The first commercial radios were made by Westinghouse Company for listeners of the experimental shows on KDKA Pittsburgh in 1920. Collectors today are interested in all early radios, especially those made of Bakelite plastic or decorated with blue mirrors. Figural advertising radios and transistor radios are also collected.

Addison, Catalin, Model 2, White Grate, 2 Dials, Brown, 10 ½ x 6 In.	*illus*	492
Crosley, Blue Catalin, Blue, White, Round Face Dial, 10 x 6 x 6 In.		183
Emerson, Model 5768, Molded Plywood, Bakelite, Metal, 1946, C. & R. Eames, 11 In.		250
Majestic, Model 60, Wood Case, Portable, 1930s, 10 x 14 x 9 In.		480
Microphone, Steel, Iron, Art Deco Base, Arched Top, W8GAD, c.1940, 42 In.		192
Shortwave, AM/FM, 65 Watts, Square, Push Buttons, Knobs, Brown, 1950s, 15 x 23 In.		1250
Sparton, Bluebird, Mirror Glass, Chromed Steel, Brass, Wood, Walter Teague, 1930s, 15 x 14 In.	*illus*	2250
Teletone, Model 111, Tube, Molded Plywood, Bakelite, Eames, c.1947, 12 In.		188
Trutone, Tube, Art Deco, Lacking Back Cover, 1939, 10 x 19 x 9 ¼ In.		60

RAILROAD enthusiasts collect any train memorabilia. Everything is wanted, from oilcans to whole train cars. The Chessie System has a store that sells many reproductions of its old dinnerware and uniforms.

Calendar, October, United States Express Co., Cardboard, 1907, 7 x 6 ½ In.		290
Celery Dish, B & O, Cheat River, Blue, 12 In.		30
Clock, Quarter Sawn Oak, Molded Door, Brass Button, Hanging, 31 x 37 In.		5082
Cup & Saucer, B & O, Thomas Viaduct, Blue, 2 Piece		49
Lantern, Conductor's, Brass, Etched Globe, Wire Guards, Open Sleeve, Blake's Patent 1852, 14 In.		2125
Lantern, Ruby Globe, L.S. & I. Ry, 15 ½ In.		275
Plate, Baltimore & Ohio Railroad, 10 ⅛ In.		767

Quimper, Wall Pocket, Umbrella Shape, Faience, Marked Henriot Quimper 142, 13 In.
$92

Cowan's Auctions

Radford, Vase, Radura, 4 Handles, Molded Leaves & Flowers, 10 ⅛ In.
$439

Thomaston Place Auction Galleries

Vintage Transistor Radios
Don't ignore vintage transistor radios (1955–63) if you see them at house sales or flea markets. Interest in all kinds of radios is growing and the supply of old radios is shrinking.

Radio, Addison, Catalin, Model 2, White Grate, 2 Dials, Brown, 10 ½ x 6 In.
$492

Morphy Auctions

Radio, Sparton, Bluebird, Mirror Glass, Chromed Steel, Brass, Wood, Walter Teague, 1930s, 15 x 14 In. $2,250

Rago Arts and Auction Center

Reamer, Ceramic, Country Cottage, Citrus, Juice, Lid, 1940s, 6½ In. $28

Ruby Lane

Red Wing, Figurine, Bulldog, Chestnut Brown Glaze, c.1895, 6½ x 8¾ In. $540

Rich Penn Auctions

Platter, B & O, Thomas Viaduct, Blue, 8 In.	147
Sign, Jackson 10 Miles, Lollipop Shape, Mounting Pipe, 14 x 28 In.	577
Sign, No Spitting On Stations, Platforms, Approaches, 500 Dollar Fine, Porcelain, 5 x 18 In.	1150
Sign, Pennsylvania RR, W, Train Whistle, Iron, Orange, Black, 1910s, 16 x 16 In.	650
Sign, Railway Express Agency, Porcelain, Red Ground, Black Letters, 49 x 49 In.	638
Sign, Texas Pacific, Teepee, Porcelain, Metal Ring, 42 In.	9600
Sign, Union Pacific System, Overland Route, Porcelain, Shield Shape, 38 x 42 In.	3132
Syrup, Canadian Pacific Railway, Attached Tray, Silver Plate, 1970s, 5 x 4 In.	71

RAZORS were used in ancient Egypt and subsequently wherever shaving was in fashion. The metal razor used in America until about 1870 was made in Sheffield, England. After 1870, machine-made hollow-ground razors were made in Germany or America. Plastic or bone handles were popular. The razor was often sold in a set of seven, one for each day of the week. The set was often kept by the barber who shaved the well-to-do man each day in the shop.

Bakelite Handle, Injector, Schick, 1930s	32
Bakelite Handle, Straight, Solingen, Germany	225
Celluloid Handle, Straight, Sheffield, Wade & Butcher, 6½ In.	50
Double Bladed, Brass, Gem Junior, Brooklyn, New York	17
Lucite Handle, Straight, Litt's, 1912	58
Plastic Handle, Amber, Straight, Red Injun No. 101, H. Boker & Co., Box, 6 In.	34
Slanted Head, Chrome Case, Hoffritz, Germany, 1940s	80
Twinplex Safety, Chromed Case, Purple Satin Lining, c.1920	48

REAMERS, or juice squeezers, have been known since 1767, although most of those collected today date from the twentieth century. Figural reamers are among the most prized.

Ceramic, Clown, Figural, Blue, Yellow, Ruffled Collar, Japan, c.1930, 5½ x 5⅜ In.	58
Ceramic, Country Cottage, Citrus, Juice, Lid, 1940s, 6½ In. *illus*	28
Ceramic, Santa Claus, Sombrero Style Hat, 1980s, 7½ x 6 In.	20
Ceramic, Yellow, Pink Roses, Brown Trim, Japan, c.1940, 5 x 7 In.	24
Glass, Clear, Ribbed, Footed, Federal Glass, 8 x 6 x 4 In.	12
Glass, Vertical Panels, Green, Anchor Hocking, Spout, Handle, 1940s	25
Plastic, Turquoise, Lustroware, 1950, 8 In.	12
Porcelain, Lemon, Yellow, Goebel, 2 Piece	38
Silver, Gold Wash, Loop Handle, Marked Fuchs, 1½ x 4¾ x 4¼ In.	550

RECORDS have changed size and shape through the years. The cylinder-shaped phonograph record for use with the early Edison models was made about 1889. Disc records were first made by 1894, the double-sided disc by 1904. High-fidelity records were first issued in 1944, the first vinyl disc in 1946, the first stereo record in 1958. The 78 RPM became the standard in 1926 but was discontinued in 1957. In 1932, the first 33⅓ RPM was made but was not sold commercially until 1948. In 1949, the 45 RPM was introduced. Compact discs became available in the U.S. in 1982 and many companies began phasing out the production of phonograph records. Vinyl records are popular again. People claim the sound is better on a vinyl recording, and new recordings are being made. Some collectors want vinyl picture records. Vintage albums are collected for their cover art as well as for the fame of the artist and the music.

Beatles, Love Me Do, P.S. I Love You, Tollie Records, 45 RPM	8
Bill Haley, Burn That Candle, Decca, 78 RPM	22
Chipmunks, Christmas With The Chipmunks, 1962, 78 RPM	9
Fats Domino, Here Comes Fats, Vol. 1, 1950s	26
Gene Autry, Columbia Historical Edition, Vinyl	15
Jack Wyatt Trio, Jazz Texas Style, 1984	18
Lady & The Tramp, 1962, 78 RPM	12
Liberace, Silver Anniversary Collection, 1976, 5 Records	35
Maynard Ferguson, Gonna Fly Now, Columbia Records, 45 RPM	15

Mister Rogers, Won't You Be My Neighbor, 33⅓ RPM, 1968		28
Oklahoma, Rodgers & Hammerstein, c.1955, 78 RPM		10
Ray Stevens, Woosh, Barnaby Records Inc., 1974, 33⅓ RPM		14
Wizard Of Oz, Read Along Book, Walt Disney, 1972, 7 x 7 In.		12

RED WING POTTERY of Red Wing, Minnesota, was a firm started in 1878. The company first made utilitarian pottery, including stoneware jugs and canning jars. In 1906, three companies combined to make the Red Wing Union Stoneware Company and began producing flowerpots, vases, and dinnerware. Art pottery was introduced in 1926. The name of the company was changed to Red Wing Potteries in 1936. Many dinner sets and vases were made before the company closed in 1967. R. Gillmer bought the company in 1967 and operated it as a retail business. The name was changed again, to Red Wing Pottery. The retail business closed in 2015. Red Wing Stoneware Company was founded in 1987. It was sold to new owners in 2013. They bought Red Wing Pottery and combined the two companies to become Red Wing Stoneware & Pottery. The company makes stoneware crocks, jugs, mugs, bowls, and other items with cobalt blue designs. Rumrill pottery made by the Red Wing Pottery for George Rumrill is listed in its own category. For more prices, go to kovels.com.

Beige Fleck, Relish, 4 Sections, 12 In.		24
Beige Fleck, Relish, 5 Sections, 12½ In.		32
Beige Fleck, Server, Meat, 12 In.		21
Blossom Time, Tureen, Lid, 8¼ x 12 In.		80
Bob White, Bowl, Vegetable, Divided, 14 In.		21
Bob White, Gravy Boat, & Lid, 5½ x 9 In.		28
Bob White, Server, Beverage, Lid, 15 In.		90
Bob White, Server, Hors D'Oeuvre		42
Brittany, Plate, Bread & Butter, 6 In.		9
Brittany, Plate, Salad, 7¼ In.		12
Brittany, Saucer		8
Capistrano, Bowl, Vegetable, 11½ In.		43
Crackle Glaze, Vase, Yellow, 2 Female Nudes For Handles, Marked, 11 In.		354
Damask, Pepper Shaker, 5 Holes		9
Damask, Sugar		15
Dancing Nymphs, Vase, Yellow, 9 In.		59
Figurine, Bulldog, Chestnut Brown Glaze, c.1895, 6½ x 8¾ In.	*illus*	540
Lute Song, Plate, Dinner, Hand Painted, 10½ In.		18
Lute Song, Tray, Tidbit, 10⅜ In.		35
Nokomis, Vase, Variegated Glaze, Marked, 12½ In.		413
Pepe, Bowl, Vegetable, Divided, 12½ x 6 In.		68
Stoneware, Fruit Jar, Stone Mason, Cream Glaze, Black Transfer, Zinc Screw Lid, Qt.		115
Tampico, Bowl, Cereal, 6½ In.		21
Tampico, Creamer, 4 In.		18
Tampico, Soup, Dish, 7¾ In.		22
Tip Toe, Bowl, Fruit, 5¼ In.		8
Tip Toe, Plate, Dinner, 11 In.		11
Turtle Dove, Salt & Pepper		58

REDWARE is a hard, red stoneware that has been made for centuries and continues to be made. The term is also used to describe any common clay pottery that is reddish in color. American redware was first made about 1625.

Bank, 3 Tiers, Hand, Small Chip, 10 In.		71
Bank, Apple, Red Paint, c.1800, 3 In.		108
Bear, Standing, Looking Down, 10 x 6 In.		93
Bottle, Lead Glaze, Multi-Ringed Body, Tapered Neck, Orange Green, c.1830, 5 x 3 In.		644
Bowl, Deep, Tapered Edge Rim, Slip, Green Accent, Tulip, Banded, Shooner, 13 x 2 In.		260
Bowl, Distelfink Bird, Freehand, Twig, Flowers, Banded Rim, C. Ned Foltz, 1976, 12 x 2 In.		95
Bowl, Milk, Slip Decorated, Molded Rim, Pennsylvania, 1800s, 11½ In.		153
Bowl, Mottled Glaze, Squared Rim, C.F. Bower, Bernville, Pa., 4 x 8 In.	*illus*	1121
Bust, Man, Incised Moustache & Hair, Green Glaze, c.1920, 5½ In.		84

Redware, Bowl, Mottled Glaze, Squared Rim, C.F. Bower, Bernville, Pa., 4 x 8 In. $1,121

Hess Auction Group

Redware, Figurine, Lion, Lead, Manganese, Coleslaw Hair, Lester Breininger, 1981, 8 x 10 In. $438

Jeffrey S. Evans

Redware, Platter, Yellow Slip, Coggle Wheel Edge, Pennsylvania, 1800s, 17½ In. $200

Hess Auction Group

Riviera, Green, Tidbit, 2 Tiers $86

Strawser Auction Group

Rookwood, Plaque, Scenic, Winter Enchantment, Vellum Glaze, S. Coyne, Frame, 1915, 11 In.
$5,625

Rago Arts and Auction Center

Rookwood, Tile, Tall Ship, Raised Outline, Faience, Square, Frame, Stamped, c.1910, 12 In.
$875

Rago Arts and Auction Center

Rookwood, Vase, Blue Matte Glaze, Raised Heads, 1900, 2 x 5½ In.
$240

Eldred's Auctioneers and Appraisers

Charger, Blue, Stencil, Lovebirds, Tulip, Foltz, Incised Lancaster Co. Hand Dug Clay, 1977, 14 In....	90
Churn, Barrel Shape, Slip Decorated, Dots, Leaves, 12½ In.	23
Churn, Slip Decorated, Flowers, Leaves, 10 x 13 In.	11
Crock, Apple Butter, Mottled, Pennsylvania, 1800s, 5½ In.	177
Crock, Green Glaze, Spots, On Half, Galena, 13 In.	1680
Eggcup, Lead Glaze, Manganese Mottling, John Bell, c.1860, 2 x 2 In.	468
Figurine, Dog, Spaniel, Seated, Free Front Legs, Mottled Glaze, Galena, 9 In.	420
Figurine, Lion, Lead, Manganese, Coleslaw Hair, Lester Breininger, 1981, 8 x 10 In. .... *illus*	438
Flowerpot, Mottled, Multicolor, Double Coggle Wheel Rim, 1885-89, 12 x 10 In.	1888
Jar, Apple Butter, Mottled, Bulbous, Shouldered, Handle, Pennsylvania, 1800s, 6 In.	142
Jar, Galena Glaze, Butter, Orange, Green, Spots, Tapers, 5¾ In.	1620
Jar, Galena Glaze, Yellow Over Green & Orange, 1 Gal. Script, Illinois, 1850-1900, 7½ In.........	960
Jug, Bulbous, Speckled Copper Glaze, Incised Lines Around Top Lip, 1800s, ½ Gal., 8 x 6 In.	330
Jug, Collar Rim, Tooled Body, Applied Strap Handles, Wood Lid, 8¼ In.	472
Jug, Great Road Style, Runny Paint Rock Glaze, Handle, 1800s, 8 In.	185
Jug, Green Glaze, Bulbous, North Carolina, Marked, c.1920, 9 In.	106
Jug, Molded Handle, Slip Band, Green Feather, Shooner, 1998, 6½ x 8¾ In.	210
Jug, Runny Green Amber Glaze, Manganese Daubs, Applied Handle, c.1850, 6½ In....	375
Jug, Tooled Spout, Rounded Lip, Applied Ribbed Handle, 9 In.	649
Pitcher, Bulbous, Rounded Collar, Flared Spout, Brown Glazed, 7¼ In.	295
Pitcher, Covered, Reddish Glaze, Squat, Handle, 1800s, 6 In.	71
Pitcher, Manganese Glaze, Molded Handle, c.1810, 5 In.	265
Plate, Indigenous Figure, Brown, Asymmetrical, Signed, Kalahari, Japan, 1900s, 9¾ In.........	13
Plate, Sgraffito, Glazed, Spread Wing Eagle, Yellow, Green, Brown, c.1850, 7⅞ In.	767
Plate, Sgraffito, Glazed, Yellow, Brown, Green, Figures, Fife, Drum, c.1880, 8 In......	649
Plate, Slip Decoration, New Jersey, 1800, 3⅞ In.	5000
Plate, Yellow Slip Decoration, Coggle Wheel Edge, c.1800, 9¾ In.	265
Plate, Yellow, Green, Brown, Tulip, c.1810, 7⅞ In.	826
Plate, Yellow, Patriotic Heart On Eagle, Sprig, Arrows, Spatter Rim, Russell Henry, 1973, 9½ In.....	70
Platter, Slip Glaze, Cheap & Good, 1800s, 12½ x 9½ In...........................	250
Platter, Yellow Slip, Coggle Wheel Edge, Pennsylvania, 1800s, 17½ In. .... *illus*	200
Pot, Base, Beige, Southwestern Style, 1900s, 20 In.	18
Vase, Dragon, Chinese, 9½ In..	100
Vase, Indian, Owl, 1900s, 5 In.	25

REGOUT, *see Maastricht category.*

 RICHARD was the mark used on acid-etched cameo glass vases, bowls, night-lights, and lamps made by the Austrian company Loetz after 1918. The pieces were very similar to the French cameo glasswares made by Daum, Galle, and others.

Vase, Blue Flowers, Vines, Cameo, Yellow Ground, 1920, 11 In.	185
Vase, Cobalt, Blue Violets, Cameo, Bright Orange Ground, Cameo, Signed, 4 In.	130
Vase, Red Berries, Vines, Cameo, Shaded, Cream Ground, 1920, 11 In...................	185
Vase, Slender, Cameo, Dark Red Flowers & Vines, Frosted Pink, Cameo, Signed, 8½ In.	177

 RIDGWAY pottery has been made in the Staffordshire district in England since 1808 by a series of companies with the name Ridgway. Ridgway became part of Royal Doulton in the 1960s. The transfer-design dinner sets are the most widely known product. Other pieces of Ridgway may be listed under Flow Blue.

Casserole, Lid, Simlay Pattern, Square Footed Base, c.1880, 11 x 8 In..................	545
Plate, Men In Boat, Cottage, Blue Transfer, c.1840, 7½ In.	45
Tureen, Lid, Palestine, Blue Transfer, 13½ x 9½ In.	425

RIFLES *that are firearms made after 1900 are not listed in this book. BB guns and air rifles are listed in the Toy category.*

 RIVIERA dinnerware was made by the Homer Laughlin Co. of Newell, West Virginia, from 1938 to 1950. The pattern was similar in coloring and in mood to Fiesta and Harlequin. The Riviera plates and cup handles were square. For more prices, go to kovels.com.

R

Floral, Eggcup, 2 ¼ In.		12
Green, Jug, Lid		49
Green, Tidbit, 2 Tiers	*illus*	86
Ivory & Turquoise, Bowl, Footed, 12 In.		79
Red, Bowl, Vegetable, 8 ¼ In.		15
Yellow, Creamer, 6 x 3 ⅛ x 2 ¾ In		9

ROCKINGHAM, in the United States, is a pottery with a brown glaze that resembles tortoiseshell. It was made from 1840 to 1900 by many American potteries. Mottled brown Rockingham wares were first made in England at the Rockingham factory. Other types of ceramics were also made by the English firm. Related pieces may be listed in the Bennington category.

Bank, Piggy, Figural, Streak Glaze, Top Slot, c.1880, 4 x 6 In.	365
Cuspidor, Brown Drips, Over Cream, 6 ½ x 13 ½ In.	38
Pitcher, Raised Arm, Hammer, Inscribed Protection To American Industry, 9 In.	92

ROGERS, *see John Rogers category.*

ROOKWOOD pottery was made in Cincinnati, Ohio, beginning in 1880. All of this art pottery is marked, most with the famous flame mark. The *R* is reversed and placed back to back with the letter *P*. Flames surround the letters. After 1900, a Roman numeral was added to the mark to indicate the year. The company went bankrupt in 1941. It was bought and sold several times after that. For several years various owners tried to revive the pottery, but by 1967 it was out of business. The name and some of the molds were bought by a collector in Michigan in 1982. In 2004, a group of Cincinnati investors bought the company and 3,700 original molds, the name, and trademark. Pottery was made in Cincinnati again beginning in 2006. Today the company makes architectural tile, art pottery, and special commissions. New items and a few old items with slight redesigns are made. Contemporary pieces are being made to complement the dinnerware line designed by John D. Wareham in 1921. Pieces are marked with the RP mark and a Roman numeral for the four-digit date. Mold numbers on pieces made since 2006 begin with 10000.

ROOKWOOD 1882	**RP**	(flame mark)
Rookwood 1882–1886	Rookwood 1886	Rookwood 1901

Bowl, Fern, Reticulated, Green Matte Glaze, 1912, 3 x 8 In.		531
Bowl, Flowers, Lorinda Epply, 1924, 13 In.		502
Bowl, Ginko Leaves, Brown Matte Glaze, 1910, 2 ¼ x 6 ½ In.		1000
Box, Lid, Moorish, Stylized Leaves, Square, Signed, Lorinda Epply, 1926, 5 In.		325
Cup, Twin Handle, Pilsner, Red Glaze, 1949, 8 In.		125
Figurine, Dog, Boxer, Standing, 10 ½ x 3 ¾ In.		570
Jar, Green Matte Glaze, Pierced Flowers, Interior Lid, 1931, 4 In.		118
Jug, Stopper, Indian Male, Portrait, Adeliza Sehon, Marked, 1900, 7 In.		3658
Paperweight, Baby Elephant, Black Glaze, 4 In.		142
Paperweight, Bird, Dark Over Light Blue Glaze, c.1927, 4 In.		1298
Paperweight, Coromandel Glaze, Goat Figure, Louise Abel, 1937, Marked, 6 In.		413
Paperweight, Dark Over Light Blue, Marked W. McDonald, Cast 1928, 3 In.		295
Paperweight, Dog, Dark Blue Glazed Drip, Marked, Cast In 1925, 5 In.		295
Plaque, Scenic, Evening Glow, Vellum Glaze, L. Asbury, Frame, 5 x 9 In.		1900
Plaque, Scenic, Pond, Field, Tall Narrow Trees, Ed Diers, 1912, 3 ¾ x 7 ½ In.		3000
Plaque, Scenic, Pond, Trees, Pale Blue, Gray, Vellum Glaze, 9 x 7 In.		3125
Plaque, Scenic, Trees, Hills, Vellum Glaze, Frame, F. Rothenbusch, 9 x 15 In.		3000
Plaque, Scenic, Winter Enchantment, Vellum Glaze, S. Coyne, Frame, 1915, 11 In.	*illus*	5625
Sign, Blue Rook On Branch, Name Of Pottery On Sign, 1915, 8 ½ x 4 In.		3540
Tile, Frieze, Raised Outline, Cottage, Trees, Clouds, c.1910, 12 x 60 In., 5 Piece		5000

Rookwood, Vase, Butterflies, Gold Dolphin Handles, Limoges Style, A. Valentien, 1883, 24 In.
$3,540

Humler & Nolan

Rookwood, Vase, Fish, Iris Glaze, Swollen, Edward Hurley, 1906, 6 ¼ x 5 In.
$3,000

Rago Arts and Auction Center

Rookwood, Vase, High Gloss Brown Glaze, Flowers, 3 Flames, Marked On Base, 1883, 5 ½ In.
$360

Garth's Auctioneers & Appraisers

R

Rookwood, Vase, Tulips, Iris Glaze,
K. Shirayamadani, 1907, 14 ½ x 6 In.
$6,875

Rago Arts and Auction Center

Rookwood, Vase, Turquoise Matte
Glaze, Yellow Flowers, Leaves, Louise
Abel, 1933, 7 In.
$393

Rachel Davis Fine Arts

Rookwood, Wall Pocket, Calla Lily, Blue
Green, Marked, 1920s, 16 ¼ In.
$390

Cowan's Auctions

Tile, Grapes & Gourds In Relief, Multicolor, 10 x 28 In.	750
Tile, Tall Ship, Raised Outline, Faience, Square, Frame, Stamped, c.1910, 12 In. .... *illus*	875
Tile, Windmill, Green, Yellow & Tan Matte Glaze, Square, Label, Frame, 1905, 6 In.	900
Trivet, Footed, Rabbits Seated Under Flowering Tree, Blue Matte Glaze, 1916, 5 ¾ x 5 ¾ In.	264
Trivet, Southern Belle, Parasol, 1922, 5 ¾ x 5 ¾ In.	325
Urn, Unicorn, Figures, c.1930, 25 ¾ x 18 In.	3250
Vase, Blackbird, Vellum Glaze, Tapered, Swollen Neck, Signed, Sallie Coyne, 9 ¼ In.	650
Vase, Blue Matte Glaze, Raised Heads, 1900, 2 x 5 ½ In. .... *illus*	240
Vase, Blues & Cream, Flowers, Cylindrical, Handles, Footed, 1937, 8 ½ In.	1320
Vase, Bud, Cobalt Blue, 1919, 6 ⅖ In.	75
Vase, Butterflies, Gold Dolphin Handles, Limoges Style, A. Valentien, 1883, 24 In. .... *illus*	3540
Vase, Caramel & Mottled Blue Gray, Matte Glaze, Embossed Stylized Butterflies, 1900s, 7 In. ...	219
Vase, Carnelian, Pink 11, 15 In.	562
Vase, Cream, Flowers, Signed On Bottom, 1939, 6 In.	480
Vase, Daffodils, Standard Glaze, Albert R. Valentien, 1884, 1890, 11 x 4 In.	1243
Vase, Double Vellum, Blue, Daisies, Flowers, Kataro Shirayamadani, 1932, 6 ¼ x 5 In.	875
Vase, Double Vellum, Poppies, Kataro Shirayamadani, 1944, 9 x 3 In.	937
Vase, Fish, Iris Glaze, Swollen, Edward Hurley, 1906, 6 ¼ x 5 In. .... *illus*	3000
Vase, Flowers & Birds, Stylized, Vellum Glaze, Lorinda Epply, 1916, 15 ½ x 7 ½ In.	687
Vase, Flowers, Fruit, Branches, Purple, Brown, Yellow, Green, K. Shirayamandani, c.1925, 8 In.	1210
Vase, Flowers, Pink, Blue Ground, Elizabeth Lincoln, Marked, 1928, 14 In.	1062
Vase, Flowers, Raised, Blue & White Glaze, Bulbous, Stamp 6761, 1945, 6 x 7 In.	236
Vase, Flying Geese, Iris Glaze, Oval, Lenore Asbury, 1909, 7 x 5 In.	350
Vase, Fruiting Viburnum Branches, Kataro Shirayamadani, 1889, 15 x 8 In.	1000
Vase, Gazelles, Art Deco, Bowl Shape, Signed, W. Hentschel, 1929, 5 ¼ x 6 In.	500
Vase, Geometric Design, Pink Matte Glaze, Marked Under Base, 1919, 8 ¼ x 4 In.	136
Vase, Gray Blue & Peach, Primroses, Signed On Bottom, 1905, 8 ½ In.	480
Vase, High Gloss Brown Glaze, Flowers, 3 Flames, Marked On Base, 1883, 5 ½ In. .... *illus*	360
Vase, Iris, Tapering Light Blue Glaze, Darkens To Black, Constance Baker, 1903, 8 ¾ In.	1875
Vase, Jewel, Prunus Branches, Katherine Van Horne, 1917, 7 x 7 In.	437
Vase, Koi Fish Over Waves, Stylized, Green Matte Glaze, Cylindrical, 1906, 7 ¼ In.	175
Vase, Landscape, Lake, Trees, Vellum, Ed Diers, 1931, 10 ½ x 5 ½ In.	1625
Vase, Lilac, Vellum Glaze, Bulbous, Squat, Ed Diers, 1908, 6 ½ x 8 ½ In.	550
Vase, Maroon, White Drip Glaze, 6 ¾ In.	75
Vase, Orchid, Vellum Glaze, Flared, Folded-In Rim, Janet Harris, 1928, 5 ½ x 6 In.	200
Vase, Oval Shape, Scenic Vellum, Waterside Landscape, Edward T. Hurley, 1938, 7 ⅝ x 4 ½ In.	1680
Vase, Parrots, Wisteria, Flat Rim, c.1924, 15 x 7 In.	1750
Vase, Red, Blue, Flowers Encircle Shoulder, Elizabeth Lincoln, 1923, 5 In.	354
Vase, Roses, Blue, Cream, Iris Gaze, Harriet Wilcox, 1901, 5 x 5 In.	687
Vase, Scenic, Craquelure Finish, Vellum, Incised FR Cypher, 1915, 9 x 5 In.	300
Vase, Scenic, Shouldered, Vellum, Fred Rothenbusch, 1922, 6 In.	2360
Vase, Starfish, Blue Matte Glaze, Reticulated Band, Signed, J.D. Wareham, 6 In.	950
Vase, Tulips, Iris Glaze, K. Shirayamadani, 1907, 14 ½ x 6 In. .... *illus*	6875
Vase, Turquoise Matte Glaze, Yellow Flowers, Leaves, Louise Abel, 1933, 7 In. .... *illus*	393
Vase, Water Lilies, Iris Glaze, Sara Sax, c.1908, 10 x 4 ¾ In.	1875
Vase, Wax Matte Glaze, Impressed Artist Monogram, Margaret Helen MacDonald, 1924, 7 x 3 In.	509
Vase, Yellow, Paneled Sides, Leaves, Grapes, 1945, 6 ½ In.	60
Wall Pocket, Calla Lily, Blue Green, Marked, 1920s, 16 ¼ In. .... *illus*	390
Wall Pocket, Calla Lily, Green Matte, 16 ¼ x 6 ½ In.	390
Wall Pocket, Taupe Crow, Leaves, Blue, Green, Faience, 1916, 14 x 6 In.	593

Rörstrand **RORSTRAND** was established near Stockholm, Sweden, in 1726. By the nineteenth century Rorstrand was making English-style earthenware, bone china, porcelain, ironstone china, and majolica. The three-crown mark has been used since 1884. Rorstrand became part of the Hackman Group in 1991. Hackman was bought by Iittala Group in 2004. Fiskars Corporation bought Iittala in 2007 and Rorstrand is now a brand owned by Fiskars.

Pedestal, Square Top, Masks, Majolica, Stamped, Impressed Marks, c.1910, 45 x 12 In.... *illus*	976
Vase, Blue, Uniform Vertical Lines Run From Rim To Base, Nylund, Sweden, 1930s, 5 ¾ In.	80
Vase, Cylindrical, Tapered, Vertically Striated, Blue, Nylund, Marked, c.1960, 17 ½ In.	295

Vase, Discus Thrower, Brown, Flambe, Glazed & Gilt Stoneware, 1930s, 11 x 6 In	2000
Vase, Flared Bottle Shape, Mottled Gold, Blue Matte Finish, Incised Sweden, 1950, 8 5/8 In	150
Vase, Glazed, Blue, Mottled, Carl-Harry Stalhane, Paper Label, 1950s, 9 x 5 In. *illus*	750
Vase, Impressed Design Around Rim, Smooth Blue Matte Glaze, Deep Rose Highlights, 12 In	200
Vase, Lid, Adam & Eve, Glazed, Gilt, Stalhane, Nylund, c.1940, 9 x 10 In. *illus*	1500
Vase, Lindstrum, Fall Maple Leaves, Cobalt Blue Shoulder Band, White Body, 16 In	250
Vase, Sailors, Brown, Beige, Flambe, Glazed & Gilt Stoneware, 1930s, 10 x 7 In	1625
Vase, Swollen Neck, Base, Smooth Blue Matte Glaze, Nylund, Incised, 12 In	236

ROSALINE, *see Steuben category.*

ROSE BOWLS were popular during the 1880s. Rose petals were kept in the open bowl to add fragrance to a room, a popular idea in a time of limited personal hygiene. The glass bowls were made with crimped tops, which kept the petals inside. Many types of Victorian art glass were made into rose bowls.

Cranberry Opalescent, Ruffled Rim, White Rim, Star Pattern, 3 1/2 x 4 1/2 In	50
Green Glass, Pink Flowers, Light Green Serrated Leaves, 4 x 4 1/2 In	23
Satin Glass, Pink, 4 1/2 In	12

ROSE CANTON china is similar to Rose Mandarin and Rose Medallion, except that no people or birds are pictured in the decoration. It was made in China during the nineteenth and twentieth centuries in greens, pinks, and other colors.

Bowl, Butter, Cover, Strainer, Painted Porcelain, Traditional Symbols, 1950s, 6 1/2 x 3 In	153
Bowl, Scalloped Rim, Gilt Border, Thousand Butterflies Design, 1800s, 5 x 9 1/2 x 9 1/2 In. *illus*	690
Bowl, Stand, Shallow Dish, Hand Painted, 1950s, 8 1/2 x 1 1/8 In	47
Ginger Jar, Hand Painted, Signed, Vintage, 7 1/2 In	30
Tazza, Oval, Hand Painted Highlights, Flower, Butterfly, 1900s, 10 x 7 1/4 x 1 3/4 In	47

ROSE MANDARIN china is similar to Rose Canton and Rose Medallion. If the panels in the design picture only people and not birds, it is Rose Mandarin.

Bowl, 2 Reserves, People, Landscapes, Red, Purple, Blue, Green, 10 In	1210
Bowl, Scene Around Exterior, Segmented Scenes On Interior, 1800s, 7 x 16 In	1560
Cider Jug, Women, Girls 1 Side, Man, Boys Other, Woven Ribbon Handle, 1800s, 9 x 10 x 7 In	360
Punch Bowl, Court, Carp, Naval Officer, Gilt Chain Border, c.1820, 6 1/2 x 16 In	5500
Punch Bowl, Figures, Landscape, Stippled, 4 1/2 x 10 1/4 In. *illus*	1800
Vase, Court Scenes, Gilding In Hair, Butterflies, 1800s, 8 x 4 3/4 In	225
Vase, Ornate Gilt Handles, Lobed Feet, Court Scenes, 1800s, 6 3/4 x 3 x 2 In., Pair	390
Vase, Scrolling Gilt Bronze Base, Molded Bronze Lilies, 37 In	938

ROSE MEDALLION china was made in China during the nineteenth and twentieth centuries. It is a distinctive design with four or more panels of decoration around a central medallion that includes a bird or a peony. The panels show birds and people. The background is a design of tree peonies and leaves. Pieces are colored in greens, pinks, and other colors. It is similar to Rose Canton and Rose Mandarin.

Bowl, Alternating Panels, C-Scrolls, Birds, Butterflies, Flowers, 19 In	2125
Bowl, Birds, Flowers, Figures, c.1875, 15 In	326 to 850
Casserole, Lid, Roses, Birds, Butterflies, 1910s, 5 1/2 x 9 1/2 x 8 1/4 In	390
Jardiniere, Bulbous, Rolled Rim, Tooled, 1860-90, 15 x 12 In	360
Planter, Hexagonal, Blue, White, 14 In	185
Plate, 1900s, 3 In	50
Plate, Bird, Flowers, Butterfly, Wood Stand, Chinese Export, 1800s, 8 1/2 In	71
Platter, Oval, 6 Bird & Butterfly Panels, Central Well, 16 x 14 x 2 1/2 In	360
Punch Bowl, Birds, Flowers, c.1850, 16 In. *illus*	500
Punch Bowl, Gilt, Figures In Courtyards, Flowers, Butterflies, Birds, 1800s, 6 x 14 In. *illus*	960
Punch Bowl, Interior & Exterior Figural & Floral Cartouches, 7 x 16 In	500
Tazza, Oval, Shaped, Birds, People, Interior Rooms, 4 Reserves, Multicolor, 2 3/4 x 13 In	150

Rorstrand, Pedestal, Square Top, Masks, Majolica, Stamped, Impressed Marks, c.1910, 45 x 12 In.
$976

Neal Auction Co.

Rorstrand, Vase, Glazed, Blue, Mottled, Carl-Harry Stalhane, Paper Label, 1950s, 9 x 5 In.
$750

Rago Arts and Auction Center

Rorstrand, Vase, Lid, Adam & Eve, Glazed, Gilt, Stalhane, Nylund, c.1940, 9 x 10 In.
$1,500

Rago Arts and Auction Center

Rose Canton, Bowl, Scalloped Rim, Gilt Border, Thousand Butterflies Design, 1800s, 5 x 9 1/2 x 9 1/2 In.
$690

Garth's Auctioneers & Appraisers

Rose Mandarin, Punch Bowl, Figures, Landscape, Stippled, 4 1/2 x 10 1/4 In.
$1,800

Thomaston Place Auction Galleries

Rose Medallion, Punch Bowl, Birds, Flowers, c.1850, 16 In.
$500

Eldred's Auctioneers and Appraisers

TIP

When cleaning or repairing antiques, remember less is more.

Rose Medallion, Punch Bowl, Gilt, Figures In Courtyards, Flowers, Butterflies, Birds, 1800s, 6 x 14 In.
$960

Brunk Auctions

Teapot, Drum Shape, Flared Foot, Knop Finial, Birds, Figures, 10 In.	450
Tureen, Sauce, Roses, Flowers, Birds, Insects, Strapped Handles, 1800s, 6 x 8 x 5 1/2 In.	1055
Vase, Cylinder Form, c.1840, 9 1/2 In., Pair	390
Vase, Dragons, Ball, Villagers, Birds, Leaves, 9 1/4 In.	120

ROSE O'NEILL, *see Kewpie category.*

ROSE TAPESTRY porcelain was made by the Royal Bayreuth factory of Tettau, Germany, during the late nineteenth century. The surface of the porcelain was pressed against a coarse fabric while it was still damp, and the impressions remained on the finished porcelain. It looks and feels like a textured cloth. Very skillful reproductions are being made that even include a variation of the Royal Bayreuth mark, so be careful when buying.

Cake Plate, Reticulated, Gold Rim, c.1910, 10 In.	125
Creamer, Pinched Spout, Gold Handle, 6 3/4 In.	119
Hatpin Holder, Small Holes In Bottom, 4 1/2 In.	36
Pitcher, Roses, Daisies, Pinks, Greens, Tans, 4 In.	28
Pitcher, c.1880, 4 x 4 3/4 In.	395

ROSENTHAL porcelain was made at the factory established in Selb, Bavaria, in 1891. The factory is still making fine-quality tablewares and figurines. A series of Christmas plates was made from 1910. Other limited edition plates have been made since 1971. Rosenthal became part of the Arcturus Group in 2009.

Rosenthal China 1891–1904	Rosenthal China 1928	Rosenthal China 1948

Bowl, Pale Green, Ball Feet, 13 x 3 3/4 In.	110
Creamer, Jet Rose, 3 7/8 In.	18
Cup & Saucer, King Edward	42
Figurine, Dog, Weimaraner, Tracking, 1900s, 3 3/4 x 8 3/4 In. *illus*	120
Group, Guinea Fowl, Marked, 1920s, 11 1/2 In.	125
Sculpture, Discus Thrower, Ottmar Obermaier, Signed, 1931, 16 In. *illus*	1000
Vase, Portrait, Woman, Brunette, Trees, Gilt Highlights, 9 3/4 In.	504

ROSEVILLE POTTERY COMPANY was organized in Roseville, Ohio, in 1890. Another plant was opened in Zanesville, Ohio, in 1898. Many types of pottery were made until 1954. Early wares include Sgraffito, Olympic, and Rozane. Later lines were often made with molded decorations, especially flowers and fruit. Most pieces are marked *Roseville*. Many reproductions made in China have been offered for sale the past few years.

Roseville Pottery Company 1914–1930	Roseville Pottery Company 1935–1954	Roseville Pottery Company 1939–1953

Apple Blossom, Jardiniere, Pedestal, Green Ground, No. 303, 10 x 14 In.	472
Apple Blossom, Vase, Cornucopia, Green, Blue, Pink, Script Mark, 4 x 3 x 6 In.	71
Baneda, Vase, Double Handles, Purple Foot, 12 In.	500
Baneda, Vase, Green, Marked, 7 In.	236
Baneda, Vase, Handles, No. 598, Unmarked, 12 x 6 1/2 In.	236
Baneda, Vase, Pink, 8 In.	236
Basket, Wincraft, Azure Blue, Marked, 8 1/2 In.	125

R

Bittersweet, Planter, Ceramic, Yellow Body, Marked, 1900s, 14 x 4 In.		63
Bushberry, Ewer, Flaring Spout, Pierced Neck, Round Foot, c.1941, 10 In.		187
Columbine, Wall Pocket, Blue, Signed Reverse, 3¾ x 8 x 4 In.		147
Della Robbia, Vase, Roman Battle Scene, Curled Handles, Incised G.B., c.1910, 17 x 8 In.	*illus*	5625
Dogwood, Jardiniere, Pedestal, Green, 17 x 9 In.		325
Dogwood, Vase, Green Tones, 9 In.		120
Egypto, Vase, Green Matte Glaze, Marked, 10 In.		472
Futura, Candlestick, Aztec Women, Orange, Green, Brown, 4 In., Pair	*illus*	708
Futura, Sign, Dealer's, Rainbow, Green, Tan, Black Letters, 1½ x 6 In.		1416
Futura, Vase, Arches, Orange Brown Matte Glaze, 14 In.		650
Futura, Vase, Pink, 2 Poles, Unmarked, 4 x 6 x 2¼ In.		226
Futura, Vase, Shooting Star, 10 In.		110
Futura, Vase, Twist Shape, Green, Yellow, Orange, 6½ In.		142
Imperial II, Vase, Drizzled Lilac Glaze Over Turquoise, Marked, 5 In.		212
Jardiniere, Carved Stylized Trees & Landscape, Body Of Water, Pedestal, 1920, 10 x 12 In.		706
Magnolia, Jardiniere, Pedestal, 9¾ x 15 In.		354
Monticello, Vase, Handles, Unmarked, 7 x 6½ In.		177
Monticello, Vase, Unmarked, 5¼ x 5½ In.		136
Nasturtium, Vase, Cream, Brown, Green, White, 2 Handles, 8 In.		594
Pauleo, Vase, Orange, Rust, Brown, c.1910, 6½ In.		395
Pine Cone, Jar, Brown Sand, 14 x 12 In.		295
Pine Cone, Jardiniere, Green Ground, 8½ x 11½ In.		106
Pine Cone, Urn, Green Rim, Brown Ground, Molded Handles, c.1935, 9⅛ In.		128
Pine Cone, Vase, 8 In.		172
Pine Cone, Vase, Brown, Handles, 6⅜ In.		225
Pine Cone, Vase, Green, 15 x 8 In.		354
Pink Carnelian II, Vase, 15 In.	*illus*	549
Planter, Rectangular Form, Blue, Green, Orange Matte Glaze, 1934, 5 x 15 x 5¼ In.		984
Primrose, Umbrella Stand, Incised Mark, 21 x 12 In		384
Raymor, Plate, Dinner, Gray Matte, 12 In.		28
Rozane, Pitcher, Red & Gold, Cherries, Leaves, Marked, c.1910, 10½ In.		385
Rozane, Vase, Olympic, Hours Taking Horses From Juno's Car, Red, Greek Key, c.1910, 14 x 11 In.		4687
Silhouette, Vase, Kneeling Nude Sides, Red, Marked, Crisp Mold, 10 In.		170
Stand, Blended Stork, Majolica Style Glaze, Figural Stork, Cattails Body, Leafy Design, 18 x 8½ In.		177
Sunflower, Jardiniere, Pedestal, Multicolor, 1925, 10 In.		1125
Sunflower, Vase, 1930, 9 In.		531
Sunflower, Vase, 4½ In.		266
Sunflower, Vase, Cylindrical, Swollen, 10½ x 6 In.		450
Sunflower, Vase, Original Sticker Under Base, 10 x 8 In.		706
Teasel, Vase, Light Blue Thistle Design, 15 x 8½ In		148
Topeo, Blue, Green, Pink, Marked, 15 In.		708
Tulip, Vase, Mottled Bisque Ground, Incised Yellow Flowers & Bud, Bottle Shape, 11 In.		325
Vase, 2 Handles, Pink, Purple, & Green Matte Glaze, 1934, 15 In.		400
Vase, 4-Sided, Neck Rising Up, Ball Shape, Burnt Orange, Brown Matte Glaze, 1934, 12 In.		308
Vase, Geometric Shape, 2-Tier Base, Blue To Ivory, Matte Glaze, 1934, 9½ In.		7380
Vase, Nude Patterns, Signed R, 11 x 5½ In.		424
Vase, Pedestal, 2 Handles, Unmarked, Cream Tones, Pink & Yellow Flowers, 9¾ In.		72
Vase, Red Silhouette Fan Designed, Base Signed, 7½ x 8 x 2¾ In.		254
Vase, Round Form, 2 Stylized Sea Gulls, Blue, Peach, Black, Green Matte Glaze, 1934, 10¼ x 4⅜ In.		369
Vista, Vase, Green, Trees, Unmarked, 10 x 12 In.		266
Wall Pocket, Panel, Nude, Standing, Tree, Blue RV Ink Stamp, 7¼ In.		200
Water Lily, Umbrella Stand, Fish, Majolica, 21 In.		561
Windsor, Vase, Blue Ground, Green Trees, Handles, 7 In.		384
Wisteria, Vase, Brown, Green Leaves, Lavender Grapes, Marked, 12¼ In.		999
Woodland, Vase, Irises Front & Back, Stippled Biscuit Ground, Applied Rozane Ware Logo, 8¾ In.		200

ROWLAND & MARSELLUS COMPANY is part of a mark that appears on historical Staffordshire dating from the late nineteenth and early twentieth centuries. *Rowland & Marsellus* is the mark used by an American importing company in New York City. The company worked from 1893 to about 1937.

Rosenthal, Figurine, Dog, Weimaraner, Tracking, 1900s, 3¾ x 8¾ In.
$120

Cowan's Auctions

Rosenthal, Sculpture, Discus Thrower, Ottmar Obermaier, Signed, 1931, 16 In.
$1,000

Rago Arts and Auction Center

Roseville, Della Robbia, Vase, Roman Battle Scene, Curled Handles, Incised G.B., c.1910, 17 x 8 In.
$5,625

Rago Arts and Auction Center

R

369

Roseville, Futura, Candlestick, Aztec Women, Orange, Green, Brown, 4 In., Pair
$708

Humler & Nolan

Retired Plates

When a limited edition figurine or plate is "retired," it is no longer made and will never be made again. When the figurine or plate is "suspended," it is not currently in production but may be at a later date.

Roseville, Pink Carnelian II, Vase, 15 In.
$549

Rago Arts and Auction Center

R

Some of the pieces may have been made by the British Anchor Pottery Co. of Longton, England, for export to a New York firm. Many American views were made. Of special interest to collectors are the plates with rolled edges, usually blue and white.

Bowl, Courtship Scene, Brown & White, 7 ¼ In.		60
Plate, Beauty Spots Of Niagara Falls, N.Y., Green, 6 In.		38
Plate, Cornell University, Flow Blue, 10 ⅛ In.		75
Plate, Great American Poets, Cobalt Blue, 10 In.		175
Plate, Great Poets, Blue, 7 Portraits, 10 In.		33
Plate, Landing Of Hendrick Hudson, Flow Blue, Rolled Edge, 10 In.		89
Plate, Longfellow, Blue & White, Rolled Edge, 10 In.		100
Plate, Porfirio Diaz, Mexican City Scenes, Flow Blue, c.1900, 10 In.		110
Plate, Theodore Roosevelt 26th President Of The U.S., c.1901, 10 In.	*illus*	48

ROY ROGERS was born in 1911 in Cincinnati, Ohio. His birth name was Leonard Slye. In the 1930s, he made a living as a singer; in 1935, his group started work at a Los Angeles radio station. He appeared in his first movie in 1937. He began using the name Roy Rogers in 1938. From 1952 to 1957, he made 101 television shows. The other stars in the show were his wife, Dale Evans, his horse, Trigger, and his dog, Bullet. Roy Rogers died in 1998. Roy Rogers memorabilia, including items from the Roy Rogers restaurants, are collected.

Bolo Tie, Black & White, Blinkin' Bull, Red, Yellow Card, 1950s, 11 ½ x 6 In.	*illus*	180
Figure, Horse, Standing, Fancy Saddle, Bridle, Gilt Metal, 11 x 11 In.		60
Puzzle, Frame Tray Style, Whitman, Paper Split, Punch Out, 1952, 9 ¼ x 11 In.		40
Record, Roy Rogers, Dale Evans, Happy Trails, Yellow Rose Of Texas, RCA, 45 RPM, 1952, 9 ¾ In.		45
Stop Watch, Portrait, Rearing Horse, Green Pasture, Cloth Bag, Box, 1950s	*illus*	420

ROYAL BAYREUTH is the name of a factory that was founded in Tettau, Bavaria, in 1794. It has continued to modern times. The marks have changed through the years. A stylized crest, the name Royal Bayreuth, and the word *Bavaria* appear in slightly different forms from 1870 to about 1919. Later dishes may include the words *U.S. Zone* (1945–1949), the year of the issue, or the word *Germany* instead of *Bavaria*. Related pieces may be found listed in the Rose Tapestry, Snow Babies, and Sunbonnet Babies categories.

Royal Bayreuth
1887–1902

Royal Bayreuth
c.1900+

Royal Bayreuth
1968+

Ashtray, Red & White, Clown, Holding, Hat, 2 Black Buttons, 4 ¾ In.		72
Bowl, Poppies, Red, Scalloped Rim, 4 x 8 In.		156
Candleholder, Fox, Seated, Orange Red Waistcoat, 6 ¼ In.	*illus*	750
Candleholder, Strong Pink, Orange, Yellow Tones, 6 ½ In.		210
Chamberstick, Handled, Maroon, Frog, Bee, 3 x 6 ½ In.		480
Chamberstick, Shielded, Handle, Green, Penguin, 7 ¼ In.		180
Creamer, Brown, White & Lavender Tones, Unmarked, 4 ¾ In.		108
Creamer, Santa Claus, Sitting, Brown		788
Dispenser, String, Rooster, Strong Colors, Wall Mount, 6 ½ In.		330
Dresser Tray, Blue Mark, Young Girl Walking Dog, 7 x 10 In.		84
Ewer, Teal Spout, Pink, Red & White Roses, Square Foot, 9 In.		40
Hair Receiver, Yellow Rose & Tapestry, 4 In.		24
Humidor, 2 Handles, Green, Brown, Yellow Tones, Scene, Man Training Horses, 7 ½ In.		150
Matchbox, Holder, Striker & Ashtray, Devil, Cards, 3 ¾ x 4 ½ In.		600
Pitcher, Elk, Blue Mark, 7 x 8 ½ x 5 ¼ In.		51
Pitcher, Green, Yellow & Brown Tones, Swans, 6 ¼ In.		72

Pitcher, White, Orange, Yellow Tones, 6¾ In.	330
Plaque, Rare Winged Nymph Portrait, Cobalt Blue & Gold Brocade Border, Round, 13 In.	48
Toothpick Holder, Art Nouveau, White, Pink & Yellow Tones, 3¼ In.	210
Toothpick Holder, Roses, Purple Handles, 2¾ In.	28
Vase, 2 Handles, Pink, Green, White Marbleized Luster, White Figures On Branches, 7 x 8 In.	300
Vase, Nymph, Blue Marked, Green Tone, 5¾ In.	36
Wall Pocket, Blue, Cream, Green Tones, 8¾ x 5½ In.	360

ROYAL BONN is the nineteenth- and twentieth-century trade name used by Franz Anton Mehlem, who had a pottery in Bonn, Germany, from 1836 to 1931. Porcelain and earthenware were made. Royal Bonn also made cases for Ansonia clocks. The factory was purchased by Villeroy & Boch in 1921 and closed in 1931. Many marks were used, most including the name Bonn, the initials FM, and a crown.

Charger, Charles I Of England, Blue, White, 19¾ In.	35
Clock, Cobalt Blue Case, Openwork Handles, Flowers, Marked Ansonia, 16 x 7¼ x 5¼ In.	325
Clock, French Style, Pale Green Case, Floral Transfer, Pendulum & Key, 14 x 11 x 6 In.	156
Clock, Shelf, La Cruz Case, Green & Brown Tones, Pheasant, Ansonia Works, 1½ x 8½ In.	300
Clock, Shelf, Ossipee Case, Ansonia Works, Open Escapement, Green & Cream, Flowers, 11 x 13 In.	270
Clock, Shelf, Record Pattern Case, Cobalt Blue & White, Pink Flowers, Pendulum, 11 x 12 In.	360
Plaque, Young Man & Woman, Stream, Brown Border, Gold Highlights, Giltwood Frame, 20 In.	1140
Vase, Elephant Foot Shape, Yellow Blossoms, Green Tendrils, Turquoise Ground, Marked, 5 In.	118
Vase, Flowers, Yellow Matte Ground, Green & Gilt Wrap, Tendril Rim, 11 x 13 In. *illus*	688
Vase, Gourd Shape, Earthy Colors, Stylized Flowers, Marked, 11 In.	153
Vase, Green Leaves On Yellow Ground, Pear Shape, Marked, Ruysdael, 7 In.	354
Vase, Pierced Leaf, Gilt, Apple Blossoms, Leaves, 32 x 9 In.	378
Vase, Pink Flowers, Blue Ground, Spool Neck, Old Dutch, Marked, 7 In.	118
Vase, Portrait, Woman, Flowers, Cobalt Blue & Gold Handles & Feet, 11 x 10 In.	344
Vase, Portrait, Young Woman, Green, Yellow Background, 4¾ x 4½ In.	72
Vase, Queen Anne's Lace, Yellow, Green Ground, Footed, Marked, 9 In.	177
Vase, Squat, Inverted Thistles, Lavender, Pink, Dark, Turquoise, Marked, 8 In.	295
Vase, Vines & Flowers, Red, Green, Yellow, Nouveau, Marked, 8 In.	118

ROYAL COPENHAGEN porcelain and pottery have been made in Denmark since 1775. The Christmas plate series started in 1908. The figurines with pale blue and gray glazes have remained popular in this century and are still being made. Many other old and new style porcelains are made today. In 2001 Royal Copenhagen became part of the Royal Scandinavia Group owned by the Danish company Axcel, and then sold to the Finnish company Fiskars in 2012. Royal Copenhagen became part of Fiskars Corporation in 2013.

Royal Copenhagen
1892

Royal Copenhagen
1894–1900

Royal Copenhagen
1935–present

Bowl, Blue Pheasant, 8 x 15 In.	121
Bowl, Monteith, Flora Danica, Fluted Edge, Flowers, 4½ x 9¼ In. *illus*	2857
Figurine, Elephant, c.1950, 7 x 10 x 5 In.	406
Group, Gray Eared Puppy, Playing, Deep Gray Noses, Muzzles, 2 x 4 In.	150
Tureen, Tray, Blue, White, Fluted, Half, Lace, 10 x 14 In. *illus*	512
Urn, Potpourri, Cherub Finial, Gilt, Flowers, 2 Handles, Juline Marie Mark, 20 In.	250
Urn, Potpourri, Cherub Holding Bouquet, Ribbons, Handles, Juline Marie Mark, 19 In.	468
Vase, 3 Handles, Blue Leaves At Base, White Ground, Marked, 6½ In.	885
Vase, 3 Handles, Overlap Design Blue Leaves, Backstamp, 6½ In.	750
Vase, Budding Fruit, Glazed, Signed, Axel Salto, c.1950, 4½ x 3 In. *illus*	2000
Vase, Budding Gourd, Purple, Stoneware, Axel Salto, 1966, 6 x 5 In.	3125
Vase, Oval Protrusions, Glazed Stoneware, Marked, Axel Salto, 1940s, 2 In.	750

Rowland & Marsellus, Plate, Theodore Roosevelt 26th President Of The U.S., c.1901, 10 In.
$48

Early American History Auctions

Roy Rogers, Bolo Tie, Black & White, Blinkin' Bull, Red, Yellow Card, 1950s, 11½ x 6 In.
$180

Rich Penn Auctions

R

Roy Rogers, Stop Watch, Portrait, Rearing Horse, Green Pasture, Cloth Bag, Box, 1950s
$420

Rich Penn Auctions

Royal Bayreuth, Candleholder, Fox, Seated, Orange Red Waistcoat, 6 ¼ In.
$750

Woody Auction

Vase, Scenic, Bold Lilies, Swallows, Gerhard Hellmann, Signed, c.1900, 16 In.	1770
Vase, Stick, Gourd, Blue, Brown, Axel Salto, c.1950, 9 x 4 ½ In.	2000
Vase, Tall, Lilies, Diving Swallows, Heilmann, Trees, Grassy Field, Signed, 1890-1902, 16 In.	1500
Vase, Trumpet, Fluted, Flowers, Blue, 10 ½ In., Pair	125

ROYAL CROWN DERBY COMPANY, LTD., is a name used on porcelain beginning in 1890. There is a complex family tree that includes the Derby, Crown Derby, and Royal Crown Derby porcelains. The Royal Crown Derby mark includes the name and a crown. The words *Made in England* were used after 1921. The company became part of Allied English Potteries Group in 1964. It was bought in 2000 and is now privately owned.

Royal Crown Derby 1877–1890	Royal Crown Derby 1890–1940	Royal Crown Derby c.1976–2014

Jar, Fluted Body, Red Decorated Birds & Flowers, Geometric Band, 14 x 11 In.	767
Jar, Gilt, Flower Basket, Ribbons, Cobalt Blue, 7 ½ In., Pair	484
Sugar & Creamer, Imari, Gilt, c.1925, 2 Piece .... *illus*	307
Urn, Conical, Trumpeted Stem, Gilt Figural Lion Handles, 9 ½ x 5 In.	545
Vase, Thick Gilt Flowers, Marbleized, Gold Decoration, Cobalt Blue Glaze, 7 ¼ x 4 ¼ In.	124

ROYAL DOULTON is the name used on Doulton and Company pottery made from 1902 to the present. Doulton and Company of England was founded in 1853. Pieces made before 1902 are listed in this book under Doulton. Royal Doulton collectors search for the out-of-production figurines, character jugs, vases, and series wares. Some vases and animal figurines were made with a special red glaze called flambe. Sung and Chang glazed pieces are rare. The multicolored glaze is very thick and looks as if it were dropped on the clay. Bunnykins figurines were first made by Royal Doulton in 1939. In 2005 Royal Doulton was acquired by the Waterford Wedgwood Group. It was bought by KPS Capital Partners of New York in 2009 and became part of WWRD Holdings. Beatrix Potter bunny figurines were made by Beswick and are listed in that category.

Royal Doulton 1902–1922, 1927–1932	Royal Doulton 1922–1956	Royal Doulton c.2000–present

Animal, Cat, Persian, 5 In.	68
Animal, Rabbit, Lop Eared, Flambe, Glossy, 2 ½ In.	72

 Royal Doulton character jugs depict the head and shoulders of the subject. They are made in four sizes: large, 5 ¼ to 7 inches; small, 3 ¼ to 4 inches; miniature, 2 ¼ to 2 ½ inches; and tiny, 1 ¼ inches. Toby jugs portray a seated, full figure.

Character Jug, Sleuth, D 6635, 3 ¼ In.	98
Character Jug, Confucius, Flambe, Yin Yang, D 7003, 1995, 8 x 6 In. .... *illus*	425
Character Jug, General Custer, Sword Handle, D 7079, 6 ½ In.	43
Character Jug, Groucho Marx, Cigar Handle, D 6710, 1983, 7 In. .... *illus*	75
Character Jug, Jessie Owens, Flag & Torch Handle, D 7019, 7 In.	30
Character Jug, The Genie, Ponytail & Lamp Handle, D 6892, 7 In.	55
Character Jug, The Lawyer, Feather Handle, D 6498, 7 ¼ In.	12
Character Jug, Winston Churchill, British Flag & Bulldog Handle, D 6907, 7 In.	61
Figurine, Balloon Man, Seated Man, Multicolor Balloons, HN 1954, 7 ¼ In. .... *illus*	350
Figurine, Christmas Morn, Hand Painted, Female, Chalkware, HN 1992, 1946, 7 ⅜ In.	55

Royal Bonn, Vase, Flowers, Yellow Matte Ground, Green & Gilt Wrap, Tendril Rim, 11 x 13 In.
$688

Fontaine's Auction Gallery

Royal Copenhagen, Bowl, Monteith, Flora Danica, Fluted Edge, Flowers, 4 ½ x 9 ¼ In.
$2,857

DuMouchelles

Royal Copenhagen, Tureen, Tray, Blue, White, Fluted, Half, Lace, 10 x 14 In.
$512

Susanin's Auctioneers & Appraisers

Royal Copenhagen, Vase, Budding Fruit, Glazed, Signed, Axel Salto, c.1950, 4 ½ x 3 In.
$2,000

Los Angeles Modern Auctions

Royal Crown Derby, Sugar & Creamer, Imari, Gilt, c.1925, 2 Piece
$307

Leland Little Auctions

Royal Doulton, Character Jug, Confucius, Flambe, Yin Yang, D 7003, 1995, 8 x 6 In.
$425

Ruby Lane

Royal Doulton, Character Jug, Groucho Marx, Cigar Handle, D 6710, 1983, 7 In.
$75

Ruby Lane

Royal Doulton, Figurine, Balloon Man, Seated Man, Multicolor Balloons, HN 1954, 7 ¼ In.
$350

Ruby Lane

Royal Doulton, Figurine, Pantelette, Pink & Blue Dress, Green Hat, HN 1412, c.1940, 7 ¾ In.
$500

Ruby Lane

Royal Doulton, Vase, Chang Ware, Runny Glaze, Charles Noke, Harry Nixon, 1920s, 8 ½ x 6 ½ In.
$4,375

Rago Arts and Auction Center

Character Jugs
Royal Doulton started making character jugs in 1934. Early jugs were three-dimensional portraits of famous English characters. By the 1980s, movie, television, and political figures from many countries were included. The jugs had figural handles: Long John Silver's handle was a parrot, Clark Gable's was a movie camera.

R

Royal Flemish, Vase, Round Medallions, Dragons, Flowers, Mt. Washington, 12 ½ x 7 In.
$1,800

Woody Auction

Royal Nymphenburg, Figurine, Cockatoo, Green, Orange, Blue Feathers, Black Beak, 7 ½ In.
$488

Bunch Auctions

Royal Worcester, Figurine, Cactus Wrens, Flowers, Dorothy Doughty, c.1925, 10 In., Pair
$270

Cowan's Auctions

Figurine, Flower Seller's Children, HN 1342, 8 In.	61
Figurine, Katherine, Purple Dress, Red Hat, HN 615, c.1924, 5 x 4 In.	750
Figurine, Lady With Rose, No. 2, Green & Yellow, HN 68, c.1925, 9 ½ In.	2000
Figurine, Pantelette, Pink & Blue Dress, Green Hat, HN 1412, c.1940, 7 ¾ In. .... *illus*	500
Figurine, Pierrette, Red Dress, Clown Hat, HN 1391, c.1930, 8 ½ In.	750
Figurine, Reflections, Strolling, Woman & Dog, HN 3073, 14 x 9 In.	75
Figurine, The Black Cat, Girl With One Shoe & Cat, HN 18, 1920s, 7 ½ In.	3125
Pitcher, Aubrey, Blue, White, 14 In.	168
Plate, Old Balloon Seller, 9 ¾ In.	20
Vase, Black Peacock, Red Ground, Bulbous, Marked, 4 In.	295
Vase, Chang Ware, Runny Glaze, Charles Noke, Harry Nixon, 1920s, 8 ½ x 6 ½ In. .... *illus*	4375
Vase, Flambe, Splashes Of Color, Red, Blue, Yellow, Tapered, Signed, 9 In.	484
Vase, Stoneware, Ducks Rising From Reeds, Yellow Ground, Marked, 10 ½ In.	384
Vase, Sung Flambe, Hand Decorated Male Peacock In Flight, Marked Logo, 4 ¼ In.	250
Vase, Sung Flambe, Hand Painted Barracudas Navigating The Ocean Reefs, Marked Logo, 10 In.	600
Vase, Yellow Flowers, Leaves, Blue Ground, Lambeth Faience, Marked, c.1898, 7 In.	154

ROYAL DUX is the more common name for the Duxer Porzellanmanufaktur, which was founded by E. Eichler in Dux, Bohemia (now Duchcov, Czech Republic), in 1860. By the turn of the twentieth century, the firm specialized in porcelain statuary and busts of Art Nouveau–style maidens, large porcelain figures, and ornate vases with three-dimensional figures climbing on the sides. The firm is still in business. It is now part of Czesky Porcelan (Czech Porcelain).

Figurine, Harvester, Standing, Yellow Hat, Arms Crossed, Basket, 17 ¼ x 4 ¾ In.	125
Figurine, Red Spanish Dancer, Jewelry, 22 x 13 In.	187
Figurine, Rita Hayworth, Dancing, Flowing Dress, 22 ½ x 14 In.	312
Group, Camel, Arab Rider, Attendant, Multicolor, 10 ½ x 16 In.	281

ROYAL FLEMISH glass was made during the late 1880s in New Bedford, Massachusetts, by the Mt. Washington Glass Works. It is a colored satin glass decorated with dark colors and raised gold designs. The glass was patented in 1894. It was supposed to resemble stained glass windows.

Biscuit Jar, Colorful Spider Mums, Gold Colors, 4-Sided, Silver Plated Lid, Signed, 9 ½ In.	726
Vase, Coat-Of-Arms, Scrolls, Stained Glass Panels, Oval, Footed, 10 In.	6655
Vase, Dragon Design, Stained Glass Effect, Gilded Scrolls, Swirls, 8 In.	1815
Vase, Harbor Scene, Ships, Birds, Scenes Framed In Gold, Handles, Signed, 14 In.	14520
Vase, Pansies, Gold Stencil Highlights, Marked, 8 ¾ In.	720
Vase, Round Medallions, Dragons, Flowers, Mt. Washington, 12 ½ x 7 In. .... *illus*	1800
Vase, Stick, Gold Lion, Shield, Gilded Flowers, Leaves, Signed, 14 ½ In.	665

ROYAL HAEGER, *see Haeger category.*

ROYAL NYMPHENBURG is the modern name for the Nymphenburg porcelain factory, which was established at Neudeck-ob-der-Au, Germany, in 1753 and moved to Nymphenburg in 1761. The company is still in existence. Marks include a checkered shield topped by a crown, a crowned *CT* with the year, and a contemporary shield mark on reproductions of eighteenth-century porcelain.

Figurine, Cockatoo, Green, Orange, Blue Feathers, Black Beak, 7 ½ In. .... *illus*	488
Figurine, Farmer, Hat, Scythe, Red Vest, Black Shoes, 9 ⅝ In.	317
Figurine, Stallion, Rearing, White, 9 ½ In.	72
Figurine, Victorian Woman, Fanciful Gown, Marked, 8 ½ In.	106

ROYAL RUDOLSTADT, *see Rudolstadt category.*

ROYAL VIENNA, *see Beehive category.*

ROYAL WORCESTER is a name used by collectors. Worcester porcelains were made in Worcester, England, from about 1751. The firm went through many different periods and name changes. It

R

Royal Worcester, Figurine, Lark Sparrow, Perched On Rock, Flowers, Dorothy Doughty, c.1925, 5 In.
$240

Cowan's Auctions

Roycroft, Andirons, Seahorse Shape, Cast Iron, William Denslow, c.1897, 20 x 23 In.
$13,750

Rago Arts and Auction Center

Roycroft, Lamp, Electric, Copper, Hammered, Round Shade & Foot, 15 ½ x 7 In.
$1,652

Cottone Auctions

RS Germany, Bowl, Yellow & White Flowers, Hand Painted, 11 ³/₁₆ In.
$100

Ruby Lane

RS Poland, Vase, Lion, Lioness, White, Blue, Double Handles, 6 ¼ In.
$600

Woody Auction

RS Prussia, Creamer, Gilt, Mill, Landscape, River, Green, White, Handle, 3 ¾ In.
$69

Woody Auction

RS Prussia, Vase, Hummingbirds, Brown, Tan, Blue, Red, 8 ½ In.
$600

Woody Auction

RS Suhl, Vase, Bowling Pin Shape, Hand Painted, Melon Eaters, Green, Red, Gold, c.1910, 7 ¼ In.
$155

Ruby Lane

R

375

RS Suhl, Vase, Ostriches, Walking, Black & Brown, Trees, Grasses, Handles Above Shoulder, 8¾ In.
$750

Woody Auction

RS Tillowitz, Cake Plate, Hand Painted, Roses, Pink, Shades Of Blue, Gold Leaf, c.1913
$120

Ruby Lane

RS Tillowitz, Vase, Chinese Pheasant, Blue Breast, White Flowers, Brown Landscape, 7 In.
$350

Woody Auction

became the Worcester Royal Porcelain Company, Ltd., in 1862. Today collectors call the porcelains made after 1862 "Royal Worcester." In 1976, the firm merged with W.T. Copeland to become Royal Worcester Spode. The company was bought by the Portmeirion Group in 2009. Some early products of the factory are listed under Worcester. Related pieces may be listed under Copeland, Copeland Spode, and Spode.

Royal Worcester
1862–1875

Royal Worcester
1891

Royal Worcester
c.1959+

Bowl, Sabrina Ware, Blue, Brown, Fish, 1929, 9¼ In.	153
Dish, Conch Shell Shape, White, 3½ x 7¾ In.	52
Ewer, Dragon, Handle, 9 x 5 In.	63
Figurine, Bluebirds, Dorothy Doughty, 10¼ In.	540
Figurine, Cactus Wrens, Flowers, Dorothy Doughty, c.1925, 10 In., Pair .... *illus*	270
Figurine, Crowned Kinglets, Dorothy Doughty, c.1900, 7¾ In.	660
Figurine, Downy Woodpecker, Pecan Branch, Wood Base, Dorothy Doughty c.1900, 10 In.	210
Figurine, Elf Owl, Perched On Cactus, Wood Base, Dorothy Doughty, 13 x 9 In.	185
Figurine, Golden Crown Kinglets, In Pine Tree, Doughty, 8¼ In., Pair	431
Figurine, Lark Sparrow, Perched On Rock, Flowers, Dorothy Doughty, c.1925, 5 In. .... *illus*	240
Figurine, Mallard, R. Van Ruyckevelt, Wood Base, c.1950, 11¾ In.	180
Figurine, Myrtle Warblers, Flowering Branches, Wood Base, Dorothy Doughty, 9 In.	300
Figurine, Orange Blossoms, Butterfly, Dorothy Doughty, 9 In., Pair	554
Figurine, Scissor Tailed Flycatchers, 2 In Flight, 1962, 7 x 25 In.	360
Figurine, Spring, Girl, Holding Lamb, 8¾ In.	73
Jug, Ball Shape, Gold Stencil Handle, Enamel Flowers, Small Spout, 9 In.	18
Plate, Dinner, Ivory, Cranberry Border, Raised Gilt Urns, 10½ In., 12 Piece	875
Plate, Raised Gilt Vases, Swags, Lapis Ground, Ernest Barker, Signed, c.1928, 10 In., 12 Piece..	1125
Urn, Reticulated, Knop Finial, Dome Lid, Pierced, Leaves, Flowers, 19 x 7 In.	2700
Vase, Cream Tones, Ferns, Gold Trim Highlights, 10 In.	108
Vase, Panel, Gilt, Flowers, 1891, 12 In.	150

ROYCROFT products were made by the Roycrofter community of East Aurora, New York, from 1895 until 1938. The community was founded by Elbert Hubbard, famous philosopher, writer, and artist. The workshops owned by the community made furniture, metalware, leatherwork, embroidery, and jewelry. A printshop produced many signs, books, and the magazines that promoted the sayings of Elbert Hubbard. Furniture by the Roycroft community is listed in the Furniture category.

Andirons, Seahorse Shape, Cast Iron, William Denslow, c.1897, 20 x 23 In. .... *illus*	13750
Bench, Ali Baba, Stretcher, c.1905, 18 x 36 In.	3750
Bookends, Copper, Hammered, Rectangular, Raised Fleurette, 8 In.	63
Bookends, Little Journeys, Copper, Hammered, Rounded Corners, 1900s, 8⅝ x 5⅞ In., Pair..	123
Candlestick, Copper, 3-Light, Hammered, Twisted Stem, 1920s, 20 x 9 In., Pair	625
Lamp, Copper, Hammered, Tripod Base, Steuben Gold Aurene Intarsia Shade, 16 In.	4688
Lamp, Desk, Copper, Hammered, Helmet Shade, Flared Foot, 13 x 6 In.	1500
Lamp, Electric, Copper, Hammered, Round Shade & Foot, 15½ x 7 In. .... *illus*	1652
Vase, Stick Neck, Copper, Hammered, Footed, 22 x 8 In.	3750

ROZANE, *see Roseville category.*

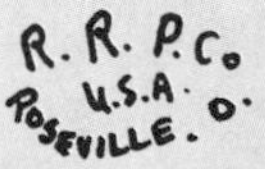

RRP, or RRP Roseville, is the mark used by the firm of Robinson-Ransbottom. It is not a mark of the more famous Roseville Pottery. The Ransbottom brothers started a pottery in 1900 in Ironspot, Ohio. In 1920, they merged with the Robinson Clay Products Company of Akron, Ohio, to become Robinson-Ransbottom. The factory closed in 2005.

Bowl, Cream, 10 x 4 In.	180
Bowl, Yellowware, Arched Shoulder, Butterfly Like Design, Brown Bands, 14 In.	68

R

Cookie Jar, Apple, Pedestal, Branch Handles, Red, Yellow, Green, 1950s, 8 ½ x 9 In.	48
Crock, Yellowware, Black & Red Bands, 4 ½ x 3 In.	35
Pitcher, Drip, Brown, 7 ½ In.	25
Planter, Sun & Moon, Brown, Dark Green Glaze, c.1900, 8 x 10 In.	75
Vase, Green & White Drip, Oval, 1950s, 22 In.	300

RS GERMANY is part of the wording in marks used by the Tillowitz, Germany, factory of Reinhold Schlegelmilch from 1914 until about 1945. The porcelain was sold decorated and undecorated. The Schlegelmilch families made porcelains marked in many ways. See also ES Germany, RS Poland, RS Prussia, RS Silesia, RS Suhl, and RS Tillowitz.

Biscuit Jar, 2 Handles, Yellow & White, Rose Design, 7 ½ In.	12
Bowl, Yellow & White Flowers, Hand Painted, 11 ³/₁₆ In. *illus*	100
Celery Tray, Yellow Background Colorful Parrot, 10 In.	60
Mustard, Green & White, Poppy Decor, Silver Spoon, 3 ½ In.	6
Plate, Parrot, Green & Dark Green Leaves, Silver Overlay, 7 ¼ In.	117

RS POLAND (German) is a mark used by the Reinhold Schlegelmilch factory at Tillowitz from about 1946 to 1956. After 1956, the factory made porcelain marked *PT Poland*. This is one of many of the RS marks used. See also ES Germany, RS Germany, RS Prussia, RS Silesia, RS Suhl, and RS Tillowitz.

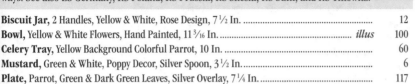

RS Poland	RS Poland
c.1945–1956	After 1956

Hatpin Holder, Chinese Pheasant, Blue, White, Green, 4 ¼ In.	209
Hatpin Holder, Windmill, Mill, Landscape, Yellow, Brown, 4 ½ In.	149
Vase, 2 Handles, Pale Green Tones, Old Cottage Scene, 4 ½ In.	120
Vase, Lion, Lioness, White, Blue, 2 Handles, 6 ¼ In. *illus*	600

RS PRUSSIA appears in several marks used on porcelain before 1917. Reinhold Schlegelmilch started his porcelain works in Suhl, Germany, in 1869. See also ES Germany, RS Germany, RS Poland, RS Silesia, RS Suhl, and RS Tillowitz.

RS Prussia	RS Prussia
Late 1880s–1917	c.1895–1917

Bowl, Basket Of Flowers, Scalloped Edge, 8 ½ In.	85
Bowl, Carnation Mold, Cobalt Blue, Gold Stencil, 15 In.	11400
Bowl, Carnation, 10 ⅜ In.	33
Bowl, Castle, Boat, Landscape, Yellow Ground, 10 ⅝ In.	81
Bowl, Cream, Brown Tones, Wild Poppy Decor, Variation Mold, 10 ¼ In.	48
Bowl, Gilt, Apples, Grapes, Cherries, White Ground, 10 In.	34
Bowl, Red Rose Swag, Green Ground, 10 ½ In.	45
Bowl, Ribbon, Jewel Mold, Dice Throwers Scenic, Gold, Opal, 11 In.	420
Bowl, Scalloped & Beaded Rim, Ship, Dock, Orange, Purple, Green, Blue, 10 ½ In.	263
Bowl, Scalloped & Beaded Rim, White & Pink Flowers, Yellow Centers, Cobalt Rim, 10 In.	128
Bowl, Shell, Floral Mold, Racamier Portrait, Green Background, Bronze Border, 10 ½ In.	330
Bowl, Water Lilies, Gold Stencil, 11 In.	48
Celery Dish, Icicle Mold, Farmyard, Pheasant, Scenic, 12 In.	270
Celery Dish, Pink Roses, Green Leaves, Light Green Ground, White Handles, 13 ½ x 7 In.	33

Rubina, Pitcher, Red & Clear, Swirl Jewel Pattern, c.1890, 8 ¼ In. $295

Ruby Lane

Rubina Verde, Pitcher, Hobnail, Square Top, Applied Handle, Polished & Ground Pontil, 1800s, 8 In. $390

Garth's Auctioneers & Appraisers

Rubina Verde, Vase, Cranberry, Green, White Birds, Rigaree Trim, c.1870, 10 In. $400

Ruby Lane

R

Rudolstadt, Ewer, Hand Painted, Textured Flowers, Violet, Gold, Green, Off-White, c.1800, 7 ½ In.
$95

Ruby Lane

Rudolstadt, Vase, Jasperware, Blue, Fairy, Classical Dress, Branches, Flowers, Handles, 11 ½ In.
$307

Forsythes' Auctions

Rug, Braided, Oval, Multicolor Bands, 7 Ft. 10 In. x 8 Ft. 9 In.
$295

Hess Auction Group

Celery Dish, Point, Clover Mold, Cream Keyhole Center, Flowers, Green Border, Gold Highlights, 13 In.	24
Chocolate Pot, Lavender, Green & Cream Tones, No Lid, Unmarked, 9 ½ In.	60
Creamer, Gilt, Mill, Landscape, River, Green, White, Handle, 3 ¾ In. *illus*	69
Creamer, White & Green Tones, Mill Scene, Gold Trim Highlights, 3 ¾ In.	72
Mustache Cup, Flower, Pink, Footed, 19th Century, 2 x 2 ½ In.	44
Plate, Cream Satin, Flowers, Gold Border, 11 In.	60
Plate, Gilt, Roses, Arcs, Arrows, Blue Cabochons, 9 ½ In.	135
Powder Jar, Lid, Iris Mold, Spring Season Portrait, Yellow, Green, Lavender, 5 x 5 In.	900
Relish, Gilt, Blue Cabochons, Red & White Roses, Handles, 9 ½ x 5 In.	101
Shaving Mug, White & Brown Luster Finish, Pink Roses, 3 ¼ In.	30
Sugar & Creamer, Pink Flowers, Leaves, Footed, c.1905	95
Sugar, 2 Handles, Green & White, Castle Scene, 5 In.	24
Teapot, Lid, Footed, Carnation, Gold Bands, c.1905, 8 x 5 In.	125
Tray, Dresser, Iris Mold, White, Lavender Satin, Winter Season Portrait, 11 x 7 ¼ In.	540
Tray, Dresser, Lily Mold, Green, Yellow, Lebrun Portrait, Iridescent Peacock, 12 x 7 ¼ In.	540
Tray, Dresser, Point, Clover Mold, Green, Dice Throwers Scenic, Gold Trim, 12 x 7 ½ In.	360
Tray, Dresser, White & Cream Center, Flowers, Tiffany Border, Myth Figure, Gold Trim, 11 In.	108
Tray, Gilt, Pink Roses, Rectangular, Pierced Handles, 11 ¾ x 7 ½ In.	90
Tray, Point, Clover Mold, Green Tones, Melon Eaters, Gold, Green Border, Opal Jewel, 9 ½ In.	300
Vase, 2 Handles, Brown Tones, Turkey, 4 ¼ In.	330
Vase, Hummingbirds, Brown, Tan, Blue, Red, 8 ½ In. *illus*	600
Vase, Melon Eaters, 9 In.	180

 RS SILESIA appears on porcelain made at the Reinhold Schlegelmilch factory in Tillowitz, Germany, from the 1920s to the 1940s. The Schlegelmilch families made porcelains marked in many ways. See also ES Germany, RS Germany, RS Poland, RS Prussia, RS Suhl, and RS Tillowitz.

Plate, 2 Tiers, Camellia Blossoms, Curled Green Leaves, 1920s, 9 In.	120

 RS SUHL is a mark used by the Reinhold Schlegelmilch factory in Suhl, Germany, between 1900 and 1917. The Schlegelmilch families made porcelains in many places. See also ES Germany, RS Germany, RS Poland, RS Prussia, RS Silesia, and RS Tillowitz.

Vase, Bowling Pin Shape, Hand Painted, Melon Eaters, Green, Red, Gold, c.1910, 7 ¼ In. *illus*	155
Vase, Ostriches, Walking, Black & Brown, Trees, Grasses, Handles Above Shoulder, 8 ¾ In. *illus*	750

RS TILLOWITZ was marked on porcelain by the Reinhold Schlegelmilch factory at Tillowitz from the 1920s to the 1940s. Table services and ornamental pieces were made. See also ES Germany, RS Germany, RS Poland, RS Prussia, RS Silesia, and RS Suhl.

RS Tillowitz
1920s–1940s

RS Tillowitz
1932–1983

Cake Plate, Hand Painted, Roses, Pink, Shades Of Blue, Gold Leaf, c.1913 *illus*	120
Vase, Chinese Pheasant, Blue Breast, White Flowers, Brown Landscape, 7 In. *illus*	350

 RUBINA is a glassware that shades from red to clear. It was first made by George Duncan and Sons of Pittsburgh, Pennsylvania, in about 1885. This coloring was used on many types of glassware.

Bowl, Ruffled, Bolted Stand, Silver Plated, 7 ¼ x 9 ½ In.	150
Pitcher, Red & Clear, Swirl Jewel Pattern, c.1890, 8 ¼ In. *illus*	295

 RUBINA VERDE is a Victorian glassware that was shaded from red to green. It was first made by Hobbs, Brockunier and Company of Wheeling, West Virginia, about 1890.

Pitcher, Hobnail, Square Top, Applied Handle, Polished & Ground Pontil, 1800s, 8 In.....	*illus*	390
Vase, Cranberry, Green, White Birds, Rigaree Trim, c.1870, 10 In.	*illus*	400

RUBY GLASS is the dark red color of a ruby, the precious gemstone. It was a popular Victorian color that never went completely out of style. The glass was shaped by many different processes to make many different types of ruby glass. There was a revival of interest in the 1940s when modern-shaped ruby table glassware became fashionable. Sometimes the red color is added to clear glass by a process called flashing or staining. Flashed glass is clear glass dipped in a colored glass, then pressed or cut. Stained glass has color painted on a clear glass. Then it is refired so the stain fuses with the glass. Pieces of glass colored in this way are indicated by the word *stained* in the description. Related items may be found in other categories, such as Cranberry Glass, Pressed Glass, and Souvenir.

Butter, Domed Cover, Dalton, Stained, Tarentum Glass Co., c.1904, 6 In.	140
Butter, Royal, Stained, Co-Operative Flint Glass Co., 1894, 6 In.	46
Cased Wine, Solid, Flashed Hobstar Base, Russian Pattern Star Cut Buttons, Fire Polished Rim, 5 In.	600
Compote, Moon & Stars, Footed, Weishar, 8 x 8 In...	22
Cracker Jar, Lid, Big Button, Stained, Crystal Glass Co., c.1912, 8¾ In.	46
Decanter, Albany, Stained, Tarentum Glass Co., 1898, 10¾ In.	35
Lamp, Wall, Oil Lamp Converted To Electric, Frosted Shades, Pair, 19 In.	121
Vase, Iridescent, Dimples, Threads, Scalloped Rim, 1920s, 4½ x 3¾ In.	750

RUDOLSTADT was a faience factory in the Thuringia region of Germany from 1720 to about 1791. In 1854, Ernst Bohne began working in the area. From about 1887 to 1918, the New York and Rudolstadt Pottery made decorated porcelain marked with the RW and crown familiar to collectors. This porcelain was imported by Lewis Straus and Sons of New York, which later became Nathan Straus and Sons. The word *Royal* was included in their import mark. Collectors often call it "Royal Rudolstadt." Most pieces found today were made in the late nineteenth or early twentieth century. Additional pieces may be listed in the Kewpie category.

Ewer, Cornucopia Body, Lion Handle, Gold, Green Highlight, 11 x 9½ In.		180
Ewer, Hand Painted, Textured Flowers, Violet, Gold, Green, Off-White, c.1800, 7½ In......	*illus*	95
Vase, Jasperware, Blue, Fairy, Classical Dress, Branches, Flowers, Handles, 11½ In..........	*illus*	307

RUGS have been used in the American home since the seventeenth century. The oriental rug of that time was often used on a table, not on the floor. Rag rugs, hooked rugs, and braided rugs were made by housewives from scraps of material. American Indian rugs are listed in the Indian category.

Abstract, Wool, Parigot, Gruber, 1970, 7 Ft. x 9 Ft. 10 In.	688
Afghan, Medallion, Red, Hand Woven, Afghanistan, 1900s, 5 Ft. 9 In. x 5 Ft. 3 In.	344
Afghan, Red Field, Gold, Blue, Barber Pole Stripes, Yellow & Brown, Wool, 3 x 4 Ft...................	325
Afshar, Boteh, Ivory Field, Panels, Hand Woven, 1900s, 7 Ft. 5 In. x 4 Ft. 9 In.	210
Afshar, Persia, Geometric Medallion, Red Field, Ivory Guard Borders, 4 Ft. 7 In. x 6 Ft. 7 In.	188
Andy Warhol, Squares, Sliced Dots, White Grid, 4 x 5 Ft.	500
Arshile Gorky, V'Soske, Bull In Sun, Wool, 1 Ft. 7 In. x 7 Ft. 5 In.	4063
Aubusson, Repeating Circles, Diamonds, White, Cream, Navy, 19 Ft. 2 In. x 12 Ft. 9 In.	6250
Bakhtiari, Flowers & Lines, Green & Gold, Beige Field, 9 Ft. 4 In. x 12 Ft. 8 In......................	600
Bakhtiari, Garden Panel, Geometric, Birds, Ivory Border, 1900s, 9 Ft. 9 In. x 7 Ft....................	600
Bakhtiari, Garden, Leafy Panels, Ivory Border, 1900s, 6 Ft. 6 In. x 5 Ft. 9 In.	450
Bakhtiari, Prayer, Urn & Flowers, Bold Colors, c.1950, 4 Ft. 8 In. x 9 Ft. 11 In..........................	180
Balouch, Persia, Ivory Medallions, Red Field, 3 Ft. x 5 Ft. 3 In.	84
Baluchi, Lattice, Diamonds, Flowers, Ivory, Russet, Aubergine, Blue, 1800s, 4 Ft. 2 In. x 2 Ft. 2 In..	54
Bessarabian, Kilim, 2 Panels, Repeating Bouquets, Brown Ground, 5 Ft. 11 In. x 8 Ft. 4 In. ...	90
Bidjar, Dark Red, Diamond Medallion, Ivory Border, Blue Field, Flowers, 2 Ft. 8 In. x 5 Ft........	144
Bidjar, Herati, Green, Blue, Red, Ivory, Pink, Navy Blue Field, 1900s, 3 x 6 Ft.	450
Bidjar, Overlapping Black, Light Blue, Ivory, Tan, Gray, Turtle Border, 1900, 4 x 6 Ft.	72
Bidjar, Persia, Circular Medallion, Anchor Pendants, Blue, Red, Turtle Border, 8 Ft. 9 In. x 12 Ft..	3000
Bird, Geometrics, Red, Blue, Green, Brown, Cream, Purple, Burnt Orange Ground, 7 Ft. 4 In. x 4 Ft. 4 In..	1995
Bokhara, Maroon Ground, 3 Rows Of Guls, c.1950, 4 Ft. 2 In. x 6 Ft.	300

Rug, Caucasian, 3 Medallions, Multiple
Borders, Red Ground,
7 Ft. 8 In. x 4 Ft. 2 In.
$660

Cowan's Auctions

Rug, Caucasian, Repeating Diamonds,
Lozenges, Red, Navy,
4 Ft. 1 In. x 6 Ft. 8 In.
$1,800

Michann's Auctions

TIP

*Don't dry-clean a
rag rug. It should be
carefully washed.*

R

Rug, Caucasian, Repeating Patterns, 3 Borders, Navy, Red, Brown, White, 3 Ft. 7 In. x 4 Ft. 10 In.
$1,020

Michann's Auctions

Fringe Determines the Value

If the border of a rug is badly frayed or missing, it dramatically lowers the value. A rug with a good fringe could be worth $1,500; without a border, the same rug could be worth only $100.

Rug, Chinese, Art Deco Design, Dark Blue Ground, Beige, Light Blue, Flower Border, 3 x 3 Ft.
$14,400

Cowan's Auctions

Rug, Chinese, Flowers, Floral Border, Dark Blue Ground, 3 x 5 Ft.
$118

Hess Auction Group

Rug, Chinese, Medallion, Light & Dark Blue Flowers, Tan Field, 1800, 11 x 17 Ft.
$300

Eldred's Auctioneers and Appraisers

Rug, Contemporary, Wool, Geometric Pattern, Flatweave, Moss, Tan, Black, 8 Ft. 2 In. x 9 Ft. 4 In.
$1,188

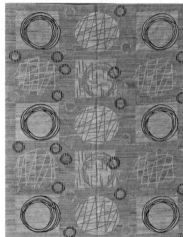

Rago Arts and Auction Center

Rug, Contemporary, Wool, Geometric Pattern, Tan, Brown, 8 x 10 Ft.
$1,000

Rago Arts and Auction Center

R

Braided, Oval, Multicolor Bands, 7 Ft. 10 In. x 8 Ft. 9 In............................ *illus*	295
Caucasian, 2 Medallions, Square, Birds, Stars, Serpent Heads, Red, Blue, 4 Ft. 2 In. x 5 Ft. 4 In..	1140
Caucasian, 3 Medallions, Multiple Borders, Red Ground, 7 Ft. 8 In. x 4 Ft. 2 In............... *illus*	660
Caucasian, 5 Medallions, Geometric, Red, Brown, Beige, Celadon, Hand Woven, 1930, 7 Ft. 3 In. x 6 Ft.	106
Caucasian, 5 Medallions, Hooked Edges, Ivory, Red, Gold Highlights, 1900s, 3 x 8 Ft.	360
Caucasian, Kuba, Kilim, Striped, Flowers, Ribbons, Red, Brown, Amber, 5 Ft. x 13 Ft. 8 In......	425
Caucasian, Kuba, Rows Of Diamonds, Geometrics, Cobalt Ground, 3 Ft. 7 In. x 6 Ft. 9 In.	1440
Caucasian, Repeating Diamonds, Lozenges, Red, Navy, 4 Ft. 1 In. x 6 Ft. 8 In. .... *illus*	1800
Caucasian, Repeating Geometric Patterns, Flowers, Red, Navy, Multicolor, 5 Ft. x 8 Ft. 3 In.	1298
Caucasian, Repeating Patterns, 3 Borders, Navy, Red, Brown, White, 3 Ft. 7 In. x 4 Ft. 10 In.. *illus*	1020
Chinese, 5 Circular Medallions, Flowering Branches, Dark Blue, Light Blue, Brown, 1900s, 2 x 5 Ft.	270
Chinese, Art Deco Design, Dark Blue Ground, Beige, Light Blue, Flower Border, 3 x 3 Ft.. *illus*	14400
Chinese, Blue, Flowers, Ivory Borders, 1900s, 7 Ft. 7 In. x 5 Ft. 2 In..........................	125
Chinese, Flowering Branches, Butterflies, Flower Vase, Blue Field, 1900s, 2 x 5 Ft...........	300
Chinese, Flowers, Floral Border, Dark Blue Ground, 3 x 5 Ft. .... *illus*	118
Chinese, Leafy Medallion, Royal Blue Field, Geometric Border, 4 Ft. x 6 Ft. 4 In.	84
Chinese, Leaves, Red, Geometrics, Blue, Ivory, 1900s, 8 x 5 Ft.	156
Chinese, Medallion, Light & Dark Blue Flowers, Tan Field, 1800, 11 x 17 Ft. .... *illus*	300
Chinese, Midnight Blue Medallion, Sky Blue Field, Palmette Border, Tan Vine, 9 Ft. x 11 Ft. 9 In.	300
Chinese, Whimsical Tiger, Wool, 2 x 5 Ft.	561
Contemporary, Wool, Geometric Pattern, Flatweave, Moss, Tan, Black, 8 Ft. 2 In. x 9 Ft. 4 In. *illus*	1188
Contemporary, Wool, Geometric Pattern, Tan, Brown, 8 x 10 Ft. .... *illus*	1000
Dargezine, Bouquets, Ivory Field, Red Border, Hand Woven, 1930, 12 Ft. x 2 Ft. 7 In.	240
Donnemara, Vines, Branches, Flowers, Green, Yellow, Wool, Charles Voysey, 1905, 13 Ft. x 12 Ft. 3 In.	8750
Hamadan, Birds, Navy Field, Light Blue Border, Red Guard, 1910, 6 Ft. 7 In. x 4 Ft. 10 In.	480
Hamadan, Charcoal Lozenge, Medallion, Gold Center, Turquoise, 1900s, 3 x 5 Ft.	216
Hamadan, Dark Red, Blue Geometric Medallions, Ivory Borders, 1900s, 4 x 6 Ft...............	168
Hamadan, Medallion, Camel Field, Geometric, Persian, 1900s, 6 Ft. x 4 Ft. 10 In..............	2280
Heriz Serapi, Runner, Indo Persian, 2 Ft. 7 In. x 8 Ft.	112
Heriz, Center Medallion, Astral Blue Ground, Burgundy Floral Border, 9 x 10 Ft...............	640
Heriz, Crimson & Navy Ground, Center Field Of Flowers, Palmette Border, 8 x 10 Ft.............	512
Heriz, Gabled Medallion, Dark Red Field, Light Red, Ivory, Spandrels, 1900s, 8 x 11 Ft.	600
Heriz, Geometric Medallions, Overlapping Blue & Dark Red, Red Field, Ivory Subfield, 1900, 6 x 9 Ft..	270
Heriz, Medallion, Golden Panels, Navy Border, 1900s, 12 Ft. 5 In. x 9 Ft.	3120
Heriz, Serapi, Blue Medallion, Brown & Red Accents, Ivory Field, 7 Ft. 7 In. x 11 Ft.	4305
Heriz, Square Medallion, Blue, Ivory & Gold, Red Field, 1900s, 10 Ft. x 15 Ft. 10 In.	960
Heriz, Stylized Flowers & Leaves, Gray, White, Red, Black, Wool, 8 x 11 Ft....................	413
Hooked, 2 Love Birds, Facing Each Other, 27 x 38 ½ In..	219
Hooked, 2-Masted Schooner, Gertrude L. Thebaud, Full Sail, American Flag, 35 x 45 In.	390
Hooked, 3 Dogs, Leaf Border, c.1920, 25 x 38 In.	300
Hooked, Bath, Black, Stylized Zigzag Border, Mounted On Stretcher, c.1915, 27 x 48 In.	390
Hooked, Burlap, Frond, Lily Pad, Water Lilies, Black, Green, Border, 18 x 29 In.	128
Hooked, Cats, Flanking Vase, Flowers, 18 x 35 ½ In...	156
Hooked, Eagle Holding Shield, Cloudy Sky, Red Border, Gold Stars, Demilune, 1900s, 27 x 39 In....	450
Hooked, Farm Animals, Alphabet, Numbers, On Stretcher, Signed Francis, c.1910, 38 x 58 In..	120
Hooked, Fireplace, Mantel, Cat, Rugs, Window, 28 x 45 In. .... *illus*	130
Hooked, Flowers, Central Cluster, Acanthus Scrolls, Red, Brown, Tan, Orange, 29 x 47 In.	42
Hooked, Geometric Field, Leaf Border, Mounted On Stretcher, c.1910, 24 x 37 In. .... *illus*	750
Hooked, Home Sweet Home, Musical Score, 28 x 54 In.	438
Hooked, Lion, Striding, Palm Trees, Shields In Corners, A.B. Frost, 1900s, 39 x 68 In.	2280
Hooked, Lioness & Cub, Tropical Background, Black & Red Striped Border, c.1890, 32 x 62 In.	240
Hooked, Log Cabin, Cows, Trees, Geese, Grass, Trees, Multicolor, 52 x 35 In.	234
Hooked, Man & Woman, Take Those Lips Away, Mounted On Stretcher, c.1910, 33 x 50 In. *illus*	1560
Hooked, Multicolor, Gray Center, Striped Border, Black Edge, c.1900, 39 x 72 In.	70
Hooked, Nautical Theme, Sailboats, Lighthouses, Round, 86 In. .... *illus*	132
Hooked, Pectoral, Lions, Palm Trees, Floral, c.1875, 30 x 60 In.........................	3125
Hooked, Portland Lighthouse, Rocky Shoreline, Burlap, c.1950, 27 x 37 In........................	263
Hooked, Sailboats, Lighthouses, Blue, White, Gray, Red, Round, 88 In......................	132
Hooked, Schoolhouse, American Flag, Light Gray Oval, Red, Green, Gray Frame, 21 x 34 In....	3720
Hooked, Tan, Acanthus Scrolls, Burgundy, Brown, Blue, Green, Pink, Orange, 1900, 24 x 36 In.	42

TIP

Turn a rug a quarter or half turn twice a year so it will wear evenly.

Rug, Hooked, Fireplace, Mantel, Cat, Rugs, Window, 28 x 45 In.
$130

Hess Auction Group

Rug, Hooked, Geometric Field, Leaf Border, Mounted On Stretcher, c.1910, 24 x 37 In.
$750

Garth's Auctioneers & Appraisers

Rug, Hooked, Man & Woman, Take Those Lips Away, Mounted On Stretcher, c.1910, 33 x 50 In.
$1,560

Garth's Auctioneers & Appraisers

Rug, Hooked, Nautical Theme, Sailboats, Lighthouses, Round, 86 In.
$132

Eldred's Auctioneers and Appraisers

R

Rug, Needlepoint, Medallion, Yellow Acanthus, Musical Instruments, 1900, 9 x 11 Ft.
$300

Eldred's Auctioneers and Appraisers

Rug, Oriental, Blossoms, Palmettes, Leaves, Dark Tangerine, 1900s, 8 Ft. 8 In. x 11 Ft. 9 In.
$600

Eldred's Auctioneers and Appraisers

Rug, Overdyed, Red & Yellow Flowers, Vines, Blue Ground, 9 Ft. 2 In. x 12 Ft.
$1,342

New Orleans Auction Galleries

Rug, Pakistani, Red, White Medallion, Blue Field & Borders, 1960, 3 x 4 Ft.
$156

Eldred's Auctioneers and Appraisers

Rug, Persian, Pictorial, Architecture, Figures, Zodiac Signs, 6 Ft. 6 In. x 9 Ft. 4 In.
$1,152

Neal Auction Co.

Rug, Persian, Wedding, Figures In Center, Flowers, Borders, 1900s, 6 Ft. x 4 Ft. 4 In.
$720

Cowan's Auctions

Rug, Pictorial, Figures, Chinese Landscape, Colored Wool, Contemporary, 6 Ft. 6 In. x 9 Ft. 6 In.
$1,342

Neal Auction Co.

Rug, Pictorial, Persian, Taj Mahal & Figures, 4 Ft. 7 In. x 7 Ft. 5 In.
$519

Neal Auction Co.

Rug, Shiraz, Geometric Medallions, Rust Field, Blue & Red Stylized Designs, 1900, 6 x 10 Ft.
$570

Eldred's Auctioneers and Appraisers

R

Isfahan, Ghaffarian, Brown Circle, White Oval, Flowers, Beige Border, Silk, 13 Ft. 8 In. x 10 Ft.	6000
Kapoutrang, Ivory, Blue Central Medallion, Flowering Branches, Ivory Borders, 1900, 8 x 16 Ft.	204
Karaja, Geometric Medallions, Brown, Gold, Red, Blue, Guard Border, Runner, 1900, 4 x 15 Ft.	570
Kashan, Central Rectangle, Navy, Urn, Trees, Flowers, Calligraphy, 4 Ft. 3 In. x 6 Ft. 9 ½ In. .	2118
Kashan, Central Red Medallion, Blue & Red Ground, Scrolling Leaves, 6 Ft. x 4 Ft. 4 In.	900
Kashan, Mohtasham, Beige Field, Navy Border, 6 Ft. 9 In. x 4 Ft. 5 In.	4375
Kasvin, Blue, Rose Red, Ivory Flower Medallion, Flowers, 1900s, 8 x 14 Ft.	360
Kazak, 2 Columns, Geometric Medallions, Red Field, Flowers, Blue, Green, Ivory, 4 Ft. 2 In. x 7 Ft.	1920
Kazak, 2 Starburst Medallions, Dark Blue Field, Ivory, Blue, Red, Tan, 4 Ft. 9 In. x 6 Ft. 8 In. .	2400
Kazak, Central Octagons, White Squares, Zigzag Border, Red, c.1900, 7 Ft. 5 In. x 5 Ft. 9 In. .	2375
Kerman, 12 Panels, Scripture, Tan Ground, Red, Green Borders, 1800s, 6 Ft. x 4 Ft. 5 In.	2178
Kerman, Central Arabesque, Blue Rose, Vines, 11 Ft. 3 In. x 18 Ft.	1512
Kerman, Lozenge Medallion, Deep Red Field, Pastels, Ivory Flower Border, 1900, 2 x 10 Ft.	120
Kerman, Tan Pendant Medallion, Flowering Vines, Gold, Gray, Green, Blue, 1900s, 7 Ft. 7 In. x 10 Ft.	204
Kilim, Flower Sprays, Pink, Chocolate Ground, 6 Ft. 1 In. x 9 Ft. 2 In.	60
Kilim, Red, Flowers, Notched Edge, Tan Band & Border, 1980s, 10 Ft. x 8 Ft. 5 In.	450
Kurdish, Blue Medallion, Red Field, Navy Border, Hand Woven, 1900s, 6 Ft. 5 In. x 4 Ft. 9 In.	219
Kurdish, Hexagonal Medallion Navy Blue, Staggered Rows, Figures, Birds, 1900s, 4 x 5 Ft.	168
Kurdish, Leafy Decoration, Red Field, Blue Corners, Multiple Borders, Kurdish, 4 Ft. 9 In. x 8 Ft. 5 In.	300
Lap, Princeton 1933, Machine Sewn Letters, Felt, Green Mountain Studios, 2 Ft. 10 In. x 5 Ft. 9 In. .	36
Lillihan, Flower Vases, Red Ground, Floral Border, 9 x 11 Ft.	3172
Mahal, Celadon Pole Medallion, Flowers, Red Accent, Ivory Corners, 4 Ft. 4 In. x 6 Ft. 6 In.	156
Mahal, Palmettes, Vines, Serrated Leaves, Blue, Gold, Camel, Green, Ivory, 1900s, 9 x 12 Ft.	1560
Malayer, Repeating Pattern, Tea, Camel, Blue, Red Ground, c.1930, 10 x 17 Ft.	6000
Modernist, Wool, Gruber, E. Lanux, 4 Ft. 7 In. x 10 Ft. 9 In.	250
Needlepoint, 20 Blocks, Animals, Aubusson Style, Linen Fold Border, Brown, 7 Ft. 3 In. x 9 Ft. 2 In.	660
Needlepoint, Medallion, Yellow Acanthus, Musical Instruments, 1900, 9 x 11 Ft. *illus*	300
Oriental, Blossoms, Palmettes, Leaves, Dark Tangerine, 1900s, 8 Ft. 8 In. x 11 Ft. 9 In. *illus*	600
Oriental, Geometric, 3 Center Medallions, Birds, 4 Ft. 9 In. x 3 Ft. 5 In.	424
Oushak, 3 Medallions, Orange Red, Olive & Turquoise Highlights, 6 Ft. 3 In. x 8 Ft. 8 In.	3600
Oushak, Oval, Indo-Turkish, 6 x 9 Ft.	60
Oushak, Repeating Triangles, Blue Ground, Green & Blue Flower Border, 2 Ft. 7 In. x 6 Ft. 3 In. .	100
Oushak, Rows Of Urns, Orange, Red, Green & Gold, Open Ivory Field, 7 Ft. 7 In. x 11 Ft.	615
Overdyed, Red & Yellow Flowers, Vines, Blue Ground, 9 Ft. 2 In. x 12 Ft. *illus*	1342
Pakistani, Red, White Medallion, Blue Field & Borders, 1960, 3 x 4 Ft. *illus*	156
Penny, Hexagonal, Multicolor Circles, Petal Border, Wool Felt, c.1900, 4 x 3 Ft.	275
Persian, Blue, Ivory Diamond, Spandrels, Peach Flowers, Wool, Hand Knotted, 9 x 11 Ft.	410
Persian, Curving Leaves, Flowers, Pastels, Blue Field, Red Outline, Silk, 1 Ft. 6 In. x 2 Ft.	531
Persian, Flowers, Soft Red Field, Navy Border, 3 Ft. x 1 Ft. 10 In.	48
Persian, Heriz, Wool, Hand Knotted, Medallion, Geometrics, Peach, Olive Green, Gray, 8 Ft. 3 In. x 11 Ft.	574
Persian, Ivory Field, Gold, Green, Sky Blue Highlights, 1900s, 4 x 5 Ft.	780
Persian, Ivory Medallion, Spandrels, Red Central Panel, Repeating Designs, 1900s, 5 x 8 Ft.	431
Persian, Medallion, Candelabra, Torches, Wool, 1900s, 10 Ft. x 6 Ft. 7 In.	2400
Persian, Pictorial, Architecture, Figures, Zodiac Signs, 6 Ft. 6 In. x 9 Ft. 4 In. *illus*	1152
Persian, Silk, Birds, Flowers, Black, White, Green Outline, Cinnamon, Inner Broken Border, 4 x 6 Ft.	767
Persian, Wedding, Figures In Center, Flowers, Borders, 1900s, 6 Ft. x 4 Ft. 4 In. *illus*	720
Pictorial, Figures, Chinese Landscape, Colored Wool, Contemporary, 6 Ft. 6 In. x 9 Ft. 6 In. *illus*	1342
Pictorial, Fish, Dots, Olive Green Field, 4 Ft. x 6 Ft. 2 In.	960
Pictorial, Persian, Taj Mahal & Figures, 4 Ft. 7 In. x 7 Ft. 5 In. *illus*	519
Pictorial, Turtles, Bubbles, Light Brown Field, Multicolor, Turkey, 4 Ft. x 6 Ft. 4 In.	1020
Prayer, Balouch, Brown Field, Geometric Medallions, Peach, Brown, 8-Point Stars, 1900, 2 x 2 Ft. .	180
Prayer, Balouch, Dark Field, Outlined, 3 Medallions, Multiple Borders, 1900, 1 x 3 Ft.	96
Prayer, Balouch, Geometric Mihrab, Red, Black, Brown, 1900, 2 x 4 Ft.	240
Prayer, Balouch, Red, Brown Mihrab, Earth Tone Borders, 1960, 3 x 5 Ft.	240
Prayer, Mihrab, Embroidered, Fan, Red, Wool, Stumpwork, Silk Flowers, 1800s, 6 Ft. 6 In. x 4 Ft. 6 In.	1140
Prayer, Mihrab, Green, Orange, Red, Silk, Fringe, Cloth Sleeve, 1900s, 3 Ft. 2 In. x 2 Ft.	96
Prayer, Mihrab, Red & White Outline, Blue Ground, Inverted Vase, Silk, 1 Ft. 11 In. x 1 Ft. 6 In. .	590
Prayer, Persian, Leaf & Limb Pattern, Fine Weave, Cobalt Blue Ground, c.1935, 4 x 6 Ft.	240
Prayer, Turkish, Red Field, Flowers, Mustard Border, 3 Ft. 6 In. x 4 Ft. 7 In.	60
Sarouk, Circular Flower Medallion, Burgundy Field, Gold Borders, 1900, 6 x 9 Ft.	600

Rug, Tabriz, Central Medallion, Flowers, Multiple Borders, Fringe, c.1910, 13 Ft. 10 In. x 10 Ft.
$960

Cowan's Auctions

Rug, Tibetan, Abstract Trees, Black, Gold, Teal, Red Highlights, Runner, 3 Ft. x 10 Ft. 6 In.
$369

Brunk Auctions

R

Rug, William Morris Style, Contemporary, Flowers, Leaves, Hand Woven, Wool, 8 x 10 Ft.
$688

Rago Arts and Auction Center

> **TIP**
> *An Oriental rug given normal wear should last over 50 years.*

Rug, William Morris Style, Stylized Flowers, Wool, 9 Ft. x 11 Ft. 8 In.
$1,875

Rago Arts and Auction Center

Rug, Wool, Geometric Shapes, Blue Heart Shape, Red Ground, 12 Ft. 4 In. x 9 Ft. 11 In.
$3,750

Heritage Auctions

Sarouk, Feraghan, Center Red Diamond, Flowers, Branches, Navy, 1900, 6 Ft. 7 In. x 4 Ft. 6 In.	2000
Sarouk, Flowering Branches, Flower Bouquets, Blue, Tan, Ivory, Green, 1900s, 9 x 12 Ft.	840
Sarouk, Red, Flower Sprays, Hand Knotted, Wool, 9 x 11 Ft.	410
Sarouk, Stepped Diamond, Spandrels, Cobalt Ground, Flowers, 1900s, 10 x 14 Ft.	875
Saruok, Lobed Diamond Medallion, Tan, Blue Green, Gold, Flowers, Vines, Palmettes, 1900s, 9 x 12 Ft.	180
Senneh, Boteh Medallions, Ivory Field, Navy Border, Hand Woven, 1900s, 6 Ft. 3 In. x 4 Ft. 6 In.	1920
Serab, Camel Ground, Ivory, Blue, Turquoise, c.1950, Runner, 3 Ft. 6 In. x 18 Ft. 6 In.	984
Serapi, Gabled Medallion, Dark Pink, Dark Blue, Beige, Ivory Subfield, 1900s, 8 Ft.	390
Serapi, Gabled Medallion, Vine, Ivory Field, Peach Subfield, Red, 6 x 9 Ft.	420
Serapi, Geometric Medallion, Pink Center, Navy Blue, Ivory Pendants, 1900s, 8 Ft.	240
Shiraz, Geometric Medallion, Red Brown, Ivory Botehs, Diagonal Rows, 1900, 5 x 5 Ft.	96
Shiraz, Geometric Medallions, Rust Field, Blue & Red Stylized Designs, 1900, 6 x 10 Ft. *illus*	570
Shirvan, 5 Medallions, Geometric, Red, 1930, 9 Ft. 8 In. x 3 Ft. 9 In.	138
Silk, Tree, Flowers, Hand Knotted, 4 x 6 Ft.	1298
Soumak Flat Weave, Dense Rows, Flowers, Vines, Red, Ivory, Tassels, 4 Ft. x 6 Ft. 4½ In.	1694
Sultanabad, Blossoms, Entwined Palmettes, Gold Field, Salmon Red Guard, 8 x 11 Ft.	840
Sultanabad, Scrolling Vine Gold, Blossoms, Palmettes, Leaves, Dark Gold, 1900s, 8 x 11 Ft.	270
Tabriz, Central Medallion, Flowers, Multiple Borders, Fringe, c.1910, 13 Ft. 10 In. x 10 Ft. *illus*	960
Tabriz, Flowers, Tan, Navy, Red, Ivory, Vines, Leaves, Vases, 1900s, 9 Ft. 4 In. x 12 Ft. 7 In.	1080
Tabriz, Scrolling Leaves, Orange Field, Sino-Persian, 6 x 9 Ft.	63
Tibetan, Abstract Trees, Black, Gold, Teal, Red Highlights, Runner, 3 Ft. x 10 Ft. 6 In. *illus*	369
Tibetan, Geometric, Beige Palette, Wool, Silk, 1900s, 10 x 9 Ft.	48
Turkish, Kilim, Geometric Designs, Brown, Beige, Red, 4 x 10 Ft.	31
Turkish, Repeating Designs Overall, Cobalt Panel, Ivory & Gold Accents, 4 Ft. 4 In. x 5 Ft.	2091
Turkish, Ushak, Angora, Gray Ground, Gray & Cream Flowers, Border, 8 x 10 Ft.	875
Turkoman, Medallions, Ivory Field, Red Border, Persian, 1900s, 6 Ft. 9 In. x 4 Ft. 6 In.	100
Turquoise, Black, Brown, Straw Color, Earth Tones, 3 Ft. 2 In. x 2 Ft. 7 In.	1295
Ushak, Gray Shape, Orange & Red Geometrics, Anatolia, c.1925, 4 x 4 Ft.	1125
William Morris Style, Contemporary, Flowers, Leaves, Hand Woven, Wool, 8 x 10 Ft. *illus*	688
William Morris Style, Stylized Flowers, Wool, 9 Ft. x 11 Ft. 8 In. *illus*	1875
Wool, Birds, Flowers Bouquet, Curving Vine, Blue, Red, Ivory, Green, 3 x 4 Ft.	236
Wool, Blue, Woodgrain Pattern, 8 Ft. x 9 Ft. 10 In.	1625
Wool, Flowers, Leaves, Blue Open Field, Outlined Spandrels, Red, Blue, White, 10 x 21 Ft.	590
Wool, Flowers, Pink, Gray, Blue, Green, Red, White, Ivory Field, 2 x 9 Ft.	413
Wool, Flowers, Vines, Red, Blue, Cream, Fringe, Rubia Carpet, Turkey, 7 Ft. x 11 Ft. 6 In.	1652
Wool, Geometric Letter Shapes, Blue, White, Edward Fields, 9 x 9 Ft.	3250
Wool, Geometric Shapes, Blue Heart Shape, Red Ground, 12 Ft. 4 In. x 9 Ft. 11 In. *illus*	3750
Wool, Ivory Ground, Meandering Designs, Cranberry Borders, 4 x 5 Ft.	148
Wool, Ivory, Red, Blue, White Ground, Red, Black Guard Borders, 5 x 10 Ft.	266
Wool, Pile, Bright Colors, After Henri Matisse, Round, 4 Ft.	250
Wool, Squiggles, Spots, Red, Brown, Cream Ground, 8 Ft. 9 In. x 11 Ft. 9 In.	875
Wool, Tribal, Geometric Patterns, Ivory Field, Blue, Red Accents, Zigzag Sides, 11 x 16 Ft.	413

RUMRILL POTTERY was designed by George Rumrill of Little Rock, Arkansas. From 1933 to 1938, it was produced by the Red Wing Pottery of Red Wing, Minnesota. In January 1938, production was transferred to the Shawnee Pottery in Zanesville, Ohio. It was moved again in December of 1938 to Florence Pottery Company in Mt. Gilead, Ohio, where Rumrill ware continued to be manufactured until the pottery burned in 1941. It was then produced by Gonder Ceramic Arts in South Zanesville until early 1943.

Vase, Matte Blue, 6 Balls Near Base, 9 In.	60
Vase, Water Lilies, Cream & Plum Glazes, Turtle Handles, 6 x 8 In. *illus*	125

RUSKIN is a British art pottery of the twentieth century. The Ruskin Pottery was started by William Howson Taylor, and his name was used as the mark until about 1899. The factory, at West Smethwick, Birmingham, England, stopped making new pieces in 1933 but continued to glaze and sell the remaining wares until 1935. The art pottery is noted for its exceptional glazes.

Bowl, Cream, Green, Flame Glaze, 1932, 12 x 9 In.	128

R

Vase, Crystalline Glaze, Shaded Blue, Salmon & Orange, Impressed, 1932, 6⅜ In.	265
Vase, Crystalline Glaze, Yellow, Aqua Crystals At Neck, Aqua Drizzled Base, 1931, 4½ In.	189
Vase, Trumpet, Blue, Orange, Green, Marked, c.1930, 9 In.	309

RUSSEL WRIGHT designed dinnerware in modern shapes for many companies. Iroquois China Company, Harker China Company, Steubenville Pottery, and Justin Tharaud and Sons made dishes marked *Russel Wright*. The Steubenville wares, first made in 1938, are the most common today. Wright was a designer of domestic and industrial wares, including furniture, aluminum, radios, interiors, and glassware. A new company, Bauer Pottery Company of Los Angeles, is making Russel Wright's American Modern dishes using molds made from original pieces. The pottery is made in Highland, California. Pieces are marked *Russel Wright by Bauer Pottery California USA*. Russel Wright Dinnerware and other original pieces by Wright are listed here. For more prices, go to kovels.com.

STERLING CHINA
by
Russel Wright

Russel Wright
1948–1950

Russel Wright
1948–1953

Russel Wright
FLAIR

Russel Wright
1959

Aluminum, Punch Set, Lacquered Wood, Bowl, Ladle, 12 Cups, Tray, Stamped, 12 x 20 In. *illus*	6250
Aluminum, Serving Set, Wood, Cork, Ball Form Server, 1930s, 4 Piece, 17-In. Tray	219
American Modern, Bowl, Fruit Lug Handle, Seafoam Green, 6⅛ In.	10
American Modern, Cup & Saucer, After Dinner, Coral	44
Coffeepot, Lid, Blue Green, Sterling China, 9 In.	174
Copper, Candelabrum, 3-Light, Round, 13¼ In.	1500
Iroquois Casual, Casserole, Lid, Parsley, Dark Green, 2 Qt.	81
Iroquois Casual, Teapot, Turquoise, 5¾ x 10¼ In.	200
Oceana, Tray, Relish, Hard Rock Maple, 4 Shaped Wells, 1930s, 18 x 7 In.	1250
Pitcher, Water, Straw Yellow, Sterling China, 9 x 6½ In.	206
Spun Aluminum, Punch Bowl Set, 8 Cups, 9 Piece	600
Spun Aluminum, Tea Set, Teapot, Sugar & Creamer, Tray, Wood Handles, 4 Piece	780

SABINO glass was made in the 1920s and 1930s in Paris, France. Founded by Marius-Ernest Sabino (1878–1961), the firm was noted for Art Deco lamps, vases, figurines, and animals in clear, colored, and opalescent glass. Production stopped during World War II but resumed in the 1960s with the manufacture of nude figurines and small opalescent glass animals. Pieces made in recent years are a slightly different color and can be recognized. Only vintage pieces are listed here.

Sabino France

Figure, Stork, White Opalescent, Paris, 4¼ In.	240
Group, Panthers, Opalescent, Marked Paris, 1928, 5¾ x 8 In.	900
Plate, Birth Of Star, Signed, 11 In.	330
Vase, Opalescent, Draped Women, c.1925, 14 In.	1500

SALOPIAN ware was made by the Caughley factory of England during the eighteenth century. The early pieces were blue and white with some colored decorations. Another ware referred to as Salopian is a late nineteenth-century tableware decorated with color transfers.

Salopian

Bowl, Cobalt Blue, Gold Trim, Fluted, S Mark, c.1795, 6 x 3 In.	172
Plate, Rural Landscape, Transfer Print, Flower & Leaf Border, 8½ In. *illus*	94

SALT AND PEPPER SHAKERS in matched sets were first used in the nineteenth century. Collectors are primarily interested in figural examples made after World War I. Huggers are pairs of shakers that appear to embrace each other. Many salt and pepper shakers are listed in other categories and can be located through the index at the back of this book.

Cactus, Potted, Orange, Brown, Green, Mexico, 3 In.	43

Rumrill, Vase, Water Lilies, Cream & Plum Glazes, Turtle Handles, 6 x 8 In.
$125

Ruby Lane

Russel Wright, Aluminum, Punch Set, Lacquered Wood, Bowl, Ladle, 12 Cups, Tray, Stamped, 12 x 20 In.
$6,250

Rago Arts and Auction Center

Salt & Pepper, Cotton Bales, Pink, Slag Glass, Metal Screw Top, 2½ x 2 In.
$36

Martin Auction Co.

Salt & Pepper, Cranberry Coin Spot, Blue Flowers, Silver Plate Lids, 3½ In.
$230

Woody Auction

New Use for Old Salts
Old salt and pepper shakers without tops can be used as small flower vases.

S

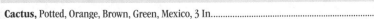

Salt & Pepper, Monks, Twin Winton, 1960s, 6 x 3 In.
$125

Ruby Lane

Salt & Pepper, Peek-A-Boo, Red, White, Van Tellingen, c.1945, 4 In.
$135

Ruby Lane

Sampler, Alphabet, Sailing, Ships, Buildings, Figures, Silk On Linen, 1815, 24 x 24 In.
$480

Garth's Auctioneers & Appraisers

Sampler, Alphabet, Trees, Gazebo, Hannah Johnson, 24 x 19¼ In.
$406

Garth's Auctioneers & Appraisers

Clown, Reamer Heads, Polka Dots, 2⅜ In.	12
Cotton Bales, Pink, Slag Glass, Metal Screw Top, 2½ x 2 In. ....*illus*	36
Cranberry Coin Spot, Blue Flowers, Silver Plate Lids, 3½ In. ....*illus*	230
Cranberry Glass, Overlapping Leaves, 3⅛ In.	17
Cut Glass, Stars & Moons, Sterling Silver Lid, 1800s, 2¾ In.	75
Esso Extra, Plastic, Premium, 1950s, 2¾ In.	65
Flowers, Etched Green Glass, Metal Top, Stand	38
Monks, Twin Winton, 1960s, 6 x 3 In. ....*illus*	125
Peek-A-Boo, Red, White, Van Tellingen, c.1945, 4 In. ....*illus*	135
Rooster, Wood, Cylindrical, 1950s, 4½ In.	17

SALT GLAZE has a grayish white surface with a texture like an orange peel. It is a method of decoration that has been used since the eighteenth century. Salt-glazed pieces are still being made.

Jar, Dog, Retriever, Fancy Collar, Blue Glaze, White's Utica, c.1860 146

ABCDE SAMPLERS were made in America from the early 1700s. The best examples were made from 1790 to 1840. Long, narrow samplers are usually older than square ones. Early samplers just had stitching or alphabets. The later examples had numerals, borders, and pictorial decorations. Those with mottoes are mid-Victorian. A revival of interest in the 1930s produced simpler samplers, usually with mottoes.

Alphabet, 10 Lines, Silk On Linen, Green Chain, Border, Frame, 1850s, 17 x 27 In.	60
Alphabet, Birds, Flowers, Rabbit, House, Portico, Dormer, 1826, 19 x 18 In.	630
Alphabet, Birds, Trees, Silk On Linen, Catherine Haines, Frame, 1825, 18 x 17 In.	454
Alphabet, Love One Another, House, Tree, Fence, Susan Griffin, 1892, 16 x 17 In.	63
Alphabet, Potted Flowers, Birds, Crowns, Baskets, England, 1846, 24 x 21 In.	219
Alphabet, Proverbs, Decorative Band, Silk On Canvas, 1800s, 12 x 10 In.	480
Alphabet, Red Buildings, 1800s, 10½ x 11 In.	117
Alphabet, Register, Family Name, Birth Dates, 17½ x 19¾ In.	688
Alphabet, Sailing, Ships, Buildings, Figures, Silk On Linen, 1815, 24 x 24 In. ....*illus*	480
Alphabet, Sarah Jane Ham, Silk On Linen, 1825, 17½ x 17½ In.	1500
Alphabet, Striped Floral Basket, Flowering Trees, Vine Border, 1822, 19 x 17 In.	1750
Alphabet, Trees, Baskets, Crowns, King, Queen, Duke, Marquess, Silk On Linen, 1836, 18 x 15 In.	240
Alphabet, Trees, Gazebo, Hannah Johnson, 24 x 19¼ In. ....*illus*	406
Alphabet, Verse, Flower, Basket, Birds, Crowns & Borders, Silk On Wool, 1796, 22 x 17 In.	406
Alphabet, Verse, Flowers, Vines, Trees, Birds, Silk On Wool, 1830, 18 x 16 In.	330
Alphabet, Verse, Margaret Collie, Wrought In The 11th Year Of Her Age, 1791, Frame, 21 x 20 In.	270
Alphabet, Verse, Owls, 1821, 15 x 16 In.	623
Alphabet, Verse, Remember Thy Creator, 12 x 12 In.	270
House, Manor, Trees, Shrubs, Urns, Flowers, Trellis, 19½ x 15½ In.	605
Pictorial, Courting Couple, Flowers, Yellow, Brown, 24 x 17½ In.	375
Pictorial, Flower Basket, Bouquets, Elizabeth Maria Puddicomb, 1828, 24¾ x 22¼ In.	281
Pictorial, Flower Bouquet, Verse, Flower Border, Mary Robinson, 1829, 20 x 18 In.	375
Pictorial, Flowers, Quaker, Catharine S. Hays, Hillsboro, Ohio, Frame, 1831, 14 x 12½ In.	225
Presentation, Adam & Eve, Snake, Tree, House, Pink, Green, 22 x 20 In ....*illus*	1440
Register, Strawberry Vine Cartouche, 16½ x 15 In.	4500
Verse, Flowers, Basket, Leaves, Sarah Jane Ham, Silk On Linen, 1826, 21½ x 17½ In.	1500
Verse, Home Sweet Home, 2 Birds, Nest, Sarah J. Harsh, Needlework, Punch Paper, 1873, 23 x 11 In.	35
Verse, House, Trees, Birds, Elizabeth Smith Cathcart, Rosewood Frame, 1842, 19 x 19 In.	1220
Verse, Landscape, Hills, Birds, Church, House, Sheep, Ship, Swans, Church, House, 17 x 17 In.	1512
Verse, Scripture, Alphabet, Vines, Numbers, 2 Flower Baskets, Bird, Silk On Linen, 1830s, 18 x 15 In.	80

SAMSON and Company, a French firm specializing in the reproduction of collectible wares of many countries and periods, was founded in Paris in the early nineteenth century. Chelsea, Meissen, Famille Verte, and Chinese Export porcelain are some of the wares that have been reproduced by the company. The firm used a variety of marks on the reproductions. It closed in 1969.

Basket, Armorial, Reticulated Edge, Crest, Eagle, 2 Handles, 4 x 8 In. ....*illus* 74

S

Sampler, Presentation, Adam & Eve, Snake, Tree, House, Pink, Green, 22 x 20 In. $1,440

Thomaston Place Auction Galleries

Samson, Basket, Armorial, Reticulated Edge, Crest, Eagle, 2 Handles, 4 x 8 In. $74

Leland Little Auctions

Samson, Figurine, Flora, Ormolu Stand, Struck X Mark, Incised AR, c.1910, 10 ½ In. $122

Neal Auction Co.

Sandwich Glass, Lamp, Clear Font, Cobalt, White Swirls, Brass Column, Marble Base, 1800s, 9 In. $780

Garth's Auctioneers & Appraisers

Sandwich Glass, Salt, Lacy, Basket Of Flowers, Cobalt Blue, 2 x 3 In. $236

Hess Auction Group

Sarreguemines, Vase, Gilt, Princess, Looking At Embroidery, Flowers, 23 ¼ x 9 ½ In. $2,280

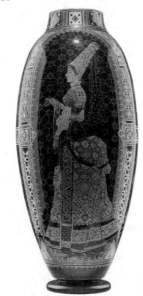

Myers Auction Gallery

Sascha Brastoff, Vase, Ceramic, Unicorn & Genie, White, Gray Gold Trim, 1950s, 9 ½ In. $495

Ruby Lane

Satin Glass, Biscuit Jar, Chrome Lid, Pink & Blue Diagonal Stripes, Ribbed, 6 In. $161

Bunch Auctions

Satin Glass, Figurine, Elephant, Trunk Up, Pink, 4 ½ x 5 In. $24

Martin Auction Co.

S

Satin Glass, Vase, Rose Shaded To Pink, White Cased, Floral Cutting, 1800s, 7 In. $114

Garth's Auctioneers & Appraisers

Satsuma, Censer, Dome Lid, Gilt Signatures On Base, Kinkozan, 7 ¼ In. $3,600

Eldred's Auctioneers and Appraisers

Satsuma, Jar, Koro, Dome Lid, Shishi Shape Handles, Figural Scenes, 3-Footed, c.1925, 25 x 19 In. $1,250

New Orleans Auction Galleries

Charger, Famille Rose Palette, Floral Border, Wood Easel, Signed, 1900s, 22 In.	750
Figurine, Flora, Ormolu Stand, Struck X Mark, Incised AR, c.1910, 10 ½ In. *illus*	122
Vase, Famille Rose, Marked, c.1900, 18 ½ x 6 In.	875

SANDWICH GLASS is any of the myriad types of glass made by the Boston & Sandwich Glass Company of Sandwich, Massachusetts, between 1825 and 1888. It is often very difficult to be sure whether a piece was really made at the Sandwich factory because so many types were made there and similar pieces were made at other glass factories. Additional pieces may be listed under Pressed Glass and in other related categories.

Cologne Bottle, Smoky Amber, Stopper, c.1850, 7 ½ In.	281
Decanter, 16 Vertical Ribs, Bulbous, 3 Applied Neck Rings, Stopper, Qt., 11 In.	2340
Lamp, Clear Font, Cobalt, White Swirls, Brass Column, Marble Base, 1800s, 9 In. *illus*	780
Lamp, Oil, 3 Printie Block, Blue, 8-Panel Stem, Square Base, Pewter Collar, 10 In., Pair	3510
Lamp, Oil, Bigler, Cobalt Blue, 8-Panel Stem, Wafer, Square Base, c.1850, 10 ¼ In., Pair	3510
Lamp, Oil, Elongated Loop, Amethyst, 8-Panel Stem, Pewter Collar, 10 In., Pair	1755
Pickle Jar, Drum, 1850-70, 5 ¾ In.	152
Salt, Lacy, Basket Of Flowers, Cobalt Blue, 2 x 3 In. *illus*	236

SARREGUEMINES is the name of a French town that is used as part of a china mark for Utzschneider and Company, a porcelain factory that made ceramics in Sarreguemines, Lorraine, France, from about 1775. Transfer-printed wares and majolica were made in the nineteenth century. The nineteenth-century pieces, most often found today, usually have colorful transfer-printed decorations showing peasants in local costumes.

Creamer, Bulldog Head, Figural, Brown, 7 In.	3932
Creamer, Horse Head, Figural, Black Mane, Brown, 9 In.	242
Vase, Cobalt Blue Coiled Base, Green Ball, Geometric Bands, Handle, 9 In.	24
Vase, Flared Rim, Flowers, Arabesques, Pierced Metal Gallery, 1900, 20 x 8 ½ In.	492
Vase, Gilt, Princess, Looking At Embroidery, Flowers, 23 ¼ x 9 ½ In. *illus*	2280
Vase, Green, Yellow, Stacked Shapes, Elephant Handles, 8 ½ In.	48

SASCHA BRASTOFF made decorative accessories, ceramics, enamels on copper, and plastics of his own design. He headed a factory, Sascha Brastoff of California, Inc., in West Los Angeles, from 1953 until about 1973. He died in 1993. Pieces signed with the signature *Sascha Brastoff* were his work and are the most expensive. Other pieces marked *Sascha B.* or with a stamped mark were made by others in his company. Pieces made by Matt Adams after he left the factory are listed here with his name.

Ashtray, Inuit Hut On Stilts, 3-Footed, 5 ½ x 3 In.	39
Ashtray, Teepee Shape, Teal, Leaves, 3-Footed, 5 ½ x 3 ¼ In.	45
Bowl, Inuit Hut on Stilts, Snow-Covered Mountains, 7 x 5 ½ In.	50
Candleholder, Rooftop, Landscape, Cylindrical, 8 In., Pair	435
Charger, Enamel, Leaves, Berries, Red, Orange, 17 In.	385
Dish, Rooftops, Signed, c.1950, 5 In.	65
Mug, Eskimo, Brown, Black, 5 In.	30
Tray, Enamel, Flowers, Green, Blue, 17 In.	165
Tray, Glazed, Modernist Decoration, Curved, Edge, Ceramic Art Co., c.1950, 3 x 17 x 9 In.	125
Vase, Ceramic, Unicorn & Genie, White, Gray Gold Trim, 1950s, 9 ½ In. *illus*	495

SATIN GLASS is a late-nineteenth-century art glass. It has a dull finish that is caused by hydrofluoric acid vapor treatment. Satin glass was made in many colors and sometimes has applied decorations. Satin glass is also listed by factory name, such as Webb, or in the Mother-of-Pearl category in this book.

Biscuit Jar, Chrome Lid, Pink & Blue Diagonal Stripes, Ribbed, 6 In. *illus*	161
Blue, White, Mother-Of-Pearl, Ruffled Rim, Silver Plate, Birds, Goodfellow & Sons, 13 In.	441
Bowl, Diamond Optic, Fluted, Peach & White Cased, 2 ¾ x 4 ¾ In.	12
Bowl, Pink, Shell Shape, Ruffles, 10 x 11 In.	30
Figurine, Elephant, Trunk Up, Pink, 4 ½ x 5 In. *illus*	24
Lamp, Ball Shade, Drape Pattern, 6-Sided Base, Nutmeg, Chimney, 1890, 4 ½ x 9 ⅜ In.	70

S

Lamp, Molded Drape, Embossed Ball Shade, Square Base, Clear Chimney, 1900, 4 x 8¾ In..... 90
Pitcher, Hobnail, Pink, Applied White Handle, 7½ In... 60
Vase, Rose Shaded To Pink, White Cased, Floral Cutting, 1800s, 7 In. .... *illus* 114

SATSUMA is a Japanese pottery with a distinctive creamy beige crackled glaze. Most of the pieces were decorated with blue, red, green, orange, or gold. Almost all Satsuma found today was made after 1860, especially during the Meiji Period, 1868–1912. During World War I, Americans could not buy undecorated European porcelains. Women who liked to make hand-painted porcelains at home began to decorate white undecorated Satsuma. These pieces are known today as "American Satsuma."

Basket, Cricket, Bouquet Finial, Flowers, Blue Handle, Multicolor, 6 In.......................... 307
Bowl, 100 Arhats, Robed, Gilt Framed Faces, Dense Design, Flared Rim, c.1915, 7 x 14 In. 1000
Bowl, Figures, Screens, Monkeys, Chrysanthemums, c.1875, 3¾ In............................... 4484
Bowl, Lobed, Figures, River Landscape, Mt. Fuji, 1000 Flower Design, 2¾ In. 420
Box, Peacock & Wisteria, Signed, c.1870, 4 In. 875
Box, Round, Kogo, 23 Figures Of Noble Men, Musicians, Shrine, Banners, Ring Of Fire, 1½ x ¾ In.. 1900
Censer, 3 Lion Heads, 2 Lion Shape Handles, 1800s, 11½ In..................................... 570
Censer, Dome Lid, Gilt Signatures On Base, Kinkozan, 7¼ In........................... *illus* 3600
Censer, Earthenware, Turquoise Colored Glaze, Ivory Covers, Yabu Meizan 2500
Censer, Rooster, Perched On Drum, 4-Footed Base, Gilt, Late 1800s, 11 In. 750
Jar, Flowers, Butterflies, Cream Ground, Handles, 6-Character Mark, 13 x 8½ In. 553
Jar, Koro, Dome Lid, Shishi Shape Handles, Figural Scenes, 3-Footed, c.1925, 25 x 19 In.. *illus* 1250
Jar, Melon Shape, Seated Figures, 13 x 11½ In.. 738
Jardiniere, Well Bucket Shape, Flowers, Bamboo, c.1900, 9½ In....................... *illus* 360
Plate, New Year Festival, Gosu Blue, Gilt Border, Signed, Late 1800s, 8½ In. 406
Plate, Porcelain, Millefleur Pattern, Marked, 1900s.. 96
Teapot, Dragon Spout, Handle, Portraits, 9½ In. 400
Teapot, Figural Dragon Handle, Spout Classic Scenes, Gold, 5 In................................ 180
Urn, Foo Dog Handles, Figures, Red, Yellow, Footed, c.1920, 27 In.............................. 125
Vase, Bucket Shape, Figural Decorations, Gilt, Pair, Late 1800s, 8 In........................... 250
Vase, Buddha, Immortals, Saints, Scrolling Dragon, Gold, White, Blue, Handles, 15½ In. 5250
Vase, Elongated, Splayed Food, Handles, Emperor's Court Scenes, c.1950, 28 x 9 In., Pair......... 2125
Vase, Figures, Eagle, Birds, Rocky Outcrop, Metal Mount, Oval, c.1925, 32 x 14 In., Pair 580
Vase, Flowers, Phoenix, 15 In.. 840
Vase, Hexagonal Meiping Shape, Shimazu Crest, 10 In... 84
Vase, Moriage, Genre Scene, Gilt Foo Dog Handles & Finial, 3-Footed, 1900, 29 In.............. 288
Vase, Peacocks, Stylized Flowers, Birds, Floral Sprays In Heavy Slip, Signed, 1927, 14½ In....... 189
Vase, Relief Demon, Brocade Patterns, Red, Tan, Gilt, 11 x 9 In. 1500
Vase, Scenes Of Emperor & Empress, Gilt Base, Mounted As Lamp, Pair, c.1950, 35½ In., Pair ... 1625
Vase, Sloping Sides, Dragons, Dogs, Leaves, Bamboo Stems, Kyoto Kinkozan Zo, 10 In............. 2242

SATURDAY EVENING GIRLS, *see Paul Revere Pottery category.*

SCALES have been made to weigh everything from babies to gold. Collectors search for all types. Most popular are small gold dust scales and special grocery scales.

Apothecary, Cast Iron, Blue & Red Paint, Brass Container, Chinese, 15 x 7 In. ..., ... 170
Apothecary, Henry Troemner, Glass Top, Marble, Ebony Case, Counterweights, 1900s, 7½ x 14 x 7 In.. 120
Balance, Brass, Gillard Dock, Harrisburg, Pa., 1820, 20 x 28½ In. 118
Balance, Brass, Round Plate, Square Plate, England, 6½ x 13 In. 30
Balance, Brass, Scrolling, Trays, Chains, Center Support, England, 25 In. 120
Balance, Double, Bowl, Pan, Iron, Brass, c.1875, 8 x 13¾ In. 225
Balance, Double, Iron, Brass, c.1800s, 7½ x 23½ In. 100
Balance, Golden Finish, Copper Weighing Dish, Computing Scale Co., 14 x 15 x 4½ In............. 360
Balance, Metal, Wood Base, c.1900, 22 x 21½ In. 100
Candy, Brandtford, Weighs Up To 3 Lbs., Black, Maroon, Golden Pinstripe Detailing, 15 x 15 x 7 In.. 1280
Commodity, Painted Wood & Iron, Walker, Marked, America, 1800s, 95½ x 115 In. 732
Postage, S. Mordan & Co., Brass, Balance, Weights, Letter Plate Marked, 1830-90, 13 x 6 x 5 In. .. 70

Satsuma, Jardiniere, Well Bucket Shape, Flowers, Bamboo, c.1900, 9½ In. $360

Eldred's Auctioneers and Appraisers

Scale, Weighing, Howe, Cast Iron Frame, Brass Scales & Iron Weights, 1800s, 28 x 44 x 9 In. $330

Garth's Auctioneers & Appraisers

Schafer & Vater, Cigarette Holder, Elephant, Howdah On Back Holds 6 Cigarettes, 5 x 3½ In. $175

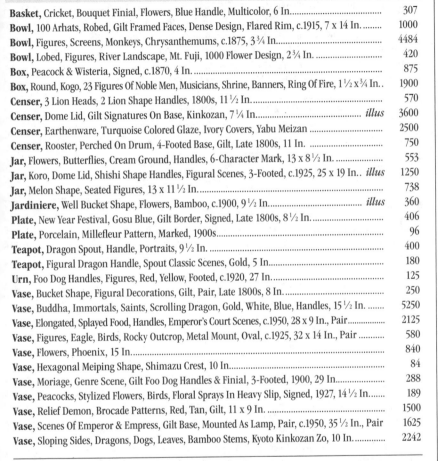

Ruby Lane

S

Scheier, Vase, Faces, Glazed Earthenware, Incised, Edwin Scheier, 1950s-60s, 10 x 10 In.
$5,625

Rago Arts and Auction Center

Schneider, Vase, Cameo, Mottled Body, Orange Art Deco Flowers, Signed, Charder, 1900s, 12 In.
$900

Garth's Auctioneers & Appraisers

Schneider, Vase, Red Glass, Yellow Spots, Mottled, c.1920, 27⅛ In.
$1,875

Heritage Auctions

Weighing, American Scale Mfg., White, 50 In.	175
Weighing, Brass, Pendulum, Bowl, Iron, 3-Footed Base, 1900-30, 6 x 4 x 11 In.	120
Weighing, Fairbanks Wood, Brass, Metal, Wheels, 58 In.	322
Weighing, Fairbanks, Cast Iron Weights, Farm, Industrial, 1900s, 43 x 27 x 3 In.	63
Weighing, Fairbanks, White, 60 In.	58
Weighing, Howe, Cast Iron Frame, Brass Scales & Iron Weights, 1800s, 28 x 44 x 9 In..... *illus*	330

SCHAFER & VATER, makers of small ceramic items, are best known for their amusing figurals. The factory was located in Volkstedt-Rudolstadt, Germany, from 1890 to 1962. Some pieces are marked with the crown and *R* mark, but many are unmarked.

Bottle, Scotch Man, Tam-O'-Shanter, With Walking Stick, Head Stopper, 5½ In.	115
Cigarette Holder, Elephant, Howdah On Back Holds 6 Cigarettes, 5 x 3½ In. .... *illus*	175
Creamer, Mother Goose, Bonnet, Handle, Blue, c.1910, 4 In.	105
Dresser Box, Bust, Woman, Pink, Green Cabochon, Bisque, 1½ x 3 In.	36
Dresser Jar, Pink, Jasperware Cameo OF Woman, 5 In. Diam.	39
Pitcher, Blue Jasperware, Ram's Head Spout, Angels, Children Playing, 4½ In.	169

Scheier **SCHEIER POTTERY** was made by Edwin Scheier (1910–2008) and his wife, Mary (1908–2007). They met while they both worked for the WPA, and married in 1937. In 1939, they established their studio, Hillcrock Pottery, in Glade Spring, Virginia. Mary made the pottery and Edwin decorated it. From 1940 to 1968, Edwin taught at the University of New Hampshire and Mary was artist-in-residence. They moved to Oaxaca, Mexico, in 1968 to study the arts and crafts of the Zapotec Indians. When the Scheiers moved to Green Valley, Arizona, in 1978, Ed returned to pottery, making some of his biggest and best-known pieces.

Bowl, Figures, Incised, Stylized, Brown, 1950s, 5¾ x 6 In.	3000
Bowl, Fish, Incised, Stylized, White, 1950s, 7 x 12 In.	3000
Bowl, Lines, Incised, Stylized, 1950s, 7¾ x 11¼ In.	1000
Charger, Figures, Incised, Stylized, Blue, 11 In.	1000
Vase, Abstract Figures, Animals, Glazed Earthenware, Edwin Scheier, 1950s-60s, 9 x 5 In.	6000
Vase, Faces, Glazed Earthenware, Incised, Edwin Scheier, 1950s-60s, 10 x 10 In. .... *illus*	5625
Vase, Figures, Faces, Glazed Earthenware, Edwin Scheier, 1950s-60s, 14 x 7 In.	8125
Vase, Figures, Glazed Earthenware, Footed, Edwin Scheier, 1950s-60s, 6 x 4½ In.	1500
Vase, Footed, Figures & Fish, Pear Shape, Blue, Glazed, Earthenware, c.1950, 6 x 4½	1500

Schneider **SCHNEIDER GLASSWORKS** was founded in 1917 at Epinay-sur-Seine, France, by Charles and Ernest Schneider. Art glass was made between 1918 and 1933. The company went bankrupt in 1939. Charles Schneider and his sons opened a new glassworks in 1949. Art glass was made until 1981, when the company closed. See also the Le Verre Francais category.

Bowl, Light Blue, Multicolor Frit Decorated Rim, Black Foot, Signed, 5 x 8 In.	424
Bowl, Low, Internally Frit Decorated, Iron Grapevine Frame, Unsigned, 3 x 9½ In.	90
Bowl, Orange & Lavender Mottled, Black Amethyst Stem, Bronze Base, Signed, 6½ x 11 In.	480
Bowl, Triangular, Cranberry, Geometric Cutting, Footed, 1930s, 4½ x 8 In.	950
Bowl, White, Pink, Amethyst Base, Signed, Marked France, 4 x 11 In.	254
Charger, Cranberry, Gilt Highlights, 16¾ In.	250
Ewer, Blue, Brown, Black Handle, Signed, 1900s, 12 x 6 In.	283
Pitcher, Mottled Pink, Purple Glass, Applied Handle, 13 In.	413
Vase, Amber, Oxblood & White Spatter, Elongated, Swollen Neck, Violet Foot, 17 In.	313
Vase, Beetle, Black, Yellow, 4¾ x 12¾ In.	1250
Vase, Cameo, Mottled Body, Orange Art Deco Flowers, Signed, Charder, 1900s, 12 In. .... *illus*	900
Vase, Epines Mounted, Blown Glass, Dark Orange & Yellow Highlights, Flared Rim, 20 In.	3227
Vase, Internally Decorated, Pinks, Red, Yellow, Signed, Marked France, 14 x 4½ In.	509
Vase, Light Green Glass Ball Shape, Drapery, Textured Ground, Polished, 6 x 6½ In.	147
Vase, Matte Finish, Blue Glass Pulled Over Red With Yellow Strands, Signed, 9¾ In.	192
Vase, Mottled Glass, White To Orange, 5½ x 17 In.	910
Vase, Mottled Rose, Amethyst, Yellow, c.1925, 19 x 9¼ In.	2375
Vase, Orange Background, Flowers, Stems, 3-Dimensional Leaves, 7¾ In.	7260
Vase, Red Glass, Yellow Spots, Mottled, c.1920, 27⅛ In. .... *illus*	1875

Vase, Trumpet Neck, Over Sphere, Orange, Yellow, Purple Base, c.1900, 14¾ x 4¾ In.............. 343
Vase, Wheel Carved, Medallion Poppy, Bulbous, Footed, Yellow Ground, Signed, 16 In., Pair 9680

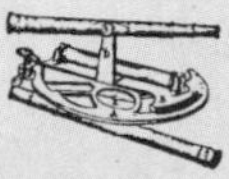

SCIENTIFIC INSTRUMENTS of all kinds are included in this category. Other categories such as Barometer, Binoculars, Dental, Medical, Nautical, and Thermometer may also price scientific apparatus.

Adding Machine, Amco, 6 x 7 In..	60
Compass, Benjamin Hanks, Surveyor, Walnut, Vernier Brass, Paper Dial, 1700s, 16 In.............	1250
Compass, Surveyor's, Alexander Megarey, c.1840, 12¾ x 5 In.	633
Compass, Surveyor's, Andrew Newell, Brass & Silver Dial, Marked, Wood Tripod, 45 x 14 In. ...	1000
Compass, Surveyor's, Brass, Screw, Sighting Vane, Wood Tripod, 1700s-1800s, 46 x 14 In. *illus*	750
Compass, Surveyor's, Engraved Face, Brass Frame, Hamlin, London, 13 In.	300
Compass, Surveyor's, Joseph Farr, Brass, Silver Dial, Inclinometer, Marked, Tripod, 63 x 13 In.	2875
Compass, Surveyor's, Paper Label, John Dupree, Boston, Wood Sighting Vanes, 54 x 12 In.. *illus*	875
Kaleidoscope, Charles Bush, Venetian Glass, Brass, 1873-1900, 9½ x 10 x 3½ In.	480
Microscope, H. Schiborr, Wood Case, 4 Objective Lenses, Electric Lamp, 12 In.	270
Model, Steam Engine, Horizontal, Dynamo Burner, 10-In. Stack, Whistle, Marklin, c.1928 12 x 12 In. .	360
Model, Steam Engine, Horizontal, Dynamo, Transmission, Water Feed Pump, Planke, 11 x 11 In.	510
Model, Steam Engine, Horizontal, Fire Box, Speed Control, Water Bucket, Marklin, c.1935, 10 x 9 In.	240
Model, Steam Engine, Horizontal, Inline Oiler, Burner, Stack, Bing Mrkt Vedes, c.1930, 13 x 11 In...	150
Planetarium, Brass Sun, Globe, Moon, Ideal Planetarium, c.1930, 12 x 20 In. .... *illus*	375
Telescope, Brass, Adjustable Stand, Working Optics, 1900s, 35 In.	360
Telescope, Brass, Tripod, Collapsible Legs, Wood, c.1980, 60 x 40 In. .... *illus*	600
Telescope, Brass, Tripod, England, 38½ In.	1500
Telescope, Brass, Wood Tripod, Collapsible Legs, 1900s, 40 In.	600
Telescope, Spotting Scope, Metal Casing, Tripod, Leather Case, 5 Lenses, 1900s, 14 In.	60
Transit, Surveyor's, Tripod, Buff & Buff..	138

SCRIMSHAW is bone or ivory or whale's teeth carved by sailors and others for entertainment during the sailing-ship days. Some scrimshaw was carved as early as 1800. There are modern scrimshanders making pieces today on bone, ivory, or plastic. Other pieces may be found in the Ivory and Nautical categories. Collectors should be aware of the recent laws limiting the buying and selling of scrimshaw and elephant ivory.

Basket, Swing Handle, Sailboats Panel On Lid, Signed, Penny Inside Base, 1987, 11 x 10 x 8 In.	480
Bowl, Relief-Carved Coconut Shell, Scalloped Border, Turned Ebony Handle, 1800, 15 In........	1080
Buckle, Silver, Leaf Accents, Jet Stones, 1970s, 2⅜ x 3 In.	110
Busk, 2 Hearts, Ship Flying 2 British Flags, Trophies Of War, 1800, 15 In.	3600
Busk, Double Arch, Potted Plant, Geometric Band, Doves, Branch, Woman, 11¾ In.	5400
Busk, Double Arch, Ship, British Flag, Drums, Cannonballs, Verse, 15½ In.	3600
Busk, Double-Arched Top, Potted Plant, Geometric Band, Oval Portrait, Leafy, 1800, 11 In......	5400
Busk, Engraved Urns, Flowers, Mother, Boy, Red, Green, Black, New England, 1845, 12 In........	938
Busk, Entwined Hearts, Geometric Bands, 1800, 13 In.	4800
Busk, Shell Inlay, Crescent Moons, Central Rectangular Panel, 1800, 15 In............................	330
Busk, Triple Arch, Entwined Arch, Island, Palm Tree, House, Hex, Crosshatch, 13 In...............	4800
Busk, Whalebone, Portrait, Young Woman, Plants, Flowers, Doves, c.1850, 11¾ In. .... *illus*	5400
Cat-O'-Nine Tails, Whalebone, 9 Hemp Tails, Sailor Knot, Crosshatched Handle, 14 x 30 In. ...	6050
Cribbage Board, Polished, Walrus Tusk, Polar Bear, Seals, 1970s, 15 In.............................	160
Figurine, Bone, Samurai, Incised Robe, Swords, Japan, 16½ In..	156
Food Chopper, Baleen Blade, Ivory Handle, Geometric, Scroll Carving, 3 x 4¼ In...................	3360
Food Chopper, Barrel Handle, Wide Blade, 7 In...	2040
Food Chopper, Double Mincing Blade, Cast Iron, Turned Hardwood Handles, 9½ x 22 In.	1000
Food Chopper, Elongated Barrel, Turned Handle, Pinned Shaft, Wide Blade, 1800, 7 x 4 In....	2040
Food Chopper, Ivory Handle, Baleen Blade, Geometric Design, Atlas N.L. Con, 3 x 4¼ In.	3360
Hippopotamus Tooth, Whaleships, Whaleboats, Whales, South Seas Village, 11 In..................	900
Panbone, American Warship, 3 British Ships, Firing Cannons, 1800, 6½ x 14 In.....................	3900
Panbone, Plaque, 4 Whaleboats, 7 Whales, Double Incised Border, 10 x 17 In.	15600
Panbone, Spouting Whale At Right, Faint Image Of A Ship, Mounting Hole, 1800, 5¾ x 10¾ In.	1680
Panbone, Whaling Scene, 5 Whaleboats, 4 Whales, Dark Roundels, 1800, 7¼ In.	9600

Scientific Instrument, Compass, Surveyor's, Brass, Screw, Sighting Vane, Wood Tripod, 1700s-1800s, 46 x 14 In. $750

Garth's Auctioneers & Appraisers

Scientific Instrument, Compass, Surveyor's, Paper Label, John Dupree, Boston, Wood Sighting Vanes, 54 x 12 In. $875

Garth's Auctioneers & Appraisers

S

Scientific Instrument, Planetarium, Brass Sun, Globe, Moon, Ideal Planetarium, c.1930, 12 x 20 In. $375

Neal Auction Co.

SCRIMSHAW

Scientific Instrument, Telescope, Brass, Tripod, Collapsible Legs, Wood, c.1980, 60 x 40 In.
$600

Thomaston Place Auction Galleries

Scrimshaw, Busk, Whalebone, Portrait, Young Woman, Plants, Flowers, Doves, c.1850, 11¾ In.
$5,400

Eldred's Auctioneers and Appraisers

Scrimshaw, Pie Crimper, Whalebone, Fluted Wheel, Turned Handle, Nantucket, c.1825, 7¾ In.
$180

Eldred's Auctioneers and Appraisers

Sevres, Vase, Black Antelope, Glazed, Gilt, Jean Mayodon, 14 x 5 In.
$1,875

Rago Arts and Auction Center

Scrimshaw, Whale's Tooth, Ship, Engraved, Pacific Of Nantucket, E. Burdett, 4¾ In.
$252,000

Rafael Osona Auctions

Sevres, Vase, Bacchanal, Nude, Horse, 2 Handles, Gilt, Signed, Jean Mayodon, 18½ In.
$4,062

Rago Arts and Auction Center

> **TIP**
> *When looking at scrimshaw, check the large hole in the tooth. Reproductions are brown, dyed to look old. Real teeth have clean root cavities.*

S

Pie Crimper, Carved Finial, Concave Scallop Shell, Fluting Identical, Crimping Wheel, 1800, 3 In.	240
Pie Crimper, Carved Handle, Whale Ivory, Pierced Ogee Design, Flower Blossom, 1800, 5 In...	2760
Pie Crimper, Curved Openwork Handle, Bamboo Shape Pillars, Wheel Mounted, 1800, 7 1/2 In.	600
Pie Crimper, Elephant Ivory, Inlaid Rectangular Shell Panels, Wheel Support, 1800, 10 1/4 In.	3000
Pie Crimper, End Of Handle Carved, Heart On Ogee Pedestal, Whale Ivory, 1800, 5 1/2 In.........	330
Pie Crimper, Fold-Out Crimping Fork, Small Spoon, Faceted Knob, Wheel Mount, 1800, 8 In.	1560
Pie Crimper, Inlaid Ebony Eyes, Nostrils, Horn, Walrus Tusk, 1800, 7 1/2 In.................	3600
Pie Crimper, Openwork Handle, Scroll At End, Pierced Heart, Red Sealing Wax, 1800, 7 In.....	1320
Pie Crimper, Pierced Heart, Cross, Diamonds, c.1820-30s, 7 3/4 In.	5100
Pie Crimper, Serpent, Nostrils, Ebony Banding, Tail End Supports Fluted Wheel, 1800, 6 In...	2160
Pie Crimper, Shaped Handle, Attached Crimping Fork, Fluted Wheel, 1800, 6 In.	480
Pie Crimper, Walrus Tusk, Unicorn Form, Inlaid Ebony Eyes, Nostrils, c.1800, 7 1/2 In.	3600
Pie Crimper, Whalebone, Fluted Wheel, Turned Handle, Nantucket, c.1825, 7 3/4 In. .... *illus*	180
Plaque, Baleen, Whaleship, Coastline, Quarter Fans, 6 3/4 x 9 In.	1080
Shell, Wood Handle, Whalebone Attachment, Bowl, 1800s, 13 In.	72
Tool, Cutting, Lignum Vitae, Dolphin Shape, Brass Tacks, 6 1/2 In.	968
Tusk, George Washington On Horseback, Doffing Cap, Eagle Grasping Shield, 1800s, 25 In.	2040
Tusk, Sailor, Woman On One Side, Sailor Holding Flag, Deer Head, 1900s, 13 In.	216
Walrus Tusk, Trophy, Tall Ships, Rope, Leafy, Flag, Drum, Musket, Eagle, Trophy, 1989, 9 1/4 In	649
Watch Stand, Whale's Tooth, Walnut Base, Star Inlay, 12 1/4 x 6 In.	3120
Watch, Whale, Ivory Panel, 2 Polished Whales Teeth, Circular Aperture, 1800, 8 x 12 x 6 In.	3120
Whalebone, Cherry, Ship's Wheel Spoke End, 1800s, 5 1/4 In.	120
Whalebone, Handle, Blubber Hook, Wrought Iron, 8 1/4 In.	540
Whalebone, Painting, Schooner Cameo, Hope Gorham Clark, c.1916, 25 In.	2117
Whale's Tooth, 2 Full-Rigged Ships, Sea, Flying Large Flags, Billowing Smokestacks, 1800, 7 In..	5400
Whale's Tooth, 4 Whaleboats Chasing 4 Whales, 1800, 6 1/2 In.	3120
Whale's Tooth, Agonies Of Death, Octagonal Cartouches, Vine Borders, Sperm Whale, 1833, 5 1/2 In.	5700
Whale's Tooth, Amorous Couple, Jack Tar Dancing, Woman Wearing Blue Dress, 1800, 7 In. .	3120
Whale's Tooth, British Ship, Full-Rigged, Flying Union Jack, Ocean, 1800, 5 In.	3120
Whale's Tooth, British Sloop-Of-War, Calm Seas, Ocean, Blue Ship's Flag, 1800, 7 1/2 In.........	2760
Whale's Tooth, Comical Scene, Woman Kicking Man In His Hindquarters, 1800, 6 1/2 In.	1020
Whale's Tooth, Compass Rose, American Whaleship, 3 Whaleboats, Flags, 1859, 6 3/4 In.	2640
Whale's Tooth, Eagle, American Flag, Sloop Approaching Land, Flowers, Red Ink, 7 In.	9600
Whale's Tooth, Eagle, Shield, Arrows, Brig, American Flag, c.1850, 7 In.	9600
Whale's Tooth, Naval Battle Scene, Ship's Hulls, Relief Carving, Waves, Smoke, 1800, 7 In.	8400
Whale's Tooth, Naval Battle, President Engaging The Endymion, British Squadron, 1800, 8 In..	6000
Whale's Tooth, Naval Engagement, British, American, Flying Flags, Carved, 1800, 5 1/2 In.	480
Whale's Tooth, Peasant Woman, Full-Length Portrait, Basket Of Berry Branches, 1800, 7 1/2 In.	1560
Whale's Tooth, Portrait, Young Woman, Black, Blue Dress, Holding Flowers, Leaves, 1800, 4 In.	1020
Whale's Tooth, Relief Carved, Pictish Warriors, Cut In Half, 7 1/4 In........................	1080
Whale's Tooth, Sailing Ship, 3-Masted, British Royal Coat, Crouching Lion, 1800, 5 3/4 In.......	1560
Whale's Tooth, Sailing Ship, 3-Masted, Rough Seas, 1800, 6 In.............................	1800
Whale's Tooth, Sailing, 2-Masted, American Flag, Spread Wing Eagle, Banner In Beak, 1800, 5 In.	7200
Whale's Tooth, Seaman Holding Cane, 3-Masted Sailing Ship, American Flag, 1800, 7 1/4 In. .	390
Whale's Tooth, Shield, Arrows, American Flag, Gaff-Rigged Sloop, Approaching Land, 1800, 7 In.	9600
Whale's Tooth, Ship With American Flag, Off Coastal Lighthouse, 1900s, 6 In..........	1140
Whale's Tooth, Ship, 3-Masted, Flying British Flag, Hull, 10 Gunports, 1800, 5 1/4 In...............	1200
Whale's Tooth, Ship, American Flagged, Coastal Lighthouse, Deeply Carved Hull, 1800, 6 In.	1140
Whale's Tooth, Ship, Engraved, Pacific Of Nantucket, E. Burdett, 4 3/4 In. .... *illus*	252000
Whale's Tooth, View Of Legendary Whaler Charles Morgan, Bow View, Signed, Dated, 7 1/2 In.	2400
Whale's Tooth, Walnut Box, Walrus Ivory, Shell Mount, 1800s, 1 x 2 3/4 x 4 In.	180
Whale's Tooth, Warship, 2-Masted, Flying 3 American Flags, Gunports, Floral Sprays, 1800, 5 In.	900
Whale's Tooth, Warship, 3-Masted, 6 Red Gunports, 1800, 6 1/2 In........................	1320
Whale's Tooth, Warship, 3-Masted, American Flag, 2-Masted Schooner, Blue Water, 1800, 6 1/4 In.	1320
Whale's Tooth, Whaleship, 3-Masted, c.1850, 6 In.	1440
Whale's Tooth, Whaleship, American Flag, Whales Off Her Bow, Whalemen, 1800, 7 In.	4800
Whale's Tooth, Whaleship, Flying American Flag, 3 Whaleboats In Water, 3 Whales, 1800, 7 In....	8400
Whale's Tooth, Whalebone Handle, Steel Ends, 1800s, 5 1/4 In.	270
Whale's Tooth, Whaling Scene, Whaleship, Whale Being Harpooned, 1900s, 5 x 9 3/4 In.	240
Whale's Tooth, Whaling Scene, Whaleships, South Seas Village Scene, 1800, 11 In..............	900

Sevres, Vase, Double Gourd, Seaside Village Landscape, Glazed, Gilt, Adrien Leduc, 1935, 15 1/2 In.
$1,375

Rago Arts and Auction Center

Sewer Tile, Figure, Pig, Brown, Salt Glaze, c.1926, 4 1/2 x 7 In.
$163

Jeffrey S. Evans

Sewing, Bird, Brass, C-Shape, Leaves, 2 Pincushions, Clamp, C. Waterman, Conn., c.1865, 5 In.
$47

Jeffrey S. Evans

This is an edited listing of current prices. Visit **Kovels.com** to check thousands of prices from previous years and sign up for free information on trends, tips, reproductions, marks, and more.

S

Sewing, Box, House Shape, Wood, Printed Exterior, Fitted, Roof Lifts, 1800s, 5½ x 6 In.
$875

Garth's Auctioneers & Appraisers

Sewing, Loom, Hand Crank, 4 Shafts, Reed, Cast Iron, Wood, Salesman's Sample, 12 x 13 In.
$2,125

Keystone Auctions LLC

Sewing, Loom, Tabletop, Wood Frame, Metal Reed, c.1950, 20 In.
$59

Jeffrey S. Evans

Whale's Tooth, Woman, Daughter, Victorian Dress, 1800, 7 In.	1320
Whale's Tooth, Woman, Full-Length Portrait, Victorian Dress, 1800, 9½ In.	3240
Whale's Tooth, Woman, Holding Bird, Blue Stripes, Feathers, Red Flowers In Her Hair, 1800, 6 In.	1200
Whale's Tooth, Woman, Holding Torch, Sheaf Of Wheat In Other Hand, 1800, 4½ In.	900

SEG, *see Paul Revere Pottery category.*

SEVRES porcelain has been made in Sevres, France, since 1769. Many copies of the famous ware have been made. The name originally referred to the works of the Royal Porcelain factory. The name now includes any of the wares made in the town of Sevres, France. The entwined lines with a center letter used as the mark is one of the most forged marks in antiques. Be very careful to identify Sevres by quality, not just by mark.

Bottle Cooler, Gilt, Feathered Flowers, Berries, Blue Tipped Handles, 1764, 7¾ In., Pair	2750
Bowl, Courting Couple, Landscape, Marked, Purple Border, Brass Stand, 12½ x 10¾ In.	54
Bowl, Lid, Gilt, Reserves, Flowers, Forest Green, Swan Handles, Stepped Foot, 5½ In.	216
Bust, Marie Antoinette, White Biscuit, Cobalt Blue Socle, 1903, 11 In.	277
Cup & Saucer, Birds In Reserves, Blue, Circles, 2 Handles, c.1790, 4½ In.	750
Cup & Saucer, Soft Paste, Flowers, Gold, Purple Shrubs, Marked, 1795, 2¾ x 6 In.	3750
Dresser Box, Blue Painted Body, Gilt Enamel Highlights, Decorated Panel, 5¼ x 11 x 7 In.	212
Goblet & Saucer, Golden Flowery Stems & Lyres, Blue Ground, Marked, 1789, 2 x 4¾ In.	2125
Goblet & Saucer, Multicolor, Stems & Palms, Marked, 1766, 2 x 5 In.	1125
Goblet & Saucer, Soft Paste, Multicolor, Animated, Marked, c.1785, 2 x 4 In.	3000
Goblet & Saucer, Soft Paste, Multicolor, Flower, Pink, Shells, Marked, 1700s, 3 x 6 In.	313
Goblet & Saucer, Soft Paste, Red & Gold Ornamentation, Leaves, Marked, 1775, 2 x 4 In.	2125
Group, Baby, Cat, Seated, Bisque, 1767-73, 5½ In.	1625
Jug, Blue, Gold Ribbons Imitating Fabric, Marked, 1765, 3 In.	1125
Jug, Flower Bouquet, Birds, Flowery Scrolls, Golden Pearls, Multicolor, Blue Background, 1788, 5½ In.	4375
Jug, Flowers, Ribbon, Pink, Dotted Circles, Multicolor, Marked, 1775, 4 In.	1250
Jug, Soft Paste, Blue & Gold Ribbons Imitating Fabric, Marked, 1765, 3¾ In.	1125
Jug, Soft Paste, Hanap Scene, Multicolor, Flower, Bird, Golden Pearls, Marked, 1788, 5½ In.	4375
Lamp, Electric, Cherub & Dolphin, Medallion Highlights, Gilt Metal Base, 30 In.	108
Perfume Bottle, Hand Painted, Flowers, Gilt, Mark, 4 x 2 x 7 In.	53
Plaque, Portrait, Profile, Man, Gray Wig, Black Coat, c.1813, 4¾ In.	1250
Plate, Courting Scene, Blue Border, Gold Stencil Highlights, Marked, Signed, De Laitre, 9 In.	150
Plate, Portrait, Poet & Comedian, Cobalt Blue, Gilt, Scalloped Border, 1853, 11 In.	1925
Plate, Portrait, Royalty, Pink Border, Signed Laure, Gilt, 1900s, 9 In.	72
Sculpture, Psyche Figural, Hard Paste, Biscuit, Marked, 1775, 12 In.	1000
Sugar, Gilt, Camaieu Rose, Cherub, Pointer, Plants, c.1760, 4 In.	500
Tray, Trefoil, Bleu Celeste, Reserve, Figure, Tree, Field, Reticulated, 8¼ In.	625
Trinket Box, Rococo Shape, Woman, Blue Shirt, Pink Skirt, Signed, Poiikel, 2½ x 3¼ In.	153
Urn, Cobalt Blue, Hand Painted, Man & Woman Seated, Lamb Scene, Signed, 23 In.	540
Vase, Bacchanal, Nude, Horse, 2 Handles, Gilt, Signed, Jean Mayodon, 18½ In. *illus*	4062
Vase, Black Antelope, Glazed, Gilt, Jean Mayodon, 14 x 5 In. *illus*	1875
Vase, Carp, Shrimp, Cream, Green, Paul Milet, Stamped, c.1900, 9⅜ x 4 In.	1750
Vase, Double Gourd, Seaside Village Landscape, Glazed, Gilt, Adrien Leduc, 1935, 15½ In. . *illus*	1375
Vase, Gourd Shape, Hunting Figures, Black, White, Gold, Glazed, Gilt, Marked, 1956, 16 x 6 In.	1500
Vase, Red, Blue Oxblood Glaze, 1892, 10 In.	1062
Vase, Roses, Violas, Daisies, Swags, 2 Handles, White, c.1774, 6½ In.	625
Vase, Urn Shaped, Framers & Animals, Celadon Glaze, France, 1951, 16 x 8 In.	1875
Vase, Viking Ships, Blue, Gold, Overglaze, Marked, France, 1951, 17 x 6 In.	937

SEWER TILE figures were made by workers at the sewer tile and pipe factories in the Ohio area during the late nineteenth and early twentieth centuries. Figurines, small vases, and cemetery vases were favored. Often the finished vase was a piece of the original pipe with added decorations and markings. All types of sewer tile work are now considered folk art by collectors.

Figure, Bird, Perched On Tree Stump, Signed, Edward Ellwood, 9½ In.	1020
Figure, Deer, Glass Eyes, c.1950, 8 x 13 In.	180

Figure, Dog, Spaniel, Sitting, Figural, Ohio, 1870s..	2287
Figure, Farmer, Standing, Hat, Holding Basket, c.1900, 11 ¼ In.	60
Figure, Frog, Sitting, Glazed, Ohio, 7 x 12 In.	550
Figure, Horse Head, 2-Tone Glaze, c.1950, 6 ½ In.	120
Figure, Lion, Reclining, Black Paint, 8 ½ x 10 In.	120
Figure, Official, Standing, Flowing Robe, Monkey, 18 ½ In................................	2420
Figure, Official, Standing, Tablet In One Hand, Snake, Stylized Waves, 17 ¾ In.	1573
Figure, Pig, Brown, Salt Glaze, c.1926, 4 ½ x 7 In. .... *illus*	163
Figure, Pig, Standing, Hollow, c.1900, 7 ½ x 13 In.	240
Figure, Squirrel, Leaning On Branch, 2-Tone Glaze, c.1925, 6 ¾ x 8 In.	531
Paperweight, Dog, Bull, Brown Salt Glaze, Ohio, 4 In.	83

SEWING equipment of all types is collected, from sewing birds that held the cloth to tape measures, needle books, and old wooden spools. Sewing machines are included here. Needlework pictures are listed in the Picture category.

Bird, Brass, C-Shape, Leaves, 2 Pincushions, Clamp, C. Waterman, Conn., c.1865, 5 In. .. *illus*	47
Bird, Brass, Tin, 5 x 4 In.	124
Box, Curved Sides, Shell Feet, Chamfered Hinged, Brass, Red, 1800s, 14 x 11 x 7 ½ In........	130
Box, Gilt, Black Lacquer, Canted, Winged Claw Feet, Interior Tray, Chinese Export, 6 x 14 ½ In.	854
Box, House Shape, Wood, Printed Exterior, Fitted, Roof Lifts, 1800s, 5 ½ x 6 In. .... *illus*	875
Box, Marquetry, Rosewood, Floral, Inlay, Divide, 1800s, 10 x 7 x 4 ¼ In.	118
Box, Needlework, Piano, Mahogany, 11 ½ In.	875
Box, White Ground, Porcelain, Multicolor, Gilding, Casket Shape, 1900s, 3 ¾ x 7 ¼ x 5 ⅛ In....	246
Cabinet, Spool, see also the Advertising category under Cabinet, Spool.	
Darning Ball, Glass Blown, White, Cranberry, Teal, c.1850, 6 In.	94
Doll, Bisque, Muslin, Painted, Pincushion Gown, Tools & Supplies Attached, 8 In.	1495
Etui, Needle Case, Agate Mount, 4 In...	813
Etui, Needle Case, Leather, Tooled, Brown, 4 ¼ In...	125
Etui, Needle Case, Leather, Tooled, White, 4 ⅛ In...	225
Etui, Needle Case, Metal, Gilt, Carnelian, Chains, Cabochons, 7 ¾ In.	750
Etui, Needle Case, Metal, Gilt, Seapod Shape, 4 In.	313
Etui, Needle Case, Silver, Shagreen, Hinge, 3 ½ In.	163
Fabric Cutter, Gear, Roller, Crank, Brass, Model, W.V. Phillips & Co., 1876, 4 ¾ In.................	75
Loom, Tabletop, Wood Frame, Metal Reed, c.1950, 20 In. .... *illus*	59
Machine, Treadle, Oak, Wheeler & Wilson, 31 x 16 In.	63
Machine, Wilcox & Gibbs, Walnut Renaissance Revival Case, Treadle, Iron, 39 ½ x 32 ½ In....	10701
Mannequin, Torso, Velvet & Satin Covered, Turned Column, Square Stepped Base, 58 In........	246
Needle Case, 9K Gold, Engraved, 4 ⅜ In.	313
Needle Case, Coquia Nut, Carved, 4 ⅛ In.	63
Needle Case, Fish, Coin Silver, Wrigglework, Tube On Back, c.1800, 2 ⅞ In...... *illus*	380
Needle Case, Porcelain, Ships, Figures, Port, White, Blue, Green, Germany, c.1890, 6 In. *illus*	230
Needle Threader, Wood Base, Magnifying Glass, Metal Arm, Spool Holder, 1916, 4 x 2 In.	50
Pincushion Dolls are listed in their own category.	
Pincushion, Bird, Fabric, Pennsylvania, 5 In.	101
Pincushion, Dog, Poodle, Bronze, Fabric Back, Marked, Geschutzt, c.1915, 6 ¾ In........... *illus*	140
Pincushion, Lion & Basket, Flowers On Pressed Glass Base, 1825, 6 ½ x 3 ½ In.	500
Pincushion, Needlework, Alphabets, Numbers, Vines, Figures, Chester Cty., Pa., 1801, 5 x 8 In..	225
Pincushion, Velvet, Graphic, Brown, Blue, 1860s, 8 In......................................	175
Scissors, Open Scrollwork, Steel, 3 ⅜ In.	63
Scissors, Openwork, Chains, Steel, 4 In.	138
Scissors, Scrollwork Handles, Steel, 2 ½ In.	50
Sheath, Knitting Needle, Fish, Wriggle Work, Silver, 2 ⅞ In.	380
Spool Cabinets are listed here or in the Advertising category under Cabinet, Spool.	
Spool Dispenser, Victorian, 3 Tiers, Iron, 10 In.	105
Spool Holder, Brass, Alternating Soldier, Woman, Children, Pedestal, Fitted Slots, 12 ¾ In.	241
Spool Holder, Brass, Cast Iron, 3 Star Shape Tiers, Claw Feet, Bone Finials, c.1890, 9 In.........	518
Spool Holder, Cast Iron, Tin, Pincushion, Thread Guides, Painted, 5 ½ In. .... *illus*	224
Spool Holder, Maple, Steel Posts, 3 Tiers, Pincushion Top, c.1885, 5 ½ In. .... *illus*	70
Spool Holder, Wood, Fabric, Pincushion Top, 6 Spool Prongs, c.1885, 7 In. .... *illus*	82

Sewing, Needle Case, Fish, Coin Silver, Wrigglework, Tube On Back, c.1800, 2 ⅞ In.

$380

Jeffrey S. Evans

Sewing, Needle Case, Porcelain, Ships, Figures, Port, White, Blue, Green, Germany, c.1890, 6 In.

$230

Bunch Auctions

Sewing, Pincushion, Dog, Poodle, Bronze, Fabric Back, Marked, Geschutzt, c.1915, 6 ¾ In.

$140

Jeffrey S. Evans

Sewing, Spool Holder, Cast Iron, Tin, Pincushion, Thread Guides, Painted, 5 ½ In.

$224

Hess Auction Group

S

SEWING

Sewing, Spool Holder, Maple, Steel Posts, 3 Tiers, Pincushion Top, c.1885, 5½ In.
$70

Jeffrey S. Evans

Sewing, Spool Holder, Wood, Fabric, Pincushion Top, 6 Spool Prongs, c.1885, 7 In.
$82

Jeffrey S. Evans

> ### TIP
> *Mayonnaise can be rubbed on water-damaged wood to restore the finish.*

Sewing, Table, Brass, Hinged, Mirror Inside, Charles Parker Co., c.1885, 31 x 12 In.
$4,480

Neal Auction Co.

Sewing, Tape Loom, Stand, Chestnut, Sawed Slots, Drilled Holes, c.1810, 37 In.
$1,298

Hess Auction Group

Sewing, Thimble, 14K Gold, Diamonds, Dots, Engraved Buildings, Steeples, c.1900, ¾ In.
$129

Jeffrey S. Evans

Sewing, Yarn Winder, Cast Iron, Brown & Sharpe, 20 x 20 In.
$150

Woody Auction

S

Table, Brass, Hinged, Mirror Inside, Charles Parker Co., c.1885, 31 x 12 In. ...... *illus*	4480
Table, Flax Break, Maple, Hickory, Poplar, 34 x 48¼ In.	59
Tape Loom, Hand Crank, 4 Shafts, Reed, Cast Iron, Wood, Salesman's Sample, 12 x 13 In. *illus*	2125
Tape Loom, Rose Head Nail, Mortise & Tendon, 16 x 22¾ In.	322
Tape Loom, Stand, Chestnut, Sawed Slots, Drilled Holes, c.1810, 37 In. .... *illus*	1298
Thimble, 14K Gold, Diamonds, Dots, Engraved Buildings, Steeples, c.1900, ¾ In. .... *illus*	129
Thimble, C-Scroll Band, 18 K Gold, Continental, 1¾ In.	138
Yarn Winder, Cast Iron, Brown & Sharpe, 20 x 20 In. .... *illus*	150
Yarn Winder, Wood, Waisted, 1800s, 30 In.	50

SHAKER items are characterized by simplicity, functionalism, and orderliness. There were many Shaker communities in America from the eighteenth century to the present day. The religious order made furniture, small wooden pieces, and packaged medicines, herbs, and jellies to sell to "outsiders." Other useful objects were made for use by members of the community. Shaker furniture is listed in this book in the Furniture category.

Abacus, 12 Rows, Steel Rods, Rectangular Frame, Multicolor, 14¾ x 12 In.	1512
Apple Peeler, Maple, Pine, Red Finish, Extended Rectangular Platform, c.1850, 13½ x 32 In.	660
Apple Slicer, Birch, Oak, Maple, Spring Action Lever, c.1870, 21 x 29 In........... *illus*	2280
Basket, Tapered, Initialed JH, 1900s, 13½ x 12 In.	46
Basket, Work, Black Ash Splint, Double Wrapped Rim, Swing Hoop Handle, 9½ x 16 In.	900
Bonnet, Sister's, Red Silk, Quilted Inside, Neck Cape, Bowtie, 9 x 8 In.......... *illus*	1680
Bonnet, Sister's, Straw, White Cotton, Blue Lace Net, Purple Silk Cape, c.1890, 7 x 7 In.	1920
Bonnet, Sister's, Winter, Iridescent Red, Silk, Quilted Interior, Neck Cape, Bow, 9 In.	1680
Box, 2-Finger, Oval, 1800s, 2½ x 6 In.	108
Box, 3-Finger, Oval, Maple, Pine, Yellow, 4½ x 11¾ In.	3000
Box, 4-Finger, Oval, Maple, Pine, Chrome Yellow, Copper Tacks, 4 x 11 In..........	6840
Box, 4-Finger, Pantry, Oval, Copper Tacks, Bentwood Maple, 1800s, 11 In.	456
Bucket, Fitted Lid, Pine, Green, Stenciled CORN, White Porcelain Knob, 3 Steel Bands, 14 x 11½ In.	1200
Bucket, Lid, Pine, Red, 3 Black Steel Bands, Turned Pull, Ebony Birch Handle, 11 x 10 In.	1680
Bucket, Tan, Aqua, Chrome Yellow, Swing Handle, Rivets, c.1850, 14 x 10 In..........	960
Churn, Rocking, Pine, Red, Rectangular Box, Turned Handles, c.1840, 29 x 29½ In.	780
Churn, Lid, Pine, Red, Horizontal Pump Handle, Fulcrum, Splash Guard, 20 x 40 In.........	600
Corn Shucker, Cherry Wood, Steel Cutting Blades, Cherry Handle, c.1875, 1¾ x 32 In.........	1560
Cutlery Carrier, Butternut, Pine, Hickory Handle, Dovetailed, 7¼ x 15½ In.	1510
Dry Measure, Maple, Pine, Yellow Paint, Copper Tacks, Canterbury, N.H., c.1840, 6 In.... *illus*	10800
Herb Carrier, Pine, Hickory Handle, Bentwood Rim, Red, Copper Rivets, c.1875, 10 x 20 In....	390
Laundry Bag, Woven Cotton Muslin, Green Vertical Stripes, Stencil CH H, 42 x 19 In.	720
Mold, Butter Pat, Maple, 64 Pats, X Design, 80 Brass Screws, 2 x 12 In.	960
Rack, Drying, Chestnut, 4 Slats, c.1850, 38½ x 24 In.	540
Rack, Drying, Handing, Pine, 6 Collapsible Arms, c.1880, 10 x 36 In.	660
Rug Beater, Loop, Handle, 33 In.....	17
Seed Box, Hanging, Hinged Slant Lid, Poplar, Gray, 3-Section Interior, 5 x 26¾ In.....	240
Seed Box, Pine, Chestnut, Wire Hinges, Shaker Garden Seeds, 9 x 16 In.	1560
Seed Box, Pine, Dark Varnish, Garden Seeds Raised By The Society Of Shakers, 6 x 14½ In....	960
Spool Carrier, Tiger Maple, 6 Carved Spool Holders, c.1840, 3½ x 4¼ In.	360
Spool Case, Walnut, Maple, Beveled Top, Canted Front, Sliding Door, Pegs For Spools, 9 x 8 In.	1020
Stoneware, Jug, Shaker Brand Ketchup, E.D. Pettengill Co., Brown Glass, Handle, c.1900, 11 In... *illus*	287
Stove, Side Rail, 4 Flat Irons, Stove Pipe, Tool Holder, Cast Iron, 62 x 17 In.	600
Washing Machine, Walnut, Brass Parts, 3 Tubs, Hand Cranked Turning Wheel, Model, 3 x 11 In.	1880

SHAVING MUGS were popular from 1860 to 1900. Many types were made, including occupational mugs featuring pictures of men's jobs. There were scuttle mugs, silver-plated mugs, glass-lined mugs, and others.

Father, Gold Calligraphy, Porcelain, Hand Painted Flowers, 1800s, 4 x 4 In.	50
Occupational, Barrel Maker, Man With Hammer, Barrel, Gold Trim, 3⅝ x 3⅝ In.	374
Occupational, Billiard Player, Gilt Inscription, Geo. Williams, W.G. & Co., France, 4 In.. *illus*	308
Occupational, Butcher, Leads Cow To Slaughter, Gilt Name, 3½ In.	70
Occupational, Carpenter, Henry Uhl, Austria, 3½ x 3½ In.....	127

Shaker, Apple Slicer, Birch, Oak, Maple, Spring Action Lever, c.1870, 21 x 29 In. $2,280

Willis Henry Auctions

TIP
A two-finger Shaker box really has three. Two are on the bottom; one is on the lid.

Shaker, Bonnet, Sister's, Red Silk, Quilted Inside, Neck Cape, Bowtie, 9 x 8 In. $1,680

Willis Henry Auctions

Shaker, Dry Measure, Maple, Pine, Yellow Paint, Copper Tacks, Canterbury, N.H., c.1840, 6 In. $10,800

Willis Henry Auctions

S

SHAVING MUG

Shaker, Stoneware, Jug, Shaker Brand Ketchup, E.D. Pettengill Co., Brown Glass, Handle, c.1900, 11 In.
$287

Shaving Mug, Occupational, Billiard Player, Gilt Inscription, Geo. Williams, W.G. & Co., France, 4 In.
$308

Shaving Mug, Occupational, Foundry Worker, 3½ In.
$47

Occupational, Fishing, Molded Handle, Brown, Blue, White, Dan Carpenter, 1995, 3 x 5 In. ...	230
Occupational, Fisherman, Flower Sprigs, Black Band, Gold Trim, Chas. Norman, 4 x 3¾ In..	295
Occupational, Foundry Worker, 3½ In. .... *illus*	47
Occupational, Hay Delivery, Open Stake Wagon, Gilt Name, c.1900, 3⅞ In.	81
Occupational, Oil Wildcatter, Outbuildings, Storage Tanks, 3¾ x 3¾ In.	150
Occupational, Railroad Passenger Car, Yellow, Blank Name, 4 In.	292
Occupational, Trolley Car Operator, Trolley With Passengers, 3⅝ x 3¾ In.	345
Occupational, Upright Piano, Gilt Name, c.1900, 3¾ In.	140
Porcelain, Hand Painted, Figures With Boat, Artist Signed, 4 x 4 In.	295
Silver Plate, Removable Soap Tray, Brush Holder & Brush, Wilcox, 3¾ x 5 In.	120
Texaco, Star Emblem, White, Green, Ironstone, Mayer China, 1930s-40s, 3½ In.	95

Shawnee USA **SHAWNEE POTTERY** was started in Zanesville, Ohio, in 1937. The company made vases, novelty ware, flowerpots, planters, lamps, and cookie jars. Three dinnerware lines were made: Corn, Lobster Ware, and Valencia (a solid color line). White Corn pattern utility pieces were made in 1945. Corn King was made from 1946 to 1954; Corn Queen, with darker green leaves and lighter colored corn, from 1954 to 1961. Shawnee produced pottery for George Rumrill during the late 1930s. The company closed in 1961.

Ashtray, Concentric Rings, Green, 8½ In.	14
Casserole, Lobster Ware, Black, White Lid, Lobster, Handle, 2 Qt.	20
Cookie Jar, Corn King, 10 x 6¼ In.	189
Cookie Jar, Puss 'N Boots, Short Tail, Gold Trim, 10¼ In.	239
Creamer, Corn King, 4½ In.	30
Creamer, Elephant, Trunk Up, Cream, Red Ears, 4½ In.	15
Creamer, Puss 'N Boots, Yellow, 4½ In.	25
Planter, Globe, Yellow, Blue, 7½ In.	65
Planter, Ivy, Yellow, 7 x 3 In.	38
Planter, Ram, Art Deco, Brown, Gold, 6 x 4 In.	29
Salt & Pepper, Corn King, 5 In.	20
Salt & Pepper, Fruit, Multicolor, 3½ In.	22
Salt & Pepper, Jack & Jill, 5¼ x 3 In.	225
Teapot, Granny Ann, Purple Apron, Gray Hair, 1940s, 8 In.	98
Teapot, Lid, Corn King, 5 x 6½ In.	110
Teapot, Lid, Rosette, Yellow, 1930s, 9 x 5 In.	31
Wall Pocket, Little Jack Horner, c.1940, 5 x 5 In.	24

SHEARWATER **SHEARWATER POTTERY** is a family business started in 1928 by Peter Anderson, with the help of his parents, Mr. and Mrs. G.W. Anderson Sr. The local Ocean Springs, Mississippi, clays were used to make the wares in the 1930s. The company was damaged by Hurricane Katrina in 2005 but was rebuilt and is still in business, now owned by Peter's four children.

Bean Pot, Multicolor Applied Slip & Ducks, Walter Anderson, Marked, 5 x 10 In.	1830
Biscuit Jar, Butterfly, Flowers, Berries, Orange, Green, Patricia A. Findeisen, 8¾ x 6 In.	125
Bookends, Pelican, Brown, Shoal Glaze, c.1960, 10½ In.	732
Bookends, Pelican, White Enamel Glaze, 10½ x 4 In.	512
Figurine, Art Pottery, Mother Goose, Frog Prince, Molds, Hand Decorated, 1930, 9 In.	125
Figurine, Reclining Cat, Cubist, Green Glaze, W. Anderson, Marked, 1900s, 8½ x 6 In.	854
Lamp, Cast, Nubian Snake Woman, With Backpack, Skirt Base, Marked, 11 x 8 In.	118
Saucer, Jiggered, Wood Duck Design, W. Anderson, c.1950, 6 In. .... *illus*	854
Vase, Storks In Trees, Brown, Tan, 9½ In.	1750
Wall Votive, Madonna, Child, Wise Men, Shepherds, Alkaline Glaze, 1960s, 12 x 14 In.... *illus*	2318
Wine Bottle, Tapered, Alkaline Blue Glaze, Figural Lid, 14 In.	490

 SHEET MUSIC from the past centuries is now collected. The favorites are examples with covers featuring artistic or historic pictures. Early sheet music covers were lithographed, but by the 1900s photographic reproductions were used. The early music was larger than more recent sheets, and you must watch out for examples that were trimmed to fit in a twentieth-century piano bench.

Bill Bailey Won't You Please Come Home, Nita Del Campo	29
Chow Chow Musical, No. 5 Dancing Wave Polka, William Hall & Son, 1853	25
Dixie For The Union, Firth Pond & Co., New York City, 1861	135
Georgia On My Mind, Tommy Dorsey, Southern Music Publishing, 1930, 12 x 9 In.	8
I'm Always Chasing Rainbows, Harry Carroll & Joseph McCarthy, 1918, 9 x 12 In.	15
Ol' Man River, Show Boat, Polygram, 1927, 8½ x 11 In.	15
She's Always A Woman, Billy Joel, 1977	12
Shine On Harvest Moon, Remick Music Corp., 1941	10
Suddenly It's Spring, Lady In The Dark, Ginger Rogers, Famous Music Corp., c.1943, 12 x 9 In.	7
Time Out For Rhythm, Three Stooges, Film Stars, Mills Music, 1941, 9¼ x 12 In.	60
White Christmas, Bing Crosby, Danny Kaye, Rosemary Clooney, Vera Ellen, 1942, 9 x 12 In.	10
Wigwam Grand March, Beardless Abraham Lincoln, c.1861, 10 x 13 In.	960

SHEFFIELD *items are listed in the Silver Plate and Silver-English categories.*

SHELLEY first appeared on English ceramics about 1912. The Foley China Works started in England in 1860. Joseph Ball Shelley joined the company in 1862 and became a partner in 1872. Percy Shelley joined the firm in 1881. The company went through a series of name changes and in 1910 the then Foley China Company became Shelley China. In 1929 it became Shelley Potteries. The company was acquired in 1966 by Allied English Potteries, then merged with the Doulton group in 1971. Shelley is no longer being made. A trio is the name for a cup, saucer, and cake plate set.

Ashtray, Rosebud, 3¾ In.	27
Bowl, Blue Empress, 4⅞ In.	65
Cake Plate, Blue Empress, Handles, 10 In.	80
Coffeepot, Lid, Wine Grape, 4 Cup, 7 In.	349
Creamer, Blue Rock, 8 Oz.	30
Cup & Saucer, Begonia, Dainty Shape	26
Cup & Saucer, Blue Daisy, Oleander Shape	185
Cup & Saucer, Laurel, Footed	38
Cup & Saucer, Old Sevres	50
Cup & Saucer, Pole Star, Footed	26
Cup & Saucer, Rock Garden	75
Cup & Saucer, Wild Flowers, Footed	46
Gravy Boat, Underplate, Harmony	174
Mustard, Lid, Underplate, Celandine	149
Plate, Bead & Butter, Margaret Rose, 6½ In.	16
Plate, Dinner, Begonia, 10¾ In.	38
Plate, Salad, American Brookline, 8 In.	35
Plate, Salad, Laurel, 8 In.	41
Platter, Wine Grape, Oval, 16¾ In.	292
Soup, Dish, Old Sevres, 8 In.	119
Sugar & Creamer, Golden Harvest	73
Teapot, Lid, Daffodil Time, Yellow Handle, 4 Cup, 5⅜ In.	438
Tureen, Lid, Underplate	498

SHIRLEY TEMPLE, the famous movie star, was born in 1928. She made her first movie in 1932. She died in 2014. Thousands of items picturing Shirley have been and still are being made. Shirley Temple dolls were first made in 1934 by Ideal Toy Company. Millions of Shirley Temple cobalt blue glass dishes were made by Hazel Atlas Glass Company and U.S. Glass Company from 1934 to 1942. They were given away as premiums for Wheaties and Bisquick. A bowl, mug, and pitcher were made as a breakfast set. Some pieces were decorated with the picture of a very young Shirley, others used a picture of Shirley in her 1936 *Captain January* costume. Although collectors refer to a cobalt creamer, it is actually the 4½-inch-high milk pitcher from the breakfast set. Many of these items are being reproduced today.

Book, Dimples, 20th Century Fox, Saalfield Publishing Co., 1936, 10 x 9 In.	48
Bowl, Cobalt Blue, Hazel Atlas, 6½ In.	20
Button, Little Miss Movie, Goldberger, Light, 1930s, 1⅜ In.	60

Shearwater, Saucer, Jiggered, Wood Duck Design, W. Anderson, c.1950, 6 In.
$854

Neal Auction Co.

Shearwater, Wall Votive, Madonna, Child, Wise Men, Shepherds, Alkaline Glaze, 1960s, 12 x 14 In.
$2,318

Neal Auction Co.

Shirley Temple, Doll, Going Skiing, Red & Brown Costume, Stand, Skis, 1972, 17 In.
$90

Ruby Lane

S

Silver Deposit, Perfume Bottle, Glass, Sterling Overlay, Etched Flowers, c.1900, 4 ¾ In.
$1,200

Ruby Lane

Silver Flatware Sterling, No. 57, Salad Servers, Georg Jensen, 1900s, 8 ¾ In.
$330

Cowan's Auctions

Silver Plate, Coffeepot, Lighthouse Shape, Hinged Lid, Monogram, G.R. Collis & Co., 9 In.
$60

James D. Julia Auctioneers

Button, Shirley Temple, Sepia Stone, Calif., Curl, 1980s, 1 ¾ In.	12
Doll, Going Skiing, Red & Brown Costume, Stand, Skis, 1972, 17 In. .... *illus*	90
Figurine, Salt, Shirley, Curtsying, Tall Basket, Flowers, White, 1930s, 4 ½ In.	95
Mirror, Celluloid, Portrait, 3 x 2 In.	79
Pin, Portrait, My Friend, Red, 1 ¼ In.	25
Pitcher, Cobalt Blue, 1930s, 4 In.	34
Trinket Box, Egg Shape, Portrait, Marked, Westmoreland, 3 ½ x 2 ½ In.	15

SHRINER, *see Fraternal category.*

SHEFFIELD, *see Silver Plate; Silver-English categories.*

SILVER DEPOSIT glass was first made during the late nineteenth century. Solid sterling silver is applied to the glass by a chemical method so that a cutout design of silver metal appears against a clear or colored glass. It is sometimes called silver overlay.

Cup, Paneled Body, Scroll Handle, Grapes, Vines, Florals Repousse, 1855, 4 x 3 x 4 In.	248
Ewer, Patina, Looped Handle, Chained Lid, Persia, 1800s, 17 In.	25
Perfume Bottle, Glass, Sterling Overlay, Etched Flowers, c.1900, 4 ¾ In. .... *illus*	1200

SILVER FLATWARE includes many of the current and out-of-production silver and silver-plated flatware patterns made in the past eighty years. Other silver is listed under Silver-American, Silver-English, etc. Most silver flatware sets that are missing a few pieces can be completed through the help of a silver matching service. Three United States silver company marks are shown here.

INTERNATIONAL SILVER COMPANY	TRADE MARK ® STERLING	RW&S STERLING
International Silver Co. 1928+	Reed & Barton c.1915+	Wallace Silversmiths, Inc. 1871–1956

SILVER FLATWARE PLATED

Bird Of Paradise, Meat Fork, Community, 1923, 8 ¼ In.	12
Dupleix, Cake Server, Christofle, Paris, France, c.1940, 6 In.	145
Eternally Yours, Pastry Server, Pierced, International Silver, 10 ½ In.	69
First Love, Dinner Knife, Hollow Handle, Rogers Bros., 9 ¾ In.	14
First Love, Iced Tea Spoon, Rogers Bros.	11
First Love, Pickle Fork, 2 Tines, Rogers Bros.	18
Friendship, Berry Spoon, International, 8 ⅝ In.	25
Friendship, Gumbo Spoon, International, 7 In.	10
Friendship, Salad Fork, International, 6 ¼ In.	9
Mayflower, Serving Fork, Rogers, 1901, 8 ½ In.	12
Morning Star, Iced Tea Spoon, Oneida	10
Niagara Falls, Serving Fork, Oneida, 8 In.	6
Old Colony, Cold Meat Fork, Rogers, 1987	35
Old Colony, Dinner Knife, Hollow Handle, Rogers, 1847, 10 In.	12
Old Colony, Gumbo Spoon, Round, Rogers, 1847, 7 In.	12
Rosemary, Serving Fork, 3 Tines, Rockford, 1906, 2 ½ In.	75

SILVER FLATWARE STERLING

Blossom, Ladle, Georg Jensen, 13 x 4 ½ In.	1180
Chippendale, Ladle, Gadroon, Double Spout, Gorham, 5 ¼ x 8 ¾ In.	247
Chrysanthemum, Ladle, Repousse, Stieff Kirk, 1900, 15 In.	195
Earle, Cheese Scoop, Frank Smith, 1890, 8 ⅛ x 1 ¼ In.	200
Floral, Lettuce Fork, Marked, Stieff, 9 ¼ In.	62
Forget-Me-Not, Cold Meat Fork, Repousse, Kirk & Sons, 9 x 2 In.	109
Francis, Butter Knife, Marked, Reed & Barton, 5 ⅞ In.	32
Francis, Cake Server, Hollow Handle, Reed & Barton, 10 In.	80
French Antique, Cold Meat Fork, Reed & Barton, 9 In.	75
French Antique, Cream Soup Spoon, Reed & Barton, 6 In.	35

S

Silver Plate, Epergne, Georgian Style, Gadroon Borders, Anglo-Irish Style Cut Glass Bowls, 13 In.
$488

Neal Auction Co.

Silver Plate, Gravy Boat, Eagle Handle, Dart Border, Christofle, France, 1900s, 6 x 9 x 5 In.
$125

Brunk Auctions

Silver Plate, Hot Water Urn, Lid, Spigot, Mushroom Finial, Scroll Handles, Sheffield, 1800s, 15 In.
$305

Neal Auction Co.

Don't Wash Silver
Some experts suggest that you do not wash silverware in the dishwasher. The detergent is abrasive and the oxidation will eventually be removed. The cement in vintage hollow-handled knives may melt, and then the knife must repaired.

Silver Plate, Pitcher, Water, Aesthetic Revival, Presentation, Pairpoint Mfg., 1880, 13 5/8 In.
$183

Neal Auction Co.

Silver Plate, Shaker, Penguin, Napier, 12 1/4 In.
$2,250

Heritage Auctions

Silver Plate, Teapot, Scalloped Body, Ash Handle & Finial, Ilonka Karasz, Paye & Baker, 1928, 5 x 6 In.
$1,250

Los Angeles Modern Auctions

TIP
Be careful how you handle clean silver. Fingerprints will show and eventually tarnish.

S

Silver Plate, Tureen, Soup, Lid, Gadroon, Shell, Handles, William IV, Sheffield, 11 x 16 In.
$1,342

Neal Auction Co.

Silver Plate, Wine Cooler, Campagna Shape, Acanthus, Old Sheffield, T. & J. Creswick, 10 In., Pair
$2,880

Brunk Auctions

TIP
Rubber bands will stain silver through several layers of paper wrapping.

Silver-American, Asparagus Fork, Applied Pine Branch, Crab, Lobster, George W. Shiebler, c.1880, 9 In.
$512

Neal Auction Co.

French Antique, Dinner Fork, Reed & Barton, 7 1/4 In.		30
French Antique, Teaspoon, Reed & Barton, 6 In.		14
King, Fork, John Bodman Carrington, 1896, 7 1/8 In.		95
Lily Of The Valley, Serving Spoon, Whiting, Marked, 8 1/4 In.		109
Louis XV, Pastry Server, Gorham, 8 In.		109
No. 57, Salad Servers, Georg Jensen, 1900s, 8 3/4 In.	*illus*	330
Repousse, Butter Pick, Twisted, Kirk & Son, 6 1/4 x 1/2 In.		80
Repousse, Sardine Fork, Kirk & Son, c.1828, 7 5/8 x 2 3/4 In.		125
Rosemary, Luncheon Fork, Easterling, 7 1/4 In.		30
Rosemary, Serving Spoon, Easterling, 8 1/2 In.		55
Rosemary, Teaspoon, Easterling, 5 7/8 In.		12
Strasbourg, Gravy Ladle, Gorham, 9 In.		100

SILVER PLATE is not solid silver. It is a ware made of a metal, such as nickel or copper, that is covered with a thin coating of silver. The letters *EPNS* are often found on American and English silver-plated wares. *Sheffield* is a term with two meanings. Sometimes it refers to sterling silver made in the town of Sheffield, England. Sometimes it refers to an old form of plated silver made in England. Here are marks of three United States silver plate manufacturers. Here are marks of three United States silver plate manufacturers.

Barbour Silver Co.
1892–1931

J.W. Tufts
1875–c.1915

Meriden Silver Plate Co.
1869–1898

Bacon Warmer, Tapering Legs, Paw Feet, Harrison Brothers & Howson, England, 13 1/2 In.	113
Basket, Handle, Pierced Border, Wilcox, Victorian, 10 x 9 1/4 In.	24
Basket, Square, Reticulated & Embossed Bird & Flowers, Unmarked, Victorian, 9 x 9 In.	120
Biscuit Jar, Blue Satin, Glass, Enamel Thistle, Spider Web Decor, Wilcox, 14 x 12 In.	780
Bowl, Acorn Shape, Squirrel & Branch Design, Middletown, 1878, 12 x 12 In.	330
Box, Relief Repousse, Figural Scene, Horse Drawn Carriage, People, 1800, 5 x 8 x 3 In.	700
Butter, Cover, Geometrical Flowers Bowl, Thistle, Lizard, Meriden, 1800s, 14 x 6 x 9 In.	41
Butter, Cow Finial, Original Insert, Unmarked, 5 1/2 x 7 In.	120
Cake Stand, Reticulated Border Bird, Butterfly, Flowers, Square, Middletown, 6 1/2 x 9 1/4 In.	150
Calling Card Holder, Butterfly, Rings, Marked Wilcox & Meriden, 4 1/2 x 4 In.	360
Casserole, Lid, Handles, Pineapple Shape, Sheffield	100
Caviar Stand, Scrolling Leaves, Ball Finial, Mappin & Webb, c.1890, 4 x 7 In.	340
Centerpiece, Applied Flowers, Leaves, Pierced Handles, Glass Liner, 8 x 22 3/4 In.	570
Centerpiece, Oak Tree, Glass Bowl, Elkington & Co., 1860, 19 In.	512
Centerpiece, Ship, Poseidon Figure, Trident, Lion's Head Feet, 25 x 17 x 9 In.	3146
Cider Jug, Embossed, Tavern, Monogram, Leaves, 9 x 6 x 8 In.	54
Cigarette Case, Embossed, Mozart & Madame De Pompadour, c.1905, 2 x 8 In.	335
Coffeepot, Leafy Design In Relief, Etched Highlights, Fruit Form Finial, 4-Footed, 9 1/4 In.	85
Coffeepot, Lighthouse Shape, Hinged Lid, Monogram, G.R. Collis & Co., 9 In. *illus*	60
Compote, Pierced, Berry Dish, Green Glass Liner, Monogram, 1863, 12 x 12 In.	100
Conch Shell, Federico Buccellati, 1 x 2 3/4 In.	188
Dish, 3 Seashells, Center Handle, Emerging Fish, Shell Feet, 8 x 14 1/2 In.	295
Dish, Buffalo Center, Etched, Textured, Geometric Design, 1970s, 6 In.	325
Epergne, Cut Glass Bowls, Israel Freeman & Son, 1928, 11 x 24 In.	256
Epergne, Cut Glass Inserts, Scroll Arms, 4-Footed Base, 18 x 16 1/2 In.	900
Epergne, Embossed Center Bowl, Leafy Scrolls, 1800s, 16 x 9 3/4 In.	118
Epergne, Flowers, Acanthus, Cut Glass Bowls, Robert Pringle & Co., 1900, 15 x 23 In.	383
Epergne, Georgian Style, Gadroon Borders, Anglo-Irish Style Cut Glass Bowls, 13 In. *illus*	488
Figurine, David, Nude, Puzzle, Nickel, Brass, Spain, M. Berrocal, c.1968, 5 1/2 x 2 In.	937
Figurine, Horse, Galloping, Marble Stand, 14 x 16 In.	75
Glue Pot, Embossed, Brush & Glass Insert, Derby, 5 In.	120
Gravy Boat, Eagle Handle, Dart Border, Christofle, France, 1900s, 6 x 9 x 5 In. *illus*	125
Hot Water Urn, Lid, Spigot, Mushroom Finial, Scroll Handles, Sheffield, 1800s, 15 In. *illus*	305

S

Ice Bucket, Shell Handles, Gorham, 8¼ x 11 In.	120
Ice Bucket, Stand, Champagne, Oval, Handle Inside Rim, Signed, 8 x 12 x 8 In.	908
Jewelry Box, Mechanical, Casket Shape, Cherub & Basket Lid, Wheeled Drawer, 9 x 6½ In.	480
Jewelry Box, Mechanical, Flower, Butterfly, Push Handle To Open, 8¾ x 4½ In.	1320
Jewelry Box, Mechanical, Flowers, Push Handle To Open, Simpson Hall, Miller, 9 x 6½ In.	300
Jewelry Box, Webster, Mechanical, Acorn Opens Up, Pushed Handle, Original Lining, 7 In.	330
Ladle, Twisted Rope Design, Reed & Barton, Marked, 13 In.	72
Mustard Pot, Blue Glass, U.S. Coast Guard Shield, Handle, Spoon, c.1905, 4 In.	850
Pitcher, Owl, Tapered, Mother-Of-Pearl Feathers, Blue Glass Eyes, Los Castillo, 10 In.	500
Pitcher, Water, Aesthetic Revival, Presentation, Pairpoint Mfg., 1880, 13⅝ In. .... *illus*	183
Pitcher, Water, Chased Fruit, Taunton, Reed, Fruit, 9 x 6½ x 9 In.	248
Platter, Grapevine Border, Pierced Edge, Acanthus, Handles, 17½ In.	180
Platter, Meat, Lid, Tree Well, Hot Water Reservoir, Handle, Smith, Sissons & Co., 26 x 19 In.	7080
Platter, Meat Dome, Shell Banding, Lion & Shield Finial, Leaf Feet, Sheffield, 20 In.	793
Platter, Meat Dome, Stag Head, Antlers, Relief, Teghini, Firenze, 1900s, 13⅜ x 28 In.	850
Platter, Palm Leaves, Fading Portrait, Figural Border, 1800s, 17 x 13 In.	36
Punch Ladle, Cut Glass Finial, Hobstar, Fan & Zipper, Marked, Watrous, 16 In.	264
Punch Ladle, Holmes & Edwards, Marked, c.1900	45
Ring, Chest, Cherub Pushing Wheeled Dolly, Carrying Suitcase, Rogers, 4¼ x 5 In.	1440
Salt, Master, Figural, Girl Pushing Cart, Cobalt Blue Art Glass, Victorian, 3¾ x 5 In.	270
Salver, Thread Molded Border, France, 1750, 11 In.	688
Sculpture, Mausoleum Shape, Columns, Abstract Figures, Nude, Italy, M. Berrocal, 1970s, 8 x 8 In.	1875
Server, Roll Top, Oval, 2 Inserts, 1 Solid, 1 Pierced, Leaves, 1872, 14 x 9 x 8 In.	336
Serving Dish, Leaves, Shell Scroll Edge, Paw Feet, Floral, 24 x 12 x 3¾ In.	177
Shaker, Penguin, Napier, 12¼ In. .... *illus*	2250
Spoon Warmer, Nautilus Shell On Rocky Base, Hinged Lid, Victorian, 5½ x 6½ In.	180
Spoon, Souvenir, see Souvenir category.	
Stand, Jewelry, Embossed Bird, Floral, Swivel Drawer, Rockford, 11 In.	1020
Tazza, Flared Rim, Twist Border, Scrolling Motif, 9 Agates, 1800s, 6¾ x 11 In.	150
Tea Set, Teapot, Sugar & Creamer, The Cube, Robert Crawford Johnson, 4 Piece	812
Teapot, Scalloped Body, Ash Handle & Finial, Ilonka Karasz, Paye & Baker, 1928, 5 x 6 In. .. *illus*	1250
Thermometer, Rabbit Looking At Temperature, Pairpoint, 6¼ x 3¾ In.	330
Tray, Floral, Scalloped Edge, Scroll, Shell Handles, Boulton, 1900s, 31 x 21 x 2½ In.	454
Tray, Reticulated Rim, 2 Handles, Dolphin Accents, Engraved, Armorial, Hodd & Son, 30 In. ..	400
Tray, Scrolled Rim, Floral, Leafy Accents, Engraved, Elkington & Co, 1853, 30 In.	246
Tray, Turtle Shell, Gadroon Borders, Sheffield, 22½ x 16½ In.	313
Trolley, Whiskey, Barrel Cart, Chain Swags, Wheels, Stopper, Tap, 9 x 16 In.	397
Trophy, Boat Race, Standing Man, Tall Reeds, Engraved, 18 x 22 x 7 In.	545
Tureen, Lid, Gadroon Rim, Griffin's Head, Coat Of Arms, Spiral Scrolls, 10 x 14¾ In.	813
Tureen, Soup, Lid, Gadroon, Shell, Handles, William IV, Sheffield, 11 x 16 In. .... *illus*	1342
Whistle, Skull Form, Snake, Anchor & Rat, Hanging Loop, 1800s-1900s, 3 In.	366
Wine Cooler, Campagna Shape, Acanthus, Old Sheffield, T. & J. Creswick, 10 In., Pair .... *illus*	2880
Wine Cooler, On Stand, Bucket Form, Stirrup Handles, Foot Ring, Christofle, 33 In.	1500

SILVER-AMERICAN. American silver is listed here. Coin and sterling silver are included. Most of the sterling silver listed in this book is subdivided by country. There are also other pieces of silver and silver plate listed under special categories, such as Candelabrum, Napkin Ring, Silver Flatware, Silver Plate, Silver-Sterling, and Tiffany Silver. The meltdown price determines the value of solid silver items. Coin silver sells for less than sterling silver. These prices are based on current silver values.

Gorham & Co.	INTERNATIONAL SILVER CO.	Reed & Barton Co.
1865+	International Silver Co. 1898–present	1824–2015

Asparagus Fork, Applied Pine Branch, Crab, Lobster, George W. Shiebler, c.1880, 9 In.... *illus*	512
Asparagus Server, King Pattern, Tiffany & Co., 7¾ x 8½ In.	750
Basket, Circular, Raffia Sides, Applied Grapevine Rim, Leaves, Bell Flowers, c.1839, 11 In.	6875
Basket, Rectangular Boat Shape, Rounded Corners, Swing Handle, Marked, 1820, 13 In.	750
Berry Spoon, Cartouche Shape Handle, W.C. Byrd, 1800s, 9¼ In.	120

Silver-American, Brandy Warmer, Turned Wood Handle, Coin, John Ewan, c.1875, 3 x 8½ In. $1,287

Jeffrey S. Evans

Silver-American, Charger, Molded Edge, Marked Shreve, Crump & Low, 1900, 15 In. $510

Eldred's Auctioneers and Appraisers

Silver-American, Compote, Repousse, Flowers, Acanthus, Inscription, Whiting, c.1890, 7⅝ x 10 In. $540

Brunk Auctions

Silver-American, Cup, New Orleans In Rectangle, Repousse, Grape Leaves, Flowers, Coin, c.1850, 4 In.
$1,875

Neal Auction Co.

Silver-American, Cup, Paneled Body, Beaded Lip, Scroll Handle, Coin, Hyde & Goodrich, c.1855, 4 In.
$610

Neal Auction Co.

Silver-American, Dish, Entree, Lid, Gadroon, Handle, Coin, Forbes, N.Y., c.1820, 9 x 12 In.
$4,575

Neal Auction Co.

Bowl, Dolphin Handles, Shell Feet, Bunde & Upmeyer Co., 4¾ x 10½ In.	1800
Bowl, Embossed Leafy Scroll Rim, Sharp Cut Glass, Shreve & Co., 1894, 4 x 10 In.	283
Bowl, Frosted Surface, Engraved Gothic, Scrollwork Cartouche, Marked, 1870, 13 In.	2500
Bowl, Hammered, Flared Rim, M. Zimmerman, c.1910, 5 x 14 In.	1375
Bowl, Horizontal S-Scroll Wire Foot, Gumps, 2½ x 6¼ In.	313
Bowl, Lid, Hammered, Folded-In Rim, Art Silver Shop, 3½ x 6 In.	375
Bowl, Lotus Pattern Watson Company, 3 x 6½ x 11 In.	125
Bowl, Monogram, Reticulated, Whiting, 10 In.	160
Bowl, Monogram, Rim, Leafy, Vine Motif, Gorham, 1921, 11 In.	277
Bowl, Monogram, Urn Form Finial, Repousse Floral Swags, 2 Scrolled Handles, 1800s, 9 In.	338
Bowl, Monteith, Flowers, Berries, Ivy, Steeple Chase 1883, S. Kirk & Son, 8¾ x 10 In.	2500
Bowl, Pierced Rim, Frank M. Whiting & Co., 4 x 11 In.	212
Bowl, Poppy Motif, Flared Rim, Art Nouveau, Gorham, 1900, 11 In.	369
Bowl, Poppy, George Shiebler, 1900, 9½ In.	461
Bowl, Repousse, Flowers, Berries, Coin, S. Kirk & Son, 4¼ x 14 In.	1920
Bowl, Repousse, Flowers, Leaves, Monogram, James Armiger Co., 7½ x 8 In.	1800
Bowl, Round, Inward Folded Rim, Swags, Shells, 4-Footed, Gorham, 1905, 4 x 12 In.	1063
Bowl, Round, Scallop Border, Scroll Flowers, Leaves, Gilt Interior, Gorham, 1892, 3½ x 8 In.	300
Bowl, Scalloped Rim, Embossed Lilies Design, Marked Meriden, 2¾ x 11 In.	207
Bowl, Shallow, Flattened Trapezoid Handles, Monogram SGK, Allan Adler, c.1950, 12½ In.	1500
Bowl, Spot Hammered, Stem Chased, Stylized Leaves, Marked, 1925, 11 In.	4000
Bowl, Vegetable, Lid, Flowers, Leaves, Loring Andrews, 10 x 7½ In.	1400
Bowl, Vegetable, Lid, Gadroon, Leafy Edge, Gorham, 10½ In.	523
Bowl, Yin Yang, Repeating Xs On Foot, W.N. Frederick, 3 x 12 In., 2 Piece	1250
Box, Book Shape, Monogram, Engraved Texts, Enameled Accents, Marked, 1938, 10 In.	8125
Brandy Warmer, Turned Wood Handle, Coin, John Ewan, c.1875, 3 x 8½ In. *illus*	1287
Bread Dish, Oval Flared, Ornate Repousse Border, Flowers, Kirk & Son, 1900s, 6 x 12 x 1 In.	277
Bread Dish, Reticulated Bread, Samuel Barbour, 1892, 7 x 13 x 2 In.	248
Buckle, Shoe, Touchmark Of Benjamin Clark Gilman, 1¾ x 2½ In., Pair	1020
Butter, Cover, Repousse, Grape Finial, S. Kirk & Son, 1846-61, 7¼ x 8 In.	1187
Butter, Dome Lid, Bands, Ball, Black & Co., 7 x 6¾ In.	437
Candelabra are listed in the Candelabrum category.	
Candlesnuffer, Curled Handle, Julius Olaf Randahl, Chicago, 9 x 1½ In.	313
Candlesticks are listed in their own category.	
Castor, Dome Lid, Baluster, Engraved Monogram, Marked, 1770, 5 In.	500
Centerpiece, Brass, Flower Grid, Reed & Barton, 6 x 11 x 31 In.	375
Centerpiece, Elaborate Cutwork, Flower Grid, Shreve, Crump, 1909, 8½ x 10 In.	500
Centerpiece, Ship, Viking, Flower Frog, Copper, Gorham, 5¾ x 13¾ In.	850
Charger, Molded Edge, Marked Shreve, Crump & Low, 1900, 15 In. *illus*	510
Claret, Jug, Hinged Lid, Duck's Beak Spout, Glass Base, T.B. Starr, 10 In., Pair	1250
Coffee Set, Coffeepot, Sugar & Creamer, Cups & Saucers, Melon Finial, New Orleans, 7 Piece	3050
Coffee Set, Coffeepot, Sugar & Creamer, Tray, Panels, Kalo Shop, 4 Piece	5000
Coffeepot, Applied Monogram, Novick, 8¼ x 4½ In.	552
Coffeepot, Repousse Flowers, Dominick & Haff, c.1890, 7 x 4¾ In.	275
Coffeepot, Swan Neck, Baluster Form, Molded Circular Foot, Marked, 1765, 11 In.	8750
Compote, Footed, Round With Scalloped Border, Marked Alvin, 1900s, 10½ In.	420
Compote, Petals, Support, Round Foot, Kalo Shop, 8 x 6 In.	468
Compote, Repousse, Flowers, Acanthus, Inscription, Whiting, c.1890, 7⅝ x 10 In. *illus*	540
Compote, Whiting Repousse, Round, Gilt, Floral, Acanthus, Bead Border, 1800s, 7⅝ x 9½ In.	540
Corncob Holders, Skewers, Cob Shape Handles, Webster, 1960s, 3 In., 8 Piece	135
Creamer, Helmet Shape, Beaded Borders, Monogram, Oval, Marked, 1785, 7⅛ In.	5250
Creamer, Neoclassical Handle, Gorham, 5 In.	49
Crumber, Rounded Handle, Coin, Curtis, 12¼ In.	180
Cup, Child's, Hammered, Cylindrical, C-Scroll Handle, Kalo Shop, 3 x 4 In.	469
Cup, New Orleans In Rectangle, Repousse, Grape Leaves, Flowers, Coin, c.1850, 4 In. *illus*	1875
Cup, Paneled Body, Beaded Lip, Scroll Handle, Coin, Hyde & Goodrich, c.1855, 4 In. *illus*	610
Decanter, Grape, Grapevine, Squat, 8 In.	132
Dish, Clover Shape, Reed & Barton, 4¾ In.	49
Dish, Entree, Lid, Gadroon, Handle, Coin, Forbes, N.Y., c.1820, 9 x 12 In. *illus*	4575
Dish, Oyster, Gilt Wash, Gorham, 5 x 2½ In.	554

SILVER-AMERICAN

Dish, Triangular, Harding, Boston, 1 ¾ x 10 ½ In.	250
Figurine, Woman, Seated, Infant In Arms, Ruffled Gown, 17 In.	12300
Fish Slice, Vine, Grape Pattern, Tiffany & Co, 12 ¾ x 5 In.	363
Flask, Horse, Jockey, Rectangle, Twist Cap, Enamel, 1900s, 7 In.	3250
Frame, Rectangular, Columns, Classical Designs, Base Metal Nuts, Marked, 1919, 20 In.	5625
Goblet, Flared, Monogram, Thin Stem, Spread Foot, Kalo Shop, 6 In., 4 Piece	350
Hot Water Urn, Swags, Flowers, Ebonized Handle, 13 In.	780
Jigger, Double, Squared Textured Handle, W.N. Frederick, Chicago, 2 ½ In.	938
Julep Cup, Engraved, Trophy, Sadie, 1961, 3 ¾ In.	108
Julep Cup, Tapered Cylinder, Beaded Rim, John Kitts, Louisville, c.1860, 4 In.	1250
Kettle, Spot Hammered, Acid Etched, Embossed Scrolls, Flower, Marked, 1881, 12 In.	2750
Ladle, Fiddleback Handle, Monogram, c.1860, 13 In.	2706
Ladle, Les Cinq Fleurs Pattern, Serpentine Handle, Wavy Bowl, Reed & Barton, 14 x 4 ¾ In.	242
Ladle, Memphis, Clark & Co., 11 ¾ In.	300
Ladle, Twisted Handle, Gilt Bowl, Fruit, Flowers, 1908, 15 In.	513
Loving Cup, Oval, Shaped Rim, Scroll Edge & Handles, Newburyport, 10 In.	1000
Mirror, Mythical Faces, Heart Shape, Birds, Medallion Crest, Dominick & Haff, 14 x 11 In.	424
Muffineer, Monogram, MP, 1700s, 7 ¼ In. *illus*	688
Mug, Anthony Rasch, Coin, c.1850, 3 ¾ In. *illus*	420
Mug, Memphis, Scroll Rim, Handle, Clark & Co., 3 ½ x 4 ½ In.	240
Mustard Ladle, Nathaniel Hayden, Charleston, S.C., Monogram, Coin, 5 ⅜ In.	540
Napkin Rings are listed in their own category.	
Pitcher, Baluster Form, Bold Fluted & Gadroon Rim, Scroll Handle, Marked, 1820, 8 In.	1250
Pitcher, Engraved & Repousse Grapevines, Pear Shape, Harris & Shafer, 11 In.	1063
Pitcher, Engraved Putto Stepping, Stylized Bright-Cut Leaves, 4 Shell Feet, 1871, 11 In.	2375
Pitcher, Flowers, Helmet Spout, Monogram, Wallace, 1900s, 9 ¼ In.	668
Pitcher, Flowers, Repousse, Kirk & Sons, c.1941	1500
Pitcher, Hammered, Lobed, Spread Foot, Petterson Studio, Chicago, 8 In.	1625
Pitcher, Pear Shape, Leafy Band, Satin Finish, Gorham, 1885, 11 x 7 In.	1375
Pitcher, Repousse Flowers, Vines, Coin, Kirk & Son, 7 ½ In.	1089
Pitcher, Repousse, Flowers, Leaves, Kirk, c. 1941, 8 In. *illus*	1770
Pitcher, Scalloped Rim, Engraved Floral Basket, Garland Design, S. Kirk & Son, 9 ¼ x 7 ½ In.	531
Pitcher, Water, Baltimore Rose, c.1903, 10 ¾ In.	2006
Pitcher, Water, Pear Shape, Flowers, Repousse, Black, Starr & Frost, 1900s, 10 In.	1680
Pitcher, Water, Repousse Flowers, Gorham, 1890s, 10 ½ x 9 ½ In.	1534
Pitcher, Water, Repousse, Flowers, Leaves, Gorham, 1884, 7 ½ In.	1125
Pitcher, Watson Company, 4 Pt., 9 x 26 In.	313
Plate, Poppy, Repousse, Wallace, 10 ½ In.	236
Platter, Oval, Flowered Rim, S. Kirk & Son, c.1950, 18 x 13 In.	1875
Porringer, Handle, Monogram FC, Engraved, Marked Jesse Churchill, 1810, 5 In. *illus*	1375
Porringer, Raised Center, Rounded Wall, Pierced Keyhole Handle, Monogram, 5 In.	484
Porringer, Shallow Lid, Round Bowl, Horizontal Handles Set, Lunt, 4 ⅜ In.	94
Pot, Paneled Body, Octagonal, Shreve, Crump & Low, 1900s, 10 ½ In.	216
Punch Bowl, Floral Swags, Waisted Foot, Frank W. Smith, c.1925, 8 ½ x 12 In.	688
Punch Bowl, Motor Yacht Repousse, Lobed Rim, Gorham, c.1925, 7 x 14 In.	1875
Punch Set, Flowers, Fronds, 6 Goblets, W.H. Manchester, Rhode Island, c.1950, Bowl 9 x 15 In.	4250
Salad Servers, Hammered, Raised D On Handle, Kalo, 10 In., 2 Piece	563
Salt & Pepper, Rose, Model 12, 4 ½ In.	300
Salt, Flowers, Loop Feet, F.H. Clark & Co., 1 ½ x 3 ½ In., Pair	720
Salver, 4 Paneled Legs, Engraved Spread Wing Eagle, Marked, 1802, 7 In.	7500
Salver, Round, Raised Ogee Border, 3 Cabriole Legs, 1817, 6 In.	393
Sauceboat, Acanthus Leaf Handle, 4 ½ x 7 ¼ In.	236
Sauceboat, Countryside, Ruins, Chased, Repousse, Oval Foot, 6 ¾ In.	1440
Serving Fork, 4 Tines, Hand Wrought, Hammered Finish, Arts Crafts, Kalo, 9 In.	74
Serving Spoon, Fiddle Handle, Merriman Byrd & Co., 1800s, 9 In.	120
Serving Spoon, Ivy, Clark, 10 In.	240
Shaker, Durgin, Cobalt Blue, 6 ½ In.	188
Sorbet, Danish Modern, Openwork Blossom Stem, International, 3 In., 8 Piece	1250
Spoon, Beaded Edge, Tipped, Monogram, William Gale, 1863, 8 In.	47
Spoon, Coin, Hayden & Gregg, 8 In.	120

Silver-American, Muffineer, Monogram, MP, 1700s, 7 ¼ In.
$688

Neal Auction Co.

Silver-American, Mug, Anthony Rasch, Coin, c.1850, 3 ¾ In.
$420

Brunk Auctions

Silver-American, Pitcher, Repousse, Flowers, Leaves, Kirk, c. 1941, 8 In.
$1,770

Alex Cooper Auctioneers

405

Silver-American, Porringer, Handle, Monogram FC, Engraved, Marked Jesse Churchill, 1810, 5 In.
$1,375

Garth's Auctioneers & Appraisers

Silver-American, Tea & Coffee Set, Monogram, Gorham, c.1916, 5 Piece
$1,020

Cowan's Auctions

Silver-American, Teapot, Straight-Sided, Acorn Finial, Wood Handle, Thumb Rest, Coin, c.1820, 6 x 4 In.
$526

Jeffrey S. Evans

Silver-American, Teapot, Urn Shape, Ivory Spacers, Coin, Marked, Bard & Lamont, c.1850, 11¾ In.
$800

Brunk Auctions

Spoon, Muddler, Flattened Handle, Monogram, Gothic S, Kalo, Felt Bag, 14 In.	375
Strainer, Circular, Pierced Rosette, Mounted Above, Openwork Handle, Marked, 1765, 4¾ In.	1500
Sugar & Creamer, Flowers On Foot, Durham, 2 Piece	177
Sugar & Creamer, Lobed Base, Gadroon Rim, Monogram, George Baker, 8¼ x 6¼ In.	594
Sugar & Creamer, Lobed, Double Handles, 1900s, 2 Piece	94
Sugar Tongs, Andrew Warner, Coin, c.1830	113
Sugar Tongs, Fiddle Handle, Claw Terminals, Merriman, c.1850, 6¼ In.	360
Sugar Tongs, Neptune Pattern, Notched Gripper, Petterson, Chicago, 4½ In.	125
Sugar Tongs, Shells, Flowers, Coin, Francis Clark Augusta, 7 In.	270
Sugar, Ladle, Shell Bowl, Pierced, Coin, Merriman, 8 In.	300
Tea & Coffee Set, Coffeepot, Teapot, Kettle, Sugar & Creamer, Waste Bowl, Schultz, 6 Piece	4500
Tea & Coffee Set, Monogram, Gorham, c.1916, 5 Piece .... *illus*	1020
Tea & Coffee Set, Pear Shape, Acanthus Handle, Lid, Bigelow & Kennard, 4 Piece	1750
Tea & Coffee Set, Teapot, Coffeepot, Sugar & Creamer, Thomas Fletcher, c.1820, 4 Piece	2375
Tea & Coffee Set, Teapot, Coffeepot, Sugar & Creamer, Waste Bowl, Gorham, 5 Piece	2117
Tea & Coffee Set, Teapot, Coffeepot, Sugar & Creamer, Waste Bowl, Repousse, 5 Piece	3304
Tea & Coffee, Set, Teapot, Coffeepot, Sugar & Creamer, Waste, Chased Flower, W. Durgin, 5 Piece	1936
Tea Caddy, Rectangular, Cut Corners, Chinoiserie Scenes, Hinged Lid, Marked, 1870, 4⅞ In.	1500
Tea Set, Teapot, Sugar & Creamer, Flowers, Leaves, Ram's Head, Castle, Bluff, 3 Piece	4235
Tea Set, Teapot, Sugar & Creamer, Waste Bowl, Repousse, Deer, Coin, Kirk & Son, 4 Piece	3025
Tea Urn, Square Base, Gadrooned Borders, Dolphin, Female Mask, Marked, 1825, 15 In.	5250
Teapot & Coffeepot, Repousse, Flowers, Twigs, Ivy, Coin, A. Jocobi & Co., 7¾ x 8¾ In.	1370
Teapot, Oval, Engraved, Ribbon Bound, Rosettes, Leafy Foliage, Cartouches, 1805, 12 In.	6250
Teapot, Paneled Body, Scroll Handle, Floral Repousse, Monogram, 1849, 10 x 6 x 11 In.	897
Teapot, Repousse, Flowers, Berries, Coin, S. Kirk & Co., 5½ In.	750
Teapot, Straight-Sided, Acorn Finial, Wood Handle, Thumb Rest, Coin, c.1820, 6 x 4 In. . . *illus*	526
Teapot, Urn Shape, Ivory Spacers, Coin, Marked, Bard & Lamont, c.1850, 11¾ In. .... *illus*	800
Tongs, Grape, Vine, Leaf, Kirk & Sons, 6½ In.	553
Tray, 2-Handles, Galleried Edge, Engraved Monogram, Gorham, 24 x 16 x 3 In.	1080
Tray, Classical Female Masks, Stylized Scroll, Oval, Marked, 1865, 33 In.	4000
Tray, Monogram, Vanity, Windsor, Reed & Barton, 10½ In.	123
Tray, Oval, Chrysanthemums To Border, Mauser Manufacturing, 1900, 22 In.	1107
Tray, Repousse Border, Engraved Field, Kirk & Son, c.1950, 17½ x 26½ In.	6500
Tray, Rococo Decoration, 4 Pierced Trellis, Oval, Marked, 1893, 14 In.	6000
Tray, Shaped Circular, Sweeping Flowers, Monogram Center, Marked, 1904, 16 In.	5000
Tray, Shaped Oval, Floral, Scroll Border, Frank Herschede, 1880, 18 x 15 In.	1088
Trophy, American Cut Glass Body, 2 Antler Side Handles, Signed, Engraved, 7 x 10 In.	2299
Trophy, Cup, Boar Tusk Side Handles, Signed Gorham, 3 Pt., 8 x 9½ x 5½ In.	1573
Tureen, Embossed Flower, Insects, Spider, Lizard, Engraved Spider Webs, Marked, 1880, 14 In.	7500
Tureen, Oval, Loop Handle, Strapwork Bands, Tiffany & Co., 1880, 8 x 13 In.	2880
Urn, Classical Style, Ribbing, Shells, Paw Feet, Tooled Grapevines, 1800s-1900s, 18 In. ... *illus*	144
Vase, Angular, Graduated, Erik Magnussen, Gorham, c.1926, 10 x 5 In.	3375
Vase, Chair Shape, Flower Sprays, Oval Windows, Applied Door Handles, Marked, 1931, 7⅞ In..	1188
Vase, Fluted, Flared, Scalloped Rim, Wallace & Co., 10 In.	390
Vase, Navarre, Shells, Acanthus Leaves, Flared Rim, Weighted Foot, Inscribed, Watson, 18 In..	660
Vase, Seashell, Scalloped, Beaded Rim, Scroll Handles, Theodore B, 12½ x 5½ In.	2520
Vase, Watson Company, Etched, Glass, 5½ x 5½ x 2½ In.	38
Wine, Repousse, Woodland Scene, Castle, Loring Andrews Co., 1910, 6 x 5 In.	800

SILVER-ASIAN

Figure, Lion, Glass Eyes, c.1950, 12 x 22 In.	1875
Punch Bowl, Leaf Band, Gold Kamon Medallion, Pedestal Base, Japan, 8 x 12 In.	2250
Vase, Etched Branches, Gilt Birds, Butterflies, Cockerel Handles, Japan, 4 x 9 In.	1875

SILVER-AUSTRIAN

Candlestick, Waisted Standard, Trumpet Foot, Karl Sedelmayer, 1817, 11 x 5 In., Pair	1188
Kettle, Stand, Chased, Flowers, 13½ In.	2040
Vase, Grid Cage, Glass Liner, Handle, Josef Hoffmann, Wiener Werkstatte, c.1910, 9½ In. *illus*	9375

SILVER-CANADIAN

Bowl, Seed Pods, Carl Poul Peterson, 6 x 10 In.	1180

SILVER-CHINESE

Ashtray, Cigarette Box, Dragon, Turquoise Cabochon, Crane Finial, 9 x 7 In. 4062
Centerpiece, Reticulated Flower Panels, Dragon Handles, Wood Base, 1 3/4 x 6 1/4 In. 3630
Cup, Irises, Double Handles, Mark Of Luen Wo, c.1900, 9 3/4 In. 1000
Tea & Coffee Set, Teapot, Coffeepot, Sugar & Creamer, Chrysanthemums, c.1900, 4 Piece 2360
Teapot, Fixed Loop Handle, Wild Roses, Champleve, 6 1/4 In. 3000

SILVER-CONTINENTAL

Biscuit Barrel, Repousse, Fruit, Deep Relief, 6 1/2 x 6 In. 687
Bowl, Acanthus, Shaped Rim, Shaped Foot, 19 3/4 In. 1375
Bowl, Filigree, Repousse, Cornucopia, Berry, Vine, Flower Bunting, 15 1/2 x 13 3/4 In. 687
Box, Repousse, Oval, Flower Sprays, Acanthus, Raised Scroll Feet, 4 x 5 1/2 In. 907
Cake Basket, Latticework, Leaf Rim, Base, Swing Handle, 10 1/2 x 12 In. 320
Chair, Miniature, Gothic Revival, Pierced Splat, Turned Legs, Enamel, Courting Couple, 2 In. ... 188
Coffeepot, Serpentine Lobed, Hinged Lid, Duck's Beak Spout, Ebonized Handle, 12 In. 336
Frame, Picture, Double, Repousse Figures, 13 x 11 In. 312
Pitcher, Engraved Flowers, Paneled, Octagonal, 8 x 8 1/4 In. 593
Platter, Battle Scene, Repousse, Fruit Border, 21 3/4 x 17 1/4 In. 1375
Platter, Meat, Dome, Lobed Oval Form, Rococo Cartouches, c.1925, 16 x 25 1/2 In. 1750
Reliquary, Crown, Flowers, Leaves, Cutwork, Round Foot, 17 1/4 In. .... *illus* 394
Salver, Knights Of Malta, Engraved Crest, Banner, c.1900, 3 1/2 x 10 In. 3500
Wedding Basket, Open Work, Scrolls, Putti Reserve, Neresheimer & Son, 12 In. 700
Wedding Cup, Woman, Arms Up, Repousse Skirt, 11 x 3 In. 167
Wine Cooler, Inverted Pear Form, Rococo Medallions, Scroll Handles, c.1950, 12 x 12 In. 1875
Wine Trolley, Wirework, Cabochon Cartouches, Wheels, c.1885, 10 x 13 In. .... *illus* 2500

SILVER-DANISH. Georg Jensen is the most famous Danish silver company.

Georg Jensen
1925–1932

Georg Jensen
1933–1944

Georg Jensen
1945–present

Bowl, Double Handles, Hallmark, 1900s, 2 x 5 1/2 In. 60
Box, Lid, Amber Finial, Footed, Georg Jensen, c.1930, 5 1/2 x 4 1/2 In. .... *illus* 12980
Box, Rectangular, Bracket Feet, Leaf Button, S. Bernadotte, G. Jensen, 8 x 3 x 3/4 In. 938
Chalice, Trophy, Shells, Seaweed, Dolphins, Anton Michelsen, 14 1/2 In. 1080
Coffee Set, Blossom, Leaf & Berry Top, Ivory Handles, Jensen, 6-In. Pot, 3 Piece 1700
Compote, Twirling Stem, Hanging Grapes, Flaring Base, 10 1/2 x 10 In. 5900
Pitcher, Large Handle, Stamped, Georg Jensen, 1950s, 11 1/2 x 8 1/4 In. .... *illus* 11250
Pitcher, Leaf, Berry Design, Handle, Georg Jensen, 1930, 5 1/2 In. 492
Platter, Circular, With A Beaded Edge, Georg Jensen, 1945, 14 In. 861
Serving Spoon, Strawberry, Etched Berries, Strainer, Holger Küster, 1800s 940
Spoon, Leaf, Berry Decoration, Hammered, Georg Jensen, 8 x 2 1/2 In. 250
Sugar, Lid, Blossom, Round, Flower Bud Finial, 3-Footed, 3 1/2 x 3 3/8 In. 719
Tea Strainer, Bottom Cup, Copenhagen Guild, Georg Jensen, c.1924, 1 1/2 x 4 1/2 In. ...... *illus* 708
Tongs, Georg Jensen, 1933-44, 8 1/2 In. 354

SILVER-DUTCH

Chair, Miniature, Ladder Back, J. Verhoogt, c.1900, 2 In., 6 Piece 281
Creamer, Repousse, Pleated Shoulder, Scalloped Rim, Animal Head, Scroll Handle, c.1900 395
Epergne, Trumpet Shape Vase, Caryatid, Flowers, Leaves, Branches, 30 3/4 x 18 1/2 In. 6875

SILVER-ENGLISH. English sterling silver is marked with a series of four or five small hallmarks. The standing lion mark is the most commonly seen sterling quality mark. The other marks indicate the city of origin, the maker, and the year of manufacture. These dates can be verified in many good books on silver. These prices are partially based on silver meltdown values.

Silver-American, Urn, Classical Style, Ribbing, Shells, Paw Feet, Tooled Grapevines, 1800s-1900s, 18 In. $144

Garth's Auctioneers & Appraisers

Silver-Austrian, Vase, Grid Cage, Glass Liner, Handle, Josef Hoffmann, Wiener Werkstatte, c.1910, 9 1/2 In. $9,375

Rago Arts and Auction Center

S

Silver-Continental, Reliquary, Crown, Flowers, Leaves, Cutwork, Round Foot, 17¼ In.
$394

Leland Little Auctions

Silver-Continental, Wine Trolley, Wirework, Cabochon Cartouches, Wheels, c.1885, 10 x 13 In.
$2,500

New Orleans Auction Galleries

Silver-Danish, Box, Lid, Amber Finial, Footed, Georg Jensen, c.1930, 5½ x 4½ In.
$12,980

Cottone Auctions

Standard quality mark

City mark – London

Date letter mark

Maker's mark

Sovereign's head mark

Basket, Gadroon Border, Engraved, William Esterbrook, London, 1824-87, 13 In.	875
Basket, George III, Gilt, Egyptian Taste, Grapevines, Scott & Smith, 5½ x 13 In.	8850
Basket, Oval, Gadroon Body, Beaded Rim, Bail Handle, George III, 1780-81, 11 In.	615
Basket, Reticulated, 2 Eagle's Head Handles, Edward VII, 1904-05, 8 In.	338
Basket, Rounded Rectangular Shape, Gadroon & Basket Weave, Heraldic, 1809, 9 x 12 x 10 In.	1020
Basting Spoon, Scottish Queen Anne, Dog Nose Handle, 1707	1500
Bowl, Dome Lid, Covered Urn, Side Handles, Flame Finial, George Fox, 17 x 10 x 7 In.	2299
Bowl, Engraved Swag, Decoration, 2¼ x 3½ In.	135
Bowl, Floral, Footed, Sheffield, 1896, 5 x 7 In.	312
Bowl, Lid, Openwork, Clear Glass Liner, 1850, 4¾ x 6 In.	431
Bowl, Shell Shape, Terminal Engraved, Rampant Lion, Rocaille, 1773, 13 In.	240
Box, Bougie, Circular Form, Swivel Action, Wick Trimmer, Engraved Crest, 1785-86, 2⅝ In.	554
Cake Basket, Oval, Chased Floral Sprays, Scrolls Centering, Engraved Monogram, 1807, 13 In.	738
Candelabra are listed in the Candelabrum category.	
Candlesnuffer, Trumpet Shape, Stamped, Sampson Mordan & Co., 1897, 12 In.	75
Candlesticks are listed in their own category.	
Cann, Cup, Acanthus-Capped Handle, Monogram, George III, 1777-78, 5½ In.	984
Cann, Cup, Monogram, Handle, George III, 1768-69, 4½ In.	523
Chalice, Gilt, Leaf & Dart Band, Buttressed Handles, Doves, Elkington, c.1875, 8 In.	1500
Cigarette Case, Curved, Gilt Wash Interior, Machined Case, Blank Cartouche, 1910, 3¾ x 2 In.	106
Coffeepot, Coat Of Arms, Ebonized Handles, Finial, George III, 10½ In.	1062
Coffeepot, Scroll Spout, Carved Fruitwood Handle, George III, 1764, 10⅜	1024
Cream, Jug, Helmet Form, Wrigglework, George III, London, c.1795, 6½ x 3 In.	625
Creamer, Embossed, Chased, Engraved, Scroll Handle, William Hunter, 1884	220
Creamer, Serpent Handle, Satyr Masks, Paul Storr, 1816, 4½ In.	1200
Cruet Stand, 5 Bottles, Pierced Caps, Samuel Wood, George II, Warwick, 1755, 9 x 7 In. *illus*	3750
Cup, Covered, Gilt, Campana Form, Regency, Robert Garrard I, c.1812	2500
Cup, Lid, Repousse Racehorses, Gilt, Handles, Paul Storr, 1809-10, 14¾ In. *illus*	10000
Cup, Presentation, Regency, Flower, Leaf Scroll Frieze, Handle, Footed, 1819, 3⅝ In. *illus*	438
Dish, Entree, Lid, George V, Sterling, Ring Handle, Sheffield, 1929-30, 11 x 9 In. *illus*	750
Dish, Hexagonal, Inset Nickel Clad, Hallmark, Elizabeth & Philip, 1973, 3⅛ In.	85
Dish, Shell Shape, Openwork Scroll, Dolphin Fish Feet, Lionel Alfred Crichton, 6 x 4½ In.	726
Epergne, Trumpet Vase, Scrolled Arms, 4 Baskets, Cutwork, Martin Hall, George V, 13⅝ In.	3068
Fish Serving Set, Fiddle Pattern, Engraved Crest, Reticulated Blade, George III, 1808, 12 x 4 In.	188
Frame, Blue & Green Enamel, William Hutton & Sons, 7 x 7½ In.	1560
Fruit Knife, Folding, Pocket, Victorian, 3¼ In.	106
Goblet, Gilt Interior, Monogram A G, Peter & William Bateman, 1808, 7 In.	320
Gong, Dinner, Figured, Child Seated, Labeled, This Way, 9 In.	300
Grater, Oval, Upper Grating, Compartment, Lower Hinged, George III, 1792-93, 2 In.	461
Hot Water Urn, Engraved, Platform Base, Marked William Holmes, 1779, 18½ In.	2500
Kettle, Stand, Thomas Whipham & Charles Wright, 1762, 20½ In. *illus*	2655
Ladle, Onslow, Scalloped Bowl, George III, 1785-86, 13 In.	861
Ladle, Round Downturned Handle, Heraldic Device, London, 1835, 13 In.	188
Loving Cup, Repousse, Applied Scroll, Acanthus Handles, 14 x 11½ In.	5747
Mustard Pot, Spoon, Rebecca Emes, Edward Barnard, George IV, 2 x 4 In. *illus*	420
Napkin Rings are listed in their own category.	
Pie Server, Reticulated Blade, Central, Floral Spray, George III, 1773-74, 11⅞ In.	738
Platter, Meat, William IV, John, Edward & William Barnard, 1835, 22 In.	2500
Porringer, Spoon, Chrysoprase, Ashbee, Guild Of Handicraft, 7-In. Bowl *illus*	7500
Pot, Greek Key, Register Neck, Engraved Acanthus, Spout, George III, 1805-06, 5 In.	492
Punch Bowl, Detachable Monteith Collar, Lion's Mask & Ring Handles, 13 In.	3000

Punch Bowl, Fluted, Drapes, Walter & John Barnard, 1887, 8 1/2 x 13 In....................................	840
Punch Ladle, Family Crest, Marked GSWF For George Smith II & William Fearn, 1794, 13 In.	170
Rattle, Georgian, Bells, Whistle, Coral Teether, Chain, Marked EF, c.1775, 5 In................. *illus*	1000
Salver, Armorial, Shell Rim, Scrolling Pad Feet, J. Robinson II, George II, 13 In.	2125
Salver, Bracketed Scroll Feet, George II, Paul Crespin, 1741, 1 1/4 x 7 1/2 In....................................	1280
Salver, George V, Presentation, Adie Brothers, 10 In.	295
Salver, Repousse Border, Engraved Field, Monogram, Jocobi & Jenkins, c.1900, 11 In....... *illus*	708
Salver, S-Scroll Rim, Ebenezer Coker, 3-Footed, George III, 1761, 11 3/8 In....................................	1750
Salver, Scalloped Shell Border, 3-Footed, Heraldic Device, 2 Sets Of Monograms, 1739, 11 In...	840
Salver, Scalloped, Cast Rim, Alternating Cartouches, Flowers, Lattice, c.1868, 9 1/4 In.	483
Salver, Scroll Rim, Flowers & Ruffled Shells On Scalework Ground, Marked, 1756, 9 5/8 In.	875
Salver, Scroll, Gilt, Irish, Dublin, Marked, George III, 1777, 13 1/2 In.	2750
Salver, Scroll, Shell Border, Acanthus Leaf Feet, 13 In...	726
Stirrup Cup, Parcel Gilt, Fox Head, Thomas Phipps & Edward Robinson, George III, 4 1/2 x 3 In.	8850
Sugar Basket, George III, Oval, Chased Flowers, P&A Bateman, 1793, 4 1/2 x 6 1/4 In.	574
Sugar Basket, Swing Handle, George III, Robert & Thomas Makepeace, c.1793, 4 x 4 1/2 In.	625
Tankard, Baluster, Scroll Handle, Flower Relief, Beaded Foot, George II, 1750, 4 3/4 In..... *illus*	854
Tankard, Coat Of Arms, Gadroon Body, William Cripps, 1700s, 7 1/2 In.	2596
Tankard, Hinged Lid, Lion Holding Sword, Henry Stratford, 1899, 6 1/4 x 7 In.	590
Tankard, Tapering Sides, Bifurcated Thumbpiece, Heraldic Device, 1667, 6 1/2 x 7 3/4 x 5 1/4 In..	6600
Tankard, Tapering Sides, Dolphin Thumbpiece, Monogram On Handle, 1683, 7 1/4 x 8 x 5 1/2 In...	6000
Teapot, Cartouche Form, Engraved Decoration, Heraldic, Wooden Handle, 1791, 6 x 10 x 3 3/4 In.	1440
Teapot, Dome Lid, Tapered Side, Beaded Edges, Knuckle Hinges, Hester Bateman, 1784, 6 x 10 x 5 In.	813
Teapot, Lid, Oval, Tapering, Beaded, 5 Knuckle, Hester Bateman, 1784, 6 1/2 x 10 x 5 In.	875
Teapot, Polygon Form, Engraved Leaves, Ivory Handle, Conforming Base, 1788, 6 1/2 x 11 x 4 In.	1046
Teapot, Scroll, Floral & Shell Decoration, Urn Finial, Wood Handle, 1849, 7 x 10 x 6 1/4 In........	1020
Teapot, Stand, 8-Sided, Engraved, Ivory Handle, Henry Green, George III, 1788, 7 x 5 In. *illus*	1046
Teapot, Wood Handle, Wreath, Monogram, Robert & David Hennell, c.1800, 6 x 11 3/4 In.	330
Toast Rack, George III, Oval, 4-Footed, 1813, 6 x 6 3/4 x 5 3/4 In...	188
Toast Rack, Rounded Rectangle, 7 Oval Dividers, Ring Handle, Shell Feet, Walton, 7 In. *illus*	336
Tray, Arms Of Lyon, Handles, George IV, Sheffield, Matthew Boulton, c.1850, 31 x 20 In............	1500
Tray, Art Nouveau, 4-Sided, Raised Rope Twist, Ball Feet, 12 In.	1512
Tray, Gadroon Border, Shells, Engraved, Henry & Arthur Vander, London, 1932, 26 In.	7500
Tray, Oval, Central Engraving, George III, 1805-06, 23 In.	3998
Tray, Raised Edge, Gadroon Border, Coat Of Arms, Paul Storr, 1798, 1 1/2 x 20 x 14 In..............	4750
Tray, Rectangular, Canted Corners, Bracket Feet, Elizabeth II, 1957-58, 14 In.	677
Tray, Rectangular, Canted Corners, Gadroon Border, Rams, Panthers, 13 1/2 x 11 In.	1512
Tray, Rectangular, Gadroon Rim, Shell Accents, George V, 1918-19, 29 In..................................	2337
Tureen, Lid, Gadroon, William Keir Reid, 1842, 16 1/4 In...	4375
Tureen, Oval, Shield, Footed, 11 1/2 x 15 1/2 In.	480
Urn, Bud Finial, 2 Reeded Handles, Eagle Spout, Ivory Finial, 4 Supports, 1808, 11 x 13 x 12 In.	5843
Urn, Cut Crystal, John Emes, London, Marked, 1805, 4 1/2 x 3 3/4 In.	183
Vase, Monogram M, Round Stepped Foot, Reid & Sons, 1989, 10 1/8 In.	2500
Vase, Presentation, Trumpet, Domed Base, Heraldic Device On Side, 1900s, 18 In.	185
Vase, Trumpet, Embossed Irises & Bamboo, W. Comyns & Sons, c.1905, 8 In., Pair....................	427
Vase, Urn Shape, Engraved, Registers Throughout, George III, 1802-03, 9 1/4 In.	984
Waiter, Circular, Openwork, Urns, Medallions, George III, Marked, c.1771, 7 In.	625
Wine Bottle Holder, Grapevine, Antler Handle, Openwork, c.1880, 8 3/4 x 7 In...........................	4500
Wine Funnel, 2 Sections, Reeded Border, P. & A. Bateman, George III, 5 1/4 In.	500
Wine Funnel, Edinburgh, George III, 1801, 4 1/2 In. .... *illus*	305
Wine Funnel, Reeded Border, Marked, Solomon Hougham, 1802, 5 1/4 In. .... *illus*	480

SILVER-FRENCH

Basket, Reticulated, Square, Tapered Openwork, Serpentine Rim, Garlands, Ribbons, 8 5/8 In.	224
Box, Painted Panel, Hinged, Minerva Hallmark, Engraved Highlights, Goat, 1 3/4 x 8 1/2 In........	605
Coffeepot, Rococo Style, Side Handle, Footed, c.1840, 8 3/8 In. .... *illus*	732
Hot Water Urn, Ivory Feet, Spigot, Insulators, Rococo, 15 3/4 In.	2280
Sugar & Creamer, Wooden Handle, Emile Puiforcat, 2 Piece	171
Teapot, Etched, Flat Disc Finial, Fluted, 10 1/2 x 5 1/2 In...	281
Urn, Belle Epoque, Oval, Panels, Cavetto Collar, Black Marble Base, c.1875, 13 x 9 In..............	1250

Silver-Danish, Pitcher, Large Handle, Stamped, Georg Jensen, 1950s, 11 1/2 x 8 1/4 In.
$11,250

Rago Arts and Auction Center

Silver-Danish, Tea Strainer, Bottom Cup, Copenhagen Guild, Georg Jensen, c.1924, 1 1/2 x 4 1/2 In.
$708

Cottone Auctions

Silver-English, Cruet Stand, 5 Bottles, Pierced Caps, Samuel Wood, George II, Warwick, 1755, 9 x 7 In.
$3,750

New Orleans Auction Galleries

S

TIP
An old hand-engraved monogram or decoration adds value to a piece of silver.

Silver-English, Cup, Lid, Repousse Racehorses, Gilt, Handles, Paul Storr, 1809-10, 14¾ In.
$10,000

New Orleans Auction Galleries

Silver-English, Cup, Presentation, Regency, Flower, Leaf Scroll Frieze, Handle, Footed, 1819, 3⅝ In.
$438

Neal Auction Co.

Silver-English, Dish, Entree, Lid, George V, Sterling, Ring Handle, Sheffield, 1929-30, 11 x 9 In.
$750

New Orleans Auction Galleries

Vinegar Set, Vine, Berry Leaves, Handle, Footed, 10¾ x 11 In.	413

SILVER-GERMAN

Basket, Fruit, Pierced Latticework, Portrait Medallions, Swags, 4-Footed, Hanau, 13 In.	549
Basket, Medusa Gorgon, Sirens, Johann S. Kurtz & Co., c.1875, 6 x 11½ In.	649
Basket, Reticulated, Pierced Swing Handle, Repousse, Garlands, Baskets, Swags, 13¾ x 10 In.	600
Bowl, Oval, Strapwork Handles, Spot Hammered, 15½ In.	344
Bowl, Scrolling Grapevines, Pierced, Shaped, 3½ x 11½ In.	437
Candy Dish, Scalloped Rim, Repousse Leaf & Swirl, 3-Footed, c.1925, 6⅝ In.	100
Centerpiece, Tapers, Acanthus, Reticulated Olive Branch, Garlands, Weinrank & Schmidt, 6 x 9 In.	413
Compote, Art Nouveau, Figural, Robes, c.1900, 13 x 10 In.	1000
Compote, Repousse, Hand Chased, 1800s, 4¾ x 10 In.	531
Condiment Holder, Handcart, Pierced, Wheels Turn, Putto, Liner, Hanau, 4 In., Pair	1342
Epergne, Trumpet Shape Vase, Fruit, Leaves, Seated Putti, Dolphin Supports, 10¼ x 10¾ In.	1250
Figurine, Knight, Shield, Sword, Glass Stones, 9¾ In.	750
Pitcher, Gadroon Neck, Banding, Cartouches, Putti, Garden, Ribbons, 9¾ In.	688
Salt, Cobalt Glass Insert, 4-Footed, Leaves, 1¾ In., 6 Piece	590
Salver, Grape & Vine Pierced Border, 3 Paw Feet, 7¾ x 1½ In.	281
Sauceboat, Underplate, Cast, Scroll Handle, Acanthus, Ruffles, Chased, 7⅜ x 9⅝ In.	377
Shaker, Dolphin Shape Handle, Ornate Repousse Decoration, 11 x 8¼ x 4¾ In.	1140
Table Ornament, Wheelbarrow, Openwork, Christoph Widmann, c.1950, 5 x 4 In.	750
Tea & Coffee Set, Gilt, Teapot, Coffeepot, Sugar, Creamer, Tray, Leafy Bands, Tiger, 5 Piece	2500
Tea & Coffee Set, Teapot, Coffeepot, Sugar & Creamer, Tray, Bruckman & Sohne, 5 Piece	2000
Tray, 4 Wells, Spot Hammered, Ball Feet, 11 In.	175
Tray, Gilt, Oval, Pierced Border, Spiral Scrolls, 16¾ In., Pair	469
Vase, Trumpet, Monogram, Henckel & Co., 22¼ In.	420

SILVER-INDIAN

Hookah, Dolphin Head Mounted, Mumbai Design, Contemporary, 19 x 6½ In.	1750

SILVER-IRISH

Cup, Double Bellied Shape, R. Williams, George III, 9 x 8 In., Pair	2835
Dish Ring, Birds, Fruit, Cartouche, Open Sides, Marked West & Son, Dublin, 1915, 4 x 7½ In.	554
Dish Ring, Potato, Spool Shape, Pierced, Birds, Castle, E. Johnson, 1910, 4 x 7 In.	1810
Salt, Gilt Wash, Garlands, Claw Feet, 1777, 4¼ In., Pair	5445
Sauce Ladle, George III, Shell Shape Bowl, Christopher Haines, Ireland, c.1780, 7 In., Pair	125
Sauceboat, Crest, Beaded Rim, Scroll Handle, 3 Shell Feet, W. Reynolds, Cork, 8 In.	1250
Sugar, 3-Footed, Ornate, 3 x 6 In.	732
Sugar, Hand Chased, Wreath Edgework, Ball Feet, William IV, c.1834, 5 x 8 In.	145
Teapot, Pricked Design, Greek Key, Gooseneck Spout, Marked, 1813, 7 x 11 In. *illus*	335

SILVER-ISRAELI

Sculpture, Houses, Stacked On Hill, 2½ In.	84

SILVER-ITALIAN

Bowl, Oval, Lobed, Upswept Ends, Rococo Rim, Footed, Stancampiano, 24 In.	1625
Centerpiece, Ram's-Head Handles, Pierced Scroll Rim, Arno Fassi, 8¼ x 19 In.	3125
Dish, Alternating Panels, Serpentine Rim, Repousse Flowers, Chased, 9¾ In.	112
Frame, Rococo Style, Repousse Acanthus Leaves, 8½ x 10½ In.	94
Ice Bucket, Lid, Repousse, Gadroon, Stepped Round Foot, David Orgell, 12 x 9¾ In.	1200
Pitcher, Pear Shape, Duck's Beak Spout, S-Scroll Handle, Footed, Buccellati, 9 In.	1250
Tea & Coffee Set, Teapot, Coffeepot, Sugar, Creamer, Lobed, Ebonized Handle, 1965, 4 Piece	3250
Vase, Poppy Flowers, Leaves, Fluted Rim, 12 x 7½ In.	750

SILVER-JAPANESE

Bowl, 5 Petals, Butterfly, Flowers, 5 In.	1140
Bowl, Liner, Writhing Dragon, Clutching Flaming Pearl, Hammered, c.1900, 8 In.	2125
Bowl, Repousse Chrysanthemum, Lobed, 4¼ x 11 In.	4687
Bowl, Shaped, Indented & Barbed Rim, Iris Flowers, Embossed, 4½ x 6 In.	1008
Box, Mums, Flowers, Doors, 2 Drawers, Flutist, Warrior, Sword, 4⅜ x 1 In.	875
Cigarette Case, Temple Grounds, Gate, Trees, Hills, Copper, Silver, 4¼ x 3 In. *illus*	172
Sailboat, In Sealed Glass, Wood Rectangular Case, Takehiko Seki, 9 x 8 x 5 In.	405

S

Teapot, Squared, Engraved Flowers, Signed Hidekuni, 5¼ In.	2040
Vase, Enamel, Sea Dragon, Waves, Sea Foam, Yellow To Pale Blue, 9¾ In.	1625
Vase, Engraved With Flowers, 7½ In.	756
Vase, Trumpet Shape, Fluted, Applied Chrysanthemums, Domed Foot, 25½ In.	1560

SILVER-MEXICAN. Silver objects have been made in Mexico since the days of the Aztecs. These marks are for three companies still making tableware and jewelry..

ChATo CASTiLLO STERLING MEXICO	 Matl STERLING MEXICO 925	 SANBORN'S STERLING H MADE IN MEXICO
Jorge "Chato" Castillo 1939+	Matilde Eugenia Poulat 1934–1960	Sanborn's 1931–present

Bowl, Oval, Floral Medallions, Sanborn's, 1900s, 14 x 8 x 2 In.	300
Centerpiece, Mayan Design, 3 Peacock Pedestal, 8 In.	2040
Centerpiece, Oval, Scrollwork Handles, Applied Leaf Border, 1900s, 21¼ In.	1000
Coffee Set, Coffeepot, Pitcher, Sugar & Creamer, Dish, Tray, Rosewood, 7 Piece	3960
Coffee Set, Coffeepot, Sugar & Creamer, Tray, Repousse, 6¾ x 15½ In., 4 Piece	720
Compote, Lobed Rim, Round Foot, 3 x 7½ In. *illus*	250
Figurine, Horse Head, Windblown Mane, Plata Artistica, 4 x 3¾ In. *illus*	118
Platter, Meat, Gadroon Rim, Tree & Well, Heather & Hijos, 23¾ In.	1125
Platter, Oval, Stylized Handles, 30¼ x 19 In.	1200
Punch Bowl Set, Gadroon Body, Monteith Rim, Footed, Tane Orfebres, 25 Piece	6250
Sauceboat, Lid, Twin Spouts, Juvento Lopez Reyes, 9 In.	250
Sugar & Creamer, Double Handles, Tapered, Big Spout, 2 Piece	259
Tea & Coffee Set, Teapot, Coffeepot, Kettle, Stand, Sugar & Creamer, Waste, Tray, 7 Piece	6500
Tray, 2 Handles, Removable Divider, Partial, Sanborn's, 18 x 11 In.	590
Tray, Pineapple Shape, 4½ In., Pair	72
Trophy, Golf, Cup, William Spratling, 1945, 6 x 3⅛ In.	590

SILVER-PERSIAN

Bowl, Repousse, Flowers, Leaves, Square, 2½ x 3¾ In.	437
Bowl, Squat, 2¾ x 7¼ In.	463
Ewer, Lobed Foot, Acanthus, Snake Shape Handle, 14 x 6 In.	1250
Plate, Repousse, Central Medallion, Flowers, Reticulated Filigree, 7 In.	437
Teapot, Concentric Circles, Square Lid, Fruit Finial, Figural Scenes, 8 x 9 In.	3125

SILVER-PERUVIAN

Bowl, Incised Oak Leaf Flared Rim, Gadroon, 9½ In. *illus*	360
Tray, Scroll Handles, Scalloped Rim, Camusso, Marked, Industria Peruana, 1900s, 15 x 25 x 2 In.	1074
Vase, Figural, Male With Ceremonial Headdress, 14 In.	563
Vase, Flower Heads, Peru, 1900, 8⅜ In.	492

SILVER-PORTUGUESE

Bowl, Shell, David Ferreira, Shell Feet, 1900s, 18½ In.	2750
Plateau, Mirrored Bottom, Rococo Shell & Scrolling Fronds, 15 In.	247

SILVER-RUSSIAN. Russian silver is marked with the Cyrillic, or Russian, alphabet. The numbers 84, 88, or 91 indicate the silver content. Russian silver may be higher or lower than sterling standard. Other marks indicate maker, assayer, or city of manufacture. Many pieces of silver made in Russia are decorated with enamel. These prices are based on current silver values. Faberge pieces are listed in their own category.

Silver–Russian Silver content numbers	 Silver–Russian 1741–1900+	Silver–Russian 1896–1908

Silver-English, Kettle, Stand, Thomas Whipham & Charles Wright, 1762, 20½ In.
$2,655

Alex Cooper Auctioneers

> **TIP**
> Don't mechanically buff silver. It will change the color and wear away bits of the silver.

Silver-English, Mustard Pot, Spoon, Rebecca Emes, Edward Barnard, George IV, 2 x 4 In.
$420

Brunk Auctions

Silver-English, Porringer, Spoon, Chrysoprase, Ashbee, Guild Of Handicraft, 7-In. Bowl
$7,500

Rago Arts and Auction Center

S

Silver-English, Rattle, Georgian, Bells, Whistle, Coral Teether, Chain, Marked EF, c.1775, 5 In.
$1,000

New Orleans Auction Galleries

Silver-English, Salver, Repousse Border, Engraved Field, Monogram, Jocobi & Jenkins, c.1900, 11 In.
$708

Alex Cooper Auctioneers

Silver-English, Tankard, Baluster, Scroll Handle, Flower Relief, Beaded Foot, George II, 1750, 4 3/4 In.
$854

Neal Auction Co.

TIP

If you break the handle on an old silver coffeepot, have it resoldered. That repair detracts little from the resale value, but a new handle lowers the value by 50 percent.

Beaker, Cyrillic, Prince Vassili Vladimirovitch Dolgorouki, Engraved, 1725, 5 1/2 In.	6000
Beaker, Gilt, Enamel, Impressed Assay, Town, Marks, Ivan Saltykov, 2 1/4 In. *illus*	400
Cigar Box, Faux Bois, Cyrillic, Moscow, 1895, 5 1/2 In.	1230
Cigarette Case, Enamel Filigree Lid, Beaded Turquoise Border, Kokoshnik, 1/2 x 4 x 3 1/4 In.	1210
Cigarette Case, Scrolling Leaf Designs, Pastel Colors, Turquoise Edge, 3 3/4 x 2 1/4 x 1/2 In.	1800
Cigarette Case, Worn Marks, Cyrillic, Interior, Cloisonne Enamel, Scrollwork, 1900, 3 7/8 In.	861
Plate, Crest, 2-Headed Eagle, Crown, Russian Seal, 12 In.	1149
Pot, Marks For Moscow, Sokolov, Engraved, Leaf Cartouche, Moscow, 1894, 6 In.	431
Salt, Pig, Gilt, Laurel Leaf Wreath, Jade Base, 3 x 3 1/8 In.	2124
Samovar, Taper, Checkered, Shield, 4-Footed, 19 x 12 1/2 In.	10710
Teapot, Paneled Sides, Parcel Gilt, Shield Cartouche, 1848, 9 3/4 In.	2006
Tray, Good Nicholas, Serpentine Sided, Rectangular, Marked, Johan F. Falck, 1844, 22 x 14 In.	1375
Tray, Oval Tray, Leafy Scroll Trim, Tane, 16 x 12 In.	472

SILVER-SCOTTISH

Basket, Rectangular, Leaves, Twist Rim, George III, 1812, 10 In.	900
Bowl, Scalloped Walls, Repousse Mythological Masks, Shells, 9 3/4 In., Pair	605
Epergne, George V, Openwork Baskets, Swags, Acanthus, Shell, Hamilton & Inches, 9 x 19 In.	3776
Teapot, Boar Head Finial, Ivory Spacers, George Fenwick, 1815, 5 1/2 x 10 In.	922

SILVER-SPANISH

Cognac Warmer, Elephant, Trunk Up, Stopper, Chain, 5 1/4 x 5 In.	218
Wine Cooler, Inverted Bell Form, Wire & Grape Base & Handles, Barcelona, 9 In.	1000

SILVER-STERLING. Sterling silver is made with 925 parts silver out of 1,000 parts of metal. The word *sterling* is a quality guarantee used in the United States after about 1860. The word was used much earlier in England and Ireland. Pieces listed here are not identified by country. These prices are based on current silver values. Other pieces of sterling quality silver are listed under Silver-American, Silver-English, etc.

Basket, Acanthus Capped Handle, Shell, Scroll Border, Coat Of Arms, 1818-19, 13 In.	1230
Basket, Egg & Dart, Chased Rim, Acanthus Capped, Lobed Interior, Bail Handle, 1823-24, 12 In.	738
Basket, Monogram, Bail Handle, Floral Motif, Rim, 1900, 14 In.	677
Basket, Shell, Scroll Rim, Bail Handle, 1818-19, 12 In.	677
Bone Dish, Canted Corners, Wide Upturned Rim, Dolphins, Vining Tendrils, 9 1/2 In. *illus*	450
Bottle, Flask, Hinged Lid, Monogram One Side, Hunting Dogs, 1800, 5 5/8 In.	738
Bowl, Chased Scenes, Peasants, Bucolic Landscape, 1700, 5 1/8 In.	492
Bowl, Chased, Various Fruit, Exterior, 1900, 10 3/4 In.	523
Bowl, Conical Finial, Projecting Leaves, Gold Washed, Mounted To Top, 1973, 5 3/4 In.	1169
Bowl, Crenulated Rim, Putti Masks, Offset By Scrolls, George V, 1908-09, 6 In.	400
Bowl, Die Cast Rim, Leaf Tips, Arabesques, Flaring Foot, 1877, 8 In.	192
Bowl, Embossed, Foliage, Shell Design, Hallmark, 1900s, 11 x 11 x 2 In.	336
Bowl, Engraved, Leaf Swags, Pendant Ribbon Tied, 3 Claw Ball Feet, 1800s, 7 1/2 In.	400
Bowl, Flared Rim, Repousse, Flowers, Oval, Monogram Kirk & Son, 1900s, 11 In.	395
Bowl, Fluted Rim, Lion Heads, Ring Handles, Medallion, 1903-04, 11 In.	1722
Bowl, Hammered Surface, 2 Reticulated Handles, Arts & Crafts, 1900, 11 In.	369
Bowl, Hand Hammered, Felt Bag, 1900s, 6 In.	120
Bowl, Hexagonal, Molded Rim, Monogram, 1907-47, 8 1/2 In.	300
Bowl, India Style, Chased Figural Scenes, Engraved, Armorial, 1872, 4 3/4 In.	492
Bowl, Lobed Form, Tooled Floral Sides, Conforming Pedestal Base, 1926, 6 5/8 x 9 In.	369
Bowl, Pierced Rim, Gadroon Body, Central Monogram, 1900s, 10 1/2 In.	144
Bowl, Repousse, Leaves, Floral Rim, Monogram, Flat Piece Metal, 1914, 11 x 11 x 1 1/2 In.	513
Bowl, Rococo, Oval, Floral Scroll, Shells, 1895, 5 x 10 x 8 In.	2880
Bowl, Rose Border, Rounded Square, Rose Relief Border, c.1870, 2 3/4 x 11 x 11 In.	369
Box, Bougie, Hinged Side Handle, Swivel Action Wick Trimmer, Engraved Register, 1792, 2 In.	677
Bread Tray, Beaded Edge, Monogram, 13 In.	148
Butter, Ornate Floral, Ribbon Scroll Border, Removable Pierced Drain Plate, 1890, 6 x 6 x 1 1/2 In.	153
Cake Basket, Pierced, Swing Handle, Aldridge & Stamper, George II, 1757, 13 x 11 In. *illus*	1188
Candelabra are listed in the Candelabrum category.	
Candlesticks are listed in their own category.	

Silver-English, Teapot, Stand, 8-Sided, Engraved, Ivory Handle, Henry Green, George III, 1788, 7 x 5 In.
$1,046

Brunk Auctions

Silver-English, Toast Rack, Rounded Rectangle, 7 Oval Dividers, Ring Handle, Shell Feet, Walton, 7 In.
$336

New Orleans Auction Galleries

Silver-English, Wine Funnel, Edinburgh, George III, 1801, 4 ½ In.
$305

Neal Auction Co.

Silver-English, Wine Funnel, Reeded Border, Marked, Solomon Hougham, 1802, 5 ¼ In.
$480

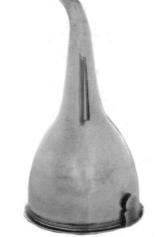

Brunk Auctions

Silver-French, Coffeepot, Rococo Style, Side Handle, Footed, c.1840, 8 ⅜ In.
$732

Neal Auction Co.

Silver-Irish, Teapot, Pricked Design, Greek Key, Gooseneck Spout, Marked, 1813, 7 x 11 In.
$335

New Orleans Auction Galleries

Silver-Japanese, Cigarette Case, Temple Grounds, Gate, Trees, Hills, Copper, Silver, 4 ¼ x 3 In.
$172

Bunch Auctions

Silver-Mexican, Compote, Lobed Rim, Round Foot, 3 x 7 ½ In.
$250

Crescent City Auction Gallery

Silver-Mexican, Figurine, Horse Head, Windblown Mane, Plata Artistica, 4 x 3 ¾ In.
$118

Burchard Galleries

S

SILVER-STERLING

Silver-Peruvian, Bowl, Incised Oak Leaf Flared Rim, Gadroon, 9 ½ In.
$360

Michann's Auctions

Silver-Russian, Beaker, Gilt, Enamel, Impressed Assay, Town, Marks, Ivan Saltykov, 2 ¼ In.
$400

Cowan's Auctions

Silver-Sterling, Bone Dish, Canted Corners, Wide Upturned Rim, Dolphins, Vining Tendrils, 9 ½ In.
$450

Eldred's Auctioneers and Appraisers

Silver-Sterling, Cake Basket, Pierced, Swing Handle, Aldridge & Stamper, George II, 1757, 13 x 11 In.
$1,188

New Orleans Auction Galleries

Silver-Sterling, Pitcher, Flutter Rim, Squat Body, Monogram, 1887, 5 ¾ In.
$390

Eldred's Auctioneers and Appraisers

Silver-Sterling, Salver, Molded Edge, 4 Hooves, 1900, 12 In.
$510

Eldred's Auctioneers and Appraisers

Silver-Sterling, Tankard, George II, Dome Lid, Tapered, Applied Girdle, Chased, Flowers, 1752, 6 ⅞ In.
$1,216

Neal Auction Co.

Silver-Sterling, Teapot, Enamel, Rosewood, Tentacle Handles, Stamped Banner, 1960s-70s, 18 x 10 In.
$7,500

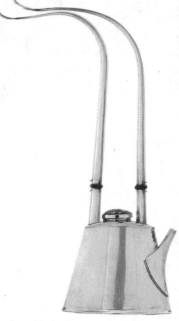

Rago Arts and Auction Center

Silver-Sterling, Urn, Mappin & Webb, Surmounted By Lion, Leaves, 4 Leafy Feet, 1907, 14 In.
$1,800

Eldred's Auctioneers and Appraisers

S

Candy Dish, Ornate Pierced Rim, Base, Monogram, 1900s, 7 1/2 In.	270
Canister, Monogram, Urn Shape, Chased Architectural, 2 Lion Head Handles, 1900, 5 1/4 In.	800
Canister, Neoclassical Designs, Armorial To Reverse, George III, 1700, 4 1/4 In.	400
Casket, Chased, Leafy, Scrollwork, 5 1/2 In.	1968
Chamberstick, Removable Bobeche, Drip Pan, Engraved Armorial, 1819-20, 2 1/2 In.	523
Charger, Edward Jr., Molded Scroll, Borders, Engraved Crown, 1843, 9 3/4 x 21 In.	313
Coffeepot, Paneled, Scroll Handle, Floral Repousse, Monogram, 1849, 10 x 6 x 10 In.	897
Compote, 2 Lion Head Handles, Die Cast Borders, Foot Rim, Monogram, 1860, 6 3/4 In.	861
Compote, Bearing Character, Petal Panels, Featuring Buddhist, Figural Stem, 1900s, 6 5/8 In.	400
Compote, Oval, 2 Upright Handles, Engraved Name, 1867-74, 7 In.	369
Creamer, Cow, Tail Forms Handle, Hinged Lid, Engraved Bee, c.1905, 6 In.	3900
Cruet Set, Castors, Silver Mounts, Glass Cruets, Laurel Swags, Neoclassical, 1773-74, 11 In.	3998
Cup, 2 Scrolled Handles, Grapevine, Engraved Coat, 1807-08, 9 3/4 In.	1968
Cup, Lid, Cartouche, Urn Shape, Engraved Armorial, 2 Acanthus, Capped Handle, 1768, 13 In.	2214
Cup, Ribbon Tied, Floral Swags, Vacant Cartouche, 1792-93, 6 In.	277
Dish, Cut Glass, Heart Shape, Handles, 5 3/4 In.	74
Dish, Dome Lid, Pea Blossom, Shell Form Handles, Chased Scrolls, 1850-51, 12 x 6 1/2 In.	2337
Dish, Entree, Lobed, Topped, Flower Blossom Finial, Grapevine Rim, 1834, 6 x 9 In.	677
Dish, Octagonal, Monogram, Etched Border Design, 6 In.	74
Dish, Relish, Etched Glass, 4 Sections, Well, Laurel Leaf, Floral, Well, Watson, 1900s, 9 x 9 x 1 In.	59
Ewer, Vase Shape, Faux-Bois Handle, Grapevines, Engraved, Leaf Swags, 1860-61, 14 In.	1107
Grape Scissors, Figural, 1860, 7 1/2 x 2 1/2 In.	236
Ice Cream Spoon, Gilt Wash Bowl, Tiffany & Co., 9 1/2 x 5 1/2 In.	334
Ladle, Hawthorne, Cut Floral, Scalloped Bowl, Monogram, 1885, 12 x 4 x 4 In.	153
Miniature, Car, 4 Wheels, Original Patinas, 1977, 2 1/4 x 1 1/4 In.	395
Mirror, Pierced Filigree, Purple Velvet Wrapped Body, Easel Stand, 23 x 18 In.	2118
Mirror, Vanity, Relief Filigree, Dark Blue Velvet Back Panel, Marked, 18 x 13 In.	242
Mustard Pot, Scrolled Handle, Cobalt Blue Glass, 3 1/4 In.	49
Napkin Rings are listed in their own category.	
Pill Box, Inlaid Abalone, Purple Highlights, Snaps Closed, 1960, 1 1/4 In.	35
Pitcher, Baluster, Leaves, Flowers, Matted Ground, 1880-1890, 8 x 7 1/2 x 5 In.	2250
Pitcher, Baluster, Slender Handle, Hammered Surface, 1945, 8 3/4 In.	3690
Pitcher, Cherry Blossoms, Extending, Handle Across, Hammered Body, 1915, 8 5/8 In.	3690
Pitcher, Circular, Wide Mouth, Upright Handle, Stepped Foot, 1900, 11 1/4 In.	554
Pitcher, Elongated Spout, Continuing Downward, Pear Shape, 1949, 10 7/8 In.	1046
Pitcher, Flowers To Rim, Handle, Pendant Floral Swags, Monogram, 1900, 9 3/8 In.	677
Pitcher, Flutter Rim, Squat Body, Monogram, 1887, 5 3/4 In. .... *illus*	390
Pitcher, Pear Shape, Floral Shape, Twig Style Handle, Monogram, 1800s-1900s, 9 In.	780
Pitcher, Rococo Style, Pear Body, 1929-42, 9 1/4 In.	720
Pitcher, Squat Form, Scroll Handle, 5 x 16 1/2 In.	188
Pitcher, Urn Shape, Gadroon Border, Scroll Handle, Shell Decoration, 1900s, 9 3/4 In.	738
Pot, Bamboo Design, Graces The Body, Handle, Spout, 8 1/2 x 4 x 5 In.	1295
Pot, Circular Form, Engraved Rocaille, Scrolls Centering, Cartouche, 1773-74, 4 3/4 In.	369
Pot, Egg Form, Lift-Off Lid, 3 Crowns, 1896-1954, 5 1/4 In.	360
Pot, Engraved, Decoration, Neoclassical, 7 3/4 In.	246
Pot, Lid, Monogram, Wood Scrolled Handle, 6 In.	123
Pot, Lighthouse, Wood Handle, Finial, 1959-60, 11 In.	523
Pot, Neoclassical Designs, Centering, Monogrammed Cartouche, 1787-88, 14 In.	1353
Pot, Oval, Neoclassical Swags, Centering Medallion, Engraved Armorial, 1796-97, 5 3/4 In.	277
Pot, Scrolled Handle, Chased Vertical, Decoration, 1757-58, 10 1/4 In.	1107
Pot, Urn Shape Finial, Acanthus Capped Spout, Monogram, 1744-45, 9 1/4 In.	800
Pot, Wooden Scrolled, Knop, Monogram, 6 1/4 x 10 3/4 In.	246
Pot, Worn Marks, Vase Shape, Acanthus Capped Spout, Wood Handle, Monogram, 1700, 11 In.	554
Pudding Spoon, Medallion Handle, Reefed Stem, Ball Black, 1860s, 10 Piece	1560
Punch Bowl, Repousse, Floral, Scroll Overall Deco, Gilt Interior, 1800-1900s, 6 1/4 x 11 In.	1968
Purse, Art Deco, Coin, Monogram, Webster, 1920s-30s, 3 1/2 x 2 1/2 x 1/4 In.	130
Salt & Pepper, Acorn, Scalloped Base, 2 1/2 In.	172
Salver, Engraved Coat Of Arms, Later Rim, 1808-09, 13 In.	984
Salver, Gadroon Edge, Engravings To Rim, Initial, Scratch Weights, 1788-89, 9 5/8 In.	431
Salver, Molded Edge, 4 Hooves, 1900, 12 In. .... *illus*	510

Slag Glass, Lamp, Brass Frame, Metal Base, Pittsburgh Lamp, 21 In.
$469

Garth's Auctioneers & Appraisers

Slag Glass, Lampshade, Leaded, Tulips, Scrolls, 12 x 25 In.
$1,800

Garth's Auctioneers & Appraisers

Sleepy Eye, Pitcher, Indian Chief Profile, Blue & White, Stoneware
$84

Martin Auction Co.

S

Smith Brothers, Biscuit Jar, Cream Colored Opal Glass, Floral, Gold Decoration, c.1880, 9 ¼ In.
$300

Ruby Lane

Snow Babies, Figurine, 2 Children, Sliding Down Brick Ramp, Germany, c.1910, 2 x 2 In.
$65

Ruby Lane

Soapstone, Carving, Foo Dog Buddhist, Flowers, Vines, Chinese, 1900s, 7 In., Pair
$300

Brunk Auctions

Salver, Oval, Shell, Scroll Rim, 4 Scrolled Feet, 1914-15, 13 In.	738
Salver, Shell, Scroll Rim, Engraved Coat Of Arms, 1808-09, 10 ¾ In.	1169
Salver, Shell, Scroll Rim, Rocaille Surface, Engraved Crest, 4 Bracket Feet, 1808-09, 19 In.	2583
Sauceboat, Gadroon Rim, Scrolled Handle, Shell Shape, 1765-66, 8 ⅛ In.	492
Serving Fork, Stem, Terminal, Seaweed, Starfish, Middle Tine, 1900s, 6 ⅝ In.	1169
Silent Butler, Sunnie O'Dea, Miniature, Monogram, Leaves, 1940s, 3 ¼ x 1 ¼ In.	71
Skewer, Loop Terminal, Shell Joint, Engraved Armorial, 1811-12, 13 In.	400
Spoon, Souvenir, see Souvenir category.	
Stuffing Spoon, Shaped Bowl, Stalk, Leaf, 5 In.	135
Sugar Tongs, Georgian, Marked, 1791	100
Tankard, Barrel Form, 2 Reeded Bands, Hinged Lid, 1818-19, 5 ⅜ In.	584
Tankard, Dome Lid, Scrolled Thumbpiece, Monogram, 1765-66, 7 ⅞ In.	2337
Tankard, George II, Dome Lid, Tapered, Applied Girdle, Chased, Flowers, 1752, 6 ⅞ In. .. *illus*	1216
Tazza, Beaded, Molded Rim, Border, Flower, Leaf Design, 1907-47, 4 ¾ In.	3 00
Teapot, Beaded Rim, Central Monogram, 4 Scrolled Feet, 1908-15, 6 ½ In.	120
Teapot, Enamel, Rosewood, Tentacle Handles, Stamped Banner, 1960s-70s, 18 x 10 In.... *illus*	7500
Tongs, Starfish, Spatula, 12 ½ x 3 In.	590
Tray, 2 Handles, Engraved Floor, Tongue, Dart Border, Bead Handles, Oval, 1859, 31 ¾ In.	3600
Trivet, Pressed Butterflies, Flowers Under Glass, 1900s, 10 In.	168
Trophy, Loving Cup, Base Engraved, Wood Base, 1900s, 25 x 8 x 8 In.	720
Tureen, 4 Paw Feet, Lion's Heads, 2 Leaf Handles, Cartouches, Gadroon Borders, 1810, 15 In..	5625
Urn, Dome Lid, Rubbed, Knopped Finial, 2 Lion's Heads, 1900s, 13 In.	1107
Urn, Mappin & Webb, Surmounted By Lion, Leaves, 4 Leafy Feet, 1907, 14 In. *illus*	1800
Vase, Flutter Rim, Conical, Engraved, Garlands, 8 ½ In.	228
Vesta Case, Acid Etched, Engraved, Lid, 3 Owls In Tree, Featuring A Frog, 1887, 3 ¼ In.	461
Wax Jack, Engraved Crest, Base, Later Monogram, 1793-94, 4 ¼ In.	369

SILVER-SWEDISH

Bowl, Glass, Grape Clusters Handles, 1930s, 11 ½ x 6 ⅜ In.	455
Coffee Set, Coffeepot, Sugar & Creamer, Art Nouveau, 3 ½ x 6 ½ In., 3 Piece	188

SILVER-TIBETAN

Prayer Wheel, Gilt, Bands, Turquoise, Coral, Sanskrit, Lotus Petals, Chain, Ball, 8 ¼ In.	501
Seal, Round Handle, Amber, Incision Work, Tibet, 1800s	114

 SINCLAIRE cut glass was made by H.P. Sinclaire and Company of Corning, New York, between 1904 and 1929. He cut glass made at other factories until 1920. Pieces were made of clear glass as well as amber, blue, green, or ruby glass. Only a small percentage of Sinclaire glass is marked with the *S* in a wreath.

Flowerpot, Hobstar, Strawberry Diamond & Fan, Engraved Border, Hobstar Base, Signed, 6 ½ x 6 In.	240
Pitcher, Bengal Pattern, Triple Notched Handle, Hobstar Base, 7 In.	250
Teapot, Engraved Leaf & Blossom, Diamond Cut Band Ray, Pattern Cut Lid, 5 x 9 In.	1020
Urn, Potpourri, Putti, Roses, White, c.1925, 16 In.	125

SKIING, *see Sports category.*

 SLAG GLASS resembles a marble cake. It can be streaked with different colors. There were many types made from about 1880. Caramel slag is the incorrect name for chocolate glass made by Imperial Glass. Pink slag was an American product made by Harry Bastow and Thomas E.A. Dugan at Indiana, Pennsylvania, about 1900. Purple and blue slag were made in American and English factories in the 1880s. Red slag is a very late Victorian and twentieth-century glass. Other colors are known but are of less importance to the collector. New versions of chocolate glass and colored slag glass have been made.

Caramel Slag is listed in the Imperial Glass category.

Purple & White, Dish, Lion Lid, 6 ½ x 7 ½ In.	34 to 60
Purple, Bowl, Swan Shape, 5 x 9 ½ In.	35
Purple, Jar, Owl, Head Lid, 6 ¾ x 3 ½ In.	30
Lamp, Brass Frame, Metal Base, Pittsburgh Lamp, 21 In. *illus*	469
Lampshade, Leaded, Tulips, Scrolls, 12 x 25 In. *illus*	1800

S

SLEEPY EYE collectors look for anything bearing the image of the nineteenth-century Indian chief with the drooping eyelid. The Sleepy Eye Milling Co., Sleepy Eye, Minnesota, used his portrait in advertising from 1883 to 1921. It offered many premiums, including stoneware and pottery steins, crocks, bowls, mugs, pitchers, and many advertising items, all decorated with the famous profile of the Indian. The popular pottery was made by Weir Pottery Co. from c.1899 to 1905. Weir merged with six other potteries and became Western Stoneware in 1906. Western Stoneware Co. made blue and white Sleepy Eye from 1906 until 1937, long after the flour mill went out of business in 1921. Reproductions of the pitchers are being made today. The original pitchers came in only five sizes: 4 inches, 5 1/4 inches, 6 1/2 inches, 8 inches, and 9 inches. The Sleepy Eye image was also used by companies unrelated to the flour mill.

Fan, Sleepy Eye Mills, Sleepy Eye Cream, 9 In. Diam.	40
Label, Sleepy Eye Mills, Sleepy Eye Cream, Round, 16 In. Diam.	150
Mug, Indian Chief, Teepees, Cobalt Blue, Thumb Rest, 4 3/4 In.	72
Pitcher, Indian Chief Head, Teepees, Cobalt Blue, 8 3/4 In.	80
Pitcher, Indian Chief Profile, Blue & White, Stoneware, 4 In. *illus*	84
Pitcher, Indian Chief Profile, Blue & White, Stoneware, 8 In.	397
Salt Crock, Indian Chief, Scrolls, Fleur-De-Lis, 4 x 6 1/4 In.	225
Sign, Chief, Tin, Oval, 14 In.	300
Vase, Cattails, Blue, White, 8 1/2 x 4 In.	136
Vase, Indian Head, Cattails, Cobalt Blue, Cylindrical, 8 x 4 In.	120

SLOT MACHINES *are included in the Coin-Operated Machine category.*

SMITH BROTHERS glass was made from 1874 to 1899. Alfred and Harry Smith had worked for the Mt. Washington Glass Company in New Bedford, Massachusetts, for seven years before going into their own shop. They made many pieces with enamel decoration.

Basket, White Opaline, Blue Enameled Flowers, Silver Plate Swing Handle, 3 1/2 In.	60
Biscuit Jar, Cream Colored Opal Glass, Floral, Gold Decoration, c.1880, 9 1/4 In. *illus*	300
Biscuit Jar, Daisies, Ribbed Swirl, Silver Plate Lid & Bail, 6 3/4 In.	175
Bowl, Round, Lobed, Oak Leaves & Acorns, Metal Rim, c.1890s, 4 x 8 1/2 In.	50
Salt, Enameled Flowers, Multicolor, 1 1/2 x 2 1/2 In.	84
Sweetmeat, Melon, Ribbed, Gold Enamel Branches & Blossoms, Lid, Bail, 4 In.	215

SNOW BABIES, made from bisque and spattered with glitter sand, were first manufactured in 1864 by Hertwig and Company of Thuringia. Other German and Japanese companies copied the Hertwig designs. Originally, Snow Babies were made of candy and used as Christmas decorations. There are also Snow Babies tablewares made by Royal Bayreuth. Copies of the small Snow Babies figurines are being made today, and a line called "Snowbabies" was introduced by Department 56 in 1987. Don't confuse these with the original Snow Babies.

Figurine, 2 Children, Sliding Down Brick Ramp, Germany, c.1910, 2 x 2 In. *illus*	65
Figurine, Baby, Red Airplane, Germany, 1930s, 2 1/2 x 2 In.	225
Figurine, Baby, Seated, Arms Raised, 1 7/8 In.	85
Figurine, Boy, Getting Bitten By Dog, Holding Skis, 22 x 1 3/4 In.	125
Figurine, Child On Sled, Outstretched Arms, c.1910, 3 1/4 In.	110
Group, Hugging Skaters, Germany, 2 1/8 In.	68

SNUFF BOTTLES *are listed in the Bottle category.*

SNUFFBOXES held snuff. Taking snuff was popular long before cigarettes became available. The gentleman or lady would take a small pinch of the ground tobacco or snuff in the fingers, then sniff it and sneeze. Snuffboxes were made of many materials, including gold, silver, enameled metal, and wood. Most snuffboxes date from the late eighteenth or early nineteenth centuries.

Biblical Subjects, Flower Sprays, Wavy Interior, Rectangular, 1700s, 3 1/8 In.	438

Souvenir, Button, Aviation Contest, Los Angeles, Orange, 1910, 1 3/4 In.
$390

Hake's Americana & Collectibles

Souvenir, Scarf, Silk, California, Map, Yellow, Red, Green, Blue, 1950s, 31 1/2 x 35 In.
$45

Ruby Lane

Broken Dishes

The French term for a mosaic made from broken dishes is *pique assiette*. The term is also used by English-speaking artists.

Spangle Glass, Pitcher, Amber, Multicolor, Gold Mica, Handle, Twisted Pattern, c.1890, 8 1/4 In.
$395

Ruby Lane

Spatter Glass, Biscuit Jar, Lobed, Clear Finial, Brown, Green, Red, Yellow, c.1900, 9½ In.

$81

Jeffrey S. Evans

Spatter Glass, Vase, Tango Orange, Multicolor, Kralik, Czechoslovakia, c.1925, 11⅛ In.

$75

Ruby Lane

Spatterware, Creamer, Rainbow, Brown & Tan, 4¾ In.

$443

Hess Auction Group

Brass, Hammered, Lift Lid, Oval Cartouche, Beaded Frame, Hungary, c.1905, 2 x 3 In.	65
Enamel, Flowers, Diagonal Gold Bands, Silver Mount, France, 1756-62, 3 In.	875
Hardstone, Moss Agate, Gold Cagework, Flowers & Rococo Elements, Unmarked, 2¼ In.	3750
Silver, Cartouche, Painted Pastoral Subjects, Strapwork, Marked, 1730, 2⅝ In.	625
Silver, Oval, 2 Hinged Compartments, Engraved Medallion, 1796-97, 4 In.	677
Softwood, Embossed Child & Chickens On Lid, 1800s, 3½ In.	30
Tortoiseshell, Boat Shape, Scattered Stars Decoration, Gilt Bronze, 1900, 3½ In.	1125

 SOAPSTONE is a mineral that was used for foot warmers or griddles because of its heat-retaining properties. Soapstone was carved into figurines and bowls in many countries in the nineteenth and twentieth centuries. Most of the soapstone seen today is from Asia. It is still being carved in the old styles.

Carving, Figure, Guanyin, Immortal Goddess, Robe, Facial, Tones, Red, 1½ x 1¼ x 5¾ In.	17
Carving, Foo Dog Buddhist, Flowers, Vines, Chinese, 1900s, 7 In., Pair .... *illus*	300
Carving, Mountain, Sages Playing, 11 In.	720
Figure, Flower Maiden, Carving, Black Soapstone Base, c.1875, 10 In.	228
Figure, Guanyin, Headdress, Turquoise, Cherry Amber Cabochon, Coral, Lotus, 1800s, 9 In.	3125
Figure, Old Man, Carving, Flower, Staff, 1900, 14½ In.	45
Figure, Old Man, Peach Tree, Seated Dragon, Rocky Base, Chinese, c.1905, 6 x 6 In.	950
Group, Reclining Woman With Attendant, Carving, Basket Of Fruit, Dragon Head Tip, 5 In.	281
Vase, Flowering Mum Plant, Openwork, Carving, Chinese, 1800s, 7½ x 2¾ x 3½ In.	177

 SOUVENIRS of a trip—what could be more fun? Our ancestors enjoyed the same thing and souvenirs were made for almost every location. Most of the souvenir pottery and porcelain pieces of the nineteenth century were made in England or Germany, even if the picture showed a North American scene. In the early twentieth century, the souvenir china business seems to have been dominated by the manufacturers in Japan, Taiwan, Hong Kong, England, and the United States. Souvenir china was also made in other countries after the 1960s. Another popular souvenir item is the souvenir spoon, made of sterling or silver plate. These are usually made in the country pictured on the spoon. Related pieces may be found in the Coronation and World's Fair categories.

Badge, Atlantic City, Next, Bathing Girls, Woman, Swimsuit, Navy, White, 2¾ x 1¾ In.	82
Ball, Astronauts, Apollo 13, 11 Signatures	420
Bracelet, Cuff, Travel Landmarks In Austria, Sterling Silver, Enamel, c.1905, 2 x 7 In.	460
Button, Aviation Contest, Los Angeles, Orange, 1910, 1¾ In. .... *illus*	390
Button, Fred Astaire, Portrait, Celluloid, 1960s, 2 In. Diam.	15
Button, I Attended The Circus, Jester, Hoop, Ehrman, 1900s, 1¼ In.	18
Button, I Say No Daylight Saving, ⅞ In.	65
Button, Nelson Mandela Tour Of USA, United Auto Workers, 3 In.	9
Cup, Saucer, Canadian Flag, Leaves, Canada, From Sea-To-Sea, Royal Albert	20
Glass, Tsarina Alexandra Feodorovna, Wearing Traditional Kokoshnik, Gilt, 1896, 3⅝ In.	575
Mug, New Glarus Hotel Restaurant In Wisconsin, Swiss Style, Glass, 1950-65, 6 x 3 x 4 In.	8
Plate, Mt. Rushmore Monument, South Dakota, Ceramic, Judy Kirk, 1950s, 7 In.	9
Plate, Pewter, Engraved, Picture Of Times Square, New York City, 1950s, 2 x 5 In.	5
Scarf, Silk, California, Map, Yellow, Red, Green, Blue, 1950s, 31½ x 35 In. .... *illus*	45
Shoe, Mohawk Trail, Glass, Blue, Gold Flower, 1960s-70s, 4½ x 1¾ x 2¾ In.	16
Spoon, City Of Angels Plaza, Los Angeles, Sterling, 1891, 5 In.	124
Spoon, City Of Churches, Brooklyn Bridge, Sterling, Gorham, 6 In.	42
Spoon, Massachusetts, Star, State Seal, Sterling, 4⅜ In.	20
Spoon, Staunton, Virginia, Seashell Bowl, Flowers, Mermaid Handle, Silver Plate	40
Spoon, Thailand, Elephant, Mountain, Enameled Brass, 5 In.	5
Spoon, Washington, D.C., White House, Eagle In Wreath, Sterling, Watson Co., 4⅞ In.	40
Toy, Flute, Empire State Building, Blue & White, Plastic, 1950s, 11½ In.	12
Tray, Marlborough-Blenheim Hotel, Aluminum, 1950s-60s, 6 x 2½ x ½ In.	10
Vase, Urn, Glass, Kiawah Island, South Carolina, 5½ x 5½ x 9¾ In.	53

S

SPANGLE GLASS is multicolored glass made from odds and ends of colored glass rods. It includes metallic flakes of mica covered with gold, silver, nickel, or copper. Spangle glass is usually cased with a thin layer of clear glass over the multicolored layer. Similar glass is listed in the Vasa Murrhina category.

Bowl, Crimped Ruffled Edge, Brown, Blue, Yellow, White, c.1900, 10 In.	50
Pitcher, Amber, Multicolor, Gold Mica, Handle, Twisted Pattern, c.1890, 8 ¼ In. .... *illus*	395
Vase, Pink, Mica Flakes, Crimped Rim, Clear Glass Trail, c.1890, 10 ¼ In.	350

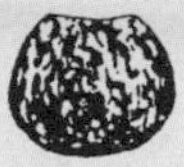

SPATTER GLASS is a multicolored glass made from many small pieces of different colored glass. It is sometimes called End-of-Day glass. It is still being made.

Basket, Ruffled, Vertically Ribbed Base, Thorn Handle, Green, Yellow, Orange, 1920s, 6 In.	145
Biscuit Jar, Lobed, Clear Finial, Brown, Green, Red, Yellow, c.1900, 9 ½ In. .... *illus*	81
Bowl, Piecrust Rim, Ruffled, White, Red, Blue, Gold, c.1890, 8 ½ x 4 In.	115
Pitcher, Ribbed, Crimped Rim, Pink, White, 9 In.	175
Rose Bowl, Pinks, Baby Blue, White, Burgundy, 1900s, 3 ½ x 4 ½ In.	49
Vase, Bulbous Cup, Oval Body, Applied Feet, Red, White Green, Yellow, c.1930, 7 In.	167
Vase, Shouldered, White Pearlescent Ground, Rust, Green, Red, Blue, M. Miller, 7 In.	55
Vase, Spiral Columns, Wafer Base, Fluted Top, Multicolor, 1930s, 8 ½ In.	125
Vase, Tango Orange, Multicolor, Kralik, Czechoslovakia, c.1925, 11 ⅛ In. .... *illus*	75
Vase, White Spatter, Green, Bulbous, Tapered Neck, 8 In.	25

SPATTERWARE and spongeware are terms that have changed in meaning in recent years, causing much confusion for collectors. Some say that *spatterware* is the term used by Americans, *sponged ware* or *spongeware* by the English. The earliest pieces were made in the late eighteenth century, but most of the spatterware found today was made from about 1800 to 1850. Early spatterware was made in the Staffordshire district of England for sale in America. Collectors also use the word *spatterware* to refer to kitchen crockery with added spatter made in America during the late nineteenth and early twentieth centuries. Spongeware is very similar to spatterware in appearance. Designs were applied to ceramics by daubing the color on with a sponge or cloth. Many collectors do not differentiate between spongeware and spatterware and use the names interchangeably. Modern pottery is being made to resemble old spatterware and spongeware, but careful examination will show it is new.

Creamer, Rainbow, Brown & Tan, 4 ¾ In. .... *illus*	443
Plate, 6-Point Star, Red, Green, Blue, Ironstone, 9 ⅝ In. .... *illus*	472
Plate, Gooney Bird, On Branch, Green, Red, Blue, Ironstone, 8 ½ In. .... *illus*	826
Plate, Peafowl, Red, Branch, 6 ⅜ In.	767
Plate, Rainbow, Blue, Red, 8 ½ In.	425
Plate, Rainbow, Red, Green, Bull's-Eye Center, 7 ½ In.	324
Plate, Red House, Yellow Roof, Green Tree, Black Foreground, 8 ½ In.	649
Plate, Tulip, Red, Green Leaves, 8 ⅜ In.	472
Platter, Peafowl, Octagonal, Blue, 12 x 15 ½ In.	244
Soup, Dish, Tulip, Red & White, Blue Tips, Green Leaves, Red Border, 10 ½ In.	122

SPELTER is a synonym for a zinc alloy. Figurines, candlesticks, and other pieces were made of spelter and given a bronze or painted finish. The metal has been used since about the 1860s to make statues, tablewares, and lamps that resemble bronze. Spelter is soft and breaks easily. To test for spelter, scratch the base of the piece. Bronze is solid; spelter will show a silvery scratch.

Bust, Arab, Cloak Wrapped, Holding Handkerchief, Signed, G. Wagner, 29 x 14 x 12 In.	1210
Bust, Woman, Hat, Off-The-Shoulder Dress, Flowers, c.1900, 11 x 6 ¾ In.	60
Clock, L. Marti, Case, Floral Garland, Mother & Child, Porcelain, Dial, Arabic Numerals, 48 In.	354
Group, Women, Carrying Torch, L&F Moreau, 27 In.	77
Group, Women, Classical Dress, 1 Seated, 1 Standing, 18 ½ x 12 In.	121
Lamp, Electric, 1-Light, Curious Dog, Filigree Lining, 4-Petal Flower, Unsigned, 8 x 12 x 5 In.	303
Lamp, Woman, Seminude, Jeweled Sphere Shade, Rocky Base, 1920s, 30 x 13 In.	2750

Spatterware, Plate, 6-Point Star, Red, Green, Blue, Ironstone, 9 ⅝ In.
$472

Hess Auction Group

Spatterware, Plate, Gooney Bird, On Branch, Green, Red, Blue, Ironstone, 8 ½ In.
$826

Hess Auction Group

Spelter, Sculpture, Man Playing Clarinet, Standing, Basket Of Apples, 25 In.
$495

Hess Auction Group

Spinning Wheel, Castle, Ebonized Wood, Bone Accents, Initials BK, England, 1800s, 50 In.
$88

Garth's Auctioneers & Appraisers

Spinning Wheel, Wood, Painted, Carved, Heart Decoration, 1800s, 46 In.
$265

Hess Auction Group

Sculpture, Horse, Stopping, 8 ½ x 8 In.	23
Sculpture, Man Playing Clarinet, Standing, Basket Of Apples, 25 In. .... *illus*	495
Sculpture, Painted, Young Maiden, Signed Verso, 14 In.	118
Sculpture, Scotsman, Horse, Black, Green, Wood Base, 14 x 7 x 18 In.	71
Tray, Lion, Standing, Bean Shaped Recess, 3 x 6 ¼ In.	30
Vase, Nymph, Dress, Wheat Stalks, Poppies, 15 ⅜ x 7 In.	424

SPINNING WHEELS in the corner have been symbols of earlier times for the past 150 years. Although spinning wheels date back to medieval days, the ones found today are rarely more than 200 years old. Because the style of the spinning wheel changed very little, it is often impossible to place an exact date on a wheel. There are different types for spinning flax or wool.

Castle, Ebonized Wood, Bone, Initials BK, England, 1800s, 50 In. .... *illus*	88
Flax, Oak, Maple, Chip Carved, Molded Edge, Punched, 52 ½ x 20 ½ In.	94
Flax, Oak, Maple, Ring-Turned Spindles, Marked, E J Miller, 1864, 38 x 22 In.	322
Flax, Wood, Red Stain, Weaver's Bobbin, Turned Legs, c.1850, 38 x 31 In.	580
Maple, Treadle Wheel, Turned Legs, 50 x 16 In.	96
Mixed Wood, c.1810, 43 In.	90
Mixed Wood, Red Paint, 41 In.	60
Wood, Painted, Carved, Heart Decoration, 1800s, 46 In. .... *illus*	265
Wool, Oak, Maple, Pewter Collar, 58 ¼ In.	47
Wool, Oak, Maple, Signed B. Sanford, 59 x 46 In.	293
Wool, Painted Flowers, 41 x 29 In.	55

SPODE pottery, porcelain, and bone china were made by the Stoke-on-Trent factory of England founded by Josiah Spode about 1770. The firm became Copeland and Garrett from 1833 to 1847, then W.T. Copeland or W.T. Copeland and Sons until 1976. It then became Royal Worcester Spode Ltd. The company was bought by the Portmeirion Group in 2009. The word *Spode* appears on many pieces made by the factories. Most collectors include all the wares under the more familiar name of Spode. Porcelains are listed in this book by the name that appears on the piece. Related pieces may be listed under Copeland, Copeland Spode, and Royal Worcester.

SPODE		ROYAL WORCESTER SPODE
Spode	Copeland & Garrett	Royal Worcester Spode Ltd.
c.1770–1790	c.1833–1847	1976–present

Pitcher, Blue & White, Glade, Buildings, Trees, 9 x 14 In.	119
Pot, Upturned Loop Handles, Heart Shape Piercings, Blue Ground, Diceware, 1800s, 2 ½ In.	800
Teapot, Hexagonal, Black Floral, Foliate Relief, Foo Dog Finial, 1800s, 8 In.	1599
Vase, 2 Handles, Cobalt Blue, Chinoiserie, Flared Rim, Gilt Deco, Asian Scenes, 1910, 13 x 16 x 13 In.	660
Vase, Chinese Landscape, Tapered Lobes, Gilt Handles, Stamped, c.1910, 14 x 17 In. .... *illus*	660

SPORTS equipment, sporting goods, brochures, and related items are listed here. Items are listed by sport. Other categories of interest are Bicycle, Card, Fishing, Sword, Toy, and Trap.

Baseball, Ball, American League All Star, 28 Signatures, Cream, 1936-37	1968
Baseball, Ball, Autographed, Babe Ruth	5400
Baseball, Ball, Autographed, Babe Ruth Singled, Light Brown, 1947	246
Baseball, Ball, Autographed, New York Team, 26 Signatures, Cream, 1949	2700
Baseball, Ball, Autographed, Ted Williams, Bobby Brown Official, 1990	788
Baseball, Ball, New York Yankees, Top Hat, Bat, 10K, 1970	1476
Baseball, Ball, Trial Of The Century, 6 Signatures	372
Baseball, Jacket, Negro League, Leather, Wool, Letterman, Patches, 1900s	113
Baseball, Sign, Little Leaguers, Player At Bat, Crescent Shape, Wood, 1950s, 10 x 20 In.	55
Basketball, Sneakers, Converse, Worn By Michael Jordan, 1984 Olympics .... *illus*	190373
Boxing, Bell, Cast, Pull Chain, Mounted On Board, 1900s, 10 In., 20-In. Board	144

Climbing, Mountaineering Pack, Wood Board, Webbing & Straps, 1940s, 27 x 15 In.	265
Clubs, Juggling, Wood, Carved Rings, Brown Patina, Black Paint, c.1910, 16 In., Pair	480
Football, Helmet, Leather, Red Paint, Stamped Logo, Spalding, c.1935	144
Hunting, Gig, 4 Prongs, Spear Head, Frogs, Fish, Black Metal, Tubular Base, 1930s, 10 x 4 In.	20
Ice Skates, Wood Platform, Wrought Iron Scroll Tip Blades, 12 In.	177

STAFFORDSHIRE, England, has been a district making pottery and porcelain since the 1700s. Thousands of types of pottery and porcelain have been made in the many factories that worked in the area. Some of the most famous factories have been listed separately, such as Adams, Davenport, Ridgway, Rowland & Marsellus, Royal Doulton, Royal Worcester, Spode, Wedgwood, and others. Some Staffordshire pieces are listed under categories like Fairing, Flow Blue, Mulberry, Shaving Mug, etc.

Bowl, Vegetable, Suspension Bridge, Pink, Green, 8⅞ In.	*illus*	130
Bust, Milton, Pearlware, Multicolor Enamel, Tapering Plinth, c.1800, 11¼ In.		431
Bust, Milton, Pearlware, Overglaze Enamel, Flaring Plinth, Pink Luster, c.1820, 10¾ In.		369
Bust, Minerva, Overglaze Enamel, Marbleized Flaring Plinth, 1800, 12 In.		431
Bust, Plato, Overglaze Enamel, Flaring Plinth, 1800, 12 In.		984
Candlestick, Tapering Stem, Molded Base, Applied Satyr's Masks & Flower Heads, 1760, 8 In.		6875
Cheese Dish, Figural Cow Head Lid, Painted, 1800s, 7⅜ x 9½ In.	*illus*	354
Coffeepot, Dome Lid, Lafayette At The Tomb Of Franklin, Clews, 11½ In.		1298
Coffeepot, Dome Lid, Palestine Pattern, Purple Transfer, 10¾ In.	*illus*	350
Coffeepot, Pear Shape Body, Painted, Floral Bouquet & Scattered Sprigs, 1765, 8⅜ In.		375
Coffeepot, Pear Shape Body, Painted, Leafy Flower Sprays & Scattered Cherries, 1765, 8⅝ In.		500
Creamer, Lafayette At Tomb Of Franklin, Clews, 3¾ In.		188
Figurine, Benjamin Franklin, Mislabeled, General Washington, c.1810, 15 In.	*illus*	780
Figurine, Dog, Dalmatian, Seated, On Oval Base, c.1860, 7 x 7 In., Pair		244
Figurine, English Gentleman, Holding Tricorner Hat, Standing, Gilded, 1850, 15 In.		308
Figurine, Fortitude, Holding Column, Raised Base, 1800, 22 In.		677
Figurine, Purity, Overglaze, Enamel, Painted Decoration, Pearl Glazed, 1800, 29 In.		4305
Figurine, Van Dyck, Standing By Column, Holding Scroll In Hand, 1800, 22 In.		1230
Figurine, William III, On Rearing Horse, Base, Laurel Border, 1800, 15 In.		6150
Group, Bacchus & Ariadne, Arm-In-Arm, Pearl Glazed Earthenware, 1800, 25 In.		3690
Group, Darby & Joan, Colonial Dress, c.1810, 10¼ x 6 In.	*illus*	256
Ice Pail, 4 Sections, Flowers, Scroll Handles, 13 x 9 In., Pair		900
Jug, Face, Satyr, Silver Luster, 3 Raised Masks, 5¼ In.	*illus*	189
Jug, Scrolled Handle, Leafy, Multicolor Enamel, Rural Cartouches, Bulbous, 1830, 17 In.		369
Mug, Commemorative, Portrait Of George II, Animals, Molded, 1750-60, 3¾ In.		8125
Plate, Asian Scene, Zebra, Blue, 9½ In.		150
Plate, City Hall New York, Blue Transfer, Ridgway, 9⅞ In.	*illus*	200
Plate, Landing Of General Lafayette At Castle Garden, Clews, 9 In.		165
Plate, Landing Of General Lafayette, Blue, Clews, c.1810, 10 In.		185
Plate, Scalloped Edge, Embossed Leaf Border, Whieldon, 9⅜ In.	*illus*	212
Plate, States, Blue Transfer, Scalloped Edge, Public Buildings, Trees, Clews, 6¾ In.	*illus*	236
Plate, States, Scalloped Rim, Building, Blue Transfer, Impressed Clews, 12¼ In.		189
Plate, Toddy, Eagle, Shield, Blue Feather Edge, Impressed Adams, 5½ In.	*illus*	325
Plate, Toddy, Masonic Transfer, Verse, Keep Within Compass, Embossed Border, 5 In.	*illus*	35
Platter, Beauties Of America, Pennsylvania Hospital, 18½ In.		886
Platter, Canova, Garden, Patio, Black, White, 13 x 15¼ In.		75
Platter, Landing Of General Lafayette, Clews, 1800s, 13 x 17 In.	*illus*	840
Platter, Lid, The Late Reverend Richard Jordan, c.1835, 19½ x 16 In.		325
Platter, Meat, Lozere, Blue Transfer, Ironstone, Challiner, 1862, 16 x 12 x 1½ In.		277
Platter, Octagonal, Historical Event, Clews, 1830, 19 x 14¼ In.		425
Platter, Oriental Sports, Hunting Dogs, Trainers, Blue, White, 19¼ In.	*illus*	1320
Stirrup Cup, Hound's Head, White & Brown, Green Eyes, 1800s		685
Sugar, Lid, Washington Standing At Tomb, Scroll In Hand, Impressed Wood, 6¾ In.	*illus*	94
Teapot, Bulbous, Ear Shape Handle, Leafy Molded Spout, Multicolor, 1775, 6 In.		584
Teapot, Globular, Cabbage Leaf, Molded Spout, Leafy Handle, Puce Enamel, 1700s, 8 In.		800
Teapot, Mask & Serpent Spout, Molded 2-Story House 1 Side, 3-Story On Other, 1750, 6¼ In.		4750
Teapot, Redware, Globular Shape, Elaborate Floral, Leafy Sprigs, 1700s, 5⅝ In.		461

Spode, Vase, Chinese Landscape, Tapered Lobes, Gilt Handles, Stamped, c.1910, 14 x 17 In.
$660

Brunk Auctions

Sports, Basketball, Sneakers, Converse, Worn By Michael Jordan, 1984 Olympics
$190,373

SCP Auctions

Staffordshire, Bowl, Vegetable, Suspension Bridge, Pink, Green, 8⅞ In.
$130

Hess Auction Group

Staffordshire, Cheese Dish, Figural Cow Head Lid, Painted, 1800s, 7⅜ x 9½ In.
$354

Hess Auction Group

S

Staffordshire, Coffeepot, Dome Lid, Palestine Pattern, Purple Transfer, 10¾ In.
$350

Staffordshire, Jug, Face, Satyr, Silver Luster, 3 Raised Masks, 5¼ In.
$189

Hess Auction Group

Staffordshire, Plate, City Hall New York, Blue Transfer, Ridgway, 9⅞ In.
$200

Hess Auction Group

Hess Auction Group

Staffordshire, Figurine, Benjamin Franklin, Mislabeled, General Washington, c.1810, 15 In.
$780

Staffordshire, Group, Darby & Joan, Colonial Dress, c.1810, 10¼ x 6 In.
$256

Staffordshire, Plate, Scalloped Edge, Embossed Leaf Border, Whieldon, 9⅜ In.
$212

Hess Auction Group

Cowan's Auctions

Neal Auction Co.

S

Teapot, Salt Glazed, Globular Shape, Crabstock Handle, Spout, Twig Finial, 1750, 7¼ In.	492

Toby Jugs are listed in their own category.

Trinket Box, Figural Nesting Pigeon, 2¾ x 4½ In.	60
Trinket Box, Mail Carrier Pigeon, Standing, Colored Highlights, 4½ x 4 In.	48
Trinket Box, Small Bird On Grapes, Color Highlights, 5¼ x 4¾ In.	96
Vase, Spill, Woman & Man, 1800s, 7 x 4 In.	125
Wall Pocket, Female Head Emerging From Leaves, Press Molded, 1760-65, 10 In.	750
Wall Pocket, Molded, Portrait Of Plenty, Holding Flower-Filled Cornucopia, 1750-55, 12 In.	375

STAINLESS STEEL became available to artists and manufacturers about 1920. They used it to make flatware, tableware, and many decorative items.

Cocktail Fork, Flared Times, Long Handles, Imperial, 5¾ In., 6 Piece	18
Fork, Southern Baroque, Oneida, 7½ In.	6
Salt & Pepper, No. 9064, International Stainless Deluxe, Box, 3½ In. *illus*	9
Sculpture, Renaissance Woman, With Stand, Certificate Of Authenticity, Boban Ilic, 62 In.	7800
Serving Spoon, Slotted, Venetia, Oneida, 8½ In.	9
Teakettle, Whistling, Copper Bottom, Bakelite Handle, Revere Ware, 7 x 7 In.	32

STANGL POTTERY traces its history back to the Fulper Pottery of New Jersey. In 1910, Johann Martin Stangl started working at Fulper. He left to work at Haeger Pottery from 1915 to 1920. Stangl returned to Fulper Pottery in 1920, became president in 1926, and changed the company name to Stangl Pottery in 1929. Stangl bought the firm in 1930. The pottery is known for dinnerware and a line of bird figurines. Martin Stangl died in 1972 and the pottery was sold to Frank Wheaton Jr. of Wheaton Industries. Production continued until 1978, when Pfaltzgraff Pottery purchased the right to the Stangl trademark and the remaining inventory was liquidated. A single bird figurine is identified by a number. Figurines made up of two birds are identified by a number followed by the letter *D* indicating Double.

Stangl 1926–1930	 Stangl 1940s–1978	Stangl 1949–1953

Bird, Cliff Swallow, Brown, Blue, 4⅝ In.	42
Bird, Cockatoo, Blue Crest, c.1945, 12⅜ In. *illus*	135
Bird, Cockatoo, No. 3405S, 6¼ In.	38
Bird, Double Parakeets, Multicolor, 1940s, 7 x 6½ In.	195
Bird, Double Woodpeckers, Red Heads, 7¾ In.	125
Bird, Goldfinch, Mother, Babies, On Branch, 12 x 4 In.	118
Bird, Parrot, Perch, Multicolor, Marked, 8½ In.	84
Bird, Penguin, 5¼ In.	285
Bird, Titmouse, Blue, 2⅝ In.	45
Bird, Turkey, Multicolor, 3¼ x 2¾ In.	425
Bird, Warbler, Yellow, Green, Blue At Base, 1940s, 5 In. *illus*	50
Bird, Yellow Warbler, 5 In.	50
Bittersweet, Cup & Saucer	11
Blueberry, Plate, Salad, 8 In.	27
Blueberry, Serving Bowl, 10 In.	54
Fruit, Bowl, Vegetable, Divided, 10¾ In.	47
Fruit, Bread Tray, 15 In.	41
Fruit, Creamer, 3 In.	17
Fruit, Cup & Saucer	26
Fruit, Plate, Dinner, 10 In.	60
Fruit, Plate, Salad, 8 In.	15
Fruit, Salt & Pepper	28

Staffordshire, Plate, States, Blue Transfer, Scalloped Edge, Public Buildings, Trees, Clews, 6¾ In. $236

Hess Auction Group

Staffordshire, Plate, Toddy, Eagle, Shield, Blue Feather Edge, Impressed Adams, 5½ In. $325

Hess Auction Group

Staffordshire, Plate, Toddy, Masonic Transfer, Verse, Keep Within Compass, Embossed Border, 5 In. $35

Hess Auction Group

Staffordshire, Platter, Landing Of General Lafayette Clews, 1800s, 13 x 17 In.
$840

Garth's Auctioneers & Appraisers

Staffordshire, Platter, Oriental Sports, Hunting Dogs, Trainers, Blue, White, 19 ¼ In.
$1,320

Eldred's Auctioneers and Appraisers

Staffordshire, Sugar, Lid, Washington Standing At Tomb, Scroll In Hand, Impressed Wood, 6 ¾ In.
$94

Hess Auction Group

TIP

Rubber cement solvent, available at art and office supply stores, has many uses. Put a few drops on a paper towel and rub off ink smudges, adhesive tape glue, or label glue from glass or porcelain.

Fruit, Serving Bowl, 9 In.	54
Fruit, Soup Dish, Lugged, 6 ¼ In.	35
Granada, Vase, Gold, No. 5023, Hand Painted, Marked, 9 ½ In.	55
Kiddieware, Plate, Pink Fairy, 1950s, 9 ½ In.	135
Magnolia, Ashtray, 8 ½ x 3 ½ In.	25
Prelude, Sugar & Creamer, Pink Flowers, Leaves	21
Thistle, Platter, Kidney Shape, 13 In.	21
Thistle, Saucer	4
Toothbrush Holder, Blue Spatter, 1970s	39
Town & Country, Candlestick, Blue, Spatterware, Ring Handle, 6 x 2 In.	28
Town & Country, Chop Plate, Blue, Spongeware, 10 In.	14
Town & Country, Salt & Pepper, Brown, Spongeware	35
Tulip, Teapot, Terra Rose, Yellow, Green Leaves, Leaf Finial, Lid, 6 x 10 In.	54
White Dogwood, Charger, Brown Scalloped Edge, 12 In.	35
White Dogwood, Cup & Saucer	12
White Dogwood, Plate, Dinner, 10 In.	15

STAR TREK AND STAR WARS collectibles are included here. The original *Star Trek* television series ran from 1966 through 1969. The series spawned an animated TV series, three TV sequels, and a TV prequel. The first Star Trek movie was released in 1979 and eleven others followed, the most recent in 2016. The movie *Star Wars* opened in 1977. Sequels were released in 1980 and 1983; prequels in 1999, 2002, and 2005. *Star Wars: Episode VII* opened in 2015, which increased interest in Star Wars collectibles. *Star Wars: The Last Jedi* opened in 2017. *Star Wars: Episode IX* is scheduled to open in 2019. Star Wars characters also appeared in *Rogue One: A Star Wars Story* (2016) and *Solo: A Star Wars Story* (2018). Other science fiction and fantasy collectibles can be found under Batman, Buck Rogers, Captain Marvel, Flash Gordon, Movie, Superman, and Toy.

STAR TREK

Doll, Guinan, Blue Outfit, Playmates, Box, 1995, 9 In.		24
Doll, Spock, Bisque Head, Hands & Feet, Cloth Body, Oak, 18 In.		127
Figurine, Spaceship, USS Bellwether, Lynn Norton, 18 x 11 In.	*illus*	4750
Glass, USS Enterprise, Description, Paramount Pictures, 1978, 6 ¼ In.		20
Model, Klingon Battle Cruiser, Die Cast, Blue, Dinky Toys, Box, c.1977, 9 x 6 In.		170
Ornament, USS Defiant, Deep Space Nine, 1997		18
Ornament, USS Enterprise, First Contact, Hallmark, 1998		35
Poster, Next Generation, To Boldly Go Where No One Has Gone Before, Light-Up, 36 x 24 In.		120
Stein, Ceramic, Captain Kirk, Spock, Dr. McCoy, Crew, Lid, Catch-A-Star, 1994, 6 ½ In.		155
Stein, Metal Lid, Ceramic, Limited Edition, 1994, 6 ½ In.	*illus*	155
Toy, USS Enterprise, Die Cast, White, Orange, Box, Dinky Toys, 9 x 4 In.		150
Window, Stained Glass, Figural, Lieutenant Commander Data, Brent Spiner, Frame, 79 x 36 In.		450

STAR WARS

Bank, Darth Maul, Episode 1, Interactive, c.1980		60
Bank, Interactive, R2-D2, C-3PO, c.1995, 10 x 7 In.	*illus*	36
Dinner Set, Plastic, Plate, Mug, Bowl, Glass, Crew, Deka, USA, c.1977		60
Figure, Queen Amidala, Hasbro, Box, c.1998		23
Toy, Movie Viewer, May The Force Be With You, Plastic, Red, Blue, Kenner, c.1977		30

STEINS have been used by beer and ale drinkers for over 500 years. They have been made of ivory, porcelain, pottery, stoneware, faience, silver, pewter, wood, or glass in sizes up to nine gallons. Although some were made by Mettlach, Meissen, Capo-di-Monte, and other famous factories, most were made by less important German potteries. The words *Geschutz* or *Musterschutz* on a stein are the German words for "patented" or "registered design," not company names. Steins are still being made in the old styles. Lithophane steins may be found in the Lithophane category.

Character, Alligator, Head Lid, Porcelain, Teeth, Musterschutz, 7 In.		856
Character, Billiken, Seated, ½ Liter	*illus*	2400
Character, Bismarck, Stoneware, ½ Liter	*illus*	180

Character, Black Man, Suitcase, Smoking Pipe, Pottery, ½ Liter	240
Character, Cat Holding Fish, Inlaid Lid, Pottery, Germany, ½ Liter	1002
Character, Chauffeur, Touring Automobile, Georg Dorn, Porcelain, ½ Liter	250
Character, Clown, Striped Outfit, Pottery, ½ Liter	800
Character, Dairy Farmer, Cheese Making, Porcelain, Liter	160
Character, Dairy Farmer, Karl Kauroff, Milking Cow, Lithograph, Porcelain, ½ Liter	160
Character, Fish, Musterschutz, Schierholz, Porcelain, ½ Liter	630
Character, Jester, Hands In Pockets, Diesinger Pottery, ½ Liter .... illus	1200
Character, Man, Holding Cat, Pottery, Diesinger, ½ Liter	395
Character, Man's Face, Bulbous, Pottery, 1 ½ Liter .... illus	144
Character, Martin Luther Holding Stein, Pottery, ½ Liter	250
Character, Nurnberg Tower, Pottery, 2 Liter	900
Character, Owl, Pottery, Marked M & W Gr., Lid, ½ Liter	108
Character, Pig With Pipe, Musterschutz, Schierholz, Porcelain, ½ Liter	192
Character, Queen Victoria, Silver, Glass Jewels, Hallmarks, c.1890, 8¾ In. ...... illus	2040
Character, Satan Head, Bohne Porcelain, ½ Liter .... illus	450
Character, Schaffler, Barrel Maker, Pewter Lid, Transfer, Hand Painted, Porcelain, ½ Liter	198
Character, Street Sweeper, Lithograph, Porcelain, ½ Liter	550
Copper, Diagonal Ribs, Leaf Finial, 1 ¼ Liter	150
Faience, Delft Birnkrug, Pewter Lid & Foot Ring, Vertical Handle Strap, c.1750, 10 In.	324
Faience, Horse, White, Jumping, Pewter Lid, Hannoversch Mundener Waltzenkrug, c.1820, 9 In.	275
Faience, Suddeutscher Walzenkrug, Pewter Lid & Foot Ring, c.1775, 9 In.	216
Farmer, Incised, Tapered Neck, Pewter Lid, Horses, Plow, West Germany, 13 In.	82
Glass, Blown, Amber, Pewter Overlay, Cherubs, Flowers, Gooseman Thumblift, 7 In.	180
Glass, Blown, Camel, Enameled, ½ Liter	200
Glass, Blown, Green Prunts, Hand Painted, Pewter Lid, ½ Liter	102
Glass, Blown, Ruby Stained, Wheel Cut, Dog, Stag, Inlay, Bohemia, c.1860, ¾ Liter ...... illus	9600
Glass, Clear Shading To Ruby Flash, White Enamel Scene, Clear Ribbed Handle, 15¼ In.	157
Glass, Flowers, Verse, 1852, ¾ Liter	50
Glass, Heraldic Shields, Flowers, Green, Enameled, 10 In.	225
Glass, Monk Lithophane, Figural Thumblift, Metal Lid, 2000s, 7 In.	205
Glass, Munich Child, Enameled, Green, Pewter Base & Rim, ½ Liter	109
Glass, Stag, Wood, Antler Finial & Thumblift, Pewter Lid, ½ Liter	299
Mettlach steins are listed in the Mettlach category.	
Porcelain, Capo-Di-Monte, Child Finial, Goat, Hinged Lid, Marked N With Crown, ¾ Liter illus	132
Porcelain, Lid, White Ground, Crossed Swords, Thuringen, 1 Liter, 7½ In.	720
Porcelain, Lithophane, Blue Onion Design, Hand Painted, Pewter Lid, ½ Liter	72
Porcelain, Ludwig II, 1845-86, Blue, White, Cut Glass Finial, Lithophane Base, 9 In.	72
Porcelain, Monk, Holding Glass, Gilt Grapes, Leaf Design, 1900, ½ Liter, 5½ In.	270
Porcelain, Nude Dancer, Lithophane, Personalized, 9½ x 6 x 4½ In.	63
Porcelain, Portrait, Man, Transfer & Hand Painted, Inlaid Lid, ½ Liter .... illus	180
Porcelain, Romantic Couple, Period Dress, Finial, Crossed Swords Mark, c.1850, 1 Liter. illus	900
Pottery, Diesinger Munich Child, Threaded Relief, ¼ Liter	25
Pottery, Eagle & W, Wiedemann Brewing Co., Pewter Lid, Marked, 1948, 5½ In.	531
Pottery, Hanke, Etched, Off The Trail, Jockey On Horse, Snow, ½ Liter .... illus	78
Pottery, Hausmalers, Hand Painted Faience, Germany, 1600s, 9 x 5 x 5 In.	370
Pottery, Munich Child, On Barrel, Relief, Liter	100
Pottery, Soldier, Transfer, Royal Bonn Delft, Pewter Lid, 17 In.	240
Regimental, 5 Comp, Inft. Regt. Nr. 129, Eagle Thumblift, Porcelain, ½ Liter, 11 In.	1752
Regimental, Roster, 2, Comp, Lion Thumblift, Bayr. Inft. Regt. Nr. 5, Bamberg, ½ Liter, 11 In..	216
Regimental, Roster, S.M.S. Ostfriesland, Wilhelmshaven, 1911-14, 1 Liter, 14 In. ...... illus	960
Stoneware, Blue Salt Glaze, Art Nouveau, Pewter Lid, Thewalt, 1 Liter	144
Stoneware, Carpenter, Transfer & Hand Painted, Pewter Lid, ½ Liter	252
Stoneware, Pewter Thumblift, Etched Inlaid Top, ½ Liter, 9¼ In.	75
Stoneware, Salt Glaze, 2 Figures, Flowers, 1900s, 13¼ In.	63
Stoneware, Salt Glaze, Flowers, 19th Century, 13¼ In.	230
Stoneware, Zur Erinnerung A.D. 90 Geburtstag, Transfer, Enamel, Pewter Lid, 1 Liter	144
Tankard, Mythological Figures, Ivory, Silver Mount, Nude Handle, c.1885, 18 In. ...... illus	6600
Tankard, Weller, Floretta, Incised Grapes, Marked, 17 In.	94

Stainless Steel, Salt & Pepper, No. 9064, International Stainless Deluxe, Box, 3½ In.
$9

Ruby Lane

Stangl, Bird, Cockatoo, Blue Crest, c.1945, 12⅜ In.
$135

Ruby Lane

Stangl, Bird, Warbler, Yellow, Green, Blue At Base, 1940s, 5 In.
$50

Ruby Lane

Star Trek, Figurine, Spaceship, USS Bellwether, Lynn Norton, 18 x 11 In. $4,750

Heritage Auctions

Star Trek, Stein, Metal Lid, Ceramic, Limited Edition, 1994, 6½ In. $155

Ruby Lane

Star Wars, Bank, Interactive, R2-D2, C-3PO, c.1995, 10 x 7 In $36

Ruby Lane

 STEREO CARDS that were made for stereoscope viewers became popular after 1840. Two almost identical pictures were mounted on a stiff cardboard backing so that, when viewed through a stereoscope, a three-dimensional picture could be seen. Value is determined by maker and by subject. These cards were made in quantity through the 1930s.

May Pole Dance, Children Dancing, Color, Ingersoll, 1898, 7 x 4 In.	10
Modoc War, Brave On War Path, Edward J. Muybridge	540
Modoc War, Bringing In The Wounded, Edward J. Muybridge	510
Vance's Daguerreotype Studio, San Francisco, E & HT Anthony	840

 STEREOSCOPES were used for viewing stereo cards. The hand viewer was invented by Oliver Wendell Holmes, although more complicated table models were used before his was produced in 1859. Do not confuse the stereoscope with the stereopticon, a magic lantern that used glass slides.

Graphoscope, Rosewood Tabletop Model, Fold-Away Lenses, Brass, Bone Tips, 1800s, 20 x 10 x 6 In.	203
Zograscope, Walnut, Various Heights, 1800s, 7 x 10 In. .... *illus*	305

STERLING SILVER, *see Silver-Sterling category.*

 STEUBEN glass was made at the Steuben Glass Works of Corning, New York. The factory, founded by Frederick Carder and T.G. Hawkes Sr., was purchased by the Corning Glass Company in 1918. Corning continued to make glass called Steuben. Many types of art glass were made at Steuben. Aurene is an iridescent glass. Schottenstein Stores Inc. bought 80 percent of the business in 2008. The factory closed in 2011. In 2014 the Corning Museum of Glass took over the factory. It is reproducing some tableware, paperweights, and collectibles. Additional pieces may be found in the Cluthra and Perfume Bottle categories.

Bowl, Blue Aurene, Inverted Rim, Bulbous, Iridescent, Polished Pontil, 1900-25, 4 x 7½ In.	615
Bowl, Clear, Applied Elements At Base, 6 x 13 In.	430
Bowl, Clear, Footed, Signed Under Base, 5 x 11 In.	70
Bowl, Clear, Spiral, Signed, Donald Pollard, 1954, 7 x 7 x 3½ In.	79
Bowl, Ivory Grotesque, Signed Under Base, 6¼ x 12 x 7¼ In.	311
Bowl, Leaded Glass, Devil & Daniel Webster, Scene From Stephen Vincent Benet Story, 1959, 14 x 7 In.	3900
Bowl, Trillium Art Glass, Signed Donald Pollard Under Base, 1953, 4½ x 10 In.	70
Bust, Elderly Woman, Weathered Face, Scarf, Cire Perdue, Carder 1938, 5½ In. .... *illus*	1694
Candlestand, Art Deco, Rosaline, Alabaster, Rose Foot & Cup, White Stem, 12 In., Pair	1298
Candy Dish, 2 Handles, Clear, 4¼ In.	62
Ceiling Fixture, 4-Light, Pendant, Brass Stem, Inverted Pyramidal Cap, 47 x 23 x 23 In.	605
Ceiling Fixture, 6-Light, Silver Plated, Serpentine 12-Panel, Gold Iridescent, 30 x 18 In.	1331
Chandelier, 1-Light, Moss Agate, Inverted Bell, Stylized Leaves, 27 x 14 In.	9045
Compote, Blue Iridescent Aurene, Gold Foil Sticker, Signed, 1900s, 5¾ x 8 In. .... *illus*	270
Compote, Calcite Exterior, Aurene Interior, 5 x 10 In.	325
Figurine, Peacock, Clear, Wheel Cut Feather Detail, Block Base, 8 x 14 In.	605
Lamp, Green Jade, Iridescent Lava, Molten Glass, Disc Shape, Gilt Metal Mount, 12 x 9 In.	1243
Lamp, Hanging, Domed, Gilt Fixture, Brass Filigree Chain, Inverted Rib, Marked, 39 x 20 In.	1029
Lamp, Oriental Poppy, Neoclassical Style, Triangular Base, Ram's Head, 1900s, 23 In.	660
Paperweight, Paired Hearts, Heart Shape, 4 x 3½ In., Pair	312
Pitcher, Blue Aurene, Tumble-Up, Long Spout, Applied Handle, Bulbous Base, 5 x 5 In., Pair	147
Salt Dip, Blue Aurene, Triation Mark, Fake Tiffany Mark, 2¾ In.	96
Sculpture, Artic Fisherman, Crystal Iceberg, James Houston, 6¼ x 6 In.	3125
Sculpture, Flying Duck, Spread Wing On A Wave, Metal Base, 1900s, 9½ x 10 x 8½ In.	900
Sculpture, Ram's Head, Acid Etched On Crystal Block, Lighted Stand, 1900s, 6 x 2½ In.	1200
Table Lamp, Blue Cluthra, Opal Glass M Shape Handles, Gray Metal Mounts, 30 x 10 In.	932
Torchiere, Oriental Poppy, Pink, Trumpet Form Shade, Flared Rim, 1900s, 8 x 8¾ In., Pair	1845
Vase, Applied Central Elements, Pair, 1959, 11½ x 12 In.	480
Vase, Baluster, Applied Loop, Ring Handles, 1900s, 9½ x 5¼ In.	450
Vase, Bright Gold, Blue Highlights, Tree Trunk Shape, Signed, 10 In.	605
Vase, Clear, Lid, Inscribed Psalm, Engraved Signature, Polished Pontil, 8¾ x 3½ In.	170
Vase, Dark Amethyst Optic Swirl, Signed Under Base, 7 x 6¾ In.	102

Stein, Character, Billiken, Seated,
½ Liter
$2,400

Fox Auctions

Stein, Character, Jester, Hands In Pockets,
Diesinger Pottery, ½ Liter
$1,200

Fox Auctions

Stein, Character, Queen Victoria, Silver, Glass
Jewels, Hallmarks, c.1890, 8 ¾ In.
$2,040

The Stein Auction Company

Stein, Character, Bismarck, Stoneware,
½ Liter
$180

Fox Auctions

Stein, Character, Man's Face, Bulbous,
Pottery, 1 ½ Liter
$144

Fox Auctions

Stein, Character, Satan Head, Bohne
Porcelain, ½ Liter
$450

Fox Auctions

S

STEUBEN

Stein, Glass, Blown, Ruby Stained, Wheel Cut, Dog, Stag, Inlay, Bohemia, c.1860, ¾ Liter
$9,600

Fox Auctions

Stein, Porcelain, Capo-Di-Monte, Child Finial, Goat, Hinged Lid, Marked N With Crown, ¾ Liter
$132

The Stein Auction Company

Stein, Porcelain, Portrait, Man, Transfer & Hand Painted, Inlaid Lid, ½ Liter
$180

The Stein Auction Company

Stein, Porcelain, Romantic Couple, Period Dress, Finial, Crossed Swords Mark, c.1850, 1 Liter
$900

The Stein Auction Company

Stein, Pottery, Hanke, Etched, Off The Trail, Jockey On Horse, Snow, ½ Liter
$78

Fox Auctions

Stein, Regimental, Roster, Relief Scene, S.M.S. Ostfriesland, Wilhelmshaven, 1911-14, 1 Liter, 14 In.
$960

The Stein Auction Company

Vase, Fan, Clear, Engraved Sailing Ship, Green Foot, 8 1/2 In.	72
Vase, Flemish Blue Optic Swirl, 7 x 7 In.	147
Vase, Free-Form, Rubina, Gold Ruby To Clear, Signed, 9 x 5 1/2 In.	254
Vase, Gold Aurene, 3-Ribbed Tree Trunks, Inverted Saucer Base, Iridescent Highlights, 6 In.	363
Vase, Gold Aurene, Etched Signature Under Base, 10 x 9 In.	396
Vase, Gold Aurene, Flared Neck, Rounded Shoulders, 16 1/4 x 8 In.	914
Vase, Gold Aurene, Signed, Frederick Carder, 8 x 4 1/4 In.	158
Vase, Gold Aurene, Stick, Signed, 8 x 2 7/8 In.	113
Vase, Gold Aurene, Trumpet Shape, 1920s, 7 In. .... illus	390
Vase, Gold Iridescent, Floriform, Circular Base, Aurene, 1900-25, 12 In.	1599
Vase, Gold Ruby Optic Swirl, 7 x 7 In.	170
Vase, Green & Gold, Pulled Feather Design, Cream Ground, Urn Shape, Signed 9 In.	2722
Vase, Green, Chrysanthemum, Peonies, Flowers, Ground Pontil, 7 x 8 In.	708
Vase, Green, Jade, Etched Signature Under Base, 8 x 7 In.	311
Vase, Iridescent Cylindrical Body, Flared Rim, Ribbed Sides, Green Threads, 12 x 4 In.	148
Vase, Ivory Glass, Ground Pontil, Oval, 10 x 10 In.	325
Vase, Ivory, 6 x 4 In.	136
Vase, Ivrene, Lustrous, Iridescent Double Handle, Ground Pontil, Frederick Carder, 10 x 7 1/2 In.	148
Vase, Jade Green Optic Swirl, Signed Under Base, 7 x 6 3/4 In.	113
Vase, Large Bowl Top, Polished Pontil, Aurene, 8 x 6 1/4 In.	708
Vase, Lotus Flowers, Plum, Jade, Acid-Etched Cased Glass, 1920s, 6 3/4 x 8 In.	2125
Vase, Plum Jade, Chinoiserie, c.1924, 4 1/8 In.	1404
Vase, Plum Jade, Purple Floral Medallions, 8 x 10 1/2 In.	3025
Vase, Plum Jade, Water Scene, Geese In Flight, Trees, Acid Cut, Flanked Handles, 13 In.	2500
Vase, Pomona Green Optic Swirl, 7 x 7 In.	124
Vase, Trumpet, Gold Aurene, 1920s, 7 x 7 In.	390
Vase, Verre De Soie, Optic Swirl, 7 x 7 In.	170
Vase, White, Iridescent, Marked, Foil Sticker Under Base, 8 x 6 1/2 In.	181

STEVENGRAPHS are woven pictures made like fancy ribbons. They were manufactured by Thomas Stevens of Coventry, England, and became popular in 1862. Most are marked *Woven in silk by Thomas Stevens* or were mounted on a cardboard that tells the story of the Stevengraph. Other similar ribbon pictures have been made in England and Germany.

Bookmark, Silk, Cross, Heart, Lily Of The Valley, Faith, Hope Charity, 9 x 2 In.	65
Bookmark, Silk, Queen Victoria, Prince Albert, 1862, 6 3/4 In.	672
Picture, Buffalo Bill's Souvenir Of The Wild West, Buffalo Bill, Indians, 1903, 3 1/2 x 5 1/2 In.	780

STEVENS & WILLIAMS of Stourbridge, England, made many types of glass, including layered, etched, cameo, and art glass, between the 1830s and 1930s. Some pieces are signed *S & W.* Many pieces are decorated with flowers, leaves, and other designs based on nature.

Bowl, Matsu-No-Ke, Rose, Turquoise Case Glass, Berry Mark, 1800s, 6 3/4 In. .... illus	390
Vase, Applied Yellow Flowers, Ruffled Rim, Pink To White, 9 1/2 x 4 1/2 In.	60
Vase, Cased Light Blue, Cranberry, Diagonal Ribbed, 1886, 9 1/4 In.	878
Vase, Gold Paste, Enamel, 3 Cartouches, Red, Brown Flowers, Oscar Erard, 9 In.	3630
Vase, White Cameo Cranes, Cranberry Ground, Bulged Neck, Flaring Lip, 5 In.	1815
Vase, White Opaque, Green Vertical Stripe Design, 5 1/2 x 10 In.	36

STIEGEL TYPE glass is listed here. It is almost impossible to be sure a piece was actually made by Stiegel, so the knowing collector refers to this glass as "Stiegel type." Henry William Stiegel, a colorful immigrant to the colonies, started his first factory in Pennsylvania in 1763. He remained in business until 1774. Glassware was made in a style popular in Europe at that time and was similar to the glass of many other makers. It was made of clear or colored glass and was decorated with enamel colors, mold blown designs, or etching.

Cologne Bottle, Lovebirds, Floral & Leafy Decorations, 8 In.	850
Mug, Flowers & Leaves, Design, 4 3/4 In.	275
Perfume Bottle, Enamel, Man In Colonial Dress, Flowers, Leaves, 6 1/2 In. .... illus	550

Stein, Tankard, Mythological Figures, Ivory, Silver Mount, Nude Handle, c.1885, 18 In.
$6,600

The Stein Auction Company

Stereoscope, Zograscope, Walnut, Various Heights, 1800s, 7 x 10 In.
$305

Neal Auction Co.

Steuben, Bust, Elderly Woman, Weathered Face, Scarf, Cire Perdue, Carder 1938, 5 1/2 In.
$1,694

James D. Julia Auctioneers

S

Steuben, Compote, Blue Iridescent Aurene, Gold Foil Sticker, Signed, 1900s, 5¾ x 8 In.
$270

Garth's Auctioneers & Appraisers

Steuben, Vase, Gold Aurene, Trumpet Shape, 1920s, 7 In.
$390

Cowan's Auctions

TIP
The first place a burglar looks for valuables is in the bedroom. A better choice is in your garage or freezer.

Stevens & Williams, Bowl, Matsu-No-Ke, Rose, Turquoise Case Glass, Berry Mark, 1800s, 6¾ In.
$390

Garth's Auctioneers & Appraisers

Salt, Cobalt Blue, Footed, Pontil, Master, 3 In.	142
Salt, Master, Cobalt Blue, Blown, Ribbed Body, Footed, Comet Tail Pontil, 2⅝ In. ..... *illus*	265
Shot Glass, Enamel Flowers, Leaves, Red, Blue, Yellow, 2½ In. ..... *illus*	175

STONE includes those articles made of stones, coral, shells, and some other natural materials not listed elsewhere in this book. Micro mosaics (small decorative designs made by setting pieces of stone into a pattern), urns, vases, and other pieces made of natural stone are listed here. Stoneware is pottery and is listed in the Stoneware category. Alabaster, Jade, Malachite, Marble, and Soapstone are in their own categories.

Bowl, Effigy, Human Figure, Inlaid, Shell, Beads, 1900s, 6½ x 4 x 3 In.	160
Bowl, Pedestal, Blue John Flourite, Neoclassical, 1800s, 5¼ In.	687
Brush Washer, Amethyst, Squirrels, Vines, Oval, 6¼ In.	181
Centerpiece, Rock Crystal, Gray, White, Oblong, 3 x 9¼ In.	600
Coral, Pink, Multiple Branching Sections, Teak Base, 9 In.	3150
Figure, Apollo, Daphne, White, Pietro Bazzanti, 26 In.	2000
Figure, Bear, Carved, Elford Bradley Cox, 6 In.	510
Figure, Bear, Quartz, 7 In.	2750
Figure, Bird, At Rest, Carved, Elford Bradley Cox, 4 In.	420
Figure, Birdstone, Popeye, Granite, Carved, Label, Lake Co., Michigan, 1800s, 6 In.	1200
Figure, Coral, Flower Vase, Red, Chinese, 6⅜ x 7¾ In. ..... *illus*	4500
Figure, Dragon, Seated, Lapis Lazuli, Wood Stand, 2 In.	275
Figure, Limestone, Bird & Serpent, Painted Wood Frame, 21 x 15 In.	2875
Figure, Nanny Goat, Agate, Carved, Inset Gold & Diamond Eyes, 2 x 2½ In.	1200
Figure, Parrot, Carved Feathers, Green Body, Black Beak, Amber Glass Eyes, Marble Base, 6 x 3 x 2 In.	45
Figure, Shiva, Gray Schist, Holding 3 Attributes, On Throne, Wood Display Base, 1500s, 12 x 9 x 4 In.	900
Figure, Shoushan, Boy, Buffalo, Calf, Pierced Ebony Base, Chinese, 1920, 9 x 4 x 7 In.	110
Figurine, Coral, Carved, Celestial Beauty, Stand, Chinese, 5¾ In. ..... *illus*	610
Jardiniere, Flowering Tree, Cloisonne Enamel Pot, Chinese, 19½ In. ..... *illus*	427
Lamp, Table, Quartz Crystal, Various Colors, Lucite Base, Pair, 16 x 8 In.	875
Landscape, Quing Rouge, Carved, 3 Travelers Crossing Bridge In Mountains, 1800s, 8 x 7 x 1¾ In.	450
Mask, Children, Sandstone, Piloted Holes, Mayan, 1800s	240
Obelisk, Rock Crystal, Blue John, Tall Plinth Base, 15 x 3¾ In., Pair ..... *illus*	2176
Ornament, Oval Base, Diana Holding Bow, Chains, 2 Hunting Dogs, Seed Pearl, 1800, 3¼ In.	1599
Pedestal, Onyx, Mottled Green, Brown, Caramel, Square Base, Collared Capital, 48 x 12 In., Pair..	619
Plaque, Funerary, 2 Boys Playing, Signed In Calligraphy, 1600s	144
Plaque, Pietra Dura, Birds, Branches, Moths, Gilt Frame, Italy, Signed, 1900s, 19 x 15 In., Pair.. *illus*	2684
Road Guardian, 2 Bosatsu Figures, Hands Forming Gassho Adoration Mudra, 1800s, 7 In.	700
Sculpture, Limestone, St. Martin On Horseback, 29 x 24 x 12 In.	7500
Sculpture, Tree, Agate, 50 Flowers, Jade Leaves, Cloisonne Pot, 51 In.	4750
Sculpture, Tree, Enameled Bronze, Cloisonne Pot, White & Orange Blooms, 20 In.	469
Seal, Tortoise, Hand Carved, 4 Animals, 4-Point Compass, Black, 1¾ x 1¾ x 3 In.	30
Urn, Pedestal, Blue John Flourite, George III, c.1780, 12¾ In.	3125
Vase, Hardstone, Phoenix, Dragon, Double, Stand, 7¼ In.	344

STONEWARE is a coarse, glazed, and fired potter's ceramic that is used to make crocks, jugs, bowls, etc. It is often decorated with cobalt blue decorations. In the nineteenth and early twentieth centuries, potters often decorated crocks with blue numbers indicating the size of the container. A *2* meant 2 gallons. Stoneware is still being made. American stoneware is listed here.

Barrel, Gray, Blue Incised Landscape, Horses, Floret, Leafy Banded Borders, 1886, 6 In.	615
Barrel, Stone Ground, Blue Design, Westerwald, c.1850, 7 In.	396
Bowl, Red, Black, Geometric Panels, Daoguang, Chinese, 1800s	60
Bowl, Thick Rolled Rim, Brown Drip Glaze, Horizontal Stripes, Unmarked, 1900s, 6 x 13 In.	19
Bowl, Tin Glaze, Footed, Bull, Green Leaves & Edging, Spain, 1800s, 2½ x 8⅞ In.	150
Bowl, Turquoise, Alev Ebuzziya Siesbye, Copenhagen, 1983, 4 x 7½ In.	3250
Canteen, Disc Shape, Embossed, Cobalt Blue, 8¼ x 6½ In.	509
Canteen, Embossed, Bail Handle, Blue, Leaves, Bears, 11 x 9½ In.	226
Chicken Waterer, Albany Slip Glaze, Incised Indian Chief, North Carolina, 10 In.	224

Stiegel Type, Perfume Bottle, Enamel, Man In Colonial Dress, Flowers, Leaves, 6 ½ In. $550

Stiegel Type, Salt, Master, Cobalt Blue, Blown, Ribbed Body, Footed, Comet Tail Pontil, 2 ⅝ In. $265

Stiegel Type, Shot Glass, Enamel Flowers, Leaves, Red, Blue, Yellow, 2 ½ In. $175

Stone, Figure, Coral, Flower Vase, Red, Chinese, 6 ⅜ x 7 ¾ In. $4,500

Stone, Figurine, Coral, Carved, Celestial Beauty, Stand, Chinese, 5 ¾ In. $610

Stone, Jardiniere, Flowering Tree, Cloisonne Enamel Pot, Chinese, 19 ½ In. $427

Stone, Obelisk, Rock Crystal, Blue John, Tall Plinth Base, 15 x 3 ¾ In., Pair $2,176

S

STONEWARE

Stone, Plaque, Pietra Dura, Birds, Branches, Moths, Gilt Frame, Italy, Signed, 1900s, 19 x 15 In., Pair
$2,684

New Orleans Auction Galleries

Stoneware, Churn, Cobalt Blue, Basket, Flowers, Lug Handles, T. Harrington, Lyons, N.Y., c.1860, 19 In.
$11,070

Skinner, Inc.

Churn, 2 Wheels, Metal Band, Circular Glass Window, Wood Stand, 1910, 8 Gal., 22 x 24 x 39 In.	130
Churn, Cobalt Blue, Basket, Flowers, Lug Handles, T. Harrington, Lyons, N.Y., c.1860, 19 In. . *illus*	11070
Churn, Cobalt Blue, Cylindrical, Tooled Shoulder, Remmey Pottery, Pa., 3 Gal., 14 In.	71
Churn, Cobalt Blue, Flowers, Vine, 4 Gal., 16 In.	560
Churn, Cobalt Blue Stencil, A.P. Donaghho, 1800s, 5 Gal., 18 In. *illus*	510
Churn, Freehand, Stenciled, Cobalt Blue, Hamilton & Jones, 2 Handles, 1800s, 19 In. *illus*	720
Churn, Green Tan Glaze, Strap & Lug Handles, HP, Hawkins Peaden, c.1890, 19 In.	1020
Container, Tobacco, Bristol Glaze, Old Green River, Paper, Blue Glaze, 8½ x 6¼ In.	205
Crock, Butter, Blue, Burley & Winter Co., 5 x 7½ In.	30
Crock, Churn, Semi-Oval, Semi-Rounded, Lug Handles, Shoulder, 1800s, 6 Gal., 11 x 11 x 19 In.	224
Crock, Cobalt Blue Freehand, Stencil, Lug Handles, Samuel Booker, Kentucky, 1800s, 13 In. *illus*	2214
Crock, Cobalt Blue Lady Slipper, c.1875, 3 Gal., 9 x 10½ In.	96
Crock, Cobalt Blue Spread Wing Eagle, Stenciled, 3 Gal., 12 In.	767
Crock, Cobalt Blue Stencil, Eagle, Banner, James Hamilton & Co., Greensboro, Pa., 1870s, 16 In. *illus*	3998
Crock, Cobalt Blue, Birds, Branch, 13 In., 3 Gal.	442
Crock, Cobalt Blue, Coniferous Tree, Molded Rim, Applied Lug Handles, Lyons, 8 In., Gal.	472
Crock, Cobalt Blue, Eagle, Slip Interior, Stenciled, Salt Glaze, 1870s, 16 In.	3998
Crock, Cobalt Blue, Flower, 2, Burger-Lang, Rochester, 11¾ In.	250
Crock, Cobalt Blue, Flower, 2, John Burger, Handles, 2 Gal., 12½ x 8 In.	224
Crock, Cobalt Blue, Flower, Impressed 5, 2 Applied Handles, Chips, 1800s, 16 In.	210
Crock, Cobalt Blue, Flowers, Bulbous, Handles, Wm. Moyer, Harrisburg, Pa., 2 Gal., 14 In.	3835
Crock, Cobalt Blue, Flowers, Marked Bosworth, Hartford, Ct., c.1875, 3 Gal., 11 In.	100
Crock, Cobalt Blue, Flowers, Stem, Blumenthal's Stoves Ranges & House, New York, 1800s, 2 Gal.	344
Crock, Cobalt Blue, Leafy, Potted Wreath, Center Date, 3 Gal., 1878, 10¾ In.	324
Crock, Cobalt Blue, Roses, Stenciled, Jas. Hamilton & Co., Greensboro, Pa., Handles, 14 In.	360
Crock, Cobalt Blue, Salt Glaze, Oval, Ears, Flattened Rim, Raised Neck Ring, 1840, 9 x 12 In.	90
Crock, Cobalt Blue, Tulip, Salt Glaze, Iron Washed, Rolled Rim, Daniel Shenfelder, 1885, 6 x 5 In.	260
Crock, E.D. Pettengill Co., Raspberry Preserves, Pottery Lid, Swing Handle, 6 In.	316
Crock, Lid, Printed Script, Stars, 1900s, 17 In.	690
Dish, Brushed Flowers, Underglaze Blue, Iron Brown, Japan, 2½ x 11 In.	123
Dispenser, Crock, Pale Blue, Stamped Iced Tea, Brass Spout, Lid, 1960s, 16 In., 4 Gal.	120
Figure, Rooster, Brown, Green Glaze, Marked Edwin Meaders, 16 In.	750
Flask, Oval, Rounded Bottom, Cobalt Blue Leaf Decoration, 1800s, 2¾ x 6¼ x 5 In.	900
Flask, Ring, Harvest, Glazed, 8¾ x 8¼ In. *illus*	325
Jar, Blue Stencil, Hamilton & Jones, Greensboro, Pa., 10 In. *illus*	141
Jar, Canning, Cobalt Blue, Pears, Greensboro, Stenciled, Outward Rolled Rim, Penn., 10 In.	4080
Jar, Cobalt Blue, 2 A, Stenciled, Conrad, New Geneva, Pa., 1800s, 2 Gal., 12 In. *illus*	228
Jar, Cobalt Blue, Flower, Rolled Rim, Cowden & Wilcox, Harrisburg, Pa., Gal., 10 In. *illus*	165
Jar, Cobalt Blue, Freehand, Bird On Twig, Salt Glaze, Applied Handles, 1800s, 10 x 11 In. *illus*	450
Jar, Cobalt Blue, Incised Line Bands, Flowers, Low Handles, 1800s, 6 x 10 In. *illus*	225
Jar, Cobalt Blue, Tree, Cow, Milkmaid, Salt Glaze, Marked Morgantown, 1860, 2 Gal., 13 x 6¾ In.	5850
Jar, Preserve, Brown, Glazed, Marked, Wilmington, Del., 7¼ In.	82
Jar, Salt Glaze, Green Ash & Blue Drip, Rolled Rim, Ear Handles, S. Loy, c.1850, 13 In.	660
Jardiniere, Banded Pattern, David Cressey, Architectural Pottery, 1960s, 14½ x 17½ In.	1430
Jug, Alkaline Glaze, Slightly Oval, Handle, 16 In.	185
Jug, Alkaline Glaze, W.F. Hahn, Trenton, S.C, c.1885, 13 In.	480
Jug, Brown Glaze, Booth & Brumham, Druggist, New Haven, 1839, Handle, 11 In.	690
Jug, Brown Matte, Harvest, Presentation, Handle, Spout, Elias Freyman, Ohio, 1880, 9½ In.	540
Jug, Cobalt Blue Bird, JW & HA Blunt, Grocers, Chatham 4 Cor NY 2, Handle, c.1875, 14 In.	750
Jug, Cobalt Blue Bird, Lamson & Swasey, Portland, Me., Applied Handle, c.1875, 14 In.	300
Jug, Cobalt Blue Flower, Applied Handle, Label, Lehman & Reidinger, Poughkeepsie, 1800s, 12 In.	125
Jug, Cobalt Blue Slip Decorated, Opposite Loop Handle, 1900s, 13 In.	72
Jug, Cobalt Blue Vine, Stamped, White & Wood, Binghamton, N.Y., 11½ In., Gal. *illus*	153
Jug, Cobalt Blue, Bird, Slip Decoration, Glazed, Loop Handle, 1800s, 14 In.	156
Jug, Cobalt Blue, Flowers, Foxglove, Cowden & Wilcox, Gal., 10¾ In.	295
Jug, Cobalt Blue, Foxglove, Oval, Rounded Spout, Handle, Cowden & Wilcox, Gal., 14 In.	212
Jug, Cobalt Blue, Grapes, Vine, Salt Glaze, Nichols & Boynton, Burlington, Vt., 17 In.	431
Jug, Cobalt Blue, Haxstun, Ottman & Co., 11¾ In., Gal.	130
Jug, Cobalt Blue, Incised Eagle & Liberty, Contemporary, 10 In.	212
Jug, Cobalt Blue, Peacock, In Tree, F.B. Norton & Co., Mass., Marked, 1800s, 2 Gal.	1500
Jug, Cobalt Blue, Plume, Impressed West Troy, N.Y., 1800s, 2 Gal., 15 In.	281

Stoneware, Churn, Cobalt Blue Stencil, A.P. Donaghho, 1800s, 5 Gal., 18 In.
$510

Stoneware, Crock, Cobalt Blue Freehand, Stencil, Lug Handles, Samuel Booker, Kentucky, 1800s, 13 In.
$2,214

Stoneware, Jar, Blue Stencil, Hamilton & Jones, Greensboro, Pa., 10 In.
$141

Cowan's Auctions

Cowan's Auctions

Stoneware, Crock, Cobalt Blue Stencil, Eagle, Banner, James Hamilton & Co., Greensboro, Pa., 1870s, 16 In.
$3,998

Hess Auction Group

Stoneware, Churn, Freehand, Stenciled, Cobalt Blue, Hamilton & Jones, 2 Handles, 1800s, 19 In.
$720

Stoneware, Jar, Cobalt Blue, 2 A, Stenciled, Conrad, New Geneva, Pa., 1800s, 2 Gal., 12 In.
$228

Brunk Auctions

Stoneware, Flask, Ring, Harvest, Glazed, 8¾ x 8¼ In.
$325

Garth's Auctioneers & Appraisers

Garth's Auctioneers & Appraisers

Hess Auction Group

S

STONEWARE

Stoneware, Jar, Cobalt Blue, Flower, Rolled Rim, Cowden & Wilcox, Harrisburg, Pa., Gal., 10 In.
$165

Hess Auction Group

Stoneware, Jar, Cobalt Blue, Freehand, Bird On Twig, Salt Glaze, Applied Handles, 1800s, 10 x 11 In.
$450

Garth's Auctioneers & Appraisers

Stoneware, Jar, Cobalt Blue, Incised Line Bands, Flowers, Low Handles, 1800s, 6 x 10 In.
$225

Garth's Auctioneers & Appraisers

Stoneware, Jar, Cobalt Blue, Tree, Cow, Milkmaid, Salt Glaze, Marked Morgantown, 1860, 2 Gal., 13 x 6¾ In.
$5,850

Jeffrey S. Evans

TIP

If you display your collection at a library, museum, or commercial store, do not let the display include your street address or city name. It's best if you don't even include your name. A display is an open invitation to a thief. Be sure the collection will be guarded and fully insured.

Stoneware, Jug, Cobalt Blue Vine, Stamped, White & Wood, Binghamton, N.Y., 11½ In., Gal.
$153

Hess Auction Group

Jug, Cobalt Blue, Rolled Rim, Applied Lug Handles, 1800, 9 In.	148
Jug, Face, Red Glaze, Blue Eyes, Edwin Meaders, 10 In.	1025
Jug, Flowers, Leaves, Globular, Turned Neck, Brown, Cutouts, c.1700, 4 1/2 In.	5478
Jug, John Mulvey New Brunswick Impressed, Cobalt Blue Date, 1885, 16 In.	438
Jug, P. Herrmann, From J H Goetgen Dealer In Groceries, Brown Glaze, 3 Gal.	2415
Jug, Quail & Leaves, Molded Lip & Eared Handles, 1800s, 10 In.	3000
Jug, Return To Webb's, 20 Market St., Wilmington, N.C., Cream, Handle, 8 7/8 In.	1035
Jug, Ring, Flask, Salt Glaze, Short Neck, c.1810, 7 1/2 In.	164
Jug, Ring, Salt Glaze, Stamped W.H. Hancock, c.1900, 8 In.	420
Jug, Tan Glaze, Stacker Form, Strap Handle, Hahn Trenton, S.C., 1880s, 8 3/4 In.	300
Jug, Water, Brushed Cobalt Design, Incised Wm Rowby Manufactor Middleton, 2 Handles, 22 In.	2880
Jug, Whiskey, A.P. Simms Fine Whiskey, 11 1/2 x 7 1/8 In.	125
Jug, Whiskey, Estate Charles Feahney Wholesale & Retail Grocers, 11 1/2 x 7 In.	175
Libation Cup, Schist Stone, Conical, Round-Marked Rim, Cuneiforms, 3 In.	120
Pitcher, Cobalt Blue, Flower, Feather, Tooled Rim, Applied Strap Handle, Daubs, 1850, 11 In.	675
Pitcher, Cobalt Blue, Leaves, Bulbous, Shouldered, 1/2 Gal., 9 1/2 In.	118
Pitcher, Cobalt Blue, Leaves, Tooled Shoulder, Remmey Pottery, Qt., 7 In.	1888
Plate, Stylized Cats, Black & White, Judy Kensley McKie, John Stone, Signed, 1983, 10 1/2 In.	813
Sculpture, Spaniel, Hand Etched, Eye, Nose, Collar, Unsigned, 8 x 6 x 4 1/4 In.	367
Vase, Birds, Antelopes, Glazed, Marked, J M, 14 x 8 In.	1000
Vase, City Vase, Burnished, Painted Earthenware, Lydia Buzio, 1982, 6 x 12 In.	1000
Vase, Cream, Light Tan, Wide Mouth, 16 x 13 In.	6490
Vase, Iron Splashed, Cream Glazed, Celadons, Oval, Miura Chikusen, 1912, 10 x 4 In.	295
Vase, Oval, Tapered Narrow Neck, Soft Blue Crystalline Matte, Tobo, Signed, c.1950, 8 In.	413
Vase, Piix, Glazed Stoneware Decorated In Engobe, Claude Conover, 17 x 15 In.	5313
Vase, Shino Glaze, Brushed Paint, Malcolm Wright, 9 1/2 In.	338
Vase, Sisters Of The Silver Moon, Torso Shape, Glaze, Multicolor, 1984, 29 1/2 x 26 In.	8750
Vase, Stylized Slip Decorated, Leaves, Swirls, Brown Ground, Monogram, 1800s, 15 In.	369
Vase, Tall, Sculptural, Glazed, Malcolm Mobutu Smith, 1995, 25 x 8 In.	938
Vase, Twin Handle, Enamel, Ho Bird, Chinese Buddhistic, 1912, 8 x 7 In.	295

STORE fixtures, cases, cutters, and other items that have no company advertising as part of the decoration are listed here. Most items found in an old store are listed in the Advertising category in this book.

Bin, Flour, Yellow, Semicircular, c.1900, 27 x 17 In.	187
Cabinet, Seed, Oak, Pine, Hinged Bins, c.1890, 39 x 49 x 40 In. .... *illus*	295
Cigar Cutter, Poodle, Mechanical, Tail Level, Bronze, 5 x 6 7/8 In.	661
Coffee Grinders are listed in the Coffee Mill category.	
Dispenser, Soda Fountain Ice Cream Cone, 5 Dispensing Tubes, 38 1/2 x 8 3/4 In.	165
Dispenser, Straw, Diamond, Panel, Glass, Gilt Metal, 12 In.	270
Display Bottle, Pharmacy, Rx, Red, Gold Trim, Black Base, Plastic, Light-Up, 1950s, 20 x 8 In.	250
Display, Keys While You Watch, Motorized, 4 Panels, Graham Mfg. Co., 32 In.	150
Display, Penny Candy Dispenser, Metal Stand, 15 Jars, 30 1/2 x 18 In.	409
Display, Rack, Clothing, Iron Base, Casters, 78 In.	292
Knife Sharpener, Wheel Crank, Sharpens 7 Knives, Oak, Cast Iron, c.1900, 48 x 32 In. . *illus*	600
Marker Set, Excelsior Sign & Price, Letter & Number Stamps, Ink, Wood Box, c.1900	242
Match Dispenser, Cigar Cutter, Embossed, 5 5/8 x 4 1/2 In.	259
Showcase, Mahogany, 3 Glass Sides, Wood Back Doors, Mirror Fronts, Refinished, c.1900, 39 x 30 In.	1250
Sign, Antiques, We Buy & Sell, 1900s, 74 x 28 3/4 In.	84
Sign, Apples, Sprayed, Handpicked, Apple Shape, Red, 2-Sided, Sheet Steel, 57 x 53 In.	1210
Sign, Barber Shop, Beauty Salon, Reverse Painting, Glass, 9 x 23 In. .... *illus*	211
Sign, Blacksmith, Rectangular, White, Black, Gray, Shadowing, 1860-1900, 43 x 7 5/8 x 3/4 In.	1900
Sign, Boots, Pine, Shoe Shop, Leather Hanging Loop, 25 1/2 x 17 1/2 In.	726
Sign, Cash Store, Black Letters, White Ground, Wood, 11 1/2 x 85 1/2 In.	1814
Sign, Fish, Pine, Dorsal Fin, 10 Iron Spines, 40 x 42 In.	2722
Sign, Fishmonger Age, Fish, Black Ground, 35 1/2 x 47 1/2 In.	192
Sign, Flounder, Wood, 57 In.	1800
Sign, Grocery Store, Red & White, Hangers, 2-Sided, 1970, 48 x 48 In.	4800

Store, Cabinet, Seed, Oak, Pine, Hinged Bins, c.1890, 39 x 49 x 40 In.
$295

Hess Auction Group

Store, Knife Sharpener, Wheel Crank, Sharpens 7 Knives, Oak, Cast Iron, c.1900, 48 x 32 In.
$600

Rich Penn Auctions

Store, Sign, Barber Shop, Beauty Salon, Reverse Painting, Glass, 9 x 23 In.
$211

Copake Auction

Store, Sign, Licensed Premises, Men's Entrance, Reverse Painting, Glass, 10 x 23 In.
$140

Copake Auction

S

Store, Sign, Meats-Poultry, Reverse Painting, Glass, 7 x 23 In.
$211

Copake Auction

Store, Sign, Top Hat & Glove, Sheet Iron, Wrought Iron, Scroll Bracket, 1800s, 44 x 36 In.
$1,888

Hess Auction Group

Store, Leibrant, McDowell & Co., Union Air Tight Pat. 1851, Iron, Philadelphia, 36 x 24 x 18 In.
$200

Hess Auction Group

TIP
Never use metal polish to clean ormolu or gilded metal parts. Polish will remove the top layer of color. Use ammonia.

Sign, Half Horse, Half Dolphin, Horse Head, Dolphin Tail, Metal, White, Red, Black, 28 x 32 In.	351
Sign, Hardware Bait Ice, Plywood, Single Sided, Blue, Yellow, 15 x 54 In.	200
Sign, Homemade BBQ, Pick, Wood, 28 ½ x 18 ½ In.	58
Sign, Horse Head, Figural, Smiling, Bridle Ring Mounts, 24 ½ x 17 ½ In.	3630
Sign, Ladies' Lifts, 10 Cents, Shoe Shape, 23 ½ x 34 ½ In.	300
Sign, Licensed Premises, Men's Entrance, Reverse Painting, Glass, 10 x 23 In. *illus*	140
Sign, Meats-Poultry, Reverse Painting, Glass, 7 x 23 In. *illus*	211
Sign, Mlle G.M. Lizotte, Corset Parlor, Gilt Letters, Black Sand Paint, Wood, 13 x 60 x 1 In.	719
Sign, No Admittance, Ring Bell, Wood Grain Background, Porcelain, 4 x 18 In.	460
Sign, Office, Pointing Hand, Wood, 10 x 42 In.	531
Sign, Pawnbroker, 3 Balls, Pediment, 31 ½ In.	1920
Sign, Pocket Knife, Open, Pine, Carved, 41 In.	213
Sign, Scissors, Cut Plug, Wood, Painted, Frame, c.1920, 12 x 32 In.	82
Sign, Spitting, 500 Dollar Fine, Year In Prison, Navy Blue, 5 x 18 In.	1150
Sign, Straight Razor, Pine, 1900s, 19 In.	118
Sign, Sundries, Yellow Text, Dark Red Ground, Masonite, 1900s, 33 x 90 In.	292
Sign, Top Hat & Glove, Sheet Iron, Wrought Iron, Scroll Bracket, 1800s, 44 x 36 In. *illus*	1888
Sign, Wood For Sale, Green, White, Ice For Sale, 30 x 19 In.	614
Sign, Wood, Architectural, Painted, N. Calhoun Variety Store, Cape Cod, c.1920, 25 x 49 In.	840
Sign, Wood, Canvas, Painted, Trade, Jerseys, 24 x 30 In.	472
Strawholder, Soda Fountain, Brass, Glass Cylinder, 1920, 12 ½ In.	55
Tobacco Cutter, Elf, Thumbing Nose, Cast Iron, 7 ½ x 13 In.	143

STOVES have been used in America for heating since the eighteenth century and for cooking since the nineteenth century. Most types of wood, coal, gas, kerosene, and even some electric stoves are collected.

Electric Gas & Oil Stove Works, Iron, Polar, 3 Burner Covers, 11 ¾ x 13 ¼ In.	210
Heating, Cast Iron, Single Burner, Casting, Coal Reservoir, 4 Flared Feet, 1880, 12 x 26 x 20 In.	50
Leibrant, McDowell & Co., Union Air Tight Pat. 1851, Iron, Philadelphia, 36 x 24 x 18 In. *illus*	200
March, Brownback Stove Co., Cast Iron, Round, 28 In.	35
North, Chase & North, Parlor, Cast Iron, Ornate, Pa., Patented 1875, 40 In.	189
Potbelly, Mt. Penn Stove Works, Tulip Finial, In.	150

STRETCH GLASS is named for the strange stretch marks in the glass. It was made by many glass companies in the United States from about 1900 to the 1920s. It is iridescent. Most American stretch glass is molded; most European pieces are blown and may have a pontil mark.

Compote, Mother-Of-Pearl, c.1920, 6 ¾ In.	115

SULPHIDES are cameos of unglazed white porcelain encased in transparent glass. The technique was patented in 1819 in France and has been used ever since for paperweights, decanters, tumblers, marbles, and other type of glassware. Paperweights and Marbles are listed in their own categories.

Beaker, Crucifix, France, c.1840, 3 ½ In.	270
Bottle, Stopper, Gentleman, Renaissance Outfit, 5 ¼ x 3 ¾ In.	1700
Goblet, Minerva, Conical Bowl, Strawberry Diamond &Fan, 8 In.	1200
Perfume Bottle, Woman, Greek, Seated, c.1840, 2 ¼ x 1 ⅜ In.	485
Tumbler, Napoleon, 3 In.	325

SUMIDA is a Japanese pottery that was made from about 1895 to 1941. Pieces are usually everyday objects—vases, jardinieres, bowls, teapots, and decorative tiles. Most pieces have a very heavy orange-red, blue, brown, black, green, purple, or off-white glaze, with raised three-dimensional figures as decorations. The unglazed part is painted red, green, black, or orange. Sumida is sometimes mistakenly called Sumida gawa, but true Sumida gawa is a softer pottery made in the early 1800s.

Bowl, Alligator, Children, Oval, Japan, 1900s, 7 ¾ x 2 ¼ In.	156

S

Vase, Blue Green Glaze Over Shoulders, Unglazed Body, Applied Figures, Marked, 1900s, 25 In. *illus* 500

SUNBONNET BABIES were introduced in 1900 in the book *The Sunbonnet Babies*. The stories were by Eulalie Osgood Grover, illustrated by Bertha Corbett. The children's faces were completely hidden by the sunbonnets. The children had been pictured in black and white before this time, but the color pictures in the book were immediately successful. The Royal Bayreuth China Company made a full line of children's dishes decorated with the Sunbonnet Babies. Some Sunbonnet Babies plates have been reproduced, but they are clearly marked.

Candleholder, Fishing, Handle, Royal Bayreuth, 5 In. 48
Group, Washing, Monday, Royal Bayreuth, 4 ¼ x 6 ½ In. 29
Nut Dish, Fishing, Crimped Rim, 3 Flared Paw Feet, 4 x 2 ½ In. 89
Plate, Laundry, Royal Bayreuth, 7 ½ In. 35
Sugar, Triangular Finial, Black, White, Z.S. & G. Bavaria, 1920s, 5 x 3 In. .... *illus* ¨49

SUNDERLAND LUSTER is a name given to a special type of pink luster made by Leeds, Newcastle, and other English firms during the nineteenth century. The luster glaze is metallic and glossy and appears to have bubbles in it. Other pieces of luster are listed in the Luster category.

Bowl, Luster, Transfer, Shipwright's Arms, Washington, Lafayette, Franklin, 4 x 8 In. 384
Pitcher, Luster, British Ship, Sailor's Tear Poem, Multicolor Transfer, 9 ½ In. .... *illus* 330
Pitcher, Pink Luster, Iron Bridge, Coat Of Arms, Sailor's Poem, 1800s, 8 In. .... *illus* 150
Punch Bowl, Luster, Purple, Green Leaves, 1800s, 5 ⅝ x 12 ¾ In. 305

SUPERMAN was created by two seventeen-year-olds in 1938. The first issue of *Action Comics* had the strip. Superman remains popular and became the hero of a radio show in 1940, cartoons in the 1940s, a television series, and several major movies.

Badge, Blue Stiff, Sticker Front, Vermont, Cellophane, 1973, 3 ⅛ In. 20
Toy, Superman Stopping Tank, Linemar, Lithograph Tin Army Tank, c.1958, 7 ½ In. 6600

SUSIE COOPER (1902-1995) began as a designer in 1925 working for the English firm A.E. Gray & Company. In 1932 she formed Susie Cooper Pottery, Ltd. In 1950 it became Susie Cooper China, Ltd., and the company made china and earthenware. In 1966 it was acquired by Josiah Wedgwood & Sons, Ltd. The name *Susie Cooper* appears with the company names on many pieces of ceramics.

| A.E. Gray & Co. | Susie Cooper | Susie Cooper |
| c.1925–1931 | 1932–1934 | 1932–1964 |

Breakfast Set, Egg Cup, Cup & Saucer, Plate, Bowl, Teapot, Spiral, Turquoise, 10 Piece 95
Creamer, Wedding Ring Pattern, Earthenware, Tan, Rust, Green, 3 In. 20
Pitcher, Hot Water, Baby Blue, Kestrel Shape, 5 ¾ In. 85
Platter, Wedding Ring Pattern, Earthenware, Green Yellow, 16 x 12 In. 30
Pot, Hot Water, Ceramic, Lid, Baby Blue, Kestrel Shape, 1930s, 5 ¾ In. .... *illus* 85

SWANKYSWIGS are small drinking glasses. In 1933, the Kraft Food Company began to market cheese spreads in these decorated, reusable glass tumblers. They were discontinued from 1941 to 1946, then made again from 1947 to 1958. Then plain glasses were used for most of the cheese, although a few special decorated Swankyswigs have been made since that time. For more prices, go to kovels.com.

Hey Kids, Ding Dong Ring, Clarabell, Howdy Doody, 1953, 4 In. 12
Water Lily, Blue, Leaves, 5 ½ In. 46

Sumida, Vase, Blue Green Glaze Over Shoulders, Unglazed Body, Applied Figures, Marked, 1900s, 25 In.
$500

New Orleans Auction Galleries

Sunbonnet Babies, Sugar, Triangular Finial, Black, White, Z.S. & G. Bavaria, 1920s, 5 x 3 In.
$49

Ruby Lane

Sunderland, Pitcher, Luster, British Ship, Sailor's Tear Poem, Multicolor Transfer, 9 ½ In.
$330

Eldred's Auctioneers and Appraisers

S

SWASTIKA KERAMOS

Sunderland, Pitcher, Pink Luster, Iron Bridge, Coat Of Arms, Sailor's Poem, 1800s, 8 In.
$150

Cowan's Auctions

Susie Cooper, Pot, Hot Water, Ceramic, Lid, Baby Blue, Kestrel Shape, 1930s, 5¾ In.
$85

Ruby Lane

> ### TIP
> *Don't put china with gold designs in the dishwasher. The gold will wash off.*

Syracuse, Bracelet, Plate, Ivory, Gold Band, Marked, 10¼ In.
$40

Ruby Lane

SWASTIKA KERAMOS is a line of art pottery made from 1906 to 1908 by the Owen China Company of Minerva, Ohio. Many pieces were made with an iridescent glaze.

Vase, Iridescent Metallic Glaze, c.1910, 12 In.	125
Vase, Trees, Landscape, Red Clouds, Handles, c.1906, 11 In.	300

SWORDS of all types that are of interest to collectors are listed here. The military dress sword with elaborate handle is probably the most wanted. A tsuba is a hand guard fitted to a Japanese sword between the handle and the blade. Be sure to display swords in a safe way, out of reach of children.

Broad, 2 Handles, Spurred Blade, Shaped Guards, Leather Handle, Iron Pommel, 64½ In.	2750
Cavalry Saber, Iron Pommel, Knuckle Bow, Leather, Brass Wire, Wrapped Handles, 41 x 5 x 4 In.	425
Executioner, Steel Blade, Leather Wrapping, Brass, Ngombe People, Congo, 30 x 7¼ x 3 In.	188
Pendragon, Blade, Stainless Steel, Cross Guard, 41 x 7¾ In.	94
Presentation, Celluloid Grip, Wire Wrapped, Swastika Pommel, Nazi Eagle, Germany, 15 In.	42
Presentation, Fullered Blade, Decorated Designs, US Symbols, Metal Guard & Grip, Marked, 35 In.	118
Presentation, Naval Cutlass, Double Edged Blade, Leather Scabbard, Ames Model 1840, 1873, 25 In.	354
Presentation, Officer, Single Edge Etched Blade, Hilt, Guard, Pommel, Grip Wood, 1900s, 36 In.	118
Saber, M1860 Light Cavalry, Stamped Top Edge Of Blade, Leather Grip, 43 In.	270
Talwar, Mughal, Gold Inlaid Handle, Steel Blade, Disc Hilt, India, 1800s, 36 In.	1320
Tsuba, Bronze, Openwork, Figure, Bell, Clouds, 3 In.	228
Tsuba, Copper, Gold, Silver, Birds, Netting, Flowers, Grasses, Tobari Tomihisa, 2½ In.	1200
Tsuba, Iron, Inlay, Peony, 3 In.	900
Tsuba, Iron, Octagonal, Brass, Copper, Chrysanthemum, 2¾ In.	204
Tsuba, Old Man, Waterfall, Cutouts, Marked, Japan, c.1800	2300

SYRACUSE is one of the trademarks used by the Onondaga Pottery of Syracuse, New York. They also used O.P. Co. The company was established in 1871. The name became the Syracuse China Company in 1966. Syracuse China closed in 2009. It was known for fine dinnerware and restaurant china.

Syracuse China, Corp. 1871–1873

Syracuse China, Corp. 1892–1895

Syracuse China, Corp. 1966–1970

Bombay, Plate, Dinner, 10 In.	32
Bracelet, Plate, Ivory, Gold Band, Marked, 10¼ In. _illus_	40
Imperial Geddo, Pitcher, Floral Design, Daisy, 7 x 8½ In.	95
Mayfair Green, Serving Platter, 14½ x 10 In.	24
O.P. Co., Butter, 4¼ x 8 In.	45
Pink Rose, Bread Plate, 5½ In.	10
Wayside, Bowl, Vegetable, 9⅝ In.	89
Wedding Ring, Plate, Dinner, 10 In.	14

TAPESTRY, *Porcelain, see Rose Tapestry category.*

TEA CADDY is the name for a small box made to hold tea leaves. In the eighteenth century, tea was very expensive and it was stored under lock and key. The first tea caddies were made with locks. By the nineteenth century, tea was more plentiful and the tea caddy was larger. Often there were two sections, one for green tea, one for black tea.

Abalone Veneer, House, 8½ x 7 In.	2125
Bird's-Eye Maple, Regency, Octagonal, Panel Lid, String Inlay, 7 x 7 In.	500
Bird's-Eye Maple, Sloping Sides, Ebony String Inlay, Double, 7½ x 13½ In.	605
Burl Veneer, Oval, Shell Inlay, c.1800, 4 x 6 In.	188

S

Burl, Rectangular, String Inlay, Georgian, England, c.1800, 5 x 8 In.		480
Coconut Shell, Barrel Shape, Pewter Lining, Stylized Dragons, Carved, Chinese, 3 In.		360
Fruitwood Veneer, Banded Greek Key Inlay, Compartment, 6 x 12 In.		540
Fruitwood, Apple Shape, George III, 1800s, 4 In.		1205
Fruitwood, Apple Shape, Hinged Lid, England, 4¼ x 4¼ In.		960
Fruitwood, Melon Shape, Crosshatched End, Brass Escutcheon, Wood Pull, 1700s, 5 x 8 In.	*illus*	3600
Fruitwood, Pear Form, Wooden Stem, Brass Escutcheon, England, 6¾ x 4½ In.		780
Fruitwood, Pear, Georgian, Hinged Lid, Metal Escutcheon, Lined Interior, c.1800, 6 x 5 In.		1320
Lacquer, 5 Fan-Shape Panels, Depicting Flowers, Plum, Bamboo, Orchids, 2⅞ x 2⅞ In.		1200
Lacquer, Black, Gilt, Shaped, Pewter Compartments, c.1830, 5 x 8½ In.		138
Lacquer, Dark Brown, Red, Stylized Chrysanthemums, Grasses, Inlaid Silver, 2 x 3 In.		1300
Lacquer, Gilt, Court, Veranda, Pavilions, People, Shaped Medallions, Flowers, 6 x 10½ In.		501
Lacquer, Glossy Black, Red & Gold, Crushed Blue Shell, Silver Interiors, 2¾ x 2⅝ In.		1800
Lacquer, Gold, Red, Allover Design, Japanese Crests, Kiku, Kiri Mon, 2⅞ x 2⅝ In.		1400
Lacquer, Leafy Maple Branches, Gold, Green, Black, 3 Fishes Ascending Water, Rock, 2¾ x 2⅞ In.		1250
Lacquer, Red, Stylized Chrysanthemums, Incised Lines Filled, Gold Dust, Black Interiors, 2¾ x 2⅜ In.		1500
Lacquer, Red Brown, Allover Design Of Scattered Cherry Petals, 2⅞ x 2⅝ In.		1700
Mahogany Veneer, Dome, Fruitwood Shell, 1800s, 5 x 5 In.		132
Mahogany, Banded Inlay, Basket, Flowers, Canted Corners, England, c.1820, 5 x 7¼ In.	*illus*	281
Mahogany, Canted Corners, Seashell, Lid, George III, 1800s, 5 x 7 In.		320
Mahogany, Compartments, Lids, Brass, Inlay, England, c.1810, 7 x 11 x 6 In.	*illus*	1353
Mahogany, Escutcheon, Handle, George III, 1700s, 5¼ In.		100
Mahogany, Fitted Interior, Federal, 6 x 12 In.		29
Mahogany, Inlaid, Fruitwood, Shell Inlay, Brass Handle, 1800s, 5 x 7 In.		660
Mahogany, Inlaid, Octagonal, Foil Lined, Bone Escutcheon, Handles, Georgian, 5 x 8⅜ In.		175
Mahogany, Molded Edge, Brass Bail Handle, 3 Tin Caddies, Lids, c.1775, 6 x 11 In.	*illus*	182
Maple Veneer, Fruitwood Inlay, Conch Shell, 4 x 5 In.		390
Maple Veneer, Fruitwood Inlay, Seashell, Compartments, 2 Lids, 4½ x 7½ In.		540
Molded, Shell & Diaperwork, Chinoiserie Figures, Staffordshire, 1750-60, 6⅞ In.		4375
Oak, Mahogany, Flame Grained Trim, Inlay, Bun Feet, 6½ x 9½ In.		60
Papier-Mache, Flowers, Leaves, Hand Painted Accents, 1800s, 5¾ x 10¼ In.		795
Pine, Painted, Geometric, Red, Black, Gold, Chinese Calligraphy, 1800s, 23½ x 22 In., Pair.		275
Porcelain, Compass Rose, Ship, Verse, 1800s, 4 In.	*illus*	450
Porcelain, Famille Rose, Tobacco Leaf, Chinese Export, c.1800, 5 In.		480
Porcelain, Flowers In Cartouches, Lattice, 4¾ In.		360
Porcelain, Geometric Decoration, Garlands, Ringtons Limited Tea Merchants, 12 In.		24
Rolled Paper, Flowers, Gilt Feathering, Inlaid Lid Edge, Oblong, 1800s, 5 x 7 In.	*illus*	2040
Rosewood, Abalone, Sloping Sides, Reeded, Brass Ring Handles, 8 x 14 In.		1331
Rosewood, Coffin Lid, Brass Handle, Chippendale, c.1770, 6 x 11 x 6 In.		720
Rosewood, Coffin Shape, Paneled Lid, Irish Cut Glass Canisters, 8 x 12¾ In.		600
Rosewood, Diamond Inlay, Coffin Shape, Paneled Lid, 5 x 7½ In.		375
Rosewood, Mother-Of-Pearl Flower Inlay, Coffin Shape, Paneled Lid, Disc Feet, 5 x 8½ In.		125
Rosewood, Mother-Of-Pearl Inlay, Doors, Handles, Bun Feet, William IV, c.1835, 13 x 12 In.	*illus*	580
Satinwood, Inlaid, Octagonal, Conch Shell Lid, Fan Marquetry, Diagonal Panel, 4½ 8 x 4 In.		720
Silver, Acanthus, Cabochons, Rectangular, Edward Dobson, George III, 1772, 4½ In.		812
Silver, Chased, Village, People, Trees, Oval, Lid, Continental, 3½ x 2½ In.	*illus*	222
Silver, Enameled, Jade Collar, Colorful Blossom & Birds, Chinese, 7 In.		2160
Silver, Engraved Bands, Crest, Motto, Francis Boone Thomas, 1878, 5½ In.		469
Silver, Flowers & Leaves, Marked, 5¼ In.		563
Silver, Garlands, Cherry Sprig, C-Scroll Feet, J. Wakelin & W. Taylor, George III, c.1785, 4 In.		4235
Silver, Gilt, Enamel, Double Jade Collars, Inset Stones, Chinese, 4 In.		2160
Silver, Notched Oval Shape, Charles Aldridge, George III, 1788, 5 x 5½ In.		1071
Silver, Sliding Top, Fitted Dome Lid, Rectangular, 1724, 4½ x 3¼ x 2⅛ In.		1800
Tole, Flowers, Leaves, Faux Grain Ground, Footed, 1800s, 5 x 5¼ x 3½ In.	*illus*	354
Tole, Flowers, Leaves, Japanned, Round, Lid, Pennsylvania, 1800s, 6½ In.		45
Tortoiseshell Veneer, Button Feet, Interior Compartments, Shell Lids, 1800s, 5 x 7 In.	*illus*	720
Tortoiseshell, Bombe, Cove Molded Cover, Brass Ball Feet, Regency, England, 6 In.		1625
Tortoiseshell, Brass Feet, 2 Compartments, England, c.1875, 4 x 6 In.		875
Tortoiseshell, Coffin Shape, Silver Monogram, Bun Feet, Regency, England, 6 x 7 In.		3000
Tortoiseshell, Flared Skirt, Button Feet, Silver Plaque, 2 Compartments, 1800s, 6 x 9¾ In.		1200

Fake Tea Caddies
Eighteenth- and early nineteenth-century tea caddies were sometimes made of wood. Some were shaped like apples or pears. These have been reproduced. The old ones may have cracks because wood shrinks with age. They should have a plug in the middle of the bottom and most have a lock.

Tea Caddy, Fruitwood, Melon Shape, Crosshatched End, Brass Escutcheon, Wood Pull, 1700s, 5 x 8 In.
$3,600

Garth's Auctioneers & Appraisers

Tea Caddy, Mahogany, Banded Inlay, Basket, Flowers, Canted Corners, England, c.1820, 5 x 7¼ In.
$281

Eldred's Auctioneers and Appraisal Services

Tea Caddy, Mahogany, Compartments, Lids, Brass, Inlay, England, c.1810, 7 x 11 x 6 In.
$1,353

Skinner, Inc.

T

Tea Caddy, Mahogany, Molded Edge, Brass Bail Handle, 3 Tin Caddies, Lids, c.1775, 6 x 11 In.
$182

James D. Julia Auctioneers

Tea Caddy, Porcelain, Compass Rose, Ship, Verse, 1800s, 4 In.
$450

Eldred's Auctioneers and Appraisers

Tea Caddy, Rolled Paper, Flowers, Gilt Feathering, Inlaid Lid Edge, Oblong, 1800s, 5 x 7 In.
$2,040

Garth's Auctioneers & Appraisers

Tea Caddy, Rosewood, Mother-Of-Pearl Inlay, Doors, Handles, Bun Feet, William IV, c.1835, 13 x 12 In.
$580

New Orleans Auction Galleries

Tea Caddy, Silver, Chased, Village, People, Trees, Oval, Lid, Continental, 3 ½ x 2 ½ In.
$222

Forsythes' Auctions

Tea Caddy, Tole, Flowers, Leaves, Faux Grain Ground, Footed, 1800s, 5 x 5 ¼ x 3 ½ In.
$354

Hess Auction Group

Tea Caddy, Tortoiseshell Veneer, Button Feet, Interior Compartments, Shell Lids, 1800s, 5 x 7 In.
$720

Garth's Auctioneers & Appraisers

Tea Caddy, Tortoiseshell, Swell Front, Cove Molded Lid, Silver Edges, Ball Feet, Regency, c.1815, 6 x 7 In.
$1,875

New Orleans Auction Galleries

Tea Caddy, Wood, Apple, Hinged Lid, Lock, England, 1800s-1900s, 4 x 4 In.
$1,440

Brunk Auctions

Tea Leaf Ironstone, Coffeepot, Morning Glory, White, Gold, Lid, 1850s, 10 x 9 In.
$125

Ruby Lane

T

Tortoiseshell, Matching Cover, 2 Compartments, Regency, England, c.1850, 6½ x 7 In.	1063
Tortoiseshell, Octagonal, Mother-Of-Pearl Knob, Georgian, c. 1825, 4 x 4 In.	1375
Tortoiseshell, Pagoda Top, Octagonal, Silver Cartouche, Brass Feet, 1800s, 6 x 6 x 4 In.	1440
Tortoiseshell, Pagoda Top, Silver Keyhole, Lid Cartouche, Red Lining, 1800s, 6 x 8 x 5 In.	2280
Tortoiseshell, Swell Front, Cove Molded Lid, Silver Edges, Ball Feet, Regency, c.1815, 6 x 7 In. *illus*	1875
Wood, Apple Shape, Hinged Lid, Knopped Stem, c.1800, 5½ x 5½ In.	1200
Wood, Apple, Hinged Lid, Lock, England, 1800s-1900s, 4 x 4 In. *illus*	1440
Wood, Hepplewhite Inlay, Octagonal Shape, c.1800, 5 x 8¼ In.	413
Wood, Pear Form, Hinged Lid, Wood Stem, Lock & Key, c.1800, 7 x 4 In.	1920
Wood, Pear Form, Hinged Lid, Wood Stem, Metal Escutcheon, Georgian, c.1900, 6 x 5 In.	1320
Wood, Round, Stitch Work Binding, Red, Sunflower, Butterfly, Paint, Chinese, 1800s, 13 x 9 In.	95
Wood, Sideboard Shape, Hinged, 3 Compartments, Rococo Revival, 11 x 19 In.	793
Wood, Square, Diamond Pattern, Veneer, Green Leather Trim, 1800s, 4 x 4 In.	1440
Wood, Tartanware, Allover Red Plaid, Serpentine Front, Fitted Interior, 1800s, 5 x 8 In.	854

TEA LEAF IRONSTONE dishes are named for their decorations. There was a superstition that it was lucky if a whole tea leaf unfolded at the bottom of your cup. This idea was translated into the pattern of dishes known as "tea leaf." By 1850 at least 12 English factories were making this pattern, and by the 1870s it was a popular pattern in many countries. The tea leaf was always a luster glaze on early wares, although now some pieces are made with a brown tea leaf. There are many variations of tea leaf designs, such as Teaberry, Pepper Leaf, and Gold Leaf. The designs were used on many different white ironstone shapes, such as Bamboo, Lily of the Valley, Empress, and Cumbow.

Cake Plate, Red Cliff, Handled, 8 x 8 In.	65
Chamber Pot, Lid, Mellor & Taylor	43
Coffeepot, Morning Glory, Anthony Shaw, c.1880, 9 In.	90
Coffeepot, White, Gold, Lid, 1850s, 10 x 9 In. *illus*	125
Compote, Red Cliff, 8 x 8 x 4 In.	53
Cup & Saucer, Alfred Meakin	35
Gravy Boat, Anthony Shaw, 1870s, 7 x 4 In.	60
Gravy Boat, Thomas Furnival & Sons	75
Platter, Alfred Meakin, 19th Century, 15 In.	60
Sugar, Lid, Luster Sprig, White, Gold, Handles, Alfred Meakin, c.1890, 7 In. *illus*	85
Sugar, Lid, Mellor, Taylor & Co., 6 x 4 In.	75
Teapot, Panels, Copper Luster, Acorn Finial, Anthony Shaw, c.1850, 9½ In.	79
Toothbrush Holder, Round, Scalloped, Alfred Meakin, 4⅝ In.	65

TECO is the mark used on the art pottery line made by the American Terra Cotta and Ceramic Company of Terra Cotta and Chicago, Illinois. The company was an offshoot of the firm founded by William D. Gates in 1881. The Teco line was first made in 1885 but was not sold commercially until 1902. It continued in production until 1922. Over 500 designs were made in a variety of colors, shapes, and glazes. The company closed in 1930.

Bowl, Buttressed, Green, c.1910, 6 x 11¾ In.	4375
Creamer, Incised Paddle Shapes, Green Over Black, 2 x 4¼ In.	240
Jardiniere, Curved Rectangles On Shoulder, William J. Dodd, 9 x 8 In.	1750
Mug, Molded Cattail & Leaves, Speckled Brown Matte Glaze, Marked, 6 In.	236
Pitcher, Tapered, Blue Matte Glaze, Greek Style, Footed, F. Albert, 13 x 4 In.	406
Vase, 2 Handles, Green Crystalline Matte Glaze, F. Albert, 9 In.	590
Vase, 2 Handles, Green Matte Glaze, 5 x 4¾ In.	390
Vase, 3 Lobes, Footed, Mint Green, Terra-Cotta, c.1910, 15 x 7 In.	812
Vase, 4 Buttresses, Green Matte Glaze, W.D Gates, Marked, 7¼ x 3¼ In.	1900
Vase, Flower Form, Light Green Matte Glaze, Charcoaling, Impressed, 13 In.	800
Vase, Flowers, Buds Rim, Leaf Tips, Cross Foot Base, Green Matte Glaze, Mundie, 13 x 8 In.	750
Vase, Green Matte Glaze, Marked, 7 In.	413
Vase, Green, Black, Terra-Cotta, c.1910, 7 x 3 In.	687
Vase, Holly & Berry, Green Matte, Fritz Albert, 9¼ x 2¼ In.	195
Vase, Lobed, Green Matte Glaze, Footed, Stamped, c.1910, 9 x 7 In.	2007
Vase, Pretzel Twist Handles, Charcoaling, Stamped & Incised, 11 In.	500

Tea Leaf Ironstone, Sugar, Lid, Luster Sprig, White, Gold, Handles, Alfred Meakin, c.1890, 7 In.
$85

Ruby Lane

Teco, Vase, Square, Tapered, Embossed Drape, Green Matte Glaze, 1900s, 13 In.
$1,920

Garth's Auctioneers & Appraisers

TIP
The material used to make repairs is warmer to the touch than the porcelain. Feel the surface of a figurine to see if there are unseen repairs.

T

Teco, Wall Pocket, Leaves, Embossed, Green Matte Glaze, Handles, Finial, 1900s, 15 x 9 In.
$1,200

Garth's Auctioneers & Appraisers

TIP

After you wash your old teddy bear, dry the fur and comb it with a dog comb.

Teddy Bear, Mohair, Light Brown, Excelsior Stuffed, Cast Iron Wheels, Germany, c.1915, 13 ½ In.
$300

Cowan's Auctions

Teddy Bear Fur

Teddy bears have been made with many kinds of "fur." Early bears had wool mohair fur. Artificial silk plush was used about 1930, cotton plush after World War II, nylon plush and other synthetics in the 1950s.

Vase, Ruffled Rim, Green Matte Glaze, Charcoaling, 5 In.		250
Vase, Square, Tapered, Embossed Drape, Green Matte Glaze, 1900s, 13 In.	*illus*	1920
Vase, Tapered, Horizontal Ribs, Green Matte Glaze, Rolled Rim, W.D. Gates, 5 ½ In.		313
Vase, Tapered, Leaves On Neck, Light Green Matte Glaze, Marked, 13 In.		531
Wall Pocket, Canteen Shape, Green Matte Glaze, 6 ½ x 2 In.		312
Wall Pocket, Leaves, Embossed, Green Matte Glaze, Handles, Finial, 1900s, 15 x 9 In.	*illus*	1200
Wall Pocket, Violets & Leaves In Relief, Green Matte Glaze, Oblong, Marked, 7 x 9 ½ In.		413

TEDDY BEARS were named for a president of the United States. The first teddy bear was a cuddly toy said to be inspired by a hunting trip made by President Theodore Roosevelt in 1902. He was praised because he saw a bear cub but did not shoot it. Morris and Rose Michtom started selling their stuffed bears as "teddy bears" and the name stayed. The Michtoms founded the Ideal Novelty and Toy Company. The German version of the teddy bear was made about the same time by the Steiff Company. There are many types of teddy bears and all are collected. The old ones are being reproduced. Other bears are listed in the Toy section.

Driving, Clown Doing Handstand, Cart, 3 Wheels, Spinning Disc, Germany, 8 x 4 In.		780
Farnell, Mohair Gold, Glass Eyes, Kapok Stuffed, 1930s, 16 In.		308
Hecla, Mohair, Ivory, Glass Eyes, Jointed, Humpback, 1906, 13 In.		3700
Jopi, Soulful Glass Eyes, Black Stitched Nosed, Excelsior Stuffed, 24 In.		615
Mohair, Cinnamon, Shoebutton Eyes, Black Stitched Nose, Mouth & Claws, 19 x 13 In.		5580
Mohair, Golden, Brown Glass Eyes, Black Stitched Nose, Mouth, Germany, 19 In.		95
Mohair, Jointed, Germany, 24 In.		53
Mohair, Light Brown, Excelsior Stuffed, Cast Iron Wheels, Germany, c.1915, 13 ½ In.	*illus*	300
Schuco, Yes-No, Mohair, Golden, Original Eyes, Germany, 1940s, 21 In.	*illus*	390
Schuco, Yes-No, Movable Head & Tail, 18-Tone Swiss Music Box, 1950s, 20 In.		572
Steiff, Golden Blond, Black Stitched Nose, Mouth, Claws, Squeaker, 19 In.		2460
Steiff, Growler, Caramel Color, Brown Stitch Nose, Glass Eyes, 1950s-60s, 25 In.		1054
Steiff, Growler, Red Collar, Metal Wheels, White Tires, 1930s, 18 x 27 In.		300
Steiff, Inoperative Growler, Black Stitched Nose, Glass Eyes, 1920s, 24 In.		1560
Steiff, Mohair, Apricot, Shoebutton Eyes, Black Stitched Nose, Mouth & Claws, 21 x 11 In.		6150
Steiff, Mohair, Apricot, Soft Stuffed, Original Pads, Glass Eyes, 1915-20, 15 In.		615
Steiff, Mohair, Cinnamon, Center Seam, Excelsior Stuffed, Fully Jointed, 1905, 15 In.		2829
Steiff, Mohair, Cinnamon, Extra-Large Back Hump, Original Eyes, Nose, 1910, 12 In.		492
Steiff, Mohair, Cinnamon, Fully Jointed, Excelsior Stuffed, Germany, 1905, 15 In.	*illus*	2829
Steiff, Mohair, Cuddy Koala, Squeaker, Partially Opened Mouth, 1955-61, 14 In.		519
Steiff, Mohair, Gold, Original Shoebutton Eyes, 1910-15, 17 In.		738
Steiff, Mohair, Golden, Glass Eyes, Tan, 16 In.		720
Steiff, Mohair, Golden, Jointed, Black Shoebutton Eyes, Button, c.1905, 10 In.		1088
Steiff, Mohair, Golden Brown, Jointed, Ear Tag, 19 In.	*illus*	120
Steiff, Mohair, Tan, Original Pads, Shoebutton Eyes, Germany, 1910, 13 In.		523
Steiff, Mohair, White, Swivel Head, Disc Jointed, Felt Paw Pads, Button, 1905, 18 In.		2300
Steiff, Mohair, Wood, Brown, Cream, On Wheels, White Tires, c.1950, 18 x 24 In.		246

TELEPHONES are wanted by collectors if the phones are old enough or unusual enough. The first telephone may have been made in Havana, Cuba, in 1849, but it was not patented. The first publicly demonstrated phone was used in Frankfurt, Germany, in 1860. The phone made by Alexander Graham Bell was shown at the Centennial Exhibition in Philadelphia in 1876, but it was not until 1877 that the first private phones were installed. Collectors today want all types of old phones, phone parts, and advertising. Even recent figural phones are popular.

Astral Telecom, Wedgwood, Blue Jasperware, Push Button, England, 7 ½ In.	*illus*	195
Elektrisk Bureau, Kristiania, Iron Backboard, Lighting Protection, Tin Case, Norway, c.1895		1294
Ericsson, Tin Case, Gilt Transfer Decoration, Horn, c.1902		1078
S.H. Couch Co., Wall, Shelf, Oak, Black Handset, c.1910, 24 x 8 In.	*illus*	300
Sign, Bell System, Public Telephone, Enameled Porcelain, 5 ½ x 18 In.	*illus*	236
Sumter Telephone Mfg., Oak Crank, Ledge, Bells, 24 x 9 ¾ In.		357
Switchboard, 5 Lines, Wood, Brass, Pacific RR, Western Electric, c.1880, 12 x 15 In.		600
Western Electric Rotary, Desktop, Black Metal, Bakelite Receiver, 1925		905

TEPLITZ refers to art pottery manufactured by a number of companies in the Teplitz-Turn area of Bohemia during the late nineteenth and early twentieth centuries. Two of these companies were the Alexandra Works founded by Ernst Wahliss, and the Amphora Porcelain Works, run by Riessner, Stellmacher, and Kessel.

Bust, Woman Wearing Extravagant Garments, Beaded Corset, Amphora, 19 x 16 x 8¼ In.	787
Candlestick, Figural, Maidens Rising From Lily Pond, Art Nouveau, Amphora, Signed, 11 In., Pair.	3630
Ewer, Green Matte, Copper Gilt Trim, Relief Dew Drops, Handle, 9½ In.	366
Ewer, Mermaid, Blue Body, Gilt Spider Webs, Flowers, 19 x 7½ In....................	502
Figurine, Girl Wearing Oak Leaf Crown & Cross, Carrying Basket, RStK., 25 In. .... *illus*	270
Figurine, Maiden, Bathing, Water Pedestal, Admiring Reflection, Gilt Highlights, Ernst Wahliss, 19 In.	3932
Figurine, Maiden, Blue Dress, Gold Highlights, Dancing Face On Base, Amphora, 20 x 17 In...	445
Group, Male, Female, Painted Flowers, Marked, 22 x 14 x 10 In.	160
Tray, Figural, Leaf Woman, Art Nouveau, Flowing Hair, Leaf Trays, Marked, 20 In........... *illus*	5445
Vase, Applied Gold Flowers, Leaves, Iridescent Mauve Ground, Amphora, Signed, 11 In.........	423
Vase, Confetti, Trees, Bubble Shape Leaves, Black, Gold, Brown, Paul Dachsel, 18 x 10 In.......	1375
Vase, Double Handled, Vine, Berries, Bluish Gray, 14 x 10 In....................	188
Vase, Dragonflies, Pierced Handles, Cream, Brown, Paul Dachsel, Amphora, c.1910, 6 x 4 In. ..	875
Vase, Figures, Nude, Stamped, c.1900, 9 x 8 In...................	1785
Vase, Gres-Bijou, Moths, Spider Webs, Green, Olive, RStK, c.1900, 17¼ x 11 In.............	6875
Vase, Leafy Trees, Blue, Stick Neck, Amphora, Paul Dachsel, c.1911, 20½ x 9¾ In............	1500
Vase, Mistletoe, Pierced Neck, Tan, Lobed Body, Cream, Amphora, RStK, 1900, 7 x 4½ In........	1000
Vase, Owl On Rim, Riessner, Stellmacher & Kessel, RStK, 13⅛ In. .... *illus*	885
Vase, Spanish Moss, Flowers, Art Nouveau, Filigree Handles, Signed, Amphora, 16 In.	3025
Vase, Woman, Flowers In Hair, Trees, Amphora, Stamped, 8 In........................	998

TERRA-COTTA is a special type of pottery. It ranges from pale orange to dark reddish-brown in color. The color comes from the clay, which is fired but not always glazed in the finished piece.

Box, Lid, Kneeling Figures, Green Matte Glaze, Atlantic Terra-Cotta Co., 12 x 9½ In........ *illus*	236
Bust, Bacchante, Red Marble & Gilt Bronze Column, France, 1800s, 9 In.	938
Bust, Beethoven, Blue Marble Base, 1824-87, 17 In.	3000
Bust, Diana, Fernand Cian, Marked, 1889-54, 20 In. .... *illus*	281
Bust, Eros, Young God, Holds Bunch Of Grapes, Rooster, Parted Hairdo, 3 x 2½ In.............	780
Bust, Female Head, Melon Coiffure, Bun, 1 x 3 In.....................	240
Bust, Fr. John, Gray Hair & Beard, 8½ In.	142
Bust, Michelangelo, After Albert-Ernest Carrier-Belleuse, 23½ In.	1250
Bust, Woman, Almond Shape Eyes, Prominent Nose, Archaic Smile, 3 x 4 In.	480
Bust, Young Man, Hat, Feather, Long Hair, Signed Lemaire, France, c.1880, 19½ In.	125
Bust, Young Woman, Melon Hairdo, Floral Wreath, Bun, Lidded Eyes, Straight Nose, 1½ x 3½ In.	460
Candlestick Lamp, Byzantine, Ring Base, Rim, Nozzle, Radiating Lines, Stylized Cross, 3 x 2 In. .	275
Charger, Koran Quote, Classic Iznik Palette Of Cobalt, Aqua Blue, White, 1800s, 14 In............	1200
Chimney Pot, Octagonal, Pedestal, Rectangular Base, George J. Fink, 1900, 16 x 16 x 47 In....	220
Figurine, Clown, Juggling Balls, Painted, Signed Waylande Gregory, 14 In...................... *illus*	767
Figurine, Cupid, Seated, Heart, Arrow Pierced, Signed L. Gregoire, 1800s, 11 In......................	125
Figurine, Diana, Nude, Seated, Ankles Crossed, Petting Dog, c.1900, 28¼ In.	1125
Figurine, Dog, Seated, White, 30 x 22 In....................	750
Figurine, Dwarf, Holding Plates, 27 In.....................	550
Figurine, E. Grozy, Modernist, Titled Meditate, Signed, 1963, 12 x 8 x 3¼ In.....................	283
Figurine, Flora, Nude, Crouching, Flowers In Hand, Jean-Baptiste Carpeaux, Signed, 1827-75, 8½ In.	7250
Figurine, Garden, Lion, Seated, 1900s, 24½ x 10 In., Pair....................	875
Figurine, Grouping, Roosters, Women, Scenic, A. Marchal, 20 x 17 x 11 In.	2118
Figurine, Horse Head, Hole Top, Ornamentation, 9 x 3 x 12 In....................	106
Figurine, La Frileuse, Painted Wood Base Imitating Marble, Signed, 1827-75, 17 In..................	1500
Figurine, Man, Sitting, Braiding Ropes, Long Gloves, 10½ x 7¾ In.....................	71
Figurine, Nude Male, Standing, Headdress, Musculature Chest, Long Garment, 11 In.............	1650
Figurine, Nude Nymph, Rides On Satyr's Shoulders, 21 In. .... *illus*	1875
Figurine, Porcelain, Masked, Harlequin Hatted, Signed, 1900s, 12 In.....................	30
Figurine, Seated Nude Woman, Incised, Louise Abel, Rookwood, 11 In........................	472

Teddy Bear, Schuco, Yes-No, Mohair, Golden, Original Eyes, Germany, 1940s, 21 In.
$390

Cowan's Auctions

Teddy Bear, Steiff, Mohair, Cinnamon, Fully Jointed, Excelsior Stuffed, Germany, 1905, 15 In.
$2,829

Cowan's Auctions

Teddy Bear, Steiff, Mohair, Golden Brown, Jointed, Ear Tag, 19 In.
$120

Richard D. Hatch & Associates

Teddy Bear Auction
The first "teddy bear only" auction was held at Christie's in London in 1985.

T

Telephone, Astral Telecom, Wedgwood, Blue Jasperware, Push Button, England, 7 ½ In.
$195

Bunch Auctions

Telephone, S.H. Couch Co., Wall, Shelf, Oak, Black Handset, c.1910, 24 x 8 In.
$300

Rich Penn Auctions

Telephone, Sign, Bell System, Public Telephone, Enameled Porcelain, 5 ½ x 18 In.
$236

AntiqueAdvertising.com

Teplitz, Figurine, Girl Wearing Oak Leaf Crown & Cross, Carrying Basket, RStK, 25 In.
$270

Cowan's Auctions

Teplitz, Tray, Figural, Leaf Lady, Art Nouveau, Flowing Hair, Leaf Trays, Marked, 20 In.
$5,445

James D. Julia Auctioneers

Teplitz, Vase, Owl On Rim, Riessner, Stellmacher & Kessel, RStK, 13 ⅛ In.
$885

Humler & Nolan

Terra-Cotta, Box, Lid, Kneeling Figures, Green Matte Glaze, Atlantic Terra-Cotta Co., 12 x 9 ½ In.
$236

Humler & Nolan

Terra-Cotta, Bust, Diana, Fernand Cian, Marked, 1889-54, 20 In.
$281

Copake Auction

Figurine, Sphinx, Holding 2 Vases, Blue Glaze, France, c.1900, 23 ½ x 42 ½ In.	1320
Figurine, Wood Base, Jean-Baptiste Carpeaux, Signed, 1827-75, 17 In.	3000
Garden Seat, Bat Handles, Blue, White, Japan, 18 x 14 In., Pair	250
Group, Venus, Cupid, Pedestal, Attributed To Louis-Simon Boizot, c.1775, 12 ½ In.	1250
Incense Burner, Byzantine, Red Clay, Flat Base, Cylindrical Vase, Small Neck, 6 x 4 In.	1100
Jar, Molded Dragon, Cloud, Greek Bolder, Mary Ellen Heibel, 1900s, 37 x 31 x 4 ¾ In.	118
Jar, Wine, Ring Handles, Wrought Iron Stand, 1800s, 28 ½ x 18 In.	369
Jug, Figural, Red, Spout Molded, Face, Eyes & Brows, Drawn In Black, Cream, 4 ¾ In.	295
Ornament, Stylized Flames, Blue, Round Base, 35 In., Pair	352
Pedestal, Winged Griffin, Square Top, c.1925, 31 x 11 In.	550
Planter, Eagle, Stag, Leaves, Scrolls, Embossed, I. Ober & Co., 6 x 8 In.	501
Roundel, Guy Le Gentil, Marquis, Jean-Baptiste Nini, Inscribed, c.1767, 6 In.	1000
Urn, Funeral, Bura-Asinda-Sikka Culture, Niger, 18 x 9 ½ x 10 In.	188
Vase, Nude Woman, Bull, Foot On Neck, Hand On Muzzle, E.F. Hoffman, 1956, 24 x 18 In.	375
Vase, Swan Shape, Plumb Body, Splayed Feet, Feather, Brown Glaze, 3 x 1 ¾ In.	2400

TEXTILES listed here include many types of printed fabrics and table and household linens. Some other textiles will be found under Clothing, Coverlet, Rug, Quilt, etc.

Bag, Camel, Combined Wool, Jaloors, Geometric, Red, Central Asia, 25 x 22 In.	395
Blanket, Silk Ikat Dyed, Amulet, Boteh Pattern, Green Silk Panels, Red Cotton, 82 x 47 In.	300
Blanket, Throw, Cashmere, Red, Pratesi, 5 ½ x 71 In.	510
Blanket, Wool, Cashmere, Natural, Gray, Ivory Stipes, Hermes, 72 x 60 In.	1375
Blanket, Wool, Masonic & Geometric Pattern, Pendleton, 59 x 76 In. .... *illus*	295
Blanket, Wool, Monogram, Olive Green, Black, Hermes, Scotland, 53 x 65 In.	1560
Cloth, Strips, Blue, White, Man, Kente, 63 x 106 In.	120
Flag, American, 13 Stars, Arranged Into 6-Point Star, Glazed Cotton, 11 ½ x 8 In.	2601
Flag, American, 13 Stars, Wool, Grommets, Bunting, 96 x 150 In.	3630
Flag, American, 19 Stars, Cotton, Hand Sewn, Applique, c.1866, 67 x 90 In.	3900
Flag, American, 33 Stars, Cedar Rapids, Iowa, Wool, Stars In Vertical Rows, c.1859, 71 x 139 In.	4920
Flag, American, 33 Stars, Printed, Oregon's Admission Into Union, Medallion Star, 6 x 8 In.	1599
Flag, American, 34 Stars, Linen, 1861-63, 27 ½ x 46 In.	2040
Flag, American, 36 Stars, Cotton, Linen Ground, Frame, c.1867, 75 x 45 In.	1920
Flag, American, 37 Stars, Cotton, Printed, Stars In Rows, Frame, c.1867, 29 ½ x 46 ½ In.	1320
Flag, American, 44 Stars, Hourglass Pattern, Cotton, Stick, Frame, c.1895, 27 x 24 In.	850
Flag, American, 48 Stars, 70 x 114 In.	138
Flag, Japanese, Railroad Lines, Cities From Nanking To Shanghai, 1937, 28 x 20 In.	184
Flag, Japanese, Yosegaki, Cavalry Unit, Red, White, 27 ½ x 31 ½ In.	126
Flag, Union Jack, Great Britain, Wood, Linen Liner, Frame, 30 ½ x 37 In. .... *illus*	3720
Panel, Harem Curtain, Woven, Handloomed, Arabic, 1848, 96 x 70 In.	248
Panel, Heraldic, Needlepoint, Tan, Glass Beads, Flags, Flowers, Brass Pole, Tassels, 1800s, 24 x 21 In.	455
Panel, Plain Weaves, Silk Embroidery, Metal Wrapped Threads, 37 x 20 In.	800
Panel, Suzani, 4 Panels, Red, Blue, Gold, Silk Embroidery, Uzbekistan, c.1875, 70 x 42 In.	1168
Panel, Yacht, Flags, America's Cup, Schwab & Wolf, Copyright 1907, 22 x 22 In. .... *illus*	570
Piano Scarf, Black Silk, Embroidered Pink Flowers, Fringe, Spain, 1930s, 49 x 49 In.	515
Pillow, Needlepoint, Patchwork, Geometric Design, Amish, c.1930, 18 In.	28
Pillow, Persian Mat, Geometric Medallion, Red, Blue & Tan, Turtle Border, 16 x 17 In.	75
Shawl, Paisley, Brown, Red, Green, Gothic Border, Fringe On 2 Sides, 66 x 70 In.	128
Sheet, Linen, Homespun, Needlework, Initials E. H., 78 x 96 In.	60
Table Runner, Silk On Cotton, Geometric, Blue, Green Colored Accents, 1980, 100 x 16 In.	200
Table Runner, Silk, Brocade, Pink, Gold, Continental, 10 x 8 ¼ In.	406
Tablecloth, Cotton, Red & White Checks, Scrolls, Leaves, Fringe, c.1910, 88 x 56 In.	75
Tapestry, Court Scene, Gown, Cape, Flower, Leaves, 79 x 56 In.	472
Tapestry, Court Scene, Woodland, Frame, England, 1800s, 57 ¼ x 43 In.	738
Tapestry, Deer, Forest Pond, Chased By 2 Hunting Dogs, France, 1900s, 49 ½ x 78 ¾ In.	246
Tapestry, Diana, Forest Hunt Scene, Archers, Dogs, Flower Border, Brussels, c.1825, 110 x 113 In.	7188
Tapestry, English Hunt, Needlepoint, Petit Point, 40 x 72 In.	358
Tapestry, Felt, Abstract, Beige, Orange, Blue, Black Ground, Signed A.P., 47 x 44 In.	563
Tapestry, Green, Purple & Red Rectangle, Yellow Border, After Royal Lesotho, Oval, 1970s, 80 x 62 In.	2375

Terra-Cotta, Figurine, Clown, Juggling Balls, Painted, Signed Waylande Gregory, 14 In.
$767

Humler & Nolan

Terra-Cotta, Figurine, Nude Nymph, Rides On Satyr's Shoulders, 21 In.
$1,875

Heritage Auctions

Vintage Printed Cloth
Vintage printed tablecloths and dish towels from the 1940s and '50s are being faked and reproduced today. Copycats have several differences. Vintage tablecloths have one selvage edge that shows. New ones are hemmed on four sides. Old fabrics are "overprinted," each color printed over the last one. Old fabric is "oxidized," so not as white as new textiles.

T

Textile, Blanket, Wool, Masonic & Geometric Pattern, Pendleton, 59 x 76 In.
$295

Hess Auction Group

Textile, Flag, Union Jack, Great Britain, Wood, Linen Liner, Frame, 30 ½ x 37 In.
$3,720

Thomaston Place Auction Galleries

Textile, Panel, Yacht, Flags, America's Cup, Schwab & Wolf, Copyright 1907, 22 x 22 In.
$570

Eldred's Auctioneers and Appraisers

Textile, Tapestry, Lambrizi, Maguey Fiber, Guatemala, After A. Calder, 1975, 56 x 82 In.
$10,000

Rago Arts and Auction Center

Textile, Tapestry, Men, Women, Pond, Boat, France, c.1900, 49 ¾ x 37 ½ In.
$330

Michann's Auctions

Textile, Tapestry, Woman Playing Lute, Plants, Continental, 1800s, 115 x 60 In.
$1,464

Neal Auction Co.

Textile, Tapestry, Moon, Maguey Fiber, Embroidered CA 74, A. Calder, Guatemala, 1974, 56 x 84 In.
$4,688

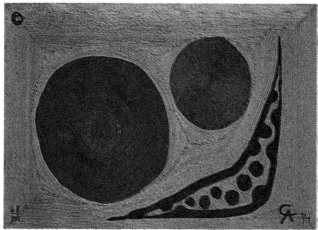

Rago Arts and Auction Center

T

Tapestry, Hanging, Wool, Weave On Back, After Pablo Picasso, 1960s, 72 x 92 In.	4063
Tapestry, Horse In The Afternoon No. 2, Wool, Calman Shemi, 62 x 91 ½ In.	601
Tapestry, House In Trees, Garden, Statue, Fountain, c.1925, 57 x 76 ½ In.	461
Tapestry, King David Entering City, Elaborate Border, Woven, France, c.1775, 107 x 114 In.	9375
Tapestry, Lambrizi, Maguey Fiber, Guatemala, After A. Calder, 1975, 56 x 82 In............... *illus*	10000
Tapestry, Men, Women, Pond, Boat, France, c.1900, 49 ¾ x 37 ½ In..................... *illus*	330
Tapestry, Moon, Maguey Fiber, Embroidered CA 74, A. Calder, Guatemala, 1974, 56 x 84 In. *illus*	4688
Tapestry, Mother & Child, Silk, Silver Thread, Ribbons, Flowers, Navy, Tan, 42 x 30 In..........	184
Tapestry, Needlepoint, 2 Maidens, Iron Rods, Classical, Victorian, 25 x 28 In.	59
Tapestry, Nun, Abbey, Courtyard, 1950, 75 x 48 In..	63
Tapestry, Portiere, Wool, Figures, Leaves, Continental, 133 x 180 In.	2750
Tapestry, Stream, Trees, Sunlight, Pheasant, 48 x 7 In...	12
Tapestry, The Lock, After Pablo Picasso, Black, Red, Cream, 1950s, 80 ¾ x 59 In.	625
Tapestry, Whimsical Portrait, Mimo's Summerhat, Bjorn Wiinblad, Portugal, 1976, 62 x 47 In.	495
Tapestry, Woman Playing Lute, Plants, Continental, 1800s, 115 x 60 In. .... *illus*	1464
Tapestry, Woman, Unicorn, Lion, Attendant, Canopy, Red, Blue, France, 1900s, 88 x 66 In......	500
Tapestry, Wool, Gentleman On Horseback, Forest Landscape, Blue, c.1790, 6 x 4 In.	2125
Tapestry, Wool, Monarch, Soldiers, Campsite, Tents, Villages, Putti, Belgium, 133 x 93 ½ In...	6875
Tapestry, Wool, Verdure, Birds, Forest, Village, 102 x 123 In.	4750
Towel, Alphabet, Fruit, Flowers, Urn, Cotton Tabs, Fringe, Needle Lace, 3 Panels, 1821, 65 x 15 In.	210
Towel, Birds, Crown, Stags, Facing, Hearts, Blossoms, 1809, 50 ⅜ x 12 ¼ In.	210
Wall Hanging, Embroidery, Foo Dogs, Flowers, Basket, 82 x 52 In.	3025
Wall Hanging, Embroidery, Phoenix, Flowers, Leaves, Japan, 80 x 53 ½ In.	1089

THERMOMETER is a name that comes from the Greek word for heat. The thermometer was invented in 1731 to measure the temperature of either water or air. All kinds of thermometers are collected, but those with advertising messages are the most popular.

American Brakeblok, Scottish Terrier, Yellow, 20 ⅛ x 5 ⅝ In.	389
Calumet Baking Powder, Best By Test, Trade Here & Save, Wood, 22 x 5 ¾ In..........	578
Cherub, Curved Feet, Victorian, Bronze, 11 ½ In...	307
Corsall Bros. Truck Lines, Mirrored, Cop, Directing Traffic, 1940s-50s, 22 x 12 In.	483
Dr. Chase's Syrup Of Linseed & Turpentine, Porcelain, 39 x 8 In...............................	1725
Figural, Brass Caution Post, Cat On Hot Tin Roof, Victorian, 6 ¼ In............................	60
Ironbound Storage Warehouses, Motorized Delivery Trucks, Wood, 21 x 8 ⅞ In.	748
Oilzum Motor Oil, Face, Logo, Wood, White & Bagley Co., 24 x 6 In............................	2250
Oilzum, Oil, Lubricants, White & Bagley Co., Wood, 24 x 6 x ¾ In.	2243
Peck's Clean Coal, Liquid-Filled Weather Predictor On Side, Wood, 6 x 7 In..................	161
Pine, Folk Art, Tulips, Birds, Pinwheels, Initials, 48 In......................................	270
Polarine, Saves The Motor, Does Not Thin Out, Wood Frame, 74 x 20 In.	3335
Prestone Antifreeze, White Dial, Red, Blue, Porcelain, Round, 10 In.	661
Red Crown Gasoline, For Power Service Economy, Polarine, 73 x 19 ¼ In.	8625
Trico Wiper Blades, Windshield Shape, Red, White, 15 In..................................... *illus*	204
Wooden, Carved, Mounted, With Brook Trout, Glass Eyes, J. Ahearn, 13 ½ In.	216
Yellow Cab Taxi, Wood, Painted, 15 x 4 In. .... *illus*	708

TIFFANY is a name that appears on items made by Louis Comfort Tiffany, the American glass designer who worked from about 1879 to 1933. His work included iridescent glass, Art Nouveau styles of design, and original contemporary styles. He was also noted for stained glass windows, unusual lamps, bronze work, pottery, and silver. Tiffany & Company, often called "Tiffany," is also listed in this section. The company was started by Charles Lewis Tiffany and John B. Young in 1837 in New York City. In 1853 the name was changed to Tiffany & Company. Louis Tiffany (1848–1933), Charles Tiffany's son, started his own business in 1879. It was named Louis Comfort Tiffany and Associated American Artists. In 1902 the name was changed to Tiffany Studios. Tiffany & Company is a store and is still working today. It is best known for silver and fine jewelry. Louis worked for his father's company as a decorator in 1900 but at the same time was working for his Tiffany Studios. Other types of Tiffany are listed under Tiffany Glass, Tiffany Gold, Tiffany Pottery, or Tiffany Silver. The famous Tiffany lamps are listed in this section. Tiffany jewelry is listed in the Jewelry and

Thermometer, Trico Wiper Blades, Windshield Shape, Red, White, 15 In. $204

Milestone Auctions

Thermometer, Yellow Cab Taxi, Wood, Painted, 15 x 4 In. $708

AntiqueAdvertising.com

Tiffany, Lamp, 6-Light, Turtleback Shade, Leaded Glass, Favrile, Bronze, c.1910, 64 In.
$30,000

Rago Arts and Auction Center

Tiffany, Lamp, Iridescent Shade, Blown-Out Bronze Base, Cabochons, Tiffany Studios, 15 In.
$6,250

Rago Arts and Auction Center

Wristwatch categories. Some Tiffany Studio desk sets have matching clocks. They are listed here. Clocks made by Tiffany & Co. are listed in the Clock category. Reproductions of some types of Tiffany are being made.

L.C. Tiffany
1848–1933

Tiffany Studios
1902–1919

TIFFANY STUDIOS NEW YORK.
Tiffany Studios
1902–1922+

Item	Price
Blotter Rocker, Bronze, Knurled Handle, Fish Swimming, Brown Patina, 5 x 3 In.	1210
Bookends, Bronze, Cats On Platform, Marked, 7 x 6 ½ In.	3327
Bookends, Dog, Reclining, Bronze, Marked, G. Gardet, 7 x 9 ⅝ In.	1200
Candelabrum, 6-Light, Bronze, Candle Cups, Glass Inserts, 21 x 15 ¼ In.	5445
Candelabrum, 8-Light, Gilt Bronze, Textured Surface, Marked, c.1925, 15 x 14 In.	1500
Candelabrum, Bronze, Jeweled, 3 Arms, Candle Cups, Green Glass Cabochons, Marked, 14 In.	7865
Candelabrum, Glass Band, Jewels, Leaf Shape, 4 Curving Arms, Candle Cups, 12 ¼ In.	9922
Candlestick, Blue Iridescent, Tulip Shape Lamp, Vertical Ribbed Body, 15 ¼ In.	4840
Candlestick, Bronze, Blown Glass, Brown & Green, Marked, c.1925, 18 In.	813
Candlestick, Bronze, Double Pivots, Retractable, Brown, Green Highlights, 7 ⅜ In.	5445
Candlestick, Bronze, Organic Form, Root Legs, Brown Patina, Marked, 9 ½ In., Pair	1210
Candlestick, Bronze, Root Form, Tapered Stem, Blown Green Glass Cup, Marked, 12 In.	968
Candlestick, Bronze, Round Foot, Slender Stem, Bulbous Candle Cup, 18 ¾ In., Pair	1512
Chamberstick, 2-Light, Bronze Lily Pad Tray, 3 Gourd Candle Cups, Glass Inserts, Marked, 6 In.	4840
Chandelier, White Glass 12-In. Globe, Gold Iridescent Leaves, Bronze Collar, Fixture, 34 In.	10285
Desk Accessory, Letter Rack, Utility Box, Grape Clusters, Gold Patina, Abalone, 2 Piece, 9 ½ In.	2420
Desk Set, American Indian Pattern, Gold Patina, Paper Rack, Inkwell, Signed, 5 Piece	1089
Frame, Acid-Etched Pine Needle, Bronze, Oval Picture Opening, Marked, 7 x 6 In.	1089
Humidor, Bronze, Shouldered, Sailing Ship Border, Stormy Seas, Lid, Glass Liner, Marked, 6 In.	968
Inkwell, Abalone, 8 Panels, Grape Leaves, Gold Patina, Signed, 4 x 4 In.	544
Inkwell, Bronze, 3 Men Tugging On Rope, Tied To Treasure Chest, Faceted Jewels, 10 In.	17545
Inkwell, Wild Carrot, Bronze, Stamped Tiffany Studios, c.1902, 4 x 5 ¼ In.	6250
Jewelry Box, Bronze, Italian Renaissance Design, Floral, Scroll Panels, Marked, 3 x 8 In.	3025
Lamp Base, Bronze, 4 Legs With Cat's Paws, Adjustable, X-Shape Base, 6 Sockets, 42 In.	9075
Lamp, 3-Light, Mushroom Shade, Urn Base, Patinated Bronze, c.1900, 21 ½ x 16 In.	12500
Lamp, 4-Light, Greek Key Shade, Patinated Bronze, Slag Glass, c.1910, 28 x 20 In.	17500
Lamp, 6-Light, Turtleback Shade, Leaded Glass, Favrile, Bronze, c.1910, 64 In. *illus*	30000
Lamp, Acorn Shade, Mottled Green Glass, Bronze Pillow Base, Ball Feet, 22 In.	7200
Lamp, Bronze Mermaid, Arms, Torso Extending Out Of Water, Raised Nautilus Shell, 15 ¾ In.	7260
Lamp, Bronze, Urn Shape, 4 Ribbed Legs, Domed Shade 7 In., Lamp 15 In.	4840
Lamp, Candlestick, Gold Luster, Twisted, Green, Electrified, Single Socket, 3 x 7 In.	410
Lamp, Desk, 3-Light, Lily, Hooked Handle, Marked, c.1925, 9 In.	4000
Lamp, Desk, 3-Light, Patinated Bronze, Favrile, c.1910, 10 x 12 x 10 In.	3000
Lamp, Desk, Gold Dore, Impressed Band, 17 x 8 In.	3025
Lamp, Desk, Turtleback, Footed, Green Cabochon Jewels, Blue Iridescent Shade, 14 In.	10285
Lamp, Iridescent Shade, Blown-Out Bronze Base, Cabochons, Tiffany Studios, 15 In. *illus*	6250
Lamp, Iridescent Stretch Glass Shade, Green Pulled Feather, Twisted Base, 3 Parts, 14 x 7 In.	650
Lamp, Lily, 3-Light, Bronze, Patina, Favrile Glass, Stamped Tiffany Studios, 13 x 8 ½ In.	2875
Lamp, Lily, 10-Light, Bronze, Gold Favrile, Gooseneck Arms, Signed, 21 In. *illus*	19360
Lamp, Linenfold Shade, Green Glass, Bronze Candlestick Base, Tiffany Studios, 22 In. *illus*	12980
Lamp, Mushrooms, Pink, Cream, Green Geometric, Shade 16 In., Lamp 21 ½ In.	8470
Lamp, Nautilus Shell, Bronze Wishbone Stand, Ribbed Base, Stamped Markings, 1904, 11 x 5 ½ In.	6215
Lamp, Platform Foot, Arched Harp, Green Linenfold Shade, Shade 6 ¾ In., Lamp 12 In.	4840
Lamp, Swirling Leaf Design, Mottled Yellow & Cream, Green Ground, 23 x 18 In.	11495
Lamp, Turtleback Shade, Bronze Base, Leaf Design, Signed, 14 In.	9680
Lamp, Turtleback Tile, Leaded, Bronze, Favrile, 1920, Pair	6250
Lamp, Weight Balance, Bronze, Tulip Shade, Gold Favrile Glass, 13 x 14 In.	2875
Lamp, Zodiac, Bronze, Gilt, Adjustable Shade, Acid Etched, c.1920, 13 ½ x 11 In.	1500

T

Tiffany, Lamp, Lily, 10-Light, Bronze, Gold Favrile, Gooseneck Arms, Signed, 21 In.
$19,360

James D. Julia Auctioneers

Tiffany, Lamp, Linenfold Shade, Green Glass, Bronze Candlestick Base, Tiffany Studios, 22 In.
$12,980

Cottone Auctions

Tiffany Glass, Bowl, Flower Frog, Heart, Vine Pattern, Blown, Wheel Carved, Favrile, c.1918, 5 x 13 In.
$938

Rago Arts and Auction Center

Tiffany Glass, Candle Lamp, Blue Favrile, Ruffled, Twisted Stem, Ribbed Shade, L.C.T., 12 In.
$3,600

James D. Julia Auctioneers

> **TIP**
> To be sure you have a genuine Tiffany lamp, you must find the words **Tiffany and Co.** printed on the metal base. The glass shades were also marked **L.C. Tiffany** or just with the letters **L.C.T.** According to the records of the Tiffany Company, all lamps were marked.

Tiffany Glass, Toothpick Holder, Lily Pads, Gold Iridescent, 1895, 2¼ In.
$380

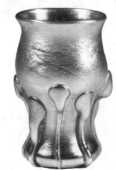

Jeffrey S. Evans

Tiffany Glass, Vase, Blue, Brown Shoulder, Footed, Favrile, Tel El Amarna, L.C. Tiffany, c.1910, 12 In.
$7,995

Skinner, Inc.

Tiffany Glass, Vase, Flower Form, Gold Iridescent, Ruffled Rim, Domed Foot, Favrile, 11 In.
$2,250

Rago Arts and Auction Center

T

Tiffany Glass, Vase, Gold Iridescent, Red, Favrile, Exhibition Piece, Louis C. Tiffany, c.1900, 6¾ In.
$33,210

Skinner, Inc.

Tiffany Glass, Vase, Gold Iridescent, Trailing Vines, Favrile, Marked, L.C. Tiffany, c.1910, 8¾ In.
$4,920

Skinner, Inc.

Tiffany Glass, Vase, Jack-In-The-Pulpit, Gold Favrile, Etched L.C. Tiffany, c.1908, 20 In.
$5,625

Rago Arts and Auction Center

Tiffany Pottery, Vase, Cypriote, Lava-Like Bands, Waves, Favrile, L.C. Tiffany, 3½ In.
$7,563

James D. Julia Auctioneers

Tiffany Pottery, Vase, Runny Glaze, Earth Tones, 3 Handles, Favrile, Incised L.C.T., c.1920, 12½ In.
$2,000

Rago Arts and Auction Center

Tiffany Silver, Candlestick, Urn Socket, Paneled Post, 6-Sided Base, Tiffany & Co., c.1950, 8 In., Pair
$1,020

Brunk Auctions

Tiffany Silver, Pitcher, Water, Repousse Band, Flowers, Marked, Tiffany & Co., c.1885, 7 In.
$1,920

Brunk Auctions

TIP

Taking part in the arts by going to shows, galleries, auctions, museums, classes, and lectures, and maybe even garage sales to search for collectibles has a positive impact on your health and well-being according to a recent British study.

Letter Holder, Pine Needle Pattern, Slag Glass, Marked, 6 x 10 In.	720
Letter Rack, Zodiac, Bronze, Gold Dore, 2 Sections, Marked, 6 x 9 ½ In.	354
Matchbook Holder, Zodiac, Bronze, Gold Dore, With Tray, Marked, 3 ½ x 4 ½ In.	295
Paper Clip Holder, Zodiac, Bronze, Gold Dore, Marked, 2 x 4 In.	236
Paperweight, Bronze, Wave Design, Iridescent Green Glass, Centered Panel, Marked, 4 In.	2722
Paperweight, Bronze, Zodiac, Gold Patina, Marked, 3 ½ x 2 In.	1210
Pen Tray, Zodiac, Bronze, Gold Dore, Marked, 3 x 10 In.	189
Sconce, 2-Light, Lily, Striped Shades, Patinated Bronze, Favrile, c.1910, 10 x 5 x 5 In., Pair	4375
Sconce, Bronze Beaded Wall Plate, Gooseneck Arm, Gold Favrile Shade, Signed, 7 ½ In., Pair	10285
Shade, Lamp, Bronze, Brown Patina, Band Encircling Rim, Geometric, Marked, 11 ½ In.	726
Torchiere, Bronze Base, Hexagonal Foot, Tall, Slender Shade, Apple Blossom, 64 In., Pair	45375
Vase, Grayish, Opal, Green Leaves, Bronze Base, Trumpet Shape, Favrile, Signed, 14 In.	1652

TIFFANY GLASS

Bowl, Blue Iridescent, Bronze Base, Louis C. Tiffany Furnaces Inc., 4 ¾ x 11 In.	600
Bowl, Blue Iridescent, Ribbed, Leaf & Vine Design, Favrile, c.1900, 10 ½ In.	2400
Bowl, Flower Frog, Heart, Vine Pattern, Blown, Wheel Carved, Favrile, c.1918, 5 x 13 In... *illus*	938
Bowl, Flower Frog, Heart, Vine, Gold Iridescent, Blown, Wheel Carved, Favrile, c.1918, 4 x 12 In.	1375
Bowl, Gold Iridescent, Scalloped Rim, Wide Ribs, Favrile, 1920s, 2 ¼ In.	210
Bowl, Iridescent, Raised, Twisted Prunts, Favrile, Bulbous, Circular, L.C.T., 2 x 4 ½ In.	181
Bowl, Iridescent, Silver Outside, Gold Inside, Undulating Rim, 3 x 7 In.	780
Bowl, Iridescent, Stretch Glass, Deep Flutes, Favrile, L.C.T., 2 ¼ x 6 In.	192
Bowl, Ruffled Flower Form, Blue, Green, Iridescent, Favrile, 3 x 9 ¾ In.	2242
Bowl, Scalloped Rim, Opalescent Light Purple, Pink Stripes, Favrile, 1896, 3 ½ x 8 ½ In.	1534
Bowl, Underplate, Finger, Blue Favrile, c.1920, Bowl, 2 x 4 In., Plate, 6 ¼ In.	500
Candle Lamp, Blue Favrile, Ruffled, Twisted Stem, Ribbed Shade, L.C.T., 12 In. *illus*	3600
Candleholder, Removable Glass Stick, Rib Swirl Design, Gold Iridescent, Signed LCT, 9 In.	270
Compote, Pastel, Yellow, L.C.T., Favrile, 3 ¾ x 8 In.	330
Compote, Sapphire Blue, Gold, Purple Highlighting, Marked, Favrile, 6 x 10 In.	767
Fireplace Surround, Marble, Mosaic Glass, Green, Blue, Gold, White Glass Tiles, 39 x 46 In.	2420
Inkwell, Bakelite Insert, Reddish-Brown, Green Highlights, 6 x 8 In.	4235
Lamp, Candlestick, Gold Favrile, Twisted Ribbed Base, Green, White, Flower Form, Ruffled, 3 x 7 In.	1416
Prisms, Favrile, Gold Iridescence, Flashes Of Pink, Blue, Green, 15 Prisms, 10 In.	1573
Shade, Linenfold, Leaded, Frosted, Gold Iridescent, Flared, 1948, 6 x 12 In.	4375
Shade, Tulip, Gold, Purple, Pink, Iridescent Waves, Green Ground, Signed, 5 In.	3630
Toothpick Holder, Lily Pads, Gold Iridescent, 1895, 2 ¼ In. *illus*	380
Vase, Bird Form, Blue Iridescent, Pink, Green, Gold, Highlights, Favrile, Signed, 4 ½ In.	6655
Vase, Blue, Brown Shoulder, Footed, Favrile, Tel El Amarna, L.C. Tiffany, c.1910, 12 In. ... *illus*	7995
Vase, Bud, Heart & Vine, Blue Iridescent, 6 ¼ In.	1404
Vase, Cypriote, Bulbous, Cylindrical Neck, Gold Lava, Purple, Green, Favrile, Signed, 5 In.	6050
Vase, Double Handle, Amphora, Gold, Favrile, 7 ½ x 6 ½ In.	767
Vase, El Amarna, Iridescent Green, Gold King Tut Design, Shouldered, Gold Design Collar, 7 In.	3025
Vase, Flower Form, Bulbous Body, Ruffled Rim, Footed, Iridescent Blue, Favrile, Signed, 5 In.	968
Vase, Flower Form, Gold Iridescent, Ruffled Rim, Domed Foot, Favrile, 11 In. *illus*	2250
Vase, Flower Form, White, Green, c.1920, 13 In.	3427
Vase, Gold Iridescent, Green Heart & Vine, Tortoiseshell, L.C. Tiffany, Favrile, 8 In.	210
Vase, Gold Iridescent, Red, Favrile, Exhibition Piece, Louis C. Tiffany, c.1900, 6 ¾ In. *illus*	33210
Vase, Gold Iridescent, Rolled Rim Bud, Ribbing, L.C. Tiffany, Favrile, 10 In.	480
Vase, Gold Iridescent, Trailing Vines, Favrile, Marked, L.C. Tiffany, c.1910, 8 ¾ In. *illus*	4920
Vase, Gold Pulled Feather Decoration, Hooked Feather Foot, Opal, L.C.T., 12 x 4 In.	1469
Vase, Iridescent, Gourd-Like, Lobed, Ribbed Cup, Scalloped Rim, L.C. Tiffany, Favrile, 13 x 5 In.	1469
Vase, Iridescent, Pulled Feather, Tapered, 6-Sided Top, Bronze Dore Base, c.1905, 13 In.	2450
Vase, Iridescent, Shouldered Form, Fluted & Coiled Handles, Circular Foot, L.C. Tiffany, Favrile, 6 x 4 In.	593
Vase, Jack-In-The-Pulpit, Gold Favrile, Etched L.C. Tiffany, c.1908, 20 In. *illus*	5625
Vase, King Tut, Gold Iridescent Body, Platinum Iridescence, Signed, 6 In.	1573
Vase, Leaf & Vine, Black & Blue, Blown, Applied, Favrile, c.1901, 6 ⅜ x 3 ¾ In.	10625
Vase, Squat, Flared Rim, Yellow Pastel, Opalescent Ribbons, Favrile, Signed, 6 In.	3630
Vase, Trumpet, Gold Iridescent, 8 Cut, Flute Panels, L.C. Tiffany, Favrile, 12 In.	480
Vase, Trumpet, Gold Iridescent, Engraved Vine, L.C. Tiffany, Favrile, 15 x 7 ½ In.	840
Vase, Trumpet, Gold Iridized, Ribbed Panels, Favrile, 12 In.	735

Tiffany Silver, Punch Ladle, Renaissance Pattern, Gilt Bowl, Marked, 1900s, 15 ¼ In.
$1,080

Cowan's Auctions

Tiffany Silver, Tongs, Wave Edge, Openwork Bowl, Claw, Monogram, 5 ½ In.
$501

Alex Cooper Auctioneers

Tiffany Silver, Vase, Trumpet Shape, Fluted, Reeded Stem, Beaded Collar, N.Y., 25 In.
$3,900

Eldred's Auctioneers and Appraisers

This is an edited listing of current prices. Visit **Kovels.com** to check thousands of prices from previous years and sign up for free information on trends, tips, reproductions, marks, and more.

Tile, Organ Grinder, Monkey, Square, Frame, Harding Black, 10 In.
$189

Humler & Nolan

Tile, Parrots, California Clay Products, Frame, 1923-33, 16 x 6 In., Pair
$875

Rago Arts and Auction Center

Tobacco Jar, Figural, Dwarf, Sitting On Stump, Terra-Cotta, Bernard Bloch, 12 In.
$390

Fox Auctions

Vase, Trumpet, Ribbed Panels, Flaring Paneled Foot, Gold Favrile, 12 In.	410
Vase, Wheel Carved Pink Flowers, Leaves, 4 Oval Panels, Signed, 6 In. Diam.	5445

TIFFANY POTTERY

Vase, Cypriote, Lava-Like Bands, Waves, Favrile, L.C. Tiffany, 3 1/2 In.	illus	7563
Vase, Runny Glaze, Earth Tones, 3 Handles, Favrile, Incised L.C.T., c.1920, 12 1/2 In.	illus	2000

TIFFANY SILVER

Bowl Fruit, Flowers, 4 Crested Feet, Monogram JLS, New York, Before 1902, 4 1/2 x 9 In.		1250
Bowl, 14 Panels, Reticulated Top Edge, Leaf & Scroll Decoration, 1907-47, 3 x 10 In.		544
Bowl, Center, Hammered, Gadrooned, Molded Rim, Flared Foot, 1918, 6 x 15 In.		3750
Bowl, Clover Leaves, Scrolls, Tiffany & Co., 2 3/4 x 10 x 18 In.		188
Bowl, Openwork Lattice Reserves, Monogram, 15 In.		968
Cake Plate, Monogram, Engraved Laurel & Rose Paneled Border, c.1922, 12 In.		750
Candelabrum, 2 Scrolling Arms, Repousse Ferns & Flowers, c.1900, 14 In., Pair		1875
Candlestick, Rococo Style, Marked, Tiffany & Co., c.1910, 9 3/4 In., 4 Piece		554
Candlestick, Tapered, Fluted, Beaded Bands, Bellflowers, Acanthus, 1914, 9 In., Pair		1000
Candlestick, Urn Socket, Paneled Post, 6-Sided Base, Tiffany & Co., c.1950, 8 In., Pair	illus	1020
Cocktail Shaker, Handle Tapering Spout, Cap Attached By Chain, 1900s, 10 1/2 In.		984
Ice Bucket, Monogram, 9 x 6 In.		1250
Italian, Serving Spoon, Pierced, Tiffany, 1870, 8 1/4 x 2 1/2 In.		350
Loving Cup, 3 Handles, Round Foot, 1900-15, 7 1/4 x 8 1/4 In.		554
Perfume, Bell Epoque Pattern, Chased Putti, Bulbous, Shaped Neck, 8 In., Pair		1464
Pitcher, Water, Repousse Band, Flowers, Marked, Tiffany & Co., c.1885, 7 In.	illus	1920
Plate, Bread, Oval, Reeded Border, Marked Tiffany & Co., 10 1/2 In.		180
Platter, Quatrefoil Medallions, Serpentine Flower & Ribbon Edge, 1921, 16 x 12 In.		1375
Platter, Well & Tree Center, Oval, 4-Footed, c.1950, 14 3/4 x 20 In.		2250
Porringer, Openwork Handle, Round, Hammered, Marked, April 3rd, Ethel, 1884, 8 In.		545
Punch Ladle, Renaissance Pattern, Gilt Bowl, Marked, 1900s, 15 1/4 In.	illus	1080
Ramekin, Rocaille Shells, Shaped Tab Handle, Porcelain Liner, c.1905, 4 In., 10 Piece		688
Tea & Coffee Set, Pear Shape, Dome Lids, Rosebud Finial, Rosewood Handle, 5 Piece		2250
Teapot, Chased, Repousse, Birds, Flowers, Branches, Ebonized Wood Handle, 7 x 10 1/4 In.		1500
Tongs, Wave Edge, Openwork Bowl, Claw, Monogram, 5 1/2 In.	illus	501
Tray, Presentation Piece, Paul Henson, Tiffany & Co., 14 x 19 In.		880
Vase, Hammered, Oval, Waisted Neck, Wavy Flared-Out Rim, 11 3/4 x 7 In.		1625
Vase, Trumpet Shape, Fluted, Reeded Stem, Beaded Collar, N.Y., 25 In.	illus	3900

TIFFIN Glass Company of Tiffin, Ohio, was a subsidiary of the United States Glass Co. of Pittsburgh, Pennsylvania, in 1892. The U.S. Glass Co. went bankrupt in 1963, and the Tiffin plant employees purchased the building and the inventory. They continued running it from 1963 to 1966, when it was sold to Continental Can Company. In 1969, it was sold to Interpace, and in 1980, it was closed. The black satin glass, made from 1923 to 1926, and the stemware of the last 20 years are the best-known products.

Black Satin, Vase, Gold Cattail, 1920s, 8 In.	85
Bull's-Eye, Biscuit Jar, No Lid, 6 1/2 In.	100
Deerwood, Compote, Rolled Edge, 1920s, 4 1/4 x 6 3/4 In.	75
Fuchsia, Bowl, Console, Flared, 12 5/8 x 3 1/4 In.	75
Minton, Pitcher, Gold Etched Band, Lid, 9 In.	89

TILES have been used in most countries of the world as a sturdy building material for floors, roofs, fireplace surrounds, and surface toppings. The cuerda seca (dry cord) technique of decoration uses a greasy pigment to separate different glaze colors during firing. In cuenca (raised line) decorated tiles, the design is impressed, leaving ridges that separate the glaze colors. Many of the American tiles are listed in this book under the factory name.

3 Ships, Santa Maria, Bounty & Mayflower, Unmarked, Moravian, Frame, 4 x 4 In.	275
Carmel Mission, Cloud, Sky, Hills, California Faience, 5 1/2 In.	437
Cockatoo, Teal Ground, Karlsruhe, 1900s, 10 In.	96
Deer, Flowers, Blue, Brown & Tan High Glazes, Moravian, Frame, 5 3/4 x 7 In.	275

Frieze, Still Life, Pitcher, Buildings, Yellow, Green, Red, Henry Varnum Poor, 16 x 37 In.	10000
Gentlemen Playing Backgammon, Green Majolica Glaze, Signed, 1890s, 4 ½ In....................	200
Horse, Brown, Rider, Red Tunic, Falcon In Hand, Blue Band, Flowers, White, Persia, 8 x 5 In.	59
Hunters, On Camelback, Decorated Bands, Multicolor, Persia, 15 x 15 In.	649
Lion, Leo, Zodiac, Unglazed Dark Gray, Molded, Arts & Crafts, 1920s, 4 In.	48
Matte Glaze, Red Clay, Arts & Crafts Wooden Frame, Alhambra Co., Marked, c.1900, Tile 6 x 6 In.	201
Minstrel, Playing Flute, Gothic Window, Blue, White, 21 ½ x 9 ½ In.	184
Organ Grinder, Monkey, Square, Frame, Harding Black, 10 In. .... *illus*	189
Parrots, California Clay Products, Frame, 1923-33, 16 x 6 In., Pair .... *illus*	875
Pink Poppy, Green, Teal, Arts & Crafts, Motawi Tile Works, 5 ¾ x 5 ¾ In.	93
Puss In Boots, Colorful Glazes, Mueller Tile Co., Frame, 9 x 9 In.	106
Puss In Boots, Colorful Glazes, Impressed 9627 On Bottom, Frame, Mueller, 6 x 6 In.......	90
Rabbit, Crouching, Lettuce Field, Dark Green On Lighter, Matte Glazes, 1904, 6 x 6 In.	2583
Rabbit, Sitting, White, Blue, Green Matte Glazes, Original Arts, 1904, 7 ¾ x 7 ¾ In.	1353
Roof, Tartar & Sumerian, On Guardian Lions, Green, Yellow Clothing, 1800s, 27 In., Pair......	1625
Stove, Girl In Bonnet, Facing Left, Light Tone Brown Glaze, 4 In.	125
Stove, Snapshot Tile Industry, 2 Triangles On Reverse, 1890s, 1 ½ In.	40
Stove, Woman Facing Right, Blue, Round, 2 ⅛ In., 2 Piece.....................	85
Woman Boiling Her Wash, Brown County Pottery, Incised, Frame, 10 x 10 In.....................	130
Woman, Washing Clothes, Blue Green Majolica Glaze, Molded, Arts & Crafts, 6 x 6 x ½ In.......	150

TINWARE containers for household use have been made in America since the seventeenth century. The first tin utensils were brought from Europe, but by 1798, tin plate was imported and local tinsmiths made the wares. Painted tin is called tole and is listed separately. Some tin kitchen items may be found listed under Kitchen. The lithographed tin containers used to hold food and tobacco are listed in the Advertising category under Tin.

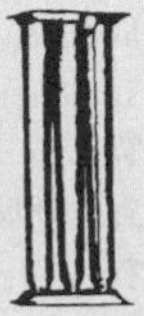

Candleholder, 2 Candles, 1800s, 34 In.	610
Coffeepot, Wrigglework, Potted Flowers, Interlacing Bands, c.1840, 11 In.	1830
Highchair Tray, Blind Man's Bluff, Lithograph, Unmarked, 10 ½ x 15 In.	396
Highchair Tray, Cat's Circus Picture, Lithograph, Louis Wain, 1860-1939, 10 ½ x 15 In.	2712
Lamp Filler, Cylindrical, Shaped Spout, Wire Bail Handle, Pennsylvania, 1800s, 9 In.	12
Parade Torch, Conical Reservoir, Stick Tube, c.1850, 10 In.	46
Sign, Painted, Lettered Hamburgers, Wood Frame, 12 x 71 ½ In.	224
Spice Grinder, Flower Spray, Compartmented, 3 x 6 In.	1037
Teapot, Swing Handle, Straight Spout, 1800s, 7 In.	305
Tub, Dark Green, Light Blue Interior, Handles, 1900s, 8 ¾ x 14 ½ In.	46

TOBACCO CUTTERS *may be listed in either the Advertising or Store categories.*

TOBACCO JAR collectors search for those made in odd shapes and colors. Because tobacco needs special conditions of humidity and air, it has been stored in special containers since the eighteenth century. Some may be found in Advertising in this book.

Coffin Shape, Burled Walnut, Mahogany, Humidor, 17 x 11 In.	96
Dog Resting On Front Paws, Hinged Head, Black Forest Style, Humidor, 1800s, 10 ½ x 6 In.	938
Figural, Dwarf, Sitting On Stump, Terra-Cotta, Bernard Bloch, 12 In. .... *illus*	390
Figural, Fisherman's Head, Sou'wester Rain Hat, Clay Pipe, Pewter Insert, Humidor, 11 In.	213
Humidor, John Bull Figure, Musical, Cylinder, Spring Driven, 15 x 5 x 4 In.............	424
Humidor, Lid, Tabac De Tonnin, Faience, c.1800, 7 ¾ x 6 ¾ In. .... *illus*	427
Silver, Cut Crystal, Lid, Repousse, Humidor, S. Kirk & Son, 6 ½ In.	369
Wood, Mixed Metals, Scottish Thistle, Humidor, c.1900, 21 x 12 ½ In.	2500

TOBY JUG is the name of a very special form of pitcher. It is shaped like the full figure of a man or woman. A pitcher that shows just the top half of a person is not correctly called a toby. It is sometimes called a character jug. More examples of toby jugs can be found under Royal Doulton and other factory names.

Guardsman, Seated, Shorter & Son, England, 1940s, 4 ½ In.	15
Man, Arms Crossed, Jacket, Hat, Portugal, 10 In..........................	62
Man, Seated, Jug On Knee, Full Length Coat, Blue & White Delft, 11 x 5 x 4 In.	350

Tobacco Jar, Humidor, Lid, Tabac De Tonnin, Faience, c.1800, 7 ¾ x 6 ¾ In. **$427**

Neal Auction Co.

Toby Jug, Man Carrying Jug Of Beer, Blue Jacket, Yellow Pants, 1900s, Staffordshire, 11 In. **$585**

Ruby Lane

Toby Jugs
The Toby jug shaped like a seated man was named for Toby Philpot, a notorious drinker mentioned in a song written in 1761. Toby jugs were popular from 1776 to 1825, but many later versions have been made.

Tole, Box, Document, Japanned, Dome Top, Wire Ring Handle, 1800s, 6 x 10 In. $236

Hess Auction Group

Tole, Box, Lid, Black, Flowers, Red, Green, Yellow Leaves, Attributed To Oliver Filley, 1800s, 8 x 10 In. $554

Skinner, Inc.

Tole, Teakettle, Hinged Lid, C-Scroll Handle, Flowers, Leaves, Japanned Ground, 1800s, 9 In. $413

Hess Auction Group

Tole, Tray, 2 Women, Neoclassical Decoration, Oval, Handles, England, 1800s, 26 x 19 In. $300

Cowan's Auctions

Man Carrying Jug Of Beer, Blue Jacket, Yellow Pants, 1900s, Staffordshire, 11 In. .... *illus*	585
Napoleon, Alfred B. Evans, Philadelphia, 11 In.	750
Napoleon, Multicolor, 9½ In.	125
Oliver Twist, Wood & Sons, 5½ In.	75
Ordinary Toby, Jug Of Ale On Knee, Blue & White, France, 1900s, 11 In.	350
Snuff Taker, Staffordshire, c.1860, 12 In.	155
Woman, Seated, Peggotty, Wood & Sons, England, 6 In.	59

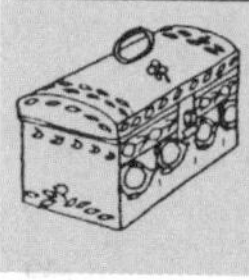

TOLE is painted tin. It is sometimes called japanned ware, pontypool, or toleware. Most nineteenth-century tole is painted with an orange-red or black background and multicolored decorations. Many recent versions of toleware are made and sold. Related items may be listed in the Tinware category.

Bin, For God For Country, & For Yale, Eagle, Shield, Black, Handle, Clasp, 14½ x 12 In.	93
Box, Document, Japanned, Dome Top, Wire Ring Handle, 1800s, 6 x 10 In. .... *illus*	236
Box, Lid, Black, Flowers, Red, Green, Yellow Leaves, Attributed To Oliver Filley, 1800s, 8 x 10 In. .. *illus*	554
Candle Box, Hanging, Canister Shape, Clasp, 11 x 9 In.	175
Coffeepot, Black, Yellow Band At Mouth, Red & Green Flower Band, 1800s, 10¼ In.	397
Coffeepot, Lighthouse Shape, Yellow Bird, Brass Mushroom Finial, C-Scroll Handle, 11 In.	649
Coffeepot, Partridge, Red & Yellow Flowers, Sheet Iron, 8 In.	234
Plant Stand, Japanned, Brass, Black, Flowers, 32 In.	234
Sconce, 3-Light, Paint & Porcelain Mounted, Bouquet Form, 1900s, 19 x 11 In., Pair	366
Teakettle, Hinged Lid, C-Scroll Handle, Flowers, Leaves, Japanned Ground, 1800s, 9 In.. *illus*	413
Tray, 2 Women, Neoclassical Decoration, Oval, Handles, England, 1800s, 26 x 19 In. .... *illus*	300
Tray, Black, Exotic Birds, Gilt Scrolls, Shaped, Raised Edge, Black Stand, Victorian, 24 In.	427
Tray, Metal, 2 Handles, Currier & Ives Style Sledding Scene, 20 x 16 In.	30
Tray, Naval Officer, Palm Trees, Decorated Border, Yellow, France, 22¼ x 17½ In.	640
Tray, Octagonal, Handle, Woman In Countryside, Holding Bird, Gold Border, 28 x 19 In.	330
Tray, Octagonal, Painted, Town, Oak Leaves, Gilt Flowers, Cutout Handles, 30 x 21½ In.	200
Tray, Octagonal, Red Border, Fruit, Leaves, 1800s, 6 x 8¾ In.	5124
Tray, Pastoral Courting Scene, Red & Black Panels, Ivy, Gold, Steel, Round, England, 1800s, 26 In.	330
Tray, Red Buds, Green, Yellow Leaves, Mottled, Rolled Rim, 8½ x 12½ In.	324
Tray, Shaped, Birds, Flowers, Mother-Of-Pearl, Multicolor, 1850-90, 24 x 17 In.	225
Urn, Asian Decoration, Black Ground, 12½ x 7¾ In., Pair... *illus*	660
Watering Can, Egrets, Grasses, Turquoise & Orange Ground, Tapered, Bird Finial, 17 In.	224

TOM MIX was born in 1880 and died in 1940. He was the hero of over 100 silent movies from 1910 to 1929, and 25 sound films from 1929 to 1935. There was a Ralston Tom Mix radio show from 1933 to 1950, but the original Tom Mix was not in the show. Tom Mix comics were published from 1942 to 1953.

Badge, Captain, Ralston Straight Shooter, Embossed, Silvered, Brass, 2 In.............................	65
Pitcher, Glass, Blue, Portrait, 4 x 4 In.	30

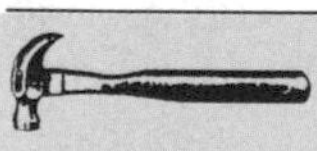

TOOLS of all sorts are listed here, but most are related to industry. Other tools may be found listed under Iron, Kitchen, Tinware, and Wooden.

Adze, Basalt Head, Carved, Reticulated Handle, Polynesia, 1800s-1900s, 28 x 10 In..................	2160
Anvil, Jeweler's, 3 x 3½ In.	88
Apple Press, Superior Drill Co., Wood & Iron, Bin, Crank, Plank Legs, c.1905, 48 x 33 In.........	1350
Asparagus Bundler, E. Watts, Iron, Patented Dec. 6, 1887, 8 x 10 In....................................	30
Bench, Cobbler's, Oak, Compartment, Tray, Leather Strapping, Box Drawer, 20 x 39 In... *illus*	1270
Bench, Cobblers, Pine, 6 Square Nailed Drawers, Lower Shelf, c.1850, 51 x 46 In.	450
Book Press, Mahogany, Mised Wood Veneers, Drawer, 1900-25, 24 x 15 In. .... *illus*	330
Carrier, Wood, Handle, 1900s, 25¼ x 9 In..	117
Chest, Oak, Pine, Other Woods, Iron Bail Handles, Multi-Drawer, 1800s, 20 x 38 In..................	960
Hairdryer Chair, Metal Frame, Vinyl, Attached Hood, Adjustable, Turbinado, 1950s................	820
Ladder, Wooden, Folding, Painted, 72 In..	132
Lawn Mower, Hand Crank, Johnson Lawn Mower Co., 1878, 47½ x 30 In. .... *illus*	960
Lens Measure, Optometrist, Metal, Glass Dial, Geneva Lens Measure, c.1910, 2 In. Diam.	45

Level, D.M. Lyon, Cherry, Brass Horizontal Sight, Hanger Hole Drilled, 30 In.	13
Level, Edward Helb, The American Combined Level, Cherry, 24 In.	25
Level, Transit, Model 320, Berger, Wooden Case	189
Plane, Molding, E. Nutting, Plank Style Jointer, 22 In.	18
Plane, Molding, E.W. Carpenter, Adjustable Sash, Knobs, Nuts	35
Plane, Molding, Stanley Bailey, No. 28, Transitional, 28 In.	30
Plane, Smoothing, Stanley Bed Rock No. 603C, Type 6, Pat'd Apr. 2-95, 19-10, c.1918, 9 In.	250
Rake, Concentric Half Circles, Shaft, 76 In.	12
Rug Beater, Metal, Looped Heart, Turned Wood Handle, Loop, 1920s, 35 x 9 In.	160
Saw, Hand, Disston & Morss, Combination Square, Level, Patented	280
Saw, Hand, Henry Disston, D-100, Aluminum, Wood Handle, 1960	13
Saw, Hand, John H. Obold, Rare, Fruitwood Carved Handle	35
Saw, Hand, Tacony Saw Co., 26 In.	8
Scythe, Farming, Wood, Metal, 1900s, 55 In.	56
Time Lock, Bank Vault, Metal Pin Dial, Sub-Dials, Spring Driven, Yale Mfg. Co., 4 1/2 x 6 x 3 In.	2178
Timer, Vault Alarm, Porcelain Dial, 72-Hour Numbers, Mahogany, E. Howard & Co., 8 x 9 1/4 x 4 In.	303
Trimmer, Lion Machine Co., Hand Miter	30
Wagon Jack, Conestoga, Iron, Wood, Closed, 1804, 29 In. *illus*	212
Wagon Jack, Iron, Wood, Initials CB, 1846, 23 In.	118
Water Filter, Ceramic, Wood Spout, Handles, British Barneveld Filter Co., 1950s, 18 In.	1500
Well Cover, Mechanical, Crank, Turned Chain, Brass, Rope, Bucket, Salesman's Sample, 11 3/4 In.	1063
Workbench, Wood, Slab Top, Square Nails, Shelf, Canted Legs, Vises, c.1840, 34 x 88 In.	780
Workbench, Woodworker, Plank Top, Drawers, Iron Pulls, Fixed Vise, 1920s, 32 x 52 In.	2950

TOOTHBRUSH HOLDERS were part of every bowl and pitcher set in the late nineteenth century. Most were oblong covered dishes. About 1920, manufacturers started to make children's toothbrush holders shaped like animals or cartoon characters. A few modern toothbrush holders are still being made.

Bisque, Figural, Dandy Dude, Luster, c.1900, 6 1/2 In.	39
Cast Iron, Ball & Claw Feet, Gold Glitter Lucite	65
Castle Scene, Cylindrical, Footed, Beaded Edge, Lion's Head Feet, c.1870, 5 In.	50
Dutch Girl, Hanging, Blue & Cream Dress, Hat, 1964, 6 3/4 In.	42
Dutch Girl, Hanging, Japan, 5 1/2 In.	64
Mother, Baby In Carriage, Oriental Scene, 4 1/2 In.	19
Pottery, Branches, Blossoms, Oranges, Transferware, Old Hall, c.1880, 6 In.	85
Spiderman, Wall Mount, Plastic, Holes In Hands, Avon, c.1979, 3 1/2 x 5 In.	35

TOOTHPICK HOLDERS are sometimes called *toothpicks* by collectors. The variously shaped containers used to hold small wooden toothpicks are made of glass, china, or metal. Most of the toothpick holders are made of Victorian glass. Additional items may be found in other categories, such as Bisque, Silver Plate, Slag Glass, etc.

Glass, Green To Cranberry Threads, Ruffled Rim, 1875-99, 2 1/8 In. *illus*	351
Silver Plate, Figural, High Wheel Bicycle, Rider Holding Barrel On Back, 6 In.	840
Silver Plate, Kate Greenaway Girl, On Sled, Hinged Open, Meriden, 3 x 4 1/2 In.	420
Silver Plate, Young Boy Training Dog, Meriden, 3 x 3 1/2 In. *illus*	125
Silver Plate, Young Girl Stands & Holds Rope Near Bag, Rogers Smith, 3 x 3 3/4 In.	84

TORQUAY is the name given to ceramics by several potteries working near Torquay, England, from 1870 until 1962. Until about 1900, the potteries used local red clay to make classical-style art pottery vases and figurines. Then they turned to making souvenir wares. Items were dipped in colored slip and decorated with painted slip and sgraffito designs. They often had mottoes or proverbs, and scenes of cottages, ships, birds, or flowers. The Scandy design was a symmetrical arrangement of brushstrokes and spots done in colored slips. Potteries included Watcombe Pottery (1870–1962), Torquay Terra-Cotta Company (1875–1905), Aller Vale (1881–1924), Torquay Pottery (1908–1940), and Longpark (1883–1957).

TORQUAY

Creamer, Applied Parrot, On Branch, Blue, 4 In.	45
Creamer, Sailboat, Red, Orange, 4 1/2 In.	75

Tole, Urn, Asian Decoration, Black Ground, 12 1/2 x 7 3/4 In., Pair
$660

Eldred's Auctioneers and Appraisers

Tool, Bench, Cobbler's, Oak, Compartment, Tray, Leather Strapping, Box Drawer, 20 x 39 In.
$1,270

James D. Julia Auctioneers

Tool, Book Press, Mahogany, Mised Wood Veneers, Drawer, 1900-25, 24 x 15 In.
$330

Leland Little Auctions

T

Tool, Lawn Mower, Hand Crank, Johnson Lawn Mower Co., 1878, 47½ x 30 In.
$960

Cowan's Auctions

Tool, Wagon Jack, Conestoga, Iron, Wood, Closed, 1804, 29 In.
$212

Hess Auction Group

Cup & Saucer, King Fisher, Blue	60
Eggcup, Waste Not Want Not, Cottage, 2¾ In.	60
Hatpin Holder, A Place For Hat Pins, Sailboat, 5 In.	100
Pin Tray, A Place For Everything & Everything In Its Place, Blue, Green, 10 x 7 In.	65
Pitcher, Deed Alone Must Win The Prize, Scandy, c.1920, 6 x 6 In.	55
Plate, Orange & Yellow, Blue Ground, Scandy, 8 In., Pair	150
Vase, Peacock, Perched In Tree, Blue Ground, 3 Handles, c.1925, 6½ In.	450

TOTE, *see Purse category.*

TOY collectors have special clubs, magazines, and shows. Toys are designed to entice children, and today they have attracted new interest among adults who are still children at heart. All types of toys are collected. Tin toys, iron toys, battery-operated toys, and many others are collected by specialists. Dolls, Games, Teddy Bears, and Bicycles are listed in their own categories. Other toys may be found under company or celebrity names.

Airplane, 4-Prop Engine, Metal Propeller Blades, 4 Side Wheels, 1 Front Wheel, 19 In.	954
Airplane, Electra 2, 2 Metal Propeller Blades, 4 Engines, Pinstriped Lines, 16-In. Wingspan	450
Airplane, Fokker, Red, Yellow, Single Prop, Windup, Tin Lithograph, TN, Japan, 7 x 9 In.	545
Airplane, Ford, Trimotor Model, 37-In. Wingspan	900
Airplane, Junker, Pilots, Passenger, Light Green, Bremen, 6½ In.	420
Airplane, Little Jim, Mono Coupe, Murray Mfg. Co., c.1929, 22½ In.	240
Airplane, Lockheed, Sirius, Black Fuselage, Red Wings, Seated Pilots, Hubley, 10½ In.	5400
Airplane, Lockheed, Sirius, Pressed Steel, White Fuselage, Red Wings, Decals, 1933, 21 In.	720
Airplane, Model, Wood, Metal, Red Paint, Engine, Propeller, Landing Wheels, 1950s, 48 In.	350
Airplane, U.S. Army Bomber, Olive, Tin, Windup, Balloon Tires, Marx, 18 In.	335
Airplane, World War II, Russian Yak, Jack Armstrong, Tru Flite, 9 x 7¼ x 1¾ In.	35
Ambulance, White, Red Cross On Side, Sturditoy, 26 In. *illus*	1800
Baseball Player, Home Run King, Windup, Tin Lithograph, Selrite Products, New York, 7 In.	265
Bears are also listed in the Teddy Bear category.	
Bear, Elongated, Pale Blue Plush, Brown Glass Eyes, Stitch Nosed, Stands Erect, 20 In.	413
Bed, Doll's, Brass, Scrolls, Spindles, Springs, Original Mattress, Silk Bedding, 6 In.	230
Bedroom Set, Doll's, Cream Wood, Gilt Applique, Canopy Bed, Armoire, 13-In. Dresser, 6 Piece	2530
Bicycles that are large enough to ride are listed in the Bicycle category.	
Bird Whistle, Tin Lithograph, Japan, 1950s, 1⅜ x 1¼ In.	15
Black Boy, Crying, Watermelon, Dog Biting His Rear, Celluloid, Windup, 1930s, 6 In.	870
Blocks, ABC Pictures, Paper Lithograph, McLoughlin Bros., Box, 12½ In. *illus*	330
Blocks, Alphabet, Wood, 2-Sided, Lid, Children Stacking Blocks, S.L. Hill, Box, c.1860, 5 x 5 In.	55
Blocks, Building, Wood Architectural, Painted, Cardboard Box, Miniature, 1950, 4 x 5 In.	30
Boat, Paddlewheel, Windup, Wooden, Cyclone, 1940s, 19 x 5 In.	40
Boat, Speedboat, Painted, Embossed, Tin Lithograph, ST, Japan, 1950s, 12 In.	55
Bonzo On Scooter, Tin Lithograph, Windup, Gunthermann, Germany, c.1924, 7 x 6 In. *illus*	480
Boy, Chalkboard, Pointer, Little Calculator Boy, Clockwork, Tippco, 7 In.	1800
Boy, Scooter, Dog Runs Beside, Multicolor, Stock, Germany, 6 In.	5700
Bulldozer, Robot Driver, Tin Lithograph, Battery, United Pioneer Co., Japan, 1960s, 7 In.	300
Bunny, Boy, Girl, Mohair, Flannel, Amber Glass Eyes, Felt Costumes, Steiff, 1950s, 10 In., Pair	460
Bus, Jackie Gleason, Wolverine, USA, 1960s, 14 In.	475
Bus, Seeing New York, Mama Katzenjammer, Happy Hooligan, Gloomy Gus, Kenton, 10½ In.	1440
Busy Lizzie, Pushing Mop, Crank, Tin Lithograph, Germany	480
Cannon, Gray & Gold Paint, Tin, Late 1800s, 11½ In. *illus*	48
Cap Gun, Metal, Plastic, Holster, Faux Stone, Hubley, 1900s, 13 In.	44
Car, Chevrolet, LaSalle, Sedan, Steel, Metal, Light Green, Yellow Wheels, 1920, 15 x 5½ In.	1495
Car, Chrysler, Airflow, Electric Lights, Rubber Tires, Light Brown, 8 In.	780
Car, Coupe, Rumble Seat, Red, Seated Driver, Arcade, 6¾ In.	270
Car, Fire Chief, Coupe, 2 Door, Pressed Steel, Windup, Siren, Marx, 1930, 13 x 5 x 5 In.	450
Car, Fire Chief, Red, Pressed Steel, Nickel Grill, Rubber Tires, Marx, 14 In.	360
Car, Fire Chief, Tin Lithograph, Friction, 1950, 3½ In.	30
Car, Fire Engine, Metal, Battery Operated, Bells, Blinking Signal Lamp, 1950, 11 x 5 In.	350
Car, Ford, TWA, Friction, 1963, 11 In.	110
Car, Lincoln, Zephyr, Sedan, Green, Hubley, 7 In.	540

SELECTED TOY MARKS WITH DATES USED

Gebruder Bing Co.
c.1923–1924
Nuremberg, Germany

F.A.O. Schwarz
1914
New York, N.Y.

Louis Marx & Co.
1920–1977
New York, N.Y.

Ernst Lehmann Co.
1915
Brandenburg, Germany

Gebruder Marklin & Co.
1899+
Goppingen, Germany

Nomura Toy Industrial Co., Ltd.
1940s+
Tokyo, Japan

Meccano
1901+
Liverpool, England

Georges Carette & Co.
1905–1917
Nuremburg, Germany

Gebruder Bing
1902–1934
Nuremburg, Germany

Joseph Falk Co.
1895–1934
Nuremburg, Germany

H. Fischer & Co.
1908–1932
Nuremburg, Germany

Ernst Lehmann Co.
1881–c.1947, 1951–2006
Brandenburg, Germany; Nuremburg, Germany

Lineol
c. 1906–1963
Bradenburg, Germany

Blomer and Schüler
1919–1974
Nuremberg, Germany

Yonezawa Toys Co.
1950s–1970s
Tokyo, Japan

Toothpick Holder, Glass, Green To Cranberry Threads, Ruffled Rim, 1875-99, 2 1/8 In.
$351

Jeffrey S. Evans

Toothpick Holder, Silver Plate, Young Boy Training Dog, Meriden, 3 x 3 1/2 In.
$125

Woody Auction

Toy, Ambulance, White, Red Cross On Side, Sturditoy, 26 In.
$1,800

Bertoia Auctions

TIP

If you want to use your old sled, yet keep it in the best possible condition as a collectible, coat it with a liquid furniture wax, then buff it, then a few days later coat it with paste furniture wax. Even the metal can be waxed after you remove the rust—and the waxing should make the sled slide even faster.

Car, Lux-A-Cab, Windup, Die Cast Tin, Decals, Strauss, 1900s, 4 1/2 x 8 1/2 In. .... *illus*	120
Car, Mercedes-Benz, Convertible, Red, Windup, Key, 1950, 10 x 4 In.	795
Car, Metal, Windup, Marx, USA, 1950s, 11 In.	120
Car, Model T, Sedan, Spoke Wheels, Gold Stripe, Arcade, 6 3/4 In.	210
Car, Racing, Driver, Disc Wheels, Open Cab, Silver, 5 1/2 In.	420
Car, Racing, Driver, Yellow, Electric, Rubber Tires, c.1920, 9 1/2 In.	7200
Car, Racing, Golden Arrow, Driver, Exhaust Flames, Orange, Hubley, 10 1/2 In.	660
Car, Riding, Seat, Steering Wheel, Rubber Wheels, 1900s, 16 x 30 In.	2000
Car, Stutz, Convertible, Cream, Green Running Boards, Nickel Grill, Driver, 10 1/4 In.	660
Car, Taxi, Yellow Cab, Cast Iron, Painted, Orange, Black, Lights, Rubber Tires, Arcade, 8 In. .. *illus*	1440
Car, Tin, Iron, Painted Wood, Windup, Stamped Bottom, 7 1/2 x 4 x 11 In.	50
Car, Torpeauto, Tin, Windup, Yellow, Original Box, 1900s	44
Car, Uncle Wiggily, Windup, Tin Lithograph, Marx, Copyright 1935, 8 In.	365
Carousel, Metal Crank, Germany, 1950s, 8 In.	120
Carriage, Doll's, Wood, Metal, Tufted Leather, 3 Wheels, Folding Sunshade, England, c.1860, 23 In.	575
Cart, Cast Iron, Front Wheels, Horse Section Removable, 1900s, 11 x 5 1/2 In.	50
Cat, Plays Violin, Tail Moves, White, Red Base, 7 1/2 In.	1440
Cat, Trying To Pounce, Mouse, Black, White, Green, Lehmann, 8 In.	600
Chair, Doll's, Original Paint, Rush Seat, c.1810, 17 1/2 In.	53
Chatter Telephone, Wood, Plastic, Metal, Push Pull, Fisher-Price, 1961 .... *illus*	30
Chickens, Pecking, Basket At Center, Green Plumes, Italy, 4 1/2 In.	270
Circus Elephant, Tin, Windup, Joseph Wagner, Original Tin Toy Factory, Germany, 9 x 10 In. *illus*	346
Clown, Juggling Ball, Tin, Painted, Gunthermann, Windup, 8 In.	660
Clown, On Pig's Back, Rocking, Pivots At Hip, 5 In.	360
Clown, Red Hat, Rides Cart, Pulled By 2 Dogs, Windup, Germany, 9 x 5 In.	600
Clown, Seesaw, Go-Cart, Clowns On Each End, Gunthermann, 14 In.	5100
Clown, Stick, Polka Dot Pants, Chasing Donkey, Multicolor, Meier, Penny Toy, 3 3/4 In.	390
Construction Set, Tractor, Trailer, Steam Shovel, Blue, Structo, 1936, 25 In.	450
Corn Popper, Plastic, Push Pull, Fisher-Price, 1980, 22 In. .... *illus*	50
Cradle, Doll's, Rocking, Red, Nail Construction, Tapered, 1890-1920, 20 x 12 x 12 In.	55
Cradle, Wood, Stencils, Papier-Mache, Shoulder Head Baby, Squeak, Germany, c.1850, 4 In.	633
Cradle, Wood, Turned Spindles, Rocks, W.H. Earnests, Steinman, Cincinnati, 1862, 37 In.	3450
Crane, Die Cast Tin, Blue & Red Paint, Partial Decal, Triang, 1900s, 46 x 34 x 19 In.	120
Crane, Overhead, End Frames, Folding, Cross Beams, Clamshell Grab Bucket, Buddy L	300
Crash Car, Indian Motorcycle, Hose, Reel, First Aid Box, Hubley, 11 1/2 In.	4800
Derrick, Vertical Boiler, Supports, Boom, Clamshell Grab Bucket, Buddy L, 1923-25, 19 In.	1680
Dog, Spaniel, Yes-No, Plush, Cut Glass Eyes, Schuco, c.1930 .... *illus*	900
Dolls are listed in the Doll category.	
Dollhouse, 2 Story, Victorian Gothic, Gables, Porches, Faux Brick Chimney, Fireplace, 45 In. .	3163
Dollhouse, 3 Story, Brick, Wood, Roof, Hand Split Shingles, Shutters, Green, 19 x 32 In.	726
Dollhouse, 3 Story, White Clapboard, Roof, Green, Porch, 38 x 36 In.	272
Dollhouse, Mansion, Side Doors Opened, Filigree Turnings, 10 x 17 x 21 In.	840
Dollhouse, Room, 3 Walls, Folds, Furniture, Drapes, Paper Lithograph, Wood, France, 1890, 22 In.	1725
Dr. Doodle, Duck, Paper On Wood, Push Pull, Fisher-Price, 1931 .... *illus*	176
Dresser, Doll's, Mahogany, Beaded Edge, Marble Top, Mirror, 9 x 15 In.	1035
Drummer Boy, Mechanical, Tin Lithograph, Marx, c.1940, 9 In.	600
Drunkard, Le Pochard, Walks Erratically With Bottle, Martin, France, c.1899, 7 In.	780
Duck, Mallard, Quack, 3 Ducklings, In Basket, Tin Lithograph, Lehmann, 7 In.	480
Elephant, Hard Stuffed, Wool, Metal Frame, Wood Wheels, Saddle, France, 1910s, 8 In.	535
Elephant, Ramp Walker, Cast Iron, Ives, Patent 1873, 3 1/2 In. .... *illus*	165
Erector Set, Zeppelin, Canvas Cover, Metal Construction, c.1930, 52 In.	510
Fawn, Felt, Stuffed, Curly Horns, Lime Green, Pink Ears, Lenci, 16 In.	460
Felix, Car, Speedy, Painted, Wood, Open Auto, Red, Decal, Pat Sullivan, c.1922, 12 In.	600
Ferris Wheel, 4 Figures, Tin, Windup, Spring Driven, Music Box, Repeats Notes, 9 1/2 x 5 1/2 In. .	484
Fire Truck, 4 Firefighters, Aerial Ladder, Pressed Steel, Red, Friction, Tonka, 1950, 10 In.	395
Fire Truck, Hook & Ladder, Marx, Box, c.1950, 33 In.	600
Fire Truck, Ladder, Open Mack Cab, Driver, Nickel Hose Reel, Red, Arcade, 20 1/2 In.	660
Fire Truck, Ladder, Red Spot Light, LaFrance, Doepke, 1950, 33 1/2 In.	275
Fire Truck, Removable Ladder, Red, Silver Trim, Hubley, 16 In.	540
Fire Truck, Water Tower, Shoots Water 20 Feet Into Air, Buddy L, c.1920	2700

T

Toy, Blocks, ABC Pictures, Paper Lithograph, McLoughlin Bros., Box,
12 ½ In.
$330

Toy, Bonzo On Scooter, Tin Lithograph, Windup, Gunthermann, Germany, c.1924,
7 x 6 In.
$480

Toy, Cannon, Gray & Gold Paint, Tin, Late 1800s, 11 ½ In.
$48

Toy, Car, Lux-A-Cab, Windup, Die Cast Tin, Decals, Strauss, 1900s, 4 ½ x 8 ½ In.
$120

Toy, Car, Taxi, Yellow Cab, Cast Iron, Painted, Orange, Black, Lights, Rubber Tires, Arcade, 8 In.
$1,440

Hot Wheels
The number on the base of a Hot Wheels car is the year it was copyrighted, not the year the car was made.

Toy, Chatter Telephone, Wood, Plastic, Metal, Push Pull, Fisher-Price, 1961
$30

Toy, Circus Elephant, Tin, Windup, Joseph Wagner, Original Tin Toy Factory, Germany,
9 x 10 In.
$346

Toy, Corn Popper, Plastic, Push Pull, Fisher-Price, 1980, 22 In.
$50

Toy, Dog, Spaniel, Yes-No, Plush, Cut Glass Eyes, Schuco, c.1930
$900

T

Toy, Dr. Doodle, Duck, Paper On Wood, Push
Pull, Fisher-Price, 1931
$176

Fisher-Price

Toy, Elephant, Incline Walker, Cast Iron, Ives,
Patent 1873, 3½ In.
$165

Hess Auction Group

Toy, Fred Flintstone, On Dino, Cloth Covered,
Vinyl Head, Tin Lithograph, Marx, 1960s,
21 In.
$357

Hake's Americana & Collectibles

Toy, Girl, Riding Hobbyhorse, Celluloid,
Windup, Platform, Wheels, Japan, Box, 9½ In.
$960

Bertoia Auctions

Toy, Henry & Henrietta, Celluloid, Suitcase,
Articulated Legs, Windup, Japan, 1934, 7½ In.
$840

Bertoia Auctions

TIP

Take batteries with you to toy sales if you plan to buy a battery-
operated toy. Check to see if the toy really works.

Toy, Grasshopper, Painted, Cast Iron, Aluminum, Rubber Tires, Pull Cord, Hubley, 12 In.
$1,200

Bertoia Auctions

Toy, Hayloader, John Deere, Cast Iron,
Painted, Vindex, 7½ In.
$5,124

Pook & Pook

Toy, Horse, Rocking, Glass Eyes, Cloth
Saddle, Platform, Black, White, Red, 1800s,
30 x 40 In.
$390

Garth's Auctioneers & Appraisers

Fox, Sly 9, Foxili, Mohair Head & Paw Tips, Dapper Fellow, U.S. Zone, Germany, c.1950, 9 In....	413
Fox, Yes-No, Tail Turns Head, Tan Mohair, Embroidered, Twill Ears, Germany, 1935, 9 In.	633
Foxy Grandpa, Skater, Yellow Vest, Glasses, Germany, 8½ In..	570
Fred Flintstone, On Dino, Cloth Covered, Vinyl Head, Tin Lithograph, Marx, 1960s, 21 In. *illus*	357
Fred Flintstone, Riding Dino, Tin Lithograph, Mechanical, Box, 7½ In.	360
G.I. Joe, Jouncing Jeep, Tin Lithograph, Windup, Unique Art, 1944, 6½ x 7½ In.....................	395
Games are listed in the Game category.	
Girl, Riding Hobbyhorse, Celluloid, Windup, Platform, Wheels, Japan, Box, 9½ In. .... *illus*	960
Gnomes, Sawing Branch, Spring-Loaded, Tin Lithograph, J. Meier Co., Germany, c.1910, 4 In.	180
Grasshopper, Daddy Long Legs, Chirps As He Crawls, Hubley, Box, 9 In.	1200
Grasshopper, Painted, Cast Iron, Aluminum, Rubber Tires, Pull Cord, Hubley, 12 In...... *illus*	1200
Hayloader, John Deere, Cast Iron, Painted, Vindex, 7½ In... *illus*	5124
Henry & Henrietta, Celluloid, Suitcase, Articulated Legs, Windup, Japan, 1934, 7½ In. *illus*	840
Horse & Rider, Balance, Man In Top Hat, Gold Paint, 1900s, 52 In...	240
Horse & Wagon, Pull, Borden's Milk & Cream, Rich Toys, 25 In..	295
Horse, Carved & Painted, Mughal Style, Patina, 1800s, 36 x 34 In.......................................	540
Horse, Civil War Era, Spring Mechanism, Glass Eyes, Crandal, 1861, 42 x 44 In......................	780
Horse, Dapple, Painted, Papier-Mache, Wood, Flax Hair Tail, Metal Wheels, Germany, c.1900, 11 x 13 In.	250
Horse, Glider, Carved, Glass Eyes, Horsehair Mane & Tail, Red, 1800s, 37 x 52 In......................	120
Horse, Jockey, Pull, Wood, Painted, Metal, Rubber Wheels, 1920, 11 In.	295
Horse, Mobo Bronco, Die Cast Steel, Mechanical, 4 Caster Wheels, 1900s, 30 In....................	120
Horse, Painted, White, Iron, Red, Hooked Pad, Saddle, Wood, 1800s..	200
Horse, Rocking, Carved Wood, Brown Wool, Glass Eyes, Leather, Cloth Saddle, 1800s, 34 x 45 In.	360
Horse, Rocking, Carved, Dapple, Hair Mane, Tail, Wood Platform, Gilt Stencils, Trian, c.1950, 33 x 40 In.	660
Horse, Rocking, Glass Eyes, Cloth Saddle, Platform, Black, White, Red, 1800s, 30 x 40 In. *illus*	390
Horse, Rocking, Painted Wood, 1900s, 24 x 37½ In.	201
Horse, Rocking, Scalloped Edges, Silhouette Neck & Head, Metal Strips, 1800s, 32 x 60 In.......	375
Horse, Rocking, Wood, Carved, Painted, Laminated Body, Leather Saddle, c.1890, 26 x 12 In..	199
Horse, Victorian Platform, Painted Wood, Leather Saddle, Horsehair Tail, 1800s, 29 x 40 In. ..	300
Hutch, Doll's, Shelf, 2 Cabinet Doors, Transfer, Girl, Teapot, Green, Cream, Wood, 1930s, 14 x 11 In.	65
Jack-In-The-Box, Head Of Man, Red Top Hat, Paper-Wrapped Spring, Civil War Era, 2¾ In...	42
Jeep, Army, Soldier, Retractable Windshield, Tin Lithograph, Box, 1960s, 6½ In.	65
Jeff On Skates, Tin Figure, Painted, Arms Up & Down, Legs In & Out, Germany, 8½ In. *illus*	510
Jester, Marching, Parade Drum, Bisque, Clockwork, France, c.1900, 16 In.	1380
Jockey, Rocking Horse, Steeple Chase Theme, Tin Lithograph, 3¾ In.	150
Kitchen, Doll's, Wood, Brass, 6 Spice Drawers, Checkered Wood, Kitchenware, Delft, c.1910, 37 In..	1725
Kitten, Curly White Mohair, Swivel Head, Glass Eyes, Jointed, Ear Button, Steiff, 10 In.	518
Ladybug, Round, Tin Lithograph, Friction, Koyo Kinzoku, Japan, 1950s, 2 In.........................	6
Maggie & Jiggs, Wheeled Base, Wire, Tin Lithograph, Clockwork, Nifty, Copyright 1924, 7 In..	540
Man, Nu-Nu, Pulling Chest Of Tea, Clockwork, Lehmann, 6 x 4 In.	1200
Man-Da-Rin, 2 Men, Carrying Sedan Chair, Enclosed Coach, Red, Blue, White, Lehmann, 7 x 5 In.	2280
Manure Spreader, Horse Drawn, John Deere, Cast Iron, Painted, Vindex, 14½ In. .... *illus*	1830
Merry Mutt, Plays Xylophone, Painted, Moving Arms, Pull Toy, Fisher-Price, 1949, 8 x 7½ In.	100
Milliner's Shop, Wood, Cabinets, Windows, Swing-Out Doors, C. Hacker, c.1880, 20 x 12 In. ..	3450
Mirror, Doll's, Psyche, Mahogany, Arched, Turned Wood Stand, Pivots, France, c.1860, 8 In....	633
Monkey Band, Tin, Painted, Mohair, Felt, 2 Drummers, 1 Plays Violin, Windup, Schuco, 5 In.	230
Monkey Clown, Drummer, Cymbals, Windup, Schuco, c.1950, 4½ x 3 In.	175
Monkey, Climbing, Pull String, Green Jacket, Yellow Vest, Box, Lehmann, 8 In........................	90
Monkey, Drummer, Uniform, Cymbal, Germany, 9 In..	570
Monkey, Weight Lifting, Plush, Felt Vest, Tin Lithograph, Windup, Japan, 1940s, 6 x 5 In.	65
Motorcycle, Cop Driver, Orange, Harley-Davidson On Tank, Cast Iron, Hubley, 5 In.	510
Motorcycle, Pea Shooter, Racing, Driver, Cast Iron, Orange & Gold Paint, Hubley, 6 In... *illus*	1320
Motorcycle, Police, Harley-Davidson, Green, Gold Highlights, Hubley, 6 In............................	720
Motorcycle, Police, Sidecar, Red, Aluminum Handlebars, Hubley, 9 In..................................	720
Motorcycle, Policeman Rider, Tin Lithograph, Siren, Clockwork, Marx, 8 In................... *illus*	330
Motorcycle, Rider, Head Moves Up & Down, Jacket, Knickers, Socks, 4½ In.	1140
Motorcycle, Speed Boy, Delivery, Driver, Embossed Wood Stake, Open Body, 9¾ In.	450
Mouse, White Fur, Blue Glass Eyes, Leather Ears, Metal Ball, Mechanical, France, c.1890, 6 In. *illus*	115
Noah's Ark, Carved & Painted Animals, Wood, Germany, 4½ x 10 In..	265
Noah's Ark, Hinged Roof, Sliding Sides, Painted Wood, Pull, Germany, 13 x 23 In.	130

Toy, Jeff On Skates, Tin Figure, Painted, Arms Up & Down, Legs In & Out, Germany, 8½ In.
$510

Bertoia Auctions

Toy, Manure Spreader, Horse Drawn, John Deere, Cast Iron, Painted, Vindex, 14½ In.
$1,830

Pook & Pook

Toy, Motorcycle, Pea Shooter, Racing, Driver, Cast Iron, Orange & Gold Paint, Hubley, 6 In.
$1,320

Bertoia Auctions

Lincoln Logs
Lincoln Logs were invented by John Lloyd Wright, son of the famous architect Frank Lloyd Wright.

T

Toy, Motorcycle, Policeman Rider, Tin Lithograph, Siren, Clockwork, Marx, 8 In.
$330

Bertoia Auctions

Toy, Mouse, White Fur, Blue Glass Eyes, Leather Ears, Metal Ball, Mechanical, France, c.1890, 6 In.
$115

Theriault's

Toy, Paddy & Pig, Irishman, On Pig, Circus Skirt, Tin, Lehmann, Germany, 6 In.
$1,320

Bertoia Auctions

Toy, Pedal Car, Chrysler, 1940 Model, Painted, Chrome, Restoration, Steelcraft, 36 In.
$840

Bertoia Auctions

Toy, Porky Pig, Holding Umbrella, Tin Lithograph, Windup, Built-In Key, Marx, Box, 1939, 8 In.
$409

Hake's Americana & Collectibles

Toy, Pull-A-Long Lacing Shoe, Wood, Plastic, Push Pull, Fisher-Price, 1960s
$49

eBay

Toy, Pull-A-Tune Xylophone, Wood, Metal, Fisher-Price, 1964
$70

Fisher-Price

Toy, Rock-A-Stack Rings, Plastic, Wood Pole & Base, Fisher-Price, 1960s
$50

Fisher-Price

Toy, Secretaire, Doll's, Bronze, Porcelain, Cabriole Legs, Hand Painted Scenes, 5 ½ In.
$2,185

Theriault's

Toy, Seed Drill, John Deere, Van Brunt, Cast Iron, Painted, 9 ½ In.
$3,172

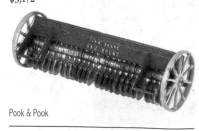

Pook & Pook

Toy, Sled, Aero, Thrill, Coaster, Stenciled, Art Deco, 29 x 40 In.
$176

Copake Auction

Paddy & Pig, Irishman, On Pig, Circus Skirt, Tin, Lehmann, Germany, 6 In. ..... *illus*	1320
Pedal Car, Airplane, Steel, Red, White & Black Paint, Chain Drive, 1900s, 23 x 47 x 25 In.	480
Pedal Car, Buick, Torpedo Style, Chrome Work, Black, Murray c.1948, 38 In.	900
Pedal Car, Chrysler, 1940 Model, Painted, Chrome, Restoration, Steelcraft, 36 In. .... *illus*	840
Pedal Car, Essex Toledo, Red, Windshield, c.1925, 36 In.	3000
Pedal Car, Fire Engine, Side Ladders, Bell On Hood, Red & White, Decals, 1900s, 16 x 41 In.	120
Pedal Car, Station Wagon, Original Paint & Decals, Red, Murray, c.1955, 48 In.	1440
Pianist, Mechanical, Plays 2 Different Songs, Martin, France, Box, c.1900, 4 In.	4800
Playset, Nurse, Uniform, Stethoscope, Reflex Mallet, Thermometer, Case, Effanbee, 1940s	390
Porky Pig, Holding Umbrella, Tin Lithograph, Windup, Built-In Key, Marx, Box, 1939, 8 In.. *illus*	409
Pull-A-Long Lacing Shoe, Wood, Plastic, Push Pull, Fisher-Price, 1960s	49
Pull-A-Tune Xylophone, Wood, Metal, Fisher-Price, 1964	70
Rabbit, Lulac, Long Limbed, Mohair Made, Squeaker, Soft Stuffed, Blue Glass Eyes, Steiff, 1960s, 20 In.	338
Robot, Astro Scout, Tin Lithograph, Windup, Spacesuit, Yonezawa, Box, Japan, 1960s, 9¾ In.	9600
Robot, Nando, Tin Lithograph, Air Pump Activated, Head Turns, Decals, Italy, Box, 1950s, 5 In.	1860
Robot, Space Explorer, Blinking Eyes, 3-D Screen, Tin Litho, Battery, Yonezawa, Box, c.1966, 12 In.	1845
Rock-A-Stack Rings, Plastic, Wood Pole & Base, Fisher-Price, 1960s	50
Rooster, Papier-Mache, Feathers, Crows Cock-A-Doodle-Doo, Mechanical, Wood Base, 14 In.	633
Secretaire, Doll's, Bronze, Porcelain, Cabriole Legs, Hand Painted Scenes, 5½ In.	2185
Seed Drill, John Deere, Van Brunt, Cast Iron, Painted, 9½ In.	3172
Seesaw, Boy, Girl, Flower Stencil, Clockwork, Tin, Ives, c.1880, 18 In.	1680
Sewing Machine, Tin Lithograph, Crank Wheel, Fisher, Germany, Penny Toy, 1920s, 3 x 4 In.	160
Sled, Aero, Thrill, Coaster, Stenciled, Art Deco, 29 x 40 In.	176
Sled, Child Cutter, Bent Oak & Iron, Branded, Maine, 9½ x 26 x 11 In.	42
Sled, Oak & Poplar, Painted, Iron Work, Maid, Stencil On Side, Child's, 1800s, 12 x 31 In.	132
Sled, Painted, Wood, Metal Runners, Signed, Francis, Child's, 35 In.	118
Sled, Painted, Yellow, Red, Black Striping, Armilda, Iron Runners, 42 In. *illus*	30
Sled, Pine & Iron, Red, Painted Swirl Decoration, 1800s, 41 In.	120
Sled, Racing, Wood, Iron, Seat, Steering Panel, 84, Original Paint, c.1915, 80 x 25 In.	531
Sled, Runner, Slats, Red, 1900s, 38 In.	23
Sled, Sno Plane, Harold Van Doren, Metal, Wood, Chrome, Patented, 1934	263
Sled, White, Floral Accents, Painted, J.L.G. Monogram, Child's, 1800s, 13 x 14 x 36 In.	120
Soldier Set, On Parade, Band, Cardboard, Lithograph Uniform, Milton Bradley, Box, c.1915, 100 Piece	950
Space Robot Car, X-9, Tin Lithograph Battery, Illuminated Balls, Japan, c.1960, 7½ In.	1200
Spaceship, Tom Corbett, Sparkling, Windup, Tin Lithograph, Marx, Original Box, 1950s, 12 In.	1265
Squirrel, Brown Velvet, Shoebutton Eyes, Button, Steiff, Germany, c. 1910, 5 In. *illus*	402
Stove, Bing, Tin, Nickel, Columns, Towel Bar, Claw Feet, Pots & Pans, Germany, 18 x 15 In.	690
Stove, Dolly's Favorite, Cast Iron, Black Paint, Nickel Doors, 1890-1925, 23 In. *illus*	439
Stove, Eagle, Cast Iron, Green & White Paint, c.1925, 9 In. *illus*	47
Stove, Gem, Cast Iron, Silver Paint, Working Baffle, 1890-1925, 8⅝ In. *illus*	199
Stove, Iron, Nickel Finish On Doors, Burner Covers, Reservoir Cover, Damper, 23 In.	438
Stove, Marklin, Tin, Nickel, Chimney, Towel Bar, Claw Feet, Pots & Pans, 1900, 18 x 10 In.	633
Stove, Quick Meal, Cast Iron, Blue Enamel, Ash Bin, Flue, Nickel Detailing, c.1910	2530
Stove, Vindex, Admiral, Iron, Nickel Plate, Light Green, Cream, Doors Open, 13½ x 15½ In.	360
Tank, Crawling, Rubber Tracks, Camouflage Green, Shoots Steel Balls, c.1930s, 8 In.	720
Taxi, Checker, Tin, Windup, Mohawk Toys, 1930s, 6 In.	225
Taxi, Seated Driver, Mesh Windows, Disc Wheels, Orange, Black, Arcade, 7¾ In.	420
Teddy Bears are also listed in the Teddy Bear category.	
Thresher, Yellow Spoke Wheels, Gray, Red Striping, Arcade McCormick Deering, 12 In.	240
Tiger, Mohair Body, Stuffed, Hand Striping, Green Eyes, Stitched, Steiff, 17 x 23 x 21 In.	300
Tool Chest, Wood, Padlock, Tools, Instructions, Buddy L, c.1927, 23 x 11 x 6¾ In.	465
Toonerville Trolley, Cast Iron, Green, Orange, Embossed, Box, Dent, 6 In.	450
Top, Spinning, Children, Dog, Chicks, Rabbit, Pig, Patriotic, Blue, Red, Star, Litho, 1950, 7½ In.	175
Top, Spinning, Clown, Elephant, Ducks, Dogs, Wood Handle, Tin Litho, Chein, 1940, 6¾ In.	165
Tractor, Caterpillar, Cast Iron, Painted, Nickel Plated Driver, Arcade, 7⅝ In. *illus*	671
Tractor, Dump, Black Rubber Tread Tires, Crawling, Tin Lithograph, Marx, 14 In.	120
Tractor, Red Spoke Wheels, Seated Driver, Gray, Cast Iron, c.1920s, 6 In.	330
Tractor, Wallis, Cast Iron, Painted, Driver, Freidag, 4¾ In. *illus*	1037
Trailer, Anti-Aircraft Gun, 4 Wheels, Military, 7-Man Crew, Green Hub, Die Cast, Dinky Toy, c.1950.	106
Train Accessory, Lionel, 140 L Tunnel, 25 x 35 In.	1200

Toy, Sled, Painted, Yellow, Red, Black Striping, Armilda, Iron Runners, 42 In.
$30

Hess Auction Group

Lego

"Lego" comes from the Danish expression *leg godt*, meaning "play well." Later the company learned the Latin word *lego* can be translated to mean "I put together."

Toy, Squirrel, Brown Velvet, Shoebutton Eyes, Button, Steiff, Germany, c. 1910, 5 In.
$402

Theriault's

Toy, Stove, Dolly's Favorite, Cast Iron, Black Paint, Nickel Doors, 1890-1925, 23 In.
$439

Jeffrey S. Evans

Toy, Stove, Eagle, Cast Iron, Green & White Paint, c.1925, 9 In.
$47

Jeffrey S. Evans

Toy, Stove, Gem, Cast Iron, Silver Paint, Working Baffle, 1890-1925, 8 5/8 In.
$199

Jeffrey S. Evans

Tractor Toys

The first tractor was built by J.I. Case in 1892, so no tractor toys were made before that date.

Toy, Tractor, Caterpillar, Cast Iron, Painted, Nickel Plated Driver, Arcade, 7 5/8 In.
$671

Pook & Pook

Toy, Tractor, Wallis, Cast Iron, Painted, Driver, Freidag, 4 3/4 In.
$1,037

Pook & Pook

Toy, Train Accessory, Marklin, Sawmill, Steam
$900

Bertoia Auctions

Toy, Train Car, Marklin, PRR Boxcar, Blue Slats, Siding Doors, O Gauge, 7 In.
$900

Bertoia Auctions

Toy, Train Car, Voltamp, 2130, Locomotive, Steeple Cab, Electric, Painted, c.1910, 11 In.
$2,280

Bertoia Auctions

Slinky

Slinky was created by Richard James. With the help of his wife, Betty, he first sold some in 1945. It cost $1. The toy was a huge success and so was the company, James Industries. In 1960, Richard decided to leave Betty and their six kids and the rest of his old life and go to Bolivia to join a religious cult. He also took a lot of the company's money. Betty, then 42, saved James Industries by making tough financial decisions and clever additions to the line of Slinky toys. There is a Junior Slinky, plastic Slinky, Slinky dog, Slinky glasses, and more. The James family sold the business to Poof Products, Inc., in 1998.

Toy, Train Car, Lionel, Locomotive 1912, Bells, Headlight, Short Crinkle Couple, Box, 16 In.
$10,200

Bertoia Auctions

T

Train Accessory, Lionel, 913 Plot, White House, Green Roof, Box, 16 x 18 In.	1440
Train Accessory, Marklin, Sawmill, Steam .... *illus*	900
Train Car, Bing, Pabst Blue Ribbon Boxcar, Beer Bottles Lithograph Sides, Germany, Box, 7 In.	1800
Train Car, Buddy L, Caboose, Pressed Steel, Red, Ladder, Decals, 18 In.	270
Train Car, Lionel, Locomotive 1912, Bells, Headlight, Short Crinkle Couple, Box, 16 In... *illus*	10200
Train Car, Lionel, Locomotive, 9E, Gun Metal, Box, 14 In.	1440
Train Car, Marklin, Locomotive & Tender, Electric Headlamps, Smoke Deflector, 21 In.	3300
Train Car, Marklin, Locomotive & Tender, Mechanical, Painted, Cow Catcher, Bell, Gold Trim.	5700
Train Car, Marklin, Locomotive, 2 Passenger Cars, Iron, Tinplate, Nickel Levers, 1898	2160
Train Car, Marklin, PRR Boxcar, Blue Slats, Siding Doors, O Gauge, 7 In. .... *illus*	900
Train Car, Voltamp, 2130, Locomotive, Steeple Cab, Electric, Painted, c.1910, 11 In. ...... *illus*	2280
Train Car, Voltamp, 2210, Locomotive, Suburban, Painted, Electric, c.1910, 13 ½ In. ...... *illus*	2700
Train Car, Voltamp, Caboose, Cast Iron, Red & Black, Lettered B & O, c.1918, 9 ½ In.	3300
Train Set, Lionel, Locomotive, 381U Kit, Green, Box, 17 In.	27000
Train Set, Lionel, Locomotive, Passenger, Tender, Flat Car, Gondola, Cattle Car, Caboose	354
Train, American Flyer, Presidential Special Set, Prewar, c.1927	2400
Train, Buddy L, Locomotive, Tender, Pressed Steel, Black, Brass Railing, Decals, Bell, 24 In.	960
Train, Bullet, Tin Lithograph, Japan, 36 In. .... *illus*	180
Train, Locomotive, Tin, Cow Catcher Front, Smokestack, Bell, Driver, Painted 14, 9 x 21 In.	300
Train, Steam Type Locomotive, Painted, Sheet Metal, Manual Reverse, Howard, c.1910, 11 In.	1920
Trolley, Pressed Steel, Green, Red, Flywheel, Reversible Bench, Friction, Dayton, c.1900, 14 In.	270
Truck, Cement Mixer, Cast Iron, Nickel Plated, Red, Green Drum Bar, Kenton, 8 ½ In.	1020
Truck, Cement Mixer, Pressed Steel, Cast Iron Wheels, Decals, Buddy L, 1920s, 14 x 24 In.	300
Truck, Chemical Pumper, American National, c.1920, 28 ½ In.	2700
Truck, Circus, Big Show, Tin Lithograph, Cage Wagon, Lion, Tamer, Marquee, Strauss, 9 ½ In.	420
Truck, Coal, Driver, Red, Yellow Coal Body, Level, Black Spoke Wheels, 15 ½ In.	840
Truck, Crank Aerial Ladder, Open Cab, Red, Buddy L, 29 In.	1140
Truck, Delivery, Milk, Borden's, Cast Iron, Painted, Embossed, Hubley, 7 ½ In. .... *illus*	1440
Truck, Driver, Blue, Flowers Embossed, 3 Wheels, Cast Iron, Hubley, c.1930, 4 In.	510
Truck, Dump, Flat Bed, Rises, Die Cast, 2 ½ x 6 ½ x 2 In.	100
Truck, Figural, Milk Bottle, Borden's, Green Paint, Rubber Tires, Embossed, Arcade, 5 ¾ In. *illus*	1200
Truck, Fro-Joy Ice Cream, Metal, Red, Yellow, Decals, Rubber Tires, Steelcraft, 1930s, 22 In.	325
Truck, GMC Missile Launcher, Pressed Steel, Green, Buddy L, 21 In.	270
Truck, Guided Missile, Unopened, Marx, Box, 1950s, 20 In.	480
Truck, Ice, Pressed Steel, Canvas Cover, Decals, City Ice Co., Steelcraft, 10 ½ x 26 In. ...... *illus*	3776
Truck, Liftgate Dump, Headlights, Hood Ornament, Turner, c.1920, 30 In.	900
Truck, Mail, 3-Panel Screen Side, Balloon Wheels, Headlights, Green, Structo, c.1920s, 16 ½ In.	360
Truck, Mail, Mail Bags, Pull Cord, Keystone Packard, c.1920, 26 In.	1560
Truck, Milk, White, Black Roof, Side Doors Open, Wood, Buddy L, c.1946, 13 In.	180
Truck, Moving Van, Opening Rear Door, Gold Stripe, Red, 13 In.	2040
Truck, Sand Loader, Yellow, Buckets, Black, Gears, Wheels, Buddy L, c.1931, 17 In.	840
Truck, Semi-Trailer, Dunwell, Land O' Lakes, Original Paint, Decals, c.1950, 23 In.	420
Truck, Steam Dredger, Clamshell, Pressed Steel, Black, Shovel, Red Roof, Buddy L, 1920s, 15 In.	510
Truck, Street Sweeper, Driver, Gray, Nickel, Rubber Tires, Elgin, Hubley, 8 ½ In.	2400
Truck, Tanker, Gasoline, Windup, Original Paint, Decals, 13 In.	695
Truck, Tanker, Oil & Gas, Green, Embossed Lettering, Water Tanks, Disc Wheels, Kenton, 10 In.	900
Truck, Tanker, Oil, Buddy L. Jr., c.1930	1320
Truck, Tanker, Oil, Red Texaco, Depicted Decal Visible, 1960, 24 x 6 x 5 ½ In.	495
Truck, Tow, Cities Service, Green, White, Original Box, Marx, 1950s, 20 ½ In.	270
Truck, U.S. Mail, Pressed Steel, Enclosed Cab, Disc Wheels, Keystone, 26 ½ In.	1020
Wagon, Auto Wheel Coaster, Wood, 15 x 36 In. .... *illus*	200
Wagon, Circus, Al G. Barnes, Backstein Circus Models, No. 119, 1980, 15 x 7 ½ In. .... *illus*	1140
Wagon, Circus, Tin Lithograph, Morten E. Converse Co., c.1925, 14 In.	177
Wagon, Farm, John Deere, Cast Iron, Painted, Vindex, 7 ¾ In. .... *illus*	793
Wagon, Wood, Framed Backrest, Spoked Wheels, Stenciled Teddy, Patented, 1900s, 46 x 18 x 24 In.	160
Wagon, Wood, Iron Wheels, Spokes, John Deere, 19 ½ x 36 In. .... *illus*	650
Wheelbarrow, Wood, Original Paint, Red, Green, Yellow, 40 In.	83
Yo-Yo, Silver, Steel Body, Hallmark, Gorham, 1930, 2 ¼ x 1 ⅜ In.	85
Yo-Yo, Tin Lithograph, Space Shuttle, Astronaut, Red, Yellow, Blue, Japan, 1950s	25
Zebra, Mohair, Glass Eyes, Steiff, 1950s-60s, 38 x 38 In.	1375

Toy, Train Car, Voltamp, 2210, Locomotive, Suburban, Painted, Electric, c.1910, 13 ½ In.
$2,700

Bertoia Auctions

Toy, Train, Bullet, Tin Lithograph, Japan, 36 In.
$180

Bertoia Auctions

Toy, Truck, Delivery, Milk, Borden's, Cast Iron, Painted, Embossed, Hubley, 7 ½ In.
$1,440

Bertoia Auctions

Toy, Truck, Figural, Milk Bottle, Borden's, Green Paint, Rubber Tires, Embossed, Arcade, 5 ¾ In.
$1,200

Bertoia Auctions

> **TIP**
> *If your battery-operated toy stops working, try sanding the terminals and the ends of the batteries. There may be slight corrosion that interferes with the battery connections.*

T

Toy, Truck, Ice, Pressed Steel, Canvas Cover, Decals, City Ice Co., Steelcraft, 10 ½ x 26 In.
$3,776

Wm Morford Auctions

Toy, Wagon, Auto Wheel Coaster, Wood, 15 x 36 In.
$200

Woody Auction

Toy, Wagon, Circus, Al G. Barnes, Backstein Circus Models, No. 119, 1980, 15 x 7 ½ In.
$1,140

Freedom Auction Company

Toy, Wagon, Farm, John Deere, Cast Iron, Painted, Vindex, 7 ¾ In.
$793

Pook & Pook

T

 TRAMP ART is a form of folk art made since the Civil War. It is usually made from chip-carved cigar boxes. Examples range from small boxes and picture frames to full-sized pieces of furniture. Collectors in the United States started collecting it about 1970 and examples from other countries, especially Germany, were imported and sold by antiques dealers.

Bank, Yew, Inlaid Matchsticks, 8-Point Star, c.1900, 6 ½ x 6 In.	*illus*	121
Box, Sewing, Hinged Lid, Green Felt Panels, Pincushion Top, Drawer, 9 x 11 ½ In.	*illus*	265
Box, Storage, Wood, Heart, Star, Geometric Design, Marked W.W., 10 x 20 ½ In.		106
Bureau, Wood, Chip Carved, Tilting Mirror, 33 x 15 x 11 In.	*illus*	189
Mirror, Wood, Circles, Rectangles, Green, Red, Yellow, 23 x 17 ½ In.		175
Mirror, Wood, Hearts, Triangles, Circles, c.1900, 52 x 34 In.	*illus*	526
Smoking Stand, Wood, Chip Carved, Red & Yellow Paint, Tobacco Leaf Finial, 38 In.	*illus*	265

 TRAPS for animals may be handmade. One of the most unusual is the mousetrap made so that when the mouse entered the trap, it was hit on the head with a mallet. Other traps were commercially manufactured and often are marked with the name of the manufacturer. Many traps were designed to be as humane as possible, and they would trap the live animal so it could be released in the woods.

Animal, Moles, Cast Iron, Spring Mechanism, Out O' Sight, Stamped, 1930s, 8 x 5 In.		65
Bear, Chain, Hand Forged, W. Virginia, 1700s, 38 In.		696
Beaver, Hand Forged, Virginia, 36 In.		580
Cricket, Kettle Shape, Landscape, Pagoda, Pierced Metal Lid, Handle, Metal		230
Eel, Basket, Splint, Oak, Woven, Native American, 20 ½ In.	*illus*	60
Mouse, Falling Block, Wood, 1800s, 8 ¾ x 16 ½ x 5 In.	*illus*	295
Mouse, Wire, Domed Cage, Wood Base, Bottom Opening, Handle, France, 1940s, 5 x 5 In.		25

TREEN, see Wooden category.

 TRENCH ART is a form of folk art made by soldiers. Metal casings from bullets and mortar shells were cut and decorated to form useful objects, such as vases.

Ashtray, Match Holder, Top Is Engraved, Shows A Crown, 1945		99
Bracelet, Iron Cross, Piece Of Shell Casing, Hinge, Engraving, 1914, 2 ¼ In.		82
Vase, Brass, Shell, Toul Spelled Out In Pattern, Hammered, World War I, 14 In.		150
Vase, Field Hospital, Army Truck, Masonic Symbols, Eagle, W.M. Morris, 1917	*illus*	540

TRIVETS are now used to hold hot dishes. Most trivets of the late nineteenth and early twentieth centuries were made to hold hot irons. Iron or brass reproductions are being made of many of the old styles.

Brass, Heart Shape, Looped Handle, c.1800, 9 ½ x 4 ¾ In.	*illus*	110
Brass, Iron, Round, Pierced, Turned Wooden Handle, 3 Legs, 5 ¼ x 13 ½ In.		23
Brass, Owl, 8 ½ x 6 In.		18
Cast Iron, Alphabet, Letter Z, J.Z.H., Union Mfg., Footed, c.1950, 6 In.		25
Cast Iron, Bonzo, Comic Dog, 3 Tapered Feet, 6 In. Diam.		165
Cast Iron, Grapes, Scrolls, Handle, Gold Color Finish, c.1950, 7 ¾ x 4 ½ In.		10
Cast Iron, Horseshoe, Star, 7 x 4 In.		14
Copper, Bear In Woods, Handle, 6 x 9 In.		65
Crocheted, Red, Christmas Trees, 1950s, 7 In. Diam.		15
Glass, Fire King, Glass Handle, Round, 6 ½ In.		10
Glass, Silver Overlay, Starburst, 1890s, 6 In.		110
Iron, Forged, Heart Shape, Turned Up Feet, 19th Century, 6 x 4 In.		195
Iron, Heart, 3-Footed, 10 ½ In.		234
Iron, Lyre Shape, 3-Footed, Hooks, Brass Handle, c.1825, 5 x 11 ½ In.		46
Iron, Wrought, Brass, Heart Shape, Folk Art, 6 x 4 ½ In.		125
Iron, Wrought, Hearts, C-Scrolls, Blacksmith Made, 15 x 29 In.		234
Lucite, Abalone Shells, Ball Feet, 1970s, 5 In. Diam.		14
Porcelain, Flower & Leaf Border, PH Leonard, Austria, c.1900, 5 x 5 In.		145
Porcelain, Pagodas, Willow Trees, Bridge & Boats In Lake, 1840s, 5 In.		250

Pottery, Brown Glaze, Round, Holes, 2 Handles, David Gill, 8 In. .... *illus* 108
Tile, Flower Basket, France, 5 x 5 In. 24
Tile, Grape Bunch, Yellow Border, Cannara, Italy, 6 x 6 In. 8

TRUNKS of many types were made. The nineteenth-century sea chest was often handmade of unpainted wood. Brass-fitted camphorwood chests were brought back from the Orient. Leather-covered trunks were popular from the late eighteenth to mid-nineteenth centuries. By 1895, trunks were covered with canvas or decorated sheet metal. Embossed metal coverings were used from 1870 to 1910. By 1925, trunks were covered with vulcanized fiber or undecorated metal. Suitcases are listed here.

Briefcase, Presto, Light Brown, 3-Digit Combination, 1900s, 14 x 18 x 4 ½ In. 66
Camphorwood, Brassbound, Lock & Key, Black Monogram Plate On Top, 1800s, 19 x 41 x 20 In. . 600
Carrying Case, Faux Snakeskin Finish, Address, Alco, Anheuser Busch Inc., 1900s, 15 x 20 x 10 In. 60
Dome Top, Baroque Leather, Brass Studs, Iron Escutcheon, Silk Damask, 17 x 35 In. 600
Dome Top, Immigrant's, Softwood, Blue Painted, Iron Mounted, 1800s, 21 x 38 In. 59
Dome Top, Medieval Figures, Brass Accents, Barley Twisted Leg Stand, Continental, 55 x 35 ½ In.. 813
Dome Top, Pine, Sycamore, Blue Ground, Birds, Crown, 1800s, 12 x 20 x 14 In. .... *illus* 750
Dome Top, Tin Mounted, Strapwork, Fitted Tray, Side Handles, c.1890, 27 x 36 x 20 In. .. *illus* 183
Goyard, Chevron Canvas Exterior, Brassbound, Leather Handle, Red, Black, 1900s, 22 x 28 x 18 In. 2214
Goyard, Chevron Canvas, Brassbound Exterior, Metal Pulls, 1900s, 14 x 40 x 22 In. 2337
Hermes, Briefcase, Suede, Light Tan, Handle, 17 x 13 In. 3750
Leather, Trimmed In Brass, Nail Heads, Multicolor, Flowers, Leaves, 1900s, 19 x 40 x 20 In..... 923
Louis Vuitton, Briefcase, Leather, Brown, Monogram, Tan Handle, 13 x 13 ⅝ In. .... *illus* 2375
Louis Vuitton, Canvas, Leather Trim, Brass Latches, Trays, Monogram Trunk, 14 x 29 ½ In. . 7080
Louis Vuitton, Canvas, Stripes On Lid, Interior Shelf, Monogram Wardrobe, 1900s, 14 x 36 x 20 In. 5228
Louis Vuitton, Garment Bag, Rolling, Wheels, 54 x 22 ¼ In. 366
Louis Vuitton, Handles, Hardware Stamped, 1800s, 22 x 44 In. 3217
Louis Vuitton, Metal-Bound, Monogram, Black, Red, White Stripes, 2 Web Trays, 1900, 22 x 43 x 23 In. 1845
Louis Vuitton, Steamer, Canvas, Brass Latches, Lift-Out Tray, Monogram, 56 ½ x 21 ¼ In...... 6490
Louis Vuitton, Suitcase, LV Canvas, Hard Sided, Leather Handle, Brass, 1970s, 19 x 19 In........ 2880
Louis Vuitton, Train Case, Stamped LV, Latch, Cream Linen Shade, 8 ¼ x 15 ¾ In. 893
Louis Vuitton, Travel Bag, Keepall, 55, Duffel, Handles........................... 343
Louis Vuitton, Trunk, Brass Handles, Leather Strap, 1900s............................. 3720
Louis Vuitton, Wardrobe, Canvas, Wood Slats, Rivets, Leather Straps & Handle, 15 x 43 In. 7500
Mark Cross Co., Leather, Nail Heads, Handles, Band, Brown, c.1950, 24 x 20 14 In.................. 688
Moroccan Hardwood, Lift Top, Brass Band & Nailhead Trim, Pierced Lock, Handles, 25 x 50 In. .. *illus* 1250
Packard Motor Car Company, Wood, Dome Top, Leather, Canvas, Chrome Plated, 23 x 36 x 21 In. 303
Red, Black, Iron Hinges, 1868, 43 ½ x 26 In.. 96
Red, Snipe Hinges, Interior Till, Key, 1800s, 12 x 34 In................................ 409
Softwood, Dome Top, Pinwheel Stamped, Rosette, Leafy, c.1810, 13 x 30 In......................... 708
Steamer, Rectangle, Tough Metal Rivet, Corner Plates, 1900s........................... 42
Steamer, Wooden, Camel Hump, Leather, Straps, On Wheels, 1900s, 27 x 37 x 21 In.............. 72
Steamer, Wooden, Rectangular, Straps, On Wheels, 1900s, 23 x 35 x 19 In.................. 100
Wood, Hinged Lid, Hand Painted, Scrolling Design On Crimson Ground, 1900s, 22 x 38 In...... 252
Wood, Spanish, Marquetry, Light On Dark, Red Lacquer, Storage, 1800s, 14 x 32 x 18 In......... 600

TUTHILL Cut Glass Company of Middletown, New York, worked from 1902 to 1923. Of special interest are the finely cut pieces of stemware and tableware.

Compote, Blackberry Pattern, Notched Teardrop Stem, 8 x 6 ½ In. 330
Nappy, Flowers, Handle, 1 ½ x 6 In. 75
Pitcher, Intaglio, Grapes, 9 In. 1200
Pitcher, Poppies, Leaves, c.1900, 7 ¾ x 9 ½ In. 375

TYPEWRITER collectors divide typewriters into two main classifications: the index machine, which has a pointer and a dial for letter selection, and the keyboard machine, most commonly seen today. The first successful typewriter was made by Sholes and Glidden in 1874.

Caligraph No. 2, Upstroke, Full Keyboard, 2 Space Bars, 1949 862

Toy, Wagon, Wood, Iron Wheels, Spokes, John Deere, 19 ½ x 36 In.
$650

Woody Auction

Tramp Art, Bank, Yew, Inlaid Matchsticks, 8-Point Star, c.1900, 6 ½ x 6 In.
$121

James D. Julia Auctioneers

Tramp Art, Box, Sewing, Hinged Lid, Green Felt Panels, Pincushion Top, Drawer, 9 x 11 ½ In.
$265

Hess Auction Group

TIP
If you are storing a large closed container like a trunk for a long time, put a piece of charcoal in it to absorb odors.

T

Tramp Art, Bureau, Wood, Chip Carved, Tilting Mirror, 33 x 15 x 11 In. $189

Hess Auction Group

Tramp Art, Mirror, Wood, Hearts, Triangles, Circles, c.1900, 52 x 34 In. $526

Jeffrey S. Evans

Corona, Metal, Black Body, Round Keys, 1900s	30
Oliver, Olive Green, Original Paint, No. 3, c.1905, 10 ¼ In. *illus*	440
Olympia, Steel, World War II Military Issue, Case, Dark Gray, Steel, Germany *illus*	1088
Royal, Quiet De Luxe, Glass Keys, 1900s, 12 x 10 x 5 ½ In.	36
Underwood, Black Frame, Round Keys, Original Box Case, 1900s	54
Wanderer-Werke, Glass Keys, Metal, Wood Case, c.1913, 18 x 28 In.	1950
Williams, No. 4, Grasshopper Mechanism, 1949	1078

UMBRELLA collectors like rain or shine. The first known umbrella was owned by King Louis XIII of France in 1637. The earliest umbrellas were sunshades, not designed to be used in the rain. The umbrella was embellished and redesigned many times. In 1852, the fluted steel rib style was developed and it has remained the most useful style.

Bone Handle, Parasol, Ivory Silk, Embroidered Leaves, Fringe, Spain, c.1880, 25 In.	560
Chanel, Black, Cream, Color Block, Logo	281
Chanel, Outline Of Flower, Cream, Black, Box	343
Clear Vinyl, Southern Belle, Domed, Pink Trim, 1960s	125
Gold Handle, Silk, Parasol, Yellow, Steel Enforcement, France, 1900s	63
Plastic, Peter Max, Stars, Circles, Figures, Yellow, Green, Pink, Clear, 27 In.	187

UNION PORCELAIN WORKS was originally William Boch & Brothers, located in Greenpoint, New York. Thomas C. Smith bought the company in 1861 and renamed it Union Porcelain Works. The company went through a series of ownership changes and finally closed about 1922. The company made a fine quality white porcelain that was often decorated in clear, bright colors. Don't confuse this company with its competitor, Charles Cartlidge and Company, also in Greenpoint.

Oyster Plate, 4 Wells, Sauce Dish, Clamshell Shape, Apricot, 8 ¼ In. *illus*	275
Vase, Monkey Heads, Flowers, Butterflies, Gold Trim, c.1900, 12 In. *illus*	2750

UNIVERSITY CITY POTTERY, of University City, Missouri, worked from 1909 to 1915. Well-known artists, including Taxile Doat, Adelaide Alsop Robineau, and Frederick Hurten Rhead, worked there.

Vase, Ivory Crystalline Glaze, Taxile Doat, 1912, 10 x 2 ½ In.	6875

UNIVERSITY OF NORTH DAKOTA, *see North Dakota School of Mines category.*

VAL ST. LAMBERT Cristalleries of Belgium was founded by Messieurs Kemlin and Lelievre in 1825. The company is still in operation. All types of table glassware and decorative glassware have been made. Pieces are often decorated with cut designs.

Bowl, Purple, Frost, Flowers, Leaves, Kidney Bean Shape, 3 ½ x 5 ½ In.	468
Candy Dish, Cobalt Blue, Acorn Shape, Spire Finial, Footed, 10 ½ x 6 In.	93
Vase, Column Shape, Green Cut To Clear, 10 In.	156
Vase, Crisscross Cuts, Green Cut To Clear, 12 In.	156
Vase, Danse De Flore, Cobalt Blue, Gilt Dancing Figures, 10 ½ In.	281
Vase, Etched Decoration, Purple Poppies, Transparent, 1900-30, 8 ½ In.	369

VALLERYSTHAL GLASSWORKS was founded in 1836 in Lorraine, France. In 1854, the firm became Klenglin et Cie. It made table and decorative glass, opaline, cameo, and art glass. A line of covered, pressed glass animal dishes was made in the nineteenth century. The firm is still working.

Dish, Elephant & Rider, Blue Opaline, 5 ¾ x 7 In.	60
Dish, Hen On Nest, Milk Glass, 6 ¾ x 5 ½ In.	96
Vase, Cylindrical, Ruffled Rim, Amber Swirl, Flowers, Grasshopper, 16 In.	812
Vase, Gourd Shape, Enameled, Curved Neck, Applied Stem, Decorated Inside, Signed, 9 In. *illus*	9680

VAN BRIGGLE POTTERY was started by Artus Van Briggle in Colorado Springs, Colorado, after 1901. Van Briggle had been a decorator at Rookwood Pottery of Cincinnati, Ohio. He died in 1904 and his wife took over managing the pottery. One of the employees, Kenneth Stevenson, took over the company in 1969. He died in 1990 and his wife, Bertha, and son, Craig, ran the pottery. She died in 2010. The pottery closed in 2012. The wares usually have modeled relief decorations and a soft, matte glaze.

Ashtray, White, Marked, 6 ½ In.	38
Bowl, Flower Frog, Mermaid, Blue Over Green Matte Incised, Logo, 1940s, 8 ¾ In.	400
Bowl, Flower Frog, Mermaid, Mulberry Glaze, Incised & Company Logo, 1920s, 8 ½ x 15 In.	600
Bowl, Flower Frog, Tulip Shape, Marked, 3 x 8 ½ In.	83
Bowl, Lotus, Ming Turquoise, Marked, 1950s, 4 ½ x 6 In.	20
Bowl, Mauve Glaze, Art Nouveau, Leaf Design, 1905, 6 In.	750
Candleholder, Mulberry, Tulip, Marked, 3 ½ x 3 In.	40
Figure, Cat, Blue Matte, 15 In.	250
Figurine, Mammy & Child, Blue, Gunmetal, c.1940, 6 ½ In.	500
Flower Frog, Blue To Green, Oval, 4 ¼ x 2 In.	42
Tile, Kingfisher, Frame, c.1915, 5 ¾ x 5 ¾ In.	1125
Vase, Compressed Pear Shape, Mulberry, Leaves, 5 In.	121
Vase, Despondency, Nude Around Rim, Yellow Matte Glaze, Blue Top, 16 In., 1970s	475
Vase, Dragonfly Handles, Mulberry Glaze, Incised Bottom, 9 ¾ In.	200
Vase, Gourd Shape, Mustard, Yellow Glaze, 1905, 5 x 3 In.	687
Vase, Gourd, Stylized Lotus Flower & Leaves, Green, Purple Matte Glaze, 1903, 10 x 5 In.	2880
Vase, Iris, Art Nouveau, Maroon, Blue, Marked, c.1920	324
Vase, Lorelei, Woman On Rim, Green Speckled Glaze, c.1905, 9 ¾ x 4 In. *illus*	10000
Vase, Molded Flowers, Shape 283, Ming Blue Glaze, Marked, 1906, 4 ½ x 10 In.	450
Vase, Poppies, Pale Blue Glaze, Stick Neck, c.1905, 9 ¼ x 7 In.	2500
Vase, Stylized Daisies, Turquoise Glaze, c.1910, 10 x 3 ½ In.	594
Vase, Stylized Flowers & Leaves, Variegated Green Glaze, c.1915, 14 x 10 In.	3375
Vase, Stylized Leaves, Berries, Pale Pink, Squat, 1905, 4 ½ x 11 In.	1500
Vase, Turquoise Matte Glaze, Marked, 1907, 5 In.	1298
Vase, Virginia Creepers, Brown, Celadon, 1904, 8 x 6 ½ In.	2500
Vase, Yucca, Mulberry & Blue Glazes, 17 In.	695

VASA MURRHINA is the name of a glassware made by the Vasa Murrhina Art Glass Company of Sandwich, Massachusetts, about 1884. The glassware was transparent and was embedded with small pieces of colored glass and metallic flakes. The mica flakes were coated with silver, gold, copper, or nickel. Some of the pieces were cased. The same type of glass was made in England. Collectors often confuse Vasa Murrhina glass with aventurine, spatter, or spangle glass. There is uncertainty about what actually was made by the Vasa Murrhina factory. Related pieces may be listed under Spangle Glass.

Bowl, Glass, Rose Color, Metallic Flakes, Gold, Silver, Copper, c.1885, 3 ½ In. *illus*	906
Bride's Basket, Pink & White Bowl, Piecrust Edge, Silver Plated Frame, Cherub Figure, 9 ½ x 9 ¼ In.	270

VASELINE GLASS is a greenish-yellow glassware resembling petroleum jelly. Pressed glass of the 1870s was often made of vaseline-colored glass. Some vaseline glass is still being made in old and new styles. The glass fluoresces under ultraviolet light. Additional pieces of vaseline glass may also be listed under Pressed Glass in this book.

Bowl, Maltese & Ribbon, Hobbs, Brockunier & Co., c.1886, 4 ¾ x 8 ¼ In.	140
Butter, Button & Daisy, Belmont Glass Works, 8 ¼ In.	90
Cake Stand, Antique & Wildflower Pattern Glass, 6 ½ x 9 ½ In.	150
Cake Stand, Button & Daisy Thumbprint Pattern, 6 ¼ x 11 In.	84
Cake Stand, Pedestal, Round Foot, 5 ¾ x 6 ½ In.	28
Celery Vase, Daisy & Button, Belmont Glass Works, 9 In.	200
Celery Vase, Pedestal, Daisy & Button, Cross Bar Pattern, 7 In.	60
Compote, 8-Sided, Daisy & Button Pattern, 7 ¾ x 8 In.	96
Compote, Daisy & Button, Crossbar Pattern, 7 ½ x 8 ½ In.	48
Compote, Daisy & Button, Openwork Scalloped Rim, Belmont Glass Works, 14 In.	450

Tramp Art, Smoking Stand, Wood, Chip Carved, Red & Yellow Paint, Tobacco Leaf Finial, 38 In.
$265

Hess Auction Group

Trap, Eel, Basket, Splint, Oak, Woven, Native American, 20 ½ In.
$60

Hess Auction Group

Trap, Mouse, Falling Block, Wood, 1800s, 8 ¾ x 16 ½ x 5 In.
$295

Hess Auction Group

U
V

Trench Art, Vase, Field Hospital, Army Truck, Masonic Symbols, Eagle, W.M. Morris, 1917
$540

Trivet, Brass, Heart Shape, Looped Handle, c.1800, 9 1/2 x 4 3/4 In.
$110

Trivet, Pottery, Brown Glaze, Round, Holes, 2 Handles, David Gill, 8 In.
$108

Compote, Opalescent, Amber, Yellow, Water Lily, 6 x 12 In.		24
Dish, Lion Lid, 4 x 5 In.	illus	60
Marmalade, Blue Ruffled Mouth, Metal Frame, 7 x 7 In.		193
Paperweight, Cat, Seated, 3 1/8 In.		29
Pitcher, Diamond, Panel-Optic, Pressed Feather Handle, c.1900, 9 3/8 In.	illus	35
Pitcher, Milk, Rose Sprig, Campbell, Jones & Co., c.1886, 7 3/4 In.		46
Pitcher, Rectangular, Hexagonal Foot, c.1975, 8 7/8 In.		93
Pitcher, Water, Rose In Snow, Applied Handle, Campbell, Jones & Co., c.1885, 8 5/8 In.		70
Salt, Clamshell, Fish, 2 1/2 x 4 1/2 In.		18
Serving Tray, Fine Cut Pattern, Bull's-Eye Border, Tab Handles, Scalloped Rim, 15 x 9 1/2 In.		48
Shaker, Flowers, Leaves, 5 x 2 1/2 In.		33
Syrup, Daisy & Button, Bird Finial, Beaumont Glass Co., 1900, 7 1/8 In.		120
Tray, Maple Leaf, Gillinder & Sons, c.1885, 13 3/8 x 10 3/8 In.		81
Vase, Jack-In-The-Pulpit, Opalescent, 12 1/2 In.		45
Vase, Squared, Rondella, Finland, 8 x 3 3/4 In.		77
Water Set, Rose In Snow, Pitcher, 6 Wine, Campbell, Jones & Co., c.1885, 8 3/4 In., 7 Piece		234

VENETIAN GLASS, *see Glass-Venetian category.*

VENINI GLASS, *see Glass-Venetian category.*

VERLYS glass was made in Rouen, France, by the Societe Holophane Français, a company that started in 1920. It was made in Newark, Ohio, from 1935 to 1951. The art glass is either blown or molded. The American glass is signed with a diamond-point-scratched name, but the French pieces are marked with a molded signature. The designs resemble those used by Lalique.

Bowl, Dark Aqua, 3 Nudes Swimming, 2 x 15 In.		180
Vase, Clear, Animal Forms, France, 1900s, 8 In.		180
Vase, Frosted Icicle Design, Beveled Square Base, Etched Signature Under Base, 7 3/4 x 5 3/4 In.		45
Vase, Lace, Acid Etched, Square Base, Verlys Of Amercia, c.1944, 7 1/2 x 5 x 3 1/2 In.	illus	159

VERNON KILNS was the name used by Vernon Potteries, Ltd. The company, which started in 1912 in Vernon, California. It was originally called Poxon China. In 1931 the company was sold and renamed Vernon Kilns. It made dinnerware and figurines. It went out of business in 1953. The molds were bought by Metlox, which continued to make some patterns. Collectors search for the brightly colored dinnerware and the pieces designed by Rockwell Kent, Walt Disney, and Don Blanding. For more prices, go to kovels.com.

Early California, Eggcup, Double, Green, 3 1/4 In.		26
Linda, Plate, Dinner, Montecito, 9 3/4 In.		8
Modern California, Serving Bowl, Azure Blue, Marked, 9 1/2 x 7 1/4 In.		23
Mojave, Bowl, Vegetable, Divided, 1950s, 11 5/8 x 6 3/4 In.		52
Organdie, Chop Plate, Marked, 13 3/4 In.		28

VIENNA, *see Beehive category.*

VIENNA ART plates are round metal serving trays produced at the turn of the century. The designs, copied from Royal Vienna porcelain plates, usually featured a portrait of a woman encircled by a wide, ornate border. Many were used as advertising or promotional items and were produced in Coshocton, Ohio, by J. F. Meeks Tuscarora Advertising Co. and H.D. Beach's Standard Advertising Co. Some are listed in Advertising in this book.

Plate, Woman, Doves, Fountain, Blue Birds, Light Green Gold Tones, Tin, 1905, 10 In.	illus	55
Plate, Woman, Flowers In Hair, Harvard Brewing Co., Tin Lithograph, 10 In.		160
Plate, Woman, Long Hair, Tin Lithograph, 20th Century, 10 In.		249

VILLEROY & BOCH POTTERY of Mettlach was founded in 1836. The firm made many types of wares, including the famous Mettlach steins. Collectors can be confused because although Villeroy & Boch made most of its pieces in the city of

Trunk, Dome Top, Pine, Sycamore, Blue
Ground, Birds, Crown, 1800s,
12 x 20 x 14 In.
$750

Garth's Auctioneers & Appraisers

Trunk, Dome Top, Tin Mounted, Strapwork,
Fitted Tray, Side Handles, c.1890,
27 x 36 x 20 In.
$183

Neal Auction Co.

Trunk, Louis Vuitton, Briefcase, Leather,
Brown, Monogram, Tan Handle, 13 x 13 ⅝ In.
$2,375

Heritage Auctions

Trunk, Moroccan Hardwood, Lift Top,
Brass Band & Nailhead Trim, Pierced Lock,
Handles, 25 x 50 In.
$1,250

Neal Auction Co.

TIP

*When starting a dirty job like cleaning metal or refinishing pewter,
try this trick. Rub your nails into a bar of soap. At cleanup time the
dirt will easily come out from under the nail tips.*

Typewriter, Oliver, Olive Green, Original Paint, No. 3, c.1905, 10 ¼ In.
$440

Ruby Lane

Typewriter, Olympia, Steel, World War II Military Issue, Case, Dark Gray, Steel, Germany
$1,088

Morphy Auctions

U
V

Union Porcelain Works, Oyster Plate, 4 Wells, Sauce Dish, Clamshell Shape, Apricot, 8 1/4 In.
$275

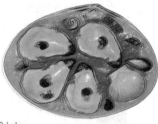

Ruby Lane

Union Porcelain Works, Vase, Monkey Heads, Flowers, Butterflies, Gold Trim, c.1900, 12 In.
$2,750

Rago Arts and Auction Center

Vallerysthal, Vase, Gourd Shape, Enameled, Curved Neck, Applied Stem, Decorated Inside, Signed, 9 In.
$9,680

James D. Julia Auctioneers

Mettlach, Germany, the company also had factories in other locations. The dating code impressed on the bottom of most pieces makes it possible to determine the age of the piece. Additional items, including steins and earthenware pieces marked with the famous castle mark or the word *Mettlach*, may be found in the Mettlach category.

Vase, Art Nouveau, Hops Design, High Glaze, 11 In.	130
Vase, Hops Design, Art Nouveau, Dark Green, Yellow Glaze, Waisted, Marked, 11 In.	153

VOLKMAR Corona N.Y   **VOLKMAR POTTERY** was made by Charles Volkmar of New York from 1879 to about 1911. He was associated with several firms, including the Volkmar Ceramic Company, Volkmar and Cory, and Charles Volkmar and Son. He was hired by Durant Kilns of Bedford Village, New York, in 1910 to oversee production. Volkmar bought the business and after 1930 only the Volkmar name was used as a mark. Volkmar had been a painter, and his designs often look like oil paintings drawn on pottery.

Plaque, First White House, Cherry St., N.Y., c.1900, 11 In.	295
Vase, Green Matte Glaze, 15 x 6 In.	550
Vase, Green Matte Glaze, Stick Neck, 15 x 6 In.	1200
Vase, Mottled Turquoise Glaze, Signed, 1931, 21 x 16 In.	720
Vase, Oxblood, Shouldered, Signed, 4 1/2 In.	240

VOLKSTEDT was a soft-paste porcelain factory started in 1760 by Georg Heinrich Macheleid at Volkstedt, Thuringia. Volkstedt-Rudolstadt was a porcelain factory started at Volkstedt-Rudolstadt by Beyer and Bock in 1890. Most pieces seen in shops today are from the later factory.

Figurine, Courting Couple, Plumed Hat, Birdcage, Flower Basket, 8 x 6 In.		77
Group, Bacchic Cherubs & Goat, Oval Base, Blue Crown Mark, 9 x 12 3/4 In.	*illus*	305
Plate, Napoleon Portrait, Geometric Border, Flowers, Gold Trim, 10 In.	*illus*	563

WADE figures c.1936+   **WADE** pottery is made by the Wade Group of Potteries started in 1810 near Burslem, England. Several potteries merged to become George Wade & Son, Ltd., early in the twentieth century, and other potteries have been added through the years. The best-known Wade pieces are the small figurines called Whimsies. They were first were made in 1954. Special Whimsies were given away with Red Rose Tea beginning in 1967. The Disney figures are listed in this book in the Disneyana category.

Creamer, Luster, Acorns, 1940s, 5 In.		59
Figurine, Budgerigar On Floral Branch, Pink, Green, Faust Lang, Marked, 5 In., 1930s	*illus*	333
Figurine, Danny Boy, 3 1/2 In.		38
Figurine, Goldfinch, Head Down, 1930, 4 In.		145
Figurine, Paddy Reilly, Dog, 3 3/4 In.		18
Figurine, Pierette, Seated On Plinth, Tambourine, Multicolor, c.1936, 6 In.		586
Mug, Fox Hunt, 4 3/4 In.		15

WAHPETON POTTERY, *see Rosemeade category.*

WALL POCKETS were popular in the 1930s. They were made by many American and European factories. Glass, pottery, porcelain, majolica, chalkware, and metal wall pockets can be found in many fanciful shapes.

Beadwork, Metis, Brown Velvet, Flowers, Multicolor, Glass, Polished Cotton, 1800s, 15 x 6 3/4 In.		120
Porcelain, Mosaic, Cherubs, Flowers, 6 1/4 In.		10
Porcelain, Urn, Pink, Scrolling Prunus, Reserve, Woman & Child, In Garden, 7 3/4 x 4 In.		1500
Pottery, Kite Shape, Blue, 16 In.	*illus*	35
Walnut, Reticulated, Grapes, 1900s, 27 1/2 x 20 1/2 In.		165
Wood, Birds, House, Fold Art, Nailed Construction, c.1880, 16 x 10 In.		198
Wood, Dog, Cattails, 1800s, 11 In.		531
Wood, Scrolls, 2 Ledges, Mirror, Victorian, 14 3/4 In.		35

WALLACE NUTTING *photographs are listed under Print, Nutting. His reproduction furniture is listed under Furniture.*

WALT DISNEY, *see Disneyana category.*

WALTER, *see A. Walter category.*

WARWICK china was made in Wheeling, West Virginia, in a pottery working from 1887 to 1951. Many pieces were made with hand painted or decal decorations. The most familiar Warwick has a shaded brown background. The name *Warwick* is part of the mark and sometimes the mysterious word *IOGA* is also included.

Grill Plate, Tudor Rose Pattern, Blue & White, 1928	25
Mug, Tommy Snooks & Bessy Brooks Were Walking Out On Sunday, 3 ¼ In.	14
Pitcher, Flowers, Stems, Leaves, Red, Orange, Scrolled Handle, 9 ½ In.	54
Pitcher, Gypsy Girl, 14 ¾ x 7 ¼ In.	55
Tankard, Friar Monk, Hold Beer Glass, 12 In.	30
Vase, Clover Shape, Blossoms, Leaves, Yellow, Orange, Embossed Feet, 10 ½ In.	300
Vase, Flared, Flowers, Brown, 12 In.	65
Vase, Hibiscus, Brown Tones, Bulbous, Handle, 7 ½ In.	50

WATCH pockets held the pocket watch that was important in Victorian times because it was not until World War I that the wristwatch was used. All types of watches are collected: silver, gold, or plated. Watches are listed here by company name or by style. Wristwatches are a separate category.

Ancre Droite, Silver Case, Swiss, Remontoir, Paris, Doule Plateau	83
Bakelite, Ehor Sport, Retractable, Black, Nickel, France, 1950	30
E. Howard, Open Face, 14K Gold, White Porcelain Dial, Arabic Numerals, c.1914, 2 In.	540
E. Mathey, Animated Repeater, Sub Seconds Dial, Multicolor, Enamel, 14K, Pocket	4410
Enamel, Case, Gray Flower, Yellow Leaves, Fob, Green, Fleur-De-Lis Shape, Woman's, 1 In., Lapel *illus*	256
Gold, 18K Tricolor, Machined, Engraved Wreath, Flowers, Pearl, 1 ¾ In. *illus*	1140
Gubelin, 14K Yellow Gold Open Face, 15 Jewel, Subsidiary Seconds Dial, 2 Adjusts, Stem Set, 1 ¾ In.	600
Hampden Watch Co., Railroad, Open Face, Marked Railway, 15 Jewel, 1880	153
International, Lever Set Movement, Engine Turned Case, Gold Filigree, 2 ⅛ In., Pocket	1500
Omega, 14K Bumper Automatic, Silver Dial, Yellow Gold Hour Markers, 1 ⅜ In.	570
Open Face, 18K Yellow Gold, Engine Turned, Cartouche On Case Back, 2 In., Pocket	1800
Open Face, 18K Yellow Gold, Engraved Dial, Flowers, Leaves, Engine Turned Back Cover, 2 In.	1200
Open Face, Enamel Dial, Moon Phase Calendar, Masonic Symbols, Swiss, 1800s, 3 In.	725
Patek Philippe, Chronometer, Porcelain Dial, Spring Driven, 18K Gold Case, Marked, 1885, Pocket	3328
Patek Philippe, Open Face, 18K Yellow Gold, 20 Jewel, Monogram, Engraved, 1 ⅞ In.	1800
Paul Maillardet, Porcelain, Enamel Face, Engraved, Mehun Sur, France, 1 ¾ x 1 ¾ In.	83
Piaget, Model No. G 34, Stainless Steel Case, Gray Dial, Silver Baton Hour Markers, 1 ⅜ In.	660
Pierpoint, Incabloc, Yellow Gold-Filled Chronograph, Baton Hour Markers, 17 Jewel, 1 ⅜ In.	215
Rockford, White Dial, Chapter Ring, Arabic Numerals, Blued Spade Hands, 21 Jewel, c.1910	677
Waltham, 14K Gold Open Face, Riverside Model, Roman Numerals, Seconds Dial, 1 ⅞ In., Pocket.	600

WATCH FOBS were worn on watch chains. They were popular during Victorian times and after. Many styles, especially advertising designs, are still made today.

5 Plaques, Art Nouveau Scrolling, Round Links, Sterling Silver, 5 ¼ In. *illus*	123
Bat, Suspended Baseball, Bone, Brass Mount & Chain, 1890s, 5 ½ In. *illus*	354
Bloodstone, Carnelian, Gold Swivel Mount, Link Chain, T-Bar End, Victorian, 11 In.	255
Carnelian Tablet, Cut Corners, Rose & White Gold Chain, 10 ½ In.	461
Carnelian Tablet, Serpentine Chain, Bicolor Chain, T-Bar End, 10 ½ In.	461
Link, Alternating Round & Oval, 18K Gold, England, 17 In.	2000
Quartz, 14K Gold, Square, Shell Scrolls In Corners, Swivel Mount, 1 ¼ In.	544
Victorian, Rolled Gold, 5 In.	51
Yellowstone National Park, Bear, Red, White & Blue Bands, Brass, Scalloped Rim, 1 ¼ In.	72

WATERFORD type glass resembles the famous glass made from 1783 to 1851 in the Waterford Glass Works in Ireland. It is a clear glass that was often decorated by cutting. Modern glass is being made again in Waterford, Ireland, and is marketed under the name Waterford. Waterford merged with Wedgwood in 1986 to form the Waterford

Van Briggle, Vase, Lorelei, Woman On Rim, Green Speckled Glaze, c.1905, 9 ¾ x 4 In.
$10,000

Rago Arts and Auction Center

Vasa Murrhina, Bowl, Glass, Rose Color, Metallic Flakes, Gold, Silver, Copper, c.1885, 3 ½ In.
$906

Ruby Lane

Vaseline Glass, Dish, Lion Lid, 4 x 5 In.
$60

Martin Auction Co.

W

This is an edited listing of current prices. Visit **Kovels.com** to check thousands of prices from previous years and sign up for free information on trends, tips, reproductions, marks, and more.

Vaseline Glass, Pitcher, Diamond, Panel Optic, Pressed Feather Handle, c.1900, 9 3/8 In.
$35

Jeffrey S. Evans

Verlys, Vase, Lace, Acid Etched, Square Base, Verlys Of Amercia, c.1944, 7 1/2 x 5 x 3 1/2 In.
$159

Ruby Lane

Vienna Art, Plate, Woman, Doves, Fountain, Blue Birds, Light Green Gold Tones, Tin, 1905, 10 In.
$55

Ruby Lane

Volkstedt, Group, Bacchic Cherubs & Goat, Oval Base, Blue Crown Mark, 9 x 12 3/4 In.
$305

Neal Auction Co.

Wedgwood Group. Most Waterford Wedgwood assets were bought by KPS Capital Partners of New York in 2009 and became part of WWRD Holdings. WWRD was bought by Fiskars in 2015 and Waterford glass is still being made.

Bowl, Colleen, 9 In.	75
Cake Stand, Starburst Pattern, 4 5/8 x 11 In.	53
Candelabrum, Crystal, 2 Serpentine Arms, Candle Cups, Bobeches, Prism, 1900s, 18 x 14 In.	125
Decanter, Lismore, Octagonal Stopper, 13 x 4 In.	50
Jar, Glandore, Round, 7 1/2 x 5 1/2 In.	62
Lamp, Table, Lismore, Bulbous, Marked, 1900s, 15 In.	62
Vase, Trumpet, Starburst Foot, 6 1/4 x 5 In.	28

WATT family members bought the Globe pottery of Crooksville, Ohio, in 1922. They made pottery mixing bowls and tableware of the type made by Globe. In 1935 they changed the production and made the pieces with the freehand decorations that are popular with collectors today. Apple, Starflower, Rooster, Tulip, and Autumn Foliage are the best-known patterns. Pansy, also called Rio Rose, was the earliest pattern. Apple, the most popular pattern, can be dated from the leaves. Originally, the apples had three leaves; after 1958 two leaves were used. The plant closed in 1965. Reproductions of Apple, Dutch Tulip, Rooster, and Tulip have been made. For more prices, go to kovels.com.

Apple, Bowl, No. 73, 3 Leaf, 9 1/2 x 3 7/8 In.	58
Apple, Mixing Bowl, 2 Leaf, Marked, 5 3/4 x 8 7/8 In.	95
Creamer, Rooster, No. 62, 4 In.	95
Dutch Tulip, Pitcher, No. 15, Marked, 5 1/4 In.	140
Rooster, Pitcher, Red, Green, Black, 1955, 5 1/2 In. ..... *illus*	75
Starflower, Pitcher, No. 17, Marked, 8 x 9 In.	100

WAVE CREST WARE **WAVE CREST** glass is an opaque white glassware manufactured by the Pairpoint Manufacturing Company of New Bedford, Massachusetts, and some French factories. It was decorated by the C.F. Monroe Company of Meriden, Connecticut. The glass was painted in pastel colors and decorated with flowers. The name Wave Crest was used starting in 1892.

Bell, Dinner, Scroll Mold, White, Blue Flowers, Ornate Gilt Metal Base, 3 1/2 x 3 3/4 In.	480
Biscuit Barrel, Blue Flowers, Green & Orange Leaves, White Ground, 10 x 6 In.	34
Box, Square, Hinged Cover, Cigars, Blue, Cream, Flowers, 6 1/2 x 5 In.	300
Dresser Box, Egg Crate Mold, Hinged Cover, Green Border, White, Pink Roses, Lion's Head Feet, 6 x 7 In.	660
Dresser Box, Helmschmied Swirl Pattern, Enamel, Satin Lining, 3 1/2 x 5 3/4 In.	102
Dresser Box, Open, 2 Mirrors, Pink, White, Blue Flowers, 6 3/4 x 6 In.	210
Dresser Box, Round, Hinged Cover, White Puffy Mold, Pale Blue, Cobalt Blue Trim, 3 x 7 In.	180
Dresser Box, Square Egg Crate Mold, Hinged Cover, Yellow Tones, Flowers, 3 1/2 x 6 1/2 In.	150
Dresser Box, Swirl Mold, Round, Hinged Cover, Cream, Lavender, White Flowers, 4 x 6 1/2 In.	150
Dresser Jar, Acid Etched Finish, Blue Shading, Yellow Roses, 1800s, 6 x 8 In. ..... *illus*	240
Ferner, 8-Sided, Footed, Pink, Cream Tones, Flowers, 6 x 8 In.	30
Flask, Pink, White, Castle Scene, Homestead Fine Bourbon Whiskey, 6 In.	300
Flask, Pocket Whiskey, Blue, White, Castle, Mountain Scene, 6 In.	150
Flask, Pocket Whiskey, Green, White, Scene, Child Flying Kite, Flowers, 6 In.	120
Inkwell, Blue, White, Pink Floral, Mold, Silver Plate Flip Cover, Glass Insert, Footed, 4 x 4 In.	600
Jar, Cigarettes, Hinged Cover, Cream & Pink Tones, Blue Flower, Shell Mold, 4 x 3 In.	330
Jewelry Box, Egg Crate Mold, Hinged Cover, Green Border, White, Pink Roses, Dolphin Feet, 5 3/4 x 5 In.	420
Jewelry Box, Hinged Cover, Maroon & Marbleized, Zinnia On Cover, Round, 2 3/4 x 4 1/4 In.	150
Jewelry Box, Hinged Pansy Cover, White, Blue, Round, 2 1/2 x 3 3/4 In.	210
Jewelry Box, Round, Hinged Cover, Pansy Mold, Cobalt Blue, Yellow & Pink, 2 1/2 x 4 In.	240
Lamp, Cream & Blue Tones, Floral Wreath, Woman Near Tree, Electrified, 20 In.	84
Plaque, Queen Louisa, Portrait, Gilt Metal Frame, 10 In. ..... *illus*	2750
Powder Box, Hinged Cover, Orange, Purple Iris, Brass Band, Mirror, 1800s, 4 x 6 In.	500
Vase, 2 Handles, Blue, White Scroll Mold, Pink Flowers, Gilt Metal Feet & Handles, 8 In.	180

WEAPONS listed here include instruments of combat other than guns, knives, rifles, or swords, and clothing worn in combat. Firearms made after 1900 are not listed in this book. Knives and Swords are listed in their own categories.

Ax, Battle, Naval, War Of 1812, Stamped, U.S., NYW, JT, 5-In. Blade	*illus*	20125
Ax, Ceremonial, Bentwood, Bolt Head, Mende People, Sierra Leone, 10 x 3 x ¼ In.		60
Club, Aboriginal, Hardwood, Ribbed Striking End, Double Cuffed, 1700s, 40 x 1⅞ In.		1140
Club, Paddle Shape, Carved, Serrated Edge, Raised Rib At Crossbar, Cuffed Butt, 1800s, 43 x 15 In.		7800
Mace, Hardwood Handle, Stone Disc Head, Vegetable Fiber Binding, Chief's Club, 1800s, 38 In.		540
Mace, Steel, Ball Shape Head, Brass Rivets, Continental, 22 In.		1187
Signal Cannon, Mounted On Newer Wood Carriage, Continental, Bronze, 1800s, 14 In., Pair.		1750

WEATHER VANES were used in seventeenth-century Boston. The direction of the wind was an indication of coming weather, important to the seafaring and farming communities. By the mid-nineteenth century, commercial weather vanes were made of metal. Many were shaped like animals. Ethan Allen, Dexter, and St. Julian are famous horses that were depicted. Today's collectors often consider weather vanes to be examples of folk art, even though they may not have been handmade.

American Indian, Silhouette, Feather Headdress, Bow, Arrow, Sheet Metal, 34½ x 30 In.		5015
Angel, Blowing Horn, Sheet Metal, 25 x 31 In.	*illus*	140
Artist Palette, Brush Though Thumb Hole, Gilt, Repousse, c.1950, 13 x 17 In.		786
Automobile, Full Body, Stick Shift, Steering Wheel, Spare Tire, Copper, 11 x 24 x 7 In.		156
Banner, Copper, Old Verdigris Surface, Quatrefoil Tail, Zinc Arrow & Ball, 1800s, 17 x 32 In.		660
Banner, Cutout Date, Verdigris, 1896, 13¼ x 34½ In.		960
Banner, Sheet Iron, Red, 34 In.	*illus*	1204
Banner, Sheet Metal, Gold, Verdigris Patina, 19 x 23 In.		281
Belle Epoch, Reticulated Wind Indicator, Reeded Post, Mount Cover, Green Patina, 1890, 60 In.		600
Biplane, Copper, Polished, Cast Iron, Iron Base Stand, 49 x 22 x 22 In.		399
Biplane, Sheet Steel, Painted Verdigris Color, Directionals, c.1950, 39 x 19 x 20 In.		360
Bull, Zinc, Full Body, Gold Leaf Surface, Wood Block Stand, 1800s, 17 x 23 In.		3300
Chicken, Painted, Sheet Iron, Directionals, 23 x 25 In.		99
Cow, Full Body, Harris & Co., Boston, c.1890, 23 x 34 In.	*illus*	3932
Cow, Iron, Glass Lightning Rod Ball, 1900s, 69¾ In.	*illus*	96
Crane, Folk Art, Heron In Flight, Directionals, 1900s, 25 x 49 In.		720
Dog, Setter Long Hair, Walking, 32 x 15 In.		3510
Dragon, Flying, Wings, Claws, Tin, 1900-50, 23 x 29½ In.		450
Eagle, Ball, Copper, Verdigris Patina, Wingspan, 20 In.		702
Eagle, Directional Arrow, Copper, Gilt, c.1950, 20½ x 20 In.		281
Eagle, Gold, Verdigris Patina, Ball, Arrow, 25 x 17 In.	*illus*	236
Eagle, Spread Wings, Directional Arrow, Ball, Copper, 1900-50, 24 x 35½ In.		420
Eagle, Spread Wings, Globe, Flagpole Topper, Figural Lion Heads, Folk Art, Metal Spike, 17 x 20 In.		563
Eagle, Spread Wings, Open Beak, Gilt, Sphere & Arrow, 36 x 22 In.		4400
Fox Hunt, Horse, Fence, 2 Dogs, North Directional, Sheet Metal, 1800s, 28 x 14 x 48 In.		650
Fox, Running, Full Body, Copper, Dark Verdigris Patina, Wooden Base, 8 x 23 In.		9000
Gamecock, Copper, Molded, Gold Paint, Wood Base, France, 1800s, 23 In.		812
Gamecock, Gilt, Copper, Mounted, 16 x 18 In.	*illus*	4956
Grasshopper, Copper, Sheet Metal Body, Green Plastic Eyes, 19 x 24 x 1 In.		126
Hand, Pointing, Copper, Cast Lead, 36 x 28 In.		2723
Helicopter, Whirling Blades, Wood, Steel, Painted, Red, Black, 1900s, 25 In.	*illus*	96
Horse & Jockey, Full Body, Directionals, Post, Copper, Fiske, c.1890, 60 In.		2125
Horse, Black Hawk, Gilt, 26 x 19 In.		4248
Horse, Black Hawk, Yellow, 22 x 17 In.		5664
Horse, Body, Molded Mane & Tail, 1860, 15 In.	*illus*	6250
Horse, Dexter, Full Body, Gold Paint, Copper, Soldered Seams, Cast Iron Head, 21 x 40 In.		330
Horse, Galloping, Dexter, Jockey, Attributed To Fiske, 15 x 33 In.		3630
Horse, Galloping, Regilded, Attributed To A.L. Jewell, 25 x 42 In.		2723
Horse, Gray, Black, Sheet Tin, 23 x 15½ In.		496
Horse, Leaping, Full Body, Gold Patina, Copper, 30 x 17 In.		5310

Volkstedt, Plate, Napoleon Portrait, Geometric Border, Flowers, Gold Trim, 10 In.
$563

Wade, Figurine, Budgerigar On Floral Branch, Pink, Green, Faust Lang, Marked, 5 In., 1930s
$333

Wall Pocket, Pottery, Kite Shape, Blue, 16 In.
$35

W

WEATHER VANE

Watch, Enamel, Case, Gray Flower, Yellow Leaves, Fob, Green, Fleur-De-Lis Shape, Woman's, 1 In., Lapel
$256

Morphy Auctions

Watch, Gold, 18K Tricolor, Machined, Engraved Wreath, Flowers, Pearl, 1¾ In.
$1,140

Cowan's Auctions

Watch Fob, 5 Plaques, Art Nouveau Scrolling, Round Links, Sterling Silver, 5¼ In.
$123

Antiques & Art International

Watch Fob, Bat, Suspended Baseball, Bone, Brass Mount & Chain, 1890s, 5½ In.
$354

Hake's Americana & Collectibles

Watt, Rooster, Pitcher, Red, Green, Black, 1955, 5½ In
$75

Ruby Lane

Wave Crest, Dresser Jar, Acid Etched Finish, Blue Shading, Yellow Roses, 1800s, 6 x 8 In.
$240

Garth's Auctioneers & Appraisers

Wave Crest, Plaque, Queen Louisa, Portrait, Gilt Metal Frame, 10 In.
$2,750

Woody Auction

Weapon, Ax, Battle, Naval, War Of 1812, Stamped, U.S., NYW, JT, 5-In. Blade
$20,125

James D. Julia Auctioneers

Weather Vane, Angel, Blowing Horn, Sheet Metal, 25 x 31 In.
$140

Copake Auction

W

Horse, Prancing, Sulky, Sheet Tin, Metal, Iron, 38½ In.	496
Horse, Running, Copper, Gilt, Steel Rod Base, 1800s, 17 x 32 In.	540
Horse, Running, Full Body, Cast Zinc Head, Verdigris Patina, Harris & Co., 1800s, 30 x 34 In.	2280
Horse, Running, Full Body, Copper, Zinc Head, Molded, c.1890, 42 In. .... *illus*	4305
Horse, Running, Nelson, Solid Head, Copper, Verdigris Patina, Mott, 41 x 30 In.	7080
Horse, Running, Solid, Verdigris Patina, Copper, 27 x 16 In.	991
Horse, Running, Wood, Sheet Metal, Angel Blowing Horn, 26 In.	70
Horse, Trotting, Molded Tin, Wrought Iron, Wood Stand, 19 x 30 x 1 In.	625
Indian, Silhouette, Iron, Pontiac Dealership, 32 x 28 In.	1380
Pig, Curly Tail, Copper, 34 x 22 In.	1287
Pig, Wood, Worn Surface, 22 x 16 In. .... *illus*	1699
Rooster, Arrow, Verdigris Patina, Copper, 1800s, 24 x 18 In.	2832
Rooster, Full Body, Zinc, Wood, 22 x 28 In.	531
Rooster, Iron, Sheet Metal, Rochester, 35 x 31 In.	4956
Rooster, Strutting, Cast Iron Legs, Gilt, c.1880, 18 x 14 In.	1815
Rooster, Verdigris Patina, Copper, 54 x 57 In. .... *illus*	3398
Rooster, Zinc, Cast, Sheet Metal Tail, 23 In.	960
Ship, 3-Masted, Sheet Iron, Old Silver Paint, c.1910, 30 x 41 In. .... *illus*	510
Sperm Whale, Wood, 13½ In.	360
Stag, Leaping, Copper, Cast Zinc Head & Antlers, c.1890, 25 x 31½ In.	1560
Steam Tractor, Wagon, Spoked Wheels, Sheet Steel, 18 x 53 In.	423
Steer, Standing, Mottled, Copper, 18½ x 28 In.	1080
Whale, Spouting, Sheet Metal, 1900s, 28 x 30 In.	200

WEBB glass was made by Thomas Webb & Sons of Ambelcot, England. Many types of art and cameo glass were made by them during the Victorian era. Production ceased by 1991 and the factory was demolished in 1995. Webb Burmese and Webb Peachblow are special colored glasswares of the Victorian era. They are listed at the end of this section. Glassware that is not Burmese or Peachblow is included here.

Webb

Bottle, Swan Head, Amber Beak, White Feathers, Threaded Collar, Silver Hallmark, 5¾ In.	6050
Compote, Alexandrite, Lavender To Yellow, Honeycomb Optic, Ruffled Rim, 5½ In.	710
Epergne, Rock Crystal, Ruby Red Fish, Carved Waves, Footed, 10½ In.	13310
Fairy Lamp, Burmese Cased, Cream Interior, Rigaree, 5⅜ x 5⅞ In.	556
Lamp, Oil, White, Red, Flowers, Yellow Ground, 3 Glass Feet, Cameo, Marked, 13 In.	2722
Perfume Bottle, Apple, Red Ground, Silver Lid, Hinged, c.1900, 4¾ In.	875
Perfume Bottle, Red, White Cameo, Silver Top, 3½ x 2½ In. .... *illus*	461
Vase, Amber, Purple, Fruit, c.1900, 5¾ In.	10000
Vase, Cameo, Flowers, Stems, Pink, White, Frosted Yellow Ground, Shouldered, Signed, 10 In.	4235
Vase, Citron Ground, White Cameo, Flowers, Butterfly, 1895-1900, 6 In.	400
Vase, Cone Shape, Cameo White Flowers, Light Blue Ground, 5 In.	2299
Vase, Cranberry, Double Band Rim, Flowers, Leaves, c.1925, 4¾ In.	250
Vase, Cream Tones, Gold Enamel Branch & Bird, 12 In.	120
Vase, Flared Rim, White Cameo, Bulbous, Honey, Accented Butterfly, 1900, 6 In.	677
Vase, Ivory Glass Cameo, Flowers, Berries, Cameo Tassels On Each Side, 6 In.	3932
Vase, Narrow Neck, Cylindrical, White Cameo, Berry Decoration, 1900, 11 In.	431
Vase, Stick, Cameo, Intaglio, Rose, Yellow, Pink, Wildflowers, Beading, 7 In.	1298
Vase, White Cameo Feathers, Leaves & Berries Encircling Vase, Red Frosted, 14 In.	2117
Vase, White Leaves, Green Satin Glass Ground, Cameo, 1881-91, 5 In.	840

WEBB BURMESE is a shaded Victorian glass made by Thomas Webb & Sons of Stourbridge, England, from 1886. Pieces are shades of pink to yellow.

Fairy Lamp, Custard Shaded To Pink, Painted Flowers, Ruffled, 3-Footed, 7 In. .... *illus*	1016
Sugar Shaker, Round, Enameled Leaves & Berries, Silver Plated Lid, 3 In. .... *illus*	738
Vase, Yellow Shaded To Rose, Stretched & Folded Rim, c.1890, 3⅜ In. .... *illus*	222

WEBB PEACHBLOW is a shaded Victorian glass made by Thomas Webb & Sons of Stourbridge, England, from 1885.

Weather Vane, Banner, Sheet Iron, Red, 34 In.
$1,204

Copake Auction

Weather Vane, Cow, Full Body, Harris & Co., Boston, c.1890, 23 x 34 In.
$3,932

James D. Julia Auctioneers

Weather Vane, Cow, Iron, Glass Lightning Rod Ball, 1900s, 69¾ In.
$96

Eldred's Auctioneers and Appraisers

W

Weather Vane, Eagle, Gold, Verdigris Patina, Ball, Arrow, 25 x 17 In.
$236

Copake Auction

Weather Vane, Gamecock, Gilded, Copper, Mounted, 16 x 18 In.
$4,956

Copake Auction

Weather Vane, Helicopter, Whirling Blades, Wood, Steel, Painted, Red, Black, 1900s, 25 In.
$96

Eldred's Auctioneers and Appraisers

W

Weather Vane, Horse, Body, Molded Mane & Tail, 1860, 15 In.
$6,250

Garth's Auctioneers & Appraisers

Weather Vane, Horse, Running, Full Body, Copper, Zinc Head, Molded, c.1890, 42 In.
$4,305

Skinner, Inc.

Weather Vane, Pig, Wood, Worn Surface, 22 x 16 In.
$1,699

Copake Auction

Weather Vane, Rooster, Verdigris Patina, Copper, 54 x 57 In.
$3,398

Copake Auction

Weather Vane, Ship, 3-Masted, Sheet Iron, Old Silver Paint, c.1910, 30 x 41 In.
$510

Garth's Auctioneers & Appraisers

Webb, Perfume Bottle, Red, White Cameo, Silver Top, 3 ½ x 2 ½ In.
$461

Cowan's Auctions

Vase, Glass, Bulbous Shape, Shades Of Pink, Gold Leaves & Vines, c.1880, 7½ In. .... *illus* 895
Vase, Stick, Ivory Casing, Gold Decoration, Asian Design, 1800s, 8 In. 120

WEDGWOOD, one of the world's most successful potteries, was founded by Josiah Wedgwood, who was considered a cripple by his brother and was forbidden to work at the family business. The pottery was established in England in 1759. The company used a variety of marks, including Wedgwood, Wedgwood & Bentley, Wedgwood & Sons, and Wedgwood's Stone China. A large variety of wares has been made, including the well-known jasperware, basalt, creamware, and even a limited amount of porcelain. There are two kinds of jasperware. One is made from two colors of clay; the other is made from one color of clay with a color dip to create the contrast in design. In 1986 Wedgwood and Waterford Crystal merged to form the Waterford Wedgwood Group. Most Waterford Wedgwood assets were bought by KPS Capital Partners of New York in 2009 and became part of WWRD Holdings. A small amount of Wedgwood is still made in England at the workshop in Barlaston. Most is made in Asia. Wedgwood has been part of Fiskars Group since 2015. Other Wedgwood pieces may be listed under Flow Blue, Majolica, Tea Leaf Ironstone, or in other porcelain categories.

WEDGWOOD & BENTLEY
Wedgwood & Bentley
1769–1780

OF ETRURIA · WEDGWOOD® · MADE IN ENGLAND · BARLASTON
Wedgwood
1940

W · WEDGWOOD · ENGLAND 1759
Wedgwood
1998–present

Basket, Creamware, Circular, Loop Handle, 1900, 5 x 7 In.	59
Bough Pot, Pierced Lid, White Relief, Amorini, Leaf Borders, Lid, 1800s, 11 In.	523
Bowl, Fairyland Luster, Fairies, Trees, Octagonal, 1920s, 4 x 8½ In. .... *illus*	2000
Bowl, Fairyland Luster, Fiddler In Tree, Ship & Mermaid Interior, 3¾ x 8½ In.	2420
Bowl, Fairyland Luster, Gilt Stamp, Marked, 1920s, 4 x 9 In.	2375
Bowl, Fairyland Luster, Gold Dragons, Blue Ground, Base, 5½ x 9 In. .... *illus*	800
Bowl, Fairyland Luster, Moorish Pattern, Crimson Columns, Arches, Octagonal, 3¾ x 8½ In. ..	4235
Bowl, Fairyland Luster, Octagonal, Gilt Stamp, 1920s, 4 x 9 In.	2750
Bowl, Fairyland Luster, Woodland Elves IV, Big Eyes, Leaves, Gilded Accents, 5½ x 9 In.	6050
Bowl, Fairyland Luster, Woodland Elves VII, Fairy In Cage, 9½ x 4½ In.	1475
Bowl, Fairyland Luster, Woodland Pattern, Daisy Makeig-Jones, 4½ x 10 In.	3600
Bowl, Fruit, Raised, Blue, Flower, Gold, Stamped Wedgwood Pearl, England, 1800s, 6 x 14 In..	120
Bowl, Scalloped Rim, Multicolor Enamel, Classical Children, Oval Medallion, 1860, 12 In.......	800
Bowl, Vegetable, Chapoo, Lid, Flow Blue, Ironstone, 12 In.	201
Box, Lid, Fairyland Luster, Willow, Bronze, Coral, Oriental Scene, Signed, 7 x 4 In.	3025
Bust, William Shakespeare, Molded Body, Titled Base, 1964, 10 In............................	185
Chalice, Fairyland Luster, Orange Interior, Cobalt Exterior, Gilt, Birds, Chased Base, 7 x 5¼ In.	180
Clock Case, Queen's Ware, Architectural, Imari Pattern, Globe Shape Finial, 1861, 13 In.	431
Creamer, Black Basalt, Bulbous Shape, Iron Red, White Palmettes, Encaustic, 1800s, 4¼ In..	738
Custard Cup, Yellow Jasper Dip, Cylindrical, Twisted Handle, White Lattice, 1700s, 2½ In......	1169
Dish, Game, Lid, Caneware, Rabbit Finial, Fowl, Grape Drapery, 13½ In.....................	135
Egret, Ernest Light, Glass Eyes, Standing Atop Pierced Rocky Base, 1913, 7⅜ In.	215
Figurine, Scantily Clad Maiden, Holding Shell, Nymph At Well, 1860, 11 In.	1046
Figurine, Sphinx, Black Basalt, Woman's Head, Marked, 1800s, 10 x 12 In., Pair................	2091
Figurine, Woman, Seated, Dog By Her Side, Sternes's Poor Maria, Edward Keys, 1855, 11 In....	861
Flowerpot, Cylindrical, Multicolor Enamel, Tall Grass, Iris Kenlock Ware, 1800s, 5 In............	492
Frame, 5 Oval Portrait Medallions, Prior, Fletcher, Congreve, Oval Plaque, 1800, 7⅜ In..........	369
Garden Seat, Majolica, Basket Weave, Molded Body, Pale Yellow Glaze, Pinkish, Red, 1800s, 18 In..	615
Jar, Jasper Dip Tricolor, Biscuit, Silver Plated Handle, Classical Figures, Lilac, 1900s, 5 In........	338
Jar, Jasper Dip, Biscuit, Silver Plated Rim, Handle, White Classical Figure, 1800s, 6 In.........	861
Jardiniere, Copper Clad, Classical Decoration, Grapes, Lion's Heads & Figures, 1800s, 4¼ x 5 In. .	60
Jardiniere, Majolica, Multicolor, Molded, Arched Floral Panel, Ribbons, 3 Scrolled Feet, 1892, 13 In..	338
Jug, Jasperware, Red, Classical Figures In Relief, Impressed Mark, 1920, 4⅞ In.	308
Lamp, Female Figure, Seated, Pouring From Jug, Fluted Neck, Acanthus Leaves, 1800, 8⅜ In.	1968
Mold Stand, Pearlware, Pyramid Shape, Multicolor, Floral Festoons, Ribbon Ties, 1800s, 8½ In...	431
Plaque, Allegorical, Figure, Winter, Darker Blue Wash, Applied White, Oval, 1775, 3 x 4 In........	1599

Webb Burmese, Fairy Lamp, Custard Shaded To Pink, Painted Flowers, Ruffled, 3-Footed, 7 In.
$1,016

DuMouchelles

Webb Burmese, Sugar Shaker, Round, Enameled Leaves & Berries, Silver Plated Lid, 3 In.
$738

Forsythes' Auctions

Webb Burmese, Vase, Yellow Shaded To Rose, Stretched & Folded Rim, c.1890, 3⅜ In.
$222

DuMouchelles

W

Webb Peachblow, Vase, Glass, Bulbous Shape, Shades Of Pink, Gold Leaves & Vines, c.1880, 7 ½ In.
$895

Ruby Lane

Wedgwood, Bowl, Fairyland Luster, Fairies, Trees, Octagonal, 1920s, 4 x 8 ½ In.
$2,000

Rago Arts and Auction Center

Wedgwood, Bowl, Fairyland Luster, Gold Dragons, Blue Ground, Base, 5 ½ x 9 In.
$800

Cottone Auctions

Plaque, Bert Bentley, Jasperware, Oval, Light Blue, White Relief, Ebonized Wood Frame, 1920, 8 In.	1046
Plaque, Classical Relief, Green Ground Center, Flowers, Leaves, Lilac, Oval, 1800s, 4 x 6 In.....	677
Plaque, Gilt Printed History, Structure Relief, Giltwood Frame, Rectangular, 1972, 11 x 12 In.	215
Plaque, Hercules, Garden Hesperides, White Relief, Ebonized, Gilt, 1970, 5 x 15 In..................	277
Plaque, Jasper Dip, Green, White Relief, Ebonized Wood Frame, Rectangular, 1800s, 8 x 19 In..	461
Plaque, Jasperware, Green, Bacchanal Scene, 4 x 12 In.	200
Plate, Fairyland Luster, Thumbelina, Maiden At Center, Twyford Border, Signed, 11 In.	6050
Plate, West Point, As Seen From Across The Hudson River, Blue Transfer, Shield Logo, 1933, 10 In.	25
Platter, Molded Fish Shape, Leaves, Decorated, Brown, Raspberry, Oval, 1879, 25 In.	338
Platter, Peace Pattern, Dove, Torch, Quiver, Garland Border, c.1880, 17 x 14 In........................	495
Pot, Fairyland Luster, Malfrey, Big Eyes, Elves, Green Fairies, Orange Ground, Marked, 4 In.	2117
Pot, Mottled Blue Ground, Gilded, Multicolor Birds, 1920, 9 ¾ In.	523
Potpourri, Pierced Lid, Mushroom Handle, Intertwined, 1900s, 9 ½ In.	281
Stand, Bidet, Queen's Ware, Mahogany, Deep Welled Body, 1800s, 17 In..........................	86
Tazza, Rope Borders, Palmette Motifs, Jasper Medallions, Classical Figures, Flowers, 1800, 12 In. ..	523
Teakettle, Black Basalt, Scalloped Bail Handle, Circular Shape, Sybil Finial, Leaves, 1700s, 7 In.	431
Teapot, Black Basalt, Widow Finial, Engine Turned, Cylindrical Pot, Scalloped Rim, 1700s, 7 In. ..	492
Tray, Am I Not A Man & A Brother, Abolition Of Slavery In Britain, Cream, Black, Round, 1900, 4 In.	492
Tureen, Queen's Ware, Hand Painted, Black, Cream, Ladle, Underplate, 13 x 8 In. .... *illus*	316
Tureen, Sauce, Underglaze Blue, Acorn Finial, Footed Bowl, Double Looped Handles, 1800s, 7 ⅛ In.	246
Tureen, Soup, Underglaze Blue Decoration, Oval, Scrolled Handles, 1914, 13 x 16 In................	111
Urn, Crater, Loop Handles, Circular Bowl, Multicolor Enamel, Flowers, 1800, 12 In.	738
Urn, Crater, Pierced Lid, Black Basalt, Circular, Upturned Loop Handle, Enamel, 1800s, 13 In.	677
Urn, Dome Lid, Jasperware, Black, White, Square Base, Classical Maidens, Marked, c.1850, 10 In.	330
Urn, Jasperware, Tricolor, Sage Green, White & Tan, Classical Decoration, 1800s, 12 In.. *illus*	1063
Vase, Bacchus Mask Head, Horn Handles, Engine-Turned Striping, Drapery Swags, 1961, 8 In.	554
Vase, Banded, Blue, Gray Matte, Wide Mouth, Tapered, Marked, 11 In...........................	443
Vase, Banded, Blue Gray Matte Glaze, Impressed Bottom, Murray, England, 11 In.	375
Vase, Black Basalt, Lekythos Shape, 2 Loop Handles, Iron Red, Black, White, 1800s, 9 ½ In.....	615
Vase, Bowl, 3 Sybil Finials, Single Pawed Leg, Winged Lions, Triangular Base, 1800, 11 In.......	4613
Vase, Encaustic, Black Basalt, Amphora Shape, Upturned Loop Handles, Iron Red, 1800s, 9 In..	2214
Vase, Fairyland Luster, Goblin Pattern, Signed, 7 In.	10890
Vase, Fairyland Luster, Torches, Cylindrical, Flared Rim, Multicolor, 11 ¼ x 5 ½ In.	2875
Vase, Glazed White, Terra-Cotta Body, Maiden Head Handles, Swirled Fluting, 1775, 11 In.	2583
Vase, Jasper Dip, Black, White Classical Figures, Man, Phrygian Cap, 1800s, 10 In.	1599
Vase, Jasper Dip, Tricolor, Diced, Blue, White, Yellow, Flower Frog, 5 ¼ x 4 ½ In............... *illus*	402
Vase, Jasper Dip, Tricolor, Torches, Light Blue Body, Lilac Dip, Leaf Borders, 1700s, 6 ¼ In.......	615
Vase, Jasperware, Blue, Gilt Bronze Mounts, Lion Mask Handle, Classical Figures, 1700s, 9 ⅞ In.....	738
Vase, Jasperware, Light Blue, Pierced Cover, Scalloped Rim, White Relief, Acanthus Leaves, 1800s, 7 In.	800
Vase, Jasperware, Light Blue, Potpourri, Pierced Lid, Oval Shape, Socle, Plinth, Ram Head, 1900s, 14 In.	369
Vase, Jasperware, Solid Black, Relief Figures, Man Wearing Phrygian Cap, 1880, 10 x 13 In.....	1046
Vase, Maiden Head Handles, Swirled Fluting, Drapery Swags, Elongated Gadroons, 1775, 10 In.	1722
Vase, Pierced Grid Lid, Blue Acanthus, Bellflower, 1800, 5 ⅛ In.................................	677
Vase, Squat, Bulbous, Concentric Bands, Green Matte Glaze, 1900s, 6 ¾ In.	584

WELLER pottery was first made in 1872 in Fultonham, Ohio. The firm moved to Zanesville, Ohio, in 1882. Artwares were introduced in 1893. Hundreds of lines of pottery were produced, including Louwelsa, Eocean, Dickens Ware, and Sicardo, before the pottery closed in 1948.

LONHUDA

Weller Pottery
1895–1896

Weller Pottery
1895–1918

Weller Pottery
1920s

Ardsley, Bowl, Cattail, Kingfisher Flower Frog, Marked, 16 x 9 ½ In.	300
Arts & Crafts, Vase, Hexagonal, Green Matte, 7 In.	236
Aurelian, Vase, Nasturtiums, Leaves, Signed, M. Lybarger, 11 In............................	295

W

Barcelona, Vase, Handles, Marked, 18 In.		212
Brighton, Flower Frog, Pheasant, Blue, Ivory, Red, Marked, 7 x 11 ¼ In.		165
Brighton, Parrot, On Stand, High Glaze, Stamped, 7 ½ In.		650
Burnt Wood, Vase, 2 Handles, Oxen Driven By Egyptians, 9 In.		165
Chase, Vase, White Equestrian Hunt Scene, Matte Glaze, Cobalt Blue Ground, 9 x 4 ½ In.		79
Clinton Ivory, Umbrella Stand, Cylindrical, 1900s, 21 In.		84
Coppertone, Vase, 2 Fish, Green, Yellow, Half Kiln Ink Stamp, 8 ½ In.	*illus*	1180
Coppertone, Vase, Tapered, Frogs, Logo Stamp, 11 ½ In.		415
Creamer, 2 Trees, White Leaves, Green Trunks, Blue Ground, Brass Lid, 4 In.		225
Dickens Ware, Jardiniere, Black Ground, Yellow Poppies, 10 In.		142
Dickens Ware, Tankard, Chief Little Wound, Marked, 1901, 16 x 6 In.		2200
Dickens Ware, Vase, Pair Of Woodpeckers On A Tree Stump, Marked, 9 ¼ In.		590
Dickens Ware, Vase, Portrait, White Swan, Marked, A. Dunlavy, 1901, 11 ½ In.		472
Dresden, Vase, Dutch Windmills, Rolling Landscape, Marked, 7 In.		212
Eocean, Vase, Pink & Green Flowers, Glazed, Marked, c.1910, 7 ¾ In.		90
Eocean, Vase, Portrait, American Staffordshire Terrier, Marked, 10 ½ In.		236
Figurine, Elephant, Cactus Line, Yellow Glaze, Brown & Black Eye, Impressed Mark, 4 x 5 In.		102
Flemish, Tub, Planter, Basket, Pink, Flowers, Leaves, 1800s, 4 ½ x 9 In.		143
Floral, Vase, Flared Rim, Tapered, 1900s, 12 In.		156
Floretta, Vase, Handles, Fluted Flared Rim, Rust Brown Glazed Body, 1900s, 10 x 3 In.		100
Forest Sand, Jar, Trees, 13 In.		649
Fru Russet, Vase, Eagle, Rooster, Hen, Brown, Small Mouth, Round, 1905, 15 x 12 ¼ In.		8125
Fru Russet, Vase, Nude Male, Grapevines, Incised, E. Pickens, 1905, 18 In.	*illus*	6875
Fru Russet, Vase, Raised Drips, Blue, Purple, Small Mouth, Long Neck, c.1905, 11 x 5 ¾ In.		375
Gardenware, Gnomes, Toadstools, Yellow, Rose, Green, Incised, 16 ⅝ In.	*illus*	4130
Glendale, Vase, 2 Tree Trunks, Blue Bird, Yellow Butterfly, Marked, 7 In.		200
Glendale, Vase, Double Bud, Gated, Goldfinch & Nest, Marked, 5 x 8 In.		266
Grapevine, Jardiniere, Pedestal, Bowl, Twisted Rib Form, Yellow Glaze Background, 12 x 15 In.		484
Grapevine, Vase, Etched Matte, Brown & Cream Ground, 8 ⅜ In.		1121
Hudson Light, Vase, Pink Irises, Marked, 14 ½ In.		177
Hudson Perfecto, Vase, Pink Hollyhocks, Marked, Claude Leffler, 12 In.		177
Hudson Perfecto, Vase, Pink, Green, Clematis, Marked, Dorothy Laughhead 13 In.		265
Hudson, Vase, Bearded Iris, Cream, Blue, Yellow, Green, Sarah Reid McLaughlin, 1920s, 15 x 6 In.		1020
Hudson, Vase, Butterfly, 1940, 12 In.		1404
Hudson, Vase, Garden Flowers, Black Outline, Creamy Ground, 5 ¾ x 7 In.		250
Hudson, Vase, Handles, Yellow Roses, Leafy Stems, Marked, Mae Timberlake, 9 ½ In.		425
Hudson, Vase, Irises, Blue & Yellow, 2 Handles, Mae Timberlake, 13 ⅝ In.	*illus*	3540
Hudson, Vase, Irises, Marked, Mae Timberlake, 9 ¼ In.		265
Hudson, Vase, Leafy Stem, Yellow Roses, Handles, Marked, 8 In.		201
Hudson, Vase, Roses, Leafy Stems, Marked, Mae Timberlake, Handles, 9 ½ In.		502
Hudson, Vase, Stems, Flowers, Raspberries, Marked, Eugene Roberts, 8 ¾ In.		82
Lasa, Vase, Gold, Green, Reddish, Tropical Sky & Palm Trees, Marked, 5 ¾ In.		354
Louwelsa, Humidor, Green, Brown Tones, 2 Pipes, Matches, Scenic, 6 ¾ In.		420
Matte Ware, Pitcher, Lizard Climbing Up The Side, Green, Marked, 4 ¾ In.		885
Matte Ware, Vase, Arrowroot Plant, Light Green Matte, Elongated Oval, Marked, 16 In.		590
Matte Ware, Vase, Shades Of Green, Rose, Black, Fru Russet, Marked, 5 In.		1180
Matte Ware, Vase, Squat, White Daisies, Matte Green Ground, 3 x 5 In.		189
Muskota, Figurine, Hunting Dog, Seated, Impressed Mark, 5 ¾ In.		384
Muskota, Flower Frog, Turtle, Brown To Green, Walking, 5 ½ In.		144
Muskota, Flower Frog, Turtle, Pale Green To Green, Walking, 4 ¾ In.		120
Raceme, Vase, Light Blue & Black Ground, Flowers, Marked, H. Pillsbury, 5 ¾ In.		200
Roma, Jardiniere, Stand, Cream, Lions' Heads, Flowers, Fluted Column, 1900s, 34 x 15 In.	*illus*	156
Selma, Vase, Daisy & Butterfly, Marked, 4 ⅜ In.		118
Sicard, Box, Covered, Daffodil Design, Bright Green, Gold, Purple, Marked, 6 In.		826
Sicard, Vase, Art Nouveau, Corn, 4 ½ In.		975
Sicard, Vase, Daisies, Reddish Copper, Gold & Blue Matte, Marked, 5 In.		265
Sicard, Vase, Mistletoe, Purple, Gold, Green, Marked, 5 ¼ In.		354
Silva, Figurine, Dancer, Yellow Glaze, Marked, 7 ⅝ In.		413
Silvertone Vase, Kiln Mark Ink Stamp, 5 ½ x 4 ¼ In.		102
Stellar, Vase, Blue, White Stars, Marked, Hester Pillsbury, 6 ¼ x 3 ¾ In.		445

Wedgwood, Tureen, Queen's Ware, Hand Painted, Black, Cream, Ladle, Underplate, 13 x 8 In.
$316

Copake Auction

Wedgwood, Urn, Jasperware, Tricolor, Sage Green, White & Tan, Classical Decoration, 1800s, 12 In.
$1,063

Garth's Auctioneers & Appraisers

Wedgwood, Vase, Jasper Dip, Tricolor, Diced, Blue, White, Yellow, Flower Frog, 5 ¼ x 4 ½ In.
$402

Bunch Auctions

W

Weller, Coppertone, Vase, 2 Fish, Green, Yellow, Half Kiln Ink Stamp, 8 1/2 In. $1,180

Humler & Nolan

Weller, Fru Russet, Vase, Nude Male, Grapevines, Incised, E. Pickens, 1905, 18 In. $6,875

Rago Arts and Auction Center

Weller, Gardenware, Gnomes, Toadstools, Yellow, Rose, Green, Incised, 16 5/8 In. $4,130

Humler & Nolan

Weller, Hudson, Vase, Irises, Blue & Yellow, 2 Handles, Mae Timberlake, 13 5/8 In. $3,540

Humler & Nolan

Weller, Roma, Jardiniere, Stand, Cream, Raised Lions Heads, Flowers, Fluted Column, 1900s, 34 x 15 In. $156

Garth's Auctioneers & Appraisers

TIP

Iridescent pottery like Sicardo should be carefully cleaned. Wash in mild detergent and water. Rinse. Dry by buffing vigorously with dry, fluffy towels. Then polish with a silver cloth as if it were made of metal. Buff again with a clean towel.

Weller, Vase, Cylindrical, Dark Gray To Light Gray Flowers, 1900s, 12 In. $150

Garth's Auctioneers & Appraisers

Wemyss, Figurine, Pig, Raspberries, Leaves, Blue Eyes, Hand Painted , Signed, Joe Nekola $472

Humler & Nolan

Umbrella, Stand, Green Matte, Molded Poppy & Sunflower Decoration, 20 x 10 In.	408
Vase, Arts & Crafts, Green Matte, Corset, Geometric, 1900s, 10 In.	72
Vase, Cylindrical, Dark Gray To Light Gray Flowers, 1900s, 12 In. .... *illus*	150
Vase, Dandelions, Purple, Blue, Gold Swirls, Flared Mouth, 1903-17, 15 x 11 In.	2000
Vase, Tapered Rim, Slender Body, Rose, 1900s, 14 In.	120
Velva, Vase, Tapered, Round Foot, Low Relief Leaves, Flowers, 1935, 9 ½ x 5 ½ In.	157
Wall Pocket, Squirrel, Tree, Leaves, c.1930, 9 ¾ In.	140
Woodcraft, Flower Frog, Kingfisher, Marked, 9 In.	201
Woodcraft, Jardiniere, Woodpecker, Squirrel, 9 ½ In.	150

WEMYSS ware was first made in 1882 by Robert Heron & Son, later called Fife Pottery, in Scotland. Large colorful flowers, hearts, and other symbols were hand painted on figurines, inkstands, jardinieres, candlesticks, buttons, pots, and other items. Fife Pottery closed in 1932. The molds and designs were used by a series of potteries until 1957. In 1985 the Wemyss name and designs were obtained by Griselda Hill. The Wemyss Ware trademark was registered in 1994. Modern Wemyss Ware in old styles is still being made.

Figurine, Pig, Raspberries, Leaves, Blue Eyes, Hand Painted, Signed, Joe Nekola........ *illus*	472
Figurine, Pig, Roses, Crazed White Glaze, Signed, Nekola Pinxt, c.1940, 11 x 17 In. ...... *illus*	1220
Figurine, Pig, Seated, Ear Up, Green Clover, White, 1900s, 6 ½ In.	188

WESTMORELAND GLASS was made by the Westmoreland Glass Company of Grapeville, Pennsylvania, from 1889 to 1984. The company made clear and colored glass of many varieties, such as milk glass, pressed glass, and slag glass.

Westmoreland Glass
c.1910–c.1929, 1970s

Westmoreland Glass
Late 1940s–1981

Westmoreland Glass
1982–1984

Biscuit Jar, Lid, Ruby Stained, 1896, 8 ¾ In.	468
Blue Milk Glass, Eagle On Basket, Amber Glass Eyes, c.1960, 7 ⅞ x 6 ⅜ In. .... *illus*	175
Bowl, Buffalo Hunt, Chocolate, 6 ¾ x 12 ¼ In.	40
Candy Dish, Lid, Kissing Doves, Oval, Milk Glass, 1970s, 5 ½ x 6 In.	45
English Hobnail, Pitcher, Vaseline, Applied Reeded Handle, c.1975, 10 In. .... *illus*	58
English Hobnail, Vase, 3 Handles, Strawberry Diamond Shape, Crimped Rim, c.1917, 8 ⅝ In. .. *illus*	45
High Hob, Pitcher, Water, Gilt, Ruby Stained, c.1912, 8 ⅞ In.	128
Orange Peel, Cup & Saucer, Petal Rim, Roses, Scalloped, 1906, 4 x 6 In.	110

WHEATLEY POTTERY was founded by Thomas J. Wheatley in Cincinnati, Ohio. He had worked with the founders of the art pottery movement, including M. Louise McLaughlin of the Rookwood Pottery. He started T.J. Wheatley & Co. in 1880. That company was closed by 1884. Thomas Wheatley worked for Weller Pottery in Zanesville, Ohio, from 1897 to 1900. In 1903 he founded Wheatley Pottery Company in Cincinnati. Wheatley Pottery was purchased by the Cambridge Tile Manufacturing Company in 1927.

Vase, Applied Cherubs, Incised, T.J. Wheatley Pottery, 1880, 9 ¾ In. .... *illus*	1534
Vase, Leaves, Brown Glaze, c.1905, 8 x 4 ½ In. .... *illus*	625
Vase, Leaves, Green, Thick Walls, 7 ½ x 9 ¼ In.	312
Wall Pocket, Molded Flowers, Green Matte Glaze, 8 x 9 ½ In.	767

WILLETS MANUFACTURING COMPANY of Trenton, New Jersey, began work in 1879. The company made belleek in the late 1880s and 1890s in shapes similar to those used by the Irish Belleek factory. It stopped working about 1912. A variety of marks were used, most including the name *Willets.*

Vase, Exotic Birds, Flowers, Parcel Gilt, Gold, Green, Purple, Belleek, 18 In.	450
Vase, Purple Flowers, Green Leaves, Blue Band, Willets, 12 x 4 In.	132

Wemyss, Figurine, Pig, Roses, Crazed White Glaze, Signed, Nekola Pinxt, c.1940, 11 x 17 In.
$1,220

New Orleans Auction Galleries

Westmoreland, Blue Milk Glass, Eagle On Basket, Amber Glass Eyes, c.1960, 7 ⅞ x 6 ⅜ In.
$175

Ruby Lane

Westmoreland, English Hobnail, Pitcher, Vaseline, Applied Reeded Handle, c.1975, 10 In.
$58

Jeffrey S. Evans

W

Westmoreland, English Hobnail, Vase, 3 Handles, Strawberry Diamond Shape, Crimped Rim, c.1917, 8 5/8 In.
$45

Ruby Lane

Wheatley, Vase, Applied Cherubs, Incised, T.J. Wheatley Pottery, 1880, 9 3/4 In.
$1,534

Humler & Nolan

Wheatley, Vase, Leaves, Brown Glaze, c.1905, 8 x 4 1/2 In.
$625

Rago Arts and Auction Center

WILLOW pattern has been made in England since 1780. The pattern has been copied by factories in many countries, including Germany, Japan, and the United States. It is still being made. Willow was named for a pattern that pictures a bridge, birds, willow trees, and a Chinese landscape. Most pieces are blue and white. Some made after 1900 are pink and white.

Bone Dish, Buffalo Pottery, c.1910, 6 1/2 In.	75
Bowl, Vegetable, Churchill, 9 1/2 In.	28
Bowl, Vegetable, Divided, Oval, Churchill, England, 10 x 7 In.	30
Bowl, Vegetable, Lid, Pumpkin Stem, John Steventon, c.1920, 9 x 9 In.	99
Creamer, Bakewell Brothers, 3 x 5 In.	22
Dish, Shell Shape, Footed, Fluted, c.1820, 5 3/4 x 5 3/4 In.	186
Gravy Boat, Newport Pottery, 7 3/4 In.	34
Grill Plate, 3 Sections, Ideal Ironstone, 10 1/4 In.	26
Muffineer, Pedestal, 5 In.	59
Mug, Georgian Shape, Ear Handle, Churchill, England, 4 In.	8
Oil & Vinegar, Stick Neck, 6 x 4 1/4 In.	125
Pepper Pot, Ribbed, 19th Century, 3 In.	45
Pitcher, Ashworth Brothers, England, c.1910, 6 1/4 In.	38
Plate, Bread & Butter, Johnson Brothers, 6 In., 4 Piece	25
Plate, Scalloped Bow Knot Border, Booth, England, c.1915, 9 1/2 In.	35
Platter, Allerton, c.1930, 15 x 12 In.	495
Platter, Gravy Well, Staffordshire, c.1830, 19 x 15 In.	240
Platter, Occupied Japan, c.1950, 14 x 10 In.	135
Platter, Oval, Bourne & Leigh, Staffordshire, 12 x 8 In.	60
Relish, Diamond Shape, 7 1/4 x 10 1/2 In.	180
Salt & Pepper, 4-Sided, Japan, 2 1/2 In.	25
Salt & Pepper, Egg Shape, 3 1/4 In.	17
Tankard, Gold Trim, c.1930, 8 x 4 3/4 In.	195
Teapot, Lid, Sadler, England, c.1940, 5 In.	45

WINDOW glass that was stained and beveled was popular for houses during the late nineteenth and early twentieth centuries. The old windows became popular with collectors in the 1970s; today, old and new examples are seen.

Grates, Bats, Semicircle, 47 1/2 x 23 In.	3802
Leaded, 2 Swans On Lily Pad, Signed, 2 Panels, 1900s, 42 x 39 In.	4200
Leaded, 4 Panels, New York, Statue Of Liberty, Yellow, Red, Blue, France, 1960s, 48 1/2 x 12 In.	7500
Leaded, Arched, Slag Glass, Flowers, Blue, Tan, Amber, Pine Frames, 1890, 89 3/4 x 28 1/2 In., Pair	800
Leaded, Arts & Crafts, Arched Central Pane, Leaves, Slag Glass, Wood Frames, c.1925, 31 x 17 In., Pair	250
Leaded, Caramel Opalescent, Triangles, 17 x 44 In.	357
Leaded, Carpenter, Yellow Hat, Twig, Column, Multicolor, 38 x 23 In. *illus*	570
Leaded, Christ, Purple Medallion, Yellow, Brown, 55 1/2 x 34 1/2 In.	192
Leaded, Columns, Pots, Topiary, Blue & Purple Skies, 33 x 26 In., Pair	416
Leaded, Confederate Flag, Red, Blue, Stars, 1900s, 24 x 30 In.	576
Leaded, Elliptical Repeating Pattern, Oak, 1900s, 16 x 47 In.	144
Leaded, Fleur-De-Lis, Red, Pink, Amber, 21 1/2 x 39 1/2 In.	467
Leaded, Flowers, Bands, Border, 50 x 26 In.	224
Leaded, Flowers, Blue Border, Yellow, Pine Frame, 22 1/2 x 36 1/2 In.	77
Leaded, Glass, Geometric Shapes, 1900s, 32 x 36 In.	228
Leaded, Mountains, Trees, Turquoise Border, 42 x 30 In.	106
Leaded, Poppy, Mirrored Glass, Slag Glass, Oak, George Washington Maher, 23 x 51 In.	4587
Leaded, Purple Flowers, Yellow Ground, Green Border, Parcel Gilt Frame, 25 x 18 In., Pair	704
Leaded, Red Roses, Green Leaves, Amber & Cream Panel, Wood Frame, American, 30 x 20 In.	2420
Leaded, Slag Glass, Cut Glass Bull's-Eyes, Purple Irises, 49 1/2 x 42 3/8 In.	375
Leaded, Slag Glass, Peacock, Green, Amber, Teal, 1900s, 38 x 26 1/4 In.	325
Leaded, Slag Glass, Red & White Flowers, Urn, Lavender Border, Frame, 22 3/4 x 22 3/4 In., Pair	500
Leaded, Stacked Rectangles, Frank Lloyd Wright, Dana House, 1902, 27 1/2 x 62 1/4 In.	8125

Window, Leaded, Carpenter, Yellow Hat, Twig, Column, Multicolor, 38 x 23 In.
$570

Michann's Auctions

Wood Carving, Angel Wings, White, Gilt, 1900, 32 x 9 In.
$2,407

Copake Auction

Wood Carving, Artist's Model, Horse, Removable Rider, Articulated, **Iron Rod, c.1810, 21 x 24 In.**
$10,800

Brunk Auctions

Wood Carving, Artist's Model, Fruitwood, Articulated Ball Joints, Incised Facial Features, Spain, 32 x 10 In.
$1,875

New Orleans Auction Galleries

Wood Carving, Bull, Resting, Japan, 1900s, 7 x 3 ½ In.
$500

Brunk Auctions

Wood Carving, Cat, Playing Violin, Nova Scotia, 35 In.
$456

Copake Auction

Wood Carving, Chalice, Ashleaf Maple, Turned, Marked, Ed Moulthrop, 14 x 12 In.
$7,500

Rago Arts and Auction Center

TIP
Don't store wooden bowls and other pieces on their sides. This can cause them to warp.

Wood Carving, Duck, Gesso, White Painted Surfaces, Custom Wood Stand, Chinese, 1900s, 12 x 11 x 7 In.
$554

Brunk Auctions

Wood Carving, Eagle, Pine, Banner, Gilt, Blue & Red, John Haley Bellamy, 1800s, 25 In.
$875

Garth's Auctioneers & Appraisers

Leaded, Star Of David, Green, Purple, Triangular, 55 x 45 In.	155
Leaded, Transom, 3 Panels, Green, Cranberry, Amber, Woman, Garden, Bridge, Bird, 44½ x 34½ In.	1890
Leaded, Transom, Slag Glass, Beveled, Green & Red Border, Scroll, Leaf, Berries, 22¼ x 36¼ In., Pair.	175
Leaded, Tulip, Mirror Image, Teal, Pink, Amber, Green Border, 52 x 28 In.	200
Leaded, Wreath, Bell, Green, Gold, Pine Frame, 40 x 14¼ In.	62
Leaded, Yellow Scrolls, Half Moon Shape, Wood Frame, 27 x 60 In.	288
Stained Glass, Cruella De Ville, Black, Frame, Ruth Elizabeth Green, 1900s, 52 x 36 In.	180
Stained Glass, Erte, Woman, Flowing Dress, Dog, Ruth Elizabeth Green, 1900s, 37 x 37 In.	156
Stained Glass, Pink & Amber Panels Inset, 3 Multicolor Rose Clusters, Wooden Frame, 28 x 66 In.	360
Stained Glass, Woman, Alphonse Mucha, Ruth Elizabeth Green, Frame, 1900s, 73 x 30 In.	360
Stained Glass, Woman, Ram Horns, Metal Mesh, Embellishment, Frame, 1900s, 56 x 36 In.	228

 WOOD CARVINGS and wooden pieces are listed separately in this book. There are also wooden pieces found in other categories, such as Folk Art, Kitchen, and Tool.

2 Monkeys, Patina, Sacrificial Tool, Baule People, Cote D'Ivoire, 13 x 11 x 6¾ In.	240
Angel Wings, White, Gilt, 1900, 32 x 9 In. .... *illus*	2407
Antelope, Spirit Mask, Kurumba People, Burkina Faso, Painted Wood, 2 Eyeholes, 54 In.	7200
Artist's Model, Horse, Removable Rider, Articulated, Iron Rod, c.1810, 21 x 24 In. *illus*	10800
Artist's Model, Fruitwood, Ball Joints, Incised Facial Features, Spain, 32 x 10 In. *illus*	1875
Bible, Geometric Designs, Spine, Sliding Lid At Top, 1800s, 2 x 7 In.	330
Bird, Beak Functions, Paper Clip, 1900s, 7 In.	96
Blocks, Square, Ridges, Tunnels, David L. Deming, 8 x 9 In.	177
Bolo Bian, Standing, Senufo People, Burkina Faso, 39 x 6¼ x 8 In.	150
Bosatsu, On Lotus, 1800s, 9 x 78½ In.	280
Box, Hand Crafted, Lid, Red, Eagle, Stamped, 1900s, 10 x 8 In.	225
Box, Rosewood, Dragon, Cloud, Metal Mount, Lock, 1900s, 6 x 13 x 8 In.	144
Bull, Resting, Japan, 1900s, 7 x 3½ In. .... *illus*	500
Bust, Santo, Jesus Christ, Paint Remnants, 10 x 7 In.	100
Bust, Woman, Torso, Figural, MCM Fashion, 1900s	75
Card Butler, Standing Extravagant Garments, Turned Tray, Seated Dog, 34 x 20 x 12 In.	1331
Carrier, Tool, Pine, Painted, Black, Banner, Scrolls, I.F. Betz, Top Handle, 12 x 33 In.	252
Cat, Playing Violin, Nova Scotia, 35 In. .... *illus*	456
Chalice, Ashleaf Maple, Turned, Marked, Ed Moulthrop, 14 x 12 In. *illus*	7500
Cricket Cage, Carved Chinese Chestnut, Gourd Shape, Pierced Lid, Bats, 1800s, 3 x 3 x 6 In.	224
Dentist, Pulling A Tooth, Knee On Chair, Signed J. Pinal, 9¾ In.	120
Dog, Black Paint, Seated, Paws Out, Collar, 21¾ x 47 In.	3750
Dog, Hunting, Black, France, 21¾ x 47 In.	3750
Dog, Reclining, Applied Beaded Collar, Trace Red Paint, Asian Style, 1900s, 22½ In.	180
Dog, St. Bernard, Barrel On Collar, Glass Eye, Dark Brown Finish, 7¾ x 9¼ In.	1150
Dog, Whippet, Pine, Sitting, Pair, c.1875, 35 x 21½ In.	5000
Duck, Bird Mount, Brown Feathers, Iridescent, Plumage, White Eyes, 8½ x 12 x 14 In.	177
Duck, Gesso, White Painted Surfaces, Custom Wood Stand, Chinese, 1900s, 12 x 11 x 7 In. *illus*	554
Eagle, Head, Glass Eyes, Feather Detail, Ron Marino, Marked RM, 6 x 8 In.	237
Eagle, Pine, Banner, Gilt, Blue & Red, John Haley Bellamy, 1800s, 25 In. *illus*	875
Ear Shape, Abstract, Chester Pfeiffer, 1900s, 19 In.	780
Element, Architectural, Human, Animal Figures, Column Supports At Each End, 1900, 72 In.	312
Falcon, Folk Art, Outstretched Wings, Piercing Eyes, Branch, Talon, Unsigned, 1900s, 21 x 22 x 17 In.	125
Female, Abstracted, Fragmented Form, 1900	12
Fertility, Cylindrical, Glass Beads, Necklace, Zaramo People, 5¾ x 2¼ x 2¼ In.	125
Frame, Board, Trees, Dugout As Leaf Form Decorations, 1900s	24
Gondoliers, Painted, Venetian, Blackamoor Style, Pair, c.1900, 11½ x 6 In.	1750
Goose, Protecting Hatching Eggs, Ferret, Realistic, Mahogany, Abe Rissler, 1960-90, 41 x 23 x 15 In.	325
Guanyin, Oriental Goddess Of Mercy, Love, Contemporary, 12 In.	180
Guanyin, Seated, On A Lotus Throne, Detailed Robes & Jewelry, 1900s, 40 x 24 x 11 In.	390
Hand, Dove, Varnished Patina, Commemorative, 1916, 7 In.	250
Happy Buddha, Lotus Throne, Walnut, Inlaid Stone Eyes, c.1900, 8 In.	150

Headdress, Mask, Mother Of Fertility, Baga People, Guinea, Guinea Bissau, 45 x 33 x 8 In.	1920
Headpiece, African, Ekoi Ejagham, Leather, Basket Weave Helmet Liner, 1900s, 20 x 10 x 11 In..	360
Helmet, Fiber, Beard, Fiber Head Pan, 1850, 13 ½ In.	88
Horse, Caparisoned Beast, Hogged Mane, Turned Head, Gilt, Multicolor, Tang, 18 x 8 x 18 In.	224
Kangaroo, Hardstone, Diamond Eyes, 2 ¾ In.	625
Koshin Akiyama, Female Ko-Omote Mask, Signed, Silk Cord, 5 ¾ x 3 ½ In.	600
Lamp, 3-Light, Mahogany, Silk Shade, Beaded & Fringed Drop Border, Ram Heads, 23 In.	1210
Lion, Patinated Black Green Finish, 1800s, 5 x 8 In.	108
Lion, Reclining, Mouth Open, Ears Alert, Wooden Plinth, 37 x 24 In.	6655
Lohan, Head Of A Temple Guardian, Remnants Of White Ground & Paint, 1 Of 18, 1700s, 16 x 9 ½ In..	420
Madonna & Child, Extravagant Robe, Crown, Fleur-De-Lis, 60 x 16 x 13 In.	4538
Madonna & Child, Multicolor, Salvator Mundi, Germany, 1400s, 44 x 10 In.	15000
Man, Resembles Caricature Of Bing Crosby, 1900s, 14 In.	144
Mask, Antelope Headdress, Shells, Beads, Kurumba People, Burkina Faso, 64 x 10 x 27 In.	1680
Mask, Bamileke, Buffalo, Cameroon, Sign Of Power, Painted Detail, 1960s-70s, 17 x 10 In......	1920
Mask, Bobo Helmet, Multicolor, Pigment, 14 In.	188
Mask, Bull, Horns, Scarification Marks, Yaure People, Cote D'Ivoire, 18 x 7 ½ x 4 ¾ In.	313
Mask, Chameleon, Multicolor, Crest, Bobo People, Burkina Faso, 9 x 8 ½ x 35 In.	150
Mask, Cloth, Cowries, Pigments, Patina, Dan Peoples, 1900s, 10 ¾ In.	50
Mask, Cowries, Metal, Bells, Hair, Cloth, Sewing, Ear Flaps, 15 ¾ In.	563
Mask, Dance, Multicolor, Zoomorphic, Mossi People, Burkina Faso, 39 x 21 x 5 ¾ In.	270
Mask, Feather Crown, Fiber Ear Tassels, Inlaid Cowrie Shell Eyes, Mouth, 1900s, 32 x 10 In. ...	360
Mask, Grain, Yellow Hibiscus, Balinese Princess, 10 x 6 ½ x 3 ¼ In.	135
Mask, Hand Carved, Painted Long Face, Small, 1994, 12 x 8 In.	300
Mask, Hand Carved, Painted Red, Cedar, Kwactulth Speaker, 1982, 9 x 8 In.	400
Mask, Inuit, Painted Soft, Eye, Nose, Mouth Openings, Holes At Side, 1900, 10 ½ x 7 ½ In.	6000
Mask, Spirit Dance, Ammassalik, Scorch, Fossilized Ivory, For Drum Dances, 1930, 15 x 8 x 3 ½ In.	660
Miniature, Paddle, Haida, 1 Spirit Eye Painting, Blue, Black, Natural Colors, Classic, 1900s, 20 In..	300
Model, Spiral Staircase, Circular Base, 24 ½ x 10 ½ In., 1900s.	688
Monk, Raising Glass, Black Forest, c.1950, 23 In.	420
Monkey, Baule Gbekre, Both Hands Holding Bowl, Ivory Coast, 40 In.	570
Monkey, Oak, Venetian, Carved Base, c.1875, 29 x 6 ½ In.	1000
Mourning Doves, Sculpture, Fisheries, Waterfowl, Songbirds, 1983, 14 x 8 x 12 In.	543
Night Watchman, Black Forest, Metal Lantern, Germany, c.1950, 42 In...................	690
Offering Bowl, Kneeling Women, Painted, Yoruba People, Nigeria, 16 x 7 ½ x 8 In.	192
Our Lady Of Guadalupe, Alabaster, Glass & Mahogany Case, Baroque, 1800s, 17 ½ x 9 In.....	1125
Our Lady Of Guadalupe, Woman, Serpent, Painted, Mirrored Base, 1800s, 16 x 7 In..... *illus*	2250
Owl, Painted, Marked, Robert & Virginia Warfield, 1981, 11 In................................	1375
Owl, Perched On Wooden Stump, Horizontal Line Through Them, 2000s, 20 ½ x 8 In.	76
Owl, Straight Face, Perched On Wooden Stump, 1900s, 21 x 11 x 8 In...................	192
Panel, Chinese, Decorative, Precious Objects, 25 In.......................................	1600
Panel, Figural, Scrolling End, Pierced, Chinese, 1900s, 16 x 39 In................................	38
Panel, Gilt, Battle, Horses, Warriors, Trees, Pagoda, Chinese, 32 ½ x 23 ½ In.	687
Panel, Hand Carved, Yellow, Cedar, Shaman, Killer Whale, Watchful Eye Of The Sun, 1983, 23 x 16 In..	225
Panel, Morrill Michael, Divided Square, Acrylic, Canvas, 1989, 72 x 72 In.	813
Pedestal, Octagonal Top, From Wine Press Screw, Walnut, France, 1800s, 47 x 13 ½ In.	312
Pedestals, Round Top, Fluted Columns, Vitruvian Scrolls, 32 ½ x 14 In.	2000
Perkeo, Holding Goblet, 5 ¾ In..	40
Pig Head, Wall Mount, Open Mouth, Paint Accent, Stain, Indonesia, 1940s, 6 ½ x 10 x 4 ½ In. ..	35
Pig, Laminated Construction, Brown Paint, 1900s, 7 ¼ x 11 In.	330
Pipe Rack, Black Forest, Wall Hanging, 4 Figural Carved Devil's Face, Signed, 3 ½ x 8 x 2 ¾ In. .	686
Plaque, Archer, Black Forest Marquetry, Germany, 1900s, 8 x 12 In.	48
Plaque, Eagle, Crest, In Talons, Furled Flags, 11 ½ x 30 In................................	1452
Plaque, Hunter, Holding Goose, Black Forest, c.1950, 14 x 8 In................................	60
Plaque, Man, Overcoat, Knickers, Top Hat, Raised Bottle, Chalice, 1900-30, 12 x 33 x 1 In.	30
Plaque, Openwork, Deer, In Forest, c.1950, 24 In.	396
Plaque, Pine Eagle, Painted, c.1875, 25 In.	923
Plaque, Putto, Multicolor, Continental, 1800, 5 x 23 In................................	369

Wood Carving, Our Lady Of Guadalupe, Woman, Serpent, Painted, Mirrored Base, 1800s, 16 x 7 In.
$2,250

New Orleans Auction Galleries

Wood Carving, Propeller, Airplane, Metal Tips, Decal, Sensenich Bros, Pa., 70 In.
$472

Hess Auction Group

This is an edited listing of current prices. Visit **Kovels.com** to check thousands of prices from previous years and sign up for free information on trends, tips, reproductions, marks, and more.

W

Wood Carving, Vase, Orangewood, Turned, Doughnut Shape, Ed Moulthrop, Signed, 4 1/2 x 6 In.
$1,476

Wood Carving, Wall Sconce, Chinoiserie, Walnut, Floral, Chinese Clothing, 1800s, 18 x 11 x 9 1/2 In., Pair
$1,800

Wooden, Bowl, Burl, 1800s, 5 1/4 x 12 1/2 In.
$840

Wooden, Bowl, Burl, Deep, Oblong, Rectangular Cutout Handles, 1800s, 15 x 11 In.
$1,230

Plaque, Solid Mahogany, Figure Of King Saul, Chin Resting On His Hand, 1800s, 19 x 55 x 3 In..	3900
Press, Specimen, Walnut, Dovetailed Case, Threaded Post, D. Bork, c.1960, 3 x 15 In.	63
Priest, Crimson Cape, Carrying Bible, Incense, Glass Eyes, 1800s, 13 In.	1000
Print Block, Metal Plate, Art Nouveau, Alphonse Mucha, 5 x 2 x 1 In.	156
Propeller, Airplane, Metal Tips, Decal, Sensenich Bros., Pa., 70 In. *illus*	472
Puffin, On A Rockery Base, Al Jordan, New York, 11 1/2 In.	420
Putti, Carved Oak Nude Figure, Gadrooned Block, Serpentine Form Base, Tassel, 40 x 12 x 12 In..	7260
Putto, Standing, Looks Down To Side, Lyre, 22 In.	124
Rack, Dog Head, Figural, Carved Walnut, 7 Spindles, Turned Coat Hanger Posts, 35 x 5 1/2 In.	968
Riding Crop, T Handle, Smiling Human Head, Fez Cap, Painted Teeth, Home Tanned, 1905, 27 In..	60
Romeo, Juliet Design, Yellow Hibiscus, Balinese, Mask, 8 1/2 x 8 x 5 In.	250
Saddle, Camel, 14 1/2 x 21 1/2 In.	33
Scarecrow, Green, Articulated Arms, Signed, George Colin, 40 In.	125
Shou Lao, Deity Of Longevity, Staff, Pumpkin Gourd, 1930-50, 22 In.	248
Shouxing, Holding Dragon Staff, Looking Down At Seated Lamb, Inlaid, Chinese, 11 In.	123
Soldier, Roman, Sleeping, Red, Green, Gold Leaf, Continental, 1800s, 29 In.	500
Sperm Whale, Open Mouth, Teeth, Black, Clark G. Voorhees, 17 In.	1815
St. Anthony, Flint Eyes, Chubby Child, Fed Halo Iron, Wire Staff, 1890, 18 x 8 In.	1395
St. Francis Of Assisi, Patina, Robes With Tassel, c.1800, 17 In.	1125
St. Luke, Multicolor, Bolivia, 1800s, 24 x 10 x 8 In.	720
Stand, Classic Ming Form, 6-Sided Marble Inset Top, Pierced Skirt, Arched Brackets, 32 x 16 In..	84
Stand, Neoclassical Woman, Chiton, Round Platform On Her Head, Red Walnut, 1800s, 26 x 9 1/2 In.	240
Stand, Plum Trees, Flower Petals, Circle Groove, 3 1/2 x 4 3/4 x 1 1/2 In.	15
Statue, St. John The Evangelist, Holding Chalice, Multicolor, Germany, 1400s, 23 x 7 In.,	4500
Target, Black Forest, Schutzen, Night Watchman, 1929, 19 In.	138
Temple, Chinese, Attendants, 1800s, 16 In.	600
Urn, George III, Mahogany, 28 x 11 1/2 In., Pair	3250
Vase, Ash Leaf Maple, Elliptical, Repeating Lozenge, Wood Grain, Ed Moulthrop, 6 1/2 x 13 1/2 In.	2625
Vase, Black Walnut, Round, Wood Grain, Glossy, Ed Moulthrop, 9 1/2 x 12 In.	3250
Vase, Hardwood, Aesthetics, Persian Iranian Design, Uzbekistan, 1990, 8 1/2 x 3 In.	120
Vase, Orangewood, Doughnut Shape, Lined Wood Grain, Glossy, Ed Moulthrop, 5 1/2 x 9 In.	2125
Vase, Orangewood, Turned, Doughnut Shape, Ed Moulthrop, Signed, 4 1/2 x 6 In. *illus*	1476
Vase, Streaked Georgia Pine, Turned, Flared, Philip Moulthrop, 14 x 11 In.	3625
Vase, Tulipwood, Elliptical, Hourglass Wood Grain, Glossy, Ed Moulthrop, 8 1/2 x 15 In.	3250
Vase, Turned Wood Burl, Signed & Dated, Melvin Lindquist, 1980, 20 x 12 In.	6875
Vase, Walnut, Turned, Inlay, Banksea Pod, Red Bud, Turquoise, Resin, 10 1/2 x 28 In.	4687
Vase, White Pine, Turned, Matt Moulthrop, 5 1/4 x 10 In.	3250
Wall Box, French Pyrography, Double Gothic Arc Backboard, 2 Mid Drawers, 1800s, 12 x 7 x 4 In.	113
Wall Hanging, Cherub, Paint, Gilt, Wings Wrap & Spread Out, 1800s, 9 x 12 In.	615
Wall Plaque, American Eagle, U.S. Shield, Cross Flag, Pine, Multicolor, Paint, 1900s, 18 x 60 In.	5760
Wall Sconce, Chinoiserie, Walnut, Floral, Chinese Clothing, 1800s, 18 x 11 x 9 1/2 In., Pair *illus*	1800
Wall Sconce, Federal Style, Gilt, Gesso, Torch Form, Candle Cups, Floral, 1900s, 31 x 11 In., Pair.	1800
Warrior, Mohawk, Kneeling, Lowered Bow, Bracket Shelf, 1993, 22 x 29 x 21 In.	450
Warrior, Nubian, Cast Glass, Oil Paint, Clifford Rainey, 1990, 70 x 18 x 14 In.	2375
Woman, Arms Raised, Dogon People, Mali, 32 x 6 1/2 x 6 In.	63
Woman, Horns & Tusk, Religious, Songye People, Congo, 19 x 5 1/4 x 5 1/2 In.	870
Woman, Kneeling, Fertility Fetish, Luba & Yoruba, Nigeria, 1900s, 24 In.	118
Woman, Standing, Colonial Dress, Baule People, Cote D'Ivoire, 13 x 4 x 4 In.	125
Woman, Standing, Headdress, Yoruba People, Nigeria, 20 x 6 x 6 In.	63
Woodpecker, On A Birch Branch, Al Jordan, New York, 12 In.	312
Zen Courier, Seated Buddhist Image, Legs Of Horse Sculpture, 6 In.	350

WOODEN wares were used in all parts of the home. Wood was used for many containers and tools. Small wooden pieces are called *treenware* in England, but the term *woodenware* is more common in the United States. Additional pieces may be found in the Advertising, Kitchen, and Tool categories.

Basket, Lid, Rice, Leaves, Painted, Chinese, 14 x 14 x 10 In.	36

Wooden, Bucket, Kerosene Oil Stenciled Black, Green, Black Bands, Handle, 1800s, 10 In.
$156

Eldred's Auctioneers and Appraisers

Wooden, Bucket, Zinc Liner, Green & Red Paint, White Stenciling, W.H. Dickenson, 1900s, 15 x 16 In.
$600

Garth's Auctioneers & Appraisers

Wooden, Cup & Saucer, Poplar, Painted, Pussy Willow, Signed, Joseph Lehn, 1890, Saucer 3 In.
$767

Hess Auction Group

Wooden, Eggcup, Poplar, Turned, Painted, Decal, Pussy Willow, Rose, Joseph Lehn, 3 ½ In.
$189

Hess Auction Group

Wooden, Hall Tree, Black, Bear, 80 In.
$5,664

Copake Auction

Wooden, Hibachi, Tree Trunk Shape, Burl, Copper Liner, Japan, 1900s, 13 x 30 x 28 In.
$1,722

Brunk Auctions

Wooden, Lamp, Metal Scroll Arms & Candle Sockets, 1800s, 14 x 21 ½ In.
$875

Garth's Auctioneers & Appraisers

Wooden, Pail, Pine Staves, Interlocking Lap Joint Bands, Bentwood Swing Handle, 1800s, 14 x 13 In.
$70

Hess Auction Group

W

Wooden, Tray, Utensil, Center Handle, Vertical Stripes, 3 1/2 x 13 1/2 x 8 3/4 In. $106

Hess Auction Group

Wooden, Watch Hutch, Star Shape, Applied Decoration, c.1890, 13 x 12 In. $180

Garth's Auctioneers & Appraisers

World War I, Helmet, Saxon Shako, Black Leather, State Of Saxony, Starburst $324

Michann's Auctions

World War II, Boots, Paratrooper's, Leather, Brown, Laces, Angled Heel, Size 13 $240

Milestone Auctions

Bird Call, Crow, Stamped Perdew, 5 1/4 In.		120
Bowl, Burl, 1800s, 5 1/4 x 12 1/2 In.	*illus*	840
Bowl, Burl, c.1810, 4 3/4 x 13 In.		354
Bowl, Burl, Deep, Oblong, Rectangular Cutout Handles, 1800s, 15 x 11 In.	*illus*	1230
Bowl, Burl, Scrubbed Surface, Flared, Notch In Rim, 1800s, 5 1/4 x 15 1/4 In.		540
Bowl, Duckbill, Carved, Geometric Motif, Cedar, Continental, 9 x 3 1/4 In.		60
Bowl, Macassar Ebony, Shaped, Rough Edge, Rude Osolnik, 6 3/4 x 11 1/2 In.		875
Bowl, Maple, Turned, Original Salmon Paint, c.1810, 5 1/2 x 18 In.		129
Bowl, Oval, Burlwood, c.1825, 5 x 14 In.		767
Bowl, Salad, Oak, Silver Plate, Trophy Shape, Cartouche, Pedestal, c.1890, 7 x 10 In.		600
Bowl, Silver & Coral Lid, Cabochon, Bronze Animal, Asia, 1900s		192
Bowl, Treenware, Stylized Flowers, Yellow, Red, 7 x 17 In.		875
Bowl, Turned Ash Burl, Raised Rim Ring, Beautifully Figured & Formed, 1800s, 4 3/4 x 13 In.		1440
Brushpot, Bamboo, Continuous Landscape, People, 6 1/2 In.		363
Bucket, Iron Banded, Swing Handle, 11 x 12 In.		50
Bucket, Kerosene Oil Stenciled Black, Green, Black Bands, Handle, 1800s, 10 In.	*illus*	156
Bucket, Sap, White Pine, Firkin, Red Paint, Finger Jointed Banding, Wash Interior, 1800s, 12 x 14 In.		570
Bucket, Zinc Liner, Green & Red Paint, White Stenciling, W.H. Dickenson 1900s, 15 x 16 In.	*illus*	600
Chicken Coop, Rectangular, W.J. Carpenter Co., 16 1/2 x 35 1/4 In.		81
Compote, Peaseware, Maple, 5 3/4 x 8 3/4 In.		510
Cup & Saucer, Poplar, Painted, Pussy Willow, Signed, Joseph Lehn, 1890, Saucer 3 In.	*illus*	767
Cup, Kero, Dark Colors, Multicolor, Ceremonial, 4 In.		350
Cup, Lehnware, Saffron, Blue, Green, Red, Pedestal, Cabbage Rose, Berries, 1870, 2 3/4 x 4 3/4 In.		1200
Cup, Willow Wood, Medicinal, 3-Tier Base, Brown Bands, Red Stain, 1880, 2 1/2 x 3 3/8 In.		190
Eggcup, Poplar, Turned, Painted, Decal, Pussy Willow, Rose, Joseph Lehn, 3 1/2 In.	*illus*	189
Firkin, Stave, Finger Lap Bands, Bent, 1900s, 12 x 8 1/2 In.		57
Hall Tree, Black, Bear, 80 In.	*illus*	5664
Hibachi, Tree Trunk Shape, Burl, Copper Liner, Japan, 1900s, 13 x 30 x 28 In.	*illus*	1722
Lamp, Metal Scroll Arms & Candle Sockets, 1800s, 14 x 21 1/2 In.	*illus*	875
Pail, Pine Staves, Interlocking Lap Joint Bands, Bentwood Swing Handle, 1800s, 14 x 13 In.	*illus*	70
Propeller, Laminated Wood, Sensenich Brothers, 98 1/2 In.		1089
Salad Servers, Rosewood, Silver Band, W. Spratling, Mexico, 1931-67, 12 In.		336
Salt Box, Painted, Brown, 1800s		12
Shrine, Tabletop, Green, Blue, Leopard Accents, 11 x 8 x 17 In.		366
Tankard, Burl, Wood Handle & Lid, Lion Feet Thumblift & Feet, Norway, c.1800, 9 In.		180
Tray, Black Forest, Marquetry, Flowers In Center, Handles, Germany, c.1990, 16 x 11 In.		42
Tray, Breakfast, Bamboo, Woven, Cutout Handles, Front Drawer, 1940s, 11 x 17 In.		165
Tray, Nail Construction, Red Milk Paint, Extended Bottom, 1850, 14 x 6 1/2 x 4 In.		270
Tray, Utensil, Center Handle, Vertical Stripes, 3 1/2 x 13 1/2 x 8 3/4 In.	*illus*	106
Trencher, Mahogany, Oblong, Handles, Marked, Kimball & Co., 1800s, 2 1/2 x 17 1/2 In.		177
Watch Hutch, Star Shape, Applied Decoration, c.1890, 13 x 12 In.	*illus*	180
Wig Stand, Georgian, Circular Top, Copper Bowl, Lid, 2 Diminutive Drawers, 1900, 32 x 13 In.		81

WORCESTER porcelains were made in Worcester, England, from 1751. The firm went through many name changes and eventually, in 1862, became The Royal Worcester Porcelain Company Ltd. Collectors often refer to Dr. Wall, Barr, Flight, and other names that indicate time periods or artists at the factory. It became part of Royal Worcester Spode Ltd. in 1976. The company was bought by the Portmeirion Group in 2009. Related pieces may be found in the Royal Worcester category.

Bowl, Dr. Wall, Blue Flowers, White Ground, 3 x 6 3/4 In.		84
Cachepot, White, Floral Band, Gold Trim, Tapered, Ring Handles, Flight & Barr, 6 In., Pair		1920
Ewer, Domed, Figural Winged Griffin Handle, Yellow Matte Body, 7 1/2 x 7 In.		152
Plate, Red Flowers, Green Leaves, 9 1/4 In.		125

WORLD WAR I and World War II souvenirs are collected today. Be careful not to store anything that includes live ammunition. Your local police will tell you how to dispose of the explosives. See also Sword and Trench Art.

WORLD WAR I

Button, Bulldog, Balancing Victory Ball, Wearing Flag, A.W. Patrick, Australia, 1 ¼ In.	25
Button, Die Cut, Metal, Paint Accent, Russian War Relief, Chute, ¾ In.	18
Canteen, Galvanized Tin, Fabric Cover, Canvas Strap, Metal Cap, Boyco, c.1910	60
Helmet, Saxon Shako, Black Leather, State Of Saxony, Starburst ...... *illus*	324
Paperweight, Iron Cross, First Class Award, Medal, Highlight In Soldier's Life, 1914	77
Pillow Top, Silk, Embroidered, Lace, Flowers, Flags, Eagle, c.1910, 17 x 18 In.	360
Poster, Gee I Wish I Were A Man, Female Sailor, Lithograph, 1918, 27 x 41 In.	1107
Poster, If You Want To Fight, Join The Marines, Woman, Dress Blue Uniform, c.1915, 38 x 27 In.	1638
Poster, Join, Army Air Service, Bald Eagle, Midair Strike, Orange, c.1917, 26 ¾ x 20 In.	1111
Poster, Recruitment, Canada, Are You One Of Kitchener's Own?, 1918, 28 x 42 In.	2740
Poster, Third Liberty Loan, Lady Liberty, Fight Or Buy Bonds, Lithograph, 42 x 31 In.	156
Poster, Uncle Sam & Britannia, Side By Side, Frame, J.M. Flagg, 1918, 19 x 26 ½ In.	840
Poster, Uncle Sam, I Want You For U.S. Army, J.M. Flagg, c.1917, 39 ¼ x 29 In.	5265
Poster, Victory Girls, Patriotic Lithograph, Young Woman, Rowing Boat, 27 x 22 In.	1480
Poster, Victory Liberty Loan, Doughboy, They Thought We Couldn't Fight, Lithograph, 44 In.	96
Relief Compact, Brass, Enamel, Henrietta, Mirror, Gold Sticker, Sole Case, 3 x 3 x ¼ In.	35
Tin, Bacon Rations, Embossed, Model Of 1916, Green Paint, Flip Lid, c.1910, 2 ½ x 7 In.	15

WORLD WAR II

Bayonet, Police Dress, Stag Grip Panels, German, Original Eickhorn Solingen, 14 In.	189
Boots, Paratrooper's, Leather, Brown, Laces, Angled Heel, Size 13 ...... *illus*	240
Button, Volunteer Observer, Horizontal Bar Pin, Celluloid, 1 ¼ In.	45
Figure, Hitler, Noose, Around Neck, Uniform, Jointed, Rivets, Cardboard, 11 ¼ In. ...... *illus*	420
Grenade, US Training Kit, Japanese Type 97, 2 x 4 In.	224
Helmet, Fixed Bale Chin Strap, Marked, 11 x 10 x 6 ½ In.	94
Jacket, Leather Bomber, Authentic Patches, Lined Collar, Cotton Wrist & Waist Bands, 24 In.	1770
Patch, Air Force, Peregrine Falcon, Holding Camera, Photographing The World, 5 ¼ In.. *illus*	195
Photograph, Parade, Soldiers, Car, American & Don't Tread On Me Flags, 1945, 3 x 4 In.	10
Poster, Red Cross War Fund, Military Doctor, Nurse & Soldier, Jes Wilhelm Schaikjer, 1943, 22 x 28 In.	142
Poster, Remember Pearl Harbor, Japanese Soldier In Crosshairs, Signed, Lt. Crouch, 1941, 14 x 16 In.	420
Poster, This Is The Enemy, Arm, Sleeve, Nazi Swastika, GPO, c.1943, 28 x 20 In.	222
Sword, Navy, Office Albert Beaupariant Finely, Steel Blade, Shagreen Hilt, 32 In. ...... *illus*	349
Tunic, 5 Buttons & 3 Hooks, Collar, 2 Interior Breast Pockets, No Tags, 18 In.	130
Uniform, Tunic, 5 Buttons & 2 Hooks, Collar, Pants, Tapered Legs, 30 In.	142

WORLD'S FAIR souvenirs from all of the fairs are collected. The first fair was the Great Exhibition of 1851 in London. Some other important exhibitions and fairs include Philadelphia, 1876 (Centennial); Chicago, 1893 (World's Columbian); Buffalo, 1901 (Pan-American); St. Louis, 1904 (Louisiana Purchase); Portland, 1905 (Lewis & Clark Centennial Exposition); San Francisco, 1915 (Panama-Pacific); 1925, Paris (International Exposition of Modern Decorative and Industrial Arts); Philadelphia, 1926 (Sesquicentennial); Chicago, 1933 (Century of Progress); Cleveland, 1936 (Great Lakes); San Francisco, 1939 (Golden Gate International); New York, 1939 (World of Tomorrow); Seattle, 1962 (Century 21); New York, 1964; Montreal, 1967; Knoxville (Energy Turns the World) 1982; New Orleans, 1984; Tsukuba, Japan, 1985; Vancouver, Canada, 1986; Brisbane, Australia, 1988; Seville, Spain, 1992; Genoa, Italy, 1992; Seoul, South Korea, 1993; Lisbon, Portugal, 1998; Hanover, Germany, 2000; Shanghai, China, 2010; and Milan, Italy, 2015. Memorabilia of fairs include directories, pictures, fabrics, ceramics, etc. Memorabilia from other similar celebrations may be listed in the Souvenir category.

Bandanna, 1876, Philadelphia, Buildings, Sepia, Blue & White Ground, 24 ¼ In.	819
Bandanna, 1876, Philadelphia, Federal Eagle, Shield, Building, Blue Star Border, 19 ¾ x 21 ¾ In.	198
Bandanna, 1893, Chicago, Fairgrounds, Celebrity Bust Portraits, Red, 21 ⅝ x 23 ⅝ In.	234
Bookmark, 1934, Chicago, Century Of Progress, Metal, Gold Finish, 4 ½ In.	30
Coffee Tin, 1903, St. Louis, Blanke's World's Fair Roasted Coffee, Picture, 11 x 3 ¼ In.	776
Handkerchief, 1905, Exposition Universelle, Liege, Stitched Picture Of Building, 15 x 15 In.	30
Key Fob, 1939, New York, Trylon & Perisphere, Keychain, 1 ⅝ In.	35
Pears, 1893, Chicago, Glass, Peachblow, Libbey, 4 ½ In., 4 Piece	130

World War II, Figure, Hitler, Noose, Around Neck, Uniform, Jointed, Rivets, Cardboard, 11 ¼ In. $420

Milestone Auctions

World War II, Patch, Air Force, Peregrine Falcon, Holding Camera, Photographing The World, 5 ¼ In. $195

Blackwell Auctions

World War II, Sword, Navy, Office Albert Beaupariant Finely, Steel Blade, Shagreen Hilt, 32 In. $349

Milestone Auctions

W

World's Fair, Pin, 1904, St. Louis, Louisiana Purchase, Jefferson, Livingston, Napoleon, 1 3/4 In. $487

Hake's Americana & Collectibles

WPA, Figurine, Fisherman, Blue Jacket, Red Hat, Basket Of Fish, 1930s, 16 x 5 In. $100

Ruby Lane

Wristwatch, Hamilton, Platinum, Diamonds, Blued Steel Hands, 17 Jewel, Manual Wind, Woman's, c.1935 $390

Cowan's Auctions

Pin, 1904, St. Louis, Louisiana Purchase, Jefferson, Livingston, Napoleon, 1 3/4 In. .... *illus*		487
Sculpture, 1904, St. Louis, Roaring Tiger, Front Paws On Rock, Marble, 23 x 14 In.		2040
Tray, 1964, New York, Syroco, 2 Finger Grip Holes, Federal Pavilion, 10 x 11 x 1 In.		20

WPA is the abbreviation for Works Progress Administration, a program created by executive order in 1935 to provide jobs for millions of unemployed Americans. Artists were hired to create murals, paintings, drawings, and sculptures for public buildings. Pieces are marked *WPA* and may have the artist's name on them.

Button, Works Progress Administration, 1 3/4 In.	23
Doll, Little Red Riding Hood, Papier-Mache Head, Cloth Body, 1930s, 14 In.	110
Figurine, Fisherman, Blue Jacket, Red Hat, Basket Of Fish, 1930s, 16 x 5 In. ...... *illus*	100
Lamp, Bronze, Seagulls, Adjustable, Robert Garret Thew, c.1928.	1230
Lamp, Nude, Holding Wheat, Cast Plaster, Gilt Finish, 1930s, 44 In.	495
Painting, Oil On Devoe Board, Lumberjacks, Frame, 19 x 22 1/2 In.	345
Painting, Still Life, Flowers, Multimedia, Signed, August F. Biehle, Frame, 32 x 26 In.	995
Painting, Watercolor, Boat On River, Winter Scene, Gustavo Cenci, Frame, 22 x 28 In.	140
Poster, Gay Nineties, Couple Holding Hands, Silk Screened, 1935, 18 x 23 In.	225
Puppet, Goldilocks, Papier-Mache, Painted Face, 18 In.	125
Puppet, Wolf, Papier-Mache Head, Cloth Body, Multicolor, 18 In.	250
Sketch, Crossing The Andes, c.1930, 8 x 18 1/4 In.	401
Sketch, Men, Laying Down Railroad Ties, T.S., 1930s, 15 x 12 In.	625
Sketch, Pencil On Paper, Woman Hanging Laundry, Signed, Charles S. Truman, 1938, 7 x 6 In.	125

WRISTWATCHES came into use during World War I. Wristwatches are listed here by manufacturer or as advertising or character watches. Wristwatches may also be listed in other categories. Pocket watches are listed in the Watch category.

Accutron, Diamond Bezel Chronograph, Black Dial, Stainless Steel Case, Baton Hour Markers, 1 1/2 In.	156
Angelus, Chronodato Rose Gold, Stainless Steel Case, Smooth Bezel, White Dial, Month & Day.	1152
Audemars Piquet, 18K Gold, Cream Dial, Batons, Quartz, Bamboo Link Band, Woman's, 7 In.	6250
Baum & Mercier, 14K Yellow Gold, Crosshatched Dial, Case Stamped, Woman's, 1 In.	1440
Baum & Mercier, 18K Yellow Gold, Diamond Set, Mother-Of-Pearl Dial, Woman's, 1 In.	1216
Baum & Mercier, Geneve, 18K, Engraved, My Devotion & Love, H.M, Italy, Woman's, 1 x 7/8 In.	1560
Baum & Mercier, Stainless Steel Catwalk Bracelet, Caseback Stamped, Woman's, 1 In.	861
Baum & Mercier, Stainless Steel, Square Face, Roman Numerals, Swiss, 1900s	360
Baylor, Yellow Gold Filled Chronograph, Blue Dial, Square Hour Markers, Stainless, 1 1/2 In.	185
Breitling, Navitimer, Stainless Steel Case, Relumed Dial & Hands, 1 1/2 In.	2520
Breitling, Superocean, Stainless, Blue, Numeral, Uni-Directional Timing Bezel, 1884	2160
Bulgari, Automatic Chronographe, 18K Yellow Gold, Italian Oyster Style Bracelet, Woman's, 1 3/8 In.	7800
Bulova, Accutron, Astronaut, Stainless Steel, Black, Linked Band, Woman's, 1900s	563
Bulova, Accutron, Stainless Steel, Astronaut, GMT, Black Matte Dial, Triangular Lume Hour Plots	338
Bulova, Ambassador, 18K Yellow Gold, 30 Jewel Automatic, 1 In.	2500
Cartier, Panther, Yellow Gold, Diamond Bezel, White Dial, Roman Hour Marker, Woman's, 1 In.	3000
Cartier, Pasha, 18K Gold, Sapphires, Ivory Dial, 3 Blue Subdials, Quartz, Woman's, 1989	3000
Cartier, Roadster Automatic, Stainless Steel Case, Roman Numerals, Black Leather Strap	2040
Cartier, Santos Galbee, Stainless, Screw Down Bezel, Off White Dial, 15/16 In.	1250
Cartier, Tank, 18K Yellow Gold, Off-White Dial, Black Roman Hour Markers, 1 x 1 1/2 In.	2250
Cartier, Tank, Stainless Steel, White Dial, Roman Numerals, Signed	2500
Concord, Quartz, White Dial, Roman Numerals, 14K Gold, Tapered Mesh Band, Woman's	720
Corum, Bubble Royal Flush, 18K Rose Gold Bezel, Care Deck Dial, Black, Red Hour Markers	3840
Corum, Zodiac, 18K Gold, Symbols On Dial, 21 Jewel, Mesh Band, Woman's, 6 1/2 In.	2400
Elgin, Naval, 21 Jewel, Lever Set, Engraved U.S. Navy, Box, Leather Strap, 1911, 3 In.	531
Fabre-Leuba, Stainless Steel Duomatic, Gray & Blue Dial, 2 In.	150
Geneve, 14K Gold Mesh Band, Diamond Crusted Bezel, Quartz Movement, Inscribed, 1 In.	968
Girard, Open Face, 18K Gold, Green Guilloche, Seed Pearl Border, Fusee, Paris, Woman's, 1 In.	584
Gruen, Curvex Precision, 14K Gold, 17 Jewel, Satin Dial, 3 Diamonds, Sword Hands, Woman's	246
Hamilton, 14K Gold, Rectangular Face, 4 Diamonds, Clasp, Woman's, 1900s	390
Hamilton, 14K Gold, Round Case, Gold Hour Markers, Link Band, Italy, Woman's, 7 1/2 In.	660

Hamilton, 14K White Gold, Diamonds, 22 Jewel, Woman's, 6 ⁵⁄₈ In.	875
Hamilton, Platinum, Diamonds, Blued Steel Hands, 17 Jewel, Woman's, c.1935 .... *illus*	390
Hermes, Stainless, White Dial, Circular Hour Markers, Leather Wrap, 1 In.	780
Jaeger-LeCoultre, Automatic, Date, Alarm, Silver Dial, Black Hour Markers, 1 ½ In.	1680
Longines, Stainless Steel, Engraved Bezel, Off-White Dial, Black Hour, 1 ⁹⁄₃₂ In.	1476
Longines, Wittnauer One Button Chronograph, Movement Signed	861
Lucerne, 18K Yellow Gold, Round Cream Color Face, Stamped, Woman's, 7 In.	572
Movado, Automatic, 14K Yellow Gold, Smooth Bezel, White Dial, Subsidiary Seconds Register.	882
Omega, 14K Gold, Diamond Set Bezel, Gold Dial, Baton Hour Markers, Woman's, 1 In.	523
Omega, 18K Gold, Cream Dial, Gold Hour Markers, Seconds Hand, Mesh Band, Woman's, c.1970...	1560
Omega, Speedmaster Professional, Tachymeter Don Bezel, 3 Subsidiary Chronograph, 1 ¾ In..	3690
Patek Philippe, 18K Yellow Gold Calatrava, Date, Stamped Inside, 1 ¼ In.	7800
Patek Philippe, Geneve, Tank Head, 18K Yellow Gold, Seconds Dial, White Dial, Hallmark Case....	5700
Patek Philippe, Platinum, 6 Marquise Cut Diamonds, Link Bracelet, Woman's	7500
Pery, White Dial, Black Arabic Numerals, Single Cut Diamonds Around Case & Bracelet, Woman's	2500
Rolex, 14K Yellow Gold Thunderbird-Turnograph Datejust, Champagne Dial, 1 ¼ In.	2460
Rolex, 18K Gold, Custom Diamond Set, White Dial, Yellow Gold Hour Markers & Date, Woman's, 1 In. .	2160
Rolex, 18K Yellow Gold, Oyster Perpetual Datejust, Roman Numeral Markers, Swiss, 1 In.	7200
Rolex, 18K Yellow Gold, Stainless Steel Datejust, Smooth Bezel, Baton Markers, Woman's, 1 In.	1680
Rolex, Datejust, 14K Yellow Gold, Stainless, Black Dial, Self-Winding	1465
Rolex, Datejust, Stainless, White Dial, Square Markers, Smooth Bezel, Woman's, 1 ¹⁄₃₂ In.	1800
Rolex, Oyster Perpetual, Day-Date, 18K Gold, Black Dial, Baton Numerals	5256
Rolex, Stainless Steel, Blue Dial, Jubilee Band, Folding Clasp, Box, 1 In. .... *illus*	1792
Seiko, Automatic Turtle, Black Dial, Large Circular Hour Markers	640
Seiko, Pepsi Chronograph, Red & Blue Tachymeter Bezel, Inner Gray Rotating Bezel, 1 ½ In. .	384
Seiko, Stainless Steel Chronograph, Black Dial, Lume Hour Markers, Tachymeter, 2 In.	570
Tag Heuer, Carrera Automatic, Black Dial & Bezel, Stainless Hour Marker, 1 ¾ In.	1088
Tag Heuer, Link Chronograph, Stainless, Matte, Smooth Bezel, Black Dial, 1 ⅔ In.	1088
Technos, Stainless Steel Chronograph, Fading Blue Timing Bezel, Matte Black Dial, 1 ¹¹⁄₁₆ In.	554
Tudor, Oyster Prince Submariner, Stainless, Blue Bezel, Black Dial, 1 ⅔ In.	3438
Tudor, Stainless Steel Oysterdate, Black Dial, Baton Hour Markers, 1 ⅓ In.	1020
Tudor, Stainless Steel Prince Oysterdate, Black Dial, Smooth Bezel, 1 ⅜ In.	1134
U-Boat, Left Hook Auto Stainless Steel, Lume Numeral, Baton Hour Markers, 2 In.	630
Ulysse Nardin, 14K Gold, Yellow Gold Hour Markers, Salmon Color Dial, Woman's, ¹⁵⁄₁₆ In.	688
Universal Geneve, 18K, Secondary Seconds Dial, Gold Hallmark, Brown Band, c.1945, 1 ⅜ In.	720
Universal Geneve, Automatic Day Date Month Moonphase, Stainless Steel Case, 1 ⅓ In.	1080
Vacheron & Constantin, 18K Gold, 17 Jewel, Bracelet, Swiss, Woman's, 7 ½ In.	2280
Vacheron & Constantin, Gents Stainless Steel, Automatic, 36 Jewel, Anti-Magnetic Protection	5100
Vacheron & Constantin-LeCoultre, 14K White Gold Mystery Diamond, Woman's, 1 In.	1536
Vacheron, 18K Yellow Gold, Constantin Tank, 15 Jewel, Arabic Numerals, ¾ x 1 In.	1800
Waltham Vanguard Co., Gold Filled, Open Case, Lever Set, 23 Jewel, c.1941	366
Wittnauer, Geneve Panda Chronograph, Black Dial, Stainless Steel Case, 1 ½ In.	2125
Wittnauer, Stainless Steel 2000 Automatic Calendar, Silver Circle Hour Markers, 2 In.	420
Zenith, El Primiro Chronograph Day-Date Month Jump Hour Moonphase, Stainless Steel, 1 ½ In.	4160

YELLOWWARE is a heavy earthenware made of a yellowish clay. It varies in color from light yellow to orange-yellow. Many nineteenth- and twentieth-century kitchen bowls and jugs were made of yellowware. It was made in England and in the United States. Another form of pottery that is sometimes classed as yellowware is listed in this book in the Mocha category.

Bank, Pig, Cobalt Blue Vines, Flowers & Verse On Back, Ohio, 8 x 3 In. .... *illus*	1169
Bowl, 3 Wavy Bands, Embossed Leaf Border, Square Base, 6 x 10 ½ In.	60
Mixing Bowl, Brown & Cream Bands, Flared, 7 x 15 In. .... *illus*	113
Pitcher, Green Seaweed Band, Bulbous, Loop Handle, 4 ½ In. .... *illus*	234
Sugar, Lid, Blue Seaweed Bands, Flattened Knob Handle, 3 ¾ In. .... *illus*	399
Tea Dispenser, Teapot Shape, Bakelite, Spigot, Ice Tea, Brown Glaze, Cordley Hayes, 15 x 10 x 9 In.	53

Wristwatch, Rolex, Stainless Steel, Blue Dial, Jubilee Band, Folding Clasp, Box, 1 In.
$1,792

Morphy Auctions

Yellowware, Bank, Pig, Cobalt Blue Vines, Flowers & Verse On Back, Ohio, 8 x 3 In.
$1,169

Forsythes' Auctions

Yellowware, Mixing Bowl, Brown & Cream Bands, Flared, 7 x 15 In.
$113

Stony Ridge Auction

Yellowware, Pitcher, Green Seaweed Band, Bulbous, Loop Handle, 4 ½ In.
$234

Hess Auction Group

Yellowware, Sugar, Lid, Blue Seaweed Bands, Flattened Knob Handle, 3¾ In. $399

Hess Auction Group

Zsolnay, Vase, Lizards, Cutout Rim, Eosin Glaze, Raised 5 Churches Seal, c.1900, 7¾ x 11½ In. $31,250

Rago Arts and Auction Center

Zsolnay, Vase, Stylized Flowers, Eosin Glaze, 4 Handles, 5 Steeple Mark, c.1900, 13 In. $15,000

Rago Arts and Auction Center

ZSOLNAY pottery was made in Hungary after 1853 and was characterized by Persian, Art Nouveau, or Hungarian motifs. A series of new Zsolnay figurines with green-gold luster finish is available in many shops today. Early Zsolnay was not marked, but by 1878 the tower trademark was used.

Zsolnay Porcelanmanufaktura 1871+

Zsolnay Porcelanmanufaktura 1899–1920

Zsolnay Porcelanmanufaktura 1900+

Basket, Centerpiece, Bowl, Bird, Floral, Mounted Ornate, Gilt Metal Frame, 14 x 12 In.	180
Bowl, Figural, Woman Riding Back Of Dolphin, Tulip Shape Planter On Dolphin's Tail, 15 x 11 In.	1560
Bowl, Reticulated Warriors, Iridescent Green, Eosin Glaze, 4¼ x 8¼ In.	93
Centerpiece, Boat Shape, Gilt, Reticulated, Purple Flowers, 11½ x 4¼ In.	281
Ewer, Handle, Reticulated Body, Floral, Cream Tones, Cobalt Blue, 12 In.	360
Figurine, Nude Woman, Kneeling, Arms Behind Her Head, Eosin Glaze, 9 In.	125
Group, Woman, Child, Iridescent Green, Eosin Glaze, 12 In.	93
Hair Receiver, Pheasants, Vines, Eosin Glaze, c.1900, 3¾ x 3½ In.	1000
Invalid Feeder, Half Cover, Side Handle, Flowers, Transfer Decoration, 3½ In.	70
Match Holder, Stylized Flowers, 1890s, 3 x 5½ In.	938
Rose Bowl, Tapered, Woman, Tending To Garden, Cherub, Multicolor, 7 x 8 In.	2375
Sleigh Bowl, Cherub, Brass, Copper Mounts, Ormolu, Stamped, 6¾ x 4¾ x 14 In.	400
Tray, Diamond Quilted, Ducks On Edge, Eosin, 4 x 6½ In.	384
Tray, Figural, Lobster & Snake, Green Iridescent, Marked, 7 In.	72
Tray, Iridescent, Figural, Woman Filling Water Jug, 3¾ x 6¼ In.	30
Tray, Pool, Frog On Edge, Birds, Marked, Eosin, 4 x 7 In.	413
Vase, Bird Skulls, Eosin Glaze, Blue, Green, Hungary, c.1900, 7¾ x 6½ In.	8125
Vase, Butterflies, Flowers, Blue, Green, Red Ground, 1890s, 3¼ x 5¼ In.	1250
Vase, Double Gourd, Stylized Flowers, Eosin Glaze, 1890s, 5½ x 3½ In.	1625
Vase, Flower Twist, Spiral Vase, Eosin Glaze, 13 x 4½ In.	5937
Vase, Jug Shape, Iridescent, Purple, Tan, Spotted, Twisted Body, 9¼ In.	1250
Vase, Lizards, Cutout Rim, Eosin Glaze, Raised 5 Churches Seal, c.1900, 7¾ x 11½ In. .. *illus*	31250
Vase, Moon, Cream, Pink, Cobalt Blue, Flowers, Fischer J., Budapest, 14½ x 11½ In.	330
Vase, Roosters, Reticulated, Eosin Glaze, Handles, c.1906, 5 x 2½ In.	1500
Vase, Stylized Flowers, Eosin Glaze, 4 Handles, 5 Steeple Mark, c.1900, 13 In. .... *illus*	15000
Vase, Stylized Panthers, Eosin Glaze, c.1900, 7 x 5 In.	2500

PHOTO CREDITS

We have included the name of the auction house or photographer with each pictured object. This is a list of the addresses of those who have contributed photographs and information for this book. Every dealer or auction has to buy antiques to have items to sell. Call or email a dealer or auction house if you want to discuss buying or selling. If you need an appraisal or advice, remember that appraising is part of their business and fees may be charged.

Ahlers & Ogletree Auction Gallery
715 Miami Circle, Suite 210
Atlanta, GA 30324
aandoauctions.com
404-869-2478

Alex Cooper Auctioneers
908 York Rd.
Towson, MD 21204
alexcooper.com
800-272-3145

Allard Auctions
P.O. Box 1030
St. Ignatius, MT 59865
allardauctions.com
406-745-0500

AntiqueAdvertising.com
P.O. Box 247
Cazenovia, NY 13035
antiqueadvertising.com
315-662-7625

Antiques & Art International
3600 S. Congress Ave., Suite A
Boynton Beach, FL 33426
antiquesandartinternational.com
561-806-6560

Bertoia Auctions
2141 DeMarco Dr.
Vineland, NJ 08360
bertoiaauctions.com
856-692-1881

Blackwell Auctions
10900 US Hwy 19 N, Suite B
Clearwater, FL 33764
blackwellauctions.com
727-546-0200

Brunk Auctions
P.O. Box 2135
Asheville, NC 28802
brunkauctions.com
825-254-6846

Bunch Auctions
1 Hillman Dr.,
Chadds Ford, PA 19317
williambuchauctions.com
610-558-1800

Bunte Auction Services, Inc.
755 Church Rd.
Elgin, IL 60123
bunteauction.com
847-214-8423

Burchard Galleries
2528 30th Ave. North
St. Petersburg, FL 33713
burchardgalleries.com
727-821-1167

Christie's
20 Rockefeller Plaza
New York, NY 10020
christies.com
212-636-2000

Clars Auction Gallery
5644 Telegraph Ave.
Oakland, CA 94609
clars.com
510-428-0100

Copake Auction Inc.
P.O. Box 47
Copake, NY 12516
copake.com
518-329-1142

Copley Fine Art Auctions
268 Newbury St.
Boston, MA 02116
copleyart.com
617-536-0030

Cordier Auctions
1500 Paxton St.
Harrisburg, PA 17104
cordierauction.com
717-731-8662

Cottone Auctions
120 Court St.
Geneseo, NY 14454
cottoneauctions.com
585-243-1000

Cowan's Auctions
6270 Este Ave.
Cincinnati, OH 45232
cowanauctions.com
513-871-1670

Crescent City Auction Gallery
1330 St. Charles Ave.
New Orleans, LA 70130
crescentcityauctiongallery.com
504-529-5057

Crocker Farm
159 York Rd.
Sparks, MD 21152
crockerfarm.com
410-472-2016

DuMouchelles
409 East Jefferson Ave.
Detroit, MI 48226
dumouchelles.com
313-963-6255

Early American History Auctions
P.O. Box 3507
Rancho Santa Fe, CA 92067
earlyamerican.com
858-759-3290

Ebay
ebay.com

Eldred's Auctioneers and Appraisers
P.O. Box 795, 1483 Route 6A
East Dennis, MA 02641
eldreds.com
508-385-3116

Etsy
esty.com

Fisher-Price
636 Girard Ave
East Aurora, NY 14052
fisherprice.com
800-747-8697

Fontaine's Auction Gallery
1485 West Housatonic St.
Pittsfield, MA 01201
fontainesauction.com
413-448-8922

Forsythe's Auctions
206 West Main St.
Russellville, OH 45168
forsythesauctions.com
937-377-3700

Fox Auctions
P.O. Box 4069
Vallejo, CA 94590
foxauctionsonline.com
631-553-3841

Freedom Auction Company
1601 Desoto Rd.
Sarasota, FL 34243
freedomauctions.com
941-725-2166

Freeman's
1808 Chestnut St.
Philadelphia, PA 19103
freemansauctiion.com
215-563-9275

Garth's Auctioneers & Appraisers
P.O. Box 369
Delaware, OH 43015
garths.com
740-362-4771

Glass Works Auctions
P.O. Box 38
Lambertville, NJ 08530
glswrk-auction.com
609-483-2683

Hake's Americana & Collectibles
P.O. Box 12001
York, PA 17402
hakes.com
717-434-1600

Henry Aldridge & Son Auctioneers & Valuers
Unit 1
Bath Road Business Center
Bath Road
Devizes
Wiltshire
SW10 1XA
henry-aldridge.co.uk

Heritage Auctions
3500 Maple Ave., 17th Floor
Dallas, TX 75219
ha.com
214-528-3500

Hess Auction Group
768 Graystone Rd.
Manheim, PA 17545
hessauctiongroup.com
717-898-7284

Humler & Nolan
225 East Sixth St., 4th Floor
Cincinnati, OH 45202
humlernolan.com
513-381-2041

I.M. Chait
9330 Civic Center Dr.
Beverly Hills, CA 90210
chait.com
301-285-0182

James D. Julia Auctioneers
203 Skowhegan Rd.
Fairfield, ME 04937
jamesdjulia.com
207-453-7125

Jeffrey S. Evans & Associates
P.O. Box 2638
Harrisonburg, VA 22801
jefffreyevans.com
540-434-3939

John McInnis Auctioneers
76 Main St.
Amesbury, MA 01913
mcinnisauctions.com
978-388-0400

Julien's Auctions
8630 Hayden Place
Culver City, CA. 90232
juliensauctions.com
310-742-0155

Kaminski Auctions
117 Elliott St.
Beverly, MA 01915
978-927-2223

Keystone Auctions LLC
218 E. Market St.
York, PA 17403
auctionsbykeystone.com
717-755-8954

Leland Little Auctions
620 Cornerstone Ct.
Hillsborough, NC 27278
lelandlittle.com
919-644-1243

Leslie Hindman Auctioneers
1338 West Lake St.
Chicago, IL 60607
lesliehindman.com
312-280-1212

Los Angeles Modern Auctions (LAMA)
16145 Hart St.
Van Nuys, CA 91406
lamodern.com
323-904-1950

Martin Auction Co.
P.O. Box 2
Anna, IL 62906
martinauctionco.com
864-520-2208

Michaan's Auction
2751 Todd St.
Alameda, CA 94501
michaans.com
510-740-0220

Mike Clum Auctions, Inc.
7795 US Highway 22 NE
Rushville, OH 43150
clumauctions.com
740-536-7421

Milestone Auctions
3860 Ben Hur Ave., Unit 8
Willoughby, OH 44094
milestonesuctions.com
440-527-8060

Morning Glory Jewelry
12815 Central Ave. NE
Albuquerque, NM 87123
morninggloryjewelry.com
505-296-2300

Morphy Auctions
2000 North Reading Rd.
Denver, PA 17517
morphyauctions.com
717-335-3435

Morton Subastas
Calle Monte Athos 179
Colonia Lomas de Chapultepec
Mexico City, Mexico 11000
mortonsubastas.com

Myers Auction Gallery
1600 4th St. North
St. Petersburg, FL 33704
myersfineart.com
727-823-3249

Naudeau's Auction Gallery, Inc.
25 Meadow Rd.
Windsor, CT 06095
nadeausauction.com
860-246-2444

Neal Auction Co.
4038 Magazine St.
New Orleans, LA 70115
nealauction.com
800-467-5329

New Orleans Auction Galleries
333 St. Joseph St.
New Orleans, LA 70130
neworleansauction.com
504-566-1849

Palm Beach Modern Auctions
417 Bunker Rd.
West Palm Beach, FL 33405
modernauctions.com
561-586-5500

Phillips
450 Park Ave.
New York, NY 10022
phillips.com
212-940-1200

Pook & Pook
463 East Lancaster Ave.
Downingtown, PA 19335
pookandpook.com
610-269-4040

Potter & Potter Auctions
3759 North Ravenswood Ave., #121
Chicago, IL 60613
potterauctions.com
773-472-1442

Rachel Davis Fine Arts
1301 West 79th St.
Cleveland, OH 44102
racheldavisfinearts.com
216-939-1190

Rafael Osona Auctions
P.O. Box 2607
Nantucket, MA 02584
rafaelosonaauction.com
508-228-3942

Rago Arts and Auction Center
333 North Main St.
Lambertville, NJ 08530
ragoarts.com
609-397-9374

Replacements, Ltd.
P.O. Box 26029
Greensboro, NC 27420-6029
replacements.com
800-737-5223

Rich Penn Auctions
P.O. Box 1355
Waterloo, IA 50704
richpennauctions.com
319-291-6688

Richard D. Hatch & Associates
913 Upward Rd.
Flat Rock, NC 28731
richardhatchauctions.com
828-696-3440

RSL Auction
P.O. Box 635
Oldwick, NJ 08858
rslauctions.com
908-823-4049

Ruby Lane
381 Bush St., Suite 400
San Francisco, CA 94104
rubylane.com
415-362-7611

Selkirk Auctioneers & Appraisers
4739 McPherson Ave.
St. Louis, MO 63108
selkirkauctions.com
314-696-9041

Shannon Fine Art Auctioneers
49 Research Dr.
Milford, CT 06460
shannons.com
203-877-1711

Skinner, Inc.
274 Cedar Hill St.
Marlborough, MA 01752
skinnerinc.com
508-970-3000

Soulis Auctions
529 W. Lone Jack Lee's Summit Rd.
Lone Jack, MO 64070
dirksoulisauctions.com
816 697-3830

Specialists of the South
544 E. 6th St.
Panama City, FL 32401
specialistsofthesouth.com
850-785-2577

Stony Ridge Auction
4230 Fremont Pike
Lemoyne, OH 43441
stonyridgeauction.com
419-297-9045

Strawser Auction Group
200 North Main St.
P.O. Box 332
Wolcottville, IN 46795
strawserauctions.com
260-854-2859

Susanin's Auctioneers & Appraisers
900 South Clinton St.
Chicago, IL 60607
susanins.com
312-832-9800

The Stein Auction Co.
P.O. Box 136
Palatine, IL 60078
TSACO.com
847-991-5927

Theriault's
P.O. Box 151
Annapolis, MD 21404
theriaults.com
800-638-0422

Thomaston Place Auction Galleries
P.O. Box 300
Thomaston, ME 04861
thomastonauction.com
207-354-8141

Treadway Gallery
2029 Madison Rd.
Cincinnati, OH 45208
treadwaygallery.com
513-321-6742

Uniques & Antiques
30200 Euclid Ave.
Wickliffe, OH 44092
uniquesandantiques.com
440-944-0133

Weiss Auctions
74 Merrick Rd.
Lynbrook, NY 11563
516-594-0731
weissauctions.com

WestLicht Photographica Auction
Westbahnstrasse 40
1070 Vienna, Austria
westlicht-auction.com

Willis Henry Auctions
22 Main St.
Marshfield, MA 02050
willishenry.com
781-834-7774

Wm Morford Auctions
RD #2 Cobb Hill Rd.
Cazenovia, NY 13035
morfauction.com
315-662-7625

Woody Auction
P.O. Box 618
317 South Forrest
Douglass, KS 67039
woodyauction.com
316-747-2694

Wright
1440 West Hubbard St.
Chicago, IL 60642
wright20.com
312-563-0020